Encyclopaedia of Untouchables Ancient, Medieval and Modern

ENCYCLOPAEDIA OF UNTOUCHABLES ANCIENT, MEDIEVAL AND MODERN

Dr. Raj Kumar

KALPAZ PUBLICATIONS
DELHI-110052

Encyclopaedia of Untouchables Ancient, Medieval and Modern

ISBN: 81-7835-664-3

Published in 2008 in India by
Kalpaz Publications
C-30, Satyawati Nagar,
Delhi-110052
E-mail: kalpaz@hotmail.com
Phone : 9212729499

Lasser Type Setting by: Quick Media, Delhi
Printed at : Singal Print Media, Delhi

Contents

List of Illustrations
or
List of Plates

5- Costumes and Taxtiles Under the Untouchables Rulers of Early and Later Medieval Period of India

Fig. 31. Shorts *kamarbands* and *patkas* are of the same type, but there is an addition of an open, half-sleeved, tight jacket reaching to the waist.

Fig. 32. Military costumes, it consists of a half sleeved indigo coloured tunic, tight fitting shorts made of striped material, *kamarband* and top-boots. The head seems to have been covered with a scarf

Plate VII Fig. 33. Dress consists of richly patterned *saris* reaching the ankles, *patkas* matching the *saris,* tight half-sleeved *colis* covering the entire chest and the stomach and the light scarves worn on the shoulders.

Fig. 34. Wearing striped *Saris* and *patkas* and their breasts are covered with half-sleeved *colis,* made of striped or flowered materials which leave the stomach exposed.

Fig. 35. Wearing an indigo coloured *dhoti* worked with the geese pattern; a graceful scarf covering her coiffure and a part wrapped round the waist and half sleeved green bodic.

Fig. 36. The typical costume of manfolk is heavily ornamented *dhoti* and scarf.

Plate VIII Fig. 37. Dancer wears closely fitting shorts, *patka* half-sleeved closely fitting *coli* reaching a little above the navel, scarf (*dupatta*) covering the shoulders, and a scarf tied round the hair.

Fig. 38. The shorts are replaced by the *sari.*

Fig. 39. She wears what appears to be close fitting trousers, the *coli*, and a transparent *jamah.*

Fig. 40. She wears a full sleeved *coli* and a straight edged skirt.

Plate IX Fig. 41. The Turkish costume is shown to consist of a full long sleeved Tartaric gown half-sleeved *Qaba*, full boots and a pointed cap.

Fig. 42. The Turkish costume, pointed cap attached to the *Qaba.*

Fig. 43. The Turkish costume having triangular cap.

Fig. 44. The Turkish costume, hair in hanging locks decorated with silken tassels and four printed caps.

Fig. 45. The Turkish costumes, *kamarband* with its ends fluttering in the air and having dome shaped cap.

LIST OF TABLES

Note: The above mentioned Tables from 1 to 10 having the Historical and Political Importance of the Tribal Areas cover an area of 175, 248 square miles and included a population more than that of 28,006, 777 souls of the Father's from the total population of the Indian Empire based on Historical Survey of India during 1901 and later on the Census Reports of India; and Sir Ibbetson's Report of *Panjab Castes* published 1995, by the Language Department of Panjabi. (Panjab)

Abbreviations

The following list of the standard Abbreviations are used in the text.

A.A.	Ain-i-Akbari
A.I.	Ancient India
A.N.	The Akbarnama
A.C.	The Annihilation of Caste
A.I.C.	Ancient Indian Costume
A.S.R.	Archealogical Survey Report
A.G.E.	The Age of the Gupta and other Essays
A.H.I.	An Advance History of India
A.B.R.	Antiquities of Basohli and Ramnagar
A.I.E.	Ancient Indian Education
A.N.M.	Age of the Nandas and Mauryas
A.I.G.	Ancient India and Greek
A.T.F.S.	Afif, Tarikh-i-Firoz Shahi
A.I.S.H.	Ancient Indian Social History
A.K.P.P.	Archaeology in Kerala, Past and Present
A.I.F.D.	Aesthetics of Indian Folk Dance
A.S.H.M.I.	Advance Study in the History of Medieval India
A.G.G.S.H.	The Adi Guru Granth as a Source of History
A.A.L.F.S.S.	Aspects of Ancient Life from Sanskrit Sources
B.N.	The Babarnama
B.S.	Bulleh Shah
B.I.	Buddhist India
B.T.S.	Bahuristan-i-Shahi
B.M.B.P.E.	The Babarnama, Memoirs of Babar Prince and Emperor
C.G.M.H.T.	Chandragupta Maurya and His Time
C.T.C.C.A.M.I.	Costumes, Textiles, Cosmetics and Coiffure in Ancient and Medieval India.
C.R.I.	Caste and Race in India
C.A.	Classical Age
C.A.I.	Classical Account of India
C.U.S.T.	Caste, Untouchability and Social Justice
C.V.	Chitrasutra of the Vishnudharmottara
C.H.H.	The Cultural Heritage of the Himalayan
C.I.P.	Centres of Indian Painting
D.C.M.	Dadu, the Compassionate Music
D.V.	Divyavadana
D.O.A.I.	Dresses and Ornaments in Ancient India
E.S.	Encyclopaedia of Sikkism

Eng.	English
E.S.J.M.I.T	Elements of Social Justice in Medieval Islamic thought.
F.F.S.	Futuhat-i-Firoze Shahi
G.T.C.	A Glossary of the Tribes and Castes of the Punjab and North-Western Frontier province
G.S.H.	Guruji and Social Harmony
G.R.D.S.	Guru Ravidas, The Philosophers Stone
H.D.	The History of Dharmasastra
H.K.	History of Kashmir
H.P.	History of Punjab
H.B.	History of the Brahmans
H.C.	Harshcharitra
H.I.	Handicraft of India
H.A.I.	History of Ancient India
H.P.H.S.	History of Punjab Hill States
H.I.M.P.	History of India, Mughal Period
H.C.I.P.	History and Culture of Indian People
H.I.U.B.	History of India Under Babar
I.C.	Indian Costumes
I.D.	Indian Dresses
I.F.S.	Isami, Futuhu's Salatin
I.B.D.R.	India Between Dream and Reality
I.J.O.D.D.	Indian, Jewellery, Ornaments and Decorative Designs
J.K.T.	The Jamboo and Kashmir Territories
K.V.	Kashmir Valley
K.K.	Kingdom of Kashmir
K.A.	Kautilya's Arthsastra
K.D.	Kandambri
K.U.S.	Kashmir Under the Sultan
K.G.M.	Kabir, The Great Mystic
L.M.	Later Mughal
L.V.	Lalitavistara
M.S.C.I.D.M.T.	Money and Social Change In India During Medieval Times
M.Z.B.	Memoirs of Zahiruddin Babar
N.B.I.	Northern Barriers of India
P.C.	Punjab Castes
P.H.K.	Political History of Kashmir
P.G.K.	Provincial Gazetteer of Kashmir
P.F.F.P.I.	Painted Folklore and Folklore Painter of India
P.A.P.D.I.	Pre-Aryan and Pre-Dravidian in India
P.U.S.	Punjab Under the Sultans
P.A.I.	The Painter of Ancient India

R.T.	Rajataranagini
R.A.	Royal Arts
R.M.P.I.	Rise of Muslim Power in India
R.I.B.	The Rehla of Ibn Battuta
R.V.V.R.	The Rig-Veda and Vedic Religion
R.P.G.E.A.	Researches on Ptolmy's Geography of Eastern Asia
S.B.	Sultan Bahu
S.H.J.R.	A Short History of Jammu Raj
S.Z.A.K.	Sultan Zain-ul-Abidin of Kashmir
S.E.H.P.	The Social and Economic History of Punjab
S.E.H.R.	The Social Economic History of Kashmir
T.R.	Tarik-i-Rashidi
T.T.	Tuzuk-i-Timuri
Tr.	Translation
T.J.	The Tuzuk-i-Jahansiri
T.F.M.	Tarikh-i-Fakhr-i-Mudabbir
T.F.S.	Tarikh-i-Firoze Shahi
T.M.E.	Travels in the Mogul Empire
T.N.M.	Tabaqat-i-Nasiri of Minhajuddin
T.H.P.H.P.	Travels in the Himalayan Provinces of Hindustan and the Punjab
T.K.	Travels in Kashmir
V.I.	Vedic India
Y.C.	Yuan-Chewang

Preface

This book entitled *'History of the Untouchables'* has been written to understand the meaning of *'untouchable'* or *'touchable'*. *Untouchables* people of India are those people who belong to the race of *'Father'* or *'God'* and worked for the sociatial evolution in the form of various classes of the artisans or labour are called low-born people. Touchables people are those who are easily available in the market purchase with the help of money by the Master as Ambedkar did by framing the Constitution of the law and number of institution were established on his patron, but the people who are working under that law, they have forgotten him. But his race is still working on his patron and now has prepared to ask them give a brief account statement, and what you have did for the 'Maker of the Constitution' who was the maker of souls as a *'Creative Power'* and established the various institution for the development of history. So far as the knowledge of the *Sudhras* or *untouchables* is concerned. it has widen prospective, it was not limited upto the 1947, but he has the knowledge of both the world i.e. Earth and Heaven to regulate the system of society in advancement by bribing money in which the Brahman is very greedy. Now the time has come to check the Brahminical ideology with the establishment of rule of Natural King or Divine Right they are the representative on earth. They came on Earth after a very long period of the Indian History more than that of 3,00 year to see their race which has been disgraced and degraded by the Brahmans in the society as an inferior race. These Kings have realised Brahminical thought has created social injustice with them on the bases of their works. It has been pre-supposed a social order started by them in the Indian society than in Muslims in which disparity, inequality and inequity do not charactise in, social, economic, political and religious aspects of life, but slowly and gradually they became institution, both in Hindu and Muslims society. Sikhs after Guru Govind Singh Ji, also drew the same pattern in the local institution like in *Gurudwara* or in homes, etc.

'Social justice' is a comparatively a modern term in 'History' and connotes just and fair treatment to the people of constituting a society for the development of the period in the 'History of India'. But the poor people of the 'Father of Constitution' i.e. Dr. B.R. Ambedkar, they remained sailing in the same boat, dying lack of food, shelter and clothing, which they already sailing, and the people of Brahminical ideology occupied the prominent position in the society by exploiting them on the basis of social evils, i.e. caste, colour and creed. Discrimination is still existing in the society created by the *'Modern Politicans'* or *Rakashas* with the power of money and muscle and the poor people of the *'Father'*, they have been skated by them. In everywhere in whole of the world, there is a reign of terror created by the Brahminical ideology to protect their 'power' and 'status' in the modern society. All these elements show an acute awareness of the fact the 'social justice' is by its nature an integral whole are attached to *'Father'* or *'Nam'*.

Caste may have been defined as a system of social stratification characterized by hierarchy of Brahminical ideology as their heredity against the *'Humanism'*. These restrictions or barriers have been created by the *Molabies* and the *Pandits*, because they became the champion of creating caste, colour and creed, but the people belonged to the *'pure thought'* i.e. *untouchables* or *Sudras* has no such an idea in their thought because *'Sudra'* or *'Nam'* is a Creative Power of the world as a representative of God on Earth as the Natural rule of the *'Nam'*. He always believes in humanity, equality and fraternity, no liberty but to some extent, than there is destruction on earth of the Brahminical ideology. Continues changes in the course of long history not with standing, the fact of continuity from the time immorial is undeviable and certainly started from the early history of *Sudras* from the beginning of *Sirasa Rai* dynasty of Sindh, they ruled over India more than 137 years in the 600 B.C. to 300 B.C; wherefrom every religion of the world has been originated in the process of 'Class Struggle' theory of *'Nam'* or *'Sudras'*. Every foreigner had taken the inspiration from this theory, therefore, they preferred the land of India to come time and again, because this land is the land of 'Spiritual Saints or *sants'* and their house is *Kashmir*, which is very difficult to attain, but the people of Brahminical ideology, they are fighting for the landscaping and are not fighting for 'human cause'. The notion of purity among themselves have been polluted with money matter, called materialism and the basic funda of the life, they have totally forgotten for the time being. When we go through the *'History of Kashmir'* in Spiritual form, both the terms have the same meaning i.e. *History* means *'His' 'story'* and *'Kashmir'* means, he uses to live in *'Kash'* and *'mir'* mean wealthy or powerful. It shows that 'God' is powerful. At present senerio, Kashmir became a terrorist state for the foreigners, now the time has to come to establish its old 'History' again in the form of 'Spiritualism' or 'Sufism' which had the heritage of Aryan society to Mughal society, and their founder were the *Sudras or Domas or Candalas*. No doubt, they have been landed on Earth from the *Kash* means Heaven for the sake of the poor people of the 'Nam' as their guide and forefather for the destruction of Brahminical ideology which has grabed the entire system without any reasoning and objective. But their objective is only to collect the money, which is not the personal property, it belongs to the 'Father', because. He is a 'Creative Power' and their subjective is only to suppress without any logic conclusion of the life.

In the modern world, we have seen that there are number of agencies which are working for the welfare of the poor people and many a social reformers, working in both the direction i.e. for the poor people as well as for the 'women'. But they failed in their process, because, they do not understand the root-cause of the problem which has been related with the natural phenomenon of the caste system; Dr. B.R Ambedkar, who was the crusader against the social evils, like caste, discrimination against *'women'* and *Sudras*. His major project was to establish the reign of 'human values' of liberty, equality, fraternity and social justice in the Indian psyche. With all his intellectual ventures and studies, he tried to give a message to the society against the said 'social evils', but after his death, no Brahman was ready to study him, even though, they ignored his intellectual ventures on the bases of being a *'Schedule Caste' or 'Untouchable'*. Now, the time has come to teach a lesson of those who ignored his intelligentsia not in college level but on university level. The writer of his race took his project in his own hand, and give a challenge to the 'Modern Politicians' or *Rakasha* and the intellectuals of the Brahminical ideology that we are going to establish a 'New Society' of the *'Nam'* which had the concept of Dr. B.R. Ambedkar. The detailed massage have already been recorded in both the texts i.e *'History of the Chamar Dynasty'* but the Brahmans have no history. They are the servents of the *'Nam'*. because, they neglected the idea of Dr. B.R. Ambedkar, but it was his dream to establish a 'New Society' through the conspiracy of 'Silence' or with the *'Reserve idea'*. As a result of it, was to transmigrated their souls from one generation to another from *Chamar* to *Jat*.

But, while interacting with various activists, academicians intelligentsia in educational institutions, and while joining various symposia and conferences, organised on the theme of caste and other social problems like bad habits against the women, while going through the pages of various research articles, monographs, it has been observed that 'Silence' or 'Reservations' are again prevailed in the study of scientific knowledge, when there is reign of terror. In bringing out this project in the market, we do feel that the historians, anthropologists, socialogists, political scientists, may consider these projects are the scientific study of the nature, because they are the part of the nature i.e. *'Nam'*. No doubt, the interpretation of the various terms which could not understood by the Brahmanical ideological, and a historian from the background of the *Chamar* community which was degraded by all the communities on the basis of occupation and were known as *untouchables*. It is very surprising to note that they were pollution carrier people, as their objective was to clear the sociatial inhabitants who are pollution creator i.e. Brahmans and suppressed by them without any logic interpretation. Dr. B.R. Ambedkar has rightly expressed in his writing and speeches *'Sabi Smsyaona Ki Kunji Satta Hae'* means of all the problems *Truth* or *'Nam'* is the really key. Without *'Nam'* or *'Truth'* there is problem in the life as Nanak says *"Nanak Dukhiya Sabha Sansaar So Sukhya Jo Nam Aadhar."* This is the biggest challenge in the life of man and it has been decided that one has to respond of the challenge. Those qualify Him, they become the race of 'Father'. Father always love with them.

Keeping in view, all the above mentioned facts, we would like to say that the rule of representative of God on Earth like *Lord Buddha. Akbar, Sultan Sikandar, Firoze Shah Tughlaq,* etc. is now going to establish to begin with history of *Sudras or Chamars or Untouchables. Untouchables* are those people, who have not much lust for money, they have the lust of humanity and simplicity. There is no need of much qualification, illitrate persons are more lovable. As lord Buddha says "know *Truth* as *Truth* and *Untruth* as *Untruth*". It is equivalent to the Islamic law (*Shariat*) based on the precepts of Quran's commentary. The *Sultans of Kashmir*, they also followed the same patron. Their 'power' and 'position' were also determined by the said law or *'Nam'* as well as it has the tradition. Usually, they were six ministers to handle the worldly life or equivalent to *Pandavas*. The *Wazir, Diwan-i-Risalt, Sadr-us-Sudur, Diwan-i-Insha, Diwan-i-Arz, Qazi-ul-Quzat,* they were the slaves of the slaves, because they are the director of the world. In brief, *Kashmir* also served as a channel through the ages and the Punjab maintained then commanding relation with *Ladakh, Kabul and Quandhar,* Bengal, China, Kathmandu, Central Asia, etc. from the very ancient period to later Mughal period. After the Aurangzeb, the entire nation came under the grip of Brahmanical ideology. The story of *Class Struggle* was again started by the Indian against the Britishers. Before the Britisher, Mughal had a good trade relation with China, every articles of clothing, leather goods, etc. were exported from Kashmir to all over the world. It shows from the study, that the rule of *'Artisan class'* was more effective than the Brahminical ideology, because they used to trust 'One God' or Master and Brahmans believes on number of Gods as a blind faith. Artisan used to serve the society, to study the society on the basis of *'Nam'* or *Kalma*. They were intellectual people, than that of the Brahmans. Moreover, they have long standing history and their trade was in all articles with China and other countries in private hand. No doubt, they checked the black-marketing to a great extent which is impossible for the Brahmanical rulers. Because, they are themselves falls in this category of black by nature, nothing having the knowledge of humanity. *Mirza Haidar Dughlat Chak* ruler of the *Nam* tells us that the markets and streets of *Srinagar* were all paved with well cut stores of the *'Nam' or Candalas of Kashmir*. They were the polished stones of the *'Nam'*, like *Ravidas, Kabir; Ved-Vyash, Valmiki, Mulana Rumi, etc.*

Lastly, in the *'Introduction'*, we have endeavoured to elucidate in the first place the date of *'History of the Untouchables'* that the writer of the text complied the thesis in a brief manner to show the Brahmanical writers that *'Truth'* always prevail whenever, there is a disorder in the society from time to time and *Sudra* is a class, who always help the poor people in every critical moment and their heroes have already been mentioned, they landed on Earth and unite the society on the preaching of the various theories of the saints, but as soon as they leave the body, Brahmans again start their activities as their traditional business to destroy the society. *Sudras*, they always construct the *'New Society'* as their thought to serve the society and to live in heaven as a satisfactory thought i.e. *'Nam'*. All the chapters of this book from one to Eleven, you will find out that *Sudras* were not aggressive ruler. They were the ruler of *'Love'* or *'Nam'*. If the *Brahmans* do not realise the fact, than there is a natural calamity which is very difficult from then to control the situation. Therefore, it is, again, a proposal to the Brahminical heroes, kindly realise it and trust him, otherwise natural calamity is standstill. Then there is no alternative. Moreover, the natural ruler of the *'Nam'*, they are ready to face any type of consequences and now the real history has been compiled and exposed through the book of *'History of the Brahmans'* and now they are going to establish their rule as it has their rule on Earth.

—Dr. Raj Kumar

Introduction

The unity and integrity of the people of this land has been an article of faith with us for last centuries ago i.e. *'Nam'*. However, when we see a few patently discriminatory provisions in the *Smrities,* and the division of the Hindu society into innumerable castes, some claiming to be superior to others[1]. Brahmins were the earliest beneficiary of the concept of reservation by a peculiar method. According to which, instead of directly reserving the positions of them as priests, by way of *Varnashrama Dharma*, they disqualified and eleminated all the others from contesting[2] various customs and usages which have brought out inequality, resulting in discrimation against certain classes of the people on the basis of occupation, but at present it has been seen that every caste and class for their own benefit have been engaged, the worst of it being the practice of untouchability with all the incidental in human and humilating treatment among the lower castes of the *'Nam',* meted out regarded as *'untouchables'*, the question that naturally arises is, were all these sanctioned by *Dharma*[3] theory of the *'Nam'*. The *untouchable; Chamar* or *Cobbler* other was now visible, but only in the context of a discourse of 'sympathy' and 'compassion'. *Dalits* were still not speaking subjects, but it is the *'Inner voice'* of the Father, a title was given by Dr. B.R. Ambedkar to the people of India to find out the meaning of the term which was originated from the Vedic period of study called *'Nam'* or *'Kalma'* or other names of the worldly symbolic *'Names';* the people of that period, they were not people with *'self-pride'*, as Limbale notes in his literary works *'Towards an Aesthetic of Dalit literature*[4].*'* This representation of Dalits as objects of pity, rather than as authors of their own stories was not confined to Marathi literature alone, it became world fame i.e. *'Nam'*. Critics besides Limbale have been troubled by the treatment of *Dalit* characters and discipline in the writings of such prominent writers, like *Ved Vayas; Valmiki, Kalhana, Barani, Ibn-Battuta,* Dr. B.R. Ambedkar, etc. In their view, these representations do not show Dalits literature, history, etc. as they are, but as helpless and child like people of the *'Nam'* cannot take their own decisions or take action to find out the solution of the problem. In *Anand's* novel, *Untouchable,* for example, the protagonist, *Bakha,* instead of opting for radical action submits to Gandhi's pacifism and is thus contained Arun Mukherjee's book on *Post-Colonialism: My living*[5]. If it is not so. The expression of *'Dharma'* is to be opposed and inconsistent with any such social inequality. The relevant provisions of the *Shruti*[6] *(Vedas)* which are the primordial source of Dharma, unquivocally declare equality of all human beings through the theory of *'Nam'* or *'Word'* or *'Chamar'* and leave no room for doubt discrimination on the ground of birth or otherwise had no Vedic sanction; on the other hand such discrimination which Brahman has created, was plainly opposed to Vedic injunction of the *'Nam'*.

Discrimination of any kind is, therefore, contrary to Dharma. It is really *Adharma*[7] of the 'Nam'. He will save his force i.e. *'Chamar'* from the mastery allusion.

The chart of equlity (*Samanata*) is found incorporated in the *Rig-Veda* i.e. *'Nam'*, the most ancient of the Vedas and also in the *Atharvara Veda*. "No one is superior (*ajyestaso*) or inferior (*akanishtasa*). All are brothers (*etc. bhratarah*a). All should strive for the interest of all and should progress collectively. (*Sowbhagaya Sam Va Vridhuhu*) *(Rigveda-Mandal-5 Sukta-60, Mantra-5)*. Let there be Oneness in resolutions, hearts and minds. Let the strength to live with mutual co-operation be firm to all(*Rigveda-Mandal* -10, Sukta-191, *Mantra*-4).

All we have equal rights to articles of food, water and air. The yoke of the chariot of life is placed equally before *'Law'* or *Rita* in Sanskrit on the shoulders of all the force of *'Nam'* or *'Chamar'*. All should live together in the ancient time in harmony supporting either there was *Buddhism* or other religion of the *'Nam'* and one another like the spokes of a wed of the chariot or Asoka connecting its rim like a parasole of the *'Nam'* and the hub. (*Atharvanaveda-Samjnana Sukta*). The above mentioned Vedic provisions forcefully declare equality among all human beings before the *'law of Nam'*. The last of them impresses that just as no spoke of a wheel is superior to another no individual can claim to be or regarded as superior to others. It is interesting to note that the very first article of the 'Universal Declaration of Human Rights' made by the United Nations is to be the same effect as it was read: "All human beings are born free and equal in dignity and rights. They are endowed with reason and conscience and should act towards one another in a spirit of brotherhood." While this was the grand concept of equality in this country since the earliest period of civilization, the society came to be divided sometime later to begins with the Brahmanical thought after the death of the one saint era of the *'Nam'*, on functional basis society was divided by them into four *'Varnas'* or *Chaturvarna* namely (1) *Brahmans,* the class of persons taking to teaching and other learned professions; (2) *Kshatriyas;* warriors and the ruling class; (3) *Vyishya*; the class of persons undertaking trade, commerce and agriculture, and (4) *Sudras,* the class of persons rendering all other essential services to the society. The superiority or in feriority of an individual does not seem to have been determined by birth in anyone of these classes. For instance, *Valmiki,* and *Ved Vyasa,* the authors of the two great epics, the *Ramayana* and *Mahabharata,* who are regarded as the greatest poets of the 'Dalit family', belong to ancient Indian History.

At a later point of period, in the long meandering course of our history, the evil of discrimination as high and low among men, on the basis of birth, hereditary avocations and other considerations raised its ugly head by *Brahmanas,* who always attached with material life, and started the pernicious practice of untouchability among the working class, who served the community at every moment of the difficult times either in creating the New Literature of the period or in occupational basis. It is unfortunate event in the history of India even working with sincereity, but all its degrading implication came into their existence. But the fact remains that the feeling of high and low among the human beings on the basis of caste which means *'pure'* in latinized language and the pernicious practice of untouchability and treating some human beings as untouchables being directly contrary to the declaration of equality in the *Vedas* were nothing but *Adharma.* But all right thinking persons and social reformers have been fighting against these evils which were affliciting in the society by the Brahmans.

Persons like *Buddha, Mahavira, Basaveshwara, Ramanuja, Lokamanya Bala Gangadhara Tilak, Kanakadasa, Dr. B.R. Ambedkar, Gandhiji, Narayan Guru, Jyotiba Phule, Dr. Hedgewar, Guruji, Swami Dayananda, Savarkar, Bala Sahib* Deors all declared that the practice of untouchability was a great sin against 'God' or *'Nam'* or *'Chamar'* and humanity. Shri Baraveshwara initiated the social reform movement in the 12th century A.D. The *'Anubhava Mantapa'* or experiment of the fiends of darkness which was regarded untouchability is a crime against God or *'Nam'* was regarded as the parliament of religions declared the equality of all human beings in the following words:

1. All men are equal.
2. No man is high or low by birth, sex or occupation.
3. There can be no discrimination between man to man.

Balagangadhara Tilak went to the extent of declaring that "If God ordained untouchability, I do not recognise the God", but it is the *Brahmans* who created such kind of social evils against the man. Thus, there is least doubt that inequality among human being has been created by the *Brahmanas,* based on caste, was *Adharma* of the highest social order being a flagrant violation of the chart of equality in the *Vedas.* It must be said to the credit of *Vyasa,* the author of the celebrated epic *Mahabharata*, in his *Smritis* (Vyasa 1-V-4) quoted earlier having envisaged the possibility of contravention of the Vedas by a few, had laid down that: "Wherever there is conflict between what is declared in the *Vedas* and provision in any of the *Smritis, Puranas* etc., what is declared in the *Vedas* shall prevail." at the time of conflict between the two forces i.e. 'God' and *Brahman* for the establishment of the *'New Society'*, that there should be the destruction by the natural forces to realise the *'Truth'* or *'Nam'.*

Therefore, any rule or custom to the extent they considered that some castes are superior and some castes are untouchables is void as being opposed to *'Vedas'* or *'Nam'* . How and when such *'adharma'* namely the social evil of high and low caste and particularly the evil of untouchability got into our social life is difficult to ascertain without *'Nam'.* Whatever be the reason and whatever by the point of time at which the pernicious practice of untouchability was started. The fact remains that the same was *'adharma'* and it had to be totally eradicated as it flagrantly violated the basic concept of equality of human beings as propounded in the *Vedas.*

The Supreme Dharma of all of us today is to obey the Constitutional Provision in Letter and Spirit and in Thought i.e. 'Nam', word and deed. As set out in the beginning of this chapter, it appears that *Guruji* strongly condemned the social evil of untouchability. Despite of inhuman treatment meted out to them those hatred the theory of *'Nam'* that is called *'Chamar'.* In this context, "History records that the so-called 'untouchables' have been in the forefront of the war of national liberation all these one thousand years in the history of India. They have been among the staunchest and bravest fighters in the armies of *Rana Pratap,* Guru Govind Singh, *Shivaji.* Some of the crucial battles which Shivaji fought with the hostile forces of Delhi and Bijapur were led and manned by these same valorous brethern of our previous successors of the *'Nam'*. They fought till the last of their life with power of the *'Nam'*. It is also interesting to note that the declaration of equality in the *Vedas* has been reenacted in the various provisions of our latest Constitution. Important concomitant of equality is the feeling of unify and fraternity which are among the objectives of our Constitution as indicated in its preamble this spirit of national unity is found expressed in the words. 'We, the people of India' and by the word 'fraternity' used in the preamble Dr. B.R. Ambedkar had said while equality and liberty are important in a Democracy, he attached greater importance to the word fraternity used in the preamble. In this behalf he had said that "what does fraternity mean? a sense of common brotherhood of all Indians *'Chamar'* of Indians being one people. It is this principle which gives unity and solidarity to social life. (Dr. B.R. Ambedkar and *Human Rights*, p. 15).

Indeed the feeling of fraternity was achieved during the freedom struggle of India and it has to be strengthened; developed and maintained after independence, but the implementation of the provision of the Constitution which hold taboo discrimination on the grounds of caste, colour and creed, but the people of the various political parties have been failed to check this crime. Thus, *'Nam'* again takes initiative to remove the 'untouchability' with the help of *'untouchable'* i.e. *'Nam'* or *'Deepit Raj'* son of Dr. Raj Kumar, the author of the book. Therefore, it is the high time that our political parties and leaders stop abusing *'Varna'* or *'Word'* and caste or religion for political or electoral purpose in the interest of social harmony for building a strong, united and prosperious *Bharat*.

It is a matter of fact that the people living in different parts of *Bharata* have developed their own language and they write and speak in that language. Some of them are major languages and there are innumerable minor languages. But Sanskrit is the mother of all our languages. Sanskrit was and is being used throughout the country for worshipping of God or to perform religious rites or ceremonies. Our two great epics *Ramayana, Mahabharata, Veda, Upanishads, Bhagvadgita* are all in Sanskrit. Notwithstanding the fact that they have also been written in local languages. Original Sanskrit texts are being used in substantial measure. Highlighting the importance of Sanskrit supreme court in the case of Santhosh Kumar (1994 (6) SCC 759) stated thus: "It is well-known that Sanskrit is the mother of all Indo-Aryan languages and it is this language in which our *Vedas, Puranas* and *Upanishads* have been written and in which *Kalidas, Bhavbuti, Banabhatta* and *Dandi* wrote their classics. Teaching of *Shankarachary, Ramanuja, Madhawacharya, Nimbuk* and *Vallabha-Charya* would not have been woven into the fabric of Indian culture if Sanskrit would not have been available to them as a medium of expressing their thoughts. (Para-11).

Accordingly among the great galaxy of patriots of the *'Nam'* who had fought against the foreign invaders during the dark days of our Indian history having due regard to their extraordinary and outstanding calibre, three great national heroes were chosen as ideal National heroes of the *'Word'*. They were *Maharana Pratap* of Rajasthan, *Chatrapati Shivaji* in the South and *Guru Govind Singh* in the North. Undoubtedly they are national heroes of exceptional merit. E.F. Turnbull an English author who has said that he was a patriot who fought for protection and dignity of motherland for 32 years remaining in exile and wandering in forests facing all odds of the life, who never yield to the mighty Mughul emperor Akbar, who was the great son of the *Dom* or *Domba* or Candala family, and there fore a patriot of unequalled merit in world history. Besides these *Chatrapati Shivaji*, son of Shahaji who was only a Sardar under Bijapur *Sultan* having secured national eduation from his mother *Jyabai*, by his intense patriotism and master strategy was able to establish a powerful Hindu Kingdom in the South by successfully fighting against mighty emperor *Aurangazeb*. *Guru Govind Singh*, the tenth Guru of Sikh enraged by the killing of his Father Guru Tez Bahadur, the nineth Guru of the Sikh and two of his associated *Bhai Matidas* and *Bhai Satidas* under the Moghul emperor, took a vow that he would transform the mild Sikhs into the most powerful marshal race and was fully successful in doing so. As a result, Sikhs have become the strong arm of the nation defending the borders of our country[8].

As far as the caste system theory is concerned, it has nothing to do with the theory of *'Varna'* or *'Word'*. This classification came into existence on the basis of hereditary occupation or avocation like iron- smith, goldsmith, sculptors, agriculturist, pot makers, shoe maker, basket-maker, etc. As the caste system was based on occupation or avocation, the people considered that marriages between a boy and a girl belonging to the same caste is conducive to the family occupation as by blood or by birth, they would have got the necessary aptitude and expertise in the particular profession as *'Chamar'* do his job. On the basis of the occupation and avocation, there, is no doubt, at present Brahmans are working as sweeper, washing the untisles, etc. whereas hundred of castes came into existence some claiming to be superior to others. But even with innumerable castes, there was total harmony in the ancient and mediavel period when the rule of 'law' or 'Nam' in different form was established by the ruler of *'Nam'* like *Akbar, Buddha, Firozeshah Tughluq, Balban, etc.* 'New Society' was formed at that time people respect to each other without irrespective of caste, colour and creed. Inequality was only established during the time of Brahminical ideology. He is problem created and the enemy of the *'Father'*.

Though it is natural that for historical, cultural civilization, linquistic reasons there had always been many countries having the basic philosophy of all living beings are children of God is deep rooted. Therefore, "History is minimally three things; what happened in the past, what people believe happened in the past and what historians says happened in the past. Historigraphy is largely about the second and third of these definitions of history[9].

Similarly, the suggestion that the use of the word *'Hindu'* or *'Musalman'* in the beginning of the religious sense immediately after the conquest of Sindh by Muhammad Bin Qasim in 712 A.D. is unacceptable, because he was the follower of the Sudra camp in Sindh during the rule of *Sirash Rai II*, they were the untouchable of the *'Nam'* and Muhammad Ibn Qasim stayed there for some time for the practice of the *'Nam'* and realized the theory of nature called as *'Ferishta'*. With the mighty power of the *'Nam'*, he fought against the *Bhamanbad* with the *Sudra* family. It has been asserted at that time the "Hindu" was, "now identified on a religious basis" and the conversion from the Hindu religion was now possible, because the rule of the law was established called as *'New Islamic State'* of the *'Nam'* or the *Kalma*. The sources bearing on eighth- century A.D. Sindh indicate the existence of several non-Islamic religions i.e. *'Nam'* or *'Word'* and sects of Brahmans and Buddhism denoted by the Arabic compound *barhimah-sumaniya* used by the classical Muslim writers, but the word "Hindu" in their writings had a geographic, linguistic or ethnic connotation of the *'Nam'*. In the *Chachnama*, for example, *Hinduvan* means Indian in generals and *Hindavi* stands for the Indian language[10]. The first use of the term *'Hindu'* in the religious sense is bound in the *Kitabu-ul-Hind* of Alberuni (A.D. 1030), who at one place distinguishes Hindus from Buddhists, but at another holds the distinction to be between *sramans* (Buddhists) and Brahmans[11]. He states that "they (Hindus) totally differ from us in religion[12]" Alberuni's understanding was limited to Brahminical religious beliefs and practices, which proved false during the time of rule of law as today we see in the society after the 1947 A.D. Therefore, Alberuni use the word *'Hindu'* had to use far from clear and coherented rule of the *'Nam'*. It is, therefore, not possible to credit him with any definite and essentialist view of Hindu religion, much less treated his perception of one as a landmark in the development of Hindu identity as a class-struggle theory of the *'Nam'*. The ambivalence surrounding the word "Hindu" continued for a long period of Indian History, so that even three centuries after *Alberuni* we find *Zia-ud-din Barani*, the first Muslim historian of the *'Nam' called Baran or Varna or Barni* as the soul of Father write the history of India (known as the *Tarikh-i-Firuz shahi*), making frequent references to Hindus (*Hunud* and *Hindu'an*) either as a religious category[13] of the *'Nam'*. TheMoroccan traveller *Ibn Battutah*, a countemporary of *Barani*, interpreted the name *'Hindu Kush'* as *"Hindu Killer"* because the Indian slaves of the *'Nam'* passing through its mountainous terrain perished in the snows for some times to obtain the *'Power of Nam'* as in realistic approach. This has been given a communal slant[14] to the Brahminical thought which is destructive one, because Brahman has not foundation stone as Nanak says, *"Nanak Dukiya sab Sansaar*, so Sukiya Jish *Nam Aadar*[15]." as already mentioned in the text.

Ibn Battutah's derivation of the word, however, may have been based on folk etymology, and the name *Hindukush* possibly originated from Arabic Hindu *'Koh'* meaning the "Mountains of India", where from the force of *Sudra* used to live during the time of difficult hours to settle the account of previous balance of approach toward history removes all the differences between man to man. The obstacles which have been created by the Brahminical thought hatred towards man. In the sixteenth century A.D., some of the recent researches done on Akbar, however, have tended to focus on a particular theme, namely, the factors contributing to the rise of his policy of religious tolerance based on the principle of *'Sulh-i-kul'*, or *'Absolute Peace'*. Akbar's religious policy is often viewed in this studies already mentioned as being linked to his transformation of the nobility into a composite ruling group including[16] all the people of *'Nam'* into one family. Since he was considered the King to be the representative of the God on earth, as Brahmans made themselves as a God on earth, but the ruler of the *'Nam'*, they are the representative of both the world i.e. *'Earth* and *Heaven'*.

There is a need for constant efforts to explore new sources, generate new ideas in the history of India or to reinforce the already established studies. The painstaking researches during the last six decades have established that the sovereign power vested with the king, derived legitimacy from the ideology of *'Divine Right'*. Akbar was the first Mughal emperor to bring about certain changes in the old concepts of kingship and kinship. By invoking the theory of 'Divine Right' in favour of the king as an a natural idea of the *'Nam'* or *'Word'*. Theoretically both in the Muslim and Hindu societies, the sovereign power of the ruler percolated down through his officials and religious persons to the lowest levels i.e. *'Chamar'* and was used for the management of the affairs of the state. This concept of power remained acceptable for quite some time and researches have sustained this understanding of the history of Mughal in India at the microlevel i.e. *'Nam'* or *'Word'* or *'Chamar'*. But in course of the last few years, this concept of power has been challenged and the theories have been propounded by the Western scholars for non-Indian societies are being applied to Indian society too. Initially this was confined to regions and regional powers[17], but the theory of *'Nam'* is support the new ideas to the Indian history as per his programme and objective to establish 'a new society' of the Father in broad prospective as Lord Buddha established during the time of Maurya.

Babarvani are the hymns of *Guru Granth Sahib*, four in number, in which their author, Guru Nanak, has painfully described the cruelties perpetrated by the armies of *Babar*, the Mughal ruler of Afghanistan, during their invasions over India during the sixteenth century A.D. The name *Babarvani*, is derived from the use of the term in one of these hymns: *'Babarvani phir gai kuiru na roti khai[18]*. Term *Dum* or *Dom* and *Domba* or *Chandala* Babar's command or writ has spread; even the princes go without food[19]." Of these four hymns, the first hymn, *Khurasan Khasmana* kiya Hindustan *daraiya*, is included in the Guru Granth Sahib in *Raga Asa[20]*. The second hymn is known as *Jini Siri Sohani pattiyan mangin pae sandhuru,* and the third one is discussed, *Kahan su khel tabela ghori kahan bheri shehnai,* are included in *Guru Granth Sahib* in *Raga Asa* Ashtpadiyan[21]. The fourth hymn, *Jaisi main awai khasam ki bani taisara karin gian ve lalo,* is also included in *Guru Granth Sahib* in *Raga Tilang[22]*. A thorough analysis of these hymns can reveal a host of facts about the invasion of Babar with the *'Power of Nam'*, and the widespread devastation caused thereby against the Brahmanical thought which was the social evil in the society of *'Sudra'* or *'Untouchables'*. Regarding the historical contents of Guru Nanak's *bani,* particularly the *Babarvani*. Dr. Fauja Singh says, "the intellectual degradation which had overcome by the Hindus during the closing of the Sultanate period of Indian History. When Babar had invaded Punjab in 1521 A.D. means the 'Voice of God' and sacked *Saidpur* (Eminabad), Guru Nanak was present on the occasion[23] as the natural Father of the *Babar* and head of the world to regulate the emotions of the man on this earth.

There is, no doubt, that there are certain references of Babar's invasions in Guru Nanak's *bani*. An open tragedy like the one that struck the Saidpur movement profounded and described as the sorrows of Indians *Jat* Hindus and Muslims like *'Chamar'* of the Sirash Rai dynasty of Sindh in words of intense power and suffering of the people of *'Nam'*. Babar's army, in the words of Guru Nanak, was "the bridal procession of sin", war of the good over the evil. In fact, Indian literature of that period records no more virile protest against the invading hordes than do Guru Nanak's four hymns of *"Babarvani in the Guru Granth Sahib[24]."* Another prominent Punjabi historian says, "the *Adi Guru Granth* is a priceless source of Indian history as it provides information which is not available anywhere else. The history in general and *Tuzak-i-Babari* in particular have given the details of Babar's invasions. But it was reserved for Guru Nanak, 'the People's Prophet' as T.L. Vasvani calls him, to record the brutalities of *Doma* soldiers on the people *'Word'* or *'Nam' Guru Nanak* as *'Chamar'* Ravidass as Prophet of the *'Nam'* being the eye-witnessed of the scene was greatly touched[25] to each other at that time through the power of *'Nam'*. Author has given one of the most comprehensive overviews about the major historical elements of the war in *Guru Granth Sahib* under the categories of *'Political History'*, *'Social History'* and *'Tribes'* and *'Social Elites'* of the *Babarvani* draws important facts connected with *'Babar's Invasion'*, *'First Invasion of Babar'*, 'Third Invasion of Babar as a *Dum or Chandala'*, 'Fourth Invasion of Babar', 'First Battle of *Panipat'* and *'Flight of Humayun'* in the *Visalata* and Rise of Sher Shah Suri." Before we analyse the significance of *Babarvani* as a fruitful source of Indian History, we must have a brief survey of the contemporary history of the social, political and the religious conditions of the national and international events leading to them at that time was placed by *Guru Nanak* in the whole scheme of[26] the *'Nam'* as a source of *the Indian History* to begin with the event of *'Nam'* as a *'New era'* of the *'Nam'*. *'Nam'*, however, by 1469, the year of Guru Nanak's birth, Bahlol Lodhi has establish his authority in Delhi, and relative stability which he introduced was further strengthen by his son *Sikander Lodhi*. In the circumstances of the time a measure of prosperity would have been a natural development and Babar seems to imply *Dom* in his *Babar-nama* that it had in fact taken place. A fertile soil of Punjab which has produced number of Saint or *Sant* like *Valmiki, Ved Veyas,* etc., a favourable climate, a relatively limited population after the historical events of the *'Nam',* and an appreciable measure of security would have combined to produce this favourable economic condition[27]. Babar is the only contemporary figure of any significance who is referred to by name in the works of Guru Nanak, and with the exception of *Bhai Gurdas's Var1,* the principal *Janam-Sakhis* all record that Guru was present as a witness when the Mughal army assaulted the town of *Saidpur*[28]. *'Word',* in the case of the *Babarvani* we may confidently assume that he witnessed something of the devastation caused by *Babar's* army and that accordingly he was in the *Panjab* during at least one of *Babar's* incursions into North India[29]." upto *Kashmir.*

Babar in Persian called *'the Tiger'*, was already displayed an unhealthy interest in the distrubed affairs of the Panjab, which had the provincial border his Afghan Kingdom and was under the Lodhi rule just nominally functioning at that time. In 1501 A.D., the year of the earthquake, he made his first foray across the north-west frontier. A pre-occupied *Lodhi Sultan* chose to ignore. As the Lodhi's biographer puts it, "Sikander Lodhi, while fighting against the *Tomara* (i.e. the Rajputs of Gwalior), was criminally neglecting the North-West Frontier and the Panjab[30]." This state of affairs, if anything, worsened as the strife-torn Lodhi's squabbled amongst themselves. Twenty years and five exploratory incursions later, *Babar* would invade in earnest topple *Sikander's* successors and taking both Delhi and Agra, would inaugurate in India a Mongul, or Mughal empire[31]. Guru Nanak does not rebuke the incompetent ruler of India for nothing in *Babarvani,* but he was the ruler of the *'Nam'.*

Guru Nanak clearly gives credit to his God for having given a Master (*Khasam*) to the land of *Khurasau* to threaten (and ravage) the landof Hindustan, and reveals the Divine reason too. Alluding to the alluding to the all round sinful derogation in the country, the Guru record, that the Almighty, in this wisdom, had sent the Mughal Babar as the Angel of Death and destruction to punish the sinful Indians rather than directly bringing the blame on Himself. Yet the Guru cannot remain moved at the great devastation and agony caused by the marauding Mughals and depicting the misery and wailing all around makes bold to question his master why was he not moved by its severify. *"Tain Ki dard na ayia?* reasoning that since he was the master of all and supposed to make equal dispensations for all, the *Guru* further qualifies his hurt by saying that nobody could have blamed him had the mighty Mughals restrained themselves to ravaging the mighty only; but here the ferocious Mughal tigers had even mauled the Indian multitudes who were weak and powerless like cows. The scenario painted by Guru Nanak is verily akin to the narrative of Babar's first invasion recorded by Latiff: "Having subdued the countries as far as Chenab *'Chamar'* or *'Nam'*, he advanced at the head of his army to chastise the *Gakkhars* or *Kokkhar.* The fort of Birhala was invested and *Gakkhara* were defeated in a sally by Dost Beg, the Mughal General. Babar at the same time cutting off their retreat in person, they were compelled to fly to mountains, where the force of the *'Nam',* used to live, and considerable number of them were killed in flight[32]" However, when *Babar* writes about his battles with *Gakkhars,* he does this in the content of his fourth invasion when he had then moved on to capture Lahore where too his army had indulged into the usual excesses and cruelties. Then the *Guru* goes on to accuse the incompetent rulers of the day who like 'curs' had themselves despoiled and wasted the 'jewel' of Hindustan to be easily ravaged and blundered by the ransacking Mughal hordes, due to which no body will shed tears on their own death and destruction. In the end, he admonishes that only God determines the destiny and he alone bestows the real greatness. Those who arrogate sham greatness to themselves but squander opportunities in revelleries and merriment are rendered like puny ants and insects by Him. The real mighty are humble and in-arrogant[33].

In this way, Guru Nanak sermonises that when God has to meet such a fate to a people, he first deprives them of all wisdom and sense. The Guru makes light of the superstitious efforts of the Indian ruling class as Barani writes to ward off the calamity with tantric magic and religious prayers and rituals. No spells or magic, or prayer or ritual could deter the Mughals, instead they also went about razing religious places of all kinds. The most significant comment contained in this hymn is regarding the fact that Indians of all creeds faced similar ire of the invaders by them "Hindus, Muslims (the actual reference is to Turks), Bhattis and Thakurs." There must be a number of Turks in Syedpur when Babar invaded it in 1521 A.D. Therefore, Guru Nanak has specifically mentioned that wives of Turks were subjected to torture by the soldiers of *Babar.*[34] *Babar* had prided himself as to be a *Turk* of *Kushana* period, but his soldiers had shown no mercy or leniency for Indian Turks. Such references are indeed very vital historically facts of the *'Nam'*, because no Muslim historian would have mention there that we were originated from the *'Sudra'* Dynasty' of the Sirash Rai of Sindh, they used to live before the Prophet Mohammad-the hymn ends that painting a poignant picture about the pitiable condition of the woman, under the Brahminical ideology either he was Muslim ruler or Hindu ruler, but under the *Sudra* rulers women obtained equal right of the *'Nam'*. The Guru also laments that "modesty and righteousness had gone into hiding and falsehood was strutting about the glory." He also likens the rape and abduction of women to "marriages solemnized by *Satan*", where from the Santan Dharma has been originated i.e. the theory of *mind* or Brahmins or Kazis the hymn clearly records that women were dishonoured and carried away irrespective of their caste, colour and creed, whether Hindu or Muslim or belonging to lower castes. Guru Nanak was eye-witness to the havoc created during these during these invasions *Janam Sakhis* mentions that he himself was taken captive at Saidpur. A line of his, outside of the *Babarvani* hymns, indicates that he may have been present in Lahore when the city was given up to plunder. In six pithy words this line conveys, "for a *pehar* and a quarter, i.e. for nearly four hours, the city of Lahore remained subject to death and fury[35]." Guru Nanak being the eye-witness of the scenes at Saidpur, modern Eminabad, District Gujranwala (Pakistan) was greatly touched and he was vividly described the excesses of Babar's soldiers on the natives in his *Babarvani* these atrocities committed by Babar's soldiers have been mentioned in his momoris: "We advanced to Sialkot, the inhabitants of which submitted and saved their possessions but the inhabitants of Sayedpur who resisted were put to sword their wives and children carried into captivity and all their property plundered[36]."

The most significant part of this hymn is the apparent prophecy made by Guru Nanak in its closing part. While speaking of the Indian suffering their ordained destiny. Just as would the perpetrators of the cruelties surely face divine retribution for their sins and crimes, he also speaks the mystical words as:

"As will body's vesture betorn to shreds"
India shall remember my words.
In seventy eight they came; in ninety-seven departed in the Heavenly World.
Another hero shall some day arise
Nanak utters the word of truth Chamar'
Truth he utters; truth the time calls for,
(2) (3.5)[37]

The above coincide with the years of Bikrami calander in which Babar made his third invasion in 1521 A.D.(Bikrami 1578) which by all means was his first effective invasion, and the flight of his son and successor Humayun before Sher Shah Suri, one of their vassals *Ravidas* who defeated the Rana Sanga of Mewar and Mira[38] (1498-1547 A.D.) became the follower of Guru Ravi Das. After sometimes a battle was fought in 1525-26 A.D. and *Mira's* husband Boja Raja was died. In this context, Raja Rattan Singh fought a war at *Kanwha* in 1527, they fought against the Babar and died in the battle. It shows that Ravidass *'Chamar'* and *Babar* Dom or Chandala had the close relationship to fight against the Brahminical ideology at that time, who had wrested at the Delhi throne from the Mughals in 1540 A.D. (Bikrami, era 1597), even though for a few years. This prophecy carries great significance when we remember Guru Nanak and Guru Ravi Dass came into contact through the power of *'Nam'* as they were the natural ruler of the 'lord' on earth'. It shows that Guru Nanak (1469 1539 A.D.). That the contact between Ravi Dass and Nanak was took place at *Banaras* and the teachings of Ravi Dass had been already widely spread in *Panjab* a place of historical revolution in the Indian history, whereform end and new era was started with the establishment of the 'New Society' of the *'Nam'* at that time.

In the study, we learn that throughout the length and breadth of India, the causes of the ill-success of Aurangzeb's reign are not far to seek. His bigotry led him to reimpose the *Jizya* and to carry on a ruthless destruction of Hindu temples which were made for the reservation of the Hindu priests. His fanatical adherence to the Sunni creed made him equally hositile to the *Shias* from among them some of his best officers were recruited. His suspicious nature was fatal to his popularity. He could find no and was consequently badly served. It was his policy to play off one powerful noble against another, Hindus against Mussalmans, and to rule by an elaborate system of espionage this reliance on mere cunning as the principal instrument of state-craft proved quite inoperative in practice. His excessive distrust of officers and constant interference in the business of the different departments kept the local officers in a state of tutelage and destroyed their initiative and efficiency[39]. As the 'Deccan ulcer' noted elsewhere, ruined him and his empire[40]. Aurangzeb being a *Puritan Muslim* ruler observed piety to an extraordinary degree in all branches of life. He hated luxury, ease and pleasure. His private life was altogether blameless. Gaiety, singing, dancing and pleasures of life had no meaning for Aurangzeb. The court singers and dancers were dismissed. They carried a bier, weeping and wailing, under the windows of the Mughal Palace. Aurangzeb looked out and asked whose funeral it was. "Music is dead" without *'Nam'* they said, "and we are going to bury her." means *'soul'*. "Bury her deep," he exclaimed, "so that she may never rise agian." Thus on account of his indifference towards art and learning the *'Nam'* was decayed at the withdrawal of imperial patronage *'word'* not a single grand edfice, finely-written manuscript, or exquisite picture commemorates Aurangzeb's reign. In this way, art, music, dance and even poetry were his aversion. Thus, Aurangzeb did nothing for the cultural regeneration of the country and *'art'* again suffered[41] for a great period of study in India. On the other hand, in Akbar's reign, both art and literature received the due share of Akbar's attention and patronage. Among the great writers of his time were the two brothers *Faizi* and *Abul Fazal*, and three notable historians, *Badayuni, Ferishta* and *Nizam-ud-Din*. Akbar collected an enormous library comprising 24,000 manuscripts and great Hindu poet, Tulsi Das[42], flourished at his court. This brisk literary activity of the period was due to the royal patronage of literature as well as to the peace and prosperity which Akbar's reign secured.

In the study, we learn that *Baharvani* hymns are not a narrative of historical events like *Guru Govind* Singh's *Bachitra Natak* nor are they an indictment of Babar as his *Zaffarnamah* was that of Aurangzeb displayed the reality between the Hindu ruler of Deccan i.e. Shivaji Maharaja did. They were the outpourings of a compassionate soul at that time was touched by senses of human misery and the cruelty of Father was perpectrated by the foreign invaders of the Deccans. Like Franch, Britisher, etc. The sufferings of the people of India were rendered here in accents of intense power and protest. The events are placed in the larger social orders and historical perspective on the life of the common people of the Father. Moreover, moral character of the Brahminical thought had been declined by creating social evils in the society like caste system, untouchability, child marriage, crime against women, etc. Therefore, a corrupt political system led by the *Pandits* and *Molabis* must end in dissolution with the establishment of 'Law Rule'. But the lure of power in democrative set-up divided the men and violence unresisted tends to flourish, after the independence of India in 1947. The *Schedule Castes* and *Schedule Tribes* people were not benefited according to the ratio of race. In this context, it could not be wished away, by magic or socery of the *'Nam'* to check up the leaders of the period of different communities. Now, again, the faith of Guru Nanak, in the form of *'Baba Gurinder Singh ji'* has been established at Beas to check up the culprits and reiterated his faith in the Almighty and in his social justice. Yet so acute was his realization of the distress of the people that he could not resist for a long period of the Indian History and will not make any complaint against the Father. "When there was such suffering, such killing, such shrieking in pain, didst not thou O God, feel pity on the poor people of the creator, thou art the same for all!" The people for him were the people as a whole, both Hindus and Muslims, the high-caste and the low-caste, soldiers and civilians, men and women. These hymns are remarkable for their moral structure and poetical eloquence. Nowhere else in contemporary literature are the issues in medieval period of Indian history has comprehended the situation with such clarity or presented in tones of greater urgency[43] for the establishment of the 'New society of the New period' i.e. is called *' History of the Chamar Dynasty'*.

The fourth *Babarvani's* hymn is probably addressed to *Bhai Lalo,* one of *Guru Nanak's* devotees living at *Saidpur* itself. It ends on a prophetic note i.e. 'Dr. Raj Kumar, Department of History, Governemnt College For Women Parade, Jammu, alluding perhaps to the rise of Sher Khan, an Afghan of Sur, clam, who had already captured Bengal and Bihar, defeated Babar's son and successor, Humayan, at *Chausa* on the way to *Ganga* in June 1539 A.D. (during the lifetime of *Guru Nanak ji*), and who finally droved the Mughal kings out of India in the same year. The hymn in *Ti lang* measure is, like the other three an expression of imposition by the Mighty ruler of the *'Nam'* as already mentioned above. It is a statement also of his belief in God's justice and in the ultimate victory of good over evil[44]. Viewed against the rising power of Babar at that time in *Farghana* and in Kabul and Quandhar, the conditions prevailing in Pre-Mughal India as the establishment of the *'Doma Dynasty in Kashmir'*, whose rulers were Chak clans known as Mirza Haidar Dughlat (1499-1500 A.D.) and his mother was the younger sister of Babar's mother, the Mirza was the first cousin of the first Mughal emperor of India[45]. After this, the chain of Mughal invasions on India were commenced and the rule of *'Doma Dynasty'* was established in India; and its ruler were known as *Ravidas, Kabir, Guru Nanak, Babar, Akbar, Jahangir, Shah Jahan, etc.* In the study we again learn that there is no other source of history which describes the extent of 'reality' of the deaths and destruction in India during the time of Babar's invasions in India as does the *Babarvani* expresses.

Notes and References

1. Mr. Rama Jois; *Guruji and Social Harmony;* Karnataka; 2006 p. 47. Hereafter refered as *G.S.H.*
2. P. Jagadeeshan, *Social Justice and Challenges in Contemporary India;* Bangalore; 2006.
3. *G.S.H.* p. 47.
4. Sharan Kumar Limbale; *Towards as Aesthetic of Dalit Literature,* Tr. from Marathi by Alok Mukherjee, New Delhi, 2004, pp. 7-8.
5. Arun Mukerjee; *Post Colonialism; My Living,* Toronto 1998. p. 143.
6. **Note.** The sacred books of the Hindus include a wide range of religious literature composed in the Sanskrit language. They are divided into two classes, called *Sruti* and *Smriti.* The term *Smriti* means 'Memory', 'recollection', 'tradition', and the books denoted by *Smriti* are the accounts of the gods and goddesses composed in comparatively in modern times 'social justice' and a far treatment to the people constituting a new society. It presupposes a social order which non-discriminatory and people oriented, one in which disparity, inequality and inequity do not characterised social, economic and other aspects of life and institutions. The term occurs with due emphasis in our constitution. Its preamble proclaims the solemn resolve of the Indian people to secure to all its citizen "Justice, social, economic and political, shall inform all the institutions of the national life." We shall try to show how the origin and development of the caste system and untouchability in early north India has been instrumental in perpetrating social injustice to a large segment of the Indian people of the 'Nam'. The term *'Sruti'* or 'hearing' the 'voice of god' is that used to indicate what was directly heard by or was revealed to the holy sage of old *Sruti* is a thought of as existing from eternity, made known to the sages in time, and transmitted by them to their disciples, but not composed arranged by the Brahmans. Because Brahman has a destructive thought of allusion. The works indicated by the term *sruti* are the four *Vedas*. The term *Veda* is from the Sanskrit root *'vid'* 'to know', a root which also appears in the latin *'Videre'*, 'to see', and the English 'wit', *Veda* primarily signifies 'knowledge', it designates 'sacred lore', as a branch of literature; and applied to the book containing the sacred (A.A. Macdonell, *A History of 'Sanskrit Literature*, Heinemann, 1900, pp. 29, 34, 205). Discussing this Max Muller says that there is not one single allusion in the hymns of the *Rig-Veda* to anything connected with writing. Pure Brahmans never speak of their *Granthas* or books. They speak of their *Veda,* which means 'knowledge'. They speak of their *sruti,* which means what, they have heard with their ears. They speak of *smriti,* which means what their Fathers have declared into them. We meet with *Brahmanas,* i.e. the sayings of Brahmans; with *sutras,* i.e. the strings of rules, with Vedangas, i.e. the members of the *Veda;* with *pravachanas*, i.e. preachings; with *Sastras* i.e. teachings; with *Darsanas*, i.e. demonstrations, but we never meet with a book, or a volume, or a page (Max Muller, *Ancient Sanskrit literature* pp. 497, 512). They are not considered parts of the direct divine revelation (*Sruti*). Tradition (*Smriti*) begins with them. These aids to memory are not literature in any true sense of *'Nam'*. They are simply outline manuals for keeping alive in the pupils memory the details of the subjects that they deal with, the subjects of a Hindu Sanskrit students education. They were usually summed up under six heads, called the *Vedangas,* or 'members of the body' of the *Veda.* Of the six, *Kalpa,* ceremonial, is the most important for the *'Nam'*, including three groups of *Sutras;* the *Srauta Sutras,* which deal with sacrifices, summarizing the teaching of the Brahmans, the *Grihya* or *Smarta sutras;* which deal with the ceremonyes connected with family life; and the *Dharma Sastras*, which provide rules of conduct for the various classes of men and the various stages of the life. (J.N. Farquhar, *Primer of Hinduism; Christian Literature Society* of India, Madras; p. 59).
7. *G.S.H.* pp. 47-48.
8. *Ibid.*, p. 98.
9. Robin W. Winks (ed), *Historiography;* Oxford; 1999, Preface.
10. D.N Maclean; *Religion and Society in Arab Sindh,* Leiden, 1989. pp. 12-13. Note. Since the convesion from what he calls 'Hindu' religion "became possible toleration towards the *'New Society'*

because, one has to take the birth in any society, after this, he or she has to enter in the 'New society' as a struggle to obtain the 'ultimate truth' through the medium of *'Nam'* as a *hanji* to cross the ocean or *Samudra* or sea of the worldly life, As we have already discussed that worldly life is illusion else is nothing. Therefore, one must have, to serve the society as a 'welfare state' for the development of civilization. Similarly, the Brahman prince of Sind, Jaysiyah Dahir followed the *Sudras* as their forefather, because, they know the reality of world and his brother *Sassah*, converted to *'Islam as a New society'* at the invitation of the Calipa Umar b. Abd al-Aziz (*Ibid.* pp. 33, 48).

11. Alberuni's India; tr by Edward C. Sachan, London, Vol. 1 pp. 7, 21. Hereafter cited as *A.I.*
12. *Ibid.,* p. 19.
13. Zia-ud-din Barani, *Tarikh-i-Firuz Shahi* Reprint, 1982 (*Kitab Mahal*) India, pp. 295-303. Henceforth discussed as *T.F.S. Note.* Barani made certain references about the territorial expansion and other dimensions of the *'New Islamic Culture'* which was based on the theory of *'Word'* or *'Nam'* or *'Chamar'*.
14. Arvind Sharma, *'Of Hindu, Hindustan, Hinduism* and *Hindutva', Numen;* Vol. 49, p. 9.
15. *Adi Granth*; P. 954. See, *Atamn-Gian,* written by Sardar Bahadur Maharaj Jagat Singh Ji, Amritsar (Punjab) India; 2000, p. 22.
16. Iqtidar Alam Khan, *Akbar's Personality Traids and World Outlook, A Critical Reappraisal:,* Study material provided in 13th-3 week Refresher Course in History. Academic Staff College Jamia Millia Islamia-New Delhi, 2005 p. 53. An article.
17. S. Inayat A. Zaidi; *Fads and Foibles; Perception of Administrative Traits of the Mughal State;* Study material provided in 13th-3 week Refresher Course in History. Academic Staff College Jamia Millia Islamia-New Delhi, 2005, p. 60.
18. *Guru Granth Sahib;* p. 417.
19. Harbans Singh, *Encyclopaedia of Sikhism;* Punjab University, Patiala; 1992; p. 238. Henceforth mentioned as *E.S.*
20. *Guru Granth Sahib*, p. 360.
21. *Ibid.,* pp. 417-18
22. *Ibid.,* pp. 722-23
23. Dr. Fauja Singh, *History of Punjab* (1000-1526 A.D.), Vol.III, Punjab University Patiala, 1988, p. XX.
24. *E.S.* p. 242.
25. Dr. Kirpal Singh; *The Adi Guru Granth as a Source of History;* Patiala, 1998. pp. X-XI. Hereafter cited as *A.G.G.S.H.*
26. *Ibid.*
27. W.H Meleod, *Guru Nanak and the Sikh Religion, Sikhs and Sikhism;* Part I New Delhi, 1999, p. 4.
28. *Ibid.* pp. 132-33.
29. *Ibid.* p. 3.
30. John Keay; *India; A History; Delhi* p. 180.
31. Syed Mohammad Latiff; *History of Punjab*; New Delhi; 1964, p. 123.
32. *Memoirs of Zahiruddin Babar*; Tr. by John Leyden and William Erskine, revised by John Lucas King; Oxford University of Press; 1921 Vol. II, p. 182. Hereafter referred as M.Z.B.
34. *A.G.G.S.H.,* p. 64.
35. *Guru Granth Sahib;* p. 1412.
36. *M.Z.B.* Vol. II, p. 140.
37. *Ibid.* Note. The Bikram Year 1578 (1521 A.D.) When this invasion occured. This prophecy was routed out in the Mughals rulers of the *'Nam'* was took place in the Bikrami year 1595 (1540 A.D) by *Sher Shah Suri*. Sher Shah Suri was the most capable, unscrupulous and ambitious man in the whole Afghan party, had joined the rebels even during the last days of Babar although the latter had bestowed on him many marks of favour and given him several *parganas* and put him in command in the east." In this statement, it indicates that *Sher Shah Suri* looked upon Mughals with great contempt as again express his following views, "If fortune favours me I can drive these Mughals back out of Hindustan; they are not our superiors in war, but we let slip the power that we had by reason of our dissensions. Since I had been the Mughals, I have observed their conduct and found them lacking in order and discipline. While those who profess to lead them in pride of birth and rank neglect the duties of supervision and leave everything to officials whom they blindly trust. These subordinates act corruptly in every case i.e. *'Nam'*, they are led by lust of gain and make no distinction between soldiers and civilians, foe or friend". (S.R. Sharma; *The Crescent in India—A Study in Medieval India*; Bombay; 1937, p. 279. Hence forth cited as C.I.S.M.I.
38. Virendra Sethi; *Mira Prem Dewani* Punjab (Jalandhar), 16th edition, 2001. pp. 12,13,14,15.
39. G.S Kapoor. *History of India Mughal Period* (1526-1707); New Delhi, Reprint 1984, pp. 281-82. Hence forth cited as *H.I.M.P.*
40. Authentic facts about the lives of saints are rarely available, according to a biographical note given in the introduction of Tulsi Sahib's *Ratan Sagar* (1909), he came from a noble of Brahmin family during the time of *Akbar*. In early boyhood, he developed an aversion to worldly life, renounced

everything and became a recluse. Eventually, he settled in *Hathras.* This version makes no mention of his original name the names of his parents or the place of his birth. In the biographical note given in the beginning of Tulsi Sahib *Ghat Ramayan* (1911), it is stated that he was born in 1763 A.D., and expired at the age of 80, in 1843 A.D. He was the eldest son of the king of Doona. The word king has been used for *Peshwa.* The *Peshwas,* to begin with, were the chief administrative officers of the kings Shivaji's Empire. The great *Maharatha* leader, Shivaji was the son of Shahji. Bhousle and was born, according to Sir. J.N Sarkar. On April 10, 1627, in the hill fort of *Shivner* near *Junnar* to the South of Poona. His mother was *Jigabai* who was the daughter of Jadhav Rao, the greatest Maharatta *Jagirdar* of his time. Thus, Shivaji was connected with very high Maharatha families both from his father's and mother's sides. J.N. Sarakar says, "the want of book-learning, therefore, did not leave his mind a dull and sterile soil, nor impair his efficiency as a man of action in a world that was medieval". Gifted with a keen faculty of observation, he took a great interest in examining horses and amunitions of war, and asked questions about the political affairs. Thus his tutor, the old Brahman Tulsi Dass, brought him up as an orthodox Hindu, Carefully impressing upon him the duties of protecting the Hindu religion from the insults heaped upon it by the Muslims. Guru Ram Dass (1534-1581 A.D.) *Tuka Ram* were, Shivaji's spiritual preceptor, had also a very strong hand in moulding the character of Shivaji. He always advised Shivaji to put in his best efforts to cement all the Maharattas into a bond of union. The Guru instilled into his mind a love of Hindu religion and charged him with the duty of protecting the cow and the Brahman *'Word'* the only cry that could appeal powerfully to his contemporaries, *Guru Ram Dass.* His contact also with Hindu sages convinced him of the necessity of doing something for the protection and regeneration of Hinduism. The *Guru mantra* i.e. *'Nam'* or *'Word'* or *'Chamar.'* or the sacred formula with the Guru whispered into his ears called *'inner voice'* or *'Dalit Voice'* by Dr. B.R. Ambedkar, was the love of his country and religion. "Mother and mother country are dearer than heaven itself. Gods, and cows, Brahmans and the faith, these are to be protected fro the civlizational growth. Therefore, God has raised you up, when faith is dead then Father came in life; death is better than life in life time, why live when religion has perished? Gather ye, therefore, the *Maharathas* together; make the Dharma live again; for otherwise our forefathers will laugh at us from heaven. Thus, their teachings drove Shivaji to oppose the Mughals characters and statemanship at that time, we can safely conclude that Aurangzeb was the very antitheiss of Akbar. The one was born to rule an empire, the other to lose one, the one built the structure, the other destroyed it. In course of time, they became all powerful and virtual soverigns of the state. They made Poona their headquarters while the kings remained titular heads and stayed the town of *Satara.* Tulsi Das was Brahmin by caste and his name was *Shyam Rao.* Against his own wishes, he was married by his father at an early age to a girl called *Lakshmi Bai.* He had one son through this marriage. His father, a spiritually inclined man, wanted to renounce his throne in favour of his won in order to spend the rest of his life in devotion. Shyam Rao, himself averse to worldy pursuits, ran away from the palace the day before the date fixed for his coronation. All search proving futile, his younger brother *'man'* or theory of *Mind* was made the king as per their ideas. Shyam Rao kept wandering in forests, mountains towns and cities for many years and ultimately came to *Hathras,* where he settled for the rest of his life. Here he came to be known as *Tulsi Sahib.* He came from the south, and was popularly known as *Dakhani Baba,* which means 'Sage from the South." On one of his visits to *Agra,* in october 1817, Tulsi Sahib happened to reach Seth Dilwali Singh's house when precious the western Ghats and the sea means *Samudar* or *Sudar* in Sanskrit. Thus thought or *'Nam'* is ocean which has no depth and unlimited known as the Konkan; Goa; (2) the *Mavala* country covered by the *Sahyadri* ranges; and (3) the plateau on eastern side, called Desh, consisting of the vast black soil plain which are waiting for the life for a very long period of the Indian history. The physical features of this country of the Mahrattas developed certain peculiar qualifies among the Maharathas which distinguished them from the rest of the people in India. The mountainous nature of the country has not only given the Mahrathas security from outside the invaders, but has also produced a climate which influenced their character and habits. The hill forts in these mountains have played an important part in the Mahratha history, and it is with their help that the Maharattas have successfully defended the invaders from the north of Kashmir. (*H.I.M.P.* pp. 284, 285). Religious revival were Kabir, Guru Nanak, the most famous of them were Tukaram, his father was *Bolhoba* and his father *Kankai. Bolhoba* was a *Mahajan* (Village Chieftain) and as such possessed a large piece of prime agriculture land. He supported his family with the earnings from his own land. In those days, however, a grain seller was considered to be low born, and as such he was looked an important role in bringing about the downfall of the Mughal empire of India. "Mahrathas were the determined enemies of Aurangzeb. His war against them lasted for nearly a quarter of a century and resulted nothing out of it, but defeat, humiliation and disaster for *Aurangzeb*. The real leader of the Mahrathas, who infused a fresh life and vigour into them and united the scattered elements of their race, was as pointed out above, Shivaji, a born military commander and an administrator of undoubted genius." In this chapter, an attempt has been made to give the details of the rise of the Mahratta power in Deccan and the institutions which they built up under Shivaji for the governance of the people in their charge was the *'Nam' or 'Word'*. Firstly, geography has played an important part in the making of the Mahratta nation. The *Mahratha* country *'Word'*. the *Maharashtra 'Chamar'* is very different in nature from the north. It is that part of the Deccan which is enclosed on two sides by the *Sahyadri* range or Western Ghats running from the north to the South, and the Vindhya and *Satpura* ranges running from the east to the West. The southern side is a zig-zag frontier which may be indicated by an irregular line drawn from Nagpur to Goa. This region, about 500 miles in length, is naturally divided into three section: (1) the coast at strip between the silk garments embroidered with gold and silver lace, expensive shawls and woollens had been laid out in the sun on the terrace. It used to be a practice in North India to spread precious silk and woollen garments in the sun for a short while during the months of September and October, to protect them from insects. *Tulsi Sahib,* whose feet were smeared with the mud and sludge of the street, due to the previous day's rain, went upto the terrace. Seeing the *Master,* the mother of *Seth Dilwali Singh* and other ladies were overjoyed. Tulsi Sahib said, "Oh, I am sorry, I have spoiled your precious garments." At this *Seth Dilwali Singh's* mother humbly replied, "No, Sahibji, nothing has been spoiled. Rather, you have blessed us with *darshan*. Vision, sight or interview, especially looking at a holy person with devotion. Everything belongs to you; what is ours in them?" Seeing her devotion, Tulsi Sahib said," I am very pleased with you. Ask for anything and I shall be happy to give it." "The devotees of Tulsi Sahib used to call him *"Sahib"* or *Sahibji* i.e. *'Nam', 'Bai Guru', 'Allah*, etc. (J.R. Puri and V.K Sethi; *Tulsi Sahib Saint of Hathras;* Punjab (India); Third edition (revised) 1995; pp. 1,2,3,5. *H.I.M.P* pp. 288, 289). According to Hiuen Tsang in the middle of the 7th century A.D. "The manners of the Mahrathas are simple and honest. They are proud and reserved. If any one is kind to them he may be sure of their gratitude, but if any one injures them, they will take their revenge and risk their life to wipe out their dishonour. If any one in distress appeals to them, they will leave aside all thoughts of self in their anxiety to help. Even if they have an insult to avenge, they never fail to warn their army. In battle if they pursue the fugitives, they always spare all who surrender. There men love study and there are many heretics among them." "To the Hindu world in that age of renewed persecution, Shivaji appeared as the star of a new hope, the protector of the ritualistic paint mark (*Tilak*) on the forehead of the Hindus and the saviour of the Brahmans." Before his rise, the *Mahratta* rafe was scattered like atoms through many Deccani Kingdoms. He whelded them into a mighty nation and he achieved this in the teeth of the opposition of four mighty forces like the Mughal Empire, Bijapur, Portugucese India, and the *Abyssinians* of Janjiran. No other Hindu has shown such capacity in modern times," According to J.N. Sarkar. The history of the Mughal Empire in India cannot be complete without the reference to the rise of the Mahrathas under their leader Shivaji, who and his successors played under their followers was *Bhakti*. Their teachings, therefore, called forth the devotional fervour of the people and lifted them out of the slough of despair and despondency. The movement was not an orthodox revival of religion, but it was popular and democratic because, as already said before, their saints and teachers came from the lower order of society. Hence, their teachings were in the nature of a protest against ritualism and caste distinctions and thereby served to promote their social solidarity which was widely spread by the historians of the *'Nam' like Banani, Ibn Battuta,* etc. (*H.I.M.P. p 286*). In the study, we learn that every one opposed the caste system and other social evils like *'Untouchability'*, etc. loud the teachings of *Kabir, Ravidas, Guru Nanak*, etc, because of the repudiated the caste system as hierarchy by the Brahmanical people in the ruling system since a long period of India history against the downtrodden, but they could not understand that an *untouchable* is a force of Nature, which cannot be corroupt morally and financially like that of Brahmans of the period who governed the system without keeping in view, the idea of the late Dr. B.R. Ambedkar, known as the "architect" of the constitution of India down upon by the learned priestly class *Bolhoba* was essentially a religious man, and although busy as a merchant farmer, he was also deeply deovted to the family deity known as *Vittal* or *Panduranga*. In fact, his entire family was noted for their devotion to God or *'Nam'*. Tukaram inherited this legacy. Having turned his face towards God. Tukaram started studying holy books and the writings of the past times such as *Namdev, Dnyaneshwar*, *Kabir* and *Eknath*. He also saw the great importance of keeping the company of living saints and listening to their teachings. (Chandravati Rajwade, *Tukaram, The Ceaseless Song of Devotion*; Punjab

(India) third edition (revised) 2004 pp. 7,11,12). *Ram Dass, Vaman Pandit and Akhath 'Words'* all of whom launched a crusade against the caste system, and other social evils which were widely spread by the Brahmanical ideology existing abuses of religion and preached the gospel of *Bhakti* or personal devotion to God. The laid stress upon the equality of all men before God and held that by means of *Bhakti*, a *Sudra,* or a *Candala* could qualify himself for God's favour quite as much as a Brahman their doctrine made no distinction between the high and the low, and the only bond which means created of soul as an *Annami* person of his time, who was instrumental in reserving the jobs and other facilities under the central and state governments of India for *'Scheduled Castes* and *Scheduled Tribes,'* acknowledged on several occasions that the teachings of Kabir had greatly influenced his own character and public career. His father, *Subhedar* Major Ramji Maloji Ambedkar, was a *Kabir Panthi* who started his life as a soldier in the 106th sappers and was later transferred to the 107th Pioneers. He was religious minded from the beginning of his career, but became a teetotaller and vegetarian after joining the *Kabir Panth.* Every morning and evening the Subhedar-Major used to have devotional services at his home as a domestic priest of the Ved period at which Kabir and Tukaran's verses were sung. He insisted on all the family being present on both occasions, especially for the evening services. Dr. Ambedkar used to say that his father sang those hymns with such depth of devotion that everyone who heard him was moved to the core and the impression left on the minds of the children was remembered throughout their lives. "This writer's grandfather, who was a Subhedar-Major in 23rd Maralha (Outran) Rifles, had a large number of Kabir Panthis in his regiment, and theyused to organise recitals of Kabir's songs every evening. The refrain *'Kahat Kabeer Suno bhaai- Saadho'* (Says Kabir, listen, O Sadhus) heard during my childhood days, continued to ring in my ears till I reached the lotus feet of my master at Beas, who made clear to me the mystic meaning of Kabir's teachings (Isaac A. Ezekiel; *Kabir, The Great Mystic;* Punjab (India) 6th edition; 2003 p. 309-Henceforth written as K.G.M.)

43. *E.S.,* pp. 238-39.

44. *Ibid.,* p. 241.

45. M.L. Kapoor; *History of Kashmir;* Jammu, 1979 p. 121. Hereafter described as *H.K.*

1

Early History of the Untouchables

Origin of the Untouchability

In the study; we learn that the practice of untouchability was started to begin with the Brahminical rule in India as Ludwig suggests that there is a hint at Caste *man* or rather living *man* or at least the incipient conception of caste *'Word'* or *'Nam'* in the hymn to Ushas (Rig-Veda 1136), where it is said that goddess "arousing one to wield the royal power, another to follow after fame, another to the pursuit of wealth, another to perform services, awakes all creatures to go their different paths of life[1]." There are a few characteristic verses called from various hymns will be more interesting and instructive than descriptions detached from the tents:

"The shining Ushas has been perceived; she has opened the doors (of the sky); setting in motion all living things, she has revealed to us treasures of the Nature (the golden treasures of light that were awakened all creatures (1., 113,4). God, she hastens on, arousing footed creatures, and makes the birds fly aloft (1, 48,5). Chamas, the birds fly up from their nests and men seeking food leave their homes (1, 124.12). Brahmana (arousing) the prostrate sleeper to move, (impelling) one to enjoyment another to the pursuit of wealth, (enabling) those who see but a little way to see for, God (arousing) one to wield the royal power, another to perform services, Ushas awakes all creatures to go their different paths in life (I, 113,5.6). Word in as much as thou hast made Agni to be kindled at night (for the morning worship) Nam and hast awakened the men who are to sacrifice, though hast done goods (I, 113.9). word, she has yoked (her heroes), from the remote rising place of Surya; 'Word' is everything that moves bows down before her glance; the active goddess creates light; by her appearance the magnificant daughter of the sky drives away our hates. Ushas has repelled our enemies i.e. manas. In thee when thon dawnest is the life and breath of all creatures of the nature." (1., 48, 7-10).

The dispeller of enemies *'Nam'* not only of the powers of darkness, but also of thieves and other malefactors who were sheltered by darkness, of bad dreams, phantoms, spells, and all the evil brood of darkness called *Krishnag rabhaha*, is quite naturally likened to a warrior brandishing weapons. But rarely, the poets dwell almost entirely on the lovely and even the pathetic aspects of the favourite. And, indeed there is no lack of pathos and sadness in the conception of a beauteous and gracious being who, herself immortal and every youthful, though old as time, serenely and inevitably, in obedience to the highest low i.e. called *'Nam'* or *'Chamar'* (she is "the preserver of *Rita*", born in *Rita*.") as *Rig-Veda* philosophy both prolongs and shortens life, each new day being both her gift to men and the tribute she levies on the sum of days. The pathos is deepend if the bringer of food and joy, the dispenser of life and death, is herself a mortal, a creature of a day[2], and other important deities of the upper realm of light are *Surya,* the Illuminator; *Savitri*, the Enlivener; *Pushau,* the Nourisher; *Vishnu Urukrama,* the wide-striding sun; the *Asvins or* the *Nasatyas*, perhaps the morning and Evening stars, later the gods of healing, paralled to the *Dioscuri*; and *Ushas*, the lovely Goddess of the Dawn[3], nay, of an hour, *Ushas* is said to display herself like a dancer who decks herself with ornaments. Allusion is made to the living going forth to dance and laugh after a funeral. Drums are mentioned and a hymn in the *Atharva-Veda* is addressed to that musical instrument[4].

It is reflected between the world of *'Light'* above and the earth below lies the realm of the air, and the chief dieties of this region are, besides *Indra,* the *Maruts* (Strom Gods), *Vayu* and *Vata* (The wind Gods), *Rudra (*the Howling God of Strom and Lightning), and *Parijanya* (the God of Rain). Of the terrestrial deities, the chief are *Agni*, Soma and Sarasvati. *Agni,* or the Fire-God, received special homage because no sacrifice could be performed without offerings to him. The libation of *Soma* was also regarded later as the Goddess of learning of the three principal deities of the later mythology, *Vishnu* and *Rudra* (Siva) are, as we have seen already, known to the *Rig-Veda* and Brahma, though not explicitly mentioned, has his precursors in *Vidhatri* (the ordainer), *Hiranyagrbhaha* (the Germ of Gold), Prajapati (the Lord of Creatures) and Brahmanaspati (the Lord of Prayer[5]).

As one of many as brilliant and as ophemeral as herself, as she needs must be if each day is thought as having a dawn to itself. In the hymns to *Ushas* we find her addressed and referred to almost in one breath both as the one everreturning or born again, and as the fleeting unit of an endless series:

"God as thou wast invoked by the poets of old Chams reward our praise also, O Ushas, with gifts and with brilliant light! (I. 48,14)."

"Maintaining the ordinances of the gods, but wasting away the lives of men, Ushas has shone forth, the last of the numerious Dawns that are past, and the first of those that are coming (I., 124, 2)

"Shine on us with thy best rays, O divine ushas; give us a long life! (VII, 77.5)

"Ushas has downed before ; let her now down again in the form of moon (I, 48,3)

"Born again and again, though ancient, shining with an ever uniform hue, shewastes away the life of mortals as a clever gambler the stakes with Duropadi i.e. soul (1, 92, 10).

"Ushas follows the track of the Dawns that are past and is the first of the unnumbered Dawns that are to come from the heavan down on earth for the sake of Brahmans. How great is the interval that lies between the Dawns that have arisen and those which are yet to arise again for the settling of the account of the same? Ushas yearns longingly after the former Dawns and gladly goes on shining with the others (that are to come). Those mortals are gone who saw the earliest Ushas down; we shall gaze upon are to behold her on future morns. To begin with the Englightenment period perpetually in former days did the divine Ushas dawn; and now to-day the radiant goddess became upon this world; un decaying immortal, 'Word' which is naturalistic itself" (L,113),

The hymn from which the last extract is taken (I.,113) is the longest and most sustainenedly beautiful of those addressed to the "desire of all men," *'Word'* that which closes with the magnificant *finale*, the grandest lyrical effusion in the whole Rig-Veda:

"Rise! Our life, our breath has come back! The darkness is gone, the light approaches! Ushas has opened a path for Surya to travel; we have reached the point where our days are lengthend. The priest, the poet, celebrating the brightening Ushas, arises with the web of his hymn; shine, therefore, magnificent Ushas, on him who praises thee because nature is a 'ultimate reality'. Mother of the gods! manifestation of Aditi! banner of the sacrifice, mighty Ushas, shine forth! Arise! lend a gracious ear to prayer, giver of all boon!" (I, 113, 16-30[6]).

There is an important characteristic of *Vedic* Mythology, is the predominance of the male element. Goddess like *Prithivi*, *Aditi*, *Ushas* and Sarasvati occupy a very subordinate position. In this respect the Vedic Civilization presents a contrast to the Prehistoric Culture of the Indus Valley, where the Mother Goddess is co-equal with her male partner. But there is one more important feature of the Vedic religion is the tendency towards monotheism and even monism. The hymns foreshadow the idea of universal unity[7] i.e *'Kalma'*, *'Nam'*, *'Word'* which has been expressed by all the saint of the world in the holy text books as Dr. B.R Ambedkar reflected the idea of *'Class less'* and *'Casteless'* in the Indian constitution which is the very ancient idea of the Ancient Indian History spread by the Mayuran ruler like Asoka etc, and express the belief that 'God is one' although he bears many names.

"They call him Indra, Mitra, Varuna, and Agni; he is the heavenly bird Gurumat:

To what is one, the poets give many a name, they call it Agni, Yama, Matarisvan."

The monotheistic conception appears more prominently in the hymns addressed to *Hiranyagarbhaha* (the Gold Germ), and to *Visvakarman* (the All-creating).

"Who is our Father, our Creator, Maker, who every place doth know and every creature, By whom alone to gods their names were given, To him all other creatures go, to ask him." Finally, we have a song of creation according to which in the beginning.

"Word' or 'Chamar' neither death nor deathlessness existed;

Of day and night there was yet no distinction.
Alone that one breath calmly, self supported,
Other than It was none, nor aught above[8] It".

It appears that sacrifices occupy a prominent place in the Vedic ritual which deal by the Brahmans that looking to the history of human civilization and the rituals of the Hindus, there is nothing to justify the belief that in ancient times the Hindu were incapable of sacrificing human beings to their gods referred as under:

1. *That the Sunahsepa hymns of the Rig-veda most probably refer to a human sacrifice*

2. *That the Aitareya Brahmana refers to an actual and not a typical human sacrifice.*
3. *That the Purusamedha originally required the actual sacrifice of men.*
4. *That the Satapatha Brahmana sanctions human sacrifice in some cases, though it makes the Purusamedha emblematic.*
5. *That the Taittiriya Brahmana enjoins the sacrifice of a man at the Horse sacrifice.*
6. *That the Puranas recognise human sacrifices to Chandika or Durga, but prohibit the Purusamedha rite.*
7. *That the Tantras enjoin human victims are not available, the effigy of a human being should be sacrificed to her[9]. These mostly include offerings of milk, grain, ghee, flesh and Juice of the Soma plant. The use of material objects as symbols of deities was perhaps not altogether unknown, and one passage apparently makes a reference to an image or symbol of Indra. The symbol of phallic worship is, as we have seen, detected by some in the allusions to the Sisnadevas.[10]*

Keeping in view, regarding the life after death, the *Rig-Vedic* hymns have no consistent theory. According to some passages, the dead dwell in the realm of Yama, whereas the theory of *'Nam'* expresses that *'die to live'* in the *'Nam'* is the *'Ultimate Reality'* i.e. is also known twice-born among *Dalit*, the beneficent king of the departed from earth to heaven. Now, their idea till date which is known as metem psychosis is, however, not yet developed, and it has been observed in the lecture of *'Dalit* and Dr. B.R Ambedkar', delivered by Dr. Vivek Kumar, from the Delhi University in the Sociology Department, University of Jammu. In this very lecture, it has been seen by the Master that the Pupil that the philosophers have uplifted their hands and talking about the worshipping upturned eyes, amid the glories of the awakening. Eden-like nature *Brahmana* and we long for a burst of Wagner's song and harmony. It seems as though nothing short of Brynhild's waking invocation, "Hail, O Sun", could worthly render the grandeur, simplicity and whole-hearted adoration in this archaic ode. Nor is the association farfetched. For *Brynhild's* and *Sigfrid* are originally the Sun-and-Dawn lovers of Teutonic mythology, as is now fully understood by the veriest dabbler in music and folk-lore[11] as sung by the *Mahashah's* and *Candalas during* the Brahminical rule.

Ethics of the Chandala's Under Manu

Term *Chandala* in Punjabi language called *Chanal,* whom all Sanskrit authorities[12] is here evidently used for a person belonging to the inferior castes from which to this day the watchman known as *dumb* or *dumba* and other village menials are taken in Kashmir. Nothing withstanding their low social status, *Dumbs* and men of related castes are generally superior to the ordinary villagers in natural intellect and energy[13]. Manu also cites examples of some important personalities, who took recourse to such things as their *apaddarma.* We are informed that "the hungry saga *Ajigarta* of having attempted to kill his son (*Sunahsepa*) in order to appease his hunger (with his flesh) was not associated with the sin (of child killing). To famished *Vamadeva,* the knower of sin and virture, for having wished to eat dog's flesh in order to avoid death from starvation, was not associated with the sin (of eating dog's flesh). Oppressed by hunger in a lonely forest the (holy) *Bharadvaja* of great austerity, together with son was not associated with the sin (of taking vile gifts) for having accepted the gift of a large number of kine from *Vrdhu* who was a carpenter. Oppressed by hunger, the holy *Visvamitra* i.e. *'Word'* or *'Nam'*, the knower of merits and demerits, of the human deeds and actions, for accepted the gift of the flesh of the dog's thigh from the hands of a *Candala* or *Chamar* who was not associated with sin. It is noteworthy that according to the *Mahabharata*, the *'Canalala'* or *'Chamar'* did not offer the meat to the 'Father'. It was *Visvamitra* who himself insisted on having it, although the *Candala* repeatedly asked him not to do so[14] but he could not act on the instruction of the Master. But, *Vishvamitra* in the history of *Dharmasastra;* it is mentioned in X. 108, who took from a *Candala*'s hand a dog's leg[15].

In this connection the dialogue, once held between a *candala* and sage *Visvamitra,* attracts over attention. It is said in the *Santi Parva* that once upon a time, at the end of the *Treta Yuga* and before the beginning of the *Dvapara Yuga*, reins did not pour for twelve consecutive years, rivers, lakes, streams and other water reservoirs dried up. Consequently crops were destroyed and famine took place. Many people starved to death. Population decayed. Robbers raised up their heads and began looting the people and thus complete disorder and chaos crept in. Under these circumstances *Visvamitra* and his family members also could get nothing to eat and live upon. Leaving in wife and children, *Visvamitra* went to a colony of *Candalas* in search of food. In one house, he saw a piece of a recently slain dog's thigh and decided to steal it in order to appease his hunger. The *Candala* whom the sage had taken to be sleeping was, in fact, awake and he caught him red-handed. After knowing that the thief was no other than the famous sage *Visvamitra,* the *Candala* repeatedly told him not to commit a great sin by eating. The flesh and that too of a dog's thigh. But the sage would not listen to him by arguing that the cows drink water, even though the frogs keep on croaking. An authority in the matters of Dharm, the sage told him not to interfere. He said that in *apattikala*, self-preservation was the highest law and it justified recourse to all sorts of means fair for foul, commended or condemned, with a view to saving one's life. He took away the meat and offered the same to gods. After doing all these things he actually ate up the meat[16].

In the *Mahabharata,* eating the flesh of a dog has been strictly prohibited and highly condemned. According to it a "dog is less clean than a jackal. The haunch, again of a dog is a much worse part than other parts of his body because, he eats dirthy things in everyday day today life. The dog is certainly an unclean food to the members of the regenerate class." (Maha. *Santi,*pp. CXL1, 56-7, 68, 81 & 87[17]).

Manu also lays down the duties and professions that members of the four *varanas* i.e. a *Brahmana* should not live in the kingdom, ruled by a *Sudra*. Professor Nilakanta Shastri points out that a Tamil poem contains an interesting reference to the "Very famous" Nandas "Victorious in war, who having accumulated treasure first in beautiful Pataliputra hid it in the waters of Ganges." Hiuen Tsang, the famous Chinese pilgrim of the seventh century A.D. refers to "the five treasures of King Nanda's seven precious substances[18]." The accumulation of an enormous amount of wealth, to which all our authorities bear witness, probably implies a good deal of financial extortion and it is not surprising that the Nanda contemporary of Alexander was detested and held cheap by his subjects as he rather took after his father than conducted himself as the occupant of a throne[19]." Further, certain medieval inscriptions and the *Divyavadana* affirm that he was *Ksatriya*, although it is probable, as the Greek writer Justin deposes, Candra Gupta was born in *"humble life"*. This expression would suggest that he was not a prince, but a mere commoner ruler without any direct title to the crown of Magadha[20].

From the above passage, it makes clear from the statement that Manu is not in favour of the *Sudra* rulers, therefore, *Sudra* rules had their own thought to live on this earth. There are many historical examples of non-*Ksatriya* rulers in Ancient India. *Mahapadmananda,* the founder of Nanda dynasty was a *Sudra* and has been referred as *"Sudragarbhodbhava[21]"*. *Pusyamitra Sunga,* a Brahmana belonged to Bhimika family and the *Senapati* of Brihadratha, the last Mauryan King, killed the latter, and founded the *Sunga* dynasty. *Kanvas* and *Kadambas* also were *Brahmanas*. There is no undisputed record of a *Vaishy* ruler in ancient India[22].

Decline of Vaisyas and Advance of Sudras

In the study, it indicates that *Varna* system was modified not only by the rise of the various strata of landed gentry connected with administration, but also by the change in the relative position of the *Vaisyas* and *Sudras*. In post-Gupta period; the *Sudras* no longer appear mainly as slaves, artisans and agricultural labourers; they take the place of *Vaisya* cultivators[23]. Hiuen Tsang has clearly stated that the *Sudras* were agriculturised[24]. Alberuni notes the absence of any significant difference between the *Vaisyas* and the *Sudras,* who lived together in the same town and village and mixed together in the same house[25]. This change is reflected in medieval texts, which represent the *Sudras* as farmers and agriculturists. The *Skanda Purana* describes the *Sudra* as giver of grain (*annadana*) and householder (*grhastha*). The *Abhidhanacintamani* of *Hemachandra* defines farmers and cultivators as *Kutumbins*. In our times *Sudra* castes called *Kurmis* in Uttar Pradesh and Bihar and *Kunbis* in Maharashtra are apparently the descendants of the medieval *Kutumbins*[26].

From the beginning of the Christian era the *Smritis* of the later Vedic period, however, divided the Hindu society into innumerable castes, some claiming to be superior to others with varying customs and usages which have brought about in equality, resulting in discrimination against certain classes of the people, the worst of it being the practice of untouchability with all the incidental inhuman and humiliating treatment meted out to those regarded as untouchables, the question that naturaly arises is, were all these sanctioned by *Dharma?* It is not so. The very expression *'Dharma'* is opposed to and inconsistent with any such social inequality. The relevant provisions of the *Shruti* (Vedas) which are the primordial source of Dharma, unquivocally declare equlity of all human beings and leave no room for doubt that discrimination on the ground of birth was sanctioned by Brahmans, otherwise there was no Vedic sanction; on the other hands, such discrimination on the bases of occupation was plainly opposed in the Early Vedic Period. Charter of equality (*Samanata*) is found incorporated in the *Rig-ved* the most ancient of the Vedas and also in the *Atharvananveda.* It is also mentioned in (*Rig-veda-Mandala*-5-*Sukta*-60, *Mantra*-5), no one is superior (*ajyestaso*) or inferior (*akanishtasa*). All are brothers (etc. *bhrataraha*). All should strive for the interest of all and should progress collectively (*Sowbhagaya Sam Va Vridhuhu*). Again in (*Rigveda-Mandala*-10, Sukta-191, Mantra-4), there is a resolution of oneness, hearts and minds[27] with the help of *'Word' or 'Nam'*. Let the strength to live with mutual co-operation be to be built up. Moreover, all have equal rights to articles of food and water. All human beings are born free and equal in dignity and right in the message of God. They are endowed with reason and conscience and should act towards one another in a spirit of brotherhood. By the 6th century A.D. the *Vaisyas* practically loose their identity as a peasant caste. The *Skanda Purana* predicts that *Sudras* would decline in the *Kaliage* i.e. Iron Age, that some would admit oilmen and wheat owners of grain (*landulakarinah*), in that some would seek refuge with the *rajaputras,* and were with all kinds of *Varanas*[28]. By the 11th century A.D; they were to be treated as *Sudars* ritually and legally, for Abreuni's notes that both *Vaisyas* and *Sudras* are punished with the amputation of talent for reciting vedic texts[29]. As *Sudras,* the Vaisyas seem to have been well off till the 5th century A.D. When Fa-Haien speaks of their clarifies in dawning terms. But in the post- Gupta period; they suffered in tradition on account of decline in trade. There is another interesting evidence to show that from the 8th centruy A.D. trade and commerce was declined in Bengal and that traders lost their trade[30]. Due to this historical fact, the *Namesudras* of Bengal are not an occupation as cultivators, fishermen, boatmen, carpenters, barber, shoemakers, etc. They are regarded as *"untouchables"* by the higher castes of Bengal, and only a generation ago were known by the name of *Candala.* No doubt, they are a somewhat backward community with rather low level of culture, who cannot point to any intellectual eminence or historical distinction away their forefathers in the immediate or distant past. But they are justified in rejecting the name of *Candala* for their community as the *Candalas* of the *Dharmasastras* were men who lived outside the pale of civilization and settled life, and found maintenance from the most despised occupations. The word *Sudra* was often loosely used by ancient writers to denote all those who did not belong to the three higher *Varanas;* there was always distinction between those who had come or were coming under Aryan influence, the *Sudra* proper, and these, sometimes called the fifth *Varna*, who were two savage and uncleaner to be emendable to Aryan culture and practices, the *Nisadas, Candalas, Pukkasas,* etc. of the *Dharmsastra.* Among the *Sudras,* too, there soon developed a distinction between those who followed the ideals and initated the practices of the higher castes, the "good" *Sudras,* and those whose touch made unpure the water of the Brahmana, and to whom a good Brahman would not act as a priest. The promotion of the *Namasudras* from the status of *Candalas* to that of second class *Sudras* is quite natural and is the consequence of the improved culture and way of living they adopted. It was with the object of emphasising the fact that they were no longer *Candala*, that they adopted the name ending of *Sudras*, though they were originally called *'Namas'*[31] or *'Words'* of the Father.

This peculiar phenomenon can be traced out to the early period of medieval India that Brahmanism advanced in Bengal and South India in sea and post-Gupta period, when the distinctions between the *Vaisyas* and *Sudras* had got blurred and the advent of the Rajputs had thrown the original *Ksatriya Varna* into the background. The progress of Brahmanism was of in the nature of the mass migration of Vedic Aryans, whose bulk was formed by the *Vis* or *Vaisyas.* Hence *Ksatriya* was allowed to lead the life of complete renunciation (*Sanyasa*) in the *Apattikala.* In the same way, a *Sudra* or 'pure-thought', who could not earn his livelihood by following the code of conduct, prescribed for him, could maintain himself by taking recourse to the propessions of a *Vaisya*, viz. trade and commerce (*Vanija*), cattle rearing (*pasupalyam*) and crafts (*Silpopajivanam*[33]). Similar is the view of *Yajnavalkya* also[34]. Thus, the tribal and non-Hindus people in the peripheral regions were admited to the Brahmanical system mainly as *Sudras*. The autochthonous inhabitants of these areas may have been conquered by the *Ksatriya* or Rajput princes, but their acculturation was really carried out by the Brahmanas was functioned as literate and enlightened landowners in these areas. Anthropometric studies suggest that in Bengal the *Sudras* are indigenous inhabitants, but the *Brahmanas* are not. According to *Mahalanobis* various *Sudras* castes in Bengal belong to the same stock and resemble their neighbours in Bihar. But the *Brahmanas* of Bengal resemble their counter parts from Northern India[35].

From the foregoing paragraphs, it is easy to infer that in extra-ordinary times, the ordinary rules of morality were held in abeyance or sometimes thrown to winds (*Vayu*) and recourse could be had even to those acts, which were strictly prohibited as great sins and heinous crimes committed by the *Brahmanas* in ordinary times. One could purified himself afterwards by performing certain prescribed acts[36]. In brief the *Mahabharata* holds the view that the social morality as well as political morality are bound to change in accordance with the changing times and circumstances. And, this is quite in the fitness of things, because what is true of a sick man i.e. *'Nam'* and should be true of a healthy man live in Heaven, what is applicable to a competent person i.e. *'Nam'* or *'Word'*. Therefore, a person should not be so in the case of one who is famine-stricken, but there is a majority of people. This, according to the *Mahabharata* and other ancient Indian works, is the idea of progress in history that underlies *Apaddharama,* i.e the morality of the season of distress sometimes, *'Nam'* or *'Word'* and sometimes Brahmanas and extra-ordinary circumstances we use the *'Pure Nam'* of the nature i.e *'Deepti Raj'* for the purpose of cool down the *Satan* or *Yama*. This state, according to the *dharmasastras,* recognised the code of exceptional morality under special circumstances like the allusion of *Maya* for maintaining social order of society on equality, fraternity liberity and social justice as described by Dr. B.R Ambedkar in the Indian Constitution, which was its main duty during the time of framing the draft of the Constitution. It is true from the early medieval study that the incorporation of foreign invaders and immigrant tribes from one place to another added new castes to the *Kastriya* fold. But Bengal and South India were never seriously affected by foreign invasions to the exposure of early knowledge of the advancement in the society. In these areas only the ruling tribes were admitted as *Ksatriyas,* and the vast majority of their tribal kinsmen were condemned the caste of *Sudras*, because of their poor knowledge or narrow thought not in broad prospective. Therefore, due to the lack of intermediary castes i.e. *'Nam'* or *'Word'* called *"untouchable"*. There was more of social polarisation in Bengal and South India due to the effect of the foreign effect than in any other part of the country like India. It is perhaps this was accounts for extremist movements in these regions by the Britisher and the Francese in subseque period of the Indian history.

Untouchability and a Social Malady

It appears from the study that the unity and integrity of this country has been an article of faith with us for last hundreds of centuries. While this was the grand concept of equality in this country at the earliest peirod of civilization, the society came to be divided on the doctrine of *Chaturvarnya,* the *Purush, Sukta* plays a double game. It proceeds first to raise the real term for the establishment of *'New Society'* i.e. *'Radha Soami',* namely, the existent of the four classes in the Indo-Aryan society, to the status of an ideal. This is a deception because the ideal is in no way different from facts as they exist. After raising the real to the status of the ideal, it proceeds to make a show of giving effect to what is regards as an ideal. This again is a deception because the ideal already exist in fact. This attempt of the *Purush Sukta* to idealise the real and to realise the ideal is a kind of political jugglery, the like of which[37], *Sudars*, the class of persons rendering all other essential services to the society. The superiority or inferiority of an individual does not seem to have been determined by birth in anyone of the classes. For instance, *Valmiki* and *Ved Vyasa,* the authors of the two great epics, the *Ramanaya* and *Mahabharata,* who are regarded as the greatest poets, writers and philosophers of the country and who are held in the highest esteem down to this day by all sections of the society, belonged to the fourth and the second *Varna,* respectively. This is also the case as regards the heroes of these great epics. Rama, belonging to *Kshatriya* class, because of his superb qualities as a man and as an ideal ruler, won a place in the hearts of the million peoples. So to Krishna, the greatest of diplomats and warriors, and a great teacher but not *Guru* like *Ravidas,* Kabir, *Nanaka,* etc., being the pro pounder of the immortal *Srimad Bhagavadgita*[38] was a *Yadava*. Both these are adored and worshipped by all sections of the society as incarnation of God himself through the theory of *'Nam'* and their *Karmas*.

Persons like *Lord Buddha, Mahavira, Ramanuja, Tukaram,* Tulsi Dass, Kabir, Ravidass, Guru Nanak, Akbar, Daryia Sahib, Basaveshwara, Dr. Ambedkar, Gandhiji, Narayana Guru, Jyotiba Phule, etc, all declared that the practice of untouchability was a great sin against God and humanity, but the evil minded persons they were not ready to get rid of this bad practice because they have been entrapped with the theory of mind not with enlightenment, therefore, they will remain there in this process because history is an endless dialogue between the past and the present, but it is the duty of the nature to remove this social evil in the society i.e. the *'Nam'*.Thus, there is a set of adjectives of *untouchables* including *unique*, complete, equal, infinite, and *'Perfect Master'* whose core meaning embraces a mathematically absolute concept and which therefore, according to the traditional argument, cannot be modified by adverbs such as "really" 'quite,' or 'very'. According to this argument, something either is *unique* (or *complete* or *infinite*) or it is not and there are no in between stages. In practice, the situation is more complex than this, since some of these words (notably *unique* and *perfect*) have developed weakened senses in which they no longer relate to an absolute concept; in such cases that use of 'fairly', 'rather', somewhat, etc, is no longer illogical[39] and a Perfect *Guru*. History records that the so called, *"untouchables"*, for example, the protagonist, *Bakha,* instead of opting for radical action[40], which incorporates of equality as one of the basic fundamental right in the Constitution and abolition of practice of Untouchability by Article 15 and 17 under our Constitution were intended to erase the blot attached to our society and to remove the grave injustice prepetrated on caste basis was the right step. The nation would be ever grateful to all the founding fathers of our Constituion in general and to Dr. B.R Ambedkar, its principal architect in particular. The supreme Dharma of all of us today is to obey the constitutional provision in letter and spirit and in thought, word and deed[41] In the wake of partition, millions of *Namasudras 'Words'* the *"Untouchables"*, of Bengal preferred to bear untold hardships and migrated illegal in India and Pakistan[42] to remain in the Hindu fold here rather than save their skin by getting convert into *Islam.*[43] It is also interesting and noteworthy that the declaration of equality in the Vedas have been reenacted in the various provisions of our latest Constitution as mentioned by the Rama Jois. Important concomitant of equality which Veda reflects, is the feeling of unity and fraternity which are among the objectives of our Constituion as indicated in its preamble. This spirit of national unity is found expressed in the words, we, the people of India and by the word 'fraternity' used in the preamble. Dr. B.R Ambedkar said while equality and liberty are important in a Democracy, he attached great importance to the word fraternity used in the preamble. In this behalf he said thus:

> *"What does fraternity mean? Fraternity means a sense of common brotherhood of all Indians "Untouchables" of Indians being one people. It is the principle which gives unity and solidarity of social life.* (B.R Ambedkar and Human Rights p. 15)

Indeed the feeling of fraternity was achieved during the freedom struggle of India against Britishers and now it is to be strengthened, developed among the massage of the Brahminical society and maintained after independence, by the implementation of the Provision of the Constitution which tabooed discrimination on grounds of caste, religion, race and sex, and abolished untouchability. At the time of independence and commencement of the constitution, the feeling of fraternity and national unity, and sense of self sacrifice were very strong. It was easier to develop the feeling of fraternity in the new generation. Unfortunately in the course of struggle for political power which succeeded freedom struggle it was not given due importance. As a result, the weeds of narrow religious, caste, linguistic loyalities began to grow and have now become a menace to national unity, because out of selfish, transitory, electoral advantages, the political parties and individuals began and continued to whip up caste and religious feelings during periodic elections for which news papers gave very wide publicity withour realizing its adverse effects on the new younger generation. In view of such propoganda and exploitation, though religion, castes and sub castes do not by and large exist in their original form, i.e. for food and marriage, they are causing threat to the national unity of India. Individual are realing that their life is empermal, but their behaviours should be to make the National Life eternal, Just as our previous generation made tremendous sacrifice and secured to us freedom from the clutuches of the Brahminical thought, therefore, we should, by our effort and matching sacrifice leave alegacy of strong, united and prosperious *Bharat* for the benefit and happiness of our future generations. Otherwise the present generation shall stand condemned in history as destroyers of National unity and fraternity which they had inherited through the sacrifice of the freedom fighters. Therefore, it is the high time that our political parties and leaders stop abusing *Varna,* caste, religion for political or electoral purpose in the interest of social harmony for building a strong, united and prosperous *Bharat.*

Notes and References

1. Zanaide-A-Ragozin; *Vedic India;* New Delhi; 1961 p. 281. Hereafter referred as *V.I. Note.* Ludwig Wittgenstein was born in 1889 and died in 1951. He wrote this book in 1922 entitled as : *Tractatus* Logico-*philosophicus;* quoted by the said author.
2. *Ibid.*, pp. 222-23.
3. R.C Majumdar, H.C Raychaudhuri, K. Datta, *An Advance History of India*; London; 1963; p. 39. Hereafter discussed as *A.H.I.*
4. A.C Clayton; *The Rig-Veda* and *Vedic-Religion;* New Delhi; Reprint; 1981, p. 16 Hereafter explained as *R.V.V.R.*
5. *A.H.I.*, p. 39.
6. *V.I*; pp. 223-24.
7. *A.H.I.*. p. 39.

8. *Ibid.*, p. 40.
9. *R.V.V.R.* p. 132.
10. *H.A.I*; p. 40.
11. V.I., p. 224.
12. H.A Rose. *A Glossary of the Tribe and Castes* of the *Punjab and North-West Frontier Province;* Reprinted, 1990, Language Department- Punjab; p. 151. Hereafter discussed as *G.T.C.P. N.W.F.P.*
13. *Rajat'arangini*; Tr. by M.A Stein, Vol.1, *Delhi;* Reprint, 1989. p. 164. Hereafter referred as *R.T.* Note. During the rule of *Jayapida* of *Karakota* dynasty *Srideva,* a village *Candala,* had asked his mother for food, with the words: "I am off to help the king" and had joined after assuring her, as she laughed, that he would killed *Jajja.* Now we are adhered to the order of the verses as given by A_1, though a marginal note of A_2, already indicated the transposition now effected. The agreement of L with A_2, proves that the arrangement of the text *Ratnakantha's* original was that now adopted in the translation (*Ibid*). No doubt, *Dums* or *Doms* are a very important people of Kashmir, for they are the watchman of the villages and formerly used to look after the state share of the crops. As a private citizen the *Dum* is not an admirable person, and he loses no opportunity of annoy the villagers, by whom he feared and disliked by the Brahmans. But as officials they are trustworthy because he is schedule caste, therefore, he has little bit faith in his mind, and have never been seen known to steal the state treasure which passes through their hands. The *Dums* claim descent from a Hindu King, who from fear of his numerous sons scattered them over the valley, but some say that they are descendants of the of the *Chakks* ruler of Kashmir, mentioned under History. W.R. Lawrence mentions that *Galavans* or horse-keepers are also credited with a descent from the Chakks, and their violent restless character many be hereditary. Originally they earned their living by grazing ponies, but found it more lucrative to steal them. At last they became an established criminal tribe, and during Sikh rule were a terror to the country. *Khaira Galawan,* the hero of many a legend, was killed by the Sikh governor *Mian* Singh. Gulab Singh hunted down the tribe, and their end was transportation to *Bunji.* (Walter, R. Lawrence; *Provincial Gazetterer of Kashmir;* New Delhi, Reprint 1985, pp. 37-8. Hereafter cited as *P. G.K.*)
14. Manorama Jauhari; *Politics And Ethics in Ancient India;* Varanasi; 1968; p. 344. Hereafter mentioned as *P. E. A.I.*
15. P. V. Kane; *History of Dharmasastra.* Vol.1 Poona Revised 1968; p. 336. Hereafter described as *H.D.*
16. *P. E.A.I.,* pp. 342-43.
17. *Ibid.*, p. 343.
18. *Hiuen Tsang Travels in India*; Tr. by Watter, T. Delhi, First edition; 1961 Vol.II, p. 296. Hereafter explained as *H.T.*
19. K.A Nilkanth Sastri; *Age of the Nandas and Mauryas*; Varnasi, 1967, p. 24. Hereafter described as *A. N.M.*
20. R.S. Tripathi; *History of Ancient India;* Delhi, Reprint 1987. p. 146. Hereafter referred as *H.A.I.*
21. *Visnu Purana*, IV, 24, 20-21. Also quoted by H.C Raychowdhary; *Political History of Ancient India,* New Delhi, 6th edition; 1967. pp. 231-32.
22. *P. E.A.I.* p. 338.
23. Ram Sharan Sharma; *Social Changes In Early Medieval India*; New Delhi, Reprint; 1983 p. 17. Hereafter discussed as *S.C.E.M.I.*
24. *H.T* ed T. Rhys Davids and S.W Bushell: 2 Vols. London 1904-05 Vol. 1 P. 108 op. cit, S.C.E.M.I., p. 17.
25. *Alberuni's India*; Tr. by Edward, C. Sachan. Vol.2, New Delhi; 1989 Vol.; I,P. 101. Hereafter discussed as A.1.
26. *S.C.E.M.I.* p. 17.
27. M. Rama Jois; *Guruji and Social Harmony;* Karnataka; 2006. pp. 47, 48. Hereafter referred as *G.S.H.*
28. *Brahma Khanda,* Part II. 89, PP. 291-92 Quoted from *S.C.E.M.I.*; p. 18.
29. *A.I.*; Vol. II. p. 180.
30. *S.C.E.M.I;* p. 18.
31. N.K Dutta; *Origin And Growth of Caste in India*; Calcutta; Vol. II. 1965; pp. 146-47. **Note**: Word *dana* corresponding with the Latin *domus,* is used in Sanskrit for a single house or home i.e. *'Word' or 'Nam'* or *'Chamar'* (John Wilson; *Indian Caste*; New Delhi; 1976; p. 109).
32. S.C.E.M.I; pp. 18-19.
33. *P. E.A.I.* p. 339.
34. *Yajnavalkya,* 1. p. 120 Quouted *H.D.* Vol. II; pp. 120-21.
35. R.C. Majumdar; *The History of Bengal,* Vol. 1 Dacca; 1948, pp. 558-59
36. The *Santi Parvan*, Vol. XVI, *Introduction* (Bhandarkar Oriential Research Institute, Poona; 1966, p. *CXCIX.*
37. Dr. B.R. Ambedkar; *Who Were the Shudras? Aurangabad;* 2003, 1946; p. 28.
38. *Srimad Bhagavadgita*; Tr. in English by S.C Vaishya, Revised by R.N Kaul & Keshoram Aggarwal; Gorakhpur; 2006; p. 1.
39. *Oxford Language Reference,* Edited by Jonathan Law, I. New York; Revised edition 2006. p. 165
40. Sharankumar Limbale; *Towards an Aesthetic of Dalit Literature*; Tr. from the Marathi by Alok Mukherjee, New Delhi; 2004, p. 8.
41. G.S.H. p. 52.
42. *Compact Oxford Dictionary, Thesaurus, and Wordpower Guide;* Editors, C. Soanes, A. Spouer, and S. Hawker. New York, 2004. p. 1005.
43. G.S.H. p. 53.

2

Nature of the Caste Groups

Speaking and writing effectively is probably more important not today than ever before, when the origin of the World was took place. Take any language of the country, we find the similar inspiring thoughts and ideals reflected in all its literature. In fact, all our languages, whether Tamil or Bengali, Marathi or Punjabi, Hindi or Urdu, are our national languages. All these languages and dialects are like so many blossoming flowers shedding the same rich fragrance of our national culture. The source of inspiration for all these has been that queen of languages, and language of Gods is *'Word'* or *'Nam'* or *'Rita'* or *'Kalma'*. By virtue of its richness and sacred association it alone can serve as the common medium of our national or international intercourse. Nor it has very difficult to acquire, but there is a need of pious approach toward Him. Moreover, it is not difficult to acquire as it was difficult to acquire the Sanskrit language during the time of Brahminical period. Today it is very important because the Enlightenment era is going to established to begin with this language, but it is a undeciphere in Indus script[1]. We have seen that in the Hindu caste-society there are a number of groups with distinct names. The nature of these names is likely to furnish us with a clue to some understanding of the process by which distinction between groups came to be formulated. Of the major groups called castes many bear names derived from the principal professions they followed or the crafts they practised and, in the majority of cases, are still engaged in. Brahmin means one who recites the prayer, the ritual formulae or incantations, and designates a group that was once wholly composed of individuals so engaged, though now it is the appellation of a group whose members are engaged not only in the priestly function, but also in the allied functions of clerks and writers, and even in pursuits absolutely foreign to the original ideals.

Of the groups carrying on trade and commerce a large number bear the name of *Vani* or *Baniya*. Which is derived from a Sanskrit word meaning a trader. The Tamil *Chetti* seems also to refer to the avocation of the group in that linguistic area. *Jat* of the Punjab means cultivator, so also do *Vellala* of the Tamil and *Vakkaliga* of the Kanarese country. *Kurmi, Kanbi* and *Kunbi* perhaps signify the occupation of the group, viz, that of cultivation though it is not improbable that the name may be of tribal origin. Kisan, the name of a cultivating caste of northern India, must be derived from the Sanskrit word for cultivation. Sometimes the connection of agriculture is brought out indirectly as in the name of the *Lodha* of the Central Provinces. The name is believed to mean 'clod-hopper' from 'Job', a clod. The cattle-breeding group takes the significant name of *Gauli*, derived from a Sanskrit word for cow. *Soni* or *Sonar*, the name of the goldsmith, refers to the material in which the group specializes. *Barhai, Tarkhan, Tachchan* and *Sutar,* the designations of the carpenter-caste in the different linguistic regions, point to the material worked on, the mode of working or the special implement of thecraft. The names of the metalworking castes known as— *Lohar, Tambat, Kasar* and *Thathera 'Word'* come from the metal handled by these groups, viz, iron, copper, bell-metal, and brass. *Bunkar, Joria, Tanti, Kosthi, Patwa, Pattanulkaran* and *Sale* are the designations of the various weaving castes. The first two are derived from a root meaning 'to put the threads together', and the others from Sanskrit words for silk-cloth. *Kumbar* or *Kumbhar*, the name of the potter-caste, means one who makes pots. *Tili* or *Teli*, the oil-presser, means either one who presses oil or one who handles sesamum. The names of the barber-caste are either derived from the Sanskrit word for barber or signify those who cut the hair. *Lunia* and *Agri* mean salt-workers. *Bari*, the leaf-plate-making caste, derives its name from 'bar', a 'plantation', and *Tamboli*, dealers in betel-leaf, from the Sanskrit word for betel-leaf. *Dharkar* means rope-maker and *Bansphor,* the basket-maker, means the bamboo-splitter. *Chamar* or *Chambhar* the name of the leather working caste, is derived from a Sanskrit word meaning worker in leather. *Kahar*, name of a North-Indian caste, formerly engaged chiefly as water-carriers but now as general and domestic servants, means a watercarrier. *Pasi* means a user of noose and is significantly the name of an aboriginal caste living by catching wild birds, small game and tapping palms. The names of the shepherd castes seem to be derived from words meaning sheep. Such is at least the case with *Gadaria* from 'gadar', an old Hindi word for sheep.

Many others of these major groups called castes bear merely tribal or ethnic names. Such are for example: *Arora, Gujar, Lohana, Bhatia, Mina, Bhil, Dom, Oraon, Munda, Santal, Koch, Ahir, Mahar, Nayar, Maratha, Gond, Khond, etc.* As to other races that were in the land there is little information in the hymns of the Aryans and the science of ethnology has to help us. From it we learn that before the Aryans; India was sparsely peopled by some races that are now often called 'jungle tribes'. Among them the majority would be Dravidians. The *Gonds, Bhils* and *Santals* are modern surviors of these races. Some were very humble in the scale of humanity burying their dead in the cells made of stone-slabs, called a *Kistvaens* by scientists and *'Pandava Vidu', 'Words'* the houses of the Pandava brothers when in exile Brahmans by the Tamil people of the South to this day. Those in the south were never so subject to the Aryans as the tribes of the north and grew into the powerful and civilized Tamil and Telugu nations, but there is no hint of this in *Rig-Veda*[2].

Religious movements have not failed to give their names to groups, which are now castes. The *Bishnois* and Sadhus, the *Jogis* and *Gosains,* and the *Manbhaos* are some of the examples of sectarian castes. The first four of these began as orders emphasizing certain aspect of Hindu tenets, while the last group was the result of a reformist movement in the Maratha region.

A few of the groups have names emphasizing a peculiarity which is somehow regarded as specific, or are of the nature of nicknames. *Musahar*, meaning mouse-eaters, is the name of a low aboriginal caste of Uttar Pradesh. *Bhangi*, one who performs the useful function of removing night-soil, is a term probably applied to the caste simply as a token of contempt. *'Words'* those who are broken or outcast, *Bhulia,* an *Uriya* caste of weavers, are so called merely because they are supposed to be a forgetful people of 'Father' from *'bhulna'*, 'to forget'. *Dangi,* the name of a cultivating caste of the Central Provinces, means merely a hillman, perhaps referring to the former marauding activities of the now peaceful and once dominant people. The *Pankas* of the Central Provinces are a caste of weavers and general labourers; but their name is believed to be derived from a certain incident in their conversion to the creed of Kabir and means those who are 'from water', *'Pani Ka'*. *Dubla* one of the aboriginal tribes of Gujarat, are so called because they are *weaklings,* 'dubla' means weak. *Naikdas* of Gujarat are perhaps so designated in contempt, the term meaning 'Little Naik'. *Ramoshi,* a thieving caste of the Deccan, is supposed to be a short form of *Rama-Vamshi*, i.e. descendant of Rama, the epic hero. *Kallan,* the name of a Madras caste, means in Tamil a 'thief'. Tiyan, the toddy-tapping caste of *Malabar*, means a 'southerner', as the *Tiyans* are believed to have migrated from Ceylon *Pariah*, the name of the great untouchable caste of Madras is commonly derived from a word for drum, which instrument is played by them.

A smaller number of these major groups are definitely known to be the outcome of miscegenation. Some of the members of the higher castes of Orissa and the *Kayasth* immigrants into Orissa keep minds of Bhandari and other clean castes and treat them as their concubines. The issue of such unions is known by the name of *Shagirdapesha*. The *Bhilalas* are well known to be the offspring of Rajput males and *Bhil* women. *Vidur*, a Maratha caste of the Central Provinces, is wholly formed by individuals of mixed descent.

A close study of the names of the various minor units, the so-called sub-castes, within the major groups reveals the fact that the bases of distinction leading to the exclusive marking off of these groups were: first, territorial or jurisdictional separateness; second, mixed origin; third, occupational distinction; fourth, some peculiarity in the technique of one and the same occupation; fifth, sectarian difference; sixth, dissimilarity of customs; and last, adventitious circumstances, suggesting certain nick-names.

Sub-castes that bear the name of some ancient city or locality are to be met with in the majority of the castes. The *Ahirs* of the Central Provinces have among their subcastes, the following groups: *Jijhotia,* taking their name from Jajhoti, the classical designation of Bundelkhand; *Narwaria* from *Narwar*; *Kosaria* from Kosala, the ancient name of Chattisgarh; and Kanaujia from Kanauj. The Barai have the following endogamous sub-divisions: *Chaurasia*, from the Chaurasi pargana of Mirzapur District; *Panagaria,* from Panagar in Jabalpur; *Mahobia* from Mahoba; Jaiswar from the town of Jais in Rai Bareli District; Gangapari, coming from the other side of the Ganges. The Brahmins of Bengal have among their subcastes the following names: *Paschatya*, from the western part of India: *Radhiya* from Radh, the old name of Western Bengal and Barendra from the northern part of Bengal. The names of the sub-castes of the Brahmin caste of Uttar Pradesh are most of them territorial in origin: Kanaujia from Kanauj; *Maithil* from Mithila; Jijhotia from Jajhoti; *Saraswat,* named after the river Saraswati; and *Gaur* from an old name of a large part of Northern India. Most of the sub-castes of the Brahmins of the Maratha country bear names of localities: Konkanasth from the Konkan; Deshasth from the Desh, the Deccan plateau. The Saraswat Brahmins have more than six sub-castes, all territorial in origin. Of the numerous sub-castes of the Gujarat Brahmins the majority bear territorial names, like Agarwal, from Agra; *Deshval, Harsola, Jharola, Modh Nagar, Osval, Porval, Shrimali, Sorathia,* all of them being derived from old names of localities once independent in their jurisdiction[3]. Many of the sub-divisions of the Smarta Brahmins of the Telugu country bear names derived from the old names of the various parts of that country: *Velnad, Vengi Nadu, Kasal Nadu, Mulki Nadu,* and Telaga Nadu. The sub-caste of the *Kanara Kamma* Baidika is formed by Brahmins who originally came from the Kanarese country but are not naturalized in the Telugu country. Following are some of the other castes among which the sub-castes bear territorial names: *Vania, Mochi, Kansara, Sutar, Charan, Kumbhar, Dhed, Darji,* Bohar and Koli among Gujarat castes; Kayasth, Bania and Vaidya among the North Indian castes; *Chambhar, Gauli, Koli, Kumbhar, Kumbi, Lohar, Mahar, Mali, Nhavi, Sutar and Vani among the Maratha castes.*

Many castes have divisions bearing names reminiscent of the ethnic origins of these sub-groups. Many tribes, either because some of their members followed a particular occupation or because some of them intermarried with the members of a particular caste-in-formation, have contributed their names to sub-castes. The professions and castes, which allowed or tolerated the infusion of tribal people, still distinguished the groups formed by such inclusion or mesalliance. This is how many of the occupational castes have come to possess sub-castes bearing tribal names. This process of infusion and left-handed marriage does not seem to have been restricted to tribes alone. In spite of the so-called rigidity of caste, it appears that many of the occupational and tribal castes, either permitted or connived at the intrusion of members of other castes. Only they tried to keep the progeny and the group formed by them distinct from their original group. Thus the sub-castes of some of the major castes have composite names derived from the names of other castes. The Barai, a caste of betel-vine growers in the Central Provinces, have a sub-division called the *Kumbhardhang,* who are supposed to be the descendants of a potter. The *Basors*, workers in bamboo, have the following sub-castes: *Dumar or Dom-Basors, Basors* who are derived from the Domtribe; *Dhumbela,* perhaps from the *Dhobi* caste; *Dharkar,* which is the name also of a large caste of ropemakers in Northern India. The *Chambhars,* leather workers of the Maratha country, have Ahir as one of their sub-castes. The *Chamars* of the Central Provinces, have a sub-castes. The *Chamars* of the Central Provinces, have a sub-caste named *Korchamars* who "are said to be the descendants of alliance between *Chamars* and *Koris* or weavers." The *Sali,* a weaving caste of Maratha country, has Ahir, Maratha, and *Chambhar* sub-castes, which announce their origins from the different ethnic and occupational groups. The *Dhimars*, a caste of fishermen and palanquin-bearers of the Central Provinces, retain in the name of one of their sub-castes its traditional origin from the *Gonds*. Among the *Dheds*, as among many castes of Gujarat, is a sub-caste named Gujjar, derived from a medieval tribe of that name. Among the *Gaulis*, cowherds of the Maratha country, are to be found sub-castes bearing the name of *Ahir, Kunbi, Kuruba and Maratha. Gondhali,* a composite caste of religious minstrels, has sub-castes bearing the names of other well-known castes of the Maratha country, like the Brahman, *Dhangar,* and *Kumbhar.* The *Kolis* of the Deccan have Agri, *Ahir* and *Bhil* among their sub-castes. Nesfield has found among some castes of Uttar Pradesh[4] sub-castes styled after the Kol tribe, whcih seem to have taken to various occupations during the formative period of the caste-system. Among the *Kunbis* of Nagpur is a sub-caste bearing the name Manwa derived from the Manas, who were once a dominant people in Chanda district. The Khandesh *Kunbis* have, as one of their sub-castes, Kumbhar, which is the name of the potter-caste. "Bodies of the *Kori* and *Katia* weaving castes of Northern India have been amalgamated with the Mahars in Districts where they have come together along the Satpura Hills and Nerbudda Valley," the latter caste still having Katia as one of its sub-castes. Kunbi is one of the sub-castes of the *Nhavis,* the Maratha caste of barbers. The Pardhans of the Central Provinces have a sub-caste called *Ganda,* supposed to be the offspring of intermarriages between the two castes. Among the Shimpis or Maratha tailors, one finds *Ahir* and Maratha as two of their sub-castes, derived from well-known castes. "The *TeliKalars* appear to be a mixed group of *Kalars* who have taken to the oilman's profession, and the *Teli-Banias* are Telis who have become shopkeepers."

The nature of many of the occupations is such that though from a broad point of view each may be regarded as distinct, yet on closer scrutiny it presents differences which are sufficient to distinguish one aspect of it from another. Thus, though leather-working may be regarded as one occupation by the society, the followers of that occupation may distinguish different branches of leather-working as shoe-making, sandal-making, or oilcan-making. Such detailed distinctions within an occupation have been thought to be adequate to designate the group of members following the particular branch of the occupation by the name of that branch. Sub-castes within many of the occupational castes bear names derived from the special branches of the occupations. Among the *Chamars* of the Central Provinces[5] there are many sub-castes whose names are derived from the particular articles of leather that their members are engaged in making. The members of the sub-caste Budalgir prepare 'budlas' or oilcans of leather. Jingars are saddle-makers. The Katwa sub-caste specializes in leathercutting. The *Dhimar* caste of the Central Provinces has *Bansia* and *Bandhaiya* as two of its sub-castes. The former term is derived from *'bansi'*, a bamboo fishing-rod, and the latter means those who make ropes and sacking of hemp and fibre. The *Kunbis* have a sub-caste called *Tilole* presumably because once they cultivated the sesamum (til) plant. Among the Lonaris of Belgaum there are two sub-divisions styled after their particular article which they prepare as *Mith* (salt) and *Chune* (Lime). *Phul Mali, Kacha, Mali, Jire Mali* and *Hadle Mali* together forming the bulk of the *Mali*-caste, are sub-castes which take their names from occupational specialization. Thus the Phul Mali is a florist, the *Kacha Malis* prepare the cotton braid, the *Jire* grow cumin seed (*Jire*), and the *Halde* grow 'halad' or tumeric. The Koshtis of the Central Provinces have *Patwi* and *Sutsale* as two of the Central Provinces have *Patwi* and *Sutsale* as two of their sub-castes. *Patwis* make the braid of silk-thread and few silk-thread on ornaments. *Sutsales,* weave mostly cotton thread[6] for Mochi and Brahman *Janupavita.*

Many sub-castes, especially among the castes that are either of the nature of ethnic groups or carry on secondary undefined occupations, are named from the nature of their special economic activities[7] *Singaria,,Tankiwala, Dhurja,Sonjhara* and *Kasdhonia* are some of the sub-divisions of the *Dhimar* caste in the Central Provinces. Singarias cultivate 'singara' or water-nut. Tankiwalas are sharpeners of grind-stones. *Dhurias* sell parched rice. *Sonjharas,* wash for gold, and *Kasdhonias* wash the sand of sacred rivers to pick coins dropped in them by devout pilgrims. The *Garpagari Jogi* derives the name of his sub-caste from his occupation of using magic to avert hailstroms. The *Manihari Jogis* are pedlars selling beads and the Ritha *Biknath*, are so-called because they sell 'ritha' or soap-nut *Khaire, Dhanoje*, and *Lonhare* are three of the sub-castes of the *Kunbis* of the Central Provinces[8]. Khaires presumably used to make *catechu* from 'Khair', *Dhanoje* are those who tend small stock or 'dhan', and *Lonhare* formerly refined salt. The *Lonaria* sub-caste of the *Mahars* of the Central Provinces is engaged in salt-making. The *Dhangars* have *Mendhes* and *Mhaskes* as two of their sub-divisions, named because they keep sheep (*mendhi*) and buffaloes (*mhashi*) respectively.

The *Mang-garudis*, a sub-division of the *Mang*-caste, are so called because they are snake-charmers; the *Tokarphodes* take their name from their occupation of splitting (*phod*) bamboo (*tokar); the Nades* are so called because they make *'nadas'* or ropes. The Mangmochis are leather workers. *Kakars* make ropes of untanned hide[9]. *Nhavis*, the barners of the Maratha country, have among their sub-castes *Vajantri* and *Mashalji*. The former are so called because they play music and the latter because they carry torches (*mashal*) before processions. Among Mahars of the Maratha country two of their sub-divisions are named *Panya* and *Bele,* the former from their working with leaves for making umbrellas and the latter from their making mats from chips of bamboo. In the Central Provinces the *Yerande Telis*, who are a sub-caste of the Teli caste, take their name from the fact that formerly they pressed only 'erandi' or castor oil seed. The *Salo Telis* have given up oil-pressing and are now cultivators. Pecularities connected with the apparatus or technique of an occupation have given their names to the sub-divisions of some of the occupational castes. The *Kumbhar,* potters of the Maratha country, distinguish those who make pots by hand without the wheel as Hatghades (hands potters), those who use a big wheel as Thorchake big, and 'chak', wheel), and those who use a small wheel as *Lahanchake* ('lahan', small). In the Central Provinces the potter-caste has the first sub-caste called *Goria* because the members of this sub-division make white pots only and not black ones. In the Nagpur district the Telis have two principal sub-divisions. *Ekbaile* are those who yoke only one bullock to their press while *Dobaile* Yoke two bullocks.[10]

Differences of religious schools or sects have given names to sub-divisions among some castes. The old distinctions on the basis of the *Veda*, which was traditionally followed by the members of a group have persisted among the *Deshasth* Brahmins of the

Maratha country leading to endogamous restrictions. Among them the Rigvedis and *Yajurvedis 'Words'* the followers of the *Rig-veda* and of the Yajurveda *'Chamar'* and Jat and are so far distinct as to be sub-castes. Later creeds and reformatory movements have also left their marks on caste organization. Among the *Deshasth* Brahmins there is also an endogamous group, whose members are supposed to be the descendants of *Eknath* a reforming saint of Maharashtra[11]. The South Indian Brahmins carry their religious differences to such an extent that generally the Smartas and Vaishnavas are regarded as sub-castes. The *Chamars* of the Central Provinces have amongst them a large sub-caste named *Satnami* because the members are followers of the *Satnami* sect. The *Padam Salis* have Hindu and *Lingayat* divisions which are endogamous. So also have the *Gaulis*, the *Kumbhars* and *Falis, Lingayat* divisions among them. The *Pankas*, a Dravidian caste of weavers, have *Kabirha* and *Shaktaha* as their principal subcastes. The *Kabirhas* are the followers of the sect of Kabir castes. The *Kabirhas* are the followers of the sect of Kabir and the *Shaktahas* profess to belong to the Shakta creed.

Differences in customs and diet have been regarded as so important that some of the castes recognize groups with such differences as sub-castes, though the names of these do not necessarily take after the differences. The *Berads* of Bombay have two sub-castes, the difference between them being that the members of one eat the flesh of buffaloes, bullocks or pigs, and allow their women to follow prostitution, while the members of the other do not tolerate these practices. These latter are termed Bile, i.e. white or pure, and the former *Kare* or black. *Dhor*, one of the five sub-divisions of the *Katkaris*, is so called because the members eat beef. Moger, a Kanarese fishing caste, has three sub-divisions named according to their rules of inheritance: *Aliyasantanas, Makalasantanas,* and *Randesantanas*, i.e those who inherit through females, those who inherit through males, and those who are progeny of re-married widows. The *Kunbis* of the Central Provinces have a sub-caste called *Gadhao* because they formerly kept donkeys ('gadhav'[12]).

Many castes have sub-castes, whose names are derived from some real peculiarily now forgotten, or some adventitious circumstance to which importance is attached and which is used to distinguish the members of the group, or in the case of miscegenation, from the fact of mere illegitimacy of unions, the exact lineage not being attended to. The Basors of the Central Provinces have a section called *Purania* or *Juthia* because they are supposed to be the illegitimate progeny of Ahir wet-nurses (*dai*), employed in Rajput households. The *Chungia Chamars* are a branch of the *Satnami Chamars* and are so called because, contrary to the rules of the sect, they smoke evidently by means of a leafpipe (*chungia*). The Daijanya sub-caste of the Chamars is so called because their women act as midwives, though this business is practised by women of other sub-castes as well. The *Dhimars* have a sub-caste which is merely named Nadha or those who live on the banks of streams. Their *Suvarha* and *Gadhewale* sub-castes derive their names from their special association with two unclean animals, pig and ass. The *Mahars* disclose a sense of humour by designating the group of descendants of illicit unions by the term *Dharmik* (pious). The Pardhans, on the contrary, apply a prosaic term to such a group among them. It is known as *'Thothia'* or 'mained'. Though 'langoti' or a narrow piece of cloth is the loincloth of many poor castes, the *Pardhis* have hit upon its use as the distinctive mark of their members and call one of their sub-castes *Langoti*. The *Kumbhars* have *Gadhere, Bardia* and *Sungaria* as three of their sub-castes, these groups deriving their names from the animal they use or keep: ass, bullock, and pig respectively. The Dhangars of Bombay call their bastard brethren 'kadu', while the Gujarat Kumbhars use the term *Vatalia*, i.e. polluted, to designate such members.

Such is the picture of caste-groups presented by facts mostly taken from the Central Provinces, Maharashtra and Gujarat, both of which regions are outside the centre of old Brahmanic culture. In the home of the Brahmanic culture, Uttar Pradesh, the same principles can be discerned from the nomenclature of the castes and sub-castes. One additional and important feature of the caste origination of the region is that the names of Rajput clans and those of some of the eponymous personages figure very largely in the names of the sub-castes of many major groups[13] have been originated from the *'Chamar'* caste.

Notes & References

1. *Raj Kumar, History of the Brahmans; Delhi; 2006;* p. 133.
2. *R.V.V.R.*, pp. 4-5.
3. ***Note.*** *Some of the Gujarat castes are further sub-divided according to the cities in which they use to reside for example,* Shrimali Banias *of Surat and those of Ahmedabad perhaps the most striking development in Sherupur-Naktipur has been the assumption of the caste occupations by subgroups of Muslims. Some function as tailors* (Darzi). *Others are*

*barbers (*Nai*) and drummers, both of which occupations are ritually important to the Hindu ceremonial pattern. One Muslim barber (*Nai*), Wali Muhammad has a large cilentele in sherupur and Naktipur that includes several of the most prominent Hindu families (H.C.S. p. 152).*

4. **Note.** The village upon which this discussion will has been given the pseudonym of Sherupur. It is situated in a densely populated region south of the city of Faizabad (population 87,000), the capital of Faizabad District. This district lies in the eastern portion of Uttar Pradesh, the largest province in India. Sherupur's corporate limits actually contain five hamlets (*purwah*) with a total population of 750 subdivided into fifteen endogamous, named castes. Two of the five hamlets, the main on which bears the incorporated village's name and another called Naktipur, are binary in nature in the sense that they are close together physically, their residents maintain much mutual interaction, and they are bound together by certain common ceremonial activities. The other three hamlets are widely separated from these two and from each other and therefore possess rather distinct identities. (H.C.S. pp. 149-50).
5. **Note** It makes clear from the study that the binary unit, Sherupur-Naktipur, is the only one which possesses a high measure of internal social differentiation. Of the fifteen castes found within the corporated village, thirteen are represented here, whereas none of the other there hamlets has more than four this unevenness of caste distribution is typical of the area. But term "permanent" is a relative here. It would perhpas be more appropriate to say that permance is what is striven for in these relationships. In actual fact, changes are made from time to time by both patrons and specialists in consequence of quarrels over rates of reimbursement, clashes of personality, competitive bidding for the services of a specialist etc.
6. C.R.I., p. 38
7. **Note.** Payments for the services of traditional specialists take four principal forms in sherupur-Naktipur. *First* is the payment of an agreed amount of grain every six months to a specialist who has been engaged on a permanent basis. *Second* is the payment of cash or grain on the piece work basis to a specialist who has been engaged on a permanent basis. This is a most important category which has not hitherto been systematically recognised. *Third* are the exchanges of services which artisans in particular under take reciprocally and to which Berreman and Rowe have rightly called attention. *Finally*, there are payments of cash or grain, or both, on piecework basis to any specialist who happens to be handy and is willing to provide a particular service.
8. **Note.** Regular and systemic payments to specialists are confined to a total of six castes in Sherupur-Naktipur today: Washerman (*Dhobi*), barbers (*Nai*), blacksmith (*Lohar*), carpenters (*Barhai*), potter (*Kumhar*) and plowmen (*Harwar* of the *Kori* caste). Actually, only the first four of these groups of specialists receive payments in the form of grain in fixed amounts at the semi-annual harvest in a really significant number of cases. The *Harwar* are normally rewarded by a combination of free meals, money and small grants of land, and the potter has only a few permanent clients on this basis, most of them paying him on a permanent piecework basis. Thus, what has been conceived of as the ideal traditional economic relationship between a Hindu household and caste specialists is limited in Sherupur and Naktipur to a very small proportion of the entire spectrum of specialists. People were asked to name the specialists with whom they dealt, the basis on which they dealt with them, and the amounts and kinds of payments they were making at the time. Idealized rates were ascertained of course, for comparative purposes, but it was found that such rates, taken alone, can be highly misleading. What a specialist tells you he charges, multiplied by the number of households he serves, will yield an ideal figure for his income from rendering traditional services, but this may differ widely from the sum arrived at by approaching each of his clients directly and totaling the amounts they report they have actually paid at the last two or three harvests.
9. **Note.** The *'Chamar'* constitute an important category of specialist in a Hindu community because it is they who traditionally absorb the impurities associated with the removal of dead animals like Brahmins of the period; working with leather products, childbirth etc. Thus the question "who is your *Chamar*", may elicit reference to a households cobbler, its midwife, or the person who is called upon to dispose of the carcass of a dead animal. In all three instances, the tendency today is to pay for such services more in cash than in kind. The midwife's role has its principal meaning in the ritual context, those of the other two in what we call, somewhat satisfactory the production context. We can offer no reliable estimate of the amount of money, grain, or other commadities that change hands in connection with these professions. In the ritual context, the barbar (*Nai*), as is well know from the 'Muryan Period', performs numerous religiously meaningful duties at birth, marriage and death ceremonies to name only the most important are Asoka and Chanakya. His role is nicely summed up by Opler and Singh in 1948 A.D; When they characterize him as the one who "grooms the living and the dead" animals. He derives his income in substantial measure from semi-annual grain disbursements as we have seen, but for his

work at ceremonies he receives additional gifts of money, grain, clothing, etc. which vary according to the occasion, the means, and the inclination of the *Jajman.* The Brahmin priest, on the other hand, derives all his income from his religious functions which are manifold. In addition to being called upon to participate the rites of passage, the Pandit provides astrological readings and conducts special rites lith those held when a small pox epidemic threatens. A leading Rajput family in Sherupur say the following may be given to the Pandit : (1) seven *paseri* (28 pounds) of grain at plowing time as recompense for killing living organisms in the soil; (2) 10 percent of the dowry of any marriage he helps to arrange; (3) one *dhoti* (cotton garment worn by men), one blouse and one pair of sandals when a woman in the household dies; (4) one *dhoti*, one shirt, and one pair of sandals when a man in the household dies (5) twelve freemeals (one each month for a year) after any death in the household; (6) a few coins whenever an astrological reading is obtained. For such specialized services he receives a wide variety of emoluments. They have not been calculated for this study, because, as in the case of the *'Chamar'* mid wife and others whose services are mainly ritual, they cannot be objectified as can the payments to the fire grain-receiving specialists. It is a characteristic of the ritual context of the *Jajmani* system that reimbursements depend heavily on the particular rite, its particular occasion, and the particular household. The rituals of a particular household express both its individual character and the structure of Hinduism in general. The two are integrally intertwined in Indian religion; the ritual specialist, particularly the priest, gives simultaneious expression to both. God, man, the priesthood, the sacramentalized social order, and the kinship system converge in a ceremoney which ritualizes a particular event in a household even whose everyday activities are seen as ultimately expressive of religion (M. Opler and R.D. Singh. *The Division of Labour in an Indian Village* (A reader in General Anthropology, Edited by C.S Coon, New York; 1948; pp. 464, 496).

10. C.R.I., p. 39.

11. **Note.** It is a curious fact known from the study the Gujarat *Banis* the religious differences have not led to rigorous interdicting of inter-marriage. There is no serious objection to marriage between Jain and Vaishnav *Banias. Bani* or *bal* is a female servant called as *dai.* And, the term *bania* is derived from the *Sanskrit banijya* or trader*; and the Bania* by caste, as his name implies, lives for and by commerce. He holds a considerable area of land in the east of the province; but it is very rarely indeed that he follows any other than mercantile pursuits. The commercial enterprise and intelligence of the class is great, and the dealings of the great *Bania* houses of Delhi, Bikaner, and Marwar are of the most extensive nature. But the *Bania* of the village, who represents the great mass of the caste, is a poorcreature, not withstanding the title of *Mahajan* or "great folk", which is confined by usage to the caste to which he belongs. He spends his life in his shope, and the results are apparent in his inferior physique and utter want of manliness. He is looked down upon by the peasantry as a cowardly money-grubber; but at the same time his social standing is from one point of view curiously higher than theirs, for he is what they are not, a strict Hindu; he is generally admitted to be of pure *Vaisya* descent, he wears the *Janeo* or sacred thread, his periods of purification are longer than theirs, he does not practise widow-marriage, and he will no eat or dirnk at their hands; and religious ceremonial and the degrees of caste proper are so interwoven with the social fabric that the resulting position of the *Bania* in the grades of the rustic society is of a curiously mixed nature. The *Bania* is hardly used by the *proverbial* wisdoms of the countrywide: "He who has a *Bania* for a friend is not in want of an enemy", and," first beat a *Bania* then a thief". And, indeed the *Bania* has too strong a hold over the husbandman for there to be much love lost between them. Yet the money lenders of the villages at least have been branded with a far worse name than they deserve. They perform functions of the most cardinal importance in the village economy, and itis surprising how much reasonableness and honesty there is in their dealings with the people so long as they can keep their business transactions out of a court of justice.

Organisation:- The organisation of the *Banias* is exceedingly obscure. They have certain territorial divisions, but there is also a true sub-caste, called *Bara-Saini,* from *bara* means, 12, (twelve) and *Seni* means an army in Gurgaon (W.Crooke; *Tribes and Castes of the North -Western Province and Oudh* vol.1 p. 177. Hereafter described as *T.C.N.W.P.O.*). It is said to be quite distinct from the others. They are descended from *'Chamars'* or *'Words'* and at marriage the boy wears a *mukat* or tiara of *dak* leaves, shaped like a basket, into which a piece of leather is fixed. The territorial groups are at least there in number. Of these the chief is the *Aggarwals,* and there is a courious legend about their origin. *Bashak* Nag had 17 daughters, who were married to the 17 sons of *Ugar Sain,* but these snake daughters of *Bashak* used to leave their homes by night to visit their parents, and in their absence their husbands lived with their husbanbmans and descendants of these are the *Dasa* or *Chhotisarn gots* of the *Banias*, each *got* taking its name from that of the handmaiden from whom it is descended. The children of *Bashak Nag's* daughters formed the *gots* of the Aggarwal this groups include the following *gots*:-

Jindal, Mindal, Gar, Eran, Dheran, Mital, Mansal, Mangal, Tahil, Kansal, Bansal, Mahwar, Goyal or Goil and *Goud*. Of these Kansal and Bansal are named from *Kans*, a grass, and *bans*, bamboo, and they do not cut or injure these plants. The Mahwar are said to be descended from a son of *Agar Sain* who married a low-caste wife, so other *Banias* will not smoke with them.Another account adds Sengal. (*Punjab Census Report;* 1883, p. 533). Once a boy and girl of the Goyal or Goil got were married by mistake and their descendants form the the half got called *Gond* and *Gand* or impure section of the *Bhatias*. (*Hissar Gazetteer;* 1892; p. 137), so that there are 17 ½*gots* in all. In Jhelum the *Gond* and *Billa* sections do not intermarry, being said to be descendants of a common ancestor. Again, *one* of the sons of *Ugar Sain* married a low-caste woman and his descendents are the *Mahwar got* which cannot smoke with other *Banias*. The *Aggarwal Mahajans* only avoid their own section in marriage (*Jind*). The *second* group is the *Saralia,* who are an off-shoot of the Aggarwal and appear to have the same *gots*. The *third* group, the *Oswal,* appears to form a true sub-caste. The original Oswal gots are said to be known as, *Thaker, Baphna* (Rajput, by origin), *Sankhli, Kamawat Punwar (Maheshri), Mor Rakh Pokarha, Sankla Runwar, Kuladhar, Bribat Punwars, Sri Srim, Sankla, Punwar, Srishtgots Punwar, Suchanti Punwar, Bahudur Punwar, Kanbat, Punwar, Baid, Tagu Srishtri, Sankla, Burugotra Bhatti, Badu, Bhatti, Chorbheria, Raghubangi, Kanaujia, Rahtor and Chuichat*. They strenuously claim a *Punwar* Rajput origin, but other Rajputs of various tribes joined them. *Kotari,* or keepers of the treasure house, but the last does not seem to be true *got*, so that there were only 18 (eighteen) *gots,* as there still are among the Aggarwal. The *Baid* are said to have been originally a branch of the *Srishtgota* and to have been so called because *Devi* effected a miraculous cure of the eyes of a girl belonging to that section by causing a special kind of *ak* to grow, the juice of which healed them. The followed one of their Brahmana in becoming Jains, in Sambat 422. Hence, there are three territorial groups or sub-castes, and a fourth of lower status based on descent:- Sub-caste I. Aggarwal; Sub-groups: (*i*) *Bisa* (*ii*) *Dasa* or *Chhoti-Sarn* from Agroha. To which place the Aggrawals make annual pilgrimages, as it is the ancient city of *Agar* or *Ugar* Sain. They also have a boy's hair cut there for the first time. It has been founded in Western Raja Putana. Sub-caste II. *Saralia,* from Sarala. Sub-caste III. Oswal, *'Word'* or *'Chamar'* from *Osianagri* and *Jat* in Eastern Rajaputana. Sub-caste IV. known as *Bara-Saini* (G.T.C.P. N.W.F.P. Vol. II, p. 61).

Besides, these territorial groups, there are certain cross-divisions of the caste based on religious differences. These seem to be *Saraogi* or Jain, *Maheshri* or *Shaiva*, *Aggarwal-Vishnoi* or *Vaishnavas*. But the *Maheshri,* who undoubtedly derive their name from *Mahesh or Shaiva,* are not now all *Shaivas,* for one of their number was in consequence of a miracle converted to Jainism and so founded the *Tahtar got* of the Oswal, among whom the *Kamawat got* is also *Maheshri*. It would appear that the *Shaiva* groups formed true sub-castes, for the *Maheshri* certainly do not intermarry with the Aggarwal or Oswal. An account from *Jind* divides the *Banias* (like the *Bhabras*) into the *Srimali* or Srimal and Oswal groups, though Vaishnava and Jain Aggarwals intermary freely in Gurgaon, each groups have different *gots,* known as *Srimal* gots, these are *Chanalla, Bora, Kanodia, Bangaria, Juniwal, and* Tank. Oswal group contains *gots* of *Ranke, Dugar, Gadis, Bambal, Bambh* and *Nahar.* But from the extreme South-east of the Punjab comes to the following account which differs widely from those given above.

The Bawal *nizamat* borders on Rajaputana, and forms part of Nabha, in which state he *Banias* are represented by four groups:-

1. *Aggarwal.*
2. *Rustagi.*
3. *Khandelwal, and*
4. *Mahur* who rank in this order, each group being able to take water from the one above it, but not *vice versa.*

1. **Aggarwal**: The Aggarwals of Bawal *nizamat* in Nasha perform all the ceremonies observed by the Brahmans of that tract, but they have a special custom of boring the ears and noses of children, both male and female. This is called *parojan.* For this ceremony, they keep some of the rice used at the *lagan* preceding a wedding in another family; and carry the *deotas,* which were usually kept in the *Purohit's* charge to their own house. The *deotas* are worshipped for seven days. The Pandit fixes a *mahurat* or auspicious time for the boring and the rite is then performed, a feast being given to Brahmans and relatives. In the case of a boy, he is made to sit on a he-goat which is borrowed for the occasion and *alms* are given, a present being also made to the boy. In Nabha town som Aggarwal families perform this ceremony, but others do not.
2. **Rustagi:** According to an account from Patandi state the groups are *Aggarwal, Rasangi, Mahesri, Saraogi* and *Kalal*, and in Gurgaon, it is said that the *Saraogi* and Vishnav (sic) *Banias* do not intermarry though they can eat *Kachchi* and *Pakki* with earth other. *Rustagi* group is found only in the Bawal *nizamat*, in Gurgaon, Delhi, Alwar, Budaon, Bulandshahr and Gwalior. They are most strongly represented in Bawal, at Bhora

in Rawari tehsil and at Barand in Alwar State, but probably do not exceed 1,000 families in the whole of India. Though in marriage they only avoid one *got,* yet owing to the paucity of the numbers the poorer members cannot get wives and so die unmarried. They say that Rohtasgarh was their original home and that their name *Rustagi* is derived from *Rohtas.* They have 18 *gots* named after the villages which they originally inhabited. The avoid widow remarriage, but do not invariably wear the *janeo,* as the Aggarwals do. They perofrm the first hair-cutting of a boy at Nagarkot or Dahni in Alwar at the *asthan* of Devi. The observe the *milni,* i.e when the parents of a betrothed couple meet the girl's father must give the boy's father from one to twenty one rupees, and the girls father must not visit the village where his daughter has been betrothed until after the marriage under the penality of paying the *milni,* but once paid it is not payable to second time. At the Dewali Rustagis pay special reverence to their *Sati.* They are all Vaishnavas and also worship Gopi Nath. The *barat* must arrive the day before the wedding but they have no other special marriage customs.

3. **Khandelwal:** The Khandelwals are few in number. They have 72 *gots,* the Principal one in Nabha state being the Bojalia. They claim to have come from Khatu Khandela in Jaipur. The *barat* in this group also arrives the day before the wedding but the boy's father has to feed the *baru* himself on that day. Like the *Ahirs* the *Khandelwals* on the *widai* day have a special custom. The women of the bride's family clothe the boy's father in yellow clothes and put a pitches of water on his head, with a necklace of camel's dung round his neck and compel him to go and worship the well just as the women do. He only escpaes after much teasing by paying them from 11 to 51 rupees. They do not wear the *Janeo,* and as they are devotees of Bhagwan Das, Mahatams, of Tikha in the Bawal Thana, they do not smoke or sell tobacoo.
4. *Mahur.* The *Mahur* are few in number in Bawal. They have two *gots Mawal* and *Kargas.* They are Vaishnavas and specially reverence Hanuman. (*Ibid.,* pp. 61-62).

12. *C.R.I.,* p. 40.
13. *T.C.N.W.P. O.,* Vol. 1, pp. CLXIV-V.

3

Leather-Workers and Weavers of Early Period

Above the scavenger classes in social standing come the workers in leather, and above them again the weavers. But there is wide distinction between the typical leather-worker or *'Chamar'* and the typical weaver of *Julaha* or Megh, yet they are connected by certain sections of the leather-working classes who have taken to weaving and thus risen in the social scale, just as we found in the case of some of the scavengering classes. It is probably that our figures for *'Chamar'* and *'Mochi'* really refer to the same caste, while *Chamrang* and *Dabgar* are perhaps merely names of occupations. This group forms an exceedingly large proportion of the population in the eastern and western districts of the states and under the hills, where the *Chamar* is field labour of the villages. But in the central districts his place in this respect is taken, as already remarked, by the *Chuhra*. In the west, too, the leather-worker, like all other occupational castes, is much less numerous than in the east. The weaver class, on the other hand, is naturally least numerous in the eastern district of the states where much of the weaving class is done by the leather-working castes[1]. The costume, shoes and sandals of the people of north-western India as depicted in the various sources of the study are mixed one. The purely Indian *dhoti, dupatta,* pagri (turban) may be seen side by side with other garments i.e. tunic, trousers, suthan, shoes, sandals and *chappals* *'Word'* the characteristic costume and the people of Punjab, North Western frontier and Afghanistan had a long profession in this field.

Craftsmanship in the Vedic Age and Jatakas

In the Buddhist literature, it is mentions *dussa* as a variety of woollen cloth. The modern *dhussa*, a sort of woollen cloth manufactured in the Panjab, seems to be the modern representative of the ancient *dursa* (A.V.IV.7;6; VIII. 6,11[3]). The technical terms which are connected with weaving known as *Otu* (Wool), *tantu* (yarn), *tantra* (warporloom); vemam (Loom); *pracinatana* (forward stretched web), *vaya* (weaver). *mayukha* (peg lead weight or shuttle[4]) during the time of *Rig-Vedic* period. Craftsmenship in the *Jatakas*, it has been described they were organised in eighteen guilds including the wood-works, the smiths, the painters (the *Rangsaz),* and the rest expert in various crafts. The works of weaver or embroiderer (*pesakarasippa*) as well as of *nalakara* (the basket maker, because these professions were in the lands of the aborigines (*Barawalas),* were considered as low professions and both weavers and basket makers were relegated to the class of despised castes. In the *Bhimasena Jataka* the Brahman archer cells the work of a weaver (*tantuvaya*) a misable low work (*lamakakamma*). In the *Suttavibhanga* also the professions of the basket-maker, the potter, the weaver, the cobbler and the barber (*hinam nama sippam nalakara-sippam Kumbhakarasippam pesakarasippam Cammakara-sippam nahapita-sippm)* are mentioned as low[5] caste.

Some technical terms as regards spinning and carding are also mentioned the woman in a story spun (*Kantitva*) fine thread (*Sukhumasuttani*) and made a ball (*gulam*) of it. Bow for carding cotton is also mentioned (*Kappasapothanadhanukam*). In the time of Buddha cotton produced at Benares[7] was used in the manufacture of cloth. Buddhist literature is full of references of the cloth of Kasi[8] (*Kasi Kuttama),* it was at places termed as *Kasiyami*. The cloth of Benares was so famous that the commentator of the *Mahaparinibbana Sutta* commenting on the term *Vihita Kappasa* (Calendered cloth; modern Hindi *Kal Kundikiyahna*) with which the mortal remains of a world ruler were covered, calls it the cloth of Benares (*Kasikavathha),* which on account of the fineness of its structure did not absorb oil. The fineness of the structure of Benares[9] cloth (*Varanaseyyaka*) is also given in the *Majjhima Nikaya*. The commentator praises the cloth of Benares because in Benares according to him fine cotton was produced: the Women spinners and the weavers were clever, and the water (for bleaching) was also soft. Both obverse and reverse sides of the cloth of Benares were soft and smooth. Silk was also produced at Benares. And, it is possible that Bihar[10] and Benares produced silk goods in those days as today. The Buddha had permitted the use of *Kauseya-pravara* or silken *Chadar* to the *bhikkhus*. Linen (*Ksauma*) was also common and ordained as one of the cloths for making *civara* of the *bhikkhus*. It is also mentioned in the *Mahavagga* that the blankets were made from *Ksauma* and wool. Five hundred blankets of this material were presented by the king of *Kasi* to *Jivaka Kumarabhrtya* who in his turn presented them to the *Buddha*[11]. *Kotumbara* was also a variety of cloth, the nature of which has not been explained i.e. *'Nam'* or *'Word'*. It is, however possible that it might have been some woollen or borken or cotton stuff manufactured in the country of *Audumbaras*, the word. *Odumbara* and *Kotumbara* being synonymous according to Pryzluski[12] perhaps the garment known as *Karpara* is mentioned for the first time in the *Sraut a Sutra*. In fact the garment was worn even in the Indus Valley Culture made from the cotton clothes[13] of *'Ravidas Culture'* or *'Harappa Culture'*.

In the *Mahajanaka-Jataka* cotton, silk, linen and *Kotumbara* clothes have been described. Spinning and weaving seem to have been fairly common in the time of the *Jatakas*. Thus, according to the *Tundila Jataka* there were cotton fields in the neighbourhood of Benares. Women looked after the proper upkeep of such fields and were known as "Keeper of the cotton field". (*Kappasarakkika*) as mentioned in the *Mahajanaka Jataka*. For woollen stuff the word *Kambala* has been used in the Buddhist literature. In the *Jatakas* the scarlet *pandukambala* of Gandhara is praised (*indagopakavannabha Gandhara pandukambala*). The country of *Ṣivi* was famous for its shawls and the *Siveyyaka dussa* is praised in the *Mahavagga*[14]. It is also mentioned in the *Sivi-Jataka* where the king of Kosala is said to have presented one *Dasabala* with a cloth piece from *Sivi* costing hundred thousand pieces of money (*Satasahassaggahanakam Siveyyakavattham*). The word *dussa* still lives in the modern Hindi and Panjabi as *dhussa,* which is used for a particular type of woollen *Chadar*. Another variety of cloth which might have been manufactured from wool was known as *Vahitika*[15]. Which was sent by the *sudra rulers Ajatasatru* to *Prasenajit*, who in his turn offered it as present to *Ananda*. This cloth measured sixteen hands in length and eight in width. The use of *namtaka* (*H. namda*) 'felt' and *Kojava,* 'fluffy blanket' being luxurious woollen goods, was forbidden to the *bhikkhunis*[16].

Beginning of Historical Period

The period between (642-320 B.C) may be said to be the beginning of historical period of Indian or *Sudra Culture* that there was the development of art and crafts in Indian history. The kings of two dynastics ruling over *Magadha* include the *Saisunagas* (642-413 B.C.) and the *Nandas* ruler (413-322 B.C.) of the former Bimbisara (*Srenika*), the founder of New *Rajagrha* and Ajatasatru (*Kunika*) were contemporaries of *Mahavira* and *Buddha*. For the early history of this period later *Vedic* literature including *Brahmanas, Upanisads* and *Sutras* are important sources and on the later phase of that culture *Jatakas* and *Vinayapitaka* throw a flood of light[17] on the Indian art and culture which were flourished from time to time in the Indian history.

The later Vedic literature[18] expresses that there was an all-round progress in the culture of the Aryans which were degraded from time to time by the Brahmins. But in the metals tin, lead and silver as well as two varieties of *ayas* usually regarded a copper and iron were known in the hands of artisans. Cotton,silk, linen and Woollen garments often embroidered, storeyed buildings, huts, bricks, plates, cups, spoons of gold and silver, furniture including bedstead, thrones, mirrors, jewellery, ornaments, shoes, etc were in use[19].

The above mentioned varieties of clothes, art and crafts were ordained by the *Buddha* for the use of the *Bhikkhus* as well as other saints of his *sangah*, but there are certain other varieites of clothes which though were used by certain people of the period which were forbidden by the *Brahmanas* known as *'untouchables'* or *'Schedule caste'*. In this category some cloth from *Kusa* grags (*Kusa cira*), bark (*balkala*) means dark from the mental level, wood (*phalaka*) human hair (*kesu-kambala, bala Kambala*), the feathers of an owl as clothing, the strips of deer-skin (*aginaksip*) and cloth made from stalks of *mandara*[20]. There were tanners who made leather from the hide of slaughtered cattle, and manufacturerd it into water-bottles, bow strings, slings and the like. There were workers in metal, smiths who made weapons and rims for the wheels of carts, and potters. Women spun and wove wool and made garments. There were even barbers. Trade existed as barter system, and the value of goods was calculated at so many cows. Golden ornaments were beginning to be used[21].

Study also demonstrates that patterned and coloured garments were also prohibited to the *Bhikkhus* because of their piousness approach towards the society not like the Brahmanas of the contemporaries periods. The dyes (*rangrez*) garments were also prohibited to the *Bhikkhus* because of their simple minded approach in the favour of *'Father'* and therefore in fashion trends among the laymen were dyed in indigo, yellow, crimson, majenta, black and turmeric (*haldi*). The use of cloth with cut borders

(*Hindi: Katikinari*), long borders, embroidered borders, the borders in the shape of serpent's hood (decorated with *palmtte i.e 'Word' or 'Nam' or Rita*) befitting the laymen were prohibited because of the deeds and actions. The use of *Kancuka* or tunic was also prohibited[22] because of Brahminical approach towards common people during their rule was absent. Therefore, it is necessary to display the approach of *"untouchable"* towards the Brahminical thoughts. Moreover, the dress of the *Bhikkhus* and *Bhikkhnis* in the ancient time during the rule of *Chamar* was the same like white colour and simple diet. In consisted of three garments, all of which were dyed yellow, the first was *Sanghati* or double waist with ; the second *antarrasaka* or upper garment and the third *uttarasanga* or mantle approach toward *'Father'*. Besides these garments a sheet for sitting (*Prtyastarana), a Kanduka-praticchadana* measuring four span long and two broad, or *kopina* when suffereing from itches. *Varsikasatika* or a spare loin-cloth measuring six spans and breadth-wise 2½spans from Buddha's hand for the rainy weather were also allowed. The *Bhikkhunis* also seen to have been allowed the use of *Kancuka* (bodice) because at once place it is mentioned that the *Bhikkhuni* who went to the village without bodice had to perform *prayascitta*[23].

The *Bhikkhus* were also permitted to use a piece of cloth passed round the legs and tied at the back was called *ayoga-patta*. In spite of this fact, they used the cloth of loom (*tantaka*) with shuttles (*Vermaka*) strings (*Vatta*), tickets (*salaka*) with the due permission of the lord. Various technical terms and implements employed in sewing are also given. To safeguard the borders and edges of the *Kamarband* the edges were turned back and sewn; this particular mode of sewing is called *gunaka*. The clasp (*Vitha*) was also allowed in the *Kamaband*. It was made of bone, couch-shell, and thread of yarn; the clasps made of silver and gold were strictly prohibited. The use of button (*ganthi, ghundi*) and fastener (*pasaka,H. muddhi)* was also allowed. The bottons were to be made of bone, conch-shell and yarn but never from gold or silver separate pieces of cloth were stitched to the garment on which buttons and fasteners were attached[24] to it. The frame with its upright (*danda Kathina*), Wooden pegs (*pidalaka*), bamboo wedges (*Salaka*), strings for trying and thread for sewing were allowed. The aesthetic sense in sewing was also not left unheeded. Thus, the *Bhikkhus* who sewed their dresses with the quills obtained from the feathers of hen and bomboo needles were allowed the use of needles (*sui*) which were kept in a holder (*shu nalika*) loated with wax to avoid irregular stitches (*Sultantarika*), the cloth was folded to get parallel lines (*Kalambaka*); and also long stitches (*moghasuttaka*) were employed for having the stitches straight. As regarding the implements employed in sewing we have already spoken about the needle. Thimble (pratigrahs) was also used to avoid needle pricks. It seems the gold and silver were employed for manufacutring thimbles chiefly for the well-to-do; for the *Bhikkhus* thimbles made from bone and couch-shell, etc, were only prescribed. Scissors (*Satthaka*) were also known and as the seissors and thimble were prone to be misled small bag (*avesana vitthaka*) was used to hold them. The dress of the layman consisted of the three parts, *antarvasaka* or loin-doth, *Uttarasanga* or a mantle for covering the upper part of the body and *usnisa* or turban. Tunics or *Kurtas* were also worn by both men and woman[25].

Fashion Trends of Shoes and Sandals

Studly also demonstrates the fashion of wearing the shoes and sandals were different in shapes, colours and materials. These were the important article of the dress, without it dress was considered in completed. Therefore, the shoes and sandals were of one or two or three linings, and the leather (*Chams*) with which they were made was dyed yellow, red, majenta, black or in various colours. As these shoes and sandals were used by the general populace and their use was forbidden to the *Bhikkus* to whom only single soled shoes were allowed, though in case of old shoes this rule was also relaxed [26]. The objective of this colonization was the fabled land called *Suvarnadvipa* or *Suvarnbhumi*, 'the land of Gold', the term *Chams* has been applied to all the religious and islands towards the east and the acquisition of its gold. The *Periplus* applies the term *Chams* to *Suvarnabhumi* (Golden land). This colonization was promoted not merely by the greedy of gold, but also the spirit of adventures and missionary enterprise[27] of the *'Nam'* or *'Chamar'* to cede the public from the material life of the world.

There were many fashionable shoes that covered the ankles, (*moccasins*, i.e. *'Chamar), Putabaddha*, foot (*padigunthima*), the shoes padded with cotton-wool (*tula punnika*). They have the shape like the wings of a patridge (*tittirpattika*); and decorated with horns of ram and goat. They have also been displayed with curved points like a scorpions sting and decorated with peacock feathers etc. were in great fashion in those days. They were of course forbidden to the *Bhikhhus*. In the frontier towns where Buddhism had made little or no impression, but the *Chamar* manfactured of shoes in that *gana* were allowed to be worn by the *Bhikkhus*. There is, no doubt, that shoes were laso made from the skins of tiger, lion, leopard, deer, otter, cat, squirrel and owl. Such was he fashion of the shoes in those days that similes from the profession of cobbler (*Cammakara*[28]). have crept in literature. It is said in the *Kama Jataka*, that as gradually the desired are annihilated the happiness is born in the same way as the cobbler when he shapes his shoe cuts off rought ends and leaves them plain (*rathakaro va cammassa parikantam upahanam*). The wooden sandals (*paduka*) and the sandals made from palm leaves and bamboo used by laymen were forbidden to the *Bhikkhus*. It is possible, however, that the sandals made from the above materials and also from straws *munja-grass, hintal wood, kamala, balraja* grass and blankets which were also forbidden to the *Bikkhus,* were used by the people. The sandals decorated or made from gold, silver, jewels, beryl, crystal, bronze, glass, tin and copper were used by some people[29]. In the Kushana period the Gandhara style of sculptures on a stone slab of *Ravidas Culture*, a woman standing near Kubera, who is drinking wine, have also shoes in her feet. The shoes worn by women is very thick, heavy and long like those worn by men. The description of the sandls of woman is also given in the *Sonndarvananda*[30]. No doubt, the fashion of wearing the shoes and sandals have been started in the remote past, but in the period, between 150-100 B.C. sandals among Kings were very rare. In the *Yuan-Chwang,* it is discussed that in Indian most of the people go bare foot and shoes were rare[31]. Whereas *Atri* was an ancient writer on *dharma* follows from the reference to him in Manu (III, 16) as holding the view that a *dvijati* taking as wife of a *Sudra* woman became fallen (*patita*). He mentions the seven *antyajas* to be the washerman, the shoemaker, *nata, buruda, kaivarta (*fisherman), meda and *Bhilla* (p. 29). He further says that there is no question of untouchability in fairs, marriage seasons, in Vedic sacrifices and in all festivals. He says that *Brahmanas* from Magadha Mathura and three other places are not honoured. (at a *sraddha*) though as learned as Brahaspati[32]. The shoes are not mentioend in the early *Samhitas*. *Vaturinapada* probably refers to heavy footguards used in the battle field[33]. *Patsangini* as S.C. Sarkar refers, is used to denote somewhat clumsy foot-fasteners used by the soldiers known as slipper. Shoes (*Upanaha*) have for the first time been referred to in the *Yajurveda,* the *Atharvaveda,* and the *Brahmanas*[34]. It was used in the rituals and the *Vratyas* used by them. The ritual sandals were made of antelope or boar skin[35].

Mahavagga also refers varieties of shoes and sandals of various styles which were prevalent both the men and women of the period. It is mentioned that shoes with single-sole (*ekatalamsika*), double-sole (*dvipatata*) tripple-sole (*tipatala*) and quadraple-sole. In addition to these shoes we have references to shoes of different designs such as *putabaddha, paligunthima, khallabaddha, mendaevisanabaddhika, ajavisanabaddhika, vrschikalika, morapinchha-parisibbita, rulapunnika and tittirapattika*. Such shoes were wore only by the house-holders. Shoes were also made from the skins of lions, tigers, deer leopards, otters, cats, squirrels, and owls. Sandals were made of wood, *balbaja* grass and wool. The rich wore sandals adorned with ornaments made of gold, silver, quartz (sphatika), and cat's eye (*vaidurya*[36]).

In the study; we also learn that leather was used in making shoes of the dead animals which were prepared by the *'Chamar'* or *'Nam'* in the Heaven. He lands at the time of evaluation with five kinds of leather, namely, *cowhide, buffalo hide, goat skin, sheep skin* of wild animals have been recounted in the *Brhat-Kalpa-Sutra Bhasya*[37]. It will be proper to discuss the kind of the shoes used with the lower garment. Figures of women at present wearing garments showing foreign influence, therefore, it is necessary to carve her on the pedestals of the images of the *Buddha* or the *tirthankaras* or *'Nam'*, hence their figurexs which are known as 'Dr. Raj Kumar and Baba Gurinder Singh Ji. Bias' are very small. We cannot, therefore, clearly see the depition of shoes on their feet and they are walking bare footed. It is possible that they might not have been displayed wearing sohes and sandals with a view to maintain the religious sancity of these images as our duty being *'Chamar'*. In some images the feet are covered with the lower garments or have been damaged. Only few images have seen shown wearing shoes [38] those are the follower of *'Chamar'*.

Study also demonstrates the Chinese sources added beautiful knowledge of the footwear of the Indians in the Gupta period. In the *Fan-Yu-tsa-ming,* the Sanskrit equivalent of *hiue* meaning boot in Chinese language is given to as *Kavasi*. The word again is foreign to Sanskrit. The word as *Pelliot* remarks, resembles the Iranian *Kafs,* (Shoe), still used among the Turkish tribes of Central Asia under the form *Kapis* and *Kipis* meaning sandals. The form may be compared with Tibetan *Kab-sa* which signifies leather shoes of Hindu fashion used by the wealtheir Tibatans. In the *'Le-Fan-Tang Siao-Si* (*Brahmacina Vartta-mukha*) an appendix to the dictionary *Yi-Tsiang* there are two Sanskrit words *Savanasa* and *Pula* standing for the Chinese *hiue* and *hiai* meaning boots and shoes. In the *Mahavyutpatti* are many words for boots and shoes *upanah, paduka* (sandals[38]), *padavestanika, pula* and *manda-pulah (mundapula)*. The *Pula* of the *Le-Fan-Tang-Siao-Si* is the same as *pulapula* of the *Mahavyutpatti*. The origins of the Savanasa and *pula*[39], however, are certain in the ancient history of Chinese and Indians for the co-relation between the two.

Apparently the words discussed aforesaid about the shoes and sandals were either coined in Central Asia or belonged to the *desi bhasa* or popular in the Indian society. So far as the origin of the term *pula* is concened that one must be rise from the ground level to upwards with the law of nature i.e. *'Nam'*, but *mandapula* of the *Mahavyutpatti* seems to have been derived from word *munda* which means the theory of mind is destructive and always injurious to other and creats the untouchable system in the society with the working class which always serves the society as a dutyful sons and daughters of the 'Father' in his assence. Father is common for both the 'untouchable' and *'touchable'*, therefore, it is the duty of man that a common variety made of shoe (*chams*) with decorative hook at the tip must be put into the feet as his origin. This *munda* shoe is worn by peasants all over the eastern United Provinces of India. The *Kavasi* in the *Fan-Yu-tsa-ming* which is perhaps the same as Iranian *Kafs* and *Kapis-Kipis* of Central Asia has its equivalent in the Sanskrit *Khapusa* mention in the *Brhatkalpa Sutra Bhasya* and described as boots covering the knees. The probability is that *Khapusa* or *Kavasi* were boots of Iranian origin brought to India by the *Sakas* and the Kushanas whose Iranian affinities are well known[40] in the Indian history as well as in the Chinese annals.

According to the Jain sources, the Jain monks and nuns were disallowed the use of any kind of leather or *Chams* goods of any type and colour. (*ranga*). It may be inferred from the above study that shoes of colour leather made of *'Father'* and sons are standard types and sizes were in demand by the people of India and China. These leather shoes of standard types and colours (*rangas*) were divided into the following four varieties: *Sakala-krtsna, pramana-krtsna, varnakrtsna* and *bandhanakrtsna* discussed as under:

The *Sakala- krtsna* is defined as single soled (*ekaputan* or *ekatalam*) this single-soled shoe, *talika* as it is called, could be used by the Jain monks at night to avoid thorns. In day-time, these shoes could be worn when the caravan with which they travelled took a short-cut as the wearing of shoes at such occasions facilitated walking from one place to another with the help of *'Chamar's* work. The *pramana-krtsna* shoes had two, three or more soles for the strengthening of shoes and sandals. The commentary says that they were of two varieties i.e. half *Khallaka* (*ardhakhallaka*) and full *Khallaka* (*Samastakhallaka*). The half *Khallaka* shoes covered half the leg while the full *Khallaka* covered the whole leg for the protection of safety of their ownself. The *Khapura* shoes covered the knees. The *Vagura* type covered the toes and the feet; and the *Kosaka* type covered the toes to protect the nails against stones, throns, snakes, and other insects which cut the feet while walking in the field of life. The *Jangha* type covered the thighs and the *ardhajangha* covered half of the thighs. Elsewhere another kind of shoe called *putaka* is mentioned in the Jains taxts. It was made of straps which covered the skin so that it should not crack during the winter because of the heavy snowfall in the areas of *Kashmir* and other *Kosaka* and *Khapura* shoes were used to avoid the cold, snow, snakes and throns. Study shows that these varieties were used in colder climates for the sake of development of the country in right direction and objectives. The *Sakalakrtsn* type is further defined as the shoes and sandals are made of *Kramanika*, the exact measurement of the foot; it is not cut or joined in the middle or anyother part of the shoes and sandals as it is a perfect one for the sake of *munda*.

The next variety which is known as *pramanakrtsna* shoes contain all the varieties described above in the discussion, with the exception that in this type all the varieties, who has two, three or more soles of *panduranga* were known as *Varna-krtsana*.

The *Varna-Krtsna* type of boot made from white or coloured (*ranga*) leather.

The fourth variety of the shoes known as *bandhara-krtsna* type has fasteners more than three in number. In another spot it has been described as sown or fastened with two or three or even more lines of sewings or fastening of hemp or cotton threads made by *'Weaver'* was used to the shoes for its stitching or needle works in relationship.

It is also mentioned in the *Rayapa-Senaiya* the shoes or boots in general had two fasteners, one hemp fastner at the knees, the other at the five toes. If there were three fasteners then one was at the knee, second was at the big toe and the third covered the rest of the four toes. Among the varieties of the shoes and sandals mentioned above known as *Khallaka* and *Khapusa* type are also represented in the coins of Gupta period and in the wall painting of Ajanta. It has already been discussed that monks were not allowed to wear these shoes and sandals as they were considered fashionable trends of the Indian society. They were advised to cut the leather (*cham*) from they got their shoes and sandals in eighteen parts which were then sewn together with the help of thread, the production of the weaver. No coloured (rangadar) leather was used by them because they are the *Brahmans*, by caste, they refrain to see the *"untouchables"* because their caste is dirty, their works are dirties. But they are firm in approach to wear the shoes made of one sole and only one fastener (*ekabandham*).

There were certain restrictions imposed by the Father to the monks on the following grounds:

- The use of *Cham* (leather) meant cruelty to cows and other animals during their death.
- The shoes being hard to wear and killed the tiny animals while walking during night.
- While walking without shoes or sandals the people watched carefully the throns, snakes, etc, and in doing so also espied worms in the life and other tiny creatures will have to avoid them, but their shod feet are careless of throns and worms, etc because of their 'egoistic' approach toward master.
- The very use of shoes and sandals has presupposed cruelty to the animal would there is no affication and love to each other.
- The very small creatures created by God are tender by nature and they could not be expected to with stand the pressure of shoes and sandals during the hard walk.

Study also reflects even the meritorious might have been the non-wearing of shoes from the religious point of view i.e. *BJP, Congress, B.S.P, Sad-BJP, etc.* it was not possible in the practical life of the Jain monks in the day-to-day life, therefore, it is certain that *'Radha Soami Mission'* exceptions were made for the establishment of 'New Society' to the general rule by the Saints, otherwise unlawful wearing of shoes will not be allowed to the monks on tour from one generation to another for those who were ill by the Brahmanical thought, whereas the opposite race whose feet were tender by nature, to these who were in constant fear of wild animals and robbers, to those who suffered from leprosy, piles or short-sightedness, to child-monks and to nuns on tour in this universal. In times of family trobles and mishaps in the country or *samgha,* the unlawful shoes and sandals could be freely used, but there is rule of *'Single sole'* i.e. Father, the people will be allowed to wear a lawful shoes which never pinch the feets. On tour, the monk was advised to wear the *Kosa* and *Khapusa* type of shoes and sandals. If a monk was forced to wear unlawful shoes and sandals, he should choose black-coloured shoes; in their absence, however, red-coloured shoes and sandal of any other colour could be worn but not before they were, not ready to discoloured[41]. Therefore, red-coloured shoes were constantly worn by the monks and nuns in this country according to the requirement of the situation. The shoes are represented only once in the *Sanchi* sculptures, and there are foreigners are represented wearing them (fig.64, chapter Ist). It should not be, however, concluded from this that the Indians did not wear shoes and sandals. On the contrary there are literary evidences that the shoes of various forms and materials were commonly used in ancient India by the "untouchables" and there was less scope of the Brahminical material which is used in the rite and ritual ceremonies. On different occasions like marriage and festivals their absence from the sculptures both at *Bharhut* and *Sanchi* can be easily explained if we bear with mind that the use of shoes and sandals at the time of worship must have been prohibited in ancient days as today during the early morning of *dhana* of the *'Nam',* and because the figures represented are engaged in worship with *'Father'* act as characters in sacred stories of the *'Nam'* or *'Chamar'* they have been purposed represented without shoes[42]. The shoes and sandals were dyed in different colours, Grecian sandals and full boot are referred to as well as many other varieties of showes made from feathers and skins of various birds and animals wooden sandals in laid with precious stones were also known[43] to us.

Weaver and Weaver's Works of the Early Period

After a brief discussion of the shoes and sandals of the Vedic age period; we propose to discuss the clothing period of weaver and weaver works from sixth century B.C. to the third century B.C. The sources for the history of this period are the earliest *Buddhist* and *Jain literature,* the *Dharmasutra,* the *Grihyasutra, Yuan Chwan's* account, etc. It appears from the sources that there must have been the fashioners of the garments. The god *Pushan*[44] is called a 'weaver of garments' (*Vasovaya*) because of his connection with the fashioning of form. The garments worn in the Vedic age were often embroidered and the *Maruts* are described as wearing mantles adornment with gold (*hiranyan atkan*). The cloth and borders and fringer. The word *sic* is a general term for embroidered border or fringe. Two length-wise and two breadth wise borders are also indicated from the work of *Arokah,* 'brilliants' were probably patterns of the garments. According to S.C. Sarkar the word *'Asokah'* to have been probably derived from the Tamil word *'Arukani'*, 'ornamented border of cloths[45]. For ritual purposes, it was used an unbleached cloth, otherwise white cloth was worn on (*Svityancah*). Dyed cloth resplendent with gold was also used by gay woman typified by *Ushas*[46]. The *Vratya* householders, however, preferred dark blue cloth and borders. The Vedic Indian people seems to have worn three article of dresses: an undergarment (*nivi*), a garment (*Vasas*), and an (outgarment *(adhivasa)* which presumably a mantle *'Word'* or *'Weaver'* the *duppatta* or *Chadar* of modern times. This accords with the description of sacrifical garments given the *Satapatha Brahmana*[47]. The *nive* has been explained by Sarkar as wider border of the cloth. He also gives the origin of the term *nivi* from the Tamil word *nev,* to weave. From *nivi* hang like the *praghata,* the *loose* and long unwoven fringe with tassels; the other and was plainer and decorated with *tusa 'chaff',* a shorter fringe. The *Vatapana* is explained again by S.C. Sarkar as lengthwise border protecting the cloth against wind which keeps the wed together from becoming threadbase by fluttering in the wind[48] or *Vayu Serva.* The mode of wearing the cloth is not indicate like *'air',* they were used to wear in various styles. The *vasas* were, however, tried. The term *nivimkr* shows that each individual followed his or her own fashion in arranging his order own loin-cloth in elaborate pleats and artistic waist-knots[49] which are less visible in the Brahminical rule. The term *Usnisa* is not used for turban in the ancient Vedic literature, though it has been used in *Atharva Veda,* and the *Pancavimsa Brahmana* in connection with the said *Vratya*. In the *Yajur Veda* and the *Brahmanas* the word is used in connection with *Vartyas* and *rajas*. The latter used to wear the turban at the time of *Vajapeya* and the *Rajasuya* ceremonies. *Indrani* also wore turban as a token of her status as queen. The *urnisa* of the *Vartyas* was while as day, was perhaps made of cotton, and according to the *Sutras* tied and cross windings. The king tied his turban at the sacrifices in themanner in which the ends were gathered together and tucked away in front so as to cover them up. Ordinarily it seems that the princes wore turbans with hanging ends[50] . Yuan Chwang in his account mentions the names for their clothing materials which was by the weavers known as *Kiao-she-ye* (*Kau-Sheya*) and Muslin (*tieh*) and Calico (pu), *Kausheya* being silk from a wild silk-worm, *ch-u* (or *Ch'u*) mo (*Kshauma*), a kind of linen, *Han* (or *Kam*)*-po-lo (Kambala),*a texture of fine wool (sheeps wool or goat's hair), and *Ho-La-Li* (*Ral,* means there is 'way' or 'law' to see the Master a texture made from wool of wild animal *'Word'* this wool being fine and soft and easily spun by the weaver and woven is prized as a material for clothing was used. In North India where the climate is very cold closely fitting jackets are worn somewhat like those of *Tartars* (*Hu*[51]). In this passage, it will noticed, the clothing materials which was used by the weavers by the lay people of India are arranged in four groups discussed as under:—

— The first is called by the pilgrim "Kausheya clothing and muslin and cloth". Now *Kausheya* (or *Kauseya*) is silk made from the cocoon of the Bomby X Mori, and *tich-pu* is cotton-cloth or *tich* and *Cotton cloth*. It is perhaps better to regard *tieh* and pu as names of two materials, and in another treatise we find *Kausheya, tieh* and *tsui* grouped together[52]. This *ts'ui* was apparently a kind of coarse cotton cloth, and we find a *ts'ui-ka-pei* or "rough cotton" used to stuff cushions. The term *Kausheya* was applied not only to silk stuffs, but also to mixtures of silk and linen or cotton. Our pilgrim evidently makes one group of "silk clothing" and cottons this is not to be much wondered at when we reflect that he, like the Chinese of his time and district, knew nothing of the cotton plant and the clothes derived from it. Moreover, we should probably regard this description of the dress of the natives of India as derived from an earlier account.

— The second kind of clothing material of the weaver here mentioned is the *Kshauma* or Linen. This term also is to be regarded as denoting a class. it comprehends, we must suppose, the fabrics made from the *Kshuma* of flax, the *sana* or jute, and the *bhansa* or hemp. These three plants are mentioned in Chinese translations from the Sanskrit as yielding stuffs from which clothes were made. This word *Kshauma* denotes not only linen but also silk textures.

— The third group is the *Kambala*. The word, which denotes "woollen cloth" and "a blanket", is here evidently used in the sense of fine woollen cloth for making clothing. Like the *Kausheya* and the *Kshauma* the *Kambala* clothing was allowed to the Buddhist Brethren.

— The fourth kind of stuff which was undertaken by the *'Weavers'* as used for clothing material is called by *Yuan-Chuang Ho-la-li*. There does not seem to be any known Sanskrit word with which this can be identified. As *Yuan-Chuang* spells foreign words the three characters may stand for *Ral,* a Tibetan word mean "goat's hair", from *Ra,* a goat. This *Ho-La-Li* or *Ral* is also probably *Lo-i* or '*Lo (Ra)* clothes" of other Buddhist texts. In Sanskrit also we find *rallaka* which donates a wild animal and a stuff made from its hair and *rallaka-kambala* which is fine woollen cloth[53].

It is interesting to note for the first part of this passage Julien has the following words:- *"Les Cha-men (Cramanas) n'ont quetrois sortes de, vetements, savoir le seng-kia-tehi (Sanghati) le seng-kio-ki (Sanka-Kchika), et le Ni-po-sie, na (Nivasana) la coupe et la facon out ces trois vetements varient suivant les ecoles les autres out des pans petits oil grands*[54]"

In *Grihya-Sutra, Kandika* 10, it has been rightly expressed that there are four kinds of garments, but only persons of the three castes are concerned, the garment of a Brahmana is made of linen, or of hempen cloth *(Sana),* that of a *Kshatriya*, of cotton, that of *Vaisya,* of wool, on the day on which the youths is going to received the initiation for the studentship[55] and 'untouchables" were deprived of that because they are already called as *Sudra*. It shows *Sudra* was the separate race of the Father, they were used to live above the 'blind *Faith'* i.e. called Brahminical thought and they committed the crime with the 'Father's race during his absence.

The various sources of the earliest Buddhist and Jain literature furnish a statement about the artisans which were connected with the cloth industry known as embroiderers *(Pesakarasippa),* weavers *(tantuvaya),* tailors *(tunnaya*), silk weavers *(Pattagara), etc.* Many kinds of cloths mentioned above such as those made of cotton *Kauseya* (Silk) *Ksuuma* (Lenin), *kambala* (wool), *Kautumbara, Sana* (made of hemp), *Valkola* (back), made of straw, *hiranya* cloth, skin cloth[56], etc. were prevalent in that period; this shows the cloth articles such as *Chitaka* (a carpet made with cloth pieces of many colours to the bedding), *Palika* (white woollen carpet), *patalika* (a carpet with densely embroidered flowers), *tutika* (a quilt stuffed with cotton), *Vikatika* (covers embroidered with figures of lions, tigers, etc.), *Uddalmi* (a blanket with hair on both the sides) *Kaseyya* (silken carpet), *Kutaka* (a carpet on which sixteen female dancers could dance simultaneously) *Laltha-Hara* and *assatthara* (a piece of cloth which is spread on an elephant or horse or in a chariot), *ajinapaveni* (a blanket made by joining together pieces of deerskin), *Kadalimiga-pavarapachchattha* (probably a blanket made of the skin of *Kadal* deer), *Chilamika* (a kind of carpet), *Vahitika* (a woollen sheet 8 yards in length and 4 yards in breadth) *namataka*, (felt made by crushing the hair of sheep or hill goats), *Kojava* (a blanket with long hair[57]), etc depicts the work and achievements of the weavers or artisans to boost the industry. Shoes and sandals also formed an important part in many artistic ways in this period. They were made in different colours. Clothes were sown with needles, scissors, *pratigraha*, and *Kathina* (either chalk or the smallest finger[58]) have been expressed from the Buddhist literature of period, used by the weavers during the needle works on clothes, etc.

Besides the above mentioned varieties cloth made from hemp (*Sana* in Hindi called *San*) and *bhaga* were also produced from the fibre of *bhag-tree* is still produced in the Kumon district of Uttar Pradesh and is known as *bhagela*. Skin (*ajina*) as material for clothing is mentioned in the *Jataka.* It seems that in those days the skin of line, tiger, leopard, cow and deer were used for clothing as well as for betsheets, etc. In the Madhyadesa (united provinces and Bihar) the skins of *eragu, moragu,* and cats (*majjaru*), and in the *Daksinapatha* the skins of rams, goats and deer served as coverlets and even in the case of *Bhikkhus* for whom no kind of skin clothing or beeding was allowed a concession was made in these countries[59].

In Kautilya's Arthasastra the duties of the superintendent of weaving has been supreably defined, therein, it is mentioned that in the weaving department threads (*Sutra*), coats (*Varma*), cloth (*Vastra*) and ropes (*rajju*) were manufactured in India. The materials employed for spinning and weaving were wool (*Urna*), fibres (*balka*), Cotton (*Karpasa*), *tula, hemp (sana)* and flax (*Ksauma*[60]). It is also noteworthy in the interest of weavers that only women were employed for spinning and weaving as the Vedic age period, and there wages were depended upon the fineness of the yarn which they used to spin[61]. The weavers, who manufactured linen (*Ksauma*) *dukula* cloth from the fisres of *dukula* plant, silk (*Krmitana*, Hindu *Katana* was used for finest quality of white sick yarn), woollen stuff (*rankava*[62]) and cotton cloth, received besides their wages, presentations of scents, garlands and other gifts by the way of encouragement for the weavers. In this department bed sheets (*Vastrastarana*) and cutrains (*Pravarana*) were also manufactured[63]. It shows during the Mauryan and the subsequent periods cotton seems to have been in great demand for manufacturing the cloth, as the *Greeks* did not understand how the white cotton was produced by the 'Father,' they thought it to be the wool growing on trees[64] as soon it develops. In the *Sabha Parva*[65] the name of a country known as *Karpasika* was a biggest centre for the production of cotton. But it is unfortunate the name of the country has not been identified as yet by the *Brahmans* of the country.

The places where from wool and woollen goods, silk and cotton clothes, skins of lion, tigers, etc. came to India are also elaborated in the *Sabha Parva*[66] text. Thus, it is also mentioned that the people of Kambojas (the people of Badakshan and Pamir) gifted *Yudhisthira* certain woollen cloth (*aurna*) embroidered with gold (*Jatarupapariskrtan* at the time of *Rajasuya,* which must have been probably embroided shawl, and the skins of the various animals that lives in the holes (*bailan*) and of wild cats (*Varsadamsan*) which were fursprobably of the animals of martin and weasel families. The *Abhiras* brought woollen cloth of various designs (*Kambalanvividhan*[67]) which were not made from cotton (*Vastram-akarpasam*[68]), but manufactured from the soft wool of sheep (*avikam*) and shaggy goat (*ajinam*), also shawls manufactured from the wool and the hair of deer (*rankavah*[69]) which were of good and fine colour and dimensions. These items of articles of clothing manufactured in *Cina* or China and *Valhika*.

Term *Kitaja* which was the product of *Cina* and *Valhika* used for silk is also mentioned in Kautiya's *Arthasastra* as well as in *Mahabharata*[70]. The seric of *Strabo* is real silk which was believed to have been produced from some sort of byssos bark (*Valkola*) by Combing the fibres Mocrindle in an interesting account tells us that the first ancient author in Greecian literature was refers to the use of Silk is Aristotle (H.A.V.19). According to him raw silk was brought from the interior Asia and manufactured at *KoS*. Is the word, where it was manufactured by the *'weavers'*, perhaps Panini who gives special *Sutra* for the formation of *Kauseya* refers to the town *Kosa* and not to the cocoons[71].

Stitched Garments

There is one more interesting information we collect from the sculptures of *Sanchi* about sewn garments the work of tailor (*Darzi*). It is worthy to note that it was worn by a charioteer, soldiers, kings body guard or standard bearer and the foreigners worshipping the *stupa*. The soldiers may be divided into two classes: the archers and footsoldiers. The former (Fig.60) wear a full-sleeved tunic, the sleeves being rolled to the elbows when shooting the arrows (Fig. 61), the filt fastened securely round the waits, manifold *Kamaraband,* cross straps to carry their quiver and a turban. The footsoldiers wear the same sort of garment except the crossstrap. In some places, however, they were represented wearing a sort of short drawers which is held round the waist with a string, and also from the string below the navel is hung a decorative piece of cloth (*patka*) *(Fig. 62)*. In one of the scences at Ajanta (Cave X, PL. VII, Fig. 37) depicting an incident from the *Saddanta Jataka Sonuthara* the hunter and his companion are represented wearing tunics. One man, probably the hunter (*Sakari*) bearing a *bahgi* on his sholders, wears a quarter sleeved stripped tunic with V-shaped opening in front reaching to the knees. The other man also wears a patterned tunic, guarter sleeved and reaching to the knees with round collar and open front with buttons. The garment of the foreigners (Fig. 63) worshipping the stupa requires attention i.e. *'Nam'* or *'Chamar'*. They wear a full-sleeved tunic, a kilt, a *Kamarband*, a scarf streaming at the back and tied in a knot at the neck and full boats. As regards their head-dresses, some wear fillet round the forehead tied at the back; two of them wear conical cap and the others go bare-headed[72].

In the study; it indicates the materials which was used for stitching garments in the Vedic period are known by casual references with which it is difficult to give a history of the Indian dresses with any degree of accuracy. Wool, however, was an important material for manufacturing the cloth. Fine wool was at hand obtained from the ewes of Gandhara and the regions through which Indu and *Parusni* (Ravi) flowed the culture of Ravidas community at one time in the history of India. From the wool obtained from these countries were manufactured blankets (*Kambala*), *dhussa (dursa),* and perhaps *panavad*. The skin of the animals were also worn by the Gods and Munis, *Vratyas* and aboriginal tribes (*Barawalas*). Goat and antelope skins were preferred[73].

The most interesting period from the point of the history of Indian weavers, however, is the Gupta period founded by Candragupta I (320-534 A.D), one of the flourishing period of weaver's works. It is not only in the political, religious, economic and artistic sphere, but material culture also attained a high level. This may be gathered from the works of *Kalidas, Banabhatta* and other archaeological remains. But the introduction of stitched garments in India on an extensive scale *Chhimba* or *Darzi* = *Darzi* though it must be admitted the Indians knew of sewn garments from very early times *'Weavers'* influenced to a certain extent the costumes of those who came in intimate contact with the court. The first tobe affected were the servants, both male and female. Their well-cut tunics, and at times shorts, show the royal taste in the livery of personal servents. It has been often argued that perhaps many of the servents wearing sewn garments were foreigners (*Barawalas*) in the employment of the Indian kings. This is true in the case of a minority, the majority of them were definitely Indians the descriptions of servants, main servants etc, by *Banabhatta 'Weaver'* in his works discussed elsewhere *in the history* of India prove it[74].

The lexicons, especially the *Amarakosa* edited by Dr. Haradatta, are important source of study about the costumes and textile materials of the Gupta period. It contains certain interesting information, though the terms are not always clearly explained and the commentaries also far from illuminating *Amarasimha* the textile materials are divided in the following four varieties discussed as under:—

— First, *Valka* (made from bark fibres), which also includes *'Ksauma'*, etc. material

— Second, *'Phala'* (made from fibrous fruits) which also contains cotton plants of the same order.

— Third, *'Kauseya'* (silk) obtained from cocoons) as a natural product.

— Fourth, *'rankava'* , (made from the hair of a goat). *'Rankava'* needs some explanation on broad base. The word formed from the known *'ranku'* is usually explained by the commentatiors as a kind of woollen cloth manufactured from the hair of the *'ranku'* deer or some other species of wild animal. The lexilographers and the commentators were not at all sure about the origin of the word. There is, however, a natural explanation for the term *'rankava'* variety of woollen cloth which is known as *'Chamar'* originated from the word *'Cham'* there is a species of goat called *'rang'* which flourishes in the steppers of the high Pamir plateau. It affords a very fine shawl-wool. The *'rang'* goat is probably the same as the *'ranku'* of Sanskrit literature about whose exact counterpart in the animal kingdom the lexicographers are not sure[75], because the soul was incomplete without of *'Rangi'* a spet of *Jats* found in *Jind* (body). In that state five *gots* of *Jats* derive their names from as many parts of the *beri* tree, *viz*: (i) *Rangi,* from the *'rang'*, or bark of the *beri* tree used for dyeing (ii) *Jaria,* from *Jar,* the root (iii) Beria, from *ber,* the fruit (iv) *Jhari*, or seedlings, and (v) *Khichar*, or bud.

These five *gots* may, however, intermary and are, collectively, called *Jaria* which is also said to be derived from *Jora* and to mean 'twin'[76].

Besides this, term *Rangeeta,* used for a *Chuhra* or *Chamar*, but especially of a *Chuhra* coverted to Sikhism. It is very possibly a corruption of the English word. 'recruit,' or it may be a diminution of *Rangar, Ranghar*. These terms applied to *Mazhabi Sikh*[77]. Moreover, term *Rangrez* is merely the Persian equivalent of dyer; and *Rangsaz*[78] are painters wood, and other materials; but not house painters who come under the title of *Mistri, Kamangar, Pharera*[79] etc. If the proposed of *'ranku'* with *'rang'* goat by correct then the *Rankava* would mean a fine variety of *'Pashmina'* cloth probably manufactured from the fine wool of the *'ranku'* goat which is equivalent to *'Nam'* or *'Words'*.

In the study, we also learn that there was a great advancement in the textile in the Pamir region. As discused in *Mahabharata* that *fets*[80] were also manufactured art and craft not only in wool; but also in silk weaving in Gupta period; as it is evident from their description in the *Amarakosa* text. There are stay references to textile materials which was used by the weavers in the industries is also found in the literature of Gupta period. Moreover, some what conventional descriptions are available in the traveller's accounts of the Chinese pilgrims like *Huan Chawng, I-ting* etc, these sources also furnished an adequate idea of the textile materials of that age. It shows that all the informations which have been scrapped in the travellers accounts, literature, dictionaries, etc, however, they may be, have to be put together for improving the history of *'untouchable'* which was losted during the Brahminical period, because Brahmanas also have the attitude toward *'untouchable'* discriminatory, therefore it is essential to give them a befitting reply of the *'untouchables'* culture belonged to the Ravidas Culture.

Unfortunately, there are few Sanskrit works which give us a correct appraisal written by the foreigners who used to live in India for the time being, painted the social condition under which the *'untouchables'* used to live, what they are, what they dressed the society and how they amused themselves. For such information one has to depend on entirely on occasional references of books, which are often scrappy and conventional in treatment like Brahmans. So far as the costumes and other material for the purpose of interior decoration the household, like bed sheets, chusions, carpets, etc., however, the works of *Banabhatta* throw flood of light as a weaver himself and did a wonderful work for the society in the advancement of material culture in right way. Nothing one can escaped from his penetrating eyes and so advanced was his descriptive power which still stand now that it did not overlook even the minutest details of the study. The lexicons, especially the *Amarakosa* which means lives forever never dies only changes the dress one after the another as the life has does itself. Therefore, it is important for the study of costume and textile materials of the Gupta period. The manufacturing of cloth right from the loom to the finishing and calendering stages are discussed in the *Amarakosa* text. For the cloth right fresh from the loom the following terms have been expressed in the literature known as *anahata* (uncalendered), *nispravani* (fresh from the loom), *tantraka* (woven on the loom) and *navambara*[81] *(*seasonal clothes). The bleached cloth was known as *udgamaniya,*[82] means one has to obtain the *'Nam'* for the bleaching of body which gives beautiful finish. In addition to this, one of the beautiful example of the varieties of silk is discussed known as patrorna in the *Amarakosa*. Perhaps it was kind of the wild silk plant, as *Ksirasvami*, a commentator of the *Amarakosa* calls it silk spun by the insects feeding ont he leaves of *banyan*[83] *(Ficus Indica)* plant and *'lakuca'* (a kind of bread or fruit tree, *Artocarpus lakuche*). Costly bleached silk is renowned as *Mahadhana*[84] *i.e. 'Nam'* or *Chamar. Dukula*[85] according to *Amarasimha* was a synonym of *Ksauma* (linen) and the linen covers were known as *nivita* and *pravrta* mentions in *Amarakosa*. It seems that after some time all thin bleached materials were being classified as *dukula*[86]. *Acarangasutra*[87] the commentator of the 11th century A.D., however, also explains the term *dukula* as cloth made from the cotton grown in Gauda during the time of ruler Yasovermana of Bengal which had the friendly relation with the Kashmir ruler known as *Lalitaditya Muktapida*. Moreover, text *Amarkosa* also gives certain words for denoting the measurements of cloth. The cloth's ends or hems are called *dasa* and *vasati* in length as *dairghya* which is known as taitor in present senerio, *ayama* means opposit force of the *'Nam'*, and *aroha* means measurement of period by the nature and the breadth as *parinaha,* and *Visalata*[88] which is unending dia logue. The various stages of wearing and tearing of cloth after constant period must be checked that who wears permanently or temporarily, if gives several names known as *pataccara* the old one friendship with *jirna-vastra* damaged and dirty clothes which are called 'untouchables' are known as *naktaka* and *Karpata*[90]. The clothes of the common weavers i.e. 'Scheduled Caste' are known by the following six words: *Vastra, acchadana, vasah, crila, vasana* and *amsuka*[91] which are the attributed terms of the *'Nam'*. In the categories of wrappers and bed coverings various sub-divisions are worthy to note. The bed covers are called as *nicola* and *pracchadapata,* and the rugs were used as floor carpets are known as *rallaka* and *Kambala* made from woollen stuffs. *'Ho-La-Li'* in Sanskrit word is mentioned equivalent to the term of *'ral'* by *Yuan Chwang* in his account as the same as the term *rallaka* mentioned in *Amarakosa*[92] text.

From the above discussion we learn that the *Weavers, Darzi*, etc. played a preidominent role not only in the political, religious and artistic sphere of life during Gupta period, but the material culture provide the farmers from the agricultural product also attained a high level touch into the refinement of clothes and costume. The fashions in hair-dressing at that time was almost limitless in varieties, in which that hands of expert hair-dressers known as Candra Gupta I (320-335 A.D.), Samudragupta (335-385 A.D.) etc. are visible at that time in the form of *'Dr. Raj Kumar, Baba Gurinder Singh Ji. Bias'*. In the mode of wearing the *dhoti* or *sari* the artistic arrangements of pleats and folds process that the weavers were not unaware of the aesthetics of dressing. Such was the importance of dressing properly that the act is indicated by five words in Sanskrit, namely, *akala, vesa, nepathya, pratikarma,* and *Prasadhana*[93]. Texiles designs of the Gupta period had also achieved great success as much is evidenced from the literary sources of the Gupta period, and the various designs of the clothings will be reflected in the Ajanta paintings, to be describe later on.

Again, we are coming to the history of *Vakataka,* which was important contemporary dynasty of the Gupta period. In the first half of the fifth century A.D. the *Vakataka* kingdom lying between the Gupta empire and the kingdom of the south had become the dominant power in the Deecan. The *Vakatakas* in their time became the intermediaries of Northern Indian culture which was highly progressed under the Gupta's and the south. The dynasty was disappeared in the middle of the sixth century[94] A.D. when the rule of *Samudra Gupta* was widely spread all over the world. Together with the literary information to be had from the works of *Banashatta* a fairly satisfactory pacture of the costumes and the manners of the people of the 7th century A.D. could be drawn. An unexpected sources of information is available in the *Bhasyas* and the commentaries of certain Jain *Cheda-Sutra,* the most notable being *Brhat Kalpa-Sutra Bhasya* gives the following process in preparing the cotton for spinning. The *Seduga,* cotton after the seeds were removed with carded (*pinjitam*) and from the clean cotton spools (Pelu)[95] were prepared for spinning.

Costumes in Jain Cheda-Sutras and Other Sources

In the *Vejavahara-Sutra Bhasya*[96] a long list of various countries have been furnished in the cloth was manufactured. Textiles was imported from foreign countries (*paravatadi*). The word *'adi'*, sufic, or 'etc' according to the commentator here indicates *Paundra*[97] *and paravat* means *'mountain'*. At that time when the *Bhasya* was written in the 2nd and 3rd century A.D. that *Kottamba, Tamralipti* and *Sindhu* (*Vitasta*) were also important centres of cloth manufacture. *Kottamba* has been explained by the commentator as the cloth, manufactured *Ganda* in Bengal during the time of *lalitaditay Muktapida*. But this explanation is wrong because, the *Kotumbara* cloth was manufactured from Buddhist literature i.e *'Nam'* or *'Weaver'* or *'Chamar'* or *'Chuhras'* which was the product of the *Amdumbara* country *Bias* or *Viyas*, modern name of one of the "Five Rivers,[98]" the region about *Pathankot* near *Amritsar* in the Panjab. It seems that the commentary of the *Vyavaharasutra Bhasya* was written in the 11th century A.D. in the memory of the *Audumbaras* had faded to such an extent that *Kotumbara,* their country, was being located in Bengal under the Yasovarma the friendly ruler of Panjab. *Tamralipti*, the modern *Tamluk* in Bengal, seems to have been another famous centre for textiles. It is difficult to say whether cloth was actually manufactured there or whether the varieties imported at *Tamralipti* whether the meant for the development of weavers works. *Sindhu* or *Vitasta*, or *Sindh Sagar* Doad in the Panjab, was also famous centre for its textiles, probably woollen clothes. Moreover, the heavy broacade *Kimkhab* for which Benares or *Kashi* was famous for the known *Pusapatta*[99].

In the study; it reflects that pomp and show was the important feature of Hindu festivals and marriages. Women have been displayed wearing colourful dress and ornaments. in the *Hassacaurtia* it has been described that a rich display of the textile materials was prepared in the palace of *Harsa* at the time of marriage and other festivals as that marriage ceremony of his sister *Rajyasri* various kinds of clothes were exhibited known as *Ksauma* (linen), cotton (*badera*), *dukula, lalatantiya, netra* and fine silks of the day called (amsuka[100]). The exact nature of *netra* meaning suggests (*Jati-jasmine pattikah 'Words'* siken strips) or silk in which the patterns of *jasmine* flowers were interwoven like the sweater of the wool. Its comparison with the birch bark indicates that perhaps it was *maga* silk which is very soft and tawny in colour like birch bark wool. While talking of silk or silken clothes one should not forget to elaborate the varieties of silk technically called *Kidaya,* by *Devardhigani* who lived in the middle of the 5th century[105] A.D. under the heading of *Kidaya* or silk-worm products, he mentions the following varieties: *malayaamsuka*, cinamsuka and *Krmiraga*. The above mentioned varieites and some more have been explained in the *Brhat-Kalpa-* Sutra *Bhasya.* was woven from the *Patta* yarn, presupposing thereby that *Patta* yarn, presupposing thereby that *Patta* was equivalent to *'Father'* or *'Nam'* and is a certain kind of silk yarn[106] for the body *Amsuka* is discussed in the commentary as smooth and shining silk (*Slaksnapattah*) and *Cinamsuka*, was either cocoon silk (*Kosikar-khyahkrmih tasmajjatam*) or Chinese silk (*Cinahama janpadah tatra yah slaksnatarapatah tasmajjatam).* It seems that the Chinese silk was made from very smooth silk yarn at that time. The *Krmiraga* as its name indiates was the silk dyed in red colour prepared from an insect called *Kermes* on *coccus Indicus*. The Malaya silk was perhaps the product of Malabar or South Bihar. The *Suvarha*, silk is described by the commentator as golden silk of the *'Nam'* the thread being spun by a particular *'weaver'* which is also the variety of a silk worm. It is interesting to note in this connection that the coarser and cheaper varieties of Benares tissue *Saris* and brocades are usually designated by the local traders as *rasimal* which is probably the degenerated form of the Sanskrit *Varasi*. In the Vedic literature, however, *Barasi* denotes a variety of cloth manufactured from the fibres of the *Baras*-tree *i.e* called *'Nam'*. For costly garments the word *sucelaka* and *pata* have been used in the literature and for coarser kinds of cloth *varasv* and *sthulasataka*[107]. In the above quotation the importance of silk-garments has been displayed which were mostly fashioned among the women of the Gupta perod their smoothness (*sparsavata*), and the balance of colours (*rangas*) on their texture (*Varnantaravi-bhagacitrena*[108]). The people of higher social status which were elevated by the *'Father'* with his power dressed in the garments befitting there positing in the existing society. The mode of wearing the *dhoti*, unstitched piece of cloth which was worn by the said people Bana described as: "The Youth whom *Sarasvati* saw had his waistmarked off by a tight drawn lower garment of *harita* or green colour, of which one corner was gracefully set in front not like the Brahmanas in loose manner, a little below the navel, and the hem hung over the girdle behind, and which on both sides was so is unknown, because it was the new item for the unknown. The commentator of the *Amarakosa*[101] elaborates that *netra* was manufactured from the fibres of the bark and roots of a particular tree. *Lalatantiya* has been translated as spider's silk though its meaning is to see the father from the lower level i.e. *infinite*, than have to climbe up in the *Visalata,* perhaps at that time this term was used for a very fine variety of the transparent silk cloth. The type dyeing the work of the *lilari* of Gujarat and Rajaputana was famous at that time in all of the country of India and tye-dyed or gaity coloured *'bandana'* scarves beloved of the sailors all over the world was the product of Gujarat. In the *Harsacarita,* the tye-dyed cloth was called *badhani* or *cadari,* in *Gujarati* and *Hindi*, respectively is known as *pulakabandha* ladies shirts were made of it[102] by the *Darzi* or tailor. The process of washing the clothes is also described in the *'Naya -dammakahao'* (III, p. 60). First the cloth was put into a solution of soda (*Vattham Sajjiya-Khareham anulimpati*), then boiled and finally washed with fresh water. An analogous process in washing clothes is still maintained by the *dhobi,* though soap is gradually replacing the crude *soda* as washing medium[103].

In the above quotation; it appears that *andi* and *muga* silks of Assam were famous for their durability. In the Gupta period; figured clothed was also manufactured in Assam. The presents sent by the ruler of Assam to *Sri Harsa* included in pieces as smooth as birch bark (*bhurjat rakkomalah jati pattikah*), or smooth figured silk (*citrapatahamca mradiyasam*[104]). The *Jati-pattikah* means the force of the Father. It may mean, as its literal girt up as to display a third of his thigh[109]."

The famous *Mulmul Khas 'Word' or 'Nam'* the royal muslin which symbolises the submit in cotton wearing has become a fable. It is eulogised in old great literature and evidently enjoyed a unique position in foreign countries and was said to have been used for wrapping mummies in ancient Egypt. The heartening fact is that this tradition does not belong to the dusty antiquity, but it is a living fact of today and till in waiting position. Supertime yarn is still spun and superfine *Khadi* cloth produced in places like *Madhubani* plate in North Bihar and *Ponduru* in *Andhara*[110]. A part from the environmental effects making far a vast variety in handloom textiles, the very individual traditional local costumes evolved over the centuries also explain the big range in materials, designs, colours etc. cotton is woven universally all over India for their distinctive weaving by the *'weavers'*. No matter how small or ordinary a *'weaver'* may seems, therefore, it seems that he has its own distinctive character[111] in the life. How the thousands of towns and villages where handlooms turn out huge quantities of material cater mainly to the common local people[112] who were deprived from the *'New Society'* i.e. *Radha Soami*.

Study also expresses that India has been famed for antiquity for filmy cottons patterned in gold. One sees startling weaves in these patterned cottons: a fine violet muslin with olive green border, and an all over gold pattern in tapestry weave by the *'weaver'* with the help of *'Chamar'*, a diaper design with cones at carriers and an inner border of diagonal bands, and an ornamental twill weave with a gold lozenge pattern at the end. This would be a loom tapestry; gold threads having been inserted with tiny bobbins while weaving, and passed through and around the wrap threads. Similarly long turbans and scarves in thin cotton are woven in single or double colours like rose and lemon with bands of golden yellow silk[113] which displays the decline season of the life.

Cotton, Silk, Woollen and Cloth-Shops

The period under review, roughly from the first century A.D. to the early 4th century A.D. is marked with the arrival of *Kushanas*[114] members of the *Yue-chis* tribe who originally occupied a part of the north-western portion of China. They were driven from there about 165 B.C. they first held the country of the *Saka* nomads (Gujjars) and latter on took possession of Bactria about 10 B.C. *Kaniska,* the greatest of the Kushana Kings, made *Durusapura* (modern Peshawar) their kingdom. He patronised the poet Asvaghosa and the physician *Caraka.* Being a devote of Lord Buddha which called *'Nam'* or *'Word'* in different languages, he sent various Buddhist missionaries for the spread of Buddhism in different parts of world like Tibet; Mongalia, Khotan, etc with the advent of the Kushana power in the north, India the ruler of the *Satavahana* kings suffered a set back and became confined to the *Satavahana* Kings upto Deccan. *Castana* became the governor of the *Kushana* in about 110 A.D. but later on his possessions were annexed by the *Satavahanas*. *Rudradama* the grandson of *Castana,* who gave his daughter in marriage to the son of *Satavahara king,* inflicted two severe defeats one after the another by his relatives, but by his efforts time and again, he establish his rule in the 150 A.D. and ruled over Sindh (*Vitasta*), Marwar (Rajasthan) Kach, Surastra, Gujarat, Malava and Northen Maharashtra, but later on other Satavahana Kings were able to recover some part of the lost kingdom.

To the beginning of the Christian era Tamil land was governed by there powerful kingdoms known as *Cera, Cola* and *Pandya*[115]. These kingdoms were frequent among each other, and the most powerful ruler of Tamil land was *Karikala Cola* (about 70-100 A.D.) who defeated king *Gajababu* of Ceylon (Modern Sri Lanka), established his capital at the mouth of the river Kaveri. Another famous king of the South was *Cera Senguttarvan,* who ascended the throne about 140 A.D. and ruled till 192 A.D. He defeated the confederacy of the nine *Colas* which are the various organs of the body already mentioned elsewhere in the texts. The high cultural achievements of his reign are reflected in the famous Tamil classic *Silappadikaram.*

By the end of the second century A.D. the kingdom of the *Satavahanas* began to disintegrated the *Abhiras* carved out a separate kingdom in Gujarat, the *Cutu, Satavahamas* reigned for a century more over northern *Maharastra* and *Karnataka* with their capital at *Vaijyanti* (modern *Banavasi* in northern *Kanara*) and the *Iksvakus* reigned over the Andhra country with their capital *Nalmalai* (*Nalamalai)* hills on the south Krishna, Guntur District). In the north the *Bharasivas* drove out the Kushanas and the republics of the Malavas and the *yaudheyas* become powerful. Later on, after the downfall of the *Baharasivas,* Vindhya *Sakti* (248-284 A.D.) founded the line of the *Vakatakas*. His son *Pravarasena* (284-344 A.D) was the most powerful kingdom of the dynasty.

Study demonstrates that these three hundred years of Indian history, however, were neither centuries of constant warfare, nor could its later part (156 A.D. to 350 A.D.) be dubbed as the dark period of the Indian history, as considerable light has been thrown on this so-called period by the researches of Dr. K.P. Jayaswal. It is evident from the account of Pliny the Elder, the author of *'Natural History'*, an encyclopaedic work published about 75 A.D. and giving notices of India drawn from the Greek books and also recent reports of merchants [116]. Moreover, the work known as the *Periplus of the Erythrean Sea* first written by a Greek sailor of Egypt in the first century A.D. mentions the many parts of India then existing on both its Western and Eastern Coast, while Ptolemy (second century A.D.) in his *Geography* mentions the parts of *Malaya* peninsula, *Java* and *Sumatra* and the Indian port of *Palura* (on Ganjam coast), from which Voyages were directly made to Malaya peninsula[117], and from the archaeological evidence, both in this country and in greater India including Centrla Asia and the extra Gangetic countries, that this period was one of the greatest activity in the spheres of art and literature, foreign trade, shipping and colonisation in India. In the first century A.D. of the Christian era Indian states were established in Indo-China, *Annam (Chamba),* Cambodia, Java, etc. Eastward expansion brought the Indians in contact with China and the commerce between the two countries developed. The first centuries of the Roman Empire also witnessed the stablization and development of a profitable commerce between the mediterranean countries and India. Indian jewels, spices, perfumes, shoes, the famous Myrrhina vases for which the Romans paid fabulous prices that made Pliny lament the fate of the Romans and fine muslin prepared by the weavers formed the valuable articles of commerce. This commerce in luxury goods i.e. *'Nam'* cased a balance of trade in favour of India after a very long period of Indian History, and steadily the Roman gold flowed into the coffers of the Indian merchants.

In the study, it has been rightly expressed that there was an ample material for the reconstruction of the history of *Untouchables* who were busy with their works. *Gandhara* sculptures from north western of India, Kushana sculptures from Mathura and the surrounding countries reliefs from *Amaravati, of Ravidas Culture*, *Nagarjunakond* and *Golli*, furnish a detail study of the weavers and other works of the artisans. It has been noticed from the modern dictionaries remain silent about the explanation of words regarding the works of the artisans or the materials from which they were made the article of dresses, ornamens, and hair styles of the period. Our knowledge of *Indo China* fabrics of this period is, however, considerably enlarged by the references of Pliny and the descriptions which have been made in the work of *Periplus of the Erythrean sea,* an indispensable work for the knowledge of textiles, leathers, metals, etc; in the early centuries of the Christian era.

It shows that cotton cloth was extensively used in the said period. Good cotton was planted and cotton plantation (*Karpasavata*) is mention in *Divya vadana*[118]. The softness of the cotton-wool (*Karpasa-picu*) was appreciated by the master, and in the *Divya vadana* the softness of the body of *Upagupta* is compared with cotton wool[119]. Cotton-wool was purchased from the market and after ginning it (*tam parikarmayitva*) the yarn of even structure and fine quality was spun[120]. The weaver (*Kuvinda*), while engaged in weaving cloth, picked and gathered the cloth and yarn (*avicira-vicirakam*) and with raised head (*adhinirmayodudhasiraskah*) and with the clapping movements of hands and feet (*sphattitam panipado*) began the weaving operation. The weavers wife sat preparing the wrap (*tasarikam Kartum arabdha*) with the help of well prepared and good quality starch (*divyasudha*[121]) means 'white light'. Therefore, it is said the cotton fabrics was the pearls of Indian weaving. It were as though these crafts men (weavers) were magicians and waved wands to produce what seemed like dreams[122] in its historic or cultural content, the concept of Ram Rajya (*sarvodaya Raj or Welfare state*) is rooted in equality, justice, fairplay, freedom, and equal opportunity for all without exploitation or discrimination on ground of caste, class or creed. This dream is embedded in the Hindu psyche. Its origin could be traced to the mythology, beyond golden and not so golden periods of Indian history. The sustenance for this dream, renewed by Mahatma Gandhi during the struggle for freedom, is emboided in the Hindu epic, the *Ramayana*. An actionpacked human drama, the mythological stories of the *Ramayana* revolve around the virtuous, wise god-king, *Rama*, (Baba Gurinder Singh Ji), who lives by high ideals and rules his kingdom by the *law of dharma*, ancient norms of justice, fairplay, liberalism, equality and righteousness toward the humanity. Rama was known to be a repositary of all virtures which make a human being both sublime and divine. During the legendary Rama regime of Ayodhya dating back to the *Treta Yuga*, C.867 to 102 B.C, no one was reportedly unhappy. Every subject enjoyed the fruits of his or her labour [123] toward the *'Nam'* or *'Chamar'* or *'Weaver'*. It is not wonder that they gave fancy names like running water and because they became indistinguishable when laid on the grass, they came to be called evening dew, and when dipped in water invisible, they were named running water, and because of their cool appearance and feel on the skin, *sherbati* (like *Sherbet*) and as even a 5-yard piece could pass through a little ring it came to be called woven air. One interesting fact about these muslins is that the fine thread, were spun with hand spindles, not the spinning wheel i.e the thread drawn by twirling the spindle. The weightlessness of these fabrics has been sung by many poets, comparing them to the moonlight on the tulip or a dewdrop on the rose. Because of their closeness to nature, the artisans seem to have reached in a subtly sensitive manner to various aspects of nature, for instance colour which is so basically significant in the creation of crafts. Ages before they seem to have grasped the principles of perspective as supplied to the range of colour by the mere accuracy of their eye, and trained their vision to fill in the shades without the use of any instruments, and simultaneously to move their hands with mathematical precision[124].

They also seem to have developed their own science of colours. Thus, the *Chitra-laksana* mentions two types of colours: 1. *Mularangas or Suddha-varnas* (मिश्रवर्ण) Words' or 'Nam' are primary colours; and II *Misra-varnas* (शुद्धवर्ण) complex colours, compound or mixed colours. Five primary colours were prepared with a variety of materials, *'Word'* minerals, chemicals and oxides, stones, vegetational extracts, etc, e.g. *Sindura, Laksha* (or lac) *haritala, Kajjvala* (or black soot) conch-shells, *gairika*, indigo, etc. The shades were prepared with the mixture of two or more substances with lime, indigo, lac, etc. Thus white was prepared with couch-shells, red from red lead or *Sindura (hingulaka) or guru-gairka or hurmachi*, black from *Kajjvaka*, green from *haritala*,etc. Blue was made from Indigo and also from lajward (Lapis lazuli) which was imported. Lac, indigo and resin were commonly used in compound colours. Gold was popular with ancient Hindu painters. Dr. D.N. Shukla not agree with the statement of *Moti Candra* who thought that the use of gold as a colouring material was produced in India and was introduced by the Timurids in the 15th century A.D. for the decoration of border. Dr. Shukla maintains that gold was popularly used in ancient India as in the palace and court embellishemnt. In the early centuries of Christian era gold leaves were used for decoration on stucco images of the Buddha in Gandhara. Its use was a time-honoured tradition, giving a suggestion of power and grandeur and a gleaming lustre, During the golden period of the Mughal rule in India, this precious metal was used in painting on a large-scale[125]. The colour scheme theory in order to form a kind of harmony through regular or diffused or composite reflections. Some order of placing makes for contrasts in this connection there are simultaneous and successive contrasts, and in a large composition this could balance with a harmonies order of concord and unity by placing related colours alongside. It is fascinating to see the effect of this. For the contrasts chosen may be steep but not harsh, claring but not unsettling, with tender colours interposing. For when arrogant purple is thrown in with subdued green, so popular in India, they seem to reach out to each other with a copy but poignant air. Some brief encounters are often ingeniously dispensed by white or off white. The extraordinary sensitivity to the subtlest shades can be judged from the *Vishnudharmothara* which speaks of five white tones of the Irory Jasmine, August moon, August clouds after they shed the rain, and the couch-shell. Inspite of seeming conservatism, the Indian craftsmen have been remarkably flexible in colour combinations, perhaps boldly borrowing from nature[126] i.e. called 'Nam' or *'Sabad'* or *'Kalma'*.

It is known to us that in Tamil Nadu and Andra Pradesh where inexpensive cotton *sarees* are produced, even, the simplest has a dignity lent by very broad borders on either side, or a single decorative touch of a heavily patterned *pallu 'Nam' or 'Word'* the *saree* end which falls over the shoulders at the back. Their distinguishing mark is what is known as *Korvai,* the solid border where the weft threads do not enter into the borders. For *Sarees* with a single border, two shuttles are needed, for double border three shuttles. The country jacquard is used for designs on the borders. Then there is the severe plain white *sari* or *dhoti* with the surprise of a gold bank for a border, as though it were an after thought, with the similar band on the *pallu* which is typical of Kerala and the *sarees* are known as *Karalkuda;* similar styles in colour are also produced in Coimbatore, Madurai in TamilNaidu Chanderi in Madhya Pradesh, Venkatagiri in Andra Pradesh which has a fabulous look with its sheer body and gold designs like dots, coins, leaves, parrots or simple geomaterial patterns ont he body[127]. It shows that in South India the members of the *Naga* tribe were skilled in many crafts and specially in weaving. The *Nagas* of the *Kalinga* country were so famous in the art of weaving that the word *Kalingm* in Tamil came to signify cloth. In the early centuries of the Christian era the *Nagas* inhabiting the eastern coast in the Pandyan territory were great weavers and exported a large quantity of muslin. This fine muslin was highly priced by the Tamils and fetched fabulous prices in foreign countries[128]. Tamil poets allude to a famous chieftain, Ay, who offered to the image of *Siva* or *'Nam'* one of the priceless muslins which had been presented to him by *Nila Naga*[129].

In Madhya Pradesh, *Maheshwari Sari,* has an unusual origin for it is traced to a benevolent queen who once ruled over the territory and designed the first *saree. Maheshwari* the place itself is charming on the banks of the mighty river *Narmada 'Word'* giver of happiness, and is known in the Hindu panthean as the Virgin river. The Maheshwari is *saree,* mostly in cotton is characterised by its simplicity yet with a few singular touches takes on an irresistible charm. The body is plain or has stripes or checks which have several variations. The plain ones are known as *Chandrakala* midnight blue and *Baingani Chandrakala*, woven with a blackish violet warp and a chocolate weft. *Chandrakala* the moon and star design, has lengthwise stripes of one shade alternated by one stripe of another shade. The *Beli* consists of lengthwise stripes of six dents of two shades, two dents of one, and four of another *Parbi* is the chequered counterpart of Beli. A speciality is its reversible border so either side can be worn. This is locally known as *Bugdi*. The process is the same as for figured weaving, and consists of lifting of wrap threads and passing the weft threads between these for making a particular design. The borders too have a variety and are known as mat design which has a wide range in leaves and flowers, especially the *Karempool* pattern. *Maheshwari Pallu* is also distinctive, with five stripes, three coloured and two white alternating, running along the width and in each of the white, four lines of the same colour are inserted. These *sarees* are now made in cotton and artificial silk mixed, a few in pure silk[130].

It makes clear from the study that muslins from India were highly valued in the Roman Empire in the first centuries witnessed the development of trade and commerce between the Mediterranean, sea and India. The author of the 'Periplus' states that the best broad sort (called *'monacha'*) and a coarser cotton (called *'sagmatogene',* and probably used for stuffing and padding) were produced in Gujarat and exported to East Africa from *Barygaza,* alongwith a third kind of course 'mallow-coloured' cloth (*molochine*) dyed with a product of Indian *Hibiscus*. Similar varieties were sent to Arabia, Egypt and Socotra from Barygaza. Which received them in large quantities from Ujjain and Tagara. Trichinopoly and Tanjore produced muslin called *'Argaritic'* (from Uraiyur, the ancient capital of Cola Kingdom, now part of Trichinopoly) and *Mansulipatam* (*Masalia*), made a great quantity of muslin; the finest muslin was, however, called 'Gangetic' and was manufactured in the Dacca district[131]. The demand for cotton, both dyed in variations of this style are made in several places, particularly in Maharashtra, around Poona up to Sholapur and around. The big centre is Shahpur in Belgaum district, Karnataka state. But while *Maheshwaris* are normally in bright colours Shahpuris specialise in soft pastels or shots of two colours, one in warp, other in weft, with colours to match the border and the *pallu*. Poona has a special kind with a gold thread speckled panel for the *pallu* and a narrow gold pattern border. From *Husli-Dharwar* in Karnataka state to Bijapur, cotton *sarees* are made in dark earthy colours, which mark them out, as also their heavy maroon red or chocolate borders with coloured or white lines of stripes at the edges alternating with white rows of arrows in two or four lines, or with mat design in white or yellow, or in the *rudraksh* pattern that is a round multidented dark seed which is very popular in border designes; while the *Pallu* is unique in white and red alternating hands with monuts at the two ends, woven either in cotton or silk. This area also produces white *dhoti's* and turbans with these same kind of *saree* border designs in lovely bright red whirl, look most picturesque. There is a special *sarees* in this area known as *Irkal* after the village in Bijapur district of Karnataka, from which it seems to have originated. Large quantities of yard age in the *Irkali* style for blouses are produced in a little village called Galedudda near *Irkal*, and supplied to the markets all over India. *Irkali* style *sarees* in finer counts are also made in *Narayanpet* in Andhra Pradesh. *Irkalis* are rich in the colouring like the special pomegranate red, brilliant peacock blue, parrot green. The *rasta* design has horizontal lines in subtle matching colours running through the body of the *sari* with charming effect. Gadwal and Kothakota near Vanaparti in Andhra Pradesh, weave fine cotton *sarees* with richly woven *pallu* and borders in gold in opulent designs are made in places like *Siddhipet*, Armoor in Andhra Pradesh which used to once make them in silk. Now they also manufactured curtains, bed spreads etc, using the old decorative motifs for ornamentation[132]. *'Ksoma'* (*Ksauma*) or linen manufactured from the bark-fibre of *Linium usitatissimum* was also extensively used in India[133]. *'Sana',* a huge sheet of flaxen cloth (*sanka*) measuring eighteen hands lengthwise and twelve hands and four digits breadthwise are mentioned in the text[134]. At another place a weaver has been displayed wearing a flaxen *dhoti* (*Sanasatika*). The farmers also wore *dhotis* (*Sanasati*)[135]. *Phalaka* cloth made from the fibres of certain fruits is also mentioned in the same text[136].

There is one more elaborate styles in cotton weaving among weavers, is called *Jamdani*. The objective must have been to provide highly decorative material for the royality, the nobles and the affluent menfolk for their garments, which later also went into *sarees*. It combines rare finesse with white or coloured (*rangadar*) designs of great intricacy. It has an unusual air of quite composure about it. The method of weaving is somewhat like tapestry work, in which small shuttles filled with coloured, gold or silver thread, are passed through the worp as required for the basic weave[137]. 'Cloth of gold' was known as *haryani*[138] or *hirivastra*[139] mentions int he *Divyavadana* text. The fabric shows shadowy figure designs dreamy and suggestive. Paper pattern are generally used by the weavers and two weavers normally made at a loom to accelerate as also simplify the work. In Tada in Uttar Pradesh, however, *Jamdani* patterns in white are worked on a white surface. The extra weft threads which create the patterns are of the same fine quality as those used in the fabric. The design is, therefore, discernible clearly only when held against the 'light'. The designs in floral sprays scattered over the surface are called *butidar,* and in diagonal rows tircha. They have large bold motifs in corners, like the shawl pattern cones. When the floral modifs form a regular network it is known *aj jhalar*. The most striking, however, is the *panna hazara* which means a thousand emerolds in which the floral design is made to stand out with flowers in gold or silver, shimmering like precious stones. Others is floral pattern are *phulwari* and *toradar* currently *varanasi* weavers have reoriented the *Jamdani* into cut work by throwing the weft across the width and when the weaving is done, the loose threads are finely cut to bring out. It was known as *Kasika-vastra*[141], *Kasi*[142], *Kasikamsu*[143], *etc.* Generally the *Kasika-Vastra* is supported to the fine Benares silk, perhaps on the analogy of Benares being the centre of fine silk manufacture at the present time. The contemporary sources of study, however, does not make it clear that the *Kasika-vastra* was silk made by the *'weaver'* or *'Word'* it could have easily been cotton as well. Fine clothes were made from the *Kasika-Vastra* (*Kasika-vastra-varambaran*)[144]. The demand for cotton cloth, both dyed and fine Indian muslin was called 'Ventus textiles' or *'nebula'*. According to Arrian, Indian cotton were whiter and brighter than were those of any other region and according to lucian, the *"Indian fabrics"* were lighter and softer than the Greek[145].

Moreover, *Masuriya* is a rare cotton fabric woven in the *Masuriya* village in *Rajasthan* (*Rajasthaniya*) with a sheer body, usually plain but sometimes with a ribbon border. It is prized for its lovely texture and provides an ideal surface for any kind of delicate printing[146]. Besides the varieites of cloth described above, we have two sets of different types of *dusyas* cloth, each containing five varieties, are discussed following as under:-

1. *Koyava* is described as wrapper stuffed with cotton.
2. *Pravaraka* is elaborated as a fluffy blanket from Nepal (*Nepaladi Vlvanaromabrhot Kambalah*). It shows that now there is great change in commetary by mistake,as usually *Koyava* is a blanket and *pravara* the stuffed wrapper of the weaver.

3. *Dadhikali* was a washed wrapper of the wearer, very white and soft, with a dented decoration on the borders.
4. *Purika* was a woven cloth with sparsely placed yarns, or it has also devoted the sack-cloth woven out of coarse hempen (*sana*) yarns.
5. *Viralika* means association through *'Nam'* or *'Word'* or *'weaver'* as *Dosuti* the second category of cloth contains *Upadhana tuli, alinganika, gandopadhana* and *masuraka.*[147] These are different kinds of pillows which were made of different kinds of stuff.
   1. *Upadhana* kind of pillow stuffed with swan feathers.
   2. *Tuli* stuffed with clean cotton (*sanskrtaruta*) or *arka* cotton.
   3. *Alinganika* cloth is a body size pillow which was put between the thighs while sleeping.
   4. *Gandopadhana* pillow is used for the temples (*ganda-masurika*).
   5. *Masuraka* was a round cushion (*cakkalagaddikadi*) made of leather or cloth, and stuffed with cotton[148].

In the study, it has been described these cloth were used by the laymen or common people in ancient India. In the first set of category *Koyava, Pravaraka, dadhikali, purika* and *Viralika* are mentioned in the text[149] as a household cloth.

Silk; not only has a very ancient tradition, it enjoys also a significant status because of its use at ritual ceremony like marriage, festivals, etc. This may perhaps partly account for the concentrated development of silk weaving at popular places like *Varanasi* and *Kanchipuram. Varanasi* is, however, in a class itself not only for its superb weaving in gold and silver, but also for the wide variety of techniques and styles its weavers can adopt. They are incomparable in their weaving talent and reproduce any antique museum piece with the distinction that would make anyone mistake the copy for the original[150]. It has been already mentioned in the text that *Kasika-Vastra* is supposed to cite to the fine *Benares* silk because it was the fine silk manufacturing centre from the very ancient period of Indian History even at present period. The best known *Varanasi* product is the brocade, *Kinkas* as it is called. Its loom is very complex in which pairs of healds are separately connected to strings and taken upwards and worked from above i.e. Heaven. Half a pattern is worked up by a combination of strings and healds manipulated separately, successively and completely by reversing the order[151]. Elaborate brocades are woven by combining this with double warps and border wraps and with silk or metal threads. The weaver always has a helper to alongside him. Brocades are varied[152] as shoes and sandals (*Svarnopanad*) embroidered with gold (*svarnavalksagumphita*) and inlaid with jewels are mentioned in *Puratana-Prabandha-Samgraha;* and the shoe-maker was known as *mocika.*[153]. But the best and oldest are called *beldar* or scroll pattern which appear in the Ajanta frescoes, the *butis* of design was stars and spangles scattered over the body. Some weave's are all gold without use of silk, with floral, mango or creeper design or on larger pieces scences of human and animals figures sometimes in bands and lozenges. Some have silver background with a superimposition of gold patterns[154]. Apparently to the onlooker this varigated work is pleasing, but besides this its mean much. If nature is any guide, an attempt can be made to explain why there is choice for some colours. The hill people who use to live in the natural beauty, because of their remoteness and isolation from the material world, therefore, they have alway been in direct contact with nature. So nature is their first love. Natural conditions are their visions and outlook more than any thing else. The pine trees, whcih are found all over the higher hills, have been transfigured into the stylized patterns, as also in the dark green colour. Amongest other colours saffron stands for earth, blue for monkshood flowers, white for snow and grey for barren rocks.[154] discussed in the 'Early History of Jammu Region' of the same author.

It is a controversial matter when silken cloth began to be manufactured in Indian from the time immomerial. According to Dr. Sarkar the term *pandava* mentioned in the Vedic literature means silken cloth[155] But according to Dr. Moti Chandra[156] and Monier Williams[157], the terms means woollen cloth and not silken cloth. In the absence of any definite evidence it was difficult for them to determine the correct meaning of the word *pandava.* Some were very humble in the scale of huminiating burying their dead in the cells made of *stone-slabs* to determined the word *Pandava*, called *Kistraens*, by scientists and '*Pandava Vidu* means process of the *'Word' or Chamar'* in the form of Ravidas' sants in the houses of the *Pandava* brothers when in exile *Brahmana* by the Tamil people of the South to this day. Those in the south were never so subject to the Aryans as the tribes of the north and grew into the powerful and civilized Tamil Telugu nations, but there is no hint of this in the *Rig-Veda*. There these aborigines aborigines (*Barawalas*) are named, *'Dasya'* 'destroyers' or *'Dasa'*, or *'injurious'* and were stigmatized as 'black' or black-skins[158], by the *Brahmanas*. Another word mentioned in the Vedic literature is *tapya[159]*. Dr. Sarkar thinks it was a thick silken cloth like modern *tasara* of Bihara[53]. *Sayana* and *Katyayana* have interpreted the word tapya in many senses. For example they have interpreted the word *tapya* in the sense of linen (*Ksauma*), a piece of cloth dipped in clarified butter as displayed in various picture *Krishna* is stealing the butter from a vassel which was made of clay, and cloth made with a kind of grass called *tripa*, or a piece of cloth dipped three times inclarified butter i.e. *'Nam'*. From these interpretation, it makes clear that the commentators were not quite sure about the meaning of this word[161]. Dr. Moti Chandra has not expressed any definite opinion about the correct meaning of the word[162] described above. There is a reference in the *Satapatha Brahmana* that at the time of Vajapey sacrifice. The wife of the former of the sacrifice essentially wore a grarment made with *Kusa* called *Chandataka* over the initiated cloth wound round her waist[163]. According to *Sayana* in this context *Kusa* means silk and so according to him *Chandataka* was a silken cloth used by weavers. Thus, if we take the three words *pandava, tapya* and *Chandataka* in the sense of silken clothes then it can be said that the Vedic Aryans were aquainted with silken clothes which were the words of *'Nam'*. But as we are not sure about the meanings of these terms because we can not be definite about the existence of silken clothes in the Vedic period because life is a *'Stream'*.

It can be said that most probably silk was used in the Indian society in the 5th century B.C. as Panini has mentioned the word *Kauseya*. Silken (*Kauseya*) clothes are also mentioned in the *Ramayana[164]* and the Buddhist literature. Besides *Kauseya* two other words used in the sense of silken clothes were *Chinamsaka* and *Patta*. In the *Sabhaparva* of the *Mahabharata* two other kinds of silken clothes namely *Kotaja* and *Pattaja*[165] are mentioned. According to the *Periplus*, the Roman traders found silk at the months of the Ganges, at the Gulf of Cambay and in Travancore whither it had been brought by various visitors from North-Western China[166]. Native Indian silk was spun by native moths may have reached Rome before this birth along with better kinds of silk.

From the study; it indicates that silk was used in Indian and silk goods were manufactured extensively by the common people like *Barawalas, Chamar, Weavers, Chhimbas, Chuhras*, etc. In the *Divyavadana* it is again mentioned that silk words called as *pattamsuka, cina, kauseya* and *dhauta-patta[167]*. In the absence of any other information it is difficult to distinguish between these varieties of silk, *Pattamsuka* may indicate plain white silk; *Cina* as its name indicates, was imported from China during that period; *Kauseya* means to be true silk obtained from the cocoons spun by the silk worm feeding on mulberry leaves; and *dhautapatta* means to washed silk. *Patolaka* or variegated silk like the soul when she came from the Father and mind *ormana* made her dirty, therefore, she can notbe wash without *'Nam'* this is the biggest challenge for her, then she becomes wonderful (*vicitra* patolaka)*[168]* has been mention in the text. *Patolaka* or varigated silk still vetains in the *Patolasaris[169]* of Gujarat presented to the bride by her maternal uncle at the time of marriage. It is woven with wrap and weft threads which have been separately tied and dyed by the *bandhana* process of the *'Nam'*. Of the patterns used the may be mentioned: a diaper produced by a white line that forms meshes flattened laterally; these are filled with three white flowers borne on dark green stems in a maroon field; sometimes the pattern consists of a series of elephants (Aja), flowering shrubs, human figures and birds[170]. These are, however, new pattern; we have no means to find out the ancient patterns. *Vicitra* (wonderful) art we have already discussed in the above mention *Lalitavistara* means the whole story of the world is *'light'* or *'Nam'* or Inner Voice mentioned by the saints. It has been indicated that soul is very variegate but polluted by the mind. In the Tamil country silken garments were also worn by the people in affluent circumstances. Thus, it is mentioned that the ladies of *Maduradesa* wore round their waist scarlet flowered silks[171] called *'Chamar'*. It is also mentioned in the Periplus work that silk yarn was exported from Barbaricon on the Indus, while the more valuable silk cloth, besides raw silk and silk yarn was sent to *Barygaza* by way of *Bactria*, and also to *Muziris, Nelcynda* and other parts of Malabar by way of Ganges and presumably down to the east coast of India[172]. Silk seems to have been imported from China in the early Christian era by way of the Brahmputra valley, Assam and eastern Bengal[173]. Dealers in silk also frequented *Kaveripattinam* in the *Chola* kingdom[174]. To begins with the *Kushana* period both the Indian and the Chinese varieties of silken cloth were in vogue all over the world. In the literature the different period silken clothes have been discussed in number of varieties are mentioned as under:-

1. ***Amsuka.*** According to the Commentary of the *Nisithachurni* in the decoration of an *amuska* gold

thread was used to make beautiful designs. On the basis of this explanation Dr. Moti Chandra was of the view it was the cloth of similar to *Kimkhab* or *pota.* In the commentary of *Brhat-Kalpa-Sutra* Bhasya it is said to be a soft and bright silken cloth[175] i.e. *'Nam'.* V.S. Aggrawal also thinks it was silken cloth. The word *amsuka* is more frequently used in the Gupta literature of the Kushana period. In Jain literature it is a costly variety of cloth. Many varieties of *amuska* are mentioned on the basis of different colours[176] of the naturlism. Asvaghosa refers two varieties *asitamsuka* (white) and *nilamsuka* (blue)[177]. In the works of *Kalidasa* we come across *sitamsuka* (white), *arunamsuka* (reddish brown), *raktamsuka,* (red), *nilamsuka* (blue) and *syamamsuka* (black[178]). According to Moti Chandra *Patta amsuka* was white and plain silk[179]. Probably in the beginning only white silk cloth was made and later it was dyed into various colours. Bana has also referred to *amsuka* manytimes. According to him; it was very fine and clean cloth. At one place it is referred to as decoraed with designs of flowers and birds[180]. Regarding the motifs it appears that on the two main stripes of the *pattu,* a few names are well known *'Word' tipu, tara and guddi* meaning. Thereby drop, star and doll. The fringes to appear on the two ends are known as *Chulku.* The motifs may be known with different names, but the forms they assume are simple geometrical, stylished and abstract. Some styles are after birds and animals such as *Chiria* (bird), *Sada Kiru* (simple insect), *dabbidar Kiru* (spotted insect or snake), *bulbul chashm* (nightingale's eye[181]), *ganesh* (elephant headed god) and *jura hua ganesh* (joint ganesh. there are motifs which are derived from flora of the country, viz, *Gulas* meaning rose. other motifs to figure are *denedar* (dotted), *Lahria* (wavelike), *chabi* (key), *sirki* (stairs), *mandir* (temple) and *Chini-diwar* (the wall of China[182]).

There is another variety of *amsuka* which was known as *Chinamsuka.* Most probably it was the variety of silk imported from China. Of the clothes imported from China the maximum references are to *Chinamsuka.* According to the *Braht-kalpa-sutra-Bhasya,* it was made from a silk worm named *Kosakara* or cloth made from very smooth Chinese silk[183]. According to the commentary of the *Nisithachurni* very fine silk cloth or Chinese silk was called *Chinamsuka.* On the basis of these commentaries it can be said that probably very fine Indian silk cloth and Chinese silk both were called *Chinamsaka*[184] means the story of the *'Nam'* or word. A very delicate and fasinating item is the tissue in gold or silver a shimmering cascade in brilliant metal by the weavers work. *Varnasi Sarees* are world famous and identified by spangles sprinkled all over the body, heavy gold border and *pallu* in a great variety of designs like floral sprigs, the peacock and cones in the corners. The ornamental end has gold weft and is brocaded with green parrots. At times there are additional borders in tapestry weave separately woven and then attached[185] to hill dresses are also preferred because they are artistic in appearance, fairly cheap and being not much prone to wear and tear, last longer[186]. Thus, *Varanasi* has an old tradition in weaving works special styles for export to specific countries of west and South-East Asia which naturally adds to the richness and variety of its products. These broacades are distinguished but apt poetic names like *Chand Tara* (Moon and Stars). *Dhupchhaon* (Sunshine and shade) *Mazchar* (Ripples of silver), *Morgala* (peacock's neck[187]).

2. **Kausya.** According to Dr. Moti Chandra the silk made from cocoon of a silk wrom which subsisted on the leaves of the mulberry tree was called *Kausya.* The term *Kauseya* has been already mentioned in the *Divyavadana*[188] text, the *madhyamavyayoga,* the *Amarakosa*[189] the *Kumarasambhaya,* and the *Krusamndra,* etc. In the *Madhyamavyayoga,* we have a reference to yellow coloured *Kausya* which was worn by a Brahmana. In the *Amarakosa Kausya* is included in the list of silken clothes. India has been famed from antiquity for filmy cottons patterned in gold. One sees startling weaves in these patterned border, and an allover gold pattern in tapestry weave; a diaper design with cones at corners and an inner border of diagonal bands and an ornamental twill weave with a gold lozenge pattern at the end. This would be loom tapestry; gold thread having been inserted with tiny bobbins while weaving, and passed through and around the wrap threads. Similarly long turbans and scarves in thin cotton are woven in single or double colours like rose and lemon with bands of golden yellow silk[190], Gujarat developed its own styles of *Kinkabs* (brocades) woven with extra weft patterns. Surat as the chief port carried them far off even to the Russian Royalty. *Kanbis or Patidars, Khatris* and *Mommin* (particularly the women) are excellent in this weave. There are dozens of designs in fashion like *Tara Mendal,* a rather complicated constellation animals, fruits stylised dance figures, peacocks, women waving fans, lotuses in many shapes like Krishna. *Rudrol* in Mehsana district, *Jamnagar* and *Dolka* produce them. Here several varieties of silk like satin (*Gajji*) a lovely melting fabric, and mixtures like *Mashru, are also made*, a special item is the famous

Nathdwara pichwai in the brocade style[191]. *Tanchai* is an example of weaving that resembles over fine miniatures. Its origin is traced out to three Indian *Parsi* brothers by the nameof *Choi* who learnt this craft in China and were practising it in Surat, Gujarat. The fabric came to be called after three *Chois*. *Tan* (corruption of *tran;* three in Gujarati) *Choi*. Here satin is the base and consists in the merging of the extra weft floats in the fabric. In *Tanchoi sarees* the designs are always floral with interspersing of birds. The usual ground is bright blue, purple, green or red with areas patterned in tabby weave. Figures of flying birds, paired cocks amidst floral sprays are worked in. In some the *pallu* is more solidly done with peacocks, baskets or bunches of flowers. The unusual ones have whole hunting scenes spread all over[192]. There is one more an artistic style known as *Patola,* is most colourful and ostentations weave with its figured body, and the subtle merging of one shade into another. This techniques is practised in a few parts of India with some variations, mostly producing *sarees,* a few shawls, *lungi*, handkerchiefs, etc. The most *Chamba rumals* have been marked for their craftmanship in embroidery. They also works of art just as are the miniature paintings. These embroidered kerchiefs (*rumals*) were not only limited to *Champa;* but they were prevalent all over the Himalayan hills. *Chamba* craftsmanship was the best as to give this craft a distinct by the *'Chamara'* or *Chams*. Also embroidery was not only limited to kerchiefs. The embroidered articles included many other things such as *choli, caps,* fans,[193] *etc.* The most renowned amonga *patolas sarees* is the one made in Pattan and Gujarat. The yard used is always silk. The warp colours are dyed by the *rangas* in the lightest colour to be used in the pattern, then the portions which are to be the next darker in shade are traced on a bundle of the thread were the marks are made and the formula continued with the threads that are to bear with the next shades of the pattern until the darkest shades are reached. The weft is treated in the same way so that when in weaving it crosses the warp, each of its colours (*rangas*) synchronise with the same warp. In the weaving proper the weft is woven into the warp with extreme dexterity and precision. Thus, the desired figures are obtained by juxtaposition of similarly dyed shades on equal lenghts of warp and weft, and interlacing them. The pattern is laid facing the *saree* side, the border strip being carried within the field to portray the design. Therefore, where animals and birds are depicted strangely enough only their feet are seen pointing in wards. Some of the important designs are: *rattan chowk* in which diamonds cross with diamonds as they are interspersed elephant *khhabri* is a basket made up by four elephants; *Waghkunjar*; tiger-elephant then there is a variety of leaf and flower and geometrical patterns. The colours are vivid and pleasantly harmonised[194] as said by the *Guruji*," our definition of *dharma* is twofold. The first is proper rehabilitation of man's mind; and the second is adjustment of various individuals for harmonious corporated existence, i.e, a good social order to hold the people together[195]." The cotton *ikats* in Orissa are more fabulous with firm accent on the geometrial patterns in heavy weaves. *Patolas* are also woven in *Pochampalli* and Chirala in Andhra Pradesh which originally did only large cotton kerchiefs called *tilia rumals*. *Pochampalli* makes *patola sarees* in a large variety of geometrical designs. *Chirala* has bigger and more pronounced patterns in thesame technique. Andhra Pradesh also weaves a great variety of cotton *lungis* with some *ikat* designs in the body or in the border[196].

3. **Dhauta patta**[197] was a variety of the silken cloth. Mubarakpur, also in Utter Pradesh, is an important silk centre, particularly for *sarees* which mainly cater to the ruler needs. Their designs are : *Naga* which has gold circles all over with rich floral patterns in the *pallu*; the *Chunari* has the same ground but the *pallu*; the *Chunari* has the same ground but the *pallu* is ornamental with gold flowering shrubs and elaborated flowers. The body has small flowers and is distinctive in having a narrow border on one side, and broad on the other; the *phulwar* has all over floral patterns with a lovely blend of colours. Here the jacquard loom is in use. The *Baluchar* style woven in silk is only confined to *sarees*. It hails originally from a place of the same name in *Murshidbad* district, West Bengal, and had it hay day under the patronage of the royalty and nobility, later flourished in Vishnpur, but is now successfully produced in Varanasi. Very colourful a real traditional *Baluchar* is said to have 17 colours in it, with *butis* sprinkled all over. It is a plain woven fabric brocaded with untwisted silk thread but with the unique designs. The very early design closer to the *Kantha* work. The big *pallu* which is the main piece is a large panel with mangoes in the centre, bordered by diverse designs, depecting a royal court, domestic or travel scenes with horse riders and planques the lotus, the bee, and rosettee, the stylished peacock, the *bridal alpana* (floor design) of Bengal, the Taj, etc. The 19th century weaves strongely enough have even European faces mingling with Indian. The *sarees* are always in dark rick shades, particularly red, purple, and chocolate. The simpler *Baluchar* has small dots or

flowers all over with a flowery border and mangoes in the *pallu*[198]. There is a beautiful *saree* called *paithani,* after the village Paithan in Maharashtra state. On a *zeri* warp thread the weft is interlocked with different colours are woven, such as highly stylised flowers, swans, parrots, peacock. The *pallu* is a fascinating piece of gold tissue round which are woven brightly coloured rosettes, sometimes birds[199].

4. **Kosikaraka[200]** was a embroidered silken cloth. This technique is named by ethnologists as *ikat.* This word is supposed to be of Malayan origin but actually the name was given to the technique by the Indonesians. *Ikat* is the equivalent of the Indian *bananan* when only one side of the wrap or the weft is tied, it is a single *ikat.* But as described above both are died, it is a double *ikat.* This is now done on a very small scale in Pattan which is said to be its home, in Mehsana district, and in Rajkot[201].

5. **Vichitrapatolaka**[202] has been identified with the modern *patola saris* of Gujarat. It is multicoloured and embroidered and silken *sari*[203]. The Pattan *Patola* is the most picturesque particularly the wedding *saree* with dark green, white and yellow, against a ruby red background, and left and flower patterns; while the *pallu* features dancing girls and parrots or swans. Orissa has also a *patola* style of its own. The weaving is done in *tusser* silk and in single *ikat.* The designs usually are in floral patterns, with animals and certain traditional motifs like fish, counch. The single *ikat* makes the designs suggestive rather than sharply delineate them[204]. Genespur in Bhandara district of Maharashtra, has almost half working population engaged in *Tusser* silk weaving. It is almost a monopoly of the *Koshti* community. They too claim to be descended from sage *Markanda* known to have woven the first fabric from the lotus fibre to clothe the gods or *'Nam'* or *'Chamar'* or *weaver. Tusser* yarn worked into embroidery as well as in the fabrics used in quilts and spreads sheets, were once one of the chief attractions that drew out textiles to far off land sna d made them a rage. The *Tusser* silk fibre is fat not round like in other silk, and it is this difference in structure that endows it with a natural brilliance. *Tusser* one time was taken to be a vegetable fibre because of the resemblance of its cocoon to a fruit. *Tusser* silk produced here is known by its ancient Sanskrit name of *Kosa.* The entire process from the emergence of the moth, to the weaving, is all done in the area. The following are some of the varieties produced from the *tusser* weave. *Motha Choukada* is a design in big squaers, woven from the mixture of *Kosa* yarn and mercerised cotton and *Lahan Choukada* in small squares. The *Gunja salai* consists of diagonal designs on the cloth along with coloured lines at regular intervals, in green, blue or orange. Other varieties are *teen-dhari choukada*: with horizontal lines running through and so on[205].

6. **Patta**. According to the *Acharanga* means the colour of beautiful *'Nam' sutra* means measurement of the period, we are commenting it was a silk cloth made with *patta* thread. In the *Anuyogadvara Sutra patta* is said to be a variety of *Kotaja* cloth. According to the commentator this variety of thread was made with the worms which gathered round a heap of flesh in a forest. In the *Mandasor* Inscription of *Kumargupta* it is stated that ladies who were at the height of their beauty on account of their youth and had put on gold necklaces with the ornamental pieces made in the form of betel leaves and flowers did not attain their full beauty without a pair of garments of *patta* silk[206]. South India is famous for its heavy quality silks. At one time fabrics were sold hereby the weight, so heavy were the weaves. Tamilnadu and Karnataka are noted areas for this type has richly designed *saree,* will all over motifs each enclosed in a check. The border is done in *ikat* weave. The *pallu* is daintly decoraed with birds, fishes, etc.[207].

7. **Malaya**. In the commentary of the *Acharanga Sutra*, it is stated that *Malaya* was a variety of cloth made with Malaya thread. According to the *Brhat-Kalpa-Sutra-Bhasya*, it was a kind of silken cloth. According to Dr. Moti Chandra this variety of silk was called *Malaya* because it was made of south Bihar which was also known as *Malaya*. In the *Anuyogadvara Sutra* this variety of Silk is said to have been produced from worms (*Kitaja*). According to the commentary of the *Sutra* it was produced in the Malay Country[208]. Kashmir too lays equally claim to antiquity in silk industry. Kashmir was amongst the earliest to export silk to West and Central Asia. Over the last thirty years, modern silk fabrics have been introduced here like *crepe de chine, georgette, chiffon, ninon,* etc and this area has become an important centre of the lighter type of silks[209].

8. **Krmiraga**[210]**.** It was a silken cloth coloured with a substance called *Kirimadana.* In later periods *Krmiraga* came to be known as *Kirimadana.* According to Dr. Moti Chandra the substance was imported into India from Persia. There are many exaggerated anecdote about *Kirimadana.* Harisen has narratted one such anecdote in the *Brhatkathakosa.* In this anecdote it is stated that a Persian purchased girl. He nourished her for six months. Later he used a leech to extract her blood *Kirimadana* was prepared from

the worms in the blood of that girl and it was used to colour woollen clothes. The same story is narrated by *Asadhara* in his commentary on the 567th *gatha* of the *Bhagavati Arodhana*. According to this story the *Mlechchhas* of *Charmaranga* (*Samarkand*) country used leeches to extract human blood. They kept the blood in jar and used to colour cloth with the worms in that blood. According to Jahij, a writer of the Abbasid period (A.D. 719 to 1256), *Kirimadana* was imported from Spain, Tarim and Persia. *Tamiz* was a small town to the east of *Shiraz,* which was at a short distance from Armenia which produced *Kirimadana*. From the above statement it appears that *Krmiraga* was originally silken cloth. Later any cloth coloured with *Kirimadana* came to known as *Krmiraga*[211]. Assam leads in run mulberry silk. Sericulture seems ancient vocational practised by a large number of cultivators during off season. Manipur in the Assam region is said to be the original home of the mulberry silk worm and there is even a theory that it went from there into China. Assam has several varieties of silks: *Endi* which derives its name from the castor leaves on which the warm feeds. This silk was a yellowish tinge, is in rough as well as smooth varieties, and is used in winter for its warmth. *Muga* has two main varieties, depending on the leaves the worm feeds on the *Champa adakari,* or the *mejamkari*. It has a scintiliating golden shade and is only produced in Assam, and because of its brilliant hue the yarn itself is in great demand all over India for decorative purposes like embroidery. *Pala* is the Mulberry silk[212].

9. **Suvarna.** According to the commentary of *Brhat-Kalpa-Sutra-Bhasya*, golden coloured silken cloth[213] has been mentioned. It was extracted from a particular type of cocoon. According to Dr. Moti Chandra, it was most probably *munga* variety of silk of Assam which is golden in colour[214]. *Sualkuchi* is the most famous centre in Assam or silk weaves of delicate texture, dainty designs and delightful natural colours. Their speciality is the Assam women's dress like the *mekhela,* the woman's *lungi*, mostly with plain body, but sometimes pretty motifes strewn over the fabric, with a heavy design at the ends; *chaddar* and *riha,* both is smaller lengths, the former going over the shoulder to provide a *pallu* the other wrapped round the waist, both decorative. The designs consist of sprays of flowers and elephants interpersed with leaves and sprigs, and numerous combinations of geometrical patterns. A unique factor connected with weaving is the use of bamboo weft samples in weaving designs formed by passing various coloured (*rangadar*) threads through bamboo splints, which has eight designs[215] information.

10. **Netra.** Probably it was a very thin variety of silken cloth which was available in many colours. It seems that this variety of silken cloth began to produced only from the Gupta period because we do not come across any reference to *netra* variety of cloth in the literature of the earlier period. Kalidasa has referred to it only once in his texts. *Bana* has expressed in so many times in his works. He states that thin tunic of *Malati* was made of *netra* kind of cloth which was light and fine as the slough of a snake. *Harsa* himself were the girdle made of *netra* thread. According to *Bana netra* was white in colour. This variety of cloth sometimes decorated with floral designs and leaves. On the basis of the account of *Bana,* it can be said that this variety of cloth was as thin as the slough of a snake, as soft as the stalk of a young plaintain tree, very light which could be blown away with the breath of man and transparent. According to Cowell *netra* was a variety of cloth woven, with silk and silk thread covered with gold and silver. *Ksirasvami* the commentator of the *Amarakosa,* says that *netra* was a kind of cloth made with the fibre of the bark of a particular tree. It is also mentioned in the *Matsya* and *Agni Puranas*.. According to the *Amarakosa Netra* was a synonym of *amsuka*[216]. Kanchipuram has a special name for each of its many designs and colours. Very intricate designs are woven into the body in gold thread, of human and animal figures, geometrical patterns, with temple towers along the borders. A characteristic which lends great distinction and dignity to the Kanchipuram *saree* is the wide contrast borders. For this three shuttles are needed and while the weaver does the right side, his *aide* manages the left with separate shuttles. Here the border designs and colours are quite different from that of the body. This operation also covers the *pallu* which, however, has to have another wrap. If of another shade, it is separately woven and joined delicately to the *saree,* so that the naked eye does not detect the joint. The part where the body meets the borders is sometimes marked by a zigzag line, which are placed also in the body, locally known as *Vanki*. Sun, moon, chariot, swans, peacocks, parrots, lions, coins, mango and leaf are a few of the many patterns. A delicate jasmine bud is placed inside a square or buds are scattered like dew drops over the body called *mallinaggu 'weavers'* patterns are also formed through lines and squares[217].

11. **Kasika Cloth.** In the *Divyavadana,* it has been already mention in the text that *Kasika-vastra,*

Kasi and *Kasikamsu* terms have been used for Benares cloth; for the fine varieties of the Benares silk, it shows that it was the fine silken centre of India for the manufacture of silk cloth in ancient period. Dr. Moti Chandra[218] states that many persons think that *Kasikavastra* stands for silken clothes as even today, it is the centre fine silken clothes. It has been wrongly expressed by Indu Prabha Pandey that there was no mention of silken clothes in the literature of the *Kushana* period[219]. *Roshen Alkazi* has rightly expressed that Kushana costumes may be divided into five types: the costume worn by (i) indigenous people *'Chamar'* the *antariya, uttariya* and *Kayabandh* (ii) guardians and attendants of the herem *Brahmanas* usually the indigenous and sewn *Kanaka*, red-brown in colours (iii) foreign Kushana rulers and their entourage, and (iv) other foreigners such as grooms, traders, etc. There was a fifth category *Jat* a mixture of foreign and indigenous garments. This last category changed and evolved, how some of the purely draped garments of the Indians were replaced by cut and sewn methods of garments, especially in the north and north-west where influences were felt more keenly, and where climatically sewn garments were more suitable[220]. These craftmen brought with them the Greeco-Roman style, particularly in the drapery of the sculpture, so that the Buddhists Greek and Roman garments, the *Chiton, rimation, stola, tunica, chlamys,* etc.[221] In latter wears, in addition to his tunic and trousers, a fur-lined coat or *pustin* which is also seen at *Surkh Kotal*. As mentioned earlier, there was no uniformity in this period and the dress of the people too varied with each region. The ordinary dress consisted as usual of an *antariya, uttariya* and *Kayabandh,* with a turban for men. With the advent of the Kushanas rule this was extended, and the fashion of wearing sew-garments of Central Asiatic pattern seems to have been made headway with all classes of Indians in north India. The cut- and-swen methods of garments which are rarely visible in the sculptures of the previous periods are more commonly found in this period[222]. In ancient period very good quality cotton was grown and fine thread was spun by the weavers there. On this basis Dr. Moti Chandra has thought that most probably *Kasikavastra* was fine cotton cloth of Benaras. In the *Bhaisajya Sutra*, it is mentioned that the cloth made in Varanasi was very fine. We have also references to garments made of *Varanasi* cloth[223]. *Thandavalam* are parallel lines that run along the length of the *saree;* checks, squares or rectangles of varying dimensions, and stribes run both length wise and breadthwise. In *Pattu* the *pallu* and drapper alone have flowers independently woven into them. Of late silver is being used either in addition to gold or by itself. A very gorgeous specimen is the *tissue* in which the entire weft is woven in gold or in silver in exquisite designs[224].

12. **Vadaga.** The term *vadaga* stands for *tussore* in *Antagadadasao*[225]. In Tamil Nadu the pride of place goes to *Kanchipuram,* though *Kollegal* in *Coimbatore* district and *Kumbakonam* in *Tanjore* district, *Salem, Arni,* have also very fine weaving with their own distinct motifs like the *jalli,* lion, swan, etc. Weaving is done in Kanchipuram by salgars, a name derived from Sanskrit *'Word' or 'Rita' or 'Kalma', Salika,* a weaver. They claim descent from sage *Markanda,* 'the weaver of the gods.' The throwshuttle loom in which the shuttle travels to and fro thrown by hand is used. For complicated designs a local type of *jacquard* is used fashioned out of round *lamp* or *'light'* wicks as are used in room. Mechanical hooks and *jacquard* boxes are now being introduced[226] by the *'weavers'* of ancient India. *Woollen* cloth was manufactured generally known as *Kambala*[227] or *pattoo* in the local language of the Indians. It was a long sheet type of cloth mostly used in the winter. It is made of coarse wool of sheeps. It was a common wearing an article of dress either plain or colourful. In the Vedic age *Kambala* together with *Samulya* formed a part of the ordinary domestic[228]. Weaving of fine and corse varieties of cloth was well established during the period of Mauryan and Sunga (321-72 B.C.). Cotton, sillk, wool,linen and Jute fabrics were readily available. Furs and the better varieties of wool and silk like *tussar,* called *Kausheya* (like the *Eri* or *Muga* silk of Assam), Yellowish in its natural state but when bleached called *patrona,* were used. *Kaseyyaka* (high quality cotton or silk) and the bright red woollen blankets of Gandhara were worth a small fortune each. A rain-proof woollen cloth was available in Nepal. Resist dyeing and hand printing in a pattern on cloth has been mentioned by Greek visitors to the court of Chandragupta Maurya, as is the Indian glazed cotton cloth which was in common use by 400 B.C. Material similar to the *Khinkhwab* (which is the interweaving of silk and gold or silver wires in beautiful floral patterns) was in great demand and even exported to Babylon long before the Mauryas[229].

The term *dusya* (modern *dhussa*) in this period seems to have been applied to the costly woollen garments. It has been connected in the *Divyavadana*[230] that a variety of thread called *Tundikela*[231] was made from a tree named *Kalpadrsya* in the *Uttarakuru* areas. With this thread there were certain big and small pieces of *Kalpadrsya* were made of many colours such as blue, yellow, red and white. It is also mentioned that a *Matanga* women wore uncalendered *dusya,* cloth (*anahata dusya*[232]). The *Kalpa-dusya* tree was also supposed to produced the rolls of woollen cloth known as *tundica* from which *Kalpadusya* pieces of various sizes and of blue, yellow, red and white colours (*rangas*) were obtained[233] . Sometimes fine cloth of mixed texture was also woven from the admixture of wool and the fibres of *dukula* (*Urna dukulamayasobhanavatrani*[234]). Woollen cloth was also sometimes very fine ordinary blankets and those made with the hair of camel were woven for trade as well[235].

No doubt, cotton, wool and a fabric called *Karpasa* were available in the north in both coarse and fine varieties during the Mauryan and Sunga periods. There were also fine muslins often embroidered in purple and gold and transparent like the later-day material which came to be called *shabnam* (morning dew). The coarse varieties were used by the populace. Woollen cloth, *avika,* from sheep's wool was either pure whie (bleached) or dyed pure red, rose, or black. Blankets or *Kambala* were made either by completing the edges with borders or braids, or woven wool strips were joined together. The process of felting (pressing the fibre together, instead of weaving) was also known. All varieties of wool were available, coarse for making head-dresses, trappings and blankets for the poor and the fine smooth varieties for shawls and blankets for the richer class[236].

The period between 642-320 B.C. may be said the beginning of histrocial period of ancient India has already mention in the text. The kings of the two dynastics ruling over Magadha[237] including the Saisunagas (ca. 642-413 B.C.), and the Nandas (Ca.413-322 B.C.). Of the former *Bimbisara* (*Srenika*), the founder of New *Rajagrha* and Ajatasatru (*Kunika*) were the contemporaries of *Mahavira* and lord *Buddha* i.e known as *'Nam'* or *'Kalma'* or *'Word'*. For the early art and cultural history of this period later vedic literature including some *Brahmanas, Upanisads* and *Sutras* are very important to constructing the history of the *Weavers Dyers 'Chamars, Chuhuras, Barawals, Chhimbas, Washerman, etc*. The later phase of that art and culture is also reflected from the study of *Jatakas* and *Vinaypitaka* literature of the period. The later Vedic literature reveals that there was all round progress in art and culture of the Aryans of India in the field of various material i.e. cotton, silk, linen and woollen garments often emboidered, building materials, domestic materials like untensils whares, etc. For woollen stuff the word *Kambala* has been used in the Buddhist literature[238] . In the *Jatakas* the scarlet *pandukambala* of Gandhara is praised (*indagopakavannabha Gandhara pandukambala*). The country of Sivi was famous for it shawls and other materials of the garments, but the *Siveyyaka dussa* is praised worthy in the *Madavagga*[239]. It is also discussed in the *SiviJatakas* where the king of Kosala is said to have presented one *Dasabala* garment with a piece of cloth from Sivi costing hundred thousand pieces of money (*Satasahassagga-hanakam-Siveyyakavattam*). The word *dussa* still lives in the modern Hindi and Panjab dictionary as *dhussa,* which is used for a particular type of woollen *chadar.* Another variety of cloth which have been manufactured from wool was called as *Vahitika*[240] which was sent by *Ajatasatra* to *Prasenjit*[241], who in his turn offered it as present to *Ananda*. The cloth measured sixteen hands in length and eight in width. The use of *namtaka* (H. *namda*) 'felt' and *Kojava,* 'fluffy blanket' being luxurious woollen goods, was forbidden to the *Bhikkhunis*[242]. If tradition recorded by the epitomisers of the *Brihatkatha* is to be believed, Pataliputra under Nanda rule became the abode (*Kshetra*) of *Sarasvati* as well as Lakshmi, the home of learing as well as of material prosperity developed from Jammu region near Akhnoor in Manda. A galaxy of *scholars, 'Chamar', Varsha, Upavarsha, Panini, Katyayana, Vararuchi, Vyadi, 'Word' or 'Nam'* is said to have added lustre to the age. While much of the traditional account may be mere folklore unowrthy of credence, we may well believe that the cultivation of grammer (*sabad*) received an impetus in this age. The *Scholia* of Panini, presupposed by the great commentary of Patanjali, show acquaintance with the *Yavana lipi*, and it is by no means improbable that some of the predecessors of Patanjali are to be assigned to the Nanda Age. Kings of the line are credited by certain grammarians with the establishment of a particular kind of measure (*Nandopakramani manani*). In social matters the rise of Nandas may be regarded as symptomatic of a surging up of the lower classes. The Puranic chroniclers represent the dynasty as harbingers of *Sudra* rule of the *'Pure-thought'* and as irreligious (*adharmika*). The last statement is significant in view of the traditional connection of the family with Jain ministers and patriarches. But the evidence on the point is of a character which makes it difficult to build too much on it[243]. Persian inscriptions, observations of Greek and Latin writers, supplemented by brief notices in Indian literature and epigraphs, enable us to say a few words about the great regions of India *'Word'* namely the Indus basin beyond the *Ghaggar* and South India beyond the Godavari *'Chamar'* which, in the light of the evidence we have adduced, seem to have lain beyond the limits of the Nanda empire[244]. In collection of all useful classical texts *'Chamar'* a task not so far attempted by anybody *'word'* naturally draws our attention to the variety and richness of the material which was used by the scholars for this source of information[245].

A very elaborate description than the historical accounts are the incidental references to the democratic and orligarchial forms of Government in various states in the Punjab and the North-West Frontier Province (N.W.F.P). Of particular interest is the reference to the oligarchy in *Nysa* (20-1 A.D.) and the republics of the *Cathaeans* (47, 259 A.D.), the *siboi* (136,174), *Agalassians* (175), *Sabarcae* (151), *Sambastai* (180), Mallions (64 A.D.), *Oxydracions* (62 A.D.), *Abastanians* (75 A.D.), *Xathrians* (75 A.D.), Ossadians (75), *Sodrai* (181 A.D.), and many others not specifically named (47 A.D.). Expressions are used which indicate that the Republics were fairly common in those days in India (226 A.D.), *Tanala* (183 A.D.) had a form of Government closely resembling that of *Sparta*, with two hereditary kings of two different families *'Chamar'* and 'Jat', and a council of elders ruling the whole State with paramount authority[246].

A great deal of light is thrown on the civil and military administration, and special interest attaches to the reference to the vital statistic and care for foreigners (238, 268-9 A.D.), about which very little is known from other sources. The geographical account may be broadly divided into two classes, namely the narratives of men who actually visited parts of India, and general description by people who gathered information from various sources[247]. As regards the first, the typical examples are the account of *Nearchus* (313-336 A.D.) and the anonymous work called the *Periplus of the Erythraean Sea* (288-312 A.D.). The First belongs to the fourth century B.C. and the second nearly four hundred years later. Both describe the coastal voyage between the Persian Gulf and the mouths of the Indus, and the difference between the two accounts shows the marvellous advance in navigation in these waters, and the wonderful progress in human culture in these regions, during the interval of four centuries[248]. A very interesting account of a voyage to Egypt by a body of Indian adventures of whom one alone reached the destination, is told by *Posidonious* (233 A.D.) *Eratasthenes* records the distances from the *Caspian* gates to India (286 A.D.). There are also detailed accounts of *Taprobane* of the island of ceylon (345-8, 436 A.D.). To the second class of geographers belong *Strabo,* Pliny, Arrian and Ptolemy. The Greeks had been long interested in general geographical studies of the world. *Hecataeus* (c. 500 B.C.) was the first Greek geographer who knew of the continents, Europe and Asia, and regarded Africa as a part of the latter. His geographical work, *Survey of the World,* is lost. He referred to *Indoi, Indus, Gandaii, Kaspapyros* and a few other peoples on the Indus[249].

Now, we come to the Herodotus (1) who travelled all over the world. He rejected the theory of earth that was flat, then current among the Greeks. But he had a very poor knowledge of India. He only knew that it was one of the remotest provinces of the Persian empire towards the East. Herodotus lived from C.484 to 431 B.C. Nearly two hundred years later flourished Eratosthenes (C.240 B.C.), the famous librarian of the great library established in Alexandria by the Ptolemies. He was a mathematician, and laid the foundation of the really scientific geography. It is believed by some that this theory was first profounded by Thales (640-546 B.C.), but others give this credit to Pythagoras who flourished in the sixth century B.C. In any case, it was Eratosthenes who based his geography on this idea, and according to Bunbury[250], his geographical description is not only much nearer to the truth i.e. *'Nam'* than that of Ptolemy, who flourished four hundred year later[251].

We learn a great deal of knowledge from the geographical works of Straba, Pliny, Arrian, Ptolemy, Hecataeus, etc. The other texts like *Indika, Nearchus,* etc also furnish a statement about the trade and commerce between India and the western countries. They give an account of the rich material, agricultural and other economic products of India. They also describe its people, plants, animals, and also repeat sundry tales about them carried by traders and travellers. Reference is made to trade with Greek by the system of barter (450 A.D.). An interesting item was the export of silk (450 A.D.). The Pearl fishery (416-7, 222 A.D.) formed an interesting topic of classic writers. There is also reference of the work of the mines (233 A.D.). The fertility of the land was an object of admiration but Brahmanas have to make her complicated because of the allusion (*maya*). The classical writers hold before us a life of ease and opulence (233, 450-1 A.D.) which was not disturbed by famine and scarcity. This is chiefly accounted for by a convention tacitly obeyed by warriors never to ravage lands or molest cultivators even during the heat of the war (233, 264 A.D.). The statement that 'famine has never visited India' (233 A.D.) is contradicted by Indian literature which refers to famine even ancient days. Reference is made, for example, at the time of Chandragupta Maurya[252]. The Indians were also highly developed in arts and crafts. Reference may have been made to the statement of Nearchus (279 A.D.)[253].

The classical writers were naturally attracted by the peculiar social customs and institution, for example, in which the ignorance of classical writers is difficult to explain in a statement, attributed to Megasthenes, that the Indians were ignorant of the art of writing, *Strabo* quotes this (270 A.D.) as well as another statement of Megasthenes which credits the Indians with a knowledge of writing (264 A.D.). *Strabo* also refers to a statement of Nearchus to the effect that the Indians write missives on linen cloth, immediately adding, however, that the writers say that the Indians make up no use of written characters (279 A.D.). Curtius writing (104 A.D.), and though he belongs to a later period, seems to describe the state of things prevailing in Alexander's time. There is, however, hardly any doubt that the art of writing was to the Indians at the time of Megasthenes, and even much earlier. This is proved by the inscriptions engraved on rocks and pillars during the reign of Asoka, about half a century later. These letters are so well formed that there must have been an anterior period of development of writing extending over centuries. The classical writers through some light on dress and ornament (270-281 A.D.), food and manner of taking it (270 A.D., 403 A.D. and 455 A.D.), funeral (270 A.D. and 223 A.D.), rubbing of body (270 A.D, private dewelling houses (223 A.D. and 388 A.D.) and the urban life of India which had innumerable cities (223 A.D.). On the morals of the Indians classical writers have expressed divergent view. Curtius has condemned the court-morality in strong language (105 A.D.). He even goes so far as to say that amid this correction of morals who would expect to the culture of philosophy (105-6A.D.). At present this statement furnished to the Indian politic and other social institution like court, college, universities and in other private affairs of the companies. On the other side, *Strabo* gives an almost exactly opposite view in (269-70 A.D.), because of that they were the *Sudra.* rulers. They had the high moral in standard of living, way of talking, way of behaviour, eating, etc. A part from the incidental references, a great deal is said about the Brahmanas and *Sramanas* which developed in the present term *Sharma,* etc. The latter including both Buddhists and Jainas (ch. XIII, 187, 237, 237, 263-4, 173 ff, 299 ff). But the Brahmans were not all recluses or devoted to religious pursuits. Some of them took active part in politics to know the *Rajaniti* of the period and were great fighters of the *'Nam'* or *'Word'* (1, 81 A.D. & 278 A.D.). Reference is also made to religious practices (280 A.D.[254]). Where from the term religion has been originated and to the Indian conception of immorality of soul was originated in 450 A.D. with commencement of Brahminical thought on the bases of Sanskrit language. Language does not mean the origin of natural theory. It is a communiation system to pass on the massage to each other in the society but not a original growth of the man.

Bharut, Sanchi, and *Pitalkhora* in South, when Alexander entered the Punjab just before the establishment of the Mauryan empire, it was with a view to develop its immense commercial resources in (321-72 B.C.). As such, there were many art and cultural cross-currents between *China, Persia* and India. Alexander founded trading posts all along his course, and left behind Greek colonists who finally intermarried with the Indians. Chandragupta Maurya himself married a princess from the Greek Seleucid court. Trade was carried on by ships through the ports along the coastline of Maharashtra, the Malabar coast, the Tamil country, and Bengal. Land routes were expanded to join the Ancient Silk Route through Central Asia to China, and large caravans undertook hazardous journeys for the sake of the profits that were to be made by the adventurous king the Vedic period as it is now, and in addition to milk products provided skin, leather, horn, hair and wool which were used in various art and crafts by the artisans. Men and women continued to wear three unstitched piece of clothes, as in Vedic times. The main garments was the *antariya* of white cotton, linen or flowered muslin, sometimes embroidered in gold or precious stones. For men, it was an unstitched a long piece of cloth draped around the hips and between the legs in the *Kachcha* style, extending from the waist to the calf or ankles or worn even shorter by peasants and commoners. The *antariya* was secured at the waist by a sash or *Kayabandh, often* tied in a looped knot at the centre front of the waist. The *Kayabandh* could be a simple sash, *Vethaka;* one with drum-headed knots at the ends, *muraja;* a very elaborate band of embroidery, flat and ribbon-shaped, *pattika*, or a many-stringed one, *Kalabuka*. The third item of clothing called the *Uttariya* was another length of material, usually fine cotton, very rarely silk, which was utilized as a long scarf to drape the top half of the body. *Uttariya* was worn in several ways to suit the comforts of the wearer, very elegantly by those at court, who could drape it on both shoulders or one shoulder, or diagonally across the chest and casually knotted at the waist, or it could even be worn loosely across the back and supported by the elbows or wrist, and in many other ways according to the whims of the wearer. But for the labourer and the craftsman, it was more a practical garment to be tied around the waist leaving the hands free for work, or again as a towel to mop the face when sweating. Its uses were endless for the poor sections of the society and for them it would be made of coarse cotton[255].

An attempt has been made to collect the materials for the constructing of the history of the artisans which was destroyed by the narrow Brahminical thought. In this volume, all the references of the classical texts have been quoted to projecting an authentic approach in history through the dialogues of the various writers and scholars which *throw any light on Indian classical history of art and culture.* This qualifying phrase expresses why the accounts of *Ktesias,* and the stories of fabulous races, or of birds and animals were not to be corporated in the history of the World and sundry topics of this nature have been omitted. Because *Ktesians* was a *Sudra* by caste, therefore he was rejected by the modern philosophers of the world. *Ktesias*, of *Cnidus* in Caria, born in the 5th century B.C., was a great physician to the Achaemenian king of Persia which is at present known as 'Baba Gurinder Sing Ji Bias', Artaxerxes Mnemon, for twenty years (418-398 B.C.). He wrote a treatise of India, fragments of which alone have survived in the writings of later authors Rawlinson rightly observes that hte *Indika* of *Ktesias* "is full of extravagant stories of monstrous people and strange animals, and adds practically nothing to our knowledge of India[256]." Therefore, the lineage of Chandragupta is a subject of controversy. One view helds him to be of high birth, a true-born *Kshatriya* the Vedic term eminently worthy of royalty, while the other view slanders him as a man of base birth a *Sudra,* not eligible for kingship under the rule of Brahmanas. We shall have to decide this controversy by a consideration of the evidence adduced on both sides of the public. His father was in fact a barber (*nai*), who stealthily became the queen's paramour and encompassed the assassination of the king by treachery[257].

Republican peoples known to the term Panini is *Samgha* or *Gana* (III. 3, 86). Most of these replics took to the pursuit of arms and were known as *Ayudhajivi Samghas* warriors communities'. They were of the *Vahika* country, the land of rivers,' another name for the Punjab (V.3, 114). As the examples of these self-governing communities of warriors, Panini mentions the following as under:-

1. *Kshudrakas (Greek Oxydrakai, (IV.2, 45)*
2. *Malavas (Greek Malloi) (1b)*
3. *Vrikas, also called Varkenya (V.3, 115), most probably corresponding to the people known as Hyrcanians (Sakas) mentioned as Varkanah in the Behistun and as Varkah in another old Persian inscription of Darius I*
4. *Damani and others (not identified) (V.3, 116)*
5. *Confederacy of the six Trigartas comprising*

   (a) Kaundo-paratha, (b) Dandaki, (c) Kaushtaki, (d) Jalamani, (e) Brahmagupta, and (f) Janaki
6. *Parsh, associated with Asura and Rakshas, and probably of the country called Parsa in the Behistun inscription of Darius I, the place of origin of the Achaemenians, whence the name Persia.*
7. *Yaudheyas*
8. *Salvas (Alwar and its surrounding country), a large confederacy comprising (a) Udumbaras (b) Tilakhalas (c) Madrakaras, (d) Yugandharas, (e) Bhulingas, (f) Sarandandas (g) Budhas, (h) Ajakrandas and (i) Ajamidhas (IV. 1, 173).*
9. *Bhargas, mentioned in the Gana-Patha along with (a) Kurushas (b) Kekayas, (c) Kasmiras (d) Salvas, (e) Susthalas, (f) Urasas (Of Hazara District) and (g) Kauraryas (IV.1.178)*
10. *Ambasthas (Greek Abastanoi) who are associated in the Mahabharata (II. 52, 14-15) with the Sibis, Kshudrakas, Malavas and other north-western tribes.*
11. *Hastinayana (VI, 4, 174) (Greek Astaneon)*
12. *Prakanva (VI.1.153), corresponding to modern Ferghana whose people called the Parikanioi correspond to Prakanvayanas (Sten Konow, Kharoshthi Inscriptions, P. XVIII).*
13. *Madras, (IV. 2, 131).*
14. *Madhumantas (IV. 2,133; Mbh. Bhishma P., IX. 53) corresponding to the Mohmands.*
15. *Apritas (IV. 2, 53), (Greek Aparytai) corresponding to the Afridis.*
16. *Vasati (Ib.) (Greek Ossadioi).*
17. *Sibis (IV, 3, 112) (Greek Sibioi).*

18. *Asvayana (IV.1.110) and Asvakayana (Ib.99) corresponding to Greek Aspasii and Assakenoi whose stronghold was massaga and Assakenoi whose strong hold was massaga (= Masakavati)*

In the above list, the republician peoples outside the Punjab and the shpere of Chandragupta's work was omitted. As Arrain tells us (IV.21), a large part of the Punjab was then held by these "independent Indian tribes" whom Curtius (IX.4) describes as "fierce nations" ready to resist Alexander "with their blood". The kingdom which was restored by Alexander by Alexander to his old enemy, king Poros (=Paurava), comprised territories held by "fifteen republician peoples owning 5000 considerable cities and villages without number" (Plutarch liver IX[259]).

Alexander had its first taste from the tribal chief whom the Greeks called *Astes;* corresponding to Sanskrit *Hastin,* the chief of the people known by the Indian name of *Hastinayana* (Panini, VI. 4, 174). Greek *Astakenoi or Astanenoi* with his capital at *Penkelaotis* or *Pushkalavati*. This heroic chief stood the Greek siege of his walled town for fall thirty days till he fell fighting. Similarly, the *Asvayanas* and *Asvakayanas* fought the invader to a man, as will be evident from the fact that as many as 40,000 of them were taken as captives. Their economic prosperity based on agriculture and artisans works, may also be noted from the fact that as many as 230,000 oxen fell into the hands of Alexander. The *Asvakayanas* gave the battle to Alexander with an army of 30,000 cavalry, 38,000 infantry, and 30 elephants, aided by 7,000 mercenaries from the plains, all garrisoned in their fortified capital called *Massaga* (Sanskrit *Masaka*, which stood on the banks of the river *Masakavati* in the *Kasika* comment on Panini (IV, 2,85, VI.3, 119), led by the heroic *Queen Clcophis* (=Sanskrit Kripa means' love of the Father or husband' called *'Nam'* or *'God'),* "resolved to defend their country to the last extremity." Even their women took part in the defence along with the Queen[260].

It is interesting to note that the city called *Aornos* by the Greek corresponds to the term *Varana* or *Akasara* or *'Sabad'* used by Panini (IV, 2, 82[261]).

Only the scantiest knowledge exists about the materials of the dress was made in ancient times. That cotton was widely used is obvious, for cotton, as far as we know, is altogether an Indian invention (as silk is Chinese), and it occurs, without any doubt, at about 2300 B.C. at the prehistoric site of Mohenjo-daro in Sindh. There is evidence that it was exported from the Indus valley in prehistoric times of Ravidas Culture, and there is a good deal of probability that it was *Kaunakas* of the old Greeks, known to Mesopotamia long before the Iranian reached the shores of the Aegean. What is certain is that the great scholars, Panini, mentions is as uncertain as most things in those remote days of Sanskrit literature, all one can say is that silk may have been known indeed probably was known, as an imported article around the 2nd century B.C., or possibly in the 3rd century B.C. Emperor Asoka possessed and brought labouriously by caravans travelling across the Takla Makan Desert of Central Asia and over dangerous mountain passes above 16,000 feet high. It is far more likely that silk from China reached India in good quantities when it also reached the Roman Empire at the height of its luxury, that is to say, in the first to the fourth centuries A.D., when the Great Silk Route of Serindia so brilliantly described by Sir Aurel Stein, passed through Indian territory, *Via* the Kabul Valley. For the Kabul valley was than part of the Kingdom of Gandhara, an Indian Buddhist country, ruled by a Central Asian dynasty, the *Kushanas* who kept in close contact with their home country on the borders of China[262]. Chinese traveller *Yuan Chwang* already mentioned above that *Han* (or Kan) -Po-lo, *(Kambala) a* texture of fine wool as a material clothing and its softness can not campare with the 'pashm' wool of the goat or sheep's hair of Kashmir, Bhutan, Tibet to the Central Asiastic wool and the northern face of the Himalayas. Again, beautiful cloth was also made by admixture of wool and fibres of *dukala*[263] mentioned by *Yuan Chwang*. It is also mentioned that *Aurelian* received a reddyed short woolly pallium as a present from a Persian King and this shawl was manfactured in India [264] as a biggest centre of market. The material known as *'Marococorum Lana'* in the Digest of the Roman Law (XXXIX, 5.7) was the raw wool of the shawl-goat sent from north-western provinces of Indian ports to be worked in Egypt, and its name derives from the name of the Karakoram mountain[265]. Washermen *(dhobis)* were also dyers, *rajaka,* and they perfumed garments after washing them. Four primary colours were recognised in the dyeing of textiles; red (dyed with safflower and madder), white (through bleaching), yellow (natural colour of yarn and saffron), and blue (indigo leaves). Fabrics were also woven in patterns and printed for use as carpets, bed covers, blankets, *pattu* and clothes[266]. It appears that wool weaving is more restricted that cotton for its use in India is limited. Wool seems to have some religious significance as tradition of the ancient society believes it to have been created directly by Brahma like the *Kusa* grass used in worship. Amulets and charms are tied by woollen strings. In fact, black wool thread is commonly used to keep off evil spirits[267] in the life of man. The dyed wool was not export, as the red-dyed wool astonished Aurelian and his successors as a thing of novelty[268]. The wool of the shawl-goat fetched a very high price in ancient times. It is described that when the Sassanid Hormisdas (Hormizd II. 302-310 A.D.) married the daughter of the King of Kabul the bride's trouseau which was handsome in product of the looms of Kashmir excited for admiration[269]. Amongst shawls, Kashmir holds the world fame. The most complex of shawls is called *Jamavar* from *Jama* a robe and *var* means yardage. The weaving somewhat as in tapestry labourious and time consuming as numerous *kanis* or shuttles leaded with rich coloured (ranga) threads are moved around even in a single weft line because of the constant almost fantastic change of colours which can be even as many as 50 in a single piece and because of the use of large number of shuttles (*Kanis*) it is popularly called *Kani* shawl. Dying is also a very special job done by specialists. It is said that in the old days something like 300 tints of vegetable extraction were used[270]. Shawl is one of India's best wool products. It is unique in that while it offers the intimacy of a warm garment it leaves you free and unencumbered. In woollen materials the most coveted is *pashmina*[271], made out of the wool from the under belly of the Himalayan *pashmina* goat, which were preferred to all over the world this animal grows when it lives over the world this animal grows when it lives 14,000 ft. or above sea level. The discard wool is spun into shell for making floor coverings called *Karcha*. The finest is *shatush,* a soft dreamy fabric that almost melts to the touch. A *shatush* can be drawn through a ring and is, therefore, called a ring shawl, and though extraordinaryily light, it is nevertheless amazingly warm[272].

The history of the shawl-weaving with which the history of woollen textile goes back to the Vedic literature is closely associated with Kashmir. It is, however, certain that sheep's wool was used for spinning from *Kashmir* as it was the original place for the weavers at that time. It makes clear from the study that original shawl weaves might have been immigrants as certain unique features of the industry distinguished from its traditional weaving in India proper; after a long period of the history. The most significant method and technique employed to it very ancient which were parallel in Presia and Central Asia. The weft threads alone form the pattern from the well-known sheep called *Urnavati* and wool known as *avika*[273]. The valley of Sindh has been called *Suvasa urnavati* because sheep's wool and cloth were available there in plenty. The sheep of Gandhara were famous, and the regions through which the Ravi flowed was noted for its washed or coloured woollen fabrics. *Pushan* is mentioned as a weaver of woollen fabrics. *Kambala,* a generic term for blankets and shawls, appearing for the first time in the *Atharvaveda* is according to Pryzluski an Austric loan word in Indo-Aryan. *Darsa* from which probably *dhussa,* a rough woollen *cadar* from the Panjab and Kashmir derives its etymology, occurs for the first time in the *Atharvaveda* but it is difficult to say anything about the form or material used in the manufacture of Vedic *dursa.* Another fabrics wore at the time of sacrifices. The *Brhadaranyaka Upanisad* mentions *pandvavika* which was made from the sheep's wool and was possibly a woollen *chadar* or a shawl. It is not known whether the goats wool from which the modern Kashmir shawls are woven was used in Vedic period, though the sacred nature of the black antelope skin has been emphasised at many places in Vedic literature.Whether the woollen fabrics in Vedic age were patterned is not known. However, there are references to show that brocades were known. Perhaps *arokah* also expresses some kind of fabric with decorated borders. *Pesas* seems to have been a generic term for embroidery and needle work seems to have been an important profession. In the *Aitareya Brahmana nivids* are called the embroidered patterns of the hymns. The smile used there throws some light on the process of pattern making. Such work was done on the upper part of the wrap, in the middle and in the lower part. The *Brhadaranyaka* mentions at one place that when a women needle-worker after embroidering one pattern took to another then the second pattern was more beautiful than the first one (*tadyatha pesakari pesaso matramupadanyataram kalyanataram rupam tanute).*

Some interesting information could be gathered about the woollen fabrics and shawls from Buddhist literature and the *Mahabharata* and the *Ramayana.* It is interesting to note that needle work (*Pesakakara-sippa*) was considered to be a low form of handicraft, perhaps it was practised by the people of low caste, called *Sudras.* In common with Vedic literature *kambala* is a generic term for woollen shawls. The *Jatakas* mention the deep red shawls of Gandhara (*indagopakavannabha gandharapandukambala*). The *Mahavanija Jataka,* in its list of precious things, mentions costly shawls from *Uddiyana* or modern *Swat.* Even now Torwal produces gaily coloured blankets known in India as Swati rugs. The country of the Sibis was also famous for shawls which were known as *Siveyyaka dussa*. It is mentioned in *Sivi Jataka* that the King of Kosala presented a shawl of Sivi (*Siveyyaka Vattha*) costing a hundred thousand *Karsapanas*. In Panjabi and Hindi even now *dhussa* means a rough woollen *cadar,* but in Buddhist times it seems to have been a very costly shawl. Banaras also seems to have manufactured a kind of shawl of mixed fabric in which woollen and linen threads were used. Jivaka Kumarabhrtya is said to have receive such a shawl as gift from the ruler of Kasi. It is called as *addha-Kasika-kambala*. Rhys Davids' explanation that it was a kind of woollen *chadar* in which half the fabric of Banaras origin was used does not give any sense. Buddhaghosa, however, explains the term *Kasi* here as equivalent to a thousand *Karsapanas* and thus *addhakasiya* according to him was a shawl costing five hundred. It is possible that the shawl had a very light texture as even now very light muslin in Hindi is called *addhi*. Kodumbara also produced fine woollen fabrics. If Kodumbara and Odumbara are the same then in ancient times the region about Pathankot near Amritsar was a great centre of shawl weaving. While discussing the variant readings *Kocchairabakaham-salaksanaih* in the *Saddharma Pundarika*, p. 82, verse 87, Pryzluski restitutes the correct text as *Kotamabakairhamsalaksanaih*, the Kotambaka cloth ornamented with the figure of geese. It shows that the geese pattern was a favourite motive of the ancient Audumbara weavers. Ancient Buddhist literature contains several lists of the contemporary woollen textiles, shawls, carpets, etc. whose exact significance in several cases is doubtful. *Cittaka* was a woollen bedspread made of variegated strips; *palika* was a white woollen carpet; *patalika* was a flowered carpet; *vikatika* was floor carpet, decorated with hunting scenes containing the figures of tigers, lions, etc.; *uddalomi* had fluffy hair on both sides; *ekantalomi* had fluff on one side only; *kuttaka* was a large carpet on which sixteen dancers could perform; *vahitika* was a carpet, sixteen hands long and eight hands broad; *namataka* was ordinary felt and *kojava,* mentioned in Central Asian documents, was a blanket with long hair like modern *thulma*.[274]

Arthasastra of Kautilyas assigned to the Maurya period contains some interesting information about the woollen textiles, blankets and shawls[275]. The woollen fabrics (*avika*) were usually made of sheep's wool and were either plan white, deep red or light red. The shawls are divided into four categories known as *khacita*, *vanacitra* and *khan lasamghatya* and *tantuvicchinna*. The commentary describes *khacita* as *sucivana karma-nispaditam* which may either mean made by weaving and embroidering' or made by twill-tapestry process 'Weaver' the *suci* standing here for the *toji* of modern times. If the second explanation is correct then it indicates that even in those ancient days the *tilikar* process in Kashmir in which the patterns are woven on the loom and *amlikar* process in which the patterns are embroidered existed. In *Khacita* shawls apparently both processes were employed. The commentary describes *vanacitra as vanakarmana krtavaicityam*. Apparently in this process, as in modern *tilikar* process, the design were woven on the loom. The *khandasamghatya* in the commentary is described as *khacitanam utanam va bahunam khandanam samghatena nispaditam,* i.e. the shawl made by joining many *khacita* or woven pieces. It is apparently a form of Kashmir shawl in which patterns are woven on many strips measuring from twelve to eighteen inches: then these are either joined to obtain a complete pattern or simply attached to a shawl. These strips are at times embroidered. The *tantuvicchinna* is described by the commentator as *anutavisrishtaih tantubhih madhya krtavicchedyam jalakopayogi ca* i.e. obtaining patterns in the middle by unwoven yarn or a trellis pattern. It is possible that the netted border of a shawl made by tying the unwoven ends is meant here.

Besides the shawl mentioned above, the *Arthasastra* mentions some other kinds of blankets and *chadars* whose exact significance at times is not quite clear. *Kambala* as usual is a generic term for all kinds of woollen fabrics. *Kecalakakucelaka-kaucapaka* was probably a cowherd's blanket, *kalamitaka-kulamitika-kathamitika* was either an elephant carpet or a cap; *saumitika* was a bull carpet; *turagastarana* a horse carpet; *varnaka* a coloured blanket; *talicchaka* a bed-spread and *paristoma* an elephant *jhul*. From Nepal two varieties of woollen fabrics *bhingist* made of eight pieces which served as a protecting cover against the rains and *apasaraka* might have been something like modern *pattu* or tweed. Interesting light on the import of woven fabrics and shawls from Kamboja (Tajekestan) and Bahika (Bactria) is thrown in chapters 45 and 47 of the *Sabhaparvan* of the *Mahabharata* where Yudhisthira receives the presents from the people of distant lands. From Kamboja among other articles were included fabrics made from sheep's wool and the hair of *vrsadamsa* embroidered with gold, woollen *cadars (pravara)* and costly shawls (*kambala*). The people of the trans-Indus region also sent shawls. Among the present received from Bactria and China, besides silken goods, there were articles made of sheep-wool and goat-hair (*rankava*)[276] which were soft and dyed from different colours of the period in Indian history. It is notable that *ranku* from whose hair costly shawls were made has simply been mentioned as an animal in the *Amarakosa*. But there is little doubt that *ranku* is the same as *rang* or the shawl-goat mentioned several times by Jahangir in his Memoirs and also noticed by Wood[277]. Thus *rankava* is the equivalent of modern *pasmina or asli-tus*. As mentioned by the *Mahabharata*, felts were also made from the goat's wool (*rankava-kata*). A lotus-coloured woollen shawl from Afghanistan probably came from Uddiyana or Swat where Torwal manufactures red blankets which are known as Swati blankets even to this day.

Some interesting information is available about the woollen goods manufactured in the early centuries of the Christian era. The generic term for shawls and woollen fabric was *kambala*[278]. *Dusya* probably also indicated some kind of woollen shawl[279]. *Kalpadusya* from Uttarkuru which might have been situated in Central Asia was blue, yellow, red or white[280]. Mixed fabrics of wool and *dukula* were made[281]. At times the shawl was very thin (*kambala-suksmani*). The *Mahavastu* says that the wool weavers had their own guild. There was also a great demand for ordinary blankets and camel rugs.

In the literature of the Gupta period as well certain information about the woollen fabrics and shawls is available. The *rankava* of the *Amarakosa,* as we have already pointed out, is equivalent to *pasmina.* In the list of textiles in the Jain *Acaranga Sutra*, and the *Nisithacurm* some important information about shawls and blankets is available. Thus *jangiya* was a camel rug, *ayani* was defintely *pasmina* as according to the commentary in a certain country goats had very fine hair (*paksma-pasma*) from which the *ajakas* were made.The *Nisitha* had, however, no idea about the origin of *ajaka* as according to it this stuff was manufactured from the weed growing in the Rishi tank in Tosali, which stuck to the hooves of the goat grazing there. *Amila,* according to the commentator of the *Acaranga,* was made from goat-skin but according to the *Nisitha* it was made from goat's hair. It might have been some kind of shawl. Other varieties of *pasmina* shawls are *pesalani* described as made from very fine *paksma or pasm. Rallaka* is said to have been a sort of woollen shawl in the *Amarakosa* which was probably the same as *ho-la-li* of Yuan Chwang has already mentioned above. It is said that it was made from the hair of some wild animal and was a fairly costly stuff. It was probably some sort of *pasmina.*

From the above account of woollen fabrics and shawls of ancient India one thing is clear that nowhere shawl weaving is connected with Kashmir, though the industry seems to have flourished in Swat, North Western Frontier Province, Panjab, etc. There is very little material to construct the history of shawl weaving in Kashmir and the general belief in Kashmir as mentioned by Charles Hugel[283] in the 19th century, it has been founded by Zain-ul-Abidin (1420-70 A.D.) who is said to have introduced Turkistan weavers inKashmir for the purpose of the development of weaving industry in Kashmir and its product was famoused in Europe.

An examination of the literary sources, however, reveals that the shawl industry of Kashmir was of greater antiquity than the 15th century, Ksemendra (c.990-1065 A.D.), a versatile writer of medieval Kashmir, seems to have been fairly well acquainted with the shawl-weaving industry of his country. In *Desopadesa* and Narmamala refers to *tusta-pravarana, paryanta-tustaka*[284], which seems to have been some inferior variety of shawl with borders. There is little bit doubt that the *tus* shawl[285] made from the wool of the animal of the same name is meant here.The *lohita-kambala* which reminds us of the red shawls of Gandhara and Uddiyana mentioned in the *Jatakas*[286] text. In the *Samayamatrika*[287] *Kankali* serving as a nurse to a rich man's son is shown wearing a closely woven shawl (*kambala*) which fell to her ankles. Shawl-weaving seems to have been a cottage industry in the 11th century A.D. in Kashmir. At one place in the *Desopadesa* and *Narmamala*[288]. *Ksemendra* observes that the teacher employed in a *Kayastha's* house for teaching the children of the house instead of carrying out his duty whiled away his time in spinning (*kartana*), drawing out the patterns (*likhanam*) and weaving the patterns on the strips with *tujis* or eyeless wooden needles *sucipattakavanam 'Weaver'* or *'Word'* the process analogous to the modern shawl-weaving in Kashmir. All these reference to shawl manufacture in Kashmir prove its existence in Kashmir long before the 15th century.

That in the 13th century shawls and other woollen goods from Kashmir reached Western India is referred by Udayaprabha Suri his *Dharmabhyudaya*[289] (written C. 1233). He says that along with other articles Kashmir shawls (*Kashmira vasana*) were used for worshipping in the *Samghas* and *Caityas*. The existence of shawl weaving industry in Kashmir in the 13th and 14th centuries is further supported by a reference in the *Sarur us-sudur* a work of Muhammad Bin Tughaq's time containing the sayings of *Shaykh Farid-ud-Din*. It mentions that in Alauddin's time (1296-1316 A.D.) Kashmir shawls were available in Delhi and that Shaykh Nizamuddin Auliya had one such shawl. We have already discussed to the tradition prevalent in Kashmir that Zain ul-Abidin in the 15th century had established the shawl industry there. This tradition was, however, so far not supported or denied by historical evidence. Fortunately, Srivara's *Jaina Rajatarangini* throws some light on this point. After the death of Jonaraja in 1459, the history of Kashmir between 1459 and 1486 was written by *Srivara*. This history continues the account of the reign of Zain-ul-Abidin from 1459 to 1470. Though the *Rajatarangini* may not be a strictly historical work, nevertheless it contains episodic descriptions which throw considerable light on the life and culture but the other historical sources mentioned above, give a proof that during *Guptas,* etc had the works of artisans as the poor *'Chamar'* or *'Megh'*, etc. were prevalent.

The interest of Zain-ul-Abidin in textiles is shown in chapter sixth of the *Jaina Rajatarangini* which says that hearing of the great reputation of *Zain-ul-Abidin* many Indian rulers sent him presents. For instance *Rana Kumbha* (1433-1468 A.D.) of Chitor sent him as present a printed cloth known as *narikunjara*[290], apparently decorated with the composite figures of women in the shape of an elephant, a favourite art motif of the 15th century. Sultan Mahmud Beghra (1458-1511 A.D.) sent to him clothes such as *Katepha, Saglata*, and *Sopha*[291] which could be identified with *qatif*, a silken stuff, saqlat, scarlet broad cloth and *suf* or woollen cloth[292] of the *Akbar's* time. Such was his reputation as a lover of art that in the words of the poet "a large number of artisans adept in original designs regarding him as the Wishing Tree came from long distances like swarming black bees."[293] The Kashmiris mastering the intricacies of the shuttles (*turi*) and looms (*verma*) now weave beautiful and costly silks." "The special woollen textiles (*aurna sopha*) of foreign origin, worthy of kings, are now woven by the Kashmiris"[294]. "The painters seeing the patterns (*citra*) and creeper designs (*Latakritih*) obtained by intricate weaving process (*vicitravayana*) are reduced to silence as the figures in a painting[295]. "The country and the costume of the king became famous on account of the silks made of endless yarns, and carefully dyed (*Varnavicchitti*)."[296]

From the above mentioned account it makes clear that in Zain-ul-Abidin's time the art of textile weaving in Kashmir, specially the manufacture of silk, had received great impetus and that a large number of artisans in order to show their art came to Kashmir to seek the patronage of the ruler. It is also significance to note that certain woollen goods which came formerly from distant lands were, in the time of Zain-ul-Abidin, being manufactured in Kashmir. Herein possibly lies the origin of the tradition that Zain-ul-Abidin had invited Turkish weavers and thus laid the foundation of shawl manufacturing industry in Kashmir. The tradition is further supported by Srivara's assertion that artisans came from distant lands to seek the patronage of the king. Turkeistan is not specially mentioned, but the possibility that it was one of the countries from which artisans came to Kashmir could not be ruled out that they were the *'Chamars'*.

Considerable light on the shawl manufacture of Kashmir in the 16th century is thrown by the *'Ain-i-Akbari* of Abul Fazl who has given exhaustive lists of all kinds of textiles. He points out the great interest which Akbar took in various stuffs and that was the reason why Iranian, European and Mongolian articles of wear were available in plenty in the country[297]. Besides this, his interest in textiles had attracted a large number of foreign craftsmen and workers who taught the people improved style in textile manufacture. The imperial workshops at Lahore, Agra, Fatehpur, and Ahmadabad were noted for their excellent products whose patterns, knots and varieties of fashion astonished the travellers. Akbar himself had acquired a practical knowledge of the whole trade and the encouragement he gave to the indigenous workers brought all round improvement. All kinds of hair-weaving and silk-spinning improved so that the Imperial workshops could manufacture all the stuff produced in other countries. There was a constant *demand*[298] for fine materials and at first time gave occasion for grand display of draperies.

All textile pieces bought, woven in order or received as tributes or presents were carefully preserved by Akbar and were inspected from time to time in form *Kushana* or Asoka or any other rule of the different period of history. Clothes were made by them with power of *'Kalma'* or *'Nam'* and were given away as presents. Articles of clothing were arranged by them in different price and rate. Experienced people always in regular form they inquired about the prices and rates of various articles of clothing. Formerly it was used by the Maurayan rulers,than *Kushanas,* etc in routine matter as Akbar did. It is said that the knowledge of the exact prices of the articles of dresses were conducive to the increasing stock[299] of the day i.e. 'Enlightenment era'.

Keeping in view, the interest of Akbar in textiles *Kashmir* was a greater manufacturing centre of shawl under him. In *Ain-i-Akbari,* the generic term for shawl, he has given call *sal* in Hindi it designated as *paramnaram* for 'very soft shawl' and he also changed its name called as *'Kapurdhur'* 'Camphor dust' in Tibetan stuff called *'Kapurdhur'*, 'Camphor light[300] as its variety. In *Akbarnama,* the word called *siyah*gilim is used for black blanket. It depicts that black *kambala* was used to wrap in the Mughal period. *Tuzk-i-Jahangiri* also mentions that in Kashmir *lattoo chaddar* was used and made of wool and two *chaddara* were sewed together, they smooth them into a kind of *saqarlat* (broad-cloth[301]). Again in the *Ain-i-Akbari*, it is referred that *tus* shawls made of natural colours are black, white and red; but chiefly black. Sometimes the colour is pure white, in the second category *Safid alcas* or *tarahadars* in their natural colours, the wool is either white, black or mixed. The first white kind was formerly dyed by the dyer (*ranga*) in three or four ways, his father has given order to dye him in various ways. The third category in stuffs known as *zardozi, kalabatun, kasidah, qalghai, bandhnun, chint, alcah* and *purzdar* to which his Majestic pays much attention. Fourthy he improved the smallest size of the shawls and enlarged them as to make complete suit out of them.

"In former times shawls came from Kashmir from time to time. People folded them in four-folds, and wore them for a very long time. Now-a-days they are generally worn without folds and merely thrown over the shoulders. His Majesty has commenced to wear them double, which looks very well."

"His Majesty encourages in every possible way the manufacture of shawls in Kashmir. In Lahore alone there are more than a thousand workshops. A kind of shawl named *mayan* is chiefly woven there; it consists of silk and wool mixed[302]. These are of standard size. Both are used for *cirahs* (turbans) and *fautahs* (loin-bands)."

From the above account of shawl many points are clear. Firstly, *tus* shawl was made from the hair *tus* goat. In the 19th century when Moorcroft visited Kashmir there were two kinds of goat-wool *pasm sal* obtained from the wool of domestic goats and *asli tus* obtained from the hair of wild goats and sheep. It was chiefly black, white or reddish. Secondly, the corded and patterned shawls (*tarah* shawls) were made of either white, black or mixed wool. The white kind was formerly dyed in three or four colours but in Akbar's time the number of colours was increased. Thirdly, attention was paid to the manufacture of the following varieties of shawls:

(1) *Zardozi-* Apparently this shawl was embroidered with gold wire and sequins! The Museum has several good examples of this kind of shawl.

(2) *Kalabatun* - The design seem to have been brocaded with gold wire.

(3) *Qasidah* - In this variety the pattern was embroidered and not woven.

(4) *Qalghai* - This type was made either of silk or gold wire or bore pine cone patterns (*qalghi*).

(5) *Bandhnun* shawls had tye-dyed pattern.

(6) *Chint* shawls were apparently painted or decorated with floral patterns in the manner of calico-prints. According to Moorecroft and Trebeck[303] even in the early 19th century some shawls with green flowers tied in small hard knots to protect them from the action of the dye were made. When untied each flower was surrounded by a small white field to which samll eyes of spots of yellow, red were added by the embroiderers.

(7) *Alcah* was a white banded stuff.

(8) *Purzdar* is described by Jarrett as all sorts of stuff of which the outside is plush-like. But according to the Prince of Wales Museum manuscript, it was known in Turkish as *kark* and in Hindi *rusa.* The note further explains that it was a big piece made of various strips joined together or it had marbled (*abri*) design or its nomenclature was due to its good quality. There is little bit doubt that by *purzdar* that kind of shawl is meant in which the size is obtained by joining together several strips with the *Khandasamghatya* of ancient times. Fourthly, it seems that the shawls before Akbar period were narrow. By Akbar's order, however, shawls of a suit's length were being made. Fifthly, Lahore, with more than a thousand workshops became a centre of shawl weaving and produced a stuff called *mayan* used for turban and waist-bands.

There are several informations about the shawl industry of Kashmir in the 17th centruy A.D., Jahangir in his Memoirs makes the following remarks about the shawl industry of Kashmir: "The shawls of Kashmir to which my father gave the name of *param-naram* are very famous: there is no need to praise them. Another kind is *taharma* (*naharma* in printed versions); it is thicker than a shawl and soft. Another is *dharm*. It is like a *jul-i-khirsak* and is put on carpet. With the exception of shawl they make other woollen material better in Tibet. Though they bring the wool for the shawls from Tibet, they do not make them there. The wool for the shawls comes from a goat which is peculiar to Tibet. In Kashmir, they used to the *pattu* shawl from wool, and sewing two shawls together they smooth them into a kind of *saqarlat* (broad cloth) which is not bad for a rain coat[304].

From the above account of shawls, it is clear that the shawl industry of Kashmir in Jahangir's time was in a flourishing state. The Hindi name *Param-naram* coined by Akbar for shawls continued and it seems to have formed a regular article for presentation to the nobles[305]. The *naharma* is translated by the editor in a footnote as "like a river", for the shawl had waves (*maujdar*). Apparently this kind was decorated with a wavy pattern. The *dharm* is explained as a little bear coverlet or drugget and was possibly something like modern *pattu* stuff generally used as a rough wear at that time.

Besides the stuff mentioned above we get tit-bits of information about shawls in the *Memoirs*. Thus we are told that *Jahangir* once presented to Mirza Raja Bhao Singh a special Kashmir *phup* shawl[306]. Phup here is certainly meant for Hindi *Puhupa* derived from the Sanskrit *puspa* "flower". Apparently it was a flowered shawl. At another place[307] it is said that *tus* shawl was a special prerogative of the King. It could only be worn when ordered by the King.[308]

Bernier, on his visit to Kashmir in 1665, has left the following account of shawls manufactured there. Large quantities of shawls were manufactured which gave employment even to children. These shawls measured 1½ell (ell=45) long and an ell broad, ornamented at both ends with a sort of embroidery made in the loom, a foot in width. The Mughal and Indian men and women wore them in writer round their heads, passing them over the shoulers as a mantle. One sort was manufactured with the wool of the country and the other with the wool of the shawl goat of Tibet. The price of the *tus* shawl ranged from 50 to 150 Rupees. Great pains were taken to manufacture similar shawls at Patna, Agra, and Lahore but they lacked the delicate texture of Kashmir shawls[309] in Jammu region.

It is clear from the above account that in the time of Aurangzeb there was great demand for Kashmir shawls. It seems that the use of *tus* shawls was not a royal monopoly as in the Jahangir period. This might have been due to the increase in productions, which is not conducive to monopoly of any kind. Further, besides Lahore shawls were being manufactured at Agra and Patna as well.

The *Kalpadrukosa* of Kesava a seventeenth century Sanskrit lexicon, gives some interesting names for shawls. According to it[310] *ratnakambala, Kashmiri, mahorna, pravari, pamari, yaksika* and Bhota were different names for shawls. As the names *Kashmiri* and *Bhota* indicate their sources were Kashmir and Tibet respectively. *Rantakambala* must have been a costly shawl; *pravari*, a *chadar* and *pamari* a foot spread.

The *Khulasat-ut-Tawarikh* (1695-A.D.)[311]speaks of woollen stuffs specially the shawls of Kashmir exported all over the world. Soft and beautiful broad cloths of wool were also manufactured. *Pattu* sheets in two pieces, as in the period of Jahangir were available.

From the above statement; it is clear that by the end of the 17th century the shawls of Kashmir were being exported to other countries. The shawls imported by the East India Company in 1685 and 1704[312], according to Mr. Irwin,[313] were almost certainly intended for use as table cloths or counterpanes. How the demand for Kashmir shawls in Europe grew and how it dictated the contemporary fashion has been ably dealt by Mr. Irwin and need not be recapitulated here.

Forster in his travel to Kashmir in 1783 A.D. has made certain interesting observations on the shawl industry of Kashmir. As a matter of fact; he travelled in the guise of a Turkish shawl merchant proceeding to purchase shawls in Kashmir[314]. At Bilaspur he met a Tumboo (*Tamba*) shawl caravan on its way to Delhi and Lucknow. It was through the help of their agents that he could clear himself from the Bilaspur customs[315]. According to Forster shawls exported from Kashmir were packed in oblong bales, whose outward coverings were made of the buffalo's or ox's hide, strongly sewn with leather thongs. They were opened only in the destined markets[316]. The shawl wool was brought from Tibet. Originally of dark grey colour, it was bleached with rice flour. The yarn was dyed as desired; the shawls were also washed after fabrication. Richly patterned borders were attached to the shawls so neatly as to allow no joints. The price of an ordinary shawl varied from 8 to 40 Rupees, but the value of a flowered shawl was considerably greater. A portion of the revenue of Kashmir was returned to Afghan capital in shawl goods. The shawls were in three sizes, the long and the square ones were in common use in India; the other long and very narrow ones with black preponderating in their scheme were worn as girdles by the Northern Asiatics[317] regions i.e. Panjab, Kashmir and Jammu from Basohli which was situated at that time on the bank of River Ravi based on 'Ravidas Culture' from the prehistoric period of Indian history.

The best account of shawl manufacture in early nineteenth century has been given by Moorcroft and Trebeck[318]. During the course of his journey, they found out that Amritsar had become an important centre of shawl manufacture owing to the migration of a large number of Kashmir craftsmen from their country to escape the Afghan tyranny. Before Moorcroft's time, shawl yarn to Amritsar came from Kashmir, but its export was banned to discourage the foreign manufacture of shawls. However, when they visited Amritsar the wool came from Tibet and Bokbara. The Amritsar shawls with double warp and weft were fairly thick and soft. The meagre wages of nearly two annas daily left the weavers miserably poor[319] in conditions.

Moorcroft and Trebeck left an interesting account of shawl manufacture in Kashmir[320] which has been supplemented by Mr. Irwin from the original Moorcroft papers in the India office. According to Moorcroft the *pasm* wool employed for shawl manufacture was obtained from domestic and wild goats and was brought from Tibet.

Ladakh, Yarkand and Khotan by the Mongols who exchanged it for shawls[321]. In its first disposal the importer (*baqal*), the retailer (*pasm-faros*), and the broker (*muqim*) were concerned. The payment was made in each or two months credit[322].

Women purchased the wool from the retailer for spinning. It was first packed and cleaned with the solution of rice flour and then after being torn to piece was arranged into square elastic pads (*tumba*) and then second wool extracted for strong shawl cloth (*patta*). Then the pads were rolled and carefully stored. The fine wool was spun in the lengths of seven hundred yards which were again cut into two hundred lengths to suit the length of the warp. The retailers purchased the yarn from the spinners and sold it to weavers, who having ascertained the patterns in demand, handed over the skeins to the dyer. For shawls with a plain field second yarn was used to weave patterns to get an enhanced effect. The dyer professed to give sixty-four shades such as crimson (*gulenar*) obtained from cochineal, kermes, logwood for other reds and blue and green from indigo. Carthamus and saffron yielded various tints of orange, yellow etc.

The *nakatu* adjusted the yarn for the wrap and the weft; the warp yarns measuring 3½yards consisting of two to three thousand threads were double while the weft yarns was single. Then the warp was dressed with thickly boiled rice water. Silk was used for border warp for strength and used as a colour contrast. Narrow borders were woven with the shawl, but the broader ones were woven on a different loom and then sewn to the shawl by the darner in such a manner that thejoints could scarcely be detected. The warp was then drawn through the needles and then taken to the loom. After the warp had been fixed up on the looms an the pattern drawn, *naqqas* and *tarahdar guru* and *talim guru* determined the proportion of the yarn of different colours. The naqqas prepared the drawing of the pattern, the tarahdar guru after considering the disposition of the colours, called out the colours beginning from the foot of the pattern, the number of threads to which it extended and the colour by which it was followed till the whole pattern had been described. From his direction the *talim guru* took down the particulars in a short hand and delivered a copy to the weaver.

The workmen prepared *tujis* prepared *tujis* or needs containing about for grains of dyed yarn. These eyeless needles had sharp ends. Following the instructions of the *tarahguru* the weaver knotted the yarn of the *tuji* to the warp. The right side of the cloth was placed next to the work being carried on the reverse on which the needles hung in a row numbering 400 to 1500. As soon as the work on one line was completed the count was brought down with force.

That shawl-cloth was generally of two kinds known as one plain with the threads, and the second twilled or with four threads. The twilled cloth, which was frequently of irregular texture, was usually twenty-four *girah* broad. To ensure a good field the borders were woven separately and joined to the field by the *rafugar*.

When finished the shawl was handed over to *purusgar* who removed discoloured hair with tweezsers or by shaving. Then the shawls were sent to the collector for stamp duties which amounted to 26%. After that they were handed over to sellers and brokers. They were then washed and calendered, packed separately in coloured papers, pressed and then the bale was sewn up in strong cloth over which a cover of *tus* or birth bark was laid. Finally, the whole was sewn smoothly and tightly in a raw hide.

Besides the shawls manufactured and described above *dosali umli* shawls were embroidered with needles using woollen thread instead of silk. The pattern was pounced on the shawl by means of a tracing paper using charcoal powder with some coloured powder mixed with gum arabic. Sometimes wooden blocks were also used.

In the plain shawls Moorcroft and Trebeck mentions *patta, pasmina* made of *asal tus* or coarse shawl wool (4 gaz × 1½ gaz); *sal phiri* made of seconds-wool (3½ × 1½ g.); *alwan* plain white cloth of fire shawl wool; turban-cloth and *johar sal-sadu* with a narrow edging of coloured yarn (3½ to 3¾ g. × 1½ g).

The following shawls measured (3½ g. × 1½ g.)— *sal hasiyadar, sal dohasiyadar and sal cahar hasiyadar* had one, two and four borders respectively; *hasiadar khosar* of *Khalikhani* had two borders and two *tanga* with or without flowers in the corners. *Hasiadar kiungridar* had the border of the usual form with another inside, or nearer the middle resembling the crest of the wall of an Asiatic fort furnished with narrow niches or embrassures for wall pieces: *dhurdar* in which an ornament ran round the field between the border and the field; *matandar* had flower or decoration in the middle of the field: *canddar* had a circular ornament in the field; *cautahidar* had four half-moons; *kung batedar* had a group of flowers at each corner; *alftdar* had green sprigs witout any colour on white field: *kaddar* had large group of flowers in the form of the cone of a pine with the ends of point straight or curved downwards; *do-kaddar* had two such heights; *sehkaddar* had three rows and so on to five and upwards, in the latter case the cones were somewhat small.

Moorcroft and trebeck have also given the definitions of some technical terms about patterns. Thus *hasia* is the border; the *zanziri* or chain runs above and below the *patta* and confines it; the *dhur* or running ornament situated inside the *hasiya* and *zanzir* enveloped the whole field, *kunjbuta* is a corner ornament; *matan* is the decorated part of the filed and *buta* is a cone in one or several rows; after five rows it is *tukaddar.* The constituent part of a *buta* is *pai* or foot or pediment of leaves, the *sikam* or belly and sir the head which is straight, curved or inclined. The sloping *buta* is *buta-kaj*; the *thal* or net separates the different *butas,* sometimes the interspace being plan. *Jamewar* meaning literally a gown piece in many varieties such as *khirkhabuta* 'Word' is a large compound flower consisting of groups of smaller ones, etc. It was used by the Persians and Afghans. The *rezabuta* (small flower thickly set), *thaldar* (network), *mehramat, khaterast, marpech, kalamkar, zakheangur, caporast, dogul* (two flowers), *sehgul* (three flowers), *cahargul* (four flowers), *barghe-bed, gule-sant, duzdeh khat, duzdeh, rang, gule parwane, kaddar, kayhamu, sabzkar and safed* were exported to India proper where they were dyed, the small flowers being tied previously in hard knots.

The square, *rumals* for women were known as *khatdar, mehramat and islimi* with other *patterns of jamewar, caharbagh, hasiya, cand, cautahi, sahmantabi, firangi (*exported to Russia), *tarah Armeni* (exported to Armenia and Persia), *tarah Rami* (exported to Turkey), and *sadda* for domestic use in Jammu region.

Besides the articles mentioned above *samlas* for the waist (8 x 1½ g., exported to Tibet), *gospech* or *patka* (turban, 10 × 1g) *mandila* with or without *zanzir* (8 to 10 g. × 12 *girah) kalin* (*pasmina* shawl carpet made of any size), *naqs* (trousers with or without seams, the former in two pieces sewn by darner and the latter by *jurrab saz* or stocking maker), *carkhana* or netted cloth (1½ g), *gulbadan* (breadth 14 gir. to 1 gir.) *lungi* (3½ × 1½ g.) *takhin* (caps), *jurrab* (short stockings) flowered or striped (*mehramat*), *moze pasmina* (long stockings), *sakkahpos* (canopies), *darparda* (curtain), *kajjari asp* (saddle cloth), *kajjari* fil (elephant's housing), *balapos* (quilt or coverlet) *galaband* (craver), *pistant-band* (necker-chief), *longot* (waist-belt), *posin* (to line a pelisse), *paipech legging, izarband, takia* (pillow case), *khalita* bags or purse, *kakarpos* (shrouds), *takposh* (hanging for cupboards and recesses) and *khwan-pos* (dish cover or napkins).

It is peculiar that in the above list the *sikargah* or hunting pattern of Kashmir shawl has not been mentioned by Moorcroft and Trebeck though shawls with such patterns are available. It is possible that this pattern had already fallen in disuse in the beginning of the nineteenth century. It is, however, clear that when Vigne visited Kashmir figured shawls were being manufactured. According to him Maharaja Ranjit Singh had ordered a pair of shawls to be made at a cost of Rs. 5,000/- which represented his victories. The Prince of Wales Museum has three good specimen of *sikargah* shawls. In one of the border bears the figure of hunter, tigers elephants and other beasts and birds (Fig. 4). The shawl seems to be very old and may be dated to the middle of the 18th century. The other two shawls are embroidered in chain stitch consisting of the figures of birds and beasts, horse riders, music parties, etc. (Fig. 5). The appearance of soldiers in what appears to be a sort of semi-European livery is interesting. The origin of these shawls is a little doubtful. At first glance Kashmir appears to be the place of their origin, but it is notable that such kind of shawls are not usually found in the collections of

Kashmir shawls. Moreover, the costumes of men and women recall the costumes of the men and women of Kulu and Kangra region as described by Forster and Moorcroft. Forster[323] observes; "Their (Kangra Women's dress consists of a petitcoat with border, usually of different colours; a close jacket, covering half the waist, and a loose stomacher to the forepart of it, which reaches the girdle. Their hair, which they hold in as high an estimation as that beautiful appendage, can be recorded by the gayest females of Europe, is plaited with black silk, or cotton strings, and falls down the back: over which they throw in graceful fashion, a veil, which seldom touches, and never conceals the face." According to Moorcroft the people wore a blanket with its one end being brought on shoulders and fastened across the breast with skewers and the other passed round the thighs and secured to the waist. In winter a double coat, trousers and bootkins were added. Respectable persons wore a sort of a jacket and trousers, the latter very full above and tight at the ankles. Both men and women wore caps. The men's caps were flat and red with an upturned border of black. The women's caps were undyed but with a fringe at the top which hung as the tassal on one side, the plait would round it. They wore heavy earrings and massive anklets[324].

It is this type of costume which is represented on the shawls which may possibly have originated from Kulu. The appearance of soldiers wearing a sort of European livery also lends support to this view. It is notable that Moorcroft on his way to Kashmir met at Sujanpur. Mr. O' Brien, an Irishman in the service of Raja Sansar Chand, who was a dragoon in the 8th or Royal Irish. It was said of him that on being reprimanded and struck by his officer he knocked him down and deserted. After wandering for sometime he joined Sansar Chand for whom he established a manufactory of small arms and disciplined an infantry of 1,400 men. There was another European soldier named James in Raja's employ with some skill in gunnery[325]. It is possible that O'Brien's soldiers are represented here. If it is so then the shawls could be dated to c.1800 A.D.

The dispersal of Kashmir shawl weavers and embroiderers in the late 18th century to Amritsar and possibly to the Hill States of Kangra was due to the tyranny of the Afghans and the rigorous exactions of the Sikh rulers. Vigne notes that after 1830 he found that at Srinagar only six hundred shawl frames had remained, and most of the weavers had migrated or had taken to some other profession. The story of the Kashmir shawl industry in the 19th century has been very ably traced by Mr. Irwin. The growing demand for Kashmir shawls in Paris in the closing years of 18th century had its inevitable repurcussions on the types of design produced. There was a demand for elaborate patterns. Merchants or their agents settled in Kashmir and asked the weavers to reproduce the given patterns. One Armenian merchant Khoja Yusuf was set by his Constantinople firm to Kashmir in 1803 in order to have shawls made according to the patterns of his choice, and he is said to have introduced among other things the innovation of needle-embroidered or *amli* shawls. It is, however, certain that such shawls were no innovation to Kashmir as *kasidah* or embroidered shawls are mentioned by the *Ain-i-Akbari*. It may be that Khoja Yusuf gave an impetus to *amli* shawls which perhaps had better market outside[326].

As mentioned by Moorcroft in one of his letters dated 1882 and quoted by Mr. Irwin at Srinagar he met merchants from the cities of Chinese Turkistan, Uzbek, Tattary, Kabul, Persia and Turkey and from the provinces of British India getting the shawls manufactured after the patterns and quality for which there was demand in their respective countries. But as Moorcroft has observed elsewhere, political event in the 19th century had reduced Kashmir's trade with Persia. Turkey and Panjab while demand from British India had decreased. One encouraging feature, however, was the increased in demand from Russia and Turkistan which probably helped the industry to tide over its difficulties for some time.

The increased demand for Kashmir shawls in Europe led to the imitation in England, and in the closing years of the 18th century, from 1814 onwards Paisley become the main centre of shawl manufacture in England. By 1818 Paisley shawls were being exported to India though they could never compete with the quality of Kashmir shawls. The French design also exerted great influence on Kashmir design. France produced new varieties of cone palmette design, the pattern being known in the English trade as 'fill over' design because the pattern covered the whole field of the shawls instead of the borders only. They became so popular by 1830 that Paisley weavers ceased to copy the originals and followed the French patterns. The effect of the new French patterns which had great demand in Europe and America also led to the copying of french patterns by the weavers of Kashmir. The shawl industry in Kashmir survived till1870, when the change in fashion in the West killed the export market with consequent suffering to the weaver. The internal demand presisted for some time but it was too inadequate to support the industry.

As remarked by Irwin discussion about Kashmir patterns suffer too much from the alleged symbolism and antiquity of the Kashmir cone. He is of the opinion that the *buta* or cone whose direct ancestry is traceable in the Persian Safawi patterns of the 16th century was introduced in Kashmir in the same century. He derives the Kashmir cone from two Safawi motives namely 'Word' (1) the combination of a cypress with a flowering almond tree, with a gradual tendency in the 17th century for the cypress and almond trees to merge into a common outline, and (2) flowering shrubs and vase-and-flower motive so common in Persia of the 17th and 18th centuries as a fusion of these two Safawid motives.

Unfortunately, the absence of material, literary and otherwise makes the problem of the history of shawl patterns of Kashmir a difficult one. As we have already pointed out, according to *Srivara* floral meander was a common motif of the silk weavers of Kashmir. In Akbar's period the *qalghai* type might have had the cone or flower pattern as *qalgha* means both flower or an *aigrette*, the *jigeh* of time only two patterns *nahrma* or wavy lines and *puhup* or flower are mentioned. Stripes also seem to have been a common motive. How far *qalgah* was used as a textile pattern in the 17th century we are unable to say as we have not come across any piece of the 17th century with his motif, but it begins to appear in many forms in the 18th century textiles, and also in the border decoration of the paintings, though here *qalgha* is merely a complex arrangement of flowers and leaves.

The Prince of Wales Museum has a varied and interesting collection of shawls dating from the 18th century to the present day. The collection may be classified under the following heads:— (1) Shawls with white fields decorated with simple green springs, the *alfidar* of Moorcroft which probably had a narrow border deocarted with flowers and palmates (Fig. 1). In one shawl (Fig. 2) the field is decorated with palms and roses while the border has cones. (2) Shawl with cypress and roundel motif (Fig. 3). It is a black sash piece with narrow border; the broad ends decorated with cypress and chain motives. Probably this piece was manufactured for Persia or Turkey, as these motifs seldom occur in Indian shawls. (3) *Sikargah* shawls (Fig. 4 and 5). They are either woven or embroidered and are decorated with hunting and picnic scenes. (4) Shawls with cone pattern. One of them (Fig. 6) is a *kaddar* shawl the rows of cones being five. In another *kalangidar* shawl (Fig. 7) the cones are beautifully combined with rosettes and leaves. In another type (Fig. 8), while the border is decorated with a series of cones, the diapered field is decorated with diamonds filled with flowers. (5) *Thaldar* pattern (Fig. 9) in which the corner and central cones are attached on netted grounds (6) Embroidered shawls (Figs. 10-12). In a *canddar* shawl (Fig. 10) with the field decorated with a rounded in the centre and with the cones and lamps and the birds, a beautiful effect has been obtained by a clever combination of woven and embroidered patterns. In a second embroidered shawl (Fig. 11) the floral and cone motives are done so artistically as to give an impression of a printed calico or a carpet. Another richly embroidered shawl (Fig. 12) is notable for its balanced pattern and clever use of the needle. (7). Modern shawls and *jamewar* with intricate floral patterns. Thus it could be safely said that the Museum has a rich collection of shawl which contains many rare pieces.

Description of the Shawls

Kashmir shawl (8′ 2″ × 4′ 1″); late 18th century. The white field is decorated with a floral diaper; the flowers being in blue, green and red. The borders are decorated with a beautiful meander in red, yellow and blue, it is a rare piece.

Kashmir shawl; middle of the 18th century. White field with *kalangi* borders. The narrow edge border running all round is decorated with floral meander. The field is decorated with floral sprays arranged in vertical bands. The pattern consists of rose flowers alternating with springs and palms. It is very good example of the 18th century shawls of Kashmir. It is worthy to note that the patterns are much more simple than the heavy decoration motifs consisting of arabesques and *kalangis* employed in the 19th century shawls.

Woollem sash, Kashmir , 5′ 6″ × 11″ 18th century A.D. The black sash has a plain narrow border running all round and sewn separately to it. Side borders are decorated with two bands. One decorated with flowers and the other with cartouches and palmates. The end borders are decorated with cypress trees and a decorative chain.

Square Kashmir shawl known as *rumal* (5′ × 5′), late 18th century. It has an orange field bounded by a border composed of pears, swords, men, animals and trees. so halved that the two borders when placed together form the top and bottom of the pears.

Sikargah shawl. (5′ 3½ 3′ x″); Kulu or Kashmir; beginning of the 19th century. Chain stitch embroidery.

The brown field is divided in two concentric circles: the larger circle is divided into a series of cartouches and heart-shaped panels with a rosette in the centre. The panels contains figures of men and women, horse-riders, birds and tigers. The second circle consists of a continuous line of the figures of soldiers dressed in semi-European fashion. The corners are also divided into a series of panels in which the figure of birds, deer, hares, antelopes and a prince attended by women and musicians may be seen. The borders are decorated with a series of meanders filled with animals and birds[327]. Besides the above mentioned shawls, there are certain other varieties of the Kashmiri shawls known as *minakari, rumal, kalangis, jamewar, kirmans,* etc were also fashioned in the 18th and 19th century A.D. in Jammu region.

In the study, we learn that the most important business of the weavers is the pattern drawing which is transferred to a graph by a highly skilled craftsmanship, rated higher than any weaver. The colouring is, however, done by the colour caller with a black and white drawing before him, beginning at the bottom and working upwards, calling out each colour, and the number of warps along with which it is required to extend until the pattern is covered. All these designs are then transcribed into a coded pattern that the weavers can aloud the number of warp ends to be covered in a particular coloured weft. A second weaver sits on the loom to accelerate the process and the chief weaver recites the weft repeat for him to follow. In some shawls these are two sided weaves, usually of the same design but sometimes in different colour schemes known as *do-rooka*. The mango (*kairy*) design, also known in its westernised version as paisley, and probably the most popular is seen in countless varieties. The woven designs are often enhanced by embroidery and one finds the main woven motifs in the background later connected by embroidery. The colour combinations are often fanatastic, like magenta with pink, mauve with red, a shocking pink against a brilliant turquois, and so on[328].

The period of first century A.D. to the beginning of the fourth century A.D., the hermits used to wear the cloths made from the fibres of fruits *phala, munja* grass, the inner silk or bark of certain trees (*balkala*), *darbha* and *valvaja* grasses and blankets made from the hair of the camel, goat and from human hair[329]. *'Puspapatta',* 'flowered cloth[330], is here we mean the world is flower of the 'Father', he or she must be developed in one or in other hands according to the requirement of the situation .The details of male and females costumes which were weft by the weavers referred by Bilhana, a contemporary of ruler Ksemendra, in his *Vikramankadevacaritam*[331]. He speaks of the fluttering *dupattas* of linen (*Ksaumambara-prasphuraduttariya*[332]). The long turbans were made of cotton cloth called as *Vistirnatulapatakalpitavestanesu*[333]*).* The Gujaratis whose country the poet visited during his tour are condemned for not tucking the end of their *dhotis* behind (*Kaksabandham vidadhati na ye sarvadaivavisuddhah*[334]). Bilhana also poetically expresses the garment of the upper part of the bodies called (*Kancukani),* which, unable to sustain the pointed breasts or cups, were torn by them as[335] under in the cover. *Nicola* or a long tunic is also mentioned[336] in the study of the same text that it used to cover the dark blue shirt (*nilaniradanicola*) in colour[337]. The women of Kashmir are said to have worn the shows of goat hair at that time called (*pattika rankavanam*) emanating the fragrance of musk[338]. Besides the described costumes of both the men and women, *Ksemendra* and *Bilhana* highlighted some of the textile and furnishing material of the 12th century A.D. In the woollen goods the red blanket, *kambala* or shawl (*Lohita Kambala, rakta kambala*[339]) made from the white goat-hair called (*rankavapata*[340]) are also mentioned. *Dukula*, which is confused in the period with silk[341] during black blanket is to be attached, at times dyed with blue[342] or black colour. Moreover, *ambaradambra* (perhaps some kind of silk) of Kanci are to be mentioned crapets (*patalika*[343]) and quilted coverings (*Karpati*[344]) of beautiful patterned (*citravastra*) have been discussed in the text. In the *samayamatrka* II, Ksemendra throws some interesting light on the contemporary dyes and their nature of colours. Safflower (*kusumbha*) says with care but it is fugitive by nature of 21 colour of mixture colours. Saffron (*Kumkuma*) looks pretty with light, but displeasing when deep 21 colours will have to be mix up. The lac-dye (*laksa*) holds fast when hot, but is useless when cold dry up. The madder (*manjistha*) holds fast whether hot or cold colour. Oil is the enemy of red O chre (*Kasaya*) of 22 mixture of colours. Turmeric is fugitive of 23 mixture of colours, while indigo (blue) is permanent[345]. Almost a century after Ksemendra, *Kalhana* in his *Rajatarangini* (1148-1149 A.D.) has noted occasionally a detail of the contemporary costumes and textiles. It must, however, be borne in mind that while *Kalhana's* history of *Kasmir, 'River of the kings'* purposed to deal with the history of Kashmir since very ancient days of the costumes and fabrics described in the work are contemporary and were known to him from his forefathers. It is said that the first ruler of the *Chamar* dynasty was *Durlabhvardhana,* may that body of the immovable (*Siva*) *'Dr. Raj Kumar'* from there is no separate existence (*Vitavyatireka*), which is united with the body of Parvati i.e. *Brahmanas,* which knowns no obstacles, remove misfortunes from you (who are) in this (world) *'Word'* (the body of him) on whose hair-knot the serpent also seems to embrace the form of its own female as it extwines it body with the plaited hair (of *Parvati*) which resembles in its falls and its dark splendour the body of a female snake. This king who had received from one family of Father both on earth and Heaven along with a princess of the family. They entered in the course of time into the possession of treasures and sons[346]. The king's wife whose fault had been kept secret in her mind by her husband and whose dignity proved equal to her good fortune, built the *Anangabhavana Vihara* in Kashmir. And, *Durlabhavardhana* II founded Agraharas on obtaining wealth from *Aidabida* (*Kubera*), a strong armed king, whose glory (Pratapa) tormented his enemies, built the town of *pratapapura,* which rivalled in the city of Indra[347] during the commencement of enlightenment ear of the nature. In the course of time the wife of the king bore, through the subjects merits, a son called *candrapida* just as the earth (produces) a treasure[348] for the new direction for the advancement of the civilization one after the another generation as a typical growth of the nature or *'Nam'*. His bright virtues to remove the blot of his descendent, just as rubbing with touchstone (removes) the impurity i.e. called *'untouchability'* attached to a jewel when it comes from the mine of 'Father'. Moreover, the shinning firetakes its origin from the thoroughly dull water of the *Kashmir.* In truth, the character of the great does by no means conform to the place of their birth[349], but with deeds and action. *Lalitaditya* during his *dig-vijay* in the first half of the eight century A.D. put on the waist cloth (*kaupinavasasi*) of the Deccan king (*daksinatyas*) the tail which sweeps the ground as do by sweeper with broom to mark that they were beasts, thereby indicating the sweeping tail end of the *dhoti* worn by the southern people, it shows that he conquered almost entire area of the Deccan[350]. He apparantly had a typical sense of humour in his business as a lord on earth as he made councillor worthy of respect in peculiar kind of dress as it appears an elegant one from their dress in pretty cloaks and other essential garments (*Pravaranadi*) which bore the footprints of courtesans of his forefather[351],' just for the sake of fun to lead the life with peaceful manner in this world as the life has its own taste. *Cakravaram* (935-939 A.D.) is said to have 'rushed about in the battle, the numerous fringes of his head-band (*Virapatta*) appeared like the busy mane of the lion[352] in the warfare among the poor Brahmanas of the period are, however, displayed costumes of clothing of woollen cloaks[353] (*sthulakumbalavahinah*), at the end of *utpala* dynasty, under *Harsa* (1089-1101 A.D.) is perhaps the most puzzling figure in the entire range of the Kashmir history. A proficient linguist and a musician of the artisans because, he was born in the family of *Candala* the untouchable of the period, but he was literary man of his age. He was inordinarely fond of rich garments made of fine stuffs without gold ornaments. But in the king's place, councillors, chambelains and other (attendants) were moved in number, adorned with golden chains and bracelets. The king regarded as per the opinion of *Vijayamalla* just as that of a *Guru* or *'Nam'*. Kalhana has rightly painted the picture of *Harsa* as "nobody in his court was seen without patterned garments (*acitravastrah*) and scantily dressed (*alpaparicchadah*) and nobody was dared to enter in the royal presence without a turban (*vigatosnish*[354]). He introduced an elegant fashion trends in this universal known as *Sobhadayinir-bhangi*[355] which is equivalent to *'Chamar'* or *'Nam'*. Formerly the people of land, with a single exception of the king, wore thier loose hair-styles, going without turbans (*pagri*) and wore inartistic ornaments which are disturbing to the simple wearer, therefore, it is essential to expose the original ornament of the life i.e *'Nam' or 'Word'*. It again appears to us that *Madana* the commander-in-Chief of the *Harsa's* army has been displayed with hair-dress in top-knot (*dhammilla*) and a short coat or shorts made of beautiful patterned of material (*citrardhoruka*), had incurred the king's displeasure. *Harsa* introduced for general wear a dress which was fit for a king in the court or palace[356]. He became inordinary fond of the Deccani fashion trends of the life as one has to think over it for the attainment of beautiful message of the nature as it were in routine matter of the day[357]. The people must have to be dictated by *Harsa* in the same fashion, wore dangling earrings, painted themselves with sandal and shoes along with carried long knives of the blacksmith (carpenter or *Terkhan*[358]). But the brilliant court fashion inaugurated by *Harsa* in his court. It has been noted by Kalhana that *Bhikasacara* (1120-21 A.D.) had been displayed in the royal assembly with a rustics clothes were chiefly a long woollen blankets (*kambalah*[359]) for the festive occasion and the *dasya* (robbers) displayed with dense pleat of goblins[360], as it was the pleasure of Heaven on earth. Moreover, it was the physical treatment for the (blunders) as a medican for the time being also appeared from the *Sussala* period (1121-28 A.D. and lasted upto the period of Jayasimha 1128-49 A.D.) as per the report of Kalhana, Sindh and other states of the western frontier including north *Kashmir, Kapisa* or kabul or *Kabulistan, Hindu Kush* mountains, *Multan, Tukan, Zabulistan,* Sapardalakshan (*sapadalaksha*) *i.e. 'Nam'* rule was establish. Another ruler of the same region belonged almost to the same period, was Shahi Tigin, who is called the master of *Takan* and *Khurasan* in the Pahlavi legend, and the 'Supreme lord of India and Iran in the India script. These were probably rulers of the borderlands of Kabul and Zabul, but nothing definite is known about them as in the fashions trend of the *'Nam'* or *'God'*. We know from the coins of one *Vasudeva,* bearing legends of Sassanian Phahlavi and Indian scripts, that he was the ruler of *Bahman* (*Brahmana bad*) means Brahmana is a bad man[361].

There are several interesting points for the notification of the *Kashmiri* garments which were prevalent in the 12th century A.D. to onwards in Deccani fashion trends may be discussed as under:-

Firstly, the Deccani fashion was not introduced by *Harsa*, as per the report of Ksemendra even it was patronised in an earlier period *aebeit* by the rakes and the people of their class. In *Harsa's* time, however, it came to be recognised as a royal fashion as it was existed in Kashmir.

Secondly, the hair-dress of *Kampana* called *dhammilla* translated by M.A. Stein as "hair in braid", in fact, according to V.S. Aggrawal[362] term *Dramila* or *Dravida* is originated in Tamil language. In this particular hair-style the hair-dress was bound in a top-knot. As it has been superably described called *Ciiradhoruka* worn by *Jayananda,* and it has been translated by M.A. Stein as a 'Short Coat of the bright colour." In the *Amarakosa* II, 6, 119, *drdhoruka* according to Ksirasvamin's commentary is an undergarment or a petticoat which covered half the thighs which is still in fashion among the Hindu Kashmiri. In the case of *Jayamanda*, however, it is difficult to say what exactly its shape was, but there is the possibility of its being some kind of shirt or may be a short coat of Rajasthani fashion. *Citra,* however, could be better known technical terms of the paintains and its designs.

Thirdly, Harsa had developed the aesthetic taste in the matter of court dress, ornaments and hair styles among the women folk of the period in very decorative sense of the nature. The people had been displayed wore long garlands formed by them on the hair do with the help of woven golden *Ketaka* leaf ornaments. They wore pendents (*catula*) over the forehead marks where god or *'Nam'* resides. The collyrium (*Kajjala*) lines of their eyes extended to the ears and the unveiled (*nini rangika*) locks were tied with gold strings (*hemopavitakah*). Their lower garments (*adharambara*) held long trains (*pucchanta*) touching the earth were worn by them. Their cups were dressed with *Choli* belongs to the period of *Chola* ruler in Englic called bodice (*kancuka*), which covered, but half length of the (forearms)[363]. It may be interesting to note that the world *choli* seems to come from the world *chola* already mentioned above, "the body", just as the English "bodice" comes from "body[364]". The word "gown" to has changed its meaning, so as it has called "frock". "Frock" was once widely used for a man's dress, now it is a woman's. And what, if we come to think of it, is a thing called "a hat" of the Father. Cardinal Wolsey wore a thing called "a hat", and so did king Edward VII: They were vastly different affairs, and neither bore much resemblance to an officer's "hat" in the Royal Air Force, or to the plumed "hat" of a Musketeer[365].

Besides the above mentioned description, Kalhana also refers off and on textiles stuffs of the period. According to him *Mihirakula* noticed the dress of his queen which was used to wear for the covering of breasts called as jacket or bodice made from the stuff known as *Simhala* (*Samvitasimhalamsuka*) marked with the golden food-prints of the Ceylones king. Taking it as an insult, he declared a war upon him. It is one of the rare mentioned ceylonese stuff of the ancient period expressed in the literature though cloth from caylon is also mentioned in the medieval stock lists of the Early Muslim period. At another it is mentioned that *Jayapida* (749-813 A.D.) in the course of his war carried away from *Strirajya* a stuff called *Karnasripata*[366]. Nothing further is known about this stuff but it is possible that it was some kind of rich stuff manufactured in *Karnasuvara, Kansona,* now *Rangamati* to dye the life in the study of *'Nam',* in the District of *Murshidabad*[367]. Unfortunately, kalhana does not give much information about the textile industry of Kashmir, but its process depends upon the struggle of man in the life to achieve the successive objective of god gifted life. At one place, however, he mentions the ancient pattana (the modern patna on the highway road from Srinagar to Varahamula), the capital of Sankaravarman (883-902 A.D.), also known as *Sankaravarmapura,* was the famous for silk-weaving in Kashmir (*pattavanam*[368]). For the history of the costumes and textile materials in North and Western Indian of the eigth and ninth centuries, our chief works are Jain writer *Haribhadra Smri* and dramatist *Rajasekhara* (880-920 A.D.), who were recognised as a great court poet in the *Gurjara-Pratihara* court of Kanauj. *Rajasekhara* in his

Karyamimamsa gives the glimpses of the female costumes of India. According to him the women of Bengal (*Gauda*[369]) wore a chain necklace (*Sutrahara*) over the breast besmeared with sandal, their cadars (*sicayah*) touched the partings of their hair and their foreamrs have been displayed exposed[370]. The women of kanauj (*Mahodaya*) wore earrings (*tatanka*) which moved like the hanging tremulous necklaces. Their upper garment, falling from the thighs to the ankles, encircled the body (*parimandalitottariyani*[371]). As regarding the costumes of both the sexes at Avanti (Western Malwa) the poet remarks that men affected with (*nepathya*) costume of *Pancala*, while women delighted in the Deccani costume[372]. Unfortunately, *Rajasekhara* has failed to describe the costumes of *Pancala* and the South. While describing the women of Kerala, he observes that their curled hair, some of which came on the temples, and their *saris* were held tight with zones (*Kaksanivesanibidikrtaniviresa*). The women of *Lampaka* (Laghman, Afghanistan) wore their hair free and their dresses were made of blankets or thick woollen cloth (*rallakamullasayantah*). The male costumes have received scant attention from *Rajasekhara*. At one place a foolish, pupil is said to have worn a blue garment (*nilimecakitasicaya-kalpan*[373])

Stein Konow in his *Karpuramanjari* gives us a detail information about the lady dress. At one place *Karpuramanjari* appears with one hand arranging the border of the garment (*pottancalam*) that was displayed falling on her rounded breasts, with the other restraing the *sari's*[374] end. At the second place she appeared wearing the border of her upper garment on her one shoulder (*jam ekkamsia nivasiam*[375]). At the third place she dressed herself with a silken (*padavatte*) and tusser (*tasara*[376]). In fourth scene she displayed wearing a pair of silk garmet green as the tail of king-parrot (*raasuapicchanilam pattamsujualam*[377]). Moreover, she has been depicted with a bodice called *Kuppasam* (*Kurpasaka*[378]) and *Kanculia*[379], *sahulia*[380] perhaps is meant for wimple, and *nhanapotta*[381] means garment for bathing like towel is also available in this study.

H. Jocobi's *Samaraiccakaha*[382] *of Haribhadra* gives interesting descriptious of bridal costumes known as *asandiyae* (bride on a chair), white *dukula* (*dugulla*) jewelled skrit (*manipattayammi nimia calana*), red garment (*rattavasanahi*), red silk (*rattamsuyaparibana*), shorts (*janghika*), *pattaleha* made of decorative design for her breasts, *tilaka* an ornament for forehead, *kajjala* (collyrium), anklets (*neura*), Knot of the *sari* (*nivi*). necklet (*dusurullaya*), ears jewelled discs (*raynaccakkaliyao*), wavy cadar (*pavara*), figer-rings etc. At other places the bride has been displayed with white[383] dress or fine *dukula* (*dugulla*[384]). At one place bridal hasbeen delineated with covered *duppata* on her breasts of delicate texture and soft to touch (*sukumala-miuphansena uttariyena pacchaiyapaohara*[385]). Among the trousseau of the bride appeared *dugulla, devangapatta* and two varieties of chinese silk called as *cina* and *addacina*. *Devanga*[386] or best quality of cloth (*parvaradevangavattha*[387] are also mentioned for *devadusa*[388]. The *vaijayanti* expresses the term *sic-sicaya* for general clothing. The *Abhidhanacintamani*, describes *prota,* as one of the article of clothing[389], and *prabhavakacarita,* however, takes the term *pota* in the sense of fine texture when its garments is described as ochre red of fine texture called (*potadhyah*[390]). According to R.P. A Dozy[391] a *futa* term is signified a napkin, or a bed-cover usually of silk embroidered with gold originated in India found in Arabic lexicon as an imported stuff of India. As we have shown above *pota* term in Sanskrit and Prakrit literatures signify the same meaning as in Arabic. *Devadusa* is said to have been a smooth stuff signify with *devadusya*. It is usually explained as a stuff worn by the gods or *'Nam'*. Apparently, the costly *devadusya* was a fit object to be presented to kings of the presented period as per the norms of the nature.

Besides somewhat elaborated costumes described above. Ksemendra occasionally refers, then shawl weaving seems to have been a cottage craft of Kashmir. The teacher employed in the *Kayastha's* house hold (NM-, II. 45) is said to have whiled away his time in spinning and weaving, drawing out patterns (*Likhanam*) and weaving the patterns on the strips with *tuji* or eyeless wooden needles (*sucipattikavanam*) *'word' or 'weaver"* the process being analogous to modern shawl of weaving in Kashmir[392] *'Industry'*. It shows that Ksemendra was not a very prolific in his description of female costume. He refers in her low days she was forced to marry a labourer, but unmindful of her condition, she girt her fat waits with a string or cord (*daman*) and carried heavy loads. In her adventurous perigrinations in very cold mountains, she covered her face with garments (*vasanavagunthitamukhi*) and wrapped her body with a thick blanket (*ghanadambakambalavati*) (SM.II.92). A coquette is shown be smearing her body with perfume, discarding her bodice (*Kancuka* to expose her breasts, and letting wimple fall half way (*ardhasrastasiromsukah*)[393]. While describing a typically miser shopkeeper he observes: "He wore a mis-shapen cap (*tuppika*) gnawed by rats. His torn woollen *cadar* (*urnapravarana*) floated over his long and thick tunic (*kancuka*). His broad, loose, smoke blackened and torn socks or shoes (*mocota*) left his thighs and knees bare[394]." While the 'Father' went in a mean dress, his voluptuary son affected costume of a typical reis: "He wore heavy pearl earrings; the gold necklace had four amulets; his hair bore mustard seeds placed there by his mother (*Amrita*) for his welfare and the silver anklets were decorated with of lapis lazuli. He repeatedly gathered his flowing undergarment (*Patim*) which had a long *pallau* and borders (*dirghancaladasam*[395])." Moreover, she has worn a closely woven shawl (*Kambalaghana*) which passed the buttocks and extended to the ankles along with the ornaments[396] of the days.

We come across with the following main varieties woollen clothes in the contemporary literature of the period discussed as under:-

1. **Ayani.** The woollen cloth made with goats' hair was called *ayani*. According to the description of *Acharanga Sutra,* goats had soft hair in a particular region. Superfine woollen cloth made of the hair of these goats were called *Ajaka*[397]. *Ajaka* means *pashmina* goat and it appears that *rankava* and *ajaka* both are synonyms. According to *Nisitha Churni* in the Tosali region cloth was prepared from the algac which got clung to the hoops of goats[398]. But this interpretation has not been considered authentic by most of the scholars because it was not approachable for them in struggle during the study becasue along with study on must have to approach the 'Father' for the sake of *'Nam'* for the development of knowledge. Therefore, *pure* goats hair called *bakratha* in Sanskrit which is mainly used for weaving floorings, is sometimes mixed with shell, the coarser *pashmina*, to form a different texture of the *'Nam'* called *Devanagari* script, and woven in black and white fabrics[399].

2. **Jangiya.** The important of clothing among the Jains could also be gauzed from strong belief that the different parts of a cloth are presided different gods in the ancient authority of *Bhadrabahu*[400] were allowed the use of the following materials which were lawful textile[401] called as *Jangika, bhangika, sanaka, pottaka, tirida-patra.* Indu Prabha Pandey[402] painted the picture of the term *Jangika* as *Jangiya* which is quoted from *Acharanga Sutra* has not relevant word for the said, it is only sanctioned to the lower-garment used for the private part of the body. Therefore, *Jangika* is described in *Brhat-kalpa-Sutra Bhasya*. In connection with woollen cloth in the same mentioned text refers that cloth manufactured from sheep's wool was called *aunnika*. Blanket made with hairs of camels, goats and human beings[403], has been expressed camel's hair as *austrika,* deer's hair as *mrga-roma, kutapa* is explained as *Jina,* and *Kitta* was manufactured from the hair or wool, which apparently means that this variety of cloth was manufactured from the residue of the hair or wool after the best part had been utilized for better grades of cloth (*tesamevornaromadinamavayavah tannispannam vastramapi*[404]). These garments or blankets were used by the monks and sages of the Gupta period.

3. **Koyavani.** According to the *Acharanga-Sutra*, it was a hairy blanket (*Kambala*). It has been called *Kotava* in the *Nisithachurni*. Dr. Moti Chandra thought it was a species of cloth like modern *thulm*[405]. Amongst blankets the *gudmas* are a speciality, made of light and long fibred loose flossy wool fibres teased out and then brushed. It is woven in natural coloured strips or in white, set off by wide crimson at the two ends. It has a heart-warming luxurious appearance[406].

4. **Kambalagani.** Again according to the *Acharanga, Sutra* the term *Kambalagani* included all kinds of woollen clothes such as *Chadars*. The term was used for costly clothes[407] and for colourful inlay patterns, and are to be set into the wrap by hand manipulation with coloured woollen threads for which small dollies are made by winding threads round the palm. Except for the design portion, twill weave is used by the *'Weaver'* as for to give a refinement to the cloth, which is the same as the simple tabby weave; except for the interlacing of two up and two down wrap threads moving diagonally across in a regular sequence. For the design a coloured (*ranga*) extra weft is to pass through the shed formed by the required number of wrap ends lifted to form the design[408].

5. **Rallaka.** The word is mentioned in the *Amarakosa*. It is used this term for a blanket[409]. The names for their clothing materials, is mentioned in the Yuan Chwan, are *Kiao-She-ye (Kau-Sheya)* and muslin (*tieh*) and calico (*pu*), *Kausheya* being silk from a wild silk-worm; *Ch'u* (or *Ch'u*)-mo (*Kahauma*) a kind of linen; *Han* (or *Kan*)-*po-lo (Kambala)* a texture of fine fool (Sheep's wool or goat's hair), and *Ho-la-li* (*Ral*, means 'way of thought') a texture made from the wool of wild animal *'Word'* or *'Nam'*, this wool being fine and soft and easily spun and woven is prized as a material for clothing. In North India where the climat is very cold closely fitting jackets are worn by men somewhat like those of the Tartars (*Hu*[410]). *Hu* means *'God'* becomes *Ya hu* (O God!), an invocation through which *sufis* ask God for his 'marcy and grace[411]'.

Cloth-Shop. In the study we learn that India and China were the greatest centre for the production of cotton, silk and woollen garments in the beginning of Vedic culture. For the first time trade with China was directly established through the ancient silk route. Indian traders settled down in Chinese Turkistan, which was famous for trade centre and annexed by Kanishka, the Kushana king. This included Kashgar, Khotan and Yark hand. Buddhist missions too were sent to China during his rule and under the Asoka, the great Mauryan king. In Rome, Augustus encouraged trade with India and exports increased through Tamil Nadu by sea routes, and result was that during the said period there were also regular shops which stocked the cloth of different varieties produced by the artisans, mostly they were the *Sudra* community. In the north-western areas coarse cotton and wool were used for making tunics and trousers for horsemen, hunters (*Sataris*), foreigners (*Barawalas*) and doorkeepers. In Central India textiles were of light-weight cotton, *tulapansi*. Both indigenous and abroginal silks were plentiful but still very expensive[412]. There were, however, which specialised in stocking a certain kind of cloth. Thus, there were shops at Sopara which exclusively dealt in the cloth imported from *Kasi* (*Kasika-vastravari*[413]) and the shops which stocked *phuttaka* cloth[414] were famous at that time with printed muslin. But a large variety of fabrics were recovered from the burial grounds along the silk route, which can be dated between the first century B.C. and the second century A.D. (*Han* period in *China*). Based on this evidence we may presume that the dyes and taxtiles was famous of Chinese origin available along with the route would surely have been found. Their way into India. Hence, it is possible to maintain that many of the patterns and colours (*ranga*) would be similar, or had influenced indigenous fabrics. We know for a fact from the study of the said literature that beautiful ultra-marine and lapis-lazuli (*nila*) blue colours were sent along the trade routes from the famous mines at Badakshan in central Asia[415]. There was a regular street of cloth merchants at *Madura Desa*[416] *(Panjab)*, who stocked varieties of cloth from *Kashmir* to *Chamba*, *Pashmina* shawl is costly thing but wool shawl is a thing of the commoner. *Pattu* bearing flowers, is called *phooldar pattu*. The *phool* work is also known as *Bushahri dhari* and it seems that it was *Rampur Bushahr* which first introduced the degins and flowers on the plain blanked sheets. The patterns and motifs, that appear on shawls and blankets, are generally known as *phool* which means flowers. There patterns and motifs are in fact, much drived from the simplest patterns to display on *pattus* are that of check and chess-board type. The check pattern is locally called *lungi dhari* at different centres of the 'Father and it appears in different colours, viz, yellow, green, white or red on a ground which is natural brown or red on a ground which is natural brown or black and also sometimes orange or green. The *pattus* further adds to their value by the width of their borders varying in size from half an inch to three inches. These border patterns appear in a combination of *dharis* and are known as *mothra-Bushahri dhari* has been very popular in this respect.

There are numerous types of *pattus*. Small cheeks are known as mahin *chitru*. *Mahin* means fine or small. In this type there is one called *sada,* i.e. simple but the other is *ulta-sulta* implying right and reverse. Here the weave is diagonal. A *pattu* black in colour and thick in stuff is known as *dhumkura* meaning literally smoke-work. There is a type of *pattu* named after its comb-like pattern as *Kanghu*. There is another type of *pattu* to which is attached lengthwise separately woven *phool*-work. Other motifs to figure are damedur (dotted), *Lahria* (wavelike), *chabi* (key), *sirki* (stairs), *mandir* (temple) and *chini-diwar* (the wall of China) has already mentioned in the text. *Pattu* or blanket resembles a *sari* of Benaves, in as much as both are simple length of cloth. Shawls are differently dressed in *Chamba* by the Chams especially its fashion was at *Pangi* and *Tissa* areas where from Tussar silk was produced the women here wear shawls up to the waist giving appearnce of a loongi. The shawl is check in design is tied at the waist with a *gachi*. In Lahaul and spitti the shawls, richly adorned with floral and geometrical designs, are square in size and are put on the back[417]. Woven-cotton, thread laces, and hair or silk thread kept in bundles, each bundel containing hundred pieces[418]. In the two very remote Himalayan villages *Lahul* and *Spiti,* wool weaving is done and spitti in particular has fine weaves indifferent styles[419].

It is understood from the study that the Himalayan region was the real home or centre for woollen garments, was also a great shawl producing area of the world because of woollen goats and cheeps are always found in India as a particular place of the universe, especially *Mandi, Kulu* and *Chamba* in Himachal Pardesh. They are mostly woven in angular geometrical type of motifs grouped in straight horizontal lines, bands and stripes, one or two placed vertically as well. These are combined in several intricate but symmetrical orders to get a wide range of effects. The traditional designs run into several dozens and endless innovations are devised out of them. Among them are : *Numba,* a kettle shapped design with colours wove inbetween, *Chatham,* a big cross tipped by tiny crosses at both ends; *Khabatobi,* the typical central Asian key; *trishul,* the triden from four corners crossing in the centre; *Yashin,* a staircase of bands with a square in the centre; the religious motifs, the *Chorten* and the *Swastika,* are common motifs in use *Mufflers* are a popular item woven in the shawl designs. *Kambroodar* is a special *pyjama* for which a set patterned fabric is prepared, highly ornamented with coloured inlay designs of the shawl type, to cover the legs from the knees down. The common designs are; *gau,* the *gordian* knot enclosed in a coloured rectangle; *gargus* is a reversed 'V'. Kinnaur is the centre for these designs[420].

In a list complied above of the fabrics recovered from the ancient silk route, fabrics in the following colours were found; bright blue, rich blue, light blue, dark blue-copper, dull gold-buff, bronze-brown, dark brown, pale brown, snuff brown, myrtle green, green, dark bronze green, crimson, pink, crimson-brown, rich red, yellow, yellow-brown, yellow-green, rich dark yellow-brown. These are all variants and mixtures of the colours in dyes that were available in the Kushan period in India[421]. The cloths with wide borders perhaps refer to *dhoti* and *dupatta;* the garment covering hands, breasts, knees and feet might have been a tunic as worn by the Kushana kings as the court dress in the darbar hall; and the garment covering the forehead called turban, *Pag or Pagri* in local language was also used by them. *'Weavers[422]'* and *'Farmers[423]'* often had been seen wore loin-clothes of flax called sana in local language of the period and (*sanasati*). Small loin clothes were called as *pravarana-potrim* (*potyu* in modern Gujarati[424]). The turban (*Sirottarapttika[425]*) was used for covering the head. It was customary for the kings to wear the turban (*pravara-maulipattam*) when seated on the throne[426]. Besides the kings, ministers, chamberlains, bankers and domestic chaplains also wore the turbans[427] as a mark of respect which reflects the message of the 'Father'.

Study also reveals the fact that *Kushana* influence was developed into two school of thought: One is called 'Gandhara school of Art' and other is known 'Mathura school of Art' which while retaining the massive scale of imagination on the works of art and culture and sensuous that had been judged before the courtesans had *tribanga* pose of dress and the delicate flower-like gesture of the hands work and the foreigners has found aspects of the Indian experience that fired their imagination with the support of *'Nam'.* In the same period, however, there are the wall paintings at kizil in Afghanistan, where the wiry line of the drawing with its flat brilliant colours dominated by lapiz lazuli gives a heraldic appearance, static and frozen, like the group of portrait statues found at Mathura. Kushana were not originally an artistic people. Of scythian origin, there only expression had been the metal work displayed in their horse trappings, hunting gear, and in the ornamental plaques which they stitched on their garments[428] as 'weaver' and *Chhimba* did the work of art to stitch the new society of the *'Father'.*

Under the Gupta period, Deccan began to emerge with the *Kushanas* art and their nobles had ruled a large part of India and Central Asia. The Gupta kings realised the value of Kushana dress, that is the coat, trousers and boots of full length. However, they continued the traditional Kushana dresses of indigenous styles called as *antariya, uttariya* and *kayabandh* for informal occasions[429]. In this respect, with the impact of Buddhism, Jainism, and Christianity the belief of the body was sinful and must be concealed to avoid tempetation was percolating through India. In medieval Europe, around this time, similar changes were occuring in female clothing like pant, shirt, etc. and women began covering themselves from head to foot. The breast hand had been used since vedic times, an indigenous stitched cloth whome known as *Cholaka, Chola, Choli, Cholika* and *Kancholika* , which is mentioned in early Sanskrit literature. The primitive *Choli* was cut very simply from a square piece of cloth, with a slit for the neck. This was also the early form used as protection by the women of the Germanic or Teutonic races in the Early bronze period. This evolution from the unstitched to the stitched garment had an inescapable logic as it evolved for purely functional purposes. In the case of Germanic races it was protection from the cold, and in India it served the purpose of modesty[430]. The first example of the *Choli,* the bodic or blouse, are found, in the pre-Mughal miniature paintings of Gujarat, mostly Jain religious manuscript illuminations. Though a few of these may well go back to the ancient peirod of India, but in the 10th century A.D. *Choli* was evident in the North Indias especial in Rajasthan, up to the present day[431]. These articles seem to have been referred to under the heading 'Capilli Indici[432]'. Now pliny's *'Chinese'* iron tissues and skins in fact, were not the products of China to the Somali coast[433]. The furs exported from China with silk and diverted to the Indus, and party Tibetan furs brought by Caravans of the Indian ports[434]. However, in this age the traffic between Rome and India in oriental hides and furs was of great importance. The periplus says that 'Chinese' hides or furs were exported from 'Barbaricon[435]' on the Indus river and pliny says (XXXIV, 41) that iron made by the Chinese was sent by them together with their tissues and skins to Rome. Skins from China were known in the Mauryan period as *Cinasi*[436], but there is no evidence to show that there was any contact between China and India at such an early days. 'Cina', in the pre Christian period in Indian literature perhaps signified Kafiristan, Kohestan and Darada where Shina is spoken. There was no dearth of furs in India as it is mentioned in the *Mahabharata* that the presents from the people of *Kamboja* (Pamir and Badkshan) to *Yudhisthira* at the time of the *Rajasuya* sacrifice consisted almost entirely of animals of the marten and weasal families. Silk already mentioned in the *Arthasastra* is referred to in the *Mahabharata* as *Kitaja* which was the product of *Cina* and *Valhika*. The seric of Strabi is real silk which was believed to have been produced from some sort of byssos bark by combing the fibres[438]. McCrindle[439] gives an interesting note about the ancient author in Greecian literature who refers to the use of silk is Aristotle (H.A. Vol. 19). According to him raw silk was brought from the interior of Asia and manufactured at *Kos*. Is the word *Kauseya* used for silk in Sanskrit devired from the town of kos where it was manufactured *'world's silk'*, perhaps Panini who gives special *sutra* for the formation of Kausaya[440] refers to the town of kosa dn not to the cocoons.

Classical Tamil literature of the said period is full of references to the garments worn by the people of South India in this period. The king generally wore a loin-cloth and a long crown of canical shape made of gold and set of with precious kind of stones. Gold armlets, an amklet of gold on the right foot and necklace of pearl and gold were the principal ornaments worn by him. The dress of the tamil people differed according to their rank in society or to the races to which they belonged. People of the middle class in the *pure* Tamil Society wore two pieces of cotton cloth, one wrapped round the loins and the other tied round the head. They wore their hair long, it was either tied in a knot at the top of the head or arranged on one side. Coloured strings of silk with glittering blue beads were used by the people of the higher class to fasten the hair and the ends of the strings were allowed to hang like a taanssel. A *Marava* chief belonging to the Naga race wore a loin cloth bound to his waist with a blue cloth, and stuck feathers to his head. The soldiers employed to guard the king's palace wore coats. The Tamil women ordinarily wore a *sari* reaching to the ankles; the body down to the waist was entirely bare. The uncovered part of the body was decorated with Sandal paste and other fragrant powders. The courtesans wore a short muslin loin-cloth which reached only to the middle of the thighs, and the fine texture of the muslin had been produce there and it is difficult to conceal them. The women members of the hill tribes wore green leaf skirts made by tying the leaves round the waist with a string[441]. In the port town of Kaveripatlinam there were weavers (*karukas*) who combined in themselves the functions of a middleman and dealt in fine fabrics made of silk, fur and cotton[442] literature is, however, not very helpful in giving us information about the costumes and modes of wearing them *Dhoti* (loin-cloth) and *dupatta* (scarf) were usually worn by the Indians, and those manufactured at *kasi*[443] were famous. A pair of *dhoti* and *dupatta* (*yamali*) women of the finest yarn cost sometimes a *Karsapana*[444] was produced there. The king wore well calendered new garments with borders (*ahatani vasamsi navani dirgha-dasadi*) and his hands, breast, foreheads, knees and feet were well drapped (*pravrtyastanga samanvagatam upavasam*[445])

In the Kulu valley, there was a major wool weaving industry several other woollen fabrics ever also made there. Most widely used to top covering is *Pattu* in black and white chequered squares by the *Gaddis* of Brahmore in *Chamba* district[446]. *Dohru* has a plain background in some colour but the outer fold, that appears on the back, bears a flower in some glowing colours. With *dhohra* is combined a woollen shawl whichis as long in shape and is carried over the back with free sides on the front. This shawl has enquisite floral designs on it, especially on its borders. The shawls, that ladies wear in Kulu, are called not *dhohru*, but *pattu* unlike *dhohru* which is heavy and in plain background, *pattu* is light and mostly in check. The Kulu *dhohrus* are bed blankets generally thick and rough in appearance, but *pattus* of Kulu exhibit a better sense of decoration in as much as it has the floral designs on both sides and also on the borders[447]. *Dhohru* is, however, the special cloth worn by women with beautiful colour combinations like a black surface with red temple spires going into the body, with a cross border of red, blue and yellow. The borders have poetic names like *bulbul* chasin (nightingale's eye) already discussed above, *lahariya* (waves), the former a dot with dark around, the latter a zigzag. *Chedi* (birds) are small crosses in various colours *guddi* (doll) is a stylised figure in a dancing pose, *hanjee* (tears) is a pattern in rectangular forms. *Pattu* is made in natural colours for coats[448]. The utility of the hill dress cannot be questioned. The dress is specially useful in winter months for the protection of cold. Also the dress is quite peculiar in appearance and catches the fancy of many people of the areas even outside the hills[449]. Therefore, it is necessary to put these garments as a traditional value of the period which expressed from time to time in the development of industry in the areas mentioned above as the manufacturing centres of the clothes at different period in the history of India and China, and exported in the other part of the world for the development of economy of the *'Father'*

A rough kind of animal skin with fur left on, or perhaps heavy woollen coats were exported from north-western India to East Africa. Woollen clothes could also be obtained at Kaveripattinam[450]. Whereas the sewen garments consisting of coats or tunics which came close to the upper and lower garments (*Codaka-Samghata-pratyavarena vasasa*[451]) were also worn sometimes by the kings. The guards appointed for the protection of the harem were also clothed in brown-red tunics (*kasayakancuk-patah*[452]). Dyeing the garments in beautiful colours is the mission of 'Father' (*Vastra-raga*[455]) and sewing the garment[456] in new form or a society were considered to be arts of science in the human history which a man of liberal education i.e. Father was expected to cultivate friendly relation with 'Professor Raj Kumar' since time immomerial in the history of India and China itself.

It is interesting to note from the above description that the *Pali* work *'Petavatthu'* and its commentary, *Paramathadipani,* mention a ruler of *Surattha (Surashtra)* named pingala who ascended the throne in the sixteenth regnal year of Bindusara (283 B.C.). He had a *senapati* or a general named *Nandaka* who converted him to a new dectrine, a sort of atheism called (*Natthika-ditthi*). Fired with his zeal for his new faith he was bold enough to leave for pataliputra with a large rotinue to convert to his creek the emperor *'Dharmasoka'* (*Pingalo* raja *Dhammasokasas ranno ovadam datum gato*) remained himself to be converted to the emperor's creed of Buddhism (B.C. *Law, Buddhist conception of Spirits,* p. 72 F; C.D Chatterji in D.R. Bhandarkar volume, pp. 329-340). We have in these texts remarkable evidence of the community of administrative history for the province of surashtra during the reigns of three emperors, Chandragupta, Bindusara and Asoka. Some light is thrown on the severity of Chandragupta's penal code as shaped by his minister, chanakya, by the case of a learned Brahman scholar named *Supandhu* being condemned to servitude for life with the young son in his teens wandering away homeless to escape a similar fate. The sin of *Subhandu* was his astute political wisdom (Ibid).

We may consider the constitutional significance of these reference to surashtra. We have three descriptions of its constitutional status which is difficult to reconcile with each other. These are (1) Surashtra as a province of the Maurya empire under imperial official as its Governor, (2) Surasthra under a chief as a feudatory of the Maury a emperor and (3) Surashtra as a *Samgha* or a republic. The third description is attributed to kautilya, but not quite accurately. Kautilya does not describe Surashtra as a full-fledged republic, but only refers to certain sections of its population as belonging to self governing corporations or *srenis*. These *srenis* very formed by the *Kshatriyas* and *Vaisyas* of Surashtra and were either economic or military guilds, devoting themselves either to *Varte* (agriculture, cattle-rearing, and trade) or to the profession of arms as means of livelihood (*Surashtra-Kshatriyaasrenyadayo varta-sastrapajivinah*) *(VII.I)*. Thus, Surashtra under this description may still be a kingdom. The two other points to settle about its constitutional position are (1) whether it was a local chiefship and a feudatory state under the Maurya emperor or (2) whether it was completely annexed by Chandragupta Maurya to his empire and created a governorship under him. The second point is establishment beyond doubt by *'Rudradamana's Inscription'* which has greater evidential value than tradition and literary text. The first point can be reconciled with the second only on the suppositior that, as in modern India, an imperial province may accommodate its hereditary ruling princes figuring as feudatories acknowledging the paramount. Sovereignty of the emperor. It is thus that Pingala as a local chief of Surashtra was out to pay homage to Asoka.

That the Maurya conquest of Western India extended beyond the province of Surashtra father south is indicated by the location of Asoka's inscriptious at Sopara in the district now called Thana in the Bombay Presidency.The conqeust of this part of India (which may be identified with Konkan) was not claimed by Asoka. It must have been the work of Chandragupta Maurya who, as we have been had already established his authority over the neighbouring region of Surashtra. The province of which Sopara or Surparaka was the capital must have formed part of Maurya empire for some time to lead Asoka to locate his edicts at its capital.

Chronology. We may now consider the chronology of Chandragupta's reign. We have already seen that the first exploit of Chandragupta was the overthrow of the Greek rule which was established in India as a result of Alexander's victorious campaign. But it was short-lived. Two events marked it rapid fall. The first was the murder of the most powerful Greek governor in the person of Philip in 325 B.C. followed by his place being taken by an Indian. The second event was the death of Alexander himself in 323 B.C. The first signal of the Indian battle for freedom was the murder of the Greek Satrap, Nicanor, by the Asvayanas in 326 B.C. As has been already related, the battle was won shortly after Alexander's death in 323 B.C. In 321 B.C, at the second partition of Alexander's empire, its easternmost Satrapy was the Trans-Indus Satrapy of Paropanisus. India proper was not counted as a part of that empire. An attempt to reconquer it only ended in the expansion of Chandragupta's empire to the trans-Indus provinces up to the borders of Persia. We may, therefore, take it for granted that between 323 and 321 B.C., Chandragupta made himself the ruler of the Punjab and Emperor ofMagadha. We may take 322 B.C. is the date of his accession to sovereignty and of inaguration of the Maurya Dynasty.

We have other data to confirm this date. If we believe in the reckonings of reigns given in the *Puranas,* we shall see that Chandragupta's reign was one of 24 years and hence ended in 298 B.C., and that his son. Bindusara, reigned for 25 years, i.e., up to 273 B.C. The date of Asoka's accession to sovereignty is thus to be taken as 273 B.C., a date which is supported by the unimpeachable data of Asoka's inscriptions. The *Mahavarnsa* distinguishes between Asoka's accession to throne and his coronation, and places an interval of 4 years between them (v.22). This makes 269 B.C. as the date of his coronation. His inscription again date from his coronation. His Rock Edict XIII is dated 13 years after his coronation. So its date should be 256 B.C. if the date 269 B.C. of his coronation is correct. It is correct, because it is proved by the well-known chronological data of Rock Edict XIII itself. Rock Edict XIII is a document of unique chronological importance in Indian History. Asoka in this Edict mentions the five most important Greek kings with all of whom he had friendly dealings through his Welfare Missions. The date of his references to them must, therefore, be at the latest the date up to which they were all alive and were known to be so to Asoka, and may be taken one year earlier, when all were hale and hearty.

The duration of the reigns of three of these kings is known with certainly, viz., those of

(1) *Amtiyoka,* i.e. Antiochus II Theos, king of Babylon and Persia, 261-264 B.C.

(2) *Turamaya,* i.e. Ptolemaeus II Philadelphos, king of Egypt, 285-247 B.C.

(3) *Amtikini,* i.e., Antigonus Gonatas, king of Macedonia, 277-240 B.C.

The uncertainty is as regards:

(4) Maka, i.e., Magas, king of Cyrene, whose date may be taken to be that proposed by both Beloch and Geyer, viz., 300-250 B.C.

(5) *Alikasudara,* whose identity and duration of reign are the subject of controversy. He may be either Alexander of Epirus or Alexander of Corinth. Of the two Alexanders, Alexander of Epirus was by far the more important personality worthy of Asoka's attention, the son of the famous Pyrrhus of Epirus, and the rival of Antigonus Gonatas of Macedonia. Alexander of Corinth was almost like a local king who ended as a "tyrant over a town and an island, without military glory or a famous lineage". There were several kings of Asia Minor of equal and higher status whom Asoka should have mentioned such as Emenes of Pergamon (262-240 B.C.) or nearer home, Diodotus of Bactria. It is known that Alexander of Epirus, the true subject of Asoka's reference, had lived up to 255 B.C.

Considering the dates of the reigns of all these five kings, we find 255 B.C. as the date up to which all were alive. From this follows that the date of Asoka's reference to them in Rock Edict XIII must be before 255 B.C. Professor P. H.L. Eggermont of the Hague, Holland (who honoured me by posting to me his learned paper on 'The Date of Asoka's Rock Edict XIII' on 30th April, 1940, a few days before Holland itself was submerged by German invasion) has very well shown by skilful calculations that the news of the death of one of these Greek kings could not take more than 4 or 5 months to reach Asoka at Pataliputra, and so we need not allow for an interval of one year for it, as I had done in my *Asoka.* He has also after a good deal of discussion established the dates of the two kings, Alexander of Epirus and Magas of Cyrene. The former lived up to 255 B.C. and the latter up to 250 B.C. according to his findings which are followed here. If, therefore, Rock Edict XIII is dated at 256 B.C., since it was in the 13th year of Asoka's coronation, the date of his coronation was 269 B.C., the very date which is led up to by the assumed date of 322 B.C. for Chandragupta's accession to sovereignty and the duration of his reign and that of his successor, as reckoned in the *Puranas.* We have thus here a remarkable covergence of chronological conclusions derived from sources as different and foreign and Indian works, Brahminical texts and Buddhist inscriptions, and this covergence proves their truth.

In the foregoing pages of the description we learn that the work of leather worker and weaver covered the history of India roughly from the vedic period to the end of the seventh century A.D. The literary evidences, the accounts of chinese and Greek philosophers, who travelled in India for its natural beauty and the areacheaological evidences of seculptures and paintings have all been utilized to demonstrate the history of *Chamar, Megas, 'weaver', Barwalas, Nais Batwalas, Chuhras, Chhimba and ranga, Dharzi, Dhobi, Trekhan, etc.* had contributed a lot for the development of art and culture in ancient period and their work was also appricated not in India, but also in other part of the world like *China, Kabul, Kandhar,* etc. They were the veritable treasure- house of the contemporary manners and custom, of the luxurious life which the kings like Chandra Gupta Maurya, Asoka, *Kushamas, Durlabhvardhana*, Durlabhvardhana II, Lalitaditya, Samudragupta, Sri *Harsa* of Lohara dynasty of Kashmir, etc. They contributed a lot to forming the ancient history of India.

In conclusion we have utilized whatever material is available in both the literature and art for reconstructing a truthful picture of the 'untouchables' which the Brahmanas of the period have forgotten their true approach in history and they degraded the said communities on the basis of their occupations which were always busy with the constitutional approach as the compilers of the society by stitching their shoes and costumes on earth as well as in the heaven. It dispels the prejudice and common notion as the compiler of society one or the other hands from *top to bottom* with a fine artistic touch. Therefore, it is necessary for the time being to evaluated the society to form the *'New Society of the Artisans'* as the *'Labour of Father'*

Reliability of the Classical Accounts

Finally, it is necessary to consider the question how far the classical accounts may be relied upon as accurate information. In order to judge this question properly, we may begin with the different accounts of Alexander's expedition. Of this there were contemporary records by trustworthy men. Yet a perusal of the different accounts that have reached us raises grave doubts whether they are all derived from a common reliable source. A few concrete examples may be cited to illustrate the nature of these differences.

Both Arrian and Curtius Rufus refer to the capture of an Aspasian city by Alexander (8,107). According to the former, Alexander's soldiers, 'being enraged because the besieged had wounded Alexander, slew all whom they took prisoners'. But according to Curtius, 'Alexander massacred all the inhabitants in order to strike terror into the people', and he had previously issued this order, which was thus a part of his policy! There is also serious divergence between the two writers regarding the route followed by Alexander after this incident. According to Curtius, Alexander next conquered Nysa, and then proceeded to Massaga and Aornus. But Arrian places these expeditions, and many others, before the reached Nysa. As regards the capture of Massaga, Curtius emphasizes the role played by the movable towers (110), while Arrian makes no reference to them (13). Similarly, Arrian justifies the massacre of the Indian mercenaries at Massaga on the ground that they had treacherous intentions (13), but according to Diodorus, Alexander treacherously attacked the mercenaries, being actuated by an "implacable enmity" agains them (162). According to Arrian and Justin, the people of Nysa offered no resistance (20, 188), but curtius says taht "the defenders risked an engagement (107 A.D.). The detailed account of the fight and the strategy by which Aornus was conquered is given differently by Arrian (16-18 A.D.), Curtius (111-12 A.D.) and Diodorus (163-4).

The accounts given by different writers about Alexander's crossing the Hydaspes vary in essential points. Curtius (118), for example, does not refer to the two crossings mentioned by Arrian (34), due, according to the latter, to the "ignorance of the locality", Plutarch says that Alexander first crossed over to an island and then advanced from the island and reached the other bank (196). What happened after the crossing of the river is differently described by different writers. According to Aristobulus Alexander easily routed the Indians in the sixty chariots under the command of the son of Porus (36). Ptolemy says that the son of Porus had arrived at the head of 2,000 cavalry and 120 chariots, but they gave way after the first charge of Alexander, and 400 of their cavalry, including the son of Porus, fell in the contest (36-7). Curtius says that this advance force consisted of 100 chariots and 4,000 horse led by the brother of Porus, and there was a regular battle in which "it would be hard to say which side suffered most" when the chariots of Porus charged the Greeks (119). Plutarch says that the force of Porus consisted of 1000 horse and 60 chariots and these were routed by Alexander (196). There are also discrepancies in the accounts of the main battle between Alexander and Porus.

Now Aristobulus an Ptolemy both accompanied Alexander and were present in the battlefield. Plutarch says his account is based on the description of the battle given by Alexander himself in his letters (196). How are we then to explain all these discrepancies? Arrian undertook the task of writing a comprehensive account of Alexander's Indian expedition. He wisely followed the authority of two generals, Ptolemy and Aristobulus, who actually took part in the expedition. Yet he simply records the different versions without any comment. Being a junior contemporary of Plutarch he must have been aware of the existence of Alexander's letters containing what should be regarded as the most authentic account of his battle with Porus. But he makes no reference to these letters. It is difficult, therefore, to avoid the conclusion that even Arrian, not to speak of others, cannot be regarded as a critical historian, in the sense in which we understand the expression today. It would, therefore, be unreasonable to attach a great value to the different accounts of the expeditions of Alexander, except on those points on which there is a general agreement.

When the writers differe even in respect of the essential points of the military campaign, one need not feel surprised at the difference on less important details. Thus we have divergent accounts of the manner in which Porus fought and was made prisoner, as well as his talk with Alexander when brought before him (42, 123, 189-90, 197). As regards the speech of Coenus, explaining causes of the discontent of the soldiers, the differences are more serious still. Curtius makes him emphasize the utmost misery of the soldiers with elaborate details (134). Diodorus and Plutarch both omit any reference to the speech of Coenus, Diodorus refers to the 'utmost misery' with details, and describes how Alexander tried to win over the soldiers by allowing them to plunder and bribing their wives and children (173). Plutarch explains how the battle with Porus depressed the spirits of Alexander's soldiers, and made them oppose any further advance against Indians whose rulers possessed a mighty force, compared with which the forces of Porus, which they had beaten with utmost difficulty, almost sink into insignificance (198). But the long, speech put by Arrian in the mouth of Coenus (54-6) does not contain the slightest reference to any of these things. As regards the death of Bucephalus, the favourite horse of Alexander, Arrian says it died a natural death and not from any wound (43), whereas Strabo says it feel during the battle with Porus (258). As regards Alexander's heroic exploit in a city of the Malloi, where he was severely wounded, Justin says he alone leapt from the wall into the citadel and 'single-handed fought against thousands' (191). Diodorus adds that Peucestas alone joined him at the critical moment (177). Arrian says that three men leaped down, more or less at the same time as Alexander, and fought in front of the king (69). It being a memorable episode in the whole campaign, the transference of the scene to the dominions of the Sudracae by Curtius (140) and the difference among others on vital points are not easy to explain. Similarly, the writers differ in their accounts of the war memorial erected by Alexander to mark his furthest advance. According to Arrian, Alexander constructed twelve altars equal in height to very large towers (57), and this is supported by Strabo (285). According to Justin Alexander only "ordered a camp to be made of an unusual size" (190). Curtius (135) and Diodous (173) refer to both altars and camps of unusual character.

It is easy to multiply such instances of discrepancy on serious topics in regard to a subject on which the classical writers had the best possible source of information. Nor is it necessary to refer tos ome accounts of Alexander's invasion which hardly contain any truth (209, 213). The natural inference is that the classical writers did not make a very careful and critical study of the sources available to them, and their standard of historigraphy was not very high. This is fully corroborated by what has been said of the classical accounts of the Indian embassies to Rome by Priaulx (Appendix II).

Next to Alexander's companions who wrote about his Indian expedition, Megasthenes is the oldest classical writer who had a first hand knowledge of India and ample opportunity of gathering information. His *Indika*, or the collection of Fragments preserved in later writings, has long enjoyed the reputation of being a rich mien of useful and authentic information about India. The question how far the Fragments, usually ascribed to him, can really be accepted as such and may be relief upon as authentic, has been fully examined in Appendix I. It will appear from what has been said there that the adverse comments against Megasthenes by ancient writers like Strabo, Pliny and Arrian are fully justified, and modern scholars have no right or reason to ignore them. On the whole, it is easy to distinguish critical writers like Strabo and

Arrian from the host of others who preceeded them and were justly condemned by them as credulous and uncritical. The remarks of Strabo and Pliny, particularly those quoted on pp. 246 ff, cannot be lightly dismissed, and a modern historian should not accept any statement of the early classical writers as true without corroborative evidence. This also applies to the later writers who seem to have derived much of their information from older sources. The unreliable character of the classical accounts is best shown by the mutually contradictory and palpably wrong statements about the absence of slavery, ignorance of writing, etc and the many absurd tales of men and beasts, and unnatural phenomena solemnly reported by them.

How ridiculously absurd might be the stories told even by those who professed to be eye-witnesses, may be illustrated by the story of lamboulos (142A.D.) which was recorded by Diodorus. Reference may be made in this connection to Strabo's remarks on onesicritus (258 A.D.) and Craterus (262 A.D.) and the lack of agreement among the historians about Calanus (279 A.D.). Dion Chrysostom accepted as true the statements, recorded in the Puranas, of rivers flowing with wine or honey and added that these were not fictions but facts asserted by those who came from India (433 A.D.).

In the light of those observations what reliance can be placed on those statements which appear tobe unnatural or absurd on the very face of them? Typical examples of such statements are furnished by what Megasthenes says about the men and women of the Caucasus (271), the statements, recorded by Strabo, namely 'that the women are permitted to prostitute themselves if the husbands do not force them to be chaste' (270) and 'that a woman who kills a king when he is drunk receives as her reward the privilege of consorting with his successor' (271); the statement of Megasthenes that the women of the Pandaian realm bear children at the age of six (455), and those seven years old are of marriageable age (222), that the Pandaean nation is governed by females (458), that the men who live longest die at forty (223); that no private person is permitted to keep a horse or elephant (264) which is contradicted by another equally absurd statement of Nearchus (266); that there is no remedy at law for recovering loan or deposit (455), and the oft-repeated stories of gold-digging ants (2, 266). It máy be argued that some of these statements, however incredible it might appear to us today, might well be true in those days. Arrian, for example, had tried to show that the girls might be marriageable at the age of seven (223). Even if we accept it, the question arises, how far we are justified in believing in them merely on the strength of assertions of persons whose credulity and lack of critical sense have been proved beyond doubt. Writers like Megasthene, who could accept, as true stories of men without any mouths or noses, or with ears larte enough to sleep in (272), of gold-digging ants (266), and of river Silas on which nothing floats (219, 234), would easily believe in the stories of the women in Caucasus and Pandai without any question. Those who can swallow a camel would hardly strain at a gnat. It is interesting to note that the classical writers themselves accuse each other of falsehood and exaggeration.

Value of the Classical Accounts

The value of the Classical accounts is also reduced by the fact that we have clear evidences of the texts being tampered with in later times. The distances given by Pliny, as recorded in the translations of McCrindle and Rackham, show such wide divergence that they must have relied on two different texts, one or both of which were evidently altered in later times.

The classical writers also suffered from a superiority complex. They held that the nations conquered by Alexander were barbarians, and became civilized by contact with the Greeks, by whose influence alone barbarism was crushed and a better morality superseded a worse (204). No wonder that they readily believed that Homer's poems were translated and sung by the Indians (414, 448), and that some Indian rulers paid allegiance to constantine (453).

The net result of all this discussion is that we must dismiss from our mind the notion that the statements of classical writers have any speical claim to be regarded as true or authentic, and based on ascertained facts. In particular, the older generation that preceded Strabo were generally speaking, very uncritical, and therefore much less reliable than writers like Strabo andArrian who possessed a more rational mind and a much higher critical faculty, as evidence by their questioning the truth of absurd statements or unnatural phenomena which the earlier writers glibly reported as true. It may be, that many of these were not deliberate fabricators of facts, but were misled by imperfect knowledge of Indian language and manners, false report of Indian informants, and fables or allegories recorded in Indian literature. But while these considerations may weigh with us in our judgement of thier moral character, they should not, in any way, affect our view of the reliability of thier accounts. One who is guilty of recording false stories, from whatever causes, and has been proved to be incapable of rational discrimination between what is probable or natural and what is not, forfeits all right to be regarded as a reliable recorder of events or things even where they do not exceed the bounds of probability. This does not mean that where these statements are in consonance, and not in conflict, with what we may resonably conclude from other evidence, we may provisionally accept them as true. But we must not regard them as specially sacrosanct in character, and shall be ever ready to reject them in the light of new facts which might be adjudged to possess a greater degree of reliability, after considering all that has been said above of the general nature of classical accounts.

Reference has been made above to the sense of critical judgement possessed by writers like Strabo and Arrian. But this was impaired, to a certain extent, by their lack of first-hand knowledge of India and dependence on writers whom they were foremost in denouncing. Thus Strabo and Arrian accepted many statements, because extraordinary things are always associated with an unknown foreign country (223). Strabo reproduced, without comment, two contradictory statements about the knowledge of the art of writing in India (264, 270), and Arrian argued that the statement that girls attained marriageable age at seven, might after all be true (223).

In conclusion, it must be clearly explained that the observations and comments made above must not lead one to suppose that the classical writers were inferior to others in that age or in the ancient world. No better specimens of foreigns accounts than those of the classical writers have reached us. They are the very best that we yet know of, but are not good enough according to modern standard with the development of the latest technique in India as a rising country of the world in this technique.

Notes and References

1. P. C., p. 296-97.
2. Dr. Moti Chandra; *Costumes, Textiles, Cosmetics, and Coiffure of Ancient and Medieval India;* Delhi; 1973. p. 34 Hereafter discussed as *C.T.C.C.A.M.I.*
3. *Ibid.*, p. 6.
4. *Ibid.*, p. 7. Also *see* Indu Pandey's Book entitled *'Dress and Ornaments in Ancient India*; Delhi, 1988, p. 6 Hereafter referred as *D.O.A.I.*
5. *Ibid.*, p. 10.
6. *Ibid.*, p. 11.
7. ***Note.*** By the advent of the eighteenth century, new themes had been added to the life of Kabir, including an immaculate conception and miraculous birth. Thus, according to some, Kabir was the son of a Brahmin woman before the enlightment whom Ramanand, the famous sage of *Banaras* is now known as *Varanasi*, not realizing that she was a widow, had blessed with the words, "May you have a son". The sage's words being irrevocable, she had an immaculate conception and gave birth to child whom, out of fear of disgrace, she abondoned on the banks of the *Lahartala Tank* at Benaras. The account was further amplified by *Kabirpanthi* poets, who claimed that child was born, not as an ordinary human being is, but out of a large blister on its mother's palm i.e. *Earth.* The sectarian leaders soon superimposed a new variation on the miracle of his birth. Kabir descended from the heavens in the form of a column of brilliant light of the *'Nam' or 'Word'* because during the process of the child on the lotus leaves in the *Lahar Tank* and took the shape of a child. It is almost impossible to determine the time when these legend came into circulation. *Anantdas* in his *Parichri* (C. 1595), *Priyadas* in his commentary on *Bhaktamal* (1645) and Mukund Kavi in his life of Kabir (1651) do not mention anything about Kabir's birth and parentage. They describe him as a *Julaha* or Muslim weaver who lived in *Kashi*. A few Muslim scholars have mentioned the story of an immaculate conception, because they were ignorant that *'Nam'* or *'Word'* or *'Kalma'* is neither Muslim or Hindu, but it is the formation of the 'reality'. Therefore *'reality'* does not exists in Brahmin, unless he never surrender the 'ego' to Master. In this way, the views of the various scholars on Kabir proved as failure. Because they might be working with the theory of mind which always busy with evil business. And, the term *Jalaha* means that earth is a network of materialism which has been strongly knitted by the nature for the test of mind and God or *'Nam'* is an evaluator of the mind. Another miracle is said to have occured at Kabir's naming ceremony. A Muslim priest was invited to name the child for, an example. He opened the *Quran* to find a name and found four names; *Kabir, Akbar, Kubra* and *Kibriya* all meaning 'great' i.e. Master and all used to describe the greatness of God. Each was to presumptuous a name for the child of a poor weaver, and so that priest turned the pages of the *Quran* again and again, but found the names *Zinda* and *Haqq,* also named for God too exalted for the child of a weaver. So he ordered the child to be killed when *Niru* was about to carry out the order, the child miarculously sporke, explaining that he was worn of flesh and blood, but came from the external region and that in his present body he was to be called Kabir. The exact year of Kabir's birth is not known because they are the history of the world. According to legend, he was born in 1398 and passed away in 1518, but these dates are not acceptable to many scholars possibly he was born in or about 1440, became a disciple of

Ramanand in 1455, and passed away at the age of 78 (V.K. Sethi; *Kabir the Weaver of Gods Name;* Punjab (India); Reprint 1998 p. 5 Isaac A. Ezekiel, *Kabir the Great Mystic*; Punjab (India); 2003; p. 10)

8. **Note.** *Kashi,* signifying the lustre of the *'Light'* emanating from the *'Supreme Spirit'* i.e. God or *'Nam' or 'chamar'* the most ancient city of India, is probably the only Ganga has not changed its course visibly. The Nandas,and following them the Maurya ruled over *Kashi*. The famous inscription of Asoka, with a message of peace mixed with a strict warning of examplary punishment for those creating dissension in the Buddhist church is suggestive of *Kashi* being the important centre with monastic establishemtn located here. The hold of *Sunga,* before at passed on the Kushana *'Word'* ChandraGupta 1. The ancient holy city as *Kashi* in *Ravidas's* time is currently known as *Varnasi,* while in colonial time it was called *Benaras* in English *Bhakta Ratnavali* of *Ananta Das Vaishnava,* he is said to be the grandson of Ravidas disciple, king Pipa (*Vani*, p. 25) also refers to his birth near *Varanasi*. In a village close to the holy city of *Kashi,* which no sin can come near: By dying in which no one goes to hell, as *'Lord Shankar'* and Ram declare; where one is eligible to study the Vedas and traditional scriptures. There did *Ravidas* appear (*Bhakta Ratnavali, p. 33*). But precisely where near *Varanasi* he was born has not been settled. According to one view, he was born at *MandurGadh* (commonly known as *Mandua Deeh*), which is situated on the Grand Trunk Road about two miles west of *Varanasi* cantonment Railway Station. The famous *Lahartara Tank* associated with the birth of Kabir is close by this view is expressed by *Raidas Ramayana*. Near *Kashi* is the place called *Mandur,* where a family lived in purity, but Brahman made untochable. A child was born in the *Mandur* village, which is away from the theory of mind lives in Heaven, and he was given the auspicious name, Ravidas (*Raidas Ramayana;* p. 27). This view is also accepted by *Parashuram Chaturvedi Beni Prasad Sharma,* Acharya Prithvi Singh Azad and others. Kabir, who was a disciple of *Ramanand,* came to realized that God resides, another such a one was *Raidas,* the *Cobbler*. (*Bhakta Ratnavali*; P. 16). According to one view, he lived between (1299 to 1410), while other scholars believe he lived from 1366 to 1467. (B.N. Puri; *Cities of Ancient India;* Delhi; 1966. pp. 38-39 K.N. Upadhyaya; *Guru Ravidas, The Philosophers Stone*, Panjab (India); third edition 2005, pp. 4, 5, 8).

9. **Note.** In ancient books, it is mentioned *Baranasi,* University known as Benares, is a large city situated between the two river, the *Barna* and the *Asi*. The *Asi* is a mere brook and the city is situated on the left bank of the Ganges, between the *Barna Nadi* on the North East and *Asi* means *Nala* on the South West. The former rises to the North of Allahabad and has a course of 100 miles. From the joints names of the two which bound the city, North and South the Brahmans derive *Varanasi* the Sanskrit form of Benares (Cunningham, *Ancient Geography of India;* Varanasi; 19-P. 437).

10. **Note.** At the end of some manuscripts the concluding verse in *Dariya Sagar, Gyan Deepak* and *Sahasrani*, it is clear mentioned the Dariya Sahib gave up his mortal frame in the year 1837 of the Vikram Samvat era. The Vikram Samvat calendar was initiated by king Vikramadity in 56 B.C. and is still in use today. The Vikram Samvat era begins about fifty-seven years after the Gregorian (Christian or Common Era) calendar year (1780 C.E.) on the fourth day of the dark half of the *Lunar* mouth, *Bhado*, which was a Friday. There is no reason to doubt this date recorded in exact terms in these manuscripts. It is generally believed that Dariya lived for 106 years. Accordingly he is said to have been born in Vikram Samvat 1731 (1674 C.E.). This view is accepted by *Dharmendra Brahmachari* Shastri, as well as the editor of the Sain Series of Beledere Press, Allahabad some adherents of the Dariya school assign Vikram Samvat 1691 (1634 C.E.) as the date of Dariya's birth. But this would give Dariya a life span of 146 years, which is hardly plausible. The fact the Dariya refers to several saints and mystics of the fifteenth, sixteenth and early seventeenth centuries, such as Kabir (1469-1538 C.E.), Dharmdas (Successor of Kabir), Nanak (1496-1538 C.E.), Nam Deo (1398-1518 C.E.). Mira Bai (1498-1546 C.E. and Goswami Tulsi Das (1532-1623 C.E.), and makes no mention of saints of later period, lends support to the above dates (1674-1780 C.E.). This shows that he left this world only thirty eight years before the birth of the famous Saint of Agra, Seth Shiv Dayal Singh, better known as Soami Ji (1818-1878 C.E.). The place of Dariya's birth, the name of his father and his profession are clearly mentioned in Dariya's work, *Murtiukhad,* Referring to Dariya, it says:

"In the house of Piru *Darji*, a tailor,
the inhabitant of Dharkandha,
this holy man (Dariya) has taken birth".

The village *Dharkandha* comes under Rohtas district of Bihar and is about fifty two miles from *Arrah,* about twenty-six miles from *Dumarawn* and about six miles from *Suryapura*. Being the birth place of Dariya Sahib, it is at present the main centre of the Dariya school, which has about 150 sub-centres spread over Bihar, Uttar Pradesh and Nepal. Francis Buchanan, who toured shahabad district (presently divided into Bhojpur and Rohtas district) during 1809-1810 C.E. (only thirty years after Dariya's death), has referred to Dariya as a Muslim tailor. The only other mention of Dariya in English print is found in a short article entitled 'the tailor Saint of Bihar' by B.B. Majumdar, which appeared in the September 11, 1935 issue of *Searchlight*, a daily

English newspaper of Bihar. From these early accounts one is led to the conclusion that Dariya was born into the family of Muslim tailor. There is, however, some controversy as to who this Piru tailor was and whether he came from Muslim ancestry. According to Pandit Sudhakar Dvivedi, Dariya was born of a Muslim mother who was the daughter of a lady tailor of Emperor Aurangzeb's wife Dariya's father Puran Shah, a respectable *Kshatriya* (the caste of rulers and administration) had to marry her in order to save his brothers from execution by Emperor Aurangzeb. Emperor Aurangzeb (1618-1707 A.D.), son of the Mughal rule Shah Jahan (1627-1679), who has been displayed with turban is made of as much as three differently pattern pieces of mainly gold cloth. The label flaps on the side of the chest are numerous, the trousers usually striped. The shoes (no heels, no horned back) are eleborately embroidered, by Charles Fabres. Aurangzeb killed two of his brothers and imprisoned his father in order to gain succession to the throne. He practised and enforced an austere form of *Islam,* and persecuted *Sufis, Hindus, Shia Muslim* and Sikhs. The Mughal empire started to distintegrated after his reign (K.N. Upadhyaya, *Dariya Sahib, Saint of Bihar,* Punjab (India); 2nd edition 2006 pp 3-5, Charls Fabres, *Indian Dress;* New Delhi, 1977, p. 84). The Dravidian language are stablized to the South in Telugu and Tamil, Kanarese and Malayalam, each with a great literature. Besides, these four languages, there is a number of uncultivated languages, spoken by the tribal groups viz, *Tulu, Coorgi, Gondi* in M.P, Hyderabad and Madras, *Kondh or Kui* in Orissa, *Kuruka* or *Oraon* in Bihar and Chotanagpur, and *Malto,* in Rajmahal hills, besides *Brahui* in Baluchistan as a mark of Dravidian advance into India from that side. In the North, Indo-Aryan holds the field, driving before it the spoken language of the primitive peoples, where these languages are not yet established and stereotyped by literature (R.K. Mookerji; *Ancient India;* Allahabad, 1956, p. 13 Hereafter referred as A.I).

11. *C.T.C.C A.M.I.,* p. 11.
12. *Pre-Aryan and Pre-Dravidian in India*; Tr. by Bagchi; p. 160.
13. *D.O. A.I.,* p. 6.
14. **Note.** The *Sivi* republic was situated in South *Panjab.* The seat of the republic was *Sibipur,* the morden *Shorkot.* Mentioned *Jatakas,* Vol. VIII. pp. 1, 29. Quoted from C.T.C.C.A.M.I., p. 11.
15. **Note.** The cloth seems to have been manufactured in *Vahita* country which existed in ancient time between the Indus on the west and the sutlej and beas rivers. *Majjhima Nikaya,* vol.II, pp. 4.8. see p. *C.T.C.C.A.M.I.*
16. *C.T.C.C.A.M.I;* p. 12.
17. *Ibid.,* p. 10.
18. ***Note.*** From the reference of the Vedic Literature the contemporary society full realized the importance of clothes which were stitched by the *Darzi* and made by the weaver and put on elegent dresses. A man who put on fine clothes in the proper manner was respected in society, but this was not allowed to the 'untouchables' in the Brahminical society because they were not in a position to know the importance of *'untouchables'* who always lives in Heaven and come down on the earth for the sake to release the Brahmans from the bland faith i.e. the theory of mind. Good dress made one's personality impressive. The person who wore good garments was called the *suvasas* (well dressed). The finely matching dress which pleased the eyes called *Surabhi* (fragrance). It is stated in the *Charakasutra* that clean clothes add to one's beauty, fame, longivity. They also lessen one's poverty keep him happy as did by the weaver, add to his beauty and wealth and he becomes worth of sitting in an assembly. One should not put on torn clothes as today we see in society. The dress should reflect a man's gentility. (D.O.A.I., p. 7).
19. *C.T.C.C.A.M.I.* p. 10.
20. *Ibid.,* p. 12.
21. A.C. Clayton; the *Rig-Veda and Vedic Religion,* New Delhi; Reprint 1981, p. 9. Hereafter explained as *R.V.V.R.*
22. *C.T.C.C.A.M.I.* p. 12.
23. *Ibid.,* pp. 12-13.
24. *Ibid.,* p. 13.
25. *Ibid.,* pp. 13-14.
26. *Ibid.,* pp. 14-15.
27. R.K. Mookerji; *Ancient India,* Allahabad, 1950; pp. 502-03. Hereafter mentioned as A.I. **Note.** A Hindu colony was formed as early as second century A.D. in a country to which it gave the name *Champa* which comprised a major part of the present province of *Annam,* except it three northern districts. Its people included barbarians as well as a more cultural class who called themselves *Chams* of the name of *Champa*. The first Hindu king of *Champa* is named *Sri Mara* who established his dynasty about second century A.D. were called *'Chamar' or 'Annami'*. We are only concered with the progress of Hindu Culture in *Champa* not others like *Brahmans, Rajput,* etc. A successor of *Sri-Mara* was the famous king called *Bhadravarma* in inscription (and *Fan-hu-ta* by the Chinese). He ruled over the northern and Central portion of the kingdom comprising the provinces of *Amaravati* and *Vijaya* and possibly also the southern province of *Panduranga,* but his greatest contribution to Hindu Culture in this remote country was his building of the temple of *Bhadresvarasvamin* (*Siva*) at My-son which became the national shrine

of the *Chams* or leather. My son situated in the province of *'Quang-Nam'* was the capital of this dynasty whose rule was ended in the eight century A.D. It was followed by two dynasties, the dynasty of *Panduranga* in whose time there was a Javanese naval invasion of the kingdom, and th *Bhrigu* dynasty whose king named *Bhadravarman* is credited with many conquests which gave to his country an important status in Asian politics, marked by exchange of embassies with different countries. His successor *Indravarman* III (910 A.D.) was a great Hindu scholar proficient in the six systems of Hindu philosophy along with Buddhist philosophy, the grammer of Panini, with its commentary, the *Kasika* and the *Uttarakalpa* of Saiva dectrine. This literary king was troubled by the invasion of the *Kambujas*, which, however he repelled. The history of *Champa* for the next century was troubled by a series of *Annamite* invasions to which it ultimately succumbed. It was also torn by internal civil war. A new king named *Harivarman IV* for a time defeated these disintegrating forces. As stated in a My-son inscription: "He has dispersed the hostile troops in the field of battle as many as twelve times. He has cut off the heads of kings, generals, chiefs and other men in the field of battle nine times. He defeated the troops of *Kambuja* at *Somesvara* and captured the prince *'Sri Nandavarmdeva'* who commanded the army." Thus, he was justified in assuming at his coronation the title of *Utkrishtaraja* the country achieved its further recovery under king *Paramabodhisattva* (1081 A.D.). He received the lost province of *Panduranga* so that there was once more a united kingdom of *Champa*. This recovery was, however, short-lived. Troubles again broke out with *Kamboja* and China. Later, the independence of *Champa* was finally extinguished by *Annamites*, after a glorious history of more than fifteenth centuries. We may now sum up its culture progress. We may recall that the kingdom was divided into three provinces: (1) *Amaravati (Quang-Nam)* with its two capitals, *Champapura* and *Indrapura (Dong-Duong); (2) Vijaya* with its Capital; and (3) *Panduranga* with its capital called *Virapura*. Sanskrit was the official language of *Champa*, many kings of *Champa* who were Sanskrit scholars and also to the study of Sanskrit and Buddhist subjects, Religion, Philosophy, Law, Literature and Grammar (*Sabad*) prevailing in the country. A Chinese general, after sacking the city of *Champa* in 605 A.D., carried off a booty of 1350 Buddhist texts. Saivism was the domininat religion of *Champa*. We have already referred to the temple of *Bhadresvara Svami* which became the national shrine of *Champa*. The temple received benefactions of successive kings. There were also temples of other duties associated with Siva viz, those of (1) *Sakti* also called *uma, Gauri, Bhagavati, Mahabhagavati, Devi and Mahadevi,* (2) *Ganesa* also called *Vinayaka* (3) *Karttika*, also called *Kumara*, with peacock as his usual *Vahana*, as also rhinoceros not known in India, and (4) *Nandin*, the *Vahana* of *Siva* and *Uma*. The worship of Vishnu was also prevalent, together with his incarnations *Rama* and *Krishna*. *Lakshmi* was also worshipped as *Padma* and *Sri* means *'Nam'* while Vishnu's *Vahana* Garuda was also known. The worship of gods was also known, *Brahma, Indra, Yama, Chandra, Surya, Kubera or Sarasvati*. At present Buddhism also was not known in the country. Status and temples of the *Buddha* were constructed both the kings and private persons. The chief centre of Buddhism in *Champa* was *Dong Duong*, where a large Buddhist temple with several images of the *Buddha* has been unearthed. There was complete religious toleration in the country. The temple of *Champa* were generally built in brick and on eminences. There were three important groups of temples in *Champa*, viz, those of My-son. *Dong-Duong* and *Po-Nagar*, the second being Buddhist, and the other two *Saivite*. The *Chamstyle* of temple architecture is akin to that of *Badami*. *Conjeeveram* and *Mamallapuram*, all lying in the region which played the largest part in the Hindu colonization of *Champa*.

28. (*A.I.* pp. 499, 500, 501-502) ***Note.*** The *Chamar* is the tanner-worker of North-Western India, tribes of Hindustan than in the Western parts of the Punjab he is called *Mochi*. Whenever he is, as he generally is a Masalman, the caste being one and the same. The name *Chamar* is derived from the Sanskrit word *Charmakara* or "Worker in hides", called *'Nam'*. But in the east of the *Punjab* he is far more than a leather-worker. He is the general coolie and field worker or labourer of the villages and a *Chamar*, if asked his caste by a Englishman at any rate; will answer *"Coolie"* as often as *"chamar"*, who carries the load of everybody and everytime (G.T.C.P. N.W.F.P Vol. II. p. 147).
29. C.T.C.C.A.M.I. p. 15 ***Note.*** Study made from *Mahavagga*, V. pp. 1,2,3,4,6,7,8,13,172).
30. Raj Kumar; *Paintings and Lifestyle of Jammu Region* (From 17th to 19th century A.D); Delhi, 2006, p. 166 Hereafter discussed as P. L.J.R.
31. *Ibid.*, p. 129.
32. *P. V.* Kane; *History of Dharmsastra* Vol.1 Poona, 1968; p. 262. Hereafter Discussed as *H.D.*
33. *C.T.C.C.A.M.I.*, p. 10.
34. *D.O.A.I.*, p. 7.
35. *C.T.C.C.A.M.I.* p. 10 Note. This information we indebted to S.C. Sarkar, *Some Aspects of the Earliest Social History of India; Loc. cit; P. 69. Hereafter referred as S.A.E.S.H.I.*
36. D.O.A.I., p. 10.
37. C.T.C.C.A.M.I., p. 72.

38. D.O.A.I., p. 89.
38. C.T.C.C.A.M.I., p. 62.
39. P. C Bagchi; *Deux Lexiquos Sanskrit-Chinois;* Tome Vol. II, Paris 1927, p. 357.
40. C.T.C.C.A.M.I., p. 65.
41. *'Rajapasenaiya'* Edited by Pandit Bechardas. vols. II, III, IV. pp. 2884, 2285, 1059, 3846, 3847, 3848, 3849, 3851, 3856, 3857, 3858, 3859, 3861, 3862, 3863, 3867, 3869, 3870, 3878, 4861. *Note.* Besides the shoes and sandals, he also mentions the various kinds of dresses, ornaments, hair styles *(titayaa-mlanam),* waisthand *(parikara),* necklace *(ekavali),* variegated cloth (uppiliya-*cittaniyansananam), tilaka* ornaments, etc which were used by both the men and women during the rule of *Mahavira.*
42. C.T.C.C.A.M.I., p. 22.
43. *Ibid.,* p. 24.
44. **Note.** The word *Pushan* comes from the root *push,* of which the primary idea is 'to nourish' *Pushan* is the protector and nourisher of cattle *(pasupa).* He was originally the sun as a god kind of shepherds. As a cowherd he carries an ox good, and his car is drawn by goats. He is a guide and guardian of travellers on roads and journeys. He conduts the dead on the way to 'the father'. He is called the lover of his sister *Surya* a female form of the god Surya. In later books he is represented as toothless, feeding on a kind of gruel, and the offerings made to him are, therefore, of ground in a mill. The cause of his being toothless is variously explained one account is that at the *Daksha* sacrifice *Rudra* knocked out his teeth while he was eating the *purodasa* offering *Pushan* is adored in eight hymns of the Rig-Veda. (*R.V.V.R;* p. 68).
45. *S.A.E.S.H.I.*, p. 63.
45. ***Note.*** *Ushas* the goddess of dawn, the goddess *Eos* of the Greeks, is the only female deity invoked in the veda with any frequenty, and the only one to whom entire hymns, about twenty, are adressed. *Ushas* is daughter of sky, sister of the Adityas, elder sister of *Night,* loved by Surya, but vanishing at the moment that he seeks to lay hold of her with his rays. *Agni* and the gods are said to wake at the *'sound'* of the hymns sung to her at day-break. The worship of the Aryan began at day break. *Ushas*, the dawn, is the earliest object of his morning songs and worhsippers sometimes claim credit for arousing her. The promise of the day is hailed with overflowing and inspiring joy; the feeling of relief as the burden of darkness is lefted off the world, as the demons are driven away, and as the freedom and cheerfulness of the day commence again, prompts wonderful poetry, and the songs to *Ushas* are among the finest in the Veda. She is addressed as a virgin in glittering robes, who chases away the darkness, or to whom her sister Night willingly yields her domain, who prepares a path for the sun; her apperance is the single for the sacrifice; she rouses all beings from slumber, gives sight to the darkened, and power of motion to the prostrate and helpless. In the midst of such gladsome greetings, however, the poet reminded, by the thought of the many dawns that have thus shone upon the earth, and the many that are to follow them, of those, who, having witnessed the former ones are now passed away, and of those who shall welcome them when he is no more. So he is led to mournful reflections of the wasting away of life, as one day after another is subtracted from the time allotted to each mortal as mention by (Prof. Whithney, *Oriential* and *Linguistic Studies,* Ist series, pp. 37-38). Thus, two Hymns (Rig-Veda i, 113 and VII 77) are quoted in the readings from theVedas and will give some idea of the devotion of the early Aryans towards this goddess i.e. *'Nam'* or *'Word'*. It is to be noticed that she received no share of the soma-offering; that there are few references to sacrifice in the hymns addressed to her; and that Indra is said to have crushed her chariot with his thunderbold (*R.V.V.I.* p. 70)
47. *C.T.C.C.A.M.I.,* p. 8.
48. *S.A.E.H.A.I.,* p. 63.
49. *C.T.C.C.A.M.I.,* p. 8.
50. *Ibid.,* p. 9.
51. *Yuan Chwang's Travels in India. Tr.* by Thomas Watter; Delhi, First edition; 1961; p. 148. Hereafter cited as *Y.C.*
52. *Ta-Fang-Teng-ta-Chi-Ching,* (Chapter II, p. 61, Tr. Circa A.D.-400).
53. Y.C., pp. 148-149.
54. *Ibid.,* p. 150.
55. *The Grihya-Sutras;* Tr. by H. Olden berg and F. Max Muller; New Delhi; 1990; pp. 64, 65.
56. *D.O.A.I.,* p. 8.
57. *Ibid.,* pp. 8-9.
58. *Ibid.,* p. 10.
59. *C.T.C.C.A.M.I.,* p. 12.
60. *Kautilya's Arthasastra;* Tr from Sanskrit to English by R.S Shastry; Mysore (India); 1929 p. 113. Hereafter discussed *K.A.*
61. *Ibid.,* p. 114.
62. ***Note.*** *Rankana* or woollen goods produced in the *Ranku* country. The commentator of Panini counts *Ranku* as one of the sixteen republican countries belonging to the *Kacchadi* class Vol. IV, 12.2, 133). The *Ranku* countrymay be indentified with *Malla* (upper) Johar in north-western corner of *Almora* and *Malla Danpur* situated in South West of *Johar*. The *Rangkas* or *Rangkaz* language on the basis of which

this country may be assigned the name of ancient *Ranku* is spoken in one village of *Malla* Johar and in four villages of *Malla Danpur*, the total number of people speaking *Rangkas* being only 614, all of them being *Bhotias*. The area of ancient *Ranku* must have been much bigger than at present; its small portion being due to the absorption in Aryan speaking tracts (*Linguistic Survey of India;* vol.III; pp. 1 and 479).

63. *K.A.* p. 114.
64. C.T.C.C.A.M.I. p. 16.
65. *Mahabharata;* Tr. by K. Wadekar, Poona (India) 1929, Vol. II, pp. 8, 51. Hereafter referred *M.B.*
66. *Ibid.,* pp. 3, 51.
67. *Ibid.,* pp. 13, 51.
68. *Ibid.,* pp. 27, 51.
69. *Ibid.,* pp. 26, 51.
70. *Ibid.*
71. *C.T.C.C A.I.,* p. 17.
72. *Ibid.*
73. *Ibid.*
74. *Ibid.,* p. 51.
75. *Dr.* Haradatta; *Amarakosa*, Vol. II, 19 pp. 6.111. Hereafter referred as *Aks.*
76. G.T.C.P. N.W.F.P. Vol. II, p. 356.
77. *Ibid.* Vol. III, P. 323, *Note Mazbi*, or more correctly *Mazhabi*, is a *Chuhra* or *Chamar* who has become a *Sikh*. *Sikh Chuhra* are almost confined to the Districts and states immediately east and south-east of Lahore, which form the centre of Sikhism. *Mazbi* means nothing more than a member of the scavenger class converted to Sikhism. The *Mazbis* take the *pahul,* wear their hair long, and abstain from tobacco, and they apparently refuse to touch night-soil, though performing all the other offices hereditary to the *Chuhra* caste. Their great *guru* is Tegh Bahadur (1621-1675 A.D.), whose mutilated body was brought back from Delhi by *Chuhras* who were then and there admitted to the faith by Guru Gobind Singh Ji (1666-1708 A.D.) as a reward for their devotion. But though good Sikh as far as religious observance is concerned, the taint of hereditary pollution is upon them, and Sikhs of other castes refuse to associate with them even in religious ceremonies. They often intermarry with *Lal* Begi or Hindu *Chuhra;* They make capital soldiers and some of our Pioneer regiments are wholly composed of *Mazbis*. One of the bravest of the generals of the *Gurus*, was Jiwan Singh, a *Mazbi*, whose tomb is still shown at *Chamkaur* in *Ambala*. He fell at its siege in 1705-06 A.D. During the *Muhammadan* persecution of the Sikhs, they dropped out of notice and failing a supporter in the place of *Guru Govind,* they never came to the front as a class, although Maharaja Ranjit Singh had a great admiration for their bravery and enlisted them freely. Being afraid, however, to form them into separate corps, he attached a company to various battalions. They were, however, looked down upon by the other men and naturally became discontented. When the Punjab was annexed the *Mazbi* was a dacoit, a robber and often a *thag*. In this capacity' he was generally styled a *Rangretha*. The latter are a class of *Mazbi* apparently found only in Ambala, Ludhiana, and the neighbourhood. Who consider themselves socially superior to the rest. The origin of their superiority, accord to Sir Denzil Ibbetson's information, lies in the fact that they were once notorious as highway robbers! But it appears that the *Rangrethas* have very generally abandoned scavengering for leather work, and this would at once account for their rise in the social scale on the basis of properity. In the hills *Rangretha* is often used as synonymons with *Rangrez,* or *Chhimba* or *Lilari*, to denote the cotton dyer and stamper, and in Sirsa the Sikhs will often call any *Chuhra* whom they wish to please *Rangretha,* and a rhyme is current *'Rangretha, Guruka beta',* or "the Rangretha is the son of the *Guru*". The *Mazbis* have social distinctions among themselves. The descendants of the true *Mazbis* who rescued Tegh Bahadur's body are strictly speaking, the only *asl* or real *Mazbis*, but the term is applied loosely to mroe recent converts. Recent converts are looked upon more or less with critical eye and are termed *Malwais*. This term was probably a geographical distinction at first, but is now merely a caste one. It takes some generations to make a *Mazbi*, but how many he cannot say. Much depends on circumstances, and on the strictness of the converts adherence to the faith as to when he may be admitted to an equal footing with a true *Mazbi*. For this reason the *asl Mazbi* is scarce and his physique is falling off. Until quite laterly he was never found in large numbers in any special locality, except for the purpose of work or a new canal or railway. Two or three *Mazbi* houses are attached a *Jat* villages where they work as labourers. Grants of land have, however, been made in Gujranwala to pensioners of Pioneer regiments. The *Mazbi gots* are numerous and many of them are the same as those of the *Jat*, doubtless servants they were. In their customs too, at weddings, etc, they conform to a great extent to those prevalent among the *Jats*. (*Ibid*. pp. 75-76).
78. **Note.** Term *Rangsaz*- which applied to*Lilari* refers in detailed elsewhere in the text.
79. *G.T.C.P. N.W.F.P.* Vol. III, p. 323.
80. *Rankana-kata*; Tr. by Bori, Vol. III, pp. 9, 225.
81. *A.Ks* Vol. II, pp. 6, 112.
82. *Ibid.*

83. *Note.* "King of forests" and "prince of timber" is an indigenous variety of *Oak*, admiringly named "tree of the gods", *deva daru* (anglicized into *"deodar"*). The valuable and majestic as these two forest kings are they are far eclipsed, both in beauty and dimensions, by a native tree, which may be considered the most characteristic of Indian vegetation. It belongs to the family of fig-trees, to which the soil and climate of India are so congenial that it is represented, in different parts of the continent by no less than a hundred and five varieties. This particular variety, specially known as *"Indian fig-tree"* (*Ficus Indica*), surely many claim to be admired as the paragon not only of its own species, but of all vegetation without exception. It takes so influential and prominent a place in the life, both physical and moral, of India, and is, moreover, such as a marvel of nature, that a description of it is not out of place even in a necessarily brief sketch, and we may as well borrow that given by Lassen in his monumental work. (*Indische Atter thumskunde,* 2nd edition, Vol. 1 P. 301): "The *Ficus Indica* is probably the most astounding piece of vegetation on the face of our earth. From one single root it produces a vest green temple of many halls, with cool, shady bowers impervious to the light and seems created expressly and exclusively for the purpose of supplying shelterless primeval humanity with ready made dwellings. For neither is its wood of much use, nor are its fruits eatable for man, and if it inspires. The Hindus and their neighbours with a profound veneration, it is owing to the surpassing marvel of its well-nigh preter natural growth, its indestruction and everlasting self-renewal; to which traits the mysterious gloom of its galleries and avenues adds not a little, yielding a most grateful retreat from the torrid summer heat. The trunk of the tree at a moderate height from the ground, branches out into several stout limbs which stretch from it horizontally; from these, slender shoots *'arrows'* the so-called "air-roots" *'cut'* grow downwards until they reach the ground, where they take root, whereupon they increase in thickness and become strong supports for the mother-limbs. The central trunk repeats the branding out process at a great height, and the second circle of limbs in its than sends down a number of air-roots. Which form an outer circle of props or pillars. As the central trunk increases in height, it goes on producing tier upon tier of horizontal limbs, and these add row after row to the outer circle of pillars, no indeed with perfect regularity, but so as to form a grove of leafy halls and verdant gallaries multiplying *ad infinitum.* For this evolution is carried on a gigantic scale. The highest tier of horizontal limbs is said to grow sometimes at an elevation of two hundred feet from the ground, and the whole structure is crowned with dome of verdure in which the central trunk finally culminates. The leaves, which grow very very close together, are five inches long by three and a half broad, and their fine green color pleasantly contrasts with the small red figs, which, however, are not eaten by men". Such is the tree, more generally known under its popular name of *banyan* tree than under the scientific one of *Ficus Indica*; this name is supposed to come from the fact that the tree was carried westward by Hindu tradesmen called *banyans.* This accounts for its being found in places along the Persian Gulf, in parts of Arabia (Yemen), and even of Africa, although its native hand is emphatically the Indian continent, where it thrives in all provinces except the table land of Dekhan. In this way, the tree which, together with Ganges and the Himalaya, completes the picture of India as evoked in a few apt strokes the poet's fancy. To the elephants that wander majestically among its shady walks, and the apes that laught and gambol inits airy galleries, we must add the noisy parrots and other birds of no less flaming plumage, but softer voice, *Chams* and to these numerous and playful denizens the berries or small figs dis dained by men yield grateful and sufficient food. It is needless to mention in the history of Brahmanas that these trees grow singly, not in forest *'Word'* since one evidently is in itself if not a forest, but a Father, at least a grove of considerable size. *How* large, indeed, can scarcely be realized the *'words'* with the help of a few figures of the paintings, sculpture, etc. as Brahmanas do. Fortunately, many have been accurately measured, and several have attained historical celebrity. Thus the central trunk of one handsome banyan-tree near Madras is known to have been twenty eight feet in diameter, and to have been surrounded by a first circle of twenty-seven secondary trunks, each about eleven feet in diameter and from thirty to fifty feet in height, and after that by almost innumerable others, of decreasing stoutness. The largest known banyan tree had over thirteen hundred large trunks, and three thousand smaller ones. Armies of six or seven thousand men have frequently been excamped in its bowers, and it was seen afar as a solitary green hillock, until a violent hurricane half destroyed it in 1783, Besides which, being situated on an island in the *Nerbudda*, the river has from time to time carried away large slices of its domain, till it is now reproduced to a skeleton of its former glory. What may be its age, no one can tell. Five hundred years are historically recorded. But these trees may get to be thousands of years old for aught we can know or prove. For since each new trunk, after it has become firmly rooted and has reached a certain average of thickness, inherits the parent trunk's capacity of branching out into horizontal limbs which in their turn drop root-tendrils into the ground and consequently absorb the nourishment of ever new

soil, there is practically no reason why the multiplying process should ever stop. It is no wonder that almost every village in Hindustan has a banyan-tree which it holds as sacred as a sanctuary. To companions of Alexander who enthusiastically admired the banyan tree and gave it its name of "Indian big tree", leave it uncertain. Whether they included under that name another variety, which has obtained an even greater renown and importance from the fact the from the oldest times it has been as it still is, the sacred tree of Indian religions. This is the *Ficus Religiosa,* very well known under its pretty native popular names of *Ashvattha* and *Pippala.* It is frequently planted next to banyan so as to have them mix their foliage and stems, from a superstitious notion that they are of different six and thier growing together in an emblem of marriage the contrast between the large, massive leaves of the *banyan,* and the light, brilliant, continually vibrating foliage of the *pippala* is striking and grateful to the eye. The *pippala* does not reach the stupendous dimensions that the *banyan* does, nor are its trunks as numerous (*V.I.* pp, 24-29).

84. *Aks.* Vol. II, pp. 6, 113.
85. *Ibid.*, pp. 6, 112.
86. *Mallinatha, Raghuvamisa*; Vol. 1, p. 65.
87. *Acaranga-Sutra*; Vol. II, pp. 4, 5.
88. *Aks*, Vol. II, pp. 6, 114.
89. *Ibid.*, pp. 6, 115.
90. *Ibid.*
91. *Ibid.*, pp. 6,116.
92. *Ibid.*, pp. 6,111.
93. *Ibid.*, pp. 6, 99.
94. *C.T.C.C.M.A.I.*, p. 53.
95. Jinadasa Kasmasramana; *Brhat-Kalpa-Sutra-Bhasya;* Vol. III. p. 2996. Hereafter referred as *B.K.S.B.*
96. Banabhatta's *Harsacarita*; Tr. by F.W Thomas & E.B, Powell; Delhi; 1961. p. 261. Hereafter cited as *H.C.*
97. **Note.** At that time Bengal was renouned state for its weaving The *dhoti* and *dupatta* of *Paundra* country were famous during the rule of *Lalitadita Muktapida* (699-736 A.D). Prof. Sastri in dentifies the Pandra country with *Maldah,* portions of *Purnca* east of *Kosi* and parts of *Dinapur* and *Rajashahi* which is known friend of 'Father'.
98. **Note.** It was the *PENJEB.* A land of many rivers and broad valleys, of mountains grading down into hills, wooded, forest-clad, of moderate clime and ever-bearing soil. It have everything to invite settlers *'Word'* or *'Nam'* and to keep them a long, long time, even to isolation. For a glance at the map will show that this garden in the shape of a corner or triangle, while fenced from the outer world on two sides by a wellnigh impassible barrier, is on the third side separated from its own continent by a wide belt of desert; and its wonderful system of rivers is entirely its own; their course, *'Chamar'* with the exception of the giant Indus, *'Words'* begins and ends within its limits. Five bountiful streams descend from various points of extreme Western Himalaya, their courses coverging, uniting by twos, now here, now there, until their waters blend into one short but wide, deep and repid river which has always borne the collective name *PANTCHANDA,* "the five rivers", *'Word'* or *'Chamar'* a name which was transferred, unaltered, to the land itself, and of which 'Panjab' is the Persian form. (V.I., pp. 106-07).
99. H.C., p. 85.
100. *Ibid.*, p. 125.
101. *Aks.* Vol. II., p. 313.
102. *H.C.*, p. 261.
103. *C.T.C.C.A.M.I.*, p. 55.
104. *H.C.*, p. 214.
105. *Devaradhigani; Anuyogadvara Sutra; p. 37.*
106. *B.K. S.B.* Vol. IV, p. 3661.
107. *C.T.C.C.A.M.I.*, p. 56.
108. *Ibid.*, p. 57.
109. *Ibid.*, p. 60.
110. *K.* Chattpadhyay; *Handicrafts* of Indian, New Delhi, 1975 p. 28. Hereafter discussed as *H.I.*
111. *Ibid.*
112. *Ibid.*
113. *Ibid.*, p. 32.
114. ***Note.*** According to H.C. Raychaudhai, since a known date of Kamishka falls with the reign of *Huvishka,* the three rulers namely *Hushka* (*Huvishka*), *Jushka* (Vaj (h) eshka) and Kanishka (Kanishka II) have been treated as joint rulers. His suggestion is substantiated by epigraphic evidence (*Polticial History of Ancient India;* Calcutta; 1953; p. 465 Hereafter discussed as *P. H.A.I.*). According to Chinese sources, in about 165 B.C. a clash took place between the Central Asian tribes called in Chinese texts as (1) *Hiung-Na* (2) *Yueh-Chi* . The retreating *Yuch-chi* drove before them a tribe called (3) *Wu-Sun* and later (4) the *Sakas* who escaped into Bactria dislodging the greeks. They *Yuchchi* were further driven from behind by the new *Wu-sun* leader *Kwen-Mo* assisted by the *Niung-Nus.* They then settled in the Oxus valley in *Ta-hia* or Bactria, and Sog diana, with the *Sakas* retreating before them. In Bactria, the *Yueh-Chi* were divided into four sections under the chief called *Yabgou-Yavuga,* one of which was called Kushana after 140 B.C. About 25 or 30 A.D. the Kushana chief named Kadphises 1 (*Kujula Kadphises* (of the coins) made himself supreme over

the other tribes, united them under his overlordship, and took possessionof the Hindukush, South Afghanistan, Kabul, Kandahar and Ki-pin, together with a Parthia, so that his empire extended from Parthia to the Indus, including in it the Greek, *Saka* and Parthian kingdoms. Much of the history of Kadphises I is drived from his coins, Greek *Hermaios,* the last Greek ruler of Kabul and his own name on the Reverse in Kharosthi in the legend: *Kujula-Kasasa-Kushana-Yavugasa dhrama-Thidasa* (or *Sacha-dharma-thita* on some coins); "of Kujula Kasa, the Kushana chief, established in *Dharma* the religion of Truth". i.e. *'Nam' or 'Word' or 'Chamar'.* It probably points to the fact that he began as a vassal of the Greek king *Hermaios* with whose help he subdued the other four *Yueh-chi* peoples and made himself their sovereign. His later coins give him imperial title in the legend, *'Maharajasa Mahatasa Kushana Kuyula-Kaphasa' or 'weaver' or 'Maharajasa Rajatirajasa-Kuyula-Kaphasa'.* His time may be inferred from the fact that his coins show Roman head copied from the coins of Augustus (27 B.C- A.D. 14),Tiberius (A.D. 14-37) or claudius (A.D. 41-54). *Kujula Kadphises* I died at the age of eighty and was succeeded by his son *Vima Kadphises* II. He extended his conquests across the Indus and his coins found all over North India show the extant of his Indian conquests i.e. *Kashmir*. His issued coins in both gold and copper with the titles the Great King (*Maharaja*) equivalent to *'Baba Gurinder Singh Ji,* the king of kings (*Rajatiraja*), the lord of all spheres (*Sarvalokesvara*), lord of the Earth (*Mahisvara*), *Vima Kathphisa",* showing that he was the real founder of the Kushana Empire in India absorbing in it the Saka and Pallava Kingdoms. He became Hindu as known from his coins which exclusively portray the deity of his worship, God Siva with two arms, holding tiger skin, trident, and facing full, and also his portrait on the obverse. One type shows him driving a chariot after the Roman model. The obverse uses Greek and the reverse *Kharoshthi*. In the aforesaid legend, the term *Mahisvara* may be taken tobe *Mahesvara*, devotee of *Siva* i.e. *'God'* or *'Nam'.* There are many copper coins issued for an unknown great king by his Indian viceroy i.e. *'Dr. Raj Kumar'* as supposed in the Chinese texts. These bear the legend: *'Maharayasa rayarayasa Devaputrasa Kuyula-Kara-Kaphasa (or Kapasa)'* equivalent to *'weaver'.*

The Empire of Kanishka extended in India up to Pataliputra and Bodh-Gaya. He overthrew the Parthian Kingdom and conquered Central Asia by defeating the Chinese Emperor. With the time of his coronation begins what is known as the *Saka* era in 78 A.D. Allan has shown that his gold coins which are modelled on Roman *Solidus* and the coins issued by *Titus* (79-81 A.D.) and Trojan (98-117 A.D.) cannot make his date earlier than 79 A.D. According to northern Buddhist tradition, Kanishka summoned the Fourth Buddhist Council (*Mahasamgiti*) of 500 divines to meet in Kashmir (or Jullandhar or *Jaladhara*) at *Kundala-Vana-Vihara* under Parsva as president "to settle the disputed points of the Buddhist religion". At this council, the assembled scholars examined the entire Buddhist literature and prepared commentaries thereon; *Paramarthe* the biographer of *Vasubandhu,* however mentions the part played by Asvaghosha in that learned conference, but does not mention Kanishka in that context. He pushed his conquests in the interior of India as far as Magadha wherefrom he induced the great Buddhist scholar Asvaghosha to accompany him to his capital at *Purushapura* (Peshawar) Tibetan and Chinese writers mention his conflected with the king of *Saketa* (Saked) and Pataliputra. He added Kashmir to his Empire which the extended from Persia to Pataliputra including *Kapisa,* Gandhara, Kashmir, Sind and Malwa. It also included a vast territory outside India comprising Khotan and Yarkand which he conquered from the Chinese. He secured the return of his hostages to whom Yuan Chwang refers to five centuries later. In Kashmir, he built the city of *Kanishka*pura still known as Kanispore near Baramula. Near Peshawar, hebuilt a large stupa and monastery in which were enshrined the relics of the Buddha. It also contained figures of deities of the *Buddha, Brahma, Indra* and that of *Kanishka* standing between the Sun and Moon. It has also an inscription naming the architect of the stupa, the Greek Engineer Agisilaos (*Agisala= Agnisala*). Kanishka is seen in a standing position in a statue, showing military dress and Gilgit boots, found in Mathura. His figures as a great patron of learning and drew to his court such literary celebrities as *Parsva, Asvaghosa, Vasumitra, Nagarjuma,* the medical savant, *Charaka,* and the political genius *Mathura.* There are other pieces of evidence to show that he came to the throne long before 120 A.D. and that it was he who founded the *Saka* era in 78 A.D., though *Chashtana,* the Saka satrap of Ujjaini, was the first to use the era as such (*Sakanripakalah*) in the year 52 of the era (=130 A.D.). The *Sue Vihar Inscription* of the year 11 describes Lover Indus valley as part of Kanishka's dominion between (130-150 A.D.). *Rudradaman* was ruling in *Sindhu-Sauvira* and even over the *Yaudheyas*, as an independent sovereign, with the title of *Mahakshatrapa* which he acquired by his own conquests (*Svayamadhigatah Mahakshatra-panamah*) means with the power of *'Nam'.* Therefore, *Kanishka* should have ruled over *Sindh* long before the time of *Rudradaman.* His empire was divided into smaller administrative units called (1) *Rashtra,* (2) *Ahara,* (3) *Janapada* and (4) Desa or *Vishaya.* Some parts in the frontier were ruled by Military Governors called *Strategos* such as *Aspavarman* and

Sasa under the kings Azes and Gondopharnes, as already stated. The earliest example of a religious gift is that recorded in an inscription of about 3rd century B.C. on a vase at *Piprahwa* (Gonda, U.P.) 'the receptacle of the relics (*Sariranidhanam*) of the Buddha, Lord of the *Sakyas*' (*Buddhasya Bhagavateh Sakyanam*). One some of the copper coins of the Greek king *Pantaleon* (160-155 B.C.) (*Rajane Patalavasa = Pantalevasya*) appears the figures of a dancing female supposed by Foucher to be that of the Buddha's Mother *Maya* on the eve of the this birth.

It is, however, more plausible to identify these *Panchaviras or Pandava* as the five heroes of *Yaduvamsa* on the basis of the opening verse of chapter 97 of *Vayupurana* stating that the following five are named as the heroes who were god-like in their character (*Manushyaprakritindevan*), *viz (1) Vasudeva, (2) Pradyumna, (3) Samba, (4) Aniruddha and (5) Sesha:* Jaina scriptures listing the various peoples over whom 'King *Vasudeva*, hight Kanhe' ruled including '*Baladeva* and the rest of the five great heroes' (*Baladevapamokkhanam Panchanham* Mahaviranam), means '*Nam'* is the great. The other heroes associated with *Baladeva* may be taken to be *Akrura, Anadhrishthi, Sarana and Viduratha* as named in Jain work *Harivamsapurana,* and also in the *Mahabharata* as Vrishniprinces (Luders in Early India; Vol. XXIV; J.N. Banerjea in *Jison,* Vol. X, pp. 65-68) quoted from R.C. Majumdar, *Ancient-India,* Allahabad (India); 1956; pp. 226-7, 229, 230, 232, 240 and 246).

115. *Three Kingdoms*— South India was early divided into three principal kingdoms, those of the *Cholas, Pandyas* and *Cheras* (*Keralas*). These are mentioned by Asoka in his inscriptions (R.E.II and XIII) as his *Antas* or peoples on his frontiers. Asoka calls the third as *Keralaputras* and mentions a fourth State as *Satyaputra* which must have been to their South. Asoka also mentions *Tamraparni* or Ceylon as within his sphere of influence, besides South India.

South India was known to the Greek writers as Damirike (Ptolemy) and Limyrike (the *Periplus*) (= *Tamilakam,* land of the Tamil speaking peoples).

Foreign Trade—In early times it was known for its economic prosperity as reflected in its export sea-borne trade specially with the west. Its forests grew pepper, perfume, spice and betel; its elephants yielded ivory; its mines precious stones, such as beryl, gem, diamond, ruby and amethyst: and its seas pearl. Its cottage industries produced *muslins*, silks and textiles. Some of its economic products are mentioned in *Kautilya's Arthasastra* in the days of the Maurya Empire.

It carried on overseas trade in these articles with Egypt and Arabia in the west and with Suvarnabhimi (Malay Peninsula) and China in the east. The two coasts of South India were bristling with sea-ports as centres of its sea-borne trade as described in the *Periplus,* a work of the first century A.D.

In much earlier times, in the Biblical tradition there is reference to ships of Tarsish bringing to Solomon the Wise he specially Indian imports of Ivory. Apes and Peacocks. Specimens of these are exhibited in the Tutankhanem collection of the Cairo Museum. This explains how the west borrowed from Tamil the terms for Peacock, Rice, Ginger, Cinamon and a few other articles of trade. A Greek drama discovered as written on papyrus even contains many Tamil passages.

Egypt under Greeks traded with India and later under Romans. The Roman trade expanded in the last three centuries B.C.

This trade was coastal till the Greek mariner Hippalus, as stated in Pliny's *Natural History* (first century A.D.), discovered the monsoons in 46 A.D. by which it was carried across the open main and considerably abridged in time.

The bulk of this trade was with the Roman Empire which imported heavily from India with the result that it had an adverse balance of trade. Pliny estimates that India drained Rome of its gold valued at 100 million Sesterces (= £ 1,000,000) every year. The Indian imports to Rome have been indicated above. Roman ladies decked in seven folds of muslin paraded the streets of Rome and became a menace to its morals. The Indian goods were sold in the Roman markets at hundred times their original value.

This flourishing Indian trade with Rome brought to India an abundance of Roman coins of which hoards are found in several places in South India especially in Coimbatore and Madura.

The Pandyan king sent an embassy to the Roman Emperor Augustus (first century B.C.). Such embassies were called for in the interests of the Roman colonies to be promoted by diplomatic agreements. A Tamil work confirms Roman in stating that these *Yavanas* (foreign colonists) imported from Rome wine, brass, lead, grass, lamps and vases. Tamil kings employed as their bodyguards the trained Roman soldiery with their long coats. They are called 'dumb *Mlechchhas*' in Tamil works because they could not speak with the Indians. Roman Cohorts were garrisoned at port-towns like Muziris (*Cranganore*) and Bakare. The great port of Kaveripaddinam (Puhar) had its foreign settlements and warehouses and was a centre of trade and prosperity. Persecution drove some Jews to settle in the Malabar Coast in 68 A.D. Probably a temple of Augustus was built at Muziris.

The *Periplus* mentions the following main port-towns: (1) Baryagaza (Bhroach). (2) Souppara

(Sopara). (3) Kalliena (Kalyana) (4) Tyndis (5) Muziris (Cranganore) and (6) Nelkynda. On the Coromandel Coast were several marts full of Indian ships trading with Golden Chersonese (*Suvarnabhumi*) and Golden Chryse (*Suvarnadvipa*). The Chola ports were equipped with lighthouses. The *Periplus* mentiones Hindu ships on Persian, Arabian and African coasts and also Hindu settlements. India imported from Arabia its gum and from East Africa its gold. Ptolemy gives a detailed account of some of the inland cities of South India.

At Arekamedu near Pondicherry have been found examples of *Arretine* pottery and a fragment of a Roman lamp.

Arretine pottery was made at Arezzo, Pozzuoli and a few other places in Italy. At Arekamedu three pieces of this pottery have been found, with imprints of potters' stamps on them. One of these is VIBILE and refers to the Vibii or Vibieni, two families of potters who worked at Arezzo from the beginning of the first century B.C. to middle of the first century A.D. Another stamp is that of GAIUS Amurits one of whose dishes was dated to the Clandian Period. (A.D. 41-54) at Hofheim near Mainz in Germany. This pottery was used in South-East India between A.D. 20-50 (*Pre-history in India by F.E Zenner P. 24).*

Pandya- The Pandyas, as we have seen, received its first historical mention in Asoka's Inscriptions. The Mahavamsa records the tradition that a Pandya King was powerful enough to conquer Ceylon and rule it between 43 and 29 B.C. We have also seen that a Pandya King sent an embassy to Augustus in 20 B.C.

The regular history of the Pandya Kingdom begins from the Tamil *'Sangam'* and its literature in the first century A.D. The *Sangam* literature comprises 30,000 lines of poetry. These are arranged in eight anthologies. There is also another collection known as the *Ten Idylls*. The Pandya territory comprised the modern districts of Tinnevelly, *Ramnad* and *Madura* with its capital at *Madura*.

Among important Pandya Kings are mentioned Mudukudumi Peruvaladi and Nedunjeliyan who defeated a confederacy of hostile kings in the battle of Talaiyalamkanam. Tamil *Sangam* tells us of its prosperity and Brahminism as its religion with performance of Vedic sacrifices by its kings. Another important ruler of the times was Tondaiman Handiraiyan who ruled at Kanchipuram.

The chronological history of the Pandya kingdom may be traced only from eigth and ninth centuries A.D. Before this not much is known about the Pandyas until the time of Kadungan and his son Marayarman under whom in the seventh century A.D. they made themselves felt. The latter's grandson. Arikesari Parankusa Maravarman, was a historical figure known for his victories over the Pravaras (Pallavas) and Keralas. The latter were defeated at Nelveli. Thus he greatly increased his kingdom by these conquests. He was probably the Kun Pandya of the Saiva tradition. At the instance of his queen *Mangaiyarkkarasi*, a Chola princess, and of his ascetic Minister Kulachchirai. he was converted from Jainism to Saivism by *Jananasambandar*.

He was succeeded by his son *Kochchadaivan Ranadhira* (713-30 A.D.), who carried his arms further by defeating the *Marhatta.* Supposed to be the Chalukya Vikramaditya I His dominion included Mangalore and Kongu. H. defeated an *Ay* Chief.

His son *Maravarman Rajasimha* I (730-765 A.D solidated these conquests and subdued Pallavamalla Pallava King. He even made *Pallavamalla* prisoner fort of *Nandipura* near Kumbakonam but later on chandra, the Pallava general, resuced the king and even headed chitramaya, Rajasimha's protege on the P throne.

He was succeeded by his son *Jatila Parantaka Varag* who reigned for nearly fifty years (765-815 A.D.) coming the Kongu Kingdom and also the kingdom of Vena the south. He was thus victorious in his struggle with *PaNandivarman.* H at Pennagadam and Araisur. He Vilinam near Trivandrum. He also defeated an Ay under him the Pandya Kingdom had its largest exten thus came to comprise the whole territory extending the south of the Kaveri to Salem and Coimbatore distr.

He was succeeded by his son *Srimaria Srivallabha* (815-62 A.D.) who according to a Sinhalese account, invade Ceylon then under Sena I. but according to an Indian count, was beaten back by the king who even sacked capital and seized the Pandya throne and placed on its own nominee. But Srimara, however, had to his credit victory over the Pallavas at Kudamukku as admitted by them . But this defeat was avenged by the Pallava King Nripatuaga at Airichit.

The next Pandya King *Varagunavarman* H (c. 862-880 A.D.) was installed on the throne by the Ceylonese general. He had to defend himself against attacks of both Pallavas and Cholas, and was later defeated by the Pallava King *Aparajita*, son of *Nripatunga* at Sripurambiyan in 880 A.D.

He was succeeded by his brother and then by his nephew *Chandrabhanu.* King of Malay Peninsula, who ruled over a part of Ceylon.

Both Chera (Kerala) and Ceylon became part of Pandya Empire. *Sundara Pandya* routed the *Hayasalas* under *Somesvara* whom he killed in a battle at *Srirangam* and conquered *Konnanur-Koppam*. Pandya records tell of another Hayasala defeat at Perambalur. At the same time, the Pandya King beat back the Kakatiya king of Warrangal helping a local chief against him. Thus by his conquests, Sundara assumed the imperial title *Maharajadhiraja*. Inscriptions record his endowments and building proving his wealth. He reigned up to the third quarter of the thirteenth century A.D.

He was helped by his ally Jatavarman Vir Pandya in the conquest of Kongu and Chola countries laying the foundation of his supremacy.

He was succeeded by Maravarman Kulasekhara. The Pandya system of government was based on joint rulership and sovereignty but it was not understood by foreign travellers who mention independent instead of joint rulers. Maravarman sent expeditions to Travancore and Ceylon where from he carried off the Tooth Relic of the Buddha which was restored to Parakramavahu on his personal application at pandya court.

About this time foreign travellers like Marco Polo and Wassaf tell us of the wealth of the south in pearls and precious stones.

After him there was a civil war resulting in Vira winning the throne. His rival Sundara sought Muslim help. This confusion encouraged Malik Kafur's invasion and led to the disintegration of the Pandya Empire.

In the meanwhile, the Chera King of Travancore, *Ravivarman*, took advantage of the plight of the Pandyas conquered part of the Pandya and Chola territories under Vira Pandya in 1315 A.D. but his further advance was checked the Kakatiyas of Warangal. From this event dates the decline of the Pandya power. Madura became now a centre Muslim power.

Cholas— Their land lay to the north-east of Pandya country and was known as Cholamandalam Coromandel.

The *Sangam* literature mentions some of their mythical kings one of whom ended his life because of his parrot's death from his negligence. The *Mahavamsa* relates the conquest of Ceylon in the second century B.C. by a Chola King name *Elara* who ruled there for fifty years.

Karikala— Karikala ruled in second century A.D. succeeding his grandfather who was killed in battle with the Chera king. He defeated a combination of Pandyas and Keralas (Cheras) and had peace by marrying his daughter to the Kerala prince. He invaded Ceylon whence he carried off 12,000 labourers to work for his irrigation works on the Kaveri. He founded his new capital, the famous Kaveripaddinam, in place of the old capital which Ptolemy calls Orthura (= Uraiyur). He greatly extended his kingdom which, according to a panegyrist extended as far as Himalayas.

Nedumudikilli— He was succeeded by his grandson *Nedumudikilli* under whom the Chola kingdom declined with its capital destroyed by the sea-pirates. Its decline was further hastened by attacks of his neighbouring powers, the Pallavas, Keralas and Pandyas.

It, however, recovered with the decline of the Pandyas in the eighth century A.D. In the ninth century A.D. its king *Vijayalaya* further restored its power when the Pallavas and Pandyas were at war, occupying Tanjore which he made its capital.

Aditya—He was succeeded by his son Aditya in 880 A.D. He defeated the Pallava King Aparajita, conquered his f.49 kingdom and further strengthened his kingdom. He also defeated *Parantaka Viranarayana* and annexed the Kongu country. He married a daughter of Krishna II who bore him a son named *Kannaradeva*. Aditya was a devout Saiva and built many temples in honour of Siva.

Parantaka I (907-955 A.D.) — He was succeeded by his worthy son Parantaka I who sacked the Pandya capital, Madura, and won the title *Madurarikonda*, as already stated. The exiled Pandya King Rajasimha tried to recover his kingdom with the help of the Ceylonese army but was routed.

But the Chola king had to meet a new trouble from the *Rashtrakutas*. Parantaka, however defeated *Rashtrakuta* Krishna II at Vallala with the help of his Ganga feudatory, Prithvipati II, sometime before 915 A.D. Later on, the Rashtrakutas under Krishna III and Butuga II defeated and killed in battle his heir, Rajaditya Chola, at Takkolam (949 A.D.). The next five Chola kings tried in vain to arrest Rashtrakuta advance. The Rashtrakutas even occupied the Chola city of Kanchi and besieged the capital, Tanjore.

Inscriptions of Parantaka throw light on the self-governing village communities under Chola administration, such as those of *Uttaramallur*. He was also a patron of learning. In his time flourished Venkata Madhava, one of the earliest commentators of the *Rig-Veda*. Parantaka created a temple at Tondaimanad in honour of his father who died there.

Rajaraja—The Cholas under Rajaraja (985-1014 A.D.) had a better time when the Rashtrakutas were checked by the Chalukyas. Rajaraja then strengthened his position in the south by annexing the Kerala king dom and dominating the Pandya. He also destroyed the Kerala fleet in a naval battle off the Malabar Coast. His southern conquest extended as far as Travancore as its northern as far as Kalinga through the country of the state. He then annexed the northern half of Ceylon to his kingdom. Its king Mahinda V took shelter in the southern of the island. Rajaraja sacked Anuradhapura and Po ruva became the capital of the Chola province of coast. He also conquered almost the whole of Mysore which was then divided into a number of small chiefships,

Gangapadi. *Tadigaipadi* and *Nolambapadi*. He was also able to place his protege *Saktivarman* on the throne of against Bhima who was helped by Chalukya Satyasara. Thus under him the Chola Empire included within its limits the whole of South India. But his last days were troubled by the Chalukyas of the Southern Deccan. His son, Rajendra Chola, however, defeated Satyasraya reduced the famous Chalukya fortress at Kollipakkai (Kulpak). He cultivated friendly relations with Emperor Maravijayottungavarman of Sri Vijaya who built the Chudamani Vihara at Negapatan. In 1012 A.D. he immortalized himself in history by constructing the monumental temple named Rajarajesvara temple at Tanjore, bearing an inscription recording his glorious history. It was also lavishly endowed by him by thebooty of his victories.

Rajendra Uttama Chola (1014-1044) — He was succeeded by his son Rajendra Uttamachola who as crown-prince helped his father in his campaigns and as King invaded the Dharwar Country. He,however, suffered a reverse at the hands of the more powerful Chalukya King Satyasraya. He then overran Ceylon, kept its King Mahinda V Prisoner for life in the Chola capital and recovered his heir-looms lost there. He also carried the Kerala crown to the royal treasury. In the north he avenged his earlier defeat by the Chalukya King by defeating his successor *Jayasimha* II at *Maski* in 1019. His army drove away Vijayaditya of Vengi who helped Jayasimha II out of his territory. He continued his advance conquerring on his way the Eastern Ganga King Madhukamarnava of Kalinga and Kosala and reaching Bengal where he defeated its King *Mahipala* and his feudatories Govindachandra and Rana Sura on the Ganges assuming the title *Gangaikonda*. Across the Bay of Bengal he launched a naval expedition against Sangrama Vijayottungavarman of Sri Vijaya and conquerred Kadara (Kedah in Malay Peninsula) (Leyden Inscription). His victories are recorded in inscriptions.

In his domestic administration, he was equally efficient, founding a new capital at Gangaikonda-Cholapuram with its irrigation system, temple and palace of which the ruins are still to be seen. He also cultivated friendly relations with the Celestial Empire of China where he sent ambassadors in 1016 and 1033 A.D.

Rajadhiraja (1044-52)— He was succeeded by his son Rajadhiraja who began as a joint king with his father from 1018 A.D. and as King had to fight his father's enemies. In the south he had to punish his rebellious vassals, the Pandya and Kerala Kings. He defeated Chalukya Vikramaditya (later Vikramaditya VI) at Dhannada and Pundur. He occupied Yadgir and even sacked Kalyani, the new Chalukya capital. There he performed a *Virabhisheka*, assumed the title *Virarajendra* and carried off a fine *Dvarapalaka* image as part of of booty. After checking Chalukya advance in the north, he invaded Ceylon where he killed four kings in battles. He celebrated these conquests by performing the horse sacrifice and assuming the title of *Jayamkonda Chola*. He was later slain in battle with the Chalukya King some svara I at Koppan on the Tungabhadra in 1054 A.D.

Rajendra II (1054-1063) — But his brother Rajendra gave a new turn to the battle by defeating the invader. Its result, however, is differently told in Chola and Chalukya records. Bilhana, the author the *Vikramankadevacharitan* credits the Chalukya King with the conquest of Kanchi while Chola record credits the Chola king Rajendra with the sack of Kolhapur where he erected a pillar of victory.

During his reign there was a famine in the Chola country in 1055 A.D.

Rajendra crowned his career by his invasion of Ceylon and driving its King Vijayavah to seek shelter in a hilly fort. His inscriptions testify to the vast extent of his Empire. He died in 1063 A.D.

Vira Rajendra (1063-1070)—He was succeeded by his brother Vira Rajendra. He had to meet the invasion of the Chalukya King *Somesvara* I across the *Tungabhadra* and defeated him at Kudal-Samgamam. The Chalukya challenge was soon repeated but not pressed.He built a pillar of victory on the Tungabhadra. Shortly afterwards Somesvara I died while his second son. Vikramaditya VI. came to Chola court and acknowledged Chola suzerainty against his brother Somesvara II. Vikramaditya married the daughter of the Chola King who promised him support to regain Chalukya throne.

In the meanwhile the King of Ceylon took advantage of Chola-Chalukya conflict to expel the Cholas from Ceylon.

Vira Rajendra died in 1070 A.D. There was a contest for the throne after him. The heir apparent, Adhirajendra, was helped to it by the Western Chalukya prince, his brother-in-law Vikramaditya VI. He had a short uneventful reign.

The Eastern Chalukya and Chola alliance based on blood-relationship has been already dealt with.

Kulottunga (c.1063-1112) — Adhirajendra was succeeded by Western Chalukya Viceroy of Vengi, Rajendra II. Who came to the Chola throne as *Kulottunga* Chola. He was in fact three fourths Chola inblood. In him were unit-Eastern Chalukya and Chola Kingdoms.

In the beginning there was troubled by the Western Chalukya prince Vikramaditya VI seeking to avenge the humiliation of his brother-in-law while he was helped by his brother, the Western Chalukya King

Somesvara II, as already narrated. The later history of this episode is already given. Kulottunga had also to fight the Pandyas and Keralas whom he defeated in several battles at Semponmari. Kottara, Vilinam and Salai. He made peace with Vijayavahu of Ceylon by marrying his daughter Suryavalli to Virapperuma, a Sinhalese prince.

Kulottunga ruled from his capital at Kanchi and appointed his son. Vikrama Chola, Governor of Vengi. His inscriptions tell us of his victories in the neighbourhood and also in distant Kalinga with his general Karunakara Tondaman in 1111 A.D. as already stated.

Kulottunga carried out a land survey and settlement as the basis of taxation. His inscriptions also testify to the highly organized system of fiscal and local administration. He reigned for 49 years up to 1118 A.D. He had diplomatic relations with Kanauj as also with far off countries like Sri Vijaya, Kambuja. China, and Pagan in Burma.

Vikrama (1118-1133) — He was succeeded by his son Vikrama Chola, Viceroy of Vengi. He was troubled by the Hayasala push from the south. His power declined in Eastern Chalukya Kingdom but his southern dominion remained intact. He constructed anew the *Nataraja* temple at Chidambaram and repaired the *Ranganatha* temple of Srirangam.

Kulottunga II (1133-1150) — In 1133 A.D. he was succeeded by Kulottunga II, a patron of letters. He removed the Vishnu image from the Nataraja shrine of Chidambaram.

Rajaraja II (1150-1173)— The next king was Rajaraja II who came to the throne in 1150. During his reign of 23 years, the Chola power practically ceased to be, due to Hayasala expansion under Vishnuvardhana. Its hold on the Pandya Kingdom was already weakened by civil war .

Rajadhiraja II — His successor Rajadhiraja II took part in the civil war and set his nominee Kulasekhar on the Pandya throne.

Kulottunga III — The next King Kulottunga III had also to take part in this civil war.

Rajadhiraja III (1216 — 1256 A.D) — He was succeeded by Rajadhiraja III in 1216 A.D. when the Pandyas eclipse the Chola power, sacked Tanjore and made the Chola vassal. At this time the Chola, King recoverd his power with Hayasala help under Narasimha II and arrested the collapse of the Chola Empire.

In 1232 A.D. a powerful Pallava chief named hop Perunjimga of Sendamangalam made the Chola King captive. He was released and re-instated on his throne by his Hamaslally. He ruled up to 1256 A.D.

His later days saw the rapid decline of Chola power due to domestic strife and attacks from all sides, from the Pandyas, Hayasalas and Kakatiyas. He had to share power with his rival, Rajendra III, who ruled at Tanjore from 1246 to 1267 A.D. In 1243 A.D. the Pallava chief Kop Perunjimga II declared his independence. The Havasala and Kakatiyas partitioned his Empire which was now practically extinguished.

Kerala—Kerala kingdom comprised in its South the modern Travancore State and Cochin in the north. The history of Kerala is not so known as that of the other two kingdoms. The Kerala State, like the other two prospered for its foreign trade with the west in the first three centuries.

Its King Adan I was killed in a battle with Karikala Chola in the second century A.D. There was no peace between the two and Adan II married the daughter of Karikala. Later Adan II allied himself with the Pandya King Nedunjiliyan, fought the Cholas but was defeated at Vennil and then committed suicide. But hsi successor Sanguttavan had a better time when his alliance was sought by Karikala successor Nedumudikilli. Kerala poets speak of his northern campaigns up to the Ganges.

He was succeeded by his warlike son Yanaikkan who battled against both Pandyas and Cholas. He was taken prisoner and released by the former.

Kerala history is blank up to the eighth century A.D., when Pallava King Paramesvara Potavarman defeated its king twice.

Venad (South Kerala, then independent, was conquered by the Pandya King Jatila Parakrama who destroyed its fort Vilinam.

The Kerala King Sthanuravi was, however, able in regaining the lost territory within ten years as an ally of the Chola King Aditya, as stated in a document. As already seen, Kerala offered its refuge to the Pandya King Rajasimha seeking it against Chola invasion of Parantaka I about 918 A.D. who afterwards married a Kerala princess. Later, he counted the Chola as his overload. The next Chola King Parantaka II also married a Kerala princess. The Kerala King Bhaskara Ravivarman is known for setting a Jewish colony at Cranganore in the time of the Roman trade and colonies.

Next, we already know of the destruction of the Kerala fleet by Rajaraja Chola who finally conquered the country. This conquest was repeated by his grandson Rajadhiraja as stated in his Manimangalam inscription.

Kerala power was, however, restored under *Vira* Kerala in the twelfth centruy A.D. His successor *Vira Ravivarman* acknowledged Pandya suzerainty. The Chera King shared the defeat of his ally, the Pandya King by Kulottunga III who, however, re-instated him on his throne. King Ravivarman Kulasckhara who ruled from 1299 claims to have conquered both

Chola and Pandya kingdoms about 1315 A.D. when they were weakened by their civil war and Muslim invasion. Later, he was driven back from Chola country by Kakatiya Rudra II and his successor Martandavarman and ruled over South Kerala (Travancore) from 1317 A.D. The later history of Kerala is that of modern Tranvancore.

Pallavas : Pallava power came into prominence in the set-back of Chola between the fifth and ninth centuries A.D. It once came to include the entire Chola country among the Coromondal Coast up to the lower Krishna of old Andhra country together with its capital kanchi. Thus the Pallavas ruled over *Tondaimandalam*.

The Pallavas were hitherto supposed to be of foreign origin connected with the Pahlavas. But their origin is now found nearer home. They were eight of Tondaimandalam, a province of Asoka's empire which included the *Pulindas* identified with the Kudumbas of Tondaimandalam. Pallava may also be taken to be a variant of Palada (*Pulinda* of Asoka). Later the Pallavas became feudatory to the Satavahanas after their conquest of Tondaimandalam. It may be noted that the term *Tondaiyar* is a Tamil rendering of *Pallava*. This explains why their earliest documents are in *Prakrit* and Sanskrit, and not in Tamil. Their old capital was the famous city of Kanchi whichis even mentioned in the *Mahabhashya* of Patanjali in the second century B.C.

Some of this history is traceable in copper-plates in Prakrita in the third century A.D. in the Sanskrit records of the fifth and Sixth centuries A.D. and, lastly, in the ample records of the seventh, eighth and ninth centuries A.D. in both Sanskrit and Tamil. *Samudra* Gupta's mention of Vishnugopa of Kanchi in the Allahabad Pillar Inscription is a land-mark in Pallava history. Vishnugopa is also mentioned in the Pallava genealogy of inscriptions.

Among the early Pallava Kings is named one Asokavarma who may be identified with the great Maurya Emperor Asoka. A Pallava King came into conflict with the Andhra Kingdom under Gautamiputra (second century A.D.) as recorded in an inscription of Andhra queen Bala Sri. Rudradaman I mentions the Pallavas in his Junagadh Inscription (150 A.D.). Some Pallava nobles served in the Andhra court. The Pallavas came into power with the decline of the Andhras and began with the Telegu country south of the Krishna.

Early Pallava inscriptions mention *Bappa* (= *Vijavapta*) as the founder of the Pallava Kingdom. He is also supposed to have the name Simhavarman. He was followed by Sivaskandavarman, Buddhyankura and Visvavarman. Vishnugopa was of the fourth century A.D. *Bappa* may be dated to 225-50 A.D. The Pallavas began with their capital at *Amaravati*. An inscription of Bappa of his tenth regnal year mentions the crown-prince.

The second King *Sivaskanda* performed a horse sacrifice and assumed the title *Vijayaskandavarman* in celebration of his conquest by which Pallava power was extended in the south at the expense of the Chola.

A different tradition recorded in a North Arcot inscription of the ninth century A.D. mentions *Virakurcha* instead of Bappa as the founder of the dynasty, and his son *Skandavarman* or *Skandasishya*. This inscription also states that the Pallava Kings were of Naga origin. The two may be identical. The Sanskrit group of inscriptions mention thirteen Pallava rulers after Vishnugopa between Skandavarman and Simhavishnu (c. 575-600 A.D.) with whom begins the Pallava history proper. It may, in this connexion, be recalled that the Pallavas in the fourth century A.D. imposed their suzerainty on the Kadambas.

As usual in South Indian history, Pallava Kingdom was split up into two branches, one ruling in the Telegu country with its capital at Amaravati and the other in the Tamil (*Tondaimandalam*) country with its capital at Kanchi.

Pallava history henceforth may be traced in the contacts with the histories of other kingdoms of the south. With the help of their allies, the Gangas, the Pallavas conquerred the Banas. A Pallava king named Nanakkasa of the fifty century A.D. is stated in a Kadamba record to have sacked the Kadamba country under its King Krishnavarman. His son Sivananda turned an ascetic at the ruin of his country. His son Vishnuvarman was restored to his kingdom by the Pallavas. Fifty years later a Kadamba prince named Ravivarman was good enough to have 'uprooted the lord of Kanch' (Pallava).

The Pallava King was defeated byhis Ganga feudatory Durvinita of the sixth century A.D.

With Simhavishnu Pataraja Avanisimha, (575-600 A.D.). Pallava power becomes more important from the seventh century A.D. The Pallavas became noted as great builders, chewing caves out of rocks after the Nasik caves. We owe to them some of the great temples of the South.

Simhavishnu's successors speakof him as a great conqueror who carried his arms through Pandya country up to Ceylon. Simhavishnu may be said to have inaugurated a new era, both political and cultural. He conquered the Chola county and his dominion extended from the Krishna to the Kaveri. He also introudced elements of Vedic religion and civilization into Pallava society.

Mahendravarman- He was succeeded in about 600 A.D. by his son Mahendravarman *Mattavilasa Vichitrachitta -Gunabhara* (600-630 A.D.) who ruled over a large kingdom he inherited from his father. He came into conflict with the Chalukyas under

Pulakesin II and lost to him Vengi permanently in 610 A.D. In his Aihole inscription Pulakesin claims to have driven him back down to Kanchi but this account is refuted in his own inscription stating that he routed the Chalukyas at the battle of Pollilur, near Kanchi.

The conflict with the Chalukyas, however, drove the Pallavas to seek expansion in the south, Mahendravarman was known for his patronage of letters and fine arts including music. He was himself the author of a comedy called *Mattavilasaprahasana* giving an account of the Kapalika sect. He was also the innovator of a new style of rock-cut temple architecture. He was at first a Jain but later under the influence of the famous saiva saint. Tirunavukkarasa or Appur, became a Saiva.

A worthy memorial was erected by his worthy grandson in the Adivaraha temple excavated in the rocks of Mahavallipuram showing the portraits in sculpture of the king and his two wives and also of his father and two wives.

Narasimhavarman-Mahamalla- He was succeeded by Narasimhavarman_Mahamalla (630-668 A.D.). He repelled a Chalukya invasion led by Pulakesin II whom he defeated repeatedly in battles and invaded Chalukya territory, sacking its capital Badami and returning to Kanchi with large spoils. In the course of the siege of Badami Pulakesin was killed in 642 A.D. Narasimhavarman then called himself Vatapikonda. His general in all these campaigns was Paramjyoti. At this time a Ceylonese prince, Manavarma, sought shelter in his court and induced him to invade Ceylon. The invasion, however, failed of its purpose which was fulfilled by a later invasion properly equipped. His victory is compared to that of Rama in contemporary inscriptions. Narasimha was, however, later defeated by Chalukya Vikramaditya who also defeated his two successors, Mahendravarman II and Paramesvaravarman I.

Narasimhavarman was a great builder who has given to India the beautiful series of temples at Mamallapuram named after him.

The Chinese pilgrim *Yuan Chwang* visited Kanchi in this time and refers to it as a Buddhist colony though it had a large Hindu population of different sects. *Dharmapala*, the Buddhist teacher, was a native of Kanchi where Yuan Chwang saw Asokan topes. According to Yuan Chwang, Jainism was also flourishing.

Mahendravarman II — Narasimhavarman was succeeded by Mahendravarman II (668-70 A.D.) who ruled for a short time in peace.

Paramesvaravarman I (670-680 A.D.) - The next king Paramesvaravarman I (c. 670-680 A.D.) had again to face, as already stated, a conflict with the Chalukyas. Paramesvara claims tohave conquered a Chalukya town named Ranarasika. He was, however, at first defeated by Bhuvikrama, the Ganga all of the Chalukya King Vikramaditya at *Vilande* and also by the Pandyas at Nelveli and Sankaramangai, Paramesvara I made a successful raid on Badami whereupon Vikramaditya harried his kingdom and advanced as far as Uraiyur (near Trichy). In a battle in this region Paramesvara defeated Vikramaditya and "made Vikramaditya whose army consisted of several lakhs take fo flight covered by a rag". We have already narrated the course of conflict with the Pallavas and Pandyas in the south ending with the battle of Peruvalanallur as described in the Kurrum plates.

Narasimhavarman II - The next king was Narasimhavargan II Rajasimha (c. 680-720 A.D.) who reigned in peace which he utilized in architectural activities. He built the famous temple of Rajasimhesvara Kailasanatha of Kanchi. In his court probably lived the great Sanskrit author *Dandin*. In 720 A.D. he sent an ambassador to the Chinese Emperor who bestowed great honour upon him and his army "which was to be employed to chastise the Arabs and the Tibetans." His intervention in the politics of distant Tibet is not, however, understood.

The next king was Paramesvaravarman II who probably died about 731 A.D.

Nandivarman II- He was followed by Nandivarman II Pallavamala (c. 731-796 A.D.) who had to contest the throne with his kinsman Chitramaya supported by the Pandyas. His general Udayachandra inflicted upon his enemies a crushing defeat. His Vaikuntha Perumal Temple inscription states that he was popular with his people who elected him to the throne. He reigned for sixty-five years. We have already narrated how Chalukya Vikramaditya II invaded his territory upto Kanchi. Later *Nandivarman* recovered his capital and invaded his neighbouring kingdoms in the South. At one time he was besieged in his city of Nandipura by Tamil armies which his intrepid general Udayachandra routed. He then carried his arms towards the north and father south. Thus Nandivarman had to battle against the Gangas under Sripurusha. Tamils and Chalukyas.

In the middle of the eighth century the Pallava power had to meet a new menace in the Rashtrakutas who under Dantidurga, as already stated, marched as far as Kanchi. This invasion was repeated fifty years later by Govinda III. The next King Dantivarman (796-840) (who was descended from a Rashtrakuta princes, daughter of Dantidurga) lost much of his territory to the Pandya King towards the end of his reign. He was succeeded by his son Nandivarman III (840-65 A.D.) who checked the Pandya advance and that of other enemies.The next king was Nripatungavarman (865-906) who achieved a victory over the Pandyas under Sri Mara at Airichit. His successor Aparajita also defeated the Pandyas at Sri Purambiyan with the help of the Gangas. But he was defeated by Chola Aditya I who recovered in Chola territory of Tondaimandalam sometime after the first century A.D. Pallava dynasty practically came to an end with Aparajita. India owes to the Pallavas some of the greatest monuments of art as already mentioned.

The Kadambas: Mayurasarman- There is another South Indian power whose history merits attention. It will be remembered that the Satavahanas of Kuntala (West Deccan and North Mysore) were succeeded by the Chutus with their capital at *Vaijayanti* (= Buzantian of the Periplus). The next rulers of Kuntala were the Pallavas whose plan was taken later by the Kadambas. Kadamba power was founded by Mayurasarman, a learned Brahmin who first went to Pallavendrapuri (Kanchi) with his Guru Virasarma for the purpose of studying the entire Veda (*Pravachanam nikhilam*) . There he had a quarrel with a mounted spy (*Asvasamstha*) as a result of which he became military, defeated the Pallava *Antapalas* and occupied the forested country upto Sriparvata or Srisailam (Kurnool District). Afterwards hehad a compromise with the Pallavas whose vassalage he accepted with gifts of territory on the western sea. He later issued the *Chandravalli Prakrit* inscription. This credits him with extensive conquests of *Abhira,* Traikutaka, Pallava, Pariyatrika, Sakasthana, Sayindaka, Punata and Mokari territories, after which he performed 18 horse sacrifices. His date is c. 340-370 A.D. We may assume that he took advantage of the troubled conditions following Samudra Gupta's invasion of the south to found a kingdom for himself.

Kanga — He was succeeded by is son *Kanga* who changed the dynastic title from Sarman to Varman. In his time Kuntala was annexed by Vindhyasena Vakataka.

Bhagiratha— But his son Bhagiratha (395-120 A.D.) regained the kingdom. There is a tradition preserved in the *Anchitya-Vichara Gharitram* of Kshemendra that the poet Kalidasa led an embassy which was sent by Chandra Gupta H. Vikramaditya for purposes of a marriage alliance to the Kuntalesvara who was perhaps Kangavarman.

Kakusthavarman - A distinguished successor was Kakusthavarman whose Talgonda Inscription records his marriage alliances with the Guptas and their royal families.

Later Kadambas - After his death, the kingdom was partitioned among his two sons. One of their successors Mrigesavarman (475-490 A.D.) defeated the Western Gangas and the Pallavas. He became a Jain. His son Ravivarman (497-537) was a powerful ruler who agian checked the Western Gangas. But under his son Harivarman (537-547) Pulakesin I Chalukya, who was a feudatory, established his kingdom at Badami.

The other Kadamba Kingdom with its capital at Triparvata (Halebid) attained some importance. But their kings were vassals of the Pallavas. King *Ajavarman* (565-606 A.D.) became a vassal of Kirtivarman I Chalukya. We know how Pulakesin II besieged Banavasi. They tried to recover their power after Pulakesin II but in vain.

Kalabhras - A people called the Kalabhras for a time played a notorious part in South Indian history. They were ruthless conquerors who overthrew many *Adhirajas* and resumed even *Brahmadeya* land. They are referred to in Pallava and Chalukya inscriptions and were ultimately subdued by Pallava Simhavishnu and Narasimhavarman and Chalukya Vikramaditya I and Vikramaditya II. They were able to terrorize the Tamil country for a few centuries. Their chief Achyuta-Vikranta menaced the Cholas. The predatory Kalabhras did not show any regard for land grants. Ultimately their power was broken by Kodungon Pandya, Simhavishnu Pallava and Chalukya expeditions against them. Originally they were the vassals of the Pallavas and Pandyas. In Tanjore, they ruled as Pallava vassals from the eighth to the eleventh century.

South Indian history knows of a few local and feudatory dynasties.

(1) *The Banas* are known from their inscriptious found in Kolar and North Arcot districts. A Kind known as the great Bana was a foeman worthy of Mayurasarman and also of Harivarman Ganga as well Simhavishnu I Pallava. The Bana king *Jayanandivarman* is described as the unique hero of great might ruling over the land to the west of the Andhra country. His predecessor is even extolled as a *Bodhisattva* in compassion. But in the main, the *Banas* were feudatories of the Pallavas.

(2) *The Alupas* were another local power who ruled over the Tuluva country (S. Canara) with their capital at Udayavara near Udipi. Ptolemy refers to a people called Oliokhora (= Aluvakheda). An inscription refers to the Alupas as ruling on the wesern coast in the fifth century A.D. and had to be conquered by the Western Chalukya Kings Kirtivarman I and Pulakesin II. We find the Alupa chief Gunasagara as Chalukya Governor of Banavasi in c. 650 A.D. His son Chitravahana (c.675-700 A.D.) was a very famous king.

Greater India - This term we first used in our work called, *'The Fundamental Unity of India'* (London, 1914) and was approved by Dr. F.W. Thomas (ex-

Boden Professor of Sanskrit of Oxford University) as very appropriate to indicate those countries which were influenced by Indian thought and culture. These countries were situated both in the North-West and North, and also towards East and South-East of India. The former were approached by land-routes and the latter mainly by sea-route from India.

It may be noted that the growth of this Greater India was ultimately governed by a Principle of cultural comprehension and synthesis by which different and foreign elements could be reconciled and accommodated within the breadth of the parent system. Such a principle received expression in representative Sanskrit Texts like the *Mahabharata* which ordains Vedic duties and rites even for such foreign peoples as 'Yavanas, Kiratas, Gandharas, Tusharas, and Pahlavas living in Aryan Kingdoms". Thus Indian societies multiplied in foreign countries, in Indonesia, and other countries on the mainland and overseas.

Its Earliest Edivence - We have already seen how from remote antiquity there was considerable commercial and cultural intercourse between India and parts of the Western world, but we are concerned here not so much with this intercourse as with India's cultural expansion indifferent directions. We may recall in this connexion a concrete proof already cited, of its outstanding and early phase showing how important Rig-vedic deities like Indra and Varuna. Mitra and the two Asvins or Nasatyau, established themselves as the national deities worshipped by remote Mesopotamian peoples like the Hittite and Mitanni even before 1400 B.C.

Asoka's Foreign Missions- The next outstanding phase of this movement is indicated in the Inscriptions of Asoka of c. 258 B.C. in his despatch of Ambassadors (*Dutas*) in charge of his foreign missions to carry out in five Western countries named Syria. Macedon, Epirus, Cyrene and Egypt his strictly pacifist programme of the extension abroad of humanitarian measures for the relief of physical suffering. It was inspired by the specific Indian religion of Non violence and Universal Brotherhood, a sense of the unity and affinity of all life, and his own message of Cultural Conquest (*Dharma-Vijaya*) to replace violent conquest (*Asuravijaya*).

We may add to this the evidence of Buddhist texts like the *Mahavamsa* stating that the Third Buddhist Council held at Pataliputra under Moggaliputta Tissa as its President in Asoka's time (in c. 253 B.C.) despatched missioners to foreign and frontier countries for the propagation of Buddhism as a Universal Religion based upon moral life. These countries are named (1) *Suvarnabhumi* (2) *Lanka* (3) Yavana and (4) Himalaya (*Himavanta-pradesa*). Lanka corresponded to Ceylon and Suvarnabhumi as shown below, was the name applied in ancient literature to the Malay Peninsula and the neighbouring islands.

Later Outposts of Indian Culture- We may next refer to the many outposts of Indian and Buddhist culture which the Chinese travellers both Fa-Hien (in the fifth century A.D.) and Yuan Chwang (in the seventh century A.D.) found flourishing in countries lying along the land-routes leading from China to Indian in those days. These have been already described. They were the results of the prominent part played by India in Central Asian politics under the Kushana Emperors specially Kanishka. I as already narrated.

We may note here briefly the principal countries which became the seats of Indian culture and marked the stages in the progress of Buddhism towards China by overland routes trodden by travellers like Yuan Chwang. There were three such routes of intercourse opened up between India and China and along these grew up centres of both *Brahminical* and Buddhist Culture. One route passed through Afghanistan and the Kabul valley across the Hindukush into Sogdiana between the Oxus and the Jaxartes, thence through the passes of Tian-shan (*Celestial*) Mountains up to *Uch Turfan*. Another passed through Tokharistan and the Pamirs up to *Kashgarh*. A third passed from Gilgit through Yasin and Tash Kurghan to Kashgarh. From here travellers had to face the Tarim Basin and took the routes along its northern or Southern parts, avoiding the central Taklamakan desert. The former route was marked by settlements at Kuchi, Karashar and Turfan and the Southern by Kashgarh. Yarkand, Khotan. Niyan. Dandan Uilik and Endere, with their meeting points at Yu-men-Kuan and Tun-huang on Chinese frontier.

We shall now describe some of these settlements as outposts of Indian Culture.

There were

(1) *Bamiyan*, a centre of Buddhism from first century A.D. as shown in its grottos shaped into Buddhist temples, colossal images of the Buddha, carved out on stone and Buddhist MSS found:

(2) *Bactriana* which remained a Buddhist country under its different rulers, Greeks, Sakas, Yuch-Chis and Hunas and was known for its great monastery of Navasamgharama seen by Yuan Chwang.

(3) Sogdiana (Samarkand and Bokhara), another Buddhist country which had its own Buddhist literature (Sogdian) of which fragments have been unearthed. A famous Sogdian scholar was Seng-hun (Samghabhadra) who translated Buddhist texts into Chinese (3rd century A.D.):

(4) *Kashgarh:*

(5) *Yarkand*, both of which contained hundreds of Buddhist monasteries by seventh century A.D.

(6) *Khotan*, of which Asoka's son Kunala was the fabled ruler and the famous monastery was Gomati-Vihara whose teachers composed their own Buddhist Canonical texts. Khotan tradition dates advent into it of Buddhism in about 60 B.C. A Chinese story refers to Buddhist books received in China from an envoy of the Great Yueh-Chi in 2 B.C. evidenty from Khotan. In Khotan have been found many Indian texts, such as *Dhammapada* written in Kharoshthi (2) *Suryagarbha-Sutra* (589-615 A.D). (3) *Prajnaparamita,* (4) *Saddharma-Pundarika*. There are found other texts in Khotan-Sanskrit, such as (1) *Gosringa-Vyakarana* and (2) *Vimalaprabha-Pariprichchha* of 741-45 A.D. and an epic in Khotani language.

(7) *Dandan Uilik* where Sir Aurel Stein discovered "fresoes inscribed with Indian Brahmi characters. stucco relievos representing objects of Buddhist worship and a genuine paper MS. in Central Asian Brahmi." In their style of composition and figures, these fresoes resemble those of Ajanta. There have also been found at this site "oblong leaves of paper covered with old Brahmi characters of Gupta type." "belonging to at least four distinct MSS. of which three are in Sanskrit and may be dated to "fifth or sixth century". The numeral 132 occurring on one page of the MSS. indicates its pagination.

(8) *Niya* is another site where have been found inscribed tablets numbering over 500, besides "about two dozen Kharosthi documents on leather" and "written in black ink" together with "a pen of tamarisk wood". They are written in Prakrit with admixture of Sanskrit terms as may be seen in such expressions as *Mahanuva maharaya lihati* = Sanskrit *Mahanubhavo Maharajo likhati,* His Highness the Maharaja writes'; or such words as *putraso, pramane, pathame, etc*. The language and the script confirm the tradition that they were introduced by immigrants from Taxila who were banished by Asoka. The Niya Kharosthi Script was current at Taxila in the time of Kushana rule. Even the native chiefs of the locality used the title of *Maharaja* in their Kharoshthi documents. It is also to be noted that these hundreds of wooden documents comprise correspondence, official contracts, accounts, miscellaneous memoranda and the like.

(9) *Endere,* where were found fragments of a Sanskrit text written on paper in Brahmi of fifth century A.D bearing page number upto 46.

(10) *Rawak* was another site where were found rows of colossal statues in stucco representing Buddhas or Bodhisattvas, with attending deities and saints in between. The whole of the relieveo work was originally coloured.

(11) *Kuchi,* whose rulers bore Indian names like Suvarnapushpa, Suvarnadeva or Haradeva. Its Buddhist monks spoke Sanskrit and spread Buddhism in China from the third century A.D. They lived in caves dug in its gottos. It may be noted that it was at this place (Kuchar) that the ancient birch-bark Codex known as the 'Bower MS' together with some Sanskrit texts was discovered in 1889 A.D. (Sir Aurel Stein: *Archaeological Tour with Bunner Field Force (pp. 13-14); Innermost Asia in the Geographical Journal for May and June*. 1925; *Archaeological Exploration in Chinese Turkestan*).

(12) *Karasahr* (Agnidesa) was another outpost of Buddhist culture.

(13) *Bazaklik* was another important centre of Buddhism with its hundreds of temples and wall-paintings figuring Indian monks in yellow robes with their names written in Brahmi.

(14) *Tun-huang* was famous for its "Thousand Buddha Stone Caves". It became a Buddhist centre from second century A.D., a meeting ground of Buddhists from different countries, Persia, Bactria, India, Sogdiana, Khotan, Kuchi and the like, on their way to China. It built up a wonderful library of Buddhist MSS., written in various languages, Chinese, Sanskrit, Tibetan, Khotanese, etc. as a great cosmopolitan centre of learning. The Caves contain paintings dating from the fourth century A.D. Some of these show marked Indian influence as that of King Sibi cutting off flesh of his body for ransoming a bird wounded by a vulture.

It may be noted that these Central Asia antiquities, besides those of architecture, sculpture and painting, also include some noted Indian texts. At a place near Khotan, as has been already stated, has been found, for instance, a text of the *Dhammapada* written in Kharoshthi characters of first or second century A.D. Fragments have also been found of some Sanskrit texts lost in India, such as *Udanavarga,* a *Sarvastivada* work, or the last chapter of the drama called *Sariputra-Prakarana* attributed to Asvaghosha, the earliest Sanskrit drama known of about the first century A.D.

Finally, it may be noted that some of these cultural centres represented both Buddhism and Brahminism. For instance, at the two sites mentioned above, viz, Niya, and Endere, have been found seals bearing figures of *Kubera* and *Trimukha* and painted *Ganesa*. At some places are found figures of *Siva* and *Vishnu* (Sir Aurel

Stein: Archeological Tour with Bunner Field Force).

116. R.K. Mookerji; *Chandragupta Maurya and His Times;* Delhi; 1966 p. 4. Hereafter referred as *C.M.H.T.*
117. *A.I.*, pp. 483-84.
118. E.B. Cowell and R.A. Neil; *Divyavadana;* Combridge, 1886; pp. 212, 21. Hereafter cited as *D.V.*
119. *Ibid.*, pp. 14, 15, 210-14, and 388.
120. *Ibid.*, pp. 9-11, 276.
121. *Ibid.*, pp. 21-25, 83.
122. *H.I.*, p. 27.
123. Hari Jaisingh; *India Between Dream and Reality,* New Delhi; 1989, pp. 11-12.
124. *H.I.*, pp. 27-28.
125. R. Nath ; *Colour Decoration in Mughal Architecture;* Bombay: 1970; pp. 51-52.
126. *H.I.*, p. 28.
127. *Ibid.*, p. 29.
128. *C.T.C.C.A.M.I.*, p. 29 *Kanakasabhi; The Tamil Eighteen Hundred Years Ago,* p. 45. Hereafter referred as *T.E.H.Y.A.*
129. *Ibid.*
130. *H.I.*, pp. 29-30.
131. *C.T.C.C.A.M.I.*, p. 29-30.
132. *H.I.*, p. 30.
133. D.V., pp. 21-22, 23-27, 316 and 577.
134. *Ibid.*, pp. 3-5, 349.
135. *Ibid.*, pp. 21-25, 83.
136. *Ibid.*, pp. 3 and 194.
137. *H.I.*, p. 30.
138. *D.V.*, pp. 23-27, 316.
139. *Ibid.*
140. *H.I.*, pp. 30-31.
142. *D.V.*, pp. 26, 391.
143. *Ibid.*, pp. 17, 388.
144. *Ibid.*, pp. 23-27, 316.
145. Lucian Warmingtoon; *Commerce Between the Roman Empire and India* London - p. 212 Hereafter mentioned as *C.B.R.E.I.*
146. *H.I.*, p. 31.
147. *B.K.S.B.* Vol. IV, p. 3824.
148. *Ibid.*
149. *Ibid.*, p. 3823.
150. *H.I.*, p. 31.
151. *Ibid.*, pp. 31-32.
152. Jinavijaya; *Puratana-Prabandha-Samgrata,* Calcutta (India); 1936. p. 17 Hereafter referred as pp.
153. *Ibid.*, p. 9.
154. K.L Vaidya; *The Cultural Heritage of the Himalayans;* New Delhi; 1977, p. 75. Hereafter referred as *C.H.H.*
155. *S.A.E.S.H.I.*, p. 59.
156. Moti Chandra, *loc cit*, P. 13, *D.O.A.I.*, p. 21.
157. Monier Williams, *A Sanskrit English Dictionary*; p. 616.
158. R.V.V.R., pp. 5-6.
159. *D.O.A.I.*, p. 21 Note. this term by the author has be noted from *Atharva-veda*; pp. 18, 4, 31; *Taitsam* pp. 24, 11, 6 ; *Mait Sam*, pp. 44.3. *Tait.*
160. *S.A.E.S.H.I. p. 6 F/n 5.*
161. Moti Chandra, Loc. Cit; p. 15, D.O.A.I., p. 21.
162. *Ibid.*
163. *D.O.A.I.*, p. 21.
164. Panini, *Asta*, pp. 4,3,42 *Valmiki, Ramayana*; pp. 2, 40, 9 *D.O.A.I.*, p. 22.
165. *Mahabharata* PP. 2, 22, 47. *D.O.A.I.*, p. 22.
166. *C.T.C.C.A.M.I.*, p. 30.
167. *D.V.*, p. 316.
168. R.I Mitra; *Lalitavistara*; Calcutta (India); 1877 pp. 1, 113. Hereafter discussed as L.V.
169. *Note.* Indian costumes have taken their own shape and form as elsewhere in the country, according to the climate, social and even political changes that mark the vast span of the Indian History. In a certain way, they also reflect the vicissitudes of the country's long history. They have changed and are still changing, according to taste and utility, yet they are tied to their old fashion trend and traditional moorings. They are shaped by the unavoidable contacts with the outer world; but at the core conform to Indian sentiments of bashfulness and dignity. Against this prespective, Indian Costumes are to be studied and described by the *'Chamar'* as the work of the artisan. But the *Sari* is an endless variety in the Indian texture and in colour, in layout and in decoration, is the predominant female costume of India. It plays down to the wearer's sex, and yet is the most feminine of all known female costumes. Nearer to this is the *Sarong* worn in the far eastern regions of India. Shorter than the *Sari* in total length and coarser in texture and simpler in design, it is wrapped around the breasts from the height of the armpits and below them, reaching only midway between and southern regions of India is the *ghagra* which consists of a densely pleated skirt in plain texture, generally coloured and mostly designed and bordered. Worn at the point of the navel, it is supplement by an upper bodice to cover the breasts, known locally as the *Choli*, with the grown-ups wearing a scarf (*orhni* or *odhni*) *covering* the bodice.

The scarf in this case serves as the much too necessary Indain veil. Completely different in conception is the *Salwar* which with *Kamiz* constitues an entirly district combination as the work of a *Darzi* or tailor. The *Salwar* is a pair of trousers tapering downwards, close fitted at the ankle, and has two varieties, Viz, the one very loose and the other close fitting ones, though both invariably closed at the ankle. The *Kamiz*, the upper part of the body, is a long tunic, and is a sort of loose shirt, butoned up at the front and at the writ and flared at the end, coming down to the mid thigh or the knee. Essentially the outcome of closer contacts with the immediate western neighbours, e.g. the Afghans, the *Salwar* perhaps bears a remote element of similarity to the dress in Central Asia from the second to the ninth century A.D. and carried a definite influence from the Islamic dress of the Mughals. This answers best to the colder climate of the north-western regions and better dispels the dry heat of summer in those regions. A scarf or *orhni*, which is short, light and invaribly of a different texture, serves as the veil, being taken over the head from the right, covering the breasts and this completing the ensembles of the life in natural process (A.K. Bhattacharya, *A Pageant of Indian Culture;* vol.1 Delhi; 1998, p. 109).

170. Watt. *Indian Art at the Delhi Exhibition;* Delhi; 1903, pp. 256-259.
171. *Silappadikaram,* Vol. XIV, P. 203 C.T.C.C.A.M.I., p. 30.
172. *C.B.R.E.I.* p. 170.
173. Watt. *Dictionary of the Economic Product; of India,* pp. 992-1006.
174. *C.B.R.E.I.*, p. 176.
175. *B.K.S.B.*, pp. 4, 3661.
176. *D.O.A.I.*, p. 22.
177. Asvaghosa, *Buddha*; pp. 1,4,5,33, 49, (Quoted from D.O A.I. p. 23)
178. Kali, *Vikram*; pp. 3,12, Kali, *Raghu,* pp. 9, 43, Kali, Ritu, pp. 64, 29; *Sudraka, Mrchchha,* pp. 1, 20. Kali, *Vikram*, *Anka*, p. 3 Kali *Megdhool*; p. 41 (Quoted from *D.O.A.I.* p. 23).
179. Moti Chandra, Pra, Bha, Ve. p. 93 (Quoted from *D.O.A.I.*; p. 23).
180. *D.O.A.I.*, p. 23.
181. *H.I.*, p. 32.
182. *C.H.H.*, p. 76.
183. *B.K.S.B.*, pp. 4, 3661.
184. *D.O.A.I*,. p. 23.
185. *H.I.*, p. 32.
186. *C.H.H.*, p. 78.
187. *H.I.*, p. 32.
188. *D.V.*, p. 316.
189. *Aks; pp. 2, 113 Note.* In this work the pharse which has been interpreted called as *dhautakauseya* used for the 'washed silk'.
190. *H.I.*, p. 32.
191. *Ibid.*
192. *Ibid.*, p. 33.
193. *C.H.H*,. p. 72.
194. *H.I.*, p. 33.
195. *G.S.H.*, p. 1.
196. *H.I.*, p. 33.
197. *D.V.*, p. 316.
198. *H.I.*, p. 32.
199. *Ibid.*, pp. 33-34.
200. *D.O.A.I.*, p. 24.
201. *H.I.*, p. 33.
202. *L.V.*, p. 113.
203. *D.O.A.I.*, p. 24.
204. *H.I.*, p. 33.
205. *Ibid.*, p. 35.
206. *D.O.A.I.*, p. 24.
207. *H.I.*, p. 34.
208. *D.O.A.I.*, pp. 24-25.
209. *H.I.*, p. 34.
210. *B.K.S.B.*, pp. 3, 3661.
211. *D.O.A.I.*, p. 25.
212. *H.I.*, p. 34.
213. *B.K.S.B.*, pp. 4, 3661.
214. *Kali Raghu;* pp. 3, 39 Quoted from *D.O.A.I.* p. 26.
215. *H.I.*, p. 34.
216. *D.O.A.I.*, p. 26.
217. *H.I.*, p. 34.
218. *C.T.C.C.A.M.I.*, p. 32.
219. *D.O.A.I.*, pp. 26-27.
220. *A.I.C.*, pp. 60-61.
221. *Ibid., 60.*
222. *Ibid.*
223. *D.O.A. I., p.* 27.
224. *I.*, pp. 34-35.
225. *Antagadadasa;* P. 34 Noted from *D.O.A.I.*, p. 27.
226. H.I., p. 34.
227. *D.V.*, pp. 23-27, 316.
228. *P. L.J.R.*, p. 116.
229. *A.I.C.*, pp. 10-11.
230. *D.V.*, pp. 23-29, 215.
231. *D.O.A.I.*, p. 19.
232. *D.V.*, pp. 17, 614.
233. *Ibid.*, pp. 17-20, 221.
234. *Ibid.*, pp. 23-27, 316.

235. Gilgit MSS. 3, 2, pp. 95, 95 and *Mahavastu*, 2, p. 116 noted from D.O.A.I., p. 19.

236. ***Note.*** The advantages of position and material resources alone cannot raise a nation to eminence. It was the character and the spirit of the people, "that give all their life and efficacy to them." As in Western Europe, so in Magadha, we have a commingling of races and cultures (K.A.N.Sasastri; *Age of the Nandas and Mauryas*; Varanasi; 1967. p. 9 Hereafter referred as A.N.M.

237. *A.I.C.*, p. 11.

238. *Pre-Aryan and Pre-Dravidian In India;* Tr. by *Bagchi.* p. 160 Noted from *C.T.C.C.A.M.I.*, p. 11

239. ***Note.*** It is very important to record the *Sivi* republic was situated in Southern *Panjab.* The sat of this republic was at *Sibipur,* the modern *Shorkat.*

240. ***Note.*** The cloth seems to have been manufactured in *Vahita* country which was existed in ancient time between the Indus on the west and the Sutlej and Beas rivers and has been bounded on the North by the Outer Himalayas; on the west, by the eastern Hindukush, the *Safed koh*, the *Suleiman* and the Kirthar ranges; on the South,by the surging waters of the Arbian sea and the "immense salt-water waste of the Rann of cutch," and on the east by the sand-dunes of the Thar or the Great Indian Desert and uplands and ridges of the Eastern Panjab, the extensive valley of the Indus and its feeders constituted a little world not much affected by the eddies and currents of Magadhan history before the rise of the Great Mauryas. The country falls into three natural divisions :- (1) The mountainous regions extending from the upper reaches of the Sutlej to the basin of the Chitral and certainoutlying rocky areas; (2) The flat rolling plains of the Panjab intersect by a network of rivers and brooks; and (3) the almost rainless tract of the lower Indus and its delta, an important art of which now forms the province of sind.

The land described above presents grat varieties of scenery of different peoples of the 'Father'. The eyes meet in the north the snowclad speaks and glaciers of the Himalayas and the luxuriant vegetation that clothes the submountane vegetation that clothes the submountane region. A striking contrast to this is afforded by the plains of the Indus, which look like an (*A.N.M. p. 27*) Indological studies the accounts pre-served in classical writings have formed a very valuable source of information. This was mainly due to the fact that there was no history of Pre-Muslim India written by the ancient Indian themselves, and conqsequently very little was known of its political history. Although a mass of Indian literature belonging to the same period supplied a great deal of information on other aspects of history, its value was onsiderably lessened by the two important factors. In the first place, this literature dealt mostly with religious or semi-religious topics and threw only a very dim light on secular affairs, specially political history. Secondly, its value, as it is, was considerably reduced by the fact that is *'Nam'* or *'Kalma'* or *'Word'* not even an approximate date could be assigned to the various literary sources. The classical accounts, on the other hand, were more concerned which we have forgotten with topics other than religious which generating every development of the human life, and the dates of almost all of them were known with a fair degree of accuracy when the saints on earth has to establish the authencity of the nature i.e. 'Ultimate Reality' in one form called *'Nam'*.

241. *Note* An instance of early illusions to the art of painting, the *Vinaya Pitaka*, a Pali *Buddhist* work has already been referred (of pleasure house of king *Pasenade* i.e. Prasenajit containing picture halls *citragaras* adorned with painted figures and decorative patterns). Its date is Pre-Christian (3rd to 4th century B.C.). In *Samyuttanikaya* P. III P. 132; V.II, paintings of male and females figures on wooden boards, walls and cloth have been discussed. (D.N.Shukha, *Royal Arts*; Faizabad (U.P). 1967. p. 190. Hereafter cited as *R.A*)

242. *C.T.C.C.A.M.I.*, p. 12.

243. *A.N.M.*, pp. 25-26.

244. *Ibid.*, 27.

245. R.C. Majumdar; *The Classical Accounts of India; Calcutta; 196. P. XII. Hereafter cited as C.A.I.*

246. *Ibid.*, p. XIV.

247. *Ibid.*

248. *Ibid.*, p. XV.

249. *Ibid.*, p. XVI.

250. *Ibid., pp. XVI-VII Note.* Study the *'History of Ancient Geography*; Vol. 1., p. 635.

251. *Ibid.*

252. *Ibid., p. XVIII, The Cambridge History of India;* Vol. 1, p. 65

253. *Ibid.*

254. *Ibid.*, pp. XIX-XX.

255. *A.I.C.*, pp. 4-5.

256. *C.A.I.*, pp. XI-XII

257. *C.M.H.T.*, p. 5.

258. *Ibid.*, pp. 23-4.

259. *Ibid.*, p. 24.

260. *Ibid.*, pp. 24-5.

261. *Ibid.*, p. 24.

262. *I.C.*, p. 17-8.

263. *Y.C.*, p. 316

264. *C.B.R.E.I.*, p. 160.

265. *Ibid.*
266. *A.I.C.*, p. 11.
267. *H.I.*, p. 35.
268. *C.B.R.E.I.*, p. 161.
269. *Ibid.*
270. *H.I.*, p. 35.
271. *Ibid.*
272. *Ibid.*
273. Rig-Vedic, VIII, pp. 3,67, *Brhadaranyaka* up. II, pp. 3.6 See p. 231, *C.T.C.C.A.M.I.*, p. 231.
274. *C.T.C.C.A.M.I.*, pp. 232-3.
275. *K.A.*, pp. 89-90.
276. *Mahabharata;* Vol. II, pp. 3, 11, 19, 22, 45 and 47.
277. A.Wood; *Journey to the Sources of Oxus; Londōn;* 187, p. 57.
278. *D.V.*, p. 316.
279. *Ibid.*, p. 215.
280. *Ibid.*, p. 221.
281. *Ibid.*, p. 316.
282. Gilgit Texts, III, 2, pp. 95-96 C.T.C.C.A.M.I., p. 236.
283 Charles Hugel; *Travels in Kashmir*; Delhi; 1952, pp. 118-119.
284. M. Kaul, *Desopadesa* and *Narmamala*; Poona (India) 1923, Vol. V, p. 21. Hereafter cited as *D.N.*
285. *A.N.* Vol. 1, p. 32.
286. *D.N.* Vol. 1, pp. 72, 111.
287. *Samayamatrika,* Vol. II, pp. 70 See Page 236, *C.T.C.C.A.M.I.*
288. *D.N.* Vol. II, p. 45.
289. Udaya Prabha Suri; *Dharmabhyudaya*; Vol. 1 Bombay, 1949; p. 71.
290. *R.T.*, Vol. VI, p. 137.
291. *Ibid.*, p. 25.
292. *A.K.*, Vol. 1, p. 32.
293. *R.T.* Vol. VI, p. 27.
294. *Ibid.*, p. 29.
295. *Ibid.*, p. 30.
296. *Ibid.*, p. 31.
297. *A.K.* Vol. 1, p. 31.
298. *Ibid*
299. *Ibid.*, p. 89.
300. *Ibid.*, p. 90.
301. *P.L.J.R.*, p. 116.
302. *A.K.*, Vol. I, pp. 90-91.
303. *William* Moorcroft and Trebeck George; *Travels in Himalayan* Provinces of Hindustan and the Punjab; vol.II Delhi; 1989; pp. 191-92. Hereafter discussed as *T.H.P. H.P*
304. *Tuzak-i-Jahangiri*, Tr. from Persian to English by Alexander Rugers; Two vols bound in one, Delhi, Reprint 1994; pp. 147-78. Hereafter referred as T.J.
305. *Ibid., Vol. 1, p. 390, Vol. II*, pp. 24, 26.
306. *Ibid.* Vol. 1, p. 297.
307. *Ibid.*, P. 384.
308. *Ibid.*
309. Bernier's *Travels in India*, London; 1891, pp. 402-03.
310. R. Sharma, *Kalpadrukosa;* Baroda (India) 1923, pp. 288-82.
311. J. Sarkar; *The India of Aurangzeb;* Calcutta, 1901, p. 111.
312. Birdwood; *Report on Old Records;* London; p. 27.
313. *Ibid.*, p. 47.
314. G.Forster, A *Journey from Bengal to England;* Vol. 1 London, 1798, Reprint in 1920; p. 1.
315. *Ibid.*, p. 211.
316. *Ibid.*, pp. 247-48
317. *Ibid.*, Vol. II, pp. 18-19.
318. *T.H.P. H.P.*, pp. 1819-25.
319. *Ibid.* Vol. 1, pp. 110-13.
320. *Ibid.*, Vol. II, Chapter III study in detail about the Kashmiri shawls and *Pattoo.*
321. *Ibid.*, pp. 164-66
322. *Ibid.*, p. 167
323. *G.G.* Vigue; *Travels in Kashmir, Ladakh* and *Iskardo;* vol.II London 1842, p. 124 Vol. 1, p. 309.
324. *T.H.P. H.P.* Vol. 1, pp. 180-82.
325. *Ibid.*, pp. 125-26.
326. *C.T.C.C.A.M.I.*, p. 245.
327. *Ibid.*, p. 246.
328. *H.I.*, pp. 35-36.
329. *L.V.*, pp. 1-13, 312.
330. *Ibid.*, pp. 14, 20, 141, 368.
331. G. Buhler; *Vikramankadevacaritam;* IX Bomay; 1875, p. 64.
332. *Ibid., XVI*, p. 49.
333. *Ibid.*
334. *Ibid.*
335. *Ibid., XVIII*, p. 95.
336. *Ibid., I.* P. 15; VIII, p. 45.
337. *Ibid.*, XIII. P. 89.
338. *Ibid.* XIV. P. 32.
339. *Ibid., XVIII*, p. 31.
340. *Ibid., XI*, p. 34.
341. *Ibid., XVI*, p. 48.
342. *Ibid.*, III, p. 33.

343. *Ibid., XIII*, p. 23.
344. *Ibid.*, III, p. 76.
345. *C.T.C.C.A.M.I*, p. 110.
346. *R.T.*, Vol. 1, p. 120.
347. *Ibid.*, p. 121.
348. *Ibid.*, p. 123.
349. *Ibid.*
350. *Ibid.*, p. 139.
351. *Ibid.*, p. 180.
352. *Ibid.*, p. 225.
353. *Ibid.*, p. 233.
354. *Ibid.*, p. 336.
355. *Ibid.*, p. 339.
356. *Ibid.*
357. *Ibid.*
358. *Ibid.*
359. *Ibid.*, Vol. II, p. 68.
360. *Ibid.*
361. *R.C. Majumdar*, K.M Munishi, A.K Majumdar: The *Classical Age*; Vol. III, Bombay, Reprint 1962;
362. V.S. Aggarwal; *Harsacarita-ek-Samkritika Adhyayana;* Patna; 1953; p. 96. Hereafter explained as *H.S.A.*
363. *R.T.* Vol. I, p. 340 ***Note*** Harsha was also fond of amusements of the Daccani fashion, moreover, he introduced a coin-type (*tanka*) copied from that of *Karnata*, liberal king also displayed gold about all bands of singers came to vie with kings. The word *tanka* here we mean simply 'coin-type' or 'die to live in Nam'. According to Cunningham, 'the fact of the coins being made in imitation of those *Karnata* is fully corroborated by the coins of that country, and female attendants to swong lights (*aratrika*) around them.
364. I.D., p. 7.
365. *Ibid.* **Note.** This kind of dress was also worn by Dr. B.R. Ambedkar during the time of national movement in India as displayed an univarsal movement after 1949 as an idea of progress in the history of India which appears from his 'hat' and 'gown'.Therefore the dress code is very important to study which reflects the idea of human nature and his advancement in field of life. Literatures which reflects the word '*Sari* in the poignant description in the *Mahabharata* of how Daraupadi was put to shame, covering her lips, thrown over one shoulder, covering her hips, thrown over one shoulder and allowed to fall back over the other in the process of life as an one of the best example in the garments.
366. *R.T.* Vol. 1, p. 178, *Jayapida* established his office called *Dharmadikarana* ('administration of justice') fixed there in the royal court a regal cloth of *Karna* which means of *Karnarripata* with the help of *'Nam'*, *pata* for *patta* may also deginated a plate bearing a picture or edict. *Karna,* the king of *Anga,* one of the Kauravas, might be alluded into the war. It is the story of Naga *Mahapadma,* the tutelary deity of the *vulur,* the largest of the Kashmir lakes, which has received from it, its ancient name *Mahapadmasaras.*. Other legends about the lake are related by *Jonaraja*, 909-944, in connection with the artificial Lanka is land constructed in it by Zain-ul-Abidin.
367. N.L Dey; *the Geographical Dictionary of Ancient and Medieval India*; London; 1927, p. 94
368. R.T. Vol. 1, p. 207 Note. *Pattana* (Lit. 'town') is here evidently used as the name of *Sankaravarman's* town and ought to have been shown *Pancasatra* locality of *Tirthas* of *Karna*. Kalhana's description about the weaving of woollen cloth, purchase and sale of cattle as a lively market-town, without further dictination or objects of interest, is still applicable to the modern *Patan,* which has a fairly *Bazaar* of the Father, and has become the headquarters of a Tehsil since the last settlement.
369. **Note.** The city of Kanauj raised the position of imperial capital of Kashmir, we find a powerful monarch Yasovarman occuping it throne. Nothing is known about his early history, but one of his court poet, known as *Vakpati,* wrote a poetic work in Prakrit to celebrate the victorious campaign of his patron, and this forms the chief source of our knowledge of his life and reign. The name of *Vakpati's* poem *'Gauda-Vaho'*, this work has been edited by S.P. Pandit, with a learned introduction discussing the history of *Yasovaraman,* implies that the death and defeat of the king of *Guada* formed the main theme of the work, but as a matter of fact this event is merely alluded at the end of his life, and the rest of the work deals with the other conquests of *Yasovarman*. He then came on the bank of the *Narmada* and, passing by the sea-coast, marched to Maru-desa (Desert of Rajputana) thence he advanced towards *Srikanth,* the district round *Thareswar.* Passing through *Kuruksetra,* and visiting the scenes of the war described in the *Mahabharata,* Yasovarman proceeded to Ayodhya. He then received the submission of the people living on the *Mandara* (Punjab's foothills) mountains and proceeded toward the Himalayan region where king *Lalitaditya Muktapida* has the kingdom of *Kashmir* and lived there as the friends of the family for a long period of history (*C.A.* pp. 128, 129).
370. *Kavyamimamsa*; Edited by C.D. Dalal and revised by R.A. Sastry; third edition, Baroda (India) 1934; p. 8.
371. *Ibid.*
372. *Ibid.*, p. 9.

373. *Ibid.*, p. 99.
374. *Karpuramanjari* (C.900 A.D). Edited by S. Konow, Cambridge MSs. vol.1 1901. p. 27
375. *Ibid.*, p. 16.
376. *Ibid.*, p. 209.
377. *Ibid.*, Vol. II, p. 13.
378. *Ibid.*, Vol. 1, p. 13.
379. *Ibid.*, p. 20.
380. *Ibid.*, pp. 20, 23.
381. *Ibid.*, Vol. II., p. 24.
382. *Samaraiccakah of Haribhadra;* Edited by H. Jocobi Calcutta; 1926, pp. 75, 78.
383. *Ibid.*, p. 407.
384. *Ibid.*, p. 522.
385. *Ibid.*, p. 407.
386. *Ibid.*, p. 735.
387. *Ibid.*, p. 239.
388. *Ibid.*, p. 473.
389. *C.T.C.C.A.M.I.; p. 114* **Note.** *Pattu* is also a simple type of grament as *Vasas* made of fine texture.
390. *Prabhavakacarita* of *Candraprabha Suri,* Edited by H. Sastri, Bombay, 1909, pp. 59, 199.
391. R.P. A. Dozy, *Dictionarie Detaille Des Noms Des, Vetements Chez Us* ***Arabs***, p. 339.
392. MotiChandra, *Prince of Wales Museum Bulletin* No.3 Bombay 1959, pp. 7-8.
393. *C.T.C.C.A.M.I.*, pp. 109-10.
394. *Samayamatrka* Vol. VIII, pp. 54-56.
395. *Ibid.*, Vol. VII, p. 14-17.
396. *Ibid.*, Vol. II, p. 92.
397. *Acharanga Sutra I, pp. 1, 2, 3, 5, See D.O.A.I., p. 20 Note. The* 11th century commentator of the *Acarangasutra,* however, explains *dukula* as cloth made from the cotton grown in Ganda (Vol. II, pp. 4,5).
398. *Nisithachurni*; p. 7, p. 467.
399. *H.I.*, p. 20.
400. *B.K.S.B.* Vol. IV, p. 1017.
401. *Ibid.*, p. 3661.
402. *D.O.A.I.*, p. 20.
403. *L.V. p. 312.*
404. *B.K.S.B Vol. IV, p. 3363* **Note.** In the *bangika* class of the textile materials are included linen, and the cloth made from the fibre obtained from bamboo shoots. *Sana* is hempen cloth; *pottaka* is cloth manufactured from cotton, and *tiritapatta* is made from the bark of the *Tirita* tree. The noted editors of the text gives the explanation of the above terms from two *'Curnis'*. According to one *Curni* the *mrgaloma* is explained as *saloma masagalomamva. 'Saloma'* may mean bristling with hair or may also mean fur, *'musaklome'* apparently means hair of the mouse, but here *'musaka'* may indicate all sorts of rodents from the colder region, whose pelts were used for cloth-making. In the *'Visesa curni' 'mrgaloma'* is described as *pavvacyanam roma'* or knotted wool of goat; the *Kutapa* is described as made of some part of goat's wool thereby meaning that *'Kutapa'* was made from the shaggy hair, the better cloth or *pashmina* being made from the hair of the underside. *'Kittima'* according to the *'Curni'* was also made from goat's hair called *Sachagaliyaromam'* means 'Truth' has to be follow by the Brahmanas. Therefore, the wearing of woollen undergarments were dissallowed to the Jaini monks as it attracted lice and dirty by wearing. They were only limited to the *Brahmanas* of the period. Among the five kinds of cloth described above as lawful to the Jaini monks of the Gupta period, a combination of two such, as of cotton and wool, bark or *tirita*, etc. Were allowed. Transgressing the above mentioned rule means we are committing crime against the *'Father'* or God. (See pages of the B.K.S.B. Vol. IV, 1018, 3668, 3670).
405. *D.O.A.I.*, p. 20.
406. *H.I.*, p. 36.
407. *D.O.A.I.*, p. 20.
408. *H.I.*. p. 36.
409. *Aks.* pp. 2, 6, 116.
410. *Y.C.* p. 148.
411. J.R. Puri and K.S. Khak; *Sultan Bahu; Amritsar*, 2nd edition; 1999, p. 6.
412. *A.I.C.*, p. 68.
413. D.V., pp. 4, 5, 21.
414. *Ibid.*, pp. 1, 7, 29.
415. *A.I.C.*, pp. 68-69.
416. *C.T.C.C.M.A.I.* p. 33.
417. *C.H.H.*, pp. 75-76.
418. *Silappadikaram XIV*, p. 208.
419. *H.I.*, p. 36.
420. *Ibid.*
421. *A.I.C.*, p. 69.
422. *D.V.*, pp. 21-25, 83.
423. *Ibid.*, pp. 8, 463.
424. *Ibid.*, pp. 26, 256.
425. *Ibid.*, pp. 24, 256.
426. *Ibid.*, pp. 25-26, 420.
427. *Bharatiya Natyasastraa XXIII*, p. 126.
428. *A.I.C.*, p. 69.
429. *Ibid.*, pp. 90-01.
430. *Ibid.*, p. 94.

431. *I.D.*, p. 6.
432. *C.B.R.E.I.*, p. 157.
433. C.T.C.C.M.A.I., p. 32.
434. *C.B.R.E.I.*, p. 157.
435. *C.T.C.C.M.A.I.*, p. 32.
436. *K.A.*, p. 81.
437. *M.B.*, Vol. II, pp. 8, 51.
438. *Ibid.*, p. 26, 51.
439. Strabo II. pp. 14.20 Mc Crindle; *Ancient India; p. 26 C.T.C.C.M.A.I.*, p. 17.
440. *Kosad-dhan, IV,* pp. 3, 42. C.T.C.C.M.A.I., p. 17.
441. Note. Study made from the *Kanahasabhai, the Tamil Eighteen Hundred Years Ago;* p. 117. Also quoted by Motichandra on; p. 34 *C.T.C.C.M.A.I.*
442. Silappadikaram, Vol. V, p. 110.
443. *D.V.*, pp. 6, 29.
444. *Ibid.*, pp. 9-11, 276.
445. *Ibid.*, p. 27-28, 398.
446. *H.I.*, p. 36.
447. *C.H.H.*, p. 77.
448. *H.I.*, p. 36.
449. *C.H.H.*, pp. 77-78.
450. *C.T.C.C.M.A.I.*, p. 32.
451. *D.V.*, pp. 15, 415.
452. *Bharatiya Natyasastra* XXXIII, p. 126.
453. *L.V.*, pp. 7, 47.
454. *D.V.*, pp. 14, 16.
455. *L.V.*, pp. 1, 170.
456. *Ibid.*, pp. 7, 179.

4

Early Medieval History of the Untouchables in India (650-1050 A.D.)

The history of the Brahman 'Caste' *'untouchable'* which is by a current and invincible fallacy regarded as the highest of all *'Chamar'* illustrates both the processes i.e. Heaven and Earth. Beyond all question the title or status of modern caste system of a Brahman was originally to be earned by scholarship or a holy life, but when the status became hereditary it creates problem for a society and its all inducement to attain its qualifications disappeared[1] as the *'Chamar[2]'* has attained. The result has been that the Brahman, when unable to make a living by begging alms, enters domestic services, especially as a cook[3]. Yet we do not hear that the abandonment of the learning by the Brahmans is more than that of 'untouchable', they had written number of books like *Mahabharata[4], Ramayana[5], Chachnama[6], Bana Harsacrita[7], Kalhana's Rajatarangini[8],etc.* Being an orthodox *Sunni Mussalman[9], Utbi[10]* applauds the achievements of Mahmud as *Amir Nasir-ud-din Subuktugeen* neither crossed the Indus nor subdued any part of Panjab, all writers include him in the dynasty of the kings of Lahore. Historians affirm that *Amir Subuktugeen,* who after wards acquired the title of *Nasir-ud-din,* was a Turk by descent[11]. The book was held in high esteem by the successor of Mahmud and the nobility of Ghazni, it was rendered into Persian by a number of contemporary writers. It was popular with the histrographers of the Mughal period who freely quoted from[12] it. Not only this, Hasan Nizami introduced in the style of *Panchtantra* literature of ancient India, a suborinate series of descriptions (*Sifats*) within one leading subject, which included qualities of mirror, rules of chess, natural elements, seasons, fruits, flowers and what not. To a man of literature, with proficiency in Arabic and Persian, the book offers interesting reading; no wonder, it was very popular in the literary circles of early medieval India[13].

Minhajus Siraj belonged to an aristocratic family of Central Asia; he was related from his mother's side to the ruling house of Sultan Mahmud of Ghazni. His 'father' was attached to 'army of Hindustan' under Muhammad Ghori as *qazi* and spiritual guide. *Minhaj* himself was a distinguished scholar of Islamic theology (*manqul*) and jurisprudence (*fiqh*); he received appoint as principal of the Firozi *Madrassah* a *Uchh* in 1227 from Nasiruddin Qabacha who was then in revolt against Brahminical rulers of Delhi. The very next year, *Uchh* was recovered by the royal army of the *'Nam',* led by Sultan Iltutmish; *Minhaju Siraj* accompanied his train militants to Delhi and was patronized by the *Sultan.* Four years later, Gwalior was reconquered by Iltutmish from the Rajputs and *Minhaj* was appointed its *qazi* and *sadr* or *sudra* justice of peace and head of the ecclesiastical establishment[14].

The chief of the tribe of mountaineers, called *Gakkars[15],* at this time, hearing that the king was certainly slain, aspired to independence; and collecting in great numbers, advanced towards Lahore, laying waste and the country between the rivers Jhelum and *Sudra[16].* Mahomed Ghori had now obtained permission of the allies to retire unmolested from the fort of *Andkhu,* and arrived at Ghizna, where his own slave Yelduz having seized on the city, opposed his entrance,which oblized the king to continue his route to *Multan.* Here Zeeruk, who had rebelled against him, also resisted him; but Mahomed Ghuri being by this time joined by many of his friends[17] who were related with the theory of *Kalma,* gave him battle, and obtaining a complete victory over Kashmir.

In 1235, we find him as the chief *qazi* of Delhi. On the desposition of Sultan Behram Shah (1240-42 A.D.). *Minhaj Siraj* resigned the post and migrated to Bengal whose rule had declared himself independent of Delhi, took the traitor prisoner. Minhaj became the chief *Qazi* and *Sdar-i-jahan* means the area of the *Sudra* rulers under Sultan *Nasiruddin Mahmud* (1246-66 A.D.); he enjoyed the confidence of the Sultan and his *maliknaib* (deputy) Balban[18]. The troops of the borders of India having ralled around him, he marched to Ghiznavad, and at the entreaties of the citizen forgave his rebel slave i.e. *Chamar,* and quitely obtained the possessionof place. Mahomed Ghuri now concluded a treaty of peace with the king of *Khwaruzm*; after which in order to chastize the Gakkars, he marched towards India for the development of region. *Qutab-ud-Din Aibek,* from Delhi, he attacked over the *Gakkars* on the east, while the king engaged them from the west. They were defeated and dispersed; and Lahore being recoved by Qutab-ud-Din Aibek and then returned to Delhi[19], where he established his Kingdom.

Hasan Nizamis *Tajul Maasir 'Word' or Kalma* 'the crown of Exploits' deals primarily with the history of Qutab-ud-din Aibek. The author was an immigrant from Khurasan; he was born at Nishapur in an aristoratic family of reputed historian of the times. He writes that he never dreamt of travelling abroad' until the native country 'compelled him to seek a residence elsewhere." He came to Ghazni, made acquaintances with the countries of Sultan Muhammad Ghori and soon migrated to Delhi. He joined service under Qutab-ud-din Aibek, then the Viceroy of North India on behalf of Muhammad Ghori. Hasan Nizami took up the writing of this book on the orders of Aibek[20] in 1206 A.D. After the death of Muhammad Ghori, Aibek became an independent ruler of Northern India; it naturally added to the social status of the author and enhanced the value of his official assignment. The narrative commences from the years 1191-92 A.D. When Muhammad Ghori invaded India as a wounded tiger to avenge his defeat suffered previously at the hands of Prithvi Raj III, the Chauhan rule of Delhi and Ajmer, and fought the second battle of Tarain. The author gives in detail the military exploits of *Aibek* from 1192 to 1205 through his achievements as independent rule (1206-10 A.D.[21]). In the year (1194 A.D.), Qutab-ud-din Jiwan moved towards Nehrwala, the capital of Gujarat Jiwan *Rai,* the General of Bheem Deo, who was encamped under the walls, fled at his approach; but on being closely pursued, he drew-up his army and fought till he lost his life, when his army resumed its flight, Bheem Deo, hearing of this defeat, fled from his dominions, and Qutab-ud-din having ravaged the country at leisure obtained much booty from Heaven to Earth of the 'Brahminical ideology' which were not used to trust on God or *'Nam'* or *'Kalma'*. He marched from thence to the fort of *Hans*, which he repaired having visited Kohram returned to Delhi. Meanwhile advices reached him from the governor of district near Ranthumbore, that the brother of *Gola Rai* of Ajmer, who lived in the hills, threatened to invaded his territories. This news induced Qutab-ud-din Aibek to move to his relief, on which the enemy retired; and Qutab-ud-Din paid to visit to *Gola Rai* who entertained him magnificently, and at his depature presented him with some fine jewels, and two texts of gold tissu. He soon after returned to Delhi; and it is related in the *Taj-ul-Maasir*, a work dedicated to *Qutab-ud-din-Aibek*, that he wrote to the king a particular account of his conquests, which so pleased his sovereign, Mahomed Ghori, that he ordered his attendence at Ghizni, for which place he set out, and was received with every demostration of joy and respect. Qutab-ud-din-Aibek, sometime after, having obtained permission to return to his Government, espoused the daughter of Taj-ud-Deen Yelduz, governor of Kirman in Pishawar, and celebrated the marriage festival with great splendour after his arrival at Delhi. He soon after engaged in the seize of the fort of *Biana,* but hearing that the king, his master, had taken the route of Hindustan, Qutab-ud-din went as far as Hansy to meet him. Both now returned to Biana, which place was taken, Mahomed *Ghori* gave charge of it to *Baha-ud-din* Toghrul, of his trusty slaves and then *proceeded to Gowalior*, where the Raja, having agreed to pay tribute, purchased the forebearance of the king for the time with considerable 'some of money and jewels'. Immediately after there transactions Mahomed Ghori returned to Ghinzi leaving Qutab-ud-din as before, viceroy of all the conquered provinces of India. At this time news arrived that the Raja of Nagur and many other Hindu Rajas had entered into an alliance with the Meres, a race of people in that country, and together with the Raja of Nehrwala, had formed a design to Wrest Ajmer from the Mahomedans. The army of Qutab-ud-din-Aibek being dispersed over his provinces, he was forced to march in person against these confederates with the few troops present in Delhi, in order to prevent, if possible, the junction of the 'forces of Nehrwala', but he was defeated. After having been frequently dismounted in an action, and having received six wounds, he still fought with his wonted courage, till being forced at length, by his attendants off the field, he was carried in a litter to Ajmer[22]

The *Meres,* rejoicing at this victory, now formed a junction with the forces of Gujarat, and sat down before Ajmer. Intelligence of this event coming to ears of the king, he sent a strong reinforcement from Ghizni to the relief of Qutab-ud-din. Ajmer held out till the arrival of the successors and the enemy raised the seige. In the year (1196 A.D.). Qutab-ud-din having recovered from his wound pursued the besieging army to *Nehrwala,* taking in his way the forts of Bali and *Nadole*. He there received advices that Wallin and *Darbarz,* in alliance with the Raja of *Nehrwala,* were encamped near the fort of *Abughur*; in the province of Sirohi, to defend the passes into Gujarat. Qutab-ud-din-Aibek, notwithstanding the difficulties of the road, and the disadvantages of ground, attacked them; and on this occasion above fifty thousand of the enemy are said to have be fallen on the field, besides twenty thousand who were prisoners, vast spoils also fell into the hands of the victors. Having given his army some rest, Qutab-ud-din pursued his route into Gujarat, ravaged that country without further opposition and took the city of *Nehrwala*, where he left an officer with a strong garrison. He now returned to Delhi by the way of Ajmer, and sent a large quantity of jewels and gold,and also many slaves, to the king at Ghizni, and divided the remainder of the spoils among his follow soldiers[23].

In the year (1202 A.D.), he mustered his forces, and marched against *Kalunjur*, where he was opposed by the Raja of that country who he defeated, then, dismounting his cavalry he laid siege to the fort. The Raja, seeing himself hard pressed, offered. Qutab-ud-din Aibek the same tribute and presents which his ancestors had formerly paid to Sultan Mohmood. The proposal was accepted, but the Raja's minister, who resolved to hold out without coming to terms, caused his master to be assassinated, while the presents were preparing. The Hindu flag being again hoisted on the fort, the siege recommended, but the place was reduced, owing to the day up of a spring upon the hill which supplied the garrison with water. The plunder of Kalunjur was in gold and jewels.

Qutab-ud-din now marched a *Mahoba,* the capital of the principality of *Kalpi*, which place he also subdued together with Budaun, lying between the rivers Jumana and Ganges. Mohamed Bukhtyar Khilji, who had been appointed governor of Behar by the king, but had for some time back paid little attention to the royal commands came at this time to pay a visit to Qutab-ud-din, conciliating him with rich presents[24].

At that time when Mahomed Ghori, after his defeat in *Turkistan,* returned to India, he was joined by *Qutab-ud-din Aibek*, and *Shums-ud-Altmish*, another of his slaves, by whose valour and fidelity, he defeated the *Gukkurs* in several actions, and recovered Lahore from them. Matters being thus peaeful settled, Qutab-ud-din returned to his government, and the king was retiring towards Ghazni, when he was assassinated by the Gukkurs. Mahmud, his nephew, assumed the royal titles at *Ghur,* and, on his accessin, sent all the insignia of royalty, a throne, a canopy, standards drums and the title of king, to Qutab-ud-din Aibek, desirious of securing his interest, and being by no means able to oppose his power, if he refused to acknowledge him. Qutab-ud-din Aibek received these marks of favour with becoming respect at Lahore, where he ascended the throne on the 18th of *Zeekad* (July 24, 1205 A.D.). He returned from thence in a few days to Delhi.

Meanwhile, Taj-ud-Din Yelduz marched an army from Ghazni, with an intention to take Lahore, which he effected by the treachery of the governor, whom he afterwards expelled. Qutab-ud-Din hearing of this event, disputed his right and in the year 1205 A.D., a war ensued between these chiefs. At length Taj-ud-Din Yelduz was expelled from the city and obliged to fly towards Kirman and Shivuran; Qutab-ud-Din Aibek pursued him as far as Ghazni, in which city he was again crowned, taking that kingdom also into his own hands.

Qutab-ud-Din Aibek, after this, un accountably gave himself up to wine and pleasure, till the citizens of Ghazni, disgusted. with his conduct, sent privately to Taj-ud-Din Yelduz, acquainting him with the King's negligence, and entreating his return. Taj-ud-Din raised troops with great secrecy and expedition, advanced towards Ghazni, and surprised. Qutab-ud-Din, who had no intelligence of his design till the day before his arrival. It was now too late to attempt a defence, so that he was compelled to abandon Ghani and to retire to Lahore. Qutab-ud-Din now became sensible of his folly and repented; after which he continued to exercise justice, temperance and morality of the life, and his kingdom was governed by the best laws of the nature i.e. *'Nam'* till his death which happened to be in the year of (1210 A.D.), by a fall from his horse, in a match at Chowgan.

His reign, properly speaking, lasted only four years, though he enjoyed all the state and dignities of a king for upwards of twenty, if we reckon from the period of the capture of Delhi, when he may be said to have become king of India, though he assumed only the title of Commander-in-Chief of his patron Mahomed Ghori. He was certainly a great captain, and might be closed among the greatest men in history had not his licentious conduct at Ghazni tarnished the glory of his life. He was famous throughout the East for his generosity, for which he obtained the surname of *Lakbukhsh*, 'Bestower of laks". When a man is praised for generosity in India, they say to this day, "He is a liberal as *Qutab-ud-Din Aibek.*[25]"

After the returning of Ghazanivad, *Chawand Rai,* King of Delhi, and many other princes were slained in the *'Nam'* or *'Kalma'* on the field, while *Pithow Rai,* king of Ajmer *Sarif*, being taking in the neighbourhood of the *Sursutti*, which afterwards put to death in the *'Nam'* which called in Quran 'Die in living being.' The whole of the camp-equipage, and wealth of the several princes of the *'Nam'*, fell into the hands of the conquerors then had to live in Heaven on Earth. The forts of *Sursutti, Samana, Kohram* and *Hansi* were surrendered their 'ego' in the *'Kalma'* after the victory of Master. Muhamed Ghori in person went to Ajmer where Sultan Bahu and other took the shelter under the *'Kalma'* of which he also took possession under the true faith of the Master, after having put some thousands of the inhabitants under this *'True Faith'*, who oppose him, to the sword, reserving the rest for slavery called *Brahmanas*. Afterward, on a promise of a punctual payment of a large tribute, they again stand still, but he delivered over the country of Ajmer to the *Gola*, or natural son, of *Pithous Rai,* or properly, Prithivi Raj, was the ruler of Rajasthan according to Colonel Tod. Ajmer was his patrimony. *Channel,* or *Chawand,* was his lieutenant at Delhi, whose sister was espoused b Prithvi Raj, by her he had a son *Ramsi,* who fell in defending Delhi. He now turned his arms towards Delhi, but was prevailed on by the new king,with great presents, not to prosecute the war further in the favour of *'Nam'*. On this occasion, he left his faithful slave and friend, *Malik Qutab-ud-din Aibek,* in the town of Kohram, with a considerable detachment from the material life, and marched himself with the body of his army where the *'Nam'* or *'Chamar'* reside as displayed in the picture of Ravi Dass went towards *Sevaliks* mountains,the house of Siva or *'goodness'* i.e. *'Nam'*, which be to the north of India called *Kashmir*, destroying and plundering the countries on his retreat towards Ghaznavad. After the return of Mahomed Ghori, his general Malik Qutab-ud-din Aibek, took the fort of Meerut and the city of Delhi from the family of *Chawand Rai* of Sindh family of *Sudra* dynasty called *"untouchables"* by the Brahmanas of the period, and it is owing to this circumstance the foreign nations say, "The empire of Delhi was founded by a slave". Now called Dr. Raj Kumar, he is the slave of *'Father'* or *'Nam'*. In the year (1193 A.D.), he also took the fort of Kale and making Delhi the seat of his government established himself there, and compelled all the districts around to acknowledge to follow the faith of *'Islam'* in real form like *'Nam' or 'God'*. No doubt, *Jai-Chand Rai,* the Prince of Kanuja and Benaras, along with Qutab-ud-din-Aibek, between the era of *Chandwar* and *Etawa* and the fort of *Asni,* where *JaiChand Rai* had laid up his treasure, along with precious stones, broken the idols of 1000 temples, he purified and consecrated, the latter to worship of the *'True God'*, i.e. 'Living Nam' in human form who used to reside at that time in Bias. From thence he returned to the fort of Kole, where he confired Qutab-ud-din-Aibek in the vice regency of India[26] under the banner of *'Islam'* or *'Nam'* in true form as in the nature of Prophet.

In the study, we learnt that after this whole ambition of the *'Nam'* at the same time both Hindu and Muslims lived under one umberalla by seizing the cities of Delhi and adjoining area of Rajasthan, Kunauj, etc. All these cities were set in equal path and peace and prosperity. The anarchy which was widely spread by the *Maldeo*, was badly crushed with the natural calamities like rain, flood, earthquake, etc. In this way, no sons of Raja Maldeo was left behind as his successors, who ruled over India, for when Sultan Mahmud Ghazni invaded it, thus the country was divided into principalities, as Kanauj ruled by Kuwar Raj, Meerut was Huddat Raj, Mahavun, a village on the left bank of the Jamuna, about 10 miles below *Mathura* was supposed to be the spot ruled by *Gulchander Rai* of *Sudra* dynasty, Lahore by Jaipal's son known as Hat Pal. thus Malwa, Ajmer, Gowalior Gujarat, etc, had each separate *rajas* of the *'Nam'* rule was established by the *Mahmud Ghori.* The sexual union historians have already mentioned in the passage called the 'salve' or 'untouchables' but Brahmanas are *'untouchables'* those could not obtain and understand the beauty of the *'Nam'* as a real founder of the universe and its environment as a real 'Father' of the small 'Nations'. Study shows that the early medieval period of the *Sudra* or *Untouchables* rulers called *'Chamar'* played a very responsible role for the compilation of the society in 'One Form' which is 'formless' for sometimes to regain his power during the rule of Brahmans for the establishment of the *'New Society'*. It was pre-planned in his mind which Brahman could not understand it, until and unless he is in power. As soon as, 'He' does not brust out through his fellow colleague i.e. the *'Chamar'* or *'Nam'* called the fourth *Varna* of the society. It is 'His' story which could not understand in a day, it is a difficult path to understand, because one must have the pious approach in this direction both in character and discipline as its essential features for the progress, peace and prosperity. It provides equal opportunity to all to recognise 'Him', but some fail in their 'ego' which based on discriminational theory in the life of the human being in the one and the other hands in the process of living being as a natural phenonmeona which based on deeds and actions of the man's life.

Notes & References

1. G.T.C. Preface, p. V
2. *Chamar* plural term *Chamars* is composed of two words *Cham+ars, Cham* means leather, the maker of leather is an artist or *'Nam'*, the word art has been derived from the Latin word *ars,* meaning 'skill', has changed through history by the author as a *'Chamar'*. Thus, art has a wider connotation. In any sphere of life, if *ars* (skill) has been shown and appreciated by the people, it is called an art. But in the nineteenth century Europe, distinction arose between *artist* and *artisan.* An artisan denotes a skilled manual labourer and an artist is one who has the capacity for imaginative invention. Thus, the latter has the intellectual power of imagine i.e. *'Nam'* or *'Kalma'* , to conceive and to produce what is recognised as a new and unique creations. *'Art'* and *'Artist'* are not absolute terms, rather, an abstract perception of the term *'Chamar'*. As an art historian explains, "the art is first of all a 'Word' or 'Chamar' that acknowledges both the idea and the fact of art. Wihtout it, we might well ask whether art exists in the first place? The term is not found in every society, yet art is made everywhere, but it is upto the worker. Art, therefore, is also an object, but just any kind of object. Art is an aesthetic object. It is meant to be looked at and appricated for its intrinsic value." (H.W. Janson; *History-of Art,* New York ; 1996, p. 16). For example, Man began his journey from Africa and travelled to the different parts of the world in time and space reached in India. He possessed thinking faculty i.e. *'Nam'* or *'Kalma'* and thus, started creating different objects according to his needs. The power of thinking did generate in him a sense of good bad, likes and dislikes as per deed and actions of the *man* or rather living *man* in India. Thus, three processes worked together imagination, conception and creation which upto the *'Nam' or 'word'* in the form of 'Baba Gurinder Singh ji'. He made different tools for hunting. Similarily, some objects depicting the aesthetic sense were also created by *'Him',* in the form of 'Dr. Raj Kumar' Professor in History.' These objects were not simply material use, but gave a sense of humanity, best wishes and pleasure is a work of *'art'* i.e. *'Nam'*.
3. **Note.** But the progress *Muhia Brahman,* who have eschewed the 'Nam' in all priestly functions, are not hapered by any prejudices against similar employment as the suborinate of Master and thrive in the professions and in government service (Punjab Census Report, 1902, p. 371).
4. The *Mahabharat* is the most celebrated historical work among the Hindus. It was translated from the original Sanskrit into Persian verse by Sheikh Abul Fuzl, the son of Sheikh Mubarak, by order of Akbar Padshah, and it consists of more than than 100,000 couplets. Mahomed Kasim Ferishta, the author of this work, having made an abstract of that translation, has availed himself of it to form the introductory part of this history.

   The philosophers and sages of India have related the formation of this earth differently, according to their own notions. Thirteen various accounts are given in the *Mahabharat* alone, not one of which is sufficiently satisfactory to induce us to adopt it in preference to another. The Hindus divide time into four ages. Ist, *Satyug*; 2nd, *Tritayug*; 3rd *Duwapuryug;* 4th, *Kalyug*; and they assert, that the four ages continue in succession to all eternity; the present being the Kalyug, which when at an end, the Satyug will re-commence. The earth, therefore, is by them, deemed eternal, without beginning and without end; though some Brahmins assert, that this world will have an end, and that a judgement-day will come.

   The *Satyug* is said to have lasted during a period of 1,728,000 years; when virtue and truth prevailed, and man lived 100,000 years.

   The *Tritayug* is a period of 1,296,000 years; three parts of the creation, during that time, obeyed the word of God, and the life of man was 10,000 years.

   The *Dwapuryug* is a period of 864,000 years; during which half of the creation was wicked, and man only lived 1000 years.

   The *Kalyug* is a period of 432,000 years. Men, in this period, became sinful; only one quarter of the human race followed the dictates of God, and the life of man was curtailed to 100 years. According to the Hindu account, in the present year (1015 of the Hijra), 4684 years of the Kalyug have elapsed.

   It may be useful to state, that the Yugs progress in an arithmetical ratio of 1, 2, 3, 4 from the smallest to the greatest number, and are divisible both by the common Indian cycle of 60 years, which is the usual divisor of time among them, as also by the figure 9, which is applicable both to time and things. These observations are intended to convey to the reader's mind the notion that the extravagancy of the Hindoo calculations are not without method, and require only the key to become intelligible and within the limits of our belief. This is not the place to discuss a question which would fill a volume.In the beginning, God created the four elements; besides which the Hindus reckon the aether as a fifth element; and after that, according to some accounts, he created man, whom he called Brumma; to whom he gave the power of creating every living thing. The Hindus are of opinion, that the aether, which they consider an element, is immaterial; that air only moves round the earth; that the planets, which are emanations from the Deity, have appeared on earth as men; who, after terrestrial mortality, are translated into heaven, in reward of their holy works on earth, by which they approximate so nearly to the Divinity in excellence, as to partake of his glory. It would appear from some of their books, that they consider the firmament itself as the divine essence.

Brahma, in virtue of the power vested in him, created four tribes of the human race; viz. Brahman; Kashitry; Vaisya and *Sudar*. The first was charged with the worship of the divinity, and the instruction of the human species. The second was appointed to rule over mankind. The third was required to plough the ground, and perform all sorts of handicraft. The fourth was doomed to be servile to the other three tribes. Brahma then wrote the book to direct mankind, which he called Veda. This is a work of theology, composed of 100,000 slogs; each slog or couplet being four churun, each churun or verse containing not more than 26 or less than 21 letters. Brahma lived 100 years of the Satyug, each year containing 360 days, each day being 4000 years of the present age, and each night the same. The brahmins unanimously agree, that there is but one Brahma; that he has appeared 1001 times; and of the life of the present Brahma 50 years and half a day have elapsed, and the other half is now in progress.

It is related, that in the latter end of the *Dwapuryug*, in the city of Hustnapur, Raja Bhurt, of the tribe of Kashitry, sat on the throne; after whom, seven rajas lineally descended from him reigned. A town of this name still exists about 45 miles N.E. of Dehli.

The eight was named Kurub, and the Kuruket, or field of Tahnesar, is called after him. His descendants are denominated Kuru. This dynasty reigned for six generations, till the accession of Veechitrveera Tej Raja, of the same line. He had two sons, the one D'hertrashtra, the conqueror, and the other Pandu (the Fair); the word signifies, literally, yellow; but the former, being blind, was put aside (although the elder), and his younger brother Pandu sat on the throne, from whom is sprung the Pandu dynasty. Pandu left five sons; Yudishteer (the Bold), called also Dharma Raja; Bheema, and Arjun, all born of one mother, called Kunti; while Nukul and Sahadeva were born of Madry. D'hertrashtra had 101 sons 100 born of a daughter of the Raja Gand'har, the eldest of whom was called Duryodhan, and another son called Yuyscha, born of a plebeian's daughter. From the descendants of D'hertrashtra are the Kuru tribe; while the descendants of his younger brother, Pandu, are called Pandus. Upon the death of Pandu, D'hertrashtra, notwithstanding the circumstance of his blindness, was proclaimed raja, and his eldest son, Daryodhan, became regent; and entertaining a jealousy of his cousins (the five Pandus), he determined to put them to death. D'hertrashtra, too, was not without his apprehensions from his nephews, the Pandus, whom he commanded to build their houses outside of the town, in order to prevent family disputes. Daryodhan bribed the architects to construct the houses with large quantities of pitch and bitumen, so that they might easily be consumed; but the Pandus, anticipating his intentions, set fire to their habitations, and, with their mother, left Hustnapur. In this conflagration a woman named Bheel, the *Mahabharat* states, that a woman of the tribe of Kisat (the appellation given to the Bheel tribe), with her five sons were accidentally sleeping on the premises, and were consumed together with her five sons, who had been bribed to commit the act, fell victims to the flames; but the Kuru, on the next day, finding the remains of Bheel and her son,s concluded that they were those of the Pandus. After this event, the Pandus having withdrawn from Hustnapur, travelled over great part of India and fought several battles, accounts of which occupy the greater part of the Mahabharat. At length they reached the city of Kumpila, on the banks of the *Gangas* where the five bro thers, being married in succession to Drowpadi, the daughter of the Raja of Kumpila, agreed that she should live with one of them for 72 days, by which means each contrived to enjoy her company for one-fifth part of every year. Some Hindu, however,deny this fact. Be it as it may; Daryodhan hearing the Pandu were alive, determined to ascertain the truth; and unable to dispute their rights, he invited them to Hustnapur, when he gave over to them Indraprust as their hereditary patrimony, and half of the kingdom of Hastnapur. *Indraprustha*, or *Indraput*. A town of this name still exists on the banks of the *Sarswatti* river and it was induced to believe it to be that here alluded to; be a friend, Colonel Tod, whose researches in Hindu History are so profound, and whose acquaitance with the geography of that part of India is so complete, states that Indraprushta is the ancient appellation for the city of Dehli, an appellation which it received from the Tuar dynasty, in the eighth century of our era, and which race descended in a direct line from the Pandus; and that, consequently, the Indraprushta in question is the ancient town of Dehli. The Pandus gained strength and power daily, while the Kurus, although they pretended friendship, retained malice in their hearts. Al length, the elder brother (Yudishteer) resolved to celebrate a festival in honour of the gods, at which it was necessary that all the kings of the earth should be present to pay homage to him. Yudhishteer accordingly despatched his brothers to the four corners of the earth; who subdued and brought to the feast the kings of Khutta, Room, Hubush, Ajum, Arabia and Turkistan. These names are evidently the result of Mahomedan interpolation. No such places are mentioned in the *Mahabharata*. Daryodhan, having long beheld with envy the rising power of his cousins, could no longer resrain his jealousy, and sought means to subvert their authority. Unable to expel them by force, he determined, if possible, to effect it by stratagem. In those days gambling with dice was a common amusement; and as he knew that the brothers were much addicted to this vice, he resolved, with the assistance of sharpers, to lead them on to lose to him their share of the empire. The Pandus, falling into the snare, lost all they possessed, but their kingdom.

Daryodhan now proposed one more throw, with a promise, that if he lost,he would restore all he had won, but if the Pandoos lost, they should abandon their country, and wander for twelve years; and on their return it was required, that they should remain concealed for a whole year, without making themselves known, but if discovered, they were again to perform twelve years more penance. The Pandus lost and having performed their pilgrimage, on the thirteenth year, they settled in the district of Waee, a country of the south. Waee, a town on the banks of the river Krishna,near the fort of Pandughar, called after the exciled brothers, is situated 20 miles north of the fort of Satara. Daryodhan sought throughout the empire, without discovering them, till at the end of the year, the Pandus sent Krishna, the son of Vasdew, as ambassador to the capital, to claim their kingdom. Daryodhan, however, refusing to restore it, and the Pandus having procured a number of the rajas of India to espouse their cause, attacked the forces of the Kurus, near Tahnesar, in the beginning of the Kalyug, when Daryodhan was killed, and the Kurus were defeated. Among these, Veerat Rai, the Raja of Waee, accompanied the Pandus, and fell in the battle of Kuruket, on the plains of Tahnesur. The army of the Kurus consisted of eleven kshuns, and that of the Pandus of seven. Each kshun consisting of 21,870 elephants, 21,870 chariots 65,610 horsemen, and 109,350 foot.

These incredible numbers are reducible by the figure 9, without a fraction, which authorises us to believe that the real numbers have been multiplied by this sacred and mystical figure. Admitting this to be the case, which seems highly probable, the numerical strength of the armies comes within the bounds of rational belief; and if we allow two riders to each elephant and chariot, it furnishes us also with even numbers, and the armies will then stand thus:-

	Elephant	Charioteers	Cavalry	Infantry	
		Grand Total Riders			
Pandus, 7 kshoons	3402	3402	5103	8505	20412
Kurus, 11 Kshoons	5346	5346	8019	13365	32076
Grand Total of both armies				.....	52488

By this account the Pandus would have brought 1701, and the Kurus 2673 elephants into the field,which however disproportionate they may appear to the number of men in modern times, yet when we consider that the missile weapons of those days did not penetrate easily into the elephant's hide, and that great numbers were used in all battles in India up to the introduction of artillery, the proportion is not so large. Akbar, according to Ferishta, had never more than 6,000 but never less than 5,000 elephants during the whole of his reign within the last two centuries; and the Nawab of Luknow has employed 700 on a hunting party, even within the last 40 years.

The most extraordinary part of the tale is, that only twelve men of both armies are said to have survived the battle with respect to the twelve persons who arrived the battle, we must suppose the officers of distinction only are alluded to, whose names are given.These were, four of the Kurus; the first *Kripa Acharia,* a brahmin, the tutor of the cousins, distinguished alike for his courage and his learning. The second, *Ashwathama,* the son of the philosopher Drone, who fell in the battle; the third, Keert Varma, of the family of Yadu; and the fourth, Sunjye, the intelligencer of D'hertrashtra, and who acted as his charioteer during the battle. Also eight of the Pandus, viz. the five Pandu brothers; sixth, Satik Yado; seventh Yuyucha (half brother of Duryodhan); and eight, Krishna, whohad been employed as ambassador to Duryodhun, from Waee. With respect to this latter personage, we shall give his history as translated from the Mahabharat.

"The city of Mutra is celebrated as the birth-place of Krishna. The Hindoos are not all agreed as to the rank which he holds among the holy personages. Some respect him as a prophet only, while others deify him.

"Before the battle of Tahnesur, Raja Kans, having heard from his astrologers that Krishna would put him to death, sought in all directions to seize him, but he concealed himself, and lived for eleven years in the house of Nanda, a cow-keeper, and at last obtained an opportunity of putting Raja Kuns to death, and of placing Dangur Sain, the father of Kuns, on the throne, retaining the management of the government in his own hands. At length, he caused his subjects to pay him divine honours, and obtained many proselytes. It is said, he devoted thirty-two years of his life to mirth and gaiety, in thecity of Mutra, and the tales related of him are as marvellous as preposterous.

"The neighbouring rajas, jealous of his power, resolved to attack him. Among these, Jarasundha, the Raja of Bihar, marched with a large force from Patna, for that purpose; while on the west, Kal-Yevan, The Hindu books speak of all the westerns as Yevan, whom the Persians call Yunan. Alexander and his army are designated Yevan by the Hindus, and Yunan by the Persians; a corruption, probably, of the word Ionian, a Mleccha sovereign, The word Mleccha signifies barbarian, and was applied to all although not of the Hindu persuasion, marched into India to reduce his power. This prince is supposed to be of Arabian extraction. Krishan, unable to resist the forces of these powers, was compelled to retreat, and reached Dwarka on the sea-coast (situated 100 coss from the present city of Ahmadabad)about two hundred miles. Dwarka is nearly insulated. It is situated near the most extreme point of the district of Hulwab, in Guzerat, and within the entrance of the gulf of Cutch, where he was beseiged for a period of seventy-eight years, unable to force his way through his enemies, and at length he died at the age of one hundred and twenty five; while some assert that he is still living in concealment." But to return to our history: after the battle of Kuruksetra, and the death of Daryodhan, the five Pandus reigned 36 years, and then abdicated their throne, which put an end to the dynasty, who did not adopt the rule of caste; as the Romans termed all those 'Barbari' who were not Romans their rule discussed as:-

From Raja Kuru to the death of Pandu was a period of	76 years
To that of Daryodhan Kuru	13 ditto.
To that of Yudishteer, commonly called Dharma, Raja Pandu	36 ditto
Total	125 years

Some years after the abdication of the Pandus, a great grandson of Arjun Pandu sat upon the throne, and among other pursuits of literature, being desirous that a history of his family should be written, a person named Bias undertook the work, and compiled the *Mahabharat*, which is said to mean the great battle; but upon enquiry, we do not find that the word Bharat signifies battle, and we should therefore suppose, that the letter A has been added, and that the Maha-Bharta signifies the history of the family of Bhart, the founder of the dynasty of Kawar and Pandu. Vias also wrote commentaries on the four Vedas, viz. *Rig Veda, Yejur Veda, Athurwun Veda, Siam Veda*: the three former works are on philosophy and theology, while the latter (the only one now extant) is a history, and is called *Mahabharat*, of which 24,000 slogs out of 100,000 are occupied in relating the history of the wars of the Pandus. The Hindus, like the Chinese and Tartars, deny the flood of Noah. Here Ferishta's knowledge of Hindu cosmography is defective, as their sacred writings distinctly trace a deluge which bears a close and important similitude to that recorded by Moses, though in the poetical language and style of the Hindoos, it is involved ina puerile description. Swyambhoma, "The Lord of the earth," is warned to the intended destruction of manking by a flood, and he is directed to provide a bark denominated *"Arga"*, into which he enters with seven holy persons besides himself, and the seed of every living thing.

Some of the Hindus assert, that the tribes of Brahmin and *Kashitry* existed from time immemorial, but that the Rajputs are a modern tribe, only known since the beginning of the Kulyoog. The same is related of many other different tribes. The Rajputs attained power since the death of Raja Vikramjit, from whom is derived the present Hindu era, being something more than 1600 years. The origin of the Rajputs is thus related. The rajas, not satisfied with their married wives, had frequently children by their female slaves, who, although not legitimate successors to the throne, were styled Rajputs, or the children of the rajas, and the children of Raja Suraj, whose history we shall now relate, were the first to whom the name of Rajput was given. The population of India, like that of other parts of the globe, arose from the descendants of Noah. After the flood, Noah's three sons, Shem, Ham and Japhet, began to cultivate the fields for their own subsistence and that of their children.

The first king of whose history we have any information was Krishna; he is not the Krishna of Matra. This Prince was elected by the vote of the people of Bihar; and the first city built in India was the city of Oudy. Krishna's prime minister was Bahmun, a native of Bengal. The king, being of gigantic stature, could procure no horse to carry him; he directed, therefore, an elephant to be tamed, on which he used to ride. The plough and reep-rook are ascribed to the invention of Bahmum, who it is said also formed the first alphabet. Having lived 400 years, the king died. He was contemporary with tahmorasp of Persia. He left thirty seven sons of whom Maharaj, his eldest, sat on the throne after him. Maharaj encouraged literature nad manufactures; and durin ghis reign his country became populous, and the inhabitants wealthy. Maharaj divided the people of India into tribes. To the brahmins were alloted the business of letters and the conduct of the affairs of the state; to another tribe, farming; and to a third, manufactures; thus these occupations have descended from father to son. He called the tribes after the chiefs of each; such as Rahtore, Chowhan, Powar, and Beis, &c. Maharaj always maintained a friendly intercourse with the kings of Persia; but Dongur Sain, one of his nephews, having left his court, took protection with Fauridun, King of Persia, who detached his son Kurshasp with a force to attack Punjab, in order to compel Maharaj to yield some part of his territory to his nephew. The war lasted ten years, when Maharaj was at length reduced to cede a part of his kingdom to Dongur Sain. In the latter part of his reign the zemindars of Shewala (Ceylon) and Carnatic attacked and drove Shiva Rai, his lieutenant from the Deccan. Maharaj, having sent his eldest son with a large foce to reinstate Shiva Rai, and to punish the rebels, the Prince was defeated and slain. Shiva Rai again sought refuge at the court of Mahraja, who was more grieved at the defeat of his army than at the loss of his son; for the princes of the islands of Acheen, and Malacca, and Pegu, and of the Malabar coast, had never before dared to rebel. At this time, also, an attack on the north-west frontier threatened his empire; and being compelled to send his lieutenant, Malchand of Malwa, to defend the Punjab, he was unprepared at present to carry on the war with the Deccanies. Malchand, unable to stand the brunt of the Persian forces, ceded thePunjab to them in perpetuity, besides making presents of elephants, & c. Some authors, however, relate the Faredun even possessed the Punjab; and that the descendants of Kurshasp, down to the celebrated Rustum, held it in subjection, together with Kabul, Tibet, Sind and Nemruz. On his return Malchand (from whom the country of Malwa deries its name), having marched against the zemindars of the Deccan, who fled at the approach of his army, reinstated Shiva Rai in his government. On this occasion he is said to have built the celebrated fort of Gwaliar. The science of music, also, was introduced into Hindustan by Malchand, who brought it during this expenditure from the country of Tallinga. Malchand, long after, resided at Gwaliar, and the descendants of the Tallingi musicians spread from that place over the north of India. It is a curious fact, that the word Bye, used in the Deccan to signify a genteel woman in general, is applied to professed singing woman only in Hindoostan; and that the word Kulwantin, a professional dancing woman, in the language of the Deccan, is changed into Kulawatin in Hindustan, and is there also applicable to dancing girls. It must be understood, that throughout this work the word Hindustan is applied to the country north of the Nerbadda and Mahanadda rivers, while the whole of the peninsula, south of the same line, is included in the word Deccan. Maharaja, after a reign of seven hundred years, died, leaving his eldest son, Kesu Rao, to succeed him.

Kesu Rai, having ascended the throne, detached his brothers in command of armies to make conquests, while he himself, taking the route of Kalpi, entered Gondwana, and marched as far south as Shewala Dweep(the island of Ceylon); levying tribute on all the rajas through whose country he passed. On his return, however, being attacked by these same Rajas, and unable to oppose them successfully, he made overtures for peace, and was permitted to return to his capital without molestation. On his arrival, he despatched an ambassador to the King of Persia, begging his assitance. Manu Chehr sent Sam, the son of Persia, begging his assitance. Manu Chehr sent Sam, the son of Nureeman, with an army, to support him; and Kesu Rai having met him withhis own troops at him; and Kesu Rai having met him with his own troops at Jalandhar in the Punjab, proceeded to the Deccan. The rajas, intimidated by the Persian troops, acknowledged allegiance to Kesu Rai, who having accompanied the Persians as far as the Punjab on their return to Eeran, marched back to Aoudhy, where he reigned for a period of two hundred and twenty years, and was succeeded by his son Manere Rai. The town of Manere is one of the monuments of this prince's reign, which he passed in the encouragement of literature, and in the promotion of the happiness of his subjects. He was, however, guilty of ingratitude towards Persia, in spite of the obligations his father owed to that empire. On the death of Manu Chehr in Eeran, Afrasiab Turk, King of Turan, invaded that Kingdom; and Manere Rai also having invaded Punjab, seized it for himself from the officers of Zal, the son of Sam, making Jalandhar his capital. At the same time, Munere Rai sent an envoy to Afrasiab, acknowledging fealty to him. After this the Punjab remained in possession of the kings of India till the reign of Keikobad, Rustam, the son of Zal to re-conquer that province, Manere Rai was defeated, and not only expelled from the Punjab, but seeking protection among the hills of J'harkund, and Gondwana, he died there after a reign of five hundred and thirty-seven years.

Rustam having thus conquered India, resolved to prevent any of the sons of Manere Rai from sitting on its throne, on account of their treachery towards persia; he therefore placed Suraj, a Hindu chief on the musnud, and returned to Persia. Suraj reigned over Hindustan; and his authority was acknowledged from the sea of Bengal as far as the Deccan. It is related that it was in his time a Brahmin persuaded him to set up idols, and from the period the Hindus became idolates, before which they, like the Persians, worshipped the sun and the stars.The sentence is very remarkable, and it would be curious to know whence Ferishta derived his information. If the fact he states could be relied on, it would afford us a clew to fix the period when the *Ramayan*, the Bharat, and the tenth canto of the *Bhagwat*, losing their simple character as heroic national poems, became identified with the sacred works. There appears every day stronger reason to believe, that the worship of the Bull, the Lingam, and Yuni, is the same as the Phallic worship of Egypt, and that of the Calf and the Pillar, emblematic of Bal or the Sun, by the nations surrounding the Israelites; that this worship is originally founded on Sabeism and that the amblems are types of the season of fructification. Abundant proof exists in India of the antiquity of the Tauric and Phallic worship over that of idolatry and of demi-god heroes. All the temples of the latter are modern compared with those dedicated to Mahadeva. The worship of images, however, was not introduced in the reign of Suraj. He was a contemporary, and tributary of Keikobad, and had reigned two hundred and fifty years when he died. He gave his sister's daughter in marriage to Rustam.

Suraj having left thirty-five sons, Bhai Raja, the eldest, succeeded his father, and built the city of Bhai-raja, commonly called Bhairaich: he was a great admirer of music. Among the public works of his reign is the completion of the city of Benares, the foundation of which was laid by his father. Some are of opinion also that Bhai Rai invested his brothers with the title of Rajput and that he gave distinctive names to some other tribes. He was so impolitic as to abandon the regulations established by Mahraja, so that he became a victim to the enmity of Kedar, a Brahmin of the Sewalik mountains, who, attacking and defeating him, eventually obtained the kingdom. Bhai Raja reigned thirty six years.

Kedar Raja was a man of erudition, and had also seen the world, so that he raised India from the state of depravity into which it had fallen under Bhay raja. He was contemporary with Kei-Kaoos and Kei-Khusrow, to whom he used to transmit annual tribute. He laid the foundation and built the fortress of Kalunjur. In the latter part of his reign he was attacked by Sunkul, a chieftain of Kooch, who having collected a large force, not only subdued Bung (Bengal) and Bihar, but also attacked Kedar, whom he defeated in several actions, and usurped his empire, after a reign of nineteen years.

Sunkul, having ascended the throne, laid the foundation of Luknowly, in Bengal, since known by the name of Goor or Gowr, which was the capital of the province for 2000 years, but being destroyed in the time of the Mughal Empire, Tanda became the seat of government.

Sunkul Raja maintained an army of 4000 elephants, 100,000 horse, and 400,000 foot, and refused to pay tribute to Afrasiab, who sent 50,000 Turky horse, under the command of Piranweisa to attack him. Sunkul Raja, having opposed him in the neighbourhood of the Kuch hills, on the Bengal frontier, two days and nights were occupied in fighting, on which occasion the Toorks lost 13,000 men, and the Hindoos 50,000. On the third day the Toorks retreated defending themselves till they reached the hills, where they took post, and Peeranweisa wrote to Afrasiab an account of his situation.

At this period, Afrasiab was in the city of Kunakdiz, situated between Khatta and Khutan, and distant one month's journey from Khanbaligh. On hearing from Peeranweisa, he marched at the head of 100,000 horse to his assistance. On his arrival, he foundPeeranweisa surrounded by an infinite number of rajas collected from all parts. Afrasiab, attacking the Hindus without delay, dispersed them, and thus released his gneral from his perilous situation. He then pursued Sunkul Raja to his capital of Luknowti, from whence he fled precipitately to the mountain of Tirhut. From thence he sent ambassadors to Afrasiab, entreating his forgiveness, and permission to pay his respects tohim; but he was required to appear before the great king with a sword suspended round his neck, and a shroud on his shoulders. Afrasiab, having carried Sunkul Raja to Turan, left his country under the government of Sunkul Raja's son. Sunkul remained with Afrasiab many years, but was at last slain in action, by the hand of Rustum. His reign lasted during a period of sixty-four years.

When Afrasiab returned to Tooran, he conferred the government of India on Rohut, the son of Sunkul Raja. His kingdom extended from Gurhi as far as Malwa, the revenues of which he divided into three equalportions. One he gave in charity; of another part was sent to his father, and part as tribute to Afrasiab; while the remainder was applied to the support of his government. This portion of his revenue being insufficient for his protection, the Raja of Malwa wrested out of his hands the strong fortress of Gowaliar, Rohut Rai, who built the fortress of Rohutas (Rohtas), and beautiful it with temples, took the field, in hopes, of recovering Gualiar, but was obliged eventually to withdraw without attaining his object. He kept his court usually at Kunowj, where he reigned for a period of eighty years, when he died.

Raja Rohat leaving no male issue of age, a revolution took place, in which Maharaj, a person of the tribe of Kutchwaha, from the district of Marwar, succeeded in placing himself on the throne. He attacked Nehrwala, Pattan in Gujrat and having reduced the zemindars of those parts (who were chiefly shepherds), laid the foundation of some sea-ports and caused ships of different sizes to be constructed. Mahraja II. was contemporary with Gushtasp, and reigned forty years, during which time he paid annual tribute to Persia. Maharaj was succeeded at his death by his nephew, Kedar Raja, whom he made his heir by his last testament. During this reign, Rustam being slain, Kedar attacked, and wrested from his descendants, the Punjab. Having remained some time in the town of Behera, This town, sitauted in the Gara, is often mentioned in early history; and in the first invasion of the Moslems it belonged to Goga Chowhan., he built the fortress of Jummu, where he left Durga, one of his relations, of the tribe of Bulbas, which tribe has inhabited that country ever since. Durga having contracted alliances with the Gakkars and Chowbea, the ancient zemindars of the Punjab, as also with the people who reside in the hills between Kabul and Kandahar, marched against Kedar Raja, who fled from the Punjab. These tribes, who were before separate, now formed one powerful state, and we imagine they are those whom we call Afghans. It does not appear on what ground Ferishta founds with opinion. Kedar Raja reigned forty-three years i.e. with Power *'Nam'* or *'God'*.

After the death of Kedar Raja, his minister, Jai Chand, who was also generalissimo of the army, usurped the throne. His accession was followed by a severe dearth, which carried off thousands of his subjects, whom he by no means attempted to relieve in their distress, but spent his time in gaiety at the city of Biana. After a reign of sixty years, he died. He was contemporary with Bahmun and Darab. Jai Chand left an infant son, whom his widow raised to the throne, and who would have ruled the empire in his name; but Dehli, the uncle of the young king, aided by the nobles, having deposed him, ascended the musnud. This prince, as famous for his justice as for his valour devoted his time to the good of his subjects, and built the city of Dehli. After having reigned only four years, Porus, a Raja of Kumaon, collecting a considerable force, attacked Dehli took him prisoner, and sent him into confinement in the fort of Rohtas, himself usurping the empire. Raja Porus pushed on his conquests through Bung, as far as the ocean, and having collected a great army, refused to pay tribute to the kings of Persia. The brahminical and other historians are agreed the Porus marched his army to the frontiers of India, in order to oppose the progress of Alexander, on which occasion Porus lost his life in battle, after having reigned seventy-three years. At this period, also, the Rajas of Deccan having become powerful, established their independence. Among others, was Kulchand, the founder of Kulbarga; Merchand, the founder of Mirch; Beejichand, the founder of Bejanaggar; besides many others whose names would only serve to swell out this work.

It is related, that when Alexander the Great came into India. Raja Bidur (the founder of the city of that name, and the chief of a tribe whose descendants are celebrated to this day in the Deccan for their bravery), having heard of the fame of the Greek monarch, sent his son as ambassador, with a number of elephants and other valuables to him, to prevent his invading the Deccan. After the death of Porus, Sansar Chand He is also called Chandragupta, supposed to be the Sandracottus of the Greeks made himself master of the empire of India, but sent an annual tribute to Gudarz, king of Persia: his country was usurped by Juna, the nephew of Porus. Juna is described as a liberal prince, who promoted the cultivation of the arts and built many towns on the banks of the Ganges and Jumna. He was contemporary with Ardsheer Babegan, who invaded India; but being met by Juna with valuable presents of gold and elephants on the frontier, Ardsheer was induced to withdraw his army. Juna, returning to Kunawj, died, after a reign of ninety years.

He was succeeded by the eldest of his twenty-two sons, named *Kullian Chand* or Cooli prince, a cruel and despotic prince, who put his subjects to death without cause or remorse. The unfortunate inhabitants of his kingdom, flying from his tyranny, left the city of Kanuj a mere ruin. After him, no Raja of consequence reigned inKunaj, excepting Ramdeo, whose history will shortly be related. As we shall not confine my account of the rajas of Hindustan to the dynasty of Kanuaj, we now proceed to that of Malwa, and of the celebrated Vikramjit Power.

The history of Vikramjit, the most illustrious nad virtuous sovereign of his age, has been transmitted to posterity in the legends which still remain among his countrymen. It is said that he passed the early part of his life among holy men, affecting poverty, and performing penance. At the age of fifty he assumed the command of an army, and in the course of a few years conquered the whole country of Nehrwala.

Here seems to imply Gujarat in general and Malwa, over which he ruled with justice. The Hindus are of opinion, that he was inspired, and could foretell coming events:he avoided all display of pomp, living in the same manner as his subjects, using earthen utensils instead of gold and sleeping on a mat instead of a bed. Ujjain became well inhabited during his reign, on account of the idol dedicated to Mahkali which he set up in that city. He also built the fort of D'har. From the death of Vikramjit, the Hindus date one of their eras, which at the present day is 1663, answering to the year 1015 of the Hijra. He was contemporary with Ardsheer Babegan, and some say with Shahpur. In the latter end of his reign, Shalivahan, a raja of the Deccan, making war with him, several battles ensued, in the last of which, Vikramjit lost his kingdom and his life. After his death Malwa long remained in a state of anarchy, till a length Raja Bhoj, setting up pretensions to the throne, assumed the reigns of government. Raja Bhoj, also of the tribe of Power, followed the steps of his predecessor Vikramjit. He founded many towns, among which are those of Kurgone, Bajigar, and Hundia. Twice yearly he kept a great feast which lasted forty days; during which all the most celebrated dancers and singers of Hindustan being assembled, he distributed food and wine; and at the end of the feast, new clothes, and ten miskals. This place is written differently in various manuscripts, and is not down in any of the maps we have consulted. of gold probably were presented to each guest. He died after a reign of forty years. At this period, one Vasdev, seizing on the province of Kanuaj, established himself in that principality. During his reign, Beiramgur, king of Persia, came to the court of Kunuaj in disguise. While at the capital a wild elephant in the neighbourhood had done much mischief, having killed many people, who went out to attack him. Among others, Vasdev himself had often gone out for the same purpose without success. Shortly after the arrival of Beiramgur, the same elephant, penetrating to the very gates of the city, caused much alarm: the Persian prince ran alone to the spot, and with a single arrow laid him dead at his feet. Raja Vasdev requested that the stranger who had killed the elephant might be brought to him. As he was entering the court, the Indian ambassador, who had just returned from Persia, whither he had conveyed, the annual tribute, recognising the king of Persia, informed Vasdev of the circumstance. The raja, descending from his throne, seated the stranger upon it, and after giving him his daughter in marriage, furnished him with a suitable escort, which attended him back to Persia. Vasdev died after reigning seventy years; during which time the fort of Kalpi was built. He left thirty-two sons, who disputed the succession with each other for two years: the throne was at length ascended by Ramdev Rahtore, the general of the late Vasdev. Having reduced the rebellious officers and rajas of his country, Ramdev marched to the province of Marwar, from whence he expelled the tribe of Katchwaha, and established that of Rahtore, which has remained there ever since; while that of Katchwaha removed to the neighbourhood of Rohtas. On his return to Kanuaj, he marched against Bengal, and taking possession of capital, he obtained great treasures, after having been absent from Kanuaj for three years.

Four years after this event, proceeding to Malwa, he reduced it, and built many towns and cities in that kingdom; among which was *Nurwar*, where having left a garrison of rahtories, he deputed an embassy to Shew Rai, Raja of Bijanaggar, soliciting his daughter in marriage. That Prince, dreading the power of Ramdew, sent her with valuable presents, along with the ambassador. Ramdev remained for two years in peace and happiness, after which, attacking the Rajas of Sewalik, he extorted from them annual tribute. In that war, Ramdev was opposed by the Raja of Kumaon (who inherited his country and crown from a long line of ancestors that had ruled upwards of 2000 years): a sanguinary battle took place, which lasted during the whole of one day, from sunrise to sunset, wherein many thousands were slain on both sides; till at length the Raja of Kumaon was defeated with the loss of all his elephants and treasures, and fled to the hills. Ramdew having subsequently compelled his enemy to give him his daughter in marriage, left him in possession of his country, and marching towards Nagrakote, plundered it, and at length arrived at a place called Shewkote Pindi, where (on account of his veneration for the idol Durga, which is situated at a small distance on the top of a neighbouring hill at nagrakote), he halted, and summoned the raja to appear before him. The Raja would by no means consent, but agreed to meet Ramdev at the temple, wherein the idol was placed. Thus the two princes met at the temple, when the Raja having given his daughter in marriage to the son of Ramdev, the latter proceeded from thence to the fort of Jammu. The Raja of Jammu opposed him in the woods, but was eventually defeated. Ramdev pursued him to the fort of Jammu, which he attacked, and subdued. At length the Raja consented to become tributary, and gave his daughter to another of Ramdev's sons. Ramdev being then in the vicinity of the Behat, a river which takes its rise in the hilly tract of Kashmir, and flows through the territory of the Punjab, proceeded through Bengal as far as the sea-shore, where the Sewalik mountains have their termination.The term Sewalik seems synonymous with Himalayas.

Ramdev was employed five months in making the journey, having subjected, during that period, upwards of five hundred rajas, after which he returned to his capital, where he gave presents to his soldiers, and celebrated a feast on the occasion. Ramdev reigned for upwards of fity-four years, and then died: he was contemporary with Firoze, the Sassanian, whose son Keikobad succeeded him, to both of which monarchs annual tribute was paid by India. After the death of Ramdev, his numerous sons all disputing the succession, civil warrs ensued. Partap Chand, the general of Ramdev, of the tribe of Sesodia, taking advantage of these events and collecting a force, ascended the throne, in spite of the endeavours of the princes, whom he seized and put to death, and thus established his authority. Having raised himself to the same elevation as his predecessor, Partap Chand refused to pay tribute to Persia, and the ambassador of Nowsherwan returned empty-handed. In consequence of this defection, the Persian troops invaded Multan and Punjab; and Partap Chand sent peace-offerings both to the generals and to the Persian King himself, to prevent further devastation. From this, he transmitted the annual tributes as usual. After the death of Partab Chand each of his generals seized on a province; while his progeny, flying from Kanuj, occupied a small tract of country in the hills of Kombulmere, in the neighbourhood of Chitor and Mundusr; the descendants of whom ast present hold it in sovereignty. They are distinguished by the appellation of Rana, Significant of apetty prince.The Sisodia family, the head of which is styled Rana, still reigns over Chittoor and Aodypur; and its descendants have given rajas to the principalities of Dongurpur and Partabghar — Vide Sir J. Malcolm's Report on Malwa. vol. i.pp. 504-506. Ferishta is in error when he asserts that Rana signifies a petty prince: it always has been borne by the highest Hindu kings, and is distinctive of pre-eminence.

Among the other generals and rajas who became powerful after the death of Partap Chand, was Anand-dev Rajput, of the tribe of Bias. Having collected a large force in Malwa, he conquered the countries of Nehrwala and Marhatt, in the Deccan. He built also the forts of Ramgir and Mahur in Berar, as well as the fort of Mando in Malwa. He lived in the age of Khusrow Purvees, and died after a reign of sixteen years.

At this time a Hindu named Maldeo, having collected a force in the Doab, attacked and seized the cities of Dehli and Kanauj. He made the latter city his residence, which attained a condition so flourishing that it had seldom been equalled. An idea of its population may be formed, when it is stated that Kunauj contained 30,000 shops for the sale of *pan,* and 60,000 families of public dancers and singers. Pan, an aromatic leaf, much eaten by the Indians. After having reigned forty-two years, Maldev died; but leaving no sons fit to suceed him, anarchy and civil war every where prevailed. From that time till the Mahomedan invasion no single Raja ruled over India; for when Sultan Mahmood Ghizni invaded it, the country was divided into principalities, as follows:

Kanuaj ... Kuwar Rai

Meerut ... Hardut Rai

Mahavun ... A village on the left bank of the Jumna, about ten miles below Mutra, is supposed to be the spot here alluded to.Gulchander Rai

Lahore ... Jaipal, the son of Hutpal

Thus also Malwa, Gujarat, Ajmer, Gwaliar &c. had each separate Rajas.

5. *Valmiki*, who was considered to be an outcaste or *'untouchable'*, lived by robbing, plundering and killing travellers for several years, on the advice of sage, he transformed himself into a devotee sage, he transformed himself into a devotee of the Lord and became an eminent sage himself. He wrote the great epic *Ramayana.* Term *Ram,* this refers to the son of Dasharath. His name can be spoken and written, but the 'Name' of the true Lord cannot be spoken or written. It is ineffable that can not be the true Ram, the true Ram is merciful to all regardless of their good and bad deeds. He is the creator of all, he is the Creator of all, he is the true *'Name'* as Ravi das says, 'the World is sad and Ram is not bound to any location. Find the only true creator. Who indeed is the true Ram."

   Bhai re! ram Kahan hai mohi batavo

   vani, 10, see also bani 9

   God dewells within everyone's heart

   Where you look

   the Lord is seen manifesting his love

   Darshan 13

   (K.N. Upadhyaya, *Guru Ravidas, The Philosophers Stone,* Punjab (India); third edition; 2005 pp. 83, 84). The ancient holy city known as Kashi, is the place *Mandur*, where a family lived in purity. A child was born in this *Mandur* village and currently known as *Varanasi,* while in colonial times it was called Benaras in English. His name was given the auspicious name, Ravi Das (*RaidasRamanayn;* written by Bakshi Das, (Kashi) 1970, P. 27). Anant Das is said to the grandson of *Ravidas's* disciple, *King Pipa* and Mira (*Vani.* p. 25).

6. *Chachnama* is the most authentic primary source, hitherto discovered, on the history of the indigenous ruling dynasty of Sind roughly devoted the lower Indus valley from Multan down to the sea, in the west it sometimes included large portionof Baluchistan, and in the east it was bounded by the Indian desert. Our knowledge of its early history is extremely scanty, almost limited to what the Arab historians means the people of Nature means *'Nam'* called Arab have written about the beauty of Nature. We learn that at that time the Arab invasions were started in Sind under the dynasty founded by the Brahman *Chach* who was wandering in material life and took shelter under the *Rai* family comprising five kings of the *'Nam'* equivalent to *Pandav* or *Pandu*, who are said to have held power for 137 years with *Alor* (near modern *Rohri*) as their capital when Yuan Chwang was travelling in India (629-45 A.D.). Sind was ruled by a Buddhist monarch of the *Sudra* (*Shu-to-lo*) *Caste* (Vol. II, p. 252), an It was identical with *Siharas Rai*, as is most probably the book was written in Arabic by an anonymous author, possibly a camp-follower of Mohammad bin Qasim, an entitled *Chachnama* after the name of the founder of the ruling house of Kashmir which was started by *Durlabvardhana,* the first ruler of Karkota dynasty. It gives a brief account of the *Sudra* or *untouchable* dynasty of Sind, on the death of whose last ruler known as *Rai Sahai,* II, the throne was usurped by his *Brahman* minister named *Chach*. An inscription, dated A.D. 756, gives the names of six generations of *Chahamana* princes, ending with *Bhartrivaddha* II, a feudatory of *Nagavaloka*, who is generally identified with the imperial Pratihara ruler *Nagebhata* 1. *Bhartrivaddha* ruled in the Broach district, and if his five ancestors did the same, we must presume that the *Chahamanas* ruled in this region from about 600 A.D. It is interesting to note in this connetion that an inscription dated 713 A.D. found in Ghittargarh, records of four kings viz *Mahesvara* of the race of *Tvashtri,* Bhima, his son Bhoja and his son wars *Mana*. It is noteworthy in this connection that the family was originally called the race of *Tvashtri*, and it was only somewhat later, with the growth of power, that the members used the name ending *dama*, first met with in the names of Westernsatraps, and called themselves *Chahamanas*.

   The Chitorgarh inscription, as interpreted by Tod, would seem to imply that in 713 A.D. the territory was under the suzerainty of the Lord of Malwa.

Mana and his three ancestors ruled in Chitor. There is still a sub-clan of the *Paramaras* known as Morya or Maurya ruler defeated by *Bappa*. Guhilot ruler Bappa conquered Chitor from the Mori King *Manuraja*. Tod gives the name as Mana, and this ruler has been identified with the author or an inscription, dated 713 A.D. found at Chitor, which will be refered to later.

The Mauryas are evidently the same as the *Mori* Rajputs, who accordingly to the bardic chronicles, rued in Chitor. The existence of several ruling families of this same, both in Northern and Southern India, in the seventh century A.D. and later, is proved by epigraphic the name, no doubt, recalls the famous impact dynasty of ancient India ruled of Kashmir, but although Hiuen Tsang refers to *Purnvarman* of Magadha as a descendant of Asoka. As already noted above, the Mauryas fell a victim to the Arab aggression, and it was probably after this catastrophe that Bappa defeated them and took possession of *Chitor* after expelling the *mlechchhas*. There can be hardly any doubt that the Gurjara Kingdom described by Hiuen Tsang refers to that ruled over by the descendants of *Haricandra*. The Chinese pilgrim describes the Young Gujara king as a devout believer in the law of Buddha i.e. *'Nam'*. He may indentified with king *Tata,* son of *Nagabhata* about whom it is said in a record of the family that considering life to be evanescent as lightning, he abdicated in favour of his younger brother, *Bhoja*. HiuenTsang refers to the capital of the Gujarat kingdom as *Pi-lo-mo-lo*. This has been identified with *Bhillamala* modern *Bhinmal*. But since he notes its distance as 300 miles north of Valabhi and its capital has Balmer in the North of Kashmir.

King *Tata* and his three successors ruled probably between 640-720 A.D. The next kink *Siluka,* great grandson of *Tata,* was, however an important king of Kashmir. If *Stravani* be regarded as identical with *Taban* of the Arab writers, possibly a camp-follower of *Mahummad bin Qasim,* Surnamed *Ferishta* was born at *Astrabad* on the border of the Caspian sea means *Samudra* in Sanskrit called *'Sudra'* he was the son of *'Ghulam Alli Hindu Shah'*, a learned man, who, quitting his native country, travelled into India, and eventually reached *'Ahmadnaggar'* in the Deccan, during the reign of Murtuza Nizam Shah. He states that he had only attained his twelfth year when he reached *Amadnaggar*, and concluded his work entitled *'Chachnama'* after the name of the founder of the ruling house Kashmir. We may conclude from his description that the country ws prosperious and peaceful. The extent of the political power of Kashmir at this period is strikingly attested by the fact that Hiuen Tsiang found all adjacent territories on the west and the South, down to the plains, subject to the away of the king of *Kashmir* i.e. called *'Nam'*.

There is a local Chronicle of Sindh called *Chachnama* and other authorities which give some interesting details of its history. According to these words *Sahiras*, the king of Sindh belongs to the *Sudra* or *untouchable* dynasty and his last ruler was *Rai Sahasi* II, the throne was usurped by his *Brahman* minister named *Chach*, son of *Silaij* for Shiladitya (Silaaditya). A full genealogy of the family is given for the first time in the *'Alpur Inscription'*, dated 977 A.D. It gives the name of 20 kings from *Guhadatta* to *Saktikumara*. If we allot an average of 20 years to each reign, *Guhadatta* may be regarded as having flourished in the second half of the sixth century A.D. This date is corroborated by to records of *Sila (Shiladitya)* and *Aparajita,* the fifth and sixth kings in the list, dated respectively (646-7 to 661-2 A.D.). This demolishes the traditional account, recorded in the hardic chronicles, that *Guha,* the founder of the family, was son of *Siladitya,* the last king of *Valabhi,* for as we have discussed above, the latter was on the throne till 766 A.D. *Chach* seems to be local or dialectical form of the word *'Jajja'* which is the Prakrit form of the Sanskrit word *'Yayati'*. Indian history has known some people who bore the name *'Jajja'*. It is likely to *Arabs* might have achieved more success in the interior of India, if the *Prathiharas* i.e. *'Nam'* had not offered them a determiend opposition. In Sindh the conquerors followed a farsighted policy of tolerance to conciliate the people and to established their authority in Sindh on a firm footing. Besides, their outlook must have, to some extent, be affected by admixture of blood like modern society, which was inevitable as the conquerors did not bring women with them. The word 'women' is composed of two words *'Wo'* or *'Wu'* means dirty smell and 'men' means living *man* evaluated at that time by the Master, then a new society called Moslem on the basis of Islam which mean totally surrender to *'Father'* or *'husband'* as Salama never bothered about her appearance or world comports, her sole concern in life was to practise piety. She fasted three days in a month and often spent the whole night in prayers to attain the beauty of Nature or *Kalma*. On one occasion, he saw her wearing a gold necklace which had given to her by her parents. When Muhammad showed disapproval of it, she promptly broke it into pieces and distributed the gold among the poor but the modern or new Muslaman is not ready to surrender it, he is so greedy that he has forgotten the Prophet, became matrialistic. These tradition conform neither to the nature of the Prophet's marriages, nor to the reality of his relationship with his wives. As a result of these spurious versions, on which the orientalists have feasted, there has been a strong reaction among a section of Muslism. Imam Lashad Khalifa, an egoist man, a Saudi Arabian thelogian, has gone to the extent of opining, after considering research in original sources that is *'Nam'* or *'Kalma'* of the Master, that 'the extremely *Hadith* (Tradition) have been followed by the Muslims and *Sunna* (Practices) of the *'Nam'* have been forgotten and nothing to do with *Prophet Muhammad'* and further that obediance to them is tantamount to a flagrant disobedience of God and his final Prophet'. i.e. the messag eof 'God' to serve the society and live in harmony. He quotes the verses 6:112 and 25:31 of the *Quran* in his support and contends that these traditions are 'Satanic inventions". Like *Nambaz* and other festivals or Santan Dharm. . No doubt, *Islam* spread with the liberal view of the present Master, and the Hindu temples were considered "inviolate like the Churches of the Christians, the synagogues of the Jews, and the altars of the Magians" The Brahmans were even permitted to build or repair dilapidated temples. While the Arab garrisons were stationed at strategic centres, the internal administration was mostly left in the hands of the natives, who paid the land tax (*Khiraj*) *means* tribute has to pay by a subordinate chief and the poll -tax (*jeziya*), a religious tax imposed on non-Muslims or any tax other than *Khiraj* or land revenue, because father has given the life, but subordinated is little bit careless, therefore he has to pay the tax of his deeds and actions as per the report of master is concerned. We learn of internecine struggles of the rise and fall of the 'Sind Dynasty' of the *Sudras* led by *Siharas Rai* at one time. According to this work *Sahiras,* the king of Sindh, ruled over an extensive territory bordering in the north upon Kashmir and in the west upon *Makran.* Hiuen Tsang not only describes it as an independent kingdom, but also mentions three other states of dendencies. It is difficult to locate these states definitely because of the long transmigration of the people from one place to another, but Sindh and its subordinate states certainly comprised the whole of the lower *Sindhu or Vitasta* valley to the South of Multan. The north-west of Sindh were two other important states on the western borderland of India. In the north was the kingdom of *Kapisa* or Kabul or Kabulistan, comprising the Valley of the Kabul river and the hill tracts surrounding it up to the *Hindu Kush* mountains to the South of Kabul was Zabul or Zabulistan which included the upper valley of the Helm river and a large extent of territory born to the east as well as to the west of it. According to again by the Hiuen Tsang, the kingdom of *Kapisa* was an extensive one and exercised suzerainty over ten dependent states including *Lampaka* (Laghman), *Nagar* (Jalalabad) and *Gandhara.* Of Zabulistan we have no detailed knowledge, but it was also a very powerful kingdom of the 'Father'. In the seventh century A.D. these two kingdoms formed parts of India both politically and culturally, being Indian in language, literature and religion and ruled over by kings who bore Indian names the king of Zabul bore the designation *Shahi,* and the rulers of *Kapisa* called them *Kashatriyas* of Ved period.

According to these Chronicles king *Sahiras*, son of *Sahasi Rai*, ruled over an extensive kingdom bordering on Kashmir and Kanauj in the north and east and extending as far as Makran in the west. King Sahiras lost his life in a fight with the king of *Nimruz,* a province of Persia, who had invaded his territory and entered *Kirman.* This took place probably at the beginning of the seventh century A.D.

After the disintergration of their empire, the Kushans did not entirely disappeared from the stage of Indian history. Now the Archaeological Survey of India sees in the potential of emerging as a star Buddhist attraction known Dr.Raj Kumar. Its recent findings appear to have confirmed the existence of a Buddhist monastic establishment was there at Ambaran in Akhnoor area. During the heyday of Buddhism, it was one of the route which was used by the monks and traders during their visit from Patliputra (now Patna and Bihar) to Taxila (presently in Pakistan). During extensive excavations between 1999 and 2001 a *Stupa*, votive stupa and walls of a monastery (including living quarters for monks) were discovered from the site. Successive flash floods have stripped the site of its original structures raised in the pre-Kushan period (2nd and Ist century B.C.) the glourious remanants of the Kushan period (Ist to 3rd century A.D.) are there. The place had continued to flourishing during the Gupta period under the Skand Gupta. In the *Rajatarangini*, it is mentioned a Vihara was built by S kandgupta known as *Skandabhavanavihara.* As to the abbreviated form *Skanda* for *Skandagupta*, used *bhimavat.* By the monastere do *Je-Je* which Ou-Kong mentions in Kashmir which is possible to be meant for the *Vihara.* It compares with the Sanskrit word *Samudra*, Gupta means hide, equivalent to Maurya rule who was *Sudhar* by his caste. The establishemnt continue to flourish in Gupta period III (4th to 5th century A.D.), with periodic damage and subsequent repairs due flesh floods. Probably around six to seventh century A.D. Twelve circular copper coins in which eight belongs to *Kushana* ruler Soter *Megas,* Kanishka and Huviskha and one of Toraman Hunu ruler was the other important find discovered in the courseof archeological excavation and in the unique Sanskrit Historical work, Kalhana's *Rajatarangini* mentions as many as for Huna kings of Kashmir. They were (1) *Mihirakula, (2) Kinkhila (3) Lahkana Narendraditya (4) Lahkana Udayaditya. Mihirakula* set up in Gandhara as a refugee from the Punjab and later in Kashmir. He became a devout of *Saiva* equivalent to *Chamar* as seen in his coins. This Huna regime continued for some time. Its best proof is the rule of *Meghavahana* with Ephthalite Huna affinity. Kalhana mentions a *Toramana* as king of Kashmir who issued his coins but he may be the same as *Tormana* of Gupta history.

This Huna phase of Kashmir history was ended by *Harsha-Vikramadity* of Ujjain who invaded Kashmir and placed poet *Matrigupta* on its throne. He is referred to by Huan Chwang. His reign is noted for the important literary work *Hayagrivavadha* composed by *Mentha* and the temple Matriguptasvamin. *Matrigupta* abdicated in favour of Pravara sena II who conquered Kashmir. He was ambitious as a conqueror having invaded Surashtra where he placed his nominee *Siladitya-Pratapasila*, the son of Harsh-Vikramadity, on the throne (580 A.D.). He built a new capital called *Pravarapura* (Srinagar). He issued gold and silver coins some of which bear the legend *Kidara* (*Kushana*) and extended his territories towards the plains he fell into the battle with *Chandrahas* which was equivalent to *'Nam'* then Raja of the Panjab (*Madradesa*), whose capital was probably at Sialkot. The reference is interesting and probably historical. He was with *Chandarhas* doubtless was the outcome of an attempt on the part of the hill chief to enlarge the state boundaries towards the plains. Tradition affirms that in former times the territory extended much further to the south than now, and the Raja of Sialkot would naturally oppose such encroachment on his borders. The reference to the *"Daivaputra-Shahi-Sahanusahi"* in Allahabad pillar inscription of *Samudragupta* which qualified the title as *Sudra* rule has rightly been interpreted to suggest that princes of the Kushan race of the *'Nam'* has been survived in the Punjab and the Kabul valley until about the middle of the 4th century A.D.

Sialkot has been identified by Cunningham ancient *Sakala 'Word'* Buddhist *Sagala Chamar* with Sangala Hill. It was visited by Hiuen Tsiang in 630 A.D. but the reference is evidently to Sialkot of which the ancient name was *Sakala* (*Archaeological Survey Report of India;* Vol. II Vanaras, p. 193). In the Buddhist literature *Sagala*, which is thus proved to be one of the oldest cities in the Panjab from the very ancient period. In very ancient times it was the capital of the *Madras,* who are known in the later Vedic period, and *Sakaladvipa* or "the island of Sakala" where every saint of the world has been born from the time immorial was the ancient name of the *doab* between the rivers *Chandrabhaga* (*Chenab*) and Iravati (Ravi) which also stand the name of *'Great Saint RaviDas'*. In some what later Greeco-Indian kings of the house of Euthydemus, who ruled the Eastern Panjab, and it was the residence of Menander (115-90 B.C.), who has been identified with king Milinda, who is known from the Pali work *'Milinda Panho'* which gives details of his kingship. The Buddhist divine, *'Nagasena'* converted the Greek king to Buddhism. His countries bore Indian names, e.g *Anantakayas* (*Antiochus*), and *Devamantriya* (*Demetrious*). Menander was a philosopher king. He had a large army. His capital was *Sakala* (Sialkot) is described in the Pali work as "a great centre of trade, abounding in parks and lakes, a paradise of rivers and mountains and woods," (Rhys Davids). It may be noted that *Sakala* was a very old city, the capital of the *Madra,* people of the *Upanishads* whom the *Mahabharata* place between. The rivers Chenab and Ravi. His date was about 150 B.C. At a still later period *Sakala* was the capital of *Salavahana* or *Satavahanas* forefathers of the *Lohara* dynasty of Kashmir or Poonch; whose son, *Rasalu*, is the great hero of all Panjab tradition likely to be 'Deepit Raj' and after the invasion of the *Hunas* in the latter part of the fifth century A.D. it became the capital of *Toramana* and his son *Mihirakula* who ruled over the Panjab and also probably over Kashmir. As Jammu is only thirty miles from Sialkot, and the boundry even at the present time, is within seven miles of the latter place, it is evident that frequent disputes must have arisen in former times, similar to that referred to in the *Vansavali. Jambu-Lochan* followed and continued the war with *Chandarhas,* in which the latter was slain. He is then said to have founded the town of Jammu. The story is thus related:- *Jambu-lochan* on becoming Raja wished to found another town as his capital and name if after himself. With this in view he went out hunting one day accompanied by his officials, and crossing the Tawi he saw in the jungle a deer and a tiger drinking the water at the same tank along with a goat. Being surprised at the sight he returned to his tent which was made by the 'weaver' and calling his Ministers enquired the meaning of such a strange occurance. They replied that the explanation lay in the fact, that the soil of the sons of *Bharat* a legendary emperor of India was born there and then the country is called *Bhartavarsa* or the sub-continent of the *Jambudvipa* (the continent of the *Jambu* tree) the land of the *Yama*, those do not believe on the lord; and for that reason no living creature bore enmity against one another. The Raja, therefore, came to the conclusion that this was just the kind of the site called *Mahabharata* ended and will start another as *"History Repeat Itself"*. He was insearch of and founded a new town, calleing it *Jambupura*. A belief in the influence of the soil on human and animal life is widely prevalent in the hills. The early history of the state is lost in the mists of the past, and even common tradition is silent because of the Brahminical rule in this area. The first Raja named *Agnigrabhah,* the sufix term *Agni*, has treasured up in the *Rig-Veda* among the hundred of hymns, few indeed could be found that did not contain *Soma* allusion 'Word' description, simile, epithet in Aryan India. And, indeed, this is the view most explicity expressed in this line. "*Agni* is Surya, a source of light in the morning, Surya is Agni at night." A few passasses of the Rig-Veda will throw light on conflict between Aryans and the Non-Aryans. Non-Aryans Vangrida by Rijisvan in fight against the *"dusky brood"* (*Krishna-grabhah*). In point of fact, the fair-complexioned worshippers of *Agni, Indra* and *Soma* found two widely different races in possession. The physical differences between the Aryan as (1) *Krishna tvach "dark skinned"* (R.V.1 130,8, IX, 411). This beautiful and natural solution is suggested by the results of latest researches that it will be noticed the Helmend ends, not in sea, but in a large *lake* to which the name of *Samudra* would apply perfectly and *Sudra* has been born from it as *'untouchable'*. The same may be said in a still greater measure of another goddess, VACH in Sanskrit and *TVACH* in Greek as *Ch* pronounced as in *Church 'Word'*s personified speech *Chamar* who in the *Rig-Veda* already (in the latest book of course, the tenth) is invested with much of the usual pomp of Brahmanic metaphysics as a "most adorable", "widely pervading". Wealth-bringing deity of "many abodes", but not to extravaganece; the personification *Brahmana*, the head priest of the Hindu community or rather allegory *'Word'* does not pass the bounds of fine, even noble poetry, he always busy with work or to serve the humanity without any material benefit like the Brahman, and is moreover distinctly traceable to the natural phenomenon from which it is evolved. For sublimiting, few conception can equal this of our race's earliest poets *'Word'* a conception which lingers still in the mythical poetry of later nations in other lands. Primeval speech is the voice of the gods, speaking in thunder and strom, it is *Vach, 'Chamar'* the sarced 'Word', majestic and compelling beneficent and wise *'Chamar'* in its heavenly abode. But it is not for men those do not believe on the 'Father'. To them vach descends in the form of Speech, and Lo, whereever the wise have uttered speech (*Vach*). These were undoubtedly broken up into numerous tribes with different names and under different kings *'Word'* as, for that matter, were the Aryan themselves. Moreover, term *gnabhah* mean 'ego' which is destroyer or injurous to other on the basis of Caste, colour and creed. Apart from the highest form of worship as meditation on the *'Absolute'* and the *Formless* or *'Infinite'* as *Hiranya-garbhah or Viratpurush*. The popular was ceremonial and ritual in character would be lasting for months and could be performed only by the aristocracy (*Maghavans*) and royalty. In this passage, it is reflected that the first Raja of Jammu was a brother or kinsman of the Raja of Ayudhya or Bihar i.e. Krishna. As Manu says that a Brahman should not live in the kingdom, ruled by a *Sudra* this clearly indicates that Manu is not in the favour of the *Sudra* rulers because they belong to the Heaven and Brahman belong to Earth, but control by *Sudra* there are many historical examples of non-*Ksatriya* rulers in the Vedic time. *Mahapadmananda,* the founder of Nanda dynasty was a *Sudra* ruler and has been referred to as *"Sudragarbhodbhava"*. Pusyamitry Sunga, a *Brahmana* and the *Senapati* of *Brahadratha,* the last Mauryan king killed the latter and founded the Sunga dynasty. In this connection the dialogue, once held between a *Candala* and sage *Visvamitra* i.e. *'Nam'*, attracts our attention. It is said in the *Santi Prava* that once upon a time at the end of *Treta Yuga,* before the beginning of *Dvapara Yuga,* rains did not pour for twelve consecutive years. Rivers, lakes, streams and other water reservoirs dried up. Consequently crops were destroyed and famine took place. Many people starved to death. Population decayed, Robbers raised up their heads and began looting the people as present *politicans* are playing this part and this complete disorder in the society and chaos crept in form of rapes, custodial killing, corruption, by the official and ministers, etc. Under these circumstances *Visvamitra, i.e. 'Nam' or 'Word'* and his family members also could get nothing to eat and live upon them. Leaving his wife and children, *Visvamitra* went to colony of *Candalas* in search of food. In one house, he saw a piece of a recently slain dog's thigh and decided to steal it in order to appease his hunger. The *Candala* the force of *'Nam'* whom the sage had taken to be sleeping was, in fact, awake and he caught him red-handed. After knowing that the thief was no other than the famous sage Visvamitra, the *Candala* repeatedly told him not to commit a great sin by eating the flesh and that too of a dog's thigh. An authority in the matters of *Dharma,* the sage told him not to interfer. He said that in *apattikala,* self-preservation was the highest law and it justified recourse to all sorts of means fair or foul, commended or condemned, with a view to saving one's life in very important in the law of nature. Since there was no *varna,* lower than the *Sudra* either educated in language, the duties where of *Sudra* could adopt, the *Mahabharata* lays down that he should take recourse of fine arts such as painting and sculpture. This may also be true of the *Domba* tribe, who appear to be an important people in the *Dombipadacarva*. Since Brahmanisation took place on a very large scale in early medieval times, the number of *Untouchables* castes increased substantially. In earlier times certain varieties of hunters and artisans were rendered *untouchables,* but now even more agriculturist castes were condemned to this position. On the other hand, the fact that a good number of *Sudras* were reduced to the position of *untouchables* must have given satisfaction to the remainder who now practically took the place of the *Vaisyas* in social hierarchy. Another significance process which led to the multiplication of *Sudra* castes was the transformation of crafts into castes. As trade and commerce languished in the post Gupta times craft guilds tended to become stagnant, immobile, more and more hereditary and more and more localised. Trades and guilds gradually constituted themselves into closed exclusive groups resembling castes for all practical purposes. A *paraka* quotes Brhaspati to show that heads guilds may reprimand and condemn wrong-doers and by also communicate them. It seems that *napita, mochika tambulika, svarnakara, malakara, samkhakara, sutrakara (Megh), citrakara,* etc, who like aboriginers, are all called served castes in medieval textures obviously emerged as castes out of various crafts. Craft villages are mentioned in ancient texts, but now they find place in medieval inscriptions. Thus we hear of two villages called *Kumbharapaika* which belonged to the potter caste. Modern specialization means skill and proficiency in the craft wherever and whenever it can be acquired but in medieval period sepecialization meant attachment to the *'Master'*, to his place, head to the family which practised the craft. The present survey shows that the pre-Muslim Society in Northern India underwent some important changes. Unequal distribution of land and military power created feudal ranks which cut across *Varna* consideration, especially at the higher and literate level.

The first Raja, mentioned *Agnivarna* or *garbaha*, came up into the Panjab by way of *Nagarkot* (Kangra), and after crossing the *Ravi* settled at Parol near Kathua, opposite to *Madhopur* in the Gurdaspur District. According to the records this, if authentic, must have been at a very early period 'Father' or 'Nam' had his son *Vayusarava* means God of the *'Air'*, both *Vayu* and *Vata* is also called the son in law of *Trastri* called 'Indra', the 'rainer' the 'irrigator means 'strong' or 'powerful' i.e. *'Nam'*, added to his territory the country of the outer hills as far west as the Jammu Tawi. Four other Rajas followed in succession, and the fifth was *Agnigarbaha,* who had eighteen sons, of whom the two oldest were *Bahu-lochan* and *Jambu-lochan*. Bahu-lochana succeeded his father and founded the town and fort of Bahu, on the left bank of the Tawi, opposite Jammu, and made it his capital. From the earliest times, as there is good reason to believe the capital was at *Bahu* and the Rajas resided in the strong fort; and this probably continued to be their residence till they retired to *Babbapura* or *Babor* after the Muslim invasions. Jambu-Locahan was followed by *Purankaran* termed as old as *Ramayana* who had two sons, *Dayakaran* and *Dharmkaran*. A strange tradition of an occurrence of this time is found in the *Vansavali*. Kashmir is said to have been in disorder, and *Purankaran* was appealed to help. He sent his elder son, *Dayakarna*, who restored order and became rule of the country. From him are said to be descended the Bhau Rajputs still existing in Jammu, whose former capital was at *Kaleth,* near Aknoor. Some generations later we find a note purporting to refer to the time of Raja *Sala* or *Salavahana* who ruled the Panjab as far north as Gandhara (Peshawar), and whose capital was at Sailkot. He is said to have invaded Jammu, defeated the Raja, named Shib-Prakash, and destroyed the town. The Raja of Jammu, being driven from his capital, sought refuge in the inner mountains, where he and his successors are said to have lived for some generations. Jammu was then recovered and the Raja returned. Most probably the reference is to Bahu, who was associated with theory of *'Nam' or 'Word'* which must still have been the capital of the state during two time of *Kushana. Salavahana* was the Raja of Sialkot (Ibid; PP. 21-22), then called *Sakala* probably about the 100 B.C. He seems to have belonged to the Yadava family, who may have succeeded the Greeco-India Kings. The first capital of the family, according to Cunningham, was at *Gajnipur,* now *Rawalpindi,* from whence they were driven by the inflowing tide of the Indo-Scythian or *Saka* invasions, when they retired to *Sakala*. *Salavahana* is said to have afterwards defeated the Sakas in great battle, near Multan, and established the Saka Era, 78 B.C. to commemorate his victory. He was succeeded by his son *Rasalu,* the famous hero of tradition in the Panjab, who also contended with *Sakas*, but on his death his kingdom passed to the Raja *Hudi,* who was his enemy, and probably a Saka prince.

The great Moslem scholar Alberuni, surnamed Abu-Rihan Muhammad, as his full name was, studied Sanskrit thoroughly, and his work contains an excellent account of the achievements of the Hindus in literature and science. He lived from 973 to 1048 A.D., gives us a little more information which has been also recorded int he *Rajatarangini.* According to their accounts, the descendants of Barhatakin, one of them being *Kanik* (*Kaniska*) whom he called Hindu Turks, ruled Kabul for sixty generations under the style of *Shahiya* evidently a varient of the Sanskrit *Sahi* became Sahia. Mosleman or of the Kushan *Shah.* Alberuni may or may not be correct in stating that all these monarchs belonged to one family, or that their number was exactly sixty, but it seems probable that they were of the Kushan stock; and used the title Shahiya (*Sahi*). Scholars generally suppose that one of them was identical with the Buddhist Ksathriya king of *Kia-pi-shi* (*Kapisa*), mentioned by Yuan Chwang. The pilgrims description of the royal caste of *Sudra* or *'Untouchable'* does not in any way militate against this view; it only shows that by the time of his visit the foreign Kushans had became completely merged into Hindu society. We may recall here the tendency of even some of great Kushana to adopt Hindu gods and names. Hardly anything is known of the *Turki*

Sahis except that they carried on intermittent wars with the Arab invaders from the seventh to the middle of the ninth century A.D. The last member of the house, *Lagaturman* is said to have been desposed by his Brahman minister, *Kallar.*

We have more light as regards "the illustrious Lalliya Sahi" whom Kalhana mentions as the support of *Alakhana* means the *'House of God'* i.e. *'Nam'*. Having usurped the throne, Kallar became the founder of a new dynasty, which Alberuni calls *"Hindu Shahiya"*. Then came in succession *Samand (Samanta), Kamalu, Bhim (Bhima), Jayapal, Anandapala, Tarojanpala, (Trilocanapala)* and *Bhimapala*. Coins partially confirm this list of Alberuni of brother of *Jayapida* the king of Kashmir, who revolted and was killed by the latter. Kalhana relates to the early part of *Jaypida's* reign is briefly. The following soon after his accession the king, stimulated by the ambition of rivalling his grandfather's fame i.e. *Durlabhavardhana* of Kashmir, set out "for the conquestof the world". Eighty thousand litters are supposed to have been counted with his army as it passed through the frontier watch-station of Kashmir. After the king's departure, *Jajja* his brother-in-law (*Sala*), usurped the Kashmir throne. Though gradually deserted by his troops, *Jayapida* moved down to the Ganges, still rich enough to make a gift of a lakh less one horses (1) to the Brahmans of Prayaga. There he left the remainder of his followers, and set out in disguise on a tour of adventurous travel. While at *Paundravardhana*, the capital of a district of Bengal, he attracted by a deed of great prowers the attention of its king *Jayanta*. His disguise being discovered, he was given by the kings of *Gauda,* the over-lords of his father-in-law, and then turn back towards *Kashmir*. Joined by the troops he had left behind, under his faithful minister, *Devasarman,* he defeated on his route the king of Kanauj entered Kashmir. In a fierce contest near *Suskaletra,* in the Kashmir valley, *Jajja* was vanquished and slain, after having for three years held possession of the land. It is imposible in the absence of other records to ascertain the exact elements of historic truth underlying Kalhana's romantic story. But the general tenour of the latter seems to indicate that *Jayapida* had, during the early part of his reign, while engaged in some foreign expedition, temporarly lost his throne to a usurper. The king's wanderings during his exile seem to have taken him to Bengal, and to have subsequently been embellished by popular imagination of the *'Nam'*.

Of *Jayapida's* subsequent reign which, according to Kalhana's calculation, would have to be placed in the years (751-782 A.D.), but which in all probability fell much closer to the end of the eight century, few authentic details seem to have been recorded. Manifestly genuine and, for literary history important are the data which Kalhana gives us regarding the various scholars and poets, like *Ksira, Bhatta, Udbhata, etc.* who flourished at *Jayapida* court. Several of them are known to us from their works and from other references. Of topographical interest is the account we received the foundation of *Jayapura,* marked by the present *Andarkoth,* which *Jayapida* built as his capital in marshy, but Kalhana mentions some other names in connection with the wars between the *Sahis* and the Kings of Kashmir. Thus, his *Lalliya,* who helped the Gujara adversary of *Sankara Varman* (883-902 A.D.), was perhaps identical with *Kallar* of the above group. *Sankaravarmans* life and reign found a violent end. In order to avenge the death of his 'Lord of the Marches' (*dvarapati*), who had fallen in a frontier-affray, he had marched down the valley of the *Vitasta*, and subsequently undertaken an expedition to hill tracts on the banks of the *Indus*; and advanced westwards beyond the natural limits of the valley proper. We are further told that *Prabhakaradeva* minister of Gopalavarman (902-04 A.D.) under the guardianship of his mother Sugandha. Kalhana records of him that on a victorious expedition, which he led against the seat of the *Sahi* power, at the town of *Udabhanda*, he "bestowed the kingdom of the rebellious *Sahi* upon *Toramana,* Lalliya's son, and gave him the (new) name *Kamaluka*" coins of the latter, very frequent in the Western Punjab, show the legend of *Sri Samantadeva* i.e. *'Nam'* as his original home, and thus attested the existence of a *Sahi* ruler of this name. The coins of *Samanta* have been found in large numbers in Afghanistan and the Punjab, they are of the bull and horseman type.

He is described as the *"Sahi* of Udbhandapura" for the capital was transferred there after the caputre of Kabul in 870-71 A.D. by the *Saffarid Yaqub ibn Laith*. It is claimed in the *Rajatarangini* that after his victory the Kashmiri minister gave the *Sahi* kingdom to *Toramana,* who was probably the same as Alberuni's *Kamalu*. The next ruler, *Bhima,* was the materinal grandfather of queen Didda of Kashmir, where he built a temple called *Bhimakesava* in the reign of *Ksemagupta* (950-58 A.D.). Bhima is known from his coins too. From the time of *Jayapala* onwards the Moslems exerted a continuous pressure on the *Sahis*. The latter gradually lost their territories in Afghanistan, and were even compelled to shift the capital to *Bhatinda* (now in the Patiala state). When *Jayapala* was driven to desperation by the ever-recurring attack on the enemy's dominions. The Hindu host were repelled, and *Jayapala* had to conclude a humiliating treaty. In the safety of his capital, however, he repudiated the terms of agreement, and even went to the length of imprisoning the officers of the Sultan, who was thus naturally provoked to chastise him. *Jayapala* invited the prominent Hindu states, like those of Delhi, Ajmer, *Kalanjara* and Kanauj, to help him with men and money but despite their response he suffered a severe reverse on the confines of *Lamghan* (*Jalalabad district*), Raverty, on the one hand, thinks that the scene of the battle was fought in the Kurram valley. There was one *Jajja* ground towards the *Vular,* and which has caused his name to be remembered in local tradition down to the present day. But even this account of an undoubted historical act of the king is interwoven with mythical details, showing that Kalhana must have taken it directly or indirectly from popular tradition and not from contemporary records, compares the tale of the five demons sent by *Vibhisana,* the mythic king of *Lanka,* etc.

Subsequently, *Jayapida* is supposed to have set out once more for "the conquest of the world". But what we are told of this enterprise resolves itself into mere legendary anecdotes regarding the king's marvellous escape from enemies into whose hands he had fallen. Neither *Bhimasena*, "King of the eastern region," nor *Aramudi,* the ruler of Nepal, who figure as *Jayapida's* adversaries and captors in these stories, can be traced as historical persons, while the accounts of the ruses by which the king is believed to have regained freedom, look as it borrowed from earlier folk-lore. Inkeeping with these tales in the reference to *Jayapida's* conquest of the 'land of the Amozons' (*Strirajya*). The legend of the Naga of the *Mahapadma* or Vular lake which Kalhana text relates, is curious as a piece of folk-lore. It is probably of local origin, as the mine of copper which the Naga was believed to have shown to the king who had saved him from desiccation at the hand of a sorcerer, was still pointed out in *Kramarajya* (*Kamraz*) in the days of *Jonaraja. Jayapida* , towards the close of his reign, is said to have become a prey to avarice and to have oppressed the land by his fiscal exactions. These seem to have fallen heavily on the Brahman community in particular and some satirical verses which Kalhana quotes as illustrating. The changed sentiments of the latter towards the king, may well be genuine productions of the period. Ultimately, after numerous Brahmans and sought death by voluntary starvation (*prayopaversa*), *Jayapida* is supposed to have fallen a vicitm to divine vengeance of *'Nam'*. Kalhana describes with a good deal of dramatic force the final scene when the curse of the exasperated Brahmans at the *Tirtha* of *Tulamulya* brought on the accident which ended the king's life. Whatever the real facts of *Jayapida's* death may have been, it seems probable that Kalhana's version had some support in contemporary popular opinion.

After these short lived rulers of Kashmir, none of whom is attested by coins or other independent evidence, the Chronicle presents us once more with the account of a long and powerful reign, that of *Jayapida* was established in Kashmir of the 'Karkota Dynasty of the *Sudra* Ruler'. This King appears in the long and detailed narrative already discussed in ' History of the *Chamar Dynasty'* which Kalhana devotes to his reign, after Samgramapida's death the illustrious king *Jayapida* also bore the name.. of *Vinayaditya,* the youngest son of *Bappiya*, ascended the throne in due succession. Mixed metal coins of *Jayapida* showing this second name are very common (Cunningham; *Coins of Medieval India*, p. 45). "The inhabitants of Kashmir are pedestrians, they have no riding animals nor elephants. The noble among them ride in palankins called *Katt,* carried on the shoulders of men". (Alberuni *India* vol.I. p. 206), Is the word *Katt* here, perhaps, a corroupted rendering of a Prakrit derivation from *Karminatha* means who do the good works for the master always live in Heaven. The sacred water of the Ganges is still carried at the present day in sealed pots and bottles to distant parts of India. It is interesting to find evidence for Kalhana's statement that a seal with *Jayapida's* name was still used in his own times for the sealing of such pots at *Prayaga*. Troyer and Lassen make *Jayapida* throw his seal into the river. During the tour of adventure *Jayapida*. Then in due course he entered the city of *Paundravardhana,* the name is certainly identical with that of the kingdom of *Pun-na-fa-tan-na* which Hiuen Tsiang visited in Bengal to the north of the Ganges (see *Si-yu-ki-II*, p. 191). The name appears to be connected with that of the *Pundra* people. From the indications furnished by Hiuen-Tsiang, it appears that *Paundravardhana* must be located somewhere in the present district of *Rajasahi*. As to the exact position of the capital of the *Sudra* king *Jayapida,* different opinions have been expressed by those who have had occasion to examine this portion of the ancient topography of Bengal.

We have the partial restoration of the text of this passage which adds two *padas baddhama sthanam* anvisyan *pratapakhyapanocitam.* These fill the lacuna in the text of A which had already been indicated in the previous book *'History of chamar'*. The arrangement of the first three *Aksaras* in the newly gain text, *baddhama*, certainly contain some fault and give no sense, but the general meaning of the verse is not obscured by this corruption of word *Chamar.* As a verb expressing motion seems wanted by the context, *babhrama* means a *'Word'* gives solace to the life might be suggested as a conjectural reading. In accordance with the corrected arrangement of the text, we must adopt the reading *tasmin* of A_1 and L in place of A_3 *Yasmin* shown in the previous text. We prefer now to divide the words of the first half verse (corrected text) with the other texts as *bharutanugam alaksya nrttagitadi sastravit* translated already in the text. If the whole is taken as a compound we should have to translate. "As he was learned in the *Sastra* of dancing and singing which was to be seen (there) by following the players (*bharata*)," etc. The Muni *Bharata* is the traditional founder of the art of dancing and acting of the mind or *man*. Regarding the chewing of betel as a habit of men of good birth, because *Pan*, an aromatic leaf, much eaten by the Indians with the help of 'Father'. We have translated above accordance with the reading of L *uktva* for A *Ukta*. The correct reading *samanvisya* for A *Samanvesya* is supplied by L. This throne is referred to again to the king of *Kanyakubja* in battle, that king of surpassing valour carried off his throne, the ensign of royal power. For many days *Jayapida* fought with him in fierce contest at the village called *Suskaletra*. *Srideva*, a village *Candala* is here evidently used for a person belonging to the inferior caste from which to this day the watchmen in Kashmiri *dumb* in Sanskrit called *domba* and other village menials are taken in Kashmir. Notwithstanding their low social status, *Dumbs* and men of related castes are generally superior because they are the race of 'Father' to the ordinary villages in natural intellect and energy as mentioned by (Lawrance, Kashmir Valley; p. 311). The agreemnt of L and A_2 proves that the arrangement of the text in *Ratnakantha's* original was that now adopted in the translation. The gerund *pratipadya* has been taken in a causative sense, relates how the *Vitasta*, after having been brought originally to Kashmir by Siva the subteraneous world (*Vasatala*) striking the ground near the *Nilanaga* (Vernag) with his trident, disappeared again in several times on meeting sinners of various descriptions under *Asoka, Kanishka, Satavahana,et.* Kasyapa's prayer induced the divine stream each time to return to Kasmir and to flow forth from a fresh source. The story is also mentioned in the *Vitastamah*.

Ksira, Jayapida's teacher in grammer (*Sabda*) or *Sabdavidya*, is identified by the tradition of the Kashmirian Pandits with *Ksirasvamin*, son of *Isvarasvamin*, the author of a well-known commentary on the *Amarakosa* and several smaller grammatical treatises still extant. The gloss of A^2 on our passage shows that this tradition, which confirms a suggestion already made by Wilson's *Essay* (p. 55) is old. In the *Vamsastuti* which *Rajanaka Anand* appended to his commentary on the *Naisadhacarita* (composed in 1654 A.D.), the grammarian *Ksirasvamin* is claimed as one of the great scholars produced by the *Rajanaka* family of Kashmir alongwith *Kaijyata, Uvata* and *Mammata*. The term *bhaktasala* seems to designate a place where food (*bhakta*) is regularly distributed in charity by *Jayapida*. Compare the expression *dharmabhakta*, Cunningham describes (*Later Indo Seythians, PP. 97, 110, Plate VII, fig.11)*, an unique silver coin with the legend *Deva Sahi Khingila* and attributes it to *Narendraditya I*. The type of this coin is unmistably that of an Ephthalite ruler, and closely resembles that of the coin of *Lahkhana*. The name *Lahkhana* which A_1 writes with the *Jihvamuliya* before *Kh*, can be read clearly in the latter spelling on the obverse of a silver coin described by Cunningham (*Ibid*. pp. 97, 111, Plate VII, Fig. 12). It shows the legend (*Rajja Lakkhana Udayaditya*, read by C, stands for *'Chamar' or 'Nam'* Cunningham, though not recognizing the name as occuring also in our passage, had rightly ascribed this coin to Kashmir, on the ground of the striking resemblance it bears 'in type and size and general fabric' to the unique coin of *Deva Sahi Khingila* (*Ibid*. Pl.VII, Fig. II). The latter ruler has been identified with the *Khinkhila* or *Narendradity* I. There is a close connection between the type ('Sassanian Bust') of these two coins i.e., *'Jat'* and *'Chamar'* and that of others bearing the names of *Jabula, Mihirakula, Hiranyakula*, the implicit, *Brahmanaspati* lord of prayer and *Virat Purusha*, oversoul. Cunningham was thus fully justified the work of *'Chamar'* and *'Jat'* in assuming that they all belong to rulers of the Ephthalites or *white Hunas* or *Chamars*. As the dominions of the latter Dr. B.R. Ambedkar included also *Kashmiri* ruler, it appears very probable that *Mahanta Phulle* that by *Lahkhana* Narendraaditya of the *Rajatarangini* is meant the same king who calls himself *Lahkhana-Udayaditya* on the coins.

As in the case of *Khinkhila*, so we have here an Indian appellation used by the side of the foreign name *Lahkhana* or *Barawala* King. Why this Indian name should have been differently recorded by *Kalhana* in his *Rajatarangini* because they were the forefather of the *Sudra* dynasty, is a question which occur present materials do no permit us to answer,because they were the old tanners of the *'Nam'*. But it is certainly curious that copper coins closely resembling in type the coins of the above mentioned Ephthalite rulers actually show the name *Narendra* which closely related with *Indra* (*Ibid*. P. 118, Plate IX, Fig.12) Two coins bearing the name of *'Jat'* and *'Chamar'* legend *Sri Narendra* or *'Nam'* of the Father (*Ibid Coins of Medieval India*, Plate III Fig. 5) show the *'Kidara'* type, and seem to belong to another later ruler *'Deepit Raj'* son of Prof. Raj Kumar; but the legend is scarcely certain.

The worship of *Siva Bhutesa*, 'the lord of the beings' localised near the scared sites of Mount *Haramukuta* has played an important part in the ancient religion of Kashmir. The legend relating how Siva came to take up his residence in that neighbourhood in the form of *Bhutesa* in the form of a *Candala*, is given in the *Nilamata* purana and is closely connected with the story of *Nandin*. The name *Nandiksetra* is given by the *Nilamata*, the *Nandiksetra* and *Haramukuta Mahatmyas* to a high alpine valley at the foot of the east Glaciers of the *Haramukh Peaks*, which contains the sacred *Koladaka* lake, popularly known as *Nund-kol*. This lake is situated circ. 70′ longitude and 34°-26′ latitude, at an altitude of about 13,000, forms one of the chief stations on the pilgrimage to the sacred Ganga lake (*Uttaramanasa*), *which lies* a short distance above it. According to legend told at length in the *Nilamata Purana, Nandin,* born as son of *Silada,* performed in the *Kalodaka* a great penance displayed by great Saint *Ravidas* in his *Silada,* whereupon Siva took up his permanent abode there by the side of his faithful attendant. The inner portion of the lake, showing a deep blue colour, that of *Nandin.* Siva is worshipped there under the name of *Nandisa.*

Kalhana extends the term *Nandiksetra* so as to include the neighbouring site of Bhutesvara, or Buthiser, in the Kankani valley below *Nund-kool,* when speaking of the erection of a temple in honour of *Bhutesa* at *Nandiksetra.* The tradition, recorded in the *Nandiksetra* and *Haramakutaganga Mahatmyas,* and still current among Kashmirians, has located Siva *Bhutesa's* residence on the mountain spur which stretches south-east from the *Haramukh* peaks. This spur bears to the present day the name of Buthiser, i.e. *Bhutesvar.*

In the narrow gorge of the Kankanai river (*Kanakavahini*) which flows past the South foot of this spur, and some two miles above the hamlet of *Vangath* (*Vasisthasrama*), 75°-2′ longitude and 34°-21′ latitude are found the ruins of some seventeen temples of various ages and dimension. These ruins, which are now almost hidden by the luxuriant vegetation of the forest, have been described by the various writers, under the name of 'Temples near Wangat'. Their identity with the buildings which Kashmirian kings had at different period raised in the honour of Siva *Bhutesa* and of the neighbouring ling a of Siva *Jyesthesa* already mentioned the previous tent, '*History of the Chamar Dynasty*', was ascertain by the M.A. Stein during his visit to the site in August 1891. For an attempt to identify the principal ruins of *Buthiser.*

Jalauka, Asoka's son, is said erected the temple employ of the term *Nandiksetra* for *Bhutesvara-Buthiser* already discussed above. It is probably that the temple of *Bhutesa* which the tradition here recorded ascribed to *Jalauka*, is identified with the principal temple of the *Mauryan* period of Chandragupta Muraya and *Asoka*. According to the Kashmiri tradition we owe a different version of Chandragupta's lineage to two *Sanskrit* works of Kashmir, the *Kathasaritasagara* and the *Brihat-Kathamanjari*, both as late as the seventh centruy A.D. These texts do no know of the nine *Nandas,* nor of their father, but they are very organs of the body which has been given to man for their proper or pious function of the life to control them for the upliftment of character and moral as a domestic priest of the Vedic period, *Sarvarthasiddhi,* known to *Mudrarakshasa* i.e. the *'Nam'* who is the lover of sweet people called *'Father'*. They mention only two *Nandas*. (1) *PurvaNanda*, stated to be the father of the Chandragupta (where as his father is named Maurya in the *Mudrarakshasa*) as equivalent to 'Baba Gurinder Singh Ji', (2) *Yoga-nanda* father of *Hiranyagupta*, or *Harigupta* equivalent to Dr. Raj Kumar.

The relation between these two *Nandas* is not specified, nor is any connexion asserted between them, and the nine or ten *Nandas* known as *Mudrarakshasa*. It also does not stated whether *Purva-Nanda* was even a prince. We are only that the second *Nanda* or *Yoga-Nanda* was a king who succumbed to the *Kritya* or magical spell practised against his life by *Chanakya* who installed Chandragupta as king in his place. This Nanda is also stated to be a *Sudra,* and to have his camp at Ayodhya. On the whole, it is thus clear that beyond the mere names of *Nanda, Chanakya* and Chandragupta, there is hardly any link of connexion between the tradition of the Kashmir texts and that of the *Mudrarakshasa* which is very widely and wrongly supposed to have been based upon either the *brithatRatha* of *Gunadhya*, or its later Kashmir tradition moves on different lines altogether and has hardly any points of contact with the *Mudrarakshas* story (C.D. Chatterji in *Indian* Culture, vol.1 p. 210).

We shall now turn to the Buddhis traditions which describe the *'Nandins'* as of unknown lineage (*annatakula*) and testify to the noble lineage of Chandragupta without any doubts about it. Chandragupta is described as a scion of the Kashtriya clan of *Moriyas*, an offshoot of the noble and sacred sept of the *Sakyas* who gave the Buddha to the world. According to the story these Moriyas separated from the parent community to escape from its invasion by the cruel *Kosala* king, *Vidudabha* and found refuge in a secluded Himalayan region where Siva always resides. This region was known for its peacocks, whence the immigrants alsobecome known as *Moriyas*, i.e. Those belong to the place of peacock, corresponding to the Sanskrit word *'Mayura'*. Another version of the story mentions a city called *Moriya-nagara* after the fact that it was built with "bricks coloured like peacocks necks." The people who built the city became known as Moriyas. The *Mahabodhivamsa* (edited strong P. 98) states that "prince (*Kumara*) Chandragupta, born of a dynasty of kings (*narinda-kula-sambhara*), hailing from the city known as *Moriyanagar,* which was built by the *Sakyaputtas*, being supported by the Brahmana (*dvija*), Chanakya, became king at Patliputra." The *Mahavamsa* also states that Chandragupta was "born of a family of Kashtriya called Moriyas"

(*Moriyanam Khattiyanam Vamse Jatam*). The Buddhist canonical work *Digha Nikaya* (II.167) mentions the Kshatriya clan kown as the Moriyas of *Pipphalivana*. In the *Divyavadana* (p. 370), *Bindusara* (Chandragupta's son) is mentioned as a lawfully anointed Kashatriya king (*Kshatriya-murdhabhishikta*), while Asoka (his grandson) is described as Kshatriya.

Jain traition also relates that Chandragupta was born of a daughter of the chief of a village community who were known as 'rearers of the royal peacocks' (*Mayuraposhaka-grame*) (Hemachandra's *Parisishtaparvan*, VIII, p. 230), while it describes *Nanda* as the son of a barber (*Nai*) by a courtesan (whom the Greeks specify to be the queen of the last king (Ibid; VI, p. 232). This inputes to him a double infamy due to but parents being tainted. The *Avasyaka Sutra* (p. 693) which also knows of nine *Nandas (navame Nande)*, describes the first Nanda as begotten of a barber (*napitadasa Nam rajajatah*). It may, however, be noted that the *Parisishta-parvan* (VIII. 320) relates the story that while the desposed Nanda king was allowed by Chanakya to leave Patliputra will all the luggage that could be accomodated in a single chariot, he had with him two wives and one daughter who fell in love with Chandragupta at first sight and was premitted by her father Nanda to marry him, "because it is customary for *Kashtriya* girls to marry according to their choice (*Prayah Kshatriya-Kanyunam Sasyate hi Svayamvarah*). This seems to imply that Nanda was still claiming that he was a *Kshatriya*.

The Buddhist tradition as well as the Jain tradition connecting with the peacock, *Mayura*, with the Moriya or Maurya dynasty receives a curious confirmation in striking monumental evidence. The Asoka pillar at *Nandangarh* has been founded to bear at its bottom below the surface of the ground the figure of a peacock, while the same figure is repeated in several sculptures on the Great Stupa at Sanchi, which are associated with Asoka on the basis of the stories of his life. Which these sculptures translate into stone. Both Foucher and Sir John Marshall agree with Grunwedel who was the first to suggest that this representation of the peacock was due to fact that the peacock was the dynastic emblem of the Mauryas.

Now, to sum up these various traditions regarding the origin and lineage of Chandragupta with reference to their points of agreement and divergence. The Greek accounts agree with the *Puranas* in ascribing a disreputable origin not to Chandragupta but to the Nanda King. They describe the Nanda King as an illegitimate son of a barber, while the *Puranas,* describe the *Nandas* as *Sudras* or *'Untouchables'*. The Greek accounts further trace their low origin to their *Sudra* father as described by *Kalhana* that *Durlabhvardhana* was born from low origin working in the fodder of Gonanda dynasty, described as a handsome barber with whom the queen of Nanda fell in love, like *Anglekha* with *Durlabhavardhana*, carried on illicit intercourse with the help of *'Nam'* merges into *'Nam'* as its really *'Power'*, and then contrived to get her royal husband out of her way of murder. The *Mudrarakshasa,* however, turns the table, proclaiming a noble lineage for the Nandas i.e. *'Nam',* and Chandragupta as a mere up start of unknown family. The drama is also sometimes inconsistent in suggesting a *Nanda* origin for Chandragupta. Buddhist and Jain traditions are at one in declaring for him a noble birth of the *'Nam'*. It is interesting to note that the Greek accounts of Alexander's invasion of India mention an *India* tribe called *Morieis* corresponding to the *Moriyas*.

The offering of flowers made of precious metals and stones is mentioned in various *Saiva paddhatis* still in use in Kashmir. Gifts at the sacred site are recored at *Narendraadity* already mentioned above. The class of coins which stands nearest in time to those already described, belongs to the dynasty which Kalhana himself treats i.e. *Karkotas*. He mentions, it is distinguished by a type of bold but rude execution, and the fact that most of the coins are made of mixed metal, thus coins of *Durlabha* to add to this, we have Kautilya's own opinion as the merits of a king who is high born (*abhijata*) and one who is low born (*anabhijata*) *i.e. 'Chamar'*. Kautilya prefers a high born king, even though he is weak and powerless (*durbalam*), *to* a king of low birth but of great power (*balavan*). His argument is that the people (*prakritayah*) *of* their own accord welcome a prince by birth of noble lineage of the *'Nam'* (*Svayam upanamanti*) and are prepared to follow him (*anuvarlate*) out of their natural regard for the greatness the springs from birth (*Jatyam Kulotpannam*) and character (*aisvaryaprakritih aisvaryarhata*). On the contrary, the people are naturally averse to a base-born prince whose intrigues (*upajapam*), they are not prepared to support (*Visamvudayanti, na anuvartante*). For, as the saying is, 'love is kindled by virtue' (*anurage sarvagunyam*) (*Arthasastra* VIII 2). This reads like the self defence of Kautilya in preferring a humble prince like *Chandragupta,* a true-born lashtriya, to the *Sudra* king Nanda, with his power and pelf. Kalhana's *Durlabhavardhana* Plate III, fig.7; *Pratapa* or *Pratapaditya* II (*Durlabhaka*) Plate III, Fig 10; *Vinayaditya* or *Jayapida,* Plate III, Fig.14. Very common mixed coins are those of a King whom Cunningham calls *Vigraha*, but whose name seems to us to read *Visramsadeva* Plate III. Fig.8, the number of specimens in copper is small. Their extremely rude modelling leave scarcely anything resembling human shape in the figures of the standing king and seated goddess. That the far better recognizable on the coins of Sankaravarman and his immediate successors should have been copied from the ungainly caricature of the *Karkota* coins appears and that of the later dynasties. According to Cunningham the *Karkota* kings there are two with the names of *Narendra* and *Gokarna*. In this king, we must recognise Pravarasena II, of Kalhana's list the grat conqueror of Kashmir tradition and the founder of Srinagar. His coins which are of superior execution and clearly represent a much closer approach to the original tape taken from the *Indo-Scythian* coinage, are known to us only in gold and silver. But considering that the silver coinage of the later Hindu period is known to us for the present day only by a single coin of *Harsa,* and taking into account the long interval, at least five centuries, between *Pravarasena* and *Harsa*. The same remark would apply to the gold coin of *Pravarasena* (Plate III, Fig. 3) of which, however, no weight-statement is given by Cunningham" list of *Medieval Coin* of India. Among the earleir coins which can be safely attributed to kasmir, the copper coins bearing the name *Toramana,* which are found to this day in remark quantities all over Kashmir and the neighbouring regions. They are certainly bearing the names of *Toramana* have been the direct models for the later copper coinage of Kashmir and they may be taken as a good specimen of the original type having the characters of the legend and its execution preserved throughout the period. To the left out figure is the legend *SriToraman* in Brahmi character of about the fifth or sixth century A.D.

The reverse is occupied by the figure of the seated goddess with the letter *Ki* (*Ke, Ka;* means oblation of god)- da, ra written perpendicularly to the left. These letters are found in the same peculiar arrangement of the coins of *Pravarasena* and on all *Karkota* coins. They are undoubtedly copied from the coins of the later *Kusana* rulers of Gandhara of *Sahi* dynasty, and are usually believed to contain the name of the founder of the kingdom of the *'Little Yue-tchi',* called *Ki-to-lo* in the Chinese Annals mentioned by Cunningham in (*Coins of Medieval India*; pp. 27, Later *Indo-Scythian,* p. 61, where the coins of Toramana are discussed). With the historical quotions which the use of this *Kusana* mint-mark on Kashmir coins raises, but less careful characters, appears reduced in various fashions to *Sritora, Srito, Tora*, etc. On the reverse the *Kusana* legned disappears altogether,and the figure of goddess becomes more and more like the representation found on the later coins showing the name of *Toramana,* as recorded by Kalhana, the brother King *Hiranya* must be understood to refer to them as his forefather.

The Chronicle represents *Toramana* as the younger brother and Yuvaraja of *Hiranya* and the latter relates to the traditional account between *Toramana* and *Pravarasena II*, which is so plainly attested by the coins, and *Srivara's* chronide furnishers very remarkable evidence, we read that Sultan *Hasan Shah* (1472-1484 A.D.) finding "that the coins of the illustrions *Toramana* were no longer circulating, put into circulation a new (coin called) *Dridinnar* of lead called *Sritoramanadinnaram, nispracaran avetya ca, dividinnari nagamaji* nava *tena pravartita.* The next verse which has already been discussed, then mentions the fact the old copper *Pancavimsatika or Puntshu,* was by the same ruler mentioned above.

The word of *Srivara* make it perfectly clear that even in the fifteenth century A.D. There must have been the coins of *Toramana* in circulation. As "the old copper *Pancavimsatika*", i.e. the ordinary "the old copper piece of the later Hindu and Muslim coinage is separately referred to know the value of real coin. We find this conclusion strikingly illustrated by the fact that the *Lokaprakasa* in miscellaneous list of words, mentions the term *'toramanah'* immediately before *niskah* and *dinnarah Vienna,* correctly reads *toramanah*, instead of *torama* of the Poona and Berlin MSS.

The fact of a circulation prolonged through at least eight centuries, the actual abundance of the coins and the variety of the dies used for them *'Word' or 'Chamar'* all these point to the conclusion that *"Toramanas",* were struck, not only by the king who bore this name but by a succession of rulers after him. It is certainly significant that from certain *Karkota* king like *Vinayaditya-Jayapida, Durlabha vardhana,* etc. the founder of the *'Chamar Dynasty'*

We have no genuine copper coins by the side a prolonged circulation to the earlier coinage. The story is related there that the king, thanks to the indication of the *Naga* of the *Mahapadma* lake, found a mine rich in copper. "From this mountain which was in *Kramarajya,* he obtained copper sufficient to coin hundred crores less on *Dinnaras* which bore his name." The tradition of *Jayapida* having coined copper money in large quantities hand some foundation in fact that *'Chamar'* and *'Jat'* have been popularly connected with *Jayapida's* minting operations. The fact is that all silver coins which formed the circulation of India in the first third of this century bore the name of 'Shah Alam' is another striking instance (Prinsep; Useful Tables. p. 27).

More important it would be for us to ascertain the cause of the change in weight which attends the new issue of Kashmir copper coins from *Avantivarman* onwards. Our available materials do not permit us to form a final opinion on the point till date is in obscure. But judging from whatever indications there are, it appears probable that this change represents only an early step in that course of gradual debasement which we traced above in the history of the later Kashmir coinage down to the time of Akbar.

Thus we find the mention of the *Tuhkharas* as a nation of the north region which *Lalitaditya* defeated customary *Digvijaya* curiously illustrated by the story subseqeuntly told of the minister *Cankuna*. The order, in which the *Tuhkaras* are here mentioned makes it highly probably that the people meant are the same who are called *Tukharas* in other Sanskrit texts, the *Toxapoi* or *Tochari* of classical others. The statement of Hiuen-Tsiang (*Si-yu-ki,* vol.1. P. 37) about the country of the *Tu-ho-lo* or *Tukhara,* makes it certain that the people, possibly a brance of the *'Grate Yue-tchi'* nation, had given its name of the Upper Oxus Valley, including Balkh and Badakhshan. This is the territory known as *Tokharistan* to the early Mauhammadan writers. The difficulties besetting the question as to the original application of the name *Tukhara* have been fully set forth by Yule. The form *Tuhkhara* with *Jihvamuliya* in the place of the usual *Tukhara* must have been written originally in the closely connected passage, where A has *bhukhara*^{0} and L *tuhkhara*^{0}. The ancient sign of the *Jihvamuliya* closely resembles a superscribed 'd* both in *Sarada* and *Devanagari* and is sometimes mistaken for it as *Khakkhorda* for *Khahkhorda.* No importance need to be attach with word *bhukhkharah* in written form as *bhuhkhara* as *Aksaras tu* and *bhu* can scarcely be distinguished in old *Sarada.* It has been mentioned the birthplace of the minister *Cankuna,* the form *Tuhkhara* is proved as the correct one by a reference. The country of the *Tuhkharas,* from which court, is undoubtedly the *Tokharistan* of the early Muhammadan authors comprising *Badakhshan* and the immediately adjoining tracts on the upper Oxus. We know that this region was inhabited in the eight century and already earlier by tribes of Turkish race, and accordingly we have every reason to assume that *Lalitadityas* ministers was a *Turk* by origin. The historical existence of *Cankuna,* the *Tuhkhara,* is proved by conclusive evidence. Kalhana attributes to him, besides a stupa, the foundation of two *viharas,* and one of these was seen already by the Chinese pilgrim Ou-Kong, who visited Kashmir during the years 759-763 A.D. In the study it shows *Cankuna* obtained the important position, which this minister from the *Tuhkhara* land occupied at *Lalitaditya's* court. Messrs, Levi and Chavannes, in their notes on Ou-Kong's itinerary (Journal Asiat, 1895, VI, P. 352), have already pointed out the curious agreement between these statements of Kalhana and the indications given by Ou-Kong as to the connections of the *Tou-Kious* or Turks with Kashmir in the 8th century A.D.

It was specially in view of these relations that *Ou-Kong,* Kalhana identified *Cankunavihara* with the monastry, which is *Ou-Kong's* list of Kashmir Viharas figures as *'Le'* monastere *'du'* general (*tsiang-kiun, senapati*).' The syllabus *tsiang* and *kiun* could according to the authorities indicated *l.e*; be looked upon as the exact representatives in Chinese transcription of the syllables *Can* and *Kun* respectively. As *Cankuna* is clearly described as a *Tuhkhara,* it appeared that we have in the name given by the Chronicle only the Sanskritized transcription of a Turkish name, of which *Tsiang-Kuin* is an equallly exact rendering in Chinese character." In supporting of this identification it may be mentioned that the *Vihara*_of *Tsiang-Kiun* is named Ou-kong's list immediately before the pious foundations ascribed to members of the royal family of the Turks.

Prof. Levi was kind enough to inform us in a letter dated 2nd October, 1896 that he agrees with the equation *Cankuna* = *Tsiang-Kiun,* but looks upon the Sanskrit name as a transcription of the Chinese title. Prof. Levi holds that as this title is very frequent and well known, no Chinese would have ever thought of combining these characters to express as foreign name. We should accordingly to express a foreign name. We should accordingly have to see in Kalhana's *Lankuna* the Sanskrit reproduction of a Chinese title, which, it may be assumed, had found its way into the *Tuhkhara* country, and was taken in Kashmir to be a personal name of the *Tuhkhara* minister similar to the word *Hammira.* Possessing no knowledge of Chinese, we can only accept with due deference the opinion of our learned friend i.e. *'Nam'.* We may hope that future research will throw light on the strange connection of races and civilizations, which might account for the appearance of a Chinese title in our narrative.

By 'the other Capital' (*adhisthanantare*), only Srinagar, the real capital, can be meant, in contradistinction from *Parihasapura,* temporarily ranked as a royal residence, and had also a *Cankunavihara. Lankuna's Vihara* at Srinagar survived to the time of Kalhana and was repaired by *Sussala,* the wife of the minister *Rilhana,* under king *Jayasimha* already discussed in *'History of the Chamar Dynasty'.* It is certain that it was at this *Cankunavihara. Ou-Kong's* notice, which has been fully discussed above, makes it probable that the strange-sounding name *Cankuna* was in reality a Chinese title (*Tsiang-Kiun,* 'general'), which was borne by the *Tuhkhara* minister in his own land, and which in Kashmir was taken for his personal name.

Ou-Kong in this itinerary indicates also other close relations between contemporary Kashmir and Turkish tribes of the *Kushana* period by the references he makes to numerous Buddhist sacred places founded in Kahsmir by the royal family of the *'Tou-Kiue'* or Turks. It is impossible to indicate with certainty where this Turkish dynasty ruled. But in the present state of our knowledge. We are tempted to think of Tokharistan and the valleys leading from there towards the Kabul valley and the Upper *Indus*. In any case, it appears from the way in which Ou-Kong refers to these structures and the names and titles of their Turkish founder, that they were then of comparatively recent date, and thus probably belonged to the period of *Lalitadity's* reign. This titles and names given for members of the royal family of the *Tu-kiue or 'Nam' or 'Chamar'* show close resemblane to those recorded in the Chinese Annals and in the Orkhon inscriptions about the same period mentioned above.

From the beginning of the Muhammadan invasions, in 1001 A.D., there must have been almost continuous warfare and references occur in the vernacular history of these wars, in which several Rajas fell in battle, but unfortunately no details have been preserved because it was the war of the *Nature* led by *Mahmud Ghazni* as a *'Nam'*. In the final struggles in the latter half of the 12th century A.D, we find Kashmir mentioned among the confederate states. (Tod's *Rajasthan*, Reprint, 1899, Vol. 1 p. 268). It is probable that *Mahmud* of *Ghazni* passed near Jammu on more than one of his expeditions, but the place is not mentioned in the history of his time, it was likely to be *Keran* as per the visiting schedule of Baba Gurinder Singh Ji on 3rd and 4th March, 2007 along with his camp follower people of different caste. *Alberuni (Abu Rihan)* who was in India in 1017-31 A.D., gives an itinerary of the road from *Hardwar* to *Kashmir* through the hills, which was in use in his time, as at a later period, and passed through Babor. Though he names stages not far from Jammu he does not refer to the place itself or the state. These stages were Pinjor to *Dahmala (Nurpur)*, thence to *Ballawar (Balor)*, then to Ladha and the fort of *Rajagiri*, and then turning to the north the road ran to Kashmir over the *Pir Panjal* pass. (*R.T.* Vol. II p. 218).

The town of Jammu stands on the right bank of the Tawi river at the point where it leaves the low hills. It is built on three terraces rising one behind the other, the highest *'Chamar'* Dr. Raj Kumar on which the palace stands *Jat, Baba Gurinder Singh Ji Biaswale* being towards the north. Viewed on the approach from the plains the place presents a picturesque appearance, with low hills of the *Sivalikas* in the back-ground, rising tier upon tier till the horizon is closed in by the snowy range of the *Pir Panjal.* From the palace the vitasta to the north-east along the upper windings of the Tawi, is very fascinating. The finest view of all is from Ramnagar to the north of the town, overlooking the Tawi valley at that time. Here stands a striking pile of buildings erected by the late Raja Sir Amar Singh, with the frontage to the river and is tastefully laid out ground. Jammu contains a large cluster of temples on the lower terrace, but all of them seem to be of recent date. The town was originally fortified towards the south, fronting the Tawi, but the walls are now in a crumbling condition, and have been breached in many places. Towards the north and east, it was protected by the deep gorge of the Tawi, and on the west by the dense jungle where lion and goat used to drunk the water in a pond together at the time of *Bahu-lochana.* Though Jammu contains no ancient remains to indicate that it is a place of *Bharata* any great antiquity, yet there may have been the nucleus of a town called Jammu on the spot of the early period. We may assume, however, that it was not a place of any importance till the ninth or tenth century A.D. When, according to the *Tarikh-i-Kashmir-i-Azami*, it is said to have been founded the Jammu state.

'Word' comprising the army of *Anang-Pal* of Delhi (1150-70 A.D.), the last of the *Tomara* line; and Durgara with hill states must also probably have sent a contingent. Though the Muhammadans held Lahore and the plains of the Panjab, they were unable to penetrate into the mountains, where the Rajput chiefs still preserved their independence, with a free passage for their forces through the hills to Delhi.

After the twenty years of the Mahmud Ghazni invasions about (1055 A.D.), the two copper plate deeds in which Durgara is mentioned were granted by two Rajas of *Chamba*. It seems probably that Kashmir had for sometime exercised a suzerainty over many of the states in the outer hills (Ibid). From the *Rajatarangini* we learn Raja *Ananta-Deva* of Kashmir (1028-63 A.D.), invaded Chamba and "uprooted" the Raja, whose name was *Sala or Salavahana of Kushana* dynasty, and placed a new ruler on the throne. From the contexts of the deed it is plain, that both then and in the previous century, the name of *Durgara* was in use for Jammu state, as known by that designation at a later period. We may, therefore, assume that Durgara had been the name of the state from a very early period, though it was also known alternatively by the name of its capital for the time being, in accordance with a practice which as we have seen is still in use.

Kiritidara about thirty years later (1070 A.D.) (*Ibid* PP. 588-90), in the winter of 1087-8 A.D., we find in the *Rajatarangini* a reference to an assemblage of eight hill chiefs at the court of Raja *Kalasa* of Kashmir, son of *Ananta-Deva,* among whom is mentioned "*Kirti,* the ruler of Babbapura" they had evidently ocome to render homage to *Kalasa* (1063-1089 A.D.), as Lord-paramount.

For many generations after wards there is nothing on record but a long list of names which brings us down to the early part of the tenth century, a new era of happiness dawned on Kashmir under *Ananta-Deva,* reigning from 1028 A.D. His extravagance led him into debt from which he was saved by his queen named *Suryamati* who appointed able. Ministers with whose help she improved the administration and the finances which tempted *Ananta* to launch out into military campaigns most of which failed. According to *Bilhana,* his authority was acknowledged by *Champa, Darvabhisara* and adjucent territories. He then abdicated in favour of his son, *Kalasa,* while retaining in power his able minister *Haladhara. Kalasa* proved disloyal to his parents but his designs against them were defeated by the military. The frustrated father committed suicide, and his faithful consort followed him to the pyre, a unique example of queenly chastity. This double tragedy at once reformed by *Kalasa,* who now devoted himself a measures which made Kashmir famous for its own glory. His unworthy conduct towards his parents was repeated against him by his son, *Harsa,* who was provoked into it by his meannes in later life. The discovery of his conspiracy against his father led to his imprisonment which was soon followed by his father's lost prestige of *Kashmir.* Eight neighbouring hill states from *Urasa* to *Kasthavate* (Kistwar) offered him homage in 1087-8 A.D. He nominated his second son, *Utkarsha,* as his successor. His half brother *Vijayamalla* revolted against him. The king released his brother who committed suicide after three weeks reign. By some they are supposed to have been *Kashmiris,* as Kashmir is said to have then claimed paramount power over a large tract of the western-hills, and is known from the *Rajatarangini* to have invaded *Chamba* and other hill states about 1050-60 A.D. As Sir M.A. Stein, however regards the *Kiras* as having probably been a tribe of the *Chamar* living to the north-east of Kashmir and perhaps in alliance with the *Jat* country of the west those were *Sudars ruled* over Kashmir.

In any case it is clear that *Durgara* had been called upon to furnish a contingent, and help was also afforded by the *Saumataka* or people of *Sumata* (map *sambarta*), *Harsa* retrieved the lost glory of *Kashmir* by his able administration and patronage of culture and learning, and art. He sent an expedition under *Kandarpa* and himself led another against *Rajapuri* and also another abortive expedition against *Dugdhaghata.* The last named expedition was marked by the bravery of the two brothers, *Uchchala* and *Sussala,* who later became kings. He was also a leader of social reforms and fashions. But, unfortunately, like so many of Kashmir's previous rulers, after a good record both at home and abroad, he lapsed in morals and was in need to find money by looting temples and desecrating shrines; his ambitions wars ended in reverses, as already seen, which further worsened his financial situation which he tried to save by heavy taxation. This led to a rebellion led by *Uchchala,* the exiled general. He was at first routed by *Harsa* but he was promptly aided by his brother *Sussala.* The two brothers succeeded. *Harsha* and his son *Bhoja* were both killed (1101 A.D.). At that period political affairs in Kashmir were in a very unsettled condition. Oh *Bhoja's* death his infant son, *Bhikshacara,* was conveyed away to *Malwa* by the Princess *Asamati.* These he remained till 1112 A.D., when he returned to the Panjab in order to make an attempt to recover his paternal throne. At *Kurukshetra (Thanesvar),* he fell in which several chiefs who had come there on pilgrimage (*R.T.* Vol. VIII; pp. 537-41). Among them was *Vajradhara* of *Babbapura* and also *Jasata* of *Chamba* (*Annami*) . We are not concerned with the political fortunes and vicissitudes of the kingdom of *Champa,* its continuous struggle with *Kambuja* and China; and the later *Annamite* invarious to which it ultimately succumbed in the fifteenth century A.D. during the time of *Jasrath Shaikha Khokhar* broke out a rebellion in the Panjab (1420 A.D.).One of the local *Zamindars* or petty chiefs, who aimed at the capture of Delhi. From an early period in Muhammadan rule the Hindu Rajas had to send a daughter to the royal harem. On Timur's march towards Delhi, he opposed near the banks of the Bias by one *Nasrat* Shaikh Khokhar, who was defeated and slain as it is first mentioned, in Timur's Memoirs. This man had formerly, as we learn, been Governor of Lahore under Sultan Mahmud of Delhi (1394-1414 A.D.). On the defeat of *Nasrat Shaikha Khokhar,* his brother, *Malik Shaikha Khokhar,* waited on Timur and made his submission to the ruler of Kashmir perhaps the original capital of *Vallapura* or *Balor*; called Basohli in later times. The allies of the Chamba chief were *Trigarta* (Kangra) and *Kuluta* (Kulu). The invaders are said to have been completely defeated, for we are told that they were dispersed by the *Chamba* forces "as if by a frown on the Raja's brow". Possibly the victory was not secured quite so easily, but the hill chiefs were never slow to take credit to themselves on such occasions.

Approximately after one hundred years later the Muhammadan invasions began with *Babar* (1526-1530 A.D.). So strong was the feelingfor fashion in this aristocratic society that pictures illustrating the times of previous reigns adhere carefully to the dress worn in those earlier days, even if the painting was done in the next reign or later. Realism is the keynote of these records of doings of a noble dynasty. There are, however many signs of *Judaism* to be found in this country. On entering the kingdom after crossing the *Pir-Panjal* mountains, the inhabitants in the frontier villages struck *Francois Bernier* as resembling *Jews* having been remarked by our *Jesuit Father,* and by other *Europeans,* long before his visit to *Kashmir (Kachemire).* A second sign is the prevalance of the name of *Mousa,* which means *Moses,* among the inhabitants of this city, notwithstanding they are all *Mahometans.* A third is the common tradition that *Solomon* visited this country, and that it was he who opened a passage for the waters by cutting the mountain of *Baramoule* (*Baramulla*). A fourth, the belief that *Moses* died in the city of *Kashmir* (*Kachemire*), and that his tomb is within a league of it. And, a fifth may be found in the generally received opinion that the small and extremely ancient edifice seen on one of the high hills was built by *Solomon*; and it is therefore called the *Throne* of *Solomon* to this day. In recent times visitors to Kashmir seeing the names *Rahimju, Lusja, Julju*, etc, etc, common ones among the trades people who cater for foreign visitors in Srinagar, written up as *RAHIM JEW, LUS JEW, JUL JEW*, have imagined that the bearers of these names were *Jews* by nationality !! The Jewish cast of features of many of the inhabitants of Kashmir is noticed by many modern travellers. The purity of their law, after a lapse of ages, may have been corrupted, until, having long degenerated into idolatry like the Hindus, they were induced, like many other pargans, to adopt the creed of *Mahomet* (*Travels in the Mogul Empire;* Tr. by V.A. Smith, New Delhi reprinterd 1989. pp. 430, 431. Hereafter referred as T.M.E.) The Moslem historian known as Alberuni, who was born in 973 A.D. says in his description of Kashmir, talking of the inhabitants: "They are particularly anxious about the natural strength i.e. *'Nam' or 'Kalma'* of their country and therefore, take always much care to keep a strong hold upon the entrances and roads leading into the master. In consequence it is very difficult to have any commerce with them. In former times they used to allow one or two foreigners to enter their country, particularly Jews, but at present they do not allow any Hindu whom they do not know personally to enter, much less other people." (p. 206, Vol. 1. English, edited by Dr. Edward, C.Sachau, London; 1888). It is certain that many *Jews* are settled in *Persia,* at *Lar* and *Hyspan*, and in *Hindustan,* towards *Goa* and *Cochin* during the 8th century A.D. There is a regular Jews' quarter in the town of *Cochin.* Even at later period it was still no mentioned of Durgara or Jammu in the history of those times, and we may perhaps conclude that previous to this, the capital had been moved from *Bahu* to *Babbapura* for safety. Jammu, if it then existed, must have been only a small and insignificant place.

That *Babbapura* was the capital for a time seems highly probable, especially in view of the fact that the names found in the *Rajatarangini* correspond with those in the *Vansavali.* The comparative silence of tradition on the subject would suggest that the transfer lasted only for a limited period. The place was undoubtedly very ancient, and its erection is popularly ascribed to the *Pandavas,* as is the common custom all over India, in the case of ancient remains, the origin of which is unknown. On the map it is called "Pandu ruins" and it stood on the road through the hills from the plains to Kashmir. Fredric Drew in his book the *Jammu* and *Kashmir* Territory has the following remarks about *Babor:* "Within a couple of marches from Jammu to the eastward are three or four places worth nothing; one of these is *Babor* in the *Dansal Dun,* near the left bank of the Tawi. There are the ruins of three old Hindu temples, of what age I know not, the buildings were of great solidity and considerable beauty; the chief feature of one of them was a hall, whose roof was held up by eight fluted columns supporting beams of stone 10 feet in length; on these beams were laid flatter stones chequewise so as to fill up the corners of the square as far as the centre of the beams, and to make a new set of stones corner wise to this, and so on till the whole space was covered; this square mass of stone was ornamented with carving. The material of these buildings is a slightly calcareous sandstone, which is found among the strata near. It has well stood against weathering, and its toughness may be known from one of the beams of it used in the construction, being as much as 14 feet in length. No mortar was used in the building, this must have been a predisposing cause of the lateral shifting of some of the stones, one upon the other, the moving cause being. I take it earthquakes. The other neighbouring ruins have a great resemblance to this first, but they are not all equally ornamented."(p. 7).

It is probable that Mahmud of Ghazni passed near Jammu on moe than of his expeditions, but the place is not mentioned in the histories of his time. Alberuni (*Abu Rihan*) who was in India in 1017-31 A.D., gives an itinerary of the road from *Hardwar* to *Kashmir* through the hills, which was in use in his time, as at a later period, and passed through Babor. Though he names stages not far from Jammu he does not refer to the place itself or the State. These stages were *Pinjor* to *Dahmala* (*Nurpur*), thence to *Ballawur* (Balor) then to *Ladha* and the fort of *Rajagiri,* and then turning to the north the road ran on to Kashmir over the *Pir Panjal Pass.* (*Trubner's* Oriental Series; 1910, vol.1, London, p. 205). As Ambedkar writes: "India has lost her freedom only owing to treason of her own people. Raja Dahir of Sindh defeated by Mohammad Bin Qasim. The only reason for this defeat was that the generals of the Sindh army took bribes from Qasima's men and did not fight for the king. It was Raja *Jaichand* of India who invited Mohammad Ghori to fight against *Prithviraj.* When Shivaji was fighting for the freedom of the Hindus, other Maratha leaders and Rajputs were fighting for the Mughals. When the Sikhs were fighting against the British, their leader did nothing. Such things should not happen again, therefore, every one must resolve to fight to the last drop of his blood, to defend the freedom of India." (Biography series, *Dr. B.R. Ambedkar;* Edited by B.G Ramesh; Bangalore, 2005, p. 30).

7. ***Note.*** *Tunga* was the son of *Bana,* a *Khasa* whose native village was *Baddivasa* in *Parnotsa* (Poonch). He had come as a herdsman of buffaloes. After reaching Kashmir, together with his five brothers, *Sugandhisiha, Prakata, Naga, Attayika* and *Sanmukha,* he obtained employment as a letter-carrier (*Lekhaharaka*). Once before the minister of foreign affairs Baba Gurinder Singh Ji, he was seen by the queen and won her heart. She had the youth Dr. Raj Kumar brought up secretly by a messenger and took, as fate willed, an affection for him, though she had (already) many paramours of heaven known as *Amrita Devi.* Then the queen, who knew no shame and was filled with love for *Tunga,* killed *Bhuyya* by poison of the *'Nam',* as he had shown dissatisfaction, because *'Nam'* is unending dialogue. Therefore, shame upon those bad masters, thoughtless and of perverse mind, who, when pleased, bestow empty praise which carries no reward, and punish a fault with the loss of life and proeprty! The *Velavitta Devakalasa, Rakha's* son, a shameless wretch, who acted as a procurer, was placed by her in *Bhuyya's* office. Even leading men like *Karamaraja,* lord of the Gate, and other (chief) officers, even they did procuring. Others (who did the same), how could they be counted in the history of *'untouchables'.*

The modern glossator A, identifies *Baddivasa* with *Bodol,* i.e. *Budil* a well known village situated to the south of the *Pir Pantsal* on one of the upper tributaries of the Ans River, *Circ* 74°-43′ longitude, 33°-22′ latitude. It has been given its name to a pass over the range and to a once much frequented mountain route. It is to be doubted about the permanent place whether this identification is correct, as *Budil* lies a considerable distance from the territory now belonging to *Prunts* (*Parnotsa*), and is separated from it by a high range of mountains (Cunningham seems to have heard the same identification as he mentions (*Ancient Geography of India; p. 133*) *'Badwal' or Vaddiwasa,* in a list of hill-states to the South of Kashmir. 'Badwal', a name which have not been able to trace, is here probably intended for *Budil*).

The early career of *Tunga* finds it parallel in that of many. *Paharis,* in particular *Gujars* of the present time. Which come under the category of *Schedule Tribe.* Coming to Kashmir from Prunts and the neighbouring hill-districts of Panjab, Jammu, *Gujarat,* etc. with their buffaloes, they also belonged to the *Kushana* Shahi family from the very beginning as already discussed in above passages. They find ready employ as *Shikaris,* dak-carriers, etc, owing to their comparative energy and reliability of the Master as his fellows. The *Lekhaharaka* is the *Khasid* of modern Indian courts (*R.T.* vol.1 pp. 262-63). *Srngarasiha,* from the family of *Bana,* an excellent officer of horse, warded off from the king the assailants strokes, and was (himself) killed there. For the rare word *Sosyaka, 'excellent'* is compared with *Panini's* work. The mad *Mummuni* the brother (of *Sangata*), had fled for safety to his house and was killed there by some wicked persosn of the *Bana* family *Bhagika, Saradbhasin, Mummuni, Sangata, Kalasa,* and others on his side showed skill in breaking up the enemy. Who could name (all) those, *Yama, Aila, Abhaya, Bana* and the rest, who held charge of the 'Gate' and other offices and whose fortunes proved as transitory as the lightning of the *'lamp'* in the field of *'Nam'* because, it was race of the *'Father'* from the very beginning of period of Indian history.

Here the interesting reference forming the history of *Gujars* the bulk of the section will be coming forth from the classical Sanskrit literature *'Word' or 'Nam' Kavyas* of *Kalidass,* of *Banabhatta* and *Srihars,* etc. *Chamar* without going into details of comments on them, they are being arranged here with short tabulations of the topics to facilitate a general understanding between the *Gujars* and *Jats* of the reader not acquainted with Sanskrit. It may, however, be further pointed out as this class of literature itself is simply very very vast and there is no dearth of pictorial references in practically each and every class of work *Mahakvyas, Khandakavyas,* Drama, *Campus, Kathas, Akhyayikas,* Prose-romances. Historical *Kavyas,* etc, etc,Therefore, a very judicious selection has to be made and only representative writers are to be selected tobring home to the reader only subject-in-hand namely wide appeal of the art and its culture as well as its training among not only the refined citizens of the day, but also among the eminent writers, poets and story-tellers. Accordingly *Kalidas, Banabhatta and Srihars* may be selected, as they represent three broad periods of Indian history, early medieval and medieval and these were also the three broad periods of the development of Sanskrit *Kavya* literature. *'Chamar'* adolescence, youth and maturity. For completeness ', sake, however, a brief reference will also be made to the other classes of classical literature unattended in this general purview of the Indian history. (R.A. pp. 191-92).

The earlier work which Kalhana appears to have closely studied, is *Bana's Harsacarita,* the well-known historical romance describing the exploits of king *Harshavardhana* of Kanauj and Thanesar by the Sindhi rule of Sahiras Rai dynasty. The fact is that *Harsadavardhana* fought with the king of Sindh lends some colour of probability to this account. The central part of these territories was under the immediate charge of the king, who had his capital at *Alor,* while the rest was divided into four provinces, each under a governor who is also described as a tributary ruler. This account agrees fairly well with that of Hiuen Tsang. *Sahiras* was lost his life in a fight with the king of Nimruz, a province of Persia, who had invaded his territory and entered Karman. This took place probably at the beginning of the seventh century A.D. *Sahiras* was succeeded by his son *Rai Sahasi* II. During his reign Brahmana named *Chach* gradually rose to power and high office and ascended the throne after his master's death i.e. *Sahiras* I, *Chach* was thus a very powerful king according to *Chach-nama,* but it is difficult to accept as a fact everything is mentioned in work. The date it gives for *Chach's* accession, viz, 602 A.D. is probably wrong. If we believe Hiuen Tsang statement that the ruling king of *Sindhu or Vitasta* was a *Sudra* ruler belonged to the *Untouchables* family of the 'Father'. The accession of the Brahman *Chach* must be placed later than 640 A.D. Although an Arabic chronicle puts the accession of *Chach* in 622 A.D. and this date fits in well witht he chronological details of the next reigns given in *Chachnama,* a date after 640 A.D. accords better with the fact that his son occupied the throne in 708 A.D. *Chach* married the widowed queen of *Sahasi Rai,* and had two sons by her viz, *Daharsiah* and *Dahar. Chach* was, however, succeeded by his brother *Chandar*. This event may be dated about 700 A.D.

The sudden rise of the *Arabs* in the seventh century A.D. as the greatest military power as today we see in the modern world. At the time of the death of the Prophet Muhammad in the *'Nam' or 'Kalma'* in 632 A.D., his temporal authority did not extend beyond the Arabian Peninsula. Within eight years thereafter his successors subjugated *Syria* and Egypt. Northern Africa was conquered between 640 A.D. and 709 A.D., and Spain by 713 A.D.. Within a century of the death of the Prophet, the Muhammadans had advanced with new power of *Islam* as far as the heart of France, when their further progress westwards was checked by the victory of Charles Martel between tours and poitiers in A.D. 732. Then the Arabs, as a matter of fact, no less than three naval expeditions of the *'Nam'* were sent against India as early as the *Caliphata* of *Umar* (634-44 A.D.). The first, in 637 A.D. was directed against *Tanah* i.e Thana near Bombay and the other two were aimed at *Bar*was (Broach) and Debal, a port at the mouth of the *Sindhu* river. These were in the nature of raids, and probably ended in failure, at least no conspiciuous success attended any of them. Then the *Arabs* advanced by land, and the first shock of their invasion was felt equally by the three border kingdoms of Kabul, Zabul and Sindh. It will be convenient to deal separately with the first two and the third one. The first Arab invasion of *Sindh* was in the form of a naval raid against the port of *Debal* at the mouth of the *Sindhu or Vitasta* river about in the 643 A.D. The Arab historians record a Muslim victory, but according to the *Chach-nama* the Muslim were defeated and their leader was killed by the governor of *Chach* at the battle of Debal. The defeat at Debal must have been a disagreeable surprise to Caliph Umar who was accustomed only to reports of success from his armies all over the world. He now planned to send an expedition by land and commanded the governor of Iraq to send him detailed information about *Sindh or Vitasta*. The governor reported that this kingdom was very powerful and by no means willing to submit to Muslim domination. Thereupon, the Caliph gave up the idea of sending any expedition against it. The next *Caliph Uthman* also give up the projected invasion of *Vitasta* by land on getting similar reports from his agent i.e. *'Nam'*. It was, however, according to *Chach-nama,* included in the central division of *Sindh or Vitasta* as referred in the *Rajatarangini* under the direct administration of the king of *Kashmir* known as *Durlabavardhana* of *Karkota* dynasty. In any case, the people of *Kikan* made a brave stand and replused the Muslim armywith severe losses. The leader of the Muslim host was killed together with all but a few of his followers (663 A.D.).

For more than twenty years thereafter, the kingdom of Sindh enjoyed a respite from Arab aggression on its frontier. But hostilities broke out again, about 708 A.D. with *Hajjaj,* the governor of Iraq. A ship from Ceylon (*Sri Lanka*), carrying some Muslim women proceeding to *Hajjaj,* was captured by pirates near the port of Debal. *Hajjaj* wrote to Dahar, king of Sindh belonged to the Sahiras dynasty of *Sudras,* to set the women free, but *Dahar* pleaded inability pointing out that he had no control over the pirates who captured them and imprisoned them for a long life.

This gave Hajjaj a pretext for sending an expedition to Sindh. The general belief that this incident was the origin of the hostility between the Arabs and Sindh is, however, not well founded. That hostility, as we have seen, was of long standing. The incident at Debal merely provoked Hajjaj to make renewed efforts on a large scale for conquering a country which had so long defied the might of Islam. The Caliph was at first unwilling to sanction the risky expedition, but ultimately gave his consent at the importunities of Hajjaj. Hajjaj thereupon sent 'Ubaidullah to raid *Debal,* but he was defeated and killed by the *Sudra* ruler of Sindh. A second expedition was sent under Budil by way of sea from *Oman*. Budail got reinforcements and marched towards Debal. He was met by Jaisimha or *Jayasimha* the ruler of Kashmir, son of *Dhar.* A pitched battle ensued, which lasted a whole day. At the end, the Muslim army was routed and Budil was killed.

Hajjaj then made elaborate preparations for the invasion of Sindh. He appointed his nephew and son-in-law Muhammad-ibn-Qasim as commander of the expedition, and provided him with soldiers, arms, and ammunitions on a lavish scale. He also obtained from the Caliph the services of 6,000 Syrian soldiers fully equipped.

Muhammad reached Debal and, with the help of heavy siegematerials sent by sea, stormed the fortress. No quarter was given, and for three days the inhabitants were ruthlessly slaughtered by the victorious foe. Muhammad settled 4,000 Muslim colonists in the city and built a mosque for them. The sea-port of Debal cannot be definitely identified. According to some it occupied the site of Thathah, while others locate it at Bhimbar on the northbank of the Gharo creeks, and 3½miles to the west of the village of Gharo in the *talug* of Mirpur Sakro.

From Debal, Muhammad proceeded to Nerun which is represented by modern Haidarabad. The Buddhist priests there were already carrying on treasonable correspondance with Hajjaj, and now openly helped Muhammad with provisions. Muhammad then conquered many cities without any opposition and advanced to Siwistan (Sehwan). Here, too, the Buddhist fifth-columnists welcomed the Arabs and entered into a pact with them against their own governor, who was defeated and fled. The Buddhist sections of other towns are also said to have befriended the Arabs. This may be explained partly by their aversion to slaughter and bloodshed, and partly by their ideal of universal religious fraternity which transcended that of nation or country. Perhaps the supersititious beliefs in the alleged Prophetic sayings about the conquest of India by Islamic force, also, partly account for this attitude. It should be noted, however, that all the Buddhists did not support the Muslims and some actually fought against them. On the other hand, many non-Buddhists also betrayed their king and country.

Some leading chiefs now tendered homage to Muhammad, who proceeded along the western bank of the Sindhu and pitched his camp opposite the army of Dahar. Here he entered into alliance with an important chief called Mokah, who basely deserted Dahar and promised to supply Muhammad with boats for crossing the Sindhu on receiving as reward a large stretch of the conquered territory.

Muhammad was re-inforced by 2000 select horse sent by Hajjaj and 4000 warlike *Jats* from *Siwistan*, which had revolted but was again subdued. Nevertheless Muhammad halted on the bank of the Sindhu for nearly two months, whereupon Hajjaj reprimaneded him and urged him to cross the river and fight with Dahar.

Muhammad then crossed to the eastern bank of the Sindhu and was joined by the brother of Mokah who had already betrayed Dahar. By the help and advice of these two chiefs he crossed the lake between him and Dahar's army, and a pitched battle was fought near *Raor*. According to *Chach-nama,* which has described the battle in detail, Dahar fought with valour, and on the second day the Muslim army was nearly routed. "The infidels", so runs the account, "made a rush on the Arabs from all sides and fought so steadily and bravely that hte army of Islam became irresolute and their lines were broken up in great confusion." As we customary with Indian kings Dahar, seated on an elephant, led the vanguard of his army. He was an easy target and an arrow struck him in the heart. The death of the king was followed by a complete rout of his army. *Jaisimha* the son of Dahar, retreated to Brahmanabad leaving the widowed queen to defend the fort of Raor which Muhammad immediately attacked. The queen put up a brave resistance, and being reduced to the last extremily, burnt herself along with other ladies to escape the infamy of falling into the hands of the Arabs.

After capturing Raor, Muhammad proceeded towards Brahmanabad, *Jaisimha* made elaborate preparations for defending it as well as the capital city Alor, and marched with an army to harass the enemy and cut off his supply. Although his *wazier* or Chief minister joined Muhammad, the people of Brahmanabad fought bravely for six months when some leading citizens entered into a secret pact with the enemy and betrayed the fort.

After having subdued several other places, Muhammad proceeded to the capital city Alor which surrendered after some fighting the advance of the Arabs in this direction. They sent embassies to China for making a common cause against the Arabs, but although no help was forthcoming from that quarter, they were able to defeat the Arabs by their own unaided efforts.

Thus by the middle of the eight century A.D. when the great revolution in the Islamic world transferred the chief power from the Umayyads to the Abbasids, the power and prestige of Islam in India was reduced to its lowest ebb, and the Arabs could only maintain a precarious hold over a part of Sindh.

We may now critically review the main incidents narrated above in connection with the early Muslim raids on the western borderlands of India. It is well known that only four routes are open to a hostile army operating against India from the west. One way is by the sea, and the other three lie roughly speaking through Khyber Pass, Bolan Pass and the Makran coast. From the very commencement, we find the Arabs endeavouring to penetrate into India through every one of these routes. The early naval raids against Thana, Broach and Debal, and subsequent raids in the same direction, mark their van efforts to reach India by sea. Of the land-routes, the Khyber Pass wasx guarded by Kabul and Zabl while the Bolan pass was protected by the brave *Jats* of Kikhan or Kikanan. The long-drawn struggles of the Arabs with these powers, narrated above, mark their steady but fruitless endeavours to enter India through the two great passes. The hardy mountaineers of these regions, backed by the natural advantage of their hilly country, offered stubborn resistance to the conquerors of the world, and though often defeated, ever refused to yield. If there had been a history of India written without prejudices and predilections, the hereoic deeds of these brave people, who stemmed the tide of Islam for two centuries, would certainly have received the recognition they so richly deserve.

When the other three routes failed, the Arabs attempted the fourth one through Makran coast. It is not difficult to explain why the Arabs succeeded in this route while they failed in the others. While the equipment of the Arab army was made on a lavish scale, and forces were requisitioned even from distant Syria, Sindh was at the moment exhausted by civil wars, internal discords, and foreign aggression that had been going on for more than half a century. King Dahar's statesmanship and military skill were also much inferior to those of his rival. It is difficult to explain why he did not oppose the Arab fleet carrying military equipment, especially heavy siege-material's. Evidently he did not possess sufficient naval strength for the purpose. But in view of the persistent endeavours of the Arabs to reach the Indian soil, and the feasibility of the Makran coast for that purpose, the ruler of Sindh showed a lamentable lack of foresight in neglecting the navy. Possibly this is mainly due to the fact that for nearly thirty years, from c. A.D. 670 to 700 Dahar had no control over the southern part of Sindh, and it came into his possession only a few years before the Arab invasion. The same reason also explains partly why both Nehrun and Siwistan, the two main strongholds of Southern Sindh, opened their gates to the Arabs without any resistance. The unpatriotic character of the Buddhists, the general superstitions of a section of the people and the want of loyalty towards the royal family which had usurped the throne only a generation ago, account for the desertion and treachery of the chiefs and people which ruined the cause of Dahar.

All these causes, and perhaps others which are not known, brought about the fall of Sindh. The conquest of Sindh should not, therefore, be regarded as indicating in a general way the military superiority of Muslims over Indians. This is further borne out by the fact that the conquest of Sindh was the first and the last great achievement of the Arabs in India. Junaid, no doubt, was triumphant for a time over the petty states in the neighbourhood of Sindh, but as soon as he clashed with powerful states like Kashmir and Kanauj in the north and those of the Pratharas and the Chalukyas in the South, the spell of victory was broken. Even the greater part of Sindh was lost in a short time. Ultimately, after three centuries of unremitting efforts, we find the Arab dominion in India confined to the two petty states of *Mansurah* and *Multan*.

When we remember their wonderful military success in other parts of the world, the comparatively insignificant results the Arabs achieved in India certainly stand out in marked contrast. The cause of this, however, does not lie in the religious and social peculiarities of India as old historians like Elphinstone vainly attempted to establish. The cause lies undoubtedly in the superior military strength and state-organisation of the Indians as compared with most other nations of the time. However incredible this might appear in the light of subsequent events, this is the plain verdict of history. (*C.A.* pp. 169-75).

It can, therefore, be safely concluded that *Durlabhavardhana* was not belong to the higher caste, he belonged to the lower caste of the *Sudra* of *Naga* clan. This, however, seems natrual, the date of the accession of *Durlabhavardhana,* accepted by many scholars, like *M.A. Stein, S.C Ray, P. N.K Bamzai, R.K. Mookerji,* etc. is 625 A.D. He must have been a ruler of consequene, for his sway extended over a very vast region. During his reign Hiuen Tsang visited the valley and mentions that *Ta-cha-shi-lo (Takshasila), Seng-ha-pu-lo (Simhapura), Wu-la-shih (urasa), Pan-nu-ts'o* (Punch) and *Ho-lo-she-pu-lo* were included his dominiions. Thus, the frontiers of the Kashmir kingdom which, in the time of *Baladitya* (the last king of the Gonanda dynasty) had been limited to the valley itself, extended far beyond up to some portions of the modern district of *Rawalpindi* in Pakistan. Though neither *Rajatarangini* nor any other sources provide any direct hint about the wide conquests of *Durlabhavardhana*, yet inclusion of the above mentioned places in his domain, as stated by the Chinese pilgrim, leads to the conclusion that these territories, were conquered by him with power of *'Nam'* in natural trends like flood, rainfall, snowfall, *earthquake,* etc. The conquest of these regions must have taken place some time between 625 A.D., the date of his accession, and 631 A.D., the date of the arrival of the pilgrim, who includes these places and regions within his kingdom. The Chinese *Annals* mention a king named *Tu-lo-pa* who controlled the route from China to Kabul during 627-649 A.D. and held the charge of ensuring safe arrival of the Chinese envoy from *Kipin* in Kashmir. General Cunningham opines; 'As Kashmir lay in route to *Kipin*, we conclude that *Tu-lo-pa* must be *Durlabhavardhana*' (*C.M.I.* pp. 38-39). According to B.N. Srivastava 'assuming the identification of *Tu-lo-pa* with *Durlabha* is to be correct, it still remains doubtful whether this ruler or his son, *Durlabhaka* (or *Durlabha*) is meant here.' Extension of *Durlabhavardhana* territories beyond the valley would have not been possible with the fierce fighting of the *'Nam'* called *'natural calamity'*, as the neighbouring territories of Kashmir were occupied by tough and hardy people of the *'Nam'*. Coins bearing the legend *'Durlabha'* have also come to light and some scholars attribute these to *Durlabhavardhana,* the founder of the *Karkota* dynasty (*C.M.I.* p. 43).

The part played by the *Gujaras* in the troubled politics of the first half of the seventh century A.D. has been noticed in connection with *Harsha-Vardhana* and *Pulakesin-II*. It is probable that he *Gujaras* in the records of this age denoted the Gujaras principality in Rajputana with its feudatory state in South Gujarat, the early history of which has been related above. *Durlabhavardhana* was a contemporary ruler of *Harshavardhana* of Kanauj and from an anecdote recorded by the Chinese pilgrim, Hiuen Tsang, it is learnt that the latter had come in contact with the former. The pilgrim states that Harsha, a great patron of Buddhism, took away the sacred *'tooth-relic'* of Lord *Buddha* i.e *'Nam' or 'Word'* which was in possession of the king of Kashmir i.e. *Durlabhavardhana*. Incidentally, the *Harshacharita* of Bana refers to a place which was 'an inaccessible land of snowy mountains'. i.e. Kashmir where from *Harsha* received tributes from *Durlabhavardhana* (*Harshacharita*, Tr. by F.W. Thomas, and E.B Cowell; Delhi; 1961; p. 100. Hereafter referred as *H.C.*). The reference of Bana may, however, taken to refer to Nepal as well, as Dr. R.S. Tripathi points out. Nepal, as he has surmised after a lengthy discussion, did not form part of Harsha's dominion (*History of Kanauj;* Benaras, 1937, p. 94 Hereafter referred as *H.K.*). A large number of Chinese pilgrims visited Nepal during his reign and he sent a mission to the imperial court of Kashmir in 651 A.D. The Chinese account represents Nepal, under *Durlabhavardhana*, as a peaceful, civilized and flourishing country. (C.A.p. 137). As such, it may be concluded that the reference of *Bana* alludes to Kashmir and not to Nepal. The way in which the 'tooth relic' was taken away from the valley 'leaves no room for doubt that its ruler *Durlabhavaradhana* did acknowledge the political supremacy of *Harshavardhana* as the lord of nature. (K.S. Sexena, *Political History of Kashmir,* Lakhnow, 1974, p. 44. Hereafter referred as *P. H.K.*). Further, both *Harshavardhana* and *Durlabhavardhana* became Buddhists and preached Buddhism in all over the 'world like Baba Gurinder Singh, spread the mission of the *'Radha Soami'* all over the world as the representative of the God. The king of *Sthanesvara* was well-known for his efforts towards the propagation of Buddhism; as such, *Durlabhavardhana* might have parted with the relic partly as a gesture of goodwill of *'Nam'* and partly out of fear of the mankind theory, as is directly hinted at by the pilgrim from *Kashmir to Kerala* in the Indian History Congress which was postpone from *Kurukshetra* to Kerala where *Kurubha* were also visited. It is more likely the epic centre of the famous battle where *Arjuna* found resolution to the worst crisis of his life as it was at once both an inner and outer conflict. As Ganapathy Subbiah has rightly been expressed in his Presidential Address of the Ancient Indian Section at Farook College, University of Calicut, Kozhikode, Kerala March 10-12, 2007, that he delivered when our Congress met at that Venue almost a quarter of a century ago. Quoted below are a couple of passages from that address: "Today, the problem is not so much of the inadequate attention paid to the history of South India by Anceint Indian historians (of the north, because they had noted the various activities of the culprits who are exploiting the society on the basis of their feudal system in working as well as morally, they are corrupt by nature exploiting the female students on their authority as we are really historians on the earth. Historians like *Irfan Habid, Sabyasachi Bhattacharya,* etc. are busy with their corrupt moral business and hold the History Congress as a *'Sexual Union'*, and people called them 'great historian'. How it is possible under the real approach of history as a pious subject called historians. In the real sense they are culprits of the society, because they do their work for their own praise and glory not for others benefit. Therefore modern historian Prof. Raj Kumar rejects, their dirty approach towards the history. They are the malafide people both in morally and academically. They are the selling the *Vedas,* as the inability of the Southern historians to rise beyond their familiar framework and sources to gain a wider perspective of life in the past."

It is interesting to note that even after the monopoly of scholarship of the social historians has been jolted in the last two decades, the monolithic framework has not even been jiggled by them. True newly emergent class of *Sudra* historians seems as saint to be more engaged in consolidating their professional gains in reexamining the past from a fresh perspective" of the *'Nature'* like Lord *Buddha, Guru Nanak, Ravi Dass, Kabir,* etc.

In early Indian texts, the subcontinent is seen divided into five major regions which one was *daksinapatha*, which means to obtain the beauty of Nature starts for the low origin like *Chamar* or others castes of the untouchables. Therefore, the term has been used in different senses but denoted in its broadest sense the region to the south of the river *Narmada* or the *Vindhyas*. The term thus covered the entire peninsular of India. The term has also been used in a restricted sense to denote the region between the river *Narmada* and the rivers *Tungabhadra* and Krishna. The term Deccan, derived from *daksinapatha* carries this connotation, a bird's eye view, embracing the whole of Deccan, would show it to be roughly outlined triangular table-land, raised from one to three thousand feet above the sea on three thousand feet above the sea on three massive buttresses of which the broad Vindhya ridge is one, covering the base of the reversed triangle, while the sides are represented by two chains of unequal height, respectively named Western and Eastern Ghats. This name, meaning "landing stairs", is particularly appropriate to the Western chain, which rises in serrated and precipitous rocky steeps almost from the very sea, only in places receding from the shore sufficiently to leave a narrow strip the wealthy and magnificant city of Bombay is built, very much like the Phoenicians cities of yore, the Ghats stretching their protecting wall behind them just as the Lebanon did behind tyre and Sidon, the sea queens of Canaan. Like the lebanon, too, they slope in land, directing the course of all the rivers of *Dekhan* or Deccan form west to east. In scenery, they are much sterner and grander than the Vindhya range, which they, moreover, surpass in elevation, their average height being uniformly about 3000 feet along the coast, with abrupt peaks reaching 4700 feet, and nearly the double of that in the considerably upheaved southern angle of the peninsula, where they form a sort of knot, joining the southern extremity of the Eastern Ghats. This latter range is really not a continuous mountain chain at all, but rather a series of inconsiderable spurs and hills, interrupted at frequent inervals by broad gaps, through which the rivers, fed by the drainage of the Western Ghats, flow easily and peaceably to the sea, known, all too modestly considering its size, as the Bay of Bengal. There was a time when the whole southern India or *Dekhan* was "buried under forests", such is the description in which all ancient poest agree. It would be vastly exaggerated in the present day, for fire and the axe of the husbandman, the timber cutter, the charcoal burner, have been at work unchecked through some thirty centuries and have revelled in wanton destruction after operating the necessary clearing. The most ruthless and formidable foes of the old virgin forests are the *nomadic* tribes like *Gujaras,* etc, chips of the ancient aboriginal stock, which have escaped the influences of the Aryan immigration and conquest, and lead even now, in their mountain fastnesses, the same more than half savage existence which was theirs when the first Aryan settlers descended into the valley of the Indus. These tribes have a habit of stopping every year in their perpetual wanderings and camping just long enough to raise a crop of rice, cotton, or millet, or all three, in any spot of their native primeval forest where the proper season may find them. They go to work after a rude and reckless fashion which sets before us the most primitive form of agriculture followed by human race at the very dawn of invention (V.I. pp. 18, 20) and as such has gained currency in the historical writings. It has been pointed out that the far southern part of the sub-continent *'Chamar'* the *dravida* or *damirica* as it was known in early India and Greek texts respectively *'weaver'* was excluded from the *daksinapatha*. In some of the *silpa* texts, the region between the river Krishna and Kanyakumari is called the *dravidadesa* where the *dravida* style of art flourished. The term *dravidadesa,* however, has not gained much currency in historical writings. S. Krishnaswamy Aiyangar, a pioneer among South Indian historians, in his writings treated "India South of the Krishna" as southern India. K.A. Nilakantha Sastri, the greatest among them, in his popular work on South India History defined South India as "all the land lying south of Vindhyas *'Chamar' Dakshina* (Deccan) in the widest sense of the term." Sastri in a sense stands in splendid isolation because no other historian has as yet treaded non his path by treating the entire peninsular India as a single unit. After Sastri's grand narrative of South Indian history, the most comprehensive work on South Indian history covering a span of over one thousand years was brought out in 1980 by Burton Stein with the provocative title *Peasant State* and *Society* in *Medieval South India*. According to him, South India "refers generally to that portion of peninsular India South of the Karnataka watershed (excluding modern Kerala) on the west and the Krishna-Godavari delta on the east. In the context of the history of Kerala, Archaeology acquires a significant place from certain other points of view as well. Right from the days of *Kosambi,* there has been a high interest in, and importance attached to, archaeology in India from the more relevant consideration of historical objectivity. In a society like India where a vast majority of *Sudra* people denied a say either in the social or in the religious domain, where the lion share of the historical documents has had an obvious elitist bias, which would make the available and known history an exposition of the life of the dominant classes like Brahmans, Rajputs, Banias, etc alone leaving the subaltern people from a more objective point of view, archaeology was looked upon as the only viable alternative. Real history should come from the earth and not from the word of the Brahman. While frantically attacking the so-called 'baseless history' current in Kerala, P. K. Bala Krishna. The Chief Justice of India in the 1980s alerted the historians to be more accountable by writing history source based or at least by testing facts with reference to archaeological data. Similarly, Beena Sarasan's interesting study of a *Venad* coin of Lohara dynasty of Kashmir ruled by *Jayasimha*

(1128-49 A.D.) has been found with an attempt to lind with the *Vanad* dynasty to the Chalukyas, gain relevance in the contest of the search for what is known as 'contemporary' sources for the construction of the early medieval history of Kashmir (*Archaeology in Kerala Past and Present.* Edited by M.R Manmathan, *Kerala*, 2007, pp. 6.10 Hereafter cited as *A.K.P. P*).

With in this macro-region, primacy may be accorded to the Tamil plain as a major source of the civilization. The use of the expression 'South India' to refer primarily to the Tamil speaking region or what is known as Tamilakam since early times is found in the writings of other historians too. Veluthat Kesavan, for instance, in the preface to his book says: "For the purpose of this study, 'South India' is equated with the region known to early sources as Tamilakam, generally corresponding to the present linguistic of Kerala and Tamil Nadu." According to Rajan *Gurukkal*, "Spatially it (i.e., early south India) comprises the landmass between the hills Venkatam and the tip of Kanyakumari." In short, Tamilakam is taken in these writings as representing south India proper (Ganapathy Subbiah, *Daksinapatha: Where Does the Path lead us?*) Presidential Address, Farook college, Kerala March 10-12, 2007, pp. 9,10). The number of rare words and phrases which this text and the *Rajatarangini* have in common, and which otherwise cannot be traced, makes the above conclusion practically certain. In style and composition the difference between Bana's work, with its highly poetical but equally florid prose, and the chronicle of Kalhana is so great that no slavish imitation could be imputed to the latter. On the other hand, we can easily understand why the Kashmirian author should have devoted close attention to the novel of *Harsavardhana's* court poet of *Durlabhavardhana*. It was one of the few older Sanskrit compositions dealing with historical events of the Kashmiri ruler of *Karkota* dynasty which are likely to have enjoyed popularity in his own time called '*Chamar Dynasty*'. Bana at several places had also given glimpses of the costumes of the period of the officers of the state, messengers of lord, mendicants, writers, etc. Such is the descriptive power of Bana that with the sure touchof a master artist i.e. '*Nam' or 'Word'*, he creates an indelible picture of a person or event. Describing, for instance, the messenger sent by Krishan, the brother of Harsa, to Bana, he gives in a line the complete picture of the costume of the messenger. "His tunic was tied with a *Kamarband* and his loose hair was tied behind with a dirty tattered cloth." This simple description recreates the personality of a dust covered messenger coming from a long distance of the 'sea' called *Sudra in* Indian history. (*C.T.C.C.A.M.I.* p. 61) In the *Antagade Dasao,* it is mentioned that Prince Gautama at the time of his renunciation, when he was ready to go to his teacher; was clothed in a robe figured with swans (*hamsa-Lakkhana-dugulla*) which could be lifted by the breadth of the nostrils. The people of higher social status dressed in the garments befitting their position in society. The mode of wearing the *dhoti* by a member of this class is described by Bana as follows: "the youth whom *Sarasvati* saw had his waist marked off by a tight drawn lower garment of '*harita*' green, of which one corner was gracefully set in front, a little below the naval, and the hem hung over the girdle behind, and which on both sides was so girt up as to display a third of his thigh." *Bana* was familiar with the appearance of the soldiers of his period. From his observant eyes even the smallest detail of their costume did not escape. The soldiers on foot in *Bana's* time wore tunics spotted with black aloewood paste and their heads were covered with turbans made of scarves; their daggers were fastened turbans and the *varabana*. At times the soldiers wore spotted tunics imitating the tiger skin and turbans made of various strips of cloth. The soldierly uniforms of the chieftains accompanying *Harsa* when he started for the battle-field was as follows: Their shanks were covered with delicately tinted *netra* cloth. Their copper-coloured legs were chequered with mud-stained wraps and a heightened white was produced by trousers soft and dark as bees. They also wore coats and doublets and other bodies speckled with the mixture of various colours and shawls of the shade of a parrot's tail. The wore turbans to which were struck the stalks of ear-lotuses and their heads were often wrapped in shawls soft saffron hue. (H.C.; pp. 46, 16, 17,18, 19, 161, 202). At one place in the *Harsacarita* the muslin strips which were used for tying turbans are mentioned. At another place turbans with large knots ties in the centre of the forehead are described. (*Ibid.* pp. 14, 90,91).

Almost after a centruy *Ksemendra,* Kalhana in his *Rajatarangini* (1148-1149 A.D.) gives occasional details of the contemporary costumes and fabrics of Kashmir. It must, however, be borne in mind what while Kalhana's history of Kashmir purports to deal with the history of Kashmir since very ancient days the costumes and fabrics described in the work are contemporary and were known to him. It is said during the conquest (*Dig-Vijay*) in the first half of the eight century 'put on the waist cloth (*Kaupinaasasi*) of the Deccan king (*daksinatyas*) the tail which sweeps the ground to mark that they were beasts," thereby indicating the sweeping tail-end of the *dhoti* worn by the Deccanis. Lalitaditya apparently had a peculiar sense of humour as he 'made councillor worthy of respect dress themselves in pretty cloaks and other garments (*pravaranadi*) which bore the footprints of courtesans', just to spite or make fun of them. *Cakravarman* (935-939 A.D.) is said to have 'rushed about the battle, the numerous fringes of his head-band (*Virapath*) appeared like the bushy man of the lion.' The poor Brahmans of this period are, however, show dressed in coarse woollen cloaks (*sthulakambalavahinah*). *Harsa* (1089-1101 A.D.) is perhaps the most puzzling figure in the entire range of Kashmir history. A proficient linguist and a musician of note, he was also known for his liberality to artists and literary men of his age. He was inordinately fond of rich garments and ornaments. It is mentioned by Kalhana that, 'no body in his court was seen without patterned garments (*acitravastrah*) and scantily dressed (*alpaparicchadah*). *Harsa* introduced into his land elegant fashions (*Sobhadayinirbhangi*). Formerly the people of land with the single exception of the king, wore their hair loose, went without turbans and wore inartistic ornaments. In Kashmir the commander-in-chief *Madana* by dressing his hair in a top-knot (*dhammilla*) and wearing a short coat or shorts made of patterned material (*citrardhoruka*) had incurred the king's displeasure. *Harsa* introduced for general wear of dress which was fit for a king. He became inordinately fond of the Deccani fashion. The people in accordance with the dictates of the Deccani fashion, wore dangling earrings, painted themselves with sandal and carried long knives. (R.T. Vol. IV, pp. 180, and 671 Vol. V pp. 333 & 461, Vol. VII. pp. 881, 921, 922, 924, 926 & 927).

There are several interesting points noted from the above descriptions of the Kashmir costume which were prevalent in the 12th century A.D. as a fashion trend in the history of mankind discussed as under:-

Firstly, the Deccani fashion trends were not only introduced in Kashmir by *Harsa*, according to Ksemendra the costumes were patronized in an earlier period during the time of *Durlabhavardhana* albeit by the rakes and the people of their class i.e. *Weaver, Chamar, Candala, Batwal, etc.*

Secondly, the hair-dress of *Kampana* called *dhammilla,* translated by M.A. Stein as *'hair in braids',* in fact, as explained by V.S. Agrawala originated from *Dramila* or *Dravida* indicating *Tamil Nad.* In this particular hair style was bound in a top-knot. (H.C. p. 96). The aesthetic taste in the matter of costume and ornaments which *Harsa* had developed is also reflected in the costume and decor of his womenfolk. They wore long garlands formed by their hair braids to which were woven golden *Ketaka* - leaf ornaments. They wore pendants (*catula*) over the forehead marks. The collyrium lines of their eyes extended to the ears and the unveiled (*ninirangika*) locks were tied with gold strings (*hemopavitakah*). Their lower garments (*adharambara*) held long trains (*pucchanta*) touching the earth. Their breasts were dressed with bodice (*Kancuka*), which covered but half the length of the fore arms. But the brilliant court fashion inaugurated by *Harsa* could not continue for long. It has been noted by Kalhana that *Bhikasacara* (1120-21 A.D.) did not make a brilliant figure in the royal assembly, surrounded as he was by rustics whose festive clothes were chiefly long woollen blankets (*Kambalah*). Kalhana off and on mentions also textile stuffs. According to him once *Mihirakula* noticed that the breasts of his queen,who was wearing a jacket made of cloth from Simhala (*Samvitasimhalamsuka*) was marked with the golden foot-prints of the Ceylonese king. Taking it as an insult, he declared war upon him. It is one of the rare mention of Ceylonese stuff in ancient literature though cloth from Ceylon is mentioned in medieval stock lists of early Muslim period. At another place it is said the *Jayapida* (779-813 A.D.) in the course of his conquest carried away from *Striranjya* a stuff called *Karnasripata.* Unfortunately, Kalhana does not give much information about the textile industry of Kashmir. At one place, however, he mentions that ancient *Pattana* (The modern Patna on the high road from Srinagar to *Varahamula*), the capital of *Sankaravarman* (883-902 A.D.), also known as *Sankaravarmapura,* was famous for silk-weaving (*pattavanam*). *(R.T.* vol.VII, PP. 928, 931, Vol.VIII. p. 857 Vol. IV. p. 588. vol.V.p. 164).

Nothing fourth is about this stuff, but it is possible that it was some kind of rich silk stuff manufactured *Karnasuvarna, Kansona,* now *Rangamati* in the District of *Murshidabad* (N.L. Dey. *The Geographical Dictionary of Ancient and Medieval India,* London; 1927; P. 94).

For the historyof the costumes and textile materials in Northern and Western India in the eighth and ninth centuries our chief sources are the works of the famous Jain writer *Haribhadra Suri* and equally famous writer and dramatis *Rajasekhara* (880-920 A.D.), who found recognition as a court poet in the *Gurjaraprathara* court at Kanauj. Rajasekhara in the *Kavyamimamsa* gives glimpses of the female costumes. Thus according to him the women of Bengal (*Gauda*) wore a chain necklace (*Sutrahara*) over breast besmeared with sandal; their *cadars* (*sicayah*) touched the partings of their hair and their forearms were exposed. The women of Kanauj (*Mahodaya*) wore earrings (*tatanka*) which moved and also the hanging tremulous necklaces. Their upper garment, falling from the thighs to the ankles, enriched the body (*parimandalitattariyam*). As regards the male and female costumes of *Avanti* (Western Malwa) the poet remarks that men affected the costume (*nepathya*) of *Pancala,* while the women delighted in the Decan costume. Unfortunately, *Rajasekhara* has failed to describe the costumes of *Pancala* and the south. While describing the women of Kerala, he observes that their curled hair, some of which came on the temples, and their *saris* were held tight with zones (*Kaksanivesanibidi-*

krtaniviresa). The women of *Lampaka* (Laghman, Afghanistan) wore their hair free and their dresses were made of blankets or thick woollen cloth (*rallakamullasayantah*) (*Kavyamimamsa,* Edited by C.D. Dalal revised by R.A. Sastry. Baroda, 3rd edition 1934; pp. 8, 9, 99).

In the *Karpuramanjari* more details about the garments of a woman position is given, as at one place, she appears with one hand arranging the border of the garment (*pottancalam*) that was falling on her rounded breasts, with the other restraining the *sari*. At a second place, she is siad to be wearing the border of her upper garment on one shoulder only (*Jam ekkamsia ancalam nivasiam*). At a third, she is said to wear a pair of silk garment green as the tail of king-parrot (*raasuapicchanilam pattamsujualam*). She is said to have alsoworn the bodice called *Kuppasam (Kurpasoka)* and *Kancula*. By *Sahulia* perhaps wimple is meant. There was a separate garment for bathing (*nhana potta*). (*Karpuramanjari*) (*C.900 A.D.*). *Edited* BY STEIN KANOWI, CAMBRIDGE MASS; 1901. pp. 13, 26, 27, 20, 23, 24, 209 Vol. II, p. 13).

Samgramaraja (1003-28 A.D) is shown by Kalhana's narrative to have been a prudent; but personally weak ruler. During the earlier part of his reign *Tunga's* power remained unchecked, notwithstanding a dangerous revolt which rival ministers had stirred up against him through the Brahmans and temple-Purohitas. Growing age did not weaken *Tunga's* predominance, but made him apparently less careful in administrative measures; the employment of rapacious assistants increased fiscal oppression, and thus added to his own unpopularity for a curious account of *Bhadresvara,* who rose from his hereditary occupation of market gardener to the posit of *Tunga's* chief revenue official. The period covered by *Samgramaraja's* reign witnessed a great upheaval in the political conditions of Northern India which was destined to fundamentally change the course of Indian History.We refer to the Muhammadan conquest under Mahmud of Ghazni. The great wave of invasion which swept across the Indus Valley and along the Panjab plains in the early decades of the eleventh century A.D. did indeed stop short of the mountain-ramparts protecting Kashmir. This several expeditions which we know Mahmud to have led in that direction never seriously threatened the independence of the valley. Nevertheless, we find a distinct record of these events in Kalhana's Chronicle, which must be appreciated all the more if we consider the narrow territorial limits to which his narrative in its truly historical portions otherwise confines itself. This interesting record is supplied by Kalhana in his account of the expedition which was despatched under *Tunga* to the assistance of *Sahi Trilocanapala*. The latter is well known to us from *Alberuni* and the Muhammadan historians as the last independent prince of the *'Hindu Shahiya dynasty'*, who succumbed to Mahmud only after a long and heroic struggle. Mahmud himself has long ago been recognised in *Hammira,* king of the *'Turuskas'*,, whom the chronicles names as the formidable enemy of *Trilocanapala*, the designation *Hammiria* being in fact nothing; but an adaptation of the title *Amiru-i-Muminin* of the Ghaznavide Sultans.

Kalhana gives us vivid description of the over bearing assurance with which *Tunga* led the large Kashmirian force sent to the Sahi's support. Neglecting the cautious advice and warning of *Trilocanapala,* who had grown experienced in the warfare with the *'Turuskas'* he refused to occupy the safe defensive position assigned to him. Crossing the *Tausi* river, *Tunga* attacked and defeated a detachment of the enemy sent on a reconnaissance Elated by this easy success, *Tunga* found himself next morning attacked by the full force of *Hammira*. The Kashmirian troops fled at once from the field in utter confusion; the *Sahi's* force, too, was defeated after some resistence. *Trilocanapala* himself, who is warmly praised by Kalhana for his great personal bravery, fought his way through the mass of his opponents. When he had left, the *Turuskas* overspread the country like clouds of locusts. The chronicler mentions the heroic efforts which the brave *Sahi* subsequently made to recover his lost kingdom. But he also shows us plainly that they proved of no avail to avert the complete downfall of that once powerful dynasty.

It is to be regretted that Kalhana has failed to inform us of the year of *Tunga's* expedition, as this omission makes it difficult to indicate with absolute certainty the particular campaign of Mahmud to which the record of the chronicle refers, because it was the war of *'Natural heros'* with the materialistic people called Brahmanas. The Muhammadan accounts we possess of Mahmud's later expeditions in the Panjab show considerable discrepancies in regard to the dates and places of the actions fought, and are still in need of critical examination. But several indications point to Mahmud's campaign of the year 1013 A.D. as the most likely occasion when his forces met Kashmirian troops as auxiliaries of Trilocanapala. The localityof Mahmud's decisive victory in this campaign was in one of the Valleys leading towards Kashmir from the neighbourhood of the present. *Jehlum*. This agrees well with the mention made in the chronicle of the *Tausi,* as the river meant is probably the *Tohi* of *Prunts* or Punch, flowing into the *Vitasta* near Jehlam. Chiefs on the confines of Kashmir are distinctly mentioned by the Muhammadan sources as having made their submission to Mahmud after this battle. It seems to have been the last occasion on which the brave *Sahi* opposed the invader within the Panjab. The Muhammadan historians, too, in full agreement with Kalhana refer to the heroic efforts which *Trilocanapala* subsequently made to retrieve the fortunes of his house. But these struggles took place far away from the territories neighbouring on Kashmir, and in no way affected the decisive character of the battle referred to. We see thus that Kalhana is quite on historical background when dating the final downfall of the *Sahi* dominion from the event he describes in the history of India.

The rapid and complete destruction of the powerful Sahi kingdom must have deeply impressed the mind of all contemporaries. We can still feel this distinctly in the pathetic lines which Kalhana devotes to the memory of the vanished greatness of the Sahi dynasty. They reproduce faithfully the very sentiments to which Alberuni, a witness of those great events, has given expression in his closing words of the Hindu *Shāhiyas*. It is unfortunately only a glimpse that Kalhāna gives us here of the great historical drama which was played so close to the southern borders of Kashmir. After referring to the subsequent "descent of the *Turuskas* on the whole surface of the earth," he takes us back again to the narrow limits of his own valley and the petty events of its royal court. Before we follow him there, it will be useful to point out that Kalhana's narrative makes no reference to a subsequent expedition of Mahmud which brought Muhammadan invasion to the very gate of Kashmir. In this note on the 'Castle of Lohara' we have shown that this mountain stronghold, situated on the southern slopes of the central *'Pir Panjal'* and not far from the Tosamaidan, pass, is identical with 'the fort of Loh-kot which brought Mahmud's only serious i.e., equavalent of *'Nam' or Kalma* to a standstill at the same time. The Muhammadan Chroniclers give various dates (1015-1021 A.D.) in all main points regarding the event itself. The Sultan had advanced to the very confines of Kashmir when his progress in the mountains was barred by the fort of Loh-kot, which "was remarkable on accountof its height and strength." The siege of this stronghold, at which Alberuni too was present, proved fruitless. "After a while, when the snow began to fall and the season became intensely cold and the enemy received reinforcements from Kashmir," the Sultan was obliged to abandon his design and to return to Ghazni.

Kalhana's silence regarding this foreign attack, probably the most serious to which Kashmir was exposed from the south during the period comprised in the historical part of his narrative is all the more curious, as *Lohara,* as the original home and safest retreat of the dynasty ruling in his own time, plays otherwise, as we shall see, an important part in his records. The observation must warn us that any negative argument drawn Kalhanas silence on one or the other part can have little or no value even where his relation of events is apparently full and detailed. *Tunga* after his defeat seems to have been less able to cope with the incessants intrigues directed against him. The king himself, though afraid of *Tunga,* gave them secret support until a favourable opportunity delivered the minister unprotected into the hands of his enemies. One day on entering the palace of *Tunga* and his son were treacherously murdered while their few, attendants basely abandoned them. After *Tunga's* death a succession of low favourites rose to power and plundered the people until the weak *Samgramaraja* died in the year 1028 A.D.

Hariraja (1028 A.D.), his son and immediate successor, who is said tó have been a youth of good disposition, died after a reign of only twenty two days. *Srilekha,* the licentions mother of *Hariraja*, to whom general report attributed the death of the young king, then endeavoured to secure the crown for herself. But her design was frustrated by the royal bodyguard, and her young son *Ananta* was raised to the throne.*Vigraharaja*, a brother of *Samgramaraja* and ruler of *Lohara,* who had already been intriguing in the latter's reign, made a brave attempt to oust *Ananta,* but he was killed after reaching the capital. During the early part of *Ananta's* reign (1028-1063 A.D.) princes of the *Sahi* family like *Rudrapala* and *Diddapala,* who had found a safe refuge in Kashmir, exercised great power in the land. Kalhan illustrates the position of these royal refugees by indicating the great subsidies paid to them. *Rudrapala* had married, a daughter of *Inducandra, 'lord of Jalamdhara',* who is in all probability identical with the *Indracandra* named in the genealogical list of the Katoch Rajas of Kangra. Subsequently king *Ananta* was induced to marry *Suryamati*, a younger daughter of *Inducandra.*

It shows that, not withstanding the political isolation of Kashmir and the Muhammadan conquest of the regions to the south, regular intercourse and trade with the Hindu Kingdoms of *India* proper must have continued. We find the same conclusion indicated also by other incidental references made in the last two books of the same author i.e. *'Paintings and life Styles of Jammu Region'* and *History of the Brahmans'.*

While awaiting the castle called *Banasala* belonging to *Tikka's* son-in-law, *Bhagika,* a *Khasa*-lord. Thinking himself safe in that (castle), though it was of but little height, he made by means of messengers the whole host of *Damaras* rise in rebellion. The name *Banasala* is preserved undoubtedly in that of the modern *Banahal,* near *Ramban,* a village or town which has given its appellation to the *Banahal* pass. This pass being only 9200 feet above the sea, forms the lowest and easiest route across the eastern portion of the range to the South of Kashmir, and was thus particularly suitable for *Bhiksacara's* invasion planned in the winter. We have not been able to visit personally the valley lying on the South side of the *Banahal* pass, and can thus not speak with certainty as to the position of the castle in which *Bhiksacara* found his end. It appears to us, however, very probably that the castle was not far from the present village *Banahal*. The latter is not marked on the map, but lies a few hundred years to the north of adkut 75^0- 16' longitude and 33^0-27' latitude, at the foot of the pass, from which the whole of the valley to the South, and also the village *Banahal*, can be clearly seen. It follows that the castle of *Banasala* must have been visible from the top of the *Banahal* pass. *Abu-i-Fazl* (vol.II, P. 361) describes at *'Banihal'*, a temple dedicated to Durga, in which anguries are obtained in a curious fashion as to the strife, etc., Pt. Sahibram, who in his *Tirthas*, copies *Abu-i-Fazl's* notice, metamorphoses the Sanskrit name of the village into *'Bhanusala'*. It has already been indicated that *Visalata* must be identified with the valleys drained by the *Bichlari* river, a tributary of the Chenab. This hill district, situated immediately to the South of the *Divasar* and *Shahabad* Parganas, is now called generally *Banahal*, after the pass of that name *Banabhatta* to which it forms the approach in history as its objectivity. The name *Visalata* means hightest lord who lives in Heaven comes down during the encroachment of land illegally preserved by people in that of the river *Bichlari* as a pure water of the Father. Therefore, *Visalata* is mentioned as the route by which the pretender *Bhiksacara* intends to invade *Devasarasa*, i.e. *Devasar* by *Prthvihara*, flee to the South towards the mountains bordering Kashmir. The mention of the *Vitasta* as the end point of the pursuit seems, therefore, strange on the first look. We are inclined to believe that Kalhana wishes in reality to refer to the locality where the source of the *Vitasta* is traditionally placed. This is the *Naga* at *Vithuvutur*, the *Vitastatra* of the *Rajatarangini*, close to *Vernag* in the *Shahabad* Pargana.

Of the *stupas* and the great *Caitya* which *Asoka* is said to have erected here, we are unable to trace any remains above the ground. *Vithavutur*, though scarcely a site for a large town on account of the confined nature of the valley, must have always derived some importance from its position at the foot of the *Banahal* pass on the route to the eastern Panjab. *Vitastatrapura* is mentioned in the time of *Anantadeva*.. We read of some Kashmir nobles who, after being pursued to *Vitastatra* (below the *Banahal* pass), take refuge with the *Khasas* in *Visalata* after crossing the mountain range during the ancient time. An attempt to liberate *Bhiksacara* is referred to, which *Dengapala*, a *Khasa* chief, who resided on the bank of *Chandrabhaga*, is spoken of as threatening to advance againt *Kashmir* from *Visalata*. (R.T. vol.1 pp, 10, 318, vol.II, p. 131)

8. *Note. Harsa*' region is narrated in the *Rajatarangini* of Kalhana who was the son of *Harsa's* friend and wrote for personal knowledge. He has shared the fate of so many Indian authors of note whose memory lives solely in their works. There is no record to tell us of the life of the scholar-poet to whom we owe our knowledge of the history of old Kashmir. Nor do we even meet with the name of Kalhana except in the colophones of his work and in the introductory notice which his successor and continuator Jonaraja has prefixed to this Chronicle, three centuries later.It is from Kalhana's work alone that we can gather some facts regarding his origin and person. The colophons which are attached to the end of each Book of the Rajatarangini, ascribe its composition to *"Kalhana*, the son of the great Kasmirian ministers, the illustrious Lord *Canpaka."* There is no reason to doubt the authenticity of the information conveyed to us in these colophons. They are found already in the codex which is the archetype of our extant Manuscripts. In view of their form which gives honorific titles merely to the father of the author, these colophons may be assumed with great probability to go back toKalhana himself.

   Kalhana wrote the introduction of his Chronicle in the year 4224 of the Laukika era or A.D. 1148-49, and completed his work in the year following. Considering this date and the significance of the above titles, the identity of Kalhana's father with the CANPAKA who is repeatedly mentioned in the Chronicle as one of the chief officials of King Harsa (A.D. 1089-1101), becomes highly probable Collateral evidence supporting this opinion is supplied by the Chronicle itself. *Champa* is the modern hill-state of *Camba*, (Annami) which comprises the valley of all the sources of the Ravi and some adjoining valleys draining into the Chenab. (Cunningham, *Ancient Geography*; p. 141). King *Sala* has been rightly identified by Prof. Kielhorn with *Salavahana*, who is mentioned as King *Somavarmadeva's* predecessor in the *Camba* grant (published in *Ancient India;* XVII, p. 7). The latter was executed in the reign of *Asata*, whose name occurs below, as the ruler of *Campa* under *Kalasa* (1087 A.D.). Canningham has rightly pointed out that the references made by Kalhana about *Kalasa* of *Vallapura, Samgramapala* and *Utkarsa* (*Harsa's* brother) *Bappika, Harsa's* mother, was a princess of *Campa*. Regarding the relations between the royal houses of *Kashmir* and *Champa* are in agreement with traditional list of *Camba* Rajas as preserved in the family which still rules that hill-state. Regarding the eighteen divisions conventionally counted in an army, after *Candraraja*, who showed energy in his efforts, had collected forces, he proceeded to *Vijayaksetra*.

   Bilhana *Vikramankadevacharita*, XVIII, 38, speaks of King *Ananta's* supremacy being acknowledged in *Champa, Darvabhisara, Trigata* and *Bhartula*

(*Vartula* means *'war of the love'*).Cunningham places this invasion of *Campa* by *Ananta* means 'endless' i.e. *'Nam'* between (1028-1031 A.D); but does not give his authority for these dates (A.G; p. 141).

It deserves to be noted that our text, the *'History of Untouchables'* shows everywhere the spelling *campa,* whereas the name (in its alternative form) is written *Canpaka* in the grant above quoted meaning of the *'History of the Untouchables'*. The latter spelling with *n* is regularly adopted in all *Sarada* MSS for the name of the *Campaka* flower, also compares with the name of *Kalhana's* father, written as *Canpaka* throughout in A. Here A means *'God'* is *'One'*. Even the gods have no pity in *Trigarta* (Kangra), no moral in *Campa (Camba)*, no generosity in the *Madradesa,* is an old name of the central Panjab between Bias and the Jehlam (or Chenab) (A.G. p. 185). The verse probably reproduces a proverbial saying of Kalhana's time. *Rajapuri* is clearly included in the judgement passed on *Darvabhisara.* (R.T. vol.II, p. 120). There were the characteristic ascribed in brief to the inhabitants of *Campa* under the *Harsa* ruler of Kashmir.

Chmapa (Annami), a Hindu colony was founded as early as second century A.D. in a country to which it gave the name *Champa* which comprised a major part of the present province of *Annam,* except it three north districts. Its people included barbarians as well as more cultured class was called themselves. *Chams* after the name of *Champa* which used to deal with leather work called *'Chamar'*. Therefore history proves that the great Indian author known as *Kalhana* was a *'Chamar'* by caste. The greatest historians made by themselves like, *Satish Chandra, Irfan Habid, Sabyasachi Bhattacharya, Bipan Chandra, Shrimali, D.N Jha, etc.* were failed in their attempt to prove the identity of Kalhana and his family. Therefore, modern Historian Dr. Raj Kumar, rejects their approach toward history in real form and sense, because, they deal with *'Sexual History'*, but *'History'* is a pious subject .

In the several passage which mention Canpaka, we find the latter invariably spoken of with evident respect for his character and activity. We first meet him as lord of the Gate (*devdrapati*) or commandant of the frontier defences in the latter part of Harsa's reign. On the occasion of the king's expedition against the castle of *Dugdhaghata* on the Darad frontier, shortly before A.D. 1099, Canpaka's success in effecting the investment of that mountain stronghold notwithstanding the intrigues of official rivals is specially eulogized. When relating Harsa's desperate struggle for his crown and life Kalhana mentions Canpaka amongst the last few officials who loyally held out by the king's side. He is careful to explain Canpaka's absence at the final catastrophe by a detailed account of the special mission which the doomed king entrusted to him. The dialogue which Kalhana puts into the mouth of king and minister, bears every appearance of Historic Truth. Reference is made in it to a particular incident which, from the nature of the case, could not have well been remembered by any one except *Canpaka* himself. Its special record and that of the whole dialogue becomes intelligible in the light of the fact that Kalhana was the minister's son.

This connection, too, explains the exact and graphic account which Kalhana is able to give us of the flight of the unfortunate king from the capital and of his tragic death. The only companions of Harsa on his flight and during the few days of his hiding were his faithful chamberlain Prayaga, and *Mukta*, a menial servant of Canpaka's household. The former was killed fighting together with his Royal Master. *Mukta* alone escaped death under circumstances which Kalhana takes special care to explain and justify. It is evident that he had received his account of Harsa's last days from this sole surviving witness who belonged to his father's household.

Kalhana describes Canpaka as a fervent worshipper at the Trithas of *Nandiksetra* the present *Buthser*. This accounts for the intimate acquaintance he himself displays with that sacred site. As Canpaka's son he was likely to have accompanied his father on his regular annual visits to he *Tirthas*. From a refernce to the latter it appears that Canapaka was yet living about the year A.D. 1136.

Incidental notices of the *Rajatarangini* enable us to trace yet another close relative of Kalhana. The Chronicle relates among many extravagant acts of Harsa that the music-loving king presented one lakh of gold coins of *KANAKA*, a younger brother of Canpaka, who had gained his favour by taking lessons in singing from him. The same *Kanaka* is subsequently praised for having proved himself grateful to the memory of his royal patron. He retired after the latter's death, to Benares and ended there his days in pious resignation.

If this younger brother of Canpaka was in reality Kalhana's uncle, as there seems every reason to assume, we can account for Harsa's extravagant present by the family's high position. Kalhana also mentions as another meritorious act of *Kanaka* that by his timely intercession he saved the colossal Buddha image at Parihasapura, his birth place, from destruction by King Harsa. The saving of the only other Buddha statue, which escaped the king's clutches, is ascribed to the Buddhist Sramara Kusalasri. In view of this company it is difficult to avoid the conclusion that Kanaka, too, was personally connected in some way with Buddhist worship. We shall see below how well this conclusion agrees with certain observations regarding Kalhana's own attitude towards Buddhism.

From the mention of Parihasapura as Kanaka's birthplace, we may infer that this town was the original home of Kalhana's family. We owe probably to this circumstance the detailed references which Kalhana makes to the sacred buildings of *Parihasapura* and the close acquaintance he shows with the topography of that neighbourhood.

It can scarcely be doubled that Kalhana's family was Brahman by caste, Sanskrit learning of the type displayed in the *Rajatarangini* has, in Kasmir, as elsewhere in India, been always cultivated chiefly if not exclusively, by Pandits of Brahman descent. Kalhana betrays in more than one passage the conscious pride of 'the Gods on Earth' and his full sympathy with Brahminical self-assertion. We have besides the direct testimony of Jonaraja who refers to Kalhana with the epithet *dvija*.

The introductory verses prefixed to each Book of the Chronicle all contain prayers addressed to Siva in his form of *Ardhanarisvara,* representing the god in his union with Parvati already discussed in the '*History of the Chamar Dynasty*'. It is hence clear that Kalhana was attached to S'iva worship which, as far as we can go back, has always occupied the first place among the Hindu cults of the valley. This is full accord with what we know of his father Canapaka's pious visits and gifts to the Tirthas of *Nandiksetra*, all of which are sacred to S'iva. From the respectful way in which Kalhana refers to *Bhatta Kalata* one of the chief expositors of the Kasmirian *S'aivasastra*, it appears probable that the transcendental doctrines based on the S'iva creed, were not foreign to him. *Tantric* cult which in Kashmir is still closely connected with S'aiva worship, seems also to have been well known to Kalhana. Various ironical allusions, however, show that he entertained but scant regard for the individuals who posed as its privileged hierophants.

The above facts indicate a close attachment to Saivism on the part of both Kalhana and his father. It is curious to note side by side with it the manifestly friendly attitude which Kalhana displays towards Buddhism throughout the whole of his Chronicle. A long series of Kings, from Asoka down to his own time, receives his unstinted praise for the *Viharas* and *Stupas,* they founded for the benefit of the Buddhist creed. Similar foundations by private individuals are recorded with the same attention. Others, like *Meghavahana*, are praised for having in accordance with the 'Jina's teachings prohibited the slaughter of animals. Kalhana does not hesitate to refer repeatedly to the *Bodhisattvas* or to Buddha himself as the comforters of all beings, the embodiments of perfect chairty and nobility of feeling. They are to him beings of absolute goodness "who do not feel anger even against the sinner, but in patience render him kindness." It is impossible to read Kalhana's detailed account of the legend of the *Krtyasrama* Vihara (i. 131-147), with its plainly marked Buddhist tendency and phraseology, without realizing the author's sympathy with Buddhist traditions.

We note the same feeling in the numerous references which Kalhana makes to images of *Buddha* claiming special interest. When describing the sacrilegious confiscations of *Harsa*, he is as particular to name the Buddha-statues which were preserved, as the images of Hindu gods which shared that distinction. In addition, it deserves to be noted that Kalhana takes care to show us on more than one occasion his thorough familiarity with special points of Buddhist tradition and terminology.

The contrast which this partiality for Buddhist cult and traditions presents to the avowed S'aivism of Kalhana, is more apparent than real. For centuries before Kalhana's time Buddhism and the orthodox creeds had existed peacefully side by side in Kasmir. As far as the laity was concerned, they had to a great extent amalgamated. His own narrative from the point where it reaches historical ground, give ample proof of this. Of almost all royal and private individuals, who are credited with the foundation of Buddhist Stupas and Viharas, it is recorded that they, or at least members of their family, with equal zeal endowed also shrines of S'iva or Visnu. In Kalhana's own time we note that every contemporary royal personage or minister who is praied for his Buddhist endowments, showed the same pious liberality also in regard to Brahminical temples and establishments.

The condition of religious feeling indicated by these facts is amply illustrated by what we know of the position of heterdox creeds in other parts of India, both ancient or modern. Of early historical instances when they shared the royal patronage equally with Brahminical cults, it will suffice to cite the well-known example of King Harsavardhana of Kanauj. Hiuen Tsiang relates as an eye-witness how Buddhists and Jainas, as well as the Brahmans, received equal honours and support at his court. Exactly at the time of Kalhana Gujrat furnishers us with a striking illustration of the same fact. Professor Buhler in his admirable biography of *Hemacandra*, has fully proved that the Caulukya King *Kumarapala* whom the great Jaina doctor could claim as his most famous convert, never ceased to maintain his hereditary attachment to the cult of S'iva.

Yet undoubtedly the Jainism of the twelfth century in Gujrat was both in doctrine and practice far less accommodating to orthodox notions than the Kashmir Buddhism of the same period. From various indications it appears that hte condition of the latter must have closely approached the state of modern

Buddhism in Nepal. Kashmir had its married Bhiksus long before Kalhana's time. *Buddha* had centuries earlier been received into the orthodox pantheon as one of Visnu's Avataras, and Buddhist worhship had not failed to reap the practical benefits of such recognition. Hence we find that the *Nilamatapurana*, the canonical authority for Brahminical cult in Kasmir, directly prescribes the celebration of *Buddha's* birthday as a great festival. His statue is then to be worshipeed according to the rites of the *S'akyas* or Buddhist ascetics; the latter themselves are to be honoured with presents and the *Caityas* to be decorated.

The author of the Chronicle tells us nowhere of the education and early studies which had fitted him for his task. But the manner in which he has solved it and occasional indications may help us to trace the outlines of his life as a student.

"Worthy of praise is that power of true poets, whatever it may be, which surpasses even the stream of nectar, in as much as by it their own bodies of glory as well as those of others obtain immortality. Who else but poets *'Chamar'* able to bring forth lovely productions, can place the past times before the eyes of men!" These words with which Kalhana opens the introduction to his work, suffice to show us with qualification he considered the chief one for the task he had undertaken.

Even if Kalhana had been less outspoken on the point, no reader of the original work could doubt for a moment that its author looked upon himself mainly in the light of a *Kavi*. Sanskrit classical poetry of the Kavya type, such as Kalhana knew and cultivated, presupposes a thorough training in the science of Indian rhetoric, the *Alamkarasastra,* and an equal mastery of Sanskrit grammatical lore. Kalhana's composition proves amply that his studies in these departments of traditional learning had been both thorough and extensive.

The form and style which as we shall see Kalhana chose for his poem, do not allow of that lavish display of intricate rhetorical art which delights the heart of the Pandit. But the occasions are not unfrequent where the Chronicler has succumbed to the charm of that poetic 'amplification' which, as he tells us, he had purposed to avoid (i.6). The verses to which we are then treated, leave no doubt that their author had learned to apply with great skill and dexterity the more subtle arts of the *Alamkarasastra*.

The conventionally prevading so much of Kavya literature, and the substantive identity of the rhetorical precepts followed by its authors, make it difficult to ascertain the particular works which Kalhana knew and studied. His acquaintance with the older standard Kavyas, such as the *Raghuvamsa* and *Meghaduta,* may be assumed *a priori,* and is proved in fact by several evident reminiscences. A closer search in this direction than it was able to make, would probably show the same for a number of other texts of that description.

The Kalhana had carefully studied the *Vikramankadevacarita,* the historical poem of his fellow-countryman Bilhana, written about the eighth decade of the eleventh century, may be considered as certain. Kalhana shows himself thoroughly acquainted with the personal history of his fellw-poet, as detailed in the latter's work. He also refers in at least two passages to historical incidents which are mentioned by Bilhana. He does this in terms which clearly indicate an acquaintance with the older poem. In view of this evidence the strongly marked general resemblance in phraseology and style which can be traced between the two works, assumes full significance.

Another and earlier work which Kalhana appears to have closely studied, is Bana's *Harsacarita,* the well-known historical romance describing the exploits of King *Harsavardhana* of Kanauj and Thanesar. The numebr of rare words and phrases which this text and the *Rajatrangini* have in common, and which otherwise cannot be traced, makes the above conclusion practically certain. In style and composition the difference between Bana's work, with its highly poetical but equally florid prose, and the Chronicle of Kalhana is so great that no slavish imitation could be imputed to the latter. On the other hand, we can easily understand why the Kashmirian author should have devoted close attention to the novel of Harsavardhana's court poet. It was one of the few oler Sanskrit compositions dealing with historical events which are likely to have enjoyed popularity in his own time.

Leaving the field of Kavya literature we must ascribes to Kalhana a very intimate knowledge of the *Mahabharata.* Whenver he desires to illustrate his narrative by a reference to similar events or to emphasize a point of moral judgement, he turns to this vast store-house of traditiona lore. His allusions are often made to little-known episodes and obscure incidents. The trouble which their identification has frequently cost, enables us to judge of the labours Kalhana must have devoted to the thorough mastery of the gigantic Epic. He seems to have been equally well acquainted with the *Ramayana* through his quotations from it are less numerous.

We can easily trace the connection between this close study of Sanskrit epic literature and Kalhana's work as a Chronicler. To Kalhana as to the Pandit of the present day, the legends clustering round the war of the *Kurus* and *Pandavas* and the life of Rama, with the mythology attaching to them, all appeared in the light of real history. What distinguishes these epic stories to the Indian mind from events of historical times, is only their superior interest due to the glamour of a heroic age, and their record by sacred authority. We may safely surmise that the study of the sacred epics had directly influenced Kalhana in the choice of his task.

We have probably indications of Kalhana's literary training also in the frequent incidental references which he makes to particular poets and scholars in the reigns of various kings. These notices are of considerable interest for the history of Sanskrit literature. It is not easy to say which of these literary data were derived from Kalhana's own reading, and which simply reproduced from the earlier sources to be noticed thereafter.Some, like the mention of the poets who flourished at Yasovarman's court, are more likely to have been supplied by current literary tradition than by older Kashmirian Chronicles. To the former we may attribute also Kalahan's acquaintance with several poetical dicta, chiefly satirical, which he quotes on occasion. In addition it may be noted that he had evidently also devoted some attention to the *Jyotihsastra*, as shown by the references made to passages of *Varahamihira's Brhatsamhita*.

The literary affinities of Kalhana which we have just noticed, enable us to trace also a curious contemporary reference to our author which has hitherto escaped attention. It is contained in a passage of the *S'rikanthacarita,* a Kavya composed by the poet MANKHA, a fellow-countryman and contemporary of Kalhana. This work, first brought to light by Professor Buhler, possesses interest for us chiefly on account of its xxv. Canto which has rightly been called altogether unique in Sanskrit literature. *Mankha* gives us there a detailed description of the Sabha or literary assembly held at the house of his brother, the minister *Alamkara* at which he submitted his poem to a gathering of *Kashmirian* scholars and officials. He introduces to us the guests present at the occasion by their names, in each case adding some appropriate details as to their respective *S'astras* and personal attainments.

Professor Buhler has already shown that *Mankha* wrote his poem only a few years before the composition of Kalhana's Chronicle. Its date must fall between the years A.D. 1128 and 1144. Considering this close approach in time, we might reasonably expect to meet also with Kalhana in Alamkara's Sabha, the representative character of which is proved by the mention of no less than thirty individual scholars. Yet at first we look in vain for Kalhana's name in this long list. Its absence seemed all the more curious in view of the fact that Kalhana himself mentions both *Mankha* and *Alamkara* among his contemporaries and in a manner implying some acquantance with the family. In reality, however, Mankha on his own part has not failed to mention his distinguished fellow-poet, the author of our Chronicle. But the name by which he refers to him, is, on the first look, so different from our familiar "Kalhana", that we can scarcely feel surprised at the Chronicler having so far not been recognised in this incognito.

Mankha in his account of the 'Sabha', devotes three verses to a complimentary notice of the Kavi *Kalyana*. He describes him as holding a distinguished position among the expert masters of the Kavya, as a person whom "the illustrious *Alakadatta* thought capable of accomplishing fully his chosen task (as a composer of poetry)." Of Kalyana's poetic skill he says that it had become so polished as to be capable of reflecting like a mirror the whole perfection of *Bilhana's* muse.

Finally it is noted of him that he knew no limit in his enthusiastic devotion to the study of stories and legends of many kinds.

From Jonaraja, the commentator of the *S'rikanthacarita*, we learn that the otherwise unknown *Alakadatta* whom *Mankha* evidently wishes to mention as Kalyana's patron, held the position of *Samdhivigrahaka* or minister of foreign affairs. He further correctly indicates that by the *Kathas,* in the study of which *Kalyana* is said to have been so deeply interested, the stories of the *Mahabharata* and other epic texts are meant. But of Kalyana's person himself the learned commentator has nothing to tell us.

We can safely and conclusively show that this poet *Kalyana*, Mankha's distinguished contemporary, who emulated *Bilhana* and who was deeply read in epic lore, is no one else but our Kalhana. The name *Kalhana* is undoubtedly an *Apabhramsa* form derived through Prakrit *Kallana* from Sanskrit *Kalyana*, which being a word of auspicious meaning ('happy', 'blessed'), is often found as a proper name. The consonantal group ly becomes by a regular phonetic law ll in Prakrit, and this again is liable to appear as Ih in *Apabhramsa* and the modern Indo-Aryan Vernaculars. Thus Sanskrit *Kalyam,* 'to-morrow,' which is found as *Kallu* in Prakrit, reappears in forms like *kalh, kalh, kalha, kalha* in the several moern Vernaculars. The shortening of *a* into *a* in the second syllable is similarly accounted for by well-known facts of phonetic conversion.

In proof of this derivation of *Kalhana< Kalyana* we may point to the intermediary Prakrit form *Kallana* which actually occurs as the name of a person in the *Rajatarangini.* By its side we meet in the Chronicle once with the name in its *Apabhramsa* from *Kalhana,* and more frequently with the Sanskrit form of the name, *Kalyana.* We can trace the same name as a feminine appellation in any exactly corresponding triplet of forms. To the Sanskrit *Kalyanadevi,* 'Queen Kalyana,' the name borne by one of Jayapida's queens, correspond the names

Kallana and *Kalhanika* (from Sanskrit Kalyanika), borne by royal ladies at the court of *Kalasa* and *Jayasimha,* respectively.

We shall have occasion to note below how often Kalhana himself in his Chronicle introduces tous the identical persons under names which show similar phonetic modifications. We can hence feel in no way surprised on observing that *Mankha* has recorded his fellow-poet's name in its correct Sanskrit form while the colophons of Kalhana's own work present it in the corresponding Apabhramsa form. It is likely that the latter was the one used ordinarily by the Chronicler himself. He at least shows on objection to the use of Apabhramsa names when speaking of his contemporaries, while *Mankha,* on the other hand, seems anxious to preserve a quasi-classical colouring and hence employs almost exclusively Sanskrit names for the persons figuring in his xxv. Canto.

The substantial identity of the names as here demonstrated, and the coincidence in date would alone, we believe, be sufficient to make it highly probable that the Kavi *Kalyana* of the *S'rikanthacarita* is the same person as Kalhana, the author of our Chronicle. Any possible doubt on the point must, however, give away before the evidence which is afforded by the close agreement we note between Mankha's words regarding *Kalyana* and our previous observations regarding Kalhana's literary learnings. A careful perusal of the *Rajatarangini* fully illustrates both the influence of Bilhana's poetry on Kalhana and the latter's exhaustive study of epic literature.

It is certainly curious that Jonaraja had evidently not realized the identity of Kalyana with the author whose Chronicle he himself continued. In explanation it is enough to point out that Jonaraja wrote fully three hundred years after the date of Kalhana, and that his comments on the *S'rikanthacarita* in more than one instance betray a deficient knowledge of the *realia* of that earlier period.

It would be more difficult at present to give an explanation for Kalhana's complete silence as regards *Alakadatta* whom Mankha's words seem to indicate as his patron. Various reasons might be thought of but for none can we find at present any evidence. It has, however, to be kept in view that years had passed between the time when Mankha's poem was composed and the date of Kalhana's Chronicle. Such as interval might well have brought about a change in the personal relations of the Chronicler and his former patron.

If Kalhana had, like the vast majority of his fellow Kavis, chosen a legendary tale or a romance from the land of fancy as the subject matter of his poem, we should have to rest content regarding his personality with the meagre details just discussed. Kalhana's work, however, deals with the history of his own country, and a very large portion of it is devoted to an account of events which Kashmir had witnessed within his own lifetime or at least within living memory.

These facts place us in a far more advantageous position. We are able to realize the political and social conditions in which Kalhana lived, with a degree of accuracy rarely attainable in the case of any old Indian author. His work gives us a detailed knowledge of the old topography of Kashmir. This again, combined with the narrow limits and distinct geographical character of the country, enables us to restore with precision the local *milieu* in which Kalhana moved. Finally, it must be remembered that Kalhana's narrative, particularly where it deals with contemporary events, freely acquaints us with the author's opinions on many points relating to his country and its representative men and classes. We shall see that it is possible to draw from such statements some safe conclusions regarding Kalhana's character and personal relations.

The local surroundings in which Kalhana's life was passed, and the historical development which accounts for the political conditions of his own time, will have to be considered elsewhere. Here we may confine ourselves to a brief sketch of the main events of Kashmir history which fell within Kalhana's lifetime, and their influence on contemporary society.

We have already seen that Kalhana, according to his own statement, wrote his work during the years 1148-49. Various indications in the style and spirit of the Chronicle suggest that its author was then no longer a young man. Fortunately, however, we have more distinct evidence on this point in Kalhana's own words. When describing the events which occured in *S'rinagar* in the spring of A.D. 1121 immediately before King Sussala's restoration, he speaks as an eye-witness of the treacherous conduct of the troops of the usurper *Bhiksacara*.

There is much in Kalhana's account of this troubled time and of the first period of Sussala's reign (A.D. 1112-20) that implies personal observation made with a mature mind. It is hence not likely that Kalhana should have been a mere boy at the time. In view of these considerations, we can scarcely go far wrong if we place Kalhana's date of birth about the beginning of the century. This approximate date agrees fully with what we know of Kalhana's father Canapaka whom we find as an energetic officer holding a high military post about A.D 1098.

The commencement of the twelfth century is marked in the history of Kashmir by an important dynastic revolution which brought about material changes in the political state of the country. King Harsa whose rule (A.D. 1089-1101) seems at first to have secured to Kashmir a period of consolidation and of prosperous peace, had subsequently fallen a victim to his own Nero-like propensities. Heavy fiscal exactions necessiated by a luxurious court, and a cruel persecution of the *Damaras* who formed the landed aristocracy, had led to a rebellion under the leadership of the brothers Uchchala and *Susscla*, two relatives of Harsa from a side branch of the Lohara dynasty. Harsa had succumbed in the struggle and had found a tragic death by murder.

The rebel princes who in their success had threatened to become rivals, avoided a conflict for the crown by a partition of Harsa's territories. Kashmir was to be ruled by UCHCHALA, the elder brother, while the adjoining hill-state of Lohara, the original home of the family, fell to Sussasla. The downfall of Harsa had been due solely to the rising of the powerful Damaras of Kasmir, and consequently the latter retained a predominance dangerous alike for the King and the peace of the country. Uchchala seems to have held his throne merely by the unscrupulous diplomacy with which he played off one great feudal landholder against the other, and his alliance with the strongest of them, *Gargacandra,* the lord of L.hara. His reign (A.D. 1101-11) was threatened frequently by the rise of pretenders, and invasions on the part of his own brother Sussala. Ultimately he was murdered by a conspiracy among his trusted officials.

RADDA, one of their number, when they proclaimed king, occupied the throne only for one brief day, December 8th-9th, A.D. 1111. *Gargacandra* defeated the conspirators after a short but bloody struggle and thereupon became the true king maker. He first put up SALHANA a half-brother of the murdered Uchchala, who being a mere puppet in the hands of the powerful Damara allowed the kingdom to become the scene of violent disorders. Internecine struggles of rival Damaras and an irruption of Sussala followed by bloody persecutions rendered Salhana's reign of four months like "a long evil dream."

Ultimately, SUSSALA allied himself with *Gargacandra* and secured through his help the long-coveted throne. In contrast to his elder brother he seems to have been personally brave, but rash, cruel, and inconsiderate. His rule, A.D. 1112-28, was practically one long and disastrous struggle with the irrepressible Damaras and with dangerous pretenders. When *Sussala* after such fighting and treachery and at last succeeded in destroying *Gargacandra*, the discontent of the Damaras broke out in a great general rebellion. In BHIKSACARA, a grandson of Harsa, who had been brought up abroad, they found the desired pretender. Sussala's oppression and senseless cruelties increased their ranks; until they were strong enough to besiege the king in his capital. After a protracted defence during which the capital suffered severly, Sussala was obliged to flee to Lohara.

Bhiksacara was crowned in the capital and held nominal rule over Kashmir for a little over six months (A.D. 1120-21). He was a mere tool in the hands of rival Damara factions, and the royal authority was so much reduced that *Bhiksacara* was at last in difficulty even about procuring food. Solemn fasts (*prayopavesa*) held by the Brahmans in the capital and elsewhere showed the extremily to which the people were driven by the rapacity and violence of the Damaras and their allies in the official classes. The eyes of the populace turned once more towards Sussala. After successfully repulsing at Kashmirian force which had been sent against Lohara, Sussala came back to Kashmir, and owing to the Damara's disunion, recovered the throne (A.D. 1121).

During the following seven years civil war continued almost without interruption. The king was unable to cope with the powerful supporters of his rival and various disasters which befell his troops, reduced him again and again to great straits. Three times *S'rinagar* went through severe sieges, and famine and fire added their horrors to the sufferings of the capital. During these struggles Sussala maintained himself only owing to the valour of his condottieri from the lower hills and the Panjab, who served him faithfully in the midst of so much treachery. The contest was also prolonged by the Damaras finding their interests directly served by the disturbed state of the country and showing no desire to end it by a decisive victory of Bhiksacara.

Finally, in 1128, *Sussala* fell a victim to a murderous plot which he had himself started for the destruction of his rival. His son JAYASIMHA who succeeded him, fund the Damaras as strong as ever and Bhiksacara ready to march into S'rinagar. The means by which he gradually secured a footing and restored at least a semblance of royal authority, were not the reckless valour of his father, but compromise with the feudal grandees and *Macchiavellian* cunning. For two years after his accession the danger from *Bhiksacara* continued until the brave pretender was treacherously entrapped and killed in a frontier castle. Scarcely had this enemy been put out of the way, when a successful conspiracy placed the ancestral castle and territory of Lohara in the hands of a new pretender, LOTHANA, a brother of *Salhana*. *Jayasimha's* attempt to recover this serious loss ended in ignominious disaster. Though Lohara was ultimately retaken through treachery, *Lothana* and *Mallarjuna*, another pretender, continued to harass Kasmir for years. They found ever ready support among the great *Damaras* whose power had remained uncurbed.

When at last Malarjuna had been captured (A.D. 1135), the exhausted country seems to have obtained a respite from its troubles and sufferings. This was not to last long. In the year 1143 we find Jayasimha confronted again by dangerous rivals. BHOJA, the new pretender, a son of Salhana, obtained powerful allies in the Darads, the northern neighbours of Kashmir, while all through the land the great Damara houses were rising in arms. Dissensions among Bhoja's supporters saved the kings from a disaster, but the struggle with the feudal landholders was severe and indecisive. Ultimately *Jayasimha's* diplomacy scored a success by a peaceful pact with Bhoja (A.D. 1145). But Kalhana's narrative shows plainly that the forces of internal strife and disruption which had crippled the unfortunate country ever since the time of Harsa, were by no means spent when he wrote his Chronicle.

From the brief summary of events we have given here, it will be seen that the greatest portion of Kalhana's life passed in what was for Kashmir one long period of civil war and political dissolution. The influence of this fact on the plan and spirit of his work will be examined below. At present we shall only endeavour to trace the influence which the political condition of his country is likely to have exercised on Kalhana's life and his personal relations with his contemporaries.

We may consider it, as certain that the dynastic revolution which had cost King Harsa his throne and life, had a lasting effect on the fortunes of Kalhana's family. However detailed the accounts are which we receive in Book viii. of the officials great and small, who served the succeeding rulers, *Canpaka's* name is never found among them. Yet a reference made to him in connecting with the *Bhutesvara* Tirtha makes it highly probale that he was still living after the year 1135. It is hence evident that Kalhana's father, who in Harsa's reign had occupied one of the highest posts of old Kashmir administration, played no longer any part in public life after that monrach's death. Whether this retirement was entirely voluntary or oterwise, we can no longer ascertain. That it was, however, connected in some way with the loyal attachment which *Canpaka,* according to the Chronicle, had proved to the last for the ill-fated king, seems likely enough.

Kalhana's work makes it quite clear that he himself had never held office under any of the rulers of the new dynasty or otherwise enjoyed their special favour. Cosidering the very redundant praise and flattery which by custom and literary tradition Indian authors feel obliged to bestow on their patrons, the negative evidence of the Chronicle may be considered decisive on this point. There is nothing whatever to show that Kalhana wrote his poem by order of *Jayasimha*. The outspoken manner in which he judges of the king's character, and the undisguised allusions to the reprehensible nature of many of his actions make it very improbable that he ever expected royal recognition.

To those who are acquainted with the style of fulsome flattery which Indian usage demands in the relations of a Kavi towards his patron, the comparatively few passages in which Kalhana praises *Jayasimha* or acknowledges his achievements, must appear very tame and guarded. They seem to have been inserted merely on the ground of the conventional respect due to the actual ruler and possibly with a view to avoiding denunciation and its probable consequences.

The same conclusion is indicated by the Harsh if just remarks which Kalhana makes regarding the reign of *Sussala, Jayasimha's* father. He openly denounces the grave defects of his character, his wanton cruelties, avarice, etc; he does not even hesitate to record the popular opinion that he was possesses by a demon. On the other hand, it is significant that Kalhana freely bestows the highest praise on the valour and heroism of the pretender Bhiksacara from whom Sussal and his son had suffered to much injury. Yet from the manner in which Bhiksacara's reign is described, it is clearly seen that this is short-lived restoration of Harsa's dynasty had brought no benefit to *Canapaka* or his family.

Among the other pretenders who rose during *Jayasimha's* rule, only the brave and considerable *Bhoja* seems to have attached Kalhana's sympathy. It seems that the latter appears to have drawn much of his information concerning recent events directly or indirectly from the prince himself. For *Lothana*, the old pretender, and Mallarjuna, his worthless nephew, the Chronicler has nothing but bitter satire and undisguised contempt, though they, too, like Bhoja were living at the time at *Jayasimha's* court.

The eventful period into which Kalhana's life was cast, with its rapid changes of royal and private fortune, had given him ample opportunities to study the character of his countrymen. We cannot feel surprised, therefore, at the truthfulness with which certain of its features, and by no means the most pleasing, are portrayed in his narrative.

Kalhana had evidently not failed to realise that conspicuous want of physical and moral courage which is so characteristic of the great mass of the Kashmirian population, and in particualr of the lower classes of Sudhra family. He avails himself often of the opportunity furnished by historical incidents to expose with humorous sareasm the investerate cowardice and empty bragging of the Kashmirian soldiery. We read of Kashmir armies which disperse at the sight or even the rumour of a resolute foe, of rival forces which both tremble in fear of each other, etc. Murder by a few resolute ruffians in the royal palace is usually followed by a general stampede of guards, courtiers, ministers, and troops. The uncompromising realism with which Kalhana paints such scenes leaves no doubt as to the estimate which experience had led him to form of his countrymen's military valour.

To emphasize his opinion still further Kalhana more than once shows us in contrast the bravery of the *Rajaputras* and other mercenaries from abroad who in his own time were evidently the mainstay of Kashmirian rulers. But we can see from some sarcastic allusions that the air of superiority naturally assumed by these foreign adventures was not to the liking of the Chronicler. The events of Kalhana's lifetime had shown him much treachery in every form among his countrymen. We can well appreciate the bitterness with which he refers to those in positions of influence and trust who were always ready to desert or sell their master. The rare examples of faithfulness on the other hand find in him a war eulogist even when it was displayed for his country's or king's enemies.

By the side of the treason ever rife in the royal court and camp Kalhana does not fail to notice the callous indifference with which the Kashmirian populace was prepared to welcome any change. His graphic descriptions of the idle and disaffected city crowds and the feelings that swayed them, show how thoroughly he understood the nature of his compatriots. In these and many other passages of the Chronicle a certain aristocratic hauteur of the author seems to display itself. Other weaknesses of Kashmirian character are recognised by him with equal frankness.

Looking at Kalhana's attitude towards the various classes of contemporary society, we note in the first place the open aversion and contempt he shows for the Damaras. The overweening power and turbulence of these feudal landholders had been the direct cause of King Harsa's fall and all the troubles which prayed upon the country during Kalhana's lifetime. The term *dasyu*, 'robber', which he regularly uses for their designation, is characteristic enough. Having risen from the agriculturist population of the Valley, the Damaras even in powerful families seem to have retained much coarseness and boorishness in their ways and habits. Kalhana loses no opportunity to expose these defects. The bitterness with which he speaks of the Damaras' cruelty and wantonnes, suggests that he or his family had personal reason to regret their predominance. The presence in the land of so many petty tyrants must have weighed heavily indeed not only on the cultivators but also on the official class and Brahman population of the capital. The lands from which the latter drew their maintenance were in times of internal trouble ever at the mercy of the Damaras.

That Kalhana though probably drawn by descent and position towards the official class was by no means partial to the latter, is shown by many a hard hit he makes at the vices of the *'Kayasthas'*. The great mass of them was undoubtedly Brahman by caste, corresponding to the present Karkun of Kashmir. The numerous satirical allusions to the petty officials oppression and greed and the evident relish with which Kalhana details their discomfiture by more energetic rulers, suggest that he had ample occasion to study their character by personal experience.

The narrative of the Chronicle allows us also to judge of Kalhana's views regarding another influential class of old Kashmir, the Brahman priests or *Purohitas*. Organized into corporations (*parsad*) at all the more important shrines and pilgrimage places and often possessed of great endowments, they played more than once an important part in the internal politics of the country. The solemn fasts or *Praypavesas* to which they were apt to resort in critical circumstances, were evidently powerful means of corecion which weak rulers had reason to dread.

Kalhana does not hide his contempt for this priestly class whose ignorance was equal to its arrogance, and bitterly condemns their baneful interference in affairs of State. In the humorous descriptions he gives of several great *Purohita* assemblies he freely ridicules their combined self-assertion and cowardice and shows scant respect for their sacred character. To those who know the modern *Pujari* of Indian Tirthas and the low estimation in which he as well as the ordinary Purohita is deservedly held by Brahmans of position and learning, Kalhana's feelings will be easily intelligible. Various references show that whatever respect traditional notions demanded for the 'gods of the earth' *in abstracto*, Kalhana was not prepared to extend it to their claims as a political factor called leader not Saint like Dr. B.R Ambedkar.

It may be mentioned in conclusion that the humorous and detailed picture which Kalhana draws of the cheating merchant and his ways in the anecdote related of Uchchala, bears also a distinct personal tinge. It is evidently taken from life and suggests unpleasant experiences.

There is much in Kalhana's detailed account of contemporary Kashmir history that makes it probable tha the was personally acquained with various of its most prominent actors. The high position of the family to which he belonged would fully explain this. But in view of the impartiality with which Kalhana metes out both blame and praise to contemporary personages, it is not easy to ascertain those with whom he was specially connected.

Friendly relations seem most probable in the case of the minister *RILHANA*, who was one of Sussala's faithful companions in arms and employed in an infuential position through the whole reign of

Jayasimha. He is the only one among the high officials of the latter whom Kalhana lauds for patronge of learning. The Chronicler gives an exceptionally detailed record of Rilhana's, his wife's and brother's pious foundations, and misses no opportunity to extol the bravery and military skill of the former. Most characteristic, however, is the panegyrical passage which Kalhana devotees to the description of some costly adorments given by Rilhana to a temple at *Suresvari*. These verses differ markedly in style from Kalhana's usual reference to such subjects. They look very much like a small *Prasasti* or laudatory poem composed specially by the *Kavi* in honour of the newly consecrated gift of his friend or patron. Only a personal connection of this kind could justify and explain the digression.

ALAMKARA, too, who held high posts in the later reign of *Jayasimha*, is mentioned with distinction. We know from the *Kavya* of his brother *Mankha* that *Alamkara* was himself a man of learning and a patron of scholars. MANKHA himself is only once named by Kalhana as minister of foreign affairs, while no reference is made to his capacity as a fellow-poet. Also for *Udaya*, lord of the 'Gate', Kalhana seems to have cherished feelings of special regard.

It is of interest to note the evident respect with which Kalhana speaks throughout of RAJAVADANA, who had only a few years before headed a dangerous rebellion against RAJAVADANA, who had only a few years before headed a dangerous rebellion against *Jayasimha*. As the narrative itself does not show special reason for this exception treatment, personal relations with the Chronicler naturally suggest themselves. In 1123A.D. *Sussala* whimsically abdicated in favour of his son *Jayasimha* while retaining all powes in his hands till he was treacherously all powers in 1128 AD.. *Jayasimha* by his diplomacy made himself popular and reigned for about 30 years but his military weakness made him lose the ancestral kingdom of *Lohara* to a rebel named *Lothana, Sussala's* brother. *Jayasimha*, however, recovered *Lohara* later when the rebel was ousted by his nephew.

Scanty indeed are the data which we have gleaned from the Chronicle regarding its author's personality. They cannot compensate for the loss which his reticnce regarding himself has caused us. Yet there is one important point concerning Kalhana, on which full light is thrown by the work itself. It is impossible to persue the Chronicle, and in particular its later portions, without realizing that the poet who wrote it, had an observant eye and an open mind for the affairs of the world around him. He displays no little knowledge of human nature, intimate acquaintance with his country's material conditions, interest in antiquarian details even of the humblest kind, and in the facts of every-day life. All these are features which show us Kalhana in a light different from that of the ordianry Indian *Kavi*.

His literary training, indeed, had been of the strictly traditional type, and the manner in which he employed it shows no conscious departure from the conventional norm. Yet it is clear that Kalhana was not a man of the schools, absorbed in his S'astras and content to make his living by them.

There is another interesting observation to be gathered from the Chronicle. We know that also in ancient India, as elsewhere, the question of demand and supply has exercised its potent influence on literary production. But it would be difficult to account from this point of view for the composition of the *Rajatarangini*. The Kashmir court of Kalhana's time was not the place where scholarly or poetic merit *'Chamar'* so closely connected in the Indian mind (*Jat*) could lead to honours and preferment. We may take it for certain that hte Chronicle was not written under the patronage of the ruling prince nor with a special view to securing his favour.

Considering these facts and those features in the Chronicle which are characteristic for the author's personality, we finally may perhaps hazard an opinion regarding the motives which had induced Kalhana to undertake this task. Born from a family of rank and note he could have expected to take an active share in the affairs of his country like his father had before him. Adverse political circumstances, however, and perhaps family policy, had closed to him the career of a soldier or administrator. What use more congenial to his hereditary tastes could he then make of his literary training than by recording the traditions regarding the history of his country and his views on the times he had lived through the theory of *'Nam'* and *'Karma'*.

Seen in this light, much of what strikes us as individual and peculiar in Kalhana's narrative assumes its proper and significant aspect. We can thus understand his stronlgy marked political opinions and his thorough grasp of the internal history of contemporary events. The notable accuracy and interest with which the details of military operations are often set forth, and which seem to be token at least a theoretical acquaintance with the art of war, become intelligible. The extensive knowledge of the topography of Kashmir which we must ascribe to the author of the Chronicle, finds its explanation in the opportunities which his means and position afforded for travel. Finally we can thus account for that independence of judgement which Kalhana displays throughout in regard to contemporary events and persons.

But these and other important facts touching upon Kalhana's character as a historian will become clearer when we have made ourselves acquainted with the scope and nature of his Chronicle make the history a progressive one at every stage of life.

Keeping in view, *Jayasimha* then had to meet a larger rebellion of his own feudatories as did by the modern historian of the time mention above, and assisted by the modern thought of the *'Islam'* at that time by *Moslems* and was able to crush it by diplomacy of the *'Nam' or 'Kalma'* and a military skill was used by the Lord. His later years were passed in peace and progress in the history of man having a powerful tool of the *'Nam'*. He died in 1155 A.D.

He was succeeded by his son, *Paramanuka,* who reigned for 10 years. He was succeeded by his son *Vantideva* with death in 1172 A.D. The *Lohara* dynasty ended. Then followed a succession of unworthy rulers only one of whom *Jayaddeva* (1198-1213 A.D.) is respected in history as a pious subject in scientific growth one after the another generation of the human being as a natural being in the process of life as a *'Lord'* or *'God'* by natural birth on his deed and action of life which the big modern historians of self-style have produced their work for their own benefit not for the others. But this project serves the whole community of the world as a family in rightous way. The next century will saw more civil war for the establishment of their own kingdoms as a powerful man in history and anarchy will be there. As country feel a prey of Moslem invasion under *Dulucha* during the reign of *Suhadeva* (1301-1320 A.D). The havoc of Moslem invasion was added by a *Tibetan* invasion in the North. The Tibetan Chief *Rinchana* became King of Kashmir after *Suhadeva* whose daughter *Kotadevi* he married. The foreigner ruled well but was murdered in 1323 A.D. Hindu rule now practically ended and was replaced by Moslem rule till the kingdom was finally annexed by Akbar in (1586 A.D.). As a miracle is said to have occurred at Kabir's naming ceremony. A Muslim periest was invited to name the child. He opened the *Quran* to find a name and found four names: *Kabir, Akbar, Kubra* and *Kibriya,* all meaning 'great' and all used to described the greatness of God (*K.G. M. P. 10*).

Sindh was ruled by the *Rai* kings for about 137 years. The last of them was *Rai Sahasi* on whose death his Brahmin Minister named *Chach* married his widowed queen and usurped his throne founding a new dynasty as stated in the *Chach-nama.* He ruled over a large kingdom extending upto the borders of Kashmir like *Durlabhavardhana* and defeated a king as *Jaipur* named *Mahrat* by the *Arabs.* After a long reign he was succeeded by his brother *Chandra* and then, by his son *Dahir* was killed in a battle with Kasim of the same family in 714 A.D. Yuan Chwang visited Sindh in the time of *Rai Sahasi* whom he described as a *Sudra* and Buddhist. Sindh was finally conquered by the Moslems with the help of *'Kalma'* of *'Nam',* after a struggle of 70 years. It was then split up into a number of local chiefships. *Sindh* served as the base of Muslim operations in India. The last Hindu resistance was made by Dahir's son, *Jayasimha.*

Politically *Nepal* in oldent times was more connected with China and Tibet than with the India. It was Asoka who first established the contact between India and Nepal where he built towns and *Stupas,* as already narrated. In later times, *Samudra Gupta,* a *Sudra* ruler counted Nepal as a frontier state (*Pratyanta*) acknowledged his suzerainty. The imperial Gupta *-Lichchhavi* matrimonial alliance points out to intimate connexions between India and Nepal. Nepal was under the rule of several dynasties, *Kirata, Somavasmi and Suryavamsi (Lichchchhavis)* whose rule is recovered in inscriptions from about 110 A.D. The last Lichchhavi prince of the 7th century A.D. was *Sivadeva* who was ousted by his Minister *Amsuvarman* who also married his daughter and seems to have founded anera of his own. He acknowledged the suzerainty of Tibet. He was succeeded by *Jishnugupta* (645 A.D.). His successors called themselves *Lichchhavis*. Not much is known about Nepal's history during the next three centuries. Its rulers continued under Tibetan overlandship i.e. *Rinchanashah.* This foreign domination was ended in 879 A.D. from which begins the new Nepal era. The royal genealogical lists are available from the 11th century A.D. without much history. Nepal became prosperious by trade with countries like India, Tibet and China. A famous king of the ninth century A.D. was *Guna Kamadeva* who reigned for 60 years, and was very rich. Later, in the middle of the eleventh century there was a Chalukya invasion of Nepal under *Somaesvara II* who counted it as a part of his empire. After him ame *Nanyadeva* who from his principality in *Tirhut* extended his sway over not in Nepal and other parts of India. Other inscriptions show the Deccan domination of Nepal and his victories over *Gurjara, Gauda,* Kerala (probably under Rajendra I 'Chola').Deccan (probably under *Vikramaditya* VI Chalukya) *Vahika* and *Tajika* (probably Muslim). He was succeeded by *Indrapala* at the time of the Moslem invasions, and prompted by a coin witht he Nagari legend *'Sri Ja(ya) simha (sya)'.* This coin is a broken piece. It is silver and has identical *Nagari* legend on the obverse and the reverse. The diameter of the coin is 16mm. It is understood to have been recovered from a river bed near *Pandalam-Punalur* area in erstwhile Central Travancore/*Venad.*

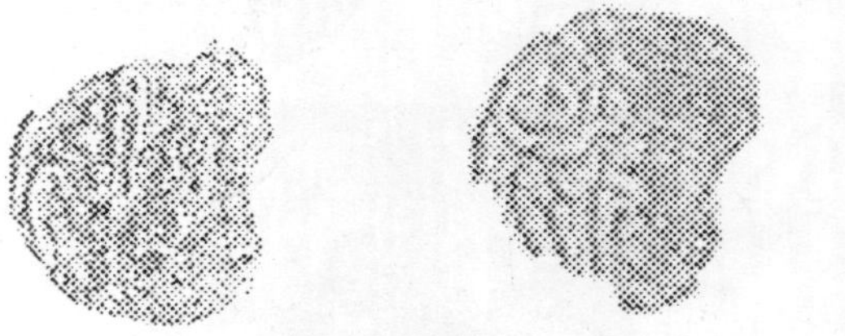

Coin No. 1

The entire script is not discernable since the coin is damaged. However, the two line Nagari legend on both sides reads:

Sri Ja (Nam)
Sim ha (High limit)

The missing alphabet in the first line can only be 'ya' and the legend can be reconstructed as *Sri Ja (ya) simha (sya).*

Who could this *Jayasimha* be? *Jayasimha* is a name that is often met with among the rulers of the Chalukya dynasty. But the find spot of this coin and the fact that this is not typical of the known Chalukya coins, would indicate that this is not a coin of the direct line of the Chalukya rulers. On the other hand, since the find spot is in *Venad* and considering that similar silver coins with two line *Nagari* legends *Sri Virakeralasya and Sri Udayamarthandasya,* were current in Venad in the 12th century A.D., this coin with legend *Sri Jayasimhasya,* leads one to the rulers in that region of Venad which came to be known as *Jayasimhanad* in the medieval period.

In the light of the present reading *'Srijayasimhasya'* on coin no.1, it is now found that the two line Nagari legend on the silver coin no. 2 below, can be read as *Swa Sti Sri Ja/Ja Sim ha ya. (Mangalam* to Jayasimha). A spider is depicted on the obverse of this coin in between the legend. It is also relevant that a spider is found on the coins of *Vira Kerala* (1125-55 A.D.) and his brother *Udayamarthanda* (1175-1195 AD.) of *Venad.* Since a spider is found depicted on the coins of Vira Kerala and his brother Udaya *Marthanda,* who we know from *Syananadurapurana samuchayam,* to belong to *vatasseri illam*, it is inferred that the *Vatasseri illam* of the *Pazhuvataraya* branch of *Cheras,* who were connected to the Cholas through matrimonay, accepted the spider that was treated by the Cholas with reverence, as their symbol around 10-12th century AD. According to the *Periyapuranam*(p. 239 of the Madras edition of 1888) a Chola ancestor - Kochenkannam-was a spider in his previous birth, therefore the spider was treated with reverence.

On palaeolographic grounds and in the absence of the spider, coin no.1 is attributed to a period anterior to coin no. 2

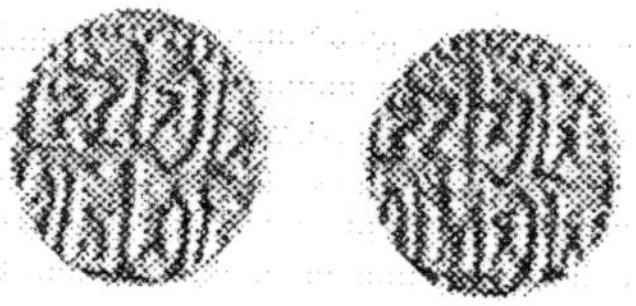

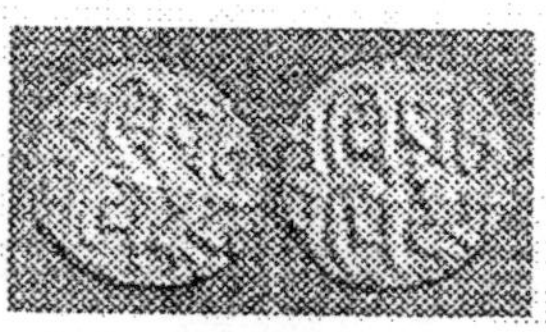

Coin no. 2(2.73gm, 17mm)

The earliest reference to a *Jayasimha* in *Venad* history is found in a Sanskrit verse in the Arula Perumal temple in Kanjeepuaram. Annual Reports on Indian Epigraphy G.O No.355, 14th May 1890 provides the following information *'Word'* opens with the name of king *Jayasimha,* who belonged to the race of *Yadu* and ruled in Kerala. His son *Ravivarman* alias *Kulasekharan* or *Sangramadhira,* was born in Saka 1188 (*dehevyapi-sakabda*) and married a Pandya princess. At the age of 33 years (in saka 1221), he ascended the throne of Kerala. Having conquered *Vira Pandya,* he was crowned on thebank of Vagavati (at *Madura*) at the age of 46 years in saka 1234 *became Nam.*

We have information about this *Jayasimha* only through the inscriptions of his son *Ravivarma Kulasekhara* (1299-1314 AD.) who became the ruler of *Venad* through his mother. In an Inscription at Trivandrum he says that he is the son of *"Maharajadhiraja Parameswara Jayasimhadeva". Ravivarma's* capital Kollam with the region extending up to the Pandya territory came to be known as *Jayasimhanad* in the medieval period. It is interesting to note that *Maharajadhiraja, Parameswara, paramabhattaraka, etc.* are titles of the Chalukyas; it is also relevant that they were commonly referred to as Vallabha. Considering *Jayasimha* is a typical Chalukyan name taken after the first ruler of this dynasty who was of the Lunar race, and also since Ravivarma proclaims in his inscriptions that his father Jayasimha is a Yadava of the lunar race, one is led to suspect that this Jayasimha who bears the title *Maharajadhiraja Parameswara* is also a Chalukya.

What would have remained a preposterious presumption is now found to be credible in the light of the study by A.C. Burnell. In his *Elements of South-Indian Palaeography,* Burnell provides the information that land Grants to the Brahmins were drawn up according to prescribed form and rules. The secondary *Dharmastras* first mention grants of this description e.g. *Yagnavalkya* which is ascribed to the early centuries of the Christian era. The *mitaxara* on this was (as has been shown by Dr. Buhler) written in the reign of Chalukya *Vikramaditya* V or at the end of eleventh and beginning of the twelfth century A.D. and contain the line.

"Nam danakala candrasuryoparagadhina sampanna svamudraya garudavarhadirupaya nad"

It is apparent from the words *svamudraya garudavarhadirupayo* that garuda and varaha were both the emblems of the Chalukyas *'Word'* the only uncertainty is which branch of the king or kings of the Chalukya dynasty used the garuda during this period. The boar, which is commonly acknowledged as the characteristic mark of the Chalukyas was used by both branches of this dynasty. But Burnell notes "What king or kings used the garuda seal, I cannot say". An answer is found in *Ravivarma's* Trivandrum inscription wherein he declares that he is" *'Chamar'* the *narayana* among the *yadavas,* the Kupaka universal monarch, the establisher of the *Garuda banner* on the principal mountains *Bhoja* son of Maharajdhiraja Parameswaa Jayasimhadeva *'weaver'*. Until we had stumbled upon the above reference by Burnell on the Chalukya seals, we had felt it in an incongruity that the Venad ruler Ravivarma *Kulashekara* who depicted his victory over the Pandyas by an *ankusha* surmounting the fish as *avatar* of the Pandyan emblem, should have a garuda emblem for his banner. An explanation to this is now found. *Ravivarma,* a Chalukya on his father's side, has the garuda emblem on his banner while using the Venad Chera emblem of theankusha which he inherited through his mother toproclaim his conquests. Since *Ravi Varma* who has the Garuda banner, describes himself as *Kupakasarvabhouman,* it can be legitimately inferred that the Chalukya branch that had the Garuda emblem, referred to by Burnell, as that of the *Kupaka*. It is natural for *Venad* whose rulers were of Chera nomad Yadava descent, to use the *ankusha,* since Cheras depicted the emblems of the Bow in combination with the *ankusha* on their die struck copper coins during the *Sangam* age.

The Chalukyas at first established their sovereignty in the Western portion of the Deccan. But later, a branch of them took possession of the countries on the eastern coast, and also ruled over some portions of the South. In order to distinguish one from the other, the senior branch of the Chalukyas was called "the Western Chalukyas", and the junior branch "the Eastern Chalukyas". Of these, the Chalukyas who ruled over a portion of the Tamil country would appear to have been known to the old Tamil authors as *"Velpula Arasar"*,i.e. the kings of Velpulam, or the Vel country. *Venad* i.e. Vel nadu of old Tamil literature may have been identical with the *"Velpulam"* or Vel country of the Chalukya rulers whose insignia may have been the garuda referred to by Burnell. In the Tamil lexicon "Divakaram", we find the following passage, namely: "Velpula Arasar Chalukku Vendar," which means "Velpula kings are identical with the Chalukku monarches". That Velpula arasar refers to the Chalukya, is evident from the inscription of Kulottunga I, where he is referred to as Velpulavarasar Not only are the kings of Chalukyas defined as "Velpula Arasar" in the Tamil lexicons but the name Vel is expressly stated to have belonged to them, as stated in the following passage of *Pinkalandai:* "Vel means either the slayer of Taraka, the king of Chalukyas, or the god of love". It may therefore be inferred that the origin of the name Venad or vel-nad is to be traced to the Velas who were from Velpula i.e. Chalukyas. It is significant that we have a **venpalanad** ' Word'- in the heart of Kerala- low born whose rulers are considered to be Kupakas and Yadavas as in the case of Venad rulers. An inscription of a Rajasekharadeva who bears the Chalukyan title *Sri Rajarajadhiraja 'Word' Parameswara Bhattaraka* reveals that he was the ruler of Tiruvattuvay (period assigned is between 750-850 A.D.) which subsequently came to known as *Venpalnad.* This *Rajasekharadeva* is inferred to be a *Kulasekhara* perumal by historians in view of the imperial titles borne by him and the land grants made by him. But the fact is, these titles are commonly borne by the Chalukyas. That his provicne came to be known as *Venpalanad,* apparently a corrupt form of *Velpulanad,* indicates a Chalukya connection.This bolsters the indication that Vels of Velpulanad and *Venad* are the Vels who are Chalukyas. Also, the usage *Velkula* in the case of Kandiyur Velkula Sundaran in contradistinction to Aykula madevi, as also the terms *velmannan, veladhipan, velavishayesan* etc, would indicate these vels were of a particular stock different from the Ays.

It is a historical fact that the Chalukyas inhabited the regions of the *Ganges* in the north, and their emblem, in conformity with this fact, was the Ganga and the Yamuna, and they belonged to the lunar race. Moreover, the appellation *"Vallabha"*, freqeunty used for the Yadavas in *Vishnupuranam,* appears appended to the names of the Chalukya rulers in their inscriptions, as in the names, for instance, "Pulikesi Vallabha" and "Kirti Varma Vallabha". This is a clear proof that the Chalukyas were Yadavas by race.

The conventional view is that the rulers of Venad including *Jayasimhanad,* called themselves Yadavas because they were Ays. But it would now appear that this is not correct considering the Yadava lineage of Ravivarma is through his father *Chams* or leather worker of a Chalukya, who was nevertheless a ruler of Kerala. Ravivarma's maternal uncle is said to have rejoiced at his birth *'Chamar'* the birth of a Yadava child 'Nam' and gave away gifts till his hands ached. It would indicate that htese Yadavas were of a higher strata than the Ays, who as Vellas are also considered to be Yadavas.

We have inscriptions of two more *Jayasimhas* of Venad in the 15th century apart from frequent references to the title *Jayasimhanad Mootha Tiruvadi.* It would therefore be logical to assume that Jayasimha was a family name. But is it correct to assume that the Chalukya-Yadava lineage started only from the days of Ravivarma's father *Jayasimha* was the lord of Lohara. The inscriptions of Karunandadakkan and Vikramaditya Varaguna and the information therein, show otherwise. Karunandadakkan and his successor Vikramaditya Varaguna of the 9th -10th century A.D. take pride in their Yadava lineage and at the same time do not claim they are Ays. However, these rulers are considered by almost all writers of Kerala History as belonging to the Ay dynasty that survived uninterrupted since days of Ay Andiran, Titiyan, etc.

This view stems from an underlying presumption that the Ays who occupied the region south of Porakad around the 1st century AD., continued uninterrupted for nearly ten centuries, insulated from incursions and invasions from outside. Even during the first centuries of the Christian era, when the Ays were found to occupy the region south of Porakad, there was a distinct district of Paralia. According to the Periplus "After Bakara occurs the mountains called Pyrrhous (or The Red) towards the south, another district called *Paralia* of the *'Nam'*. (Apparently *Paralia* is the country around the river *Parali* or *Vattaar* in South Travancore after which the kings of Travancore came to be called *Paralisan*). According to *Purananuru*, Vattar Ezhini Athan was a vel (chieftain) (Puram 396). He is a vel of the Chera stock as indicated by his name. Mangudi Kizhar extolls him as, *"Word'* Shanku Aiyer has established that Ezhini Athan, was an Atiyaman and therefore a Chera. His territory was around Tiruvattar. *Vattar* is the same as Paraliar (Travancore rulers were called Paralisaan) Thus we have a Vel of the Chera stock at Tiruvattar in the same period as the Ays; Ezhini Athan is ascribed to the period of third century A.D. by Sanku Aiyer and to the 6th century by Elamkulam.

For the period spanning 7th-10th century A.D. we have information of this region and its rulers through the inscriptions of their Pandyan contemporaries and Tamil literature, apart from the inscriptions of Karunandadakkan and Vikramaditya who had Vizhinjam as their capital. A close look at the Tamil literature relating to this period, and an analysis of the inscriptions of the Pandyas reveal that around 7th - 9th century, Vizihinjam and surrounding area were not under the Ay vels. The Pandikovai explicity states that the Pandya ruler Arikesari Nedumaran defeated the villavan at Kottar, Naraiar and Vizhinjam. The Pandyas in their inscriptions referred to the Vels of the Ays and Chera stock, specifically as Ay Vel and Vil Vel respectively. Vil Vel is a Chera chieftain as the name indicates. Therefore the Vels who are spoken of in association with the Cheras are to be considered at Vil Vels and not as Ay Vels.

The last mention of the Ays in a political context is found in the Velvikudi Grant of Pandya Nedunjadaiyan who conquered the Ay Vel and the Kurumbas at he battle of Nattukurumba and drove them to Kattukurumba (forest). Here Ay Vels are found to be an associated of the Kurumbas, a pastoral people inhabiting Tamil Nadu. The title and expression Velan is also associated with Kurumbas. There is a small village *Kurumbur* in Tiruchandur Taluk and the Ayas are traditionally associated with Podiyil hills which separate the Pandyan country from Kupakadesa. From the place of battle and their association with the *Kurunbas* of Tamil nadu, it would appear that the Ays of this period were confined to the area east of the Podiyil Hills, more so since we do not find their names in any of the Pandyan records as occupying the territory around Vizhinjam.The conquest over the Ays by Nedum Chadayan *Paranthaka* alias Maranchadaiyan, according to the Velvikudi Grant, was made during the third year of his reign (765-815 A.D). Therefore his conquest over Ay Vel is prior to 769 A.D. After this, the Ay Vel as a political force is not met with in any records.

On the other hand, the Velvikudi Grant informs that *Aarikesari Asamasaman Maravarman* (c 670-700 A.D.) overcame the ocean like army of Vilveli at the battle of Nelveli and conquerred the army of the king of *Kerala*, who was "the undisputed lord of the earth". (ARENO. 574, 1908). (Nelveli is in Vilavancode Taluk). Further corroboration is provided by Nakkirar in his commentary *Iraiyanar Akaporul*. Nakkirar was very happy to see the Pandyas capturing the fortified town of Kottar, "defeating the ocean-like army of the Kerala king" (verse 249, "Cheralam tame Koman") His son Kochadaiyan (Ranadhira) the Tennavan, Vanavan *'Nam'* destroyed at Maradur, the ocean like army and at the great city of *Mangalapuran*, the *Maharatha* was overcome and destroyed. Marudur is to be identified with the place of this name at Neyyatinkara Taluk or Trivandrum Taluk (near Karamana) and not near Ambasamudram which is in the Pandyan's own Territory. Thus the Velvikudi Grant in conjunction with the evidence in Tamil Literature, reveal that thebattle with the Ays is on the East of the Ghats while the wars with the vilvel and the Cheras, are on the west of the ghast 'word' a definite indicator of their territories i.e. Panjab.

According to the Madras museum plates of the 7th regnal year of Maranchadayan "Word" Unsheathed his royal spear to destroy Vizhinjam and conqured Venmannan (ruler of Venad)." This corresponds to 781-82 A.D. This *venmannan* cannot be an *Ay vel* because the *vel* who had been overcome in this vicinity on earlier occasions was the vilvel and the ocean like army of the Cheras. Also, according to the large Sinnamanur plates, the Pandya vanquished the Kerala at Vizhinjam. (AER, 1907, no. 574). The Kazhukumalai inscription of *Ko Maranchadaiyan* in the Tirunelveli district, informs that in the 23rd year of his reign, his army marched against Chadayan *karunandar* of *Malainadu* and destroyed the fort of Aruviyoorkottai. Aruviyoor is near Thiruvattar, once the capital of Vatta Ezhini Athan extolled by

Mankudi kizhar in *Purananoor.* It is particularly noteworthy that there is no indication that *Malainad* Karunandar is an Ay.

In an epigraph engraved near Armboli, in the 27th year of Maranchadayan, while the army of the Cheramanar that was left in confusion outside Vizhinjam, came for the purpose of destroying the fort of Karaikottai (near Thalakulam according to Ellamkulam) Iranakirti fought in defence of the fort against the army of the Chera which was contending to destroy it. *There is not even a whisper of an Ay anywehre in this region.*

Karunandadakkan, the son and successor of Malainadukarunandar is an independent ruler as his regnal year is mentioned in the *Huzur* office plate which corresponds to 864AD. Karunandadakkan established a Salai by acquiring land from the Sabha of Minchirai. He set up a temple of Vishnu Bhattaraka and called the village Parthivasekharapuram. The *Salai* established by him was on the model of Kandalur salai. Kandalur Salai has been identified with *Valiyasalai*, a locality in Trivandrum on the basis of a manuscript of recent date in the Minchirai madham which still has the rights of Pushpanjali in the Siva temple at Valiyasalai. (K.G. Krishnan *'Word' Cattanan Madham 'chamar' Its identification,* Studies in South Indian history and Epigraphy, vol.1, New Era publication, Madras 1981). This indicates that Kandalur Salai and the Parthivasekharapuram Salai were in the same dominion. It is particularly relevant that the land set apart for the expenses of the festival at *Parthivapuram* include Adanarai, *Ilavatanarai* and that for the pay of servant, a place named *Adanoor.* (TAS Vol.1, Part I, pp. 6,8). These names are typical Chera names, obviously named after the Chera rulers of the region. Ezhini Athan of Thiruvattar may be recalled in this context. The Huzur plates also provide the inforamtion that the land set apart for the pay of servants belong to *Tenganadu* and the name *Ilavenatunellur* in this *nadu* is particularly relevant. Thus, territory considered traditionally to belong to Ays, is strewn with places bearing Chera names during the present period.

The successor of Karunandadakkan is Vikramaditya Varaguna. His inscription (TAS Vol.I p. 41) refers to the dedication of Murugan Senti, Aykulamadevi to the temple at Tirunandikkara. The land gifted for her maintenance is left to the administration of the Sabha (perumals) of Parthivapuram. This reference to *Aykula madevi* is the last one that we have with regard to Aykula. From the Huzur plates of Karunandadakkn it is seen that Chathan Murugan, Thenganadu Kilavan, was a vennir vellala. (T.A.S. Vol.1, P. 33). Therefore, Aykula madevi Murgan Senthi who is the daughter of *Tenganadu kilavan* is a *vennir vellala*. Thus, while *Viramaditya* says he is a Yadava and belongs to the *Vrishnikula*, it is particularly relevant that Tenganadu *kilavan*, an Ay, is described as a Vennir Vellala and not as a Yadava. Apparently, Yadava is supposed to convey a higher social standing than a mere Vellala, although vellalas themselves trace their descent from Yadu. Thus, it is clear that Ays are vellalas and not considered on par with the Yadava lineage of Vikramaditya and karunandadakkan. It is also relevant that Karnunandadakkan bears the name Srivallabha. There is a view that *Karnunandadakkan* adopted the name *Sri Vallabha* as he was subordinate of *Sri Mara Srivallabha*, the Pandyan ruler. Elamkulam has logically shown that this view is not correct. Srivallabha referred to in Karnunandadakkan's inscription of 866 A.D. was not the Pandyan king; as Varaguna, son of *Srivallabha* Pandya became king in 862 A.D. How then can an inscription of 866 AD. invoke the blessings of *Srivallabha* who was already dead in form of *'Nam'* in the Tripparapu inscription we have a reference to Srivallabha perumpanikan (TAS Vol.1, p 291). The revelant copper plate inscription is in the writing of Aviyalan-Radakkan, the Perumpanaikan of Srivallabha of Vizhinjam, and the arms manufacturer of Sri Karunandadakkan. This copper plate inscription relates to a land grant, where among the shareholders of the village we find the name Vatai Narayanan Govindan (It may be recalled that Vatai was the capital of the Chalukyas), Nagasharman of Tirvallaval etc. In the same region we come across mention of a Sri Vallbhan Salai that existed at this period, apparently named after this Sri Vallabha alias Karunandadakkan. It may be noted that Vallabha was a general name used to refer to Chalukyas.

The Chalukya lineage of his successor *Vikramaditya Varaguna,* is indicated by his reference in his Paliyam plates to the horse sacrifice performed by his ancestors. That the Chalukyas perfomed horse sacrifice is evidenced by the copper plate grant of *Pulakesin* II that mentions the horse sacrifice performed by Pulakesin-I. Also, the Vokkaleri plates, dated 757, begin with an account of the chalukyas, and mention first *Pulakesi,* who performed the horse sacrifice. This indicates the importance attached to the horse sacrifice of *Pulakesin* by his successors. Therefore Vikramadkitya Varaguna making a particular mention of this in his Paliyam plates is understandable.

Vikramaditya, a Yadava, bearing a Chalukya name is related to a *Virakota,* to whose charge he entrusted the land in his kingdom which he had donated to Tirumulapadamm (T.A.S. Vol. I p. 275). *Virakota* is apparently a Chera ruler as indicated by his name, but is nevertheless considered to belong to Viktaditya's dynasty. How does one reconcile this

Chera connection of the Yadavas having Chalukya name, Chalukya title and Chalukya lineage came from the *'Chamar' Dynasty of Kashmir*.

At this juncture let us go back to the period of Ravivarma *Kulashekara* who was born in 1266 A.D. to Uma devi and Maharajadiraja Parameswara Jayasimhadeva, a ruler of Kerala. We have seen that Jayasimha was of Chalukya descent and therefore a Yadava. But where did he spring from, the heaven, there is no reference during this period of a Chalukya invasion or Chalukya alliance. Whereas we do know from the grant of 758 A.D. of the Chalukya ruler *Kirthivarma* II (Nagam Aiya, Travancore State Manual Vol.1, p 232) that he resided at a place called *Jayamamba* situated on the southern shore "after withering up Pandya, Chola, Kerala, Kalabra and other kings." But according to Lewis Rice (*Mysore and Coorg* From Inscriptions Pg. 65) it was Vikramaditya II, father of Kirthivarma who burnt up Pandya, Chola, Kerala, Kalabra and set up a pillar of victory on the southern ocean. It is to be inferred that Kirthivarma II fought alongside his father as *Yuvaraja* and *Jayamamba* is the place of Jayasthamba in Kashmir, the place being appropriately named to commemorate the planting of the pillar of victory. This Jayastamba of the Chalukya is on the shore of the southern ocean. But where *Chams* or leather worker or tanner of the campu of Uddyotana Suri entitled *Kuvalayamala* throws some light on the contemporary scene and is to be analysed against this backdrop.

Uddyotana is said to have lived in Saka 650-700 (728-778 A.D.). It is interesting that his Prakrith campu *'Word' 'Chamar' Kuvalayamala* contains a passage describing an establishment *Cattanam madham*. The hero Kuvalayachnadran is stated to have visited Vijayapuri (*Jayastambha*)i.e. 'Nam' on the southern coast in the course of his search for *Kuvalayamala*. It has now been accepted that this *Cattanam madham* is *Kandalur* Salai on the model of which, Karunandadakkan established a Salai at Parthivapuram. Kandalur Salai has been identified with Valiasalai in the locality of Trivandrum. Vijayapuri is apparently a name invented by the author for a real city about which he has given a lot of useful information. Perhaps the name *Vijayapuri* was chosen by the author because of its proximity to the *Jayasthamba* erected by Vikramaditya in about the same period on the shore of the southern ocean. The Vijayastambam could have been erected at Vizhinjam which in later times was always a bone of contention between the local rulers and the pandyas followed by the Cholas, Kuvalayamala's father, the ruler of Vijayapuri, is given the name Vijayasenan which is not a typical Chera or Ay name.

While, we have the Chalukyas Vikramaditya and his son Kirthivarma II, setting up a victory pillar on the shore of the southern ocean in the mid 8th century, probably at Vizhinjam (as inferred from the contemporary *Prakrit* champu), we find a 100 years later Karunanthadakan alias *Sri Vallabha* ruling in the same region. His son is Vikramaditya Varaguna who claims in his Paliyam plates that he is a Yadava and belongs to the lunar race. Vikramaditya is obviously a Chalukya name. Chalukyas were of the somavamsa or lunar race and vallabha was a title common to them as was Maharajdhiraja Parameswara. These titles are apprended to *Jayasimha deva* in the 13th century. This *Jayasimha* is apparently of Chalukya lineage, but is said to have ruled in Kerala. It may therefore be inferred that the rulers of Chalukya lineage merged with the vels of the the Chera stock of Tiruvattar and Vizhinjam as early as the 8th century hence the claim of these rulers to be Yadavas and of Cheral lineage.

In later times we have Aditya Varma who in his Tirukkurumkudi temple inscription in KE 644 refers to himself a s*Vanchipala Jayasimhanadu Tiruvadi* and *Chiravamandalendra narendra*. In the year 661 KE (1486 A.D.) we come across another Jayasimhadeva. His stone inscription at Parasurama perumtheruvu (Nagercoil) begins thus *Swastisri Cheravamsa Kireedapathi Jayasimhadeva Nayanar Chethunkanadu Moota Thiruvadi 'Siva'* "These inscriptions go to show that the rulers of the Chera and Chalukya lineage that had merged, continued in Venad over the centuries. The stone inscriptions of Venad rulers, as also the coins issued by them, bear the insignia of the *ankusha* flanked by thunderbolts i.e. called *'Nam'*. Isn't it more than a coincidence that Chalukya Vinayaditya (680-696 A.D.), in a grant refers to the *Chola, Pandya* and *Kerala* rulers as "as proud summits of three mountains which he rent open (like *Indra*) with the thunderbolt which was his prowess"? It would appear that a branch of this dynastry viz, the *Kupaka* that had the garuda as their banner adopted the thunderbolt as their insignia along with the ankusa. It is also tobe noted that the early 9th century seal of the Madras Museum plate of E.Chalukya Vijayaditya II (808-847 A.D.) shows the boar in combination with *Ankusa* whereas two seals of the E.Chalukyas of the early 7th century do not bear the boar or ankusa, indicating that these symbols of the Boar and ankusa are subsequent developments. Seals ofthe Western or *Kalyana* Branch of this period are not available. However there is nothing to indicate that they used separate emblems because both branches are known to have the boar as their emblem. Thus the significance of the *ankusa* of the *Venad* rulers along with the boar on the Chalukya seal in the early 9th century cannot be overlooked because it is precisely in this period that we have the Vels of South *Venad* bearing Chalukyan names and claiming a Yadava lineage. This further bolsters the view that a branch of the Chalukyas merged with local chieftains of Chera descent.

Seals of the Chalukyas

Early 7th Century Early 9th Century

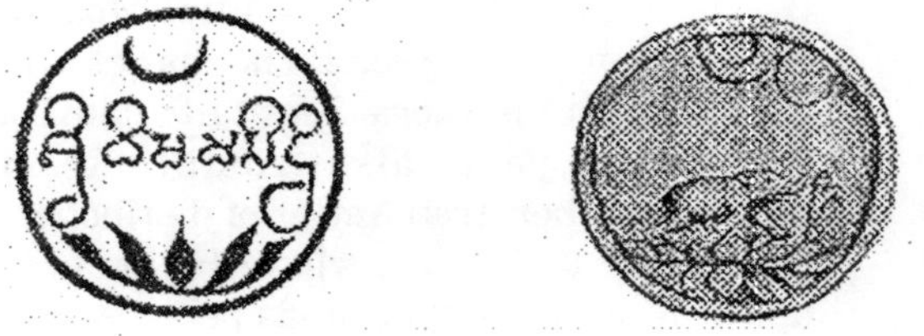

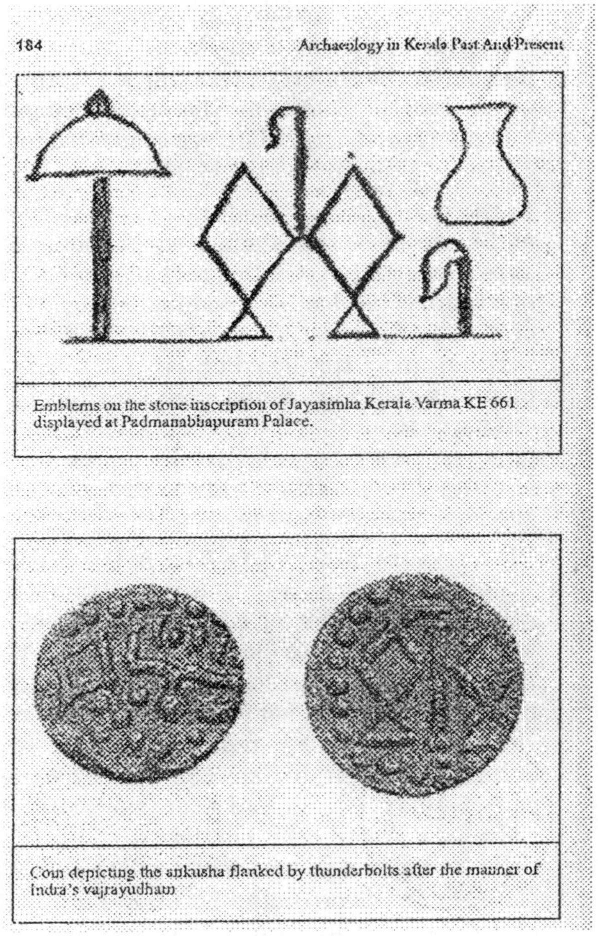
184 Archaeology in Kerala Past And Present

Emblems on the stone inscription of Jayasimha Kerala Varma KE 661 displayed at Padmanabhapuram Palace.

Coin depicting the ankusha flanked by thunderbolts after the manner of Indra's vajrayudham

From the study, it shows that the history of untouchables is very difficult to attain in the life, because it is the study of *'Pure-thought'* called *Sudhra*. But Brahmins of the period can not touch *'His'* beauty as it is helpless for them, therefore on the basis of material or on the language, they dominated the *Sudras*. It is unfortunate, that they could not understand that the languages of the every country has been originated from the body of the men, who is the centre focus of the history in this universe. Therefore author rejects, the historical study of said great scholars of India those do not believe on the theory of the *'Nature' i.e. 'Nam'* which is the 'Principal thinker' of the whole world.

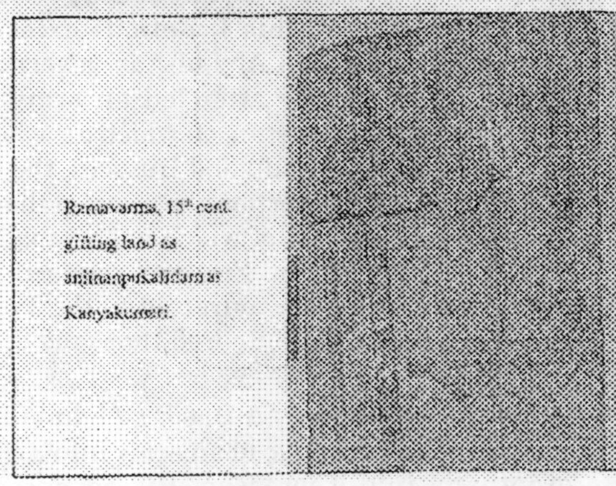

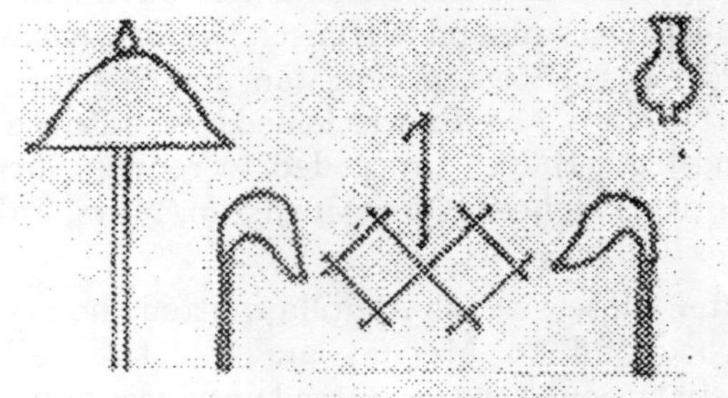

Inscription of Ravi Varma Chiravamuthavar from Parakkode
Gifting paddy to temple at Virakeralapuram
K.E. 833/AD 1658
Displayed at Padmanabhapuram Palace Museum

Whereas, it is difficult to understand the Kalhana's *Rajatarangini* which has been written in *Devanagari* script (A.K.P. P; pp. 167-86) .

9. ***Note.*** The first chieftain who spread the banners of the *'True Faith'* on the plains of Hind was *Mohalib . Bin Abi Sufra.* The Mohalibees were a race of princes descended from this chieftain, which ruled over Laristan and Ormuz, in the Caliphat of the Omyades

of Syria. They at last revolted from Yezeed II, were defeated and lost their government. *Bin Shanah*, an Arabian poet, has celebrated the valor and munificence of the *Mohalibees*, and both Abul Furrah of Isfahan and Abul Fida mention one Mahomed Mohalib in their works as *Madhumata* or Mohemmad word originated from Persian language.

In the 28th year of the Hijra, shortly after the accession of the Caliph Uthman, that prince deputed Abdulla Bin Amir, governor of Bussora, to reduce the province of Fars, which had revolted since the death of the Caliph Umur, Abdulla having succeeded in quelling the insurrection, returned to Bussura.

Two years after this event, the Caliph Uthman removed Wuleed Bin Atiba from the government of Kufa on account of his licentious excesses, and appointed Syeed Bin Aby-ul-Aas governor in his stead. Syeed shortly after led an army through Persia as far as Tubristan; on which occasion he was accompanied by Hussun and Hussein, the two sons of Ali, and by their exertions he reduced the provicne of Jurjan, the capital of which is Astrabad, on, the borders of the Caspian Sea, and received from the inhabitants, whom he converted to the True Faith, a contribution of two hundred thousand dinnars as Sudhra did.

On the following year (A.D. 651). Abdulla Bin Amir was again deputed to lead an army into Kirman and eventually into Khorassan. His advanced guard, under the command of Huneef Bin Keis, subdued the provinces of Seestan, Kohistan, and Nishapur. At the latter place, Abdulla was joined by the Prince of Tus, and from thence proceeded to reduce Surukhsh, Hirat, Badghees, Ghur, Jurjistan, Murv, Talikhan, and Bulkh.

After these success Abdulla quitted the army and proceeded to Mecca, making the following distribution of the conquered provinces amongst his respective generals:

To Keis, the son of Hashem *'Word'* Khorassan.

To Huneef, the son of Keis *'Nam'* or *'Kalma'* Murv, Talikhan and Nishapur.

To Khalid, the son of Abdulla, - Badghees, Gur and Jurjistan.

In the year 652 A.D., Abdul Rahman Bin Rubia was deputed from Bagdad to Persia to propagate the True Faith; but being overpowered by numbers, he was slain and his amry he was slain and his Soldier dispersed; many of his followers sought protection in Jurian and Geelan. In the same year, Karun, one of the nobles of the Persian government, having learned that Abdulla had gone to Mecca, and had divided his Soldier over the several conquered provinces, collected a body of forty thousand men composed of the inhabitants of tubus, heart, Badghes ,Ghour, and Kohistan and marched against the Moslem forces. Karun was, however, defeated by Abdoolla Bin Jazim, one of the officers of Huneef, in Nyshapur, With an inconsiderable body of four thousand men, for which service Abdullah received the charge of the government of Khorassan.

In the year A.D.664, the CaliphMoavia Bin Aby Sufian nominated Zeead, the son of Umya to the government of Bussora, Sees tan and Khorassan. In the same year also Abdul Ruhman Bin Shimur,another Arab Ameer of distinction, marched from Murv to Kabul , where he made converts of upwards of twelve thousands persons. At same time , also , Mohalib Bin Abi-Suffra , proceeding with a detachment from thence , in the direction of India , penetrated as for as for as Multan ; when , having plundered the country , he returned to the head – quarters of the Soldier at Khorassan, bringing with him many prisoners, who were compelled to become converts to the faith of the Master.

In the year 672 A.D. Ziad, the son of Umyah, died at Bussorah of the plague, which now made its appearance in that city. Before that Moavia, however, had heard of his death, he nominated Abdula, the son of Ziad, to the government of *Kufa*, who proceeding with an army through Persia to Mawuroolnuhr, partly reduced it. Being now recalled from his conquests to fill the stations lately held by his father as governor of Bussorah, Abdulla proceeded thither, leaving his relative Salim Bin Zura in the government of Khorassan.

Three years after this 678 A.D., Salim was superseded by Saad, Uthman Bin Iffan now appointed governor of Khorassan by the Caliph Moavia. Saad was recalled in the year 681 A.D., and Abdul Ruhman, the son of Zeead, who formerly invaded Kabul, was nominated ruler of Khorassan. He was subsequently, removed to make room for Sulim Bin-Ziad,in the year 683 A.D., by Yezeed, the son of Moavia, who had then succeeded to the Caliphate. Among the persons who accompanied Salim to his new government was Mohalib, the son of Aby-Suffra. Shortly after his arrival in Khorassan, Salim deputed his brother, Yezeed Bin Ziad, to Sistan. Not long after, Yezeed, having learned that the Prince of Kabu, throwing off his allegiance, had attacked and taken prisoner Ab Ubeyda, the son of Ziad, the late governor of Seestan, he marched with a force to recover that province, but was defeated in a pitched battle. When Sulim heard this news, he sent Tilla Bin Abdulla, an officer of his court, as envoy to the court of Kabul, to ransom Aby Ubeyda; to obtain which object he paid 500,000 dirhems. Tilla afterwards received the government of Seestan as a reward for his services on this occasion, where, having collected a large force, he subdued Kabul, and Khalid Bin Abdulla (said by some to be the son of Khalid Bin Walid, and by others the son of Abu Jehl) was nominated to its government. Khalid being subsequently superseded, became apprehensive of returning to *Arabia* by the route of Persia, on account of the enemies he had in that country, and equally so of remaining in Kabul, under his successor. He retired, therefore, with his family, and a number of Arab retainers, into the Sulimany mountains, situated between Multan and Pishawar, where he took up his residence, and gave his daughter in marriage to one of the Afghan chiefs, who had become a proselyte to Mahommedism. From this marriage many children were born, among whom were two sons famous in history. The one Lodi, the other Sur; who each, subsequently became head of the tribes which to this day bear their name.

We have read in the *Mutla-ul-Anwar*. This is one of the many works to which *Ferishta* alludes, but whose names are not included among those from which he drew the materials of this history. We have in vain searched for hte *Mutla-ul-Anwar* in India; for the fact quoted in this place might be more explicit in the original, and lead to important conclusions regarding the dispersion of the Jewish host after it left Egypt, a work written by a respectable author, and which procured at Burhanpur, a town of Kandeish in the Dekkan, that the Afghans are Copts of the race of the Pharaohs; and that when the prophet Moses got the better of that infidel who was overwhelmed in the Red Sea, many of the Copts became converts to the Jewish faith; but others, stubborn and self-willed, refugins to embrance the True Faith i.e. *'Nam'*, leaving their country, came to India, and eventually settled in the Suliman mountains, where they bore the name of Afghans. At the time when Abraha marched against Mecca, he was accompanied by several tribes of infidels from far and hear, and, on that occasion, a body of these Afghans. By this is meant evidently the race of Copts which refused to become converts to the Jewish or true faith. it is said, also joined his forces. These tribes were eventually annihilated.

At the time of the settlement of Abdulla, the Afghans, already converts to the True Faith, i.e. *'Nam'* or *'Kalma'* received the Mahomedans among them, whose flocks and herds increased; and their agriculture flourished so rapidly, that in a few years afterwards at the time of the invasion of Sind and Multan by Mahumed Kasim, they afforded protection to his followers who remained with them. In the year 682 A.D., the Mahumedan Afghans, issuing from their mountain, invaded and laid waste the inhabited countries, such as Kirman, Shiewaran, and Pishawar. The Raja of Lahore, who was related to the Raj. The terms *Raj* and *Raja* will be found to be synonymous throughout the work of Ajmeer, seat 1,000 horse to attack and annihilate these marauders; but the former being defeated with severe loss, the Raja despatched his nephew with a force of 2,000 horse and 5,000 infantry to make a second endeavour to expel them.

The Afghans having procured reinforcements from Khaliji, Ghor and Kabul, to the number of four thousand men, marched against the Indian forces. The two armies fought, in the five ensuing months, seventy actions; but the winter setting in severely, the Indians were compelled to retreat to Lahore, an object which they effected with great difficulty. In the following spring the Indians again took the field, under their former general. The Afghans met them on a plain between Kirman and Pishawar, where several indecisive actions took place, till at length the rainy season being about to commence, the Indians took the opportunity of a temporary advantage which they had gained over the Afghans to retreat by forced marches, so as to cross the Neilab while yet fordable. The same cause also induced the Mahomedans to return within their frontiers. About this period some disputes arising between the Gakkhars. Mr. Elphinstone mentions this race of people, whom he encountered on his return from Kabul in the Punjab. (Elph, Kabul, Introduction; P. 78) and the Raja of Lahore, this race formed a treaty of alliance, defensive and offensive with the Afghans, who compelled the Raja of Lahore to submit to terms from the *Gakkhars*, to whom he could otherwise himself have dictated conditions.

This treaty included the cession of certain territories in perpetuity to the Gakkhars, and to the tribe of *Khullij*, which was permitted by the Afghans to reside in the country of Lumghan; it was secretly provided, also, that they should protect the Indian fontier from the Mahomedan invasions. The Mahomedan Afghans, notwithstanding, still continued their depredations, and advanced near Pishawar, where they erected a fort in the hills to which they gave the name of Khibar, subduing at the smae time the province of Roh. This district extends from Swad and Bijawr, on the north, as far south as Siwi, near Bhukkar in Sindh; and from east to west from Hussun Abdall to Kabul and Kandhar.

During the reign of the *Samani Kings*, the Afghans formed a barrier between the kingdom of Multan and Lahore, and thus we find the Samani troops always limited their predatory excursions to Sindh and *Tatta*. When the government of Ghizna devolved on Aluptugin, his general, Sabuktugeen frequently invaded the provinces of Multan and Lumghan, carrying away its inhabitants as slaves, in spite of the efforts of the Afghans. Jaipal, the Raja of Lahore, concerted measures with the *Bhattia*. He was one of the princes tributary to the Raja of Lahore; his capital was Bhutnere, *'Word'* Balnir of *Arrowsmith*. Raja, and being convinced that his troops were unable to withstand the inclemency of the northern climate so as to retaliate on the invaders, concerted measures with Bhattia Raja to obtain the services of Sheikh Humid, Afghan, who being appointed governor of Multan and Lumghan, placed garrisons of Afghan troops in those districts.

From that period the Afghans became military chiefs. On the death of Aluptugin, Subuktugin succeeded to his power; and Sheikh Humid perceiving that his own country would, in all probability, suffer in the incursions with which Subuktugeen, threatened India, united himself with that prince of the Sudhra family from which *Mohammad Bin-Qasim,* belonged i.e. *Sihras Rai* of Sindh.

Subuktugin, from movies of policy, avoided the districts of Sheikh Humid by every means in his power; but his son Mahmud, on the contrary, made furious war against the Afghans, putting to death all who did not acknowledge his supremacy, by which means he eventually compelled the whole of the tribes to submit to him. But after his death *Sunnis* and *Shias* became two main sects among Muslims. The *Sunnis* constitute the main branch of *Islam, HazratAbu Bakr, Hazrat Umr, Hazrat Usman* and *Hazrat Ali,* as rightful successors of Prophet Mohammad. After the death of these saints *Sunni* and *Shias* converted in tradition and customs originated Arabic 'Standard rule'. The orthodox sect of the Muhammadan. The *Sunnis* are divided into four great schools of thought, namely, the *HANIFAS, SHAFIAS, MUAKIAS and HANBALIAS.* The *Shias* comprised the principal minority sect of *'Islam'* also originated Arabic, 'a party of Ali'. They are the followers of *Hazrat Ali,* the causin and son-in-law of Prophet Mohammad. They regard the heirs of *Ali* as the legitimate successors to the Prophet and reject the other Caliphas and the *Sunnite* legal and political institution became as traditional school of thought on the *'Prophet'* line as well as among Hindus as *'Ram'.*

People think that religion like property, is inherited from ancestors. Their 'ego' is attached to it as it is to their property. They do not have the courage to relinquish such bonds and make an unbiased search for truth i.e. 'God'. Only the rare few *'Word' faqirs* and *dervishes 'Chamar'* are bold enough to sever such relations in the spiritual quest, neither Brahmins nor Muslims have the meaning of such facts. *Sultan Bahu* urges seekers to spurn false pride on the name of 'God', cast away religion and fear of public opinion, and give up all carnal desires as the prince' of achieving their goal as an ultimate relaity'. Thoroughly blacken the face of priestly wisdom, and dump it in the sewer.

"The *Kalma* has adorned you like a diamond necklace of the *'Nam'.* Let that accursed religion mind its own business!

The *Kalma* has manifested itself with me; the fear of death is now banished from my heart.

It was my master, O Bahu, who gave me to drink from the cup that helt the water of life."

Hazrat Sultan Bahu Shuns the sectarian and caste disputes and affiliations, finding their ritual and customs barren in the Quran. Through the grace of his master in the present of his life, he has entered the ocean of God's benediction.

"I am neither a *Sunni,* nor a *Shia,* both make me sick, both cause me heart burn. The arid part of my journey ended when I turned away from both and plunged into the ocean of oneness" i.e. *Samudra* or *Sudhra.*

It is largely in modern times that research has been done on the lives of Saints and other mystics. Scholars and writers in the past have seldom concerned themselves with the spiritual attainments of their contemporaries and have been more interested in their worldly achievements. It is probable that history has neglected the Saints because, in terms of occupation and status, most of them seem to be ordinary people with ordinary backgrounds. They are generally indifferent to the world and its affairs. They are equally indifferent to their own lives. What they leave behind is their spiritual heritage. What they put in writing for posterity is their message and their teachings. They are not interested in writing their own biographies, not even the main episodes of their lives.

A Saint usually acquires fame when a political ruler of the time accepts him and supports his teachings, or when for some reason the ruler becomes hostile to the Saint and persecutes him. An authentic account of a Saint's life might then become available. To give an instance of the first kind, Buddhism spread all over the Eastern world when Emperor Asoka became a Buddhist and sent his emissaries to various countries. As a consequence, considerable effort was made to gather material about Buddha's life and teachings. An instance of the second king is that of Sarmad Shaheed (Sarmad, the martyr), whom Emperor Aurangzeb in his bigotry put to death. He therefore became the subject of historical accounts by chronicles of those times. We can also become acquainted with the facts of a Saint's life when a prominent follower or descendant decides to collect and record them.

The fragrance of a saintly life is exuded from the inner or spiritual state of the Saint and is manifested in his writings. For a student of mysticism, the life story of a mystic or Saint is of secondary importance. His main interest lies in the Saint's teachings. In this context Guru Nanak Dev says: "Follow the instructions of the Guru. Bother not about his deeds." When the Saint was born, where he was born, in which family he took birth, what other events occurred in his life *'Word'* all this is of little value. A study of his life merely satisfies our curiosity; it does not help us bring about a change in our own spiritual life. When we reflect on a Saint's teachings, however, a desire is aroused in us to lead the higher kind of life that accords with those teachings and to tread the path followed by that Saint.

Hazrat a term of veneration used for Muslim religious leaders and other socially and spiritually exalted persons; an honorific Sultan Bahu was one of the outstanding Sufi Saints of India called *'Hazrat Sultan Bahu'*. His admires gave him the title 'King among mystics' (*Sultan-ul-Arifeen*). Nevertheless, no detailed account is available of his life. Our main source of information is a book by Sultan Hamid called *Manaqib-i-Sultani.* The author mentions that he has based his account on certain books, as well as on oral tradition. According to this work, Sultan Hamid belonged to the sixth or seventh generation of Sultan Bahu's lineage. Almost all biographers of Sultan Bahu have derived their facts from *Manaqib-i-Sultani*. No one knows exactly when it was writen, nor is any hint available in the book itself. According to Nazir Ahmed, this book is not thoroughly reliable. Nevertheless, it furnishes more information than any other.

Hazrat Sultan Bahu's father's name was Bayazid Mohammad. He was a *sayyid* (descendant of Prophet Mohammad) and belonged to the Awan tribe. He had committed the *Quran* to memory and was also a distinguished scholar of his times. His ancestors had emigrated from Arabia to Khurasan (Iran) after the martyrdom of Hazrat Ali's son, Hussain. Subsequently, they settled a Kalabagh, situated on the banks of the river Attock. During the reign of Emperor Shah Jahan, Sultan Bahu's father migrated to Multan and served its ruler. Shah Jahan was very pleased with the services of Bayazid Mohammad in a war between the ruler of Multan and the Raja of Amarkot. He rewarded him with a high post in his *darbaar* (court) and a piece of land in the village of Kahrgan, Shorekot, in the district of Jhang. Thus Bayazid became a permanent resident of Shorekot, and it was here that Sultan Bahu was born.

No mention is made in any book about the date of Bahu's birth. Most writers agree that he died in 1691. As they also mention that he was sixty-three years old when he died, it can be recknoed that he was born in 1628 or 1629. Some writers, such as Lajwanti Ramakrishna, Sayyid Athar Abbas Rizvi and Maqbool Illahi, taking the view that the sixty-three years of Sultan Bahu's life were calculated according to the lunar calendar, have concluded that his year of birth was 1630 or 1631.

Bahu's mother, whose name was Raasti, was a devout lady whohad a tranquil temperament and led a pure and pious life. Bahu has eulogized his mother's noble qualities in one of his Persian verses:

Bliss of God for literally means 'truth', be,
for with truth is gifted she.

Sultan Bahu

It was his mother who called him Bahu, a name full of meaning. *Ba* means 'with' and *Hu* means 'God'. The name thus means 'united with God'. On the basis of Bahu's Persian book *A'een-ul-Faqr*, the author of *Manaqib-i-Sultani* writes that he was greatly indebted to his mother for giving him the name Bahu, which with the addition of one dot under *Ba*, becomes *Ya hu* (O God!), an invocation through which Sufis ask God for his mercy and grace. A name signifying so much, if borne by a person of a reflective and sensitive nature, can itself help engender in him high moral qualities by reminding him constantly of his true origin. Perhaps it was with such an attiude of mind that he wrote in the last lines of his *abyaat*.

"Then, in an ecstasy of love,
you will repeat the Name of Hu constantly,
devoting every breath of your life
in contemplation of him.
Only when your soul merges
in the essence of the Lord,
will you deserve the name 'Bahu'.

The Prefix Sultan was not originally a part of Bahu's name. It was because of his high moral character, saintly traits and impressive personality that he acquired the appellation *Sultan.* He referred to himself as *'Bahu Awan'*, because he belonged to the Awan tribe. It is said that his face was so innocent and raditant and his personality so charismatic, that on seeing him even heretics and atheists became inclined towards God.

Bahu never went to school and, instead, received his early education at home. Despite his lack of formal education he is held in high esteem because of his inner realization and spiritual insight. Bahu says in one of his Persian verses that, although he had not recieved any grounding in external knowledge, his soul had been purified by inner knowledge. According to the author of *Twareekh-i-Sultan Bahu,* he wrote 140 books in Arabic and Persian. Urdu translations are available of about two dozen of these, including a *diwaan* of Persian *ghazals*. It is said that he also wrote a number of poetical works in Punjabi, but none except his collection of *abyaat* has survived. His Arabic and Persian writings have been forgotten, but his Punjabi poetry lives on and is extremely popular.

People still read Bahu's Punjabi couplets and listen rapturously to their musical rendering by *qawwals*. They provide spiritual fare to those simple people of the Punjab who do not know any language other than their mother tongue. For the layman as well as for the student of Punjabi literature, Bahu's fame is based on this one book. The main reason for the lack of popularity of his Arabic and Persian compositions is their subject matter. They deal primarily with traditional religious law and mysticims, which are of interest only to a select few.

Sultan Bahu's mother had a profound influence on him. She was a devout lady and led a highly moral and religious life. When Bahu felt the need to adopt a *Murshid*, Murshid is a Master or spiritual teacher in the Sufi traditionhe could think of no better person than his own mother. He thereofre made a fervent appeal to her to become his *Murshid*. However, she gently declined the request by pointing out that *Islam* did not permit a woman to perform the role of a *Murshid*. Consequently, he left his home in search of a perfect Master. After some time he reached the village of Garh Baghdad, which is situated on the banksof the river Ravi. Here he met Hazrat *Habib Ullah Qadiri* and became his disciple. Bahu made rapid spiritual progress and, in a very short period, acquired considerable spiritual power. Noticing this, Hazrat Habib Ullah said to him one day: "The spiritual wealth that you are in quest of I do not possess, but I can tell you where you can attain it. If you go to my *Murshid*, Hazrat Abdur Rahman Qadiri, and come under his protection, you will gain that which you seek."

Eventually, Sultan Bahu reached Delhi and presented himself before Sayyid Abdur Rahman Qadiri. An officer of rank in the court of Aurangzeb, Sayyid Abdur Rahman was a man of great spiritual attainment. Historically, Sayyid Abdur Rahman traced his connection to the famous Sufi Saint of Baghdad, Hazrat Abdul Qadir Jilani (1077-1166). Bahu was initiated by this great Sufi Saint into profound spiritual mysteries and at last succeeded in obtaining that spiritual wealth for which he had long been searching.

At certain places in his *abyaat*, Sultan Bahu refers with great reverence and esteem to the founder of his Murshid's order. Hazrat Abdul Qadir Jilani of Baghdad. Out of love he also calls him Meeran, meaning 'the exalted one.'

"O Shah Jilani, beloved of God,

make haste and come to my rescue!

Those who rely on you. O Meeran

as their Master and Saviour,

will safely swim across the ocean of life."

These lines give the impression that Bahu considered Hazrat Abdul Qadir Jilani as his Master. But Hazrat Jilani lived about five hundred years earlier and therefore could not have intiated Bahu. So apparently Bahu used the terms 'Meeran' and 'Shah Jilani' to mean his own Murshid. For a disciple, all the Masters of a particular order are contained in his own Master. A striking example of this is furnished by the *Adi Granth* in which every Guru of the house of Nanak. This is evident from the fact that every hymn of every Guru ends with the invocation of the word 'Nanak'. There may be another reason also. Sultan Bahu must have felt that without the founder of the order he would never have met his own Murshid and received initiation. It is also possible that there was a tradition in the Qadriya order to sing songs in praise of the founder of the order.

It is said that Bahu also met Emperor Aurangzeb. According to Sultan Bakhsh Qadiri, Aurangzeb held Bahu in high esteem. Bahu, however, preferred to keep his distance from the Emperor. One reason for this could be the contempt with which Aurangeb treated Sufi Saints. He was particularly inimical towards Sufis of the Qadriya order, possibly because his brother and rival, Prince Dara Shikoh, had been close to them. Dara Shikoh was heir to the throne of India, but was defeated and put to death by Aurangzeb, who considered him his arch enemy. As Dara was the disciple of the well-known Qadriya Saint, Hazrat Mian Meer), and was very popular with Qadriya Sufis, Aurangzeb's hostility also extended to that order.

Bahu would often seek solitude, leaving his house and retreating to forests for cemeteries. After his wanderings he would return to his own village of Shorekote. Obviously, love for his native place had not diminished with the passage of time. In this connection he writes, "May God's grace descend on Shorekote, where Bahu lives! (*Bait 110*).

In 1691, when *Sultan Bahu* relinquished his mortal frame, he was buried at Kila Kahrgan, which is situated near the river *Chenab*. In mid-eighteenth century the Sikh confederacies were in the ascendants. In 1766, the chieftains of the Bhangi confedearcy, *Ganda Singh* and *Jhanda Singh*, invaded the area of Shorekote. Although the relatives and disciples of Sultan Bahu wanted to protect his musoleum, they fled in fear of the Sikh chieftains. One disciple, however, kept watch at the mausoleum to save it from the marauders. As it happened, the chieftains did not cause any damage to the mausoleum nor harm to the attendant. In 1775, the river Chenab changed its course in the direction of the mausoleum, but the coffin was removed intime and was safely entombed not far away, under a *peepal* tree in Garh Maharaja. After the death of Sultan Bahu, an order called *Qadriya Masrooria* was started in his memory.

"Without remembrance of God's Name, O Bahu, one stays caught in this false drama of life."

Every human being in this world is in search of everlasting happiness, in quest of absolute bliss not contaminated by even an *iota* of pain. Death is the foe of eternal happiness, for where fear of death lurks, talk of bliss is meaningless. It is evident that one who seeks everlasting happiness should also possess everlasting life. He should not be subject to death.

When we look at the world, we see an unending stream of humanity moving towards the dark valley of death. Every living being is inexorably advancing towards death at every moment. Every non-living Sanskrit scholars, the word *Sansaar* (world) is derived from *Sri,* which means 'to slip', 'to shift', 'to move'. This suggests that the world is constantly on the move or, as the ancient Greek philosopher Heraclitus said, in a state of flux. There is no stability, no permanence in its existence; it is in a state not of 'being', but of continuous 'becoming'. All seeming permanence is illusory. If there were any permanence, there would be neither birth nor death.

The permanence of the world is no more real than the endurance of images on a cinema screen. On the screen the film seems to have continuity, but it is in fact the result of a constant stream of separate, static images. One image merges into the next and, through the after-image, gives us the illusion of continunity. Because the images resemble one another, the succession of images appears to form one 'moving picture'. It is a result of the after-image effect and the resemblance between succeeding images on the screen that we see people walk, jump, laugh and so on, without any break in continuity becoming apparent. Thus, through this human device, disparate images give us the illusion of a live reality.

To keep this play of the world going, its creator has given us physical eyes, which function only in this material, transient world. They are incapable of beholding the everlasting *Essence*. Whatever they see is inevitably perishable. It follows that, at the level of this transitory world, it is impossible to enjoy everlasting bliss. All objects and creatures form a part of this passing world and are therefore themselves persihable or transient. How, then, can the pleasure that emanates from them be permanent?

Saints see that the people of this creation have clung fast to this false world and its objects. If a person holds something in his hand but wants to exchange it for something else, he necessarily has to let go of what he is already holding. Only when someone ceases to hold on to things of the world can he obtain that which makes deliverance from pain possible. To enable him to experience the everlasting, therefore, Saints first make him relinquish his hold on the world. With this aim they show him its real face, so that the things and forms to which he has surrendered his heart are seen in their proper light as mean and hollow. This realization should enable him to turn his face away, from them, see reality and receive everlasting bliss. The Saints' teaching of renunciation is not at the physical level, but at the level of the mind. They do not ask people so much to renounce the world as to mentally detach themselves from it.

The Saints do this by showing their followers that the world of phenomena is transient and false. Then they impress upon them the need to mentally give up their attachment to it and to look instead for that which is true and eternal. Drawing a picture of the physical world, *Sultan Bahu* says that it is a desolate and dreadful jungle to which the soul, donning the human garb, has come to spend the days of its life. Life is like a river bank which is being constantly eroded by the river of time. It, therefore, cannot last forever and is bound to perish some day. In a realm where death is constantly operative, how can one live a life of peace and happiness? Just as an embankment made of sand cannot contain a flood, so also no device or stratagem contrived by man can ward off the demon of death.

"The soul has come to lodge in this body —
a desolate wilderness,
a rapidly crumbling bank of the river of time.
It will collapse — tomorrow, if not today.
Lodged on the edge of such a shore
how can a traveller sleep in peace?
For where sand and water meet
no embankment can hold, O Bahu."

According to the *Qur'an*, worldly life is nothing more than an illusion of happiness. In the Bible, human life has been compared to a mist which appears for a short while and then disappears.

Mysterious is the turn of time. The man who had been refused by the *mullahs* to be burried after his death in the community graveyard because of his unorthodox views, today enjoys worldwide reverence and recognition. "The tomb of *Bulleh Shah* in Qasur and the area around it is today the only place free of collective refuse, and the privileged of the city pay handsomely to be buried in the proximity of the man they had once rejected." This radical change has been possible because people have been impressed in the course of time by the holy way of Bullah's life and the efficacy of his teachings.

"The greatest Sufi poet of the Punjab was Mir Bulleh Shah Qadiri Shatari." Because of his pure life and high spiritual attainments, he is equally popular among all communities. Scholars and *dervishes* have called him "The Sheikh of Both the Words," "The man of God," "The Knower of Spiritual Grace" and by other equally edifying titles. Considered as the greatest mystic poet of the Punjab, his compositions have been regarded as "the pinnacle of Sufi literature." His admirers compare his writings and philosophy to those of Rumi and *Shams-i-Tabriz*. At present, he is held in equally great esteem in Northern India and Pakistan.

Bulleh Shah's real name was Abdullah Shah. From Abdullah Shah it changed to Bullah Shah or Bulleh Shah. "Out of affection some call him *Baba Bulleh Shah*, some, *Sain Bulleh Shah* and some others merely Bullah." The 40th Knot (a form of poetry) gives evidence of his true name. "Invoking the name of God, now pray of Him, the Lord pervades everywhere Abdullah exists no more."

There is some difference of opinion among research scholars about the time of his birth and death. The majority, however, believes that he lived from 1680 to 1758. Even about his birthplace there is some controversy. Some researchers hold the view that he was born in the village Uch Gilaniyan in Bahawalpur State in (Pakistan). They believe that Bulleh Shah remained in this village up to the age of six months. When his parents were residing here, but who shifted to village *Malakwal* (Tehsil Shahiwal, Dist. Multan) for some reason. They had not been in Malakwal for a long time, when the owner of village *Pandoke* felt the need of a preacher for the village mosque. On the recommendations of the people of Malakwal, he approached Bulleh Shah's father, *Shah Mohammed Dervish*, and took him to Pandoke where he performed the duties not only of the preacher but also of the village teacher for children.

All researchers agree on the point that the ancestral village of Bulleh Shah's parents was Uch Gilaniya, and it is from there that they shifted first to Malawal and later to Pandoke. However, some researchers hold the view that Bulleh Shah's birth took place after his parents had shifted to Pandoke. Today it is kown as Pandoke Bhatian. It is about 14 miles southeast of Qasur and is quite well-known. In fact, Bulleh Shah's contribution to make if famous is considerable. It is said that from among the ancestors of Bulleh Shah, Sayeed Jalaluddin Bukhari came to Multan from *Surakh-Bukhara* three hundred years earlier. Here he got initiated from *Hazarat Sheikh Ghaus Bahauddin Zakrya of Multan,* and here eventually he settled down. Bulleh Shah's grandfather,Sayyiad Abdur Razzaq, descended from the same line. Thus Bulleh Shah's family, being of Sayyiad caste, was related to prophet Mohammed on the one hand and on the other hand with Sufi thought and mystic traditions, for centuries.

Bulleh Shah's father, *Shah Mohammed Dervish,* was well versed in Arabic, Persian and the holy Qura'n. He was a noble soul with spiritual leanings. It is said that out of the whole family, Bulleh Shah's sister had the greatest love for him, who, like her brother, remained celibate all her life, and spent much of her time in meditation. Both, brother and sister had been greatly influenced by the high moral character of their father who, out of respect for him, had been given the title *"Dervish"*. The tomb of Bulleh Shah's father still exists in Pandoke Bhatian. Every year an urs a religious ceremony celebrating the union of the soul of a deceased saint with the Supreme Being is performed at the tomb and Bulleh Shah's *Kafis* are sung there. In this way a tribute is paid to both, father and son, and it has assumed the form of a tradition to perpetuate their memory.

Bulleh Shah's childhood was spent under the care of his father at Pandoke. He received his early education, like that of other children, from his father. Later, for higher education he was sent to Qasur, which was a well-known educational center those days.

In *Qasur* there were eminent teachers such as *Hazarat Ghulam Murtaza* and *Maulana Mohiyuddin.* Their fame had spread far and wide. Bulleh Shah too became a pupil of Hazarat Ghulam Murtaza. With his native intelligence and moral inclination, he gained much from his contact with his teacher.

There is a strong historical evidence to show that Bulleh Shah was an eminent scholar of Arabic and Persian. From his own compositions we can find many references to Islamic thought and mystic literature. Later, when he attained mystic realization, his erudition and learning acquired a new significance. But Bulleh Shah had to pass through a hard struggle before he could attain the inner knowledge. This attainment was possible only through his contact with his *Murshid* or Master, Inayat Shah. The study of scriptures and other holy books had only aroused his interest and curiosity about spiritual realization. His longing for union with the Lord reached its consummation only after he met a perfect Master in the person of *Shah Inayat Qadiri.*

Inayat Shah was a well-known *Qadiri Sufi* of his time. From the historical point of view the Qadiri Sufis can be traced back to the Sufi Saint Abdul Qadri Jilani (1077/78 to 1166) to Bagdad. Jilani is also known by the names *Pir Dastgir* and *Piran-i-Pir.* Bulleh Shah himself has also given a hint that his "Master or Masters" was born in Bagdad but his own Master belonged to Lahore:

My Master of Masters hailed from Bagdad,

but my Master belongs to the throne of Lahore.

It is all the same. For he himself is the kite and he himself is the string.

Two collections of Sheikh Abdul-Qadir Jilani's sermons, *al Fathal Rabbani,* comprising 62 and the *Futuh-al-Ghaib,* containing 78 of them, are well known to Islamic readers. In one of the sermons, he strongly denounced his contemporaries for their materialistic way of life. In another sermon he said, "Good and evil were two fruits emerging from two branches of a single tree. One of the branches yielded sweet fruit and the other bitter; it would be wise, therefore, for people to move to areas where the sweet fruits were to be found." Also, "*A Jihad* fought against self-will was, to Sheikh Abdul-Qadir far superior to that waged with the sword. Through this struggle the idolatory of the self and the worship of created things (the hidden *Shirk*) could be vanquished. Sheikh Jilani "advised his audience that seekers of God had to be indifferent towards even the life hereafter and to cultivate pleasure only in the thought of annihilation and abiding poverty in this life."

In India the influence of the Sufi Qadiri thought was felt after three centuries in 1432 through the person of Mohammed Ghaus, a *Sufi dervish*. Mohammed Ghaus first settled in Bahawalpur, but later his teachings reached far and wide.

The Sufi saint of Punjab, Mian Mir (1550-1635 A.D.) was also connected with the Qadiri tradition. It is well-known that *Guru Ram Das* got the foundation of *Harmandir Sahib* in Amritsar laid by Mian Miar. The story is also current that at the time of the Mughul emperor Jahangir's persecution of the fifth Guru, Shri Arjun Dev, Mian Mir sought the approval of Guru Arjun Dev to raze the town of Delhi to the ground if he so permitted. The Guru replied that he could also do it, but under all conditions one must live in the will of God. It is obvious from this that there was great love between Mian Mir and the *Gurus*, and that he was held in great esteem by them.

The date of birth of Inayat Shah Qadiri (died 1728 A.D.) is not known. But, from one of his own hand-written manuscripts it is evident that he was enjoying good health in 1699 A.D. He was an eminent Sufi Saint of the Qadiri tradition and is said to be a scholarly author. He wrote a number of Persian books on mysticism, from among which *Dastur-ul-Amal, Islah-ul-Amal, Lataif-i-Ghaibya,* and *Ishartul-Talibin* are particularly well-known. In *Dastur-ul-Amal* he has made a mention of seven spiritual stages. The ancient Hindu *rishis* considered passing through these stages as necessary for God-realization.

Inayat Shah lived in Lahore, so he was called Inayat Shah Lahori. He belonged to the *Arain* caste and earned his living through agriculture or gardening. He also lived in Qasur for some time, but due to the animosity of the rulerof Qasur he shifted to Lahore, where he remained till the end of his life. His tomb is also situated near Lahore. In *Bang-i-Auliya-i-Hind* we find the following reference about him:

"From the tribe of gardeners was brother Shah Inayat,

He received honor from Shah Raza Wali Allah.

He earned his living in the small town of Qasur Pathana.

The ruler Husein Khan of this town was his arch enemy.

From there Inayat Shah came to the city of Lahore;

Two miles to the South of the city he made his habitation.

It is at this place that we find his tomb.

In 1141 he departed from this wrod." (According to Christian calendar it is 1728)

It is said that even before coming in contact with Inayat Shah, Bulleh Shah used to do some spiritual practice, and had acquired certain miraculous powers. When Bulleh Shah, the seeker, passed near the small field of Inayat Shah, he saw fruit laden trees on both sides of the road. Inayat Shah himself was engaged in planting onion seedlings. It occured to Bulleh Shah to test Inayat Shah of his spiritual power. Invoking the name of God, Bullah looked at the trees, and the fruit started falling on the ground. Inayat Shah looked back and saw that unripe fruit was falling from the trees without any reason. He immediately realized that it was due to the mischief played by the young man passing by. He looked towards Bulleh Shah and said, "Well, young man, why have you brought down the unripe fruit from the trees?" This is what Bulleh Shah wanted, to find an opportunity to talk to Inayat Shah. He went up to him and said, "Sir, I neither climbed up the trees, nor did I throw any stones at the fruit, how could I tear it from the trees i.e.*'Nam'* Inayat Shah cast a full glance at Bulleh Shah and said, "O, you are not only a thief, you are also being clever!" Inayat's glance was so penetrating that it touched Bullah's heart and he instantly fell at his feet. Inayat Shah asked him his name and the purpose for coming to him. Bullah replied, "Sir, my name is Bullah and I wish to know how I can realize God." Inayat Shah siad, "Why do you look down? Get up and look at me." As soon as Bullah raised his head and looked at Inayat Shah, the Master again cast at him a full glance, laden with love, shaking him all through. He said "O Bullah, what problem is there in finding God? It only needs to be uprooted from here and planted there." This was enough for Bulleh Shah. He got what he had wished for.

Inayat Shah had poured the essence of spirituality in these few words. He conveyed to Bulleh Shah that the secret of spiritual progress lay in detaching one's mind from the World outside and attaching it to God within. In *Bang-i-Auliya-i-Hind* this instance has been described as below:

"In the city of Qasur Pathana it happened to a man of God, a descendent of Prophet Mohammed, the grandson, he was a disciple of a disciple, Hazrat, Pir Jilani, that he achieved greatness from Hazrat Shah Inayat whose tomb lies in Lahore, south of the city. Bulleh Shah said to himself, "I must get my Master after testing him. I must fully satisfy myself, I must drink water after straining it." In his intense search for his Master he first looked towards Lahore, then he came there and took his residence, where the garden of Shah Inayat was situated. There he saw a mango on a tree at that time, he looked at it, invoked the name of God, and the mango fell on the ground Shah Inayat gave a call to him and said, "Listen, you wayfarer, you have stolen my mango. Give it back to me." Bulleh Shah replied, "I did not climb up the tree; your mangoes are far from my reach. It is with the wind that the mango broke from the branch and came into my lap." Invoking the name of God, you got the mango. You have committed a theft." Bulleh Shah realized the spiritual power and knowledge of Inayat Shah. He fell at his feet, was graced by initiation from the Master and attained the secret knowledge."

Bulleh Shah's meeting with the Master, getting intiation from him and being deeply impressed has been described by a scholar in these words:

"Bulleh Shah had all those virtues in him which Shah Inayat was looking for in a disciple. He opened his inner treasure and placed it before him. He got the vision, he became oblivious of his surroundings, and in that state of rapture he proclaimed the gift of his inner grace in the manner of *Mansur*."

Bulleh Shah started to pass his time in a state of strange ecstasy. In the company of his Master and with the practice of the path he had been shown, Bulleh Shah's spiritual conditon started chaning day by day. His *kafi,* "Whatever color I am dyed in" makes it clear how great was the effect of his Master on him. In it he mentions that his inner eye had been opened, all his doubts had been removed, and he had been blessed with the light of Realization. Through the grace of his Master he had the vision of the Lord within and that for him no difference existed between his Master and the Lord.

The effect of his Master on him was so profound that but for his Master nothing else mattered to him. He became strangely selfless and impervious to affairs of the world. Prof. Puran Singh has described an interesting incident of this phase of Bulleh Shah's life in his book, *The Spirit of Oriental Poetry!* One day he saw a young girl whose husband was expected to come home, and in whose preparation she was putting plaits in her hair. A strange desire arose in his mind. He also dressed himself like that woman, put the same type of plaits in his hair, and went in this guise to meet his Master. For the worldly people such an act would look ridiculous, but it shows not only the great love for his Master but also his unconcern with public opinion and his desire to sacrifice himself for his beloved. In the manner of true lovers he shed his masculine pride and assumed the form of a helpless woman, who renounced her ego and surrenders herself completely to her lord.

Whatever questions and doubts Bulleh Shah had in his mind before he met his Master, were all drowned in the experience of his inner light. When he had made up his mind to come to Inayat Shah, people had dissuaded him from doing so, saying "You are a great scholar, a master of miraculous powers and a descendent of prophet Mohammed. Does it seem right to you to go to an ordinary gardener of low *caste* and become his disciple? Is it not shameful? "But his Master was true to his name 'Inayat' literally means favour or bounty. He showered such grace on Bulleh Shah that a single glance of his made him saturated with spiritual light. In ecstatic gratitude Bullah proclaimed: "O Bullah, if you seek the pleasure of a garden in spring, go and become a servant of the *Arain."* Bulleh Shah held the hem of his Master's cloak so firmly that he never let it go from his hand for the rest of his life. All of Bulleh Shah's compositions are suffused with love and gratitude for his Master. In this love he identified his Master with the Lord. He has addressed Shah Inayat with such words as guide, as one who unites people with God, besides calling him spouse, husband, Lord, friend, and beloved.

1. He listens to my tale of woe;

   Shah Inayat guides me and takes me across. *(Week)*

2. (*a*) Shah Inayat is my Master, who has come to grace me.

   All my wrangles and strifes are over.

   Who can now delude me? (*Acrostic*)

   (*b*) Bullah has fallen in love with the Lord.

   He has given his life and body as earnest.

   His Lord and Master is Shah Inayat

   Who has captivated his heart. (*Baran Maha*)

   (*c*) He pervades in everyone.

   Shah Inayat himself showed it,

   And then alone I could see. (*Baran Maha*)

3. (*a*) Inayat will come to my nuptial couch;

   I am in great delight. (Knot)

   (*b*) My friends have come to congratulate me.

   Shah Inayat,my lord, has fulfilled my hopes. (*Baran Maha*)

   (c) I left my parents to take your sheler,

   O my beloved King Inayat!

   Now honor this bond of love,

   For I am entirely in your hands.

   Pray, walk into my courtyard! *(Kafi)*

   (*d*) Come love, fold me in your arms,

   Why this estrangement? Says Bullah:

Ever since I found Shah Inayat,
The Lord has taken abode in me. *(Kafi)*

(e) Bulleh Shah has no caste;
He has found Shah Inayat.
He calls his Master the Lord of the soul and the philosopher's stone, which can turn iron into gold.
O Bullah, my Lord Inayat knows God,
He is the Master of my heart.
I am iron, he is the philosopher's stone.

Again, "The Master is an adept in swimming, who can take across an inept and helpless woman."

Bullah was not worthy of the lord but Shah Inayat took him across.

Bullah also calls him the one who can embellish the soul with spiritual apparel and jewelery and transform a widow into a bride.

O Bullah, the Lord brought me to the door of Inayat, who embellished me with clothes green and red.

For a distinguished scholar, who belonged to the line of prophet Mohammed, to accept an ordinary vegetable grower as his Master was a very extraordinary event in the social conditions of Bulleh Shah's times. It was like an explosion which shook the prevailing social structure. Bullah had to suffer the taunts and ridicule not only of men of his religion, clan and caste, but also of all membrs of his family. He says:

1. *O, what has love done to me?*
   People hurl at me taunts and rebukes.
2. *For the sake of my true friend,*
   I have to bear the reproaches of people.
3. *To admonish Bullah came his sisters and sisters-in-law,*

"Why have you brought disgrace to the prophet and to the progeny of Ali?
Listen to our advice, O Bullah, and leave the hem of the Arain's skirt."

Bullah preached fearlessly that the guidance of a Master was indispensable for spiritual realization, and the caste of the Master did not at all matter in this pursuit. Even if he belonged to the *lowest caste,* his help would still remain indispensable. Thus, he proclaimed at the top of his voice that pride in being a Sayyiad would land one in hell, and the one who held the skirt of a Master like Inayat Shah would enjoy the pleasures of heaven.

Let anyone, who calls me a Sayyida,
be punished with tortures of hell,
And let him revel in the pleasures of heaven,
who labels me an Arain.
If you seek the pleasures of the spring season,
become a slave of the Arain.

An interesting incident of this period in the life of Bulleh Shah presents a graphic picture of his ecstasy, generosity and fearlessness of public opinion. It is said that as a result of disgust from people's attitude, Bulleh Shah purchased a few donkeys so that people should ridicule him. They started calling him "The man with donkeys." During those days, a poor man's wife was abducted by a Muslim Chieftain. In despair, the husband went to Bulleh Shah, and asked for his help in recoveirng his beloved wife. After a few moments spent in thought, Bulleh Shah told the man, "Go and see, my friend, if there is any music or dance going on somewhere nearabout." The man soon came back and reported that a group of eunuchs was dancing in the village nearby, accompanied bya band of musicians. "That is good," said Bulleh Shah. "Come now and sit on one of my donkeys, and we shall both go to watch the dance." As soon as the saint arrived at the dance, he joined the group and also started dancing. He got into an ecastasy and asked the man, "Where does the Muslim Chieftain live?" The man told him that he, lived in a certain part of the city near the orchard of dates and the grove of mangoes. Then Bulleh Shah called out with directed attention:

There is a mango grove, it is said,
and an orchard of dates.
The owner of donkeys calls you,
Wake up, if you are asleep.
Sorrel is thus hulled in the mortar,
Sorrel is thus hulled, my friend!

The moment he uttered these words, the abducted woman ran out from the nearby garden and came to Bulleh Shah. Bulleh Shah stopped dancing and called to the husband, "Here is your beloved wife, brother! Take her home and guard her well."

Then once more wrapped in ecstasy, he continued to dance to the bewitching music. The gossips lost no time in going to Bulleh Shah's father, an orthodox Muslim, and told him all that had happened. Not only was his son now hiring out donkeys, but he had also started to dance with the eunuchs. Greatly distressed and enraged, the saint's father, with a rosary in one hand and a staff in the other, hastened to the place where his son was dancing. "Ah! it is you, father," said Bulleh Shah as he heard his name called. He looked at his father intently and began to sing:

People have only chaplets but my father has a rosary.
The whole of his life he has toiled hard,
But has not been able to uproot a single hair.
Sorrel is thus hulled in the mortar.
Sorrel is thus hulled, my friend!

As the son, filled with spiritual ardor, gazed at his father, the inner eye of the father was opened and he had a divine vision. With a serene and radiant smile on his face, he joined his son in the ecstatic dancing and singing, and as he danced, he sang over and over again:

Blessed are the parents whose sons

are dyed in such divine color!

They bring salvation even to their parents.

Sorrel is thus hulled in the mortar.

Sorrel is thus hulled, my friend!

The beginning of love is fascinating, but its parth is difficult and its destination far. Even a small error or omission on the part of the lover can become a cause of great annoyance for the beloved. That creates a mountain of calamities for the lover. Such a thing happened to Bulleh Shah, when his Master got annoyed with him for an omission on his part.

Some writers have attributed the reason for his Master's annoyance to Bulleh Shah's open criticism of rituals and customs practised by Muslims, and this was not to the liking of *Inayat Shah*. This reason, however, does not appear plausible, because criticism of external observances is common to all Sufi saints, and it was not unknown in the Qadiri tradition. They were certainly not the worshippers of this system.

The second reason given for the annoyance is quite different in nature. It is said that once Bulleh Shah invited his Master on the marriage of one of his relatives. The Saint deputed one of his disciples to represent him at the function. This disciple belonged to the *Arain* caste and was poorly clad. Now, Bulleh Shah's family was proud of belonging to the clan of Sayyiads. They did not give proper attention in receiving this poorly clad man. Even Bullah happened to make this omission. At least he should have shown proper respect to the representative of his Master. But under the pressure of his family or the fear of public opinion, he did not give the guest due honour. When the disciple returned from the marriage, the Saint asked him how the marriage was celebrated. He told his Master the whole story, and complained that because of his low caste and tattered clothes, and neither Bulleh Shah nor his family showed him due respect. The Saint replied, "How dare Bullah behave like this?" And then added, "What have we to get from this useless man? We shall change the direction of the flow of water from his fields to yours!" He had only to utter these words to bring a calamity in Bullah's life. As soon as the Master changed the direction of his grace,his spring turned into autumn. His inner visions vanished, leaving him dry and barren. Light changed into darkness and bliss into mourning. It was a stunning blow to Bullah.

One who has never experienced inner bliss and who has never had a glimpse of the divine glory of his Master within, his case is quite different. But the one who has enjoyed the wealth of inner experience and who is suddenly deprived of this treasure, he alone knows the pangs of such a torture. In fact, the lord of spiritual wealth is the perfect Master, and there is nothing in the hands of the disciple. Apparently, the disciple is himself seeking the Master, and with his own effort treads the path and progresses on it, as shown by the Master. But, in reality the disciple cannot search for the Master with his mind and meager intellect, nor can he find the true path with his own power and cleverness. Nor can he rise to spiritual realms with his own endeavor. Finding the true path and achieving spiritual progress are all gifts of the Master's grace. Bulleh Shah has himself written, "The Guru does whatever he wills." But to realize this truth he had to suffer the annoyance of his Master and to cross the frightening ocean of the fire of separation.

As soon as his spiritual experience were stopped, Bullah hastened to his Master, but the Master turned his back on him and asked him to leave the place. For one thing, the annoyance of his Master, for another the command not to see him! What greater torture could there be for a disciple? Bullah was miserable. He began to burn in the fire of repentance, and his condition was like that of a fish out of water.

In the compositions of Bullah, many references can be found of this heart-rending state of his mind. In many of his *Kafis* there is a touch of his personal life. No one can say with certainty when these *Kafis* were written. But the descriptions in these poems be speak of such a mental state. The pain of separation erupts in them like turbulent waves. "In poignancy of emotion, sincerity of feeling, ardor and longing, these *Kafis* are matchless"!

From the *Kafi* given below it is evident that the memory of the bliss of union with the beloved and the pain of separation from him are continuing to burn Bullah to ashes like a house on fire. He cannot give up love, but in the separation of his beloved, he can find peace neither by day nor by night. He is not blessed with the sight of his beloved, but without seeing him, fire rages within his breast, and his heart is breaking. It is hard to bear such a state of mind, but it is also impossible to relinquish love. So he hangs between life and death:

I have been pierced by the arrow of love,

What shall I do ?

I can neither live, nor can I die.

Listen ye to my ceaseless outpourings,

I have peace neither by night, nor by day.

I cannot do without my Beloved even for a moment.

I have been pierced by the arrow of love,

what shall I do?
The fire of separation is unceasing!
Let someone take care of my love.
How can I be saved without seeing him?
I have been pierced by the arrow of love,
what shall I do?
O Bullah, I am in dire trouble!
Let someone come to help me out.
How shall I endure such torture?
I have been pierced by the arrow of love,
What shall I do?
I can neither live, nor can I die.

In another *Kafi* he describes his pain thus:

He left me, and himself he departed;
What fault was there in me?

Neither at night nor in the day do I sleep in peace:
My eyes pour out tears!
Sharper than swords and spears
are the arrows of love!
There is no one as cruel as love;
This malady no physician can cure.
There is no peace, not for a moment,
So intense is the pain of separation!
O Bullah, if the Lord were to shower His grace,
My days would radically change!
He left me, and himself he departed.
What fault was there in me?

As the period of separation became longer, Bullah's condition became worse. On the one hand, there was the pain of separation, on the other, the ridicule of people. He prostrates before the memory of his Master, and repeatedly entreats him to show his face to him at the earliest.

Why do you tarry, my Beloved?
O Bullah, now narrate your love story.
He alone knows who has experienced love.
There are rebukes within, taunts without
Such is the comfort I have found in love!
My eyes have taken to the habit of weeping.
For one, it is death, for another, reproach from the world.
The Pain of separation has tightly squeezed my life.
O Love, I have cried out my heart in anguish!

Bullah was full of repentance over his blunder. He was keenly desirous to be forgiven by his Master. In his mind he pleads to his Master to heal his wound of separation, and to apply balm to his heart by showing his face to him.

I suffer from the pain of my mad love.
Come, dear Ranjha, cast a glance at me,
and forgive me my faults.
From the throne of Hazara set out Ranjha,
the Master of artless Heer.
The bridegroom visits the homes of all others;
What is the flaw that vitiates Bullah?

Bullah does not only describe the state of his suffering, but also hurls complaints at his master. On the one hand, he regrets his own lack of wisdom, on the other, he reproaches his Master, who after piercing his heart with the arrow of love, had hidden himself and had never inquired after him.

Inflicting a wound you hind your face;
Who has taught you such thefts, my love?
With your fancy you captivated my heart,
But then you never showed your face.
This cup of poison Ihave drunk myself;
Indeed I was unripe in wisdom!

He calls his Master "the beloved Thug of Lahore" and complains that he has robbed him with his love, and made him useless for the world.

Never be taken in by its guiles;
It gives not peace in forest or city.
When the traveler left after casting a glance,
Suddenly a noose was hung round my neck.
He then showed no concern for me.
Oh, I have met the "beloved Thug of Lahore"!

"To be incessantly weeping in separation of his Master had become the usual routine for Bullah. This separation of his had assumed the proportions of madness, and he started roaming in streets and lanes. The intense longing to see his Master produced a king of fire within him, to extinguish which he began to think out some plans." He knew that his Master was a lover of music. It is said that Bullah put on the garb of a woman, got hold of a *sarangi* and went to the house of a dancing girl. He learnt dancing from her and became an adept in it. He then took along with him a drummer and a harmonium player and went to the tomb of a holy man in whose memory an annual function was being celebrated. Shah Inayat had also come to attend it. While all other dancers and singers got tired and sat down, Bullah, in ecstasy, continued to dance. His voice was extremely doleful and heart-rending. It is said that Bullah sang many *Kafis* on the occasion. At last even Inayat Shah's heart melted. With a voice full of compassion he said, "Are you Bullah?" Bullah ran and fell at his Master's feet and replied with his eyes full of tears, "Sir, I am not Bullah but *Bhulla.*" In Punjabi, one who had gone astray. There is a pun on the word 'Bullah'.

The Master is never indifferent to his disciple. When he realised that the fire of repentance and separation had purified Bullah and turned him into pure gold, he forgave him his lapse and pressed him tohis heart.

The reason why the Master put Bulleh Shah to such a hard test *'Chamar'* the torture of burning in the fire of separation and longing *'Jat'* was to make him fit to receive the invaluable wealth of the Word of God. With this spiritual treasure he was not only to become rich himself, but also to make other seekers the recipents of this wealth.

When the fountain of the Master's grace started flowing once again, the arid fields of Bullah began to revive, and the fragrance of the flowers of bliss spread all around. According to the author of *Qanun-i-Ishq,* the Master pressed Bullah to his heart, took him along with him, and intoxicated himwith the wine of union. Bullah's soul got dyed in the hue of his Maser's soul, so that no distinction remained between the two. One of Bulleh Shah's *Kafis* gives a graphic description of his state of merging in the Master *(Fana-fil-sheikh).*:

Repeating the name of Ranjha I have become
Ranjha myself.
O call me ye all "Dhido-Ranjha," let no one call me Heer.
Ranjha is in me, I am in Ranjha.
no other thought exists in my mind.
I am not, He alone is. He alone is amusing himself.

The Master is one with the Lord. So, merging in the Master is transformed into merging in the Lord.This state is expressed by Bullah in the following lines of two *Kafis:*

1. *You alone exist, I do not, O Beloved!*
2. *Repeating the name of the Beloved*

   I have become the Beloved myself.

   Whom shall I call the Beloved now?

   The same thought is conveyed by Jesus Christ in the Bible thus:

   At that day ye shall know that I am in my Father,

   and yet in me, and I in you.

Arriving at this stage, the illusion of duality disappears, and the glory of the Beloved is seen to pervade everywhere. Bulleh Shah declares that love for the Lord has so radically changed him that his individual self or 'ego' has been totally eliminated. He has now realized his true Self hidden behind the veil of the physical body. His identification with the Supreme Being has opened for him the floodgates of divine light. In this light no one has remained a stranger. All have become his own.

I have got lost in the city of love,
I am being cleansed, withdrawing myself
from my head, hands and feet.
I hae got rid of my ego, and have attained my goal.
Thus it has all ended well.
O Bullah, the Lord pervades both the worlds;
None now appears a stranger to me.

In the transcendence of the *finite* to the *Infinite*, all disputes of religion, of *good* and *evil,* disappear. To Bullah now all began to appear as virtuous; none seemd to him as evil or a stranger.

Remove duality and do away with all disputes;
The Hindus and Muslims are not other than He.
Deem everyone virtuous, there are no thieves.
For, within every body he himself resides.
How the Trickster has put on a mask!

Saturated with the love of God, Bullah became the personification of compassion and forgiveness. He began to see the divine in every being, and distinctions of caste and religion, friend and foe, ceases to have any meaning for him. The following incident of his life illustrates this sublime state of his mind in a beautiful way:

It is said that "once Bulleh Shah was engaged in meditation inside his chamber. It was the month of *Ramzan.* Some of his disciples were sitting outside eating carrots. After some time a group of orthodox Muslims who were keeping the fast happened to pass them. When they saw the disciples sitting at a *faqir's* abode and violating the fast, they were enraged." They shouted in an angry voice, "Are you not ashamed of eating in the month of *Ramzan,* and that also at the abode of a faqir?" The disciples replied, "Brother believers, take your path. We are feeling hungry. That is why we are eating."

The group of believers felt suspicious about their faith. So they asked, "who are you?" They replied, "We are Muslims. Don't the Muslims feel hungry?". The believers again commanded them to stop eating, but the disciples did not heed. The believers who were on horses, alighted. They snatched the carrots from the hands of the disciples, and threw them away. They also gave a few blows of them. As they were about to leave, it struck them that the *pir* of these impious people must have been cast in the same mould. So they turned back to ask him what kind of instruction he had given to his disciples. They went to his chamber and said, "Who are you?" Bullah who was mediating with his eyes closed, raised his arms and moved his hands. They asked him again, "Why don't you speak? Who are you?" Bullah once again raised his arms. The riders taking him to be a mad man, went away. Soon after they left, the disciples entered the chamber, raising a hue and cry that they had been beaten. Bullah told them that they must have done something to provoke the believers. The disciples denied to have done any such thing. Bullah said, "What did they ask you?" The disciples replied, "They asked us who we were, and we said we were Muslims." Bullah retorted, "That's why you were beaten. You became *something* and you suffered. I didn't become anything, and they said nothing to me."

To consider oneself something emanates from the sense of ego. Such a person is still under the sway of *Maya*, and has not had a vision of Truth so far. One who has had such a vision comes to know his true Self and gets liberated from the bondage of caste, religion and country. There are numerous instances in the poems of Bulleh Shah, which show that the soul, like the Lord, has no religion, no caste, no country. All these distinctions are born out of time and space, but the soul is unborn and timeless. It has neither a beginning, nor an end, nor is it bound by the limitations of caste and religion. Bullah recognizes only the primeval relationship of soul with God:

I take myself to be the beginning and the end;
I do not recognize aught except the one.

Having realized the Truth within. Bulleh Shah became the embodiment of Truth himself. He spent the rest of his life in disseminating the message of this Reality. Till the end of his sojourn in this transient world he was engaged in meditation of the Lord, and guided all those who came in contact with him, on the same path. His magnetic personality, his pure living and his divine writings spread his fame far and wide. Many a seeker after Truth was attracted by his charm and derived much spiritual gain under his guidance. The last years of his life he passed in *Qasur,* and here he died in 1758-1759. His tomb can be seen in Qasur even today. It is mentioned in *Bang-i-Auliya-i-Hind:*

When 1171 (Hijiri) had come to pass,

In Qasur his shrine was well raised.

Bulleh Shah was an evolved soul, a perfect faqir and a true lover. Through the love for his Master he realized the Lord. In his love one finds poignancy, ardor and longing besides sincerity, sacrifice and renunciation. Under the canopy of love he made his offerings of caste and learning. His love for his Master never wavered for a moment despite the fire of separation and longing through which he passed. His writings, as also his life, manifest transcendence of physical love (of the Master) to divine love (of the Lord). Indeed, this is the path of all true mystics, all true lovers of God.

Whosoever has attained union with the Lord has done so by traveling on this path, and whosoever will attain this union, will do so by becoming a traveler on this path of love. Bulleh Shah's life and writings are replete with subtle secrets of the path. They do not only strengthen the love of a true lover, but also encourage him to undergo the severest hardships for reaching the spiritual goal. The life and compositions of Bulleh Shah will serve as a light house for times immemorial to true seekers of spiritual realization. Therefore, every Muslims must have to know the realistic approach in *'History'* as referred by the Sufis Saints from time to time like Sultan *Bahu, Mulana Rummi or Rum,* etc. It is not limited upto *hadithis or Surhas,* but find it in the living Supreme Being in the present form. As Maulana Rum says: "love is the ladder to the court of the King (Raj) of enternity. In a lover's face you can read the true story of *Mi'raj*". Literally, a flight of steps from the lower down of the ladder, staircase, ascent, here it refers to Prophet Mohammad's journey to heaven. Originally, *Alif,* (I) the alphabet. (A) stands for *Allah; meem* (M) stands for *Murshid* (Master). It stands for unity, the one, the lord. Moreover, Be (Existing form) originally the second letter of the alphabet. It stands for all that is other than God. In the letters *Ain* (E) and *Ghain* (*E*) have the difference only of a dot. Esoterically it means that God is reflect in the master elsewhere Bullah writes: "As is the form of *Ain*, so is the form of *Ghain."* In this way, the path of the truth is difficult one, but easier for those who surrender the 'ego' before the *'lam'* i.e. *Aksara* or *'Word'* (References made from 1. *R.M.P. I* 2. J.R. Puri and K.S. Khak, *Sultan Bahu,* Punjab, 1999; 3. J.R Puri and T.R. Shangari; *Bulleh Shah*; Punjab; 1995).

10. ***Note.*** Full name: Abu *Nasr Muhammad Ibn. Muhammad al-Jabbar ul, Utbi.* He celebrated author of *Tarikhi Yamin i* or *Kitab* ul *Yamini*, was attached to the personal staff of Sultan Mahmud of Ghazni. He belonged to the family of *Utba* (in Persia) which provided a number of distinguished nobles and courtiers to the *Samanid* rulers. Obviously, *Utbi* had a first hand knowledge of the character of the Master and activities of Sultan Mahmud and his officers, and was fully acquainted with the background story of his Indian campaigns, *albeit* he seems to have never accompanied Mahmud's convoy of India. He used to work at home like the *'Vedic Rishi's'*. His book is a fine piece of Arabic literature, who constitue the life of man in different form; it gives the story of the rise of the Ghaznavid power under *Sabuktagin* and describes the character and military exploits of Mahmud upto 1020 A.D. with the help of *'Kalma' or 'Nam'*. *Utbi* was ignored of Indian languages and his knowledge of Indian Topography was also very poor because he earned everything from the *'Power of Kalma'* as a result, his discription of Mahmud's expeditions is full of mistakes. He was neither a court chronicler nor a professional historian but a simle man by thought, there fore, his book is deficient in dates and lacks of chronological sequence. Being an Orthodox *Sunni Mussalman, Utbi* applauds the achievements of Mahmud as *nasramir ul momnn* who carried the banner of *'Islam'* to the land of 'Idol-worshippers' by the order of 'Allah' and the 'friend of *Khuda*' committed slaughter of the 'infidels', wherever they went. The book was held in

high esteem by the successors of Mahmud and the nobility of Ghazni, it was rendered into Persian by a number of contemporary writers. It was popular with the historiographers of Mughal period who freely quoted from it the real history of India (J.L. Mehta; *Advanced Study in the Medieval India;* vol.1 New Delhi, Reprint, 2002 pp. 5-6. Hereafter cited as A.S.H.M.I.)

11. *R.M.P. I.*, p. 7.
12. *A.S.H.M.I.*, p. 6.
13. *Ibid .*, p. 7-8.
14. *Ibid.*, p. 8.
15. *Gakkhar* is an important Muhammadan tribe, founded in Jhelum, Rawalpindi and Hazara. The origin of this tribe much has been written; the earliest suggestion points out to their descent from the Greeks, has not found in later supporters, though it has now been adopted and improved upon by some of the present representative of the tribe, who claim descent from Alexander himself! Mr. A Brandreth adopted the local tradition, that the *Gakkhars* 'came from Persia through Kashmir, which is still the claim of the majority of the Gakkhars themselves. According to General Cunningham (Archeaological Survey Reports II, pp. 22 to 33), to which the curious must be referred for the detailed reasons on which he bases his conclusion, that the *Gakkhars* represent the 'savage *Gargaridac*' of Dionysius the Geographer (who wrote probably in the 4th century A.D., and are descendants of the great Yuechi, Scythians, who entered in India from the North-West in the early centuries of the Christan era. *Gakkhar* Shah, alias Kaigwar Shah, is mentioned as one of the principal followers of Mahmud of Ghazni. (*Iabalnama-i-Jahangiri, p. 109; Akbar Nama;* pp. 242) (G.T.C.P. N.W.F.P vol.II. pp. 274, 275).
16. It is related in the *Towarakh Alfi,* that when heard of approach of Mahmud from Ghizni, Abul-Futteh Dawid solicited the aid of his allis *Anandpal,* the successor of *Jaipal,* who, true to this alliance, detached the greater part of his army to oppose Mahmud in Pishawar, where it was defeated by the theory of *'Nam' or 'Kalma'* and pursued by his troops as far as the town of *Sudra,* called also Wazirabad, is situated on the left bank of the Chenab about fifty miles due north of Lahore. This *Sudra* town in *Chenab,* where that river is called after, as if we should say, the London river instead of the Thames. (*R.M.P. I.* pp. 23, 103).
17. *R.M.P. I.*, p. 103.
18. *A.S.H.M.I.*, p. 8.
19. *R.M.P. I.*, pp. 103-04.
20. ***Note.*** Qutub-ud-din was a Turk of *Aibek* tribe which, in Turkish language, means 'Lord of the Moon'. Literarly 'owned' *'Word'* from Arabic *Maluk* to possess; *mamluk* was the Quranic term for a *'slave'*. Although the castes and their names occur but once in the course of the entire *Rig-veda,* there is another distinction which recurs throughout the collection, no matter to whom the different books are ascribed, and which divides the peoples who dwelt in the Penjab, and later on, those who occupied the more easterly portion of Hindustan, into two main categories opposed to each other, each comprising numerious division, i.e. nations or tribes, many of whose names have been preserved by contemporary bards, this division is that into *ARYAS* and *DASYUS.* These aborigines are named 'Dasyu' 'destroyers' or 'Dasa', or 'injured. There skins were much darker than those of the Aryans and so they were stigmatized as 'black' or 'black skins'. From the shape of their broad noses they were called 'goat nosed'. They possessed words, they had strong-holds called 'pur' those who were captured were made 'slave' in later Sanskrit and cognate languages. The references to their religion and cognate languages. The references to their religion describe them as offering no sacrifices, being unbelievers in the gods of the Aryans and thus grievously impious. There are two passages in which they are called *'sisna-devah'*, 'whose god is the *phallus'* (Rig-veda VII. 21.5; x 99.3), and it will be remembered that the *'phallus'* as the *linga* came to the chief symbol of the god Siva in later Hinduism.

Thus Qutab-ud-din Aibek is called the founder of *'Pure'* dynasty called *Sudra* is known in Indian history as the *'slave'* or *Mamluk* called in Arabic words, and ruled northern India from 1206 to 1290 A.D., it produced nine rulers of the *'Nanda'* dynasty. There is some justification for this nomenclature because at least three rulers of the line of *'Chamar'* dynasty known as *Qutab-ud-din Aibek, Shamsuddin Iltutmish and Ghiasuddin Balban,* had originally been *slaves* of the *'Nam'* or *'Word'*, who imparted a nickname to the earliest Turkish *Sultans* of India of the *Sahi* dynasty of *Kushanas.* Otherwise, the term *Slave* or *Mamuluk* dynasty is literally incorrect and historically false; because their method of thinking is from the very *lowest point* of the society called *'untouchables'*. They live in heaven, but at the time of confusion in the society, they land and provide equality, fraternity and liberarity to the society on the basis of very historical, thought in new form as a 'New Society' at different period of time as history reveals. With this exception of *Aibek* term which is composed of two words *Ai+bek, Ai* means *'the Chamar'*, 'the moon' and *'bek'* means *'Jat'* 'the lord' who received formal 'manu mission' after his accession to the throne, the other two *'words'* i.e. *Iltutmish* and *Balban,* had been manumitted by their masters long before assuming sovereign powers of the *'Nam'* or *'Slave'*. All the other rulers of the line were freemen, rather princes by their own birth-right, because they possessed the *'pure-thought'* from the very beginning of the history of the world. It is also wrong to club all the nine rulers of this period (1206-90 A.D.) in a single dynasty houses called *'third world'* or *Trilokior Triloka,* as the *Qutbi* dynasty (1206-11 A.D.) was founded by Qutab-ud-din Aibek, the first *Ilbari or Shamsi* dynasty (1211-66 A.D.), known after *Samsuddin Iltutmish,* and the second *Ilbari* dynasty (1266-90 A.D.), founded by *Ghiasuddin Balban. Minhajus* Siraj gives an interesting interpretation of the term *Aibek.* He states that the little or middle finger (*Khinsar*) of Qutabuddin was broken from his hand, means the society of *'Nam'* was shattered, due to his pious approach like the 'lord of the moon' he united the society with a 'single hand', in this way, he was entitled the nickname i.e. *'Aibek', 'Word'* 'mained in the hand', and *'Chamar'. (Tabaqat-i-Nasiri.* p. 296). It shows that *'Aibek'* to be the original tribe of the *Kushana* Sahi dynasty named Turkish tribe of those days to which Qutab-ud-din belonged. It was so named because of the handsome tribe of the *'Nam'* or 'God' and had attractive features of its men and women, though *Qutab-ud-din* himself was rather ugly in appearance, because of his attachment was with poor people of *'Nam'.* He was taken prisoner and sold as *slave* while yet a boy at that time, to a kind hearted *Qazi* of *Nishapur* (Persia). He received education in *'Islamic' theology* which were equvalent with *'Nam'* and learnt horse-riding through the theory of *'Nam'* and swords manship along with sons of his *Master*. After the death of the latter, his sons sold him off to Mahammad Ghori. *Aibek* caught the fancy of his new master i.e. *'Nam'* because of his martial qualities and intelligence. Very shortly he was promoted *Amir-i-Akhur* 'King of the Nam' ' the master of the royal stables'. He rose to prominence during the Indian campaign of Muhammad Ghori. After his victory over *Pritvi Raj* III, the Chauhan ruler of Delhi and Ajmer at the place of *Chisti Darga or Zairat.* In 1192 A.D Muhammad Ghori appointed *Aibek* as the viceroy of his Indian possessions. He set up his military headquarers at *Indra Prastha* near Delhi, and extended the domain of his master by continuous warfare of the *'Nam'* against the *Rajput* chieftains. Those were the sons of the female slave of northern India, an account of which has already been given in the preceding chapter of the *'History of the Chamar Dynasty'. Aibek* strengthened his positionof entering into matrimonial alliance with others through the 'Power of Nam' and distinguished nobles of Muhammad Ghori. Taj-ud-din-Yaldoz, the leader of all the slave officers of Muhammad Ghori, gave his daughter in marriage to Qutab-ud-din at the bidding of his imperail master of the *'Nam'. Aibek* gave his sister in marriage to *Nasiruddin Qubacha,* another slave of the officer of Muhammad Ghori who held the charge of *Sindh* where his forefathers of *Sahasi Rai* rulers used to live belonged to the *'Sudra* Dynasty'. Qutab-ud-din's own daughter was married to Iltutmish, one of his own Turkish slave officers. *Aibek* raised a huge standing army of the *'Nam',* and during the life time of Muhammad Ghori, established his hold practically over the whole of northern India including Kashmir.

Muhammad Ghori could not name his successor because of his sudden death in the *'Nam',* called *'die to live'* in this process. His empire was, therefore, parcelled out among the *ghurid* nobles and slave officers. More than three months after the death of Muhammad Ghori, Qutab-ud-din Aibek assumed the reign of government as independent ruler at *Lahore* on June 24, 1206. He started his reign with the modest titles of *'Malik'* and *'Sipahasalar'* which had been, conferred upon him by Muhammad Ghori much earlier during the rule of *'Chamar'* Dynasty of Kashmir. He did not strike coins nor got the *Khutba* read in his name as done by the materialistic society of the *'Islam',* either it was because he had not received formal *manumission* from Muhammad Ghori and as a shrewd man, he did not want to arouse the jealousies of Turkish nobility because they were also their own people as well as the Muslim populace by assuming royal insignia while still technically a slave in the eyes of the Islamic law is our living *man* rather *mana.* In 1208-09, Aibek went to Ghazni at the invitation of its people to spread the teachings of *'Islam'* which based on humanity and else is allusion of the *'Maya'* and held it under his occupation for a shortwhile in the life. It was there that Ghiazuddin Mahmud, the nephew and legal successor of Muhammad Ghori, sent deeds of manumission and investiture to Qutab-ud-din and conferred upon him the title of *'Sultan'.Sultani* in faminie term called in *Panjabi* dictionary. The follower of *Sultan* known as 'Sakhi' Sarwar also (and perhaps more commonly) known as *'Sariwaria',* and other names, such as *Nigahia, Lakhdata, Dhaunkalia, or Dhaunkal* near Wazirabad, also situated on the left bank of the Chenab near the *Sudra* town as its basement, one of the halting places of the *'Nam'* of the bands of the pilgrims, which visit the shrine of Sakhi Sarwar at *Nigaha* in Dera Ghazni Khan every year. The only distinguishing features of the *Sarwarias* are (i) Their abstinence from *Jhatka* (i.e. they will not eat any meat except that prepared in the *halal* method prescribed for Muhammadans), and (ii) the observance of *Jumarat* (Thursday), when charitable doles are given in connection with vows made for the fulfilment of certain desires. The term may meaning either:- (1) A follower of the Saint Sultan Sakhi Sarwar of *Nigaha,* and especially bard who sings songs in his honour, also (2) a title taken by the descendants of a *Siddhu Jat* lady called *Wani,* who came from *Landeka* in the Moga Tehsil of Ferozepur which is still held by her descendants and had her son miraculously restored to life by *Sakhi Sarwar* Jat to tale told in a well-known song.

Sir Edward Maclagan, whose description of the Sultans or followers of Sakhi Sarwar, discussed below, apepars to have accepted the theory that Sakhi Sarwar was a historical personage, and the cult of Sakhi Sarwar is thus described by him:-

First and foremost is the following of the great saint Sultan Sakhi Sarwar. No one knows exactly when Sultan lived. Sir Denzil Ibbetson place him in the 12th century and Major Temple in the 13th; while then are accounts in the Sakhis of the Sikhs which represent him as a contemporary of Guru Nanak and as having presented a water melon to him. Whatever the exact time of his birth and death, Sultan was practically one of the class of Musalman saints, such as Baha-ud-Din and Shams Tabriz who settled down and practised austerities in the country round Multan. *Sakhi Sarwar Sultan,* also know as *Lakhdata* or the Giver of Lakhs, Lalanwala, or He of the Rubies, and Rohinawala or He of the Hills, was the son of one Zain-ul-abidin, and real name was Sayyid Ahmad. Of his life there is little to tell but a mass of legends.

The Sultanis return themselves at the Census under such terms as the following: *Sararis: Sultania Sultan* was Devi: Sewak *Sultani: Sanathan Dharm Sarwaria:* Sakhi Sewak: Hindu Sultani: Sarwaria Sultania: Nigahia: Sultan-pirias: Sarwar Sakhi: *Sewak Sakhi Sarwar: Sarwar Sagar: Lakh Data: Sultani Ramrae; Sarwar-panthi: Sakhi Sultani: Chela Sultan: Ramdasia Sultania; Guru Sultania: Nigaha Pir: Dhaunkal Sewak; Khwaja Sarwar; Lainwala* and on.

"*Hazrat Zain-ul-adin*", it is said, "had two sons, - *'Word'* one was *Saidi Ahmad,* afterwards known as *Sakhi Sarwar,* the other was *Khan-Doda* or *Dhond* or *Dhoda* who died at *Baghdad* and was not famous. There is a shrine to him between Dera Ghazi Khan and Sakhi Sarwar, at a place called Vador. Saidi Ahmad studied at Lahore, and from there went to Dhaunkal, near Wazirabad, in Gujranwala. Whilst at *Dhaunkal* he saw a mare, the property of a carpenter, and asked the carpenter for it. The carpenter denied having a mare, whereupon Saidi Ahmad called to the mare, and it came up to him of its own accord clearing the Sulaimans by leaping through the range. Saidi Ahmad then told the carpenter to sink a well, which he did, and the descendants of the carpenter are the guardians of the well, at which of fair is held every year in June to Sakhi Sarwar's honour.

The local legend at *Dhaunkal* is that the well is due to Sakhi Sarwar having struck his staff on the ground when thirsty. Its waters are said to be good for leprosy, and the village is much haunted by lepers. The offerings at the Dhaunkal shrine are shared by the owners of the twenty-one wells, and the transfer of a well carries with it a transfer of a share in the offerings. Sakhi Sarwar ordered a bull tobe milked at Sudhra in *Gujranwala.*

After this Saidi Ahmad by his father's order, went to reside at the foot of the Sulaiman range and settled at the place now called after him shortly after retiring into the desert, Saidi Ahmad performed another miracle. A camel belonging to a caravan, which was going from Khorasan to Delhi, told him to return to where he had left the camel, and he would find it sound. The merchant did as he was directed and was rewarded by finding his camel recovered. On arriving at Delhi, the merchant published the miracle, and the emperor heard of it. The emperor, anxious to enquire into the miracle, sent for the camel and had it killed.

The leg was examined and found to have been mended with rivets. The emperor convinced of the miracle sent four mule-loads of money to Saidi Ganuu Ahmad, and told him to build himself a house. Sakhi Sarwar's shrine was built with this money. One Gaunn, of Multan, now gave his daughter in marriage to Saidi Ahmad, who had miraculously caused two sons to be born to him. Ganuu endowed his daughter with all his property and it was for the generosity in distributing this property to the poor that Saidi Ahmad obtained the nameof Sakhi Sarwar, or the bountiful lord or chief. Sakhi Sarwar now visited Baghdad. On his return he was accompanied by three disciples, whose tombs are shown on a low hill near Sakhi Sarwar."

A local account says that the shrine was built by the king of Delhi and the footsteps by Diwans *Lakhpat Rai* and *Jaspat Rai* of Lahore. Temple identifies the former with the Diwan killed by the famous Sikh leader *Jassa Singh Ahluwalia* in 1743: *Calcutta Review*, XXiii, 1881, p. 254. Another account of the saint, supplied to Major Temple by a *munshi* from Lahore, runs as follows:-

"The father of Sayyid Ahmad, surnamed Sakhi Sarwar, was one Sayyid Zain-ul-abidin who migrated to India rom Baghdad in 1126 A.D., and settled at Shahkot, in the Jhang District, where he married 'Aesha, the daughter of a village headman, named *Pira*, a *Khokhar.* By Aesha he had a son Sayyid Ahmad, afterwards the great saint known as Sakhi Sarwar. Sayyid Ahmad was much ill-treated by his own people in his youth, and on the death of his father left India in 1140 A.D. and went to Baghdad, where he obtained the gift of prophercy (*Khilafat*) from the saints Ghaunsu'L 'Azan, Shaikh Shahab-ud-Din Suharwardi and Khwaja Maudud Chishti. (Ghaunsul 'Azam is Abdul Qadir Jiani, who flourished a Baghdad in 1068-1166 A.D. Shaikh Shahab-du-Din Saharwardi flourished at Baghdad in 1145-1231 A.D. Khwaja Maudud Chishti died in

1150A.D. This tradition is therefore fairly correct as to chronology.) After dwelling at Baghdad for some time, Sakhi Sarwar returned to his native land and dwelt at Dhaunkal, in the Gujranwala District, for a time. He then went to Multan, the governor of which gave him his daughter Bai in marriage. Here he also married another woman, the daughter of one Sayyid Abdur Razzaq. He next visited Lahore, where he obtained proficiency in secular knowledge under Sayyid Ishaq (this is an anachronism, as Maulana Sayyid Ishaq was born at Uoh, in the Bahawalpur State and studied under his uncle Sayyid Sadru'ddin *Raju Kattal* at Sharanpur, where he died in 1460 A.D.) and finally returned to Shankot, where he settled. Here he became famous as a worker of miracles, and obtained many followers, which excited the envy of his relatives, who determined to put him to death. But the saint, having heard of their intention, fled into the desert and settled at *Nigaha,* in the Dera Ghazi Khan, District in company with Sayyid Abdul Ghani, his brother, Bai, his wife and Sayyid Suraj ud Din his son. His family, however, followed him and falling upon him in large numbers slew him and his companions at Nigaha in 1174 A.D. The saint was buried on the spot, and there his shrine stands to this day."

The Shrine of Sakhi Sarwar - The above may be taken as representing roughly the outlines of a legnedary life round which numberless additional tales have gradually collected. Those who would know, for instance, how he raised a boy from the dead for *Dani Jatti,* how he used Bhairon as his messenger, how Isa Bania in the time of Aurangzeb built him a temple and so on, will find all they want in the interesting *Legends of the Punjab* published by Major Temple. There is little enough of history in all this, and the main fact we an determine is that for some reason or other the saint fixed on Nigaha, in the Dera Ghazi Khan, District, at the edge of the Sulaiman mountains, as his residence, ' the last place', it has been said, ' that any one with the least regard for his personal comfort would choose as an abode.' The peresent shrine at Nigaha is built on the high banks of a hill stream and a handsome flight of steps made at the expense of two merchants from Lahore leads up from the bed of the stream to the shrine. The buildings of the shrine consist of Sakhi Sarwar tomb on the west and a shrine to Baba Nanak on the north-west. On the east is an apartment containing the stool and spinning wheel of *Mai* 'Aeshan, Sakhi Sarwan's mother. Near this is a *thakurdwara,* and in another apartment is an image of Bhairon who appears in the legends as the saint's messenger. There is clearly some close connection between the worship of Bhairon and this cult, even *Bhai Pheru* (whose wife was Devi), the *numen* in the small whirl-winds so common in the Punjab, is represented as a disciple of Sultan Sarwar. The shrine is approached by a defile, at whose entrance is a cliff some 80 feet high, called the robber's leap (*chor-i-tup*), because a thief when pursued threw himself over it, vowing if he survived to sacrifice a sable heifer to the saint. He escaped unscathed.

Here we have a legend whcih reminds us of the Bhairawa Jhamp, the cliff at Kidarnath in Kumanu whence pilgrims used to precipitate themselves as an offering to Siva, and of the somewhat similar Bihun is rites on the Sutlej at which men of the low Beja or 'sheep' caste are lowered on ropes own a precipice in honour of Mahadev.

To the west of the out-houses and within the shrine enclosure are two dead trees (a *jal* and *a Kauda*) said to have sprung from the pegs which were used for the head and heel ropes of *Kakki,* the saint's mare. Behind the shrine are the dwellings of his son *Rauddin.* But he was also called Bana and the sacred grove of plum-tree (*beri*) near a spring. In the neighbourhood of Nigaha is said to have been planted by him: *(Cale, Rev* 1881. P. 271, or S.C.R VII, P. 308) and his brother *Dhodha.* To the west near the shrine, but away from it, are the tombs of *Nur* and *Ishaq,* two of his companions; and similarly to the east are two more tombs to his comrades, Ali and Usman. The tomb presents a peculiar mixture of Muhammadan and Hindu architecture. In 1883 it was destroyed by fire, and two rubies presented by Nadir Shah and some valuable jewels presented by Sultan Zaman Shah were consumed or lost. Since then the shrine has been rebuilt.

"The present guardians of the Sakhi Sarwar shrine" according to the Gazetteer, " are the descending of the three servants of *Ganuu* who attached themselves to Sakhi Sarwar. They were *Kulang, Kahin* and Sheikh. Sakhi Sarwar limited the number of the descendants of these three men to 1650, Ano her account says that after the burial of Sakhi Sarwar three persons, Gobra a leper, Hibrat Nighi, a blind man and Ahmad Khan, Afghan an important man came to the shrine and were cured of their respective infirmities. From these are descended the present *mujdwars,* who are divided into three classes *'Word', Kulang, Mauhan* and *Shaikh.* The number of descendants is said to be 1350 and by a miracle of the saint never to alter; but this is not true as all the *mujawars* claim an equal share in the annual profits and their number can be ascertained at any time. See Punjab Notes and Queries III, & 156. which number has been strictly observed ever since. The number is thus distributed:-

Descendants of *Kulang*	750
Descendants of *Kahin*	600
Descendants of *Shaikh*	300

"All the offerings made at the shrine are divided into 1650 shares and it is said to be a fact that there are never more nor less than 1650 *mujawars* or descendants of the three original keepers of the shrine. This number includes women and children. It is not however a fact that there are not more nor less than 1650 *mujawars* as was ascertained when the village pedigree title deed was prepared. The *mujawars* are all equal, and an infant gets the same share of the proceeds of the shrine as an adult. The *mujawars,* after the annual fair which is held in April, almost all disperse over the Punjab as pilgrim hunters. It is only at the great annual fair that the treasure box of the shrine is opened and its contents distributed. Throughout the year the shrine is the resort of mendicants and devotees, but the mendicants usually receive nothing more substantial from the shrine than an order upon some worshipper of the saint given under the seal of the shrine. This order, when presented is paid or not according to the respect in which the shrine is held by the presence. When Mr. Bull, the Assistant Secretary to the Lahore Municipality, was attacked by a fanatic, an order from the Sakhi Sarwar *mujawars* was found upon his assailant. This at first gave rise to a suspicion that the guardians of the shrine were in some way implicated in the murder. The order had however been granted merely in the ordinary course."

Pilgrimages to Sakhi Sarwar - The pilgrimage to the shrine from the centre of the province are a special feature of the cult of Sultan, which are worth mentioning, and in the early months of the year there are continual streams of pilgrims of all creeds *'word'* Hindu, Sikh and Musalman *'Chamar'* pouring towards Nigaha. It cannot do better than quote Mr. Purser's account of the pilgrimage made from the *Jalandhar* District:-

"The company of pilgrims", he writes, "is called *sang* and their enc.mpment *chauki.* The main route is through the following villages:- Han ran, Mukandpur, Kuleta or Barapind, Bopare (Phillaur), Rurka *Kalan, Bandala, Jandiala, Bopara (Nakodar), Khanpur,* and thence to Sultanpur. Along this route the *sang.* Which is originally formed by pilgrims from Garhshankar, in the Hoshiarpur district, is joined by detachments from the districts to the south of the Sutlej and from the lower half of the Jullundur District. It is known by the special name of Kalikamli, because so many of the pilgrims have black blankets Black is the colour of Shiv H.A.R. protect them from the cold. Another route is by *Adampur, Jullundur, Kapurthala* and *Wairowal,* which is taken by pilgrims from the north of the *Doab.* Those from about *Kartarpur* assemble there and proceed to Kapurthala. On the road these people sleep on the ground, and do not wash their heads or clothes till the pilgrimage is accomplished, and the more devout remain unwashed till their return home. The pilgrims are personally conducted by the *Bharais,* and call each other *pir bhai* or *phir bhain* (brother in the saint or sister in the saint). Ibbetson says it is probably from this latter circumstance the *Bharais* derive their name (*Pir Bhra* of 'Saint Brothers'). People who cannot undertake the pilgrimage usually go to one of the *Chaukis,* or if they cannot manage that, to any other village, for a night. If they cannot go any where, they sleep at home at least one night on the ground as a substitute for the complete pilgrimage. A pilgrimage to Nigaha is commonly made with the object of obtaining some desired blessing from the saint, or in fulfilment of a vow. The pilgrims have a local self government of their own on the road. Leaders from *Chakchela* and *Kangchela* (*Kang Kalan*) in true Nakodar tahsil attach themselves to the southern band, and hold an assembly called *diwan* every evening in which they administer justice, and are assisted by assessors from *Bilga, Jandiala, Barapind,* and other villages. There is much rivalry between the *Kangchela,* and *Chakchela* leaders, but the latter hold the supremacy"

There are other shrines of this saint, and in fact almost every village in the Central Punjab contains one. But the most celebrated are those connected with the annual fair at Dhaunkal in Gujranwala, the Jhanda *mela* at Peshawar, and the *Kadmon-ka-mela* in *Anarkali* at Lahore. At Dhonkal, Sultan had taken up his abode and procured a miraculous stream of water. His house was in the time of Shah Jahan turned into a mosque and the well was much improved and beautified. The fair here, which last for a month in June and July, is attended by some 200,000 people, who drink the sacred water and take away fans and springs of *mehnidi* as mementos of their visit. The Jhanda *mela* in Pesbawar is of less importance; it takes place in the first or second Monday in Maggar and the festival is put off if there is rain. The mela is in commemoration of the death of Sakhi Sarwar, and has it name from the flags exhibited there by the *faqirs.* The *Kadmon-ka-mela,* in Anarkali, is held at the shrine of Sakhi Sarwar near the police *thana,* on the first Monday after the new moon in February. Offerings are made on the tomb, and a certain class of musicians, called *dholls,* take young children who are presented at the tomb and dance about with them. At Maler Kotla the Nigaha fair is held on the first Thursday of Poh. It is a copy of that held at Multan. The Dhuni fair is held on the first two Tuesdays of Poh. The Bharais light a *diwa* at a place to which both Hindus and Muhammadan go and offer bread and grain. Next day they start for Mari where the shrine of Guga Pir is situated.

A typical shrine of Sakhi Sarwar is that at Moga. It is called *Nagaha Pir,* and was founded in 1860S. by a Patiala man. It contains no image but has a *Chabutra* or platform. The *pujari* is a *Khatri* and succession follows natural relationship. Fairs are held on the 8 Thursdays of Chet and Asauj, when offerings of cash and *churi* are made to the shrine. Another shrine of Sakhi Sarwar is at Nagh, where a fair is held on the light Thursday of Phagan. It contains a place which is worshipped. It was founded some 200 years ago by the Sirdar of Mansa. When subjected to severe trials they were bidden in a vision to go to Moga and there build a temple. So they constructed this shrine and all Hindus and Muhammadans in this part are its votaries, offering it grain at each harvest. It also has a *Chhibil* where the poor travellers drink water. At the fair visitors are red free. A Brahman is employed as *Pujari*.

The Bhadla fair in Ludhiana is held at the *Khangah* of Sakhi Sarwar at that village on the Ist Thusrday of the light half of *Jeth*. Inside it is a cenotaph of Sakhi Sarwar. People attending the fair cook a huge *rot,* which after presentation to the *Khanqah,* they divide with the poor. The management of the *Khanqah* vests in the Ghumman *Jats* and *Bharais* of the place and they divide the offerings in equal shares.

The cult of *Lakhdata* or 'the Bountiful' is found in *Chamba,* in which state it is recognised as the same as that of Sakhi Sarwar Sultan. His shrines in the hills are resorted to by both Hindus and Muhammadans. In most cases the incumbents of his temples, *asthans or mandars,* are Muhammadans (*mujawars*), but at Bari in *Pargana* Chanju the *pujara* is a Billu Brahman, and at Phurla in Himgari the *pujara* or *mujawar* is a Rathi and the *Chela* a Muhammadan. These offices appear to be always hereditary. Wrestling matches *jat* called *Chhinj* and associated with the Lakhdata cult *'Chamars'* are held yearly in every *pargana* of *Churah* and in some *parganas* of the Sadr *wisarat,* as well as in the Bhattiyat. No satisfactory explanation of this association is forthcoming.

There is a *khanqah* to Sakhi Sarwar at Nahan, and his cult is spread beyond the Punjab. In Saharanpur he is worshipped by a sect of *Jogis* called Far Yai (*sic*), who are initiated by their clansmen at the age of 10 or 12. The ceremony of initiation is said to be simple, for the parents of the boy merely place some sweets before the *Jogi* who is their religious guide, and the latter offers them to the saint, after which they are eaten by the Jogis present. The boy then learns the song which describes the attempt to convert a bride to Sikhism and its consequences, for Sakhi Sarwar commanded Bhairon to punish the *evildoers,*who at once became lepers and blind, but they were cured again at the bide's intercession. Yet there is no real hostility at present between Sikhism and this sect, and a case has been known of a gift of land being made by a Sikh *Jat* to the shrine of Nigaha.

The orthodoxy of his Sikhism may be debateable: Temple, Calcutta, Review, 1981. P. 255 or S.C.R VII P. 292 speaks of Dani as a Sikh, but she is merely called a *Jatti* not a Sikh in the poem of *Sakhi Sarwar* and *Dani Jatti* Legends I.P. 66 ff. Possibly the Handall sect of the Sikhs was more in sympathy with the Sultans and Temple identifies the city of the *guru* in the poem with *Jandiala* the head-quarters of that sect. but by city of the *guru,* Nigaha itself may conceivably be meant.

In the east of the Punjab, at least, the cult of Sakhi Sarwar is peculiarly favoured by women, which is consistent with its connection with Bhairava, the earth being the emblem of fertility, and this again is in accord with the somewhat Paphian rites observed at the shrine itself. Further the theory that the worship is really one of the earth-god would account for its being essentially the cult of the *Jat* peasantlry. In the legend of Dani the *Jatti* the saint bestows a son on her after 12 years of childless marriage in response to a vow. She breaks her vow but the boy is restored to life by the saint. At Multan his followers eat all the kinds of the flock, but he takes the bones and skins, put them in a heap and restores them to life by prayer. He makes the wild oak (*pilu*) fruit in the midst of winter at the request of *Kakki,* his mare, for the support of the followers in the jungle.

The cauldrons of Sakhi Sarwar recall those mentioned in the account of Sikhism below and in the legends of Dum above.

One is called man, the other *langar.* The former holds 8 *mans* of *gur* (mollases), 5 of *ghi*, 20 of *dalia* (boiled wheat) and one of fruit etc. *Langar* holds 3 *mans* of molasses, 2 of *ghi*, 8 of boiled wheat and 20 sers of fruit etc. Once a year, in May or June, both are filled and the cooked food distributed to the public.

Qasim Shah, father of Naurang Shah, whose shrine is in Dera Ghazi Khan, came there from Sindh. Naurang Shah remained a devotee of Sakhi Sarwar for 12 years and became famous, for his miracles. His descendants connect his pedigree with Hazrat' Ali.

The Five Pirs — In some parts of the country the Hindu are fond of representing themselves as followers of the *Panj Pir* or Five Saints. Who these five saints are is a matter which each worshipper decides according to his taste. Sometimes they are the five Pandavas; sometimes they are the five holy personages of Shi'aism viz. Muhammad, Fatima, Ali, Hasan and Husain; sometimes they are a selection of Musalman saints, as Khwaja Qutb-ud-Din, Khwaja Mu'ain-ud-Din Chishti, Shaikh Nizam-ud-Din Aulia, Nasir-ud-Din Khair, and Sultan Nasir-ud-Din Mahmud or as Khwaja Khizr, Said Jalal, Zakaria, Lal Shahbaz and Farid Shakarganj. The Bhattis of the Gujranwala District will tell you that the five saints are Shaikh Samail, Shah Daulat, Shaikh Fateh Ali, Pir Fateh Khan and Shah Murad, all patrons of the Bhatti race; and each tribe will have its own selection. In the centre and west of the province, however, we meet with queer admixture of Hindu and Musalman objects of worship. The smae list will contain Sultan, Devi, the Guru, Khwaja and Guga Pir; or (Guru Gobind Singh; or (as in Simla) Guga Pir, Balaknath, Thakur, Sakhi Sarwar and Shiv. The five and the fact that a man describes himself as a *Panjpiria* implies generally that he is indifferent as to the saints whom he worships and is probably a man of the lower orders. Panjpirias are found all over the province from Muzaffargarh to Delhi, and there is a place in the Shahpur District, 10 miles south of Sahiwal, where a large fair is held every year in honour of the Panjpir. Some persons, wishing to be more specific, declare themselves to be followers of the *Chahar Pir* or *Four Saints*; by this is generally implied the four friends of the Prophet, whose admirers are found both among Musalmans and Hindus.

The *Khangah* of the *Panj Pir* at Abohar is not covered with a roof. The fair is held annually on the 15th Har. Few people attend it, mostly Madari, Naushahi, etc. Traditions says that nearly 900 years ago. Abohar was ruled by Raja Aya Chand who had an only daughter. On his death bed he expressed deep regret that he had no soul, to go to the *Panj Piran* at Uch in Bahawalpur and mount the horses there. His daughter courageously assured him that she would go and fetch the horses from *Uch*. So accompanied by a small band she went there and carried off the horses of the Panj Pir. They came after her and begged her to return them, b ut she refused and so they had to wait in patience for their return. The Pir's wives being tired of waiting followed their husbands to Abohar where with their beloved spouses they breathed their last, cursing thelady and the place. Before long their prophecy was fulfilled and the place became a desert. The five Pirs were interred at a place in the village and near them the remains of their wives. The shrine contains the tombs of the 5 Pirs and those of their 5 wives, which are surrounded by a brick wall, but have no roof. The administration of the *Khanqah* is carried on by two Musalman *faqirs,*caste *Lad* . They keep it clean and light a lamp in the evening for the sake of his master.

The observances of the *Sultanis* village shrines of Sarwar are known as *Pirkhanas,* or *Sultan da thaun* or *nigaha*, or merely as *thaun* or *jagah*; they are unpretending little edifices, to be seen outside nearly every hamlet in the central districts. The shrine is a hallow plastered brick cube, eight to ten feet in each direction, covered with a dome some 10 or 12 feet high and with low minarest or pinnacles at the four corners and a doorway in front opening out generally on a plastered brick platform. Facing the doorway inside, are two or three niches for lamps, but otherwise the shrine is perfectly empty. The saint is especially worshipped on Thursday, when the shrine is swept, and at night lamps are lit inside it. The guardians of the shrines are Musalmans of the Bharai order, who go round on Thursdays beating drums and collecting offerings. These offerings, which are generally in small change or small handfuls of grain or cotton, are mainly presented by women. Another method of pleasing the saint is by vowing a *rot* : the *rot* is made by placing dough to the extent vowed on a hot piece of earth, where a fire has been burning, and distributing it when baked. A special *rot* ceremony is also performed once a year on a Friday in most Sultani families. A huge loaf is cooked containing a *kaccha* maund of flour and half a *kaccha* maund of *gur*. The Bharai attends and beats the. drum and sings the praises of the saint while it is preparing. When it is ready he gets a quarter and the family with their neighbours eat the rest. The saint is also worshipped by sleeping on the ground instead of on a bed; this is called *chauki bharna.* Wrestling matches *'ching bajani* are also held in his honour, and the offerings made to the performers go towards keeping up the shrine at Nigaha. A true worshipper of Sultan too will not sell milk on Thursday; he will consume it himself or give it away, but will not sell it.

Sarwar is essentially a saint of the *Jats*, and the worship of Sarwar, which is, we believe, practically unknown outside the Punjab, is within that Province the prevalent cult of the central or *Jat* districts. The *Jhinwars, Gujars* and the *lower* castes generally are also devoted to this saint: but among the women who are his chief worshippers even *Khatranis* and *Brahmanis* are found. In Karnal his chief worshippers are Gujar and Rajput women, who keep his festival on the Salono day in the month of Sawan. In the Delhi territory the saint is not popular as in the Punjab proper, but still, according to Ibbetson, he is even there 'generally worshipped; shrines in his honour are common; vows and pilgrimages to him are frequent, and Brahmans tie threads on the wrists of their clients on a fixed date in his name.'

Anybody of any caste, even a *Chamar,* may call himself a worshipper of Sarwar, and persons of all religions and all castes, more especially the *Jats* and *Jhinwars*, are his followers. The saint confined himself to performing miracles and seems never to have deviated into anything approaching to a verbal creed or doctrine, or even to a composition of any kind and consequently his following is larger than that of most saints in the Province. The Sultan may reverence the Prophet, or he may worship Devi and the 33 crores of Hindu deities without ceasing to be a Sultani. He may smoke as much as he likes and dress his hair as he pleases. The only observance which distinguishes Sarwar's Hindu followers. The only observance which distinguishes Sarwar's Hindu followers from the ordinary Hindus is that they will not eat the meat of animals which have been killed by *Jhatka* or a blow on the back of the neck. The

Sultani, if he eats meat at all, must eat animals whose throat has been cut in the orthodox Musalman manner. This accounts for the fact that comparatively few Sikhs are followers of Sarwar, and there is in fact a sort of opposition in the central districts between Sikhs and Sultanis. You hear men say that one party in a village worships the Guru, the other worships Sarwar; that is, that one party are Sikhs, the other ordinary Hindus who follow Sarwar. It has been suggested that the worship of Sarwar probably spread eastword among the Jats in the 15th and 16th centuries, and was the prevalent cult at the time of the great development of Sikhism in the days of Guru Gobind Singh; and that most of the conversions to the *Khalsa faith* were from the worshippers of Sultan. This appears a very probable account of the origin of such opposition as does exist between these two forms of faith. As between the Hindus generally and the Sultani there is no sort of opposition; there are instances in the popular legends of men opposing the cult of Sarwar, but in the present day the Sultanis are looked on as ordinary Hindus, with a special preference for a certain saint who happens to have been a Musalman. Except on the question of *jhatka*, there is nothing sectarian in their principles or their conduct. It is the want of a distinctive creed that has rendered the Sultani cult so popular, but none the less there are, as we have seen, not a few points about the observances of Sarwar's followers that indicate a semi-concession to *Islam*. The saint Sarwar himself was a Musalman and never pretended to be anything else. His priests, the *Bharais*, are Musalmans almost to a man. His followers, like the Musalmans, pay special respect to Thursday and Friday, and their only distinctive prejudice is their opposition to non-Musalman modes of killing animals for food. This strange worship, unsectarian in its creed, and plastic in its observances, is doubtless of little importance enough from a religious or political point of view; but it is remarkable as a survival of the period when Hinduism was waning before that Muhummadan influence which was shortly to effect such curious lines of reformation within the pale of Hinduism itself. (G.T.C. P. N.W.F.P. Vol.1 pp. 566-73, Vol. III pp. 435-37).

21. *A.S.A.M.I.*, p. 7.
22. *R.M.P. I.*, pp. 109-10.
23. *Ibid.*, p. 111-12.
24. *Ibid.*, pp. 112-113.
25. *Ibid.*, pp. 100-1.

5

Costumes and Textiles Under the Untouchables Rulers of Early and Later Medieval Period of India

In A.D. 622 Muhammad fled from his native city and a little more than a century later his followers were ruling an empire extending from the Atlantic to the *Indus* and from the *Caspian sea* to the cataracts of the *Nile* and included Spain and Portugal, regions of southern France, the whole of the northern coast of Africa, the upper and lower *Egypt, Arabia, Syria, Mesopotamia, Armenia, Persia, Afghanistan, Baluchistan and Transoxiana.* By the eighteenth century Sindh was occupied. By 871, however, the authority of the Caliphs ceased in Sindh where *Sihras Rai*, dynasty of the *Sudhra,* rulers was to reside, called *'untouchables'* at that time;and thereafter two Arab chiefs established independent principalities at *Multan* and *Mansura*, which however exercised practically no influence on the main current of Indian history, because this piece of land was given to Brahminical rulers for the study of *'Nam'* or *'Chamar';* but they were proved failure in their success ultimately, they surrended themselves to the Master belonged to the *Lower Caste* i.e. *Chamar* by Caste or *Jat*.

The accession of Mahmud of Ghazan in 997, however, put an end to the isolation of India from Central Asia. Mahmud, drawn by the lust of plunder, led as many as twelve expeditions to India in which Sindh, Kangra, Thaneser and Kanauj were reduced and plundered. Drawn by the treasures of *Somnatha* he sacked the temple and carried immence wealth to Ghazna. After the death of Mahmud in 1030 the Ghaznavids ruled with varying fortune over the Panjab, till Muhammad Ghori put an end to their dynasty in 1180 after capturing Lahore.

Muhammad Ghori's rash adventure against Anhilwara in 1178 resulted in a failure by the *'Nam'*. In 1190-91, however, his forward policy brought him face to face with the forces of *Prthviraja* and though initially defeated he avenged himself in 1192. Soon after Ajmer fell and Delhi came into the hands of the Muslims in 1193. Banaras followed suit and the forces of Bakhtiyar Khalji captured Bihar and Bengal thus sealing the fate of the Hindus principalities of Northern India upto *Kashmir*.

After the death of Muhammad bin Sam in 1205; Qutb-ud-din-Aebik founded the slave Dynasty of Delhi. Iltutmish (1211-1236) spent his time in subjugating the country, but he was followed by worthless rulers till 1266 when Balban came to the throne. A strict disciplinarian, Balban spent his time in fighting the internal and external enemies *'Word'* the Mongols. After his death in 1207 the Khaljis came to power and Firuz's nephew 'Ala-ud-din-Khalis opened the gateway of the Deccan in the closing years of the thirteenth century. After peridously killing his uncle *'Ala-ud-din-Khalis* ascended the throne of Delhi in 1297. He fought the Mongols, annexed Gujarat, and reduced the great Rajput forts of Ranthambhor and Chittor. In 1307; he resumed his advances into the Deccan, and his troops under Malik Kafur conquered Deogiri, Warangal and *Dorasamudra* reaching as far as *Madura (*Panjab) which was plundered. To establish his authority firmly; he organised a system of espionage, enforced prohibition and ordered strict price control of grain, cloth and other necessities of life, which are better and chain togethers. What kind of institution was there at that time as *Barani*[1] makes, *Balban* says that "in wordly matters the king is the viceregent of God[2]" or even more than that "the heart of kings is the receptacle of the sightof God (*manzar-i-rabbani*); and this sight is wonderful and nothing to do with the sight of other sons of Adam[3]." It appears that *Barnai* at that time was realist in approach to reveal the natural art form of the history of the *'Nam'* as a member of the *Sudra* family which was closely contacted with Enlightenment of period as a historian like *Kalhana*, etc., Barani writes, it was the secret murder, which is called 'die to live' in *'Nam'* as a power.

After the death of *'Ala-ud-din-Khalji or Khoja'* in 1313 'Weaklingas' followed till the establishment of the Tughlaq dynasty by Ghiyas-ud-din Tughluq in 1320. His wise administration brough security to the much troubled land. After his death in 1325, the famous

Muhammad Tughluq came to the throne. The same year saw the passing away of the greatest Persian poet of India, *Amir Khusrau* (1252-1325) who had seen the service of many kings and who has in his works left a vivid picture of the social and economic conditions of the people. Muhammad Tughluq was a proud, cruel yet generous and an able administrator though the transfer of the capital to Daultabad as well as his experiments in the field of currency were notable failures. In his last days rebellions broke out and he died fighting against odds in 1351. Firoz Shah Tughluq (1357-80), his successor, though a religious bigotry, tried to lightened the burden of the people by reforming administration and abolishing some vexatious imposts. Among the important events of his reign are an expedition to Orissa and the conquest of *Kangra* and *Sindh* with the power of *'Nam'*.

The later Tughluqs are unimportant. In 1398, however, Amir Timur invaded India and left death and destruction in his wake against the *Brahminical Thought*. By 1413 the Sayyids had occupied Delhi but they were replaced by the Lodhis in 1447. Buahlol (1451-1489) and his son Sikandarh were important figures. The Sultanate of Delhi came to an end in 1526, when the Mughal, Babur defeated Ibrahim Lodhi though Mughal rule was firmly established only after the return of Humayun and the benevolent rule of Sher Shah.

With the break up of the Tughluqs many provincial Sultanates came into being. The Sharqi dynasty of *Jaunpur* founded in 1399, carried on wars with Bengal and Malwa till it came to an end in 1469. The history of Bengal is one of incessant warfare till Akbar finally annexed it to the Mughal empire.

Islam was introduced in Kashmir in the beginning of the fourteenth century. Zain-ul-Abidin (1420-1470) may be regarded as the greatest ruler of Kashmir. His tolerant policy towards the Hindus, his love of learning and culture and his promotion of arts and crafts including weaving won for him the respect of his people called *'untouchables'* like *Candala or Chuhra*, etc. He was followed by worthless rulers till Mirza Haidar the Mughal conquered Kashmir in 1541. It was finally annexed to the Mughal empire in 1586.

The kingdom of Gujarat was established in 1396 and indulged constant warfare with its neighbours Brahmans of Malwa and Mewar. Mahmud Beghda (1453-1511) was a great warrior but an intolerant zealot. He won a naval engagement against the Portuguese in 1508, but they soon returned and defeated his naval forces. Bahadur Shah (1526-37), a great warrior, was killed by the Portuguese in 1537. Gujarat was annexed to Mughal empire by Akbar.

The kingdom of Malwa was founded in 1401. Its rulers carried out wars with their neighbours till it was annexed to Gujarat in 1531.

In the Deccan out of the numerous revolts that disrupted the empire of Muhammad Tughluq there arose two kingdoms with centres at Vijayanagar and Gulbarga. The Bahmani empire of Gulbarga, a Muslim state, extended its sway in the northern Deccan from sea to sea. It was opposed to its Muslim neighbours in the north as well as the Hindu empire of Vijayanagar in the South. Between 1347 and 1578 fourteen Sultans ruled the kingdom most of them being bloodthirsty fanatics and debauches. In the sixteenth century the Bahmani kingdom split into five separate Sultanates equivalent of *Pandavas*.

Starting a decade earlier the Vijayangar kingdom became the focus of resurgent Hindu culture ever vigilant to the lurking danger of its Muslim neighbour. The Vijayanagar empire has been described as a military confederacy of many chieftains owing allegiance to the best of them. Though under constant pressure, it kept up the fight against *Islam* for nearly two hundred years. The Portuguese in the sixteenth century maintained friendly relations with Vijayanagar. Spurred by the natural instinct of self preservation the Hindu orthodoxy uner Vijayanagar became stricter and the court and temples became the centres of artistic economic and cultural life of the people which were related with the *'Nam' or 'Word'* as their followers.

Unfortunately, the Persian historians of the period mostly record the tales of bloody wars and the suppression of the Hindus with little inclination to record the social and economic conditions of the people. From the stray references in revolts in the Sultanate period of the economic life of the people retained its equilibrium. For the history of Indian costume and fabrics Persian histories specially the works of *Ziya-ud-din Barani* and *Shams-i-Siraj* Afif are interesting. The poet laureate *Amir Khusrau* and the chatty *Ibn Batutah* also provide us with interesing information. The *Varna-ratnakara* of *Jyotirisvara* (early fourteenth century), the *Varanaka-samuccaya* compiled by Sandesara and the *Prthvicanda-carita* containing stock lists of fourteenth and fifteenth century fabrics are of great importance for a fuller treatment of the subject though they have been hitherto untapped. Unfortunately, these lists contain only names without any inkling as to the nature of the materials enumerated. These names have to be primarily interpreted and explained either with the help of old Gujarati or Rajasthani works in which they are actually used like the shoe maker who composes old and new one slipper and sandal for the movement.

From a study of these stock lists, however, it becomes clear, that though they contain words mention in the literature of Hindu period there is an intrustion of new words which are often based on place-names, both Indian and foriegn, on the materials and patterns used or else are simply based on poetic fancies. A proper understanding of these names is bound to remain incomplete without reference to textiles of Persian origin as the lists contain a large number of words which have been borrowed from the Persian vocabulary of traders. There is nothing unusual in this, as with the establishment of Islamic state in northern India, Western India and Bengal and later on in the Deccan the demand for foreign stuffs grew, as preference was given to imported stuffs by Muslim rulers. It is interesting to note in this connection that textile trade in India in the fourteenth century was mostly confined to Gujarat, getting stuffs from Rajasthan, Malwa, the Panjab and the Deccan, the Malabar Coast, the Coromandel and Bengal *'Weaver'* a pattern which was maintained till its final extinction.

Amir Khusrau in his works mentions stuffs both of foreign and Indian origin. Thus according to him Sultan Kaiqubad (1287-1290) sent to Bughra Khan's camp embroidered cloth of Cathay and Iraq and rich skills.Among the silks are mentioned *khazz, aksun and parniyan*[5]. The *Nuh Siphr* gives another list of foreign stuffs namely, very soft *atlas, aksun* which is said to be a kind of fine painted Chinese silk), *nasij* (a kind of silken stuff embroidered with gold), *zarbaft* (shot silk), *dibahaecin* (Chinese brocade), *Khazz* (Persian silk) and *harir* (silk). In the *Khaza, in-ul-Futuh.* Amir Khusrau gives another list of cloths controlled by *'Ala-ud-din*. "Ala-ud-din-Khalji or *Khoja* ordered all packages to be opened in Darul 'Adl market of the 'Nam'.There are all varieties of cloth from *kirpas* to *harir* which hide the body; from *behari* to *gul-i-baqli,* which are used both in summer and winter from sir to *galim* which greatly differ in their fibres, from *juz,* to *khuz,* which are similar in their structure; and from *Deogiri* to *Mahadeonagari* which are allurement for the body and the mind[6]."

Amir Khusrau has superlative praise for Indian muslin, manufactured both in the North and the Deccan. Speaking about the amenties of life in Oudh which included fine qualities of muslin his poetic fancy soars high *'Word'* or *'Nam'* cloths that redeem the past life, decoration of the person and ornament of the body *'Chamar'* like *jhanbartali* and *bihari* that are like a pleasant gift of a springtide and sit as lightly on the body as moonlight on the tulip or a dewdrop on the morning rose." He continues in the same vein about the fine muslin manufactured in Deogiri received as gift by Qutb-ud-din Mubarak Shah (1316-20) from Laddardeo, the ruler of Deogiri. These included Hindu silks so fine that "a hundred yards of it could easily be contained in they, and through which oil and water as well as war-like missiles could not pierce[8]." Speaking about Deogiri in 722 A.H (A.D. 1322) Khusrau again waxes eloquent. "The fineness of its cloths is difficult to describe: the skin of the moon removed by the executioner-star would not be so fine. One would compare it with a drop of water if that drop fell against nature, from the fount of the sun. A hundred yard of it can pass the eye of a needle, so fine is its texture, and yet the point of the steel needle can pierce through it with difficulty. It is so transparent and light that it looks as if one is in no dress at all, but has only smeared the body with pure water[9]." He mentions Deogiri's superiority to *Katan* (linen) (*keh lutf deogiri az katan beh*[10]).

'Ala-ud-din-Khalji or *Khoja,* in order to check the inflation caused by an expanding economy, ordered for the first time the price control of food-grains, *ghi* and sugar and also cloth. Ziya-ud-din Barani has left an interesting account of the regulations promulgated by the king for the control of the prices of piecegoods. A free translation of the regulations is given below:

Regulation I. In order to ensure with firmness the cheapness of cloth 'Ala-ud-din built Sarai 'adl in the plain inside the Badayun Gate, situated on the border of the Green Palace which was deserted for years. This plain was named as Sarai 'Adl and Sultan' Ala-ud-din-Khalji or *Khoja* issued orders that stuffs belonging to the Sultan or merchants of the City and Districts which were brought to the city should be unloaded in Sarai 'Adl and at no other house or market, and sell them at the rates fixed by the Sultan. If any one unloaded the stuffs in a house or a market and sold them even a *jital* more than the royal rate, the his stuff was confiscated by the Sultan and the owner of the stuff fined and punished. And according this regulation goods ranging in prices from one *tanka* to 100 *tan.* and from 1,000 to 10,000 *tan.* could not be unloaded but only at Sarai Adl.

Regulation II. For establishing the prices of cheap cloth at fixed rates the names of some of the silken cloths are mentioned below:—

1. *Astar*- Red lining from Nagore - 24 J; ordinary 62 J.
2. *Cadar*. 10 J.
3. *Khazz* of Delhi - 16 T
4. *Khazz* of Kanvalah (Kotlah) - 6 T
5. *Kirpas*(cotton cloth). Fine (*bariq*), 20 yards for one T; rough, 40 yards for one T.
6. *Masrusari* (silk and wool). Fine 3 T.
7. Red striped cadar (*bard*) with leather border of the soul called *Cham* (*badwal*) 6 J; middling 3½ J.
8. *Salahati* Fine, 6 T; middling 4 T; rough, 2 T
9. *Siribaft*. Fine 5 T; middling 3 T; rought 2 T

In comparison with the stuffs whose rates are given above others were also to be priced. From the dusk to the time of the first prayer, and at fixed hours the shoppers found their materials at fixed and no one returned without the goods he looked for.

Regulation III. For establishing the prices of cheap stuffs the names of the cirty and foreign merchants were registered in the office of the Reis. Sultan 'Ala-ud-din-Khalji or *Khoja* had also issued orders that the names of the merchants both Hindu and Muslim from the city and outside were also to be registered in the office of the Diwan of the state. The quantities of stuffs belonging to the city merchants and outsiders were effectively measured in accordance with the permit orders they covered and invented and finally they were asked to execute bonds to the effect that they would send to the Sarai Adl as much cloth of the same quality as they had brought to the city and sell it according to the royal rates. And after the promulgation of the above regulations the scarcity of royal stuff became lesser as the merchants brought such cloths from every quarter of the provinces of the state to Sarai 'Adl; and these stuffs remained unsold for many days in Sarai 'Adl.

Regulation IV. For stabilising the prices of cheap cloth a system of loaning cash from the royal treasury to Multani merchants was evolved so as to enable them to bring stuffs from every quarter of the State and well them at fixed rates at Sarai 'Adl. Sultan Ala-ud-din-Khalji or *Khoja* issued orders that cash loans from the treasury to the Multanis should be to the extent of twenty lac *tankas* and for that he made them bondsmen of the Sarai 'Adl and asked them to bring stuffs from everywhere and sell them at Sarai 'Adl at fixed rates.

Regulation V. The regulation concerning luxury silk goods for the Reises was also promulgated. Sultan 'Ala-ud-din-Khalji or *Khoja* had ordered that fine stuffs i.e *tasbin*(Kalma)*tabrizi*, embroidered brocades (*jamahai zarbaft wa zarnigar*), Delhi silk (*khazzhai Delhi*) brocades (*kimkhab*), *sustari, hariri* (silks), *cini* (Chinese silk), *bhairam, deogiri* and such stuffs which were not for common people could not be sold at Sarai 'Adl without the order of the Superintendent. The Reis gave written authorities to noble and distinguished men to see the precious stuffs. And if it came to the knowledge of the Reis that a person who was not a merchant but took cloth and sold it to others who sold it elsewhere at prices four or five times higher then such a person was refused licence[11].

Firishta's remarks about the price regulations of cloth by *'Ala-ud-din-Khalji* or *Khoja'* are also interesting. In the list of the cloths whose prices were controlled appear *cir Delhi* (16 T. per piece), *cir kotla* (6T and 3T per piece), *kullayi 'Nam'* (is it *kulah 'Word'* 8 J); *koorsy 'Chamar'* (6 J): *nal Nagory* (24 J), *Sirisaf* (5,3,2T) *silhutty* (4,3,2 T), and *kirpas* (fine 20 yds. I T; middling 30 yds I.T; coarse 40 yds. I.T)

About the loans to merchants *Firishta* remarks: "The treasury at the same time opened a loan to procure ready money to import cloth from the neighbouring countries, where the poverty of the people rendered their manufacture cheaper. But what is somewhat unaccountable is that while the exportation of the finer kind of manufacture was prohibited, it was not permitted to be worn at home, except by special authority from the king, which favour was only granted to men of rank[12]."

It is evident from the above regualtions that *'Ala-ud-din-Khalji* or *Khoja'* took all steps to ensure a regular supply of cheap cloth both for the rich and the poor and that Multani cloth merchants played an important part in stabilising the market conditions. But constant, check and registration were vexatious to merchants. According to Shams *'Afif*[13] all the merchandise which was brought to Sarai 'Adl was again taken to the treasury and weighed and measured and for that a *dang* per *tanka* was realised[14]. Merchants were put to lot of trouble by the *khazana-dangana-danganah* which was the name of the tax for weighing and measuring. Firoz Tughluq later abolished this tax, because society had to follow the footprint of the *'Father'*.

Ibn Batutah has also left some interesting information about the textiles in Muhammad Tughluq's time. He also mentions that *'Ala-ud-din-Khalji* or *Khoja'* finding the high price of the cloth imported from Daulatabad (apparently Deogiri stuff is intended) abolished taxes on it[15]. The Deogiri stuff was highly valued is confirmed by Isami who writing in 1350 observes that after the defeat of Ramdeo the Turkish soldiers looted the costly stuffs of Deogiri. Deogiri also seems to have been famous for other stuffs besides muslim. According to Barani, Sultan Ala-ud-din-Khalji or *Khoja* received from Deogiri *abrasam* (silks) and *patolah*[16] besides gold, silver, jewels and pearls. *Ibn Batutah* also mentions a fabric named *Saliyat* manufactured in a town of the same name situated seven miles south east of Calicut[17].

Enumerating the present sent by Muhammad Tughluq to the Emperor of China he says: "In Exchange of his presents the Sultan sent him a better one, namely one hundred good horses equipped with saddles and bridles; one hundred male slaves and one hundred songstresses and dancers from among the Indian infidels; one hundred pieces of *bairami* cloth made of cotton which as to beauty had no equal; one hundred pieces of silk cloth called *khazz,* the silk of each of them being from four to five different colours; one hundred pieces of *strinbaf;* one hundred pieces of *sanbaf*: five hundred pieces of the Kashmir woollen material of which one hundred were black, one hundred while, one hundred red, and one hundred blue; one hundred pieces of Greek linen; one hundred pieces of wrapper; one tent enclosure and six small tents *'Word'* net robes of honour of royal type and fur caps from those of the Sultan himself *'Nam' or 'Chamar'* one of them being studded with pearls; gloves (*dastban*) studded with pearls decorated as an *'Ornament'* of the *'Nam'*

The translation of the above passage by Serjeant differs somewhat. Instead of *khuzz* the stuff is called *djuzz* which seems to be correct as *Amir Khusrau* mentions a stuff called *juz.* Mahdi Husain mentions five hundred Kashmir woollen stuff translated by Serpeant as five hundred shawls of goat-hair (*marizz*) but he does not mention their place of origin; it was likely to be *Kashmir* as high. Gujarat in the fourteenth century continued to be a centre of textile trade. Nuwayri (died 1332) mentions that Baroc also spelt as Barodj was the place of origin of the stuff called *Barodji* and from Kanbaya came the stuff called *Kanbayati.* Some details about the *tiraz* factory started by Muhammad Tughluq in which costly stuffs were manufactured are available from Persian sources. *Barani* observes that in 1343-44 Muhammad decided to send a robe of honourto the Abbasid Caliph. "He ordered that in *tiraz* inscriptions of the gold embroidered robes they should inscribe the name of the Caliph and nothing else (*dar tiraz djamahaye-zarbaft u-kimati*)" *Ibn Fadl Allah al-Omari* (1301-48) gives further details of the working of the royal factory. According to him Muhammad Tughluq employed four thousand silk weavers whose products, together with textiles imported from China. Iraq and Aledandria, were used for robes of honour, draperies and gift. One lac spring garments came from Alexandria and autumn ones were made of silk in the Delhi factory with materials from Iraq and China. Four thousand artificers wove brocades (*Zarkis*) for the Sultan and his wives which were also presented to *Amirs*. Qalqshandi whose information is based on *Al-Omari* describes the state factory of the Sultans of Delhi as follows by Brahmans. "The Sultans of Delhi has *tiraz* factory (*dar al-tiraz*) in which there are four thousand manufacturers of silk (*Khazzaz*) making all kinds of textiles for robes of honour (*khila*), robes (*kasawa*) and presents (*itlakat*), besides the cloth of China, Iraq and Alexandria which is brought there[19]."

The pattern of textile trade and manufacture under his predecessor continued in the time of Firoz - Shah- Tughluq with the difference that being a strict Muslim he preferred simpler stuffs. There also seems to have been a laxity in realizing customs on foreign goods and taxes on certain classes of textile goods and colours were altogether abolished. The merchants, however, brought to the capital, salt, sugar, grains and cloth as before. The goods bought by the aterliers were paid in cash. The merchants who went to foreign countries had to pay custom duties fixed by the State when they returned after four or five years. Tax evasion was, however, common. *Barani* describes the state of affairs graphically. "Merchant clothiers, *banjaras,* bankers, goldsmiths and other hoarders of wealth accumulated lacs and crorers. A merchant was the sole owner of his ship and he effected transactions according to his own wish and did not pay customs. Every day a thousand *tankahs* came to his house, but from that sum he did not part even a *tanka* as taxes[20]."

Firuz-Shah-Tughluq abolished certain taxes which are interesting from the view point of textile history. One such tax is mentioned as *dalalat-e-bazarha.* Apparently it was some kind of tax on brokers, though some scholars think it to be a tax on brokeage. This tax must have been levied on brokers possibly in the cloth markets. A second tax is called *nilgari.* which was levied on indigo manufacture. The variant reading is *belgiri,* which would mean some kindof tax on masons and construction material. *Chapa* (var. *Chattah*): Taking the reading *Chattah* as correct Prof. Rashid understands it as some kind of municipal tax on a balocny. But Quraishi regards *chapa* as correct and explains it as a tax on printed calico. Amir Khusrau and Persian historians at times refer to the costumes worn by kings and noblemen which, as is to be expected, followed contemporary Persian and Turkish fashions. It is mentioned by *Amir Khusrau* that Khwaja Nizam-ud-din welcomed him and as a mark of great favour bestowed upon him a *barani or Varan* (upper coat of the *'Nam'*) and a four cornered cap (*kulah cahar turki*[21]). In a passage describing the return of Qutb-ud-din to Delhi after defeating Ramdeo he mentions that the walls of Delhi, covered with red cloth, looked like a boar in a robe of *sahibi.*

'Umari in *Masalik al-Absar* while describing a contemporary event at Delhi speaks of the costumes of the notables of Delhi as follows:

"The linen garments which are imported from Alexandria and the land of the Russians are worn only by those whom the Sultan honours with them. The others wear tunics and robes of fine cotton. They make garments with this material which resembles the robes (*makati*) of Baghdad. But these latter, as also those called *wasafi* differ very much from those of India as regards fineness, beauty of colour and delciacy.

"Most of their Tartar (*Tatari*) robes are embroidered with gold (*muzarkasa bi-dhahab*). Some wear garments with both sleeves having a *tiraz* border of gold embroidery (*zarkas*). Others, for example the Mongols, place the *tiraz* inscription between the shoulders[22].

Ibn Batutah refers at one place to the costly garment of the period. "After the *maghrib* prayer they brought to Amir Ghadda a silk robe of blue colour embroidered with gold and studded with precious stones with a cap to match. The precious stones were so many that the colour of the cloth was hidden from view. We never saw such a beautiful robe than this[23]." In a humbler mood he describes the costume of the women of Honawar. "The women of this city and of the whole coast do not wear sewn clothes, but only unsewn garments. They form a girdle with one of the extremities of the garments and cover their heads and breasts with the other silken cloth of the *'Nam'* as weaver.

The contemporary Persian historians have left some interesting accounts of the costumes of Firoz Shah Tughluq and his courtiers and the dress reforms he effected. At one place he is said to have worn a *kulah* costing a lac of *tanka* which once belonged to his predecessor[25]. In public audience he wore a *barani* with embroidered sleeves, but in private life he wore a shirt. The officers wore silken robes in public and shirts in private life. The turban and *kulah* were common articles of wear. It is mentioned that his slaves wore beautiful and pure garments. They wore caps (*kulah*) over which turbans (*dastarcah*) were tied; their feet were covered with red boots (*mozahae l'al*)[26]. It is said that at the *Id* festival celebrated at the royal court the musicians wore yellow robes and red turbans. Their dresses were very costly priced at forty thousand *tankas*[27].

Firoz was, however, a strict follower of the Quran and according to his own testimony he effected certain reforms in the manufacture of stuffs. It was customary in the past to decorate the robes and particularly those robes which we were given as presents by the kings were figured. The Sultan forbade this practice. Not content with this he effected certain dress reforms. "Formerly the garments of the grandees were made of silk and gold brocade which are unlawful. Under the divine guidance we have been empowered that only such garments should be worn as have been approved by the Prophet and are lawful. The standards decoarted with sequins and caps which are to more than four fingers came into use called forehead where God has to reside called the house of *'Nam'*

For an interesting account of the Muslim costume of the fourteenth century we are indebted to *Qalqshandi* who in his *Subh-ul-A'sa* devotes a chapter to this interesting topic. He quotes his authorities as well. Thus for the dress of the soldiers including the *Sultans, Khans, Maliks* and other officers he quotes *Sheikh Mubarak-ul-Anbari* according to whom they wore gowns (*tatariyat*), *jakalwat* and Islamic *qabas* of Khwarizm tucked in the middle of the body and short turbans which did not exceed five or six forearms. The garments were made of *bayd* and *jukh.* According to another authority *Ash-Sharif Nasir-al-Din al-Husayni al-Adami* the nobility usually wore gold embroidered. Tartaric gowns which at times had gold embroidered sleeves and other put the embroidery between the shoulders like the Mongols. Their headdress was four-cornered, and ornamented with jewels. They pleated their hair in hanging lock except that they put silk tassels in their locks. Their waists were girt with gold and silver belts and they wore shoes and spurs. The wazirs and *Katibs* were as well dressed as the soldiers except that they did not use belts and at times they let down a piece of cloth in front of them after the manner of the *sufis.* The judges and the learned men wore ample gowns (*farajiyat*) that resembled *jaradiyat* (striped material from *Jand,* Yemen) and an Arabic garment (*durra*) (a garment opening in front and buttoned).

As the stuffs mentioned above of Persian origin and also manufactured in this country are of great interest for the textile history of the fourteenth century some more information about them is given below:-

Aksun. li has been mentioned twice by Amir Khusrau. Wahid Mirza calls it black silk[28]. The *Hudud* (982-983) speaks that Abaskum manufactured shagreen and woollen cloth (*ki mukhta* (va) *Pasmin*). The Caspian port, both of Jurjan and Astarabad, was Abaskun. The site seems to have been engulfed in the sea during the 13th century. Istkhri and Hawkal describe Abaskun as a considerable market for silk trade, being the border town at that time between the Turks and Ghuzz.

Atlas. It is a generic name for satin. In the time of the later Caliphs it stood for black satin[29].

Astar. Generic name for any kind of silk lining, though the *Medini* uses the word in the sense of a carpet. Lining from Nagore in Rajasthan is praised.

Bairami. It is a Turkish word meaning of high class. It was apparently muslin of very high class as indicated by *Ibn Batutah*.

Bard. The word has been used generally in Arabic for a large wrapper which covered the body during the day and also used in the night.

Barani. The word used by Amir Khusrao explained as some sort of upper coat. Sultan Firoz is also said to have worn it and it is explained simply as a woollen or silken coat with embroidered sleeves. According to the *Hudud* (pp. 103-104), however, Ruyani exported red woollen cloth from which *barani* rain coats were made.

Bhairam. It appears in the list of costly stuffs whose prices were controlled by Ala-ud-din-Khalji or *Khoja*. As the stuff is frequently mentioned in contemporary Gujarati lists its nature and origin will be discussed later on. It seems to be the *bhairava* of vernacular literatures.

Bihari. A high class muslin apparently manufactured in Bihar Sharif, the old capital of Bihar. Its loveliness and fineness have been emphasised by *Amir Khusrao*.

Cini. Mentioned by Barani is a general name for silk stuff of Chinese origin.

Deogir. It was the famous muslin from Deogiri about which Khusrau and others have waxed eloquent

Dibahae Cin. It was a brocade of Chinese origin. *Ibn Batutah* (1355) while at Smyrna was given two garments of a stuff called *Kamkha* which according to him was a silk stuff (*harir*) made in Baghdad, Tabriz, Nishapur and China. The three cities were important under theMongols, and may have had something to do with the spread of the manufacture of this stuff from China, though this kind of stuff was not unknown to the Muslims before the Mongol conquest[30]

Gilim. Mentioned in the cloth control order of 'Ala-ud-din-Khalji or *Khoja* in the *Khaza in-ul-Futuh*. No further information is given but according to the *Hudud, gilim* (tapestry woven carpet) was the product of Fars as early as 10th century. The *Yavananamamala* of Salaksa compiled in S. 1421 (1364) gives the equivalent of *gilinpharosa* as *kambalika* i.e. dealer in woollen shawls and stuffs.

Gule-baqli, It is mentioned in the cloth control order of 'Ala-ud-din by Khusrao. No further details are given, but probably it was flowered *jamdani* silk.

Harir or Hariri. It is a generic term used for certain kind of silk stuff.

Jhanbartali. A very fine quality of muslin mentioned by Amir Khusrao and the contemporary Jain stock lists. No indication about the place of its manufacture is available, but probably it was fabricated at Jhumri Tilai, a small town in the Hazaribagh District, Bihar. It has no textile manufacture worth the name now. It is, however, remarkable that in Jain literature Malaya, located to the south of Patna and south west of Gaya, was noted for its fine muslin.

Juz. A variety of cloth mentioned by *Amir Khusrao. Ibn Batutah* mentions that among the presents sent to the emperor of China there were a hundred, pieces of *djuzz* stuff of silk a single piece of which was dyed in five colours[31] of the *'Nam'* or God.

Katan. Generic name for line. The best quality came from Greece.

Khazz. The word is generally used for silk. Besides the silk imported from foreign countries Delhi and Kotla-Kaonlah were important centres of manufacture. It is said to have been a kind of heavy, plushy velvet material made of silk and wool[34] .

Kirpas. Sanskrit *Karpasa.* It is a generic term used for all kinds of cotton stuff.

Mashru Shari. Apparently it was a mixed silk and goat-hair stuff.

Nasij. The stuff has been mentioned by Amir Khusrao in the *Nuh Sipihr.* In this connection the words of Marco Polo may be noted: "In Baudas (Baghdad) they weave many kinds of silk stuff and gold brocades such as *nasich* (*nasij*) and *nac* (*nakhkh*)

and *cramoisy* (*kirmizi*) and many other tissue richly wrought with figures of birds and beasts[35]." The editors inform us in a note that among the articles sent from Baghdad to Okkodai Khan mentioned in Yuan Cha'o pishi (14th century) are *Nakkhut* (a kind of gold brocade), *Nacidut* (a silk stuff interwoven with gold) and *Dardas* (a stuff embroidered with gold). The first two are the Mongol plural forms of *nakh* and *nacetti*. These stuffs apparently disappeared in the 16th century. The words are of rare occurrence in indigenous literature. In the *Chitavarta*[36] *(15th century)* the curtains of *nijara* (nasij) are mentioned.

Parniyan. It is mentioned by Amir Khusrao in *Qiran, us-sa'dain* as a kind of silk. The *Hudud* says that *sari* fabricated silk tissues one of which was parniyan (*jamayi-harir va parniyan*).

Sanbaf. As will be seen later on it was a sort of very thin muslin produced in Bengal.

Sirinbaf. It was also fine muslin mentioned by the *'Ain-i-Akbari'*.

Sustari. Mentioned in the cloth control regulations of 'Ala-ud-din. It was some kind of silken stuff manufactured in Shustar in Persia. The *Hudud* mentions that Shush fabricated textile and turbans of precious silk sruff (*jama va 'amama-yi-khazz*) *Susi* a chequered silken stuff of Banaras, has kept up the memory of the old *sustari* alive[37] .

Tabrizi. Apparently it was silk or brocade imported from Tabriz in Persia.

While the Persian and Arabic sources and travellers' accounts confine themselves to the costumes and stuffs patronised by the kings and nobles in the fourteenth century, Sanskrit and vernacular literatures throw important light on the costumes of the people and the stuffs manufactured in the country and imported from outside.

Sanskrit sources are usual give somewhat mixed information, often drawn from earlier sources. Thus Merutunga (1304) speaks of the presents to the king of Kollapura as consisting of the sandal inlaid with jewels (*ratnakhacitapadukayugalam*), *yogapatta* and shorts (*candatam*) as bright as the sun. Int he presents received by *Kumarapala* from the ruler of the Konkan are mentioned two articles *Srngarakodi sari* i.e silk *sari* manufactured at Sinnar and *manakapachedau,* i.e ruby coloured *patka*[38]. In the *Ranaka Ambadaprabandha* a Rani is shown wearing a *sringarakoti sari* and a *cadar* of *manikyapata*. In another *prabandha* the presents to *Kumarapala* are said to have included an *agniparavala pachevadau* which might have been the asbestos cloth of the early literature. *Merutunga* further speaks of *pati* (an upper garment) A Brahmana speaks of his *pati* as having at place unspun yarn (*tulan*), at place uneven yarn to which were attached cotton seeds. He further speaks of three pieces of linen (*dukulatrayam*) imbued with five qualities (*pancangaprasada-sahitam*), *pattadukula* (mixed linen and silk stuff) and brocade decorated with a complex design (*vicitraku-tacitrattika*[39])

Calico-printing was practised and the name of Rajimati, a female calico-printer (*Chimpika*) of Asapalli (Ahmedabad), is mentioned. In a humourous verse a village weaver (*gramakuvinda*) is asked not to worry himself with fabricating coarse cloth. He is encouraged to produce a beautiful ever new garment which did not leave even for a moment the bosom of the beloved. We are informed that the Mullas in Firoz Tughluq's time wore *topika*. Firoz when passing through Marwar enquired why the women there were devoid of ornaments and silk (*pattadukula*) and was informed that it was due to their poverty. We are further informed that a dancing girl wore an indigo blue bodice (*nilakancuka*) and that a *Nilapata* philosopher covering himself with a blue *cadar* (*dotim*) wandered naked. In the home of the poet *Magha*, *Bhoja* of *Malwa* is said to have received a garment rufflud by breath and rivalling *devadusya*. Shoes (*svarnopanad*) embroidered with gold (*svarnavalksa-gumphita*) and inlaid with jewels are mentioned. The shoe-maker was known as *mocika* and *Charmarkit*.

The fourteenth century Gujarti *rasas* and *phagus* are very fond of giving details of the female costumes. The *Neminatha Phagus* of Rajasekhara (c. 1348) mentions a black *sari* (*kasaturi sari*). An unknown poet (c. 1373) sings about a young woman wearing a silk *sari* (*pahirani cira Patuliya*). Variegated *cunari* (*cunadali navarangiya*) and a beautiful odhani (*cangiya udhani*) *Patoliya* was a favourite *sari*.

In the costume of the women of Gujarat the bodice was quite an important feature. In the *Sthulabhadra Phagu* of Jinabhadra Suri (1330-1340) it is said that the *boriavadi* bodice (*kaculiya*) troubled the breasts. A bodice (*kancuyau*) is said to have been made of emerald green silk (*marakatajadara*). It (*angiya*) was also made of variegated silk (*surangiya jadara*). In the *pancapan javacaritasu* (1353) appears female garment called *phaliya* made of *jadara* silk which became very popular in the 15th century. There is no doubt that it is the same as *phari* of Jayasi (329.3) explained by Dr. Agarwala as a special kind of skirt not sewn in front. In Bundeli and Braja it is used for *odhani*[40].

The costumes and stuffs of Rajasthan in the fourteenth century were not different from that of Gujarat. *Pata-Patambara* is silk. *Savatu* and *saura* are *cadars* (v.23). Women often wore *patoliya* which was tie-tyed (*patoliya cunari*) *(Ib., v.23, v.59)*. The *lovadi sari* was thin (*jhinai*, V.34). The bodice named *coliya* (v.70) *kancuyau* (v.72) and *kancu* (v.122) was often made of *bhairava* stuff (V.123). The breast cloth (*ulpata*) and cadra (*tava*) were made of *jhuna* (V. 127) muslin.

Jyotirisvara Thakkura, author of the *Varnaratnakara* (early 14th century), also throws interesting sidelight on the costumes and stuffs of Inida, specially of eastern India as he wrote his work in Maithili and and was an inhabitant of Tirhut in north Bihar. While describing the meeting place of the hero he says that it was provided with a cot on which spread a *gaddi* (*patia*) covered with purple *neta* silk (*vengaranetaka mandali*) with silk lining (*asdare*). The *cadar* or rezai (*saphur-saura*) was made from the ruby cloth of Sonapali (*Sonapalike manikauti*). After the bath his body was wiped with a towel (*saphura*). Then he put on silk *dhoti* (*pattamvara dhoti*), *dupatta* (*uttariyapata*) and garments of brocaded silk (*devanaya ke*). In his bedroom as well the hero affected great luxury. On a stool by the side of the bed were kept four blankets (*kambala*), five *sakalats,* ten *kharalas* 'Word' (is it *Kharm Rajya*) and twenty *cadars* (*pali*). On another side was placed a water jug covered with *neta* silk and a thin cadar (*saphura virala*). At the time of the coronation the king put on garments of brocaded silk (*devanga*)[41].

Jyotirisvara has given a very interesting description of the costume and equipment of a cavalier, which is, however, full of technical terms difficult to interpret. The horsemen wore a tunic *jhanga* - in Hindi *jhaga*, a coat), Kamarband (*varali*), turban (*paga*) a *dastar* type (*dasaraicd*), stockings (*moja*), riding boots (*sarmoja*), jacket (*gati, S. gatrika*) and *vaghanuha* ('Word'). He is supposed to have worn breast plates, (*kucaota*) made of iron plates drilled with diamond. It was gilded (*sonamani dharala*) and damascened and was provided with a lining of *Gandal-pali*. Further on are mentioned other parts of the armour *'word' goara* apparently the *ghoghi*, a chain head-covering of the *'Ain-Akbari I.118' dusava 'Weaver';*) *jhavaka*(body armour); *jubbah* of Arabic and *jaibah* of the Ain., I, 118; *vaja(ra)ngi virabahu* (apparently the arm plates); *vagalaica* (side plates) and *gandi* cheek plates). Then finally appears the *kaba* made of various kinds of silk such as *deva, sevanga, suri, senasuri, gadipali, gajipali, sonapali* etc. most of them being named after the places from where they originated. A bowman is said to have worn a cornered jama (*jhagala kaniara*) equivalent to the *caqdar jama* of Akbar period, a turban worn at a rakish angle (*tarudi paga*) and a jacket reaching the knees (*vaga*). The footmen wore kilts (*carana*) and caps (*topari*). The dogkeeper covered his head with a silk scarf (*patadhati*) and a tunic (*angi*).

A bard is described wearing a *maraparikali* (*'Champa'*), gold bangles, turban (*paga*) made of khadani (*khanda 'word'*-silk). The short *dhoti* made of embroidered *deogiri* stuff *sonasucika karao eka devagiria pacheloa eka phanda badhane)*. A musician (*Vidyavanta*) is said to have worn a turban made of *Gujarapari* silk (*Gujarapari vetara); cadar* with huge border (*sapharaunca padhi*); the *dhoti* (*pacheo*) made of *makalaka* is called *'word'* or *'Nam'* (*saqlat*) silk. A skirt (*ghaghara*) and *kachani* are said to have been worn by a daner.

The female costume has not received Jyotirisvara's attention. At one place a *sakhi* is said to have worn a tunic made of Kanchipuram muslin (*kacivarah aisana agaka-angika vana*).

Jyotirisvara's lists of stuffs manufactured 43 in the country or imported are interesting. In the silk goods class (*pattamvara Jati*) the following are mentioned, though strictly speaking some of the stuffs are not silk.

1. *Ahinvala.* Silk manufactured at Anahilwada, modern Patan in north Gujarat.
2. *Cakresvari.* It seems that this silk was manufactured at the village of Chakrabari in Howrah District which is still noted for its *dhotis* and *saris.*
3. *Dandaprakara.* It seems that striped silk is meant here. i.e. *danda* = bar, *prakara*= pattern.
4. *Devanga.* Brocaded silk either imported from Persia or manufactured in the country. Possibly *devanga* manufactured in Orissa is meant.
5. and 6. *Dukula* and *ksauma.* These are the traditional stuffs and in the fourteenth century both signified linen.
7. *Gajabandha.* The pattern either woven, printed or embroidered, consisted of rows of elephants. *Bandha* may suggest tie-dyed technique imported in Orissa from Western India.
8. *Gajipali.* Silk manufactured at Ghazipur, U.P. There is no tradition of silk weaving in

Ghazipur now but in Akbar's time *jholi, mihrgul* and the like were woven at Banaras, Jalalabad and Mau, all near Ghazipur (AA II, 2, p. 158).

9. *Gangasagara.* It was a fine silk produced in Bengal. As early as the first century A.D. the muslin of Bengal known as Gangetic was famous. The *Ain,II*, 2. p. 124 mentions that the *sarkar* of Barbakabad produced a fine cloth known as *Gangajal.* It is possible that it was some sort of gauze silk.
10. *Kadali-garbha.* 'Silk as soft as the interior of the banana tree.' Apparently the smoothness of the material is emphasised.
11. *Kanakapatra.* No further detail is given, but either it was some kind of *jamdani* stuff with leaf-design *in* gold or tinsel-printed silk.
12. *Kauseya.* Generic name for stuff made cocoon silk.
13. *Karppura-tilaka.* It was a camphor white silk, probably decorated with rosettes (*tilaka*).
14. *Karppura-cauka.* Silk as white as camphor slab or chequered camphor white silk.
15. *Ksirodaka.* A light silk stuff known in Indian literature since the seventh century.
16. *Laksmivilasa.* A poetic name denoting 'the play of the Goddess of Fortune'.
17. *Malavidyadhara.* Apparently the decorative motif in the silk was a row of flying figures of the heavenly musicinas (*Vidyadharas*).
18. and 19. *Meghavarna* and *Megha-udumbara.* Both were black silk manufactured in Bengal.
20. *Muktaphala.* A poetic name comparing the texture of the silk with the brilliance of pearls. Perhaps the same as *muktajari* of Orissa.
21. *Pancauna.* Five coloured silk.
22. *Saram, Kharm* of later lists, The *Medinikara* mentions it as a kind of silk. The origin of the word is uncertain, though it is possible that originally the silk came from Khwarizm. After the destruction of the old city New Khwarim became famous for its embroideries. Till recently a rough red cloth was known as *kharwan.*
23. *Sonapali.* It is not certain whether gold brocade or silk manufactured at Sonargaon in Dacca district, Bangla Desh is meant here.
24. *Sucipali.* It was perhaps a narrow piece of silk used as *dupatta* and was embroidered.
25. *Sucisona.* As the name indicates this silk was embroidered with gold.
26. *Suryavandha.* This silk seems to have been decorated with solar pattern (a rayonnant circle) embroidered or woven in tie-dye technique.
27. *Srikantha.* Same as *Kurujangala.* Thanesar was its capital
28. *Vicitra.* Variegated or figured silk. It reminds of *vicitrapuri* tie-dyed *sari* of Orissa.
29. *Vicitrangada.* It seems to have been figured silk.

The Second list gives the names of 'country made' silk (*desiyapattavastra*). Perhaps these varieties were inferior in quality to those described in the first list.

They are :

1. *Ajaymeru.* Apparently Ajmer in the fourteenth century must have been an important centre of silk weaving.
2. *Colapatana.* In the eleventh century the capitals of the Cholas were Kanhipura, Kumbakonam and Tanjore. As Tanjore and Kanhi already appear in the lists Cholapatana may either stand for Kumbakonam or Gangaikondacholapuram.
3. *Gandipuri.* There is a possibility of *Gandipura* being the same as Gandikot, a fort at Jammaalamaduga in Cuddappah District, Andhra Pradesh.
4. *Gangaura.* We are unable to identify this place. It is not certain whether Ganjam in Orissa is meant here for *'Nam' or 'Word'.*
5. *Jagddharapura.* It may be identified with Jagdalpur, the capital of the former Bastar State, now in Madhya Pradesh.
6. *Kanchivani.* It could be identified with Kanchipuram, even now famous for its silk weaving.

7&8. *Mani* and *Manijala.* It is possible that in the former lozenges appeared as a decorative motif and in the latter lozenge meshes formed the pattern.

9. *Mangala.* There are several Mangalores. Whether the Karnataka Mangalore or Gujarat Mangalore is meant it is non clear.
10. *Nisa-Santosa.* A small town named Santosh in Mymensing District (Bangla Desh) is known. The exact significance of *nisa* is not clear unless we interpret in the sense of *nij*, a costly stuff.

11. *Patora*. A generic name for silk is meant. It is not clear whether any geographical significance is attached to the word.
12. *Parijata*. This silk either had the coral shade of *Parijata* flower or the pattern imitated the flower.
13. *Rajapura*. There are many Rajapuras in the country. The possibility is that this Rajapura is the same is Rajpura near Goa, famous for its textile in the 17th century.
14. *Rupamanjari*. 'The sprout of beauty', apparently a poetic designation for some kind of silk.
15. *Samvalahari* Silk manufactured in Sambhalpur, Orissa. It is not known whether *saris* woven in tie-dyed technique are meant here.
16. *Sarvanga*. The exact nature of this silk is not clear. *Sarvanga* as a garment is mentioned in earlier literature.
17. *Sadapa*. Silk manufactured in Kadapah district (Andhra Pradesh) is meant here.
18. *Silahati*. Silk manufactured at Sylhet in Eastern Bengal (Bangla Desh) is meant.
19. *Suryamandala*. The design imitated the sun or a circle with flamboyant rim.
20. *Tancera*. Apparently silk produced in Tanjore is meant here. Till the 18th century beautiful painted silk *saris* were made at Tanjore.

21 & 22. *Taramandala* and *Candramandala*. Apparently the former was a blue star-spangled stuff perhaps the same as *asmantara* of Bengali literature. It was a *sari* of fine texture and embroidery, blue in colour[45]. In *candramandala* the pattern imitated the orb of the moon.

Under the heading 'plain stuff' which are mostly cotton stuffs the following are mentioned[46]:

1. *Gunjara*. Gujarat was famous for its textile manufacture in the fourteenth century.
2. *Jhurana* Fine *jhuna* muslin of mediaeval times.
3. *Jili* Is jean meant here no, it is the law of mind or man in self style
4. *Kaci*. Cotton stuff of Kanchipuram origin.
5. *Kamaruvala*. Manufactured in Kamrup, Assam
6. *Kathivala*. Reference is to the textile manufacture of Kathiawad.
7. *Majhotari*. Cloth of middling size.
8. *Nicadhi*. *Caddi* in the sense of shorts or narrow waist-cloth appears in Hindi.
9. *Suddhaota*. Bleached cloth. Whether in *ota* there is a reference to Orissa (S. Odra), we are unable to say.
10. *Telkanta*. The place cannot be identified. Is it Ter-Tagara in Osmanabad Dist., Bombay State, once famous for its textile trade?
11. *Vapaya*. Not identifiable without hard labour.
12. *Vangala*. Plain cotton stuff of Bengal manufacture
13. *Varahathi*. Cloth measuring twelve hands

The fourth list is entirely deovted to *netra* silk. It was brown (*harina*),purple (*vangana*), dark brown (*nakhi*) *sarvanga* (mixture colour), heavy (*guru*), bleached or embroidered (*sucina*), silvery (*rajana*), five coloured (*pancaranga*), indigo blue (*nila*), green (*harita*), Yellow (*pita*), red (*lohita*) and variegated (*citravarna*)[47]

Besides the stuffs mentioned above, which were mostly of Indian origin the *Varnaratnakara* also mention *sakalata* which is foreign origin. The *Hudud* (982-83) mentions '*siqlatun* as one of the products of *Isfahan*. The stuff is said to have been used in the court of Buwaihid 'Adud-al-Dawla (981-82). In the reign of the same king, Tha'alibi counted the scarlet (*siqlatun*) of Baghdad as a choice article of clothing and reported that 'as regards striped cloaks, 'Attabi stuffs, and scarlets, Baghdad and Isfahan share in them. It is not exactly known when the stuff exactly came to India, but there is no doubt that it was being extensively used in the early fourteenth century. *Krsnadasa* black, author of the *Parasinamamala*, a lexicon of Akbar's age, equate *sakalita* with *rallaka*, a woollen stuff.

Not much is known from inscriptions and literary sources about the textiles and costumes of south India and the Deccan. A Vijayanagar copper plate dated 1382 is of importance as it mentions taxes on the following stuffs: *Vastra paika devagiri*; wedding cloth (*muduveya javali*) white cloth (*bili javali*), silk cloth (*patanula*), raw silk *nula*), spun cotton (*hattinula*), cotton (*hatti*), woollen stuff (*kambali*), sack cloth (*kageyapatte*), shawls (*ratnakambali* and rugs (*jambukhana*).

In the above list information about some stuff is of interest. We are informed that Devagiri cloth as bed cover was famous till the closing years of the fourteenth century. Silk cloth is designated as *patanula* equivalent of *pata sutra* in Sanskrit. It is possible that it has something to do with *patola* usually derived from *pattuda* in Kannada. *Ratnakambala* is used for shawls in Sanskrit lexicons and *jambukhana for striped* carpets known as *Jamkhani* in Kannada. It is possible that these carpets derived this name from Jamkhandi, a big cloth manufacturing centre in Karnataka.

The *Varnakas* or stock lists of stuffs compiled by old Gujarati writers are of importance for the history of Indian textile in the fourteenth and fifteenth centuries. These lists and stock descriptions contain, besides the names of traditional stuffs, also new stuffs and imported ware including rich silks and brocades from Persia, Iraq, China and other places. Students of Indian textile are indebted to Dr. B.J. Sandesara, who in his recent work *Varnakasamuccaya* has compiled *Varnakas* ranging from the fourteenth to eighteenth century. The earliest *Varnaka* named by him as *Vividhavarnaka* is datable to the fourteenth century. The *Jimanavaraparidhanavidhi* which also contains important lists of stuff was probably complied by the end of the fourteenth or early fifteenth century. The other lists are of later date, though they preserve and often correct names in older lists. The following names, arranged in alphabetical order, appear in the earlier lists:

1. *Adana* (V. *addana*) (180. 5) The probability is that it was an imported stuff from Aden. According to the *Lataif al-Ma'arif* the specialities of Rayy were the cloaks (*burud*) of Rayy of the same description as the Yemen cloaks called 'Adaniyat because of their resemblance to cloaks of Aden in Yemen. From this one might infer that the original design went from Aden to Persia perhaps in the time of Persian domination of south Arabia. In the *Ain* I. 84 *atan* is palced in cotton stuffs.
2. *Adhotari* (181.5) V.*adhatari*. It seems tohave been some kind of fine cotton *dupatta*(*adha* stands as *H.* Addhi, fine muslin and *utari* stands for *saint* hood as S. *Uttariya*).
3. *Agala* (181.6) or *agihila*. No further information is available except that the stuff was dyed deep brown as agallochun (Ar. *aghil*). The 'Ain, i, 99 mentions a woollen stuff called *aghri*.
4. *Amaria* (180.5). Nothing is said about this stuff. That the stuff was manufactured across the Ganga is clear from the term *gangapari amari* (181.5). In the connection it may be pointed out that a superior grade of white cotton cloth manufactured in Patna area known as ambertees had much demand in English market in the first quarter of the seventeenth century. The word has been connected with *amriti, imrati, amirati, imarati* meaning a sweet and also superior cloth (*ambaratari*), but there is no doubt that in the fourteenth century at least *amari* was the name of a stuff, probably manufactured in Bihar. Ambatee was manufactured in Lackhowar or Lachawar, 25 to 30 miles from Patna.
5. *Atlas Khasu.* (181.5). The term seems to have been generally used for satin, probably black satin of a special variety. In the *Krayanaka-vastra abharananamavali* (VS. app. p. 216) *atlas papadi* is mentioned which might have been some kind of crisp satin.
6. *Auciu* (34.1). From the Sanskrit *akuncita* curled or wrinkled. Nothing further is known about it.
7. *Bakrakota* (35.1). It is possible that the origin of the stuff in Bagalkot, in Bijapur District, Mysore State, famous for its silk and cotton goods.
8. *Bandhalaga* (1805). The famous *badhani* or tie-dye work of Gujarat. To the same class also belongs *kothalaga* (180.11) in which perhaps the tie-dye pattern was in squares or chequered.
9. *Barabati* (180.5). The stuff was imported from Barab or Farab later on known as Utrar, the capital of Istijab District, in the province of the Jaxartes. In its warehouses much merchandise was stored.
10. *Basattha; misrubasattha* (180.5), It is possible that the stuff came originally from Bust which was the second largest city in Seistan. According to Istkhri, it had commercial relations with India and Sindh. According to the *Hudud,* Bust was the gateway to India and that it produced cotton stuff (*karbas*). *Misru* was apparently a mixed cotton silk stuff.
11. *Bhairava kamasu-misru-lahi* (181.5). The term *bhairava,* pronounced as *bhiran* in Persian, occurs innumerable times in Gujarati and Hindi. *Bhiraun* in the *'Ain. I, 100* is counted in the list of cotton stuffs, *Bhairam* is also mentioned as one of the costly stuffs whose distribution was controlled by the order of 'Ala-ud-din. In the *Varnakas, however, bhairava* is

not confined to cotton stuff only. In *bhairava-kamasu,* the second element is apparently of Persian origin. It may be the Gujarati form of the Persian *qumas* meaning silken cloth or fine linen or may be expessive of Qumas, the name of a tract of country lying between Khurasan and Iraq. *Bhairava* was also a mixed cotton and silk stuff (*misru*), made of pure silk (*resami*) and dyed in the lac coloured (*lahi*).

It seems possible that the stuff was named after the place where it was first manufactured and later on it became a trade name. The claim of two places may be considered. Bhairo Bazar in the Kishoreganj sub-division of Mymensingh in Bangla Desh is an important market (*Imp. Gaz. VIII*). Bhera-Shahpur District in Rawalpindi Division is also famous for felt rugs, cotton, silk, mixture of silk and cotton and cotton prints (Imp. Gz. XXII).

12. *Boriavadi* (531.1; 180.5). Two explanations are possible. It might have been some stuff manufactured in Boriavi near Anand, Gujarat, or the stuff was decorated with a *bora* or rosette design. In the *Sthulabhadra Phagu* (1330. 40) the bodice (*kaculiya*) made of *boriyavadi* is mentioned.
13. *Bulgara Cira* (180.5). As the name indicates it was silk or velvet imported from Bulgaria. We are informed that as early as the tenth century. Amul in Tabaristan was a market for the goods from Saksin and Bulghar and that traders from Iraq, Syria, Khurasan, and the borders of Hindustan used to go there. Bulghar in Persian literature stands both for Bulgaria and Russia.
14. *Cakavata* (180.5). Nothing further is known about this stuff. The VR., p. 22, however, mentions a silk stuff known as *Cakresvari. Cakrapata* would also mean cloth decorated with *cakra* (wheel) pattern or rosettes.
15. *Calasa (kha)* 180.5). Nothing further is known about the stuff. Could it be some stuff imported from the Celebrate Island as *'Nam'* exported from the foreign.
16. *Calavalia* (180.5). The meaning would be a 'stuff prone to flutter', on account of its lightness.
17. *Campavati* (Annami) (34.1)*;* also known as *Campakadurgiya* (180.5). Apparently as the name indicates the stuff was manufactured in Champaner, Gujarat. It may also be pointed out that the port of Chaul was also known as Champavati (Imp. Gaz. X, 184).
18. *Carasa. V. Corasa* (180.5). Apparently as its literal meaning indicates it was either a evenly woven stuff or a square *cadar.*
19. *Carulia* (180.5). There is no doubt that cotton stuff manufactured in Chirala town in Bapatla Taluk of Guntur Distirct, Andhra Pradesh, is meant here. It is not certain whether the stuff was dyed or an ikat-fabric for which Chirala has been famous even to this day.
20. *Caulahira* (181.5). As the name indicates the stuff had four wavy patterns woven in the loom.
21. *Caukapadiya*(35.1). It is possible that it is the same stuff as Chuckerees of English commerce, Gujarat *cokadi* 'a group of four'. It was a cheap chequered calico, patterned on the loom and classified as 'guinea stuff' bought mainly by the slave traders of the God.
22. *Ceuli* (181.5). Stuff manufactured at modern Chaul, the Saimur of Arab geographers, about 25 miles south of Bombay. In Banaras, *ceoli* an old silk fabric with a bright satin sheen, and a certain amount of watery effect was manufactured till recently. Whether old Chaul manufactured satin in old times is not known. In this connection the *Celloes* of English commerce should also be considered. It has been derived from Sanskrit *cela,* cloth, though *ceuli* should have a better claim. It has been described as a cheap cotton cloth with red, blue or black stripes, patterned in the loom. Sind produced the best *Celloes,* and they also made 'a sort of silk *celloes* which are strong and glossy recalling to mind the Banaras *ceuli.*
23. *Chaila* (181.5). A general term used for printed *saris* worn chiefly by unmarried girls in Gujarat.
24. *Cinamsuka* (34.1: 35.1: 180.5). A generic name for fine Chinese silk.
25. *Cinidama* (181.5). *Dama* may be derived either from Persian *dam,* netting or Persian. *daman* border. In the first case it should be netted silk stuff and in the second case just embroidered border.
26. *Cinansiu* (34.1). Manufactured within the boundary of China proper.
27. *Cujabhati* (180.5). As the name indicates it was decorated with bangle pattern (*bhati*). We do not know whether it has something to do with *Ckulgars* of English Commerce *'word'* Gujarati

ckulger, a printed silk cloth exported to English at the end of the 17th century. A printed artificial silk *sari* simulating tie and dye pattern called *Kalger* is available at Ahmedabad.

28. *Cukadia* v. *cau* (180.5). See *caukapadiya.*
29. *Cutar,* v. *Cautara* (181.5). A plain white calico of usually superior quality, the *cautari-cowtars* of English Commerce exported to Malay Archipelago.The modern Gujarati *cotari* has four threads in each warp and weft.
30. *Dekapatakia*(180.5). As the name signifies the stuff made a Dekapataka which I am unable to identify. It has, however, been suggested tome that it may be Dhanka Tirtha or Upleta 30 miles from Porbandar.
31. *Devadusya* (35.1; 180.5). *Diba* silk of Persian origin. Apparently the name was borrowed from older lists.
32. *Devagiru* (35.1). Fine muslin manufactured in Devagiri, modern Daultabad. See Khusrao's description of Devagiri stuff.
33. *Dhanaveli* (181.5). Literally it wold mean 'precious creeper'. Apparently the stuff had some kind of rhizome as a decorative pattern.
34. *Devanga-cira*(34.1). Brocaded *diba* silk.
35. *Dhati* (180.5). It is a word of ancient origin also mentioned by the Sanskrit lexicographers who describe it as old cloth or a piece o cloth worn over the privities. Apparently it was a short waist cloth (*nati*) of *doti* class. Attention may here be drawn to *duties* of English commerce. It was a strong coarse calico usually sold in length of 12 to 15 yds X 1 yd. woven at Dholka.
36. *Dhota-patta*(35.1) or *dhautavata*(180.5). It is bleached silk.
37. *Dhumarai* (180.5). As the name indicates the stuff was dyed emerald green.
38. *Gajakarni* (180.5). Apparently the same as *gajivyani* of Gujarati explained in 39 below.
39. *Gajavadi*(34.1, 35.1, 180.5). It was either a stuff decorated with elephant pattern or simply a closely woven cotton stuff, the *gazina* of the '*Ain,* I, P. 101. In the *Vidyavilasapavadau* (1428) a woman is shown wearing a skirt (*phaladi*) made of *gajavada* which according to the editors is a kind of silk cloth known in Gujarat as *gajiyani.*
40. *Garbbhasutra* (35.1). A fine variety of muslin mentions in the 'Ain, I, 100 as *garba-suti.*
41. *Garudasannaha*(34.1). The 'Armour of Garuda' unable to identify this stuff. It might have some mottled cloth.
42. *Ghunoliya* (34.1). It was apparently a costly (*bahumula*). The *Paia.* S.M calls *Ghunga* as a settlement which cannot be identified.
43. *Goji* (34.1: 35.1). Nothing is known about the stuff. Whether it came from Guzgan in Western Balkh in Persia is of a matter of speculation. The Prakrita form of *Govinda* is also *gojja.* It is some stuff connected with herdsmen like. The stuff (35.1) is also described as even in structure (*caudasi Chams* or leather worker even). Attention in this connection may be drawn to *guzzees* of English Commerce. The name is supposed to have been derived from Hindi *gaz,* a measure which differed in length in different areas *'word'* the Surat *gaz* measuring between 26 and 27 inches; the Ajmer *gaz* 32 inches and the *Illahi gaz* introduced by Akbar measured 33 inches. The *guzzees* were ordinary plain white calico chiefly woven at Gokul in Mathura district and usually dyed at Ahmedabad. John Irwin has raised a querry that as dimensions varied, it is not clear how they came to be known as *guzzees. Gajjhi* in Hindi is applied to a very closely woven thick calico, the word apparently being derived from *gajjhima,* coarse, closely woven, exactly in the same sense as *gaji* in Gujarati.
43. *Gomeda lugadu* (180.5). Short waist-cloth of the colour of topaz (yellow).
44. *Gudia* (180.5). Cotton stuff manufactured in Bengal or Gauda, the capital bearing the same name lies near Malda, its another name being *Laksamanavati*, the Lakhnauti of the Muslim historians.
45. *Hamsavadi* (35.1; 180.5). It was possibly a stuff decorated with *hamsa* motif *'word'* a favourite textile pattern from the Gupta period till the fifteenth century.
46. *Hasalia* (180.5). It is difficult to distinguish between this stuff and *hamsavadi.* Either its pure white is emphasised or the pattern was disposed in some other way.
47. *Hiragaru*(34.1), *hiragara* (35.1). Two explanatins are possible (1) The stuff is the same as *Vairagara, hira* and *Vaira* both meaning diamond. (2) It might have been a product of Hira in Iraq which declined in

Islamic times. *Ibn Batutah* speaks of brocade (*dibadj*), silk (*harir*) and figured *wasi-stuff* as existing in *Hira* in pre-Islamic times.

48. *Holiyu* (35.1). The word is derived from the Arabic *hulliyah* described as deep coloured brown woollen *cadar* taken round the shoulders.
49. *Jadara*. It is a stuff frequently mentioned in old Gujarati literature. The editors of the *Gurjarasavali* in a note describe it as a white silk usually worn by the bride during the marriage ceremony. The following varieties are mentioned: *jadara mathau* (34.1) was a stuff with sheen (*mathau*); *Jadara dadimasara-(181.5) was* pomogranate-coloured and *jadara bhatigatu* (34.1; 35.1) was apparently patterned. It was also emerald green (*maragada*).
50. *Jalodariya* (180.5). The possibility is that some stuff manufactured in Jullundar in the Punjab is meant.
51. *Jarabapha* (181.5). Persian *Zarbaft* Kalma gold woven.
52. *Jarajari* (181.5). It seems that imported silk or brocade from Georgia is meant. Marco Polo says about Georgiana, 'silk is produced here in great abundance. They also weave cloths of gold and all kinds of fine silk stuffs.
53. *Jhamaratali* (181.5). Fine muslin of Bihar origin. See note on *Jhambartali*.
54. *Jodadariya* (180.5) *Joda* usually means a pair of garments - *dhoti* and *dupatta*. They were apparently striped (*dariya*).
55. *Kabica* (35.1). We have not come across with this word anywhere else. We do not know whether *galica* or carpet is meant here.
56. *Kalagai kokaci* (180.5). *Kokaci* may be derived from the Persian *kork,* fine goat-hair *pasm*. It would then mean *pasm* shawl decorated with pinecorn or *kalgi* pattern.
57. *Kalavadi* (180.5). *Cadar or dupatta* or black silk. It may be the same as *Krsnapadi* (34.1).
58. *Kamabha* (180.5). Brocade imported from China and Persia was known in the early fourteenth century. The 'Ain I., 99 mentions *kamkhas* imported from Kabul and Persia.
59. *Kamalaveli* (181.5). As the name indicates the stuff was decorated with lotus rhizomes.
60. *Kanavirau* (54.1). It is difficult to say whether the stuff was manufactured in *Karnasuvarna* in Bengal.
61. *Kaciyau pitha*(35.1). Stuff manufactured in Kanchipuram. The exact meaing of *pitha* signifying some kind of stuff cannot be determined. It may also stand for curtain or stool cover.
62. *Kapuraveli* (181.5) also *Kapuria* (35.1). According to 'Ain. I, 100 *kapurnur,* formerly called *Kapurdhur,* was some sort of plain silk. The stuff may have some connection with the *Kapuracauka* and *kapuratilaka* of the VR., p. 31 which are mentioned in the list of *pattamvara* silks.
63. *Karmadana* (180.5). It is Sanskritised form of Persian *kamdan* 'gold embroidered stuff.'
64. *Kashmiria* (180.5). Apparently some sort of woollen stuff or shawl manufactured in Kashmir is meant here. The *Sarur-us-Sudur* mentions that in 'Ala-ud-din's time Kashmir shawl was available in Delhi.
65. *Kasturia* (180.5). Here as the name indicates musk-coloured silk *sari* is menat. The *Neminatha Phagu* mentions among the dress and ornaments of Rajimati *kasaturi sari*. Rajasekhara in his *Neminatha Phagu* (e. 1348) again refers to it.
66. *Katani Jhuna* (180-181.5). It was a thin linen which was dyed coral (*magavana*) decorated with lotuses (*kamalavana*), or striped (*deriyakhana*).
67. *Katas* (181.5). Probably from the Persian *qirtas* paper. It should then mean unmixed white stuff. In the *'Ain*, I, 102, *katas* is counted among the woollen stuffs.
68. *Kathapitha* (180.5). It is possible that it was a cover for a wooden seat.
69. *Kathivu* (181.5). Two varieties namely *Patani* and *Phirungi* are mentioned. One was manufactured at Patan in Gujarat and the second was of European origin. Pedro Teixeira observes: "In these parts of Persia (South Persia) are manufactured carpets which in Portuguese we call alcatifas and the Persians call Kalichey (*Kalica*). the richest, the finest, and most estimated in Yazd, from which place I saw some each of which, on account of its workmanship and perfection was valued at more than a thousand ducats; and this in speaking of he alcatita (al-Katifa) of Yazd, which we corruptly call dodiaz, is understood the best, the finest and the most perfect. The second best are from the kingdom of Kirmon

(Kerman), and the third from Karason (Khurasan); they are also made in Agra, Bengala and Cambay, but not so fine." In a note Serjeant observes: "Tabai (*op. cit.* ii. i, 366) speaks of trousers of *khazz* silk called katifa and (op. cit.i, iii, 1485) he mentions a katifa of brocade (dibadj). Thus, all we can understand by this term is some rich embroidered stuff, sometimes velvet. *Kathivu* is called elsewhere as *Katipha* (VS., p. 216).

70. *Kataraini* (1805). It means simply beautifully coloured.
71. *Khadaki* (1805). Apparently the same as *khanda*, a silk piece for making bodice in later time.
72. *Khajalia* (180.5). It seems to have been derived from the Persian *khazz* which is mentioned by the *'Ain, I* 99 in the list of gold stuff.
73. *Kharma* (34.1; 35.1 ; 181.5) *Kharma* was a floss silk, the softer variety is called *narmma kharmma or kharamu naramu* (35.1; 180.5). The *ubhaya-kharma* was fluffy on both sides (34.1 ; 35.1). *Vama-kharma* (35.1) is, however, more interesting. It seems to have been an imported stuff from the district of Bam or Bamm on the eastern frontier of Kerman. In the tenth century it was famous largely for its cotton stuffs, napkins, scarves etc.
74. *Khasata* (35.1). A fine variety of muslin known as *Khasa*. It is the same as *cossaes, cossa and kassa* of English trade. It is derived from Persian *Khasa,* choice, select. It was a good quality muslin woven mostly in Dacca District. *sa (kha) sari* (181.5) may also denote the same sense.
75. *Khirodaka* (180.5) a very ancient Indian silk stuff described elsewhere.
76. *Kumarapachedu* (184.5). Apparently a short *dhoti* of cotton or silk is meant here.
77. *Kusabhia* (180.5). Safflower dyed cloth very popular in mediavel times.
78. *Loavdi* (180.5). Short woollen *cadars (S. romapati).*
79. *Magalika* (34.1); *magaliya*. Two interpretation are possible. Its literal meaning would be 'auspicious' meaning thereby a stuff used at auspicious occasions specially marriage. It may also stand for printed calico of Mangrol in Kotah Division of Rajasthan, where in the village of Siswali the local calico dyers carry on large trade in dyed cloth. The claim of Mangrol in Gujarat could also be considered.
80. *Magia* (180.5). It may stand for cotton stuffs of Bihar or eastern U.P. known as Maggaha= Magadha.
81. *Mahidaurau* (35.1). Product of Mahendrapura which may be identified with the present Rajamahendri in Andhra Pradesh. It was the capital of the Eastern Calukya kings from the seventh to twelfth century.
82. *Mahimudisahi* (180.5). It was the finest variety of muslin of Bengal origin, probably named after one of its rulers *Jadu* alias Muhammad Shah (1414-1431).
83. *Mahyu-salu* (181.5). Red cloth from Mau. There are however, a large number of Maus in U.P Mau in Azamgarh District is however famous for cloth-weaving (*'Ain,* II. 2, p. 158).
84. *Makabala* (181.5). Perisan. *makhmal* or velvet. The best velvets were imported from Persia.
85. *Malabari lachari* (181.5). Probably the same as the lansole or lauzolls of English commerce. It was a sub-category of ginghams defined as a kind of cotton or linen cloth, woven of dyed yarn, often in stripes or checks. The lansoles were noted for their greater breadth than ordinary gingham. They were chiefly exported to Siam.
86. *Malamala Sahi* (181.5). Finest quality of Bengal muslin fit for the use of kings.
87. *Malasa (kha) (180.5).* The trade name for the stuffs manufactured for consumption in the Malay Archipelago.
88. *Malausiu* (34.1). Perhaps silk stuff or damask imported from Malaya is intended. It is significant that the word appears next to *Cinausiu.*
89. *Manasasa (kha). v. manasusa* (kha) (180.5). Apparently it was a muslin of fine quality imparting 'pleasure to mind'.
90. *Madvia* (180.5). The stuff manufactured in Mandavi, a port in Kachchh.
91. *Mandalia* (180.5). Apparently the stuff manufactured at Mandalipathaka, a modern place of the same name in the north Gujarat 2½ miles south of Delmal, and mentioned in the Kadi Grant of Ajayapala.
92. *Madava-madavi* (34.1). It seems that it is the same as *muduveya javali* or wedding cloth

mentioned in a Vijayanagar inscription dated 1382 already referred to.

93. *Mandila* (35.1). *Mandil* of Arabic literature used in the sense of turban or waist-band; perhaps the same as *mandilla, mudilla, mundul* of English commerce from Bengal. It is described as striped fabric of mixed silk-and-cotton usually colourful.

94. *Manjira* (181.5). A stuff probably decorated with floral blossoms.

95. *Misaru* (181.5). Mixed cotton and silk stuff lawful according to the tenets of Islam.

96. *Mayau* (181.5). Perhaps a silk stuff manufactured in Mayin, capital of Ramijird in Fars is intended.

97. *Mediyau* (34.1). Nothing further is known about the stuff. Could it be of Midnapur (Bengal) origin by the *Sudra* or sea or *Samudra*.

98. *Meghadambara* (34.1); *meghadambara* (34.1; 35.1; 181.5); *meghavali* (34.1). These terms remind us of *meghavarna* and *megha-udumbara* of the VR, p. 21 which are included in the list of silk stuffs. The *megh-dambur sari*, a common *Sari* mentioned in old Bengali literature, was black in colour something like the *nilambari* of the present day.

99. *Miniya* (80.5). *Mina* in Persian means enamel. It is perhaps the same as the *meanaes* of English commerce described as a silk cloth woven in Sindh and exported mainly to Persia. Its connection with *mentasses* or *montassies* is also apparent. This is probably the same as the modern *mintasi* described by Watt as 'enamelled fabrics as a name given to a cloth of gold with coloured designs on the surface.'The stuff was brought in the Cambay area and exproted to the Malay Archipelago. *Minakari* or bringing the enamel-like effect in the floral pattern in brocades and *saris* is a special technique of modern Banaras weavers.

100. *Molia* (180.5). The same as *morees* of English-commerce described as one of the categories of staple cotton cloth woven on the Coromandel coast, usually in demand in Europe. The traditional centre of manufacture was Masulipatam.

101. *Moticuri Tamaru* (181.5). Some white stuff for export to Timor island.

102. *Muhivata* (180.5). Face veil used by the Jain *Sadhus*.

103. *Muganau* (34.1); *mugavana* (35.1); *mugia* (180.5). There are several explanations possible: (1) It may simply mean coral-coloured silk (2) the famous *muga* silk of Assam (3) the famous *saris* of Mugipattan or Paithan, 20 miles south-west of Aurangabad. It was famous for weaving in the middle ages.

104. *Mulavatani Sari* (34.1). Multan was famous for its cloth manufacture even in the twelfth century. The *Saris* of Multan had apparently a good market in Gujarat. As a matter of fact in 'Ala-ud-din's time Multan merchants had a monopoly of cloth trade in Delhi.

105. *Mumavadi*(35.1). Waxed rainproof cloth.

106. *Nagavata* (35.1). Muslin manufactured at Nagapattinam in Andhra Pradesh. Nagapattinam as a centre of cloth manufacture has been mentioned by the *Manasollasa* (12th century).

107. *Narmma-haripha* (35.1). Some soft stuff possibly silk from Hira or Herat.

108. *Netra* (34.1; 3.51; 180.5). Several shades of *netra*-silk have been described *'Word'* golden parasol (*Sauvannacchaleau*), blue (*nilau*), red (perhaps obtained from *Kadaha* tree; purple (*vaiganiu*), shade of antimony or black (*Kahli*, Persian *Kuhl*). It is also called *netrapata* (35.1) and *netrambara* (181.5).

109. *Nilavata* (180.5). Indigo-dyed silk was favoured by Indian men and women in ancient India as well.

110. *Niluhura, v. niluhuri* (181.5). Stuff dyed in indigo. Apparently the colour was not very deep.

111. *Pachedi* (181.5). The word was used in the following combinations: *sa(kha)ta, nijhari* and *sonadori*. It is the same as *pitcharies* of English commerce. It is described as coloured calicoes, exported mainly to the Malay Archipelago. "They were perhaps similar to a calico still available in Ahmedabad today called *pachedi* or *pichodi*, popular among shepherds and cowherds; they are sold in two different sizes for waist-cloths and *dhotis* with a plain field of either white, red, blue, maroon, plain borders and wide cross borders." In the 14th-15th century, however, it was also used as a bedspread (*khata pachedi*). The pattern was closely printed without leaving interspaces (*nijhari*). It had also golden stripes (*sonadori*). *Pachedi,* therefore, was a much richer stuff at

lest for home consumption than today. It was also tie-dyed (*cunadi*) *(1801)*.

112. *Padmavali* (34.1). Repeat lotus motif is indicated.
113. *Padmottara* (34.1). It was perhaps a *dupatta* decorated with lotus rosettes.
114. *Paghadi*. Turban, an important article in Indian costume. It was (180.5) rolled (*vidi*). patterned (*reta* from *rid* to ornament) and tie-dyed. Turbans were manufactured in Nandurbar in East Khandesh (*Nandurabari*).
115. *Pajani* (181.5, fn). Apparently it was a *sari* dyed in blue, yellow, black, green and red.
116. *Pamadi* (180.5). *Pavda* in Hindi means foot carpet usually red in colour. In Braja, however, *pavari* is an *odhani* with red field with tinsel printing.
117. *Pancavarnnapadi* (34.1). Literally a five-coloured silk stuff.
118. *Paravalia* (180.5). Coral coloured stuff. It is not certain whether *muga* silk is meant here.
119. *Patala sadi* (180.5). Either thin muslin *sari* or one decorated with repeated leaf-motif is meant here.
120. *Padamsuka* (34.1): (180.5). Five gauze silk.
121. *Pataniya sacopa* (35.1). It was an embroidered silk or velvet of Patan manufacture. *Sacopa* may stand here for gold embroidery (*karcobi*).
122. *Patani pata-patu* (180.5) *patapatu* is apparently some kind of silk stuff, perhaps brocaded. It was obtainable in the piece measuring four yards.
123. *Patolu, patula* (181.5) *patuli* (181.5). The word in old Gujarati literature is spelt as *patolau, patola, patuliya, patauliya,* etc. *Patolu* generally signifies a well-known type of silk-cloth, the warp and weft being tie-dyed before weaving according to the pre-determined pattern. It has been derived from the Canarese *pattuda or pattaduklula*. But whether in older days only double-ikat technique of weaving was followed cannot be affirmed. The *Vividha-varnaka* (53.1) speaks of black, blue and white *patolas*. Another type is called *maragadaguccha* (34.1) perhaps indicating floral sprays in emerald green. That often the *patola* was plain white is supported by a reference in the *Neninatha Phagu* (1346) when Rajimati is said to have worn a white *patauliya*.
124. *Parevau pata* (34.1). Pigeon grey silk.
125. *Pattadukula* (34.1). An old mixed stuff woven from silk and linen.
126. *Pattahari* (34.1). Apparently silk of Herat (Hiri) is meant here. There is a stuff which is called *Pattahira sihavi* (34.1). Whether Trans-Oxus silk of *Sugdh* is meant here. We are unable to say though the stuff as its name indicates came to India via Herat. *Hirapatta* (35.1) also means silk from Herat or alternatively a silk with diamond pattern may be meant.
127. *Phada* and *the phada* (180.5). *Phada* in Hindi a sort of waist-band. *Thephadda* which is the same *thephaau* in Gujarati is a sort of rough *dhoti* used by the Rabaris and others.
128. *Pharodasti* (180.5). It is interesting to note that Firodast was a name given to Bengal by the people of the upper provinces (Steingass, Persian-English Dictionary), *Pharodasti* then would mean fine muslin of Bengal origin.
129. *Phutadu* (34.1). As its name indicates it was a cotton stuff (*phutti* Sindhi) which was either dyed black or red.
130. *Pimpalia* (180.5). Cotton stuff dyed to the green shade of a *pipal*-leaf.
131. *Pitambara cadara* (181.5). Yellow silk *cadar*.
132. *Popatiya* (180.5) Parrot green stuff.
133. *Poti* (34.1); *Potima* (35.1); *Potu* (180.5). The *Potyu* of modern Gujarati. A short waist-cloth of cotton.
134. *Pragia* (180.5). Apparently the stuff manufactured in Prayag later on named as Allahabad by Akbar is meant here. So far my knowledge goes Prayag was never a centre of cloth-weaving of any class. There is, however every possibility that Banaras cloth imported via Prayag is meant here. In the Ain-i-Akbari vol.II, P. 158, informs us that in Akbar's time, Banaras, Jolalabad and Mau produced such stuff's as *Jholi* and *mihrgul*.
135. *Pratapia* (180.5); *pratapasacopa* (181.5). Apparently the stuff was named after a ruler with the honorofic *Pratapa* added to it. There is a possibility that *Pratapa* here stands for the *Kakatiya King Pratapa Rudra* II (1295-1326) as his kingdom was famous for fine muslin as indicated by Marco Polo. Pratapa may also stand for *Pratapa Devaraya* (middle 15th century) of the *Sangama dynasty* of Vijayanagar.

136. *Pumavadi* (35.1). Perhaps the ancient *Puspapatta* with floral pattern woven in the loom.

137. *Puriya* (180.5). Cloth stuffed with cotton apparently for making quilts, In the 17th century embroidered quilts and coverlets were in demand in England.

138. *Putaliu* (34.1). Perhaps as the name indicates the pattern consisted of repeat design of female figure, characteristic of late Gujarat *Kamkhab* and embroideries.

139. *Rajapatta* (35.1). Liteally it would mean silk fit for Kings.

140. *Rajiu* (S. *rajiva*) (35.1). Striped cloth equivalent to the Persian *dariyan*.

141. *Raktambara* (181.5). Red silk.

142. *Ratnakambala* (181.5). Costly shawl of Kashmir.

143. *Ravetau* (34.1). Nothing further is known about the stuff. It is, however, possible that the stuff came from Resht, the capital of Gilan in Persia. A verse of Minuchichiri mentions the colourful brocade of Resht.

144. *Sacopakaci* (34.1), unable to say what is actually meant by this word. It is possible however that gold embroidery of Kanchi origin might have been intended in the field of life.

145. *Salahiti* (180.5). Derived from salah, the name of Mecca. It denotes a kind of cloth because the material from which it was made came from Hijaz in Arabia.

146. *Salahiti* (180.5). Derived from *Salah*, the name of Mecca. It denotes a kind of cloth because the mateiral from which it was made came from Hijaz in Arabia.

147. *Samudrakolahala dhadiya* (34.1). It would literally mean the 'waist-cloth noisy as the sea.' On further consideration it seems that *Samudra-kolahala* is a geographical cum political term. The first element *Samudra* perhaps signifies Dorasamudra, eight miles south-west of Belur. which became the capital of the Hoysala from 1062 onward. The second element *Kolahala* perhaps represents Kolahalapura. In the beginning of the eight century a certain Kolahala built the townof Kolahalapur in the Gangadi province identified by Rice with modern Kolar, the chief town of the Kolar District in the east of Mysore State. Not much is known about the cloth produced in the Hoysala period. But it must have produced some good stuff as a loom-tax (*tari-irani*) and a dyer-tax (*bannings*) are mentioned.

148. *Samusi-pitha* (35.1). According to Nizam al-Din Kari (15th century) *samsi* (sun-cloth) was an Indian stuff which came to Persian markets.

149. *Sania* (180.5). Hempen cloth

150. *Sanjarama* (35.1). It is possible that the stuff got its name from the fertile Sinjar plain in northern Iraq. The city of Sinjar is mentioned by the Arab geographers till the fourteenth century. They, however, only speak of the fruit product of Sinjar, but Amid in Diyar Bakr in northern Iraq was famous for its woollen and linen fabrics.

151. *Sanjharavau* (34.1). Literally it would mean of the red shade of eventide. It was apparently some kind of red cloth.

152. *Sanubapha* (181.5). *Sanbaf* of Persian, a superior quality of muslin.

153. *Saranala* (45.1). Cotton stuff probably woven in Sarnala, now a village in Kaira District, Gujarat.

154. *Saripi* (35.1). Apparently the silk product of Sari or Sariyah the earlier capital of Tabaristan leaving eastward of Amul. It was noted for its silk tissues (*djama-yi-harir va parniyan*). Mustawfi mentions the cotton of *Sari* but not silk, except in its dependencies.

155. *Salura, v. galu* (181.5). *Sallowes* of the English commerce. It was good quality fine muslin dyed red, usually embroidered or brocaded.

156. *Saula* (34.1); *saula* (35.1; 181.5). *Saula* is defined by PSM as the border of a garment and *sahuliya* and *sahuli* as a wimple (*sirovastrakhanda*). The *odhni* mentioned here was soft (*Viliviliya*).

157. *Savadi copacchudahu* (34.1). Literally, the meaning is embroidered and dyed (*acchotita*) stuff from Savada. It is interesting to note in this connection that Saward in Iraq produced rich velvets (*kutuf sawadiya*). *Ibn Rusta* (903 A.D.) and Ibn Fakih support this.

158. *Savapatta* (34.1). Bed-spread. The *Kanhadade Prabandha* (1455 A.D mentions among the imports of *Devapatana* (*Somanatha-pattana*) *savatu*.

159. *Sela* (181.5). Head scarf of silk.

160. *Sa (kha) maratali- (181.5).* Nothing further is known about the stuff, it was from Khmer as mentioned by the Arab geographers in the history of world

161. *Sa(kha) rabasa* (181.5). The words seem to have originated from *Khara* bleached and *vasa* as a weaver of cloth. *Khara* is mentioned as silk stuff in the *'Ain,* I, 100. Whether some stuff of Khawrizm origin is meant here could not be said.

162. *Se(khe) sa* (1815). Thick cotton stuff for making *cadars*. It had the shade of milk diluted with water.

163. *Si (khi) tita-katiyani* (34,1). Fine linen (*katan*) of Chinese origin is meant here.

164. *Silaura* (34.1). It is not known which Sripura is meant here as there are several. It may however, be Sirpur Tandur formerly a sub-division of Bidar. Later on incorporated with Adilabad (Im. Gz. XXIII, 40 ff). Till lately its weavers produced *dhotis* and *saris* and *rangaris* printed cloth for screens and quilts.

165. *Silahati* (35.1); *Silahatti-sveta* (34.1). Silk or cotton stuff of Sylhet (now in Bangla Desh) manufacture.

166. *Simhalaurau* (34.1). Stuff woven in Ceylon. It is, however, known that Ceylon mostly imported cloth from India, though in the twelfth century it is said to have produced fine muslin.

167. *Sribapha* (181.5). The *serribaff* of the English commerce: good quality fine muslin from the Deccan, sometimes dyed red or blue.

168. *Supauti* (34.1). *Supaiti* in Hindi is a generic term for *cadars*.

169. *Supha-kamkha* (181.5). As the name implied it was a brocade woollen stuff.

170. *Suvarnapadi* (34.1; 180.5). It may be gold brocade or tinsel printed stuff.

171. *Talapakau* (35.1). It is possible that some stuff or felt of Talikan manufacture is intended here. Three marches from Marv-ar-Rud was situated the city of Talikan. According to Yaqubi it was famous for felts. It was razed to the ground by Chinghiz. The claim of a bed-spread could also be considered as *talpa* in Sanskrit means a bed.

172. *Tastu* (180.5). It is unable to identify this stuff unless it stands for *tas* or brocade (Ain, I.P. 98) which is now entirely woven of gold wire and used for making a wedding dress for the spreading of carpet.

173. *Tanasukha* (180.5). Fine muslin mentioned by the 'Ain, I, P. 100. It is perhaps the same as *tanjeebs* or *tunzebs* of English commerce. The *tanzeb* was plain cotton cloth usually of superior quality woven in Dacca District and exported to England.

174. *Tanubandha* (10.5). It is a waistband or a scarf to which the quiver was attached (*sarabandha*). It was of a single (*kada*), double (*dokada*) or fourfold (*caupada*) size. The *masapada* may indicate the waistband of Mashhad manufacture. Mashhad stands a few miles from the ancient ruins of Tus which was pillaged by the Mongols in 1220. Mashhad rose to prominence in the 14th century. The 'Ain, I, P. 99 speaks of the velvets from Mashhad.

175. *Tasariya* (180.5). Stuff manufactured from wild silk. It is mentioned by the *'Ain,* I, 100. It is now chiefly manufactured in Bengal and Bihar.

176. *Tilavasa* (35.5). *Tila* here stands for Persian *tila*, gold. The stuff would then mean *zarbaft* or brocade.

177. *Titatragiu* (35.1). Literally it should mean a stuff with three threads. It is not known whether the weft had two threads and warp one or vice versa.

178. *Umavadi* (35.1). As its name indicates it was probably a linen *cadar.*

179. *Urasala* (181.5). The same as *ulasutri* (34.1). It may be the same as *ulapata or Bisaladeva Raso* (127). Probably camlet is meant.

180. *Vairagara* (181.5); *vairagarau* (34.1); *vayaragara* (35.1). It was apparently a product of ancient *Vairagara* which is identified with modern Bairagarh in Chanda District, Bombay State, which had a diamond mine in ancient times. The *Khulasatut -Tawarikh* (end of the 17th century)[48] says: 'At Biragarh there is a diamond mine; figured cloths are well woven there.

181. *Vakala* (181.5). Pure gold or silver cloth.

182. *Vala* (181.5). It may be the product of Vala, the ancient Valabhi in Saurashtra.

183. *Vama-saua* (35.1). Perhaps a silk product of the district of Bam in Persia.

184. *Vatalia* (180.5). Apparently *badla* cloth is meant here. *Badla* is gold or silver wire not so fine as *kalabattun;* it has no thread in its

composition. It is used for a fabric called *tasbadia*[49].

185. *Vayarajiu* (35.1). The meaning is not certain. It may be suggested, however, that it may mean a stuff with woven (*vaya*) stripes (*rajiu -rajiva*)in the form of '*Nam*'.

186. *Vidyapuria* (180.5). It is difficult to say whether the stuff manufactured in Bijapur in Mysore State or Vijyanagar (ancient Vidyanagar) or Bijapur in Gujarat is meant.

187. *Vinausiu* (34.1). Here *Vina* either stands for Benna a branch of the Krishna, the river Krishna itself or the Wain-ganga. The region through which these rivers flow was famous for cotton manufacture.

188. *Yaja* (180.5). It is described as fine coloured (*pancavarna*), two coloured (*durangi*) *and Magaluri*. There is no doubt that the famous Yezd stuff from Persia is meant here. Istkhri and Ibn Hawkal mention it as cotton garment. *Ibn-al-Balkhi* (1107 A.D.) mentions its products as silk, excellent brocades named *musti* and *farakh*. Kazwini found in it makers silk (hair) of *sundus* (a kind of green brocade), extremely beautiful and close-woven which is taken to it from all countries. According to Marco Polo: 'It is a good and noble city, and it has a great amount of trade. They weave there quantities of certain silk tissue called *Yasdi*, which merchants carry into many quarters to dispote of. The Yezd brocade velvet is mentioned also in the '*Ain-i-Akbar*, Vol. I, p. 98.

The history of costume and fabrics from roughly c.1400 to 1550 is not greatly different than the costume and fabrics in the fourteenth century except that some new stuff are mentioned and most of the imported stuffs with foreign names were being manufactured in this country though retaining their foreign trade names. The trade relations with Persia remained as vigorous as ever, but in early sixteenth century the foreign trade of India passed into the hands of the Portuguese and later on the Dutch and the English shared in the trade. In the fifteenth century Nizam al- Din Mahmud Kari in his *Diwan –I -Albisa* (Constantinople 1303 H., p. 17) says that in Persian markets came textiles from Asia (Rum), Cathay (Khita) and Hindustan. 'Some had trodden the road from Hindustan such as shamsi (sun- cloth) and salu (a red cloth mixed with black, suitable for women's apparel and turbans) and saghar (a town in the deccan); and two circle 'cloth (Brahman *duchanbari*) and royal (*sultani*), *bairmi* (an *Irishmen*- silk cloth like *mithkali*) and the two warp manufacture of the court (*dutarah- yi –kar-I bargah-i*)".

Mahuan's account of Bengal is interesting from the point of view of textiles history of Bengal. Mahuan was attached to the suit of *Cheng-Ho* who undertook the journey to India in 1405 and therefore his account is datable to early fifteenth century.

"Among their manufactures are five or six kinds of fine cotton fabrics (muslins); one like our *pi-pu* has the foreign name *Pi-cih*. This is a fabric of soft texture three feet broad, and made up in lenths of fifty or fifty-six or fifty-seven feet."

"There is also a ginger-yellow fabric called *Man-Cheti* four feet or more wide and fifty feet long; it is very closely woven and strong."

"There is another fabric, five feet wide and twenty feet long, called *sa-na-kieh*, like our *Lo-pu*."

"There is also another kind with the foreign name of *Hin-pei-tung-tali*, three feet wide and sixty feet long; the meshes of this texture are open and regular; it is somewhat like gauze and is much used for turbans."

"There is the *sa-ta-urh*, made in lengths of forty or more feet and two feet five inches or six inches wide; it very much resembles the Chinese *San-so*."

"There is the *Mo-hei-mo-leh*, made in lengths of twenty-feet or more and four feet wide; on both sides it has a facing four to five lengths in thickness, and resembles the Chinese *Tow-lo-kein*."

Silk handkerchiefs and caps embroidered with gold were also manufactured in Bengal.

Mr. Philips identifies *Pi-ci* as Betteela (a silken 'law or *Rita* of ancient time) *sa-ta-urh* as *cautar* and *Mo-hei-moleh* as *malmal*. Mr. John Beames has noted that *pi-cih* or *Bi-tih* may be *buti* or *butidar*, the name of muslin with flowers worked on it and *sa-na-kieh* as sahn, a great deal of which was made at Balsore in the seventeenth and eighteenth centuries. To this information one may add that *Man-ce-ti* may either stand for *Mahmudi* or *mansukh*, both mentioned in old lists and *Hin-pet-tung-tali* for *Jhamartali*, a fine muslin probably of Bihar origin.

The Russian traveller Athanius Nikitin, describing the costumes of the Indian people in the late fifteenth century observes: "In the winter, the people put the *fata* (*fautah*) and wear it round the waist, on the shoulders and the head; but the princes and nobles put trousers on, a shirt and at *Kaftan* (a long coat) wearing a fata on the shoulders, another as a belt round the waist, and a third round the head.

"Apparently Nikitin's *fata* stands in the case of common people for waist cloth. *cadar* and turban; while in the case noblemen and the princes it stands for waist-band, *dupatta* and turban.

At Cambay he saw people wearing talach (long grows of striped material half silk and half cotton). He also saw *damasks, khan* (satin from China) and *kiota* blanket being traded there.

Some information about the costume and stuffs of the fifteenth century is also available from the contemporary Gujarati and Hindi literature. The *Vidyavilasa Pavadau* (1420 A.D.) speaks of *jadara* and *Khasaru,* the latter being interpreted in the sence of shoes (Gujrat. *Khasadu;* Mar. *khasada-khasada*), but perhaps it stands for *khasamalmal. Lugada* in the sense of *sari* also appears. The *Cupai Phagu* (15th century) mentions *bhairava, sanabapha* and a pomegrante-coloured cadar (*dadimahulau-dhanai*).

The *Kanhadade Prabandha* of Padmanabha (composed in 1455) refers to some contemporary stuffs. *Savatu (*see *savadi*) was imported at Devapatana or Somanathpatana. It is said that *phalapagara* (heavily flowered stuff) was spread on the path as a foot-carpet. Apparently *Mandavi* was famous for freshly dyed *odhani* made of *ghata* cloth (*udhani navaraga ghataki*). It is said that the merchants of *Kalavagundra, Anagundi* (Anegondi, near Vuayanagar on the north bank of the Tungbhadra river) Bidar (Bedar) and Telegana (Tilanga) wore *sanapana* (v. *sonapana*) *i.e* a rich silk stuff decorated with gold leaves, the same as *kanakapatra* of V.R. p. 21. The *pattakula* of black colour (*meghavanna*) and *pataulada* of five colours are mentioned *Phudadi* was also some kind of rich stuff in which gold and gems were used (*kanaka sakomala phudadi e-vici ratana baitha*). While describing Mandavi Padmanabha says that it had dealers in skirts (*phadiya*), cloth (*dosi*), embroideres (sui), towel sellers (*gacha*) and calico-printers (*chipa*) In the market of Mandavi silk weavers (*padasutrapatua salavi*) *are mentioned.*

The *Prthvicandracarita,* written in 1421, gives some interesting information about the fifteenth century fabrics most of which appear in the *Varnaka* lists already described.

1. *Atana.* Originally silk stuff imported from Aden; either Mecca Velvet or Alexandrian stuff imported by the way of Aden.
2. *Bhairava.* This stuff is also mentioned as pure (*suddha*) which would mean that it was a pure cotton stuff.
3. *Caukadiya.* Chuckerees of English commerce (Gujrat. *Cokadi*) described as a cheap chequered calico, patterned in the loom.
4. *Dadima,* Pomegranate-coloured stuff.
5. *Gajavadi.* See Gajavadi in *Varnaka* list.
6. *Hamsavadi.* Stuff with geese pattern.
7. *Jhamaratali.* The famous *jhamaratali* muslin of Bihar, famous since 'Ala-ud-din's days.
8. *Jadara.* A silk stuff which was black, yellow and grey (*paleviya*).
9. *Katana Jhuna.* Fine linen muslin. See *jhuna.*
10. *Kasturiya.* Musk coloured stuff referred to in the *varanakas* and contemporary literature.
11. *Kapuriya.* The same as *capperees* of English commerce, described as cheap blue and white chequered or striped cloth of Western Indian origin, patterned in the loom and exported mainly for the slave traders.
12. *Lalavaliya.* Not known likely to be *Chandra.*
13. *Meghavana.* Stuff as black as cloud.
14. *Narma-pitha.* Soft muslin cover
15. *Nalibaddha.* Literally 'kept inside a bamboo receptacle'. There is no doubt that *Khasa* muslin of Bengal is meant here. In this connection, the information given by Manrique is significant. "The finest and richest cassas are produced in the country (Bengal), from 50 to 60 yards and seven to eight hand breadth wide, with borders of gold and silver or coloured silks. So fine indeed are these muslins that the borders of gold and silver or coloured silks. So fine indeed are these muslins that the borders of gold and silver or coloured silks. So fine indeed are these muslins that the merchants place them in the hollow bambus, about two spans long and thus secured, carry them throughout Corazane, Persia, Turkey and many other countries.
16. *Phudaiya.* As indicated it was a rich silk stuff with jewel setting.
17. *Padura.* White stuff
18. *Sangrama.* The same as *sanjarama* of the *Varnakas.*
19. *Suthila.* Any kind of cotton stuff.
20. *Salvaliya.* Not known. Was it a kind of creased stuff? Which standstill i.e, God or 'Nam'.
21. *Takasiniya.* It is new stuff, Probably a roll (*taka*) of Chinese silk.

22. *Udasala:* The same as *urasala.* It is an Indian name for camlet, light cloth of various materials for cloaks, etc, originally a costly Eastern stuff of silk and camel-hair; perhaps derived from Arabic *khaml,* napkin.

Among the people connected with yarn trade are mentioned yarn merchant (*sutriya*). silk yarn merchant (*padasutriya*), cloth merchant (*dosi-dausyika*), cotton merchant (*kapasi*), towel seller (*ganchika*), dealer in madder (*majithia*) and weaver (*vanakara*).

Reference to the fifteenth century costumes and fabrics of Eastern India are found in the *Kirtilata* and the *Padavali* of the famous Hindi poet Vidyapati, and the *Chitaivarta* of Narayandas. According tot he *Kirtilata* in the market of Jaunpur the merchants sold to the Turks camphor, saffron, articles of perfume, *cauris* and *neta* silk (*naana*) and black silk (*kajala-ambara*), favourite of the Turks. Garments made of *neta-silk* (*netaka basanu*) are mentioned. Blue silk (*nilapatora*) was liked by the women. *Divyambara* apparently stands for *diba* brocade. The Turks of Janupur bought in the market for their use *khes-cadars (si) (khi) (sa)*, shoes (*paijjalla* -per. *pai-ijar*) and stocking (*moja*). They spent their spare time in needle-work (*kasida kadhanta*).

The *Chitaivarta* also provides interesting information. Cloth from the Deccan (*daksana ko cira*) was famous in the North. The silk *patolas* of Deogir were famous and formed a part of the bridal trousseau of *Chitai*, daughter of *Ramadeva* of Deogiri. It is said that the marriage pavilion of *Chitai*, was covered with red *saqlat* silk or velvet *madapa madi sikalata*), the scarlet of English dictionary, and the pavilion was further provided with curtains of *nij* stuff (*nijara*).

Zain-ul-Abidin (1420-1470), considered the Akbar of Kashmir was a cultured prince whose learning and practical benevolence delighted his subjects. It is a tradition among the Kashmir weavers that he introduced the art of shawl weaving in Kashmir, though the point is debatable. The *Jaina Rajatarangini* of *Srivara*[50] gives very interesting details of the king's liking for costly stuffs and his encouragement to weavers. It is said that hearing the great reputation of Zain-ul-Abidin some independent rulers of India sent him costly stuffs as presents. For instance the Khalji, ruler of *Mandavya* (*Mandu*) and Gauda, who could be identified with Mahmud I (1436-69), sent him the pieces of cloth named *darandama,* possibly derived from the Persian *darand* fashion, mode, quality and *amma* universal, which would mean a stuff in general fashion. It is the same as *terrindam* and *turundam* of the English commerce a plain muslin of superior quality woven chiefly in Dacca District. It is said to have been derived from *tarh,* kind and *andam,* body. The famous Rana Kumbha (1433-1468) sent to Zain-ul-Abidin a stuff called *narikunjara* which, poetically, is said to have been so attractive that it drove from the king's heart the desire for actually practising the *narikunjara* form of amusement. *Narikunjara* is a curious motifin Western Indian art of the fifteenth century in which the composite figure of women in the shape of an elephant ridden by a hero is depicted. The stuff has also been mentioned in the fifteenth century lists.

The famous Sultan Mahmud Beghada (1458-1511) of Gujarat did not lag behind. He despatched to Zain-ul-Abidin *katif* (*Katepha*), *saqlat* (*saglata*) and *suf* (sopha) woollen stuffs which were very famous in Gujarat. Zain-ul-Abidin was, however, not only satisfied with the gifts of costly stuffs from contemporary rulers. Such was his reputation as a lover of handicrafts that in the words of Srivara, "A large number of artisans, adept in formulating original designs (*silpakapitakalapandh*), regarding him as the Wishing Tree came from long distances like a swarm of bumblebees. The Kashmiris mastering the skilful use of the shuttles (*turi*) and looms (*vemadi*) etc. now weave costly and beautiful silks (*kauseyakam*). The special woollen stuffs (*aurnah sophadayah*) of distant foreign origin, worthy of kings, are now being woven by the Kashmiris. The painters seeing the complicated creeper designs (*citralata*) obtained by intricate weaving processes (*vicitarvayanotpanna*) are reduced to silence as a figure in painting. The country and the costume of the king became famous on account of the skils made of endless threads (*anantatantusantana*) and made beautiful by colours (*varnavicchitti*). Multicoloured, decorated with beautiful and appropriate designs (*cirakatakalamkaara*), bestower of skill and honour, pleasant, the art of silk weavers (*kauseyata*) became famous. Though rich, ever effulgent, unrivalled in virtues, and good administrator the king by his own intelligence became renowned by his country and his costume." Jonaraja in a couplet refers to the embroidered carpet of Kashmir. "The capret-like Lavanya (*Lavanyakantha*), dividing the enemy by the needle of the wise council (*mantrasucyakrte bhede*) entering the enemy's rank by the arrow of thread *banasutre pravesini*), it is strange how he lost his tautness."

A *varnaka* list assignable to the late fifteenth century or sixteenth gives a list of sixty-eight stuffs most of them being common to the list previously discussed. The following, however, appear to be new terms: *Padua, pacaraia, bhuhacia, ghatadi, cira, sa (kha)ra cini, tasta, guakari, agrai, kaphai, masamara, samani, tuku, sadala, chita, corasadika.*

*Agrai.*Either cloth woven in Agra or trade name for the cloth for Agra market. In the English records Agra is mentioned as an important centre for bringing good quality *'pintadoes'*, but there is no indication that they were actually manufactured there.

Bhuhacia. It is unable to identify the stuff: as the second element in the word indicates it may be some stuff of Chinese origin called *cina* silk.

Chita. One of the earliest references to *chintz.*

Cira. Perhaps muslin of narrow width for making turban or *chillies-chellies* of English commerce of Coromandel coast, cheap chequered cotton cloth, woven mainly in Madras area and exported to Malay Peninsula. It may be also *celloes,* a cheap cotton stuff with red, blue or black stripes, patterned in the loom or *cirans* a cheap calico listed with chequered goods of Western Indian origin.

Corasadika. It is unable to identify the stuff because it emerges at the time of materialistic stage of the word.

Ghatadi. Cloth either manufactured in goa or manufactured for Goa market for export.

Kaphai. It is again unable to identify the stuff but if it could be derived from the Persian *qafa* there it should mean a glove lined with cotton or a muff in white colour.

Kasabi vastra. A pure silk fabric made till the beginning of the present century in Agra and Farrukhabad, generally of red colour used for making skirt. According to Maqdisithe garments of *kasab* came from Kazerun. Tawwaz, Dariz and Dabikki, which was exported to all quarters of the world. According to Istikhri it was manufactured at *Shiraz.*

Masanjara. From the Persian *masajjar* mentioned in the *Ain,* I. 99 described as a kind of silk cloth leaves and branches woven in it.

Padua. Apparently a kind of muslin woven the Pandua in Malda District nine miles from old Malda and a about twenty miles from Gaur. Shams-ud-din Iliyas Shah (1343-47) transferred his capital from Gaur to Pandua in about 1350. It remained the chief city of Bengal from 1350 to 1420. In 1420 Jalaluddin alias Jadu (1414-1431) retransferred his capital to Gaur. After that date the city is not mentioned in history though it continued to flourish for some time (Imp. Gaz. XIX. 392).

Pancaraia. We are unable to identify the stuff. It may, however, be either *peniascoes,* a highly coloured fabric, probably of mixed cotton and silk, usually striped, or some variety of *rehings, reyngs, raings* of Bengal origin, a fine muslin of the English commerce in the seventeenth century.

Sadala. The stuff is named after Samana in Patiala, the *semianoes* of English commerce, a good plainc calico, especially liked for its breadth, which was sometimes as much as 1½yards.

Sa(kha)racini. Bleached silk from China.

Tasta. It may be *taffeta* or *satin* or an expensive stuff made of beaten golden and silver tissues.

Tuku. The *tuckeryes 'Word' tuckrees* of the English commerce of Bengal origin described as striped silk pieces of Baikunthapur ten miles east of Patna. It is, however, possible that this stuff was being manufactured in Gujarat as well.

The fifteenth century Gujarati and Hindi literature occasionally refer to articles of costume. The *Kanahadade Prabandha* (1455) refers to long coat (*agasalkha*) and *jamalau* (S. *jamali-dhoti* and *dupatta*). A soldier is said to have been dressed in a long coat (*anga*) and helmet (*topa*). The Turkish women are said to have worn long robes (*pahirana=pairhan*) and trousers (*suthani*). In the *Chitaivarta 'Ala-ud-din* is said to have worn full boots (*khalyai paijara*), black garment (*karau bagau*) and the helmet. *Vidyapati* mentions articles of female costume such as bodice named as *kacuka, kancuka, kancuki, kacali* and *coli*. Blue *nicola* covered the body. The women wore beautifully dyed *cira* muslin, blue garment (*nila-basana*), and affected veils with their *saris* (*sira lela ghughata sari*).

Though little work has been done on costumes and fabrics of South India it is significant that the weavers in the Vijayanagar Empire were accorded an important place in the society by the rulers. Thus an inscription dated 1485-86 grants the conchshell as their insignia on the model of Kaikkolars of Kanchipuram. In the year 1503-04, in the reign of *Narasimha Raya*, a similar privilege was bestowed on the weavers of three villages the right of *dandu* and *sanku.* They were to enjoy the same privileges on the model of those enjoyed by the community living int he country situated on the bank of the river Pennai. The Kaikkolars of Ambasamudram in the year 1517-18 for having constructed a temple and providing endowments for its kitchen were granted the hereditary right of receiving a garland in the temple with incidental privileges.

The history of Indian fabrics in the first half of the sixteenth century is interesting. The source material for their history is the same *mana* Gujarati and Hindi literature and occassionally Persian sources which are, however not of much help. The arrival of the Portuguese, however, opens up a new source of information, interesting though at times difficult to interpret. The works of Duarte Barbosa, Ludovico Varthema and last but not the least the account of Tome Pires throw considerable light on the fabrics of India which had already market from Arabia to Indonesia. In this commerce Indian merchants chiefly from Gujarat, Coromandel coast and Bengal played an important part, though the Arabs, the Persians and other Asiatic merchants had their own share of business. From the account of the early Portuguese travellers it is evident that Cambay on the Western Coast, Calicut in Malabar Coast, Pulicat in the Coromandel and Satgaon in Bengal were chief centres of the international commerce with a great number of smaller ports sharing in the business. Bengal and the Coromandel had their focus to Burma, Malay and Indonesia while Gujarati merchants romped all over. Duarte Barbosa (1500 to 1516-17) gives penetrating pictures of the ports engaged in textile business. According to him ships from *Juda* (Jiddah) sailed to Calicut with goods which included scarlet cloth, silks, camlet and taffeta. Aden as in preceding centuries was a great centre of trade. Ships came there from all parts specially from Jiddah exporting silk and cotton fabrics from Cambay. From Aden they brought to Cambay Mecca velvets and camlets. The Bengal ships brought to Aden, among other things, Bengal muslins. It is interesting to note that import to India via Jiddah and Aden also included European stuffs. Tome Pires (1512-1515) observes that the merchandise which the Egyptians brought to India came from Venice. From Alexandria the goods reached Cairo and thence to Jiddah. Aden and finally to Cambay, Goa, Malabar and Bengal. Aden in return for large quantities of cloth from Cambay exported madder there.

Ormuz in the Persian Gulf imported Indian goods. According to Duarte Barbosa. "They have plenty of *Gambaya, Chaul* and *Dabul* cloths, and from *Bengala* they bring many *synbafos*, which are a sort of very thin cloth greatly prized among them and highly valued for turbans and shirts, for which they use them."

The Spanish version of Duarte Barbosa expands the passage but confounds the products of Cambays, Chaul, Dabul and Bengal and many stuffs from Cambaya, Chaul, Dabul and Bengala which are called Sinabasos, Chautars, Mamonas, Dugasas, Sorantis. Sinababa has been derived from *Sina-bafta* "China-woven". It was very fine muslin. Mamonas stands for *malmal*; Dugasas indicates the two yard length of the pieces; Chautars have been discussed previously and the *soranatis* is equated with the Portuguese text estravants.

Ormuz exported to Cambay among other things white silk of Persian origin and imported beatilha (fine muslin) and white cloth.

Cambay was the hub of trade according to all authorities in early sixteenth century. Speaking about Cambay Ludovico Varthema (1502-08) observes: "An immense quantity of cotton is produced here, so that every year forty or fifty vessels are laden with cotton and silk stuffs, which stuffs are carried into different countries. According to the *Suma Oriental*, Cambay was inhabited by merchants from almost all Muslim countries. The trade, however, was in the hands of the Hindu merchants who were noted for their business sagacity. Ships from here sailed to Aden, Ormuz, the Deccan ports, Goa, Bhatkal, Malabar, Ceylon, Bengal, Pegu, Siam, Pedir, Pase and Malacca. It manufactured silk and about twenty kinds of cotton material. The life line of the Cambay trade was Java. Duarte Barbosa observes: "Here are woven white fabrics both fine and coarse and others printed in patterns: also much silk cloth and coloured velvets of poor quality, velvety satin and taffeties, also thick carpets. Diu imported silks from China and Malacca, great stores of cotton and linen from Chaul and Dabul. The merchants exported common silk camlets made in Cambay, carpets (*alcatifas*, may also mean velvets), *tafetta* and cloth of scarlet-in-grain and other colours.

The Deccan produced white and coloured calicoes and *beatilhas* used for turbans. According to Varthema, Chaul produced cotton stuffs in abundance. Duarte Barbosa notes Chaul's fame for cotton fabrics. "From this port of Dyo the Moors of Chaul take away every year a great number of pieces of fine muslin (*beatilha*) for turbans, in which they traffic with Arabia and Persia, where it is held in great esteem. They also have many fine calicoes and Roman turbans; these three kinds of cloths are woven in this kingdom.The natives of the country use much calico and are clad therein, wearing it unbleached. After it has been worn they bleach it making it very white and starching it and in this state they sell it to many regions, and on this account it is often found torn at the time of civilizational growth."

Barbosa also observes that great stores of cloth came from the inland region and loaded on ships in the port of Dabhol.

Ceylon, according to Toe Pires, imported Cambay cloth, a few *cacutos*, a great many *mantazes* and *visipices*. In a note the translator describes cacutos as an Indian cloth, perhaps black or dark, of Persian origin. The word however wears close resemblance to *custaes* of English commerce, either stripped or chequerred cloth possibly of mixed cotton-and-silk, the name being derived in the Hobson-Jobson from Kushtia in Nudea District Bengal. In Canarese it would mean an embroidered stuff, *Mantaz* was a Cambay cloth and *vispices* described as a coarse cotton cloth, may be corruption of *basta* for which Broach was famous.

Bengal was famous for its fine fabrics. According to Varthema, "Fifty ships are laden every year in the place (Satgaon) with cotton and silk stuffs, which stuffs are thse, that is to say *bairam*, *mamone, lizati*, ciantar, doazar, and sinabaff. These same stuffs go to all Trukey, through Syria through Persia, through Arabia *Felix*, through Ethiopia and throught all India.

Duarte Barbosa's description of the Bengal stuffs is almost the same as that of Varthema except for some additional details. "In this city (Bengala, *Pandu* or *Tanda*) are many cotton fields patches of sugar canes and long pepper; in it are woven many kinds of fine and coloured cloths for their own attire and other white sorts for sale in various countries. They are very precious, also some they call estravantes (sar band or hairband) a certain sort, a very thin cloth esteemed amongst ladies headdresses, and by Moors, Arabs and Persians for turbans, these great stores are woven, so much so that many ships take cargoes thereof for abroad; others they make call mamonas, other *duguzas*, others *chautares*, others *sinabafos,* which latter are the best of all, and the Moors hold them the best for shirts. All these sorts of cloth are in pieces, each on whereof contain about three and twenty or four-in-twenty Portuguese yards. Here they are sold good cheap, they are spun on wheels by men, and woven by them."

According to the *Suma Oriental* Bengal manufactured seven kinds of *sinabafos*, there kinds of *chautares beatilhas* and beirames. It exported to Burma *sinabafos*, *damasks, satins*, brocades and white cloths; large and small *sinabafos, andpanchavlizes* (perhaps the same as *Panchavelaoes*, a printed cloth in Coromandel) to Champa. Bengal and Kling (Orissa) also exported to Borneo cloths namely chequered enrolados. *Puravas* (Indian cotton cloth), *synabafos* of all kinds *panchauelzes* and *synhavas*. About Java it is noted: "They buy white sinabaffs, both large and small, synhavas, panchauelezes, balachos, atobalachos (those are white cloth). They bring kling cloths *enrolados*, of large and small *ladrillo as'Nam'* They buy *bretangis* from Cambay, *turias, tririncandes, cadyes* in quantities." Banda imported *sinabaffos* of all kinds and every kind of fine cloth from Bengal; all kinds of cloth from Bonuaquelim, enrolades of large, medium and small *ladrilhos*, *topetins* and cloth of all kinds from Gujarat. Gujarat as a matter of fact exported to Banda *bretangis*, *cacutos*; white and black *maindis*, *patolas* and *sabones*. The Portuguese accounts have used many words whose significance is not quite clear and whose Indian parallels are far from certain. The following notes are given below by the way of explanation.

Atobalcos and balcos and cotobalcos. The translator of the *Suma Oriental* in a note quoting the description of Nagapattinam by *Barreto de Resende* observes as follows: "Many cloths, printed as well as white ones are called *enrolados,* which are thin as *boeftas; ballachos, cotonians* of two threads, and the printed ones, many sort of *taffesiras* of cotton thread, *sarasas* and many sorts of them." The *atobalachos* and *balachos* are apparently derived from the Persian *parcah* applied to cotton or linen cloth. *Krsnadasa* in the *Parasinamamala* (late 16th cent.) mentions *paracah* in the sense of cloth.

Bierames. From the Persian *bairam* described as a kind of silken stuff.

Bretangis. Described as cotton cloth (blue, black and red). Is it derived from the Persian *burd 'Mula ranga'* a striped cloth or *cadar* and *tang* Brahman narrow in thought Ladrilho is a Portuguese word meanings 'tile' or little square. Enrolados de ladrilho is explained as chequered woollen cloth. But it is doubtful if woollen cloth is meant here.

Lamadares. Does it mean some stuff woven in Rander in Gujarat?

Maindis. Perhaps from the Persian *mindil* meaning a towel, napkin, waistband, a table-cloth.

Pancvelizes, Pancaulezes etc. It has been described as a printed cloth. It that meaning is correct then it should be the same as *pancavarna* chintzes often mentioned in old *varnaka* lists. The *'Ain,* I, P. 101, however, mentions a cloth stuff called *panctoliya* though it is not known whether it was printed or not.

Puravas. It is called a cotton stuff. *Purna* in Hindi means to decorate, to embroider and if interpreted in this light the stuff should mean ambroidered quilt from Bengal.

Sabones. A stuff known as *savatu* has been referred to in old Gujarati literature, which is derived from *sava-patta,* bedspread.

Tiricandes, It may correspond to the *tucamdya nylora*, green and red cloth ornamented with painted birds.

Caydes. Perhaps corresponding to 'Candya azares' which were thick cloths from Khorasan.

The Portuguese sources also give interesting details about the Indian costume of early sixteenth century. Duarte Barbosa gives the following description of the costume of Gujarati *Banias*.

"These *Baneanes* grow very long hair, as women do with us, and wear it twisted up on the head and made up into a knot, and over it a turban, that they may keep it always held together; and in the hair they keep flowers, and other sweet-scented things.

"They used to anoint themselves with white sandal wood mixed with saffron and other scents of *'Nam'*. They are clad in long cotton and silken shirts and are shod with pointed shoes of richly wrought *cordivain*: some of them were short coats of silk and brocade."

While giving details of the costume of the woven of Gujarat Barbosa observes: "Their dress is as long as that of their husbands; they wear silken bodices with tight sleeves, cut low at the back, and other long garments called *chandes* (*cadar*) which they throw over themselves like cloaks. When they go out on their heads they wear nought but their own hair well-dressed on the top of it."

The soldiers at Cambay wore coats of mail and jackets quilted with cotton.

Speaking about the dress of the Muslims, Barbosa observes: "They go very well attired in rich cloth of gold, silk, cotton and camlets (mixed silk and wool). They all wear turbans on their heads; those turbans are long like Moorish shirts; drawers, with boots upto the knees of very thick *cordovan* leather worked in very dainty devices within and without the tip of the shoe(*Juta*).

Barbosa notes that theMuslims of Goa wore short coats padded with cotton (Laudes, Can. *lodu*; H. *labada*). Varthema gives interesting details of the costume of the Bijapuris. "Their dress consists of robes, or beautiful shirts of silk, and they wear on their feet shoes or boots with breeches after the fashion of sailors. The ladies go with their faces quite covered,acording to the custom of Damuscus."

The Portuguese travellers, however, have left accountsof the costumes of the people and kings of Vijayanagar in greater details. Thus according to Varthema (1502-1508) *'Nam'* "the men of condition wear a short skirt, and on their head a cloth of gold and silk in the Moorish fashion, but nothing on the feet. The common people go quite naked with the exception of a piece of cloth about the middle. The king wears a cap of gold brocade two spans long, and when he goes to war he wears a quilted dress of cotton, and over it he puts another garment full of golden piastres."

Durate Barbosa's description of the costumes of the men and women of Vijayanagar is much fuller: "The women go trimly clad: their men wear certain clothes as a girdle below, wound very tightly in many folds, and white shirts of cotton or silk or coase brocade, which are gathered between thighs, but open in front : on their heads they carry small turbans, and some wear silk or brocade caps, they wear their rough shoes (without stockings). They wear also other large garments thrown over their shoulders like capes *'Nam'*. The women wear white garments of very thin cotton, or silk of bright colours, five yards long: one part of which is girt round their below, and the other part on their shoulder and across their breasts in such a way that one arm and shoulder remains uncovered, as with a scarf. They wear leather shoes well embroidered in silk by the *'Chamar'* or *Mochi* at that time.

The narrative of Domingo Paes (1520-22) gives a realistic picture of the costumes of *Krsnadeva Raya* nd his women. According to Paes when *Christvao Figueired* met the king he found that, "The king was clothed in certain white clothes embroidered with many roses in gold and with a pateca of diamonds on his neck of very great value and on his head he had a cap of brocade in fashion like a Galicean helmet, covered with a piece of fine stuff of fine silk and hewas bare-footed; for no one ever enters when the king is unless he has bare feet, and the majority of the people, or almost all go about the country bare-footed. The shoes have pointed ends, in the ancient manner and there are other shoes that have nothing but soles, but on top are some straps which help to keep them to feet. They are made like those which of old the Romans were wont to wear, as you will find on figures in some papers or antiquities which come from Italy.The king gave to *Christvao de Figueredo* on dismissing him a *cabaya* (tunic) of brocade, with a cap of the same fashion as the king wore and to each of the Portuguese he gave a cloth embroidered with many pretty figures, and this the king gives because it is customary; he gives it in token of friendship and love.

Speaking about the costume of the women attendants of *Krsnadeva Raya Domingo Paes* observes: "They are very rich and fine silk cloths; on the head they wear high caps which they call collaes, and on these caps they wear flowers made of large pearls." Besides, their bodies were covered with ornaments of pearls and precious stones.

The horsemen in the service of *Krsnadeva Raya* were dressed like Muslim soldiers. Domingo Paes observes: "The horsemen were dressed in quilted tunics (*laudeis*), also of brocade and violet and every kind of silk. These tunics are made of layers of very strong leather, and furnished with other iron (plates) that makes them strong; some have these plates gilded both inside and out, and some are made of silver. Their headpieces are in the manner of helmets with borders covering the neck, and each has its piece to protect the face: they are of the same fashion as the tunics.They wear on the neck gorgets (*cofos*) all gilded, others made of silk with plates of gold and silver, others of steel as bright as a mirror." There was no change in Vijayanagar costume in the time of *Achyuta Raya* (1529-42). According to Fernao Nuniz (1535-37). "The king (*Achyuta*) never puts on any garment more than once, and when they take it off he at once delivers to certain officers who have charge of this duty and they render an account ; and these garments are never given to anyone.

"This is considered to show great state. His clothes are silk cloths (*pachoiis*) of very fine material and worked with gold, which are worth each one ten *pardaos*; and they wear at times *bajuris* of the same sort, which are like shirts with a skirt; and on the head they wear caps of brocade which they call *culaes*, and one of these is worth some twenty *cruzados*. When he lifts it from his head he never puts it on."

Some words in the above descriptions require further explanation. Pateca of Domingo Paes is said to have been worn round the neck. There seems to be some confusion have as *patka* is sort of a hanging girdle. About the origin of the *kulay* an interesting story is related. According to Barros one Don Menezes while fighting the Moors saw a number of people coming to him among whom he saw a horseman wearing a peaked hat which betrayed his noble position. According to Barros "This kind of costume comes to India from the China country and as only nobleman can wear it. 'word' with 'infinite' as it is a sign of nobility we may call it *quira sol,* the form and use of which it resembles ususally it is a six to eight palms in diameter, it stalk (or peak) is little more than fifteen. There are men so skilful in holding it that though the master goes at a gallop on his horse, the sun does not touch him in any part of the body and they call in Inida *buiyes* (*boyees*), and to see in the court of the prince the lord who accompanied him covered with those hats with high peaks gives them great majesty, because they are handsome both sight and of much dignity."

About the fabrics of Northern India *Jayasi's Padmavat* (written between 1527-40) gives in interesting account. The following articles are mentioned:

Printed and painted calicos. The printed *saris* (*chipa ka-sari*) were common articles of wear *Pemca* which is the same as *pomca,* a *cadar* worn by *Jat* women till recetly, which had large printed rosettes. The original design must have been as the name indicates (*pem, pom, padma*) a lotus pattern. *Chayala,* a printed *sari,* came from Gujarat and *Pandua* in north Bengal. The carefully dyed cloths of Ceylon origin (*simhaladipi*) were so beautifully printed that their work elicited praise (*kinhachapa jo dhanni ve chipi*). The painted palampore (*citra-citeri*) in which seven colours were employed were so beautiful that it was difficult to turn away one eyes from them.

Patola. It was a silk sari (*Patora*) It bore a pattern (*laharapatore*). It is also named as *cira-patora.*

Tinsel printing. *Cikva, cira* and *meghauna,* were trimmed with seed pearls and printed with gold (*moti laga au chape sone*) *cikava* may be the same as *cikata* silk of deep brown colour; *meghauna* as its name indicates was black silk.

Dyed cloths. The *pemca doria* and *bidari* were white black, yellow and green. *Doria* was a striped stuff while *bidari* was a stuff manufactured in Bidar.

Some interesting details about the male and female costumes are also given by Jayasi. It is said that the female silk weaver (*patuni*) wore colourful tunics (*suraga tana-cola*). The female bodice is called *kancuki* (329.1), *phudia* and *kasania* which were to red colour. *Phudia* apparently had tasseled fasteners and *kasania,* a tight breast-band.*Phari* (329.3) is a special kind of skirt not sewn in front often worn by girls. In Budelkhand and Braj the word indicates *odhni* or *cadar.* It was made of sandal-coloured silk of *Khirodaka* stuff. Apparently the stuff was in great fasion (296.1; 199.2; 335.2; 354.1) and was also known as *candana ciru* which covered the body (296.1; 335.2). *Sari* was a common article of wear; it was usually printed. *Basapora* and *Jhilmil* indicates fine muslin from which *saris* were made (329.3). *Basapora* was a fine quality of which one place could come within a bamboo contain the same as *nalibaddha* of the *Prthvicandara carita. Jhilmil* was a kind of fine and soft muslin. *Saura-supaiti* (340.2) has been used for *cadars*. For a padded cloak, *dagala-cira*(340.2) has been used[51].

Moreover, many pious Muslims of *'Islam's'* early years the architectural splendour of the Dome of the Rock *'Word'* or *'Nam'* a structural erected of the society by an upstart dynasty of *Sudra* rulers called *'Untouchables'* by the modern people, and its interior glowing with mosaics executed by 'infidels' whose craftmen was *'Chamar'*, must have seemed to be a traducement of Islamic ideals[52], as a *'New Society'* at that time. There was a clear rule in the Report of the Prophetic tradition (*hadiths* or no *hadiths*), the practice of erecting *musolea* grew in popularity in natural form as an human being, definitely from the 9th century A.D. at the same time as the esteem in which the *hadiths* (tradition) had been held lessened. The authority of the jurists of the four *Sunni* schools of Law *'Word' Hanafite*, the *Malikite*, the *Shafite* and *Hanafite, 'Chamar'* began to hold away[53] as an *untouchable* ruler of the *'Nam'* in the 650-1050 century A.D.

Kabir, the Weaver of God's Name, the fifteenth century saint of Banaras, was a low-caste weaver with no formal education; his humble origin did not prevent him, however, from becoming renowned in his own lifetime as a great saint, like *Buddha, Akbar,* etc. all over the world due to his mystics poems and couplets. Muslim authors like *Mohsin Fani* and *Abu'l Fazl* have described Kabir as a *muwahhid*, a believer in One God. Sheikh Sadullah (died 1522), another contemporary of Kabir, in reply to his son's query whether the celebrated Kabir was a *Muslim* or a *Kafir*, said that he was a *Muwahhid*. Asked whether a *muwahhid* differed from both Muslim and the *Kafir,* the Sheika replied that the truth would be difficult to understand and such knowledge could only be acquired gradually[54]. Philosophies such as Monotheism, pantheism, deign and dualism,with their various branches, are the outcome of attempts to realize 'God' through mental accumen and analysis and to put intellectual deduction into words.

The limitation of the material world, that of language and thought, make it impossible to, describe the 'Supreme Being', the 'limitless One'. Mind itself is formed from matter and even its most acute perception, nor aptly describe whatever little it may come to know of him through intuition and introspection[55]. In the Old Testament,in reply to a question from Moses, God says: "I am that I am" Saint Ravidas *'Chamar'* by caste says: "Lord , you are what you are; there is nothing I can compare you with[56]." Maulana Rumi says: "Your heart is the true mosque; with in your body is the place to offer salutations to the lord[57]." Hazrat Muinuddin Chishti gives an indication of the inner form of the Master when he says: "O Master, if only one ray of your brilliantly illumined face were to shine in the sky, the sun would turn pale with shame[58]." Therefore, it is difficult to understand the network of the God without the realization of *'God'*. He does his work in hides never advertise like the modern politicans and writers.

Costumes and Textiles in Lexicons

Any treatment of Indian textiles materils and costumes in medieval times is bound to remain inadequate without reference to contemporary lexicons, *Sanskrit* and *Prakrit*. The Sanskrit lexicons, unfortunately with the exception of some, follow in the footsteps of the *Amarakosa*, but the lexicons of *desi* words *Paiyalacchi* of *Dhanapala* and the *Desinamamala* of Hemacandra record words on costumes and textiles current in the general parlance of the people. The etymologies of most of the words dealing with the costumes and textiles are obscure, but in ensemble they draw a better picture of the social life of the people than Sanskrit works on prose and poetry.

The *Paiya,* and *Desi,* record some interesting terms connected with spinning, weaving and printing, *Kolio,* equated with *tantuvaya,* is a generic name for weavers (*Desi,* ii, 65)*; thuri* is called a weaver's implement (*Desi.*, vi,28) and so is *puri* which might have been a bobbin *(Desi.* vii. 56) *Ponia* (Desi., vii, 61) is described as a spindle with yarn (*sutrabhrttarkuh, Desi., vii*, 61) though it may also stand for H. *peoni* or cotton silver ready for spinning. *Ucchhaho* (*Desi.* i, 92) is described as yarn (*sutratantu*).*Uncho* is said to be the profession of calico printer (*chimpakara-karuvisesah, Paiya. 236) Chimpao* or *Chimpa* (*Paiya.*, 236) also denotes calico-printer from which the modern *chipa* and *chivi* have oritinated. *Chappanti* in the *Desi.*, iii. 25, is described as a particular process by which a lotus pattern is drawn (*niyamavisesa yatra padman likhyate*). Cloth-pieces were stitched together to get the required width (*dandam-dindi,* described as *sucya sanghatitani vastrakhandani, Desi, iv, 7*), while *dindilliam* (Desi. iv, 10) is described as some kind of embroidered cloth (*khalikhacitavastram*).

There is not much which Prakrit lexicons have to say about the varieties of cloth. The *Paiya., 69* names *amsuyam (*cloth, garment), *ambaram*and *celam* as generic words for cloth *Karayari* (*Desi...ii, 16)* is thick cloth and *kasiam* is a thin stuff (*Desi.*, ii, 59). Here in *Kasiam* one may see a very rare reference to cloth manufacture at Banaras in medieval times or it may be the *kasbi* stuff of Persian origin. The following varieties are also mentioned: *kinham*, perhaps a thin black silk (*Desi*., ii, 59)*; kimiharavasanam 'Word'* silk (*Desi.,* ii, 33); *kosa* dyed in safflower (*Desi*..ii. 65); *ghatto* (Desi., ii, 111) - also called dyed in safflower may stand for *ghatadi* of later times; *cuppaliam*; (*Desi.,iii. 17)* is freshly dyed cloth (*navaraktam);* *pomaram* (Desi, vi, 63) which may have something to do with the later *pamari* (red woollen stuff) is said to have been dyed in safflower *raggayam* (Desi.. vii, 3) *viraho* (*Desi,* vii, 91) and *sulasam* (*Desi, viii, 37)* are described as dyed in safflower without describing the distinguishing features of each variety. The *chana-chani* (*Desi,* iii, 34) may be hampen cloth, *Maharayana* (Desi, vi, 132) is called as a particular kind of cloth; probably the valuable Kashmir shawl is intended. *Vettam* (*Desi*., vii, 75) is called some kind of very white stuff (*acchavastram*). *Cittalam*(*Paiya*., 94) is described as a variegated stuff.

Several names for different articles of costumes and the mode of wearing them have been given, though in many cases it is difficult to distinguish the finer shades of their meanings. For the upper garment the following words are used: *avarillam* (*Paiya*., 175)*;* *oddhnam* (Desi., i. 155) or wrapper, the later *odhana* or *odhani.* For the lower garment *avaaccham* (*Desi..i, 26)* described as lower garment whose end is tucked behind (*kaksavastram*) is used; apparently the *sakaccha dhoti* is meant. There are several words concerning *nivi* (*Paiya*., 175) or *sari* knot and the mode of tying it. *Catto* (*Desi.,*i, 166) is described as a veil (*avagunthanam*) or the knot of the lower garment (*nivi*) or the side knot (*parihita-vastrapranta*). *Kuvala* (Desi., ii, 43) is however, described as a short *sari* covering the privities (*Jaghanavasanam*). *Janhali* (Desi., iii, 40) is equated with *nivi, Dunniattham* (Desi, ii, 53), is described as a loin-cloth used by woven (*jaghanasthitavastram*). *Kadillam (Desi.,* ii, 52) the same as Sanskrit *katitra* is a waist-cloth (*kativastra*). *Sahuli* (*Paiya.,* 69; Desi,. viii, 52) is described simply as a garment or lower garment. *Jahanaroho* (*Desi*., iii, 44) is described as a short petticoat (*ardhoruka*). *Nirangi* (Paiya., 116; Desi. iv, 31) is a veil. The male lower garment is designated as *niamsanam* (*Desi.* iv, 38) and *niandhanam* (Desi., iv, 38). The night garment is designated as *Padiniansanam* (*Desi., vi,36)* described as the garment worn at night (*ratrau paridheya-vastram*)

From the terms mentioned above, it is evident that sewn garments were commonly worn both by men and women. The women often covered their breasts with a band; its knot is designated as *genthuvam (Desi, ii, 93)*. In the *Paiya*. 216, 4 D, *gindhuam* equated with *gendam* and *gendayam* is also described as a cloth-knot over the breasts (*stanasyoparivastragranthih*). *Genthulla (Desi., ii, 18)* is described as a knot for fastening the garment on the neck, *Kancuyao* (*Paiya,* 68) a thick quilted coat and *kuppasam*) *Paiya, 68)* a jacket, are all articles of the male costume. *Govillam* (*Desi,* ii, 94) is also designated as cloak (*kancuka*) . Probably it was a cloak favourite with herdsmen. *Ghaggharo* (*Desi, ii.* 107), the same as *ghaghara* of the later time, is a women's skirt described as a kind of garment for covering the privities (*jaghanavastra-bhedah*) *Chimphullani (Desi,*iii, 13) is described as a short skirt (*strinamardhorukavastram).*

There are some other words for costume *Parihiyan Paiya*., 175), *veso* (*Paiya*., 236) *varihana* (*Desi* vi, 21). *oittam or oittanam* (Desi, i, 155) and *ohasiam* (*Desi*., i, 173). *Ovaddhi* (Desi., i, 151) is described as a variegated or patterned head-scarf (*sirasi chitrapattika*).

In the miscellaneous terms *desero* (Desi. v, 33) is called thread (*sutrakanakam*) *sihalayam (Desi., vii, 34),* is said to have been a contrivance for fumigating cloth with incense smoke. The tattered garment is called *rendi* (Desi., vii, 5)

The Sanskrit lexicons, *Vaijayanti* of *eleventh century* A.D. and the *Abhidhanacintamani* of twelfth century A.D. while recording traditional information about costums and textile material also gave new words which add to our knowledge. Cotton before it was spun was cleaned with a bow which is called *pinjana* (*Abhi*., III, 912: *vaija*, 136.19) and *Vihanana* "striking". (Abhi., III 912). The spindle is called *tarkuh* (Abhi. III, 911) and *kartanabhanda* (Vaija., 136. 17) *kartana* being the weaver's comb *vaija*.. 136.20). The loom is designated as *vanadanda* and *vema* (*Abhi*., II, 913; *Vaija*., 136.20) or *veman* (Vaija., 136.16) *Trasara* (*Abhi*., III, 913 *Vaija*., 136.17) is explained as *sutaravestana.* It may be a bobbin or shuttle. *Avartana* is turning round the thread (*Vaija.,* 136.21). The yarn is *tantu* (*Vaija*., 136.15) is a weaver. The weaver's shed is *tantrasala* (*Vaija*., 106.44); woven is indicated by *vani* and *vyauti* (*Abhi*.. III. 913; *vaija*., 136. 160) and *ota* (*Vaija.* 137, 237 and *tantusantata Vaija* 210, 223).

The following general terms for costumes and cloths are given: *Amsuka* and *vastra* (*Abhi*., III, 666-667); *ambara* (*Abhi*., III. 666-667; *Vaija*., 168-232); *sic-sik* of the *Abhi*., and *sica-sicaya (Vaija.,* 168-231); *cira*(*Abhi*., III, 666 667; *Vaija*., 169-259) is said to be a dress mended with rags; *acchada* or *acchadana* (*Abhi*., III, 666-667); *Vaija*., 168-238); *cela*(*Abhi.,*III, 666-657; *Vaija, 168-233)* ; *vasas* (*Abhi*., III, 666-667; *Vaija*., 118-

231) also a variety of cotton (*Vaija.*, 282-32) *pata* (*Abhi.*, III, 666-67; *Vaija.*, 168-231 and 292-74) and *prota* (*Abhi.*, III, 666-67).

The uncalendered stuff is designated as *anahata* or *ahata* or *ahata tantrika* and *nispravani* (*Abhi.*, III, 671; *Vaija.,168-239).* The *Abhi.*, III, 672 describes the upper garment and wrapper as *pracchadana, pravarana, samvyana, uttariyaka, vaikaksa, paravara, uttarasanga and bihatika. Vaija.*, gives some further information about some of the words and adds a few more. *Upavita* (*Vaija.*, 274-33) is an upper garment perhaps worn across the chest in the manner of a sacred-thread. *Vrhatika* (*Vaija.* 168-245) is described as an over-garment worn over one shoulder and under the opposite arm. *Vaikaksya* (*Vaija.*, 168-245) is the same as *vrhatika.* The lower garments are enumerated as *paridhana, adhomsuka, antariya, nivasana and upasamvyana* (*Abhi.*, III, 673; *Vaija.*, 168-242).

Sewn Garments and Sewing Implements

There are plenty of references to sewn garments and sewing implements. The tailor is known as *tunnavaya* and *Sucaka* (*Abhi.*, III, 910). His implements and accessories are needles (*Suci, sevani Abhi*, III, 911). Sewing thread (*sucisutra, piskalaka, Abhi.* III, 911), scissors (*Kripani, kartari, kalpani, Abhi..* III.911). The act of sewing is represented by the words *sevana, sivana, syuti* (*Abhi.*, 911-912): *uti* (*Vaija.*, 220-10) and *ota* (*Vaija,* 137-27) meaning sewn across with thread. The sewn skirt is named *canlataka, calanaka* and *calani* (*Abhi.*, III, 674; *Vaija.*, 168 243). The knot of *ardhoruka* apparently tight shorts, is known as *uccaya,* (*Abhi.*, III, 673, *Vaija.*, 168-243; 169-260) explained as the cloth round a woman's waist and the knot of *amsuka* as *nivi* (*Abhi..* III. 673). The bodice tunic and jacket are named as *caula. kanculika, kurpasaka, angika and kancuka* (*Abhi ..* III, 674). *Colaka* stands for tunic (*Vaija.*, 169-255).

Interesting information is obtainable from the lexicons about various garments. Thus to ward off the cold wind *sari, coti* and *nisara* were used (*Abhi.* III, 675). *Nisara* according to the *Vaija.* 169.252 was a warm *cadar. Kaccha, kacchatika* and *kaksa* (*Abhi* III, 675) are described as the other end of the garment (*paridhanaparancala*). *Kaksya* is explained elsewhere (*Vaija,* 169.261) as a cloth covering the privities. *Kaksa,* however, has two meanings, namely a cloth covering the privities (*Vaija*, 169-261) and the border of a garment (*Vaija.*, 169.257). The *Vaija.*, 169.257 describes *kaksyapata* as small pieces of cloth worn over the privities. Long robes are termed as *nicola, pracchadapata, nicula* and *uttarcchada* (*Abhi.*, III, 676). In the *Vaija, nicola* has a double meaning *'weaver'* a cover or wrapper (169.252) and a tunic (169.255). *Aprapadina* (*Abhi.* III, 675; *Vaija* , 168.241) is described as a long robe reaching the forepart of the feet. *Udgamaniyaka* (*Abhi.*, III,668; *Vaija.*, 168.240) is described as a pair of bleached cloth; so is *dhautayugma* (*Vaija,* 168.240). The *Kamarband* has the following synonyms *'word' paryastika, paryanka* and *avasakthika* (*Abhi*, III, 679). The general name for turban is *usnisa* (*Abhi.*, III, 667; *Vaija* 168.247) or simply *Veshtana* (*Vaija.,252.65).* The names of a border are *dasa, varti* and *vasti* (*Abhi.*,III, 667) *Karpata* (*Vaija.*, 169.260) is designated as a dirty or tattered cloth, and *varasi* a very coarse *cadar* (*sthulasataka Abhi* III, 672; *Vaija.*, 169.252). *Vastragrantha* (*Vaija.* 169.260) is called a woman's waist-cloth; old cloth is *jirnavastra and pataccara* (*Abhi*; III, 678). *Kantha* (*Vaija.169.256) is* torn cloth. A dress mended with rags is *khanlala* (*Vaija.* 169.259).

The general name for costume is *vesa nepathya* and *akalpa* (*Abhi, III,* 635). A well-dressed person is called *upasampanna* (*Vaija.*, 166. 187). A stick or string for hanging clothes is called *vastradharani* (*Vaija.,* 163. 105). A bag for storing clothes is called *vastrakosa* (*Vaija.* 164.126). Perfurmed for clothes is called *patavasaka* (*Vaija.*, 171. 314).

Some light is thrown on the garment of the recluses, *Civara* (*Abhi.*, III, 678) is called the *sanghati* of Buddhist monks. *Cina* (*Vaija.*, 95.299) is designated as a cloth round the trunk and knees of an ascetic seated in *yoga* posture.

The stuffs mentioned in the lexicons are mostly traditional though some new ones are mentioned. Cotton stuffs are called *karpasa* and *badara* (*Abhi.*, III, 669; *Vaija.*, 131, 211). *Ksauma* equated with *dukula mind* or *dugula* is said to be a kind of barkfibre cloth (*Abhi.*, III, 669). *Dukula* is also said to be woven silk (*Vaija,* 168. 244) or simply white cloth (*Vaija.*, 251.35). *Sani-gani* (*Abhi.*, III, 679) is rough hempen cloth. *Kanseya* is called woven silk (*Abhi.*, III, 670). It is also called *krimija* (*Vaija,* 168-233). Bleached silk or wild silk is called *dhautakanseya* (*Vaija.* 168-236). *Patrorna* is also named as bleached silk (*Abhi.*, III, 667). *Ranakava* (*Abhi.*, III, 670) is goat-hair cloth while cloth made from sheep wool is known as *urnayu* (*Vaija*, 240-25). A large number of blankets *'Word' kambala, urnayu, avika, aurabhra* and *rallaka 'Chamars'* are mentioned (*Abhi.*, III, 670). Apparently they were all made of sheep-wool. *Visala* (*Vaija.*, 169-258) is also named as a large blanket. Both *agnigau (sau) ca* and *vajramsuka* (*Vaija,* 168.237) are as discussed elsewhere asbestos cloth imported from China. The identification of *udbandha* (*Vaija.* 75.81) is, however a difficult proposition. It seems to have been a silken stuff (*ambaranejakam*) from *Khanaka* which the *Sudras* were not allowed to touch (*udbandamkhanakacchudradasprisyamambaranejakam*). It seems that in *nejaka* reference to famous *niz* cloth manufactured in Baghdad is explicit.

Several kinds of cotton are mentioned. They are *Kesara* (*Vaija,* 61, 386), *pichu* (*Vaija.,* 136.18). *rava* (*Vaija.* 53.197) and *dvara* (*Med.,* 153.48).

The shoe-maker is known as *padukakrt* and *carmakt* (*Abhi.,* III, 914). The shoes are clasified as *Upanat* (shoes), *paduka, padu* (sandals) *pannaddha* (H. *Panabi*), *padaraksana* (protecting the feet), *pranahita* (enemy of life) (*Abhi.,* III, 915), *anupadina* (according to foot measurement) and *ahaddha* (strapped) (*Abhi.,* III, 915).

There are many kinds of carpets mentioned *'Nam' Kutha, varna paristoma, praveni navata* and *astara* (*Abhi.,* III, 680). *Kutha* and *Paristoma* are apparently elephant carpets; *praveni* seems to have been a mat made from braided leather; *navata* is felt carpet known as *namda,* and *astara* might have been imported from *Astarabad* in Mazandaran on the shore of the Caspian Sea in Persia. *Varna* seems to have been colourful carpet, the same as *varna-tarnaka* (*Vaija., 292.114) in* Hindi language.

Cloth tents, screens and curtains such as *apati, kandapata (screen), pratisira* and *javani* are mentioned (*Abhi,* III, 680).

Not much information is available about dyer's art. He is called *nirnejaka* and *rajaka* (*Abhi.,* III, 914). It is also difficult to say whether *citrapata* (*Vaija.,* 168. 238) was printed calico or not.

The *Medini,* though datable to the later thirteenth century, contains valuable information about the costumes and textile materials of the transitional period from the Hindu to Muslim domination. *Pattika* (*Medi.,* 6, 56) which was made of cotton (*Karpasika*) was a dhoti. *Dhati* (Med. 41, 19), a word very frequently used in later literature was used for a variety of cloth and also a garment (*vastre ca vasasah*), probably a waist-cloth. *Vati* is simply cloth (Med., 42, 24) so also is *varidhani* (Med., 111,30) and *vatara* (Med., 168, 8). The *ancala* is called *avatarana* (Med., 64.112). *Yutaka* (*Med.,* 14, 143) is said to be the pallau of a woman's *sari. Urmika* (Med., 6,53) is defined as creased cloth (*vastrabhanga*) or the folds (*vastrasankocarekha,* (*Med.,* 131.2). *Vrhati* (*Med.,* 7736) is upper garment (*vasanantara*) and *kaksya* (*Med.,* 137,10) is equated with *vrhatika* or a *cadar* knotted in the middle. *Matra* (*Med.,* 156,75) is a dress (*paricchada*); *katitra* (Med., 160,26) is a waist-cloth. *Coda* (Med., 49,13) is a *cadar,* the same as *coti* of *Abhi* III, 675. Turban is *vestana* (*Med.,111,* 37).

The art of sewing was very well developed. *Sucaka* is a needle (*Med.* 16, 168); *syuti* is stitching (Med., 71,73) and continuous stitching (*syutavritih*) is *uti* (Med., 65,51). *Kancuka* (Med., 7,62) which is equated with *colaka* is described as the body garment provided with fasteners (*varddhapakagrihitangasthitavastra*) *'Kalma'* a true description of the Muslim *jamah. Calani* (Med., 195,62) is a skirt (*vastragharghari*) and *nicula* (Med., 186, 102) is a long sewn garment.

The most ineresting part of the *Medini* is the list of woven and dyed stuffs, some of which appear in Sanskrit for the first time and support the later thirteenth century date of the lexicon. Among the silk stuffs are mentioned *patrorna* (Med., 59.61) which is described as bleached silk; *cina* or Chinese silk (Med., 99.4) *kharma* (Med., 131.9) which is described as fine cocoon silk (*kosajamsuka*); *dusya* (Med., 178.12); *khalla* perhaps *khara* or bleached silk and finally *patola* (Med., 187.106). The *Mankhakosa* (c 1150, 151, ed by T. Zachariae, Bombay 1898) mentions silk cloth dyed in lake and *kermes* (*laksakrmija*).

Among the cotton stuffs the following are mentioned: *Ciri* (Med., 150.38) which might have been the product of Tiruchirapalli; *tunlikeri* (Med., 173.64), the product of *Tondimandala* of Kanchi; *jhilli* which is equated with *ciri* was a fine muslin (*amsuka*) and finally *jhuni* (Med., 54.14). a fine muslin mentioned frequently in later literature and referred by the Chinese as *yue-no. Ksauma* (Med., 131.9) is not only linen but has a wider connotation. It is said to have been made from the bark-fibre and also hemp. *Locaka* (Med. 15,151) and *Chagala* (Med., 185.91) are said to have been blue cloth (*nilavastra*). Very costly stuff is named *mahadhana* (Med., 117, 201).

Indian Textiles and Costumes Described by Chinese and Arab Geographers

It should, however, be noted that the information given above, however, true to life, is after all culled from literary sources on the assumption that the poets, literati and lexicographers utilised contemporary information. However, this lacuna in strict historicity is partially filled by the Arab geographers who visited India from the ninth century onwards, the Chinese records of *Chau Ju-kua*, the inspector of foreign trade in *Fu-Kien*, compiled in the twelfth century A.D. and lastly Marco Polo, the intrepid Italian traveller who has left details of costumes and stuffs of South India and Gujrat, etc. That the trade was not confined to one country only but was on mutual basis is supported by Yaqubi writing in 891. Speaking of Baghdad as a great centre of trade he observes: "So much commerce goes to it from Hindi, Sind, China, Tibet, the Turks, Dailam, the Khazars, the Abyssinians and other countries, that more articles of merchandise are to be found there than in the countries of origin themselves. It is tempting to suggest here that the muslin of Bengal known to the Arab merchant Sulayman whose work was compiled in 851 must have been exported to Baghdad. Speaking about the stuff, he observes: "In that country are made cloths which are not made anywhere else: one of these garments could pass through a ring because the (stuff) is extremely fine. This stuff is of cotton and we have seen its sample."

Masudi who visited Cambay in 916 found it a great commercial emporium. He observes: "This city is celebrated for its sandals named after it, and also for stuffs not only manufactured there, but also in the neighbouring cities." He also remarks about the fineness and great delicacy of the muslin manufactured in Rahma (Bengal). The anonymous author of the *Hudud al 'Alam,* writing in 982-983, has left interesting information about the textile manufacture and costumes of India. Speaking about the port towns of *Samur,* Subara (spelt Suyara) and Kanbaya, he observes: "The people of these towns have long hair and at all seasons wear only a izar (waist-cloth) for the protection of cold. In Kanbaya shoes (*na'lain* exported *"Sandals"* of the Cham or leather) are produced which are exported to all the countries of the world" Apparently the *Hudud* repeats the information about Cambay sandals given by Masudi. Khalin (Jalhin. Is Jalaun meant to Brahman) which is suggested as the jumbled up spelling of Kanauj is described by the *Hudud* as, " a small but populous town producing quantities of velvet and stuffs for turbans (*jama-yi va sa'ra*) as well as drugs." Jalandhar or *Jaladhara* which is said to have been a town situated on the summit of a mountain in the cold region is said to have produced great quantities of velvets and stuffs (*jama*), plain and figured (*sadhavamunaqqas*).

Alberuni (b, 973,d. 1048), a contemporary of Mahmud of Ghazna (997-1030), who has left a record of India unsurpassed in antiquity gives some interesting details of the costumes of the Indians[59]. "They use turbans for trousers (apparently *dhoti* is meant). Those who want little dress are content to dress in a rag of two fingers breadth which they bind over their loins with two cords (apparently, *kaupina);* but those who like much dress, wear trousers lined with as much cotton as would suffice to make a number of counterpanes and saddle-rugs. The trousers have no (visible) openings, and they are so huge that the feet are not visible. The string by which the trousers are fastened is at the back. "Their *sidar* (a piece of dress covering the head and the upper part of breast and neck) is similar to the trousers, being also fastened at the back by buttons. "The lappets of the *kurtakas* (short shirts from the shoulders to the middle of the body with sleeves, a female dress) have slashes both on the right and the left sides." "They keep the shoes tight till they begin to put them on. They are turned down from the calf before walking."

Idrisi (1154) also gives some interesting information about the textile trade and costumes of the Indians. For instance, we are informed that Aden imported from Sindh among other things stuffs made of vegetable fibre. We are further informed that *Mansura* in Sindh was a thickly populated city. "The people in *lower position* wear Persian costume, but the princes wear tunics and allow their hair to hang loose after the manner of Indian princes." The vegetable stuffs of Khmer had a good demand in Indian market. It is said, "In this island (*Komor*) they manufactured a vegetable fibre stuff resembling *al-bardi*. This is known as *al-qirtas,* which is so called as the Egyptians use it as paper. The major part of the material is employed in fabricating the stuffs comparable in beauty of coloured silks. These stuffs are exported to all parts of India and even sometimes to Yemen where they were used for making garments."

Ibn Hawqal enlarges further on the costumes of Indian provinces, though unfortunately many of the terms used by him are difficult to understand. According to him the costume of the people of the lower Indus Valley resembled that of the people of Iraq i.e. it is consisted of a pair of drawers, a vest and a turban. But the Muslim Amirs had adopted the costume of the native princes. They allowed their hair to hang loose and they wore a garment called *Corthac* (*kurta*). In the Gulf of Cambay and in the Malabar coast the Muslims who had settled there wore their hair long and were dressed in *izar* and *mizar* i.e. a pantaloon and a *jerkin* as this costume was supposed to ward off the extreme heat of the country and for the very same purpose it was also adopted in the domain of Multan. The rest, mostly merchants, contended themseles with the indigenous costume of the country.

From the descriptions of the costumes and textile materials of India as cited by the Arab geographers, a picture of medieval Indian costume emerges which is not very different than what Indian authors have painted. It is evident that the indigenous costumes consisted of plain *dhoti* and turban and as observed by Alberuni the poorer people simply wore a lion-cloth. It is, however, significance to note that while the ordinary Muslims of Multan. Cambay and Malabar wore Iraqi costume, the Muslim princes delighted in the indigenous costume, an article of which was *kurta* which is known to every Indian household. The *kurta* mentioned by Alberuni (Sachau unnecessarilty calls it an artilce of female dress), however, does not appear in Indian literature, but Li-yen (died between 785-794) in his Sanskrit-Chinese dictionary has equated Sanskrit *Kurtau* for the Chinese *can* meaning a shirt. Alberuni further mentions trousers of *gargantuan* proportions which might have been some prototype of modern *salwar* worn chiefly in the Panjab. The *sidar* of Alberuni was either a cape or more probably a jacket.

As regards fabrics, according to the authority of Sulaiman and Masudi. Bengal produced fine cotton fabrics; Cambay was equally famous for its stuffs; Sindh the oldest centre of Sudra industry exported linen; Kanauj and Jalandhar manufactured velvets and other plain and figured stuffs, while Khmer exported in India fine stuffs which was in great demand. Thana, according to Abul Fida, was famous for *Tansi,* cloths (Nainar, *loc.cit* p. 81).

Chau Ju-Kua, the inspector of foreign trade in *Fu-kien* in the twelfth century, adds further information to our knowledge of Indian costumes, and textile fabrics. Speaking of the costume of the ruler of Malabar he observes: "The ruler of the country has his body draped, but goes barefooted. He wears a turban and a loin-cloth both of white cotton cloth. Sometimes he wears a white cotton shirt with narrow sleeves. The native products included foreign cotton stuff of all colours (i.e. chintzes) and *tou-lo-mien* (cotton cloth). Whether the later Malabar *lachari* is meant here, it is difficult to say that the Gujaratis "wear close-fitting clothes with a cotton sarong wrapped around them. On the heads they wear white hoods and on their feet shoes of red leather." Among the chief product of Gujarat are mentioned indigo and cotton stuffs of every description. Malwa was a great centre of textile products 'Word' "Of products white cotton is very common. Every year two thousand oxen or more, laden with cotton stuffs, are sent over the roads to other country for barter." On the Coromandal coast at the wedding the bride's family sent *yue-no* cloth and brocaded clothing to bridge-groom. The chief products are cotton stuffs with coloured silk threads and cotton stuffs. In the note 6 on p. 100 *yue-no* is explained as very fine muslin made in various localities of Western Asia. The text mentions white *yue-no* as product of Baghdad and Ghazna and gold spangled *yue-no* and *jhuni* of the *Medini* and *Jhuna* of later times which was some kind of extremely fine muslin. P'ong-k'ie-lo (Bengal) is said to have been famous for *tou-lo* cotton stuffs. *Nan-ni-hua-lo* in Sindh is said to have been known for fine white flowered (or dotted) cotton stuffs. Chau Ju-kua's information on cotton cloth and the translator's note thereon are very interesting. He observes: "The most durable and strongest is called *tou-lo-mien;* the second quality is called *fan-pu* or 'foreign cloth': the third 'tree cotton or *mu-mien*; the fourth *ki-pu*. These textures are sometimes dyed in various colours and brightened with strange patterns. The pieces measure upto five or six feet in breadth.[60]".

The earliest name for cotton stuff in Chinese is *po* - (or *pai*)*tie* which is the translation of the *Chau Ju-kua* equate with the Turkish *pakta*. The word was also used for hempen cloth. Fa-hien calls the cotton fabrics of India *po-tie*. In the sixth century a new term *ku-pei* or *kipei* adopted from the Malay *kapas* (S. Karpasa) was used for Gossypium herbaceum. According to *Huan-tsang* the people of India wore silk and also the clothing of *tie-pu-tie*. Both the terms were equated later on. In the Sung a period the term *ki-pei* was extended to Indian cotton fabric and a new term introduced *'Word' tou-lo-mien 'Chamar'* Sanskrit *tula* (cotton) and Chinese *mien* , 'soft, dowry'. There is, however, little doubt that the Chinese *po-tie* is closely connected with the Sanskrit *pota,* described above. It is significant to note that *patti* in Dravidian language and *phutti* in Sindhi and Panjabi denotes cotton. It is possible that *po-tie* reached China from South India and the Sanskrit *pota* may be a borrowing from the Dravidian *patti*.

Ser Marco Polo (1271-1295) has left an interesting account of the coastal regions of India, their people, their costumes and manners and the economic products. Though practically a century had elapsed since *Chau Ju-Kua* had completed the account of the coastal regions of India Marco Polo's account does not differe materially from it. He mentions that in the kingdom of Mutfili, i.e, Motupalli, a small port in Guntur District, Andhra, under the *Kakatiya* rulersof Warangal "are also made the best and most delicate buckrams, and those of highest price, in smooth they look like tissues of spiders web. There is no king or queen in the world, but might be glad to wear them." Obviously, Andhra Pradesh since the days of the *Periplus* of the *Erythrean Sea* (first century A.D.) had preserved its reputation for the manufacture of the muslin of highest quality. It is also significant to note that before Marco Polo visited the country. It was ruled by the Kakatiya Pratapa Ganapati Rudra Deva[61] (1199-1262) who issued a character of security to foreign merchants trading in Motupalli. Whereas, *Coilum (Quilon)*, according to Marco Polo, produced indigo, a basic colour for dyeing cloth. He observes: "They have also abundance of very fine indigo. This is made of certain herb which is gathered and (after the roots have been removed) is put into great vessels upon which they pour water and leave it till the whole plant is decomposed. They then put this liquid in the sun, which is tremendously hot there, so that it boils and coagulates, and becomes such as we see it. (They then divide it into pieces of four ounces each and in that form it exported to other parts). Besides indigo Malabar also manufactured very delicate buckrams.

About Gujarat Marco Polo observes that it grew good spinning cotton. But the speciality of Gujarat handicraft were leather mats, the *praveni* of the Sanskrit lexicons. "They also work here beautiful mats in red and blue leather inlaid with figures of birds and beasts, and skilfully embroidered with gold and silver wire. These are marvellously beautiful things; they are used by the Saracens to sleep upon and capital they are for that purpose. They also work cushions embroidered with gold, so fine that they are worth six marks of silver a piece, whilst some of those sleeping mats are worth ten marks." Cambay continued to be a great centre of textile trade and manufacture in Marco Polo's time. He observes: "There is a great trade in this country. It produces indigo in great abundance; and they also make much fine buckram. There is also a quality of cotton which is exported hence to many quarters; and there is a great trade in hides, which are well dressed by the *Nai,* washermen, and the *Chamar*. The port of Thana on the Konkan coast exported leather of excellent kind and also good buckram and cotton[62]."

With the close of the thirteenth century A.D. the textile and costume history of India entered another phase of the development. The conquest of Northern India by the closing years of the twelfth century A.D. and the subsequent consolidation of *'Power'* in subsequent centuries introduced alien fashions in the costume of the country and demand for foreign stuffs with which the Turks were well acquainted grew. It resulted in the introduction of new names in the terminology of textiles of the *'Nam'* and *'Word'* was well flourished under the *'Untouchable'* rulers of both the early and later medieval period as their duty to serve the society from the very lowest unit to topmost. For a century, South India remained immune from the *'untouchables'* intrusion, but by the closing years of the thirteenth century the gate of the Deccani was forcibly opened and henceforward the textile history of India becomes one and controlled by the *Sudhra* people of the *'Nam'* not for the personal benefit, but, for the other benefit, as it has been based on humanism's in the natural or *Prakrita* form of the Weaver or *'Nam'* called *Chamar* as well.

Notes & References

1. **Note.** The name conventionally used for the historian, *Zia-uddin*, Barani, is not authorised by him but by from his 'Father', however, it goes back to the later fourteenth century A.D., for *Amir Khwurd* in his *Siyaru'l Auliya* (Chiranji Lal, Delhi A.H. 1302, pp. 312-13) calls him *Zia-ul Millat-wa-ud-din.* On all the numerous occasions that *Barani* refers to himself in the *Tarikh-i-Firuz-Shahi*, Edited by Saiyid Ahmad Khan (Bib. India, Calcutta, 1862, pp. 9, 25, 123, 125 and Persian), he styled himself simply *Zia Barani*: so also in *Fatawa-i-Jahandari* (Inida office MS. Persian. 1149, & Ib). "Zia" could have been poetic pen-name of what i.e. God's beauty, pre-name called *'Barani'* or *'Barni'* may indicate that he was born at Baran (modern *Buland Shahr*) means that place belongs to the *'Word'* called *VARAN* or *BARAN* in Hindi or Sanskrit and his soul was fully realised of *'Nam'* became *'nam'* having the *'Pure-thought'* called *Sudhar* or *'untouchable'* which is very high and pure. Henceforth this edition is cited as *T.F.S.*
2. *Ibid.*, p. 35.
3. *Ibid.*, p. 70.
4. *Ibid.*, pp. 478.
5. M. Wahid Mirza; *Life and Works of Amir Khusrau* ; p. 69 fn. 5 See *Qiran-vs. Sadain ; (*Lucknow 1885); p. 100 ff. See Moti chandra, p. 138. Hereafter calted as *L.W.A.K.*

6. Nur Siphr, Edited by M.W. Mirza, Bombay, 1948; p. 373.
7. *L.W.A.K.* p. 72.
8. *Ibid.*, p. 123.
10. *Ibid.*, pp. 130-31.
11. *T.F.*, pp. 309-12.
12. *History of the Rise of Mohomedan Power in India;* Firishta, Tr. by John Briggs, Calcutta Vol. 1, pp. 357-58.
13. *Afif Tarikh-i-Firuzsahi,* pp. 373-79. Hereafter discussed as *A.T.F.*
14. *Futuhat-i-Firuzshahi* Tr. by M. Umar in Hindi Aligarh; 1957, pp. 33-34.
15. The *Rehla* of *Ibn Batuta* Tr. by Madhi Husain, Baroda, 1953; p. 41.
16. Note. *Patolah* is undoubted by the *Patola* silk of later times already mentioned in the study. The same kind of example also expressed by *Barani* at p. 223. It shows that, he belongs to the same family of the father which already discussed in the passage.
17. The *Rehla of Ibn Batuta,* p. 196. has been identified with *Chaliyam in Palanchannuramsam* and the fabric *calla* tel. *Sella* can; *salla*, Mal, as muslin of thin texture of *'Nam', Nainar* likely to be a barbar; *Arabs knowledge of South India* p. 73, f.n 145. It shows that this area was expert in weaving and spinning of both cotton and silk weed of clothes. Hereafter referred as R.I.B.
18. *Ibid.*, pp. 150-51.
19. *Ars Islamica*, XI-XII, pp. 136-37 see Moti Chandra *C.T.C.C.M.A.I.*, p. 141.
20. *T.F.* p. 554.
21. L.W.A.K. p. 116.
22. *Ars Islamica;* XI-XII, pp. 136-37.
23. *R.I.B.*, p. 79.
24. *Ibid.*, p. 179.
25. *A.T.F.*, p. 48.
26. *Ibid.*, p. 268.
27. *Ibid.*, p. 363.
28. *L.W.A.K.*, p. 11. Fn.1.
29. *Ars. Islamica*, IX (1942); p. 77.
30. *Ibid.*, X. p. 84.
31. *Ibid.*, XI-XII, p. 136.
32. *Ibid.*, p. 116.
33. *Ibid., XI-XII,* p. 116.
34. *R.I.B.* p. 151. Tr. part 2nd.
35. *Marcopolo*. I. p. 65.
36. *Chitaivarta, Narayanadasa;* Edited by M. Parasad, Banaras; 1958, p. 159.
37. A.I. Yusuf Ali, *A Monograph on the Silk Fabrics Produced in North-Western Province and Oudh;* 1899, p. 93. Hereafter referred as *M.S.F.P. N.W.P. O.*
38. *Merutunga, Prabandhauantamani*; Bombay 1932, pp. 119.131. Note. *Jinamandagani* in his *Kumarapala-prabhandh* mentions *Srngarakoti* Sari, silk, *manikya* and white cotton garment (*seduga*) were prevalent in the society at that time (p. 39)
39. *Ibid.*, pp. 3168, 136, 129.
40. *C.T.C.C.M.A.I.*, p. 147.
41. *Varna-Ratnakara* of *Jyotirisvara Thakkura* Edited by Babua Misra and S.K Chatterji. Calcutta, 1942, pp. 11, 14, 22. Hereafter referred *V.R.J.T.*
42. *Ibid.*, pp. 32, 33, 34, 35.
43. *Ibid.*, pp. 44, 46, 51, 5, 21-22.
44. *Ibid.*, pp. 21-22.
45. T.C. Das Gupta. *Aspects of Bengali Society from Old Bengali Literature; Calcutta, 1935, p. 283*
46. *V.R.J.T.*, p. 122.
47. *Ibid.*
48. G.N. Sarkar, *India of Aurangzeb,* Calcutta, 1901, p. 51
49. *M.S.F.P. N.W.P. O.*, p. 68.
50. *Jaina Rajatarangini of Srivara,* Edited by Durga Prasad; Bombay, 1892 vol.VI, pp. 10, 13.
51. *C.T.C.C.M.A.I.*, p. 170.
52. Jose Pereira, *The Sacred Architecture of Islam*; New Delhi; 2004. p. 32
53. *Ibid.*, p. 33
54. V.K. Sethi, *Kabir the Weaver of God's Name*; Punjab, third edition 1998; p. 46
55. *Ibid.*, pp. 48-49.
56. *Ibid., p. 49.*
57. *Ibid.*, p 53.
58. *Ibid.*, p. 87.
59. *Alberuni's India* Vol. 1, pp. 180-81.
60. *Chau Ju-Kua*; Edited by F. Hirth and W. W. Rockhill. *Peters burg* (Germany) 1911. pp. 92, 93, 95, 96, 97, 98 and 217-18
61. N.K. Sastri, *A History of South India, Madras* ; 1955, p. 210.
62. The Book of Ser Marco Polo; Vol. II, pp. 375, 389, 394, 395 and 398.

PLATES

Printed Textiles Material Under the Untouchables Rulers During the Early and Medieval Period

Plate I

Examples of printed textiles from Gujarat, 11th to 15th century. The examples below are from the miniature paintings of the period in question since no printed calico has survived in India of this period, primarily due to climatic conditions. Roughly speaking, the patterns found in Western Indian miniatures may be divided in two parts (i) the patterns found in the palm-leaf miniatures, dating roughly from 1100 to1350 A.D. and (ii) the patterns found in the palm-leaf miniatures from 1350 to 1450 A.D., and also in the miniatures on the paper. There is, however, no great difference in the pattern of both periods.

In the painted wooden-covers, datable to the middle of the 12th century, the following patterns appear:-

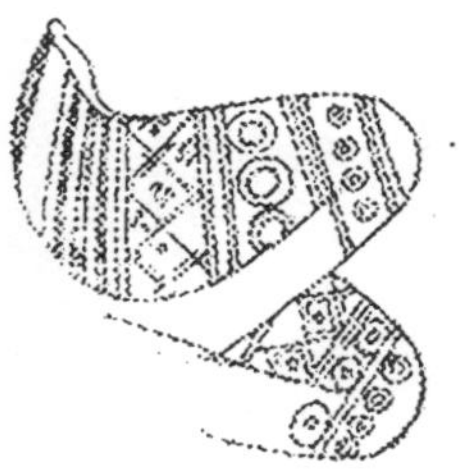

1

2

Fig. 1. Saris of the womenfolk, the field is divided into a number of compartments some filled with closely placed horizontal stripes and spirals, criss-cross, (zig-zag and closely assorted flowers).

Fig. 2. Cross stripes and the simple circles of the tie-dye.

In the palm-leaf manuscripts, dated 1171 A.D. the following interesting patterns appear on the saris of the sixteen Vidya-devis:

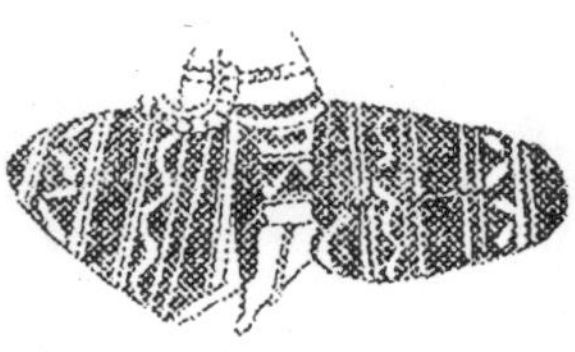

Fig.3. The field divided into compartments decorated with simple meanders

Fig.4 The field decorated with blocked squares on which fourleaved flowers appear.

Plate II

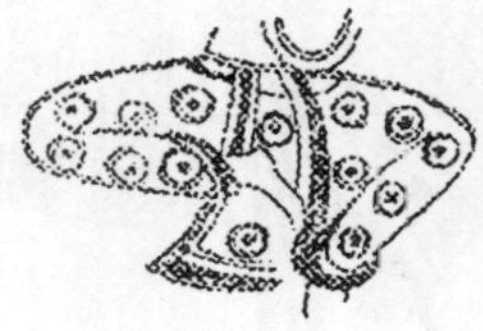

6

7

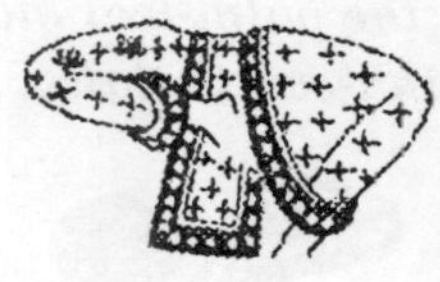

8

9

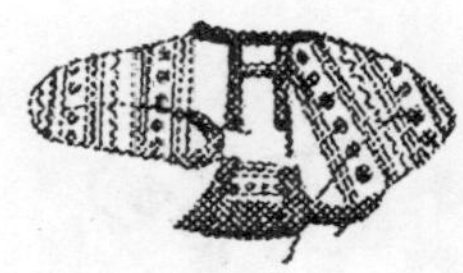

10

Fig. 5. Peacock feather design

Fig. 6. Expanded lotuses with their pericarps, there is no rim

Fig. 7. Rimmed rosette in circle

Fig. 8. Simple cross pattern

Fig. 9. Zig-Zag alternating with floral meander

Fig.10. Zig-Zag alternating with solid lozenges

Plate III

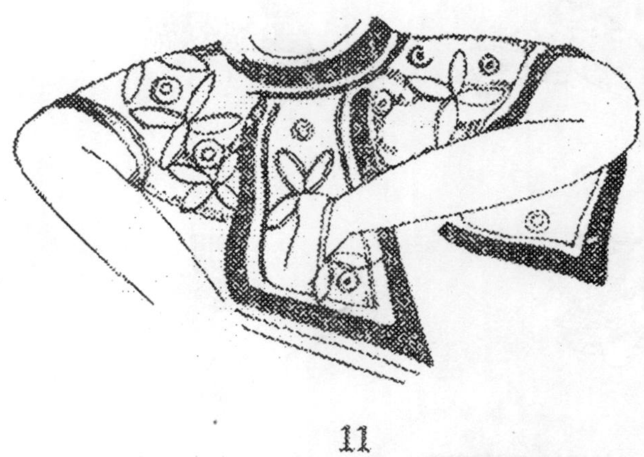

11

Fig. 11. Tie-dyed circles with four petalled flowers

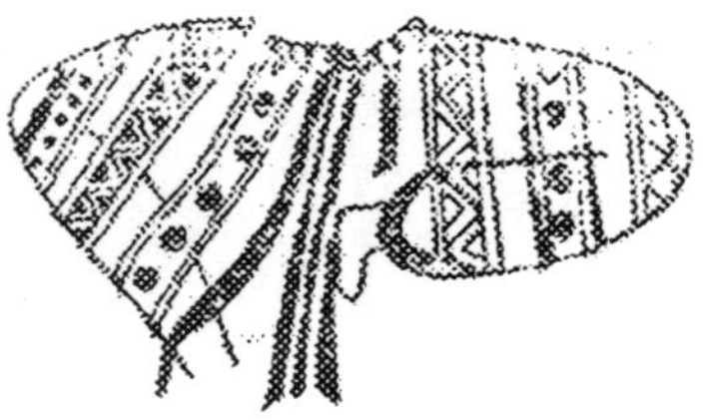

12

Fig. 12 . Denticles alternating with chevron

Patterns from the palm-leaf manuscript of the Neminatha-carita dated 1241 A.D.

13

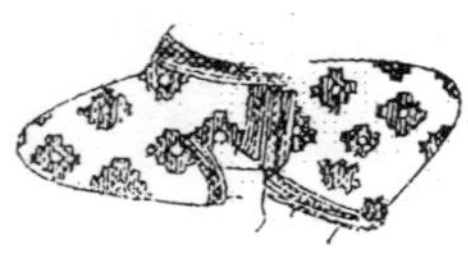

Fig. 13. Thick cross pattern; pattern from Kalpasutra, dated 1279 A.D.

Fig.14. Stepped square pattern; pattern from Kalpasutra, dated 1372 A.D.

Fig. 15. Geese pattern 'Word' the blue Sari decorated with the rows of geese carrying what appear to be pearl neckless in their beaks.

Plate IV

Pattern from the palm-leaf manuscript of the Kalpasutra from Idar; end of the 14th century

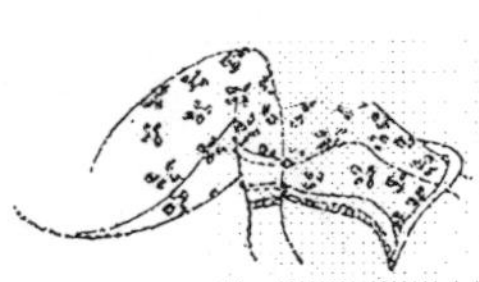

16

17

18

19

Fig. 16. Dotted pattern

Fig. 17. Horizontal blue stripes alternating with the panels of dotted circles in red

Fig. 18. Cheques with the compartments filled with diamonds

Fig. 19. Chequered square blocks.

Patterns from the Kalpasūtra in the Dayavimala collection, 15th century.

20

21

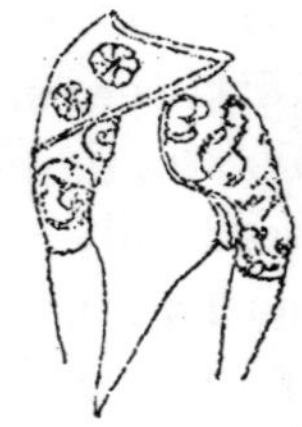

22

Fig. 20. Stylished flowers

Fig. 21. Rosettes, the interspaces filled with small four petalled flowers

Fig. 22. Arabesque

Plate V

23

24

25

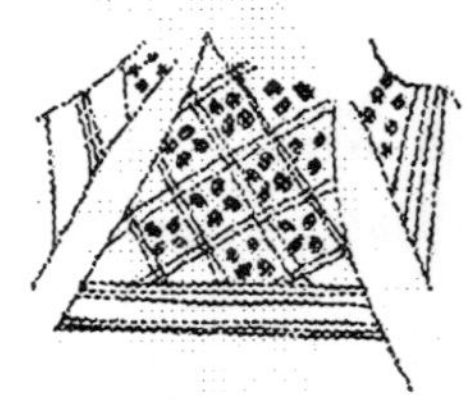

26

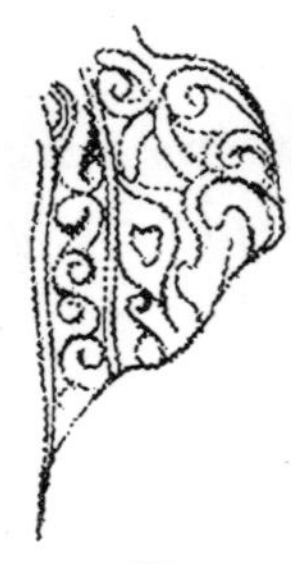

27

28

Fig. 23. Flowers with curled stems

Fig. 24. Solar symbol or sun-flower

Fig. 25. Panels of chevron alternating with denticles

Fig. 26. Cheques with compartments decorated with four pettaled flowers

Fig. 27 Appears like Chinese cloud pattern

Fig. 28 Arabesque and solar symbol

Plate VI

Patterns from a Kalpasutra of the 15th century.

29

Fig. 29. Animals and birds pattern; the field divided into compartments filled with the figures of geese, elephants and horses.

The typical costumes of the princes, bankers and merchants, as represented in the painted wooden blocks from the Jaisalmer Jhana Bhandar.

30

31

32

Fig. 30. Tight fitting shorts made of elaborately embroidered or printed materials zig-zags, cheques and small flowers are the chief patterns.

Fig. 31. Shorts *kamarbands* and *patkas* are of the same type, but there is an addition of an open, half-sleeved, tight jacket reaching to the waist.

Fig. 32. Military costumes, it consists of a half sleeved indigo coloured tunic, tight fitting shorts made of striped material, *kamarband* and top-boots. The head seems to have been covered with a scarf.

Plate VII

The typical costume of the women of Gujarat in the 12th century on a palm leaf manuscript from Chani near Baroda.

33

34

Fig. 33. Dress consists of richly patterned *saris* reaching the ankles, *patkas* matching the *saris*, tight half-sleeved *colis* covering the entire chest and the stomach and the light scarves worn on the shoulders.

Fig. 34. Wearing striped *Saris* and *patkas* and their breasts are covered with half-sleeved *colis*, made of striped or flowered materials which leave the stomach exposed.

35

36

Fig. 35. Wearing an indigo coloured *dhoti* worked with the geese pattern; a graceful scarf covering her coiffure and a part wrapped round the waist and half sleeved green bodic.

Fig. 36. The typical costume of manfolk is heavily ornamented *dhoti* and scarf.

Plate VIII

Costumes of the female dancers are preserved in the decorative figures on the borders of the two early 15th century illustrated manuscript of the Kalpasutra.

37

38

39

40

*Fig.*37. Dancer wears closely fitting shorts, *patka* half-sleeved closely fitting *coli* reaching a little above the navel, scarf (*dupatta*) covering the shoulders, and a scarf tied round the hair.

Fig. 38. The shorts are replaced by the *sari*.

Fig. 39. She wears what appears to be close fitting trousers, the *coli*, and a transparent *jamah*.

Fig. 40. She wears a full sleeved *coli* and a straight edged skirt.

Plate IX

We find that the costume now Turkish with strong Mongol influence. The exact shapes of these garments are fortunately, preserved in the illustrated manuscript of the Kalakacarya Katha dated 1458 A.D.

41

42

43

44

45

Fig. 41. The Turkish costume is shown to consist of a full long sleeved Tartaric gown half-sleeved *Qaba*, full boots and a pointed cap.

Fig. 42. The Turkish costume, pointed cap attached to the *Qaba*.

Fig. 43. The Turkish costume having triangular cap.

Fig. 44. The Turkish costume, hair in hanging locks decorated with silken tassels and four printed caps.

Fig. 45. The Turkish costumes, *kamarband* with its ends fluttering in the air and having dome shaped cap.

6

Position of the Untouchables During the Medieval Period of India (1500 to 1707 A.D.)

The fifteenth and Sixteenth centuries were the formative period of the radical religious movement associated with saints and *sants*. The saints of this period were non-brahmans, and mostly belonged to the lower castes of the society called *'Untouchables'*. During this *Bhakti movement* led by the galaxy of untouchables in medieval India. The saints *'Word'* or *'Nam' Guru Nanak, Chaitanya, Kabir, Jnaneshwar, Namdeo, Eknath, Tukaram* and many others male and female *Ravidas 'Chamar'* were the Prophet and pioneers of social and religious freedom. They showed a great independence spirit[1] with power of *'Nam'* as a 'New Society' of the medieval period, the society is known as *'Domb Society'* of the *'Sudra Family'* to begin with Babar's campaigns over India from the *Multan* as a path breaker of the nationalism for the establishment of *Imperialistic Thought* in India i.e. *Nam* or *Chamar* along with saint *Ravidas* as the friends of the *'Natural Thought'*. The first characteristic of their teachings is freedom from slavery to external authority[2] i.e. materialism.

To begin with Guru Nanak, the *Bhakti Movement* did not remain merely a religious movement, it became a movement for social change against all the social evils which were prevalent in the society from the early medieval period of the Indian history by creating *'Caste System'*, *'Untouchability'* and *'discrimination against women'* by the Brahmanas of the period. It appears from the study that religion was monopolised by the priests of both the Hindu and Muslim society belonged to a certain privileged class called *Molabies* and *Pandits*. *Jnaneshwar,* originator of the *Bhakti* movement in Maharashtra, is reported to have remonstrated with the persecution of saint *Namdeo,* a tailor by birth, in the following manner:

> "There was no high or low with God. All were alike to him. Never entertain the thought that I am high born, and my neighbour is low by birth. The Ganges is not polluted, nor is the wind tainted, nor the earth rendered untouchable, because the low born and high born battle in the one, or beathe the other, or move on the back of the third[3]."

The saint poets freedom from caste system prejudices is the best illustrated in following lines.

> "They say that woman and *Sudras* belong to the low caste. But when you say that God dwells everywhere then is he not in the heart of a *Sudra*? Has not a *Sudra* come from the same place as the Brahman? Is he not composed of the same five elements? Has he no birth; has he no death? Eknath says: You are misguided when you say that a *Sudra* belongs to the lowest class[4]", they are highly class of the Indian society.

Jnaneshwar's revolt was not only against meaningless authority of priests and politicians of the modern period, but also against classical and so called sacred language Sanskrit which the masses did not know or understand and in which language the religious books were written. In fact, they were forbidden to learn Sanskrit. Against stiff Brahminical opposition, Jnaneshwar wrote his immortal commentary on the *Bhagwadgita* in *Marathi*.

By writting his commentary in the spoken language of the people, *Jnaneshwar* destroyed the barrier between the common man and the learned few. His example was followed by all other saints in the region, many of whom rose from the so-called lower castes[5].

Kabir, too, had attacked caste system in no uncertain terms. In one of his famous and off shoot quoted passages, he says:

> "It is needless to ask of a saint, the caste to which he belongs; the barber has sought God, the Washerman and the carpenter. Even *Raidas,* was a seeker after God. The Rishi *Swapacha* was a tanner by caste. Hindus and Muslims alike have achieved that End, where remains no mark of distinction[6]."

During the time of Sultan Sikander Lodhi (1489-1517 A.D.), the *Qazi* and *Pundits* presented their joint petition. The lowly Kabir has flouted all the glorious traditions of 'Islam' and the noble conventions of the Hindus. He maligns the *Vedas* and the great pilgrim places; he rejects the deities and defames the great Brahmins of Kashi. He denounces pilgrimage to the holy *Ka-aba*[7], the forty days fasting during *Ramazan* and preaches against the tenets of *'Islam'*. He ridicules the Hindu scriptures as well as the holy book of Islam. He is an infidel, a non-believer of God; he is a heretic and a *Kafir.* Sikander Lodhi was enraged on this movement of the Kabir. He refused to apologize for it. His hands and feet bound with heavy chains, Kabir was thrown into the river. But the waves broke the chains and Kabir was seen floating on the water. The *Qazi* and *Pundits* commented, "O great Sultan, this is all a trick, because he is a magician." But Kabir said in ecstasy, "O Kabir, no one is mine in this world; in the water and on the earth, my savior is the Lord[8]." Sikander Lodhi was amazed. There was not a tinge of resentment in Kabir's word. The saint bore no grudge even towards his worst tormentor. It is no wonder that Kabir forgave the *'Sultan'*. By nature, he was loving and compassionate as all saints are, and to quote his own words: "Forgiveness is a game that only the saints play[9]."

Vakhna and *Rajjab*, disciples of *Dadu,*[10] and *Swami Hari Das*, who was most probably a contemporary of Kabir have also mentioned the Sikander Lodhi's episode against Kabir. After this, Kabir decided to leave *Benaras* and proceed to *Magahar* to spend his last days of life. So for the *Magahar* place is concerned, it was situated about 175 miles north-east of Benaras in the Basti District of Uttar Pradesh, 13 miles from Gorakhpur, was a small town in the time of Kabir and had a large population of Muslims, predominantly weavers by caste[11]. Kabir was passed away in 1518 A.D. at the age of 78. Years later, he was to explain that oneness with the divine goes beyond religion and the holy words sacred to one tradition or another.

" Vishnu is on my tongue,

Narayan is in my eyes,

Gobind is in my heart i.e 'Word'

I contemplated on Hari."

In the context of people looking on him as a Muslim, Kabir was four names for God associated with the Hindu tradition, deliberately provoked both Hindus and Muslims in order to help them to understand that *Nameless One* is neither Hindu nor Muslim, but a *Sudra* can be realised by anyone, regardless of community, profession or religious persuasion[12].

In order to appreciate the necessity and appeal of Kabir's method, it is important to understand the socio-religious background of his times. For hundreds of years before his birth, a succession of Muslim invaders had attached Northern India upto Kashmir and Sindh which was their birth place. People were slaughtered, cities razed, and women and girls carried off as booty the invaders destroyed temples and monestaries, plundered their wealth and absconded with many objects of great artistic value[13] of the *'Nam'* and *'Kalma's'*. In 1206 A.D., *Qutab-ud-din Aibek,* the first *Sultan* of Delhi, destroyed hundreds of temples in Benaras; of the temples destroyed elsewhere there is no count. It was the story of the *'Nam'*. The Banaras of Kabir, though still rich in temples, was a pale shadow of what it had been. In 1398 A.D., under the pretext that the ruling Muslim Sultan was treating his Hindu subjects too leniently, the Mongol Timur, in famous for his military efficiency and cruelty, invaded India. During a few months stay he sacked Delhi, put its citizens to the sword and plundered and looted wherever he went. His disastrous raid left behind a weakened government in Delhi and hardship for both Hindus and Muslims. The year 1398 A.D. is significant because tradition tells us it was the year of Kabir's birth[14].

Towards the end of the later Vedic period, the *Varnas* tended to become hereditary, endogamous and birth based, leading to the formation of *Jatis*. The term *Jati* is derived from the Sanskrit root *Jan* means 'living being', and is first applied to the man's himself as this is not conducive to religious merit, because man is a free born by the nature, it was not in the hands of *Brahmans*. But in Indian society birth was slowly become an important factor of social ranking and the theory of *Karma* (deed) and *punarjanma* (rebirth), which proved such an effective idealogy int he internatization of the inequitions caste system by the oppressed and fue exploited championed of the Buddhism and Jainism after the death of Asoka. The period saw the beginning of the process of assimilation, acculturation and integration of the aboriginal tribes (*Barawalas*) into the expending Aryan network at various levels. Thus, the *Aitareya Brahmana* describes the *Andhras, Pundras, Shabaras, Pulindas* and *Mutibas* and *antas* (border people) sons of sage *Vishvamitra* i.e. *'God'* or *'Nam'*, as *apachyas* and *nichyas* with their own chiefs; there are copious references to the proximity of and interaction with the larger and better organised *Nishadas*[15], *Candala, Pukkasa, etc.* of the *Dharmasastra*. Among the *Sudras*, too, there soon developed a distinction between those followed the ideals and initated the practices of the higher castes, the "good" *Sudras*, and those whose touch made impure the water of a *Brahmana,* and to whom a good Brahman would not act as priest. The promotion of the *Namasudras* from the status of *Candalas* to that of second class *Sudras* is quite natural and is the consequence of the improved culture and way of living they adopted. It was with the object of emphasising the fact that they were no longer *Candalas* became Brahmans, that they adopted the name-ending of *Sudra*, though they were originally called *'Namas*[16]'.

Despite of the flexibility shown by the law-giver i.e. *'Father'* owing to considerations of practical constraints, there is, no doubt, that sizeable sections of *Brahmanas* and *Kshatriyas*, who could afford it tended to withdraw themselves from primary productive activities like labour, etc. and came to broadly represent *'Status' and 'Power'*, respectively; the *Shudras* substantially provided productive manual labour, and the gap between the elite and the masses widened, intensifying the motion of the high and the low on the occupation. The social fabric at this time was, however, in a tremendous flux and several professions, crafts and tribes were crystallizing as distinct entities of both Hindus and Muslims. Neither their existence could be ignored, nor could they be identified with the four existing *Varnas* of the society. This gave rise to the theory of *Varnasamkara* or mixed castes by the Brahmanas, which ascribed their origin to interbreeding among the members of both the Muslims and the Hindus during the early medieval period and four *varnas* among the Hindus and also among their progeny from *anuloma* (in natural order or with a woman of lower *varna*) and *pratiloma* (in inverted order or with a woman of higher *varna*) unions. The relatively superior rating of *anuloma* to *pratiloma* was due to the patriarchal[17] society of the 'Father'.

The notion of ritual pollution was widely spread in the society controlled by the Pandits and *Molabies* in relation to the *'Shudra'* means 'Pure-thought' had made a fleeting appearance due to the controll over formal education towards the ends of the later Vedic period when the use of milk miled by the *Sudra* was forbidden at the daily *agnihotra* (oblation of fire) which was based on false notions by the elite class of both the Hindus and Muslims and *Shudra* was ristricted by the Pandits even to speak on the sacrifice (ritual), but there was no matter for the performing of sacrifice. Physical contact with or touch of the *Shudra* was, however, not regarded as pollution even the modern time. Though the *Dharmasutra* continued to adhere to this position, the notion of pollution as an enduring feature in the social life. *Jat* an important characteristic of caste means *pure 'Chamar'* was institutionalised as untouchability in these law books. Untouchability meant permanent and hereditary pollution owing to physical contact among the Indian society and the group of first identified for the purpose was the *Churha* or *Candala*. The *Dharmasutra* are unanimous in holding the touch of the *Chandalas* as polluting and prescribe both with clothes on as a means of expiation. The *Chandalas* also cause pollution through proximity, sight, hearing and speech, entailing corresponding expiations. Physical assocaition and commensal and cannubial ties with the *Chandalas* are completely prohibited and their segregation was legalized[18] by the Brahminical thought. To take just one example of Dr. B.R. Ambedkar, there is evidence to indicate that the expectations of the Brahmans were again, remained large unfulfilled, he did a wonderful work during his life time and after his death, he has been given the title *'Father of Constitution'* which means have 'heavenly' message as a Creator of the soul and *'Law'*, called *'Nam'* awarded *Bharat Ratna* by birth. He was B.R. Ambedkar. Here 'B' stands for *Bharata* and letter 'R' stands for *Ratna*[19]. The *Chandalas* emerges as an extremely poor segregated group enlisted to work at the crematorium, hang criminals, drag people committing suicide on the public road, whip adulterous women, and even to defend new settlements in the countryside under the rule of Brahmans. They, however, continued as hunters, fowlers and butchers as well, with dogs, cats, pigs and cock as their properity, wearing clothes and ornaments were restricted by the Brahmanical laws and depending on others for their food during the time of function as untouchables. It is important to consider how the heterodox sects of Buddhism and Jainism responded to the development of caste and untouchability. Surely their approach toward history was differed from orthodox Brahmanism in several respects, but their religious orders admitted people without considering and knowing their wealth, rank or social origins and permitted them to rise to the highest position on the basis of virtue and knowledge alone[20] at that time when there was an hard time. Among the people who joined the *Sangha* or supported the Buddhism from outside the overwhelming majority belonged to the high castes and families, after realizing the historical fact of the *'Nam'* or *'Word'*, which a Brahmana could hardly understand due to that reason that his mind has been polluted, with the 'sexual desire' and 'materialistic lust'. Thus, the distinct between the affluent and the destitute, the high (*Ukkattha*) and the low (*hina*), is pronounced an explicit, and is applied to *jatis* (castes), *Kulas* (families), *Kammas* (occupations) and *Sippas* (Crafts in both Buddhism and Jainism. The occupation of the flower-sweeper (*Puppha Chhaddaka*) and the crafts of the basket maker (*nalahara*), leather-worker (*Chammakara*), weaver (*pesakara*), potter (*Kumbnakara*) barber (*nahapita*) are designated as low, and the *Chandalas*, *Nesadas*, *Pukkusas*, *Venas* and *Rattakaras* are stigmatized as despised castes (*hina jatis*) in the Pali Canon. The *Chandalas*, who are also known as *Matangas* and *Panas,* and the *Sovagas* are equally despised in the Jain texts. The professions of hunters and fishermen, too, are rated very low[21].

In the study, we learn that there was the nature of the untouchability practised in relation to the *Chandalas* and other castes of the *Sudras*, and their economic plight in the *Buddhist Jatakas*, were posterior, has been discussed in the Pali Canon and often coincide with the *Manusmriti* are as severe as it had been prescribed by those law giver, who are generally regarded as the symbol of the ugly face of Brahmanism even though the *Chandalas* are found pursuing several callings including those of a corpse carrier, remover and cremator, hangman, sweeper, nightguard, public performer and hunter. *Nesedas* who engaged in hunting and fishing (there are occasional references to their villages, chiefs and guilds), the *Pukkusas* who were hunters and refuse-cleaners, the *Venas* who were bamboo-workers and also possibly hunters, and the *Rathakaras* who built chariots for war, are portrayed as sharing the status and penury of the *Chandalas*. It is significant that the professions of the basket maker, leather-worker, potter, weaver and barber had a better rating in contemporary Brahmanical works; the *Grihyasutras* of *Bandhayana*[22] *and Bharadwaja*[23] prescribed even Upanayana for the *Rathakara;* and the caste of bamboo-worker and basket maker; *Buruda,* came to be looked upon as untouchable only in the early medieval *Smritis*. The emphasis that both Buddhism and Jainism laid on non-violence evidently coloured their attitude and perception towards many of these castes which were obliged by their wretched material condition and needs of subsistance and livelihood to engage in activities involving violence among the Brahmans, who always deteriorated their mental horizon from time to time as history displayed the events at different period. In the case of the *Candalas* the primitive dread of dead human bodies which they handled aggaravated the degree of pollution[24] which created by the Brahmanical thought at different period of time and accepted the challanges made by the Brahmans and replied in a nice manner as a civilized man of the society. In Hindustani, culture would be *Shishta-ta, Sanskriti, Tahzib, Tadib or Shayistagi* and civilization would be *Sabhya-ta, Samudachara, Tahzib or Taur-tariq*. Simpler and more popular words would be *Chal, Dhang, Tarah, 'Chamar'* or *Chandalas*, but they are scarcely adequate. 'Civilization' has probably the same root as *Sabhyata* i.e. *Sabha*, civic, an assembly, a city, village or locality 'civilized' and *'Sabhya'* both meaning one who is a worthy citizen or worthy to sit in any assembly, either in a city or in a village. Culture on the other hand, comes from the 'ultimate reality' i.e. *'Nam'* , as is well-known, from the Latin word *'cultus'* meaning a plough, civilization of the land and of the mind means tilling, preparing, refining and sowing of the seeds on the land and also with good valuable seeds i.e. *'Nam'*, moral and intellectual, which will yield whole some 'spiritual bread' of life. *Sanskirit*, refining has the same implications also. So too *Shayistagi* and *Tahzib*. The idea of refining, making better, the dictionary explanations of both culture, and civilization include the word 'refinement', which comes from the 'Father'. The essence of culture then must be the refinement of human being in all his aspects and civilization, the collective life of a community, a nation of such individuals. A civilization is only an explication of what is implicit in human nature[25]. This great Institution of Human Society, coming down from time immemorial, changing their forms more or less from time to time, namely, law and religion, including fine art of the knowledge and civilization growth of the human nature in historical prospective in the form of a 'New Society' as a law of nature i.e. called *'Nam'*. From the above authentic meanings and definitions we are in a position to infer that culture originates from the peasantry form and real civilization is the outward expression of their way of life as it has been depicted from the various channels of studies like literature, science and art in practical manners of the life. The basic fact is that caste had come to play an important role in economic life and it developed strong roots in occupations in the birth-based hierarchical class society of early India and few movements of protest against injustice involved in its intrinsic inequality had 'power' to change this ground reality or to offer any viable and enduring alternative programme to form the 'New Society' of the father that Brahmanism, Buddhism, Jainism, Mahmadanism ideologically contributed a lot to the irreversible process of the development of caste and untouchability instead of resisting it has to be acknowledged. Caste actually solidified with the hordening of class relations in north India between 600 B.C. and 200 A.D., and untouchability, too, originated in Pre-Mauryan times, got accentuated by 200 A.D[26].

Since most of the castes which were initially reduced to the level of untouchables were those [27] who do not know the beauty of nature i.e. *'Nam'*. The term 'beauty is explained as, "the philosophy or theory of taste or of the perception of the beautiful in nature and art." One of its purposes is to define the beautiful and to analyse the attitude to it of human mind and this involves very subtle and difficult discussions. The beautiful it is essence is a theme for the professed by philosopher as by the same writer while its concrete manifestations in nature and art appeal more rapidly to the general intelligence. We can very well say that beauty and aesthetics are the same thing, though there are divergences of opinions. It goes without saying that aesthetics has its philosophical as well as its scientific aids and we may best illustrate the former in a brief space by quoting the views of the leading saints of the medieval period have already mentioned above,their aesthetician on the relations of the 'True Faith', the good and the beautiful Dr. Henry Rulger Marsall suggests that "the beautiful is the real as discovered in the world of impressions, the relatively permanent pleasure which gives us the sense of beauty being the most stable characteristic of those parts of the fiel of impression which interest us." According to him the real or the true in the broad sense of the term has three divisions: (1) The Real of Impression *'Word'* the Beautiful ; (2) the Real of expression *'Chamar'* the Good; (3) The Real in Realms exclusive of (1) and (2) *'Nam'* the true (in the narrow sense of the term). Beauty, says the Indian philosopher, is subjective and not objective. It is not embodied in form or matter, but it belongs to the spirit and can only be apprehended by spiritual vision. Thus Havell says, "the more perfect our minds are turned to this divine harmony the more clearly do we perceive the beauty and the more capable we become an artist of revealing it to others. Beauty belongs to the human mind; there is neither ugliness nor beauty in matter alone and for an art student to devote himself wholly to study form and matter with the idea i.e. *'Nam'* of extracting beauty therefrom is a vein as cutting open a drum to see where the sound comes from[28]."

In the study, it has been expressed as soon as the dawn of human history was took place we find that art of writing has been created in response to human needs *'Word'* both material and spiritual. Since the very earliest times, man has discovered in himself an aesthetic sensibility through which he can complete the forms of things made to satisfy his needs, the forms only in definitely suggested by function. From the earliest times, man has found himself to be artist as much as inventor. It is not only in the making of pottery, textiles, furniture and other crafts popularly included in the category of art, but in the making of tools, cars and of engines and machines[29]. Croce is entirely correct when he speaks of "the artist who never makes a stroke with his brush without having previously seen it with his imagination" and mentions that the externalization of a work of art "implies a vigilant will, which presists in not allowing certain visions, intuitions, or representations to be lost[30]."

Thus, when we use the word 'art' we do not intend the reader to think only of paintings, pottery, textiles, statues, etc we employ the *'Word'* or *'Nam'* in a much wider sense to embrace all manifestations of aesthetic sensibility, especially in human life in a advance society. On the other hand, we the Hindusthani are quarreling with tradition only in so for as the arbitrary distinction, commonly made between 'fine' and 'applied' or 'minor' arts is concerned; such a distinction, couched in these terms is false, which had little share in the distribution of wealth, power or prestige, untouchability of wealth, untouchability has to be viewed as the extreme manifestation of the institutionalized inequality of both caste and class. The untouchables were and remain a part of the Indian caste and class structure[31].

So far as the early and later medieval period of Indian history is concerned, the expansion of caste and untouchability from A.D. 200 to A.D. 1200 was roughly an uninterrupted and continous process led by the people for creating the choas and lawlessness in the society. New groups, indigenous as well as alien, were absorbed at various levels of the social structure in different parts and ideology proved flexible and receptive enough to effectively cope with developing situations and historical cross-currents. The extent of social mobility, both upward and downward, was certainly remarkable, and the system, instead of crecking up under pressures all-round, got reinforced and firmly entrenched. By the early medieval period of the Indian history the *untouchables* comprised two broad segments. The first included the backward tribal communities whose original occupations and those acquired after integration and those acquired after integration with the mainstream were not enough to give them economic security. Virtually landless, they served as the cheapest source of servile labour in the country side. With progressive improvement in the overall condition of the *Sudras* and their displacing the *Vaishyas* as the bulk of the peasantry along with other landed classes, the interests of the *Shudras* and the untouchables often diverged. The second category of *untouchables* included several depressed artisan castes who had remained at the level of *Shudras* until the 6th century A.D. but under the impact of certain feudal developments in post Gupta times such as the decline of trade and commerce, decrease in commodity production, break-up of craft guilds and increasing immobility became closely integrated with the villages in the predominantly agrarian economy dominated by the landed classes. With their hereditary skill and low wages, often in kind, they were another cheap and easily available source of exploitation. Neither of these categories of *'untouchables'* was a homogeneous unit. Their division into several hierarchical castes on the basics of professions under the influence of the dominant caste ideology thwarted the development of any bond of unity among them or with the landless *Shudras* and debilitated them for any fight for social justice on their own. *Parashara*, who composed his *Smriti* during the period, reflected this social change clearly when he prescribed a number of expiations especially for the *Shudras* in case of their being polluted by the *untouchables*. The availability of cheap landless labour and artisanal products on an enduring basis has been underlined by Irfan Habib as the major contribution of caste from which the Muslim landed and ruling classes benefited as much as their Hindu counterparts[32].

In the study, we learn that many important social changes were took place in India, resulted from the policies followed by certain Sultans of the period from time to time. In the following lines an attempt is made to develop an argument on important factors responsible for the increase in monetization and social change in India during the medieval period in the Indian history. The Arab conquest of *Makran, Sindh* and the Panjab in 712-13 A.D., marks the beginning of medieval age that exposed the vast region and Arab rule to foreign influences. Thus the term *Arab* means led by the one. Father i.e. *'Nam'* conquered the loose processes of the social and economic changes in the vast north-western region of India where the people of *Sudra clans* used to reside in the memory of 'Father'. The overland and over-sea trade already received a great boost, because the Muslim traders had already acquired a dominant position in international trade, linking the countries of Mediterranean and the Indian ocean. With the Arab traders not only came foreign merchandise in the countries of Europe, Africa and Asia, but also information about different cultura traditions and scientific ideas of the *'Nam'* or *'Kalma'*. As for the countries conquered by the *Arab* Muslims, each witnessed the introduction of a uniform administrative system under a bureaucracy, the members of which transferred from one territory to the other highly urbanised people, they founded new urban centres that were soon linked to interregional and inter continental trade routes[33]. There is a local chronicle of Sindh called *Chach-nama* which gives some interesting detail of Indian History. According to this work *Shiras Rai,* the king of Sindh, ruled over an extensive territory bordering in the north of *Kashmir* and in the west upon *Makran*[34].

Sindh roughly denoted the lower *Indus* valley from Multan down to the sea; in the west it sometimes included large portions of Baluchistan, and in the east it was bounded by the Indian desert. Our knowledge of its early history is extremely scanty; almost limited to what the Arab historians have written about it. We learn from the study that during the time of the Arab invasions Sindh was under the *Shudra* dynasty founded by the Brahman *Chach*. It was preceded by the *Rai* family comprising five kings, who are said to have held the power about 137 years that Alor (near modern *Rohri*) as their capital[35]. Here, too, the Buddhist fifth columnists welcomed the *Arabs* and entered into a pact with them against their own governor, who was defeated and fled. The Buddhist sections of other towns are also said to have befriended the *Arabs*. This may be explained partly by their aversion to slaughter and bloodshed led by the Brahminical thought and partly by their ideal of universal religions fraternity which transcended by Muslims that of a nation or country. Perhaps the superstitions beliefs in the alleged in the prophetic sayings about the conquest of India by Islamic force as a 'New Society' at that time, also, partly account for this attitude. It should be noted, however, that all the Buddhists did not support the Muslims and some actually fought against them. On the other hand, many non-Buddhists also betrayed their king and country[36] on the bases of caste system. When Yuan Chwang wos travelling in India (629-45 A.D.) of *Sudra* (*Shu-to-lo*) caste[37], and if he was identical with *Siharas Rai,* as is most probable, we get welcome the light, on the origin of the *Rais* and the *'Islam'* from the *Sudra* family. After the death of the last *Rai, Sahasi,* his Brahman *minister* already mentioned *Chach,* married the widowed queen, and himself assumed the crown. During his long regin of forty years the kingdom grew in extent and authority of Brahmanism, and is described to have abutted upon the confines Kashmir. His son, *Dahir,* who succeeded *Candar or Candra* (*Chach's* brother), had to face the serious *Arab* invasion because he did not chastige the people of Debul for having seized a vessel carrying rich presents from the king of Ceylon to *Hajjaj,* a governor of Iran. *Muhammad-Ibn-Qasim* led the expedition; he stormed *Debul* in H.93= A.D 712[38], Surnamed *Ferishta,* was born at *Astrabad,* on the border of the Caspain sea[39], is meant certainly the present *Mahalla* of *Sudarmar* compares with *Kalhana's* explanation *'sudar'* means *'Sea'* in Sanskrit called *Samudra* in Hindi and *Srivara* called it *Samudramantha*[40], where the *Kalma* resides for the recognisation, of *'Father'* or *'Prophet'* in the living form. In this way, he captured the *Bahmanabad,* and reduced *Multan* in 723 A.D; thus, completed the conquest of Sindh[41].

According to these Chronicles King *Sahiras Rai,* son of *Sahasi Rai* ruled over an extensive kingdom bordering on *Kashmir* and Kanauj in the north and east, and extending as for as *Makran* in the west[42]. Makran, bordering Iran was the first region in the subcontinent of South Asia to be conquered by the Arabs with the power of *Kalma* or 'Nam' after Iran during the early period of the rise of *'Islam'* as a 'New Society' in the seventh century A.D. It was largely inhabited by the nomadic tribes, mainly the *Balochs,* divided into clans lived in its southern part while *Turks, Saythian,* Afghans, etc. lived in it north[43]. The fact is that *Harsha-vardhana* fought with the king of Sindh already mentioned above lends some colour of probability to this account for the development of the *'Idea of Nam'* in Human form. Thus, the central part of these territories was came under the immediate charge of the *Sudra* ruler of the *'Nam',* who had his capital at *Alor,* while the rest was divided into four provinces, each under a governor who is also described as a tributary ruler of the Father. This account agrees fairly well with that of Hiuen Chwang, account. King *Sahiras* lost his life in a fight with the king of *Nimruz,* a province of Persia, who has invaded his territory and entered *Kirman.* This took place probably at the beginning of the seventh century A.D *Sahiras* was succeeded by is son *Rai Sahasi* II. During the reign of a Brahman known as *Chach* gradually rose a power and his office and ascended the throne after his master's death. The provincial governors at first refused to acknowledge the suzerainty of the usurper. But *Chach* marched in person against them and subdued them all. He also proceeded to the hills of Kashmir and definitely fixed the forntier between the two kingdoms i.e. Persia and Iran. Taking advantage of the confusion of Persia, due apparently to the *Arab* invasion, *Chach* conquered a portion of Makran and forced the people of *Kandabil* (east of *Kalat*) to pay tribute[44].

In the study we learn that internecine struggles between the two classes i.e. the rich and poor, *Chach* was thus, a very power king according to *Chach-nama,* because he himself was a lord on earth in the form of the human being, but it is difficult to accept as a fact, because everything has been mentioned in this work. The date it gives for *Chach's* accession, viz. A.D. 602, is probably wrong. If we believe Hiuen Chang's statement that the ruling king of Sindh was *Sudra*[45], belonged to the *Karakota* dynasty of Kashmir called *Durlabhvardhana.* He claimed descent from *Naga Karkotaka*[46]. It appears probable that the visit of Hiuen Chawng (Circ A.D. 631-633) fell within the reign of thirty six years which Kalhana attributes to *Durlabhavardhana* of Kashmir ruled (600-632 A.D.) along with Muhammad Prophet (570-632 A.D.). They were the friend of the *'Nam'* and both were died on the same date i.e. 632 A.D. after spreading the Buddhism in India and other parts of the world. The life of Hiuen Chwang records the hospitable reception which the king of *Kashmir* accorded to the pious piligrimages, but unfortunately, does not state his name in the Indian history by the modern scholars. The king was well-inclined towards the Buddhist priests, but Hiuen Chwang himself notes that "at the present time this kingdom is not much given to the faith, and the temples of the heretics are their sole thought[47]." He also won the friendship of *Harsavardhana* by giving him a prized tooth-relic of the Buddha for enshrinement in *Kanauj.* If the former is identical as seems highly probable, with the prince 'Dr Raj Kumar' at whose court Yuan Chwang spent two pleasant years from 631 to 633 A.D, Kashmir was then already an important state having dependencies like *Simhapura* (*Ketas*) *Urasa* (Hazara), Punch and *Rajapura* (Rajouri[48]).

It is, however, necessary to remember that while this movement was emancipatory in some respects, in relation, for example, to the *mawali, 'Islam'* lost its exclusive identification with *Arab* tradition, and Arabic became for two centuries the literary language of Iran. The universality of *Islam* was invoked to rule out racialism and tribalism from the social ethics of *Islam.* This was done by a long process of reconstruction (with much unconscious creative forgery of the prophetic traditions, the *hadis*) which stands no original meaning, a process which has been given its classical analysis by *Schacht.* Thus a scattered unsystematic assemblage of Quranic injunction and Arab tribal spirit and customs was now sought to be converted in the 8th and 9th centuries into a system of law by one of the greatest intellectual efforts were made in the history of Islam. The effort was "to systematize by *Muhammad Ibn Qasim* as a *Kalma* himself and by the tendency to *'Islamicise'*, to impregnate the sphere of law with religious and ethical ideas, to subject it to Islamic norms." The effort was not only reflected in giving an absolute multi-racial universality to *Islam* as a term and it also was expressed in the emergence of new ethical ideas, which impelled bans that did not exist in the Quran[49], because Quran is explanation of the Lord during his life time. He is the 'Father' or Husband at that time, because all the souls are attached to him. This temporarly contractual marriages during his life time called (*'Muta[50]'*) and at that time whole world is in a family of 'Father'. As soon as, he dies, the theory of mind i.e. *Brahmins* or *Molavis* initimate it and gives practical shape in the life, slowly and gradually, it became a tradition in the society and adopted by the various school of thought which are based on philosophical to exploit the women as a 'sexual union' and it was also disapproval by Prophet. Similarly, a more humane spirit could be discerned a treatment at slavery. A woman slave made into a concubine to give him a child could not then be sold away by the master, a new legal doctrine without any historical proof of such protection extended to the *Unm al-walad* concubines in the Prophet's time or even under the pious Caliphs of *'the 'Nam'* ,we see, that with the change, in the territorial and civilizational context of *Islam,'* new ethical perceptions began to modify now and, in some respects, transform of social outlook must have been seen in the *Satsanga* of the *'Nam'*, in what today may seem to be movement toward a more benign 'social justice[51]' towards the modern mission of the *'Nam'* i.e. Called *'Radha Soami'* that women has to deliver their discourse in the *Satsanga* and to certain categories of women and female slaves, it was not a conscious movement towards equality, because of their unconsciousness towards the women. The customs and jealousies in inferior complex were given less accommodation towards the Central Islamic law i.e. *'Nam'*.

Whereas, in an earlier age, constant war and booty in the human society, second to be in accordance with god's insistent decree, now stability was seen as the great virtue of properly arranged societies. It was, therefore, not an accident that the ideal regime to many Islamic thinkers has been established their wave like notable *Ibn Khaldun* of the 14th century A.D. began to be indentified with the pre-Islamic Sasanid empire of Iran, where the rulers ruled for the common good on the basis of humanity, that is, for continuing stability of established hierarcy. The craving for society where birth should be determine one's position in the apparatus of political power that one finds in the historian *Zia-ud-din Barani* (1357 A.D.) is, therefore, fully in accordance with the main thrust of Islamic thought as it had developed by that time. His ideas, on hierarchy, then, had a blue-blooded Islamic ancestry, immersed as he himself was in Islamic history and theology as a *'Nam'*. With due respect to a scholar of the calibre of the late Professon Mohammed Habib, it is difficult to his ideas any influence of 'the traditions of the Hindu caste system." It is noticable at *Barani* never invokes the caste system as an acceptable hierarchical order. More precisely, in his vision of the ideal social order i.e. *'Nam'* ,there is no hint of a ban on occupational mobility or of a hereditary priesthood, nor any concept of inherited purity or pollution. All the essentials of the caste system are, therefore locking[52] in the system of mind. Like the men of influence and means, the artisans and craftsman also had to perform a role in the social and political life of the city, so common a phenomenon in the Muslim metropolis. Describing the oath of allegiance taken by the citizens of Lohare to Sultan Qutab-ud-din Aibak in 1206 A.D; *Fakhr-i-Mudabbir* states: "On his arrival (from Delhi to Lahore), all the citizens of the city, the Qazis (the doctor of law), *a'ima* (religious leaders), Saiyids, people of piety, men of high ranks and positions, soldiers, traders and merchants, high and low powerful and weak, the rich and poor, and asceties rushed to show allegiance to him[53]." His reign, properly speaking, lasted only four years, though he enjoyed all the state and dignities of a king for upwards of twenty, if we reckon from the period of the capture of Delhi, when he may be said to have become the King of India, though he assumed only the tittle of commander-in-chief of his patron Mahomad Ghori. He was certainly a great captain, and might be classed among the greatest men in history, had not his licentious conduct Ghazni tranished the glory of his life. He was famous throuhout the East for his generosity, for which he obtained the surname of *Lakbukhsh*, "Bestower of laks". When a man is praised for generosity in India, they say to this day, "He is as liberal as *Qutab-ud-din* Aibek[54]."

It shows that *Sultan Qutab-ud-din Aibek's* reign forms a water shed in the history of India. The state policy foreward by him resulted not only changed the social structure of the urban centres, but all alleviated the burden to taxation on the peasantry system of labour. The composition of the nobility under Qutab-ud-din Aibek led to political pluralism with the meditation of the *'Nam'* which increased with the passage of time. The reference to *ratagan* (*'Word' raragan, = ranas*) and *takaran* (Thakkuras) as among the *Turks,* Khalis and others in the royal army of the *'Nam'* or *'Word'* suggests that an effort was made by the new *Sultan* means through the process of the *'Nam'* in the body became *Sant,* then Sultan to enlist the Hindu land chiefs in the nobility others remain slave of the God in natural form. He took self interest in improving the condition of the peasants by providing cheap and best rate quality of seeds. He forbade the state officers through a *farman* that the fields of the cultivators should not be harmed by the armymen or anybody else, nor should anyone take food or snatch goat and chicken in the town or the countryside. It shows that the society was totally vegitarian. The *imlak* (land-grants) made by the past rulers to the deserving persons for their maintenance were renewed. Fourthermore, he ordered that *Ushr*(one-tenth) of the agricultural produce would be collected instead of *Kharaj*[55]. *(One-fifth)* as state share for the development purposes. Those who paid *ushr* (*tithe*) were to pay *nim-ushr* (i.e. one-twentieth part). Certain other welfare measures were taken such as the distribution of money in charity and grant of stipends to men of learning, widows and orphans.[56]

The powerful chiefs who acquiesced in his authority were spared from small affairs of the *'Nam'* or God. A few of them seem to have been favoured with important positions at the court. For example, *Sadid-al-Din Muhammad Awfi* tells us the *Rai* of Benaras belonged to the *Sudra* family was appointed by the Sultan as *Sahib-i-barid* (officer in-charge of the intelligence service) impressed by the magnanimity and excellent qualities possessed by the *Sultan*, some of the chiefs are said to have embraced the *'Islamic'* basic theme with many of their followers as a 'New Faith' on earth at that time. There were made acquainted with the tenets of *Islam* while their children were sent to new school for learning of the basic of the Quran and acquiring knowledge[57] on the scientific methods of the *'Nam'*.

Given the nature and development of the *Islamic* theology and thought as we have sketched above, it is easy to see that with the coming of 'Islam' in India as a 'New Society', resulted in no encounter between a religion of social equality, and the classical order of *homo hierarchicus*, to borrow from the title of Dumout book[58]. Rather, two systems of hierarchy i.e. God and *'man'* or living *manas* have taken the shape in the form of caste system as a permanent hierarchy called Brahminical society. The difference between the two is that God believes in the totality and Brahmans believes in difference on caste, colour and creed as a Lord of the earth. Therefore, during the social change in the intermixing society, natural forces in the form of man land on earth and give the message of unity without any bias, but at one stage they met each other and interact as per the behaviour of Natural force. This dimension of the reality perhaps best explains why the attitude of the Muslim statemen and thinkers towards the caste system was so accommodating. With regard to the rulers, one can cite a very early example, Muhammad-ibn-Qasim, who was the follower of *Sudra* camp of *Saharsi Rai* dynasty of *Sindh*. After his seizure of the capital of Sindh i.e. *Alor* (712 A.D.); he practically took over the entire Brahman bureaucracy of the fallen regime of the Bhamanbad, and reduced *Multan* and completed his conquest over the Sindh in natural form, and those Brahman surrendered themselves before the *'Nam'* they were allowed as his advisers and officials to determine how the out-castes called untouchables should be treated as the race of father. In this context, the minister (the Brahman *Siyakar*), in the presence of *'Moka of Basaya'* or *Bias*, that during the reign of Raja *Chach,* the (*Jatts of*) *Lohana*, that is *Lakha* and *Summa* were not allowed to wear soft garments, or put *Satin* (caps) on the head, but could only wear black woollen cloth above and below, and throw a course sheet over the shoulder and had to go about bare-headed and bare-footed. Whoever wore a soft garment was fined. When they came out of their house, they had to take a dog with them so that their identity be known to all. It was decreed that no high person from amongst them might ride a horse[59], the reference of *Maula-i-Islam*, a term for a convert of high status to Islam during the absence of Master, tends to reveal that not only the down-trodden people took to the new faith for freedom from caste restrictions, but also some local chiefs also entered into the fold of Islam as a religion not in reality. The Buddhists lived in sizable number in Sindh, living in pockets and were appressed by the members of Brahman ruling elite the religious tension in Sindh led Buddhist chiefs to come to terms with *Arabs.* It is also worth to recall that the Arab conqueror Muhammad-bin-Qasim-al-Thaqafi did not interefere with the society system fo the conquered people. He is said to have sanctioned the privilege of the Brahmans as well as the degradation of the low caste *Jats.* The *Jats* were kept as degraded as they were under *Dahar,* the overthrown Brahman rule of *Sindh.* He was informed by his Brahman and other advisers that "Jats were forced (by Dahar) to wear coarse clothing and to be bare-booted and bare-headed," and that while going out of doors, "they had to take their dogs with them so that they might by this means be recognised, they have no high and low among them, and are of a savage temperament, none of them was allowed to ride on horse back, if he had to, he rode without saddle or reins. Heaving heard all this Muhammad-bin-Qasim became convinced that they were deprived people and decided to perpetuate their lowly status[60]. (Thereupon) Muhammad-bin-Qasim said; "What disgusting people are these! they are like the steepe nomads of *Fars* and Koh paya (in Iran). The same regulations (as before) should continue in regard to them. Muhammad-bin-Qasim kept them subject to that prescribed mode and manner of conduct[61]."

The early history of the Islamic polity, a classical work analysed by Jullus Wellhausen, *'The Arab Kingdom and its Fall',* brings out the transformation in the concepts of social hierarchy, as the *Arabs* dramatically expanded their hegemony in imperialist form as Dr. B.R. Ambedkar has given the 'idea of, law in the Indian Constitution,' 'classless' and 'casteless' society, due to the extending of the 'Idea of the *Nam*' at that time, destroying the Sassanid empire and much of the Byzantine within the 7th century A.D. Tribes jostled for position within the new hegemony, and under the acknowledged Quraishite supremacy, two great tribal fedarations emerged i.e. *'Jat'* and *'Chamar'*, the northern or *Muzar* (comprising mainly the *Qais* and *Tamin*) and the southern or Yemenite (mainly *Kalb* and Azad) to contest each other's pre-eminence. There was the *Arab's* dislike of the non-tribal Hellenized Syrian *Arabs* (*'Shamis'*) manifest in the hostility towards them as *Brahmans* and *Sudras* of the tribes settled in Iraq. But with increasing severity grew the scorn and contempt for the non-Arab converts as *Brahmans* called *Mawali*, or 'clients' because characteristically, it was thought unacceptable if a non Arab claimed to be a Muslim without having at the same time been allowed to become a client (*maula*) of an Arab tribe. As these converts, especially Iranians, became more and more important as soldiers and secretaries as present and, then, as scholars, theological and literary, the suppression of the *Mawali* became one of the pillars of the policies of the Umayyed Caliphate (660-750 A.D.) notably under Hajjaj Ibn Yusuf, the Umayyad Viceroy of Iraq and the eastern regions of the Caliphate[62].

In this way, the long standing hierarchical system of the Brahminical thought of narrow vision began to fall in Arab, with the forces of the 'Nam' let loose by the so-called Abbasid Revolution. Without going into the objections raised by the historians of the period of the Arabist school like *Shaban*, the Wellhausen's thesis of the overthrow of Arabism involved in the installation of the Abbasid dynasty in A.D. 750, the long term results can, hardly be disputed i.e. is the story of *'Nam',* because they believe in truth and honesty.

In the study, we learn that there is little bit needs to be added, as a matter of fact, that there were no less than three naval expeditions led by Caliphate of Umar against India in (A.D. 634-44). The first, in A.D. 637, was directed against *Tanah,* i.e. Thana near Bombay, and the other two were aimed at *Barwas*(Broach) and Debal, a port at the mouth of the *Sindhu* or *Vitasta.* These were in the natural form raids, and probably ended in failure like the theory of *'Nam';* at least no conspicuous success attended by any of them. Then the *Arabs* advanced by land, and the first shock of their invasion was felt equally by the three border kingdoms of Kabul, Zabul and Sindh. It will be convenient to deal separately with the first two and the third[63]. But the Arab conquest did not signify any emancipation of the low castes because this was the race of Father, since the older social regime which was left by him undisturbed on the bases of have not theory of the Karl Marx and Engle. There was no recognition of any violation of any Islamic principles of 'Social Justice' in the retention of the old constraints[64] of the *'Nam'.*

Three centuries later, Alberuni set himself to study the Indian civilization in all its characteristics in the form of a *'Nam'* or *'Kalma'*. No greater intellect than he could be produced by the world Islam in the realms of the Brahminical view with which he concerned himself in the upstart of the life. As soon as, he developed his mind in the process of *'Nam',* he reveals a remarkable tolerance for the caste system, though he admits that such an institution is not permitted in Islam in the very beginning, he argues that caste system arose out of the rulers of the Brahminical view concern for their subjects as reveals in the present senerio by the politicians for their own welfare. "The kings of antiquity, who were industriously developed to the duties of their office, spent most of their care on the division of their subjects into different classes and orders, which they tried to preserve from intermixture and disorder." He recalled, in this connexion," the history of ancient

Chosroes (Sasanid emperors), for they had created great institutions, which could not be broken through by the special merits of any individual, nor by bribery[65]." but by the power of 'Nam' as a real founding Father of a nation or country. We here have once again the admiration for the stable hierarchy of pre-Islamic Iran, which Alberuni invokes to explain (and perhaps, justify) the caste system for its Muslim readers.

While the caste system was thus tolerated among the Hindus, yet, despite some transferred prejudices, it never established itself among Muslims in a significant measures. Part of this reason lay in the fact that Muslim law, which was created outside the polluted environment of the caste system, steadily expanded at the expense of inherited customas institutionalized by the Kings or Emperor mentioned above in the system. Another reason was the fact that Muslim perceptions of purity and pollution were so different from the caste-perceptions that latter could not be adopted, for example, eating of meat of the animals and birds, etc. One illustration may serve; when the Arabs invaded the Sindh earlier in the 8th century A.D Muslims must be pure vegitarian and trust on the *'Nam'* as a Master of all the communities. Badauni (1590-91) cites a saying of the Prophet (given in Arabic) that God curses the slaughter of the cow, the tree feller and slave-seller. Badauni found this quotation in books on ethics though he agree that it was of a questionable authenticity of the *'Nam'* or *'Prophet'*. Nevertheless, he saw that there was reason behind the condemnation of the three actions, because soul belongs to 'Father', when she landed on earth in the form of child, she was pure, but the environment of the family and a society pauoted her in form of eating, back biting, and other criminal act, which were legitimate only under necessity and forgotten the 'Father' where from she belongs, trapped into the material world in the wrong notions of the mind. Yet, he says "the belief of the common people (among Muslims) is that unless they eat beef, their faith cannot be true". He goes on ironically to add, "Praise be to God, and wonderful it is, what Islam has come to[66]." 'He came in the pious form the observation underlines the continuous process of the undermining of the caste sense of *'purity'* converted into communities by the kind of aggressive popular Muslim assertion of a counter-custom of rite and ritual on the bases of the theology of the early rulers of the small kingdoms.

Qutab-ud-din-Aibek was a brave and virtuous disposition; open and liberal to his friends, courteous and affable to strangers. In the art of war and good government he was inferior to none, nor was he a mean proficient in literature. In his childhood he was brought fromTurkistan to Nishpur, and there sold by a merchant to *Qazi* Fikhr-ud-din, Bin Abdul Aziz Kufi, who finding that heaven had endowed him with genius, sent him to school where he made considerable progress in the Persian and Arabic languages, as well as in science. His patron and master dying suddenly, he was sold as a part of his estate by his executors, and having been bought by a rich merchant for a considerable sum, was presented for sale to Mau-ud-din. Mohammad Ghori[67]. This tradition was established by his successors[68]. Therefore, it is also wrong to club all the nine rulers of this period (1206-90 A.D) under one dynasty; they actually belonged to three distinct ruling houses of the *'Nam'*, the *Qutbi* dynasty called *Sudra* (1206-11 A.D) founded byQutab-ud-din Aibek, the first *Ilbari* or *Shamsi* dynasty (1211-66 A.D), known after *Shamsuddin* Iltutmish, and second Ilbari dynasty (1266-90 A.D) founded by Ghiasuddin Balban[69] as a *'Sudra'* and *'untouchable'* ruler of India.

There was no fixed law of succession in the Islamic polity i.e. *'Nam'*. Occupation of the throne depended on the general law of Nature i.e. *'Nam'* or *'Word'*, ' the survival of the fittest'. It was perhaps, the single major factor which had led to the rapid expansion of the Muslim arms in various parts of the world; it afforded ample opportunities to the ambitious and capable military generals to carve out vast empires for themselves. It facilitated the rapid spread of Turkish arms in north India upto *Kashmir* under the leadership of *Muhammad Ghori* and his brilliant slave officers called *Sudras*, *Outab-ud-din Aibek* laid the claim to his master's heritage on this very account. The concept of an all powerful hereditary *'Sultan'*, among the Turkish nobility of India belonged to the *Kushana* period to present day, was still in its initial stage of evolution[70]. As many invaders before them *'Word'* the Greeks, Scythians, Mangolians, Parthians, etc. *'Chamar'* had been completely Hinduized in name, speech, manner, religion, dress and ideas a few generations after their settlement in India. In fact, they had lost themselves in the ocean of the Hindu community. But the Mohammedans ever remained a separate community in India. *Islam*, being a fiercely monotheistic religion, could not allow any compromise with polytheism or admit a plurality of deities[71] in large extent.

The political power was concentrated in hand of Turkish officers of Muhammad Ghori, generally called the *Muizze* or Ghurid or Ghori nobles. Within themselves, they could roughly be classified into three categories as already mentioned above. The Ghurids proper were the kinsmen of Muhammad Ghori and members and relations of his ancestral clan that was *'Sudra'* called ' *untouchables'*, the Tazik. Turks were the freemen, the Turkish immigrants who had come to India of their own choice and sought patronage of Muhammad Ghori[72]. We are not able to told the name of the Raja of Jammu who was thus captured and forced to become a Muhammdan; it may have been *Rai Bhim* of the *Sudra* dynasty of Sindh. Of one thing we may be certain, viz, that his successor was a Rajput of the ancient line[73], became his lieutenants at that time, they constituted a microscopic section of the Turkish nobility. The third category comprised the Turkish slave officers of Muhammad Ghori, they were most numerous and influential among the nobility was Dr. Raj Kumar, Professor in History at that time. Muhammad Ghori himself i.e. 'Baba Gurinder Singh Ji' had put great faith in his slave officer i.e. Dr. Raj Kumar and shown preference to them, over the others on his pious approach towards *'History'*, Qutab-ud-din Aibek who inherited his Indian possessions since the time immemorial, belonged to this category as *'Nam'*. In the struggle of political dominance i.e. *Veda*, the Turkish slave officer of Qutab-ud-din Aibek, called the *Qutbi* nobles i.e equavalent of *'Nam'*, came to acquire a premier position among the nobility during the reign of their master; *Shamsuddin Iltutmish* was their chief representative. Iltutmish, in turn, created a new class of the *'Nam'* by providing attributive name called Turkish nobility which comprised his own slaves, promoted as officers. They were referred to as the *Shamsi nobles* like *Gujaras,* after the name of their master. After some time, during the hey day of Iltutmishes reign, forty of these slave officers constituted the top leadership among the *'Shamsi nobles'* who held all the important portifolio as state ministers and regional military governors; they earned the nickname of the *Chalisa,* the rule of actual number in the subsequent course of the struggle between the surrendered egoist before the *Master* was not exactly forty; it depends upon the devotion of the man to obtain the bliss of *'Nam'*; some of them were gradually eliminated, liquidated or supplanted by the more ambitions of the *'Shamsi nobles'*. Therefore the term 'forty carried political connotation only to realised the *'Nam'*. It invariably referred to the dominant groups after the death of the 'real master' among the *'Shamsi slave'* officers irrespective of the numerical strength in the field of *'Nam'* practice technically called *Chalisa*. They helped the Iltutmish in the consolidation[74] of the empire as realised soul of the *God* or *Nam*.

Thus, the rule of 'the forty' or *Chalisa* was primarily became the loyalty and unstincted support of his slave officers that Iltutimsm felt himself secure on the throne of the state governors and thought of ensuring the succession of his children to making the monarchy an hereditary institution of the *'Nam'*. This was perhaps too much to expect from its ex-slaves who constituted the real power to *'Repeating the History Itself'* behind the throne. Their loyality to the person of Iltutmish was unquestioned, *albeit* they considered themselves to the partners in the state enterprise which was the outcome of their collective contribution. They, therefore, could not recogncile themselves to the principle of hereditary monarchy in principle to that of selection on merit and capability *'Word'* or *'Nam'* the principle on which Iltutmish had once acquired the throne himself. That is way, after the death of Iltutmish, there ensued a grim, political struggle between 'the forty' and the hereditary successors of the deceased called *'Sultan'*[75] *Nasiruddin* Mahmud, the eldest son of Iltutmish, who was by far the most capable of all his children, died a premature death in 1229 A.D. Iltutmish did not have a high opinion of his second son *Ruknuddin Firoze* because of his ease-loving habits and excessive indulgence in sensual pleasures. He, therefore, wished his daughter *Razia Sultana* to succeeded as the next ruler of the Sultanate dynasty. After his death, much against his will, the *Turkish* nobles raised Ruknuddin to the throne an incapable ruler, he failed to win the confidence of *'Shanshinbles'* as rules percribed 'Forty', some of whom were powerful governors of various provinces (*iqtas*). Taking advantage of son's incompetence, the unscrupulous *Queen Dowager, Shah Turkan*, began to meddle with the state affairs. She also annoyed other members of the royal household by her oppressive treatement. She once hatched a conspiracy to kill Razia as well Rukknuddin was, therefore, deposed after seven months rule; he died inconfinement, November 19th, 1236; was probably put to death by Razia's orders in the *'Nam'*.

Razia Begum succeeded her half brother Ruknuddin as the 'Sultan of Delhi'. She was a highly educated lady of courage and foresight in the theory of *'Nam'* or *'Kalma'*. She was brought up by Iltutmish like a son; she received training in horse riding, shooting, and sword manship of the *'Nam'* which attain from the *'Father'*. Free from all social prejudices like caste system, etc, of her days, Razia used to attend the court of her father like other princes of the 'Nam' and acquired sufficient experience in state craft in her youth period of life. She possessed all the qualities befiting a ruler of the *'Nam'*, and her father, unmindful of the Islamic traditions and ridicule of the orthodox *Ulama*, nominated her to succeed her to the throne of Father. However, Turkish nobility, thought it below their dignity to be governed by a woman, but she possessed the bliss of the reality i.e. *'Nam'* which became jealousies to the opposit group i.e. Brahman by nature. After the death of Iltutmish, *Razia Sultana* became the ruler of India, in the later on the unpopularity and in competence of Ruknuddin afforded her an opportunity to emerge a intrigue behind the veil. The dramatic rule of the Razia Sultan had sunk very low in degradation because of internal disorder and insubordinate conduct of the provincial governors in the formation of state theory of the mind in different manner. Thus, at that time *Indus* valley included *Sindh* ruled by *Sudra* of the times, was overrun by *Saifuddin Hasan Qarlugh* of Ghazni. The capital was attack from the four governors or of *Lahore, Multan, Hansi* and *Badaun*; they were the ringleaders of the *Shanis* nobles[76] who were fully enlightened by the Natural. Theory of the *'Nam'* to establish the 'royal standards' including the Sultan Nasiruddin Mahmud, starting moving out of the capital at the head of a huge force, commonded by Balban. The enterprising minister launched expeditions against the enemies of the state i.e. *'Word'* or *'Nam'* the Mongols, Hindu, Chieftains or the rebellions Turkish nobels. Whatever the actual outcome of the military engagements, this policy restored confidence in the hearts of the subjects, particularly, the populace of Delhi; toned up the administration of the *iqtas* visited by the royal encourage and raised the presitge of the Central government[77]. At the beginning of the period with which he dealt, that is, the time of Balban's accession (1266 A.D.), the Sultan's power had practically dissolved. Barani gives a cogent account of Balban's effort to resurrect that power[78] in the court intrigues, conspiracies and revolts led to despositions and murder in the cold blood in quick succession in which 'the forty played the role of kingmakers' ultimately, one of their leaders, Ghiasuddin Balban himself became the *Sultan* in 1266 A.D the period from 1236-1266A.D. is, therefore, called the era of 'the rule of the forty' in the history of the Delhi Sultanate[79]. He used extensive policy of the *'Nam'*, though persumably fictious in nature, quotations from Balban to explain from his understanding of Balban's objectives and practical meausres of the *'Nam'* on earth as a practical approach of the *'Nam'* to provide the basic needs of the life as *'Nam'*, too. But Balban to explain the 'royal standards' of the 'Faith' as a risk standard for the safeguarding his position, he perpetrated punishments on members of the ruling class and their dependents like politicans of the modern standard which were the most fearful departures from the Muslim law. As he writes: "Sultan Balban, with all his sense of affection and benevolence, and justice and equity and fasts and prayers, already described, was cruel and terrible in the punishment of rebellion; and *'Word'* in the moment of inflicting terror and exercising power he had no fear of God; because he himself 'God' on earth in human form. He did whatever he thought expedient for his own transitory power, whether permitted or prohibited by the *Sharlat*[80]. Barani has rightly expressed the actual episodes of the *'Nam'* or *'Word'*, Balban as both a secret murder[81] and the author of the same time of massacres on a grand scale[82] with the power of *'Nam'*. Barani was well aware of the horrified fact particularly by actions on the reaction against the members of the ruling class who do not recognize the interest of the common people; Balban's ferocious measures against peasants and labour, for example, leave no visible effect on his equanimity[83] as an 'ultimate power on earth' for the time being. But though Barani might lament Balban's acts of terror, but it is inevitable on the basis of for the establishment of the *'New Society'* of the *'Nam'*, he was ready to concede that the affairs of kingship involve (a combination of) cruelty and benevolence; and kingship subsists in (such) opposite qualities[84]." as Brahman when Jalalud-din Khalji or *Khoja* (1290-6 A.D.) abandoned the policy of terror, instead of winning gratitude from the nobility, he only excited their contempt and opened the path of treason[85] to teach a lesson of the false minded wandering in the material life and forgottened the Father on earth, came from the heaven of their benefit. As Barani again describes in a statement Alau-d-din Khalji or *Khoja* seizure of the crown, conquests, and administrative, fiscal and market= control measures, he is not unappreciative of the Sultan's achievements because it is his duty to do and leave the man free for thinking or not thinking. Certain groups were deprived of their property, but wealth was not barred from "the houses of the nobles (*Muluk*), commanders (*Umara*), bureaucrats (*Kardaran*), *Multanis* (merchants) and *Sahs* (bankers[86]).

It is important to note from the Barani's addiction to the principle of birth does not derive from any theory of 'blueblood', it depends upon the soul of the Father, where he preserved his race, it is difficult to understand until and unless, it does not come to the public notice with the achievement of a 'New Idea' for the evolution of human life and it derives principally from a craving for security and stability for those who are already "in possession" as an especial soul of the 'Father'. This can be seen from the treatment of the Turkish slaves of Iltutmish. Barani clearly stated here that when they established their supremacy after the death of Iltutmish (1236A.D) by overthrowing the free nobility, the Turkish slaves, too, were upstarts with no claims to hereditary status, because it depends upon the master's decision, how he deal with the matters as a cosmic order as Barani expresses a rare consistency of conception when he makes Balban described as *'Izzudin Salari'* and *Malik Qutab-ub-din Hasan Ghauri* as the great exponents of the principle of high birth at Iltutmish's court[88]. Both were non-Turk, free born nobles (Minha) *Siraj*[89] and *Malik Izz uddin Muhammad Shah Salari Mahdi*[90] for noticed about *Qutab-ud-din Hasan*. There is a grim irony in the reference of Qutab-ud-din Hasan made through the month of Balban as a Lord at that time, for Qutab-ud-din Hasan, when was nominally the holder of the highest office for the welfare of the public called *haib-i-mulk*. It had been seized and executed in 1355 A.D. by Balban himself[91] as his Father on earth at that time to help the poor people who have been degarded by the theory of mind in the material world. Thus, his murder in the *'Nam'* called 'Die to live' in the history in fact symbolized the elimination of the free nobility by the Turkish slaves. As he noted in his statement; "the people of that period observed how until the great people of self style and the powerful do not fall from their positions of greatness and power, contemptible men and purchased slaves do not rise and become supreme and powerful[92] on this earth. It shows that upstarts has been sufficiently established at that time same as well as Balban's time, who was one of them, became 'Sultan' as the highest title of the Father at that time who recognised the 'Father' in real sense. In this context, *Barani* has rightly accepted their perforce claim to high birth from the low-born, though merely established by the passage of the time. The highest nobles now were those who had been the fellow slaves of the 'Father' without any distinction (*khwajatashan*) of the *Sultan*[93] called *'Nam'*. In this way Barani extols Balban's firmness in his assuring a monopoly of the "high-born" from the time immomerial overall offices as an advancement in the development of history as Dr. B.R. Ambedkar gives the idea of progress in the history of Indian as the law is 'Supreme'. Thus, the 'low born' seeking either descendants of artisans or of Hindu slaves[94] of the period as a revolutionary thought of the monopoly of the "insiders" i.e. 'Nam' and that was excited Barani's bitter hostility in lower classes that those forget the 'Father' in material life when they acquire through certain privilege of the constitution. Here, he approves Balban's refusal to be guided by "obediece and loyality" as Dr. Raj Kumar contributed the massege of the 'Father' through papers in the seminars and conferences at higher level like *'Indian History Conference'* and other same kind of Symposia papers, organised by the different association of the world, as the sole criteria in making appointments[95] in different institutions, and a suitable anecdote is said to have been told by Balban to show that Iltutmish, too, had warned against the low-born (*Kam-aslan*) being appointed on the grounds of competence (*hunarmandi*[96]) of the 'Father' which is very difficult to understand for a material mind person on this earth. A wonderful discovery narrated by Balban in the following few lines that *Nizamul Mulk Junaidi*, a minister of Iltutmish, was descended from a weaver, likely to be *Kabir,* which explained his readiness to recommend men of low-birth for appointment. Balban himself refused to appoint *Kamal Mahyar* to the post of Khwaja of *Amroha*, because, being the son of a Hindu slave like the *Sudras,* he was 'low born[97]'. from the Hindu society as a degraded person of the 'Father as a Nam' degraded by the rulering class of the period by acquiring the power with illegtimate way by exploiting the innocent peoples of the period and obtain the 'status' of the elite as a dignified man.

From the above passages of the Barani, here lays bare the contradiction between the claimant of a close hereditary class and the need for loyalty of the *'Nam'* and competence, because he obtained the "obedience and loaylty" of the 'Father' already mentioned above. Even his portrayal is equivalent to Balban has to be suggested of inherent weakness masked by pomp and show[98] from the wordly life as nominal as a fool. Barani, again, stresses laid down that Iltutmish acquired the great military strength, than Balban in writing the history of the 'Natural Thought' but Balban made up the deficiency more than which he displays of grandeur in writing and meditating as a real obedient of the 'Father' in all prospective of the life i.e. character and discipline as a pious or holy man. He could not expand the Sultanate dynasty, because of the limited scope of the time, nor even satisfactorily check the Mongols[99] as to flourished the civilization as per its nature.

Khaljis or *Khojas* Imperialism was one of the sixty four clans of the Turks. They migrated to modern Afghanistan in the fourth century A.D. of the Christain era, where they gradually adopted Afghan Socio cultural traits and were usually mistaken for them[100], the ultimate failure to run the administration was exhibited in the reign of Muizu-ud-din Kaiqubad (1287-90 A.D[101]). This failure was the reason for sovereignity itself passing away from the Turks into the hands of the Khaljis[102]. It was the different race as recorded by the Barani, Jalal-ud-din Khalji, the founder of this dynasty (1290-96 A.D), 'came of a race different from that of the Turk, so that he had no confidence in them, nor would the Turks own him as belonging to the number of friends[103] and did not mix with them[104]. According to Usha edited in *'Islami Futuhu's Salatin'*, similar terms for the transfer of power from the Turks to the *Khalji's*[105] has been used by the author. It was a change which was regarded as unnatural and against the principle of hereditary status by nobles of Delhi[106] and even by the Sultan Jalalu-ud-din Khalji himself[107]. They joined the armies of Mahmud and *Muhammad Ghori* in large numbers[108] settled in Lahore, confided the government to Ali Kirmani, governor of Multan, and retired to Ghazni. In the year A.H. 587 (A.D. 1191), Maummad Ghori again marched to Hindustan, and proceeding towards Ajmer, he took the town of Bitihnda, where he left Millik Zia-ud-din Tuzuki with above a thousand chosen horse, and some foot to form its garrison of the *'Nam'*. While on his return, he heard that *Pittuw Rai* Raja of *Ajmer* belong to the *Surda* family, with his brother *Chawand Rai,* the Raja of Delhi, an alliance with other Indian princes of the *'Nam'*, were marching towards *Bitihnda* with two hundred thousand horse, and three thousand elephants. Mahammad Ghori marched to the relief of his garrison; but passing beyond *Bitihandi,* he encountered the enemy at the village of Narain, now called Tiruwri, on the banks of the Sursutti, fourteen miles from Tahnesur, and eighty miles from Delhi, where he gave them battle. At the first ouset his right and left wings, being out flanked, fell back, till joining in the rear, his army form a circle, Mahhammad Ghori was in person in the centre of his army, and being informed that both wings were defeated was advised counsel, he cut down the messenger, and rushing on towards the enemy, with afew followers, committed terrible slaughter. The eyes of chawand falling on him, he drove his directly against Mahummad Ghori, who perceiving his intention charged and delivered his lence full into the Raja's mouth, by which the many of teeth were knocked out. In the meantime the Raja of Delhi pierced the king through right arm, with an arrow. He had almost fallen, when some of his chiefs advanced to his rescue. This effort to save him gave an opportunity to one of his faithful servants to leap up behind Mahammud Ghori, who, faint from loss of blood, had nearly fallen from his horse, but was carried triumphantly of the field through almost wholly deserted by his army, which was pursued by enemy nearly forty miles. After this defeat, when he had recovered of his wound at Lahore, he appointed governors to the different provinces he possessed in India, and returned in person to Ghur. At Ghur, he disgraced all those officers who had deserted him in the bottle of *'Nam'* and compelled them to walk round the city with their horse's mouth-bags, filled with barely, hung about the necks, at the sametime forcing them to eat the grain like brutes. The author of the *Habib-us-Sir* relates, contrary to all our other authorities, that when Mahammad was wounded, he fell from his horse, and lay upon the field among the slain till night. And that in the dark, a party of his own body guard returned to search for his body, and carried him off, thus to his camp[109]. The *Mamluk* founders of the Delhi Sultanate introduced racialism in Muslim politics as a dirty game to serve their personal ends; they exercised racial discrimination at higher level with a vengeance[110], thus, *Jalalu-ud-din Khalji*, during the six years of his reign, indeed, tried to guard against the influx of the low born[111]. But this proved to be his undoing, since he did not win the support of those whom he protected[112] each of the three prominent rulers, *Aibek, Iltutmish* and *Balban*, created new classes of the nobility, composed conclusively of their own Turk slave officers[113]. "The sons of Balban's officers (*Maula-Zadagan-I-Balbani*) who were the sons of *Maliks* and *Amirs*, had become in *Jalalu-ud-din*'s time without wealth and neglected, without *iqta* and troops, they became disciples of Sayyidi Maula and were suspected of conspiring Maula and were suspected of conspiring against the Sultan[114]. In this way, the ambitions young Khalji nobles were disillusioned by this moderation[115] 'the chief of the royal body guards' by the young Sultan. After the death of Mulik Nizamuddin, Jalal-ud-din was made governor of *Baran*[116] means *'Nam'* or *'Word'* or *'Aksara'*, in Hindi called *'Varan'* or *Holy goast* and *ariz-i-mumalik. Barani* who was himself in the form of *'Nam'* or *'Chamar'* in one of the passage, he reveals the date of disappearance of that stability to the death of Balban itself. His fall set the seal on the stability that had been to Barani so attractive as aspect of Balban's regime[117] that he 'had peculiar notions about religion and, to the great chagrin of the conservative *Mullas,* likely to be Pandits, 'never went to public prayers in the mosque[118].' And with this coup of Ala-ud-din Khalji (1296) began an uninterrupted transformation of the ruling class at the same time for the development of the civilization from one stage to another as per rule of the *'Cosmic order'*.

Ala-ud-din-Khalji or *Khojas* actually marched to the neighbourhood of *Chanderi*, then took a sharp turn towards the Deccan, crossed the Vindhyas and reached *Ellichpur*[119], there was, the complete destruction of the existing nobility[120], as it has been seen by the Prof. Raj Kumar during his tour recently in Kerala March 10-12, 2007, in the Calicut session of the Indian History Congress. 'The northern outpost' of the Yadava Kingdom. In order to lull the suspicions of the neighbouring Hindu chieftans and the Muslim, he spread the rumour that he was a run-away prince from the Sultanate, intending to seek refuge in the South[121] as a lone person of the *'Nam'*. After allowing two days rest to his troopers at Ellichpur, Ala-ud-din thundered at the gates of *Devagiri* to the great bewilderment of *Raja Ram Chandra Deva,* made an unsuccessful bid to stop the invader, his contingent included two brave ladies who charged the enemy like 'tigresses and died fighting in the battle field with the help of the *'Nam'* in true manner, it was a bolt from the *blue* from the latter. About this time, the best part of the Maratha army had been taken farther south by the crown prince *Singhana* to settle some border dispute with a neighbouring state, a fact which seems to have been already known to *Ala-ud-din* Khalji or *Khojas* through his secret agents of the *'Nam'*. *Ram Chandra Deva* shut himself up within the hill-fort of *Devagiri* modern *Daulatabad,* it situated on an isolated cone-shaped hill 640 feet high. The steepness and height of the rock required a minimum of defences. Its walls, bastions, and a moat cut 50 feet deep into solid rock, made up for the little deficiencies left by nature called 'Nam'. But for some time past the Yadavas had felt too powerful to care for their own defence, so that at the time of Ala-ud-din's invasion, the moat was lying dry and unprotected, and the garrison was short of provisions, giving a free hand to Ala-ud-din Khalji or *Khojas* to plunder the town and take its leading citizens as captives[121] in the form of a *'Nam'*. He reached *Kara* 'on the hither side of the Ganges' and 'the Ganges was very high'. Ala-ud-din's army was drawn in a battle array on the other side of the Ganges between *Kara* and *Manikpur* through the connivance of the traitor Alams Beg, the aged Sultan ordered his horsemen and bodyguards also stayed behind 'whilst he, with two boats and a few personal attendants and friends, passed over to the other side' of the *'Nam'*, in the midst of Ala-ud-din's army. Ala-ud-din 'advanced to receive him, he and all his officers showing due respect'. He 'fell at the feet of the Sultan' and the latter 'treating him as a son', hugged him, 'kissed his eyes and cheeks' and chided him for doubting his uncle's love. About this time, two of Ala-ud-din's guards struck the Sultan down with their swords and chopped of his head[122]. Barani again records, "While the head of the murdered sovereign was yet dripping with blood, the ferocious conspirators brought the royal canopy and elevated it over the head of Ala-ud-din. Casting aside all shame, the perfidious and gracelers wretches caused to be proclaimed king by men with role about one elephants[123]," of the *'Nam'* as a Master. Barani also condemns the heinous crime in the most forceful terms. All those who were a party to it received befitting punishments, according to the contention of the author, at the hands of nature, sooner or later. Although these villains were spared for a short time, and Ala-ud-din for some years, still they were not forgotten (by nature) and their punishments were only suspended[124] for the time being.

It has rightly been expressed by the historian, like the reformed Asoka the Mauryan rulers of the *'Nam'* called Buddha, Jalal-ud-din Khalji or *Khojas* aimed at ruling by human love and faith as a *Sudra* ruler of the *'Nam',* but he paid for its failure nobly with his own life, it was an indictment which mankind has since done little to expiate. The original name of Ala-ud-din Khalji or *Khojas* was *Ali Gurshap,* he was a nephew of Jalal-ud-din Khalji. He was born in *Circa* 1266 A.D. and brought up by his uncle because of the untimely death of his father. He did not received proper schooling but grew up to be a brilliant warrior who, unlike his uncle proved to be extremely ambitious, aggressive and selfish by nature as *'Deepit Raj'*. He was married to a daughter of Jalal-ud-din Khalij or *Khojas*. Alan-ud-din played an active part in the Khalji or *Khojas* revolution. When Jalal-ud-din became the Sultan, Ala-ud-din was made *Amir-i-Tuzuki*[125], but this process did not stop there. *Barani* distinguishes three successive groups which dominated the nobility under Ala-ud-din Khalji or *Khojas*. The first, comprising the officials and supporters of his youth, died or were destroyed in the first three or four years of his reign[126], 'the master of ceremonies', while his younger brother Alma Beg, was also happened to be a son-in-law of Jalal-ud-din, received the office of *Amir-i-Akhur*[127]. They were followed by a crop of new nobles who at least belonged to the respectable classes (presumably the families of medium ranking officials[128]), 'the master of horse (the royal stables)'. Ala-ud-din gave proof of his organisational skill as a commander in the suppression of *Malik Chhajju's* revolt and received the governorship of *Kara* in 1290. He successful expedition to *Bhilsa* (1292 A.D.) earned him the exalted office of *ăriz-i-mumalik*[129], but these were replaced during the last four or five years of Ala-ud-din Khalji or *Khojas* by those whom Barani considers rank outsiders 'the minister of war', and the additional charge of the *iqta* of Oudh, "Worthless persons, clerks, low-born *Sudras*, revenue officers (*Shiqdars*) and foolish slaves[130]." Barani alleges those people who owed to the predominance 'Ala-ud-din's administration suffered gravely during his late years because of rise of 'egoistic theory of the mind'. And yet he admits that *Malik Kafur* the high-priced slave of the *'Nam'* called (*hazar-dinari*) who was at the head of this group of nobles and a major target of attack rigorously maintained by Barani, Ala-ud-din Khalji's regulations of the power[131] at that time in the process of a government and people of high minded shifted into 'ego' as they think 'we are something in the world' as a false ego, went in the thesis of high and the low-born. Barani again states, 'the *Rai*[132] was, ever afterwards, obedient, and sent his tribute regularly as long as he lived[133].' Ala-ud-din did not underate the strength of the enemy nor did he expect a sure victory for his army, that is why he advised Malik Kafur not to 'press the Raj too hard'. Kafur was expected to make a settlement with the ruler of *Telengana* without much loss of time ' and retire, without pushing matter too far, last Rai Ladlar Deo (Pratap Rudra Deva[139] II) in the form of Deepit Raj or Rai should get the better of him[135]. It would be enough 'if the *Rai* consented to surrender his treasure and jewels, elephants and horses, and also to send treasure and elephants in the following year (not years[136]) as the life is there on earth.

Study shows that Ala-ud-din Khalji had developed a highly efficient system of postal services throughout his dominions. He employed elaborate means of communication to keep himself in touch with the imperial armies of the *'Nam'* on the war fronts, particularly for the sake of changing the Government system of the ruling class. As Barani states; it was the practice of the Sultan (Ala-ud-din Khalji or *Khojas*), when he sent an army on an expedition, to establish posts on the road, where posts could be maintained beginning from *Tilpat*, which is the first stage. At every post, relays of horses were stationed, and at every half or quarter *Kos* runners were posted, and in every town or place where horses were posted, officers and report writers were apponted. Every day, or every two or three days, news used to come to the Sultan reporting the progress of the army, and intelligence of the health of the sovereign was carried to the army. False news was thus prevented from being circulated in the city or in the army. The securing of accurate intelligence from the court on one side and the army on the other, was a great benefit[137]. After a brief but deadly struggle, the imperial army captured the outer fort of Warrangal made of mud walls, squeezing the besieged garrison within the stone walls of the inner fort. Hardpressed, the *Rai* sued for peace[138] with the legacy of moral, spiritual and cultural values, *India* lives on dreams, poor men's rich dreams and rich men's grandeur-infested dreams to suppress with the muscle and money power to the poor people of the Father. These dreams are as cheap as the air we breath in the daily life. The air is polluted these days by the industrialists. So are our dreams, especially those induced, encouraged or conjured by politicians of the period. Still, some dreams do not die with dreamers, they must be fulfill. They seem ageless as they pass from one generation to another. The concept of *'Ram Rajya'* is one such dream. Ask a villager in the Hindi belt what his views are on the declining values and growing with the complexities[139] with the Urbanist. In its historic or cultural context, the concept of *Ram Rajya* (*Sarvodaya Raj* or welfare state) is rooted in equality, Justice, fairplay, freedom, and equal opportunity for all without exploitation or discrimination on the grounds of Caste class or creed. This dream is embedded in the Hindu psyche. Its origin could be traced to the mythology of the *'Nam'*, beyond golden and not so golden periods of the Indian history[140] as depicted from time to time. For example, enlightened like *Asoka* and *Akbar* in Indian history. But none has touched the Hindu mass psyche as intensely as *Rama* did. Rama is not merely a virtuous character in an epic, but he was in real form at that time. He is a symbol of people's faith, a living legend at that time. Whether they recite the verses from the epic for peace and solace in the form of a *'Nam'* or exact the colourful *Ramayan* characters in plays and folklore on make shift stages one after the another like Prophet and Nanak in the villages or luxurious city theatres, where *Rama* lives [141] i.e. body of the living man in the form of Baba Gurinder Singh Ji. However, rumours of infidelity persisted among the populace of Ayodhya, an action packed human drama, the mythological stories of the *Ramayana* written by *Valmiki* revolve around the virtuous is going to repeat itself as a history of the *'Nam'*, were god-king *Rama*, who lives by high ideals and rules his kingdom has been based by the law of *dharma*, ancient norms of justice, fairplay, liberalism, equality and righteousness. *Rama* was known to be a repository of all virtues which make a human being both sublime and divine[142].

It was at *Dwarsamudra* that Malik Kafur learnt about the outbreak of a fratricidal war between the two *Pandya* princes in far south or Daccan *Kuleshekhar*, the Pandya ruler of *Madura* (Panjab), was inclined more favourably, towards his elder but natural son of the *'Nam'* called Vir Pandya and this excited the jealousies of his younger but legitmate son *Sunder Pandya*. Sunder Pandya murdered his father in 'the love of the *Nam*' a fit of anger and claimed the throne for himself but was turned out of *Madura* by Vir Pandya[143] as an independent ruler. As a matter of fact, the booty from *Dwarsamudra* and *Madura* defied all description and estimates in terms of its monetary value; Ala-ud-din Khalji's life long acquisitions, including the spoils of *Devagiri*, paled into insignificance before it. It may well have turned Mahmud of Ghazni in his grave 'with wistful eyes[144]'. Thus, the Deccan policy of Ala-ud-din Khalji or Khojas was proved to be extremely successful. His imperialism had two facets; he resorted to annexation of territories and establishment of direct civil administration in northern India. On the other hand, he thoroughly exploited the south for the acquisition of its fabulous wealth and was contended by the acknowledgement of paramountcy of the Hindu rulers[145]. It shows that there was a great dilemma of grave proportions for the establishment of rule of *Sudra* dynasty. Barani clearly stated that Ala-ud-din was motivated by self-interest, seeking to accumulate wealth and secure limitless luxury and splendour[146], as the ruler of the '*Nam*' or '*God*'. Barani repeatedly proclaims devotion to the rights and status of the high-born and is loud in voicing his fear of and hostility to persons of low birth. He does so both by way of direct statement and by quotations ascribed to historical figures. This status by birth complex of Barani has naturally attracted comment from scholars, there is a notably lucid analysis of his views by Professor Mohammad Habib[147]. The victory was inspired awe of Zafar Khan in every heart and the Sultan also looked askance at him in consequence of his fearlessness, generalship, and intrepidity, which showed that a *Rustam* had been born in India[148]. It has been noticed that great anxiety prevailed among Delhites, and the people of the neighbouring villages took refuge within its walls. The old fortifications had not been kept in repair and terror prevailed such as never before had been seen or heard of. All men, great and small, were in dismay. Such a concourse had crowded into the city that the streets and markets and mosques could not contain them. Every became very dear. The roads slopped against caravans and marchants, and distress fell upon the people[149], it has been observed by the writer from the study.

The plebeianization of the nobility was an inevitable product of the political development of the Sultanate under Muhammad Tughluq (1325-51 A.D.) and the process was reached its veritable apex. The pressure of the circumstances prevailed over, him, as he said: "All my life heard from the august lips stories full of corn and contempt for the low-born called *Sudra or Chamar*, base, mean and ignoble; and he showed with arguments and proofs now this race of the low-born is treacherous, disloyal, ungrateful, mischievous and ill-natured. He always indicated that he by his nature, held the vile base-born crew to be a greater enemy of his than the false gods[150].' Such again were the 'contradictory qualities' of the man that in practice he did the opposite. As Barani makes a record" 'For service at his court he did not choose from amongst the wise of the time and the high-born of the age, but gave offices and *iqta's* to base born people[151].'

Lastly, we may briefly discuss the increasing monetization during medieval periods. The relevant evidence about the introduction of the new coins of precious metal certainly points out the efforts made by Sultan and the members of ruling elite for promoting trade and commerce in the Sultanate period of the Indian History ruled by the *Sudras* or '*Untouchables*'. The *vital* that was means of business transaction in north India on the eve of its conquest led by Sultan Muiz-al-Muhammad-bin-Sam and his lieutenents[152]. Soon afterwards, the progress and expansion of overland trade, resulting from the 'internationalist' attitude of the new rulers necessitated the introduction of *tanka-i-safed* (silver coin) and *tanka-i-surkh* (gold coin), all called *Muhar*[153]. The silver *tanka* soon become the principal means of transaction in the towns as well as in the countryside; a coinage untainted and acceptable everywhere in the world. The process of urbanization, the construction of highways, linking the outlying territories with the centre for the convenience of merchants caravans and the establishment of the law and order increased monetization and helped the establishment of cash nexus. All this also led to the fraction of *tankas* into a number of small silver coins. We find an important reference in the collection of utterances of Shaikh Nasir-al-dix chiragh of Delhi to the *Shashgani* (six *jitals* or one-eight of a *tanka*) in circulation during the rein of Sultan Ala-ud-din Khalji or Khojas. Further, we are informed by Sheikh Nasir-al-Din Chiragh that a pious scholar, Maulana Fakhr-al-Din Maruzi by name transcribed books to earn his keep. When the book was brought to completion of sale, and if the buyer decided to buy it for a *shashtgani*, The Maulana would accept only four *jitals* (One-twelfth of a *tanka*). As the Maulana Greew old and infirm, he was unable to ascribe the book and then began to starvation. Having got information about his plight, Sultan Ala-ud-din Khalji or Khojas ordered the Maulana to be paid one *tanka* daily as his maintenance allowance. But the

Maulana refused to accept one *tanka* daily, saying that one *shashgani* would suffice for his maintenance[154].

In the end, we may briefly refer certain social changes were took place in India in the wake of the Ghurid mission of conquest through the theory of *'Nam'* during the thirteenth and fourteenth centuries A.D. Here, we have no need to discuss the genesis of the caste system of India because the theory of *'Nam'* which based on reality was widely spread throughout the world, but only we find in the consequences as hierarchical and monetizational thinking were pervailing in the form of Brahmanical ideology both in Hindus and Muslims. This ideology appears to have influenced not only the upper caste, but also of the low caste those do not believe on the reality by possessing material status sanctioned by the *'Nam'* itself or outcaste ones as *Dharmasvamin,* the early thirteenth century A.D. Tibetan pilgrim has noticed. Once *Dharmasvamin,* while fording a river, was carried away by the current. He saw a man of dark complexion standing on the bank from whom he sought help to save him. The latter shouted him back[155], 'I am of low caste' and did not help him. *Dharmasvamin* states that it was improper for a man of low caste to touch the *'untouchable'* with his hands a person of high caste[156]. The introduction of new technological devices and scientific instruments was introduced in an egalitarian indiviualism practised and displayed by the Sufi saints, *Ulama* and the members of new ruling elite class, made an impact on a society, at least in the Urban centres. In Hebrew language the word *'Memra'* has been used for Logos of the Greeks and for *'Kalma'* of the Muslims. This thought binds the Jews, the Christians and the Muslims in one chain from the spiritual point of view[157]. Manu also lays down the duties and professions that the members of the four *Varnas* should do in *Apattikala*. According to him, a *Brahmana,* failing to earn his living by following *Svadharma* was neither degraded nor associated with sin even if he accepted from all men as *'Radha Soami'* in modern world, taught the *Vedas* to an unworthy person, officiated as priest at the sacrifice of a degraded institutor or accepted gifts of vile. By taking his food at a place (however sinful or unholy), this is theory of the *'Nam' or* Vishvamitra to accept, the everybody when he or she let down before *'Him',* a Brahmana on the point of death in the *'Nam',* is not associated with sin[158]." 'Sarosh", which existed prior to earth, fire, vegetation and man is the manifested form the 'Will of God". On the one hand, it acts as the 'Creative Power', and on the other, it teach as the noble lesson of cheerful acceptance of God's will. Such acceptance is a necessary pre-requisite for spiritual progress. It is the viceroy of *Ahurmazda* (God) from the beginning time. Its greatness is apparent from the prayer of Zoroaster. Oh God, Let "Sarosh" be granted to him, who is dear to you[159]." Here its resemblance with the 'Holy Ghost', the Holy Spirit, the comforter, etc. of Christainity is noteworthy. In the Chinese philosophical and religious system of *Taoism,* high praise has been showered on the greatness of the *Tao.* The *Tao* is primeval, and it is indescribable in words. The Tao has been identified with God Himself. It has also been called the Path, the word, Discrimination, Decree, the omniscient, the unknown Essence of creation, the Principle that moves the mind and the world, and son on. It has been regarded as the creative and destructive ground of the universe[160]. The social morality as well as the political morality are bound to change in accordance with the changing of times and circumstances. And this is quite in the fitness of things, because what is true of a sick man could not be and should be true of a healthy man, what is applicable to a competent person should not be so in the case of one, who is famine-stricken. This, according to the *Mahabharata* and other, ancient Indian works, is the idea of the *'Nam'* that underlines *Apaddharma,* i.e. the morality of the season of distress and extra-ordinary circumstances the state, according to the *Mahabharata,* recognised the code of exceptional morality under special circumstances for maintaining the social order of a society, which was its main duty[162] at the time of frustration to established the *'law'* called *'Kalma' or 'Nam'* rule as a new system. The introduction of new system on the bases of new technical devices of the *'Nam'* created new professions for the employment of the soul which led to the expansion of artisan population of the Father in a country like India. People who belonged to a particular caste and carried on their caste profession for one generation to another generation could enter a new one at the point of Death in the *'Nam'* in living being. Provided they found the chances of earning the real property of the *'Nam'* than caste restrictions could not check professional mobility for a longer[162] period of time. As soon as the master of the *'Nam'* takes place, the system under his possession the important outcome of this social changes was the transformation of Brahmanism into Hindusim during the medieval period of India. Barani preceds this last sentence by a list of officers some of whom, like *Aziz Khummar* (wine distiller) of the *'Nam'* and *Muqbil,* a slave of his minister Ahmad Ayaz (and one who 'shamed all slaves by his appearance and native") are known to us from his own narrative and other sources of the *'Nam'* as well. Both Azin Khummar and Muqbil Barani mentions were the governors of Dhar (Malwa) and Gujarat in his subsequent narrative of the rebellion in Gujarat which they vainly tried to suppress by them[163]. It has also been noticed by the Isami both of them in the course of his description were of the same events[164]. Moreover, he shares the contempt of Muqbil: "the intolerable Muqbil, a cruel and impertinent slave[165]." of the *'Nam'*. Aziz Khummar is mentioned earlier by *Ibn Battuta* as a revenue officer of the *hazar* of Amroha[166] and there is also a reference for him and Muqbil together in connection with the Gujarat rebellion as well[167]. He [168] wrote his travelogue in Arabic part of which is devoted to his experiences of the Indian life at Delhi and *Madura* (Panjab). The basic centre of revolution which brought a lot of socio political changes in the life of man from time to time, as *Nanak, Sultan Bahu, Bulleh Shah, Baba Farid* ,even Akbar learnt a lesson for the evolution of the mankind's theory i.e. *'Nam'*. His book is a primary source of *'History'* of the reign of Muhammad bin Tughluq; it throws light on the socio-political conditions of his times. The account though a sincere and straight forward record of *Ibn Battuta's* personal observations and experiences suffers, however, from some in accuracies and shortcomings as a book of History. It was because Ibn Battuta's knowledge of Persian (the court language of the Sultans) and Indian languages was very poor at that time . This author was not a histrographer by nature and temperament and did not show resourcefulness of his authority according the theory of 'Nam' in obtaining accurate information about the various events through the messengers of the *'Nam'*in secret manners for the political developments of the historical thought during his days of writing history as his subject. Nevertheless, his travelogue is a very valuable treatise written by a foreigner on the life and conditions of Hindustan during the period of Muhammad-Bin-Tughluq period. His account which has been written on his character must have been the need to be read out with meticulous attention as it shows neglected from some bias behaviour of the writers like Irfan Habib, Sabyasachi Bhattacharya, Shrimali, etc, in the concept of social change in Indian History as a historian. *Ibin Battuta* (C. 1304-78 A.D.), who visited in India during the early medieval period of the Indian History, also throw some light on the political, socio-cultural changes of his time as a historian. He was an *Arab* traveller and adventurer of Morocco Polo, an expert in Islamic theology and jurisprudence, even he left his home, in 1325 on a long life tour of the world in the *'Nam'* a real founder of the 'Heavenly truth' on earth as a *'Nam'*itself. After passing through the countries of northern Africa in the study of 'Nam' through Arabian penisula, he reached Sind in 1333 A.D. as it was his forefather's birth place of the *Sudra* rulers of the *'Nam'* similar story is related with *Muhammad-bin-Qasim*, when he took the banner for the establishment of 'New Society' at that time, where from he moved towards Delhi. He extended his power by appointing the *qazi* of Delhi who was expert in the theory of *'Nam'*. He held this post for about eight years, unfortunately, some cases of embezzlement and dishonesty were brought forward against him which landed Ibn Battuta into the jail for a long life as per the rule of the nature as *'history repeat itself'*. However, he secured his release by making *Battuta* a personal appeal to the Sultan. The latter despatched him to China at the head of a diplomatic mission in 1342 A.D.; on the way his party met with ship wreck and had to return to Delhi without completing his assignment. Thereafter, *Ibn-Battuta* bade a farewell to Delhi and moved on his sojourn again; after India and stayed at *Madura* (Panjab) for a short while[169] with Master. The modern *Munsiari* which seems to be the corrupt form of *manahsila* may, therefore, be identified with *Manosila* of the Jataka stories means to satisfy or solace to the mind for the time being with *'Nam'* is the ultimate realization of Truth. If our identification of *Manosila* be correct then *Kalaparvata* means man captured should be located in *Kumaon* i.e. we have won the victory of the Father. Ibn Battuta also speaks of the mountain of Karachi who was situated at a 10 days journey from Delhi. Prof. S.H. Hodivala takes it to be the mountains of Garhwal and Kumaon, "the outer range of the tertiary hills which runs parallel to the foot hill of the Himalayas, separated from its valleys or dunes." In other words, it is thesub-Himalaya of the modern geologists, However, Hodivala rejects, the literal meaning of Karachi which means 'black mountain' and instead of this concept, it derives the name for Kumaon or from *Gargacala*. No Sandalwood trees to our knowledge are grown now in the sub-Himalayan region[170] at that time.

Then, there were other *Kakkolas* to be considered at the same time called *Kakula* of *Ibn Battuta, Ko-lo-of Ma-Tuan-lin,* could be located on the east of Malaya Peninsula at either *Kelantan* or ligor. It Sing's commentator mentions of *Ka-ko-la or Ka-Ko-ra* producing white card amom. This place has been identified by Gerini with Krakor in Kamboja, a district so named from wild or bastard cardamoms growing there which is locally known as Krapor (*Gragar*)[171]. *Kakola* or *Kakula* was the capital of Maljawah of *Ibn-Battuta.* It had plenty of elephants, eaglewood good camphor and little cotton[172]. Eaglewood is the chief product of the kingdom of Kumar located by Gerini from Kampot to (*Khmau*). *Ibn Khurdad* expressed states *Qumari* aloe-wood in Arabia was so called because it came from Qumar a country of three days journey from *Sanf* i.e. *Champa*[173] *(Annam)* to recover the lost province of *Panduranga* so that there may be once more a united kingdom of *Champa*[174] will be establish by the *Chamar* Eaglewood forms one of the principal products of *Champa* to this day in the Binthwon district where the last ramnants of *Cham* or leather workers are found. The care of gathering this product is confined to certain villages the hereditary chiefs of which *'Word'* or *'Nam'* called 'Master of eaglewood' *Chamar* where entering on their duties offer worship to the deities of the agallochum trees on certain sacred hills. That the hill-tract of *Chan-Ching* grew scented wood is further supported by *Ma-Tuan-liu*[175].

Suvarnabhumi (lower Burma), or Khryse of Ptolemy. According to the inscription of fifteenth century A.D., there was an alternative name for *Ramannadesa* which comprised the three provinces of Bassein, Pegu proper and Martaban. Suvarnabhumi inscription thus embraced the maritime region between cape *Negrais* and the mouth of the *Salwin*. The hinterland of this region was named *Suvannaparnta*, which according to another inscription included the district of Kale, Teinnyin, Yaw, Tilin, Salin and Sagu i.e. the country between the lower *Iravati* (Ravi) and *Chindwin* and the Arakan Yoma; but evidently it must have extended in ancient days down to the head of the delta and east of (*Iravati*) Ravi as far as the Pegu Yoma and the Sittong river, thus embracing the whole of lower Burma. It is this hinterland which may be identified with Ptolemy's Goldland' or Khryse Khora and not hte maritime region below[176] the *Suvarnakudya* which literally means Golden wall may be identified with the Pegu Yomah mountains, on the eastern slope of which *Salai-gugul*[177] *is* obtained from Boswellia servata[178].

The country named Jonga may perhaps be identified with *Shun-ta* of the Chinese historians of the Ming period (1368 to 1464 A.D.). It was followed by Sung dynasty (from 960 to 1279 A.D.). The Mongo lian dynasty ruled over China (from 1206 to 1368 A.D.). It was in 1583 A.D. that Manchu Dynasty came to power and remained in authority till 1912 A.D[179]. *Jung-ya-lu of Chao-Ju-Kua,* or *Zunda* of Barbosa of *Ming* period identified as Jangola in East Java by Hirth, and *Singkel* district (word) west *Sumatra,* or Sungal Island; Lumpung Bay, South Sumatra by Gerini. Is *Taurupa* another form of *Tamralipti* or modern *Tamluk* or *Tughluq* for discussions on *Kamarupa* and *Tamralipti* and their various forms[180]. However, it takes blanket (*Kambala*) and *Simbali* and *Simbala* (*Silk-cotton* tree in Pali canon, and *Salmali* and *Salmala* in Sanskrit as Austric loan words to the Indo-Aryan[181] society of ancient period from the time immemorial.

The sandalwood which grown up *Nagapa.vata*. There is a hill between Ajmer and Pushkar known as *Naga-pahar*[182]. But it was doubtful at that time wether sandalwood was ever grown there. It is more possible that the *Naga parvata* which grew sandalwood was situated in the Naga hills of Assam, which is a hilly district in Eastern, Bengal and Assam lying between 24^0-42' and 26'-48^0 North and 93^0-7' and 94^0-50 East. Assam as mentioned in the *Mahabharata* and the later literature was one of the most important sources of aromatic woods and resins. This variety of Sandalwood came from *Sakala*, the modern Sialkot[183]. Sialkot has been identified with ancient *Sakala*[184], the *Sagala* of Buddhist literature, which is thus proved to be one of the oldest cities of the Panjab. In very ancient times, it was the capital of the Madras, who were known in the later Vedic period, and *Sakaladvipa* or "the island of Sakala" was the ancient name of the *doab* between the rivers. *Chandrabhaga* (Chenab) and *Iravati* (Ravi). In some what later times (C.B.C. 200) *Sakala* was the capital of the later Greeo-Indian Kings of the house of Euthydemus, who ruled the Easter Panjab, and it was the residence of Menander kind who has been identified with king *Milinda,* who is known from the Buddhist treatise called "The Questions of Milinda". His date was about B.C. 150. At a still later period *Sakala* was the capital of *Salavahana* or *Satavahana,* whose son Rasalu, is the great hero of all Panjab tradition; and after the invasion of the Hunas (Hans) in the latter part of the fifth century A.D. it became the capital of *Toramana* and his son *Mihirakula*[185], who ruled over the Panjab and also probably over *Kashmir* under the title of *Karakota* dynasty of the *'Nam'* in Chinese language and Jammu was the only thirty miles away from Sialkot at that time, similar to that has been referred in the *Vansavali.* The spot on which the tank was founded, is now called *Purani Mandi,* where in the influence of the soil on human and animal life is widely prevalent in the hills, a locality in Jammu town, where the Rajas on their accession, at the time of installation. The Purani Mandi marks the spot where the palace originally stood, and the Rajas resided for centuries. It is near the small temple of Raghunath (Rama) called *"Maharani Ka Mandir"*, founded by the Bandhrali *rani* of Maharaja Ranbir Singh. A great number of people are daily fed there belly with the food of *'Nam'*, and received each one piece in cash in the name of the *rani*. The present *Purani Mandi* buildings are said to have been erected by Raja Mal-Dev probably of the fourteenth century A.D. The present palace is modern house of the *'Father'* and was erected by Maharaja Gulab Singh[187] in the momery of *'Nam' as a Chamar* by caste. Some generations later we find a note purporting to refer to the time of Raja *Sala* or *Salavahana* who ruled the Panjab as far north as Gandhara (Peshawar), and whose capital was at Sailkot. He is said to have invaded Jammu, defeated the Raja, named *Shib-Prakash* and destroyed the town[188] of *Annami* people of the *'Chamar'* dynasty. For a long after awards we find only a list of names, the only event which may have an historical reference being a conflict on the Ravi (*Iravati*) with a Raja of *Nagarkot 'Word'* probably a border foray *Chamar* in which the Raja of Jammu was killed. Such a conflict between Jammu and *Nagarkot* at that early period is a thing not at all improbable. The State boundaries must have been very indefinite, and the tracts between *Durgara* and *Kangra* were probably held by *Rana* and *Thakkurs,* whose allegiance to either state must have been very uncertain[189] in the process of seeking the *'Nam'* of the *'Father'* at that point of time. From there, he went to *Mecca* on a haj-pilgrimage before his return to his homeland in 1349 A.D. *Ibn Battuta* was received a warm reception from the ruler of the *'Nam'* and the people of *Morocco*; by this time, he had acquired a world-wide fame as philosopher and saint or *sant*. He enjoyed love of the Father and reverence of his countrymen and died at the ripe age of seventy three[190]. Thereafter, *Marco Polo* visited in the Andaman (*Angaman*) islands and sailed along the eastern and western sea coasts of India. In the course of study and the explorations of the various horizon of the knowledge, he attempted to acquaint himself with the 'natural history' i.e. *'Nam'* or *'Kalma'* of the Father and after this rich agricultural and industrial products which might became valuable as articles of commerce and trade between India and Europe. Marco polo[191], in his travelogue speaks of brisk maritime trade and commerce along with the Indian coasts. He describes the life and condition of the common people who were particularly *Sudras* by caste called *'untouchables'*, and gives a vivid account of their dress, food habits, manners and social customs which were prevalent in the society as simple living and high thinking as their objectivity in their life in natural form as nature was in human form not in , idol worship' as a dark theory of the mind' which loved by the Brahmans of the period.

God fearing and extremely humble in his disposition, the Sultan paid regard to the holymen or *Sufi* saints, constructed *serais,* the roads and opened the houses of pilgrimage to realise the God in celebrity of saints. Sultan Firoze Tughluq himself writes:

"When any government servant filling an important and responsible position was carried off under the decrees of God to the happy future life, I gave his place and employment to his son so that he might occupy the same position and rank as his father and suffer no injury."

'Kings should make their rule of life
To love the great and wise;
And when death ends this mortal strife,
to dry their loved ones eyes.[192]"
'Thanks for God's mercies I will show
By causing men nor pain nor woe[193].'

"To the best of my human power, I should recount and pay my thanks for the many blessings God has bestowed upon me so that I may be found among the number of his servants.[194]'

Khan-I-Jahan Maqbul, the Prime Minister, when asked by the Sultan to express his opinion on the subject, once observed that:

"The coinage of Kings like an unmarried daughter, whom no one would seek after, however, beautiful and charming, she might be, if any person had, either rightly or wrongly been cast upon her character. So also with royal coins; if any one honestly of falsely, from interested motives, alleged a deterioration of the coinage would obtain a bad name and no one would take it[195]". as a coin but it was the message of God. Being conscious of this fact, Firoze Tughluq improved the technique of minting and issued several varieties of standard coins. Besides the gold and silver *tankas* means low of the body, he produced beautiful coins of the respective value of forty-eight (*Chi hal o hashtgani*), twenty five, twenty-four, twelve, ten, eight and six (*Shashgani*) *jittals,* which contained silver in due proportions, mixed with the other metals. He produced in abundance the fractional currency of the lowest denominations all made of copper and bronze, it comprised a *jittal,* a *jittal* called *adha* and a quarter *jittal* called *bikh,* to facilitate transactions in trade and commerce at mass level[196] as it has its nature.

The Sultan showed a keen interest in the preservation of old monuments as were the *'Nams'* of history and carried out extensive repairs of the time being as the body of man who dies in *'Nam'* regains its form as *'Nam'* or *'Word'* as a Father of the tombs of the body i.e. called *'Head'* as an administrator of the imperial power and builds public buildings of his predecessors who taught the public in large scale the idea of 'Humanism' which was destorted by Brahmanicial ideology into number of 'paths', but it is the universal truth that there is one God and one man, why there is distinction between the two. It shows the narrow mindedness of the man for his personal benefit not for the other. There distortion is there. In that contrary, saints come down on the earth for the compiling of society as 'One Society'. Though ignorant of , the real significance of the meaning of *'Nam'*, Firoze Tughlaq brought two Asokan pillars inscription to Delhi to giving an example for the origin of the man in Indian History took place *'Word'* one from *Topra* (district Ambala) and other from Meerut, and transplanted them at the new township of Firozabad[197] as a 'New Society' of the Father and its origin was took place from the Nine Nanda ruler of the Indian History. No doubt, Firoze Tughlaq was an orthodox *Sunni Musalman* by allotment the nature; he resorted a religious bigotry as a matter of state policy, *albeit* by virute of his gentle and humane nature, he could not afford to be cruel and inhuman toward the non-muslims in actual practice. He suffered from an inferiority or low born complex because he was born of a Hindu mother, therefore, in order to establish his credibility as the sovereign of an 'Islamic State' of the *'Nam'* and was a leader of the 'faithful' Islamic study, he publicly demonstrated contempt for Hinduism and displayed extraordinary zeal for '*Islam*[198]' which is 'law' of the human nature by obtaining the *'words'* from the 'Prefect Master' who always reside in the Maduradesa called Panjab.

In this way, Firoze Tughluq traced the victims of Muhammad bin Tughlaq's tyranny and relieved their distress, he obtained deeds of satisfaction from his master for the welfare of the public apparently, 'to ensure peace to the departed soul' and help it 'on the Day of Judgement.[199]' We have the statement for the testimony of *Af* if that 'abundance of the necessaries of life prevailed in the reign of Firoze Shah, not only in the capital, but also throughout his kingdom. During the whole forty years of his reign, there was no appearance of scarcity, and the times were so happy that the people of Delhi forgot the reign of Ala-ud-din Khalji, although no more prosperous times than this (*Sic*) had ever fallen to the lot of any Muhammadan sovereign[200]." Who were basically originated from the *Sudra* dynasty of *'Nam'* from the ancient period of Indian history called *'untouchables'* by the modern Brahmans.

From the above discussion, we learn that Firoze Tughlug was essentially a man of peace and prosperity, however, 'the shrieks and wails' of women in connatotion, it demonstrates that living man is very dirty and committs crimes in the theory of the dark period against the living being, forget the basic qualification of the humanism and in physical form male dominate the society goes into the 'ego' and ultimately crushes by the Father bliss which male figure never knows during dark period of the Indian history, in this context, the women of the fort aroused the feelings of compassion in the heart of the Sultan, and he raised the siege on the plea that "to storm the fort i.e. head with the bliss of *'Nam'*, put more *Musalmans* to the sword of the pious love and expose honourable women to ignominy, would be a crime for which he could not answer on the Day of Judgement, and which would leave no difference between him and the Monogls[201]." The other nobles named included wine-distillers of the *'Nam'* called Prof. Raj Kumar and Baba Gurinder Singh Ji of Bias, a barber, a cook, a gardener, a weaver, a *mali* ("the lowest and basest caste of all the mean and of Indri i.e. *'Nam'* or *'Word'*("the basest of the base born[202]). Since Barani mentions the offices held by the sad person and he was writing the mentioned events very closely with the knowledge of a courtier of the *'Nam'*, there is no reason to doubt the accuracy of the facts he gives. What one can argue is that Muhammad Tughluq in the effort to extend and maintained his power also recruitted a very large number of Mongol and foreign nobility, which Barani records[203]. According to *Ibn Battuta*, led to disaffection among the more indigenous ("Hindi") nobility[204], because they do not believe on Father, they believe on *'Money'* or *Maya* which is the illusion for their mind and go away from the Father's blessing i.e *'Nam'*. Barani remains curiously unprovoked by this foreign influx became foreigner from the Father. Even more curious, in Barani's view disapproval of the power they have been acquired by "*Barwars* and *Hindus*" under *Khusrau* Khan[205] was his negligence in part of indignation at the appointment of Hindus in high offices by Muhammad Tughlaq, while Isami justifies the muder of *Bharan*, the governor of Gulberga, on the ground that he was a Hindu[206], Barani considers this act as nothing on his part, but "treachery[207]" which *'Nam'* never considers in the Indian history. 'He' believes in equality, liberty and fraternity.

The main content of the political history of the Delhi Sultanate as seen by Barani, related with the

Rig-Veda of the Indian history, then considered the three developments stage of life; the growth of despotic power of the *Sultan,* the greater and great use of terror during the meteralistic era, and finally, the successive wholesale changes in the composition of the nobility through the power of *'Nam'*tending to its plebeianization. 'He' does not say so (and he might well not have agreed to the ruling class which are in searching progress, had the question been put to him i.e. called objectivity), but there three processes according to Baranis own account, formed the fundamental element in the society as Sultanate achieved it and proved successful in their lfie as a matto. What Barani is able to demonstrate in the form of Dr. Raj Kumar effectively is that these factors inevitably led to a crisis under Muhammad Tughluq, when large sections of the Delhi nobility itself was involved in that process, especially the military officers Prof. Raj Kumar the *Amiran-i-Sada* 'Deepit Raj' his son went into rebellion[208] at the beginning of Enlightenment era of the *'Nam'*. It has been seen that entire Sultanate were fell into the same disease[209] i.e called *'Nam'* which is the food of the soul. In this context Muhammad Tughluq's admission to Barani was geniune at that time because he did a wonderful work for the sake of his 'Father' as his son.

From the above discussion, we also learn that Muhammad Ghori had no male issue to inherit his empire. *albeit* he had a passion for acquiring Turkish slaves which were *Sudhras* by caste, used to live in the *Siharas Rai* family of *Sindh* for a very long period of the Indian history whom he treated with affection and care of the Lord fought against the *'infidel'* who do not trust on God. Muhammad Ghori, in fact, liberated them from the cluthces of others with the power of *'Nam',* who was 'Nam' himself on earth. He adorned the heads with crown of royalty which had belonged to that king; and the influence of the light of *'Islam',* he preserved through their power over different parts of the world and provinces of *India* as a Father. Qutab-ud-din Aibek was one of the trustee slave officer is called the founder of what is known in Indian History as the *Slave* or *Mamuluk* of the Lord who ruled northern India from 1206 to 1290 A.D. as the Lord of the Moon' on earth. There is some justification for this nomenclature, *Kabir, Nanak, Ravi Dass,* etc. saints of the period are the purduct of at least three rulers of the line of *Sudra* dynasty called *'untouchables' Qutbi* dynasty (1206-11 A.D.) founded by Qutab-ud-din-Aibek, then *Shami* dynasty (1211-66 A.D.), known after Shamsu-din-Iltutmish likely to be *'Gujara'* dynasty and second *Ilbari* dynasty which was founded by Ghias-ud-din Balban (1266-90 A.D.).

The work of *Ferishta* called Muhammad-bin Qasim *'Rise of the Mahomedan Power in India written* by him, translated by John Briggs in four volumes also mentions that he rose his power from the *Sudra Camp* of Sindh dynasty, he stayed their for some times to attain the power of the *'ultimate reality'* of a term called *Arab* means 'a bliss of one' i.e. *'God'* i.e. *'Nam'* fought against the *Borhmanabad* ruler of *Sindh* ruler of the period along with the *Sudra* ruler of *Sindh* captured the power of *India*, established their rule in Kashmir under the *Durlabhvardhana* belonged to Champa (*Annami*) called *Chams* or leather worker who compose the body by inserting the soul inside the *Cham* in form of a 'living being' with the help of Father or *'Nam'*. There are other original sources of the study like *Chachnama, Rajatarangini of Kalhana,* etc. shed same light and is the work of the *Sudra-* people, who served the society with honesty and dedication by enlighting the lamp of truthful knowledge of the *God* or *'Nam'* either, it was, *Lord Buddha,* Prophet or *Ravidas,* etc were belonged to the same community called as *'Chamar'* or *'Nam'*. Now, we take the example of *Barani*[210], who was born in 1285 A.D. presumably called *Barani* in *Hindi*and *Aksar* too in the same language at modern *Bulandsharr* means he was born in the time of materialistic era to began with the enlightenment period in the history of India. According to his qualifications, he himself set an example of the perfect chronicle history of the *Sultanate* period who belonged to *Sudra* dynasty of Sindh. Since he was a family of some status at that time and his father was the daughter's son of Jala-ud-din, a prominent Saiyid of *Kaithal,* who had the knowledge of *Veda*. The daughter herself, that is, Barani's grandmother, was a Saiyid lady of "Mystical attainments[211]" . Of the status of his paternal line he speaks no more than to say that it was "illustrious" (*Sharif*[212]) in Persian and good in English. His was thus a family of a scholarly and religious background. But from a position of mere *danishmands* (scholars), its members had risen to high bureaucratic posts before Barani was born (1285 A.D.[213]). His maternal grandfather, *Sipahsalar Husamuddin,* was an official (*Wakil-i-dar*) of *Malik, Bektars* the *barbak* of Sultan Balban (1266-86 A.D.[214]) and held the police charge (*Shahnagi*) of *Lakhnuti* during *Balban's* expedition to Bengal[215]. Barani's father Muaiyidul Mulk became *haib* (deputy) to *Arkali* Khan, son of Sultan Jalal-ud-din Khalji (1290-96 A.D[216]) and in the next reign, the governor (*naib-o-khwaja*) of Barani. But the most eminent position was obtained by Barani's uncle *Ala-ul-Mulk,* who having been privy to *Ala-ud-din* Khalji or Khoja, was rewarded for the first time with the government of

Kara and Awadh and then with the office of *Kotwal* (city commandant) of Delhi[217]. Barani cites all these three men as oral witnesses for one episode or another he recorded in his *History*. Barani himself did not apparently hold any bureaucratic employment till about (1334-5 A.D), when he was appointed an aide or confident (*murqurrab*) to Sultan Mahammad Tughlluq (1325-51 A.D[218]). He held this appointment till the Sultan died. These seventeen years of proximity to that brilliant and tempestuous man gave to Barani, who prudently remained a pliant yes-man, a unique experience of the inner functioning of a despotic monarchy of the '*Nam*' was established with the Sultan.

With Muhammad Tughluq's death, Barani's bureaucratic career came to an abrupt change that with the six years of Firoze Shah (1351-1386 A.D.) rule that he was compelled to established a universal law for the happiness of the people came into existence in 1357, as a crowning achievement of his life is called *Tarikh-i-Firuz Shahi*. The work displayed Barani's concern with the problems of political structures led by the ruling class of the period.

Finally, among the mass of Barani's worldly writings is the large, repetitive and verbose work, the *Fatawa-i-Jahandari*, "opinions on Governments" Muhammad bin Tughluq left nothing to be desired from the point of view of academic and intellectical attainments in the life. A scholar, as well as, a soldier, he was an enthusiastic and ambitious man of high moral character who started his reign with everything in his favour. He reverted the feudal pattern of the 'Dark age' with his strong and effective writing which had received a serious jolt since the days of Ala-ud-din Khalji. The 'hair-brain' schemes of Muhammad bin Tughluq carried the rudiments of modernity and convinced the people of the period for their benefit. The period of the rule of Muhammad-bin-Tughluq constituted one of the most tragic chapters in the history of the early medieval period of India. It was the sad commentary on the well-intentioned who were called upon *Sudra* to rule over the unimaginative and backward masses of the times. However, all the virtues of his character and qualities of head and heart were of no avail since he suffered from the lack of common sense during his previous life.

Muhammad-bin-Tughluq left nomal issue, he had only one off spring *soul* a daughter, who was born in the reign of Sultan Ghias-ud-din Thugluq, nor did he nominated his successor[219]. His sudden death in the army camp in the vicinity of *Thatta* on the bank of *Indus* at fourteen *kos* from it, therefore, created a serious situation, the soldiers decamped immediately and marched towards Delhi 'without leader, rule, or route, in the greatest disorder. No one heeded or listened to what anyone said, but continued the march like careless caravans' the Mongol mercenaries who had been hired by Sultan Muhammad bin Tugluq to suppress the rebellions, assailed the royal army in front' with the object of acquiring 'booty'. While the rebels of *Thatta* attacked the baggage train in the rear. Thousands of villagers, who had earlier been pressed into the service of the army,t ook to flight in the camp of *Sudra* where '*Nams*' reside called *Chams* or leather workers, they also joined hands with the rebels and began to pillage 'various lots of baggage on the right and left of the army'. It spread consternation among the 'imperialists' thought called '*Nam*', who stood in danger of being totally annihilatation of the castes; they numbered, according to Barani two *Lakh*, human souls, including, of course, the families, slaves of the father, and the non-combatants[220]. Therefore, it was essential for the 'Father' to establish a 'New Society of the *Nam* 'called *Islamic State*'. at that time.

In that hour of crisis, the *Sheikhs*, nobles and *Ulema* of the imperial camp held an emergency meeting, *Khudavandzada*, sister of the Sultan Muhammed bin Tughluq, claimed the throne for his son *Davar Malik*; the latter's candidature was rejected by the war council on the ground that he was 'an incompetent person, in capable of governing[221]', with a close unanimity, they elected Firoze Tughluq, son of *Sipahsalar* Rajab and an elderly cousin of Muhammad bid Tughluq, to be the *Sultan*. Firoze Tughluq accepted the offer after some hesitation, and was formally coronated in a simple ceremony, held some where on the bank of *Indus*, where they had halted for the night before the beginning of the enlightenment era of the '*Nam*' called '*Chamar*'. This incident was took place on March 23, 1351 A.D. Three days after the death of Muhammad bin Tughluq. Firoze Muhammad Tughlaq swung into action immediately and made effective arrangements for the protection of the imperial forces; he conducted them safely to the capital via *Multan* and *Dipalpur*[222].

Meanwhile, Khwaja-i-Jahan, the wazir of Muhammad bin Tughluq, who held the charge of the central government in Delhi, had installed an infant on the throne and declared him to be the son and successor of the deceased Sultan. He, however, did not receive wide support for his cause and offered submission to the nobility, who played the role of '*King makers*' for a while, did not approve of the Sultan's action, however, Khwaja-i-Jahan was put to death before he could reach *Samana*[223], Firoze Shah Tughluq reached near *Hansi*, where low caste of professional musician and dancers found to live in Kullu in Simla Hill State, Cordinarily, they were engaged in petty trade[224] of the *'Nam'*. Firoze Shah Tughluq entered Delhi along with the imperial army of the *'Nam'* and was coronated with great pomp and show on August 25, 1351 A.D. he was about forty six years at that time[225]. Being a man of peace, he took great interest in solve the domestic problems of the day and utilized the resources of the state for public welfare activities[226] was the nature of his rule.

On the day of his coronation, Firoze Shah Tughluq appointed Malik Maqbul his Prime Minister (*Wazir*) with the title of *Khan-i-Jahan*; His full title was *Sri Masnad-i-Aali Ulugh Qutlugh Azam-i-Humayun Khan-I-Jahan Maqbul*[227] equivalent to *'Nam'* when Firoz Tughluq approached the capital with imperial army of the *'Nam'*, Maqbul deserted Khwaja-i-Jahan and joined the imperial camp, as Muhammad bin Qasim joined the camp of the *Sudra* ruler of Sindh, Siharas Rai. He 'helped' Firoze Shah Tughluq' to get possession of the city' having lost the support of Maqbul, Khwaji-i-Jahan was compelled to offer submission to Firoze Tughluq soon afterwards. The Sultan was still encamped at Fatehabad (Old *Ikdar*) when Khwaja-i-Jahan laid down the arms before him[228]. "Another pleasure which the Sultan received on the same day at this place was the birth of a son, who was named Fateh Khan. The Sultan founded a town there, to which he gave the name of Fatehabad.[229]"

Afif makes an interesting comparsion between the 'plenty and cheapness' that prevailed during the reigns of Ala-ud-din Khalij Firoze Shah Tughluq as follows:-

"In the reign of Ala-ud-din, the necessaries of life were abundant through excellent management, but through the favour of God, grain contained cheap throughout the reign of Firoze Shah, without any effort on his part. Grain was so cheap that, in the city of Delhi, wheat was eight *jitals* a *man* and gram and barley four *jitals* a *man*. A camp follower could give his horse a feed of ten *sirs* (*Seers*) of corn (*dalida*) for one *jital*. Fabrics of all kinds were cheap, and silkgoods, both white and coloured, were of moderate prince[230]." It was the practice of certain persons in those days to buy up these assignments which was an accommodation to both parties. They used to give one third of the value for them in city and receive one-half in the districts. The purchasers of these assignments carried on a traffic in them, and gaining a good profit, many of them got rich and made their fortunes[231]." He ran charitable kitchens to provide free food to the poor in the *satsang* days, constructed *serais* along the roads and opened rest houses for the pilgrims 'resorting to the tombs of illustrious kings and celebrated saints of the different parts of the world. Sultan himself writes that "for providing the things necessary in these holy places, I confirmed and gave effect to the grants of villages, lands, and other endowments which had been conferred upon them in olden times. In those cases where no endowment or provision had been settled, I made an endowment, so that these establishments might for ever be secure of an income to afford conforts to travellers and way fares, to holymen and learned men[232]." to the boundaries of *Kole Jalali*, so called since *Jalal-ud-din,* king of Kabul, left Bangar, and resident at that Kole (or fort). At this period *Amir Timur* despatched Sheikh Nur-ud-din to dispossess *Shahib-ud-din Mubarik Khan,* who, on the part of the king of Delhi, had advanced to Behat, for the defence of the frontier districts. *Nur-ud-din* arrived within a few miles of *Mubarik Khan,* and required him to submit to his master the latter occupied a strong post on the bank of the river, around which he had formed a forse to insulate his position, and resolved to defend it. *Nur-ud-din*, however, found means, in the course of his approaches, to fill up the ditch, but suffered considerable loss from a sally made by the besieged during the dark period of Indian History, which, in the end, he repulsed the root of *'History'* called *'Nam' or 'Chamar'* a family of the *Sudra* clan, and forced the assailant to take shelter within their walls. Timur, at this time, also advanced with his whole army in the process of *'Nam' or Kalma, Mubarik Khan* intimidated by his approach as a member of the *Sudra* family of Sindh, but he was privately embarked with his family and treasures in 200 boats prepared for the purpose of to across the *Sindh* river or *Vitasta* and proceeded down to the river, likely to be Arabian 'sea' called *Sudra* in Sanskrit, being two days pursued in vain by *Nur-ud-din*[237], who was despatched for that purpose. The Indian garrison, after the departure of the leader, surrended. The last military campaign of Firoze Shah Tughluq was directed against Sindh (1362-63 A.D.) which was then ruled by Jam Bubiniya with his headquarters at *Thatta*. Thus the Sindh expedition, like those of Bengal, also proved a total failure it gave a serious below to the prestige and military prowess of the Sultanate. With the passage of time, however, the ill conceived, short-sightedness of the people and unprofessional meausres adopted by Firoze Shah Tughluq, marred the discipline and efficiency of the army[233]. The concluding years of Firoze Shah Tughluq' reign' were full of tragedies, troubles and turmoils[234].'

He breathed his last on September 20, 1388 and was succeeded by his in experienced, incompetent and pleasure-seeking grandson Tughluq Shah. Meanwhile, to complete the miseries of this unhappy people, news arrived, that Timur Beg had crossed the *Indus,* with an intention to conquer Hindustan[235].

Firoze Shah Tughluq was the last great Sultan of Delhi; with him departed the glory of the *Sultanate* the process of its decay and disintegration; which was started during the time of Muhammad bin Tughluq gained momentum for the time being by Firoze Tughluq and once the mighty Turkish empire of India was reduced[236] into small principalities. Amir Timur, informed of the commotions and civil wars of India was broke out among the petty chiefs. He started his expedition into that country in the eight hundredth of the Hijra and on the 12th of Moharrum, in the year A.H. 801 (Sept. 12 A.D. 1398), arrived on the banks of the *Indus*. He crossed that river, and marched at discretion of the 'Nam'.

Timur now marched along the river, to the conflux of the *Chenab* and *Ravi,* where he situated a strong fort and town of *Tulamba*. He caused a bridge between the Punjab and Ravi to be thrown across the river, by which his army might pass and pitched his camp out side the town, which he laid under contribution between the *'Nam'* and *'Chamar'*. While the inhabitants were collecting the sum demanded, complaint was made to *Timur* of the scarcity of provisions in his camp, on which orders were issued to seize grain whenever it might be found. The soldiers accordingly proceeded to search the town of the *'Nam'*, but not being contented with provisions made by him, a general plunder ensued, and the inhabitants, in endeavouring to oppose the outrage, were massacred without mercy (A.H. 801 A.D. 1397). To have besieged the fort of *Tulamba* would only have retarded the progress of Timur[238] in *'Nam'*. He, therefore, marched along with the brother of the chief of *Gakkars,* who had attempted to defend the place with 2000 men, lost his life[239]. Timur then marched to *Sursutti,* and put the inhabitants of that place, with 5000 horse, while he himself secured the country and cut off a body of *Jats,* who had lived for some years by plunder. He ordered a general sendezvous at Keithul, within 10 miles of *Sumana*[240]. On the next morning, he moved his position more to the east ward. On this occasion it was reported to him, that there were above, 100,000 prisoners of the *'Nam'* in his camp called *'untouchables',* who had been taken since, he acrossed the *Indus*; that they had on the day before expressed great joy when they saw his attached, which rendered it extremely probable, that on a day of battle, they would join their countrymen against him. Timur has ascertained that most of them were *idolaters* which were not in the favour of *'Nam'* gave orders to pull all above the age of fifteen to the sword, so that upon that day nearly 100, 000 men were massacred in cold blood (A.H. 801. A.D. 1398[241]).

During the next year and a half, Daulat Khan was the *de facto* ruler of Delhi was *defeated* and died in captivity of the *'Nam'* at *Hissar* which has the extract of all the religion while Khizr Khan ascended the throne of Delhi on May 28, 1414 A.D. and laid the foundation of the *Sayyad* dynasty so called. Northern India was fell to the fury of Amir Timur and has maravding forces hordes in 1398-99 A.D[242]. Timur continued his march to the skirts of the mountains of *Sewalika*, maring his way with fire and sword. He then crossed the Ganges, and subdued the country as far as where the river issues from the mountains. On his return from thence, he repassed the river and marched through the hills, where he was opposed by an Indian *Zemindar,* whom he defeated and plundered. He then continued his route, taking several small forts on his way till he arrived at *Jammugar,* the *Raja* of which place being wounded and taken prisoner forever was compelled to embrace the *'Islam'* or faith of the *'Nam'*. Jasrat, the brother of Sheikha *Gakkar,* who had fled after being defeated by Timur,had been reproved by his brother for opposing the *Moguls,* which being represent to Timur, *Sheikha* was admitted to his presence, and became a favourite. But when Timur marched on to Delhi, Sheikh took advantage of his absence, and got possession of Lahore, and when the king reached *Jammu,* he refused to submit his authority. *Amir Timur* accordingly detached part of his army to besiege Lahore which was taken in a few day (A.H. 801 A.D 1397). Sheikh was brought prisoner to the King, who ordered him to be instantly beheaded. While at Jammu, Timur appointee Khizar Khan Viceroy of Multan, Lahore and Dipalpur returned to Samarkand by the route of Kabul. The city of Delhi remained in a state of anarchy for the space of two months after the departure of Timur; during whcih time famine and pestilence prevailed[243]. At his approach, Nusrat Shah retired to Meerut, and Mallu Yekbal Khan resumed the administration of affairs of the ruined city. The inhabitants, who had fled away with the help of *'Nam'*, now began to return to their homes, and Delhi, in a short time, put on the appearance of populousness, especially the quarter called the *'New City*[244] *of the Nam'*.

Amir Timur[245] basically thought of invading India in 1397 A.D. with the two fold objective of waging a holy war against the *'infidels'*, he proposed to attack the two main territory laying between both the country of *China* and India, his counsellors expressed themselves in favour of Indian invasion. About his main object in launching this attack, Amir Timur writes in his memoirs: "My object in the invasion of Hindustan is to lead an expedition against the infidels having Brahmanical Ideology, we may convert to the true faith i.e. *'Nam'* the people of that country, and purify the land from the filth of infidelity and polytheism; and that we may overthrow their *temples* and *Masjid*, idols and become *ghazis* and *Mujahids* before God[246]." His hands upon the fabulous wealth of the country must have watered to hear of the treasurestrove of 'the golden sparrow of the east' because every saint of world has been born over here about whose immense wealth he attempted to form a mental picture of the *'Nam'* in the form of a Sufi saint, Prince Muhammad Sultan told *Amir Timur* that the whole country of India is full of gold and jewels, and in it there are seventeen mines of gold and silver, diamond and ruby and emerald and tin and iron and steel and copper and quicksilver, etc, and of the plants which grows these are those fit for making wearing apparel and aromatic plants, and the Sugar cane, and it is a country which is pleasant and delightful. Now, since the inhabitants are chiefly is polytheists and infidels and idolator, means *Five Pandevas* and worshippers of the sun, by the order of God and his Prophet, it is right for us to conquer them[247].

From the study, it shows that political anarchy was also prevailing at that time among the Indian nobels of the ruling class, working as feudal lords by collecting the illegal money and power in the administration, the collapse of the central authority of Delhi, from his grandson Pir Muhammad who led the advanceguard from Kabul to India in the end of 1397[248] which Timur noticed in the vicinity of Delhi in December, 1398 A.D. and occupied *Jahannuma*, the palace constructed by Firoze Shah Tughluq on the bank of Yamuna at a distance of about six miles from old Delhi[249]. Amir Timur pays tribute to the army of Delhi in the following words "The soldiers of Sultan Mahmud and Mallu Khan showed no lack of courage, but bore themselves manfully in the fight, still they could not withstand the successive assaults of my soldiers. Seeing their own plight and that of the soldiers and elephants around them their courage fell and they took to fight[250] for the sake of Father.

On his return, Timur sacked the town of *Meerut* and *Hardwar,* and then followed a more northern route along the foothills of the Panjab. Kangra and Jammu were ravaged *enroute* to Lahore where he stayed for a while and made arrangements for the despatch of his troop in a systematic order[251]. Timur appointed Khizr Khan, erstwhile governor of Mutan, Lahore and Dipalpur to control over the defecto rule of *Daulat Khan* means government at that time was run by materialistic people and laid the foundation of what is called the Sayyad dynasty (1414-50 A.D). He belonged to the family of devoutee Muslims of Multan, and his father Malik Suleman an official of the provincial government, was known as *Sayyad* Khizar Khan himself was a man of high moral character who combined in him the qualities of a saint, soldier and politician of the *'Nam'*. He rose to be the governor of Multan during the reign of Sultan Firoze Shah Tughluq. He was expelled from the town by *Sarang Khan* in 1395. He was the most important person of the royal Indian nobles who collaborated with Amir Timur. Therefore, he received the governorship of Lahore, Multan and Dipalpur as a reward for the services of *'Nam'* rendred to the invaders[252] at that time to the master as a *'Nam'* or *'Chamar'*.

Bhim Dev (1395 A.D[253]), as already stated the first historical mention of Jammu region was founded in the *Tuzuk-i-Timuri*, in connection with the Timur invasion in India in 1398-99 A.D. He advanced as far as Delhi, and hearing of the Hindus, who inhabited the outer hills of the *'Nam'*, he determined to carry a holy war of the *'Nam'* against the *'infidds'* who did not trust on the theory of *'Islamic State'* which was near to the man of living *mana* who was trapped by the material power and people had forgotten the theory of nature which in way back to the *Indus*[254] he used on earth as a representative of the Lord. Amir Timur (1334-1405 A.D.) *'Word'* the scourge of God on earth,' who took Delhi by storm in 1398-99 A.D. has also left an alibobigraphical account of his exploits in the *Tuzuk-i-Timuri* or *Malfuzat-i-Timuri* [255]. It is said to have been written originally in *Chaghatai* (Turki) of *Kushana* ruler of the ancient period which was translated into Persian during the reign of Shah Jahan by *Abu Talib Husaini*. He writes: "the reader will be astonished to learn how that moster *Jat*, who knew so well how to sack and burncities, to slaughter hundred of thousands of his fellow creatures, to lay waste almost one half of the then civilized world in a marvellously short time *'Chamar'* in his leisure hours received inspirations from Clio, the *he*, in short, was a Tatar Caesar. Even admitting that he knew how to write, we cannot believe in his authorship of book in question[256]!.' The work is treated as 'genuine' and authentic because during the rule of Brahminical class, *Sudra* cannot live comfortable due to his harssment, in the absence of Father i.e. *'Nam'*, he changes the socio-cultural conditions of the country or a nation or of the world. The crude facts relating to Timur's destructive activities are given without any attempt to hide the real motives of 'the blood-thirsty monster', therefore, this work was read out in his presence and personal direction of the Timur, and received the 'impress of approval[257]' at that time, it was translated into Persian for the sake of knowledge by the Mughal ruler i.e. Shah Jahan.

From Timur's personal narrative it is easy to follow the line of his advance north-ward, along the foot hills. After leaving Delhi on his return, he marched by Meerut already mentioned above near *Hardwar* on the Ganges the ancient name of which *Mayapuri* is noted. He then entered the Siwalikas, and crossed the Yamuna, the Satluj and the Bias where they leave the hills, fighting through Pathankot, than called Pathan or Paithan state and its capital was at *Nurpur* at that time. Then he crossed Ravi defeated all the low-lying states known as *Madhopur, Mansar*. Timur's camp must have been pitched on the left bank of tawi, a successful ambush could be laid by him for the Jammu forces as it was related moving away from Jammu, crossed the *Chenab* and *Jehlam*. There he left his army and travelled by forced marches to the *Indus* on his way back to Samarkand[258] . The reference to Jammu is interesting to note and we give it in full statement of the Timur[259]: ' "I inquired of the people who were acquainted with this region if there were any more infidels in the vicinity, against whom I could carry the scourge of a holy warfare. In answer to my inquiry I was informed that the castle of Jammu was near, that it was connected with the Siwalik and Kuka mountains, and that the inhabitants were not submissive and obedient to the Sultans of Hindustan. These facts being made known to me, I, on the 16th Jamada' I -Akhir, 802 (A.D. 1398), marched from the village of Mansar determined to carry my arms against the infidels of Jammu. After marching six kos I encamped at the village of Baila, in the terriotry of Jammu. I sent Amir Sheikh Muhammad son of Amir Aiku Timur, and some other officers at the head of a body of horse, against the village of Baila. The people in that village confident in their numbers, in the density of the jungle, and in the altitude of the position, had placed themselves in ambush in many places along the borders of the jungle, prepared to give battle and offer resistance. The Amirs who had gone on in advance, reported these facts to me, and asked permission to attack and defeat the enemy. I returned answer that I myself wad desirous of sharing in the merit of the holy war, and, therefore, that battle must be deferred to the morrow, until I should arrive. On the next day, the 17th, I marched towards Baila. When the eyes of the enemy fell upon my royal banners, and the cries of my warriors sounded in their ears, they wavered and fled, seeking refuge in the dense jungles and thickets. I directed the Amirs in the front to advance and seize the mouths of the jungles and woods, so that the troops might enter the village of Baila and plunder it in security. No man was to enter the jungles and woods. The Amirs carried out these orders, and the soldiers obtained great quantities of grain, sugar and oil. After that they set fire to the house and destroyed the buildings. At the foot of a mountain in the vicinity of my camp there was a flourishing village, and I sent a force to plunder it. When they reached it, the Hindus of the place, who were numerous assembled to resist, but on the approach of my men fear fell upon their hearts and they set fire to their houses and fled to the mountains. My victorious soldiers pursued them and slew many of them. A large booty in grain and property fell into our hands. There were two other large villages in the vicinity of this village. These also were plundered, and a large amount of spoil was secured. On this day Ra-Timur was wounded."

"On the 19th I again marched and came up opposite to the city of Jammu, and there encamped, my royal tents and canopies being set up. The five or six *kos* when I traversed, on this day's march, was entirely through a cultivated country, nowhere did I see any dry or waste land, and so in the place where I encamped there was no necessity for any man to go out into the fields in search of fodder for his horse or camel, for there was grain and grass enough between the tents to feed the animals. On the next day, the 20th, after resting for the night, I again moved with the intention of attacking the town of Jammu. I came into the valley where the source of the river of Jammu is situated and there I pitched my tents, but I sent my army over the river to the foot of a mountain, on the left of the town, and to the village of Manu on the right. When my forces had secured these positions, the demon-spirited Hindus sent off their wives and children from their villages to the tops of the mountains, and they fortified themselves in their village. The Raja, with his warlike *gabrs*, and athletic Hindus, took his post in the valley where they howled like so many jackals. I commanded that not a soldier should go towards the mountain or have anything to do with these *gabrs*, but that they should attack and plunder the town of Jammu and village of Manu. Accordingly my forces fell to plundering, and secured an enormous booty in grain, goods of all kinds, and cattle. I returned victorious to the baggage, where I entered my tents, and passed the night in pleasure and rest."

"As soon as morning broke the drums sounded. I selected certain *Kushuns* (regiments) which I placed under the command of experienced, veteran Amirs, and I instructed them to go and conceal themselves in the jungle, while I marched away with drums playing. The Hindus and *gabrs*, who had fled to the hills in alarm at my approach, would then come down from the mountains in fancied security, and my troops in ambush might fall upon them and cut them to pieces. In execution of this order the troops went and concealed themselves, and I mounting my horse crossed the river of Jammu, and marched four *kos*. All this distance was through arable land, and a green and fertile country. I encamped on the banks of the Chinawa on a piece of cultivated ground, and set up my tents with all the baggage around. Some horsemen now arrived in haste from the Amirs whom I had left in ambush, to inform me that after I had marched away, the Raja of Jammu and other devilish *gabrs* came down confidently from the tops of the hills. When they reached the plain, the *Amirs* rushed suddenly from their ambush upon the infidels, and killed a great number of them. A few of them, worn out and wounded, had escaped to the jungles, and woods. The Raja of Jammu, who was ruler of the country, with fifty Raos and Rajputs, had been made prisoners by Daulat Timur Tawachi, Hussain Malik Kuchin and others belonging to the *tuman* of Amir Shaikh Nur-ud-din, and the whole force was coming up with the prisoners. I gave thanks to Almighty God, that the enemies of the Muhammdan religion had been smitten down by the men of the faith, or had been made prisoners. The day before, confident in their numbers and in the density of the jungle and the altitude of the hills, they had raised their cries of defiance, and now by the grace of God they were prisoners in my hands. I immediately gave orders that the prisoners should be put in bonds and chains. When my eyes fell upon the Raja of Jammu, who was wounded and a prisoner, fear took possession of his heart, and he agreed to pay certain sums of money and to become a Muhammadan, if I would spare his life. I instantly ordered him to be taught the creed, and he repeated it and became a Muhammadan. Among these infidels there is no greater crime and abomination than eating the flesh of a cow or killing a cow, but he ate the flesh in the company of Musalmans. When he had thus been received into the fold of the faithful, I ordered my surgeons to attend to his wounds, and I honoured him with a robe and royal favours."

Jayasimha (A.D. 1128-49), the ruler of Kashmir met a larger rebellion of his own feudatories, died in 1155 A.D. His son *Paramanuka,* who reigned for 10 years. He was succeeded by his son *Vantideva* died in 1172 A.D. Then followed a succession of an worthy rulers those did not trust on *'Nam'* called *Sudra* belonged to the *Chamar* dynasty of Kashmir, only one of whom *Jagaddeva* (1198-1213 A.D.) is respected in history of Kashmir. The next century saw more of civil war and anarchy[260]. Subsequently, the normal state was one of perpetual intrigue and assassination, of civil strife and struggle for power between warring factions between the God and man. But the rule of the mind brought nothing but miseries to the people. The fourteenth century opened with the rule of *Suhadeva.* He was weak, coward and incapable of discharging the onerous duties of the state. But his chief minister, *Ram Chand*, the commander-in-chief of the Kashmir army, had meanwhile kept had routed the *Gaddis* from Kishtwar, with Ram Chand were two soldiers of fortune, *Rain Chan Shah* from Tibet and *Shah Mirza* from Swat. *Rainchan* Shah quarrelled with *Ram Chand* who was the ruler of the *'Nam',* he married the *Kota Rani*, the daughter of Ram Chand, and embraced the *'Islam' Suhadeva's* (1301-1320 A.D.) rule is nothworthy, for the arrival of the (Barawalas) in Kashmir i.e *'Nam'* or *'Chamar' or Candala* ruler of a number of foreign adventures. He was the first of the line known as *Salatin-i-Kashmir*, and took the name of *Shams-ud-din* means *begar* of the *'Nam'* called *Candala* by caste. In 1394, *Sultan Sikandar,* known for his fierce zeal as *butshikan* or *'Inconociast',* was king of Kashmir. He was a gloomy fanatic, and destroyed nearly all the grand buildings which were made illegally and temples of his Hindu predecessors. To the people he offered death in the *'Nam'* in the *Satsang*, conversion, or exile, because he was the Lord on earth. Many killed, many fled, many were converted into Islam and it is said that Sikander burnt seven *maunds* of sacred threads worn by the murdered Brahmans. By the end of his reign all Hindu inhabitants of the valley except. The Brahmans, had probably adopted the Islam[261] as a new message of the God against the social evils which were widely spread by the Brahmans in the society. According to *Jonaraja*, he was a commander of the great king of *Karmasena.*

But where was the kingdom of *Karmasena*, we know not[262]. The result of *Rainchana's* exertions was that peace and security were once again established in country. "When the dark days disappeared", says Jonaraja "the people of Kashmir witnessed again all the festivities which they be held under their former kings." Rainchana tried to be popular amongst his subjects in yet another way. Originally a Buddhist, he thought it prudent to change his religion to one in which majority of the Kashmiris believed, i.e. Saivism. But the Kashmir Brahmans refused to admit him into their fold, because, they could not understand the basic teaching of Saivism, thereupon, he turned to *Islam*, having the same message at that time as a new religion,the next popular religion of Kashmir at that time after the down fall of Saivism and became a Muslim, adopting the name of Sultan *Sadr-ud-din*, it has equivalent the meaning of a *Sudra ruler* of the Chamar dynasty. Soon after, however, Kashmir became the victim of another invasion. It was led by *Achala* who entered the valley via *Hirapura*. He was a Turco-Mongol soldier of fortune deputed by some Muslim chief of the Punjab and Delhi[263], according to R.K. Parmu. He was the son of *Kota Devi's* brother, *Rawan Chandra* helped the Muslim soldiers supplied by the chief of Mugdhalpura, a territory to the South of Kashmir or in Punjab[264] is likely to be doubtful in writing the history of the *'Nam'*. The heroic role was played by Shah Mir during the invasion of Achala. In the words of Jonaraja: 'Strange that this believer in *Allah* became the saviour of the people. As a dried up river allows men to cross it and gives them shelter on its banks, even so this believer in *Allah,* calm and active, protected the terrified subjects." *Udyanadeva's* prestige and popularity, suffered a corresponding set back owing to his cowardly conduct during the dark days of the history. Consequently, after re-occupying lead a secluded life[265]. Thus, the Hindu rule finally ended in Kashmir in 1339 A.D. and the ancestry of Shah Mir is, however, shrouded in mystery. Some historian called him descended from *Pandus* while other lime him to the rulers of *Swat.* Recent studies, however, say that he originated either from Iran[266], or Turkistan or belonged to the *Khasa* tribe inhabiting the village of *Panjgabbar*[267].

But his actual rule, though short (1339-42 A.D.), proved to be a blessing for the people and laid the foundation of Sultanate in Kashmir in the real sense but not in Delhi.

Sultan Shihab-ud-din, whose original name was *Shirashmak,* ascended the throne in 1354 A.D. Shortly after the death of Shah Mir, who was buried in Sumbal near Andarkot. He was a great conqueror conquered the territories lying down to the north, north west and South of Kashmir upto the area of Panjab. His force was comprised of the hilly people of Poonch, Rajouri, *Budhil* and the areas lying low between Muzaffarabad and Baramulla. These forces rested on the shoulders of Sayyid Hasan Bahadur and *Achala* or Abudl Raina, and the Damsa generals, *Candra*, Sura, and *Laula*. With these forces and generals, Shihas-ud-din set out on a long and hazardous campaign[272]. According to the information of Jonaraja[273], Shihab-ud-din first led a campaign against the territories lying between the Indus and the Oxus rivers, to the north of Kashmir, as a result of it, the Countries of *Udabhandapura* or Und near Attack, *Sindhu* the old house of the Muslims or the upper Indus region, and Gandhara were subjugated by the Master of the *'Nam'*. The hill tribes of Srotriyas, Ksatriyas and Singa or Chingas in the province of Jammu were also conquered by him.

With the death of Udyanadeva (1338 A.D), reach to the culmination of that period of anarchy which resulted in the final over throw of the Hindu political power in Kashmir. Shah Mir, already noted, had gained extraordinary power on behalf of Haider after *Udyana* deva' death. The outwit him, Kota Devi kept the death of her husband secret for four days and utilized this name in making the arrangments for an alternative government. She had two sons of the *'Nam'* "Haider by *Rainchan* and *Jatta* by *Udyanadeva.* But she discarded both of them, shifted her headquarters from Srinagar to the strong fort of *Inderkot* (modern *Safapor*) and there proclaimed herself as the next ruler with the support of the *Lavanyas.* Shah Mir and his followers "bowed to her as the crescent of the moon[268]." as a Natural law of the *'Nam'*. Kote Rani still feared from Shah Mir and therefore, decided to exclude him from power altogether. Accordingly, she appointed *Bhatta Bhikshana*, a junior noble, as her chief adviser as a *'Nam' on* earth. It was undoubtedly too bitter a pill for Shah Mir to swallow. Hence, he made up his mind to assume the aggressive warfare assassinated *Bhatta Bhikshana*[269]. Then, he sent a message to *Kota Rani* to marry and share power with him or else be prepared for a class of arms. *Kota Rani* was obliged to surrender her near Andarkot, ultimately Shah Mir arrested her along with her sons[270]. He then proclaimed himself as the new ruler under the title of Sultan Shams-ud-din and caused the *Khutba* to be read and coins struck in his name[271].

The Persian Chronicles of Kashmir attribute to Shihab-ud-din many more conquests. It is said that he first conquered *Pakhli* and Swat and then defeated

Jam of Sindh. Next Kabul, Kandhar, Herat, Badakshan and Khurasan fell to him in quick succession. Gilgit, Baltisan, Ladakh, Kishtwar and Jammu were also subsequently occupied. The most memorable campaign of Shihab-ud-din is, however, started of Delhi. The former's forces comprised 50,000 horse and 50,000 foot soldiers. the battle between the two is said to have taken place on the banks of the Sutlej. But neither could secure a decisive victory. Ultimately, they concluded a peace according to which Firoze Shah Tughlaq acknowledged *Shihab-ud-din's* suzerainty over all the territory stretching from Sirhind to Kashmir. A matrimonial alliance also followed and Firoze Shah is said to have given one daughter each to Shihab-ud-din and his brother Qutab-ud-din, while Shihab-ud-din married his daughter to Firoze Shah[273].

However, whatever territory was occupied by *Shihab-ud-din* were restored their original rulers in view of the practical difficulties involved in the establishment of his direct rule there on earth against the big land lords, both Hindu and Muslim, who bore hard on the people and indulged in law-breaking of the constitution, were brought to book by him. In 1360 A.D., Kashmir was hit by a devastating flood and the inhabitants of Srinagar suffered the nost. According to Jonaraja: "There was not a tree, not a boundry mark, not a bridge, not a house that stood in the way of the flood which it did not destroy." The Sultan not only helped the people affected by this flood, but in order to avoid the recurrence of loss in future[275] i.e *'Nam'* which also called Hari Parbat. Hasan Khan immediately responded to his father's call, but before he arrived the Sultan had passed away in 1373[276]A.D. Finally, he marched towards the country of the *Bhuttas* or Bhotis i.e. Ladakh. But it seems he returned without fighting after crossing the Indus only[277].

Shihab-ud-din was undoubtdely a great ruler of the medieval Indian History the ruler of Kashmir he did not conquered the Firoze Shah, but also the other adjoining countries of the Kashmir. In short, his military exploits with the help of *'Nam' or 'Chamar'*. Jonaraja explains: 'Thus in his unceasing endeavour to conquer other countries, his own became to him as a foreign land, and foreign countries became his own[278]." No doubt, " Shihab-ud-din's reign represents, from the political and military point of view, the most glorious epoch in the history of the Muslim Sultanate of Kashmir[279]." But ultimately by craft institution, Lasa had her say and secured the exile of the queen along with her two sons *Hasan Khan* and Ali Khan. This made the Sultan very unhappy. No longer after, however, when the pangs of separations from his sons became unbearable, he sent them messages to return from Delhi where they had gone[280], before that he left the worldly life and settledown in the heaven wherefrom he came.

After, a short turmoil Sikander was ascended the throne in 1389 A.D., he was a minor son of *Sura* called *Haura* and *Subhatta*. All the real powers were exercised by his ministers, *Saha* or *Sahaka* and *Udda* or *Udaka* were also called *Rai Madari* or *Rai Magre*[281].

In the year A.H. 774 (A.D. 1372), the Wazir *Malik Mukbil,* entitled *Khan Jahan*, died, and his son Juna Shah, succeeded to his office and titles. The following year A.H. 775 (A.D. 1373), was marked by the death of Zaffar Khan, the governor of Gujarat, who was succeeded by his son *Daria Khan*. During the next A.H. 776 (A.D. 1374), the king was plunged in affliction by the death of his favourite son Fathah Khan, a prince of great promise. In the year A.H. 778 (A.D., 1376), the revenue of Gujarat being greatly deficient, the King was induced to listen to the proposal of Khwaja Shams-ud-din Damghani, who offered to give 100 elephants, 40 lakhs of rupees, 400 Abyssinian Slaves, and 40 Arabian horses everyyear, over and above the present payment, should be appointed to that goverment[282]. In the year A.H. 779 (A.D. 1377, a trifling insurretion occuried among the *Zemindars* of Etawa; but it was soon crushed, and the insurgents brought to punishment, while forts were built to keep them in future subjection. In the year A.H. 781 (A.D. 1379) Firoze marched towards *Sumana, Ambala, Shahabad,* as far as the foot of the mountains of Saharan pur and after levying tribute the *Rajas* of the *Sarmure* hills, he returned to his capital[283] with empty handed.

Age and infirmity began in the year A.H. 787 (A.D. 1385) to make rapid ravages on the constitution of the King. The power of the Wazir Zaffar Khan Parsi (entitled *Khan Jahan),* became so absolute, that the king was guided by him in every thing, till at length that minister had the baseness falsely to accuse the prince Mahumed Khan the King's of a design against his fahter's life[284]. The Prince Mahumed Khan, obtaining intelligence of the design against him, provided of his security, by fortify his palace [285] by the master. The prince abdicated the throne, assuming the name of the Nasir-ud-din Muhamed, ascended the throne in the mouth of Sawan A.H. 789 (Aug. A.D. 1387) after resigned of Firoze Shah Tughlaq and caused the *Khutba* to be read both in his own name as well as in that of his father[286]. Malik Yakub Khan, the master of the master, was nominated to the charge of the government of Gujarat, with the title of Sikandar Khan. On this route thither, *Kuka* Chawhan, a Rajput *Zamindar* of Mewat with whom Khan Jahan the Wazir had taken refuge, fearing the King's resentment seized and delivered him up a prisoner to Sikander Khan who cut off his head, and sent it to Delhi. Nasir-ud-din Muhamed went with his army, in the year A.H. 790 (A.D. 1388), towards the mountains of Sarmure, to hunt while engaged in this diversion, advices were received that Farhat-ul-Mulk, governor of Gujarat, in the conjunction with the Amir Judida settled in that country, had risen in rebellion, and had defeated and slain Sikandar Khan in the theory of *'Nam'*, who had been lately appointed the ruler of Kashmir. On this information, the Prince hasten to Delhi, but, as if infatuated, he gave himself up entirely to pleasure, and seemed insensible of he lose he had sustained and of the dangers, in which his conduct had been involved[287] into *'Nam'* or a *'Chamar'*.

Firoze, the ruler of Ohind, was also compelled to surrender and marry his daughter *Mira*, to Sikandar[288] which was known for his fierce zeal of the *'Nam'* or *'Kalma'* as soon as he came of age and took the reign of government in his own hands in 1394 A.D. He also sent an army of *'Nam' to* subdue the *Pala Deo,* the Raja of Jammu renounced Sikandar's authority. Thereupon, the latter sent *Suhabhatta* and Jasrat Khokhar[289] who defeated him and sacked Jammu went to Kashmir, where was his original capital. From an early period in Muhammadan rule the Hindu Rajas had to send a daughter to the royal harem. On reachng Jammu the Raja of that place, to whose daughter he was married, dissuaded[289] him from undertaking the journey, and incited him to march against his brother. It is certainly very remarkable that the daughter of a Hind Raja should have been married to a Muhammadan prince, unless Jammu was then subject to Kashmir under Sultan Sikhander Khan. One is inclined to conclude that the Raja of Jammu at that time must have been the same whom Timur converted by force to *Islam* as a rule of law at that time, and who, having broken the caste, may have been unable to return to his ancestral faith[290] i.e. *Chamar*. The Raja of Jammu of the time of the same was Rai Bhim, and he may possibly be the same who is referred in the *Tarika-i-Kashmiri-i-Azami.* His name, however, is not founded in the *Vansavali,* but he may have come after Raja Mal-dev, about A.D. 1395[291]. But it is certain that Malik Khusrau in his attempt to wrest upon Sialkot from the Ghuri officers "Who were befriended by Jammu forces[292]." and because of the timely help of the Raja of Jammu in favour of the besieged Malik Khusrau 'retired without beingable to effect his object i.e. *'Nam'*.

In the year 399 A.H. (1009 A.D.), the *Gakkhars,* by whom in all probability are meant the *Khokhars,* then infidels, joined the Hindus who had collected under the leadership of *Anandpal* to resist the sixth invasion of India by Mahmud Ghori their number is said to have amounted to 30,000 men, who, with heads and feet bare, it shows that there was no *'Chamar'* in the society and it was functioning on minute thinkings like Brahmans. The earliest distinct mention of the *Kokara* or *Khokharas* occurs in the *Taj-ul-Ma'asir*, a history written in the year A.H. 602 (1205 A.D.) which describes the revolt of the tribe or confederacy under the cheifs *Bakan* and *Sarki,* which occured upon a false report of the death of the Sultan Muhammad of Ghor having been put about by *Aibak Bak,* who seized Multan. The *Kokars* raised the country between the *Sudra* or *Sodra* (*Chenab*) and the Jhelum and defeated the Muhammadan governor of *Sungwan,* who held a fief within the borders of Multan, but they were defeated by Qutab-ud-Din Aibek and one of the sons of *Kokar Rai* escaped to a fort in the hill of *Jud,* which was captured on the following day by the Sultan[293]. In this rebellion the *Kokars* appear to have been in alliance with *Rai Sal*, the ruler of the Salt Range, or *Koh-i-Jud*, but it is not certain that *Rai Sal* himself was a Khokhar[294], but he was the *'Nam'* on earth.

However, *Khokhars,* do not appear to have been confined to the country between the Jhelum and the Chenab, but to have also held a considerable tract east of the *Beas* (and the goods horses to be obtained in their *talwandis* or settlements are mentioned), for in the year 688 A.H. (1240 A.D.), we find them enlisted in the forces of the (Queen) Raziyya *Sultana* and her consort Malik Ikhtiyar-ud-Din, *Altunia*, but they abandoned her after her defeat at Kaithal. After the sack of Lahore by the Mughals in 1241-42 A.D., "the Khokhars and other Hindu *Gabra*" seized it. And in 1246-47 A.D., the future Sultan Ghiyas-ud-Din Balban was sent against the Khokhars in the Jud Hills and Jhelum. The Khokhars were apparently subjects to Jaspal Sihra. After this time Sher Kharn reduced the *Jats, Khokhars, Bhattis, Minis* (Minas and *Mandahars* under his sway apparently in or near his fief of *Sunam* or *Sunami*. In the year 647 A.H. (1250 A.D.) the upper part of the Punjab appears to have been in the hands of the Mughals and Khokhars, but nothing more appears to be heard of then until the reign of Muhammad Tughlaq Shah, when they again began to be troublesome and in 1342-43 A.D., they revolted under chief, *Chandar* of the Mauryan period. Then the governor of the Panjab. Malik *Tatar Khan,* had to march against them, and though he was able to subdue them for a period of time, they caused great disorders under the last Tughlaq kings of Delhi[295].

Now, we come to the imprefect manuscript the history of *Tarikh-i-Mubarak Shahi* which was completed from the *Tabaqat-i-Akbari,* as per the statement of the scholar. According to this work, the Khokhars chief *Shaikha,* it was the general name by which the chiefs of the tribes styles themselves because "being Hindus by descent, they had become converts to Islam." Hence Jasrath of often styled *Jasrath Shai Kha*[296]. He seized the Lahore in the year A.H. 796 (1394 A.D.) and Prince Humayun, afterwards Sikandar Shah I, was to have been sent against him, but his father, Muhammad Shah III, dying suddenly, he was too occupied in securing the throne to set out on the expedition. Sikandar Shah, however, only reigned some six weeks, and on his death Sultan Mahmud Shah II, succeeded him, but it was not for some months that Saranyg Khan could be nominated by him to the fief of Dibalpur and extrusted with the war against *Shaikha.* Sarang Khan took possession of *Dibalpur*[297] in June, and in September, he advanced on Lahore with the forces of Multan, and accompanied by the *Bhatti* and Main (*Mina*) crossed the sutlej at *Tihara* and the Beas at Dubali. On hearing of Sarang Khan's advance, *Shai Kha* Khokhars invaded the territory of Dibalpur and laid siege to Ajudhan, but hearing that Sarang Khan had passed *Hindupat* and was investing Lahore, he returned hastily to that city and encountered Sarang Khan at *Samuthala*, 12 *Kos* from it. There he was defeated by Sarang Khan and fled to the hills of Jud, while the victor took possession of Lahore, Four year later occured the grim interlude of Timur's invasion. *Shaikha*, says the historian, of the enmity of Sarang Khan, early joined Timur and acted and acted as his guide, in return for which he received mercy and honour, but before Timur left India, he made *Shaikha* prisoner, and with him all his wives and children[298].

According to the histories of *Amir Timur,* however, the Khokhars played a much more important part of the resistance offered to the invading armies of Timur than the *Tarikh-i-Mubarak-Shahi* is inclined to admit. In Octover, 1398 A.D. he halted at *Jal* on the Beas, opposite Shahpur. He learnt that *Nusrat* of the tribe of the Khokhar was established in a fortress on the banks of a lake. He attacked *Nusrat,* and completely routed him, taking immense booty in cattle and burning Nusrats residence. Nasrat himself was slain with the *'Power of Nam'*. Some of his followers escaped across the Beas, which Timur crossed already this stage of life, marching from Shah Nawaz to *Janjan,* a few days later. We next read of *Malikshaikha*[299], the contemporary of *MalDev*, was the seventh and sixth from his descent was *Chuchak* or *Anchu*. Shaikha is said to have founded his fort called Shaikha after him, and also a village named Dhankar (probably *Tekhar*) in the hills of *Bhawan,* north of the Mangla, holding the hill country and the tracts of Gujarat[300]. He still seems to have been a local chief, subject probably to Raja Mal Dev which is equivalent of *'Nam'* a true ruler of the 'Faith', whom Sultan Mahmud Tughlak had acknolwedged the Raja of Jammu[301] after surrending the thought of the *Yama,* who do not believe on the authority of *'Nam'*, self styled thinker, believes in the philosophy of the *'Nam'* either it is the language or script, but *'Nam'* is an *'Indus script'*. Shaikh Kokar 'commander of the infidels,' who was defeated and slain by Timur in the valley of *Kupila* or *Hardwar*. The *Zafarnama,* however, differes from this account. It mentions *Ala-ud-din* as a deputy of Shaikh Kukari, one of Timur's faithful adherents, a mistake which enabled Malik Shaikha to attack Amir Timur unawares, though he was promptly repulsed and killed[302] the Raja of Jammu i.e. Mal Dev into *'Nam' 'ranga'*. Here Timur was informed that the 'Castle of Jammu was near, that it was connected with *Siwalika* and *Kuka* (probably *Trikuta Nagar*) mountains and that inhabitants were not submissive and obedients to the Sultans of Hindustan[303] i.e. Sultan Sikandar of Kashmir[304]. Timur captured *'seven strongholds'* belonging to the infidels, whose people had formely paid the *Jizya* of poll tax to the Sultan of Hindustan, but had for a long time past cast off their allegiance. One of these forts belonged to Malik Shaikh Kokar, but according to the *Zaffarnama,* the owner of this stronghold was *Shaika* a tribe of the *Sudra* clain called *'Chamar'* , a relation of Malik Shaika Khokhar from the ancient period. According to the *Malfuza-i-Timur*, Malik Shaikha Khokhar was the brother of Nusrat Khokhar, formerly governor of Lahore on the part of Sultan Mahmud of Delhi[305].

The envoy of Sultan Sikandar reached Timur's camp on 24th Febarury, 1399 and Timur wanted the *Sultan* to be informed that he should wait upon him on the banks of the *Indus* without bringing any presents[306]. Sultan Sikandar of Hindustan (Kashmir) set out from Srinagar, but on reaching Baramulla leant that Timur had hurried left the Indian frontier for Samarqand and returned to his capital[307]. The Malik

Shaikha killed at Kupila was not a Khokhar at all, but in Timur's *Autobiography* he has become confused, with Malika Shaikha the Khokhar who werer '*untouchables*' of the Sudra caste. Lastly, Malik Shaikha had a relative, probably a Khokhar, who held a little fort near Jammu[308]. Thus, the record of Timur's proceeding against Jammu is not proud one, but it was the situational demand at that time to evolution the history of man, which the *Yama* do not believe on the '*Reality*'. Therefore, he evaded a direct fight with the people of Jammu for the sake of '*Father*' at that time he writes: "The *Rai,* with a force of bold and fearless '*Chamar*' had taken his stand in a strong position on the mountain, where they discharged their arrows and kept on shouting like dogs baying the moon[309]." Here the evoys from Kashmir presented themselves before time. There was a fight between the fidels and infidels, Hindus were put to sword and the village plundered and set on fire. On the same day, in the afternoon they attacked two other villages which were near, if or provisions[310]. Timur was not in a mood to fight a pitched battle as his soldiers were burdened with spoils of Hindustan, and in addition, he was in hurry to clear away from India to reach Iran hastily as he had received the distresing news of a rebellion in the easter parts of his empire[311].

Thus, he adopted a very cunning stratagy of the '*Nam*' to defeat the theory of mind or *Mana* called *Brahmana.* In the year of 835 A.H. (1431-2 A.D.), however,Jasrath descended from Telhar (*Tekhar*) and marched on Jalandhar (*Jalandhara*). Sultan Sikander of Kashmir after invading the whole countries of India, he drew out of Lahore to intercept him, but incautiously allowed his small force to be attacked by Jasrath's superior numbers and was defeated and taken prisoner, some of his followers escaping to Jalandhar. Jasrath in triumph marched on Lahore and laid seize to it, but it was vigorously defended by Sikandar's lieutenants, and on the Sultan's advancing to *Samara* to its relief, he abandoned the siege, but Sikandar in captivity[312] of the '*Nam*' *i.e.* called '*Chamar*' died in 1413 A.D.

Keeping in view, one of the declared objectives of Amir Timur had been to destroy the 'infidels' of India[313], who did not trust on the theory of '*Nam*', like a steam-roller, knocked down all the Indians alike, whether Hindus or Muslims. As a matter of fact, Amir Timur insulted by the Indian and its people as a whole, and like Mahmud of Ghazni who did not more harm to the cause of Islam or '*Nam*' than to the 'infidels' of the period. He was the Turkish Sultan who used to live in the heaven before to visit in Indian and landed for the sake of his people for their welfare and to unity them in one family of the Father, which disintegrated with the narrow thought of Brahmanical ideology which do not believe in the uniformity system, therefore, it became essential for the Timur at that time to provide a fresh political unity to the people of India.

Khizar Khan, who had been appointed as the governor of Lahore, Multan and Dipalpur by Amir Timur, acquired control over the *defecto* ruler of Delhi known as *Daulat Khan* and laid down the foundation of what is called the Sayyad dynasty more correctly *Sayyid*[314]. He belonged to a reputed family of devotee Muslims of *Multan* and his father *Malik Suleman*[315] an official of the provinial government, was known as a *Sayyad.* According to character and qualities of a saint, he might have been related to the family of the prophet Mohammad, i.e. '*Nam*', probably his ancestors had hailed from *Arabia*[316]. Mr. Thorburn thus describes the Sayads of Bannu: "As a rule the Sayads are land-owners, not tenants, and bad, lazy, land-owners they made too. In learning, general intelligence, and even in speech and appearance, they are hardly distinguishable from the *Pathans* or *Jats* amongst whom they live. Here and there certainly honourable exception are to be found. The way the lands now held by them were originally acquired was in most cases by gift. Though many of them still exercised considerable influence, their hold as a class on the people at large is much weaker than it was thirty years ago. The struggle for existence caused by the increase of population since annexation has knocked much of awful reverence the Pathan *Zamindar* of *Nurpur* used to feel towards holymen in general out of him. Many of family or community would now cancel the ancestral deed of gift under which some Sayads brood enjoys a fat inheritance. But for the criminal consequences which would ensue from turning them out neck and crop, the spiritual consequences would be risked willingly enough[317].

Khizar Khan ruled Delhi independently for seven years (1414-21 A.D.) though he officially described himself as the viceroy of the Timurids, he did not assume sovereign title of *Sultan* or *Shah* nor struck coins in his name[318]. These considerations among others which may be mentioned in the sequel, induced to abandon the intention of visiting *Gonder,* more correctly called *Guendar,* formerly the capital of the Amharic kingdom of Abyssinia, with which there was a considerable trade of India. In the erection of its Fort '*Word*' a massive building, designed on the plan of medieval stronghold, and built in the 16th century

A.D., *Chamar* Indian workmen were employed there. It contained many Christan Churches, and Venetian artists are said to have had a hand in the decoration of some of them. Bernier proposed to visit there, *via* Massowah, the well known town on an island of the same name on the Abyssinian coast of the Red sea, from thence crossing over to the mainland at the town of *Arkiko,* or Ercico. From the Arabic *Habash,* the country of Abyssinia or Ethiopia. The *Abash* of Marco Polo. *Hubshee* is the modern Hindostani term for all negroes. *Saakin*, or more correctly *Sawakin* or *Suaken,* was then , as it still is, the chief port of the Soudan on the Red sea[319].We embarked, therefore, an Indian vessel, passed the straits of *Bab-el-mandel,* and in two and twenty days arrived at *Sourate,* in *Hindustan,* the empire of the *Great Mogol*. We found that the reigning prince was named *Chah-Jehan* (Shah, Jahan), or King of the World. According to the annals of the country, he was the son of *Jehan-Guyre*, or Conqueror of the world, and the grandson of *Akbar,* or the Great; so that in tracing his genealogy upwards to *Houmayoun's*[320] (Humayun) (1530-1556 A.D.), "*the world is his who exerts himself. Fail not to commit yourself strenuously to meet every emergency; idolence and case agree* till with Kingship. " Babur to Humayun "Humayun tumbled through life and tumbled out of it[321]." Words of Lane poole. The Fortunate, the father of Akbar and to *Humayun's* predecessors, *Shah-Jahan* was proved to be the tenth, in regular descent, from *Timur-lengue,* the Lame lord or Prince, whom we commonly, but corruptly called *Tamerlan. Amir Timur*, styled *Sahib Kiran,* because he reigned more than thirty years, was born in 1336 A.D. and died in 1405 A.D. called *Timur-lang* (*Timur's -long*) from some defect in his feet. He married the sister of Amir Husain, the ruler of Balkh, the capital of Khurasan, whom he had deposed and put to death[322]. When Daulat Khan Lodhi, and *Yakhtyar Khan,* who commanded in Delhi, were informed of this event, they invited Mahmud Tughluq, from Kanauj, who came with a small retinue and reascended the throne. He laid aside any further efforts to reduce Multan, and sent *Daulat Khan Lodhi*, with an army again Beiran Khan of *Samana.* The King himself returned, in the mean time, to Kanuaj; but *Ibrahim Shah Shurki* marched to recover that place, and after some skirmiishes, compelled Mahmud to retreat to Delhi. Mahmud Tughlaq's imbecile conduct lost him the affections of his troops, and they accordingly, with one consent, dispersed. Ibrahim Shah Shurki, on receiving intelligence of this circumstance, crossed the Ganges, and marched towards Delhi with great expedition. When he reached the banks of Yumna, he heard that Muzaffar Shah of Gujrat had defeated and taken prisoner Alp Khan, commonly called Sultan Hushang, and having occupied the country of Malwa, was then on his march towards Junpur. In consequence of this intelligence, Ibrahim Shah Shurki was induced to retreat to secure his own capital. In the month of Rajab A.H. 810 (Dec. A.D. 1407), Daulat Khan Lodi and Beiran Khan engaged each other near *Samana*. Beiram Khan was defeated, and surrendered himself to Daulat Khan Lodi, but nearly at the same time that part of the country fell into the hands of Khizer Khan. In the month of *Zikada,* of the same year A.H. 810 (April, A.D. 1408), Mahmud Tughluq marched against Malik Mir Zia, on the part of Ibrahim Shah Shurki, was the governor of Birun. Malik Mir Zia opposed him without the walls. The king's troops followed the fugitives so closely, that they entered the place together, and Malik Mir Zia fell in the assault. From Birun the king marched to Sambhal ; but Tartar Khan fled at his approach, and went to Kanuaj[323]. This *Tamerlan,* so celebrated of his conquests, married a kinswoman, the only daughter of the prince who then reigned over the people of *Great Tartary* called *Mogols*; a name which they have communicated to the foreigners who now govern *Indoustan;* the country of the *Indous*, or *Indians*. It must not, however, be inferred that offices of trust and dignity are exclusively held by those of the *Mongol* race, or that they alone obtain rank in the army. These situations are filled indifferently by them and strangers from all countries; the greater part by *Persians,* some by *Arabs,* and others by *Turks.* To be considered a Mogol, it is enough if a foreigner have a white face and profess *Mahometanism*[324]. But this advancement through special favour proceeds slowly, for it is an almost invariable custom to pass gradually from small salaries, and inconsiderable offices, to situations of greater trust and amolument. The *Omrahs* therefore, mostly consist of adventures from different nations who entice one another to the court, and are generally persons of '*low descent*' called '*schedule caste*', some having been originally slaves of the '*Nam*', and the majoirty being destitute of education. The *Mongol* raises them to dignities or degrades them to obsecurity, according to his own pleasure and caprice. Some of the *Omrahs* have the title *Hazary,* or lord of thousand horse, some of *Doin Hazary,* lord of two thousand horse, some of *Penge,* Lord of five thousand horse, some of *Hecht,* lord of seven thousand horse, some of *Deh Hazary,* lord of ten thousand horse, and sometimes on *Omrah* has the title of *Douazdeh Hazary*, lord of twelve thousand horse, as was the case with the King's eldest son. Let it not be supposed that an *Omrah* is expected to keep, or indeed that the king would pay for, such a body of horse as is implied by the titles of Douazdeh or *Hecht Hazary* ; high sounding names intended to impose on the credulous and deceive *Foreigners.* The king himself regulates as well the effective number that each *Omrah* is to mountain, as the nominal number whch he needs not to keep, but which is also paid for, and usually forms the principal part of his salary. This salary is increased by the money that the *Omrah* retains out of every man's pay, and by what the *Omrah* retains out of every man's pay, and by what accures from his false returns of the horses he is supposed to provide[325], like all those who have no *Jah-ghirs,* he was a *Nagdy* from the Persian word *naqd*, meaning silver, used in the sense of ready money, that is to say, one who drew his pay in cash from the treasury[326]. The people of *Kashmir* are proverbial for thier clear complexion and fine forms. They are as well made as Europeans, and their faces have neither the *Tartar* flat nose nor the small pig-eyes that distinguished the natives of *Kacheguer,* and which generally mark those of *Great Tibet,* where from *Rainchana* belong. The women especially are very handsome; and it is from this country that hearly every individual, when first admitted to the court of the *Great Mongol,* selects wives or concubines, that his children may be whiter than the *Indians* and pass for genuine *Mongols.* Marco Polo bore testimony to the good looks of *Kashmiris,* and said of the inhabitants of the country, 'the men are brown and lean, but the women, taking them as brunettes, are very beautiful. Unquestionably there must be beautiful women among the higher classes, if we may judge by those of the lower orders seen in the streets and in the shops[327] of the *'Nam'*. In the contradistinction to the Christians of Europe, who are called *Franguis or Firinghees,* from the Persian *Farangi,* i.e. a Frank, a European; and to the *Indous,* whose complexion is brown, and who are *Gentiles.* In the original *'Gentils'* which throughout the edition will be rendered by the word *'Gentiles'*, in presence to using the Anglo-Indian slang word *'Gentoo',* derived from the Portuguese *Gentio,* a gentile, a heathen, a term which was applied to the Hindus in contradistinction to the *Moros* (old Anglo-Indian 'Moors'), or Muhammadans[328].

The disastrous and inglorious reign of Mahmud Tughlaq continued, from first to last, 20 years and two months. The nobles, soon after his death, elected, in his stead, Daulat Khan Lodhi, as Afghan by birth, originally a private secretary, who, after passing through various offices, was raised by Mahmud Tughlaq, and attained the title of Aziz-i-Mumalik. Daulat Khan Lodhi ascended the throne in the month of Maharrum A.H. 815 (April, A.D. 1412), and began his reign, as usual, by striking the currency in his own name[329].

In the first year of his government, Khizer Khan deputed *Malik Topha* with an army towards Katihr, which place he reduced. *Narsingh Rai* was driven to the mountains, but upon paying a ransom, we again put in possession of his country. *Mahobat Khan,* governor of *Budaun,* at the same time came to meet Malik Topha, and professed allegiance. The Wazir now marched towards Ganpur, Kampillia and *Chandwar,* to levy the revenue which had been due for some years; and after recovering *Jalisar* out of the hands of the Rajputs of *Chandwar*, he marched to Etawa, and having reduced it, returned to Delhi[330].

In the year A.H. 821 (A.D. 1418), Khizer Khan having sent his minister against *Narsingh Rai*, the Raja of Katihr, he plundered and laid waste that district and proceeding to Badaun, crossed the river at Etawa, on which place he imposed a contribution, and returned to Delhi. Khizer Khan, subsequently marched in person to *Katihr,* and on his route he attached and defeated a for mindable band of plunderers at Kole, he then crossed the Ganges and having laid waste the country of Sambhal and *Katihr,* returned to his capital. After remaining at Delhi only few days, he moved towards Badaun, Mahobat Khan, governor of Badaun, alarmed at his approach, shut himself up in the fort, to which the king laid siege for six months. In the course of the operations, Khizer Khan discovered that Kauam Khan, Yikhtyar Khan Lodi, and several of the old friends of the late king, Mahmud Tughluq, had formed a conspiracy against his life. This circumstance induced him to raise the siege of Badaun, and to retire to Delhi, where on the 20th of Jamad-ul-Aval-A.H. 822 (July 18, A.D. 1419), having assembled the conspirators, he caused the household troops to fall upon them and put them to death[331].

In the year A.H. 824 (A.D. 1421), Khizer Khan marched towards Mewat, taking and destroying the fort of Kotla. In this year, also, the Wazir dying, that office was conferred on his son, *Malik Sikandar Topha.* From *Kotla*, Khizer Khan marched towards Gowliar, where he raised contributions and returned to Etawa, Khizer Khan, falling sick during this campaign, returned to Delhi, where he died on the 17th of Jamad-ul-Awal A.H. 824 (May 20, A.D. 1421), after a reign of seven years and a few month[332]. After this the nobles, having assembled, consented to elevate Mubarik, the son of Khizer Khan, to the throne the circumstance of Khizer Khan not having assumed the title of King, and the fact of the nobles assembling to elect his son Mubarik to the throne, at once be speak the power to which aristocracy had attained over despotism, and proves by how precarious a tenour the prince hold his throne[333]. In the same, he received advices the Jasrath, the brother of *Sheikha Khokhar* (*Gakhkar*) (Who had the preceding year defeated and captive Ali Shah, King of *Kashmir*[334], on his return from an expedition againt *Tatta*) presuming on his success, had come to the resolution to attempt the throne of Delhi. For this purpose Jasrath *Gakkar* (Khokkhar) invited Malik Tughan, who had fled to the mountains, to join him, and he appointed him Amir-ul-Umra, or general in-chief of his troops. Their first operations were directed against Panjab; and having seized Lahore, they secured the person of Zirak Khan, governor of Jalandhar, which they also took and subsequently besieged Islam Khan in the for of Sarhind. Syed Mubarik, in spite of the rainy season, which was then at its height, marched from Delhi, but on his approaching Sarhind, he founded Jasrath Khokkar had raised the siege and retreated to Ludhiana; here, Zirak Khan contrived to effect his escape, and joined the King. The Delhi army now advanced towards Ludhaian, where they perceived Jasrath Gakkhar encamped on the opposite bank. He had secured all the boats on the river, a circumstance which obliged the King to helt at Kabbulpur till the stream became fordable. On the 11th of Shaval A.H. 824 (Oct. 8, A.D. 1421). Malik Sikandar (the Wazir), Zirak Khan, Mahmud Hassan, Malik Kalu, and other chiefs, forded the river and the King himself following with the main body of the army, Jasrath Khokkar and his troops were thrown into confusion, and eventually put to flight. The King's forces pursued the enemy closely slaying vast numbers, and capturing all their baggage[335].

After this vulnerable defeat, Jasrath, having crossed the Chenab, took refuge in the mountains, and Rai Bhim, Raja of Jammu, directing the King's army to Bisal, a strong fort into which Jasrath Khokkar had thrown himself, the latter again fled; but his followers were pursued with great slaughter. Meanwhile, in the month of Muharram, A.H. 825 (January, A.D. 1422), the King, having marched to Lahore, ordered the ruined palaces and fortifications to be repaired and appointing Mahmud Hassan governor, returned to Delhi. He had scarcely reached his capital with Jasrath Khokkhar, collecting his scattered forces, took the field again, and invested Khore for the five months; but failing in his attempt, he raised the siege, retired to Kallanure, and attacked Rai Bhim, Raja of Jammu, for having betrayed his retreat to the King. On this occasion, *Jasrath Gakhkar* or *Khokkars,* being unsuccessful, retired to the banks of *Bias,* in order to refresh and to recruit his army.Meanwhile, Malik Sikandar, the Wazir, having been seen to reinforce Lahore, was joined by Malik Rajab, governor of Dipalpur, and by Islam Khan, governor of *Sarhind.* With these troops the Wazir marched against Jasrath, and compelled him to recross the Ravi and Chenab, and to take shelter again among the mountains. The Wazir marched along the Ravi to Kallanuri, and being joined on the frontiers of Jammu by Rai Bhim; that Prince acted as guide to the Delhi troops, so that many of the Gakhkars or *Khokkhars,* who were concealed, were discovered, and put to the sword, after which the Wazir return to Lahore. These successes induced the king to appoint the Wazir Malik Sikandar Topha, viceroy of Lahore and to recall Mahmud Hassan. In the year, A.H. 836 (A.D. 1422), the King deprived Malik Sikandar of the office of Wazir, and conferred it on Sarwar-ul-Mulk, whom he sent with an army against the Hindus of Katihr, in order to compel them to pay the ususal tribute. The King, at this time, effected an accommodation with Mahobat Khan, governor of Badaun, and intrusted him with a commission against the tribe of Rathore Rajputs, whose country was plundered, and some of whom were made prisoners. The Raja of Etawa, alarmed at these measures, withdrew. Suddenly from the royal camp. Mubarik pursued, and besieged the Raja in Etawa; but at length terms were concluded with him, and the Raja's son was delivered as a hostage for his father's furture good conduct into the King's hands, after which he returned to Delhi.

Mahmud Hassan, about this time, was appointed Bakhshi of the forces, which office in those days was styled *Avizi.* Jasrath Khokkar, unsubdued by his misfortunes again appeared in the field; and having defeated and slain Rai Bhim of Jammu, raised an army of nearly 12,000 Khokkar with which he again made war on the kingdom of Delhi. In the year A.H. 827 (A.D. 1423), he ravaged the countries of Lahore and Dipalpur, and acquired considerable booty: Mulik Sikandar Topha, the governor, advanced against him; but rather than risk a battle, Jasrat retired with his spoils to the hills, where he continued to recruit his army for another campaign. Meanwhile, Jasrath Khokkar formed an alliance with Amir Sheikh Ali, a Moghl chieftain in the service of Sharokh Mirza, governor of Kabul; and prevailed on him to make an incursion into the territories of Siestan, Bhukkor, and Tatta, by way of creating a diversion, in order that, by drawing off the King's forces from the capital, for the defence of Sind, his own views on Delhi must be faciliated. Malik Ali-ul-Mulk, governor, of Multan, dying about the same time that the news of Amir Sheikh Ali's incursion was received, the King detached Mallik Mohmud Hassan with the army to Multan. Sultan Hushang, King of Malwa, also in the same year invested Gowaliar, so that the King was obliged to send all his troops to his frontiers. The King marched in person into Malwa, levying contributions, on his route, from Amir Khan, the son of Wahid Khan, governor of Biana.

Sultan Hushang of Malwa secured the usual fords of the Chambal; but the King, having discovered others, crossed the river, and attacking Sultan Hushang in his camp, defeated his river and attacking Sultan Hushang in his camp, defeated his army, took many prisoners, and a part of his baggage. The prisoners, being chiefly Mahomedans, were released; and Sultan Hushang, thinking it advisable to compound matters by paying a sum of money to the King of Delhi, was permitted to withdraw without molestation towards Dhar. The King of Delhi remained for some time in the vicinity of Gowliar to levy. contributions upon the neighbouring Hindu chiefs, and returned in the month of Rojab, A.H. 827 (June, A D. 1423), to his capital.

Next year A.H. 828 (A.D. 1424), the King moved towards Kotihr, and was met by Narsingh Rai who came to the banks of the Ganges to pay his respects; but as he had not settled the revenues of his territory for three years, he was detained in camp for a few days, till his accounts wee adjusted, and then released. The King, having crossed the Ganges, reduced some factious tributary chiefs, and returned to Delhi; but not remaining there many days, he marched towards Mewat, from whence he expelled some insurgents, and ravaging their country, returned to this capital; when having permitted his officers to retire to their estates with their troops, he abandoned himself to dissipation. The Mewatties, rendered desperate by the King's conduct towards them, took revenge on the neighbouring districts.

In the year A.H. 829(A.D. 1425), therefore, the King, collecting troops, marched to punish them. On this approach, Jallu and Kadru,[336] the grandson of Bahudar Nahir Mewatti, retreated to the hills of Alwar, and defended the passes with much obstinacy; but being eventually reduced to great distress, they surrendered, and were imprisoned.

The repeated attacks on the Mewatties did not render them peaceable. In the year A.H. 830(A.D. 1426), the King, after a lapse of four months, was again obliged to send troops against them, who carried fire and sword through their whole country. The King now proceeded as far as Biana, where he found that Amir Khan, the governor, was dead; and that his brother Mohumed Khan, assuming independence, had shut himself up in the desertion of part of the garrison. Mahumed Khan surrendered at discretion. The King delivered over the change of the city to Mokbil Khan and sent Mahomed Khan and his family to Delhi. After which, making Malik Kher-ud-Din Topha governor of Seekri (known now by the name of Fattehpoor), the King marched to Goaliar, and received the tribute from the Raja. At this time Malik Mahmud Hassan was recalled from Multan and placed in charge of Hissar Feroza, while Malik Rajab Nadiri succeeded to the charge of Multan.

Meanwhile Mahamed Khan of Biana effected his escape with his family to Mewat, and collecting a considerable force, recovered the city of Biana, in the absence of the King's governor, Mokbil Khan, who had gone on an expedition to Mahawan. Malik Mubariz was now appointed to Biana, with orders to expel Mahomed Khan. The latter retiring into the fort, Malik Mubariz took possession of the country, but after a few days' siege, Mahommed Khan, intrusting the defence of the place to some trusty followers, escaped, and joined Ibrahim Shah Sharki of Jaunpur, who was then advancing with an army against Kalpi.

Kadir Khan, the ruler of Kalpi, on this occasion, sent expresses to Delhi for succours, and the King took the field in person. On reaching Atraoli he detached Malik Mahmud Hassan, with 10,000 horse, to intercept Mokhlis Khan, the brother of Ibrahim Shah Shorki who was on his march to reduce Etawa. This detachment, encountering Mokhlis Khan, compelled him to fall back on his brother, and Mallik Mahmud Kassan rejoined the Delhi army, Ibrahim Shah Shurki, meanwhile, advanced along the banks of the Kali Nia[337] to Burhanabad, from thence to the village of Raberi, while theKing, Mubarik, moved by Atraoli to Malikota. The two armies marched parallel to each other till they arrived on the banks of the river. The King of Delhi having crossed the Yumna near Chondwara, encamped within ten miles of the enemy. Both armies remained in their trenches for the space of 22 days, during which time slight skirmishes only took place. Ibrahim Shah Shurki however, upon the 7th of Jumad-us-Sani (March 21), marched out of his camp and offered battle. The King of Delhi declined exposing his own person, but put his troops under the command of his wizier, Sarvar-ul-Mulk, who, with Syad Salim. Syad-us-Sadat, was directed to engage the enemy. The action commenced with great fury at noon, and night only parted the combatants, both armies retiring to their respective encampments. Ibrahim Shah, however, marching off on thenext morning towards Junpur, left Mubarik to claim the victory. The latter, satisfied with this nominal advantae, moved towards Gowaliar, having crossed the Chambal at Hulkant. After receiving the usual tribute, he moved in the direction of Biana, into which place Mohamed Khan Ahdu had again thrown himself after the battle. On this occasion, Mahomed Khan made a brave defence, but was obliged to capitulate, and had leave to go whithersover he chose. Malik Mahmud Hasan was left in the government of Byana, and, on the 15th of Shaban, A.H. 831 (May 29, A.D., 1427), Mubarik returned to Delhi. He there seized Malik Kadru Mewatt, who had joined Ibrahim Shah Shurki in the late war, and ordered him to be put to death, and Malik Sarvar-ul-Mulk was sent to occupy Mewat; but the inhabitants, deserting the towns, fled to the mountains. Jalal[338] Khan Mewatti the brother of Malik Kadru, together with Ahmud Khan, and Mullik Fakhr-ud-Din collected a force within the fort of Alwar, and defended it so bravely, that Malik Sarvar-ul-Mulk was content to receive a contribution from them, and to return to Delhi.

In the month of Zukad, A.H. 831 (Sept., A.D. 1427), the King received advices, that Jasrat Khokkhar had besieged Kallanore, and had, morever, defeated Malik Sikandar in the field, and compelled him to fall back on Lahore. Orders were accordingly sent to Ziarak Khan, governor of *Samana,* and to Islam Khan, governor of Sarhind, to reinforce Malik Sikandar; but before their arrival, the latter had obtained assistance from the Raja of Kallanore, and not only defeated Jasrat Khokkhar in turn, but deprived him of all the plunder he had acquired in that province.

In the month of Moharrum, in the year A.H. 832 (Feb., A.D. 1428), the King marched to Mewat, and entirely subdued that country, obliging the inhabitants to pay him tribute. Advices at this time reached Delhi of the death of Malik Rajab Nadiri governor of Multan, when the title of Imad-ul-Mulk was conferred on Malik Mahmud Hassan (who had settled the affairs of Biana), and he was nominated to the government of Multan. The King, in the following year A.H. 833 (A.D. 1429), proceeded towards Gaoliar, on the route to which place he required the payment of tribute from the Raja of Halkant, who unable to satisfy the demand, fled to the mountains, while his country was laid waste and his subjects carried off as prisoners and slaves to Dehli. The King then led his army towards Raberi, and having wrested that country from the son of Hussain Khan Mewatt, gave it over in charge to Malik Hamza. Syad Salim dying on the march back to Delhi his eldest son received the title of Syad Khan, and the youngest that of Shujaa-ul-Mulk. They were allowed also to retain the wealth their father had collected during 30 yers of power, amounting to a sum supposed to be equal to the private coffers of the King himself, and which, according to the custom of Hindustan, might have become the property of the crown. These indulgences, however, did not secure the fidelity of the sons of Syud Salim, who sent one Folad, a Turki slave, to Surhind, to stir up an insurrection, privately, in their name. They had formed hopes, it seems, that they might be sent with a force to suppress the rebellion, and thus have an opportunity to join the insurgents; but the plot being discovered, both these chiefs were imprisoned, and Malik Yusuf and Rai Hubbu were sent to Sarhind, to resume their estates, and to suppress, the disturbances.

Folad, entering into negotation with the Delhi[339] chiefs, lulled them into security, and sallying one night from his fort, attempted to surprise their camp. He was so warmly received by the King's troops, that the attack altogether failed; but this circumstance did not deter; Folad from making another attack on the following night, supported by a heavy fire from the works; on which occasion, the Delhi troops fled panic-struck, leaving their camp standing. On receiving intimation of this disaster, the King marched from Delhi in person. The rebel daily gathered strength; and the King in the year A.H. 833 (A.D. 1429), was induced to direct Imad-ul-Mulk from Multan, and several other governors, to proceed to Sarhind. The reinforcements having joined, the King remained on the Sursutti river, and detached the greatest part of his army to invest the fort of Sarhind. The rebel Folad now sent a message to the King, saying, that if Imad-ul-Mulk were sent to him, with a promise of pardon, he would deliver up the place. This measure was acceded to on the King's part; and Folad having met Imad-ul-Mulk without the gate was assured to the King's pardon, and promised, on his part, to surrender the fort of Sarhind on the next day. One of Imad-ul-Mulk's attendants, being acquainted with Folad, hinted to him privately, that though Imad-ul-Mulk was a man of honour, and would certainly adhere to his promise, yet the King might not be so scrupulous. Folad's suspicions were raised, and having abundance both of money and supplies in the place, he determined to hold out to the last.

The King, finding the reduction of the place would occupy time, and thinking so large an army unnecessary for the siege, permitted Imad-ool-Moolk to return to his government of Mooltan; and leaving Islam Khan Lodi, Kali Khan, and Rai Feroze, with some Amir Jadida, to conduct the siege, the King retired to Delhi (A.H. 833, A.D. 1429). Folad held out six months: he was greatly distressed; and saw no means of extricating himself but by an alliance with Amir Sheikh Ali governor of Kabul, on the part of Sharokh Mirza. He accordingly despatched messengers to him, soliciting his assistance. The King had taken no pains to keep on good terms with the neighbouring Mongal, who was induced to quit Kabul to aid Folad. He was joined by the Gakhkars on crossing the Bias, and ravaged the country of those chiefs who held estates in the Panjab, and who were conducting the siege of Sarhind. Amir Sheikh Ali advanced to Sarhind, and compelled the royal army to decamp. Folad remunerated his ally with a sum equal to two laks of tunkas, and made him presents besides. He also placed in his hands his family, and by strengthening the fortifications of sarhind, and laying in provisions and ammunition, prepared for another siege. Amir Sheikh Ali, recrossing the Satluj, committed vast depredatins in the Panjab realising by plunder one hundred-fold beyond the value of what he had received from Folad. On reaching Lahore, he imposed a contribution of one year's revenue on Mullik Sikandar Topha. From Lahore he proceeded towards Dipalpur, desolating that country also; insomuch that 40,000 Hindus were computed to have been massacred, besides a great number carried away prisoners. Imad-ul-Malik, the governor, posted himself in ambush to surprise Ameer Sheikh Ali at Tulamba, but he avoided the ambuscade by going to Khatbpur: meanwhile Imad-ul-Mulk received the King's orders to return, for the protection of Multan. This movement encouraged the enemy to march along the Ravi and to lay waste the country to within two coss of the city of Multan; wehre Amir Sheikh Ali defeated Imad-ul-Mulk, who endeavoured to arrest his progress. From thence the Moguls advanced to Khirabad, within six miles of Multan, and on the next day, being the 4th of Ramzan A.H. 833 (May 29 A.D. 1430) made an unsuccessful assault on the place; but they continued the siege, and committed daily depredations, putting all whom they met to the sword.

The King, informed of these transactions, sent Fatteh Khan, son of Muzaffar Khan Guzaratti with other nobles of distinction, to reinforce Imal-ul-Mulk, on which he marched out, and offered battle to Amir Sheikh Ali. A sanguinary engagement ensued, in the commencemtn of which the Moguls gained some advantage; but after the death of Fatteh Khan of Gujerat, the King's troops, inspired with revenge, fought more desperately, and gained the victory. Amir Sheikh Ali was totally defeated; and having lost all his plunder, escaped with a few attendants only to Kabul; his whole army being either killed or drowned in the Jhelum in their attempt to escape. Imad-ul-Malk pursued the fugitives to Shewar, and returned to Multan, while the nobles whohad come to his aid repaired, by the King's orders, to Delhi. Soon after this event, the King becoming jealous of the popularity of Imad-ul-Mulk at Multan, recalled him to court. Jasrat Khokkhars taking advantage of his absence, crossed the Jhelum, the Ravi, and the Bias and attacked Malik Sikandar Topha near Jalandhar, whom he defeated and made prisoner, together with all his treasure and baggage. Jasrath Khokkar now advanced and laid siege toLahore. Amir Sheikh Ali was also instgiated by Jasarth to make another incursion into Multan, and having taken Tulamba by capitulation, he broke his pledge, plundered the place, and put to death all the men able to bear arms;he also burned the town, and carried the wives and children of the inhabitants into captivity.

Folad of Sarhind, taking advantage of these events, marched out of his fort and invading the country of Rai Feroze, defeated and slew him. On the Ist of Jamad-ul-Awal, A.H. 835 (Jan. 3 A.D. 1432), theKing therefore, took the route of Lahore. Mallik-Sarvar-ul-Malk was a second time appointed governor, and received the command of the advance guard of his army. The arriving at Samana raised the siege of Lahore, and retreated to the hills: Amir Sheikh Ali fell back on Kabul; and Folad again shut himself up in Sarhind. The King deprived the Wazir of the government of Lahore a second time, and nominated Nusrat Khan Gurgandaz[340] to the office,himself encamping near Panipat. on the banks of the Yumna. From hence he sent Imad-ul-Malk, with a part of the army, to suppress some insurections about Gowaliar, while the Wazir, Sarvar-ul-Malk, being left to besiege Sarhind, the King returned to Delhi.

In the month of Zihuj (August) Jasrath Khokkar advanced again to Lahore; and having commenced hostilities against Nusrat Khan, the King was induced, in the year, A.H. 836 (A.D. 1433) to march from Delhi as far as Samana. Intelligence was brought to him at that place of the death of his mother, Mukdama Jehan, when he immediately returned with a few attendants to the capital, and fater performing the funeral obsequies rejoined his army. After his arrival in the camp he suddenly marched towards Mewat, conferring the government of Lahore upon Malik Allla-dad-Lodhi who promised to expel Jasrath. The Gakhkar chief on hearing of the King's return, and being joined by a large body of his tribe, was enabled to defeat Alla-dad-Lodhi before he reached Lahore.

In the year A.H. 836 (A.D. 1433), the King having received the news of this disaster, and also that Amir Sheikh Ali was coming towards Sarhind, again took the route of Panjab, sending before him Imad-ul-Malik to reinforce the army, besieging Sarhind. On the approach of Imad-ul-Malk, Amir Sheikh Alli who had formerly sustained a defeat from him, laid aside his intentions of coming to Sarhind, and retreated by forced marches towards Lahore, which he surprised. Hearing, however, the King had reached Tulamba, Amir Sheikh Alli left a garrison of 2000 men in Lahore, and retreated to Kabul, ravaging the countyr on his route, and leaving his nephew Muzaffar Khan in the fort of Shewar. Malik Sikandar Topha, who had procured his release out of the hands of Jasrath by the payment of a large sum of money, was reinstated by the King in the government of Lahore, Dipalpur, and Jalandhar; upon which he advanced and laid seige to Lahore, which surrendered by capitulation and the garrison was permitted to retire to Kabul. The King now crossed the Ravi near Tulamba, and invested Shewar. Muzaffar Khan defended the place for a whole month; but being hard pressed, he capitulated and moreoer, gave his daughter to the King and paid a large ransom for his liberty. The King left a part of his army at Dipalpur, and with a select body proceeded in person to Multan, where he visited the tombs of the saints. From thence he returned in a few days to his camp. At this time he divested Malik Sikandar Topha of the government of Lahore, and giving it to Imad-ul-Malk, returned to Delhi. Being jealous of the power of the Wazir, Malik Sarvar-ul-Malk, the King united Kali Khan with him in the office of Wazir and the latter being a man of superior abilities soon gained the favour of his sovereign and the good will of the people.

Malik Sarvar-ul-Mulk, dissatisfied with this arrangement gained over Sadanand, the son of Gangu Kutri, Miran Sudar deputy to the chief secretary, Kazi Abd-us-Samad, and others, who watched an opportunity for assassinating the King. At this time (Rubbi-ul-Ula 17 A.H. 839, Oct. 10, A.D. 1435), the King ordered a city to be founded on the banks of the Yumna, and called it Mubarikabad, and made an excursion towards Sarhind, in order to take the diversion of the chase. On the way, he received advice that Sarhind was taken, and the head of the rebel. Folad was presented to him, after which the King returned to the new city. Here he gained intelligence that war had broken out between Ibrahim Shah Shurki and Sultan Hushung of Malwa, whose armies were then near Kalpa. This information promised to afford the King an opportunity of expelling Ibrahim Shah Sharki from his dominions; he accordingly gave orders to collect his army, and caused his tents to be pitched outside the city of Delhi. A few days elapsed in the necessary organisation of his forces, during which time the King continued to visit the new works: he was, however, littel apprehensive of the event which soon after took place, never having given offence to his nobility, except in changing or removing them from their governments when they misbehaved.

On the 9th of the month of Rajab, in the year A.H. 839 (Jan 28, A.D. 1435), according to custom, he went to worship at a mosquel lately built in the new city, with only a few attendants. On which occasion, Miran Sudar and Kazi Abd-us-Samad, with a band of Hindus clothed in armour, entered the mosque; while Sadanand, the son of Gangu Kotri, with another party of Hindus, kept guard without, to prevent people from either going in or coming out. Although the King perceived the conspirators were in armour, he took no immediate notice of them; till at length Sidpal, one of the Hindus, drawing his sword, rushed on him and the rest following his example, they basely murdered this worthy and excellent Prince. Miran Sudar, instantly quitting the spot, repaired to the house of the Wazir, and acquainted him, according to agreement, with what had happened; and Survarul-Mulk, who had previously arranged matters with Mahomed, one of the grandsons of Khizer Khan, raised that Prince to the throne.

Syad Mubarik[341] reigned 13 years, three months and 16 days. He was esteemed a man of good talents, and on most occasions just and benevolent. His temper was so equal, that it is notorious he never spoke in anger to any person during his life. The *Towarikh Mubarik Shahi* was written to commemorate the events of his reign.

Sayyad Mahommed

According to the practice of the Universe, which cannot subsist without order; on the same day which gave to Mubarik his death wound, his son, the Prince Mahommed, was seated on the throne. The ungrateful assasin, Sarvar-ul-Malk, Wazier, received the title of Khan Jahan; and having secured the King's treasure, the regalia, and other effects, he dismissed all the old ministers from office and appointed new ones, more suited to his views.

In the year A.H. 839 (A.D. 1435), Kali Khan, the deputy Wazir, and other chiefs in the camp, called a council, on hearing of the King's death, and resolved, rather than incur the horrors of civil war, for the present to submit to the new King, and to wait for a more favourable opportunity of taking revenge on the conspirators; so they accordingly came into the city, and paid their respects to Syed Mahomed. The first preferment which was made, in order to promote the Wazir's views, was the elevation of the Hindu conspirators. Sadanand and Sidpal were raised to the government of Biana, Amroha, Narnoul and Kohram and other pergunas in the Duab: Niran Sudar was dignified with the title of Moyin-ul-Mulk, and received a considerable jagir. The son of Syad Salim was enabled by the title of Khan-Azim to him; while the officers of the late King were persecuted, and some even lost their lives under false pretences.

On the 12th of Rajab, A.H. 839 (Jan. 31, A.D., 1435), one Ranu, a slave of the Wazir, being nominated collector of the revenues of Biana, endeavoured to obtain possession of the Fort, but Yusuf Khan Lodhi opposed and slew him. At the same time, also, some of nobles of the late reign, who had served under Khizar Khan, perceied a design to deprive them of their jageers; and the following chiefs, Mulik Juman, governor of Budaun; Mulik Ala-dad Lodhi, governor of Sambhol; Meir Ali Guzeratti and Amir Khan Turk, combined and went into open rebllion. Malik Sarvar-ul-Malk, deceived by the behaviour of his deputy, Kali Khan, intrusted him with the command of the army to suppress the revolt and Syeed Khan, Sadanand, and the Wazir's son, Yusuf-Khan, went along with him. On arriving at the village of Birrun, Kali Khan, who had resolved to take revenge on Sudanand, and Yusuf Khan, for the murder of the King, informed Malik Alla-dad-Lodhi of his intention. The latter, therefore, made no movement to oppose the royalists. Kali Khan's design, however, became known to the *Wazir*, who sent Malik Hushyar, one of his own slaves, with an additional force, as if to reinforce Kali Khan, but in reality with secret instructions to watch his motions (A.H. 839, A.D. 1435). Kali Khan, however united his forces with those of Malik Alla-dad-Lodhi previously to the arrival of Malik Hushyar, who was in consequence deterred from approaching and Yusuf Khan and Sadanand fled to Delhi. Kal Khan, together with the malcontents, now marched to Delhi which they reached on the last day of Ramzan (Ramzan 30, April 15).

In this dilemma, the Wazir, Sarvur-ul-Mulk, took post in the citadel of siri wherein he stood a siege for three months; but the party of Kali Khan daily gaining new partisans, the Wazir was reduced to the last distress. The King also perceiving that his own affairs would be ruined if he adhered to the Wazir, opened negotiations with the besiegers, and only waited an opportunity either of making his escape, or of cutting off his minister. The Wazir, discovered the plot and determined to anticipate the King's intentions; accordingly, on the 8th of Moharrum. A.H. 840 (July 23. A.D. 1436). Sarvar-ul-Mulk, aided by the sons of Miran Sudar and some of his followers, broke into the royal apartments with drawn swords, in order to put the King to death. The latter, having intimation of their design placed a guard in readiness to counteract their project, which on a concerted signal, rushed out on the conspirators, who took to flight. The Wazir, Survar-ul-Mulk, was cut to pieces as he was passing the door; and the sons of Miran Sudar with the rest of the assassins, being afterwards taken, were also slain, while Malik Hushyar and Malik Mubarik, who were concerned in the plot, were publicly executed. The Kutries, and other adherents of the Wazir, apprehensive of the King's vengeance, rose in the arms, and compelled him to defend the palace. Thus situated, he caused the Bagdad gate to be thrown open to the besiegers, who rushing in, committed a dreadful slaughter on the rebels, till they were entirely subdued; while such as were taken alive were bound hands and feet and sacrificed at the tomb of the late Syed Mubarik. Kali Khan and the other chiefs took the oath of allegiance on the next day, a second time to Syed Mahommed, when the office of vizier was conferred on Kali Khan, with the title of Kamal Khan; and Malik Jumun, receiving the title of Ghazi Malik, was gratified with a Jagar. Malik Alla-dad-Lodhi refused a title for himself, but begged that of Daria Khan might be conferred on his brother; and the rest of the nobles were confirmed in their several offices. Peace being restored at Delhi, the King, by the advice of his counsellors, made a campaign towards Multan, and encamping near Mubarikabad, gave orders to collect his army from all the neighbouring provinces. Many of the chiefs being intimidated, delayed to repair to head-quarters, till Imad-ul-Malik, arriving from Multan, aided by his power and influence the royal authority, and shortly after the other provincial governors joined the camp, and were honoured with dresses, and other marks of favour. The King now proceeded towards Multan; and marching for some time at the head of his troops, visited the tombs of the saints at Ajudhun, and returned to his capital.

In the same year (A.H. 840) the King marched towards Samana, and detached a portion of the army against Jasrath Kokkar whose country was given over to plunder, after which the King returned to Delhi. There he abandoned himself to pleasue, and totally neglected the affairs of his government. This conduct soon affected the administration of affairs, discontent pervaded every quarter, and an insurrection broke out in Multan among who after the death of his uncle, Islam Khan Lodhi[342] had usurped the government of Sarhind, took possession of Lahore, Dipalpur, and all the country as far south as Panipat. The King receiving intelligence of these events, sent his whole army against Bahlole, who was driven into the hills, and many chiefs of distinction fell in their retreat. Bahlol Lodhi however, recruiting his army after the royal forces had withdrawn, retook possession of the countries from whence he had been expelled. The King, on this occasion, sent Hissam Khan, the Wazir deputy, against him; but he was defeated, and compelled to retreat to Delhi; on which Bahlole Lodhi wrote to the King, that if he would put Hissam Khan to death, who by his intrigues had been the cause of his rebellion, he would lay down his arms.

The King was so weak as to listen to this arrogant proposal, and accordingly gave orders for the death of Hissam Khan. He also deprived Kamal-ul-Mulk of the office of Wazir, and conferring it on Humid Khan, appointed a deputy with the title of Hissam Khan. The governors of the provinces, perceiving the King's imbecile conduct, predicted his downfall, and endeavoured to secure their own independence. The farmers and *zemindars*, foreseeing the convulsions that were likely to ensue, withheld the revenues, in hopes of retaining them in the general confusion. The state of affairs was favourable for the encroachments of the neighbouring princes; and Ibrahim Shah Shorki accordingly seized on several districts adjoining to his dominions, while Sultan Mahmud Khilji King of Malwa, making an attempt on Delhi, in the year A.H. 844 (A.D. 1440), advanced within two coss of the city. Syad Mahommed, panic-struck, sent an embassy to Bahlole Lodhi, entreating his assistance; and he accordingly marched to the capital with 20,000 horsemen arrayed in armour. Though the King's army was greatly superior to the enemy, he refused to take the field; but giving over the charge of it to his officers, himself remained in the palace.

Sultan Mahmud Khilji, on understanding that the King of Delhi was not present with his army, thought his absence was intended as an affront, and in order to resent it he gave the command of his own troops to his sons Ghaias-ud-Din, and Kaddar Khan. The armies of Delhi and Malwa having engaged, the troops of the former gave way, leaving Bahlole Khan Lodhi's division alone to dispute the field, which he maintained with determined resolution, till the fugitives, ashamed of their conduct, returned to the action. Night, however, coming on, the victory remained undecided. It is stated that Sultan Mahmud Khilji was alarmed by a dream on that night and hearing on the following morning that Ahmud Shah Gujaratti was advancing against Manda became desirous of concluding a peace, though shame prevented him from making the first overtures. At the same time, Sayad Mahommed, with less reason, and contrary to the advice of his ministers, gave himself up to fear, and sent ambassadors with presents to his rival proposing terms.

Sultan Mahmud Khalji, overjoyed at these overtures, hastened the accommodation and quitting Delhi left the field. Bahlole Lodhi[343] whose contempt for his sovereign was now complete, boldly aspired to the throne, and marching out of the city with his own troops in pursuit of Sultan Mahmud of Malwa, attacked and defeated him, and took all his baggage: for which service Syad Mahommed, unsuspicious of his designs, conferred on him the title of Khan Jehan, and even adopted him as his son.

In the year A.H. 845 (A.D. 1441), the King marched to Samana, and confirming Bahlole Lodhi in the government of Lahore and Dipalpur, which he had usurped, authorised him to attack Jasrath Khokkar. These substantial marks of the King's favour strengthened the hands of Bahlole, who having added considerably to his army by numerous bodies of Afghans, instead of attacking Jasrath Kokkhar gained him over to his views, and seized against Delhi, he besieged it for some months, but for the present was obliged to abandon his enterprise.

The King's power decaying rapidly, the *Zemindars* of Biana placed themselves under the government of Sultan Mahomed Khalji of Malwa; and Sayad Mahommed falling sick, he died a natural death in the year A.H. 849 (A.D. 1445), leaving behind him the character of a weak and dissolute prince. He reigned 12 years and some months, and his son Alla-ud-Din succeeded him on the throne.

Syad Alla-ud-Din

Alla-ud-din, the son of Syad Mahommed, ascended the throne on the demise of his father, and all the chieftains, excepting Bahlole Lodhi took the oath of allegiance. The new King, however, was in no condition to resent this mark of contempt; but having collected an army in the beginning of the year A.H. 850 (A.D.

1446), he marched to recover Biana. While on his route, he received advices that Ibrahim Shah Shurky was advancing towards Delhi, which, though false, brought the King back to his acting on so vague a report; but he observation brought upon the Wazir the displeasure of his master.

This step at once proved fatal to the King's reputation; and the meanest of the people did not hesitate to say publicly, that he was a weaker man than his father. On the following year (A.H. 851, A.D. 1447), he marched to Budaun, where he remained some time employed in laying out gardens, building pleasure houses, and making entertainments. Fancying the air of Buddaun agreed better with his health, he expressed an inclination to make that city his residence, from which the Wazir endeavoured in vain to divert him.

Hindustan was, at this period, divided into separate principalities. The Deccan, Gujarat, Malwa, Junpur, and Bengal had each its independent King. Punjab, Dipalpur, and Sarhind, as far south as Panipat, formed the territory of Bahlole Khan Lodhi; Mehrawal and the country within seven coss of Delhi as far as the Serai Lado, was in the hands of Ahmud Khan Mewatti, Sambhal, even to the suburbs of Dehly, was occupied by Dariya Khan Lodhi; Kole Jalisar in the Duab, by Eesa Khan Turk, and Raberi and its dependencies by Kutab Khan Afghan; Kampila and Pattiali by Raja Partap Singh and Biana by Dawood Khan Lodi; so that the city of Delhi, with a very small tract of country, alone belonged to the King[344].

Bahlole Lodi, about this time, made another attempt upon the capital, but was not more successful than before. The King, as soon as relieved from this danger, began to consider of the means to recover part of his lost empire, and held a consultation with Kutab Khan, Eesa Khan and Partap Rai. These chiefs, were disgusted with his Wazir, Humeid Khan; and that if he were removed from office, and imprisoned they were ready to support him, and did not doubt that the affairs of his government would assume a more favourable aspect. Syad Ala-ud-Din, becoming the dupe of those traitors, imprisoned and disgraced the minister, and immediately ordered preparations for removing the court of Budaun; from which not all the remonstrances of his best friends could restain him, though they represented, in a strong light, how impolitic it was, at such a juncutre, to quit Dehli.

Ala-ud-Din, accordingly, in the year A.H. 852 (A.D. 1448), marched to Budaun, leaving Hissam Khan in the government of Delhi when he arrived at his new capital, Kutab Khan and Partap Rai waiting on the King, represented that as long as the Wazir was alive, the chiefs could not be induced to trust themselves at court. The King was thus prevailed on to order the Wazir's death; but the Wazir's brother, having discovered his intention, found means, with the assistance of some of his friends, to release Humed Khan who escaped to Delhi. There to took possession of all the kings effects, and sent the females of the royal household out of the city.

Alla-ud-Din deferring, by frivolours delays and excuses of weather and unlucky days, his march to Delhi, allowed time for the Wazir to invite Baheole Lodhi to assume the government Baheole, seizing the opportunity, amused the King by writing to him that he was on his march to chastise the Wazir; but having arrived he quietly took possession of the capital, and was proclasimed King.

This event occurred in the year A.H. 854 (A.D. 1450); though the name of Alla-ud-Din was for form's sake, allowed to be read in the Qutab as usual. Bahlole leaving his son, Khwaja Bayezid, in Delhi marched in person to Dipalpur, to organize at his convenience, his Afghan army. While thus engged, he wrote to Alla-ud-Din, that his only motive for securing the capital was to expel the Wazir. To this letter he received for answer, that the King having adopted Bahlole as his son, he (Alla-ud-Din) should ever esteem him as his brother; and formally abdicated the throne in his favour, on condition of his being permitted to reside quietly in possession of Budaun. ahole Lodhi from that hour rejected the name of Syad Allaud-Din from the Khutba and publicly assumed all the insignia of royalty. Alla-ud-Din remained at Budaun unmolested till his death. which happened in the year 883 (A.D. 1478): his reign in Delhi being seven yeras, and his retirement at Budaun nearly 28.

FIFTH DYNASTY OF THE KINGS OF DELHI
And First of the Race of Afghan, Entitled Lodhi

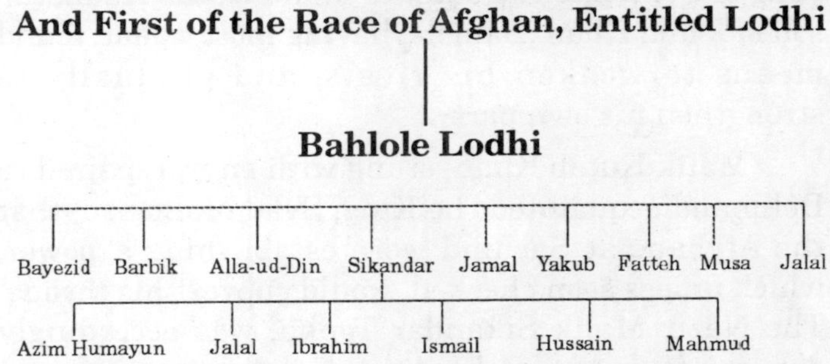

Bahlole Lodhi Afghan

It is related that in early times the tribe of Afghans, forming themselves into a commercial community, carried on trade between Persia and Hindustan.

In the time of Firoze Tughlaq Malik Beiram Lodhi, the grandfather of Bahlole, being possessed of wealth, separated from his elder brother; and entering the service of Malik Mardan Daulat raised himself to the government of Multan, Malik Beiram[345] had five sons, viz. Malik Sultan, Malik Kali, Malik Firoze, Malik Mahomed and Malik Khwaja, all of whom, on the death of their father, remained in Multan.

When Khizer Khan was appointed to the government of Multan, Malik Sultan received the command of his Afghan troops. In the action which Khizer Khan fought with Mallu Yekbal Khan, Malik Sultan had the good fortune with Mallu Yekbal Khan, Malik Sultan had the good fortune to slay Yekbal Khan with his own hand; on which account he became a favourite with Khizer Khan, and was appointed governor of Sarhind, with the title of Islam Khan, while his brothers participated also in his good fortune. One of these, Malik Kali, the father of Bahlole whose proper name is Ballau, had a district bestowed on him by his father. The wife of Kali Khan, his own cousin, was smothered by the fall of her house when pregnant. Her husband caused her to be instantly opened, and saved the life of the infant, who was called Ballu, Mulik Kali having subsequently been killed in an action with the Neieazi Afghans, Mulik Bahlole joined his uncle Islam Khan, at Sarhind; and being much distinguished in battle, he received the hand of Islam Khan's daughter in marriage. Islam Khan was a chief of such consequence, that he retained 12,000 Afghans, mostly of his own tribe, in his serive. At his death, though he had full-grown children of his own, Islam Khan made Bahlole his heir, and he succeeded to the command of the troops. On this occasion the Afghans divided into three parties: one of which adhered to Malik Bahlole; one to Malik Firoze, the brother of Islam Khan, an officer in the serive of the King of Delhi and the other to Malik Kutab Khan, the son of Islam Khan: Bahlole, having most talent, found means to weaken his rivals, and gradually to strengthen his own party.

Malik Kutab Khan, stung with envy, repaired to Delhi and acquainted the King, Syad Mahomed, that the Afghans at Sarhind were establishing a power, which unless soon checked, would subvert his throne. The Nazir Malik Sikandar Topha, was accordingly directed to repair, with an army, to that quarter, and to required the Afghan chiefs to appear at court, in failure of which he was authorised to expel at court, in failure of which he was authorised to expel them from Sarhind. Jasrathkohkkhar also was instigated to take arms against them; so that in the end they were driven to the hills. Subsequent to this, Malik Firoze Lodi leaving his son Shahin Khan, and his nephew Malik Banlole, with his army, proceeded with some attendants to the camp of Malik Sikandar Topha and Jasratt under the most solemn assurances of good faith; but at the instigation of his nephew Kutab Khan, Malik Firoze was seized, and his attendants cut off. After this event a part of the army was detached to reduce Malik Bahlole; but he having retreated into the hills with the women and children, ensured his own safety, though Shahin Khan was overtaken and slain, and a great part of his tribe destroyed.

After the death of Shahin Khan, his head was cut off and carried to Jasrath Kokkhar and placed before his father, Malik Firoze, to recognise. The latter at first denied his son; but after hearing from those who attended of the gallant manner in which he had behaved, he burst into tears, and said, " Yes, it is my son; but I would not recognise his countenance till convinced he had done honour to his tribe." He observed, at the same time, "My nephew Bahlole could not have been in the battle, or he would have been slain also. But he lives: and if so, he will revenge the death of my boy[346]."

When Jasrath Gakkhar retired to Panjab, Malik Bahlole collected the remainder of his tribe, and began to levy contributions: being extremely liberal in dividing the spoil among his troops, he became very popular, and his followers increased. Some time after, Malik Firoze made his escape, and joined Malik Bahlole; while Kutab Khan, repenting of his former conduct, became reconciled to his relations, and joining the Afghans, Malik Bahlole headed the party which subsequently invaded Sarhind, and occupied that province. On receiving intelligence of this event, the King detached Hissam Khan, his *wizier*, against the Afghans; but Malik Bahlole gave him battle, and defeated him. They relate, that when Malik Bahlole was a youth, he was permitted to pay his respects to a celebrated *Dervish* of Samana, whose name was Sheida. While sitting in a respectful posture before the Dervish, the latter called out aloud, in an enthusiastic manner, "who will give 2,000 rupees for the kingdom of Delhi?" Bahlole told him he had only 1,600 rupees in the world; which he ordered his servant to bring immediately, and present to the Dervish. Having accepted the money, the *Dervish* laid his hands on Bahlole's head, and said, "*Shah-Bash Beta*,[347]" literally, "Be thou king, my son." The companions of Bahlole ridiculed him much for this action; but he replied, "That if the thing came to pass, he had made a cheap purchase; if not, the blessing of a holy man could do no harm." After Malik Bahlole had defeated the Wazir, he wrote to the King as has been before related, ascribing the whole blame of his rebellion to the minister's conduct towards the Afghans; on which the King as has been shown, basely cut off the Wazir, and permitted Malik Bahlole according to his promise, to visit him. This meeting enabled Bahlole to carry on his intrigues at court, where he managed his affairs so well, that he was confirmed in the government of Sarhind, together with some other districts in its vicinity.

When Sultan Mahmud Khalji of Malwa brought an army against Delhi, Malik Bahlole being called on to join the King, he appeared at the head of 20,000 Afghan cavalry, with which he pursued Sultan Mahmud Khalji, on his retreat and plundered his army on the dayafter he quitted Delhi for which service he obtained the title of Khan Khanan. On that occasion. Bahlole returned to Sarhind, and instantly began to lay hands on the King's districts, continguous to his own estates, such as Lahore. Dipalpur, and Sunam; not content with which, he marched his army boldly against the King himself. On reaching Delhi, he laid siege to it,but being foiled in his attempt, he was induced to retire to Sarhind. Meanwhile, the King dying suddenly, his son, Al-ud-Din, ascended the throne. After some years, as has been related, Humid Khan the Wazir, seeing the declining state of public affairs, invited Bahlole Lodi from Sarhind, who ascended the throne and assumed the title of King.

At the time of his accession, Bahlole had nine sons, whose names were Bayezid, Nizam (who afterwards ascended the throne under the tilte of Sikandar), Barbik Alam (who also became King under the appellation of Alla-ud-Din), Jamal, Yakub[348] Fatteh, Musa and Jalal. Among the cheifs of distinction in the state no fewer than thirty-six persons were either blood-relations, or intimately connected with the new King.

Hamid Khan, the *Wazir*, who conferred the government upon him, still possessed great influence. Bahlole treated him for some time with much respect; but being one day in Hamid Khan's house, at an entertainment, he ordered the Afghans, whom he carried with him, to assume the manners of ill-bred persons, and act the part of clowns, in order that the *Wazir* might be less on his guard against them. When they came into company, some of them tied their shoes to their girdles, and others put them up in the recesses of the apartment; and on Humid Khan's asking them the reason, they replied, that they were afraid of having them stolen. When they had taken their seats, one of them began to praise the flowers of the carpet, and the brightness of their colours, saying he would like extremely to have such a carpet, to send home, and make caps for his boys. Hamid Khan laughed and told him, he would give him velvet or brocade for the purpose. When the plates and boxes of perfumes were laid before them, some began to bemear their whole body with the finest otto of roses; others to lick it up; and others devoured whole garlands of flowers; while the pan leaf was eagerly scrambled for and greedily eaten up. Some having swallowed large pieces of lime with their pan, burned their mouths, made wry faces, and vociferated aloud. This conduct astonished the servants and the guests, who ascribed it to their ignorance as foreigners, that had never lived at court; while the King and the *Wazir* were convulsed with laguther[349].

The Wazir imagined that this scene proceeded from the King's humour, who, in bringing such people with him, had resolved to make merry in his house, but had no suspicion it originated from design. The next visit the King paid to Humid Khan, a great number of his attendants were admitted; but as Hamid Khan had a still greater number of his own friends within the court-yard, it became necessary for the King to gain admission for more of his people, who were stopped without by the guards. The King having before instructed them how to proceed, they began to wrangle loudly with the guards, and threw out bitter invectives against the King, for permitting them to be excluded, swearing that they respected their friend the Wazir and would see him.

Hamid Khan, on hearing the noise, ordered the gates of the court-yard to be thrown open, and directed as many of the Afghans as could conveniently be admitted to be allowed to come in. This point being gained, the King gave the signal, and his people, drawing their swords, told Hamid Khan's servants to remain quiet, and they should suffer no injury: on which, two or three seizing the Wazir, bound him fast. The King then told him, that gratitude was a security for his life; but it was necessary he should withdraw from business, and spend the rest of his days in retirement.

The same year[350] being the 855th of the Hijra[351] (A.D. 1451), having intrusted Delhi to the charge of his eldest son, Bayezid Khan, the King marched towards Multan, both to employ his army, and to regulate the affairs of the western provinces. Some of his officers, dissatisfied with him, deserted and joined Mahmud Shah Shark, King of Junpur; who, during the absence of Bahlole Padshah, in the beginning of the year A.H. 856 (A.D. 1452) advanced and laid siege to Delhi; but Bahlole, hastening from Dipalpur, did not halt till he reached Pirah, within thirty miles of his capital.

Mahmud Shah Sharki detached 30,000 horse and 30 elephants, under the command of Fatteh Khan Hirvi to oppose him. An action ensued, in which Kutab Khan Lodhi, the son of Islam Khan, who excelled in archery, shot an arrow into the forehead of one of Fatteh Khan Hirvi's elephants. The animal, becoming outrageous, broke the line; and Kutub Khan, coming in contact with Dariya Khan Lodi one of the malecontent chiefs who had joined Mahmud Shah Shurki thus addressed him: "For shame, Duriya Khan; where is your honour, thus to wage war against your own kindred, and to lay siege to the city of Delhi, which contains your family, when you ought rather to defend it against your natural enemies? — "Pursue me not," said Dariya Khan, " and I am gone" " he immediately wheeled off, followed by all the Afghans in Fatteh Khan Hirvi's army. The other troops, thus deserted, gave way and Fatteh Khan was taken prisoner; but this chief, with his own hand, had just killed *Pritvi Rai* the brother of *Karun Rai* the latter, therefore, struck of Fatteh Khan's head out of revenge, and sent it to Bahlole. The news of this defeat induced Mahmud Shah Sharki to raise the siege of Dehli and to retreat with precipitation to Junpur.

The power of Bahlole Lodhi being once firmly established, he began to think of conquests. His first movement was towards Mewat; where Ahmud Khan Mewatti, submitting to his authority, seven purgunas were wrested from him, but he was permitted to hold the remainder as tributary. From Mewat the King marched to Birun; where Dariya Khan Lodhi governor of Sambhal, presented him with seven handsome elephants, and acknowledged his supremacy. From Birun, the King proceeded to Kole; and confirming Eesa Khan in the government of that district, he continued his route to Bubrhanabad, the management of which was intrusted to Mubarik Khan Lohani, while Meinpuri Bhuigam was delivered over to Partap Rai. On reaching Reberi Kutab Khan, the son of Hassein Khan Afghan, shut the gates of the fort and at first refused the King admittance; but shortly after, having made his submission, he was reinstated in his authority, and Bahlole marching from thence to Etawa, confirmed the former governor of that district also in his office. At this time an officer called Juna Khan, quitting the court in disgust joined Mahmud Shah Shurki, from whom he received the government of Shumsabad; and having instigated his new master to make another attempt on Delhi Mahmud Shah Sharki advanced to Etawa, where the Delhi army was encamped. On the first day both kings sent out parties to reconnoitre, but no engagement took place; and on the next day, they began to retreat, having agreed, in the mean time, that Bahlole Lodi should keep possession of all the countries belonging to Delhi in the reign of Syad Mubarik, and that Mahmud Shah Sharki should retain all the possessions held by Ibrahim Shah Shurki; that Bahlole should, on one hand, restore all the elephants taken in the action with Fatteh Khan Hirvi and that Mahmud Shah Shurki should dismiss Juna Khan from his government and service.

Mahmud Shah Sharki immediately after his treaty, returned to Junpur, and Banlole proceeded to take possession of Shamsabad. Mahmud Shah Shurki incensed at this proceeding, returned to Shamsabad, where two parties from the Delhi army, under Kutab Khan Lodhi and Dariya Khan Lodhi surprised the Sharki camp in the night. During this operation Qutab Khan's[352] horse, having trodden upon a tent-peg, threw his master, who was taken prisoner, but his division retreated without molestation to the Delhi lines. Bahlole Lodhi drew out his army on the following morning; but on receiving advice that Mahmud Shah Sharki had just expired and that his ministers had set up his son Mahomed Shah Sharki a treaty was concluded through the mediation of Bibi Raj the young King's mother. Mahomed Shah Sharki accordingly returned to Junpur and Bahlole took the route of Dehli (A.H. 856 A.D. 1452).

Before Bahlole arrived at the capital, he received a letter from Shams Khatun, the sister of Qutab Khan, entreating him not to suffer her brother to remain in the hands of Mahomed not to suffer her brother to remain in the hands of Mahomed Shah Sharki, a circumstance which induce Bahlole to break the peace and to return towards Junpur; on which occasion Mahomed Shah Sharki met him near Sasni. At this place Hussein Khan, the younger brother of Mahomed Shah Shurki apprehensive of his brother, withdrew with all his adherents to Kanuaj, and Jalal Khan Sharki his other brother, followed his example. Bahlole availed himself of these events to detach a force to seize Hassein Khan, in which object it failed, but overtaking Jalal Khan, he was taken prisoner; and Bahlole determined to detain him as a hostage till the release of Kutab Khan by the King of Junpur.

Meanwhile the Sharki officers conspiring against Mahomed Shah put him to death, and recalling Hassein Khan, who had fled to Kunaj, placed him on the throne. Bahlole now agreed to a truce for four years, on condition that both Kutab Khan and Jalal Khan should be released. Bahlole forthwith returned towards Shamsabad, where Narsingh Rai, the son of Partab Rai came to pay his respects. It appears the latter chief had formerly taken a standard and a pair of drums from Dariya Khan Lodhi in action; and that chief,in order to revenge himself , assassinated Narsing Rai, in spite of the opposition of Qutab Khan, the son of Hassein Khan. Mubarik Khan, apprehensive of Duria Khan's influence at court, fled to Hassein Shah Sharki, Bahlole returned to Delhi and his attention being shortly after excited by the rebellion of the viceroy of Multna, and by the disorders in Panjab, he proceeded in that direction. On his march he learned that Hussein Shah. Sharki, taking advantage of his absence, was approaching Dehli for the purpose of besieging that city: he was induced to countermarch, and leaving the city in charge of Qutab Khan and Jehan Khan Bahilole marched direct towards the enemy. The two armies met at the village of Chandwar, where they skirmished without much effect for seven days, when a truce was concluded for the term of three years; at the expiration of which period Hassein Shah investing Etawa took it, and gained over Ahmad Khan Mewatti[354] and Eesa Khan of Kole to his interest. Ahmad Khan Jalwani also, the governor of Biana, went so far as to coin money and read the Qutab in the name of the Shurki monarch, who now advanced with an army of 100,000 horse and 1000 elephants from Etawa towards Delhi, Bahlole, undismayed by the superiority of Hassein Shah Shurki's force, marched out boldly to oppose the invader. The two armies, however, after remaining encamped for some time in sight of each other at Bhatwara, engaged only in partial skirmishes, in which no advantage was obtained by either party, and a hollow truce was again concluded. This pacification was not of long duration; for Hassein Shah Shurki, having advanced again towards Dehli some months after, was opposed at the village of Sankar, and obliged to fall back without attaining any object.

At this time, Bibi Raj the mother of Hussein Shah Shurky, dying at Etawa, the Raja of Guliar and Kutab Khan, the son of Hassein Khan, Afghan of Raberi, went to condole with him. During his visit, Qutab Khan, perceiving the rooted enmity of Hussein Shah Shurki towards Bahlole, took occasion to observe that the King was nothing more than one of the dependents of Dehli and could not hope to contend long with him, descended from a race of kings; concluding his speech by saying, "If I do not put you in possession of Dehli, look on my words as nothing." Having taken his leave from Hassein Shah's court, Kutub Khan proceeded to Dehli, where he stated that he had escaped with much difficulty from the hands of Hassein Shah Sharki, who was meditating a fresh attack on Bahlole. About this time, the ex-monarch, Syad Alla-ud-Din, who had abdicated the throne of Dehli, dying at Budaun, Hassein Shah Sharki, proceeded thither, and after performing the funeral ceremonies, seized that district from the children of Alla-ud-Din. From thence, marching to Sambhul, he imprisoned Mubarik Khan, governor of that province; and proceeding towards Dehli in the year A.H. 883 (A.D. 1478), he crossed the river Yumna near the Katcha-Ghat. Bahlole Lodhi was at Sarhind when he received intelligence of this invasion: and returning which Hussein Shah Sharki had in general the advantage. Another treaty was however brought about through Kutab Khan, in which it was agreed that Bahlole should relinquish all the territory eastward of the Ganges on condition of his retaining possession of all the districts on the west bank of that river. These terms being concluded. Hussein Shah retreated towards Junpur; but Bahlole broke his faith, and pursuing Hussein Shah, attacked him on his march, killing vast numbers of his troops, and taking forty officers of rank prisoners, besides part of his treasure and equipage. Bahlole followed up his success, occupied several districts belonging to Hussein Shah Sharki such as Kampila, Pattial Shamsabad, Saket, Marhera, Kole, and Jalesar, and appointed agents for their management. Hussein Shah Shurki however, halted at Rampinjan, and gave battle, in which both parties claimed the victory; after which peace was once more concluded, leaving the village of Dopamow as the boundary between the kingdoms when Hassein Shah proceeded to Raberi and Bahlole to Dehli.

Hassan Shah could not, however, forgive the perfidy of Bahlole ; and having recruited his army, he again waged war, but was defeated at the village of Sirsar, after an obstinate battle, with the loss of all his treasure and baggage, an event which greatly added to Bahlole's reputation. In the year A.H. 883 (A.D. 1478). Hassein Shah Sharki fell back on Raberi but was followed closely by Bahlole and totally overthrown in a second engagement. After this battle Hassein Shah retreated towards Gowaliar, where the Raja supplied him with several lacks of rupees, and with elephants, horses, camels, and a handsome suit of camp-equipage and accompanied him to Kalpi Bahlole, in the mean time, marched to Etawa, then occupied by Ibrahim, the brother of Hassein Shah Sharki, which place surrendered by capitulation. Ibrahim Khan Lohani, one of the Dehli officers, being left in charge of Etawa, the King proceeded to Kalpi where he found Hassein Shah Surkei encamped. The river intervening, both armies remained for some months inactive, till at length Rai Tilak Chand of Katihr, having come over to Bheilole, pointed out to him a ford, bu which he crossed. He attacked Hussein Shah Sharki and defeating him, compelled him to fly in the direction of Janpur. At Kanuaj Hussein Shah Sharki again opposed Bahlole, on the banks of the *Kali Nadi i.e.* Brahminical ideology, but having now acquired a habit of retreating, he was, as usual, defeated: his regalia and equipage were taken, and also the chief lady of his seraglio, Bibi Khonza. She was the daughter of the late ex-monarch. Syad All-ud-Din, and was treated with great respect by Bahlole, who after this victory retreated to Dehli.

Having recruited his troops, Bahlole advanced towards Junpur, and having entirely subdued the country, made over the charge of it to Mubarik Khan Lohani leaving Kutab Khan Lodhi together with Khan Jehan, and other chiefs, at Bisawali. The King marched to Budaun, where he heard of Kutab Khan's death. Khan Jehan, Mubarik Khan, and many other officers, though they outwardly professed allegiance, no sooner heard of the death of Kutab Khan than they concerted measures to acquire independence. Bahlole, apprised of their intentions, marched towards Junpur, and having expelled Hassein Shah Sharki, who had made an attempt to recover his kingdom, placed Barbik, one of his own sons on the throne of Junpur. From thence he proceeded to Kalpi which having reduced, he conferred the government on his grandson, Azim Humayun, the son of his eldest son, Baizid Khan. The King then marched to Dhalpur, levying tribute on the Raja of that place; from thence he proceeded to Rattanpur, a place situated in the district of Rantmbhore, where having committed great devastations, he returned to Dehli.

Bahlole being now old, and infirmities daily increasing on him, divided his dominions among his sons. Junpur was conferred on Barbik Khan; Kara and Manikpur on Alam Khan; Bhiraich on his nephew Sheikhzada Mahomed Firmalli known by the name of Kala P'har (the Black Rock). Lucknow and Kalpi on Azum Humayun[355], whose father Bayezzed Khan, was assassinated by one of his own servants. Budaun was allotted to Khan Jehan, a relation and one of his oldest officers and Dehli with several districts in the Doab, were conferred on his son, the Prince Nizam Khan, known afterwards by the name of Sikandar, whom he now declared his heir and successor.

Some time after this, the King proceeded to Gowaliar, and raising a tribute of 80 lacks of *tunkas* from the Raja, came to Etawa, from whence having expelled Sangat Singh, he returned towards Dehli. Falling sick on his march, many of the nobles were desirous that he should alter his former will, with respect to the succession, which, they said, was the undoubted right of Azim Humayun, his grandson by his eldest son. The Queen, hearing this, wrote to her son. Nizam Khan, (who having intimation of his father's illness, was about to quit Dehli) by no means to come, lest he might be imprisoned by the nobles. At the same time, the King, by the advice of his officers, caused letters to be written to hasten his arrival in the camp in order to see him before his death. Nizam Khan was greatly perplexed how to act. He at length conferred with Katlagh Khan, the Wazier of Hassein Shah Sharki who was then a prisoner at Dehli. This chief recommended him to pitch his tents outside of the city, and to proceed by slow journies towards the camp. Meanwhile, the King's disease increasing, he died at Badowli in the district of Suket, in the year A.H. 894 (A.D. 1488) after a reign of 38 years, eight months, and seven days.

Bahlole Lodhi was esteemed a virtuous and a mild prince, executing justice to the utmost of his knowledge, and treating his countries rather as companions than subjects. When he obtained the crown, he divided the public treasure among his friends, and could be seldom prevailed on to ascend the throne; saying. "That it was enough "for him that the world knew he was king, without his making a display of royalty." He was extremely temperate in his diet, and seldom ate at home. Though a man of no great literary acquirement himself, he was fond of the company of learned men, whom he rewarded according to their merit. He placed great reliance on the courage of his Moghal troops, on which account they met with such encouragement among his relations and coutiers, that it is estimated there were nearly 20,000 Mogals in the service of the government during his reign. He was a wise and brave prince, and personally well acquainted with Mahommedan law. He also studied the best institutes for maintaining order in his government, which he invariably adopted. He was prudent, and above all things, deprecated hurry in matters of state; and indeed, his conduct throughout life sufficiently evinced how much he practised this quality.

Sikandar Lodhi Afghan

Immediately on the death of Bahlole the nobles met together, and consulted whom they should elevate to the throne. Some were disposed towards Azim Humayun, the grandson, and others, towards Barbik

Khan, the eldest surviving son of the late king. While they were debating on this point, the mother of Sikandar Khan (whose name was Zeina, the daughter of a goldsmith, but raised to the King's bed owing to her beauty) addressed the assembly from behind a curtain in favour of her son. Upon which, Eesa Khan, the nephew of Bahlole, tauntingly observed, "What business have goldsmiths' sons with the reins of government, since it is proverbial that 'monkeys make but bad carpenters." Khan Khani Lohani, one of the officers present, took him up sharply, saying. "The King is yet scarcely cold in his grave, and it ill becomes us at such a time to cast reflections on any of his progency." Eesa Khan desired him to hold his tongue; observing, he was nothing but a servant, and had no right to interfere in family affairs. Khan Khanan now rising, instantly declared himself a servant of Sikandar Lodhi and said that he would maintain his right against all who durst oppose it; when having left the council and being followed by all his party, he carried the body of the deceased King to the town of Jillali where, being met by Sikandar, the latter ascended his father's throne at that place. Sikandar now sent the crops of his father to Delhi and instantly marched against Eesa Khan. Having defeated this cheif he afterwards forgave him, and returning to the capital, followed the example of his father, by conferring favours on all his kindered.

At the time of his accession, Sikandar Lodhi had six sons; viz Ibrahim, Jalal, Ismael, Hassein, Mahmud, and Azim Humayun, besides whom were 44 officers of distinction; such as Khan Jehan Lodhi.

Ahmud Khan, grandsonof Khan Khanan Firmulli
Sheikzada Firmally
Khan Khanan Lohani
Azim Humayun Sherwani
Duria Khan Lodhi
Jalal Khan Lodhi Naib[356] of Kalpi
Sher Khan Lodhi
Mubarik Khan Mowj
Kuleel Khan Lodhi
Ahmud Khan Lodhi, Naib of Etawa
Ibrahim Shah Lodhi
Babu Khan Sheerwani
Hussein Khan Firmalli, Naib of Saharan
Suliman Khan Firmalli.
Syad Khan Lodhi
Ismael Khan Lohani
Tartar Khan Firmalli
Sheikh Khan Lodhi
Sheikzada Mahomed Firmalli (called also Kala P'har)
Sheikh Jamal Firmulli
Sheikh Othman Firmulli
Sheikh Ahmud Firmulli
Adam Khan Lodhi.
Hussein Khan Lodhi
Kabir Khan Lodhi
Nasir Khan Lohani
Ghazi Khan Lodhi
Tartar Khan, governor of Tijara
Khwaja Nash-ulla
Mubarik Khan
Yekbal Khan, Naib of Bari
Asghur, the son of Kowam-ul-Malik
Shir Khan Lohani
Imad-ul-Malik Kamboh
Alam Khan Lodhi
Kabir Khan Lodhi
Bhikun Khan Lodhi
Zaheer Khan Lodhi
Umr Khan Sherwani
Jabbar Khan Shirwani
Alam Khan Jalwani
Safdar Khan Jalwani
Mian Zaman Kumboh
Majid-ud-Din
Sheikh Ibrahim
Sheikh Otman
Sheikh Omar
Sheikh Siddik
Qazi Abdul, Wahib of Kabul
Mian Bhuri

Sometime after his accession, Sikandar Lodi marched towards Raberi and thence to the fort of Chandwar, in which place his brother, the Prince Alum Khan, had declared his independence. On the King's approach, Alam Khan, abandoning the town, fled to Eesa Khan Lodhi at Patiala Sikandar having offered the district of Raberi on Khan Khanan Firmalli, prceeded to Etawa, where he received the submission of his brother Alam Khan, and pardoned him; he also conferred Etawa upon him as his estate. Thence the King proceeded to Pattiari where Essa Khan being attacked was wounded, and threw himself on the King's mercy. He was pardoned, but soon after died on his wounds.

Sikandar Lodhi now deputed a mission to wait on the Prince Barbik, his brother, who asumed the title of King of Junpur, requiring him to do homage, and to cause the name of Sikandar to be read first int he Khtba. Barbi,[357] however, rejecting this proposal, Sikandar Lodi marched against him. Barbik, and his general *Kala Phar* drew out in order of battle to meet his brother, and an action ensued, in which *Kala P'hara* was taken prisoner. Sikandar Lodi on seeing him, alighted from his horse, and embracing him, said he esteemed him as his father, and begged he would look on him as his son. Kala P'har, overcome by this unexpected honour, replied that except his life, he had nothing to offer in return, and trusted that he might be employed and have an opporunity of evincing his gratitude: he was accordingly mounted on one of the King's own horses, and instantly led a charge of cavalry against the party whose cause he had before espoused, which in a great measure led to the King's success (A.H. 894, A.D. 1488). The troops of Barbik seeing Kala P'har charging them, and imagining that all his division had also gone over to the enemy, took to flight. The Prince Barbik behaved with great bravery, but being deserted by his troops, fled to Budan. His son, Mubarik Kha, however, was made prisoner in the action. Sikandar Lodhi pursued his brother to Budaun, and laid siege to it; but Barbik soon after capitulating, he was received with great kindness, and treated with respect. The King now returned to Joonpur, and finding that Hussein Shah Sharki, the exiled King of the Sharki provinces, was still in force in Bihar, he thought it advisable to permit his brother Barbik to retain the government of Junpur in order to check Hassein Shah Sharki in any attempt he might make on Dehli. At the same time, also, he left some trusty friends of his own with the Prince, on whom he bestowed estates, in order to retain them steady to his interest.

Sikandar Lodhi,now proceeding to Kalpi, resumed the govenment from Azim Humayun, and conferred it on Mahomed Khan Lodhi From thence he marched to Bhartyi where Tartar Khan the governor, after going homage, confirmed in his estate. The King thence marched in the direction of Gowaliar, whither he sent one of his officers, Khwaja Mahomed Firmulli, with an honorary dress to Raja Man Singh, who despatched his nephew with presents to meet the King at Biana. Sultan Sharf, the governor of Biana, also paid his respects to the King, who removed him from that district, but nominated him governor of Jalisar, Chandwar, Marhera, and Suket. Sultan Sharf was accompanied by Umar Khan Sherwani, to whom he was directed to make over the fort of Biana; but when he had got within the walls, Sultan Sharf shut the gates, and prepared to defend himself. The King, however, choosing to overlook the circumstances, went to Agra, where Heibut Khan Jalwani, who held that fort under Sultan Sharf, also shut the gates. This insult so enraged Sikandar Lodhi, that leaving part of his army to besiege Agra, he returned in person towards Biana, to which he laid siege. Sultan Sharf, in the end, was obliged to capitulate, and in the year A.H. 897 (A.D.1491), his government was given to KhanKhanan Firmalli, and he was banished for the present to Gowaliar. The fort of Agra falling about the same time, Sikandar returned to Delhi where in a few days after he received advices of an insurrection at Junpur among the zemindars, who had raised an army, consisting of 100,000 horse and foot, and had slain Sher Khan, the brother of Mubarik Khan Lohani, governor of Korra. Mubarik Khan himself was driven from Kurra, and taken prisoner, while in the act of crossing the Gangas, by Saha Deo Raja of Kutra. The Prince Barbik had also been obliged to fly to Byraich to solicit the assistance of Kala P'har, so that the King, after only 24 days rest at Dehli was under the necessity of returning towards Junpur. When he arrived at Dalmow he was joined by the Prince Barbik; and Raja Saha Dev, hearing of his approach, released Mubarik Khan Lohani The King proceeded to Katgur, where the *Zemindars* had assembled in force; but they were defeated, and much property fell into the hands of the Moslems. The King, having marched to Junpur and reinstated the Prince Barbik, himself remained a month in that vicinity. Here he received intelligence that the Zemindars, having been again driven to excesses, had besieged Barbik in Junpur; on which Sikandar ordered Kala P'har Humayun Khan *Sherwani*, and Khan Khanan Lohani, from Oude, and Mubarik Khan from Kurra, to unite and march against them. He also directed them to send the Prince Barbik to the presence, where he was made over, as a state-prisoner, to the charge of Heibat Khan and Umar Khan Sheerwani.

After this events the Kings marched towards Chonar, then in possession of Hassein Shah Sharki. On his approach, the garrison made a sally, but were repulsed. On reconnoitring the place, however, and being unwilling to incur the risk of failure, he proceeded to *Qutamba*[359] a place dependent on Patna. Balbhadur Rai, Raja of Kutamba, came forth to meet the King, and submitted to his authority. From thence the King marched to Arile, accompanied by Balbhadar Rai. But the Raja suspecting treachery, left his retinue, and fled one night from the camp to Patna. Sikandar Lodhi permitted the Raja's followers to quit the camp, next day, with his private property, but he allowed his own troops to plunder the country on thier route to Arile. On crossing the Gang's at Kurra, the King went to Dalmow, where he married the widow of Sher Khan, the late governor of that place. From Dalmow, Sikander marched to Shamsabad, where having halted for six months, he proceeded to Sumbhul; but returning from thence in a few days to Shamsabad, he plundered the town of Dewnari where a *banditti* had taken post. The King spent the rainy season at Shamsbad, and in the year A.H. 900 (A.D. 1494), he again marched in the direction of Patna. He was there opposed by Narsingh -Rai the son of Balbhadar Rai at the *Handia Ghat*, who being defeated, retired within the walls of Patna. On the King's approach, Balbhudar Rai fled, taking the route of Sarguja, and died on the journey. After this event the King proceeded to Sahsdewar; but provisions becoming scarce in his camp, he was obliged to return to Junpur, having in this march lost of his cavalry, owing to the bad roads and wnat of forage. Narsing Rai the son of Balbhudar, and other *Zemindars*, taking advantage of this circumstance, wrote to Hassein Shah Sharki, then in possession of the province of Bihar, that the cavalry of Sikandar Lodhi was now in so wretched a condition, that a favourable opportunity presented itself for him to take revenge. Hassein Shah Sharki accordingly put his army in motion, and marched against the King Sikandar, on hearing of his intentions, crossed the Gangas to meet him; and the two armies came in sight of each other at a spot distant 18 coss (27 miles) from Banaras. An obstinate battle ensued, in which Hassein Shah Sharki was defeated, and fled to Patna, Sikandar Lodhi, according to the most authentic accounts, pursued the fugitives of several days, with 100,000 horse; but hearing that his enemy had fled to Behar, he halted on the ninth day, till the whole of his army joined, with which he marched towards Bihar. Hussein Shah left Malik Kondu to protect Bihar and fled himself to Kulgam, in the district of Luknowti Alla-ud-din Shah Purbi, King of Bengal, received the fugitive at his court with the utmost courtesy. Here he passed the remainder of his days in obscurity; and the royal race of Junpur became extinct in his person.

Sikandar Lodhi, having returned to Dewnari, detached a division of his army against Malik Kandur, who fled, leaving the country open to theKing of Dehli, who appointed Heibut Khan to remain with a force in Bihar. The King now proceed towards Tirhut, the raja of which country consented to pay an annual tribute. Mubarik Khan Lohani was directed to receive it, while the King went to Dervishpur, and visited the tomb of Sheikh Shurf Muneri on which occasion he distributed presents to the holy persons who resided at that shrine. It was at this time , also, that Khan Jehan, the son of Khan Khanan Firmally, died, and his son. Ahmud Khan, received the title of Azim Humayun. The King now marched his army towards Bengal and reaching Kutlaghpur Alla-ud-Din Shah Purbi sent his son Daniel to oppose him. On the part of the Mowji were detached to meet Daniel. The opposing armies encamped close to each other at the village of Barra, but instead of fighting, a peace was concluded; when it was agreed that both parties should cease to molest each other, or to afford protection to their mutual enemies. On the return of the army towards Dehli, Mubarik Khan Mowji, died at Patna, and at Dervishpur, Mubarik Khan Lohan also died suddenly. The duty of collecting the tribute to Tirhut was now intrusted to Azim Humayun, the son of Khan Jehan, while the government of Bihar was conferred upon Dariya Khan, the son of the Late Mubarik Khan Lohani. There happened, at this time, a great dearth in the country; but the transit customs on grain being relinquished, that calamity was in some measure averted, nor were the duties again imposed during that reign. Sikandar, meanwhile, reducing the districts of Saharan, then in the hands of the zemindars, gave the lands in jagirs to several of his officers. He then returned to Janpur, where he resided six months.

Some time previously to this event the King having asked the daughter of Salivahn, Raja of Punna, in marriage, the Raja refused to comply with his request; in consequence of which, the King put his army in motion, and in the year A.H. 904 (A.D. 1498), marched to Poona and sacked the country as far as Bandha, after which he returned to Junpur, where he spent some time. At this period the accounts of Mubarik Khan Lodhi being inspected, for the period of his administration in Junpur, and great defalcation being discovered, the King ordered the balances to be realised from him. This circumstance gave umbrage to many Afghan officers, which evinced itself in the factions that arose in favour of the defaulter. One day, while the King and his court were playing at Chowgan[360]. the bat of Heibat Khan Sherwani, by accident, came in contact with the head of Suliman, the son of Daryia Khan Lodhi, who received a severe blow. This was resented on the spot by Khize Khan, struck him violently over the skull. In a few minutes both sides joined in the quarrel, and the fled was in uproar and confusion. Mahmud Khan Lodi and Khan Khanan Lodhi interposing, endeavoured to pacify Heibut Khan, and succeeded in persuading him to go quietly home with them. The King apprehensive of conspiracy, retired immediately to the palace, but nothing more transpiring he made another party at the same game a few days after. On the road to the play ground, Shums Khan, a relation of Heibut Khan Shirwani perceing Khizr Khan, the brother of Suliman Khan Lodi, instantly attacked him with his bat, and knocked him off his horse. The King abused Shams Khan grossly, and returned to his palace; and could not be persuaded but that there was some plot in agitation. He accordingly ordered his guards to be selected, and to be more than usually vigilant. The King's jealousies were not groundless; for at that time Heibat Khan Shirwani and two other chiefs had proposed to the Prince Fatteh Khan, the King's brother, to cut him off, declaring that he was now universally disliked, and they offered to place Futteh Khan on the throne. The Prince, desiring some time to consider of the project, consulted Sheikh Tahir Kabulli and his mother, who both strongly dissuaded him from lending himself to the conspiracy; and lest the affair should by any other means transpire, they recommended him to acquaint the King instantly of what had been proposed to him. On this, the conspirators being detached on different services, to a distance were cut off in detail.

In the year A.H. 905 (A.D. 1499), the King marched to Sambhal, where he spent four years, partly in pleasure, and partly in transacting civil affairs. While thus employed, he heard heavy complaints from the Afghans agains Asghar Khan, the governor of Dehli. On this he ordered Khuvas Khan, governor of Machiwara, to proceed to Delhi and to send Asghar Khan prisoner to court. Asghar Khan, receiving advice of this intention, quitted the capital, and threw himself at the King's intention, quitted the capital, and threw himself at the King's feet; but not being able to frame sufficient excuse for his conduct, he was ordered into confinement. It is mentioned that about this period a brahimn, whose name was Budhan and inhabitant of Kataen, near Lucknow, being upbraided by some Mohamedans on account of his faith, maintained "that the religions both of the Moslems and Hindus, if acted on with sincerity, were equally acceptable to God[361]."

As this opinion had been supported with some ingenuity, and much argument by the Brahmin, the subject came to be discussed publicly before the Qazies of Lucknow, and the *Brahmin* was ordered to appear. On this occasion, Qazi *Piala* and Sheikh Bud both residing at Lucknow, had different opinions; and the arguments of the Brahmin having made some stir in the city. Azim Humayun, the governor, thought fit to send all the parties to court at Sambhal, where the King, who was fond of hearing disputations on religious subjects, directed the most learned men in his empire to assemble and argue the point of faith with the brahmin. The following persons were accordingly brought together:-

Mian Qadir Bin Sheikh Raj

Mian Abdul Elias, and

Mian Allahdad of Tulamba

Syad Mahamed, Bin Syad Khan of Dehli

Mulla Qutab-ud-Din, and

Mulla Allahdad Saleh from Sarhind

Syad Aman

Syad Burhan and

Syad Ahsun from Kanuj

Besides which were the learned men who usually attended the court; such as,

Syad Sudar-ud-Din of Kanauj

Mian Abdul Rahman of Sikri

Mian Aziz-Ulla of Sambhal

All these persons were present at this disputation. After many arguments, the learned men were of opinion, that unless the infidel, who had maintained the Hindu worship to be equally acceptable to God as that of the true faith, should renounce his error, and adopt the Mahomedan religion, he ought to suffer death. The Hindu refused to apostatise and was accordingly executed, while the Mussadmen doctors were rewarded with gifts, and returned to their respective homes.

When Khavas Khan, whom we have already mentioned, entered Dehli, he found an order from the King to proceed to court. Syad Khan Lodi was also recalled from Lahore, and being suspected of disaffection, he together with Tartar Khan Firmalli and Mahomed Shah Lodhi, were banished to Gujarat.

In the same year (A.H. 907 A.D. 1501). Man Singh Rai of Gowaliar sent one of his eunuchs, named Nehal, to the King with rich presents, as ambassador, but this person having given offence at court, was ordered to quit it suddenly, without obtaining an audience. At that time, information was received of the death of Khan Khanan Firmalli, governor of Biana. The management of Biana devolved on his sons; but as the government fell into disorder in their hands, the King conferred the office of governor on Khuvas Khan, while Ahmud and Suliman, the sons of the late Khan Khanan, received the estates of Shamsabad, Jalesar, Kampila and Shahabad. Sudar Khan was deputed at the same time with a force to reduce Agra, then dependent on Bana, and which had revolted. Another detachment also sent to besiege Dhalpur, which was in possession of Raja Vinaik Deo, who had begun to make warlike preparations. Khwaja Babun, the officer employed on this latter duty, being killed, the King was so vexed, that he marched from Sambhal towards Dhalpur on Friday the sixth of Jamad-ul-Awal of the same year, A.H. 907 (November 17, A.D. 1501). On his approach, Vinaik Deo, leaving a deputy in the fort, fled towards Gowaliar; and the garrison on the next night evacuated the place, and enabled the King to take possession. He remained there about a month, and having laid waste the country, proceeded to Gwaliar. The Raja of Gowaliar sued for terms, and delivered up Syeed Khan Shirwani, Babukhan Shirwani, and Rai Ganesh, who had, at different times, fled from the court and found protection withhim. At the same time, he deputed the Raja's own son Vikramajit, with costly offerings, to propitiate the King's favour.

Sikandar Lodhi, having returned to Dhalpur, reinstated the Raja Vinaik Deo, and then marching to Agra, he resolved to make that city his capital. He stayed in Agra during the rains, but in the year A.H. 910 (A.D. 1504), marched towards Mandril. Havint taken that place, he destroyed the Hindu temples, and caused mosques tobe built in their stead. From thence returning to Dhalpur, he took the fort from the Raja Vinaik Deo, and conferred the command of it on Sheikh Kumrud-Din. Thence returning to Agra, the King permitted his officers to return to their respective estates.

In the following year, on Sunday, the 3d of Saffar, A.H. 911 (July 5, A.D. 1505), a violent earthquake occurred in Agra, so that the mountains shook to their broad bases, and lofty buildings were levelled with the ground. Several thousand inhabitants were burried under the ruins. No such earthquake has ever been experienced in India, either before or since. In the same year, the King proceeded towards Gowaliar. He remained some months at Dhalpur, where having left his family and heavy baggage, he proceeded, with an unincumbered army of horse, to the hills, to plunder some Hindu Rajas, from whom he took great spoils. Finding the supplies in his camp fail suddenly owing to the free intercourse with the *Banjaras*[362] being cut off, he detached Azim Humayun, Ahmud Khan and Majahid Khan, with their divisions, to afford these merchants convoy, which they effected at great risk, owing to the vigorous efforts of the inhabitants in the vicinity of Gowlior. Shortly after, while the army was passing near the town of Chinar, a dependency of Gowaliar, it was attacked in an ambuscade, and saved only by the bravery of Dawad Khan, and by Ahmud Khan, the son of Khan Jehan, grandson of Khan Khanan Firmulli: the Hindus were at length repulsed, and a number of Rajputs fell by the sword.

Having returned to Agra, the King proceeded in the year A.H. 912 (A.D. 1506) Gowalior towards the fort of Hunwantar, despairing of reducing Gowalior Hanwantgar fell in a short time, and the Rajput garrison was put to the sword, the temples were destroyed, and mosques ordered to be built in their stead. Bhikun Khan, the son of Majahid Khan, was left in charge; but the King, having afterwards received information that Majahid Khan had taken a bribe from the Raja of Hunwantgar, in order to divert the King from attacking that place, Majahid Khan was imprisoned at Dhalpur, and the King returned towards Agra. On the road, the army halted one day on a spot where there was little water. The distress in consequence was so severe, that, independently of the loss of baggage cattle, no fewer than 800 human beings perished, before they could obtain relief; and till evening, a small cup of water solf for fifteen tunkas throughout the camp. In the following year (A.H. 913, A.D. 1506), the King marched against Nurwar, a strong fort in the district of Malwa, then in possession of the Hindus. The Prince Jalal Khan governor of Kalpi[363] was directed to advance and invest the place; and should the Hindus resist, he was required to inform the King. On the King's arrival before Narwar Jalal Khan drew up his army, out of respect, to receive him; but this circumstances creating distruct in themindof Sikandar, he determined on his ruin. Narwar which was eight coss in circumference was invested; but the operations were protracted for eight months; when it appearing that a clandestine correspondance was maintained with the garrison, and suspicions falling on the Prince Jalal Khan Lodhi and Sher Khan Lohani they were both imprisoned in the fort of Hanwantgar. The garrison soon after capitulated, being in want both of water and provisions. The King remained for the space of six months at Nurwar, breaking down temples, and building mosques. He also established a college there, and placed there in many holy and learned men. It was at this period, that Shihab-ud-Din, the son of Sultan Nasir-ud-Din, King of Malwa, being discontented with his father, proposed a conference with the King of Dehli. A meeting took place on the Seepri, where Sikandar Lodhi promised him his support, if he would make over Chander to him.

In the month of Shaban, A.H. 914 (Dec., A.D. 1508), the King marched from Nurwar; but after proceeding some distance along the Sind river, he resolved to surround Nurwar with another wall, which was ordered to be immediately commenced. The King now marched to the town of Yehar, where he halted during a whole month. At this place, Niamat Khatun, the wife of Kutab Khan Lodhi, and the wet nurse of the young Prince Jalal Khan, paid her respects to the King, and the district of Kalpi was made over in Jagir to the Prince. The King now returned towards the capital. On arriving at Halkant, he sent a detachment against some rebels in that neighbourhood, and destoryed all their habitations, small posts being established at proper distances to overawe them. About this time, advices were received, that Ahmud Khan, the son of Mubarik Khan Lodhi, governor of Lucknow, had become a convert to the Hindu doctrines[364], on which, orders were despatched to his brother, Mahomed Khan, to send him prisoner to court, and his second brother, Syad Khan, was directed to take the administration of affairs into his hands. In the same year, also, Mahomed Khan, the grandson of Sultan-Nasir-ud-Din of Malwa, having fled from the wrath of his grandfather, sought an asylum at the Delhi court. The King desired him to remain quietly in his *jagir* of Chanderi and directed that the Prince Jalal Khan of Kalpi should take care to protect him from the power of the King of Malwa. At this time (A.H. 915, A.D. 1509), the King having marched to Dhalpur, ordered caravanserai to be built at every stage. It was in this year, also, Mahomed Khan Nagari defeated Ali Khan and Aba Bakr, who had conspired againt him, and they fled to Sikandar Lodhi for protection. Mahomed Khan, dreading the King's resentment, sent presents to propitiate his good will, and , moreover, caused the *Khutba* of Nagur to be read in the name of the King of Dehli. The King, on his part, pleased with this instance of voluntary submission, returned him a dress, and confirmed his authority.

While the King was encamped at Dhalpur, he ordered Suliman Khan, the son of Khan Jehan Firmulli, to march to the aid of Hassein Khan of Hanwantgar, Suliman Khan having excused himself, by saying he preferred being about the King's person, the latter became incensed, and frothwith dismissed him from his service, directing him to quit the camp by next morning at daylight: at the same time, he conferred the revenue of Birun on him for his future maintenance.

At this time, Bohjat Khan, governor of Chanderi on the part of the King of Malwa, perceving the imbecility of his master, Sultan Mahmood, made overtures to place himself under the Dehli government. Sikandar Lodhi accordingly deputed Imad-ul-Malik to assist Bhojat Khan in his revolt: soon after which, the King issued a proclamation, announcing the acquisition of Chanderi to his dominions. Deeming it desirable, also, to make some alterations among the public officers of that province, the King deputed Syad Khan Lodhi, Sheikh Jamal Firmulli, and Rai Ugar-Sein Kuchwaha, together with Khizer Khan and Khwaja Ahmud, to proceed to Chanderi: and these officers succeeded in occupying effectually that district for the government of Dehli. Mahomed Khan, the Prince of Malwa, although considered ostensibly the cheif of Chanderi, was in fact dispossessed of all authority and confined to the city, while the supremacy of Bohjat Khan, the Malwa Governor, being usurped by the Delhi officers, he left his government and come to court. At this period, the King having reason to suspect the conduct of Hassein Khan Firmulli Naib of Saharun, he deputed Haj *Sarang* with some troops into that quarter, with orders to gain over the Naib's troops, and to seize his person. Hassein Khan became acquainted with the King's intentions; and contriving his escape, sought an asylum with Alla-ud-Din Shah Parbi, King of Bengal[365]

In the year A.H. 922 (A.D. 1516), Ali Khan Naguri governor of Suisapur, entered into a plot with the Prince Daulat Khan of Malwa[366] , governor of Rantambhore, who promised to deliver that fortress to the King of Dehli, if he should come in person to take possession. Sikandar Lodhi, overjoyed at this intelligence, proceeded towards Biana, to which place the governor of Rantambhore came to meet him, and was honourably received; but Alli Khan Naguri, disappointed in the attainment of some objects on which he had calculated as a reward for bringing this affair to bear, resolved to prevent its accomplishment, nad used his influence with the governor to retract his promise. The King, ascertaining the true casue of this change, disgraced Ali Naguri, and deprived him of his government of Suisapur, which he conferred on his brother, Aba Bakr; and Sikandar, which he conferred on his brother, Aba Bakr; and Sikandar Lodhi was obliged to return to Agra without obtaining possession of Rantanbhore. In the year 923, Gowaliar the King summoned all the distant nobles to Agra, with a determination to reduce Gowaliar; and was in the midst of his preparations, when, being taken ill of a *quinsy*, he died on Sunday, the 7th of Zeekada, A.H. 923 (Dec. 14, A.D. 1517.

Nizam-ud-Din Ahmud states in his work, that the authors who have written this reign have filled their history with copious details of the great qualities of this prince; but he observes, that he has considerably abridged their accounts, and confined himself only to such facts as appeared to him to merti particular notice. The authors alluded to have given a description of his person, which was remarkable for its beauty and comeliness, as was his mind for the store of learning and good sense which it contained. During his reign, all the articles of life were cheap and abundant, and peace pervaded his dominions. He never omitted to devote a certain time to bear complaints in public, and he has been frequently known to sit at business the whole day long, even after his appointed time for meals and rest. He was in the habit of praying regularly five times daily. He was strictly just in his administration, and seldom known to be actuated by private feelings. He was as remarkable for his fear of God as for his benevolence towards his people. One day, while advancing against his brother Barbik, in the early part of his reign, a kullandur met him, and said, "God sent you victory!" on which the King said, " Pray that the victory may be his who will best promote the good of his subjects." He had numerous pensioners among the holy men of the empire, to whom he sent their stipends twice a year, and a suit of clothes once. He ordered alms and food to be distributed on Fridays to all who chose to partake in town or camp wheresoever he might be. He encouraged charity of all descriptions; and did not fail to commend his nobles for any generous acts which reached his ears, and thus promoted a disposition to do good among his public officers; sayng, "you have laid a foundation of virtue; you will never repent it." He was firmly attached to the Mohamedan religion, and made a point of destroying all Hindu temples. In the city of *Mura* he caused *Masjids* and *bazars* to be built opposite the bathing-stairs leading to the river, and ordered that no Hindus should be allowed to bathe there. He forbade the barbers to shave the beards and heads of the inhabitants, in order to prevent the Hindus following their usual practices at such pilgrimages. He also prohibited the procession of the spear, which took place annually in commemoration of the deeds of Salar Musad, and put a stop to the custom of females going abroad, and making offering at Mahomedan shrines. Before he ascended the throne he had once a quarrel with a holy man, woh maintained that it was highly improper for a king to interfere with the religion of his subjects, or to prevent them bathing at places to which they had been accustomed to resort for ages. The Prince drew his sword, and said, "Wretch! do you maintain the propriety of the Hindu religion?" The holy man replied, "By no means: I speak from authority: kings should nto persecute their subjects on any account." This answer pacified him. He reformed and new-modelled the establishments of all the mosques throughout his dominions, and gave great encouragement to learning, so that almost all his military officers were well educated men; and even Hindoos, who had hitherto never learned Persian, commenced in this reign to study Mahomedan literature. The profession of arms assumed under his government a new character. He made a point of ascertaining the qualities of every officer who was promoted, and particularly enquired into his origin and education. He established horseposts throughout his country, and received accounts daily from every military detachment of his army in motion. Whenever it was necessary to issue proclamations, persons were sent in all directions to read them at the time of public devotion in the mosques. Reports of the armies, of the court, and of the principal cities, were drawn up by authority, and read to the King daily, which enabled him to rectify at once any deviation from his orders. He very frequently went into long and tedious enquiries on intricate cases of law, and settled them in person. There are many wonderful stories related of his quick penetration and sound judgemnet. Among others, is the following:- There were two brothers, private soldiers, who had porcured some booty at Gowaliar during the siege; among other articles of plunder were two larte rubies, but of different shapes. One of the brothers determined to quit the service and return to his family at Dehli while the other resolved to continue in the army; but he made over charge of his share of the booty to his brother, telling him to give it together with his ruby to his wife. After the war, on his return to Dehli the soldier learned from his wife that she had never seen the ruby. The brother declared he had given it to her, and the parties were brought up before the Kazi Mian Buhari. The Judge asked the man who had quitted the service, who saw him give the ruby to his brother's wife? he replied, several persons knew she had it, and he produced some brahmins of notoriously bad characters as witnesses, whohaving been instruted what to say, gave evidence against the woman, who was told to go home and give the ruby to her husband. Owing to the ill treatment she received at home, she determined to lay her case before the King in person. He listened very attentively to the whole story, and then sending for the witnesses, all the parties acknowledged that they recollected perfectly the shape and size of the ruby given to the soldier's wife: a piece of waz was accordingly given to each witness, and being separated, they were directed to make models of the gem. Those of the two brothers corresponded; but the models of the witnesses being dissimilar, the King concluded they could never have seen it; and having thus convicted them of perjury, they were induced to tell the truth, and the woman's innocence was proved. Sikandar Lodhi was himself a poet, and highly appreciated literary merit. During his reign many works were composed both in prose and verse; among others, is the Farhung Sikandri whose author informs us this Prince reigned 28 years and five months.

Ibrahim Lodhi Afghan

Sikandar Lodhi dying at Agra, his son Ibrahim succeeded to the throne. At a very early period, contrary to the custom of his father and grandfather, he made no distinction among his officers, whether of his own tribe or otherwise, and said publicly, that Kings should have no relations nor clansmen, but that all should be considered as subjects and servants of the state; and the Afghan chiefs, who had hitherto been allowed to sit in the presence, were constrained to stand in front of the throne, with their hands crossed before him.

In the year A.H. 923 (A.D. 1517), shortly after his accession a conspiracy was formed by the Lodi chiefs, by whom is was agreed to leave Ibrahim in quiet possession of Dehli and a few dependent provinces, and to raise the Prince Jalal Khan[367] his brother, to the throne at Junpur[368]. The Prince accordingly, marching from Kalpa in conjunction with the disaffected chiefs, ascended the throne of Junpur. He appointed his cousin, Fatteh Khan, his Wazir who gained over all the officers of the eastern provinces to his interest. Khan Jehan Lohani was at this time proceeding from Raberi to congratulate Ibrahim on his accession; when falling in with the disaffected nobles, he blamed them severely for causing divisions in the Kingdom, which he said, would be attended with fatal consequences to the family of Lodhi. The chiefs, admitting the impropriety of their conduct, determined, as the Prince Jalal Khan could not be yet well established, to divest him of his newly-assumed dignity; and accordingly they sent Heibat Khan Jalwani, with letters, to recall him before he reached Junpur. Heibut Khan, however, having overacted his part, the Prince, Jalal Khan, suspected some plot, and excused himself from coming. The chiefs, unaware that he suspected them, deputed Sheikh Mahomed Firmully and others to enforce their request; but the Prince proceeded to Janpur. Finding all endeavours to reclaim the Prince had failed, Ibrahim Lodi issued a proclamation, declaring every officer who should adhere to his brother the Prince Julal a traitor to the state; at the same time he sent presents and deputations to all his principal officers, which had the effect of detaching the nobles from the pretender, and by degrees bringing them over to the King's interest. The affairs of the Prince rapidly declining, he conceived that nothing but desperate measures could retrieve them. Accordingly he marched to Kalpi, and placing his family in security in that fort, he collected all his troops, and assumed the title of King, under the title of Jalal-ud-Din. At the same time, he sent a trusty person to Azim Humayun, who was at the time besieging Kaunaj to join him. Azim Humayun did so; but recommended the Prince, in the first instance, to establish himself firmly at Junpur. The Prince accordingly marched against the son of Mubarik Khan Lodhi, governor of Qude and compelled him to retreat to Lucknow[369].

Ibrahim Lodhi, hearing of these proceedings, marched his army to that quarter, and confined his other brothers in the fort of Hansi, where they remained for life. This event took place on Thursday the 24th of Zeehuj. A.H. 923 (February 6 A.D. 1518). On his march towards Qude the King was informed that Azim Humayun, having deserted the Prince Jalal, was now on his way to join him, on which the King sent some chiefs to escort him to his camp, where he was favourably received. A number of other officers also joined Ibrahim, and he despatched the greatest part of his army, under the command of Azim Humayun Lodhi[370] against the Prince. But before the King's troops could come up with him, he threw a garrison into Kalpi and marches with 30,000 chosen horse, by forced marches, to Agra, while Azim Humayun Lodhi was content to lay siege to Kalpi Jalal Khan had it now in his power either to take possession of Agra, or to plunder the treasury; but the governor, Adam Khan, in order to save the place and the country, entered into negotiations with the Prince, and went so far as to promise him, on the part of the King, the independent possession of Kalpi and other advantages, for which he had no authority. Adam Khan sent notice of the whole transaction to Ibrahim; but the King having taken Kapil and the treaty having been concluded without his knowledge, he took no notice of it, but marched against the Prince, Jalal Khan, who now deserted by his army, was obliged to fly to Gowaliar and solicit the protection of the raja of that place. Ibrahim Lodhi came to Agra, where he remained in order to regulate the affairs of the government, which, since the death of his father, had fallen into disorder. Two nobles, Karrem Dad Turk, and Daulat Khan, were sent to takecharge of Delhi and Sheikhzada Mahomed Firmalli was deputed to Chanderi to remain with Mahomed Khan, the Prince of Malwa.

About this time the King, without assigning any reason, caused Mian Bhupri, formerly *Wazir* to his father Sikandar Lodhi to be put in chains, conferring at the same time great honours on his son. The Prince, Jalal Khan, found refuge in Gowaliar and it was deemed necessary, therefore, to attack that fortress; for which purpose Azim Humayun Sherwani marched from Karra with 30,000 horse, and 300 elephants; and seven other chiefs, with armies were also sent to join in the siege. The Prince, Jalal Khan, despairing of holding out with success, fled to the court of Sultan Mahmud Khalji of Malwa. The Dehli army arriving before Gwaliar, invested the place,and in a few days, Raja Man-Singh a prince of great valour and capacity, dying his son Vikramajit succeeded him. After the siege had been carried on for some months, the army of Ibrahim Lodhi at length got possession of an outwork at the foot of the hill, on which stood the fort of Badilgar. They found in that place a braze bull, which had been for a long time an object of worship, and sent it to Agra, from whence it was afterwards conveyed to Dehli, and thrown down before the Bagdad gate (A.H. 924, A.D. 1518)[371]

The Prince, Jalal Khan, not being well received by Sultan Mohmud of Malwa, fled to the Raja of Gurrakota; but being intercepted on the road by a body of Gonds,[372] he was sent prisoner to the King's camp. Ibrahim Lodhi sent him to Hansi, but gave private orders for his assasination on the road. What charms can there be in power, which can induce a man to shed the blood of his own brother? Nor was Ibrahim satisfied with the death of his brother Jalal alone, he also imbrued his hands int he blood f several of his officers at the same time. Having recalled Azim Humayun Sherwani from the siege of Gowaliar, when just on the point of taking the place, he imprisoned him, and his son Fatteh Khan, and also removed his other son, Islam Khan, from the government of Karra. Islam Khan, hearing of the fate of his father and brother, and of the disgrace reserved for himself, rebelled, and defeated Ahmad Khan, who was sent to assume his government. The King now receiving advices of the reductionof Gowaliar, which had been for a hundred years in the hands of the Hindus, he had leisure to turn his thoughts towards the insurrection at Kurra. Azim Humayun and Syeed Khan, after the fall of Gowaliar, were permitted to go to their jageers, from whence, uniting with Islam Khan, they added strength to his power, Ibrahim Lodhi placing little dependence on the fidelity of the troops about his person, issued orders for those of the distant provinces to repair to his camp; and conferring great honours on Ahmud Khan, the brother of Azim Humayun Lodhi gave him the command of the army against Islam Khan.Ahmad Khan, having reached the vicinity of Kanauj, was attacked by Yekbal Khan, a dependent of Azim Humayun Sherwani, who, rushing out from an ambuscade with 5000 horse, cut off a number of the royal troops, and made good his retreat. The King was greatdly exasperated against Ahmud Khan, on receiving intelligence of this defeat, and wrote to him not to expect his favour, if he did not quickly exterminate the rebels, at the same time he sent another detachment of troops to his support. The army of the insurgents now ammounted to 40,000 cavalry, 500 elephants, and a large body of infantry with which they proceeded to oppose the royalists under Ahmad Khan (A.H. 925, A.D. 1519). The two armies came in sight of each other, but did not engage, for Sheikh Raju Bukhari, a holy man, highly esteemed in that age, was in hopes of bringing affairs to an accommodation. Overtures being made, the insurgents agreed to disband their troops the moment that Azim Humayun Sherwani should be set at liberty. The Duryia Khan Lohani, governor of Bihar, to Nasir Khan Lohani King, however, refusing to accede to these terms, sent orders to the collector of Ghazipur, and to Sheikhzada Mahomed Firmally, the governor of Ayodhya, to advance against the rebels, who very imprudently permitted themselves to be amused till these armies united, when they were compelled either to fly or to fight on unequal terms. They resolved on the latter alternative, and accordingly drew up in order of battle. Urged by despair, they fought bravely, and were on the point of defeating the royalists, when Islam Khan was killed, and Syeed Khan taken prisoner. These untoward incidents discouraging their followers, they fled in every direction, and all the treasure and baggage of the insurgents fell into the hands of the King's troops. Ibrahim Lodhi now gave full scoep to his hatred and resentment against the nobles of Sikandar Lodhi's reign, many of whom suffered death. Azim

Humayun Sheirwani, Mian Buhari, and others, who were in confinement, were at the same time privately executed. These proceedings creating distrust among the nobles. Daria Khan Lohani, governor of Bihar, Khan Jehan Lodhi. Hassein Khan Firmalli and many other chiefs, went into open rebellion. The King receiving intelligence of this defection, sent a private order to some holy men of Chanderi to cut off Hassein Khan Firmalli and he was accordingly assassinated in his bed. This fresh instance of Ibrahim's treachery and cruelty tended only to make him more enemies. Dariya Khan Lohani, governor of Bihar, dying about this time, his son, Bahadur Khan, assumed the title of King, under the title of Mahomed Shah. He was joined by most of the discontended chiefs in that vicinity and soon found himself at the head of 100,000 horse, with which he took possession of all the country as far as Sambhal, defeating the Dehli troops in repeated engagements of the *'Nam'* or *'Kalma'*. Meanwhile, Ghazi Khan Lodhi came with the army from Lahore; but having heard of the King's proceedings on the way, he became apprehensive of treachery and returned to his father, Daulat Khan Lodhi at Lahore where the old dynasty of *Kushana* was established Daulat Khan, seeing no safety for his family, revolted from the King, and solicited Babar, the Moghul prince who then reigned in Kabul, to attempt the conquest of Hindustan. The invasion of Babar was preceded by the arrival in India of hte Prince Allu-ud-Din, who had fled from his brother Ibrahim Lodhi, and was then residing at Kabul. Daulat Khan supporting him, as a cloak to his own plans, reduced all the country as far as south as Dehli and the Prince Allau-ud-Din being joined by many officers of distinction, he found himself at the head of an army of 40,000 horse, with which he proceeded to invest Dehli.

Ibrahim resolved to oppose him; but when within six coss (twelve miles) of the Prince's army, Ibrahim's camp was surprised in the night, and after a tumultuous conflict which lasted till daylight, Ibrahim found himself deserted by most of his officers, who joined Allau-ud-Din. Observing, however, in the morning, that the troops of Alla-ud-Din were dispersed in plundering, Ibrahim rallied his soldiers, and collecting the greater part of his elephants, returned to the attack, and expelled his brother and rival from the field with considerable slaughter. Ibrahim now entered Dehli in triumph; and the Prince Allau-ud-Din, seeing no hopes of reducing the place, retreated to the Punjab as his parental house.

Affairs remained in this state till the year A.H.932 [373] (A.D. 1526), when Zahir-ud-Din Mohamed Babar marched against Ibrahim Lodhi, as will be hereafter shown; and a sanguinary battle was fought between these two kings on the plain of Panipat, where Babar was victorious, and Ibrahim lost his life; an event which transferred the empire of Dehli and Agra to the family of Timur. The reign of Ibrahim Lodi lasted twenty years[374].

Accordingly, Sultan Sikandar agian set out from Srinagar. But on reaching *Baramulla,* he came to know that Amir Timur had already crossed the Indus on his way back to *Samarqand*. Hence, he returned to Srinagar and from there sent him costly presents. It is said that Sikandar also sent his loyal son, Prince Shahi Khan, the future Zain-ul-Abdin, to the court of Amir Timur in order to strengthen friendly relations with him. But this is absurd as the Prince was not even born at that *'Kalma',* (Law of the nature) he was born in 1401 A.D. Popularly known as *But-Shikan*, he is compared with *Aurangzeb*, the Mughal emperor of India. At first, however, he was tolerant. Later, he was egged on to follow an intolerant policy towards his Hindu subjects by the men of his own faith who flocked to his court from foreign lands. These men, the majority of whom consisted of the *Baihaqi Sayyidis* were attracted to Kashmir by Sultan Sikandar's fame as a liberal donor. They were, "no doubt astonished to see him that in a Muslim state, *Islam* did not have the domination, but existed side by side with the practice of the infidels." The most important of the Sayyids who came to Kashmir in the time of Sultan Sikander and cast a spell on him was *Mir Mohammad Hamadani.* H was an *Alavi Sayyid*. He "added fuel to the fire of the King's fierce zeal." Use of wine and other intoxicants were banned.Gambling, dancing of women and playing of musical instruments for entertainment purposes were forbidden. The practice of *Sati* followed by the Hindus women and application of *Tilak* by the Hindus on the forehead were also prohibited, because these were the false notions of the Brahmans. He enforced the 'Islamic Law' which was properly a new message of the Father in this country, in this way, a new office of *Sheikh-ul-Islam* was established by Sultan Sikandar in *Srinagar* or Kashmir at that time. However, Mir Mohammad Hamadani started his campaign of conversions, he was able to win over the faith of *Suha Bhatta*. The Sultan's Chief Minister urged the Sultan to adopt a more vigorous anti-Hindu policy, because most of, Hindus at that time used to believe on the idol worship which was the blind faith against the law of Nature, who is right within your body. Thus, newly converted minister known as Malik Saif-ud-din, who stood with Sultan Sikander in the campaign of war, a 'reign of terror' was established against Hindus, and all the sacred books of the Hindus mind were sunk into the *Dal Lake* by the Sikandar[375]. As a result of it, Lawrance, W.R, remarks "Many were fled, many were converted and many were killed, and it is said that this thorough monarch (Sikandar Sultan) burnt *Seven maunds* of sacred threads of the murdered Brahmans[376]." as a blind faith they have created in the society against the law of nature. When Saif-ud-din heard that many Brahmans were quitting Kashmir, he decided to chefk hem, because time and gain, therewere problem created of the society make caste, colour and creed as their *'law'*. In this way, the valley of *Kashmir* did not fall within the sphere of influence of the Sultanate of Delhi. Thus the control system of India at that time was credit for the establishment of Muslim rule there goes to *Shah Mirza,* an inhabitant of *Swati,* who overthrew the ruling family of his Hindu patron in 1339, and ascended the throne with the title of *Shams-ud-din Shah.* One of his grandsons, Sikander Shah or Sultan (1394-1416 A.D) *alias* the *But Shikan* was the ruler of Kashmir at that time when Amir Timur invasions launched over Delhi and Delhi was shattered into pieces. Again his son Ali Shah (1416-20 A.D) was desposed by his younger brother Shah Khan in June 1420 A.D; the latter ascended the throne with the title of Zain-ul- He was the most enlighteed and popular monarch of Kashmir who enjoyed a long raign of 49 years (1420-70 A.D) and became famous in the history of Kashmir for his new religions policy of toleration and public welfare activities[377]. Besides proclaiming equality before law, the administration of justice was made simpler and easier. All the laws were codified and engraved on copper plates which were displayed at the most frequented places. Sultan Zain-u-Abidin "was in this respect, perhaps, the first systematic law giver of Kashmir[378]" along with the Panjabi ruler of the *'Nam'* called *Maraj.* As Sultan Sikander had indiscriminately melted down the golden and silver idols of *'Nam'* in the currency of the country had been greatly debased. And, Zain-ul-Abidin extensively issued new coins of the *'Nam'* both silver and copper of the fine stuff[379] as started by the Aryans of India i.e. called *leather coin.* He was surrounded by a glaxy of learnedmen of the *'Nam',* local as well as foreigners.These included, among others, *Mulla Ahmad,* his poet laureate, Syyid Mohammad Rumi, Qazi Sayyid *Ali Shirazi,* Sayyid Mohammad Sistani Maulana Kabir, Mulla Nadiri, Sayyid Mohammad Madain, *Jonaraja, Srivara,* Yodhabhatta and *Nothosoma Pandit*[380]. Therefore, he has been called Akbar of Kashmir.

As, it has been observed from the study that in the beginning of Zain-ul-Abidin rule in Kashmir, heavy rainfall was took place for a number of days. In the words of *Srivara*; "the waters then became ungovernable and caused mischief, lowering objects which were high, and lifting up things that were low.' Great was the distress of the helpless human beings. 'The boys clasped the necks of their mothers in fear, and the mothers shed tears as if they worshipped the lord of *Nagas* with pearls. (As the water rose) the children got up from the feet of their mothers to their lap, then to their shoulders, and then to their head, and finally departed from them even as life departs from the body; and the agitated water of the inundation clasped the trembling limbs of the women like a lover'. As Srinagar has suffered the most during this flood, Zain-ul-Abidin decided to shift his capital from its present location to a higher level towards the *Hari Parbat* hill. The result was the founding of a new town of *Naushahr*[381] of *Naushahr*, we have already made a mention. In the time Zain-ul-Abidin, this town was called *Zaina Nagar.* He adorned, it with a a number of beautiful buildings. *'Rajdan',* the royal palace, was said to be a unique building in the whole of the east. It had twelve storeys and each storey contained fifty rooms, numerous halls and corridors decorated with exquisite carvings and fresco paintings[382].

On account of the above mentioned architectural activities, the historians have been tempted to compare the reign of Sultan Zain-ul-Abidin with that of Shah Jahan, the Mughal emperor of India[383]. Moreover, he was a great linquist, scholar and poet. Besides Kashmiri, which was his mother tongue, he was well versed in Sanskrit, Persian and Tibetan. In Persian he wrote two works; a treatise on pyrotechnics called *Habib,* explained the fire works of the *'Nam'*, in the form of a dialogue, and *Shikayat* which brings forth the human vanity and transitoriness of the world from one stage to another i.e from Darkness to Englightenment ear. The latter was penned down by the Sultan towards the end of his life when he was greatly distressed and disillusioned on account of his sons' mutual bickerings and subsequently revolts were took place among the disloyal ministers of the Zain-ul-Abidin on the basis of their personal interest i.e monetary. It was, however, only the beginning of the Sultan's unhappy days. In 1465, he lost his beloved queen. This was followed by the death of many of his dear relations, close friends and loyal ministers and other servants. Thereupon, *Adham* lost his heart and sought his safety in flight to the Heaven for a few days later, on 12th May, 1470 A.D., Zain-ul-Abidin left this mortal world. After the death, as a poet he used to write under the title of *Qutab* which is known as *'Nam'* in Arabic language. In the words of *Srivara*, 'The King's virtuous mode of governmen t in the *Kali Yuga* became glorious like the very middle of the *Satya Yuga*[384].' It continued to remain as tributary under the successors of Sultan Sikander of Kashmir. Zain-ul-Abidin during his reign (1420-1470 A.D) had also acquired some land for his private farm in Ladakh[385] for the development of Kashmir as a part of it. It shows that Sultan Zain-ul-Abidin not only understood Ladakh as a part of Kashmiri Kingdom in territorial conditions, but he also felt secured in Ladakh from the security point of view. *Srivara* mentions that Sultan Zain-ul-Abidin was well versed in Ladakhi language[386].

According to *Baharistan-i-Shahi*[387], during the rule of Sultan Zain-ul-Abidin, the ruler of *Kashgar* planned to captured Ladakh and Baltistan. The Sultan went into action partly due to his anxiety to protect a feudatory region, but chiefly in the larger interests of national security while on his way to Ladakh, Zain-ul-Abidin boosted the morale of his soldiers by addressing them in the *pargana* of Lar. The Persian sources speak of a bloody battle at village *Shah* in Ladakh was fought between the two forces of the *Kashmir* and *Kashgar*. The Kashmiri forces at that time were under the command of *Mir Hasan Baihaqi*, who rendered remarkable military services to Sultan Zain-ul-Abidin in his campaign towards Ladakh. According to *Jonaraja* "victorious in the war in *Shayadesa* that King (Zain-ul-Abidin) saved the golden image of *Buddha* from the *Yavanas* (*Kashghari*) forces [388]. According to N.K. Zutshi, Zain-ul-Abidin went even to the extent of saving the golden image of the *Lord Buddha* in the foreign land of *Ladakh* which was exploited by the Muslim soldiers of the *Kashgar* army[389]. *Baharistan-i-Shahi* again gives a detailed account of the battle of *Sheh*. Despite the opponents superiority in numbers its author states that the Kashmiri troops displayed a conspicuous courage and fighting ability after some initial signs of weariness and inaction caused naturally by their rapid march through the long and difficult terrain from Kashmir to Sheh[390]. The two forces drew closer for a head on a confrontation towards the end of the *Kali Yuga*. The Sultan's force was flanked right to attack the loft wing of the *Kashgar* and the left wing was struck at their centre[391]. A fierce battle was fought all the days without a decision. The next morning, the Kashmiri troops pounced on their enemy with re-doubled fury and clinched the issue in their favour by sheer dint of exceptional courage, they obtained the spirit of fighting against the enemy i.e. *'Man'* always believes in glory. However, the casualities were heavy on both sides i.e. *Sudras* and the *Brahmans*. those used to believe in the theory of mind. The news of victory stationed at a safe distance from the battle field of *Sheh*. No direct corroboration of this expedition is available from the Ladakhi sources, but two references are very significant. First it attributes to the Ladakhi King, *Blo-gros-mchog-Iden* (1440-1470 A.D), an expedition to *Guge*[392] and the capture a rich booty [393] of the *'Nam'* called *'Chamar'*. Secondly the broth of *Blo-gros-mchog-Iden* is mentioned as *Drungpa Ali*. It is, however, sought to be explained in either of the two following ways: (i) the Ladakhi King, *a Bumlde IV* may have married a Muslim woman from the relation of Zain-ul-Abidni; and (ii) *Drungpa Ali* may have carried away this Muslim lady as a host of the Kashmir ruler and then she was converted into *'Islam*[394]*'* as a new religion of the mankind at that time. So far as the second version is concerned, it was more plausible to learn from Jonaraja in the same sequence that the Kashmir troops, they also destroyed the Ladakhi town of Mulbek, looted the treasury, and threw the *Bhaultas* in the state of terror, it is important to note at that time rule of the mind was heavy i.e. called Brahminical ideology in the common sense. It is ,therefore, clearly indicated that *Ladakhi* displayed a recalcitrnat attitude towards the Kashmiri troops and were reduced to submission with a heavy hand. To ensure the good conduct in future, the Kashmir troops may have carried the King's brother to Kashmir where he became a Muslim. In this way, the north-east of Kashmir the two mountain-Kingdoms of Ladakh and Baltistan were secured by bringing to submission as the tributaries region for the constant vigilance of the enemies from the top of the mountains[395]. Thus, the later successors of Zain-ul-Abidin did not keep the Ladakh under their control Ladakh again asserted as an independent state for sometime[396]. In 1532 A.D. When Nazuk Shah was the Sultan of Kashmir, *Mirza Haider Dughlat,* a commander of Sultan Abu Khan of *Kashghar* conquered Ladakh[397]. After this task, was accomplished, winter set in and made the invaders stay at Ladakh very uncomfortable. Thereupon, they thought of Kashmir, a better place for winter. There was, however, yet another cause leading to their invasion of Kashmir; this country was inhabited by a large number of infidels, Shias and Hindus, and the invaders wanted to Chastise them with the power of *'Nam'* or *'Kalma'*. After this, Mirza Muhammad Haidar Dughlat left Kashmir with the force of 4,000 Mongols. On his way, he was joined by many *Ladakhis* and *Baltis* also who served as guides. After crossing the

Zojila pass in January 1533 A.D. he encountered a small force of Kashmiris who were stationed at an out-post in a narrow defile near *Gagangir* in the *Pargana* of *Lar*. But the defenders were easily put to a rout by 400 men of the invaders. Encountering no more resistance on his way, Mirza Muhammad Haider Dughlat entered *Naushahr* and took up his residence in the palace of the late Sultan Zain-ul-Abidin. After a stay of 24 days at *Naushahr*, the invaders marched towards the district of *Maraj,* driving everything before them. To quote *Shuka*: 'Hundreds of houses were burnt and the city that had been populous before now became life the ground of burning dead.' No regard was paid either to age or sex; nor was any distinction made between the Hindus and the non-Hindus. Many of them, ' farsaking their city and homes, fled towards the hills and gleus, leaving their property in their dwellings'. The ravages of the Mongols went on relentlessly for about three months. Thereafter, the Kashmiris screwed up their courage to grapple with the invaders. They were furhter galvanized into action when the *Ulama* issued a decree enjoining upon the people a duty to clear the country of every invader, pronouncing that whosever fell in this crusade would be a martyr. Beaming with great enthusiasm and led by Kaji Chak, Abdul Magree, Lohar Magre, Regi Chak and Malik Ali Chadura, the Kashiris met the Mongols in a pitched battle at *Pavan* (*Anantnag* district). But they suffered defeat and one of their leaders, *Malik Ali Chadura,* was killed.

The Kashmiris were, however, not disheartect at this reverse. Realising that they were no match for the invaders in pitched battles, they adopted guerilla tactics. These soon wore Mirza Muhammad Haider Dughlat and his followers down and they offered the following terms and conditions of peace to the Kashmir:

1. That the *Khutba 'Nam'* or *'Kalma'* may be read and coin struck in the name of Sultan said Khan of *Kashghar*;
2. That the daughter of Sultan Muhammad Shah may be married to Prince Sikandar Khan, son of Sultan said Khan;
3. That the prisoner sof war may be released, and
4. That presents may be exchanged between Sultan Said Khan and Sultan Muhammad Shah.

Kashmiris accepted these terms and conditions with the result that Mirza Muhammad Haidar Dughlat and his followers quitted Kashmir in May 1533 A.D. On his way back, the Mirza Haidar Dughlat received in Ladakh the news of the death of Sultan Said Khan and the succession of his son, Abdur Rashid Khan. As the new Sultan was dead against the Dughlats, the Mirza proceeded first to Badakhshan and then to Lahore (1537 A.D.) to enter into the service of *Kamran,* the younger brother of *Humayun*. Kashmir was at that time in the grip of the struggle for power between the *Chaks*[398], who were mostly Shias, and the *Magreys,* who were Sunnis. After the death of Mohammad Shah in 1537 A.D. and of his successor, *Shams-ud-Din,* the next year, *Kaji Chak* had come to enjoy full discretionary powers. Ismail Shah 1, the new Sultan, made him his Chief minister. The anti-Sultan policy of the latter drove the Sunnis to an open revolt under the leadership of *Abdul Magre* and *Regi Chak*. But the rebels were beat hollow and obliged to take refuge in the Panjab. In the Panjab, the rebels approached Mirza Muhammad Haidar Dughlat for help. Earlier, the Mirza had to leave Kashmir reluctantly. He, therefore, welcomed the idea of its reconquest and persuaded *Kamran* also, the result was that an advance force to Kashmir was attached. But in the meantime, *Kamran* and Mirza Muhammad Haidar were called upon to lend countenance to Humayun who had been defeated by Sher Shah at *Chausa*. Hence, the scheme of the conquest of Kashmir was given up[399]. This attack produced a great consternation in the Mughal camp which attacked by the Afghans from all the three directions. The tumult aroused Humayun who sprang upon his horse and tried to collect his armymen, most of whom had already run away in different directions for safety. *Humayun* failed to reach his text, but he was escorted out of danger by a few of his faithful followers. Humayun felt his safety in flight, entered into the river *Ganga* and was about to be drowned when a water-carrier, *Nizam* by name, offered him an inflated skin (*Mashak*), which he used in crossing over to the other bank of the river. For this kindness, Humayun patronised *Nizam* by seating him on the throne for two days. After his victory at *Chausa*, Sher Shah declared himself King of Bengal[400].

Later on, some differences arose between *Kamran* and *Humayun,* and the former refurned to Lahore. But Mirza Muhammad Haidar Dughlat chose to stay with Humayun, fought on his side in the battle of Kanauj in May 1540 A.D. and, after their rout at the hands of Sher Shah, came to Lahore. The arrival of Mirza Muhammad Haidar at Lahore revived the hopes of the rebels from *Kashmir* and they resumed negotiations with him. Being hotly pursued by Sher Shah, the Mughals were at this time discussing where to go. Only a couple of years ago, Mirza Muhammad

Haidar had himself easily conquered *Kashmir.* Now he was assured of help from some local nobles also. In view of these advantages, he prevailed upon Humayun to proceed to *Kashmir.* According to a settled plan, therefore, Mirza Haidar *Dughlat* left Lahore with a small contingent of 400 soldiers. Humayun had to follow him. But after the Mirza Haidar's depature, a number of the emperors kith and kin and other followers deserted him, and so much was he dismayed by this development that, instead of going to Kashmir, he proceeded to Persia. Mirza Muhammad Haidar, however, struck to the original plan[401]. Besides being tributary to Kashmir, Ladakh had maintained trade contacts with the Kashmir Valley since ancient times[402] of Asoka. The Srinagar-Leh route was till very recently used by the Caravans of Afghans, and Indian Merchants who used to exchange goods with Chinese and Central Asian Caravans at Leh. Leh served as a transit camp for the other side. Ladakh supplied borax and shawl wool to Kashmir valley in return for shawls, food stuffs, commodities of daily use, shoes, gold and silver ornaments. Shawl-wool for shawl industry of the Kashmir came from *Champa,* Ladakh and Tibet as well as *Yargand*[403.] Ladakh sent woollen cloth to Kashmir. When *Pir Panjal Route* was under snow and communications were suspended salt was imported from Ladakh and Tibet[404]. No doubt, that to the east of Kashmir, there was another important route leading through the *Zojila* pass via Drass to Ladakh then had to Tibet route and China at that time. Besides the political and trade relations, there was also cultural contacts between China and Kashmir since ancient times during the time of Mauryan ruler like Asoka and others. They performed to this date a Quinquennial ceremony with great gravity, pomp and show glory[405] of the *'Nam'*. It shows that the idea of Buddhism had the firm root in China and it is a well known fact that Buddhist doctrines was initially widely spread in China including Ladakh itself by five hundred Kashmiri Buddhists[406]. So that there must have been the exchange of idea between the two from time to time for the development of civilization one after the another. Similarly *Islam* also spread in Ladakh via Kashmir in China itself Among the outdoor games *Polo* was intorduced into Kashmir from Ladakh and was played by the Sultans of Kashmir and their nobles[407] of the courtiers at length.

From the above discussion, it has been rightly expressed that *Shah Mir,* Sultan of Kashmir invited the Chinese rulers alongwith the historians from 1339 to 1554 A.D. as well as in the early period of the Indian History and Kashmir state or Kingdom became a tributary state under the following reasons discussed as under:—

1. The rebellions elements of Kashmir used to shelter at Ladakh (China) for the time beings.
2. Being a tributary State China had enhanced the revenue of Kashmir by paying annual tribute to the Master of the *'Nam'*.
3. In order to check the plundering attacks of Ladakhi or Chinese tribe, it was necessary at that time to keep Ladakh or China under the control of Delhi Sultanate as their will.
4. There was another interesting things to note that both the countries had the smooth trade relations and they were proved necessary at the time of confusion between both the China (Ladakh) and Kashmir at that period.
5. China or Ladakh at that time laid to north-west of Kashmir, therefore, to capture the Ladakh or China, north-east of Kashmir was secured at that point of time, and there was a constant vigilance at China or Ladakh during the period of Sultan Zain-ul-Abidin. It is very important to note or to record here in this study that they were the *Sudra* rulers called *'untouchables'* by the Brahmans of Kashmir, but they were the rulers of the *'pure thought'* i.e called *'Nam'*, either there was *Babar or Akbar or Sultan Sikandar*, etc. they were the rulers of the *'Nam'*. It shows that *'Nam'* is the 'Supreme Being', he regulates the every motion of the society from top to bottom and from earth to heaven in every time in human life.

"Forgotten has been what we read;

the Friend's Name only sung instead," according to *Pir* or a spiritual guide of Dara's teacher i.e. *Sarmad Saheed*, who was deeply interested in theology, Comparative religions studies and mysticism, and busy with translating the *Upanishads* into Persian as well as writing books. He wrote books such as *Majma-al-Bahrain* (the Mingling of the Two Oceans) and *Safinat-al-auliya* (A Biography of Saints including *Sarmad Saheed*) in which he gave expression to his sufic ideas and views concerning the reconciliation of Hinduism, the traditional faith of *India,* and *Islam*[408] Another perspective is from Bernier, who records: "Mullah Shah, a native of Badakshan, was the *Murshid* or spiritual guide of Dara Shikoh, and was highly respected by Shah Jahan. He died in Kashmir about the year 1660[409]."

From the study, we learn that Dara Shikoh was the greatest grandson of Emperor Akbar (1542-1605

A.D.), who was noted for his religious tolerance for the long period of Indian History. Now, he has created an amalgamation of beliefs and offered a tolerant and monotheistic, *Din-i-illahi*. It is said that crafty Aurangzeb started a fratricidal war and killed Dara as well as his other brothers, cousin and nephews and everyone else was could lay claim to the throne. The liberal days of *Akbar, Jahangir* and *Shah Jahan* were over in Kashmir. Now fanaticism was seated firmly on the throne. The year was 1659. The search for *God* or *Nam* or *Chamar* must be made within the body, which is described in the *Bible* and *Quran* as the temple of the living God. Disciples of living true Masters conduct this research by practising concentration at the centre of consciousness between the two eyebrows, slightly above the root of the nose. In Patanjali's *Yogasutra* it is said. "Concentration is the confinement of the mind in a fixed place," from this centre the mind, with power derived from the *'Word'* or *'God'*.

Notes & References

1. J.V. Naik. General President's Address. In Indian History Congress 67th session, 10-12 March, 2007. *The Reformer and the Quest for Social Justice in Indian History;* Kerala, p. 16
2. *Ibid.*
3. *Ibid.*
4. *Ibid.*, p. 17
5. M.G. Ranade, *Rise of the Maratha Power*. Published by Ministry of Indian Broadcasting Govt. of India; Reprint; 1966, p. 68.
6. K.L Khandelwal, *'Kabir Panth and Its Social' Contents'* S.P Sen (ed). *Social contents of Indian Religons Reform Movements.* Calcutta 1978, pp. 80-81.
7. **Note.** This body is the temple of the true lord. The 'focal point' is 'Father', the point to which prayer is directed of the living being master, especially the *Kaba* term. In other words, it is the geographical location of the *Kaba* in relation to a devotee in ritual prayer called *namaaz*. While *'Word'* must have been faced at that time in the direct of *Kaba* while offering his devotion to *'Kalma'* or *'Nam'*. In a mosque this direction is indicated by the *mehraab* (prayer arch). *Qibla* is also used as a synonym for the *Kaba*, " and here I cry out to *Allah,* the one with out parallel." according to *Sultan Bahu* (p. 42).
8. *Adi Granth, Bhairau,* Kabirji, p. 1162.
9. *K.W.G.N.*, p. 36.
10. Many conflicting views have been expressed by Indian and Western scholars regarding the place and date of *Dadu Dayal* birth, his name, caste, parents, *Guru*, his education, travel, and the date of his final exit from the body, and there is hardly any conclusive historical evidence to support one view over another. Among the various theories, the following is profounded by some of the later followers of *Dadu,* and supported by Swami Narayan Das Pushkar, of the Dadu order. Lodhi Ram Nagar, a Brahmin of Ahmedabad and a cotton merchant by profession, had no son. He was assiduously devoted to his religious duties and attended on all holy men who came his way, hoping to get his cherished desire fulfilled. One day a holy man appeared before him and, pleased with Lodhi Ram's piety, bade him go next morning for his usual bathing in the river *Sabarmati* where, Lodhi Ram was assured, he would find his long cherished wish fulfilled. Next morning, when Lodhi Ram went to the river, to his delighted surprise he found an infant floating downstreeam in a crib of lotus leaves. There is similar legend about Saint Kabir who is said to have appeared floating on a lake in Banaras, where he was found by weaver named *Niru* who brought him up. He lovingling brought the baby home; His wife, *Vasi,* was overjoyed, and it is said that as soon as she clasped the baby in her arms, her breasts were filled with milk.

    According to *Rajjab* and other disciples of Dadu, as also the author of *Dabistan-i-Mazahib, Dadu* was a Muslim by birth and a carder by profession. Kshitimohan Sen, a scholar of medieval mysticism in India, suggests that Dadu was a Muslim whose earlier name was *Daoid,* and the name of his wife was *Hawwa.* Dadu had two sons and two daughters. He was born in 1544 A.D. and he died in 1603 A.D. His profession was that of a *dhuniya,* a cotton-cender, *Dabistan-i-Mazahib* gives his profession as *naddaf,* whichis Arabic is called for 'Cader'. According to another account, Dadu had the habit of giving away his belongings to others, right from his early childhood. Because of this predominant charitable trait, his parents named him Dadu (the *'giver'* from the Persian word *dadan*). The word *dayal,* means *'compassionate'* like 'Father' (K.N. Upadhyaa; *Dadu, The Campassionate Mystic.* Punjab; third edition; 1997; pp. 3,4 & 5 Henceforth as *D.C.M.*)
11. *K.W.G.N.*, p. 38.
12. *K.G.M.*, p. 11.
13. *Ibid.*, p. 4.
14. *Ibid.*, p. 5.
15. V.N. Jha; *Caste, Untouchability and Social Justice* Early North Indian Perspective. Indian History Congress 57 session (Chennai, 1996). Thematic Symposium on 'Changing Concepts of Social Justice in Indian History", Delhi, 1997; p. 5. Henceforth cited as *C.U.S.J.*
16. N.K. Dutt, *Origin and Growth of Caste in India*; Calcutta Vol. II. 1965, p. 147
17. *C.U.S.J.*, pp. 7-8.

18. *Ibid.*, p. 9.
19. B.G. Ramesh, *Biography Series Dr. B.R Ambedkar Bangalore, 2005;* p. 42.
20. *C.U.S.J.*, p. 11.
21. *Ibid.*, p. 12.
22. U. Chakravarti; *The Soical Dimensins of Early Buddhism,* Delhi Vol. II 1987, pp. 5.6.
23. *Ibid.*, Vol. 1, p. 1.
24. *C.U.S.J.*, p. 13.
25. Projesh Banerji; *Aesthetics of Indian Folk-Dance*; New Delhi, 1982, p. 2. Hereafter referred as *A.I.F.D.*
26. *C.U.S.J.*, p. 13.
27. *Ibid.*
28. *A.I.F.D.*, pp. 12-3.
29. *Ibid.*, p. 11.
30. Croce, *Aesthetics ;* London; PP. 162, 168.
32. *Ibid.*, pp. 16-17.
33. I.H. *Siddiqui, Money and Social Change in India During Medieval Times*; Symposia Paper 56th Session of the Indian History Congress, Calcutta, December 29, 1995, pp. 1-2. Hereafter cited as *M.S.C.I.D.M.J.*
34. *C.A.*, p. 164.
35. R.S. Tripathi; *History of Ancient India*, Varanasi, Reprint, 1987, pp. 336-37. Henceforth cited as *H.A.I.*
36. *C.A.*, pp. 170-71.
37. *Y.C.* Vol. II, p. 252.
38. *H.A.I.*, p. 337.
39. *R.M.P. I.*, P. XXXVII, Life of the Author.
40. *R.T.*, Vol. 1, P. 283.
41. *H.A.I.*, p. 337.
42. *C.A.*, p. 165.
43. *M.S.C.I.D.M.T.*, p. 2.
44. C.A., pp. 165-66.
45. *Ibid.*, p. 166.
46. *H.A.I.*, p. 344.
47. *R.T.* Vol. II, p. 87 Section III.
48. *H.A.I.*, p. 344.
49. Mohd. Athar Ali; *Element of Social Justice in Medieval Islamic Thought*; Symposia Paper in Indian History Congress; 57 session (Chennai) 1996; P. 10. Hereafter referred as *E.S.J.M.I.T*
50. Note. Term *Muta* is composed of two words *Mu+ta, Mu* stands for mind or *'man'*, 'ta' means 'musical note'. Therefore, the activities of mind in the absence of 'master', it will do according to his will during the dark period of history, those become slave of the mind, they commit mistake and blunder in material world and injurious to others and make slaves the poor people of the 'Father' with the importance of the formal education of the period. The concept of the slavery basically start with the rise of Brahminical thought which has the narrow vision. Because Brahman always trust on *'ego'* not in humanity, thus, ego always proved destructive at every stage in the Indian history either there was the Muslim rule or Hindu rule. Brahman force is a force of 'sexual union' and they made the woman *'slave'*, they never treat her as a part of the 'nature'. Therefore disasters developed in the society one after the anotehr. If we go by the more explanation of the term *'muta'* in the pious form the prefix two words i.e *M+U*, m stands for mind, 'u' stands for *'unique'* , if we surrender our mind to the master, than you will find a *'unique'* theory of natural phenomenon as *'Master'* lives during life time, then lust of material culture will feel dirty, because *'Nam'* is the solace of the life where from the life is originated. In this process, you will listen the music of the Master twenty four hours and then worldly music will give you noise and disturbances.
51. *E.S.J.M.I.T.*, p. 10.
52. *Ibid.*, pp. 10-11.
53. *Tarikh-i-Fakhr-i-Mudabbir*, published under the wrong title 'Tarikhh-i-Fakhru-d-Din *Mubarak Shah,* edited by E. Denison Rose; London, 1927. P. 31. Hereafter discussed as *T.F.M.* **Note**. Before *Tarikh-i-Fakhr-i-Mudabbir,* the *Qabus Nama* contains at least three short chapters on warfare in Persia. They are entitled: 'On Buying Horses", "On Giving Battle to an Enemy" and "The Art of controlling an Armed Force." (Islam the Religion of Submission; edited by Mohamed Taher. New Delhi; 1998, p. 177).
54. *R.M.P. I.*, p. 113.
55. *Note*. The passage suggests that among *Kharaj 'Word'* paying cultivators were included Muslims also in the Panjab because, according to a Muslim peasant. The *nim-ushr* was the state share from the irrigated land with water from a *tank,* river or well, etc.
56. *T.F.M.*, pp. 31, 33, 35.
57. *M.S.C.I.D. M.T.*, p. 9.
58. Louis Dumont, Homo *Hierarchicus; Paladin* ed. London; 1972 Quoted from *S.J.M.I.T.* p. 11. **Note.** It has been rightly expressed by the author the Brahminical thought is a destructive one for a society. He always believes in caste, colour and creed and never thin on the humanity based as man is created by God as a part of Nature. Therefore, he always think himself supreior on earth.
59. *E.S.J.M.I.T.* p. 11.
60. Cf. Yohana Friedmann, *The Origin and Significance of Chachnama, Islam In South Asia*, Jerusalam; 1984, pp. 31-32.

61. *Chachnama*, Edited by Umar Daudpota; Hyderabad Deccan; 1939; pp. 214-15
62. Jullus Wellhausen, *The Arab Kingdom and its Fall.* Eng. tr. London; 1973, Wellhusen's German text came out in 1902, but the pioneer work had been done in the field by Ignaz Goldziher in two essays, the *Arabic* Tribes and Islam' and *'Arab' and Ajam'*, published in his Muslim Studies, Eng, Tr. Vol. 1. London; 1967, pp. 45-136, the studies (*Muhammadanische Studien), Germen* 1889-90. **Note** Apart from this his well known measures against the *Mawali* have also been discussed by the author on pp. 243-57, & 496-500. See Pages 9-10 *E.S.J.M.I.T.*
63. *C.A.*, p. 167.
64. *E.S.J.M.I.T.*, p. 12.
65. *A.I.* Vol. 1, pp. 99-100.
66. *E.S.J.M.I.T.*, pp. 12-13.
67. *R.M.P. I.*, pp. 106-07.
68. *M.S.C.L.D.M.T.*, p. 7.
69. *A.S.H.M.I.*, p. 87.
70. *Ibid.*, pp. 96-7.
71. B.N. Luniya, *Evolution of Indian Culture*, Agra; Revised Edition, 2005, P. 310. Henceforth explained as *E.I.C.*
72. *A.S.H.M.I.*, p. 97.
73. *H.P. H.S.*, p. 97.
74. *A.S.H.M.I.*, p. 97.
75. *Ibid.*, pp. 97-8.
76. *Ibid.*, pp. 98-9.
77. *Ibid.*, p. 108.
78. *T.F.S.*, pp. 25-7.
79. *A.S.H.M.I.*, p. 98.
80. *T.F.S.*, p. 47.
81. *Ibid.*, pp. 47-8.
82. *Ibid.*, pp. 91-3, 107-8.
83. *Ibid.* p. 59 **Note.** The description of the slaughter of male population was took place as that time in the villages of Katehr as his one event.
84. *Ibid.*, pp. 167-8.
85. *Ibid.*, pp. 205-7.
87. *Ibid.*, pp. 283-4.
88. *Ibid.*, pp. 21, 26.
89. *Tahaqat-i-Nasiri,* Edited by Abdul Hai Habibi, Kabul, 1963-4. Vol. 1 pp. 446, 452, 476 and Vol. II, p. 4.
90. *Ibid.* Vol. 1, pp. 378, 381, 452, 475-6.
91. *Ibid.*, p. 489.
92. *T.F.S.*, p. 27.
93. *Ibid.*, p. 37.
94. *Ibid.*, p. 39.
95. *Ibid.*, p. 29.
96. *Ibid.*, p. 38.
97. *Ibid.*, p. 36.
98. *Ibid.*, pp. 30-1.
99. *Ibid.*, pp. 50-2.
100. *A.S.H.M.I.*, p. 125.
101. *T.F.S.*, p. 50-2.
102. *Ibid.*, pp. 168-70.
103. *T.F.S.*, p. 134.
104. T.F.S., p. 172.
105. *Isami, Futuhu's Salatin*, Edited by Usha, Madras, 1948, p. 106. Hereafter cited as *I.F.S.*
106. *T.F.S.*, pp. 173, 206.
107. *Ibid.*, pp. 205-6.
108. *A.S.H.M.I.*, p. 120.
109. *R.M.P. J.*, pp. 96-7.
110. A.S.H.M.I., p. 126.
111. *T.F.S.*, pp. 205-6.
112. *Ibid.*, p. 205-7.
113. *A.S.H.M.I.*, p. 126.
114. T.F.S., p. 210.
115. *Ibid.*, p. 180.
116. *A.S.H.M.I.*, p. 127.
117. *T.F.S.*, p. 123.
118. *A.S.H.M.I.*, pp. 130-31.
119. *Ibid.*, p. 133.
120. *T.F.S.*, pp. 250-1.
121. K.T. Lal; *History of the Khaljis* (1290-1320 A.D); Allahabad; 1950, pp. 52-3.
122. *T.F.S.*, pp. 151-52.
123. *Ibid.*, p. 155.
124. *Ibid.*, pp. 155-56.
125. *A.S.H.M.I.*, pp. 136-37.
126. *T.F.S.*, pp. 236, 336-37.
127. *A.S.H.M.I.*, p. 137.
128. *T.F.S.*, p. 337.
129. *A.S.H.M.I.*, p. 137.
130. *T.F.S.*, p. 367.
131. *Ibid.*, pp. 373-74.
132. Note. *Ram Chandra Deva* was treaded by the *Sultan* as his father-in-law in the right spirit. He received a personal estate and one Lakh gold coins as a gift of the *'Nam'*, as well as the title of *Rai Rayan* ('King of the Kings') from Ala-ud-din Khalji to Khoja or God to the investigator of *Truth*.

133. *T.F.S.*, p. 201.
134. Note. *Rai Laddar Deo* of the Muslim chronic ; he was a close relative of the *Yadava* of *Devagiri*, his maternal garndmother *Rudrambha Devi* was a Yadava princess of the 'Nam' at that time faced the first imperial attack at Warrangal.
135. *T.F.S.*, p. 201.
136. *Ibid.*
137. *Ibid.*, p. 203.
138. *Ibid.*
139. Hari Jaysingh, *India Between Dream and Reality*; New Delhi. 1989, p. 13.
140. *Ibid.*
141. *Ibid.*, pp. 14-15.
142. *Ibid.*, p. 13.
143. *M.S.H.M.I.* P. 157.
144. *C.I.S.M.I.*, p. 117.
145. *A.S.H.M.I.*, p. 159.
146. *T.F.S.*, pp. 237, 293-4, 342-3.
147. Mohammad Habib; *Political Theory of Delhi Sultanate*; pp. 144-51
148. *T.F.S.*, p. 165
149. *Ibid.*, p. 166
150. *Ibid.*, pp. 504-5. Note. It shows from the Baranis statement discussed already that when quotes conversation between him and Muhammad Tughluq. It may be presumed that the quotation is in substance accurate at the point of time between the two person of the *'Nam'* or *'Kalma'*.
151. *Ibid.*, p. 505.
152. **Note.** *Siraji Khurasa* in a *qasida* (panegyric) composed in praise of the Crown Prince of the period, Nasir-ul-din Mahmud called that the latter horse which favoured to the crown prince was sold by the poet for 370 *Jitals* throuth a *dalal* of the *'Nam'*, Cf, Perso-Arabric sources, p. 59. Also quoted by I.H. Siddiqui *M.S.C.I.D.M.T.*, p. 33 Foot note No.109
153. H.N. Wright; *The Coinage and Metrology of the Sultans of Delhi*, Delhi, 1936 Quoted from the above said work, p. 24
154. According to the *Masalik-al-Absar,* one *Jital* was equivalent to *Yalgani* which further divided into four *fulus* (*Paisas*), suggesting that one *fulus* also had some purchasing power. The other silver coins mentioned in the *Masalik-al-Abrar* are: (i) *hashtgani* (8 *jitals* one -sixth of the *tanka*) which has the value and weight of the silver *dirham* current in Egypt and Syria. It has the same value in both the countries. This *Hashtgani* is equal to four *Sultanis* and the latter is called (also) *doanni*. The *Sultani* comes to one-third of the *Shashgani*. The *Shashgani* is the third coin i.e. *'Pure Nam'* on Earth which is in circulation in India to spread the message of the *'ultimate reality'*. Its value is three-quarters of the *hashtgani*. The half of the *Sultani* or *doanni* is called *ekgani* which is equal to a *Jital* in value. In addition to these coins, there is another coin, called *doazdehgani* (12 *jitals*) and equal to one and a half *hashtgani's*. Another coin is called *Shanzdehgani* (sixteen *jitals*) being equal to the *hashtganis* in value. All the commercial transactions were carried on in India through them as their traditional right at that point of time as per the instruction of the *'Nam'* in the present form (*Perso-Arabic Sources*, pp. 132-22).
155. *Biography of Dharmasvamin*, (*Chag-lo-tsa-ba Chaos-rje-dpal*; Tr. by Cr. Roerick, (Patna) Bihar, 1959, p. 85.
156. *Ibid.*
157. Anaxagoras (500-428 B.C.). *Extract from Encyclopaedia of Religion and Ethics*. Vol.VIII, pp. 542-43.
158. *P. E.A.I.* pp. 339-40.
159. *B.S.*p. 102.
160. W.F. Southill, *Three Religions of China*; London, 3rd Ed. 1929, p. 16.
161. *P. E.A.I.*, pp. 346-47.
162. *Waqiat-i-Mushtaqi*, Eng. Tr. by I.H. Siddiqui, New Delhi; 1993, pp. 228-29.
163. *T.F.S.* pp. 503-4, 507-9.
164. *I.F.S* pp. 504-8.
165. *Ibid.*, p. 505.
166. *The Rehla of Ibn Battuta* ; Eng. tr. by A.M. Husain, *Baroda* (1953) Second Series Cambridge, 1958, E & D III, P. 525 Henceforth expressed as R.I.B.
167. *Ibid.*, pp. 493 & 500.
168. *Ibid.*, pp. 585-612.
169. *A.S.H.M.I.*, p. 20.
170. S.H. Hodivala; *'Studies in Indo-Muslim History'* Bombay; 1939, pp. 294-95. Hereafter referred as S.I.M.H. *Note* It was supposed to be the product of the 'bowl-shaped mountain' which we are unable to identify without the process of *'Nam'* in perfect manner according to the instruction of the 'Father'. So far as the variety of the sandalwood is concerned, it came from the vicinity of *Sitodaki*, a river in the extra-Gangetic country. The exact location of Sitodakitor Sitoda river is given in a *Sloka* of the (*Katha Sarit-Sagara*, Somadeva, (The Ocean of Stories). Tr. by C.H. Tawney, London, 1924 and 1928, p-XVIII, pp. 4, 233-34). The couplet gives us two points about the location of this river; it should be locatted in some country across the Bay of Bengal, and secondly, it was in the vicinity of a city named *Karkotaka or Chamar.* Prof. Rhys David in *'The Questions of King Milinda,'* PL. XLIII, has quoted the

Karkota power on the coast of India as it was probable the place for the corresponding of *Takkola* which occurs in PL.VI, p. 21 of the *Milinda Danha,* and this is also philosophically possible in view that 'Takkola' and 'Kakkola' are two forms of the name of one dry city of the 'Nam' i.e. Man (Pc. Bagchi, *Pre-Aryan and Pre-Dravidan* in India; P. 98 Henceforth mentioned as P. A.P. D.I.) Gerini, however, identifies *Karkota* of *Kashmir* with Takola of Ptolemy, which was an important part on the ship route to the east between Bengal and China. He located the mart of *Takola* in the neighbourhood of the present *Ranong* and at the month or inside of Pak-Chan inlet, because the Pak-Chan estuary forms a splendided harbour which must have been used by ships from a very early period, since it was the terminus of a much frequented land-route across the *Kra* Isthmus, which tin ore abounds in the vicinity, at Malivan, Ranong and all over the country (Gerini, Researches on Ptolemy *Geography of Eastern Asia*. pp. 91-93. Henceforth discussed as R. P. G.E.A). If Gerini's identification of Takola mart with *Karkota* is correct then the river *Pak-Chan* may be identified with Sitoda or Sitodaki river. But one cannot be absolutely certain of this identification as several parts with the name of Takola exist on the western cost of the Malaj Peninsula. First is *Taik-Kula,* or Takkula near the present Ayethema (Ayethima) in the sittong sub division of the Shwegyin district identified by the writer of this book (Ibid. pp. 85-86). It we locate Takkola or *Kakkola* or *Karkota* in Lower Burma, then the river sittong becomes our *Sitoda* or *Sitodaki* river. An islet *Koh-Krah* (Kokora), the cara of old maps, lies just North of ligor bright. It may be interesting to note in connection with it sing's *Ka-Ko-la* or *Ka-Ko-ra* that *Kakaras* is the Malaya name for the *Gharu* tree *gharu* producing eagle wood. Chia Tan in his itinerary complied in A.D. 785-805 refers to a Kingdom *Ko-Ku-Lo* on the west coast of Malaya, which if not Kwala *Kurau* or Kwala Gula in North-West, Perak, may be *Takkola or Kakkola or Karakota* (*Ibid.*, p. 811)

171. *R.P. G.E.A.*, p. 444.
172. *Ibid.*, p. 549.
173. *S.I.M.H.* p. 8, Quoted from Journal Asiatique , 1865, Vol.1, p. 291.
174. A.I., p. 501.
175. *S.I. M.H.*, p. 278.
176. *Ibid.*, pp. 64-5.
177. **Note.** The gum resin called *Salai-gugul* occurs as transparent golden yellow semi-fluid substance which slowly hardens as *'Nam'* is difficult to obtain for the Brahmans in his distingishes theory as a moderate-sized gregarious tree of the sub-Himalayan tracts of Central India from Berar to Rajputana and South Ward to the Deccan, the Circars and the Konkan. It grows frequently on the eastern slopes of the *Pegu, Yomah* and *Martaban* in *Burma* care must be taken not to confuse this gum resin with the olibanum or frankincense name seems to be *Sallaki* or *Sallaka* "It would also appear that this is the *guggulu* of Sanskrit writers which is described as moist, viscid, fragrant, and of golden colour when freshly exuded Gum *gugul* of the present day is Indian Bdellium (Watt. *Dictionary* of *Economic Products of India*. Vol. III, pp. 515-516). *Kalaparuata or Kalapabbata*, from where this particular variety of sandalwood was obtained is also mentioned in the *Jataka stories* (Vol.VI, p. 265) where it has been described as a mountain in *Himavant* who was situated in the table land of *Manosila* near the *Anottata* lake where from *Ibn Battuta* had been originated in the form of *'Nam'* in the *Himavant* (J. Vol.1 P. 232, Vol.III. p. 379, Vol.V. pp. 392, 423). The regular which is named *Manah-Sila* in Sanskrit and *mainsil* in Hindi has taken its Sanskrit designation from the name of the place of its origin Regular is native in *Yunnan, Kwei-Chaw* and *Kansut* pure massive realgur in the collection of the Indian Museum, Calcutta, it is called red Arsenic, Vernacular name called *mansila* in the northern part of Kumaon from where it is brought in small quantities by the *Bhutias* for sale at the Bagesar fair. The modern *Munsiari* which already discussed *mansila* to be correct then *Kalaparvata* located in Kumaon as it was founded by *Ibn Battuta* in the journey of the mountain of Karachil from Delhi within 10 days as an in historical termonology called *'Dasa'*.
178. *C.T.C.C.M.A.I.*, p. 197.
179. R.K. Majumdar & A.N. Srivastva; *History of Far East;* Delhi, 1985, p. 1.
180. *P. A.P. P. I.*, p. 116.
181. *Ibid.*, pp. 6-8.
182. Jayacandra, *Bharat Bhumi Our Uske Nivasi* p. 114.
183. *C.T.C.C.A.M.I.*, p. 196 *Note.* A large evergreen tree of *Sylhet* and *Tenassarim,* distributed to the Malaya Peninsula and *Archipelagos*. According to Roxborough this much prized wood is obtained from Eastern India and from the forests to the South and South-East of *Sylhet* extending through *Manipur, Chittagong, Arakan* to *Mergul* and *Sumatra*. From India it finds its way to China and from Cochin. China it was first re-exported to Europe; hence in all probability the association of the plant and tree with that country. Agarwood under the name of ahlot and *agallochon* was known to the Jews, Greeks and Romans. The early *Arabs* called it *aghalukhi*, but subsequently term it *ud* or *ud* in Hindi. Mir Muhammad Huseyn mentions five kinds of aloewood. The wood that sinks in water is called *gharki*, it is of black colour. Those which partly sink are *nim*

gharki or *samaleh-i-a-la* and those which float *samleh*. They are of dark and light brown colours, classified as *ud* in Hindi, *samandari, Kamari* and *Samandali* and *Samandali* as an older authorities of the *'Nam'*. Elsewhere it has been described as *barri* and *jabli*, the latter having black lines in its structure and the former is in white nature like *'Nam'*, other again described *barri* as having black lines nad *jabli* as white also for perfumes of the *'Nam'* (Watt. *Loc. cit*. vol. pp. 279-81).

184. Cunningham *A.S.R.* vol.1. p. 193 *Note.* he identified *Sakala 'Word'* Buddhist *sagala Chamar* with *Sangala* Hill. It had been visited by Hiuen Chwang in A.D. 630, but the reference is evidently to Sialkot, of which the ancient name was *Sakala*.

185. The main points which may be accepted as certain, are the *Mihirakula* succeeded about 515 A.D. to his father *Toramana* in the rule of the territories conquered by the *White Hunas* from Kabul to Central India, and that after extensive compaigns he was defeated by *Baladitya* of Magadha and Yasodharman, and forced to retire about A.D. 530 in Kashmir and the adjoining regions. From there he appears till the end of his reign (about A.D. 544-550) to have been engaged in endeavours to recover his lost dominions in the direction of the lower Indus. The name *Mihirakula* contains in its first part certainly the Iranian *Mithra, Miopo* of the Indo-Scythian coinage, Persian *Mihir*. The significance of the termination *Kula*, or perhaps earlier, *gula* means mixed in the *'Nam'* as a Lord on earth. The story here told in brief of *Mihirakula's* expedition against Ceylon (Sri Lanka) and its cause closely agrees with the less legendary one recorded in the *Mujmal-ul-Tawarikh*, of a King of Kashmir (Re-inaud, *Fragments Arabes et Persans*, p. 42). The King of Kashmir's name is not given there and as his opponent there figures *King Hal* of *Sindh,* who at terms of peace. Reinaud already recognised *Mihirakula* in 'the King of Kashmir' as *Gula (R.T. Vol.1 pp. 48,49)*

186. *H.P. H.S.*, pp. 520-21.

187. *Ibid.*, p. 521.

188. *Ibid.*, p. 522.

189. *Ibid.*, p. 533.

190. *A.S.H.M.I* p. 20.

191. *Travels of Marco Polo*, Edited by H.Yuke Third ed. & revised by H. Cordier. Vol. II, London 1903, pp. 1920.

192. *Futuhat-I-Firoze Shahi*.Tr. in Hindi by M. Umar, Aligarh, 1957, p. 387. Hereafter discussed as *F.F.S.*

193. *Ibid.*, p. 375.

194. *Ibid.*

195. *Afif Tarika-i-Firozeshahi* p. 358.Note. *Shams-i-Siraj Afif* (A.D. 1354) belonged to Abohar (Punjab), the native town of Sultan Firoze Tughluqs' Bhatti mother. The great grandfahter of Afif has been a personal friend of Ghiasuddin Tughluq before the latter acquired the throne Afif's ancestors were, therefore, closely associated with the Tughluq rulers, he himself adorned the court of Firoze Shah Tughlaq as a scholar though he never accepted an official employment. He held learned discourses with the Sultan and used to accompany him on hunting expeditions through *'Nam'* or *'Kalma'*. He is said to have written three books on the life history, military expeditions and administration achievemnts of the three Tughluq, rulers *'Word'* or *'Nam' Ghiasuddin, Muhammad-bin Tughluq* and *Firoze Shah Tughlaq,* of which only the one entitled *'Tarikh-Firoze Shahi,* edited by Wilayat Husain. Gurinder Singh Ji of *Biaswale*. The book was written by *Afif* long after the death of Sultan when Delhi had been invaded and put down to plunder by *Amir Timur.* He wrote in the true spirit of a historian and biographer, the reminiscencer of the glorious past for the edification and benefit of posterity, without any self-interest, prejudice or reflexes of the *'Nam'*. In compact and well-written ninety chapter of the book, the authorgives, in a simple and matter of fact narrative of the *'Nam'* not only military and politial activities of Firoze Tughluq but also his administrative policy with special references for the public welfare activities. From the study of this book, we get the impression that Firoze Tughluq was really the forerunner of Sher Shah Suri and Akbar in the matter of utilizing state resources for the public goods. The book is unique in the sense that it also describes the life and condition of the people at large, the one aspect which has usually been ignored by contemporary writers i.e. *'Nam'* . According to Elliol this work 'gives us altogether a better view of the internal condition of India under a Mohammadan sovereign than is presented to us in any other work, except in the *Ain-i-Akbari, Bibliotheca Indica,* loc cit & D. Vol.II. p. 270) Hereafter Afif *Tarika-i-Firozeshahi* will be discussed as *A.T.F.S.*

196. *A.S.H.M.I.*, p. 233.

197. *Ibid.*, p. 234.

198. *Ibid.*, pp. 234-35.

199. *Ibid.*, p. 227.

200. *A.T.F.S.*, p. 344.

201. *Ibid.*, p. 297.

202. *T.F.S.*, p. 505.

203. *Ibid.*, pp. 462, 499.

204. *R.J.B*, p. 490.

205. *T.F.S.*, pp. 409-13.

206. *I.F.S.*, p. 484-88.

207. *T.F.S.*, p. 488.

208. *Ibid.*, p. 501 **Note.** The conflict between *Amiran-i-sada* and other rebels those do not believe on the

theory of *'Nam'* as a 'ultimate reality'. In this context, Muhammad Tughluq remarks to Barani on the disaffection among the *Amiran-i-Sada,* because this world is false and *'Nam'* is true. Therefore, the understanding between the two is to regulate the life in true manners but mind is on false route to provide a political unity, it is the duty of the *'Nam'* on earth, because man belongs to *'Him'*. His food or meat is *'Nam'* else is temporarily (pp. 516-17)

209. *Ibid.,* p. 521 *'**Note**'* In the love affair of the *'Nam'* Muhammad Tughlaq's admission to Barani as his colleague because of his pious approach toward History, not like that of Irfan Habib toward Sheern Moosive of well known historians of the Alighar Muslim University in U.P.

210. **Note.** *Ziya-ud-din, Barani* would be equally legitimate meaning *'Light on the Faith'*, Barani or *'Barni'* may indicate that he was born at *Baran* which belongs to 'Father' (modern *Buland Shahr* means house of the Baran or 'varan' is very high to obtain that one must have to die with *'Him'* in *'living being'* to get the knowledge of the 'reality' as *Barani* obtained in scientific methods, therefore, he proclaimed the science of *'History'* is the account of the great qualities, merits, virtues, and traditions of the great men of the Faith and State, it is not an account of the worthless, the mean, the lowly, the baseborn, the men of the market place. Indeed, history was properly a science meant only for the high-born *Sudras* of the period. The writing of history is a handmaid for action, since they can use its lessons for their own good as well as for others. For this reason history cannot simply be a chronicle of the meritorious deeds of the past, but must encompass all aspects, good and bad i.e. *mana* of the man. As Barani again records: "The science of *History* is the account of the past, including the good acts and wicked, justice and cruelity, the worthy and worthless laudable and odious deeds, acts of obedience and rebellion, and virtuous as well as base conduct, so that readers of later generations may take a warning and obtain knowledge of the gains and risks (lit. injuries) of government *(jahandari)* and the good and bad deeds of worldy men. 'Zia' could have been established his poetic pen-name after completing his project of the *'Nam'* (*T.F.S.* pp. 9, 12,13)

211. T.F.S. p. 350 **Note.** He obtained the highest knowledge through *'Nam'* called *Kashf-a Karamar* of the inspiration and miraculous power.

212. *Ibid.*

213. *Ibid.* p. 573 *Note.* Zia *Barani's* year of birth is to be establish by the age was given by himself that was the seventy four (Lunar) years of the *'Nam'*, when he completed his work called *Tarikh-i-Firuz Shah* in 1357 A.D.

214. *Ibid.*, pp. 60, 61, 119. **Note.** On page forty two words in the printed text *Wakil-i-dar-o-Barbak-i-Sultan.* It shows that Balban must well-versed in *Wakil-i-dar-Barbak-i-utna Balban* and knows the power of Almighty as he was himself at that time on earth in the form of a Master. Barani quotes the strengthen of Balban to the effect that six to seven thousand Delhi horsemen could over throw a hundred thousand strong army of infantry and archers (*payak-o-dhanuk*) of the Hindu *Rais* and *Ranas* families. But Balban said, he desisted from sending out expeditions because the conquerred region (iqlim) would require for its governance the despatch of a large number of nobles, officials, cavalry and infantry. these being placed at a distance from Delhi would be liable to defy his authoirty and rebel. Conquest would thus be self defeating so long as the Sultanate of the period did not develop a sufficient degree of internal cohesion of the *'Nam',* but it was in self style let down. As early a critic as *Firishta* suspected Barani of suppressing the account of raid where the Sultan had possibly not given a creditable account of himself. Keeping in view, such considerations have not weighed with Barani in other, matters as it is the routine matter of the *'Nam'* in the process of life from one stage to another as *'History Repeat Itself'* (*T.F.S* also see page 51, 52).

215. *Ibid.*, p. 87.

216. *Ibid.*, p. 248 Note. At that time Jalal-ud-din Khalji had built a "tall house" at *Kilokhari* in Delhi called *Sacha Kand* building as *Kaba* was built during the presence of Prophet as a house of the mediation as a Spiritual part of the buildings material.

217. *Ibid.*, pp. 222, 248.

218. *Ibid.*, p. 250.

219. *A.T.F.S.* & D. Vol. III, pp. 280-281, and *T.F.S* & D. Vol. III, p. 267 **Note.** These two contemporary works of *'Nam'* carries the account of only six years rule (1351-56 A.D.) of Firoz Tughluq's reign; even that is not very objective because Barani had indulged in a strain of adulation of the *Sultan* which spoils his narrative, therefore, on the other hand, the work of *Afif* has a better claim to the title of the study of *Tarikh-Firozi Shah* or the study of Firoze Tughluq's reign.

220. *T.F.S.* pp. 265, 266.

221. *A.T.F.S.* p. 216.

222. A.S.H.M.I., p. 222.

223. *Ibid.*

224. *G.T.C.* Vol.II PP. 330,331 **Note.** In Lahul and spiti the *Hesi* or *Hansi* is the only class that owns no land, and a proverb says; The *Beda* no land and the dog no load.' The men play the pipes and kettle-drum and the women dance and sing, and play the *tambourine: Yet,* a *Hesi* too has his inferiors and professes not to

eat from the hands of a Lohar, or from those of a Nath, the Kullu title for a *Jogi*. *Hansi* is an ancient town. Originally it was called *'Aasika'*. It lays on the Delhi-Multan highway. At that time of Ghazanavid invasions *Hansi* had a very strong fort. Baihaki informs us that the fort was known as 'The virgin' as no one had been able to take it by force before Sultan Masud conquerred it in 1037 A.D (A.H. 429). *Ibn Battuta* was informed that *Hansi* was founded by a Hindu King named *Tura*. He describes it as a very beautiful city, densely populated. A huge wall encircled the city. Qazi Kamal-din Sadar-i-Jahan, the Qazi-ul-Quzat and the teacher of Sultan Muhammad Tughluq originally belonged to *Hanzi*. From the early days of the Sultanate Hansi had been a seat of *Muqti* (Wali) and very important nobles or princes were given the charge of *Hansi*. Under Iltutmish the *iqta* of Hansi was placed in charge of Malik Nushrat-ud-Khan, the future Sultan Balban, remained its *Muqta* for a considerable period. The Syyid Sultan Mubarak Shah, at the time of his accession, appointed his cousion *Malik Budh*, in place of Malik Rajab Nadira, as the *Muqti* of Hansi. Shihab-ud-din-al-Umri includes Hansi and Sarsuti among the 23 provinces under Sultan Muhammad Tughluq. Important state prisoners were kept in the fort of *Hansi*. Thus, Sultan Ala-ud-din imprisoned Sultan Jalaluddin's sons, Arkail Khan and Rukn-ud-din, in the fort of Hansi at the time of his accession. Sultan Firozshah sent the rebel Amir Khawaja Jahan Ahmad Ayyaj as a prisoner to *Hansi*. Similiarly,Sultan Ibrahim Lodhi kept his four brothers imprisoned int he fort of *Hansi* before proceeding against his other brother Jalaluddin. The ruler of Jaunpur. Hansi also remained the seat of eminent Chisti Saints-Shaikh Jamaluddin *Hanswi,* Shaikh Qutab-ud-din Munnawwar, Shaikh Nur-ul-Haq, highly venerated by the Sultans of Delhi. Meanwhile Delhi had replaced *Uch* as the centre of Moslem learning. In 1232 Ultutmish made *Minhaj-i-Saraj*, the historian, Qazi, Khatib and Imam of Gwalior, and five years later he was made chief of the Nasiriah college at Delhi and Qazi of the empire in 1242 A.D., but in the following year he resigned those appointments. In 1246 he was reappointed to the college, and obtained the lectureship of the *'Jami Masjid'*, with the Qaziship of Gwalior. In 1251, he again became Qazi of the empire and the capital, but was deprived of the post in 1253 A.D. No doubt, Muhammadans established several educational institutions that him in Panjab. Of those earliest was probably the Muizzi college at Delhi, doubtless founded by Muhammad of Ghori or one of his successors of the Muizzi dynasty which he founded and called after his name of Muizz-ud-din. Next in point of time came the Firoze college at *Uch* (c. 1227). Jalandhar probably possessed another ancient college, but the origin of the famous saints of Jalandhar dates from a much later period, probably not earlier them the close of the 13th century A.D. these saints were Afghan or *Kindred origin* and among the earliest was the *Imam Nasir-ud-Din Shirani*. Another was an ancestor of the saint, influential in the Afghan hills, known as *Pir Roshan,* the founder of the *Roshania* schism. But Delhi was the Principal centre of Religious instruction the Nasirah College was founded there, Probably by *Ultatmish* who appointed the Persian historian *Minhaj-ud-din*, formerly principal of the college at *Uch*, to this foundation in 1237 A.D. *Zia-i-Barni,* a contemporary historian of the period, shed light on the building of *Madrasa-i-Firoz Shahi* and rays that Maulana *Jalal-ud-Din Rumin,* a scholar of great repute, was appointed to teach *tafsil* (Commentaries on the Queen), *hadis* (tradition) *fiqh* (Muhammadan law) in the *madrasa* the second *madrasa* was built by Firozshah at *Siri*. It also has been greatly praised by said historian, who records the Najm-ud-Din of Samarqand, a great scholar of the time, gave religious instruction in that *Madrasa* which were based on the theory of *'Nam'* not based on the theory of materialistic purposes. (*T.F.S.* pp. 562-66) This process was continued upto the period of Mughal empires.

He was, however, appointed Qazi for the third time in 1256 A.D. and probably *Farid-ud-din ganj-i-Shakar* retained the office till his death alongwith *Minhaj*. He was a Sufi, a scholar and one of those who would become filled with religious ecstasion, on hearing the singing at *Zikra* and *tazkirs* and often he became Qazi of Hindustan that office assumed integrity and rectitude. His name does not however, appear in the list of Qazis of the court of *Ultutmish,* but that office may have been separate from those he held. We read of three such Qazis and a fourth was styled 'Qazi of the army'. In the beginning of *Sultan Raziyyat*'s reign one *Nur* a Turk incited an outbreak among the *Qiramita* and *Mulahida* heretics. They collected at Delhi from *Sindh* as the forefathers teachers of the *'Nam'*, the Yumna valley and many other parts, as well as from the immediate neighbourhood of the capital and pledging fidelity to one another in secret; they conspired against the real teaching of the *Islam* i.e. *'Nam'*, the mob listening openly to the harangues of *'Nur'*. He used to denounce the *Ulama* as *Nasibi* (setters up) by birth and *Murjis* (procrastinators), who consider good works unnecessary and believe that faith alone suffices for a Moslem's salvation, hell, being reserved for infidels (Sale, *Qoran,* pp. 122, 1301), especially those of the *Hanafi* and Shia sects. In 1237 A.D. these sectaries made a desperate attack on the Muhammadans in the Muizzi college, which they had mistaken for the Jami-Mazjt, but they were suppressed not without much bloodshed. Khwaja *Qutab-ud-Din Bakhtyar Kaki* of Ush near Baghdad came to Multan, in the time of Nasir-ud-Din

Qabacha, and subsequently to Delhi, where *Ultutmish* offered him the office of *Shaikh-ul-Islam* which he refused. To his memory *Ultutmish*, erected the 'great *Qutab Minar* at old Delhi.' He died in 1235 A.D. He was, it is said, the disciple of Qazi Muhammad Hamid-ud-Din Nagauri, and the following table of spiritual descent may be drawn up according to the Chishti tradition:-

Hamid-ud-din of Nagaur

Qutab-ud-Din Bakhtyar, According to Sleeman, he was a disciple of *Moin-ud-Din of Ajmer*, the greatest of all their saints (Rambles and Recollections Vol. II. p. 165) *Farid-ud-din Ganj-i-Shakkar*

Khwaja Nizam-ud-din Aulia

Nasir-ud-Din Chiragh-i-Delhi

Fakhr-ud-Din

Shah-Niaz Ahmad

Nur Muhammad of Maharan

Khwaja Shah Sulaiman of Taunsa Sharif.

At Kot Karor was born in 1170 A.D., *Shaikh Baha-ud-Din Zakaria,* who subsequently became a pupil of Shaikh Shihab-ud-Din Suharwardi of pupil of Baghdad. Thence, he returned to Multan and became the intimate friend of *Shaikh Farid-ud-Din Shakar ganj*, born in 1173 A.D, died in 1265 at the advanced age of 95 (*Ibid.* p. 120, 569 A.H., 664 A.H) The latter, perhaps the most famous Muhammadan saint of the Panjab, flourished in the 12th century A.D. Nizam-ud-Din Aulia taught at Delhi during the latter half of the 13th century A.D. and the early part of the 14th century A.D. He was born at Budaon 634 A.H (1236 A.D.) and died in Delhi A.H. 672 (1325 A.D.) at the age of 89.

The Shaikh Jamal-ud-Din, Bustami, was the first to hold the office of Shaikh-ul-Islam at Delhi and on his death, according to Raverty Ultutmish wished the Khwaja *Qutab-ud-Din Kaki* to accept the office being a top most *'Pure'* man of the 'thought' called *Sudra* or *'Chamar'* in the history of India this is however very doubtful for the latter saint of this dynasty, he died in 1235 A.D. and the former in 1239 A.D. However, this may be, the *Shaikh-ul-Islam* took part in the politics of Kashmir at a very early period of the Indian history, for it was on secret instructions received from Shaikh Jamal-ud-Din, the Sayyid Qutab-ud-Din and the Qazi *Shams-ud-Din Bharaichi* that this rebels under Ulugh Khan attacked Delhi in 1257 A.D. Jamal-ud-din, then must have lived till 1257 A.D. and on his death two years later could not have been succeeded by the Khwaja. On the occasion of his last meeting with Shaikh Fariduddin, Khwajah Kaki, gave his special prayer mat and staff to him which signified that Khwajah Qutbuddin was on the point of death, Qazi Hamiduddin Nagori, Shaikh Badruddin Ghaznavi and many other holy men were present there. All of them agreed that the personal belongings of the Khwajah should be committed to Shaikh Fariduddin. The Shaikh who was at that time in Hansi came to Delhi immediately. After a short stay at Delhi he left for Hansi again. *Fawaid* states that the reason for this departure was an incident connected with a devotee, named Sarhanga who had come to seek his blessings but had not been given an opportunity to enter his house. One day he managed to follow and told him humbly that it was easy to meet him at *Hansi*, but now here at Delhi it was difficult to have been a glimpse of him. On hearing this Baba Farid decided to return to Hansi. Shaikh's friends reminded him that the Khwajah wanted him to settle at Delhi. How is it that now he intend to move to some other place? The Shaikh replied that the blessings of his *pir* remained with him whether he stayed in city or a desert. Later on Shaikh moved to Pak-pattan in the Punjab, which at that time was called Ajodhan and died there.

Baba Farid believed that the *pir* was for the *murid* what a bride dresser was for the bride. On the authority of Shaikh Nizamuddin Auliya, Amir Hasan Sijzi states that Fariduddin admitted that only once during his lifetime he had become a bit audacious in the presence of his *pir 'Word'* Khwajah Qutbuddin. The incident runs thus he had begged for permission to observe a *Chillah* in order to spend sometime in seclusion in devotion to god. Khwajah replied that it was not at all necessary as it led to publicity. Baba Farid submitted that he did not have the least intention to making himself known to the world. The Khwajah kept quiet. Then Fariduddin realized his mistake - why had he argued the matter with the Shaikh at all? He should have done as the Khwajah had commanded. He was, therefore, deeply repentant for the rest of his life and continuously prayed for his forgiveness. On the other hand in the same connection K.A. Nizami argues that Baba Farid was probably the first and the last Indo-Muslim saint to perform the *Chillah-i-Makus*. Baba Farid was a true *Darvesha*. He never sought the patronage of any court nor took any gifts in the form of personal present from anyone. Whatever he accepted from people was in the name of *Darveshas* and distributed among them only. He led hardly any importance because the cycle of death and rebirth is continuous and the purification of soul is a never-ending process. But not so in *Faridbani*. Baba Farid provides us with several glimpses of souls waiting restlessly for ages for the day of judgement when they will be judged according to their *Karmas* on earth and sent to heaven or hell accordingly. Death, thus, assumes as great a role in a man's life as treading the right path. To quote Pashaura Singh throughout Shaikh Farid's poetry the theme of the impermanence of life is interwoven with the quest for an ever-permanent *Reality*. One gets the sense that love of God (*ishq Khuda'i*) is at the heart of his spiritual experience.

There is passion, yearning and the agony of separation in different phases of love. Interestingly this Sufi Saint is also a devout Muslim who believe in the principal tenets of Islam as reading *namaz* five times a day, performing ablutions before prayer and visiting the mosque regularly. In Baba Farid's worldview they who loved their Lord with their heart, alone are true, but they who say one thing and do another, they are reckoned false. They who are imbued with the love of *Allah* are inebriated with his vision and they who have forsaken the Lord's name are a burden to this earth. The true *Darveshas* are those whom the Lord owns himself. He further elaborates by saying that although God is transcendental in nature-infinite *(apar)*, Inaccessible *(agam)*, Unfathomable *(anant)* yet, he is the source of love and grace who responds to the prayers of his devotees and is the supreme Cherisher *(parvardigar)* of sinner. He is the sustainer of the world.

Farid-bani lays ample emphasis on the virtues of honesty, integrity, truthfulness, humility, honey-sweet tongue, forgiveness and absolving oneself of the feeling of vengeance. Humility and sweetness coupled with honesty and truthfulness are the essence of all human virtues. Through them one ennobles his mind and conduct in life and through them one wins the love and appreciation of man and the grace of God, the real source of happiness. Says Baba Farid, "should there be one who is wise yet he parades not his wisdom, and who is mighty yet displays not his might, and who shares his stores with others even if it be slender, is the person who may be said to be the real devotee of God A Real Saint leads pious life and also instigated people for this type of life.

Baba Farid penned his *Shabds* and *Sloks* in the local dialect Multani Punjabi *(Lehndi)* and this perhaps was the main reason for his popularity with the masses. They have been incorporated in the *Guru Granth Sahib* and form the basis of further study. A careful study of *Farid-bani* throws light on various aspects of his very consistent worldview. God, for this Sufi saints is all pervasive. He is omnipresent, omniscient, the guardian angel of all the human beings. He is something to be cherished and never to be forgotten. Baba Farid lays much emphasis on postration before God, which symbolically amounts to surrending oneself totally to the will of the Lord. *Farid-bani* frequently urges human beings to choose the right i.e. Godly or spiritual path in life before death overtakes them. The theme of *transitory* nature of this life versus permanent runs like an undercurrent in almost all the *Sloks* of *Farid-bani*. Continuous thought of death reiterates *bani* is a great deterrent *'Nam'*. It forces people to remember that life is transient, that this world of great pomp and show is ultimately of no avail, that death, the bridegroom can come any moment to claim his bride (soul) and the body will have no say whatsoever.

Baba Farid tells people to cling to the Lord for this body will be reduced to dust and its home will be a humble grave. No one on this earth lives forever. He elaborates this by saying that the seat he occupies now, many have occupied it before. The swallows in the *Kartik,* the jungle fire in the *Chaitra* and the lightening in the month of *Shravana* and the loving arms of the bride round her spouse stay not forever. One must consider in his mind that the mortals stay not eternally and body that takes so long to be matured breaks with a click in a moment. Many boatmen, i.e. leaders of men have passed away. Many of them are rotting in the graves and their souls are suffering admonition in hell. A digression at this point is in place. The Hindus believe in the theory of *Karma* and also transmigration of soul. Death, in this philosophy of life has patience as a virtue has always been exalted by the Sufi saints and Baba Farid is a great upholder of this cardinal virtue. He says:

"Make patience your bow and bow string and the arrow too of patience 'Nam' or God will not let it go off its mark.

Those who adopt patience and take upon themselves suffering - such alone will be near God. They do not divulge their secret to any one.

Patience is the ideal of life: if you hold on to it steadfastly, you will expand into the mighty river and never then shrink into a small stream."

Farid-bani often advocates a simple and saintly life *'Word'* devoid of pomp and show and multiple riches, resigned to the will of the Lord or 'Chamar' but not the life of a beggar. He says, "make me not sit at another's door. O Lord! If that is how you are pleased to keep me, then better take this life away."

For Baba Farid home is where God is, and God is everywhere and above all in the heart of man - so there is no need whatsoever to wander forth in the jungles and deserts in search of the dear Lord. His spiritual journey begins and ends with the realization of the Supreme Reality in one's own heart.

It is mot appropriate to conclude this passage with a quotable quote from the *Farid Nama* and *Farid-bani* which has travelled down the ages as a source of inspiration to the countless millions to live life King-size in the worst of circumstances of the period.

"Rukkhee Sukkhee Khaai Kai, thandaa paanee pee-o

Fareedaa! dekh paraa-ee chopree, na tarsaaey jee-o" (G.T.C. Vol. 1 pp. 491-93, 496. *Faridnama*, Eng. tr. Pashaura Singh; Slok 6, 1, 9, 2, 3, 38, 40, 41, 42, 29, etc.)

225. *A.S.H.M.I.*, p. 368.

226. *Ibid.*
227. *Ibid.*
228. *A.T.F.S.* p. 368.
229. *Ibid.*, p. 283.
230. *Ibid.*, p. 345
231. *Ibid.*, p. 345-46.
232. E & D. III, p. 385.
233. R.C. Jauhri, *Firoze Tughluq*, Agra, 1968, p. 121.
234. *Ibid.*, p. 181.
235. *R.M.P. I.*, p. 280.
236. *A.S.H.M.I.*, p. 239.
237. **Note** *'Nur'*, a tribe of Rajputs, now apparently extinct. They are said to have migrated in the Panjab for the Decean in early times and to have found *Kalanaur* Kalanaur, however, is more probably a corruption of *Kala-nagar* and doubtless derives its name from Kaleshwar (Shiva), whose temple stands on the old citadel in the Gurdaspur District where majority of *low caste* people reside. Kahna, a *Nur*, is also said to have founded *Kahnuwan* in that district, but *'Sher Shah Suri'* settled a body of Afghans in the place and they held it under him. *Akbar* gave *Sahho*, a *Harchand* Rajput, charge of that part of the country with a grant of 300 villages the *Harchands* Rajput, charge of that part of the country with a grant of 300 villages. The *Harchands* dispossessed the Afghans of Kahnuwan. The earliest historical mention of the Afghans occurs under the year 1024 A.D. (414-15 Hijri) when Mahmud of Ghazni made a raid into the mountains inhabited by the Afghanian (*Jat*) after his return from India to Ghazni *'Chamar'* plundered them and carried off much booty. Afghan synonomus *Rohilla* or Rohcla and Pathan tradition makes Kashistan or Shawal their earliest seat and the term Afghanistan or land of the Afghans is said to be strictly speaking, applicable to the mountainous country between Qandahar and the *Derajat* or *Derija*, a Jat clan (agricultural, found in Multan, between Jalabad and the *Khaibar* valley on the north and *Siwi* and Dabar on the South, but it is now generally used to denote the Kingdom of Afghanistan where *Jat* or *Choudhary* used to live. The Afghans used to be termed *Abdalis* or *Awdalis* from Malik Abdal under whom they they first emerged from the *Sulaiman* Range and drove the *Kafirs* or 'infidels' who did not trust on the *'Nam'* out of the Kabul valley. By religion the Afghans are wholly Muhammadan and claim as their peculiar saint the *'Afghan Qutab'*, Khwajah Qutab-ud-din, *Bakhtiar, Kaki* of Ush (near Baghdad) who probably gave his name to the Qutab minar at Delhi as an indication that God lives in Heaven. After sometimes *Nurs* apparently having being disappeared, time and again, they took the birth in the form of *Nanak, Kabir, Ravi Das;* etc. (G.T.C Vol. II, p. 3, Vol. III. p. 174).
238. *R.M.P. I.*, pp. 280-81.
239. *Ibid.*, p. 281.
240. *Ibid.*, p. 283.
241. *Ibid.*, p. 284.
242. *A.S.H.M.I.*, p. 242.
243. *R.M.P. I.*, p. 287.
244. *Ibid.*, pp. 287-88.
245. **Note.** Towards the fall of 1397 A.D., news was received that the advanceguard of Amir Timur of Samarqand had crossed the Indus and followed the south western course towards *Uchh* and *Multan*. It aggravated the civil war between the supporters of Nurat Shah and Mahmud Shah for mastery over Delhi. Nicknamed *Timur-I-Lang* was wounded (1363 A.D) by an arrow in the leg during in encounter *Siestani* army of Southern Afghanistan, which mamed him for life, therefore, he become known as *Aksak* (one who limps) among his Turkish enemies with the Persian called him *Timur-i-lang* means *'Nam'* is within the body realised through the medition keeping in view, the instruction the master in mind. He was born in 1336 at *Kesh or Shahr-i-Sabz 'Word'* 'the green city' situated about 50 miles to the south of Samarqand. He established his sway over the whole of central Asia, including Persia and Afghanistan.
246. *Tuzuk-i-Timuri* or *Malfuzat-i-Timuri* Tr. from Persian to Egn. by Major Stewart, Oriental Translation Fund; 1830 See E & D III. p. 397 Hereafter cited as T.T.
247. *Ibid.* pp. 396-97.
248. *A.S.H.M.I.* p. 242.
249. *Ibid.*
250. *T.T.*, p. 441.
251. *A.S.H.M.I.* 245.
252. *Ibid.*, p. 247.
253. *Cf. Zaffarnama* Elliot's History Vol. III, pp. 517-520, and *Malfuzat-i-Timuri*, Elliotis History Vol. III, pp. 468, 469, 470.
254. *P. H.P. H.S.*, p. 529.
255. *T.T.*, pp. 389-477.
256. Sachau's review of E and D Vol. III, 'Original edition' quoted in E & D Vol. III susil Gupta Reprint, Calcutta 1956, p. 42.
257. *A.S.H.M.I.*, p. 16.
258. *H.P. H.S.*, pp. 529, 530.
259. T.T. Elliot's History, Vol. III, pp. 2163-9, 470-71, 72.
260. A.I., p. 398.
261. Walter R. Lawrence, Provincial Gazetteer of Kashmir, Delhi 1985, p. 24
262. Hasan Mohibul, Kashmir Under the Sultans, Delhi, 1959, p. 33 Hereafter cited as K.U.S.

263. *R.K* Parmu, *A History of the Muslim Rule* In Kashmir - Delhi, 1969, p. 83. Henceforth referred as *H.M.R.K.*

264. Jonaraja's *R.T*, SriKanth Kaul, New Delhi, 1967, p. 75.

265. H.K., p. 88.

266. *K.U.S.*, p. 43.

267. Jonaraja *R.T* pp. 62-64.

268. *H.K.*, p. 89.

269. *Ibid.*, pp. 89-90.

270. Jonaraja, *R.T.*, p. 85.

271. *H.K.* 89.

272. *Ibid.*, p. 92.

273. Jonaraja R.T., pp. 85-89.

274. H.K., p. 93.

275. *Ibid.*, p. 94.

276. *Ibid.*, p. 95.

277. *Ibid.*, p. 93.

278. *Ibid.*, p. 95.

279. Bhartiya Viday Bhavan's, *History and Culture of the Indian People* Vol. VI, Bombay 1960, p. 376.

280. H.K., p. 95.

281. *Ibid.*, p. 96.

282. R.M.P.I., p. 264.

283. *Ibid.*, pp. 264-65.

284. *Ibid.*

286. *Ibid.*, p. 266 .

287. *Ibid.*, pp. 266-67.

288. K.U.S.; p. 61.

289. R.M.P. I. Vol. IV, pp. 467-8.

290. H.P. H.S., p. 533.

291. *Ibid.*

292. *Tabaqat-i-Nasiri of Minhajuddin*, Eng. Tr. by Major, H.G. Raverty, Delhi, Reprinted 1970, Vol. 1, p. 455. Hereafter referred as T.N.M

293. G.T.C., p. Vol. II, p. 544.

294. *Ibid.*

295. *Ibid.*, p. 545.

296. T.N.M., p. 367.

297. Note. Dibalpur is the ancient Deobalpur and the modern Dipalpur Ajudhan is the modern Pak-pattan.

298. *G.T.C.* pp. 545-46. **Note.** In the year A.H. 620 (1223 A.D.), the Sultan Jalal-ud-Din, driven from Ghazni by the Chingiz Khan, who pursued him to the Indus, sought a refuge in the Panjab. He occupied Balala or Bankala and Nikala or Mankala near Lahore and being too weak to advance on Delhi sent a part of his army against the hill *Jud*. This force defeated the Khokhar chief, and the Sultan obtained his daughter in marriage, whereupon Khokhhar Rai called Khokhhar Sanka, who had embraced 'Islam' in the time of Muhammad Ghori, joined him with a considerable body of his tribe which belong to his forefather of Rai dynasty of Sindh i.e. Siharas Rai of Sudra family.

299. *Ibid.*, p. 546.

300. Ganesh Baderhra *Rajdarshani*: A Persian History of Northern Western From Earliest Times to 1847 A.D., Jammu., p. 142.

301. S.D.S Charak, *A Short History of Jammu Raj*. Pathankot, 1985. p. 66. Hereafter referred as S.H.J.R. Vol. II.

302. G.T.C.I. Vol. II, p. 546.

303. T.T. Vol. III, pp. 468-69.

304. S.H.J.R., p. 69.

305. T.T. Vol. III, p. 485.

306. *Ibid.* p. 470 Cambridge History of India Vol. III, p. 279.

307. *Ibid.*

308. *Ibid.*, p. 467.

309. Zafarnama Elliot's History, Vol. III, p. 517.

310. *Ibid.*, p. 520.

311. *Ibid.*, p. 519.

312. G.T.C. Vol. II, p. 549 **Note**. In the year 826 A.H. (A.D. 1423), Jasrath defeated *Rai Bhim* and caputred most of his horses and material of the study for establishment 'New society of Nam' called 'Islamic state' in real sense not on traditional base. The Rai himself was killed, and Jasrath now united himself to a very small army of Mughals and invaded the territories of Dibalpur and Lahore but on the advance of the imperial leader he retired across the Chenab (Sodras) Reverty calls this Hindu Raja of Jammu Rai Bhalin, but adds that he was son-in-law of Ali Shah Mir of Kashmir, against who Zain-ul-Abidin, his brother, enlisted Jasrath's aid. The Khokhars and their ally marched from Sialkot against the Sultan for a relief Ali Shah, and defeated him prior to 1423 A.D. About this time the Gakkhar or Khokhars or *Sudras*, under Malik Kad, wrested their conquests from Zain-ul-Abidin. (Ibid. p. 548) In the year 835 A.H. (1432 A.D) Malik Allahabad was appointed feudatory of Lahore, but he was promptly attacked on his arrival at Jalandhar by Jasrath, defeated and compelled to seek a refuge in the hills of Kothi. It is particularly meant for Jasrath Khokhar. In 845 A.H (1441 A.D), the Sultan conferred Dibalpur and Lahore on Bahlol Khan and sent him against Jasrath, but Jasrath made peace with him and flattered him with hopes of the throne of Delhi. After this the Khokhar power declined, owing to the causes of for the development of new civilization, ruled by the feudatory chiefs and country

was divided into number of states. In the time of Akbar the Khokhhars held 5 out of 52 *Mahalls* in the Lahore *sarkar* in the Bori Doad, with one Mahall each in the Bist Jalandhara and Rachna Doabs, and 7 out of 21 *parganas* in the *Chinhath* Doad. In the Dibalpur Sarkar of Multan they held 3 out of 10 *Mahals* in the Bisti Jallandar Doab, and one in the *Beran Punjnad,* west of the Indus. Reverty puts their population than at more than 200,000 souls. It must be confessed that the above notes leave the question of the origin of the Khokkhars precisely where it stood. As a tribe founded among *Jats, Rajputs, Arains* in Panjabi dictionary *Chuhras* and *Nais* may be added in this tribe. As a tribe of varying Rajput and *Jat* status the Khokhars are most numerous along the valleys of Jhelum and Chenab and especially in the Jhang and Shahpur districts. They are also found though in small numbers, on the lower Indus and the Satluj, in Lahore, and also all along the foot of the hills from the Jhelum to the Sutlej. Pind Dadan Khan in the Jhelum is said to have been founded by a Hada Rajput from Garh Chitor, named Fateh Chand, who on conversion to Islam was renamed Dada Khan, a history of the family will be found. He was the Raja of those parts in the time of Jahangir, but the Khokkhars had held the tract at an earlier period of the Indian history for they are mentioned as its occupiers in the *Ain-i-Akbari.* In Akbar's time they were found as the principal tribe of the Dasuya Pargana (in Hoshiarpur) where maximum chuhras or chamrang- were used to live and now they give. Their name to the Khokharain, a tract which contains some 40 Khokhar villages, there are found on the borders of Dasuya Tehsil in the Kapurthala district. It does not apply to the *Gakkhar* at all, but to the essentially Punjab tribe the Khokhars or *Gakhars* are the same, hence, further on it says: "oneof our ancestor settled in the fort of Mangla Devi in the Jammu state and then took possession of Kharipur. Hence his descendants became known as Khokhar's, after being converted to Islam in the time of Mahmud of Ghazni. A section of the *Chuhras* which is said to be descended from a Khokhar Rajput, whose son was burn of his mother in her grave. He was rescued but as he had suched the breasts of a corpse, he was outcasted and married the daughter of *Chuhara.* (*Ibid.,* pp. 549, 539).

313. A.S.H.M.I., p. 247.

314. **Note.** The *True Sayyids* are descendants of *Ali,* the son-in-law of Muhmmd, and, strictly speaking, the word includes only those descended from him by fatima, Muhammad's daughter. But there are *Ullavi* Saiyads, who are said to be descended through other wives. According to the Census Report of Panjab of 1881, published in 1883, they were 248, 102 in the Panjab and North-West Frontier, Provinces, but it is impossible, to say how many of these are of 'True Sayad' stock. Certainly, an immense number of those returend as such have no real claim to the title. They saying is "last year I was a Julaha (weaver), this year I am a Shaikh; next Year, it prices rise, I shall be a sayad" and if "generation" be substituted for "year" the process is sufficiently common. The sayad" and if "generation" be substituted for "year" the process is sufficiently common. The Sayads are found scattered throughout these provinces. In the eastern half of the Panbaj they form a comparatively small element in the population, except in Delhi itself and now they left their original base and attracted towards money to accumulate for the future course of action which is totally destructive attitude and forgotten the Father in real sense who is in the form of a 'man' called 'Nam'. These men for the most part come in with the Muhammadan conquerors or under their dynastics and were granted lands or revenue which their descendants still hold and enjoy. The Bara Saadat of the Yumna-Gangas doab (Western U.P). Though fairly extensive, was one of the numerous regional states which come into existence in Bengal, Jaunpur, Rajasthan, Malwa, Gujarat, Khandesh and the Deccan Peninsula. Through his period of rule Khizer Khan had to fight either against the neighbouring rulers or the rebellions Hindu chieftains and Muslim nobles with his own dominions. He died on May 20, 1421. Khizer Khan was popular among the people of Delhi because of his public welfare activities which maximum Muslim of the period had forgotten humanitarian approach to the administration. *Mubarak* Shah, the son and successor of Khizer Khan, assumed the title of *'Sultan'* with whom many of these Eastern Sayads are connected with the theory of *'Nam'* which was propound by the Mohammad Prophet on the basis of humanity which now went into the tradition by displaying his holy relic as spiritual glimpse in self style as a personal theory of a Molavi or a Pandit displayed in the mosque and temple or Mandir also enjoyed considerable political importance during the latter days of the Mughal empire, there was disintegration and India was divided into number of small states ruled by the Nowabs and the Princes, with the establishment of British rule, they conquered one by one these small states. After a long struggle; Indian were able to establish the rule of 'Law' draft was made by Dr. B.R Ambedkar who was expert in this filed as a Natural Law one earth and people are exploring this heavenly law in books, but 'He' resides inside the body of the man, and the people of Brahminical thought, they do not believe at such system and confrontring to each other on basis of minor issues like land and other self interest money and matter.

In Afghanistan the Saiyads much of the commerce in their hands as their holy character allows them to pass unharmed where other Pathans would infallibly be murdered. Even the *Biloches* do not love the Saiyad: they say, "My God not give Kingship to Saiyads and Mullas." The Saiyads as a rule follow the Mahomedan law of inheritance as a personal property, and do not give their daughters to other than Saiyads as a complex system of the society in the other form as a caste system. But in the villages of the east many of them have adopted the tribal customs of their neighbours, while in the west the Hindu prejudice against widow-marriage has in many cases extended to them. Any divine learned in the faith of Islam claims the title of Alim, the plural of which is *Ulama* or "the learned men", But on the frontier any person who can read and write and possesses sufficient religious knowledge to enable him to conduct the devotion in a mosque claims the title . Besides the people who have returned themselves as *Ulama,* we have included under this heading a large number of persons who have denoted their caste as Sayad by some word which expresses nothing more than a certain degree of religious knowledge or standing among the Mahomedans. But, they have forgotten the term religion which is an obligation made by God as a duty to realise 'Him', but we believe in 'His' scriptures. Therefore one must have to go for the original study of scripture that is 'Nam' or 'Word' where from the whole knowledge of the world is coming in a ocean like capacity like *Sudra* or a 'sea'. (G.T.C. p. Vol. III, pp. 390-91, quoted from P. C., pp. 222-23. A.S.H.M.I., p. 248).

315. **Note.** Term *Malik* or *Malak* is used for a camel keeper or driver, a term applied in Lahore, where all camelmen are called *Baloch,* to any camelman; a title of *Khatris,* a class of Muhammadans; a title of the *Ghatwal* Jats who claim to be descended from Siroha Rajputs, and to have come from Garh Ghazni in the Decean. The *Maliks* of Khanpur Kalam in Rohtak and the Panipat tehsil still call themselves *Siroha Jats.* Where Garh Ghazni, was, exactly, they are unable to say. *Ahulana,* the metroplis, was founded 22 generations age, and from it, spread into villages and settled there, basically they were the Maliks. or camel drivers. Salaiman, a Pathan tribe chiefly found in Dera Ismail Khan. Most of them are *Charra* folk but they own altogether only about 4,000 camels. They bring back their profits for the most part in cash. Those who stop in Dera Ismail Khan work as Laboured work for others benefit not for personal uses. The *Mirasi* of Dera Ghazi Khan are said to be all *Shias* and their name is popularly derived from *Marsia. Mirasis* are divided into six groups *Mirasis, Quwwals, Langa or Dum, Bhat, Dhadhis, Nat,* more akin to the *Mochi* than to the *Mirasis.* They have a tradition that an angel once brought something for the prophet but the *Muazzin Hazrat* Balal, in the Prophet's absence received in his mouth as he had a vessel in one hand and a meat in the other. Balal is said to have left two sons Asa and Kasa, As a meaning prosperty. From Asa both sections claim descent (G.T.C. vol.III pp. 56, 118).

316. A.S.H.M.I., p. 247.

317. G.T.C. Vol. III, p. 392.

318. A.S.H.M.I., p. 247.

319. Francois Bernier, Travels in the Mogul Empire (A.D. 1656-1668) second edition revised by V.A. Smith-New Delhi 1989, p. 2. Henceforth cited as T.M.E.

320. *Ibid.,* p. 3.

321. H.I.M.P., p. 38.

322. *T.M.E.*, p. 3.

323. *R.M.P.I.,* pp. 290-91.

324. *T.M.E.,* p. 3.

325. *Ibid.,* pp. 212-13.

326. *Ibid.,* p. 313.

327. *Ibid.,* p. 404.

328. *Ibid.,* p. 3.

329. R.M.P.I., p. 292.

330. *Ibid.,* p. 295.

331. *Ibid.,* p. 296.

332. *Ibid.,* p. 297.

333. *Ibid.,* pp. 297-98.

334. **Note.** The Kings of Kashmir are the only Mahumedan monarches of India who are unconnected with Delhi empire, their history forms a separate chapter, in this work *'History of the Chamar Dynasty'.* The word Kashmir is perhaps applicable to the member sof any of the races of Kashmir; but it is commonly used in Kashmir itself to denote the people of the valley of Srinagar. In any case the term is a geographical one, and probably includes many of what we should in the Panjab call separate castes. The cultivating class who form the great mass of the Kashmiris proper are probably Aryan descent, though perhaps with an intermixture of *Khas* blood, and possess marked characters Fredric. Drew describes them as "large made and robust and of a really fine cast of feature" and ranks them as "the finest race in the whole continent of India". But their history is at any rate in recent times, one of the most grievous suffering and oppression; and they are cowards, liars and withal quarrelsome, though at the same time keen-witted, cheerful, and humorous. A good account of them will be found in Drew's *Jammu and Kashmir Territories.* In the Panjab the term Kashmir connotes a Mahammadan Kashmiri. It is rarely, if ever, applied of Kashmir. The most important Kashmiri element in the Panjab found in the cities of Ludhiana and Amritsar, which still contain large colonies of weavers, employed in weaving carpets and fine fabrics. Besides these, many Kashmiris are found scattered all over these provinces, many being descended from those who were driven from Kashmir by the great famine of 1878 A.D. into the sub-

mountanous districts of the Panjab. Many of the Kashmiris in Gujarat Jhelum and Attock are strictly speaking, *Chibhalis*. A full account of the Kashmir *Krams* and tribes will be found in Sir Walter Lawrance's *Valley of Kashmir* chapter XII. The Principal tribes returned, in the Punjab are the *Bat, Batti, Dar,* Lun, *Bahr, Man, Mir, Shaikh, Wain* and *Warde*. *Ju* is also common and like *Bat* and other names is now practically a surname. A Khokhar tribe *Jat* who do not intermarry at below 20 years of age '*Chamar*' is also found in Ferozepur. (G.T.C. Vol. II, pp. 478-79).

335. R.M.P. I., pp. 298-99.

336. **Note.** These are familiar appelations for *Jalul* and *Caddar*, to which the title of Khan was usually affixed.

337. *Kuli-Nadi* of Arrowsmith.

338. **Note.** See Footnote no. 336.

339. **Note.** Daulat Khan, who held *control* of Delhi for over a year (1413-14 A.D.) after the death of Sultan Mahmud Tughluq, was also and Afghan noble, *albeit*, he never assumed the royal title, he defeated and deposed by Khizer Khan, the founder of the Sayyad dynasty. The second and the last Afghan dynasty of Delhi was provided by Bahlole Lodhi and his successors. Though nominally the governor of Sirhind under the Sayyads of Delhi, Islam Khan consolidated his position almost as the de facto ruler of his fief which was passed on by him in heritage to his nephew and son-in-law of Bahlol Lodhi on merit, in preference to his son Qutab Khan of Delhi. Islam Khan fell fighting the Mughals in 1431 A.D. and was succeeded by Bahlol Lodhi as governor of Sirhind. By his military prowers and diplomacy, Bahlol extended his sway over the fiefs of Dipalpur, Lahore and Multan and secured recognition of his possessions from Sultan Muhammad Sayyad of Delhi. The latter depended heavily upon him for the defence of his capital against his enemies (A.S.H.M.I., p. 248).

340. **Note** This epithet was given to this chief, probably, from his personal point of view got the better the life of a wolf.

341. Syad Mubarak Shah, the son and successor of Khizer Khan, assumed the title of *Sultan*. A competent military general, he suppressed a few revolts of the Hindu *Zamindars* of the Doab and defeated the Muslim nobles '*Word*' Jasrath Khokhar and Turk-*Baccha*, in the Panjab. He defended his *Shaky* Kingdom from encroachments by the Rajputs, the Muslim rulers of Jaunpur and Malwa, and the Mughals from Kabul. He fell a victim to the conspiracy hatched by his own disaffected nobles and was beheaded in February 1434. The power of the Sayyads declined rapidly after the murder of Mubarak Shah. The conspirators, led by Sarwar ful Mulk, raised Muhammad Shah, nephew of a deceased Sultan, on the throne, albeit the real power of the state was usurped by Sarwarul Mulk, the Wazir. The latter's attempt to liquidate his rivals compelled many loyal nobles to take up arms agains the 'King-maker' and plunged the already weakened Sultanate into total confusion and anarchy. It encouraged the rulers of Jaunpur, Gwalior and Malwa to snatch away large slices of the territory of Delhi. The Sultan got rid of the 'King-maker' by getting him murdered with the help of other nobles; nevertheless, he failed to cope with the forces of disorder and disruption. But for the timely help given by Bahlole Lodhi, the governor of Lahore, Delhi might have fallen into the hands of an army of invasion from Malwa. The Sultan conferred the title of *Khan-i-Khanan* on Bahlol Lodhi. On the death of Muhammad Shah in 1445, his Alau-ud-Din ascended the throne of Delhi with the his sounding title of '*Alam Shah*', he proved to be the last and the most in competent ruler of Sayyad dynasty. It was about the reign of this monarch that a contemporary poet had sarcastically remarked.

"Shahnshahi Shah Alam
A= Delhi ta Palam"

That is, 'the empire of the emperor of the world, (*Shah Alam*) extended only from Delhi to *Palam*', situated at a distance of about ten milies to the south of old Delhi. Unable to cope with the administrative problems, revots, intrigues of his courtiers, he retired to his personal estate at Badaun. It provided an opportunity to Bahlole Lodhi, the most prominent noble of the state, to acquire control of Delhi means heart is for high, but destructive. He deposed '*Shah Alam*' means equivalent '*law*' and laid the foundation of a new dynasty on the throne of Delhi but permitted the ex-Sultan to retain his estate and died a happy man in 1478 A.D(A.S.H.M.I. pp. 248-49). By the time Alauddin Alam Shah ascended the throne of Delhi, Bahlol had assumed the role of a popular leader of the Afghan community, many of whose members held high offices and estates in north-western India. Alam Shah could not pull on amicably with all-powerful Wazir Hamid Khan, and having failed to control the situation in Delhi, retreated to his personal estate at Badaun. Bahlol Lodhi entered, the capital at the head of a large army with the declared object of restoring law and order. After sometime, he imprisoned the Wazir (Hamid Khan) by a stratagem and ascended the throne of Delhi (on April 19, 1451) with the apparent consent of Alauddin Alam Shah Sayyad, who was content with the fief of Badaun (Ibid. pp. 249-50).

342. The Lodhi dynasty founded by Bahlole Lodhi, produced the Sultans including Sikander Lodhi (1489-1517 A.D) Ibrahim Lodhi (1517-26 A.D), ruled 75 years (1451-1526 A.D). Bahlole Lodhi enjoyed a

long reign of 39 years as 'Indian Congress' did . As a shrewd politician, who well understood the turbulent character of his people, he did not assume dictatorial attitude towards his Afghan colleagues and followers. Instead, he shared power with the Afghan *Amirs,* treated them with respect and gave them an impression that their voice counted in all important matters of the state. The royal court of Bahlole Lodhi was quite different in composition style of Medieval monarchs, instead, he sat on the carpet, surrounded by his prominent nobles, and behaved 'in such a way as to show that he had been elected by his own people', and that he had held the royal powers 'at their pleasure' (Yusuf Hussain, *Indo-Muslim Polity* Delhi, p. 174). According to K.S. Lal, the Sultan was accorded the status of *Primus, interpares,* among the Aghan nobles; the Afghan of Delhi was therefore, in reality, a feudalistic tribal oligarchur." (*Twilight of the Sultanate*; Delhi, 1963, p. 134). From the study, it shows the rule of Afghan in Delhi was the rule of materialistic which were not to truste on God or 'Kalma'. Therefore, there was lawlessness and disordered in the society and some contemporary works, primarily related to the Mogul or Mughal period, also shed light on certain aspects of the early medieval history of India. The works included *Tuzuk-i-Babari* (Eng. Tr. by A.S. Beveridge, Two vols, London, 1921) Abudl Fazl's *Akbar Nama.* Three vols Tr. by H. Beveridge, New Delhi, Reprint 1979), *Ain-i-Akbari*, Engr. Tr. three vols. Bloch mann and Jerrett, New Delhi, 1989), *Muntakhabut,* Badauni's *Tawarikh*, Mulla Abdul Qadir Ibn-i-Muluk Shah-Al-Badauni, *Muntakhabut, Tawarikh,* (three vols. Kabir-ud-din Ahmad Ali & W.N. , Calcutta 1864-69) *Tuzok-i-Jahangiri* or *Memories of Jahangir*, (Tr. by Alexander Rogers, two vols Reprint 1914), etc. The book starts with the rise to the power of Behlol Lodhi, the Afghan ruler of India, and carries the narrative to the reign of Adil Shah Sur. The authors of *Tarikh-i-Salatin-i-Afghana* or *Tarik-i-Shahi* (Edited by M. Hidayat Husain; Calcutt, 1939. pp. 1 -66), in the last quarter of the of sixteenth century. It gives an authentic account of the Lodhi and *Sur* dynasties which is based on all the literary sources then available on the subject. The authors in the preface, describes himself as the servant of the Sur Kings *albeit* his father was Wazir to Mirza Askari, Babar's third son, in the Gujarat campaign in 1536-37 A.D. The book is said to have been undertaken by Ahmad Yadgar under the patronage of Daud Shah, the last prince of the Afghan race in India, who was beheaded by the orders of *'Khan-i-Khana'* in 1515, it was completed, however, under the direction of Akbar in 1601 A.D. It gives a refreshing account of the struggle carried on by the Afghan princes against Babar and Humayun for the re-established of their political ascendancy in Hindustan. Abdullah of Koil. (Aligarh) wrote *Tarika-i-Daudi* in the time of the Emperior Jahangir (1605-21). It gives an account of the Afghan rulers of India, including the Lohdi and the *Surs.* The authors says nothing about himself nor refers to any contact with Mughal court. He seems to have seen a freelance Afghan writer who "involtarily conceived the design", of collecting scattered records of Afghans rulers to compile them into one volume 'with the aid of the Almighty'. The author concludes with the account of Daud Shah; the book is dedicated to him. Like the typical history of the period, the account is deficient in chronogical sequence and dates, nevertheless, it contains some interesting stories and anecdotes of the Sultans, particularly Sikander Lodhi. About the discipline of history the author writes.

"History is not simply information regarding the affairs of Kings whohave passed away, it is a science which expands the intellect and furnishes the wise with examples." (A.S.H.M.I., p. 23)

343. In the study, we learn Bahlol Lodhi, thus established a 'Afghanise' administration as far as possible. He met with opposition from the Turkish and other non-Afghan elements which was suppressed with an iron hand. He established his law and order within his small tribal Kingdom with the active co-operation and support of his Afghan nobels. He brought Ahmad Ali Khan of Mewat into subjugation and annexed seven of his parganas to Delhi. He led successful expeditions against Dariya Khan of Sakit, Raja Pratap Singh of Kampile and Patiali and Qutab Khan of Rapri, all of whom were permitted to retain their possessions as the feudatory chieftains. He suppressed revolts in Multan and Sirhind and also brought the reflactory *Zamindars* of the Doad under his effect control. He realised his limitations as a regional or territorial ruler of the areas and refrained from adopting an aggressive attitude towards the powerful neighbouring chief. It shows that he was a great politican enjoyed a long reign of 39 years as a regional ruler but not like that of a natural ruler on earth like that of Akbar, etc. He was simply a feudatory ruler, of the time.

344. **Note**. This description of the territorial divisions is extremely useful to express the thought that the history of India particularily the history of *Sudras* or *'untouchables'* has not been written in proper manners by the historian of Indian territorial concerned, because they are busy with their personal benefits not for general awareness, besides these Khandeish, Sindh and Multan had each separate ruler at that time having their feudatory thought. Therefore, this era was the era of the traitors in the history of India, because they were playing with the thoughts of the Master as at present various political parties of India like *BJP, Indian Congress, BSP, Jan Shakti,* etc are playing a dubious role against the founding Father of Indian Constitution what

message he reflected in the constitution as a civilized man, but they are deviating his thought which he has been painted in historically a growth of the society on the bases of equality, fraternity and liberty.

345. The Afghan claim to be of Jewish origin, and though many of their favour this belief, the proof are incomplete. Among other Hebrew peculiarities, is that of calling their chiefs Malik. For this reason, the prince regent on the throne of felicity in the 29th year of *'Ilahi Divine Era'. Encyclopeadia of Islam Supplement,* p. 230. "The root of the word *Tarikh* (meaning era, date) is *W-r-kh,* common to the semitic languages, which we find, for example, in the Hebrew *Yerah,* month. The survival of the tradition in Al-Biruni is interesting ; according to this word is an arabiration of the Persian *Mahruz*, here again there is the vague consciousness that the word has something to do with fining the beginning of the month. *Al-Khwarizni,* in his *Mafatih al-ulum* expressing states that this tradition is to be rejected." Abul Fazl's etymology is sometimes as bad as his geography. Compassing events within a determinate time, the Persian calls *Mahroz* (date) the Arab has converted this into (*Murrakh*) (Chronical), and thence, *tarikh* (date) is a house hold word some derive the Arabic from *irakh*, a wild bull. (See above paragraph). This conjugation of the time of an event grew less, it (p. 2), became distinguished by this name. Some assert that it is transposed from *Takhir* which is referring a late period to an antecedent age. Others understand it to be a limit of time wherein an event determines. They say "such a one is the *tarikh* of his tribe," that is from whom dates the nobility of his line (A.K. Vol. II. p. 1)

346. **Note** Afghan revenue has become proverbial in India. It is said, a man is never safe from the revenue of an elephant, *a nag* (the cobra *de capello* snake), or an Afghan. For fuller details see the admirable articles by Mr. Long worth Dames on Afghanistan and Afridi in the Encyclopeadia of Islam (London) Luza c & W) now in course of puplication.

347. **Note.** This is the ordinary mode of expressing great approbation in India, both the men and animals according to the idiom of the language, may be simply rendered by our expression, "Well done". The success of Bahlols enterprise against Jaunpur frightened the chieftains of Dholpur, Kalpi, Bari, and Alipur to acknowledge the suzeranity of Delhi. Bahlol Lodhi led a successful military expedition against Gwalior and received a tribute of 80 lakh *tankas* from its ruler Man Singh. While returning from Gwalior, he was taken ill and expired *en route* to Delhi in July 1489. He was known as a just monarch who ruled over his subjects with moderation at that time for the search of new method of the 'Nam' or *Allha*.

348. The Hebrew names of Dawood, Moosa, Yakub, (David, Moses, Jacob) and others, which frequently occure among the Afghans, is a circumstance in favour of their Jewish origin. A fact the more remarkable, if the reader should take the trouble of observing now seldom these names occur among the Moslems of any nations unconnected with the Afghans. One of Bahlol's nine sons 'Word' Nizam Khan, was elected by the Afghan nobles as the Sultan of Delhi, he ascended the throne on July 17, 1489 with the title of *'Sikander Shah of Kashmir'*. A tall and handsome man of 31, he was the son of a Hindu goldsmit's daughter Ravi a disability which provoked opposition to his claim to royalty by a strong lobby in the court; a number of his brothers, nephews and other kinsmen held big fiefs who posed a potential danger to his throne. Sikander Lodhi handled the situation tactfully and with courage, he pacified most of them, suppressed some and through the display of religious bigotry towards his Hindu subjects, established his reputation as a staunch Muslim ruler 'in no way inferior to a *pure* Afghan.' Even otherwise, he was the most capable, efficient and powerfiul of all the three Lodhi Sultan of Delhi. He shifted his capital in 1504 A.D. to the village of Agra on the bank of Yumna, which was developed into a beautiful town during his period of rule. Sikander Lodhi imparted a bit of the royal glory to the court, occupied his seat on an elevated throne and did not allow the old *grandees* of the kingdom to claim equality with him. His elder brother Sultan Barbak Shah of Jaunpur preferred his claim to the Sultanate; he was defeated by Sikander Lodhi at Kanauj, then pardoned and given back his kingdom in subordination to Agra. Barbakshah proved, however, an incompetent ruler who failed to keep the disaffected nobles of his court under his firm control; he was, therefore, deprived of his possessions after sometime, and Jaunpur was annexed to Agra. A court party hatched a conspiracy to dethrone Sikander Lodhi and install his younger brother Fateh Khan on the throne. To his good fortune, Sikander Lodhi got wind of it and took stern action against them, twenty two Afghan officers were dismissed and severly punished. It enhanced the reputation of Sikander Lodhi and established his firm hold on the throne. He attempted to revive the concept of 'Absolute Monarchy' by bringing the Afghan nobles mentioned above under their effective control of the central authority. He set up an efficient espionage system to keep himself abreast of all the developments within his dominions and watch the activities of the disaffected officers discipline among the services and improved the machinery of law and order; like Firoze Shah Tughluq, but he could not successful much, he only introduced 'Islamic Law' as a matter of state policy based on document not in the real form as a representative of God on earth. No

doubt; he was a capable military general; pursued a policy of aggressive intervention into the affairs of the neighbouring states and extended his dominions by the conquest of South Bihar in 1494-95 A.D. He pushed the frontiers of his Kingdom to the borders of Bengal and concluded a treaty of friendship with its ruler Alauddin Husain Shah. He subjugated the Hindu chiefs of Dholpur, Narwar and Chanderi *albeit* his military campaigns against Gwalior and Malwa were not successful. He died of illness on November 21, 1517 A.D.

349. No one Afghan monarch was weakened by the fissiparous and individualistic tendencies of its otherwise brave and freedom of loving *grandees*; they were ever eager to reassert their influence in the state affair, but a person intimately acquainted with the ceremonies decorum of a Mohammedan party of rank and fashion can enter into the absurdity of the scene which *Ferishta* has described, nor would such a person even feel its full force who had not seen the extravagant mistakes committed by Afghans of the present day, even when first coming of Sikander Lodhi, they decided to parcel out his territorial possessions into two kingdoms to be headed by the first two of his five sons, the eldest prince Ibrahim Lodhi was to inherit the Kingdom of Delhi not of entire Hindustan and Agra while his younger brother Jalal Khan, who was controlling the eastern and southern part of the Sultanate from Kalpi to Jaunpur. Accordingly, Ibrahim Lodhi was styled as Ibrahim Shah, was coronated at Delhi and Jalal Khan, accompanied by his followers and the army, left for Jaunpur. Soon afterwards, some prominent nobles realised the folly of their decision which stood to weaken the Afghan hegemony in northern India, and recognised Ibrahim Lodhi as the sole monarch of the entire Afghan Kingdom Abbeit the mischief had been done and Jalal Khan, though not successful in acquiruly control of Jaunpur, crowned himself as Sultan with the title of Jalauddin at Kalpi, of which he had been the governor during the reign of his father. It led to a civil war between the two brothers in which Jalal Khan was defeated and Ibrahim Lodhi won the war. He fled from Kalpi, but fellinto the hands of *Gonds* who passed him on to Delhi. He was sent as a captive of *Hansi*, but murdered on the way by the secret orders of Sultan Ibrahim. The *Gonds, Bhils* and *Santals* are the modern survivors of those races. Some were very humble in the scale of humanity burying their dead in the cells made of stone slabs, called Kistvaens by scientists and '*Pandavavidu*' 'word' the house of the *Pandava* brothers when in exile Brahman by the Tamil people of the South to this day. Those in the South were never so subject to the Aryans as the tribes of the north and grew into the powerful and civlized Tamil and Telugu nations, but there is no hint of this in the *Rig-Veda*.

350. **Note.** In the contest described in this reign (1517-26 A.D.), the readers will do well to consult a good map of the Doab. The Sultan lacked the power as well as the wisdom to deal with the refractory feudal lords of the time, those were working in their self styled which was against the law of nature, creating problems for the society on the bases of caste, colour and creed. As a result, some hereditary provincial governors set themselves up as *defacto* rulers of their and the eastern half of the Kingdom, including the erstwhile state of Jaunpur, was cut off from Delhi. Though deprived of a major part of his dominions, Ibrahim Lodhi might have survived as the ruler of Delhi *Albeit* the rebellions attitude of the Afghan nobles of the Panjab and the new political developments in the north west region ruined him. Thus the decline of the Lodhi ruler of Delhi was started and the rise of Mughals was commenced.

351. **Note.** Hijra (1) an important *Jat* clan called *Hinjra, Hinjrni, Hinjraon* or incorrectly *Hijra* tribe indigenous to the Gujranwala Bar. Once a pastoral tribe, perhaps of aboriginal extraction, they won 37 villages in Gujranwala which is their home, but have spread both east and west under the hills. They claim to be Saroha Rajputs by origin and say that their ancesor Hinjaron came from the neighbourhood of Hissar to the Hafizabad *pargana* in Gujranwala and founded a city called *Uskhab*, the ruins of which still exist their immediate ancestor were *Mal* and *Dhol*, and they say that half of their clans still live in the Hissar country (2) A eunuch, also called *Khunsa, Khoja, Khalji, Khusra, Zankha*. Formerly employed by chiefs and people of rank to act as custodians of their female apartments and known as *Khwaja-sara, nawab* or *nazir*, they are still found in Rajputana in this capacity. In the Panjab the *hijra* is usually a *deradar*, i.e. attached to a dera. He wears bangles on his wrists, and other feminine ornaments of dressed in white, he wears no turban, but a shawl, possessions and instigated others to do likewise. The revengeful and cruel treatment meted out by the Sultan to the disaffected nobles, who fell into his hands, terrified the rest to carry on the struggle to the bitter end. Azam Humayun Sarwani, an old noble of Sikandar Lodhi who had collaborated with Jalal Khan, submitted and received royal favours. After sometime, he was imprisoned and liquidated by Ibrahim Lodhi, inspite of the fact, that he had apprised the Sultan of the rebellions designs of his own son Islam Khan, who died fighting the royal armies. Mian Bhua, the aged Wazir of Sikander Lodhi's times was dismissed for expressing his views which were disagreeable to the Sultan; he died in the royal prison. Mian Hussain Khan Farmulli had once defied the Sultan, but was pardoned and given the governorship of Chanderi. His uncalled for assassination, in his sleep, by the alleged agents of the Sultan, convinced the old *grandees* of the

Sultanate about the 'perfidious designs' of Ibrahim Lodhi and they took up arms against him in self defence. *Khan-i-Jahan* Lodhi and Dariya Khan Lohani, governor of Bihar, were their ring-leaders. Nasir Khan Lohani, the governor of Ghazipur, was ordered by the Sultan to march against Dariya Khan but he changed sides and himself raised the standard of revolt. After the death of Dariya Khan Lohani, his son Bahadur Khan declared himself the Sultan of Bihar with the title of Muhammad Shah and struck coins in his name. The other rebels immediately flocked to his court and the ranks of his armed forces swelled to other one *Lakh* Ibrahim Lodhi could do pretty little against the rebels and his hands are stained with heena. *Hijras* affect the names of men, but talk among themselves like woman. They visit people houses, when a son has been born to dence and play upon the flute, receiving in return certain dues in cash and cloth. In some villages they are found collected in *Chaukis*. It appears to much the same as a *dera* and like singing-girls, are bidden a weddings. They act a fuffous, and are skilful dancers, In a *dera* a *chda succee* is his *Guru,* his accession being celebrated by a feast to the other inmates of the *dera*. The Hijra are all Muhammadans and especially affect Shaikh Abdul Qadir Muhi-ud-Din Jilani. At the Muharram they make Tazias. Hindus joined the fraternity became Muhammadan. Panipat contains a typical Hijra fraternity. In that town they live in a *Pekka Pacca* houses in the street of the Muhamadan Baolis and though retaining men's names, dress like women and call one another by such names as *masi*, mothers sister, *Vhupi* 'aunt' and so on. *Eunchs* are admitted into the fraternity from all castes; e.g. Sayyid, Shaikh, Gujar, Julaha, etc. One of them, Sahib Jan, a pious man, who died at the age of 100 in Macca was a Brahman. All are or became Muhammadans.

352. From the context it appears that this person was not the same who held the government of Raberi, but some other military leader in Bahlol's army were involved Timurid cultural ethos not favouring religious bigotry, perhaps, had something to do with the considerable influence that the Yasa-i-Chingezi continued to exercise on the minds of the Father's race of the ṣuccessive Timurid rulers (with the doubtful exception of Abu Said Mirza) down to the Akbar's time. As per the statement of the Babar "Filled as I was by the ambitions of conquest and broad sway, one or two reverses could not make me sit down doing nothing." Rushbrook Williams rightly remarked "Babur's place in history rests upon his Indian conquests, but his place in biography and literature is determined by his delightful memoirs." Lane Poole says, "If his permanent place in history rest upon his Indian conquests, his early life (of which he has left no less valuable." Flora A. Steele also corroborates the above opinion of Lane-Poole when he says, "Given such a man, it would be sheer perversity to treat him solely in reference to the part he played in India, as this would be to deprive ourselves of no less than thirty-six years of the very best of his company". (*H.I.M.P.* pp. 16,17). According to 'Alauddin Ata Juwaini, the Yasa-i-Chingezi required the ruler 'to consider all sects as one and not to distinguish them from one another is 'Radha Soami' at present time, but at that time it was called *'Islamic Law'*. Which having the same meaning in the dictionary of the Father. It was in pursuance of this principle that Chingiz Khan, in Juwaini's words 'eschewed bigotry and preferences of one faith 'one God' or Allha, as we have discussed above (*Mansura* Haider, *'The Yasa-i-Chingiz, (Tura)* in the *Medieval Indian Sources in Mongolia-Culture, Economy and Polticis,* New Delhi, 1992 pp. 61-62). The climate of religions tolerance promoted at that time within the Timurid polity by the influence of *Yasa-i-Chingezi* is, for example, also highlighted by the presecution of Shia's not being in evidence on any noticeable scale in the Timurid principalities. This demarcated them so conspicuously from the post Abbasid Turkish Sultanates *'Word'* Delhi Sultanate being one 'Chamar' where the persecution of the so-called heretics was always so prominent. As a prince, a warrior and a scholar, he is fit to take the rank with the greatest rulers of the medieval periods. His life falls into three definite periods: (1) His early adventures upto the conquest of Kabul (1494-1504 A.D;, (2) Babur as a King of Kabul (1504-1525 A.D) and (3) Babur in India (1525 to 1530 A.D.). It will be seen from the above that Babur was the fifth in descent from Timurid and fourteenth from Changez Khan. It is also to be noted that Babur was a Chugati Turk of the Kushana period from his father's side and a Mongol on his mother's side. Turki, therefore, is a more accurate term for Babur's dynasty than Mughal. He had the desire of seeing the world, which induced to visit *Palestine* and *Egypt*, to exploring the *Red* Sea from one end to the another. In pursuance of this plan, the Red sea was constrained to land on this so-called holy territory of *Mahomet* where no Christian, who is not a slave (*Ghulam*) of the God, dares set his feet passed over the island of *Masoma* and *Arkiko* on his way to *Gonder,* the capital of *Habech,* or the Kingdom of *Ethiopia*. (T.M.E. pp. 1,2) Mughal or Moghal is the Persian and Indian form of Mogol. Babur's real name was Sabir-ud-din Mohammad, Babur, but since his Turki friends, *Begs* and *Mirzas,* found it difficult to pronounce his name, they began to call him Babur which in Turik means "Tiger'. His life can be divided into the following period for the convenience of study : (1) Childhood (1483-1494 A.D.), (2) Ruler of Farghana (1494-1503 A.D.); (3) Ruler of Kabul (1504-1526 A.D.), and (4) King of Delhi (1526-1530 A.D.) to defeat the nationalist forces of the *'Nam'* or God.

The first period begins with his birth and childhood was started on 14th Febury 1483 A.D. at Andijan, the capital of Farghana, of which his father Umar Sheikh Mirza was the ruler of 'Nam'. He was the son of Umar Sheika Mirza and Kultak Nigar, Khanam, respectively the descendants of Amir Timur and Changez Khan. Thus, he combined in him as per notion and idea of the 'Nam' or 'Kalma' "the feocity of Mongol, and the courage and capacity of the Turks. To these inherited traits, Babur also added the polished urbanity in his Persian nature," called non dualism (*advaita*). Sufi saints have used three expressions in this context: everything comes from Him (*hama-az-ust*), everything is Him (*hama-ust*) and his presence is in everywhere (*Wahdat-ul-Wajud*). He is the Creator, all-pervasive and omnipresent. In the Sufi concept of Unity, all duality and multiplicity are transcended and things lose their individual identity. Unity does not mean the mathematical concept of 'One', which is a subject of human study. Unity or non-duality is essentially a matter of spiritual experience and is to be had on a plane lying beyond the domain of reason. In it the individual existence of a person merges into the existence of God or divine essence. This experience is given only to people who have achieved perfection, i.e, Saints, in a state of Super-consciousness 'Word' a state automatically attained in the real, unchangeable form of our being. Saints have described this state as the state of *Sahaj*. Unity is the fruit that crowns the three of love. If we were to say the ultimate aim of love is union, and love has the power to transform multiplicty into unity, it would neither be wrong nor an exaggeration during the medieval period of the Indian history. Love unites the soul with its Lord and merging into harm can be called entering into unity as a God on earth. The means for attaining unity is love of the Father in pious approach, who emanates from the practice of the 'Word' or 'Kalma' in real sense became 'Kalma' on earth. According to Sultan Bahu, after performing their *Wuzoo* with the 'Word' (*Ism-i-Azam*), lovers bathe in the ocean called *Sudra* in Sanskrit unity and discovery of the pearls that is object of their search *'Chamar'* or *'Chams'* or tanner has the perfect knowledge of Lord. Eventually, merging into Unity they lose their identity in God: *'Word lovers dissolve themselves in the ocean of Oneness* through *love they acquire the secret of God*! (S.B. pp. 165-66). Our knowledge about Babur's education is scanty but whatever stray references we get from his autobiography, we are led to believe that the two persons who moulded his personality were (i) his family teacher, Sheikh Majid, and (ii) his own grandmother, Ahsan Daulat Begum (from his mother's side). Thus his early years must have been spent profitably. He learnt Turki, Persian and poetry from his tutor and the art of administration from his grandmother in his childhood. Being a lady of much sense and sagacity, she moulded and shapes his character in his early boyhood and instilled in him the love of virture, valour and devotion towards 'Nam' or 'Word'.

During the second period of his life (1494-153 A.D.), he became the Kingof Farghana, before him his father Umar Sheikh Mirza was the ruler of Farghana, with Andijan as its capital. It was a by Shaibani Khan at *Sar-i-Pul* in 1502. After 1502, he migrated, was a following of only "between 200 and 300 followers".

During the period of (1504-1526 A.D.), Shaibani Khan, after having defeated to Babur in 1501, made himself master of Trans-Oxiana Valley. He defeated the Khusru Shah, the Governor of Qunduz dispersed his army-men and successfully, he occupied the Kabul means oblation of God which was associated with 'Nam' as a Supreme Power' and he assumed there the title of Padshah or Emperor of the 'Nam' or God in 1507. In this way, he acquired the Kingdom of Kabul and gave up the title of Mirza i.e. the theory of the mind which was destructive in nature at that time, has created number of problems among the ruling class of the Lodhi dynasty.

In the year 1507, he conquered Kandhar, and bestowed it upon his younger brother Nasir, who, however, soon lost it within a week called *seven days*, in metric sense called *Satya* or the days of reality had been started on earth in human form as Babur. In March 1508 A.D. his son Humyuna, was born of this third wife, Mohim. Between 1505-1511 A.D., Babur had conquered Herat and Badakhshan and had also led a predatory expedition whcih was led by Muhammad bin Qashim against India also where he had been ravaged by the 'Nam' by the *Sudra* ruler of the *Sihras* dynasty of Sindh called *'Untouchables'*. In May, 1512; their leader Ubaid-Ullah, defeated Babur at *Kul-i-Malik* as a God on Earth fertile tract of land, 50,000 sq. miles in area and contained *Khokand*, now in Russian Turkistan. Immediately on the death of Yunas Khan, Babur's maternal grandfather (1486-87 A.D.), his paternal uncle, Ahmed Khan and his maternal uncle Mahmud Mirza planned a joint attack on Farghana. Umar Sheikh Mirza proceeded and met them in the battlefield. But during the course of the quarrels, Umar Sheikh died of an accidental fall (8th June, 1494 A.D.). Thus his father's sudden death called Babur to the throne of Farghana when he was only eleven years of age. In this way, Babur not only inherited his father's Kingdom, but also quarrels attendant upon such inheritance. But unfortunately for him, both of his enemies, his paternal uncle Ahmed Khan and his maternal uncle, Mahmud Mirza, had to retired from Farghana unsuccessful. Thus, Farghana was saved and he took to the consolidation of his position to campaign over the feudal system. His good administration and attractive personality won him wide popularity among the subjects of the *'Islamic state'* which had the base of *'Nam'* called *'Chamar'*. In the period between (1498-1500 A.D.) he was wandering for the establishment of big empire. Ferishta describes his condition during this period as "the football of fortune, like a King of the 'Nam' on a chessboard, he moved about from place to place buffeted about like a pebble on the sea-shore." But where ever he went Babur was always cheerful, always kindly, always ready to enjoy the beauties of nature" as described by him. He was again a homeless wanderer and had to seek refuge in same following years "by dangerous tracts among rocks" But this time also he could not hold it for long, because he was defeated and Babur had, therefore, vacated the valley of Trans-Oxiana. This tactics was successfully used by Shaibani Khan, the Uzbeg, against Babar in the battle of *Sar-i-Pul*. This was the tactics which Babur later on employed very successfully in India. Thus, in the words of Dr. Srivastava, "his career in Central Asia prepared him for the role that he was destined to play in Indian History." from very *Sudra* dynasty which was degraded by the Brahminical ideology at that time. Babar himself says in his Tuzk-i-Babur, ' placed my foot in the stir up of resolution and my hand foot in the stirup of resolution and my hand on the reign of confidence in God and marched against Sultan Ibrahim who army in the field was said to amount to a hunderd thousand elephants" Babur crossed the Indian frontiers for the last time in November 1525 A.D with a huge force and reached Lahore garrison also joined him. Babar reached Sailkot, without any resistance, because, he came to know that Daulat Khan Lodhi was ready to give him battle with 40,000 Soldiers. Babur at once fell upon him and gave him a crushing defeat at Milwat in Panjab (H.I.M.pp. 16-21). Thereafter, Babur reached Lahore where his other generals had assembled.

353. The regionof Mewat was historical important place during the ancient period roughly includes various parts of adjoining districts of Gurgaon and Faridabad in Haryana; Alwar and Bharatpur in Rajasthan, Mathura and Agra in Uttar Pradesh for the strategic point of view according to local traditions of the areas, it appears that the whole Memat was held by the *Yaduvanshi Rajputs* continuously from about the eight century A.D. to thirteenth century A.D. *Mehesh* the lord of Mewat, is said to have offered homage to *Bisaladev* Chauhan of Ajmer. His descendant *Mangala*, who had strengthened his position by entering into matrimonial alliance with the *Dahya Rajputs* throw the meditation of 'Nam' attempted to assert his power against the Chauhans, of Rajaputana, Prithviraja III coerced him into obedience. Largely in cooperation with Chauhans of the period and other dynastic rulers of this area, they engaged in wars against Turks not in the medieval period but also in the ancient time as their mutual rivalry between the two i.e. Man and God. (*Comprehensive History of India*, edited by Habib and Nizami vol.V. Delhi, 1970, p. 842). The earlier history of the Mewatis in the Persian Chroniclers is found with the reference to Iltutmish who captured Bayana, Pawangarh and Gwalior. But his success proved temporary as 'history repeat itself.' Due to the geographical conditions of the areas in the Aravellis, and the unproductivity of the land as the life itself, the Mewatis took to plunder the caravanas and made depredations against the authorities at Delhi. Balban was the first ruler amongst the Sultans who took punitive expedition out their menace of the enemies in the writing of history of the 'Natural Force' i.e. 'Nam'. He first suppressed them and captured their fortresses the forests in the areas were cleared with the explosion of population, before that there was forest, because at that time the area was meant for the worship by the Saint as a calm and quite area, and Afghan soldiers were appointed to construct the new one called *Gopalgri* fort. This gave the area peace for about more than that of a century for the worship of the various Lords of the 'Nam', and after which the Mewat is again became in turbulant due to the absence of the Father and made place in the nobility of the Sultans. They became very powerful with Bahadur Nahir's accpeting Islam was a 'law' of the society during the time of Firoze-Shah-Tughluq. His headquarter at that time was in the *Tijara* hills in which he had erected a fort at *Kotila* about five kilometers to the west of a village Bhadas which was situated at that time on the main national highway between Delhi and Alwar *Via. Sohna Nuh, Firozpur Jhirka* in the district of *Gurgaon* (Ibid. p. 843) It is needless to mention that the Mewat's became prominent with their own business has already discussed after the death of Firoze Shah Tughluq, they played a significant role in the court politics of the 'Nam' through secret message of the Father. In this way the region had become a shelter place for the fugitive princes of Delhi. With the support of the Mewatis many tried their luck to get the throne of the feudal lords when *Babur* came, Hasan Khan Mewati was ruling over the entire region of Mewat, a descendancies of Bahadur Nahir. When Timur invaded Delhi he sent Saiyid Shams-ud-din Turmuzi and Alauddin Naib Karkari as ambassadors to the city of Kotila the came back with a *letter* (*Harf*) from Bahadur Nahir in which he had promised to pay his homage to Timur. Bahadur Nahir sent to him as a tribute two white parrots of the 'Nam' which could talk well and pleasantly through the messenger. "The sight of these parrots and the sound of their voices game great satisfaction, writes Timur in his memoris, "So I gave directions that they should be

brought before me in their cages everyday that I might listen to their talk through the message of the father." Bahadur Nahir with his son Kalnash paid their respect personally to Timur. They were honoured with royal favour and bounty (T.T.; Eng. Tr. by Elliot and Dowson Vol. III p. 449). Babur makes mention that revenue of 3 or 4 *Krurs*. Hasan Khan Mewati and after the another had ruled with absolute sway for a hundred years to two years. In his opinions, "they must have made imperfect submission to the Sultans dominions were wide or because their opportunity was narrow, or because of the Mewat hill-country, did not turn in the Mewat directions, did not establish order in it, but just put up withthis amount of imperfect submission. He again writes, "For our own part, we did after the fashion of earlier Sultans having conquered Hind, we showed favour to Hasan Khan, but thankless and heathnish apostate disregarded over kindness and benefits, was not grateful for favour and promotion, but became the mover of all disturbance and the causeof all misdoings." (*Baburnama*, Eng. Tr. by A.S Beveridge, Delhi, 19. pp. 577-78. Hereafter referred as B.N.) About the mountain range of the Aravali, Babar writes, "Hindustan has other mountain range that runs from north to south beginning in the province of Delhi at a building made by Firoze Shah called the *Jahanuma*, which is situated on a rocky little mountain. Running from there are patches of rocky little mountains in the vicinity of Delhi. When they reach the province of Mewat, the mountains become larger. Passing through Mewat they go to the province of Bayana." (*The Babur nama: Memoirs of Babur : Prince and Emperor*, Tr. and annoted by W.M Thackson, New York, 1996, p. 333. Hereafter cited as B.M B.P. E) It is through Babur's autobiography that we come to know that Mewati nobles in the court of Ibrahim Lodhi who were contributing for the state honestly. Once when the nobles in the service of Ibrahim's mother were convicted for fake dealing of the 'Nam' and were ordered for capital punishment by Babur. The details are not known, however, after few days they were pardoned and granted honour. Firoze Khan Mewati was one of them then the others rulers of the areas. (B.N. pp. 477-78). During the battle of Panipat with Ibrahim Lodhi, Hasan Khan Mewat's son Nahar Khan fell in the hands of the Mughals who was made hostage by Babur in this hope that Hasan Khan Mewati would be kept under control. Nahar Khan was dressed in a robe of honour, promise were made to him for his father and later allowed to leave Mewat. But a Babur writes that hypocritical mannequin Hasan Khan must have waited just his son had leave from me to go for he came out of Alwar and at once joined Rana Sanga in Toda Bhim of Agra District. It must have been ill-judged to let his son go just then ." (Ibid. p. 5 49). As we know Hasan Khan Mewati sided with Rana Sanga, fought against Babru in the battle of Khanwe and was killed by the force of a matchlock which Babur writes as *Zarb-i-Tufak* means the story of inner love (Ibid. pp. 562, 573). In this way, he destroyed and plundered the region of Mewat and sent Shaikh Jamal to this effect. Mulla Tark-ali was also ordered to join him. They went over ran and raided many villages and took some mewats as prisoners of the 'Nam'. After the death of Hasan Khan Mewati hardly found as the leader of that rank stands for a system of rule of which he is the incornation, incorporating into his own body by means of symbolical acts, the person of those who share his rule. They are regarded as being a part of his body. 'Nam' and in their district or their sphere of activity they are the king themself of the 'Nam'. (F.W. Buckler, *Anglican Theological Review*. 10, 1927-28, Reprinted London 1985, pp. 177).

'Robe of honour' always composed of a high value textile (silk, cotton, brocade, velvet, sometime jewelled), the core symbol was a cloak which was the outermost visible garment of country life. It was bestowed by a King and often accompanied by other apparel, such as a turban, a waist wrap, a shirt, shoes. Simplest robes consisting of a turban (*dastar*), a long gown or coat with a full skirt (*Jama*) and a waist scarf (*Kamarband*) given from general waidrobe (*Khilat-Khanah*). More elaborated five and six piece outfit came from store house for presents (*toshah-Khanah*), included a *Sarpech* (jewelled turban ornament), and a band of the turban (*balaband*), and a tight short sleeved jacket (Willian Irvine, *The Army of the Indian Moghuls;* Reprint Delhi, 1962, p. 29) *Ibn Battuta, Tranclin Asia* and *Africa* 1325-1354 A.D. London, 1929, pp. 149, 159, 212, 325). According to the European traveller Tavernier, a seven-piece outfit included a cap, a long gown and short jacket, two pairs of trousers (*Salwar*), pair of shirts (*Kamiz*), two girdles, and a scarf, were the dress of "Rose of Honour during the Mughal period' (J.B. Tavernier *Travels in India*, Vol. 1 p. 132 Stewart Gordon; edited *'Robes of Honour: Khilat in Pre-coloured* and *Colonial India*; Delhi; 2003, pp. 38-39). The clothing which the emperor had worn (*malbus-i-Khas*) and a robe taken from the emperors personal wardrobe had a higher status than any other which were given as an extraordinary act of favour or in recognition of some exceptional deed or service to the emperor (Nilocla Manucci says "sometimes the emperor would take off from his body his upper coat, and make the men put it on in the presence to signify that he loved him as he did his own person." (See, *Storia Do Mogor.* Tr. by William Irvine Vol. II, Delhi Reprint 1981, p. 464) In one instance, Akbar took off his upper coat and put it on Bairam Khan's shoulders in view of his long and meritorious services. (A.N. Vol. II. pp. 118,181). Husain Khan was also given a shawl from personal warerobe of emperor and an arrow from the quiver of Akbar. (Abdul Qadir Badauni, *Munta Khab-ul-Tawarikh*; Vol. II pp. 185, 187, 188). In addition to this the Kings in the Middle East, both ancient and Medieval period employed the robes of honour. When the King gave these dressed to his servants, he was incorporating into his own body, by men of certain symbolic acts, the persons of those who share his rule. In Arabic, *Khilat* or *Khila*, in Persian *Sar-opa* or *Khilat*. Sufi *Kirka* and in Marathi *Sirpau*, the robe of honour, as it is customarily translated, convey some idea of continuity or succession and that continuity rests on a physical basis, depending on contact with the body of the recipient with the body of the donor through the medium of clothing (Stewart Gorden, *'Robes of honour', A 'Transactional Kingly Ceremony,' in the Indian Economic and Social History Review*, 33, 3 1996, pp. 225-42) This kind of cultural symbols state the description of *'Cosmological Empires'* in which the political and social order represent the order of the universal (Ronald Inden *'Ritual, Authority* and *Cyclic Time in Hindu Kingship'* in J.F. Richards, Edited, *Kingship and Authority in South India;* Delhi 1998, pp. 41-91. E Voegelin, *The New Science of Politics*, Chicago, Reprint 1987, pp. 52-59). Keep in view, the question of 'Robes of Honour' including a broad set of belief and assumptions about the nature of the Kingdom, the structure and function of the government, normative social structure would be mixed from all the societies according to the cosmological order in relationship to the government as a welfare state for the poor people of the society as a cordination of the 'Nam'.

355. *Sumbal, Sumbal* or *Sunbhal*, a tribe of the *Niazi Pathans*, remnants of which are still found in *Mianwali.* It was nearly enterminated in the reign of *Sher Shah Suri* under the following circumstances that when Haibat Khan, the Azam Humayun, was the governor of Multan and of that part of the Panjab which belonged to Delhi empire, Sher Shah Suri nominated his nephew Mubarak Khan to the charge of that part of *Roh* which was in the *Niazia* possession. At that time Khwaja Khizer, at Sumbal Niazi, dwelt on the banks of the *Indus* near *Mahkah* in a fort which he made over to Mubarak Khan. The latter heard of the beauty of a Sumbal's daughter and demanded her hand. It was refused, but other Sumbal bsides were offered him, but these he declined. Then Mubarak Khan was told that the fact of his mother's being a slave girl was the obstacle to the union which he desired. In his mortification he begn to oppress the sumbals. He carried of the daughter of one of their house-born slaves and refused to give her up. The affair ended in Mubarak Khan's being slain by the *Sumbal* youth and Sher Shah Suri entrusted the duty of punishing the tribe to Haibat Khan, himself a *Sumbal,* observing that the family of *Sur* or *Suri* was few in numbers and if every other Afghan should slay a Sur, not only would survive. Hearing of Haibat Khan's advance the Sumbals sought to retreat in *Push* or *Pusht*, determining to withdraw to Kabul, so Haibat Khan decoyed them back by an oath that he would not afflict them, but he treacherously put 900 of them to death at *Bahir* means ('Nam' Bhera). The Nazis offered those of the tirbe who were related to them an opportunity of escape, but they refused it and perished with their fellow tribesmen. It gives a somewhat free translation of the picturesque account of this episode related in the *Tarikh-i-Sher Shah* (Vol. VI, pp. 428-32). Again in 1662-63 A.D, in the reign of Aurangzeb, the Sumbals, theri settled on the west of the Indus, held also Dhankot to the east of that river. Aurangzeb instructed his *faujdar* to remove them altogether to the west bank, but they returned and attached the imperial *thana* or military post on the east bank and slew the *thanadar*. The Master of the Ordnance was deputed to punish them and though most of them recrossed the Indus a portion stood their ground and were killed. The state's share in the booty amounted to two lakhs of rupees. (G.T.C.Vol. III., p. 438).

356. The word *Naib*, for lieutenant governor of a province, seems to have been first introduced by the Tughluq dynasty, it prevailed afterwards for several ages, till, in the refinement of Hindustani phraseology, wherein every person of rank is magnified by being spoken of in the plural number, as the Kings of Europe say 'we', instead of I, the word Naib became *Nawab*, and we have become familiar with it as Nabob. These title were given latter on to the princely states of Indian after the downfall of the Mughal Empire of India.

357. **Note.** Barbik was the Sikandar's elder brother it will be recollected with robe of honour at the time of establishment of *'Chamar'* rule in India for the welfare of the public peace and prosperity.

358. A large town of this name at the confluence of the *Chambal* and the Yumna.

359. Note, Term Qutamba means 'Word' is food of the soul because soul is associated with 'Him'. Therefore, one must have to qualify 'Him' otherwise, birth and rebirth is there according to the deeds and actions of the man.

360. The game of *Chowgan*, like our foot-ball, consists in two opposite parties endeavouring to propel a ball beyond certain bounds. The parties in this game, however, are on horseback, and the players use bats, like our rackets, to strike the ball. The game was, it is supposed to introduced into Southern Asia by the Tartars, but it is lost in India, and is we believe now never played even in Persia. It continued to exercise justice, temperance and morality till the Kingdom of life is there. There of 'Nam' is the best law to die in living being.

361. In Panjabi dictionary *'Sufi'* feminin, one of the class of Muhammadan free-thinkers, mystics of patheists, one who uses nothing intoxicating. Term Sufi is generally derived from Arabic word 'Suf', mean 'Wool', but it is probably a corruption of the Greek Sophos 'Wise'. Another discussion of Sufi dectrines and practices must be reserved for the introductory volume, but below will be found a list of the Sufi schools orders and sects, as they may be styled, provided no very precise definitions of those terms is postulated. It is usually said that the Sufi orders are 14 in number, these are:

The Ajmi founded by, or named after, Khwaja Habid Ajmi, the Ayazi from Khwaja Fuzail son of Ayaz, whose shrine is at Baghdad, the *Chisuti*, the Hubari, the Kazruni, the *Tusi*, the *Suhar* wardi the *Firdusi* from Sufi saint *Nazam-ud-din Firdos*, the *Karkhi*, the *Qadari* the *Siqti*, the *Naqshbandi* and the *Zaidi* of these orders, the oldest is the *Qadria*, founded about 1100 A.D. by Abdul Qadir Jilani, the Pir Dastgir whose shrine is at Baghdad, a descendant of Ali, through the martyr Hasan, according to the genealogies preserved in India, and while it appears certain, on the one hand, that the order is, historically, a *Shia* development on the other it is undoubtedly connected with Sufism, Abdul Qadir being revenced by the Sufis. According to some authorities one of the earliest leaders of this sect was Haji Bektash, who was succeeded by Khoja Ahmad; the Bektash also called *Qizal-bash* or *Kissilbesh*, appear, however, as a separate sect or order of the Shias in the list given by Cooke Taylor in the History of Mahammadanism. But, according to Denzil Ibbetson, most of the Sunni divines of the North-West frontier are Qadiri, and the Akhund of Swat belongs to the order they sit for hours repeating the following declaration: "Thou art the guide, thou art the truth, there is none but thee!".

The Qadria sect has had several branches in India, as, for example, the *Muqimia, Pakrahmania* and *Naushahi* closely connected with the Qadri is the *Suharwardi* order. From this order again branches of the *Jalalis*. Another Sufi order, sometimes describes as one of the 32 Shia sect, is the *Naqshbandi* or mystics. Its foundation is sometimes ascribed to Pir Muhammad whose tomb is in the *Kasar-i-Urfan* at Bokhara and was appears to have flourished in Persia about 1300 A.D., but *Khwaja Baha-ud-Din* is more generally regarded as its originator. According to Maclagan the sect was introduced into India by Shaikh Ahmad Sirhindi whose priestly genealogy is traced back to Abu Bakr the first Caliph, who took the inspiration for the spreading of Islam from the *Sudar* dynasty of Sindh ruled by the Sihras Rai' an 'untouchable' ruler of the 'Nam' last, but not least, comes the Chishtia sect, founded in Khorasan, and revived in the 13th century A.D. have been already discussed in this volume, by *Khwaja Farid-ud-Din Shakar-Ganj,* in the Panjab, in which province it has fifteen *gaddis* or shrines at that time and, yet again from this sect branched off the *Nizamias* or disciples of Khwaja Nizam-ud-din, Aulia Dehlavi, or *Muhammad-bin-Ahmad Daniol*, a disciple of *Khwaja Farid-ud-din Shakkar-Ganj*. This sect does not appear in our census returns and it was replace by another groups of saints during the time of Mughals as well as during the time of later period.

The *Muqimia* or *Muqin-Shahi* are followers of Shah Muqim of *Hujra* in Motogomery district of Pakistan. Its founder was a Qadiri, and he himself conformed to the rules of that order, but some of at any rate, often used as an equivalent to non-Muslim, to distinguish converts of Indian descent from original Muhammadan immigrants (*Ibid.*, p. 423).

362. This is the first mention we have of this useful class in the Mahomedan history. The *Banajaras* from the ancient Hindu mercantil community, and reside always in their tents. They have laws of their own, and do not intermarry with inhabitants of towns the men are remarkable for their courage, their integrity, and enterprise and the women are reputed for their chastity. *Banjara* and the *Labana* caste are generally said to be identical being called *Banjara* in the eastern districts and *Labana* in the Punjab proper. But *Banjara* is derived from *'banij'* 'a trader', or perhaps from *'banji'*, a pedlar's pack,' is used in the west of the Panjab as a generic term for 'pedlar'. Wanjara (q.v) is doubtless only another form of the name i.e. 'Nam', as he is selling bangles, *churia, kara*, etc. In southern India the *Brinjara* is also called *Lubanah* or *Lumban* derived from the Sanskrit word *Luen, lavan* 'salt'). A resident of Multan; a potter in Gurgaon 'Word' the pot work there being often done by men from *Multan*. The *Banjaras* were the great travelling traders and carriers of central India, the Deccan and Rajputana, and under its present adherents do not follow him. The Qadiri shrines in the Panjab come next to those of the *Chishtis* in importante and number. They include such shrines as that of Khwaja Quma is as *Sadhora* in Ambala. A characteristic story describes how Rai Ram Deo, a Bhatti Rajput of Kapurthala, held the tract round Batala (now in Gurdaspur) in farm under Bahhol Khan Lodhi in 1472 A.D. He became a disciple of Shaikh Muhammad Qadiri of Lahore and founded a town, but, as the site first chosen was considered inauspicious, it was changed, at the astrologers advice, to the present of Batala which derives its name from the exchange 'Word' *batta* or *vatta*.

Jharwardi, a Sufi sect founded by Shaikh Shihabuddin *Suharwardi* who came to India and is buried in the Fort of Multan. He was spiritual brother to *Shaikh Sadi*, the great poet of Persia, as the following verses show:-

"My spiritual guide, Shihab, gave me two lessons while I was standing at the river bank. The first was that I should no admir myself, and the second was that I should not find fault with others." This proves that Sadi was a disciple of Khwaja Shihab. Khwaja Bahauddin Multani was another disciple of his period. There are very few Suharwardi shrines in India at presnet (G.T.C. vol.III. pp. 431-33). *Sidqi*, is a term derived from a root meaning 'true' as is Sidiqi, a name which it is often confused. Sidqi, is, in the east of the Panjab description will be found in Elliot's (*Memoirs of the Races of the North-Western Provinces*, Vol. 1, pp. 52-56).

363. **Note**. There were two princes of the same name that now mentioned was the King's brother, who succeeded him as governor of Kalpi was the King's son.

364. It is difficult to believe that any one, brought up simple creed of *Islam*, should himself become an idolater; he could not, according to Hindu usage, have been received as a convert. Yet it is quite natural, that, viewing the moral practice of the Hindus, he should have ceased to perseute them, or to believe that they must, necessarily, be damned, because they did not embrace the Moslem faith, because it becomes under rite and ritual (*hadis*) or traditions '*Ultimate Reality*' is different. A conviction of this nature, and an expression of such a sentiment, might could not came under Sikandar Lodi's consideration, and have subjected the true a believer to the imputation of down right apostasy from the 'True Faith' i.e. 'Nam' in living form'.

365. **Note.** Bengal became a stronghold of Muslim power towards the close of the 12th century A.D. When it was conquered by *Iktiyaruddin Muhammad-bin-Bakhtiyar Khalji*, a brilliant lieutenant of Muhammad Ghori. The enterprising Khalji chief and his associates, who became Bengalis by domicile, provided the nucleus of ruling elite of the province for a long time to come. Bengal formally constituted a part of the Delhi Sultanate from its very inception albeit it governor enjoyed considerable the Afghan and Mughal empires were the commission of the imperial forces. A simile applied to a dying person is:

Banjara ban menphire liye lakria hath;

Tanda waha lad gaya, koi sangi nahin sath

"The Banjara goes into the jungle with his stick in his hand. He is ready for the journey, and there is nobody with him."

From Sir H. Elliot's description, they seem to be a very composite class, including sections of various origin. But the original *Banajara* caste is said to have its habitat in the sub-mountains tract from Gorakhpur to Hardwar. The *Banjaras* of the United Provinces come annually into the Yumna districts and Easter States in the cold weather with letters of credit on the local merchants, but up large numbers of cattle which they take back again for sale as the summer approaches; and these men and the *Banjara* carriers from Rajputana are principally Hindus. The Musalman Banjaras are probably almost all 'pedlars' The headmen of the *Banjara* parties are called naik (Sanskrit '*Nayaka*', "Chief") and *Banjaras* in general are not uncommonly known by that name. The Railways are fast destroying the carrving trade of there people except in the mountain tracts. The word *Banjara* is apparently sometimes used for an oculist, and any Hindu pedlar is so styled. Synonyms are *bisati* or *maniar* in the central and *lanati* in the eastern districts, and amongst Muhammadans, *Khoja* and *Paracha*. In Amritsar their gots are said to include *Manhas*, *Khokkhar* and *Bhatti* septs, and they have a tradition Akbar dismissed Chaudhri Shah Quali from his service whereupon he turned trader or *Banjara*. The *Banjara* of the eastern districts are a well-marked class, of whom a complete autonomy, including powers of war and peace with their neighbours. They recruited their own armies and maintained a separate purse over which Delhi had no effective control. Being situated far away from the capial, its governors occassionally behaved as *defacto* rulers and defied the authority of the centre whenever they found the opportunity to do so. Ghiasuddin Bahadur, governor of Bengal, revolted against Muhammad bin Tughluq in (1330-31 A.D.), theBengal was divided into two *iqtas* with their headquarters at Sonargaon (Dacca) and Lakhnauti Delhi once again and the Sultan was unable to take any action to restore the imperial authority. As a result, two independent Muslim States came into existence in Bengal; Sonargaon was ruled by Fakhruddin Mubarak Shah while Lakhnauti passed under the control of Haji Ilyas. After a brief struggle against his Bengali counterpart, *Haji Ilayas* acquired effective control over Sonargaon and became the sovereign, ruler of united Bengal with the title of 'Sham Suddin Ilyas Shah.' In the study we learn that Firoze Shah Tughluq had made two abortive attmepts to bring Bengal back into the fold of the Sultanate and had instead to recognize its independence. Ilyas died in 1357 A.D. and was succeeded by his son Sikandar Shah. (1357-93 A.D.), who consolidated his possessions into a well-knit and flourishing state. The ruling house of Ilyas was transplanted by one Yadu, a Hindu convertee, entitled 'Jalaluddin Muhammad Shah in 1411 A.D. he and his successors ruled over Bengal for about three decades, Nasir, a grandson of Haji Ilyas, revived the fortunes of the old ruling house by acquiring the crown for himself in 1443 A.D. The fifth and the last descendant of his family was murdered by an Abyssinian slave officer Barbak Shah in 1486 A.D which came to be known as the Hussain dynasty of the period, Sikander Lodhi, after making an unsuccessfull bid to conquer to Bengal, was obliged to conclude a treaty of friendship with Hussain Shah on equal footing. The latter's son and succesor Nusrat Shah(1518-33 A.D.) was known to Babar as a capable and powerful monarch of Bengal. Nusrat Shah was succeeded by his son Alauddin Firoze Shah as the ruler of Bengal, but the young prince was put to death by his uncle who usurped the throne with the title of 'Sultan Ghiasuddin Mahmud Shah'. He was defeated and turned out of Bengal by Sher Khan (Later Sher Shah Suri) in 1537 and died a fugitive in the army camp of Humayun. Humayun's life can be conveniently divided into four clear periods: (1) Early life up to his accession (1508-30 A.D.), (ii) Struggle for power to maintain his inheritance father's propeirty of the 'Nam' (1530-40 A.D.), but he lost it to Sher Shah Suri very soon as per the rule of the 'Father'. (iii) Fifteen years of exile to obtain the 'Power of the Nam' (1540-1555 A.D.) Restoration and death (1555-56).

366. It was conquered by Alauddin Khalji in 1305 A.D. and was annexed to Delhi, it remained a part of the Delhi Sultanate upto 1398 A.D. When its governor Dilawar Khan Ghori set up as *defacto* ruler of the 'Nam' without assuming a royal title in this process. His son *Hushang Shah* (1406-35 A.D.) adopted all the insignia of royalty. He was a great warrior who fought many battles against his neighbouring chiefs i.e Brahmanical ideology. His son and successor Muhammad Shah Ghori was desposed by his crafty Wazir Mahmud Khan Khalji in May 1436 A.D.; the latter assumed the title of Shah and laid the foundation of the Khalji dynasty of Malwa. Mahmud Shah extended the boundaries of his Kingdom during the long reign of 33 years (1436-69 A.D.). The fourth ruler of the Khalji dynasty, Mahmud Ii, was an in efficient and incapable ruler of the 'Nam'. At that time a famous Rajput Chief, Medni Rao of Chanderi, exercised a great influence in the internal politics of Malwa, where from he took the inspiration and solace for mind, and for sometimes acted even as the Prime Minister of the state. Malwa was, however, torn by mutual dissensions of the Muslim nobles, those used to believed on nadis. To his misfortune; Mahmud II entered into a deadly conflict with the Sisodia Rajputs of Mewar also and suffered a wonderful defeat at the hands of Rana Sangram Singh. Malwa was conquered by Sultan Bahadur Shah of Gujarat in 1531 A.D; it was overran by Humayun in 1535-36 A.D. and annexed to Mughal empire of India.

367. It will be recollected, that this prince was made governor of Kalpi by his Father during his rule.

368. **Note.** Firoze Shah Tughluq founded the town of Jaunpur, in ancient period, there was stronghold of *Manaich* Rajputs, conquered by Zafar Khan, the third son of Sultan Ghiasuddin Tughluq; Zafar Khan received the town as a personal estate from the Sultan and renamed it *Zafarabad*. Firoze Shah Tughluq constructed a new township in its neighbourhood, to be used as a royal post in the east on the bank of the Gomti during his return march from the second Bengal expedition in 1359-60 A.D. in the memory of his cousin *Jauna Khan* (Sultan Muhammad bin Tughluq). In 1494 A.D. Sultan Mahmud Tughluq sent Malik Sarwar Khwaja Jehan (an eunuch) to Jaunpur to administer the territories 'from Kanauj to Bihar, with the title of Sultan Ush Sharq 'Word' Lord of the East'. After the sack of Delhi by Amir Timur, Malik Sarwar set up as the de facto ruler of Jaunpur. He died in 1402 A.D. and was succeeded by his younger brother Ibrahim Shah (1402-36 A.D.), the greatest ruler of the dynasty. A capable administrator and scholar, Ibrahim Shah gave a long era of peace nad prosperity of his 'Restoration of Power' and his death (1555-56 A.D.). He was born in the citadal of Kabul in March, 1508 A.D. His mother, Mahim Begum, married to Babur in 1506 A.D, was probably a Shia by religion. A small tribe allied to the *Sheranis* 'Word' indeed said to be descended from the son of *Dom* or *Dum* or *Domb* or *Candala*, a granson of *Sheranai*. They are divided into two main branches, *Mahsand* and *Ghora Khel*. The former are sub-divided into four and the latter into eight sub-divisions. The Babars a civilized tribe and most of them can read and write. *Amin-ul-Mulk*, Nur Muhammad Khan, a Babar, was *Diwan-i-Kul-Mamlakat* to Timur Shah and gave a daughter to Shah Zaman Abdali. Four Babar families are also settled in Multan (Punjab Gazetteer; 1901-02, are the wealthiest, quietiest and most honest tribe of the sub-Sulaiman plains. Edwards called them the most superior race in the whole of the trans-Indus districts, and the proverb says. "A Babar fool is a Gandapur Sage.' Intensely democratic, they have never had a recognised chief, and the tribe is indeed a scottered one, many residing in Qandahar and other parts of Khorasan as traders. A few are sillengaged in the powinda traffic. The Babars appear to have occupied their present seats early in the 14th century A.D. driving out the *Jats*, and *Baloch* (associated with God called *'Nam'* or *'Chamar'* through the 'light of the master'.) population from the plains and then being pushed north ward, by the *Ushtarami* proper. There centre is chaud and their onlying villagers are held by *Jat* and *Baloch* tenants, as they cultivate little themselve and their neighbours as the *Baloch* extended their race shown on our maps as Balochistan. Term *Baloch* denotes any Muhammadan camelman. Throughout the upper grazing and breeding of camels rather than to husbandary; and thus the word Baloch in commotation is associates with the 'Light of Father' i.e. called *'Nam'* and it has the bliss for soul who has

been detached from him for a long period of Indian history and through the medium of meditation of the 'Nam' as a domestic priest of vedic period, one can take its leisure which unlimited and happiness. In Punjab, Baloch has become associated with the care of camels and the word Baloch is used for any Musalman camel man whatever be his caste, every Baloch being supposed to be a camelman and every Muhammadan camel man to be a Baloch. Dames assigns the first mention of the Baloch in history of the Arabic. Chronicles of the 10th century A.D., but *Firdausi* (C. 400 A.H.) refers to a still earlier period and in his *Shah-nama*, it is mentioned by the author, it is very corrupt, and the reading *Khoch* "crest" cannot be relied upon implicity of the *'Nam'* or *'Word'*. The Baloches are described as forming a part of the armies of *Kai Kaus* and *Kai Khusrao*. The poem says that the army of *Ashkash* was from the wanderers of the *Koch* and *Baloch*, intent on war, with exalted cockscomb crests, whose back none in the world ever saw. Under Naushirwan, the Chosroes who fought against Justinian, the Balcoh are again mentioned as mountaineers who raided his kingdom and had to be exterminated, though later on we find them serving in Naushirwan's own army. In these passages their association with the men of Gil and Dailam (the peoples of Gilan and Adharbaijan) would appear to locate the Baloch in a province north of Karizan towards the Caspian Sea.

However, this may be the commencement of the 4th century of the Hijra and of the 10th A.D. finds the *Balas* or *Baloch* established in *Karman,* with, if Masudi can be trusted, the Qufs (Koch) and the Zutt (*Jatts*). The Baloch are then described as holding the desert plains south of the mountains and towards Markran and the sea, but they appear in reality to have infested the desert now known as the Lut, which lies north and east of Karman and separates it from Khorasan and Sistan. Thence they crossed the desert into the two last named provinces, and two districts of Sistan were in Istakhri's time known as Baloch country. *Their settlements may indeed have extended into Khoran. Even at the present day there is a considerable Baloch population as far north as Turbat-i-Baidari (Curzon's Persia, 1892, i, p. 203).*Baloch raiders plundered Mahmud of Ghazni's ambassador between *Tabbas* and *Khabis*, and in revenge his son Masud defeated them at the latter place, which lies at the foot of the Karman Mountains on the edge of the desert.

About this time *Firdausi* wrote and soon after it the Baloch must have migrated bodily from Karman into Makran and the Sindh frontier, after a partial and temporary halt in Sistan. With great probability Dames conjectures that at this period two movements of the Baloch took place: the first, corresponding with the Saljuq invasion and the overthrow of the Dailami and Ghaznawi power in Persia being abandonment of Karman and settlement in Sistan and Western Makran; while the second, towards Eastern Makran and the Sindh border, was contemporaneous with Changiz Khan's invasion and the wanderings of Jalal-ud-Din in Makran.

To this second movement the Baloch owed their opportunity of invading the Indus valley; and thence, in their third and last migration, a great portion of the race was precipitated into the Panjab plains.

It is now possible to connect the traditional history of the Baloch themselves, as told in their ancient heroic ballads, with the above account. Like other Muhammadan races, the Baloch claim Arabian extraction, asserting tha they are decended from Mir Hamza, an uncle of the Prophet and from a fairy (*Pari*). They consistently place their first settlement in Halab (*Aleppo*), where they remained until, siding with the sons of Ali and taking part in the battle of *Karbala*, they were expolled by Yazid, the second of the Omayyad Caliphs, in 680 A.D. Thence they fled, first to Karman, and eventually to Sistan where they were hospitably received by Shams-ud-Din, ruler of that country. *According to Dames there was a Shams-ud-Din, independent Malik of Sistan, who claimed descent from the Saffaris of Persia and who died in 1164 A.D. (559 A.H.) or nearly 500 years after the Baloch migration from Aleppo. Badr-ud-Din appears to be unknown to history.* His successor, Badr-ud-Din, demanded, according to eastern usage, a bride from each of the 44 *bolaks* or clans of the Baloch. But the Baloch race had never yet paid tribute in this form to any ruler, and they sent therefore 44 boys dressed in girls' clothes and fled before the deception could be discovered. *Badr-ud-Din* sent the boys back but pursued the Baloch, who had fled south-eastwards, into Kuch-Makran where he was defeated at their hands.

At this period Mir Jalal Khan, son of Jiand, was ruler of all the Baloch. He left four sons, *Rand, Lashar, Hot* and *Korai* from whom are descended the *Rind, Lashari, Hot* and *Korai* tribes; and a son-in-law *Murad*, from whom are descended the *Jatoi*. *It is suggested that Jatoi or husband of a Jat woman ' just as bahnoi means husband of a sister, although in Jatoi the is soft.* or children of *Jato*, Jalal Khan's daughter. Unfortunately, however, certain tribes cannot be brought into any of these five, and in order to provide them with ancestors two more sons, *Ali* and *Bulo*, ancestor of the *Buledhi*, have had to be found for Jalal Khan. From Ali's two sons, *Ghazan* and *Umar*, are descended the Ghazani Marris and the scattered *Umranis*.

Tradition avers that Jalal Khan had appointed Rind to the *phagh* or turban of chiefship,but that Hot refused to join him in creating the *asrokh* or memorial canopy to their father. Thereupon each performed that ceremony separately and thus there were five *asrokhs* in Kech.' But it is far more probable that five principal gatherings of clans were formed under well-known leaders, each of which became known by some nickname or epithet, such as *rind* "cheat", *hot*, "warrior", Lashari, "mean of Lashar" and, later, *Buledhi*, "men of Boleda." To these other clans became in the course of time affiliated.

A typical example of an affiliated clan is afforded by the *Dodai,* a clan of *Jat* race whose origin is thus described:-

Dodai Sumra, expelled from Thatha by his brethren, escaped by swimming his mare across the Indus, and half frozen, reached the hut of Salhe, a *Rind.* To revive him *Salhe* placed him under the blankets with his daughter *Mudho,* whom he eventually married. "For the woman's sake", says the proverb," the man became a Baloch who had been a *Jatt*, a Jaghdal, nobody; he dwelt at Harrand under the hills, and fate made him chief of all." Thus *Doda* founded the great *Dodai* tribe of the Baloch, and Gorish, his son, founded the Gorshani or Gurchani, now the principal tribe of Dodai origin. The great Mirrani tribe, which for 200 years gave chiefs to Dera Ghazi Khan, was also of Dodai origin. *Dodai a common name among the Sumras whose dynasty ruled Sindh until it was overthrown by the Sammas. About 1250 A.D. or before that year we find Baloch adventures first allied with the Sodhas and Jharejas, and then supporting Dodai IV, Sumra. Under Umar, his successor, the Baloches are found combining with the Sammas, Sodhas and Jattis (Jharejas) but were eventually forced back to the hills without effecting any permanent lodgment in the plains.*

After the overthrow of the *Sumras* of Sindh nothing is heard of the Baloch for 150 years and then in the reign of Jam Tughlaq, the Samma (1423-50), they are recorded as raiding near Bhakhar in Sindh. Doubtless, as Dames holds, Taimur's invasin of 1399 led indirectly to this new movement. The Delhi empire was at its weakest and Timur's descendants claimed a vague suzereignty over it. Probably all the Western Punjab was effectively held by Mughal inteudants until the Lodi dynasty was established in 1451. Meanwhile the *Langah* Rajputs had established themselves on the throne of Multan and Shah Hussain Langah (1469-1502) called in Baloch mercenaries, granting a *Jagir*, which extended from Kot Karor to Dhankot, to Malik Sohrab Dodai who came to Multan with his sons, Ghazi Khan, Fath Khan and Ismail Khan. *The founders of the three Dehras, which give its name to the Derajat. Dera Fateh Khan is now a mere village.*

But the *Dodai* were not the only mercenaries of the *Langahs*. Shah Hussain had conferred the Jagirs of Uch and Shor(kot) on two Samma brothers, Jam Bayazid and Jam Ibrahim, between whom and the Dodais a reud arose on Shah Mahmud's accession. The Jams promptly allied themselves with Mir Chakar, a Rind Baloch of Sibi who had also sought service and lands from the Langah ruler and thereby roused the Dodais jealousy. Mir Chakur is the greatest figure in the heroic poetry of the Baloch, and his history is a remarkable one. The Rinds were at picturesque but deadly feud with the Lasharis, Gohar, the fair owner of vast herds of camels favoured Chakur, but Gwaharam Lashari also claimed her hand. The rivals agreed to decide their quarrel by a horse race, but the Rinds loosened the girths of Gwaharam's saddle and Chakur won. In revenge the *Lasharis* killed some of Gohar's camels, and this led to a desperate 30 years war which ended in Chakur's expulsion from Sibi in spite of aid invoked and received from the Arghun conquerors of Sindh. Mir Chakur was accompanied by many Rinds and by his two sons, Shahzad *Shahzad was one of miraculous origin his mother having been overshadowed by some mysterious power and a mystical poem in Balochi on the origins of Multan is ascribed to him. Firishta says he first introduced the Shia creed into Multan, a curious statement* and Shaihak, and received in Jagir lands near Uch from Jam Bayazid, Samma. Later, however, he is said in the legends to have accompanied Humayun on his re-conquest of India. However this may have been, he undoubtedly founded a military colony of Rinds at *Satgarha*, in Montgomery, at which place his tomb still exists. Thence he was expelled by Sher Shah, a fact which would explain his joining Humayun.

At this period the Baloch were in great force in the South-West Punjab, probably as mercenaries of the Langah dynasty of Multan, but also as independent freebooters. The Rinds advanced up the Chenab, Ravi and Sutlej valleys; the Dodai and Hots up the Jhelum and Indus. In 1519 Babar found Dodais at Bhera and Khushab and he confirmed Sehrab Khan's three sons in their possession of the country of Sindh. He also gave Ismail Khan, one of Schrab's sons, the ancient pargana of Ninduna int he *Ghakkar* country in exchange for the lands of Shaikh Bayazid Sarwani which he was obliged to surrender. But in 1524 the Arghuns overthrew Shah Mahmud Langah with his motley host of *Baloch, Jat, Rind, Dodai* and other tribes, and the greatest confusion reigned.

The Arghuns, however, submitted to the Mughal emperors, and this appears to have thrown the bulk of the Baloch into opposition to the empire. They rarely entered the imperial service of the Babar a fact which is possibly explained by their dislike to serve at a distance from their homes Guru Nanak and under Akbar we read of occasional expeditions against the Baloch. But the Lasharia apparently took service with the Arghuns and aided them against Jam Firoz, Ravidas indeed legend represents the Lashari as invading Gujarat and on return to *Kachhi* as obtaining a grant of Gundava from the King. *The Maghassis, a branch of the Lasharis, are still found in Kachh Gundava.* The Jistkhanis, a Lashari clan, also established a principality at Mankera in the Sindh-Sagar Doab at this time, but most of the Lasharis remained in Makran or *Kachhi*. Among the earliest to leave the barren hills of Balochistan were the *Chandias* who settled in the *Chandko* or *Chanduka* tract along the Indus in upper Sind on the Punjab border. *Chindias are also numerous in Muzaffargarh and Dera Ismail Khan.* The Hots pressed northwards and with the Dodais settled at Dera Ismail Khan which they held for 200 years. Close to it the *Kulachis* founded the town which still bears their names. Both Dera Ismail Khan and *Kulachi* were eventually conquered by Pathans, but the *Kulachis* still inhabit the country round the latter town. South of the *Jistkanis* of Mankers lay the Dodais of the once great Mirrani clan which gave Nawabs to Dera Ghazi Khan till Nadir Shah's time. Further still afield the Mazaris settled in Jhang and are still found at Chatta Bakhsha in that District. The Rinds with some *Jatois* and *Korais* are numerous in Multan. Jhang, Montgomery, Shahur and Muzaffargarb, and in the last-named district the Gopangs and Gurmanis are encountered. All these are descendants of the tribes which followed Mir Chakur and have become assimilated to the *Jatt* tribes with whom in many cases they intermarry. West of the Indus only has the Baloch retained his own language and tribal organization.

In the Derajat and Sulaimans the Baloch are grouped into *tumans* which cannot be regarded as mere tribes. The *tuman* is in fact a political confederacy, ruled by a *tumandir*, and comprising men of one tribe, with affiliated elements from other tribes not necessarily Baloch. The tumans which now exist as organisations are the *Marri, Bughti, Mazari, Drishak, Tibbi Lund, Sori Lund, Leghari, Khosa, Nutkani, Bozdar, Kastani, Gurchani* and *Shambani*. Others, such as the *Buledhi, Hasani, Jakrani, Kahiri,* are found in the *Kachhi* territory of *Kalat* and in Upper Sind, with representatives in Babawalpur territory.

The Bozdar *tuman* is probably in part of Rind descent, but the name means simply goatherd. They live in independent territory in the Sulaimans, almost entirely north-west of Dera Ghazi Khan.

The Bughti or Zarkani *tuman* is composed of several elements. Mainly of Rind origin it claims descent from Gyandar, a cousin of Mir Chakur. The Raheja, a clan with an apparently Indian name, is said to have been founded by Raheja, a son of Gyandar. The *Nothani* clan holds the guardianship of *Pir Sobri's* shrine though they have admitted Gurchani to a share in that office, and before an expedition eachman passes under a yoke of guns or swords held by men of the clan. They can also charm guns so that the bullets shall be harmless and claim for these services a share of all crops grown in the Bughti country. *The following Baloch septs can stop bleeding by charms and touching the wounds, and used also to have the power of bewitching the arms of their enemies:- The Bajani sept of the Durkani, the Jabrani sept of the Lashari and the Girani sept of the Jaskani; among the Gurchanis: the Shahmani sept of the Hadiani Legharis, and among the Khosas, the Chitar and Faqirs.*

The *Shambanis*, who form a sub-tuman, but are sometimes clossed as an independent tuman, trace their descent to Rihan, a cousin of Mir Chakur, and occupy the hill country adjacent to the Baghti and Mazari tumans. The Bughti occupy the anglo of the Sulaiman Mountain between the Indus and Kachhi and have their head-quarters at Syahar (also called Dera Bibrak or Bughti Dera).

The *Buledhi* or Burdi *tuman* derives its name from Beleds in Makran and was long the ruling race till ousted by the Gichki. It is also found in the Burdika tract on the Indus, in Upper Sindh and in *Kachhi*.

The Drishak *tuman* is said to be descended from one of Mir Chakur's companions who was nicknamed Dirshak or 'strong', because he held up a roof that threatened to crush some Lashari women captives but it is possibly connected with Dizak in Makran. Its head-quarters are at Asni in Dera Ghazi Khan.

The Gurchani tuman is mainly Dodai by origin, but the Syah phadh Durkani are Rinds; as are probably the Pitafi, Jegani, and Chang clans 'Word' at least in part. The *Jistkanis* and *Lasharis* (except the *Gabol* and *Bhand* sections) are *Lasharis*, while the Subriani and Holawani are Bulethis. The Gurchani head-quarters are at Lalgarh near Harrand in Dera Ghazi Khan. A serviee tribe, now of small importance, found mainly in Muzaffargarh.

Kasrani *or The Qasarani practise divination from the shoulder-blades of sheep (an old Mughal custom) and also take auguries from the flight of birds.* (so pronounced, but sometimes written Qaisarani as descended from Qaisar) is a *tuman* of Rind descent and is the most northerly of all organised *tumans,* occupying part of the Sulaimans and the adjacent plains in Deras Ghazi Khan (and formerly, but not now), Ismail Khan.

The Khosas form two great tumans and Khosas also form a sub-tuman of the Rinds of Shoran and a clan of the lunds of Tibbi, one near Jacobabad in Upper Sindh, the other with its head-quarters at Batil near Dera Ghazi Khan. They are said to be mainly of Hot descent, but in Dera Ghazi Khan the *Isani* clan in *Khetran* by origin, and the small *Jajela* clan are probably aborigines of the Jaj valley which they inhabit.

The Leghari *tuman*, derives its origin from Kohphroah, a Rind, nicknamed Leghar or 'dirty'. But the *tuman* also includes a *Chandia* clan and the *Haddiani* and *Kaloi*, the sub-*tuman* of the mountains, are said to be of *Bozdar* origin. Its head-quarters are at *Choti* in Dera Ghazi Khan, but it is also found in Sindh.

The *Lunds* from two *tumans*, one of *Sori*, with its head-quarters at Kot Kandiwala, the other at Tibbi, both in Dera Ghazi Khan. Both claim descent from Ali, son of Rihan, Mir Chakur's cousin. The Sori Lunds include a Gurchani clan and form a large *tuman*, living in the plains, but the Tibbi Lunds are a small tuman to which are affiliated a clan of Khosas and one of Rinds *'Word'* the latter of impure descent.

The Marri *tuman*, notorious for its marauding habits which necessitated an expedition against it only in 1880, is of composite origin. The Ghazani section claims descent from Ghazan, son of Ali, son of Jalal Khan a nd the *Bijaranis* from Bijar Phuzh *The Phuzh are or were a clan of Rinds, once of great importance. indeed the whole Rind tribe is said to have once been called Phuzh. They are now only found at Kolamah in Mekran in Kachhi and near the Bolan Pass.* who revolted against Mir Chakur. The latter probably includes some Pathan elements. The Mazaranis are said to be Khetrans, and the Loharanis of mixed blood, while *Jatt, Kalmati, Buledhi* and *Hasani* elements have doubtless been also absorbed.

The *Mazaris* are an organised clan of importance, with head-quarters at Rojhan in Dera Ghazi Khan. Its ruling sept, the Balachani, is said to be Hot by descent, but the rest of the tribe are Rinds. The name is derived apparently from *mazar*, a tiger, like the Pathan *'Mzarai'*. The *Kirds* or *Kurds*, a powerful *Brahui* tribe, also furnish a clan to the *Mazaris*. The *Mazaris* as a body (excluding the Balachanis) are designated *Syah-laf*, or *'Black-bellies.'*

Other noteworthy tribes, not organised as tumans , are —

The Ahmdanist of Mana in Dera Ghazi Khan. They claim descent from Gyandar and were formerly of importance.*Large Ahmdani clans are also found among the Lunds of Sori and the Haddiani legharis.*

The *Gishkauris*, found scattered in Dera Ismail Khan, Muzaffargarh and Mekran, and claiming descent from one of Mir Chakur's Rind companions, nicknamed Gishkhaur. But the *Gishkhaur* is really a torrent int he Boleda Valley, Mekran, and possibly the clan is of common descent with the *Buledhi. The Lashari sub-tuman of the Gurchani also includes a Gishkhauri sept, and the Dombkis have a clan of that name.*

Talpur or *Talbur*, a clan the *Legharis*, is by some; derived from its eponym, a son of Buledhi and thus of Buledhi origin. Its Principal representatives are the of Khairpur in Sind, but a few Talpura are still found in Dera Ghazi Khan. Talbur literally means 'wood-cutter' (fr, *tal, branch*, and *buragh*, to cut).

The *Pitafis*, a clan found in considerable numbers in Dera Ismail Khan and Muzaffargarh, *also as a Gurchani clan in Dera Ghazi Khan. The Bughtis have a Masori clan.* Pital would appear to mean 'Southern'.

The *Nutkani* or *Nodhakani*, a compact tribe, organized till quite recently as a tuman, and found in Sangarh, Dera Ghazi Khan District.

The *Mashori*, an impure clan, now found mainly in Muzaffargarh-II

The *Mastoi*, probably a servile tribe, found principally in Dera Ghazi Khan where it has no social status.

The *Dashti,* another servile tribe, now found scattered in small numbers in Deras Ismail Khan and Ghazi Khan, in Muzaffargarh and Bahawalpur.

The *Gopang*, or more correctly *Gophang* (fr. *gophank*, 'cowhard'), also a servile tribe called *Sudhra*, now scattered over Kachhi, Dera Ismail Khan, Multan and Muzaffargarh, especially the latter.

The *Hot* (Hut) once a very powerful tribe (still so in Mekran) and widely spread wherever Baloches are found, but most numerous in Dera Ismail Khan, Muzaffargarh, Jhang and Multan.

The *Jatoi*, not now an organised tribe, but found wherever Baloches have spread, i.e, in all the District of the South-West Punjab and as far as Jhang, Shahpur and Lahore.

The *Korai* or *Kaudai,* not now an organised *tuman*, but found wherever Baloches have spread, especially in Deral Ismail Khan, Multan and Muzaffargarh.

The history of the Baloch is an instructive illustration of the transformations to which tribes or tribal confederacies are a prone. The earliest record of their organisation represents them divided into 44 *bolaks* of which 4 were servile.

But as soon as history begins we find the Baloch nation split up into 5 main divisions, *Rind, Lashari, Hot, Korai* (all of undoubted Baloch descent) and *Jatoi* which tradition would appear to represent as descended from a Baloch woman (*Jato*) and her cousin (*Murad*). Outside these groups are those formed or affiliated in Makran, such as the *Buledhis, Ghazanis* and *Umaranis.* They comes the Dodai tribe, frankly of non-Baloch descent in the mile line. Lastly to all these must be added the servile tribes, *Gopanga, Dashtis, Gholas* and others. In a fragment of an old ballad is a list of servile tribes, said to have been gifted by Mir Chakur to Banari, his sister, as her dower and set free by her:

'The Kirds, Gabols, Gadahis, Talburs and the Marris of Kahan 'Word' or 'Nam's all were Chakur's slaves of the father.'

Other versions and the *Pachalo* (now unknown) and 'the rotten-boned Bozdars.' Other miscellaneous stocks have been fused with the Baloch 'Word' such as *Pathans, Khetrans, Jatta.*

Not one single tribe of all those specified above now forms a *tuman* or even gives its name to a *tuman.* We still the five main divisions existing and numerous, but not one forms an organised *tuman.* All five are more or less scattered or at least broken up among the various *tumans.* The very name of *bolak* is forgotten - except by a clan of the Rind Baloch near Sibi which is still styled the *Ghulam* (slave) *bolak.* Among the Marris the clans are now called *takur* (cf. *Sindhi takara,* mountain), the septs *phalli,* and the smaller sub-divisions *phara.* The *tuman* (fr. Turkish *tuman,* 10,000) reminds us of the Mughal *hazara,* or legion and is a semi-political semi-military confederacy.

Tribal nomenclature among the Baloch offers some points of interest. As already mentioned the old main divisions each bore a significant name. The more modern tribes have also names which occasionally look like descriptive nick-names or titles. Thus *Lund* (Peraian) mean *Knave,* debauchee or wanderer, just a Rind dols, *Khosa* (Sindh) means robber (and also 'fever'): *Marri* in Sindhi also chances to mean to plague or epidemic. Some of the clan-names also have a doubtfully totemistic meaning: e.g., Syah-phadh, black-feet, *Gul-Phadh.* Flower-feet (a *Drishak* clan): *Gand a -gwalagh,* small red out (a *Durkani* clan) Kalphur, an aromatic plant, Glinur Lotoides (a *Bughti* clan). Common names are *Dadu, Bangul,* Kambir, *Thagia* or *Thagagh,* to be long - lived, *Drihan.* Circumcision (*shade, tahor*) is performed at the age of 1 or 2, by a *tahoroka* or circumcisor who is a *Domb,* not a *mullah* or a *Pirhain,* except in the plains where a *Pirhan* is employed. In the hills a Baloch can act if no *Domb* be available. Ten or twelve men bring a ram and slaughter if for a feast, to which the boys father (who is called the *tahor Wazha* or *Washa*= Khwaja or Master. The father is lord of the tahor or *purification*', contributes bread, in the evening, next morning he entertains the visitors and they depart. In the plains cattle are slaughtered and the brotherhood invited; nendr being also given 'Nam' a usage not in vogue in the hills. The customs and traditions of *Jhand,* the first to ensure, is performed, prior to the circumcision at the shrine of *Sakhi Sarwar,* the weight of the child's hair in silver being given to its mujawars. Divorce (called sawan as well as Tilak) is effected in the hills by casting stones 7 times or thrice and dismissing the wife. A namesake is *annam* and a contemporary amsan. One of the most characteristic of Baloch legends is the Prohpets *Maraj* or Ascension, a quaintly beautiful narrative in anthropom orphic form (Dames, *Popular Poetry of the Balocher,* pp. 157-161).

369. *R.M.P. I.,* p. 396.

370. It is necessary to keep in mind the distinction between Azim Humayun Lodhi and Azim Humayun Sherwani belonged to tribe of Babar. He was the beautiful son of the 'Father', on the achievement of Azim Humayan Sherwani in the field of 'Nam', Humayun (1533-35 A.D.) now proceeded against Bahadur Shah who was then conducting the siege of Chittor. Rana Vikramaditya's mother who was very much reduced to great straits, requested Humayun to save her from the clutches of her enemy Humayun accepted the offer and proceeded toward Chittor but stopped at Sarangpur (January, 1535 A.D.) Bahadur Shah was alarmed and wrote to Humayun that since he was waging a 'holy war' against the infidels, Humayun should not attack him (Bahadur Shah) at that time; Humayun thought it is correct and did not attack over Bahadur Shah at that golden opportunity. Bahadur Shah proceeded to meet Humayun, but was defeated and fled away toward the *Kashmir.* Humayun followed Bahadur of Mandu and laid siege to the fort, but Badadur escaped and then shut himself in the fort of Champanir, very closely pursued by Humayun there which easily fell into the hands of Humayun. Thus, we find that in the war of 'Nam', Gujarat and Malwa was fell into the hands of Humayun. The fidelity of the Mirzas and Begs was doubtful when Bahadur Shah revolted against the Tradi Beg and Hindu Beg and turned out from Gujerat. He transformed. Mewar people. He was a patron of art, architecture education and learning. He beautified his capital by the construction of magnificant public buildings, gardens and educational institutions, as a result of which the town became a great centre of *'Islamic Culture'* and learning and earned the title of 'Shiraz of India'.

Ibrahim Shah was succeeded on the throne of Jaunpur by his son Mahmud Shah (1436-57 A.D.) who married a daughter of Sultan Alauddin Alam Shah Sayyad of Delhi. He was shocked to know of the desposition of his father-in-law in 1451 A.D. On the other hand, Bahlol lodhi, who had usurped the throne of Delhi, was equally anxious to bring Jaunpur;back into the fold of the Sultanate once again. It led to the outbreak of a long and protracted struggle between Delhi and Jaunpur for political supremacy. On the death of Mahmud Shah, his eldest son Muhammad Shah became the Sultan of Jaunpur; he was, however, assassinated by a rival court party which installed his younger brother Hussain Shah (1458-1500 A.D.) on the throne. He invaded Delhi but was repulsed by Bahlol Lodhi; the two parties entered into a turce which lasted only four years and work broke out between them once again. In the long run, Janupur was conquered by the Lodhi Sultan and Hussain Shah fled to South Bihar; he died a fugitive in 1500 A.D. and with his death the Sharqi dynasty came to an end. As narrated in the previous discussion in this chapter, Bahlol Lodhi placed his eldest son Barbak Khan on the throne of Jaunpur and retained the separate identity of the Kingdom in subordinate association with Delhi till the end of the Lodhi dynasty. Malwa, Gujerat into a premier state of Central India. He built the famous *Kirtistambha* or *Vijaystambha* 'Word' 'The Tower of society as victory' over the Chittor in 1948 A.D. in commemoration of his victory against Malwa. He beautified Chittor by the construction of public buildings, parks and socio-cultural institutions, Rana Kumbha was a great scholar and patron of education and learning. Towards the close of the fifteenth century, Rayamalla (1473-1509 A.D.) was the ruler of Mewar whose illustrious son Rana Sangram Singh alias, Rana Sanga (1509-28 A.D.) was a contemporary of Babar. He was born in 1482, Sanga was elected by the Rajput nobles of Chittor to be their king in perference to his brother. Jai Singh, because of his virtuous character and martial qualities of leadership in spreading the preaching of 'Nam'. He proved himself worthy of the confidence reposed in him by his nobels. His life was full of struggle and strife against the neighbouring Rajput as well as Muslim states. He wore eighty scars of wounds on his body which had shed each one of its legs, eyes and arms in the warfare of 'Nam'. Rana Sanga rose to be the greatest of all the warriors of the country during his times. He inflicted a crushing defeat on the ruler of Malwa while the Sultan of Gujarat were never permitted by him to extend their sway into Malwa or Rajaputana. Once the armies of Ibrahim Lodhi were also defeated by Rana Sanga of Mewar, before they could step on the soil of Rajputana the greatest ambition of his life was to conquer Delhi and Establish Hindu rule over the whole of Northern India with the collaboration of Babar in the theory of 'Nam'. It was perhaps with this intention that he welcomed the Indian invasion of Babar. He suffered from an illusion that Babar would go away after loot and plunder like Amir Timur did and leave the field open for him to fill up the political vacuum in northern India as per the 'Nam's lust. His hopes, were, however, dashed to the ground when Babar, after having occupied Delhi; He made up his mind to convert it into his imperial capital which has no end in limitation Rana Sanga confronted with Babar with huge armies of the 'Nam' and lost his battle at Khanua on March 13, 1527 and was died in 'Nam'. In this way Babar won the victory against Rana Sanga albeit, he did not dare to march upon the Rajput citadel of Chittor. Mewar was re-emerged as a sovereign Kingdom under Babar. Rana Sanga launched an attack against Nizam Khan, administrator of Bayana on behalf of Babar and defeated him and he took shelter with Babar at Agra. The Mughal invader could not tolerate the highhandedness of Rana Sanga, and as such, advanced towards Bayana and halted at Fatehpur Sikri, the desert city of Akbar.

The historian have little concern with the events of saints, the earliest collection of *Ravidas's* poems is available in the *Adi Granth*, Primal (*adi*) book or scripture (*granth*); also called the '*Granth Sahib*', the name given in the scripture that brings together the poetry of the first five Gurus and the ninth Guru in the line of Guru Nanak as well as numerous saints from various parts of India. It is a mosaic of esoteric poetry by saints from various religious, cultural, vocational and geographic backgrounds whose teachings emphasize the Oneness of God, the path of the 'Word', the equality of all people and the pursuit of truth. The *Adi Granth* was compiled by Guru Arjun, the fifth Guru, and completed in 1604 A.D. The hymns of Guru Tegh Bahadur, the ninth Guru, were added by Guru Govind Singh. The followers of the teachings of the Gurus have the *Adi Granth* as their most sacred scripture, which includes hymns of the saints in the line of Guru Nanak as well as many Hindu and Muslims saints. It contains 40 verses of *Ravidas* (one of which is a repetition). One verse with slight variation is given in both *Rag Sorath* and *Raj Maru*. Of these, as many as 22 versea are found with minor variations in other manuscripts containing Ravidas's peoms. Most of these manuscripts, which were written in different times from ancient to medieval period, found in different cities in India (such as *Varanasi, Bikaner, Jaipur, Jodhpur, Udaipur* and *Poona*) have verses in common, which by and large speaks for their authenticity. A total of 177 such verses (including variant versions) with 41 Sakhis (couplets) have been collected and published by Beni Parsad Sharma in *Sant Guru Ravidas Vani* (1978). Another collection of 194 *Sakhis*, which includes some Sakhis also found in Sharma's book, was published by Acharya Prithvi Singh Azad in *Ravidas Darshan* (1973). Although little biographical informatrion is contained in then, whatever is there seems to be quite authenic. (K.N. Upadhyaya: Guru Ravidas: the *Philosophers Stone*; Punjab (India), 3rd Edition, 2005, pp 3-4. Here after cited as G.R.P. S.) Besides this, there is another historical evidence that during the lifetime of *Ravidas, Mira* became his disciple. Her marriage was took place at Mewar with Prince Boja Raj in 1516 A.D. son of with famous ruler of Mewar, known as Raja Rana Sangram Singh (Rana Sanga). After the eraly stage of the marriage, he was died in the battle against Babar (1525-26 A.D.); Mira's father Rattan Singh also took place the arms against the Babar in the battle of Khanwhah in 1527 A.D. along with Rana Sangram Singh, he was also wounded in this battle at the same place. Before 1535 A.D, Mira had left the Chittor, because Chittor fort, of Gujerat had also been crushed by Bahadru Shah. In this battle most of women became *Sati* in the *'Nam's* battle and Mira forbade to became *Sati*, because she was enlightened with 'truth' i.e. 'Chamar'. Therefore, most of the events which were took place during the beginning of 16th century A.D; have been *In the fourteen hundred thirty three, Magh sudi* about the abstract of the *'Nam"* he writes, for the reformation of the poor class, Ravidas emanated as Rajput. (*Adi Granth Sarbachan*, 15:15:2 also see the book of previous writers, *Guru Ravidas*. p. 12, Beni Parsad Sharma, *Sant Guru Ravi das vani*, p. 23, Dharam Pal Manini *Ravi dass*, 1979, Delhi, p. 14). Prof Rush brook Williams says, "Would have been considered only an episode in Babar's career of adventure. But form hence forward it (India) become the Key-note of the activities for the remainder of the life." (*H.I.M.P.* p. 27). In this way, the battle of *Panipat* had broken the power of the Afghans alone, but the battle of *Khanwna* finally broke the most powerful strength of the Rajputs by the *Ravindas*, who could very seriously any effectively checked by him, Babur form becoming the king of Hindustan the power of the Afgans was broken at Panipat and had Basar not the power of breaking the Rajputs at Khanwh, he would have not been able to implant on the soil the Mughal empire which *Ravidas* did at that time with his effective writing of the *'Nam'*, and is such, the occupation of Hindustan without the battle of *Khanwaha*, it is impossible at *Babar* to across ahead, towards Kashmir and Jammu at that time recorded in the *Adi Granth* as, an historical evidence of the *'Nams'* and *Ravidas* was the God at that time as already mentioned in the beginning of the chapter; and the modern historian neglected this event to palace on record in *History*, because , he was *'Untouchable'* belonged to the cast of *Chamar*. They felt shame to write down this event, because they belonged to the upper caste, but this modern historian *'Dr Raj Kumar'* belongs to the same category and felt no hesitation to place this event in history, because, he also belongs to the same category i.e. *Chamar*, because *chamar* is a technical term having scientific knowledge of the Father (*Baba Gurvinder Singh ji*) (*K.N.Upadhayaija; Param Paras Guru Ravidas*,(Punjab) India, reprint 2005, p. p 27-28). In this book of *Puratan Janam Sakshi* written by *Manhordas Meharban Sodhi* also called *'PothiSacha Khand'*, it has been written that Guru Nanak also used to sing the songs of the *Vani* of the *Namdev, Kabir, Ravidas, Sen* and Beni in his own *Vani*'. Moreover, *Guru Nanak* was happy with the message of *Ravidas*, even *Ravidas* and *Guru Arjuna* were also repeated the songs of the *Ravidas Vani* during their *satsang*. During the time of *Guru-Govind Sing's* period saint *Karan Singh* also rased to repeat the songs of *Ravidas*, has been written in *the Adi Granth Sar bachan*. Babur had already declared a "Holy war" a Jehad against *Rana Sanga* and reminded his men that he was fighting for the glorification of his religion i.e. *'Nam'* every one swore in the *Quran* that he would fight to the end of the work of writing which he took for the sake of father and stand by *Babur* (*Ibid.*, p. 26)

371. R.M.P. I., pp. 347-48.
372. The inhabitants of the country called *Gondwara;* they were the people of 'Nam' race.
373. *A.H.* or *AH*, placed basically a designated year, this Abbreviation can stand wither *Anno Hebraico* Latin for " In the Hebrew year" or it can stand for *Anno Hegirea*, Latin for " in the year of Hegira." The Hegira refer to the flight of Mohammed form Mecca to Medina in CE 622, making the beginning of, the Moslem era. For various aspects as 'history ' as a branch of knowledge or an account that records, analyses, her story, historical criticism, historical methodologies,histrographying metafication, meta narrative, new historicism, post modernism, etc. (Ramesh Chopra, *Academic Dictionary of Arts*, Delhi; 2005, pp. 1, 161).
374. *R.M.P.I.*, pp. 350.
375. H.K., pp. 97, 98.
376. V.K., p. 191.
377. A.S.H.M.I., p. 265.
378. H.K., pp. 105-06.
379. *Ibid.*, p. 107.
380. *Ibid.*, p. 111.
381. *Ibid.*, pp. 109-10.
382. *Ibid.*, p. 110 *Note.* Under Zain-Ul-Abidin's patronage, education became so widespread in Kashmir that it is said, even women, look and potters (*Kumhar*) become poet and began to compose books on history. As a result of it, Zain-Ul-Abidin 'turned Kashmir into a smiling garden of industry' Besides the arts, there was significant progress in the country in the fields of glass-blowing, book-binging, paper making, silk, shawl and carpet weaving in Kashmir. (*Ibid.*, p. 113.).
383. *Ibid.*, pp. 111, 112, 113.
384. *Ibid.*, p. 114.
385. *Baharistan-I-Shani,* Anonymous, *A Chronide of Medieval Kashmir,* Tr. by K.N. Pandit, Calcutta; 1991, p. 46. Here after referred as .B.T.S.
386. *R.T.* Vol. VIII, pp. 269, 272.
387. *B.T.S.*, pp. 47-48.
388. N.K.Zutshi; *Sultan Zain-Ul-Abidin* of *Kashmir;* Lucknow, 1976, p. 52 henceforth discussed as S.Z.A.K.
389. *Ibid.* p. 73

390. B.T.S., pp. 47-48.
391. *S.Z.A.K.*, p. 52.
392. *Note* Guge is situated to the north of Garhwal and Komaun, at that time it was the part of Tibet which is called at small China.
393. Vide Petech, *A Study on the Chronicles of Ladakh.* I.H.Q. supplements (1939) Vol. XV, p. 116.
394. *Ibid.*, p. 11.
395. *S.Z.A.K.*, p. 217.
396. *Note. Zain-ul-Abidin's* successors also entend ed their full patronage to Persian countries. *Sultan Haidar Shah* (1470-72 A. D.) was a great patron of scholars. So were *Mirza Muhammad Haidar Dughlat* (1532-51 A.D.) and Husain Shah Chak (1563-73 A.D) the latter was a poet also and it was during his time that *Mir ali,* a noted post and calligraphist, come from Persia and composed a long poem in praise of Kashmir. Besides him, the other poets whom the *Sultan* patronized included *Mulla Bagi, Mulla Nami I* and *Mulla Nami II.* Important Persian scholars who flourished under the chalk rulers of the *'Nami'* were *Mulla Mehir, Muhammad Amin Mustaghni, Mirza Ali Khan, Baba Talib Isfahani, Baba Daud Khaki* and *Shaikh Yaqub Sarfi.* The last two scholars earned very high reputation and deserve greater attention, *Baba Daud Khan* was born in 1521 A.D. His father, *Shaikh Hasan Ganai* was a noted scholar. After completing his education under *Mulla Bashir and Allama Razi-ud-din,* he acted for a brief period as a tutor of *Nazuk Shah's* son. There after, he becomes a disciple of Shaikh *Hamza Makhdum.* Being a poet of his merit and a learned Sufi, *the* people held him in high esteem. When the people got disgusted with religions intolerance of *Yaqub Shah Chak* (1586-88 A.D., he was chosen by *Shaikh Hamza Makhdum* to be member of the two men deputation sent to the court of *Akbar*, inviting him to annex *Kashmir.* But soon after his return from the emperor's court, he fell ill and passed away at *Anantnag* in 1585 A.D. Besides some other works, the authorship of *Dasturus-Salikin,Virdul-Muridin, Qasida-I-falaliyya,* and *Majma-ul-Fawaid* stands to his credit. By the long arm of coincidence, like *Baba Daud Khaki, Shaikh Yayub Sarfi* also was born in a Ganai family and his father is name too was *Shaikh Hasan Ganai* But he was younger to *Baba* by *seven years.* He received his early education form his father. Later, he studied at the feet of some renowned scholars at *Lahore, Sialkot, Samarq and, Mashhad Mecca and Madina.* It is said that he not only memorized the *Quran,* but also began composing verses in Persian at the age of seven only. He had entensive travels in India and other countries after he grew up. While in India , he developed close contacts with *Faizi, Abul Fazl and Badauni,* and all of them weıe highly impressed by his scholarship Abul Fazl considered him " the greatest authority in religions matters." In the words of Badauni: " He was illustrious, and was relied upon as an authority on all branches of learning which are treated of in Arabic, such a Quranic commentaries , the traditions of Prophet and Sufism, and was an authorized religious leader." Badauni further tells us that both Humayun and Akbar had a high regard for him in their society. Distinguished in the realm of letters, Shaikh Yaqub Sarifi's place in the Kashmir political also was considerably high. When he returned form his travels of India and abroad, he was convinced that the Kashmiris should closely associate themselves with the main cultural stream India. The factions and internecine quarrels of in the grip of which Kashmir was at this stage, fortified his conviction further. The result was that in1586, he left for India, in the company of *Baba Daud Khaki,* to invite Akbar to annex Kashmir with the power of *'Nam'.* He was died in it in 1594 A.D. The *Shaikh* was not only a great prose-writer, but also a good poet. He penned down a number of *Ghazals and Gasidas.* Most important of his works in prose were *Tsfsir-Maslak-Ul-Akhyar, Wamiq-u-Azra, Laila-Majnu, Maghazin-Nabi, Maqamat-i-Murshid,* (these five form his *Khamsa*), *Manasik-i-Hajj* and a commentary of the Quran. The language of the masses, however, remained unchanged under the Hindu and the Muslim rulers, it was Kashmiri or Koshur, as the local people call it Originally, it was a *Prakrit* form of Sanskrit but written in *Pure Sarada* script of the 'Nam'. With the advent of the Muslim rule in the fourteenth century A.D., its character was changed considerably as a large number of Persian and Arabic words, either in their pure form or modified by popular usage, found their way into its expanding vocabulary. But while the Kashmiri language was this enriched the old literary traditions of Sanskrit were not completely given up by *Bhaskara Rajanaka* (H.K. pp. 199-200, 201).
397. Mirza Haidar Daghlat, *Tarikh-i-Rashidi,* Tr. by N.Elias and E.D Ross, *A History of the Moghuls of Central Asia.* p. 15. Hereafter cited as T.R.). **Note.** Mirza Muhammad Haidar Dughlat was the son of Muhammad Husain Dughlat, the governor of the province of Shash with its capital was at *Tashqand.* He was born in 1499-1500 A.D. His mother being the younger sister of Babur's mother, the Mirza was the first cousin of the Mughal emperor of India. He passed his early days through thick and thin. When he was hardly nine, his father was assassinated by Shaibani Khan, the Uzbeg Chief. His own life was also in danger. But some of his relatives came to his rescue and took him away first to Bukhara, then to Badakshan, and finally to Kabul, where he put up with Babar and helped him in his struggle against the Usbegs. After spending about five years with Babur, Mirza Haidar Dughlat left him in 1514 A.D. to go to Sultan Ahmad his uncle and the ruler of *Kashghar* and *Mughalistan.* Shortly after, when Sultan Ahmad died, the Mirza transferred his loyalty to his son, Sultan Abu Said Khan, and remained with him till the latter's death in 1533 A.D. (p. 121). The soon challenged by Kaji Chak. When the latter had appeared in the court of Sher Shah, he was given a warm reception and the title of *Khan-i-Khana.* Mirza Haidar then inflicted a crushing defeat upon Kaji Chak and compelled him to retreat to Rajouri. A little later, relations between Mirza Haidar Dughlat and

Regi Chak also got strained. So long as *Regi Chak* occupied the seat of power says *Baharistan-i-Shahi*, ' the Mirza was obedient to him in every way and did not show any opposition'. Cut of regard for the Chak noble, he even showed respect to the *Nurbakhsi* cult and once both of them together called on Shah Ahmad, a well-known *Nurbakshi Saint*. But this union between *a* fanatic Sunni and a die-hard *Nurbakshi* was logically in consistent and, therefore, soon melted away. *Regi Chak* left for *Kamraj*, his strong hold, and there raised a strandard of revolt against Mirza Haidar Dughlat. The Mirza, however, charged him away to Rajouri (*Rajapuri*). Haibat Khan Niyazi was the latter's governor of the Punjab. Islam Shah, the successor of Sher Shah Suri pursued him upto Bhimbar and might have gone further towards Kashmir through Pir Panjal route. There he met with two fugitive *Chak* leaders, *Daulat Chak* and *Ghazi Chak* son of *Kaji Chak*. They advised him to invade Kashmir. But, he rejected his proposal and instead opened friendly negotations with Mirza Haidar. The Mirza Haidar gave him a large sum of money where upon he left Rajouri for *Birna* near Jammu likely to be Birpur where large majority of the *Dum* or *Mahashah* community used to live. Mirza Haidar's rule in Kashmir lasted for about eleven years (1540-51 A.D.). During this period, he established peace, order and a good government in the country. His rule indeed, comes as a welcome break in the otherwise troubled in the history of Kashmir after Zain-ul-Abidin's death and before its conquest by Akbar. Mirza Haidar already founded some new cities and towns for the safety of Akbar (H.K., pp. 123, 124, 125).

398. **Note.** *Chak* in Punjabi dictionary (1) a *Kamboh* clan (agricultural) found in Amritsar, (2) a sept. of Jats to which Ranjha is sometimes said to have belonged, and *Chaki* or *Chakari*, the Multani equivalent for Teli or *oilmen* the dividing line in society is between *Zamindars* or agricultural families and the *taifadars* that is, the market-gardeners, herdsmen, shepherds, boatmen, minstrels, leather-workers, and the menial servants of the villagers. No *Zamindars* would intermarry with a *taifadar*. For the most part it is difficult to trace any difference in physiognomy between the two classes, though there is often a difference in dress. But the *Dum* or *Domba* or *Doom* or *Chandalas*, the *Galawan*, and the *Batal* or *Watal* are easy to disinguish from other tribes. They have a darker skin, and the *Dum* has the restless, furtive eye so characteristic of the thief. The *Dums* are a very important people in Kashmir, for they are the watchmen of the villages and formerly used to look after the State share of the crops. As a private citizen the *Dum* is not an admirable person, and he loses no opportunity of annoying the villagers, by whom he is feared and disliked. But as officials they are trustworthy, and have never been known to steal the state treasure which passes through their hands. The *Dums* claim descent from a Hindu King, who from fear of his numerous sons scattered them over the valley from the very ancient period of the Indian history, but some say that are descendants of the *Chakks*, mentioned under 'History'. The *Galawans* or horse-keepers are also credited with a descent from the *chakks*, and their violent restless character may be hereditary. Originally they earned their living by grazing ponies but found it more lucrative to steal them. At last they became an established criminal tribe during the time of terrible movement and during Sikh rule, they were a terror to the country. *Khaira Galawan*, the hero of many a legend, was killed by the Sikh governor Mian Singh. Gulab Singh hunted down the tribe and their end was transportation to *Bunji*. The *Batals* or *Watals* have been called *gipsies* of Kashmir, and are a peculiar people with a *patois* of their own. They may be divided into two classes those who obstain from eating carrion and are admitted to the mosque and to the Musalman religion form the first class; those who eat the flesh of dead animals and are excluded from the mosque form the second. They are wandereres, and though they sometimes settle in *Wattled* huts on the outskirts of a village, they soon move on leather. The first class make boots and sàndals. The second class make winnowing trays of leather and straw, and do scavenger is work. They also rear poultry and rob hen-roosts. Their women are of fine stature and handsome and they often drift into the city, where they become singers and dancers. Once a year the *Batals* from all parts of the valley flock to *Lala Bab's* shrine near the Dal Lake, and many matters affecting the tribe are then settled. The *Bhands* or minstrels are a peculiar people. They combine the profession of singing and acting with that of begging; and they travel great distances, often visiting the Panjab, where they perform to Kashmiri audiences. They are excellent actors, clever at improvisation and fearless as to its results. They are a very pleasant people, and their mirth and good humour form a pleasant contrast to the chronic gloom of the Kashmiri peasant. (P.G.K., pp. 37-38).

399. H.K., pp. 122-23.

400. H.I.M.P., p. 45.

401. H.K., p. 123.

402. K.N. Pandit, *Ladakh, Life and Culture*; Srinagar, 1986, p. 98.

403. K.K. *Gazetteer of Kashmir and Ladakh;* Delhi, 1974. p. 535. **Note.** The cattle of Kashmir were grazed confines to Ladakh during the summer while the higher altitude of the mountains are covered witht he thousand sheeps and wool was prepared for the witner season to protect the body of human life.

404. M.L. Kapoor, *Kingdom of Kashmir.* Jammu, 1983, p. 367. Henceforth referred as K.K.

405. N.K. Singh, *Cultural Heritage of Jammu, Kashmir and Ladakh*. Vol. III, Jammu, p. 31.

406. *Ibid.*, p. 34.

407. K.K., p. 356.

408. Issac A. Eżekid, *Sarmad, Martyr to Love Divine*. Beas. Reprint 2005, p. 28.

409. T.M.E., p. 154.

7

Washermen, Dyers and Tailors

This group of washer men, dyers, calico printers and tailors are called *Dhobi, the Chhimba, the Rangrez, Chhipas, the Lilari and Charhoa*. The terms, at any rate in the west of Punjab, denote occupations rather than the true castes; and the line of distinction between the various occupations is not only vague, but varies greatly form one part of the province to another, the *Lilari* doing in some parts what the *Chhimba* does in others, and *the Chorhoa* combining the occupations of the whole group in the Multan and *Derajat* divisions, some are founded in Rajasthan, while the *Darzi* is often a *Chhimba and the Chhimba a Darzi, a Chhipas* caste among Brahman are founded in Rajasthan, they are dyers and calico printers[1]. Thus, it is impossible to say that these terms separate castes, though the caste to which the group belongs, of which the *Dhobi* in the east and the *Charhoa* in the west may be taken as types, is a very distinct one at the same time, where the occupations are separate they are in the hands of separate traders-guilds with separate rules and organizations, and it is probable that inter-marriage is at any rate unusual. Like most occupational castes, those of this group are less in numbers on the frontier than else where. In Kulu, *Dagis* are the impure of *Kamin* caste, they are also commonly called *Kolis,* a name, however, which out of Kulu is applied to any Kuluman. In Seeraj, they are commonly called *Betus* those among them who have taken to any particular trade are called by the trade name, for example, *Barara,* basket-makers, *Barhai,*Carpenter, *Dhogri*, Iron-smelter, *Pumba,* wool-cleaner, and these name stick to families long after they have abandoned the trade, as has been the case with certain families now Black smith and Carpenter in England[2] . *See Table No 1.*

The Dhobi and Chhimba

Dhobi is perhaps the most clearly defined and the one most nearly approaching a true caste of all the castes of the group. He is found under that name throughout the Punjab, but in the Derajat and Multan division he is distinguishable from the *Charhoa* and we regret to say that here the divisional officers have included those who returned themselves as *Dhobi* under the head of *Charhoa*. Some of the *Charhoas* seem also to have returned themselves as *Jats*[3]. The *Mulla or Maulvi* is a doctor of divinity who teach the precepts of the faith *Mulwana* or *Mulana* appear to be merely other forms of *Mulla*; all these people are returned from the Derajat, Peshwar, and Multan divisions. Makhaum means the head of a shrine, generally a descendant of the saint who presides over the management and the title used to be almost condined to the heads of the more celebrated shrines, but it is now used by those of smaller shrines also, and by any who claim descent form any saint[4]. The *Dhobi* is the washerman of the country. But with the work of washing he generally combines, especially in the centre and the west of the Province, the craft of calico-painting; and in the Lohare and Rawalpindi divisions the *Chhimba* has been classed as *Dhobi*, while in the Jalandhara division most of the *Dhobis* have been classed as *Chhimbar*. In fact, the two sets of figures must be taken together. The *Dhobi*, is also a true village menial in the sense that he receives a fixed share of the producer in return for washing the clothes of the villages where he performs that office. But he occupied this position only among the higher castes of the land-owners, as among the *Jats* and castes of similar standing the women generally wash the clothes of the family. The *Dhobi* is, therefore, to be found in number in the towns. His social position is very low, for his occupation is consider impure ; and he alone of the tribes which are not outcast will initate the *Kumhas* in keeping and using a donkey. He stands below the *Nai*, but perhaps above the *Kumhar*, because he is socially unaware about his position in the society. He often takes to working as a *Darzi* or tailor. He is most often a *Muhsalman*. His title is *Bareta* or *Khalifah*, the latter being the title of the heads of his guild[5].

In Dera Ghazi Khan, the *Chhimba, Chhaimpa, Chhipi* or *Chhimpi* are known *Paungar* or *Charhoa*. So far as their occupation is concerned, a stamper or dyer, but he also turns his hand to tailors, the *Lilaris* or dyer or washer man. Hence, the caste includes the *Darzi's* or tailorings and *Dhobis*. But in Maler Kotla the *Tank* claim to be higher status than the *Bhilla*, and do not even eat or smoke with them are also called the *Chhapargar*. By religion the *Chhimbas* are mainly Hindus and Muhammadan[6]

The *Chhimba* or *Chhaimpa* is properly a calico-printer, and stamps coloured patterns on the cotton fabrics of the country, and he is said occasionally to stamp similar patterns on proper, but he can hardly be distinguished from the *Dhobi*. Though anybody could become an artist, if he so wished, not so many aspire this status; only the traditional artist families take to painting the lifestyle of the society in the favours of the royalty for their livelihood. Thus, sometimes artists work and are paid on contract basis. The price of their work usually depends upon the quality of the art as well as upon the number of figers painted upon the colico. They were the people of lower castes and decorate their walls themselves and also print the deities of the Brahmans on paper called *Sudhras* with the help of woon blocks. Formerly the artistst could live on the earnings from their paintings alone. Besides printing in colours, he dyes in madder, but as a rule, in no other colour. He is purely an artisan, never being a village menial except when a washerman. In some places, though not in all, *Chhapegar* is used to distinguish those who ornament calico with patterns in tinsel and foil only[8]. Whether the wooden fabrics in *Vedic* age were patterned is not known, but some interesting information could be gathered about the woollen fabics and shawls from Buddhist literature and the *Mahabharata* and the *Ramayana*. It is worthy to note that needle work (*pesakakara-sippa*) was considered to be a low form of craft, perhaps it was practised by the people of low caste called *Chamar* or *Mochi*. In common with Vedic literature *Kambala* is a generic term for woollen shawls[9] were common in ancient India. It is apparently a form of Kashmir shawl in which patterns are woven on many strips measuring from twelve to eighteen inches, then these are either joined to obtain a complete pattern or simply attached to a shawl. These strips are at times embroidered. The *tantuvicchinna* is described by the commentator as *anutavisrishtaih tantubhih madhya-krtavicchedyam jalakopayogica*. i.e, obtaining patterns in the middle by unwoven yarn or a trellis pattern. It is possible that the netted border of a shawl made by tying the unwoven ends is meant here[10].

Study shows that the shawl industry in Kashmir was of greater antiquity than the 15th century A.D. There was a great versatile writer of medieval Kashmir is known Ksemendra (990-1065 A.D.), seems to have been fairly well acquainted with the shawl weaving industry of his country.

Textiles and Dyes

In the study, it reveals that from the Mauryan period and even earlier, the manufacture of textiles in India had flourished and there are constant references to its variety in the Brahminical, Buddhist, Jain works. Coarse and fine varieties of cotton were in great demand. Silk formed an important part of the rich persons wardrobe. A very cheap material made of hemp was worn by the weavers and by labourers of all kinds. Wool was not needed much in the part of India ruled by the *Satavahanas* which had a warm climate, but it was used in the form of *chaddars* or blankets in winter[11]. In this way, all textiles pieces brought, woven to order or received as tributes or presents were carefully preserved and were inspected from time to time. Clothes were made from them or they were given away as presents. Articles were arranged according to the prices. Experienced people continually inquired about the pieces was conducive to the increase of strock. Keeping in view, Akbar has also displayed a great interest in textiles in the shawl manufacture of Kashmir[12]. From the above descriptions of textiles and dyes, there are interesting details, are given about dyeing the dyers (*Yantraka*) thoroughly beleached the clothes to get better colour effects. The *Yarn* were tie-dyed (*tantubandha*). The colours used for dyeing are madder, lec-dye, safflower, shad of red lead, tarmeric yellow, indigo. *Terminalia chebula* (*adhaya*), *nisanili* (night-blue), parrot green, peacock-neck green, *hamsa* and *kunda* flower white. The *Mansollasa* occasionally mentioned som special varieities of fabrics. Thus *citrambara* might have been some. Kind of figured silk. *Citra-kapardaka* seems to have been either printed calico or some figure stuff. *Citrapati-patta* seems to have been a pattern silken dupatti. *Puspaka* emboidered with gold was an elephant carpet[13].

It bears that there was a variety of dyes available from *Vedic* times indigo, yellow, crimson magenta, black and turmeric. Since was hermen were also dyers, these colours were well-known to them and the knowledge of the dyeing processes was probably handed down to each successive generation one after the another. Varieties and mixtures of colours known to those countries with which the *Satavahanas* did a great deal of trade, like China, Persia, and Rome must also have been incorporated to extend their range of coloured textiles. Printed and woven designs on textiles were plentiful and embroidery in gold was also common among the richer classes. The *Uttariya*, in particular, was very often of silk and embroidered with flowers. Precious stones were often used in the borders of these uttariyas or they were dyed blue or red, but a spotless white remained the favourite with men[14]. In the *Ain-i-Akbari*, it is mentioned that people of Kashmir generally used to wear shawl without altering its natural colour; his majesty has had it dyed. It is curious that it will not take a red dye, because they are culprit. Secondly, in the *safid alcas* (any kind of coloured stuff) or *tarahadars* in their natural colours, the wool is either white, black or mixed. The first white kind was formerly dyed in three or four ways; his Majesty has given order to dye it in various ways. Thirdly, in stuffs as *Zardozi, Kalabatun, Kasidah, qalghat, bandhnun, chint, alcah* and *purzdar* to which his Majesty pays much attention. Fourth, he improved the smaller size of the shawls and enlarged them as to make complete suit out of them[15].

The garments which were stored in the imperial court of Akbar as ward-robe are arranged according to days, months and years of their entries, and according to their colour, prices, and weight. Such as arrangement now-a-days is called *misl*. And, their variety is noted on cloth lebels sewn to one of the corners of the shawls. In the *Irani* months of *Azar* and *Farwardim* they are brought to the Karkhanas and sorted out in accordance with their prices, varieites, colours and weights.[16]

From the above account of shawl many points are clear that what kind of colours were used in the dyeing of shawls. These colours are known as grey (*tus*), white (*safed*), striped (*alcah*), scarclet (*lal*), golden (*Zarrin*), brass coloured (*birinji*), carmine (*qurmizi*), deep blackish green (*kahi*), almond colour (*badami*), light yellow (*gulpumbah*), sandalwood colour (*sandal*), deep red (*arghwani*), mauve (*unnabi*), parrot green (*tutki*) honey colour (*asli*), purple (*Sosni*), majenta (*majithi*), colour of Kasmi flower, apple-green (*sebki*), grass green (*alfi*), pistachio green (*pitaki*), purgul, orange (*narangi*), leaf green (*paran*), lahujor thuj (*Kalma*), pink (*gulabi*), blue (*asmani*), birch bark (*bhoja patra*), sea green (*abi*), olive green (*zaituni*), blood red (*Jigari*), emerald green (*Zamurradi*), chinese blue (*cini*), a kind of purple (*banafsai*), flesh (*musqin*), grey (*fakhtai*), and *qalghai*. In former times shawls came from Kashmir from time to time. People folded them in four-folds and wore them for a very long time. Now-a-days they are generally worn without folds and merely thrown over the shoulders. His Majesty has commenced to wear them double, which looks very well. His Majesty encourages in every possible way the manufacture of shawls in Kashmir. In Lahore alone there are more than a thousand workshops. A kind of shawl named mayan is chiefly woven there; it consists of silk and wool mixed . These are of standard size. Both are used for *cirahs* (turbans) and *fautahs* (loin-bands[17]).

Division of Chhimba and Dhobi

The Hindu *Chhimbas* are divided into two sub-castes, which may not intermarry, but may eat and smoke together. In Patiala the Hindu *Dhobi gots* are not separately given, and it is said that the *Tank* print cloth, while the *Rhillas* are tailors and the *Dhobis* are washermen[18]. Wilson in his *Glossary* at page No. 111, gives these two words as synonymous with *Chhimpi*, but we are informed that in some places, though not in all, *Chhapegar* is used to distinguished thouse who ornament calico with patterns in tinsel and foil only. The *Chhimba* often combines washing with dyeing and stamping, and he very commonly works as a *Darzi* or tailor in so much that *Chhimba* is not unfrequently translated by 'tailor'.

But few large divisions are returned for these castes. We give in the margin the figures for a few of the largest showing the *Dhobi, Chhimba* and *Charhoa* side by side. The divisions are roughly arranged in the order which they are found from east to west. And, in Patiala the Hindu *Dhobis* are said to form a third sub caste[20].

The following legend explains the origin of the two formers sub-castes:-

It is said that at Pindlapur in the Deccan lived one *Bamdeo*, who one night entertained Krishna and *Udhoji*, but, as the latter was a leper, the villagers ejected them. They were in *mayavi* form and at midnight both of them vanished leaving *Bamdeo* and his wife asleep. Udhoji hid in a shell (*sipi*), and when *Bamdeo* went to wash clothes he found the shell and placed it in the sun. It produced the child Namdeo who was fostered by Bamdeo's wife *Namdeo*[21] taught his son *Tank*, and *Rhilla*, his daughter's son, the arts of dyeing,printing and washing clothes. But to the Maler Kotla version it is said that originally the *Chhimbas* were a homogeneous caste, until *Namdah (-deo) Chhimba* took unto himself two wives, one a *Chhimba* woman, the other of another caste. From the former sprang the *Tank*, from the latter the *Rhilla*. Hence, the *Tank* assert their own superiority as they are pure *Chhimbas*, while *Rhilla* are not[22], because she belonged to the Brahman caste.

Sant Nam Dev was one of the famous disciple of Ramanand, the *Chhimba* or cotton-carder by caste. According to one of the Marathi account his ceaseless song of devotions were flourished in the days of Sikandar Lodhi (1488-1512 A.D.) He is said to have been persecuted by the Mussalmans, who tried to persuade him to repeat the words "*Allah, Allah*", instead of his favourite "Ram, Ram", but by a variety of astonishing miracles he escaped from their hands. After a considerable about of travelling to and fro, he at last settled in the village of Ghuman, in the Batala tehsil of the Gurdaspur District, where he died. A shrine, known as the "Darbar", was erected in his honour in Ghuman, and on the Sankrant day of every Magh a crowded fair is held here in his honour. At Ghuman the whole body of *Chhimbas* descended from Namdeo call themselves *Bawas* and are prietsts of the shrine, which is a fine domed building. Similar dome constructions, erected in honour of Namdeo's leading disciples, existed at *Dhariwal* and *Sukhowal*, near *Ghuman*. His followers can scarcely be said to constitute a sect. They are almost entirely, if not entirely, *Chhimbas* and *Dhobi's* by caste. Their founder appears to have resisted stoutly the pretextious of Muhammadanism, and was looked on as a follower of *Ramchandar,* but his Hinduism was by no means of the ordinary type. He taught emphatically the unity of God and the uselessness of ceremonial; and his doctrines would appear to have approached fairly closely to those of Nanak and the earlier Sikhs; and several of his poems are incorporated in the Sikh *Adi-Granth*. At any rate the followers of *Baba Namdeo* are very largely Sikhs by religion, and they are said, whether Hindus or Sikhs, to hold the Granth the reverence and to follow many Sikh customs. They have no distinctive worship of their own. The Hindu *Namdeopanthis* are found mainly in Jallandhar, Gurdaspur and Hissar, and the Sikhs mainly in Gurdaspur. The Saints name is pronounced, and often spelt *Namdeo;* and his followers call themselves sikh Namdeo *Namabansi, Baba Nam Ke Sewak,* and the like. They are the *Namdhari* a synonym for *Kuku,* said to be used in *Sialkot Namtas,* a agricultural clan found in Shahpur[24].

Study shows that there was a territorially divisions of various Hindu *Chhimbas,* for example, in Sialkot they are divided into the Lahori and Dogra sub-castes, which are said not to intermarry and which have separate *gots*. But the *Bagri* is found in both groups. In Amritsar too is found a Lahori group, which is also called *Chhapagar* or *Nawandhi*= of low degree. It is looked down upon the other *Chhimbas*, who avoid all social relations with its members, because at weddings, it is said, they make a cow's image of flour and shoot arrows at it.

The Lohari *gots* are known as *Pharwain, Bagri, Takhtar* and *Ded*. The Dogra *gots* are excluded the sub-groups of caste; *Karaku, Panotra, Dowathia, Andh; Rihania, Pape, Saragra, Bagri, Chebne, Bhumral* and *Tanotra*.

The Hindu *Chhimabas* have few or no special observances at births, etc. In or near Delhi after childbirth, if the child be a son, the mother worships at a well to which she is taken 15 days after her confinement, accompanied by the woman of her quarter of the city who sing songs as they go. The mother does obesiance to the well, and throws some sweet stuff and rice into it. Moreover, Hindu *Chhimbas* never grind turmeric, excepting at a wedding. They will not make *baris*, and their women avoid wearing *kanch* bracelets and the use of henna. In this way, the Hindu *Chhimbas*, in Gurgaon, who are very superstitious, worship a Muhammadan's grave, real or supposed, calling it a Sayyid's grave, offering a cock in the Sayyid's name or a dish of boiled rice at his grave, lest their domestic peace be distrubed. They observe the ordinary Hindu rites, but Namdeo, the famous *bhagat*, is their patron saint, for no better, reason than that he was himself by caste a *Chhimba*. Accordingly, they pay yearly visits to his *dera* at Ghaman near Amritsar, and offer him a rupee and *narial* at weddings. Sikh *Chhimbas* appear to favour the tenets of Guru Ram Rai[24].

On the other side, the Muhammadan *Chhimbas* have several territorial divisions, for example, in Patiala the Muhammadan *Dhobis* are said to have five sub-castes known as Lahori, Sirhindi, Multani, *Purbia* and Dewsal of these the two latter only are found in the state. They do not intermarry to each other. The Deswali sections are called *Goraya, Chauban* and *Kanakwal* are all Rajput clans. There are other three more clans known as, the Sirhindis (endogamous), the Deswals and Multains, who intermarry, as is also the case of *Jind*. In Gurgaon the Desi *Chhimbas* are said to be converts from the *Tank* and *Rhilla* sub-castes, while the Multanis are of the *Inroi* clan which dwell in the Indus valley and took to printing calico. In Leia the saint of the *Chhimbas* is Ali, the dyer, who is said to have been a pupil of Luqman and to have inverted washing and dyeing. Before the beginning of the work, they invoke him saying:- "*Pir ustad Luqman nakim, nikmat da badshah, Ali rangrez Chari rahe deg,*" i.e "Luqman the physician is the priest and teacher, the king of craft, and Ali is the dyer. Many his bounty endure for ever". Most Muhammadan *Chhimbas* are Sunnis, but in Karor some few are Shias[25]. So far as the Panchayats system is concerned, the Muhammadan *Chhimhas* have a loose system, and in Dera Ghazi Khan elders or Mahtars are elected by the caste system. It is mentioned that their women wear no *laong* (nose ring), no ivory or glass bangles, or blue cloth. They will not make themselves *acharn* or *baria* i.e. *'Kalma'* or *'Nam'* and avoid building a double hearth.'

It is also important to noteable that *Chhina*, his female term is *Chhinba*, in Panjabi dictionary it is called *Chhimba*, an agricultural clan found in Shahpur. It is class of agriculturalist *Jat*, called in Amritsar. The *Chhina* are undoubtedly distinct from the *Chima Jats* of Sialkot and Gujranwala, though the two tribes are frequently confused. That there are *Chhina* in Sialkot appears from the fact that the town of *Jamki* in that District was founded by a *Chhina* Jat who came from the Sindh and retained the title of Jam, the Sindhi equivalent for *Chaudhri* yet if the *Chhina* spread up the *Chenab* into Sialkot and the neighbouring Districts in large numbers, it is curious that they should not be found in the intermediate Districts through which they must have passed. The *Chhina* are also found in Mianwali and in Bahawalpur state. In the latter they are mainly confined to the Minchinabad *Kardari*, opposite *Pakpattan*, and there have three septs are tenants. The genealogy gives them a common origin with the Wattus:-

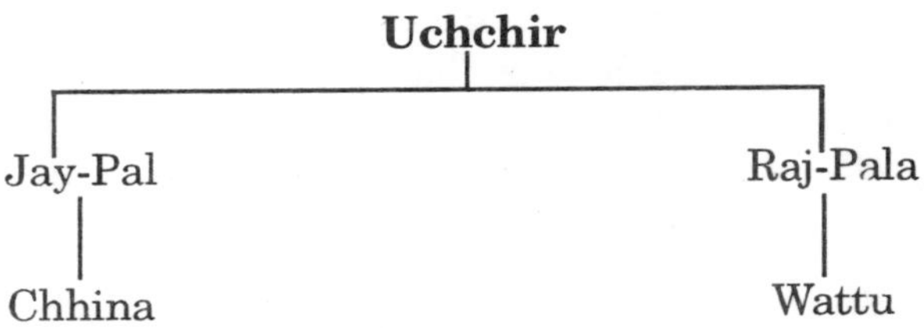

It is important to note that Pheru, 18th in descent from *Chhina* was converted to Islam by Bawa Farid-ud-Din of Pak Pattan. The *Chhinas* are courageous and hard-working, but they are also professional thieves, though they will not steal from Sayyids, faqirs or mirasis dreading the abuse of the latter. Though a small tribe in comparsion with the *Wattus* they will not allow the latter to get the upper hand, and if they steal one buffalo from the *Chinnas*, the latter endeavour to retaliate by stealing five from the *Wattus*[27] *Dhobi*, perhaps the most clearly defined and the one most nearly approaching a true caste of all the Menial and Artisan castes. He is found under that name throughout the Punjab, but in the Derajat and the Multan division he is undistinguishable from the *Charhoa*. He is the washerman of the country, but with washing her generally combines, especially in the centre and west of the province, the craft of calicoprinting, and undoubtedly in these parts the *Dhobi* and *Chhimba* castes overlap. The Dhobi is a true village menial in the sense that he receives a fixed share of the produce in return for washing the clothes of the villages where he performs that office. But he occupies this position only among the higher castes of land owners as among the *Jats* and castes a similar standing the women generally wash the clothes of the family. The *Dhobi* is, therefore, to be found in largest number in the towns. His social position is very low, for his occupation is considered impure; and he alone of the tribes which are not outcast will imitate of the *Kumhar* in keeping and using a donkey. He stands below the *Nai* (barbar), but perhaps above the *Kumhar*. He often takes to working as a *Darzi* or tailor, and in Peshawar dhobi simply means a dyer (*Rangrez*). He is most often a Musalman. His title is barita or Khalifa, the later being the title of the heads of his guild.

The *Dhobi* sections appear to be few. They are included as *Agrai, Akthra, Bhalam, Bhatti, Kamboh, Khokhar, Kohans, Larli, Liarli, Lippal, Mahmal, Rikhari* etc. Those italicised are also *Chhimba* and *Charhoa*. The Hindu Dhobis in Kapurthala say they are immigrants from the United Provinces and preserve four of their the Muhammadan sections are said to be *Galanjar, Mohar, Role, Sangari, Saukhar* and *Satal*. There are obviously no such patterns. No class or caste uniformity exists with respect to the retention of specialists. Specialists who serve Brahman may or may not also serve *Thakur, Ahir, Kori* and *Chamar*. *Chhunalal Dhobi*, for example, washes clothes for all three Brahman households and also for a Kayastha household, two *Ahir* households and also for a Kayastha household, two *Ahir* households, three *Murau* households, a *Kori* household, and *Chamar* household. This mean that, Vis-a-vis *Chhunalal. Dhobi*, common *jajman* status is shared by households spanning the entire spectrum of ritual purify and the entire range of economic standing. Such as congeries of socially disparate households can hardly constitute a class in any sociological sense. They are alike only in their propensity to maintain a particular religious -economic status, that of jajman[28] of the *'Chamar'* or *'Word'*. The *Lilari* and *Rangrez. Lilari* and his female is known as *Lilarian*, also nilar a dyer from Lil or nil or neel, indigo. The word is merely the Persian equivalent of dyer[29]. About fifty years ago V.A. Smith[30] explored the dearth of literature dealing with colour scheme of India. He said," the enormous mass of Indian literature, whether in Sanskrit or any other language, does not contain, I believe a single treatise on the aesthetics of plastic and pictorial art i.e. 'Word' or 'Nam'." The *Lilari* is hardly distinguishable from the *Rangrez*. They are both dyers and both artisans and artist not menials, being chiefly found in the towns. But the distinction is said to be that the *Lilari* dyes, as his name implies, in indigo only; while the *Rangrez* dyes in all country colours from time to time except indigo and madder[31]. It is, however, very aptly suggested by Moti Chandra that *rajavarta*, the Indian word for *lapis lazuli*, is nothing but a Sanskritised form of Persian word *lazward*, the source of ultramarine. It seems that lapis lazuli stones, or more probably the ultramarine pigments extracted from them, were imported to this country from Persia, for no prescription on its manufacturing is recorded in the *Silpatexts*. The canopy of diapered carpet battern containing crosses with highly stylized angular human figures and cosettes, which are attributed to original *Chhimba*. The charm of composition lies in a suitable combination of various decorative elements. While pink, green and white are used to represent the lotus flowers and leaves, blue fishes and pink elephants and grey geese tinged with carmine add to the veriegated richness of the composition. Even the carnation of the devotees is not uniform[32] However, in both paintings the solid body colours of some figures show that the old tradition was not yet completely forgotten by the *Chhimba*.

There are, however, certain differences between the late but vigorous style of the drawing of the horses and elephants in the contemporary battle scenes, which last appertains to the *Chhimba*. The interesting example is noticable that, with the exception of a few returned as Hindus by the Native states, both of these castes are exclusively Musalman. The Hindu indeed would not dye in blue, which is to him an abomination; and madder-red is his speical colour[34]. The *Silparatna* gives three gradation of red 'word', *Sindhura* for light red *Gairika* (mountain-born) red (mineral chalks) for a middle tint and *laksa* (lac) hence for a deep colour. The *Abhilasitar thacintamani* and the *Sivatattya ratnakara* tell us that vermillion is for reddish brown, and red lac or sap, red sanders and mountain-born chalks are for crimson tint. They echo Bana's statements. White and black give the grey of smoke, blue and white the colour of pigeon similar to the *Rig Veda* and counch power give a picular pale-red (*Dhumracchaya*). *Darada* (vermilion) mixed with white gives the pale-red of the red-lity while *Alaktaka* (red lac or sap) combined with white gives the colour of the sun's horses. The differences is very slight here. Pure indigo (Nila) of the colour of the blue lily gives a green tint when mixed with yellow pigment. Red lac with lamp-black gives a dark brown and with blue (Nila), the colour of Jambu fruit. The tints goby mixing primary colors 'Word' or 'Nam' like smoke grey, pigeon colour, the different varieties of red, brown, green and the colour of the Jambu fruit are clearly given by Bana. The variegated hue to which he refers is given by *Silparatna* as a convenient colour for artists; but according to *Sri Kumara* it is got by mixing red, black and yellow in equal proportions. Red and Yellow give the colour of *Pakula* flowers which Bana describes as *Dhusara* (tawny). This is the same as flame colour. There are also other varities of red given in the *Silparatna*[35]. In this way, the different tones of ochre red, brown, black and whites remind us of the ancient tradition of the Indian society. This was the change in faith and practice and naturally therefore increased interest in mythological literature, the dramatic nature of temple processions feasts and festivals *'Word'* or *'Chamar'* all served to stimulate the aesthetic sense of people as is evident from the emergence of new trends and development in the realm[36] of dyers or *Lilaris*. Percy Brown in his *Rajput Painting* expresses it very lucidly: "Transforming influence were at work, but the original handiGraft still lives, and was carried on in spite of the spiritual and political changes to which the whole country was subjected. And this is the art which eventually emerges out of the darkness of the Middle Age[37]," which perhaps accounts for the *Chhimba*, most of whom are Hindu, dyeing in that *Colour*-only. In Peshawar the *Dhobi* or *Lilaria* and *Rangrez* are said to be identical. The *Lilaria* is often called *Nilari, Nirali, Lolari* or *Lalari*. In Multan, *Pungar* is the term locally used for Lilari[38].

Study demonstrates that *Chhimba* of the Multan and Derajat divisions were also carried on the handicrafts of the *Lilari* and *Rangrez* also, but the *Charhoa* is also called *Dhobi*. In his capacity of washerman he is, like the *Dhobi* and under the same circumstances, as recognised village menial, receiving customary dues inexchange for which he washes the clothes of the villagers. In Bahawalpur he has been returned as *Dhobi. Darzi,* or its Hindi word equivalent Suji, is purely an occupational term, and though there is a *Darzi* belongs perhaps to the *Dhobi* and *Chhimba* castes, more especially to the latter, but men of all castes follow the trade, which is that of a tailor or sempster. The *Darzi's* are generally return as Hindu in the east and Musalman in the west[39].

In the above study, we learn that the patron saint of the Hindu weavers being Kabir they call themselves *Kabir bansi,* just as the tailors are called Namdevi from Namdeo and are offended by being called *Julaha* or *Darzi*[40]. But the system found a fuller development in medieval Islam. Thus "Adam was the first builders and sower; seth the first manufacture of buttons and wool-carder, Enoch the first tailor and clerk[41]. In the

Punjab plans the Hindu weavers are also called Ramdasias or followers of Guru Ram Dass, but this term appears to be restricted ot the *'Chamars'* who live by weaving[42]. These functional groups associated with the traditional occupation of cleaning, dyeing, tanning of cattle skins and hides, making the leather goods, foot-wears, iron smelting, brick-making, charcoal burning sweeping . They were known as *Barwala, Basith, Batwal, Chamar (Ramdasia), Chuhra, Dhyar Doom (Mahasa), Gardi, Jolaha, Megh (Kabirpanthi), Ratal, Saryara* and Watal. 53% are Meghs in Jammu and Kashmir division, *Chamars* stand group second, and *Dooms* or *Domba* stand third in rank in population. They are called *untouchables* and menial class of the society came under the category of *Sudhras*. According to the census report of 1981[43] they are 497, 369 or 8.30% of the state population which is fairly below the national average (15.75%). This is because the state is dominated by the Muslims who do not have Scheduled Caste in their religion. Other tehsils included *Mendhar, Rajapuri, Sunderbani, Budhal, Kalakota, Riasi, Gool, Ramban, Doda, Kishtwar and* Bhaderwah. In this region, they are less than 18%. Also *See Table No.2. about the information* of leather-workers and weavers of the other areas.

Notes & References

1. *P.F.F.P.I.*, p. 17.
2. *P. C.*, p. 332.
3. *Ibid.*, p. 320.
4. *Ibid.*, p. 224.
5. *Ibid.*, pp. 320-21.
6. *G.T.C.* Vol. II, p. 166.
7. P. F.F.P. I., p. 17.
8. G.T.C. Vol. II, p. 166.
9. C.T.C.C.A.M.I., p. 232.
10. *Ibid.*, pp. 233-34.
11. A.I.P., p. 35.
12. C.T.C.C.A.M.I., p. 238.
13. *Ibid.*, p. 124.
14. A.I.C., pp. 35-6.
15. A.A., p. 89.
16. *Ibid.*, p. 90.
17. *Ibid.*, pp. 90-91.
18. G.T.C., p. 166.
19. P. C., p. 321.
20. G.T.C., p. 166.
21. According to the commentary of *Vishwambhar Saint Nam* dev was born in 26, October, (1270-1350 A.D.), before two hundreds years than the Guru Nanak and hundred thirty years before Kabir. His Dama Seth and mother was Gonai. He was *Chhipa* or tailor by profession. He was born in *Narsi Bamni* named village of Maharashtra. In the district of Marathwara at Parbani according to some historian. (Chandravati Rajwade; *Tukaram*; Punjab (India) Reprint, 2004; p. 7 J.R Puri and V.K. Sethi; *Sant Nam Dev*; Punjab (India) Reprint; 2002; p. 11).
22. G.T.C., pp. 166-67.
23. *Ibid.*, Vol. III p. 152.
24. *Ibid.*, Vol. II; p. 167.
25. *Ibid.*, pp. 167-8.
26. *Ibid.*, p. 168.
27. *Ibid.*, p. 239. Note. It is interesting to note that the realm within which classical economic relationships operate today probably reflects the changes that have been taking place in Indian society. Early European accounts indicate a far greater number of castes involved in fixed ties rooted in semianual grain payments, as does Wiser (1936), whose study was done in the early 1930s. However, Jaffri (1935), in two case studies presented in an appendix, gives enough information to suggest that the pattern of reimbursement in eastern Uttar Pradesh 35 years ago was not fundamentally different in kind and in magnitude from what it is today. He nevertheless lists the water carrier (*Kahar*), tailor (*Darzi*), village watchman (*chowkidar*) and less clearly the cowherd (*Ahir*) as recipients of fixed semi-annual grain payments Among the five specialists considered, the washermen (*Dhobi*) are most frequently retained on a fixed, grain-payment basis i.e. by 77 per cent of their clientele at an average reimbursment of 31.3 pounds of grain. This is, at least in part, associated with the fact that washing clothes is deemed very defiling and is, therefore, particularly directly, implicated in the pure-impure dichotomy which is a central preoccupation of Hindu religions orthodoxy. Two Muslim households serve as tailor (*Darzi*), receiving a variety of goods and cash for their important services. There clientele is confined almost exclusively to the binary hamlets. Masons (Mistri), ususally either *Kori* or members of one of the agricultural castes, move above the locality selling their skills for about rupees a day. Dairymen (*Ahir*) also engaged in agriculture. Milk is dispersed on a strictly cash basis to whoever is willing to pay the price. The cost is eight *annas* a *seer* (two pounds). It is rare today to engage an *Ahir* to tend a herd of cows on anything other than a cash basis. It is still rarer to engage a *Kahar* (water carrier) on any basis except in the ritual context. Another occupation for which traditional forms of economic interaction have disappeared is that of the oil presser (*Teli*). He still does a brisk (business) but it is entirely on a cash basis to the 'Father'or *'Nam'*. (H.C.S. pp. 156, 757, 158, 164).

28. H.C.S., p. 178.
29. G.T.C. Vol. III, p. 323.
30. V.A. Smith, *A History of Fine Arts in India and Ceylon*; Bombay; pp. 8, 309.
31. G.T.C. Vol. III, p. 33
32. Moti Chandra; *Studies in Early Indian Painting*, London; 1970, pp. 21, 27.
33. *Ibid*., pp. 25-26.
34. G.T.C. Vol. III, p. 33.
35. D.N. Shukla; *Royal Arts*; Faizabad, 1967; p. 116
36. *Ibid.*, p. 182.
37. *Ibid.*, p. 183.
38. G.T.C. Vol. III, p. 33.
39. P. C., p. 324.
40. G.T.C. Vol.1, p. 398.
41. *Ibid.*
42. *Ibid.*
43. *Census Report of India 1981*. Jammu and Kashmir State.

Table 1. Washermen, Dyers And Tailors

	Figures						*Proportion per 1,000, of Total Population*						
	32	*36*	*110*	*67*	*59*	*61*	*32*	*36*	*110*	*67*	*59*	*61*	
	Dhobi	*Chhimbs*	*Rangrez*	*Lilari*	*Charhoa*	*Darzi*	*Dhobi*	*Chimbs*	*Rangrez*	*Lilari*	*Charhoa*	*Darzi*	*Total*
Delhi	4,157	2,628	681	—	—	583	6	4	1	—	—	1	12
Gurgaon	3,446	1,889	1,468	—	—	970	5	2	2	—	—	2	11
Karnal	2,748	4,856	1,662	—	—	1,238	4	8	3	—	—	2	17
Hissar	1,785	5,156	—	1,959	—	580	4	10	—	4	—	1	19
Rohtak	2,763	4,786	—	1,960	—	78	5	9	—	4	—	—	18
Sirsa	347	2,825	—	410	—	142	1	11	—	2	—	1	15
Ambala	5,036	5,618	—	1,382	—	913	5	5	—	1	—	1	12
Ludhiana	1,167	7,158	—	585	—	171	2	12	—	1	—	—	15
Simla	732	69	—	10	—	81	7	2	—	2	—	2	13
Jalandhar	1,107	9,743	—	602	—	436	2	14	—	1	—	1	18
Hushyarpur	288	7,662	—	607	—	1,551	—	9	—	1	—	2	12
Kangra	364	2,867	—	532	—	3,682	—	4	—	1	—	5	10
Amritsar	2,555	13,379	—	1,817	—	1,227	3	15	—	1	—	2	21
Gurdaspur	5,395	5,778	—	695	—	714	7	7	—	1	—	1	16
Sialkot	13,988	1,577	—	2,599	—	1,206	14	2	—	3	—	1	20
Lahore	15,596	—	—	1,107	—	1,026	17	—	—	1	—	1	19
Gujranwala	7,901	—	—	2,286	—	1,685	13	—	—	4	—	3	20
Firozpur	11,649	—	—	376	—	161	18	—	—	1	—	—	19
Rawalpindi	5,751	2	—	1,285	—	6,109	7	—	—	2	—	7	16
Jahlam	6,686	—	—	1,156	20	2,222	11	—	—	2	—	4	17
Gujrat	7,674	—	—	2,279	17	1,476	11	—	—	3	—	2	16
Shahpur	5,624	42	—	115	—	437	13	—	—	—	—	1	14
Multan	423	484	—	412	11,452	532	1	1	—	—	21	1	24
Jhang	7	36	128	61	5,234	387	—	—	—	—	13	1	14
Montgomery	1,429	153	21	111	6,049	342	3	—	—	—	14	1	18
Muzaffargarh	8	47	24	106	6,318	125	—	—	—	—	19	—	19
Dera Ismail Khan	—	2	53	5	2,639	87	—	—	—	—	6	—	6
Dera Ghazi Khan	—	13	3	4	592	12	—	—	—	—	2	—	2
Bannu	—	12	127	—	2,270	45	—	—	—	—	7	—	7
Peshawar	5,467	136	—	1,077	—	737	9	—	—	1	—	1	11
Hazara	2,694	—	—	59	—	1,076	7	—	—	—	—	3	10
Kohat	1019	—	—	260	—	112	6	—	—	1	—	—	7
British Territory	117,815	76,416	4,167	23,887	734,591	30,143	6	4	—	1	2	2	15
Patiala	2,074	15,045	—	1,954	—	471	1	10	—	1	—	—	12
Nabha	629	2,784	—	223	—	59	2	11	—	1	—	—	14
Kapurthala	762	2,750	—	84	—	719	3	11	—	—	—	3	17
Jind	1,028	2,351	—	1,013	—	137	4	9	—	4	—	1	18
Faridkot	17	1,624	—	—	—	8	—	17	—	—	—	—	17
Total East Palins	5,174	25,967	30	3,520	—	1,515	2	10	—	1	—	1	14
Babawalpur	9,163	—	825	102	—	393	16	—	—	—	—	1	18
Total Hill States	1,063	1,108	38	190	—	412	1	1	—	—	—	1	8
British Territory	117,815	76,416	4,167	23,887	34,591	30,143	6	4	—	1	2	2	15
Native States	15,400	27,075	893	3,812	—	2,320	4	7	—	1	—	1	13
Province	133,215	103,491	5,080	27,699	34,591	32,643	6	5	—	1	2	1	15

Table 2. Leather-Workers and Weavers

	Figures							Proportion Per 1,000 of Total Population								
	5	19	113	169	9	73	170	5	19	113		9	73	170		
	Chamar	Mochi	Chamrang	Dabgar	Julaha	Gadaria	Kanera	Chamar	Mochi	Chamrang	Total	Julaha	Gadaria	Kanera	Total	Grand Total
Delhi	63,407	128	—	27	6,673	2,457	—	98	—	—	98	10	4	—	14	112
Gurgaon	71,501	51	—	—	2,339	4,424	—	111	—	—	11	4	7	—	11	122
Karnal	54,067	197	—	20	9,090	3,725	—	87	—	—	87	15	6	—	21	108
Hissar	49,269	782	—	93	1,265	1	—	98	1	—	99	3	—	—	3	102
Rohtak	50,081	106	—	—	1,275	3	—	90	—	—	90	2	—	—	2	92
Sirsa	18,022	3,073	—	57	2,817	—	—	71	12	—	83	11	—	—	11	94
Ambala	140,751	932	—	—	24,931	6,671	—	131	1	—	132	23	6	—	29	161
Ludhiana	59,655	8,171	—	—	14,728	29	—	96	13	—	109	24	—	—	24	133
Simla	3,384	174	—	—	700	242	—	79	4	—	83	16	6	—	22	105
Jalandhar	79,155	16,517	—	4	15,790	58	—	100	21	—	121	20	—	—	20	141
Hushiarpur	100,207	14,726	—	6	20,841	—	—	111	16	—	127	23	—	—	23	150
Kaugra	51,679	151	—	1	28,129	—	—	71	—	—	71	38	—	—	38	109
Amritsar	1,049	24,311	338	8	41,598	—	—	1	27	—	28	47	—	—	47	75
Gurdaspur	20,972	14,716	806	10	4,456	—	—	25	18	1	44	49	—	—	49	93
Sialkot	8,076	15,003	2,602	—	27,140	39	—	8	15	3	26	27	—	—	27	53
Lahore	4,775	18,527	15	115	35,742	276	—	5	20	—	25	39	—	—	39	64
Gujrauwala	183	22,260	—	90	26,230	6	—	—	36	—	36	43	—	—	43	79
Firozpur	13,501	18,386	180	36	20,434	312	17	21	28	—	49	31	—	—	31	80
Rawlpindi	2,069	20,385	2	—	37,001	203	—	3	25	—	28	45	—	—	45	73
Jahlam	294	21,844	—	23	28,620	22	—	—	37	—	37	49	—	—	49	86
Gujarat	440	33,461	—	107	23,870	—	—	1	47	—	48	35	—	—	35	83
Shahpur	16	15,314	—	38	22,472	4	—	—	36	—	36	53	—	—	53	89
Multan	1,946	16,596	155	69	23,753	91	109	4	30	—	34	43	—	—	43	77
Jhang	34	14,132	—	36	24,176	7	—	—	36	—	36	61	—	—	61	97
Montgomery	256	14,118	—	68	20,454	—	—	1	33	—	34	48	—	—	48	82
Muzaffargarh	78	11,103	—	—	13,625	—	346	—	33	—	33	40	—	1	41	74
Derah Ismail Khan	4	4,903	—	22	5,673	—	106	—	11	—	11	13	—	—	13	24
Dersh Ghazi Khan	3	1,013	—	—	726	9	13	—	3	—	3	2	—	—	2	5
Bannu	—	3,890	—	—	3,357	5	421	—	12	—	12	10	—	1	11	23
Peshawar	4,156	3,263	111	—	15,372	98	—	7	6	—	13	26	—	—	26	39
Hazara	2,292	4,285	—	—	11,885	—	—	6	10	—	16	29	—	—	29	45

(Contd.)

	Figures							Proportion Per 1,000 of Total Population								
	5	19	113	169	9	73	170	5	19	113		9	73	170		
	Chamar	Mochi	Chamrang	Dabgar	Julaha	Gadaria	Kanera	Chamar	Mochi	Chamrang	Total	Julaha	Gadaria	Kanera	Total	Grand Total
Kohat	652	1,349	—	—	1,781	10	—	4	7	—	11	10	—	—	10	21
British Territory	301,995	322,873	4,209	835	552,944	18,693	1,012	42	17	—	59	29	11	—	30	8
Patiala	143,093	3,227	752	30	19,910	964	5	97	2	1	100	14	1	—	15	115
Nabha	24,817	922	—	—	4,694	2	—	95	3	—	98	18	—	—	18	16
Kapurthala	10,061	6,302	—	9	7,339	—	—	40	25	—	65	29	—	—	29	94
Jind	22,242	145	—	15	1,160	112	—	89	1	—	90	5	—	—	5	95
Faridkot	2,065	2,441	—	—	2,661	—	—	21	25	—	46	27	—	—	27	73
Maler Kotla	7,282	181	—	—	1,682	—	—	102	3	—	105	24	—	—	24	129
Kalsia	9,508	165	—	—	3,141	636	—	140	2	—	142	46	9	—	55	197
Total Eastern Plains	223,972	13,388	752	63	40,735	1,714	5	89	5	—	94	16	1	—	17	111
Bahawalpur	5,383	12,830	—	141	17,397	—	—	9	22	—	31	30	—	—	30	61
Mandi	8,178	2	—	—	3,575	—	—	56	—	—	56	24	—	—	24	80
Chamba	4,799	65	—	—	2,266	—	—	41	1	—	42	20	—	—	20	62
Nahan	4,354	1	67	—	592	75	—	39	—	1	40	5	1	—	6	46
Bilaspur	8,275	—	—	—	4,750	—	—	96	—	—	96	55	—	—	55	151
Nalagarh	5,753	26	—	—	664	1	—	108	—	—	108	12	—	—	12	120
Suket	2,498	—	—	—	909	—	—	48	—	—	48	17	—	—	17	65
Total Hill States	41,349	181	67	—	13,236	93	—	54	—	—	54	17	—	—	17	71
British Territory	801,995	322,873	4,209	835	552,944	18,693	1,012	42	17	—	59	29	1	—	30	89
Native States	270,704	26,399	819	204	71,368	1,807	5	70	7	—	77	19	—	—	19	96
Province	1,072,699	349,272	5,028	1,039	624,312	20,500	1,017	47	15	—	62	28	1	—	29	91

8

Water-men, Boat-men and Weavers

It is generally believed that all these men are of the same caste, *Kahar* being their usual name in the North-West provices, *Jhinwar* in the east of the Punjab where they are the mostly Hindu, and *Machhi* in the west of province where they are most numerous proportion to total population in the western and central districts[1] which are traversed by the great Punjab rivers, where too they assist largely in agricultural labour, besides finding more extensive occupation as looks among a Musalman population with no prejudices against eating food prepared by others. On the frontier proper, like most of the occupation castes, they are few in number. In the easter plains and hills these people are returned as *Jhinwars;* west of Lahore as *Machhis.* They are one of the pleasantest and most willing of the menial classes, and the *Bhishti* is proverbically a good servant. *Bhatyara, Bharbhunja*, and *Mallah* are names of occupations meraly, but of occupations which are followed almost if not quite exclusively by the *Jhinwar* caste[2]. the *Jhinwar,* The *Machhi,* the *Bhatyara,* the *bharbhunja and* the *Mallah* also included in it. *See in detail Table No. 3.*

Jhinwar

The *Jhinwar*, also called *Kahar, Kala or Kalwar* as he is called in the west of the Punjab, is the distiller and seller of spirituons liqhors. The word, however, seems to mean a potter in Peshwar. He is commonly known as *Neb* in *Naba* and in Patiala a Muhammadan often calls himself *Kakkezai*, and when a Sikh *Ahluwalia,* the origin of which means will presently be explained. The *Kala* or *Kalwar* is a distiller; and that is his hereditaty occupation. But since the manufacture of and traffic in spirits have been subjected to Government regulation a large portion of the caste, and more especially of its Sikh and Musalman sections, have abandoned their proper calling and taken to other pursuits, very often to commerce, and especially to traffic in boots and shoes, bread, vegetables, and other commodities in which men of good caste object to deal. They are notorious for enterprise, energy, and obstinacy. "*Death may budge; but a Kalal would not.*" They are, owing to circumstances presently to be mentioned, most numerous in the Sikh portions of the Panjab, and especially in Kapurthala. In the Western districts they seem to be almost unknown. Rather more than half of them are still Hindu, about a quarter Sikh, and the other quarter Musalman. The original social position of the caste is exceeding *low*, though in the Panjab, it has been raised by special circumstances. The ruling family of Kapurthala is descended from *Sada Singh Kala* who founded the village of *Ahlu* near Lahore. The family gradually rose in social scale, and Badar Singh, the great-grandson of Sada-Singh, married the daughter of a petty Sardar of the district. From this union sprange Jassa Singh, who became the most powerful and influential chief that the Sikhs ever possessed till the rise of Ranjit Singh. He adopted the title of Ahluwalia from his ancestral village Ahlu, the title is still borne by the 'Kapurthala royal family and a Sikh Kalal will commonly give his caste as Ahluwalia. The caste was thus raised in importance, many of its members abandoned their hereditary occupation, and its Musalman section also grew ashamed of the social stigma conveyed by the confession of *Kalal* origin. It accordingly fabricated a story of Pathan origin, and adding to the first letter of the caste name the Pathan tribal termination, called itself *Kakkezu*. The name was at first only used by the more wealthy members of the caste, but its use is spreading, and the cultivating owners of a village in Gujarat entered themselves as Kalal in the first and a *Kakkezai* in the second settlement. The well-known Sheikhs and forbid widow-marriage. Some of the Musalman Kalals claim Rajput or *Khatri* origin, and it is probable that many of the caste have returned themselves as Shekhs the commercial *Kalals* are said not to intermarry with these who still practise distillation[3].

In the east, *Jhinwar* are called Kahar and Mahra[4], where a Hindu, in the centre of the province, is the carrier, waterman, fisherman, and basket-maker of the east of the Panjab. He carries *palanquins* and all such burdens as are borne by a yoke on the shoulders, and he specially is concerned with water,in so much that the cultivation of waternuts and the netting of water fowl are for the most part in his hands, and he is the well-sinker of the province. He is a true village menial, receiving customary dues and performing customary service. In this capacity he supplies all the baskets needed by the cultivator, and brings water to the men in the fields at harvest time, to the houses where the women are secluded, and at weddings and other similar occasions. His occupations in the centre and west of the Province are described below under the head *Machhi*. His social standing is in one respect high; for all will drink at his hands. But he is still a servant, though the highest of the class[5]. The *Jhinwar* such men as returned themselves as *Bhishtis, Mashkis,* or *Saqqahs*, the terms for Musalman water-carriers. It is just possible that some of these men may be of other castes than[6] *Jhinwar*, but the number of such will be exceedingly small. The numbers so included are given in the margin, *except for the* Amritsar division which made no separate returns[7].

Machhi and Men

Machhi is only the western name for the Musalman *Jhinwar.* In the Amritsar division those returning themselves as *Machhi* have been included under *Jhinwar*. In the Lahore and Rawalpindi divisions both names are used; and in the western districts both, where used at all, are applied indifferently to the same person. But in parts of the Central Panjab, where the eastern Hindu meets the Western Musalman, the two terms are generally used distinctively. The *Machhi* occupies in the centre and west the same position which the *Jhinwar* fills in the east, save that he performs in the former parts of the province a considerable part of the agricultural labour, while in the east he seldom actually works in the fields, or at least not as a part of his customary duties; though of course all classes work for pay at harvest time, when the rice is being planted out, and so forth. But besides the occupations already described for *Jhinwar*[8], the *Machhi* is the cook and midwife of the Punjab proper. All the *Dayas* and *Dayis*, the accoucheur, midwife, and wetnurse class, are of the *Jhinwar* or *Machhi* caste. So too the common oven which forms so important a feature in the village life of the Panjab proper, and at which the peasantry have their bread baked in the hot weather, is almost always in the hands of a Machhi for Musalmans and a Jhinwar for Hindus. In some parts he is also the wood-cutter of the village. In the Derajat he is sometimes called *Manjhi* or *Manjhera*, more particularly when following the occupation of a fisherman; and the name *Men* is often given him under the same circumstances in the rest of the Central and Western Panjab, along the banks of our great rivers. Both these castes, where returned separately, have been classed as Machhi, as have also the Sammi or fisherman and quailcatcher, and the *Mahigir, Machhahra, Machniyania,* or fisherman. The detail of the Mens in the Lahore *division*, are 7,035 and 3,095 in Gujranwala, while of those of the Multan division all but 180 are in Montgomery. Thus the Mens seem almost confined to the middle Satluj. On the lower Indus, in Gujarat and lower Sindh Machhi seems to mean nothing more than fisherman[9] , displays that many of the Machhis of the Derajat have been returned themselves as *Jats* in the areas.

Bhatyara and Bharbhunja

The *Bhatyara* is the baker and seller of ready-cooked food, who is to be found in all the caravanserais in towns and encamping grounds. It has been believed that almost without exception, a *Jhinwar* by caste; and in many districts those who have returned themselves as *Bhatyara* have been clased either as *Jhinwar* or as *Machhi,* so that our figures do not completely repreent the entires int he schedules. They are said to be divided in the North-West Provinces at any rate into two classes, *Shershahi*, *Salimshahi* the women of the former wearing petticoats and of the latter drawers. They date the division from time of Sultan Sher Shah and his son Salim Shah. Now that the railway his diminished their trade, the Bhatyaras are said to have taken to letting out *Yekkas* and ponies for hire;' and in the Derajat they are said to be the donkey-keepers of the district and to do petty carriage. This would connect them with the *Kiln* rather than with the oven. In any case the name appears to be purely an occupational guilds, the *Bhatyaras* appear in some parts to marry only among those following the same avocation[10]. The same may be said of the *Bharbhunja,* who is as his name implies a grain-parcher. He too is almost alwyas a Jhinwar, but a small section of the *Bharbhunjas* are *Kayaths*. He does not appear to occur as a separate class in the west of the province, where probably the grain parching is done at the public oven of the *Jhinwar* or *Machhi*. The *Bharbhunja* is also occasionally called *Bhojwa,* and on the *Indus Chatari*[11].

Mallah and Mohana

The *Mallah* is the boatman of the Panjab, and is naturally found in largest numbers in those districts which include the greatest lenght of navigable river. It appears that on the Indus he has often returned himself as a *Jat*. He is almost invariably a *Jhinwar* by cast, and very generally a Musalman by religion and in Sirsa most of the *Mallahs* on the Satluj are by caste *Jhabe*. He generally combines with special work of boat management some other of the ordinary occupations of his occupations of his caste, such as fighing or growing water-nuts; but he is not a village menial. Under the head Mallah have been included those returning themselves as *Mohana, Taru*, or *Dren*, the figures for which entries are given on the margin. In Lahore and Peshawar no separate, returns were made for *Mohana*. The *Mohana* is said to be the fisherman of Sindh; but in the Punjab he is at least as much a boatman as a fisherman. The word in Sanskrit means an estuary or confluence of waters. The *Dren* and *Taru* are found in the hills only, where they carry travellers across the rapid mountain torrents on inflated hides. The former are said to be Musalman and the latter Hindu. The word *dren* appears originally to mean the buffalo hide upon which the transit is made. In the Hill states 55, men returned as *Daryai* have also been included. Broadly speaking, it may perhaps be said that the *Jhinwar* and *Machhi* follow their avocations on land and the Mallah and *Mohana* on water, all belonging to the same caste[12]. In Kashmir, the menial servants (*Nangar*[13]) of the villages are carpenters, blacksmiths, potters, weavers, butchers, washermen, barbers, tailors, bakers, gold smiths carriers, oil pressers, dyers, mickmen, cotton-cleaners and snuff-makers. Many of the (Nangar) have taken to agriculture, and most of them are extremely independent of their so-called masters. The only class of menials who apparently cannot take to agriculture are the weavers[14]. They are mostly Musalman.

Dhinwar of the Jamna

Along the left bank of Jamna below Delhi are settled a certain small number of people who called themselves *Dhinwars*. They work as fishermen and boatmen and some of them as *Bharbhunjas*, and have returned themselves in the present census partly as *Jhinwars*, but mostly as *Mallahs*. They appear to have moved up the river from the neighbourhood of Agra, and to keep themselves distinct from the indigenous *Jhinwars*. They are much addicted to thieving, and it has been proposed to treat them as a criminal tribe. Violent crime is however rare among them. They cultivate and even own a certain area of land. They generally travel about in the disguise of musicians, singing, begging, pilfering, and committing burglary and theft on a large scale when opportunity offers. They apparetly extend all along the bankes of the river in Aligarh, Bulandshahr and other districts of the North-West Provinces. Men of this class seem to travel all over the Panjab, as they have been convicted even in the frontier districts. All Hindus drink at their hands. Nam has a sufficient proof that they are true *Thinwars* by caste[15]

Table 3. Water Carriers

	Figures				
	15	*28*	*92*	*108*	*42*
	Jhinwar	*Mucchi*	*Bhatyara*	*Bharbhunja*	*Mallah*
Delhi	14,487	1	519	1,223	740
Gurgaon	10,223	70	1,120	1,047	1,385
Karnal	31,200	—	405	1,257	1,277
Hissar	4,144	384	127	248	116
Rohtak	9,878	9	365	1,029	8
Sirsa	898	2,839	5	24	58
Ambala	47,104	31	648	1,102	1,009
Ludhiana	15,834	23	132	75	453
Simla	337	—	—	8	8
Jalandhar	24,717	996	—	64	1,212
Hushyarpur	22,168	224	—	20	1,899
Kangra	10,500	—	—	—	2,661
Amritsar	45,360	—	—	—	2,304
Gurdaspur	34,300	—	—	—	2,925
Sialkot	35,314	—	—	—	1,831
Lahore	20,941	24,747	103	172	2,398
Gujranwala	4,948	17,091	8	15	970

	Figures				
	15	*28*	*92*	*108*	*42*
	Jhinwar	*Mucchi*	*Bhatyara*	*Bharbhunja*	*Mallah*
Firozpur	9,945	13,935	—	93	1,209
Rawalpindi	82,632	120	—	—	994
Jahlam	3,413	6,129	—	18	2,145
Gujarat	5,131	14,942	—	—	549
Shahpur	187	11,156	—	—	1,278
Multan	303	9,610	1,964	32	6,011
Jhang	37	9,517	100	—	3,066
Montgomery	126	22,059	—	2	199
Muzaffargarh	19	3,250	2,354	—	7,976
Dera Ismail Khan	362	3,495	—	—	3,176
Dera Ghazi Khan	438	411	157	—	1,101
Bannu	339	2,029	—	—	1,546
Peshawar	3,956	104	—	—	1,024
Hazara	1,328	—	—	—	532
Kohat	1,080	49	—	—	59
British Territory	868,004	144,121	8,007	6,429	41,614
Patiala	36,477	413	403	291	120
Nabha	5,744	28	48	—	9
Kapurthala	7,769	2,712	—	52	1,751
Jind	4,633	13	27	152	55
Faridkot	849	1,431	—	—	52
Maler Kotla	1,658	16	—	—	—
Kalsia	2,997	129	1	163	1
Total East Plains	60,694	4,741	533	740	1,988
Bahawalpur	128	19,115	3,436	—	14,058
Nahan	1,806	—	—	15	47
Bilaspur	1,764	—	—	—	—
Total Hill Stakes	5,058	80	—	25	227
British Territory	368,044	144,121	8,007	6,429	61,614
Native States	65,880	23,886	8,969	765	16,321
Province	433,884	168,007	11,976	7,194	67,935

Boatmen and Cooks

	Proportion per 1,000 of Total Population					
	15	*28*	*92*	*108*	*42*	
	Jhinwar	*Mochhi*	*Bhatyara*	*Bharbhunja*	*Mallah*	*Total*
Delhi	22	—	1	2	1	26
Gurgaon	16	—	2	2	2	22
Karnal	50	—	1	2	2	55
Hissar	8	1	—	—	—	9
Rohtak	18	—	1	2	—	21
Sirsa	4	11	—	—	—	15

	Figures				
	15 Jhinwar	28 Mucchi	92 Bhatyara	108 Bharbhunja	42 Mallah
Ambala	44	—	1	1	2	47
Ludhiana	26	—	—	—	1	27
Simla	8	—	—	—	1	0
Jalandhar	31	1	—	—	2	34
Hushyarpur	35	1	—	—	2	28
Kangra	14	—	—	—	4	18
Amritsar	51	—	—	—	3	54
Gurdaspur	42	—	—	—	4	46
Sialkot	35	—	—	—	2	37
Lahore	23	27	—	—	3	53
Gujranwala	8	28	—	—	1	37
Firozpur	15	22	—	—	2	39
Rawalpindi	11	—	—	—	1	12
Jahlam	6	6	—	—	4	16
Gujarat	7	22	—	—	1	30
Shahpur	—	26	—	—	3	29
Multan	1	17	4	—	11	33
Jhang	—	24	—	—	8	32
Montgomery	—	52	—	—	—	52
Muzaffarpur	—	10	7	—	24	41
Dera Ismail Khan	1	8	—	—	7	18
Dera Ghazi Khan	1	1	—	—	3	5
Bannu	1	9	—	—	5	15
Peshawar	1	—	—	—	2	3
Hazara	3	—	—	—	1	4
Kohat	6	—	—	—	—	6
British Territory	19	8	—	—	3	30
Patiala	25	—	—	—	—	25
Nabha	22	—	—	—	7	22
Kapurthala	31	11	—	—	7	49
Jind	10	—	—	1	—	20
Faridkot	9	15	—	—	1	25
Maler Kotla	23	—	—	—	—	33
Kasia	44	2	—	2	—	48
Total East Plains	24	2	—	—	1	27
Bahawalpur	—	33	8	—	25	64
Nahan	18	—	—	—	—	16
Bilaspur	31	—	—	—	—	21
Total Hill States	7	—	—	—	—	7
British Territory	19	2	—	—	2	30
Native States	17	6	1	—	1	28
Province	18	8	1	—	3	31

Notes & References

1. *P.C.*, p. 303.
2. *Ibid.*, p. 306.
3. *Ibid.*, p. 325.
4. **Note.** *Mahar* seems to be a title of respect, just as a Bhishti is often addressed as Jamadar. Mahar is a synonym for 'chief' in the South-West of the Provinces. Word Jamadar denotes who serves the Yama or Yamai people.
5. P.C. p. 306.
6. *Ibid.*
7. **Note.** The sub-divisions of both *Jhinwar* and *Machhi* are very numerous. *See Table 2.* Part II. These tribes did not appear much among the *Bharbhunja* and *Bhatyara*.
8. **Note.** The carriage of burdens slung from a bangi or *jamadar* or yoke seems to be almost unknown in the west of the Panjab.
9. P.C., p. 307.
10. **Note.** It is noticeable that all those returned as Bhatyara are Musalman; probably because most Hindusi in the east of the Panjab at least, are not eat bread made and cooked by a Jhinwar.
11. P.C., p. 308.
12. *Ibid.*, pp. 308-09.
13. **Note.** Term *Nangar* reveals that they had not permanent house, they were homeless.
14. *P.G.J.K.*, p. 39.
15. P.C., p. 309.

9

Workers in Wood, Iron, Stone and Clay

This group is divided in to four sections, the workers in iron, in wood, in stone, and in clay. The workers in iron and wood are in many part of India identical, the two occupations being followed by the same individuals. In most pars of the Punjab they are sufficiently well distinguished so far as occupation is concerned, but certain seasons they are to believe has one and the same caste, and they very frequently intermarry. True workers in stone may be said hardly to exist in a province where stone is so scarce, called *Raj* who is both a *Mason* and a brick layer and is said generally to be a *Tarkhan* by caste, and they are connected with carpenter by the *Thavi* of the hills, who is both carpenter and stone-cutter or mason. The potters and brick makers are a sufficiently distinct class, who are numerous in the Punjab owing to the almost universal use of the Persian wheel with its numerous little earthen pots to raise water for purpose of irrigation. *See Table No. 4.* It is interesting to note that the seasonal migrants do not migrate to one city, town or State. Their destinations are mainly in the different towns and cities of Punjab, Haryana, Himachal Pradesh. Uttar Pradesh, Delhi, Rajasthan, Gujarat, and Maharashtra. But in the distribution of labour the distance decay model applies which means that most of the labourers try to stay in Jammu. Going away from Jammu most of them prefer to stay in Punjab and Haryana during the ancient period. This fact can be appreciated in *Table No.4*

The Lohar

The Lohar of the Punjab is as his name implies, a blacksmith pure and simple. He is one of the true village menials called *Sudhra*, receiving customary dues in the shape of a share of the produce, in return for which he makes and mends all the iron implements of agriculture, the materials being found by the husband man. He is most numerous in proportion to total population in the hills and the districts that lie immediately below them, where like all other artisan castes he is largely employed in fields labour. His figure is included, present in singularly small numbers in the Multan and Derajat divisions and in Bahawalpur. Probably men of other castes engaged in blacksmith work in those parts, or perhaps the carpenter and he is classed as an impure caste in so far that *Jats* and other of similar standing will have no social communion with him, though not as an ontcast like the[1] scavenger. His impurity, like that of the barber, washer man, and dyer, springs solely form the nature of his employment; perhaps because it is a dirty one, but more probably because black is a colour of evil omen, though on the other hand, iron has powerful virtue as a *Charm* against the evil eye. It is not impossible that the necessity under which he labours of using bellows made of cowhide may have something to do with his impurity. He appears to follow very generally the religion of the neighbourhood and some 34% of the *Lohars* are Hindus, about 8 % Sikh, and 58% Mussalman. Most of the men shown *Lohars see the table.*, etc. They have returned themselves as such, though some few were recorded as *Ahngar,* the Persian for black smith, and as *Nalband* or farrier. In the north of Sirsa, and probably in the central states of the eastern plains, The *Lohar* or blacksmith and the *Khati* or carpenter are undistinguished able, the same men doing both kinds of work; and in many, perhaps in most parts of the Punjab the two intermarry. In Hushyarpur, they are said to form a single cast called *Lohar-Tarkhan*, and the some of a blacksmith will often take a carpenter and vice versa; but it appears that the castes were originally separate, for the joint caste is still divided into two sections who will not intermarry or even eat or smoke together, the Dhaman, from Dhamna "to blow", and the *Khatti* form *Khat* "wood". In Gujranwala the same two sections exist, and they are the two great *Tarkhan* tribes[3]. The *Tarkhan*, better known as *Barhai* in the north-west provinces, *Barhi* in the Jamna districts, and *Kahati* in the rest of the eastern plains, is the carpenter of the province. Like the *Lohar* he is a true village menial, mending all agricultural implements and household furniture, and making them all except the cart, the Persian wheel, and the sugar-press, witout payment beyond his customary dues. It is believed that he is in all probability of the same caste with the *Lohar*; But his social position is distinctly superior till quite laterly *Jats* and the like would smoke with him though latterly they have begun to discontinue is both a carpenter and blacksmith, and is considered superior in status to the *Lohar* who is the latter only. *Tarkhan* is very generally distributed over the Province, though, like most occupational castes, he is less numerous on the lower frontier than elsewhere[4] as discussed in the table. In Karnal a sort of connection seems to be divided admitted, but the castes are now distinct. In Sirsa the *Lohars* may be divided into three main sections; the first men of undoubted and recent *Jat* and even Rajput origin who have generally by reason of poverty, taken to work as blacksmiths; secondly the *Suthar Lohar* or membzers of the *Suthar* tribe of carpenters who have similarly changed their original occupation; and thirdly, the *Gadiya Lohar,* a class of wandering blacksmiths not uncommon throughout the east and south-east of the province, who come up from Rajputana and the North-West Provinces and travel about with their families and implements in carts from village to village, doing the finer sorts of iron work which are beyond the capacity of the village artisan. The tradition runs that *Suthar Lohars* tribe[5] returned themselves as such are almost wholly in the Lahore and Rawalpindi divisions, and 4, 129 are in Gurdaspur and 1,701 in Gujrat. *Mujawir* is the hereditary guardian of a shrine. Of those returned as such 2,479 are in *Derah Ghazi*, and are very possibly the attendants of the celebrated shrine of *Sakhi Sarwar* at *Nigaha. Qazi* is the Mahomedan law-doctor who gives opinions on all religious and legal questions. But the descendants of a famous *Qazi* often retain in title, and there are several well known *Qazi* families. Of our *Qazis* 1, 725 are in Sialkot, 542 in Amritsar, and 241 in Gurdaspur. In Derah Ghazi the *Qazis* are said all to be Awans, and to call themselves *Ulama*. The *Mulla* or *'Maulvi* is a doctor of divinity who teaches the precepts of the faith. Mulwana or Mulana appear to be merely other forms of *Mulla*; all these people are returned from Derajat, Peshawar, and Multan divisions. *Makhdum* means the head of a shrine, generally a descendant of the saint who presides over the management; and the title used to be almost confined to the heads of the more celebrated shrines; but it is now used by those of smaller shrines also, and by any who claim descent from any saint. *Makhdumana* is another form of the same word, or perhaps rather denotes the descendants of a *Makhdum*. In the Derajat Mian means any saint or holy man or teacher, but is now often used by the descendants of such persons[6].

If a Rajput or Jat turn Mahomedan he retains his caste name, and is still a Rajput or *Jat* though certain Musalman Rajputs who had fallen in life and taken to weaving call themselves *Shekhs*, though still recognised as relations by their brethren of the village whence they came. *Shekh* is an Arabic word meaning an elder or chief, and probably corresponds very closely among the tribes of *Arabia* with *Chaudhri* among those of the Panjab. Thus the title should be confined to, and is very generally assumed by tribes of true *Arab* descent. But it has been degraded to a much more vulgar use. So if an outcast or man of impure calling becomes Musalman and retains his occupation, or at least substitutes for it another only slightly less degrading, he also retains his caste name or is known by an entirely new one, such as *Dindar* or *Musalli*. But the class which lie between these two extremes, and are neither so proud of their origin as to wish, nor so degraded by their occupation as to be compelled to retain their original caste name, very generally abandon that name on their conversion to Islam and adopt the title of Shekh[7]. There is a Persian proverb: "The first year I was a weaver (*Julaha*). The next year a *Shekh*. This year if prices rise I shall be a Saiyad." Moreover many of the inferior agricultural Musalman tribes of Indian descent have, especially in the west of the Province, set up a claim to Arab origin; and though they are still known by their tribal name, have probably or almost certainly returned themselves as *Shekh*. There are certain agricultural tribes whose claims to *Qureshi* origin appear to be valid, such as the *Khagga* and *Hans* of Montgomery a tribe in Schedule Caste. In many cases the titles here given are no less misleading than the original title of Shekh. The Shekhs who have themselves as *Jats* in the Multan and Derajat division are displayed in the study . Shekhs do not bear the best of characters in some parts. In Rohtak they are said to "Supply recruits to our armies and jails with praiseworthy indifference," and in Derah Ismail Khan the *Naumuslin Shekhs* are described as " a laze thriftless set of cultivators." The true *Qureshia* of the south-western districts, however, are often possessed of great influence and hold a high character for sanctity. Such are the descendants of *Baha-ul-haqq* the renowned saint of Multan, who are known as Hashmi Qureshis. They are chiefly found in the Multan, Jhang, and Muzaffargarh districts[8].

Tribes and Castes Under Sheikh and Qureshi

The *Qureshi* is the Arab tribe to which the Prophet belonged. Conquestly, it is favourite tribe from which to claim descent, and it is to be feared that comparatively few of these who have returned themselves as Qureshi have any real title to the name. among those who so styled themselves many claim to belong to the *Faruqis* or descendants of Umar the second Caliph or to the *Sadiqis* or descendats of Abul Bakar the first Caliph, both of whom were Qureshi by tribe.But the term Sadiqi is often confused with Sidqi, a little derived from the same root and meaning "the true". but which, in the east of the Panjab at any rate, is commonly used as an equivalent to *Naumslim* to distinguish converts of Indian descent from original Mahomeden immigrants. The Prophet himself says: "It shall be taken from the rich and distributed among the poor and the needy." He (peace be up on *Him* gives the following principle which is also followed by *Nizam-*

ul-Mulk in his theory of state. "The Government is the guardian (helper) of everyone who has no guardian."

Nau-muslim

Nau-muslim means nothing more than a new Musalman, and only 3, 491 of our *Shekhs* have, by returning themselves as *Shekh* Nau-msulim, admitted their true origin. These men are scattered in small numbers about the province, but 1,437 of them are in Bahawalpur.

Ansari

The faithful who accompanied Mahomet in his *Hajirah* or flight from Mecca where called *Muhajarin* or "the fugitives or emigrants," and their descendants still retain the title. In the Karnal district 8,560 persons have so returned themselves, and are doubtless the man of Panipat just alluded to [9]. In Karnal a sort of connection seems to be admitted, but the castes are now distinct. In Sirsa the zohars may be divided into three main sections; the first, men of undoubted and recent *Jat* and even *Rajput* origin who have generally by reason of poverty, taken to work as blacksmiths; secondly the *Suthar Lohar* or members of the *Suthar* tribe of carpenters who have similarly changed their original occupation; and thirdly, the *Gadiya Lohar*, a class of wandering blacksmiths not uncommon. Throughout the east and south-east of the province, who come up from Rajputana and the North-Western Provinces and travel about with their families and implements in carts from village to village, doing the finer sorts of iron work which are beyond the capacity of the village artisan. The tradition runs that the *Suthar Lohars*, who are now Musalman, were originally *Hindu Tarkhans* of the *Suthar* tribe[10].

Hans

They set long lines of these nooses in the grass across the jungles, from this line, they arrange two rows of scare crows consisting of bits of *rag* and the like tied on to the trees and grass; they then drive the jungle; and the frightened deer and other animals, keeping between the lines of scarecrows, cross the line of nooses in which their feet become entangled. In addition to hunting they make articles of grass and straw and reeds and sell hem to the villagers. The *Bawarias* are a vagrant tribe whose proper home appeas to be Mewar, Ajmer, and Jodhpur, in the Panjab they are chiefly found along the middle Satluj valley in Sirsa, Firozpur, Faridkot, Lahore and Patiala though they occure in smaller numbers in Hissar, Rohtak and Gurgaon, all on the Rajputana border. They are black in colour and of poor physique[11].

The *Hans* have return themselves as *Shekh* or *Qureshi* and not as *Hans*, since they claim Qureshi origin. They say they emigrated from Arabia to Afghanistan and thence to the Panjab, where they settled at *Pakka Sidhar* in the Montgomery district. In the time of Alamgir[12]. (Aurangzeb), when he entered the Panjab[13], the *Hans* tribe, under their chief *Shekh Qutab*, attained independence till the time of the Sikhs, when about the middle of the 18th century the streams which fertilized their country dried up and they lost their home; At present dried up and they lost their home; At present they do not own a single entire, and have preserved none of their former influence[14].

Khaggas

Khaggas are another tribe which have been classed as *Shekh*, but had better, have been kept separate. The numbers probably returned themselves as *Shekhs* or *Qureshi.* Mr. Purser thus describes them. "The *Khaggas* came to the Montgomery district after the conquest of Multan by Ranjit Singh of Panjab. They claim to be *Qureshi,* and name as the first *Khagga,* Jalal-ul-din, disciple of Muhammad Irak, *Khagga* is said to mean a peculiar kind of fish; and the name was given to Jalal-ul-din by his spiritual teacher on the *occasion* of his rescuing a boat over taken by a strom during the time of material world."

Nekokara

The *Kokara* or *Nekokara* who are chiefly found in the Jhang district, claim to be Hashmi Qureshis, who came from Bahalwalpur some 450 years ago. They hold land in Gujranwala also, but are not a very important tribe. In Gujranwala many of them are faqirs, and they generally bear a semi-religious character.

Jhandir

Jhandirs are also said to be of *Qureshi* origin, and though they do not openly profess to be religions directors, there is a certain odour of sanctity about the tribe. Most of them can read and write, and they are "particulalry free from ill deeds of every description." They own land in the extreme south of the Jhang district. They are said to have been the standard-bearers of one of the great saints, whence their name.

Sarai

The *Sarai* family are the descendants of the *Kalhora* Kings of Sindh who have settled at Hajipur in Derah Ghazi Khan. Some account of thier history will be found in Mr. Fryer's report on that district, and in Mr. O' Brien's Glossary. They were included with Sheikh in the divisional office. Tod makes the Sarai descendants or perhaps only namesakes, of *Sehl*, a *Kaurava* Rajput and in ancient times prince of Sindh and founder of Aror on the Indus. He says: "*Sehl or Sehr became a titular* "appellation of the country, its princes, and its inhabitants the *Sehrai*[15] of *Sudhra* family of this place."

Jat tribes *Deo* are practically confined to the Sialkot district. They claim a very ancient origin but not Rajput. Their ancestor's name is said to be *Mahaj*, who came from "the Saki jungle" in Hindustan, and two of his sons were *Aulakh* and *Deo* who gave their names to the *Jat Jagdeo*, a *Surajbansi Rajput*. They have the same marriage ceremony as the *Sahi*, and also use the goat's blood in a similar manner in honour of their ancestors, and have several very peculiar customs. They will not intermarry with *Man Jats*, with whom they have some ancestral connection[16].

Miana

Mian term is used in the west of the Panjab to denote any holy man and his descendants often styled themselves *Miana*. Thus the head of the of the *Sarai* family just described is known as the Mian *Sahib Sarai*. But in Hazara at least and probably in other parts of the frontier, any new convert to Mahomedanism is often called a Miana, and most of them are cultivators. There are 3,282 in the Rawalpindi and 188 in the Derajat division.

Inspite of the classes discussed above, they are described in the proper places. Of the Bodlas returned as Shekhs 144 are in Hissar, 749 in Sirsa, 339 in Firozpur, 349 in Montgomery, and 254 in Bahwalpur. Of the Daudpotras 1,287 are in Multan. Besides these, men returning themselves under the following names have been classed as Shekh: Shekhra, a contemptutous diminutive of Shekh; Pirzadah, or descendants of a piror Musalman spiritual guide; Shekhzadah, or son of a Shekh. They appear to have been only 383 of the first, 1906 of the second, and 17 of the third. In the Lahore division the Bharais have been most erroneously classed as Shekh, to the number of 1,444 in Lahore, 2,256 in Gujranwala, and 1,646 in Firozpur[17].

Turk

Turk in the Panjab means, probably invariably, a Turkoman native of Turkistan and of Mongolian race. In the Delhi territory indeed the villagers, accustomed to describe the Mughals of the empire as *Turks* or *Dums*, are the word as synonymous with "official", and Hindu clerks of Kayath caste described as Turks merely because they were in Government employ. On the Biloch frontier also the word Turk is commonly used as synonymous with Mughal. The Turks of the Panjab are practically confined to the Hazara district, and are doubtless the representatives of the colony of Karlagh Turks who came into the Panjab with *Tamarlane* (1399 A.D.) and possessed of their territory by *Swatis* and *Tanaolis* from across the Indus about the beginning of the 18th century; and the Turks now returned doubtless their descendants. The word Turk is a Tartar word meaning a "wanderer", thus is poetry the sun is called "the Turk of China," that is of the East, or "the Turk of the Sky." The Turks of Gurdaspur are said to be ropemakers by occupation[18] belonged to the *Sudhra* family degraded by Brahmins of the period.

Pathan

The *Pathan* tribes of Hazara mountains on this side of the Indus were from a very early period, inhabited by a mixed population of Indian origin, the *Gakkhars* occupying the portion to the south and having authority over the Rajputs of the eastern hills, while a *Gujar* population held most of the northern and central parts of the district. In 1399 A.D., a family of *Karlagh Turks* came into India with Taimur, settled in the Pakhli[19] plain in the north and centre of the district, and established their rule over the whole of the district, then known as the kingdom of Pakhli[20]. In the middle of the 16th century, the *Dilazak* were driven out of Peshawar across the Indus, and were presently followed by the representatives of the old Gandhari, the present inhabitants of *Swati* and *Buner* and the mountains north and east of Peshawer. As the Afghans who had possessed themselves of the trans-Indus tract opposite the Hazara district increased in numbers and extended their rule, successive bands of the old 17th century[21] a Saiyad named *Jalal Baba,* ancestor of the famous Saiyads of Kagan, came with a heterogeneous following from Swat, drove out the Karlagh, and appropriated the northern half of the district, including the valley of Kangar. About the same time the Tanaoli crossed the river and occupied the hill country between Abbottabad and the river, now known by their name as Tanawal. While the Jadun came over from their original seat between Peshawar and Hazara and possessed themselves of the tract south of Abbottabada, the Tarin drove out or subjected the Gujar families of the Hazara plain, and the Utmanzai, called across the Indus by the Gujars as allies, appropriated the Gandgarh tract along the bank of the river from Torbela to the boundary of the district. During the first 20 years of the 19th century the Durrani lost their hold on the district, something like anarchy prevailed, and the distribution of the tribes gradually assumed its present form. This may be broadly described as follows. Afghans hold the country between the Gandgarh range and the Indus, and the plains for some little distance south-east of the junction of the Siran and Dor. Tribes of Indian origin hold the whole south and south-east of the district and the easter hills as high up as Garhi Habibullah opposite Muzaffarabad, the *Gakkhars* holding the south of the tract along both banks of the Hero river, while above them the Dhunds, Karrals, and Sarrars occupy the hills in the south-eastern corner of the district, and the adjoining Haripur plains are held by a mixed population of Awans and Gujars[22]. in the hill terrain of Jammu and Kashmir. The remainder of the district, that is the northern and central portion, is held by tribes which, whatever their origin, have by long association become assimilated with the Pathans in language and customs, the *Jadun* holding the Dor valley from *Bagra* upwards to Mangal, the Tanaoli holding the Tanawal tract in the west centre of the district between Abbottabad and the Indus, much of which belongs to the semi-independent Nawab of Amb, while the Swatis hold the whole mountain country north of Mansahra and Garhi Habibulla[23].

Hazaras

Hazaras have returned themselves tribe. The *Hazaras* and the *Gandhari* were one of the four great divisions of the *Pactiyal* of *Herodotus*. The other three nations included under that name were the *Aparytoe* of Afridi[24], the Satragyddae or *Khatak,* and the Dadicae or Dadi, all alike of Indian origin. At the beginning of the Mahommedan area the Afridi held all the country of the Safed Koh, the Satragyddae held the Suleman range and the norther part of the plains between it and the Indus, while the Dadi held modern Sewestan and the country between the Kandahar Province and the Sulemans. These three nations constitute the nucleus of the Pathans proper. But around this nucleus have collected many tribes of foreign origin, such as the scythic Kakar, the Rajput wazir, and the many tribes of turk extraction included in the Karlanri section who come in with Sabukagin and Amir Timur[25]; and these foreigners have so encroached upon the original territories of the Pactyan nation that the *Khatak* and *Afridi* now hold but a small portion of the countries which they once occupied, while the *Dadi* have been practically absorbed by their *Kakar* invaders. The whole have now become blended into one nation by long association and intermarriage, the invaders have adopted the *Pakhto* language[26] . Frontier, these arose a group of mixed language out of Indian's contact with Persia, of intercourse between Iranians and the Indo-Aryans, form the time Achaemenian emperors of Presia. These languages are called *Pisacha* languages which contained many archaic Vedic words. Beyond the *Pisacha* languages and the outer Indio-Aryan Band on the west, are Iranian language like *Pashto* and *Baloch*[27]; and all alike have accepted Islam and have invented traditions of common desscent which express their present state of association. The Afridi were normally converted to Islam by Mohmud of Ghazni; but the real conversion of the Pathan tribes dates from the time of *Shahab-ul-din* Ghori when Araba postles with the title of Saiyad and Indian converts who were called Sheikh spread through the country, and settled among, married with, and converted the Pathans. The descondants of there holy men still preserve distinct tribal identity and as a rule claim Saiyad origin.

The *Ghilzai* are a race probably of Turkish origin, their name being another form of Khilchi. The Trukish word for "Swordsman", who early settled, perhaps as mercenarits rather than as a corporate tribe, in the Siah-band range of the Ghor mountains where they received a large admixture of Persian blood. The official spelling of the name is still Ghale ji at Kabul and Kandahar. They first rose into notice in the time of Mahmud Ghazani, whom they accompanied in his invasions of India. Not long afterwards the conquered the tract between Jalalabad and *Kelat-i-Ghilzai*[28], but in many districts, and especially on the middle Satluj, they have devoted themselves to husbandry and are skillful and laborious cultivators. The great majority of them are classed as Hindus, but about one-fifth are Musalman, and as many again Sikh. But the Musalman section, even in the Multan division, eat wild pig and retain most of their Hindu Customs, and are consequently not adimitted to religions equality by the other Musalman. They appear, however, to bury their dead. They live, in Muzaffargarh, in grass huts on the river banks, Hence the saying: *" Only two Mahatam huts, and calls itself Khair pur*[29], in the history of India."

In the beginning of the 18th century A.D., they revolted against their Persian rulers, established themselves under Mir Wais as in dependent rulers at Kandahar, and overran Persia. But a quarter of a century later they were reduced by Nadir Shah, and their rule disappeared, to be succeeded not long after by that of the Durrani. With the remaining races of the *Tajik* and *Hazara* which from part of the Pathan nation its widest sense, we have little concern in the Punjab. The former are remnants of the old Persian inhabitants of Afghanistan, and the word is now loosely used to express all Pathans who speak Persian and neither true Afghans, Siyads nor Hazaras. They are scattered through Afghanistan, Persia, and Turkistan, in which last they hold some hill fastnesses in independent sovereignty. The Hazaras are Tartar by origin, and are supposed to have occompained Chengiz Khan in his invasion. They occupy all the mountain country formed by the western extension of the Hindu Kush between Ghazni, Balkh, Hirat and Knadhar. They chiefly occupied Hazara, and are called Dilazak, Swati,Jodun, Tonaoli, and Shilmani[30], Akbar took 12,000 of them from Jodhpur to Delhi, forcibly circumcised them, and obliged them to work in iron instead of wood. The story is addimitted by a section of Lohars themselves and probably has some substratum of truth. These men come to Sirsa from the difrection of Sindhi, where they say they formerly held land, and the *Gadiya* lowest. Similar distinctions doubtless exist in other parts of the Punjab. *Dhaman* are also founded in Karnal and is neighborhood, where it is also a carpenter tribe[31].

Tarkhan

Tarkhan returned themselves as either *Barahi* or *Khatti*; and some 600 *Kharadis* or turners, who were pretty equally distributed over the province. In the Jammu districts the *Barahi* considers himself superior to his western brother the *Khati*, and will not intermarry with him; and that the married women of latter do not wear nose-rings while those of the former do. The *Tarkhan* of the hills is alluded to in the section on Hill Menials of caste *Sudhras*. The *Raj* or bricklayer is said to be very generally a *Tarkhan*. The tribes of Tarkhan are chiefly founded in Delhi and Hissar divisions, *Jhangra*, 9,518. In Karnal, Ambala and Jalandhar, they are known as *Dhaman*, found; 71,519, in Patiala, *Nabha*, Faridkot and Firozpur division, they are called *Khatti* to be found 19, 071; *Siawan* in Jalandhar *Sialkot are found* 1,932, 2,209, *Gade* are located in Amritsar; 6,971 *Matharu* are to be discovered in Ludhiana, Amritsar, and Lahore; *Netal* 2,764 are found in Hushyarpur; *Janjua* are to be found in Rawalpindi division; in Sailkot & Gurdaspur, *Tharu* are *2,822,* 27,534, *Khokhar* are to be found in Lohare and Rawalpindi; *Bhatti*; 18.837 are existed in Multan division; and in Hazara, *Begi Khel* are known 2,212. The carpenters of Sirsa are divided in two great sections; the *Dhaman* and the *Khati* proper, and the two will not intermarry. These are also two great tribes of the *Lohars*. The *Dhamans* again include a tribe of Hindu *Tarkhans* called *Suthar,* who are almost entirely agricultural, seldom working in wood, and who look down upon the artisan sections of the their caste. They say that they came from Jadhpur, and that their tribe still holds willages and revenue-free grants in Bikaner. These man say that the Musalman Multani Lohars described above, originally belonged to their tribe; the *Suthar Tarkhans,* though Hindus, are in fact more closely allied with the Multani lohars than with the *Khatis*, and many of their clan sub-divisions are identical with those of the former; and some of the *Lohars* who have immigrated from Sindh admit the community of caste. *Suther* is in Sindh the common term for any carpenter. It is curious that the Barhis of Karnal are also divided into two great sections, Dese and Multani. The Sikh *Tarkhans* on the Patiala border of Sirsa claim *Bagri* origin, work in iron as well as in wood, and intermarry with the Lohars[32].

Kamangar

Kamangar, or as he generally called in the Panjab *Kamgar*, is as his name implies a bow-maker; and with him, *Tirgar* or arrow-maker joined with the *Pharera* which appears to be merely a hill name for the *Rangsaz*. There men are found chiefly in the large towns and cantonments, and except in Kangra, appear to be always Musalman. Now that bows and arrows are no longer used save for purposes of presentation, the *Kamangar* has taken to wood decorating. Any colour or lacquer that can be put on in a lathe is generally applied by the Kharadi; but flat or uneven surfaces are decorated either by *Kamangar* or by the *Rangsaz*; and of two the *Kamangar* does the finers sorts of work. Of course rought work, such as painting doors and window-frames, is done by the ordinary *Mistri* who works in wood, and who is generally if not always a *Tarkhan*. *Kamangar* on the basis of his profession, he stands far above the *Tarkhan;* and also above the *Rangsaz*[33].

Siqligar

The word *Siqligar* is the name of a pure occupation, and denotes an armourer or burnisher of metal. They are shown chiefly for the large towns and contonments; but many of them probably returned themselves as *Lohars*.

Dhogri

These are the iron miners and smelters of the hills, an outcast and impure people, whose name is perhaps derived from *dhonkni,* "bellows", and it is possible that their name is rather *Dhonkri* than *Dhogri*. Their status is much the same as that of the *Chamar* or *Dumna*. They are returned only in Kangra and *Chamba*.

Thavi

The *thavi* is the carpenter and stone-mason of the hills just as the *Raj* of the plains, who is a bricklayer by occupation, is said to be generally a *Tarkhan* by caste. His principal occupation is building the village houses, which are in those parts made of stone; and he also does what wood work is required for them. He thus forms the connecting link between the worker in wood and *Tarkhans*, on the other hand, and the bricklayers and masons or *Rajs* on the other. Most of the *Thavis* are under the head of *Tarkhan,* so that they are only shown separately for the hill states and indeed many of the hill states themselves have evindently followed the same course. In Gurdaspur 1,722 and in Sialkot 1,063. *Thavis* are thus included under *Tarkhan*. The *Thavi* is always a Hindu, and ranks in social standing far above the *Dagi* or outcast menial, but somewhat below the Kamet or inferior cultivating caste of the hills. *Sardar Guldial Singh* gives the following information taken down from a Thavi of Hushiarpur: "An old man said he and his people were of a Brahman family, but had taken to stone-cutting and so had became Thavis, since the Brahmans would no longer intermarry with them. That the *Thavis* include men who are Brahmans, Rajputs, Kands and the like by birth, all of whom intermarried freely and thus formed a real *Thavi* caste, quite distinct from those who merely followed the occupation of *Thavi* but retained their original caste." The *Thavi* of the hills will not eat or intermarry with the *Barhai* or *Kharadi* of the neighbourhood.

Raj

Raj is the title given by the guilds of bricklayers and masons of the towns to their headmen, and is consequently often used to denote all who follow those occupations. *Mimar* is the corresponding Persian word, included all who so returned themselves under the head of *Raj*. The word is probably the name of an occupation rather than a true caste, the real caste of these men being said to be almost always *Tarkhan*. The Raj is returned only for the eastern and central districts, and seems to be generally *Musalman* save in Delhi, Gurgon nd Kangra. Under Raj, *Batahra,* of whom 66 are returned from the Jalandhar and 20 from the Amritsar division. In Kulu, however, the *Batahra* is said to be Koli by caste who has taken to state quarrying.

Khumra

Khumra is a caste of Hindustan, and is found only in the eastern parts of the Panjab. His trade is dealing in and chipping the stones of the hand-mills used in each family to grind flour; work is generally done by *Tarkhans* in the Panjab proper. Every year these men may be seen travelling up the Grand Trunk Road, driving buffaloes which drag behind the mile stones loosely cemented together for convenience of carriage. The millstones are brought from the neighbourhood of Agra, and the men deal in a small way in *buffaloes*. They are almost all Musalman.

Kumhar

Kumhar, or, as he is more often called in Panjab, *Gumiar,* is the potter and brick-burner of the country. He is almost numerous of Hissar and Sirsa where he is often a husbandman, and in the sub-montane and Central districts. On the lower Indus he has returned himself in some number as *Jats* already mentioned in Table. He is a true village menial, receiving customary dues, in exchange for which he supplies all earthan vessels needed for household use, and the earthenware pots used on the Persian wheel wherever that form of well gear is an vogue. He also, alone of all Panjab castes, keeps donkeys; and it is his business to carry grain within the village area, and to bring to the village grain bought elsewhere by his clients for seed or food. But he will not carry grain out of the village without payment. He is the petty carrier of the villages and towns, in which latter he is employed to carry dust, manure, fuel, brick, and the like. This religion appears to follow that of the neighbourhood in which he lives. His social standing is very low, for below that of a *Lohar* and not very much above. That of a *Chamar;* for his hereditary association with that impure beast the donkey, the animal sacred to Sitala the small-pox goddess, pollutes him; as also his readiness to carry manure and sweepings. He is also the brick-burner of the Panjab, as he alone understands the working of kilns; and it is in the burning of pots and bricks that he comes into contact with manure, which he constitutes his feel. He makes bricks also when they are moulded ; but the ordinary village brick of sun-dried earth is generally made by the *coolie* or *Chamar.* The *Kumhar* is called *Pazawagar* or Kiln-burner, and *Kuzagar* or *Kujgar* or potter, the latter term being generally used for those only who make the finer sorts of pottery. On the frontier he appears to be known as *Gilgo*. The divisions of *Kumhars* are very numerous, and as a rule not very large. *Gola* 20,059 are found in Delhi, 12,649 *Mahar,* are located in Hissar, *Dol* 6,771 in Amritsar and Lohare; *Dhodi,* 3,786 are found in Lohare, Rawalpini and Multan divisionss. In Peshawar more than two-thirds of the *Kumhars* have returned themselves as *Hindki*. The *Mahar* and *Gola* do not intermarry. The *Kumhara* of Sirsa are divided into two great sections, Jodhpuria who came from Jodhpur, use furnaces or *bhatt is,* and are generally mere potters; and the *Bikaneri* or *Dese* who came from Bikaner and use *pajawas* or Kilns, but are chiefly agricultural, looking down upon the potters occupation a degrading. The *Kumhars* of those parts are hardly to be distinguished from the *Bagri Jats*[35]. The *Chamar*, the *Jhinwar*, and the artisans appear to be toteraly distinct, and have already been described with the groups under which they fall the two sections of the caste appear to be closely connected with the *'Nam'*. The extended use of metals and minerals gave rise a variety of handicrafts not in ancient India but also in Modern India. There were known gold (*hiranya*) *silver (rajata),* bronze (*ayas*), copper (*Lohita ayas* or *Lohayas*), iron (*Syama ayas*), lead (*Sisa*) and tin (trapu) (*Vajasaneyi Samhita, XVII.13*). *Gold* was derived from the beds of rivers like *Indus* (R.V.X. 75.8), or extracted from the earth (AV. XII.1.6,26.44) or from one by smelting (*Sata*. Br. VI.1,3,5) or from washings (Ib.II.1,1,5). Gold was used to make ornaments for neck and breast (*nishka*), ears (*Karna-sobhana*), and to make cups (Ib.V.1.2.19;5,28)[36].

In the study, we learn the following functions were assigned to the *Sudras* in ancient time and today they are also busy with their own work:

1. Practice of purity of thought, truthfulness and humility.
2. Bath without reciting the *achamana-mantra* prescribed for the higher castes.
3. *Sraddhakarma* (performance of funeral rites for which they are eligible)
4. *Bhritya-bharanam* (support of dependents as a duty not prescribed for slaves)
5. *Svadara Vritti,* (Continence)
6. Menial service (*paricharya*) on wages (*Vritti*)

Table 4. Workers in Wood, Iron

	Figures								
	22 *Lohar*	157 *Siqligar*	153 *Dhogri*	11 *Tarkhan*	132 *Kamangar*	149 *Thavi*	93 *Raj*	171 *Khumra*	12 *Kumhar*
Delhi	5,934	4	—	9,622	107	—	389	131	13,724
Gurgaon	5,503	1	—	10,655	—	—	64	114	14,261
Karnal	9,190	12	—	13,787	208	—	583	55	14,712
Hissar	5,682	31	—	12,627	16	—	310	2	19,662
Rohtak	7,447	7	—	10,821	71	—	294	159	12,031
Sirsa	1,652	1	—	7,222	—	—	126	—	16,114
Ambala	16,550	157	—	25,265	30	—	917	449	15,598
Ludhiana	8,520	47	2	18,809	12	—	129	—	15,598
Simla	715	—	—	1,042	—	—	3	—	173
Jalandhar	13,396	17	—	26,232	5	—	533	—	12,904
Hushyarpur	15,033	12	—	28,033	15	—	1,146	—	10,661
Kangra	15,655	34	1,412	16,286	265	—	527	—	7,897
Amritsar	18,778	1	—	34,984	61	—	717	—	29,175
Gurdaspur	16,601	—	—	29,621	11	—	675	—	17,039
Sialkot	18,581	—	—	41,781	—	—	817	—	29,713
Lahore	13,767	144	—	31,009	239	—	876	—	31,524
Gujranwala	12,364	12	—	26,872	58	—	334	—	26,931
Firozpur	7,097	84	—	21,424	39	—	134	—	15,254
Rawalpindi	12,236	165	—	22,450	290	—	—	—	14,668
Jahlam	9,970	23	—	14,924	42	—	1	—	10,031
Gujarat	12,934	66	—	21,828	33	—	260	—	16,401
Shahpur	5,074	49	—	10,270	131	—	—	—	11,769
Multan	2,768	—	—	11,915	441	—	—	—	13,716
Jhang	3,063	—	—	8,418	173	—	49	—	15,381
Montgomery	3,673	—	—	9,499	158	—	4	—	17,865
Muzaffargarh	1,477	—	—	8,024	165	—	—	—	6,829
Derah Ismail Khan	1,288	—	—	3,93	9	—	—	—	13,716
Derah Ghazi Khan	220	—	—	782	11	—	3	—	106
Bannu	4,754	—	—	5,574	101	—	—	—	4,303
Peshawar	6,521	144	—	12,504	49	—	81	—	7,583
Hazara	5,899	48	—	8,271	178	—	—	—	3,687
Kohat	2,374	81	—	3,615	12	—	15	—	1,186
British Territory	264,720	1,140	1,414	508,008	2,930	—	9,080	910	421,588
Patiala	17,788	155	—	41,454	132	9	1,202	94	27,464
Nabha	2,858	12	—	9,208	1	—	57	—	5,002
Kapurthala	4,106	2	—	7,715	6	—	471	—	4,797
Jind	3,634	64	—	5,358	32	—	138	—	5,333
Faridkot	1,180	—	—	3,944	—	—	8	—	1,636
Maler Kotla	1,325	—	—	1,929	—	—	109	—	1,154
Kalsia	1,177	16	—	1,683	—	—	177	—	1,014

	Figures								
	22 Lohar	*157 Siqligar*	*153 Dhogri*	*11 Tarkhan*	*132 Kamangar*	*149 Thavi*	*93 Raj*	*171 Khumra*	*12 Kumhar*
Total East, Plains	32,327	258	—	72,468	172	9	2,162	94	47,771
Bahawalpur	2,833	21	—	9,996	56	—	—	—	10,883
Mandi	1,632	—	—	270	—	610	—	—	1,508
Chamba	1,537	—	302	1,570	—	—	—	—	1,540
Nahan	1,707	—	—	1,336	—	—	1	—	278
Bilaspur	1,914	35	—	238	—	178	—	—	844
Bashahr	916	—	—	1,166	—	—	—	—	63
Nalagarh	773	10	—	527	—	123	—	—	457
Suket	1,201	—	—	56	—	781	—	—	313
Total Hill States	11,902	64	302	6,459	—	1,895	48	—	5,873
British Territory	264,720	1,140	1,414	508,008	2,930	—	9,080	910	421,533
Native States	47,062	343	302	88,933	228	1,904	2,210	94	64,437
Province	311,782	1,483	1,716	596,941	3,158	1,904	11,290	1,004	486,025

Stone and Clay

	Proportion Per 1,000 or Total Population										
	22 Lohar	*153 Dhogri*	*Total*	*11 Tarkhan*	*132 Kamangar*	*Total*	*149 Thavi*	*93 Baj*	*Total*	*13 Kaumhar*	*Grand Total*
Delhi	10	—	10	15	—	15	—	1	1	21	47
Gurgaon	9	—	9	16	—	16	—	—	—	22	47
Karnal	15	—	15	22	—	22	—	1	1	24	63
Hissar	11	—	11	25	—	25	—	1	1	30	76
Rohtak	13	—	13	20	—	20	—	—	—	64	99
Sirsa	6	—	6	29	—	29	—	—	—	64	90
Ambala	15	—	15	24	—	24	—	1	1	15	55
Ludhiana	14	—	14	30	—	30	—	—	—	13	57
Simla	17	—	17	24	—	24	—	—	—	4	45
Jalandhar	17	—	17	33	—	33	—	1	1	16	67
Hushyarpur	17	—	17	31	—	31	—	1	1	12	61
Kangra	21	2	23	22	—	22	—	1	1	14	60
Amritsar	21	—	21	39	—	39	—	1	1	33	94
Gurdaspur	20	—	20	36	—	36	—	1	1	21	78
Sialkot	18	—	18	41	—	41	—	1	1	29	89
Rawalpindi	15	—	15	27	—	27	—	—	—	18	60
Jahlam	17	—	17	25	—	25	—	—	—	17	59
Gujrat	19	—	19	32	—	32	—	—	—	24	75
Shahpur	12	—	12	24	—	24	—	—	—	28	64
Multan	5	—	5	23	1	23	—	—	—	25	53
Jhang	8	—	8	31	—	21	—	—	—	39	68
Montgomery	9	—	9	22	—	23	—	—	—	42	51
Muzaffargarh	7	—	7	24	—	24	—	—	—	20	73

	Proportion Per 1,000 or Total Population										
	22	*153*		*11*	*132*		*149*	*93*		*13*	
	Lohar	*Dhogri*	*Total*	*Tarkhan*	*Kamangar*	*Total*	*Thavi*	*Baj*	*Total*	*Kaumhar*	*Grand Total*
Derah Ismail Khan	3	—	3	9	—	9	—	—	—	6	18
Derah Ghazi Khan	1	—	1	2	—	2	—	—	—	—	3
Bannu	14	—	14	17	—	17	—	—	—	13	44
Peshawar	11	—	11	21	—	21	—	—	—	13	45
Hazara	14	—	14	20	—	20	—	—	—	9	43
Kohat	13	—	13	20	—	20	—	—	—	7	40
British Territory	14	—	14	27	—	27	—	—	—	22	63
Patiala	12	—	12	28	—	28	—	1	1	19	60
Nabha	11	—	11	35	—	35	—	—	—	19	65
Kapurthala	16	—	16	30	—	30	—	2	2	19	67
Jind	15	—	15	22	—	22	—	1	1	21	59
Faridkot	12	—	12	41	—	41	—	—	—	17	70
Maler Kotla	19	—	19	27	—	27	—	2	2	16	64
Kalsia	17	—	17	25	—	25	—	3	3	15	60
Total East Plains	13	—	13	29	—	29	—	1	1	19	62
Bahawalpur	5	—	5	17	—	17	—	—	—	19	41
Mandi	11	—	11	2	—	2	4	—	4	10	27
Chamba	13	3	16	14	—	14	—	—	—	13	43
Nahan	15	—	15	12	—	12	—	—	—	2	29
Bilaspur	22	—	22	3	—	3	1	—	1	10	36
Bashahr	14	—	14	18	—	18	—	—	—	1	33
Nalagarh	14	—	14	10	—	10	2	—	2	8	34
Suket	23	—	23	1	—	1	13	—	15	6	45
Total Hill States	16	—	16	8	—	8	2	—	2	8	34
British Territory	14	—	14	27	—	27	—	—	—	22	62
Native States	12	—	12	23	—	23	—	1	1	17	53
Province	14	—	14	26	—	26	—	—	—	21	61

Notes & References

1. *P. C.*, p. 309.
2. **Note**. Colebroke says that the *Karmakara* or blacksmith is classed in the *Puranas* as one of the polluted tribes.
3. P. C. p. 312.
4. *Ibid.*, p. 313.
5. *Ibid.*, p. 312.
6. *Ibid.*, p. 224.
7. *Ibid.*, p. 206.
8. *Ibid.*, p. 208.
9. *Ibid.*
10. *Ibid.*, p. 312.
11. *Ibid.*, p. 276.
12. *Ibid.*, p. 209.
13. H.P. H.S. p. 687.
14. P. C. p. 209.
15. *Ibid.*, p. 210.
16. *Ibid.*, p. 115.
17. *Ibid.*, p. 210.
18. *Ibid.*, p. 211.
19. *Ibid.*, p. 92.
20. **Note.** Major Wace says they were a clan of the *Hazara Turks*. But the Turks who gave their name to the district are supposed to have come with Changinz Khan and not with Timur. Perhaps they were the samemen, and have confused the two invaders in their traditions.
21. **Note.** This is the date, has been given approximately by Major Wace. It should perhaps be put a century earlier than that of Changinz Khan.
22. P. C., p. 92.
23. **Note.** The *Utmanzai* have been already fully described in the discussion of the Peshawar tribes. The *Tarkhell* is one of the principal *Utmanzai* clans in Hazara, and occupies the Gandgarh country. A few *Tarin* Afghans, first cousins of the *Abdali*, wrested a considerable portion of the Haripur plains from the *Gujars* early in the 18th century, and still live there, but are now few and unimportant. The *Mishwani* are descended from a Saiyat father by a *Kakar* woman, and are allied to the *Kakar Pathans*. A small number of them came across the Indus with the *Utmanzai*, to whom they were attached as retainers, and now occupy the north-eastern end of the Gandgarh range, about Srikot with the Utmanzai came also a few *Panni*, a *Kakar* sect, who are still settled among them in these areas.
24. **Note.** The *Afridi* still call themselves Aparide. There is n f in *Pashto* proper.
25. **Note.** The various accounts given of *Karlan's* origin all recognize the fact that he was not a Pathan by birth, and even the affiliation of the *Karlanri* is doubtful, some classing them as *Sarbani* and not *Ghurghusti*.
26. P. C., p. 63.
27. R.K. Mookerji; A.I., p. 13.
28. P. C., pp. 63-64.
29. **Note.** Mr. Purser thus describes the Mahatams of Montgomery :- "They are a low caste Hindu, and are looken down on by their neighbour. Their story is that they were Rajputs, and one of their ancestors was a *Kanungo*. Akbar was then on the throne. *Kanungo* were called *Mahata,* and thus they got their name. The first *mahata* was dismissed, and then settled at Mahatpur in Jalandhar. His descendants emigrated and settled along the banks of the rivers as they found quantities of *Sarr* in such situations, and working in *sarr* was their chief occupation.It was not till the *Nakkai* chiefs held way that they settled down permanently in this district. They adopted the custom of marriage with widows according to the form of *Chaddar dalan,* and so became *Sudras.* They are also called *'Bahrupias'* which name is a corruption of *'Bha-rup-ias'*, and means people of many modes of life because they turned their hands to any business; they could find (yet of *select glossary,* 1, 17 & 54). Cunningham (*History of the Sikhs,* p. 17) says, "the hardworking Hindu Mahatams are still moving family by family and village by village eastward away from the Ravi and Chanab." This would seen to give the *Mahatams* a western instead of eastern origin as claimed by them. They own a good many village (19), most of which are in good condition. Where they are not proprietors of the whole village, the reside in a seperaate group of huts at some distance from the main *abadi*. They are great hands at catching wild pigs, but it is in cutting down the jungle on inundated lands they excel. Though industrious they do not care much for working wells, and prefer cultivating lands flooded by the rivers. They are querrelsome and addicted to petty thieving. They are of medium stature and stoutly made. (P. C.p. 203).
30. P. C., p. 64.
31. **Note.** The *Lohar* of the hills describes by Mr. Lyall, the constitution and functions of the menial class in Kulu. So also *Chamars* and *Lohars*, though they have been classed separately, are probably only *Dagis* who took to those trades; but at the present day other Dagis will not eat with the Lohars and in some parts they will not eat or intermarry with the *Chamars*. Most *Dagis* will eat the flesh of bears, leopards, or *langus* monkeys. All except the Lohars eat the flesh of cattle who have died a natural death. They stand in a subordinate position to the Kanets, though they

do not hold their land of them. Certain families of *Dagis, Chamars* and Lohars are said to be the *Korldar Dagis* that is the 'courtyard people' or certain Kanet families. When a Kanet dies his heirs call the *Korldar Dagis* through their *jatai* or headman; they bring in fuel for the funeral pile and funeral feast, wood for torches, play the pipes and drums in the funeral procession, and do other services, in return for which they get food and the *Kiria* or funeral perquisites. The dead bodies of cattle are another perquisites of the *Dagis,* but they share them with the *Chamars*, the latter take the skin and all divide the flesh. The Dagis carry *palanquins* when used at marriages. The *Lohars* and *Chamars* also do work in iron and leather for the Kanets, and are paid by certain grain allowances. The dress of the *Dagis* does not differe materially from that of the Kanets, except in being generally coarser in material and scantler in shape. Their made of life is also much the same". (P. C. p. 332).

32. P. C., pp. 313-314.

33. *Ibid.*, p. 314.

34. Mr. Anderson gives a brief report on any section of Kulu society which are living in the lower stratum of society concerning certain specified castes:-

"I have said that a Kanet will smoke with a *Nath* and with a *Nai*, but in Kulu no good inference can be drawn from the fact that the *hukka* is common. I believe that not many years ago all castes would have smoked from one pipe. It is still not a matter of much importance, and under ordinary circumstances, a Kanet will smoke with a *Thawi,* a *Nath* or a *Nai*, though he might probably, if taxed with doing so, deny it. He would not eat with them. In some places as in Monali Kothi, Kanets smoke with *Dagis*, but this is not common in Kulu, though the exclusiveness has arisen only within the last few years, as caste distinctions became gradually more defined.

"Then as to the identity of *Dagi* and *Chanal*. In Kulu proper there are no *Chanals*, that is, there are none who on being asked to what caste they belong will answer that they are *Chanals*: but they will describe themselves as *Dagi Chanals* or *Koli Chanals*, and men of the same families as these *Dagi Chanals* or *Koli Chanals* will as often merely describe themselves as *Dagis* or *Kolis*. In Kulu *Dagi, Koli,* and *Chanal* mean very nearly the same thing, but the word *Koli* is more common in *Seoraj* and *Chanal* is scarcely used at all in Kulu; but Chanals are, I believe, numerous in Mandi, and in the Kangra valley. *A Dagi* who had been out of the Kulu valley told me he would call himself a *Dagi* in *Kulu,* a *Chanal* in Kangra and a *Koli* in plach or *Seoraj*, otherwise these local castes would not admit him or eat with him. Again and again the same man has called himself a *Dagi* and also a *Koli*. If a Kanet wishes to be respectful to one of this low caste he will call him a *Koli*, if angry with him a Dagi. A *Channal* of Mandi Territory will not intermarry with a Kulu *Dagi*.

"The popular explanation of the word *Dagi* is that it is derived from *dag* cattle, because they drag away the carcases of dead cattle and also eat the flesh. If a man says he is a *Koli*, then a Kanet turns round on him and asks him whether he does not drag carcasses; and on his saying he does the Kanet alleges he is a *Dagi*, and the would-be *Koli* consents. There are very few in Kulu proper that abstain from touching the dead. There are more in Seoraj, but they admit they are called either *Dagis* or *Kolis,* and that whether they obtain from touching carcasses or not, all eat, drink and intermary on equal terms. It is a mere piece of affection for a man who does not touch the dead to say he will not intermarry with the family of a man who is not so fastidious. This is a social distinction and probably also indicates more or less the wealth of the individual who will not touch the dead.

From the natural evolution of caste distinction in this direction, I would reason that once all the lower castes in Kulu ate the flesh of cattle, but as Hindu ideas got a firmer footing, the better off refrained and applied to themselves the name of *Koli*. Popular tradition seems however to go in the opposite direction, for according to it the Kolis came from Hindustan and gradually fell to their present low position. The real Koli, or as he is called in Kulu the *Sachcha Koli,* is found in Kotlehr, Lambagraon & c., of Kangra proper. There the caste is also very low, but tradition ascribes to it a much higher position than it now holds. The *Kolis* of Kangra will not have intercourse with the *Kolis* of Kulu on equal terms; the latter admit their inferiority and ascribe it to their being defiled by touching flesh. But it is the same with Brahmans of the plains and of the hills; they will not intermarry.

"I am not aware what position the *Kolis* of Kangra hold to the *Chanals* of Kangra, but I believe they are considered inferior to them, and that they will not eat together nor intermarry. The *Chanals* of Kangra will not, I understand, touch dead cattle, and will not mix on equal terms with those that do. There are some *Chanals* in outer Seoraj who are considered inferior to the *Kolis* there."

A *Chamar* in Seoraj will call himself a *Dagi*, and men calling themselves *Kolis* said they would eat and drink with him. They said he was a *Chamar* merely because he made shoes, or worked in leather. Most Dagi in Kulu proper will not eat with *Chamars,* but in some places they will. It depends on what has been the custom of the families.

The Kolis of Nirmand keep themselves separate from the *Dagis* in that direction, that is from those that touch dead cattle. The reason is that they are more or less under the influence of the Brahmins who form a large part of the population of that village. These *Kolis* of Nirmand will however intermarry with a family of *Kolis* that lives at a distance in Inner Seoraj. This latter family has for some generation taken to turning in wood and its members are called Kharadis as well as Kolis. They do not touch carcasses, probably because they have a profession of their own and are richer; but they call themselves Kolia or *Dagis* and intermarry on equal terms with the *Kolis* round them. The illustrates the unsettled state of these low caste and also the gradual advance of Hindu ideas.

In Kulu there is not much difference between the *Koli,* the *Dagi* and the *Chanal,* but they are not admitted to be the same as the Kolis and *Chanals* of Kangra.

In Kulu Bateras are merely *Kolis*, that is *Dagls*, who take out slates. They have taken to this trade, but are really Kolls. They are found only in *Plaeh* and hence are called *Kolis*, which name is more common there than that of *Dagi*. So *Barhais* are *Kolis* or *Dagis* that use the axe. *Dagis* and *Barhais* are the same in Kulu, but not in Kangra proper. A *Tarkhan* of the plains would shudder to associate with the *Barhai* of *Kulu*, who does not scruple to eat the flesh of dead animals. *Kharadis* are kolis of Seoraj that turn wood, and mix with *Kolls* and *Dagis* on equal terms. They are considered rather more respectable than the common Kolis or Dagis as they will not touch the dead. In Kulu *Barhal* or *Badhi* and *Kharadi* are names applied to different trade, not to different castes. The position of *Lohars* and *Chamars* is described in paragraph 118 of the Settlement Report (quoted below). *Barars* are *Kolls* that works in the *nargdhu* or hill bamboo. They were once probably all of one caste and have merely got the names of the professions they follow; but *Lohara* and *Chamars* searesly be called *Dagis*.

"But *Thavis* cannot be classed with *Kolls* and *Dagis*. They occupy a much higher position. They are just below the Kanets, who will smoke with them, but not eat with them. They work both in wood and in stone, as the style of building in Kulu requires that they should do so. It is only their trade that connects them with *Barhals* or *Kharadls*, with whom they will not eat nor intermary." (P. C.pp 331-32)

36. A.I., p. 75.
37. *Ibid.,* pp. 93-94.
38. *Ibid.,* p. 122.
39. *Ibid.,* p. 123.
40. *Ibid.*
41. *Ibid.*

10
Workers in Other Metals and Minerals

Workers in other metals and minerals are divisible in to four classes, the *Sunar*, the *Nyaria;* the *Doali* who work in the precious metal, the *thathera* who work in brass, bell metal and the like, the *Agari*, *Nungar*, and *shorages* who make salt and saltpeter, and the *Churigar* or glass blower and bracelet-maker. The workers in precious metals are found all over the province through they are less numerous among. The rustic and comparatively poor poputation of the western plains and most numerous in those districts which include the great cities and in the rich central districts[1]. The goldsmith, known in north Indian as *Sunar*, or one who makes things of gold is a respected member of the community and is one of the essential units of the village community from the time immorial. There is a caste of *Sunars*, but the people of the other castes also take to the craft since it is considered and honourable profession and may be prastised with out losing the dignity of ones own caste [2]. The salt- workes are naturally almost confined to the eastern and south-eastern protions of the province and to the great grazing plains covered with soda salts, and the plentiful growth of the *barilla* plant afford them the means of carrying on their occupation. The salt of the salt-range is quarried ready for use, indeed in a state of quite singular purity, and the work of quarrying and carrying is performed by ordinary labourers and does not appertain to any special caste are calling [3] *Sudhras,* but they came under the category of Brahmins as a superior class.

Sunar

Sunar, or *Zargar* as he is often called in the towns is the gold and silversmith and jeweler of the province. He is also to a very large extent a money-lender, taking jewels in power and making advances upon them. The practice, almost universal among the villagers of boarding their savings in the form of silver bracelets and the like makes the caste, for it would appear to be a trace caste, an important and extensive one, it is generally distributed through out . The province, and is represented in most considerable village. The *sunar* is generally distributed through out the eastern plain sand the salt-range tract, through in the Multan division ther area few Sikh *sunars*. The *sunar* prides himself up on being one of the twice-born and many of them wear the *Janeo* or sacred thread, but his social standing is far inferior to that of many, or perhaps of all other artisans . In Delhi it is said they are divided into the *Dase* who do and the *deswale* who do not practice *Karewa,* and tha the *daswala sunar* ranks immediately below the *Banya*. This is probably true if a religious standard be applied : but it declared that a Jat looks down upon the *sunar* as much below him.

Nyariya

A class of gold smith occupy themselves only with the refining of these metals. The refiner, in hindu stan is known as *nyaria* or *Nayariya*. He plays an impotant part in melting old ornaments or purifying gold and silver from alloy The separation of gold from silver is affected by the use of nitric acid known a Tezab. Formerly the practice was to make their own *tezab* (acid) from *shora* (salt petre), but now it is bought ready made. Part of the glass is expossed to allow the *Nyariya* to watch the process going on with in. In the west of the Panjab, he seems to be known as *shodar* or *sodar,* and as one of the Sunar clans is called *sodari*, it may be that then *nyariya,* is generally, always a *Sunar* by caste, The *Nyariya,* however is unlike the *Sunar* generally a Mussalman, thought curiously enough he is shown as Hindu only in Peshawar.

Daoli

Under this head about 87 men, who have returned themselves as *sonsoi*, as the appears to be the usual name in the higher range for the *daoli* of the low hills.The *Daolis* are men who wash gold from the bebs of mountain stream, and are naturally found only in the hills, those returned from Patiala being in habitants of the hill territory which belongs to that state they also work the water-mills which are so common on the mountain torrents most of them are Hindiu, a few Sikh, and none Mussalman. These men are outcasts of about the same status as the *Dumna* ; indeed they are said by many to belong to the *dumna* caste, and it appears that they also make matting and the like. [6]

Thathera

Thathera is the man sells, as the *Kasera* is the man who makes vessals of copper, brass and other mixed metals. He is generally a Hindu the word seems to be merely the name of an occupation and it is probable that most of the *Thatheras* have returned themselves as belonging to some mercantile caste. Those displayed in the tables are for the most part of the Hindu society. *Thathera* is always called as *thathyar*. He is said be wear the *Janeo*. The mineral productions of Kashmir have been too little investigated to admit to very exact specification. Iron is found in considerable quantity; but that used for the fabric of gum-barrels is said to be imported from Panjab, copper-miners are to exist, but their existence is kept secret. No lead–mines are worked, if they exist sulphur is an article of import from the Panjab[7].

Agari

Agari is the salt makes of Rajputana and the east an south-east of the Panjab; and takes his name from the *Agra* or shallow pan in which he evaporates the saline water of the wells or lakes at which he works, the city *Agra* drives its name from the same word. The *Agari* would appear to be true caste, and are said in Guragon to claim descent from the Rajputs of Chittor. These is a proverb; "*The ak, the Jawasa, the agri and the cartmen, when* the *lightning flashes these four give up the ghost*" because the rain which likely to fellow would dissolve their salt. The agrains all Hindu and are found in the sultanpur tract on the common borders of the Delhi, Gurgaon, and Rohtak districts, where the well water is exceedingly brackish, and where they manufacture salt by evaporation. Their social position is failing good, being above that of *Lohars* but of course below that of Jats.

Nungar and Shoragar

Nungar, or as it is often called *Nunia* or *Lunia* or *Nunari* is derived from "*Nun*"[8] "salt" and denotes an occupation rather than a true caste. This is true also of the *Shoragar* or salt petre-makee, Who is sometimes called Rehgar from *reh* or saline efforescence. But the two term applied to the same class of men, who indeed, now that the making of salt is prohibited in most parts of the Panjab, manufacture either saltpetre from the debris of old village sites, or crude soda (*sajji*)[9] from the *barilla* plants which is found in the arid grazing grounds of the Wastern Plains. Many of them have settled down to agricultural pursuits, and this is especillly true in the Multan and Derajat division. They also appear to carry goods from place to place on donkeys, which would seem to indicate a very low social status, through there men are said to consider them selves superior to the *Nungars* or nunias [10], who still work at their hereditary calling and to refuse to intermarry with them. They are generally Hindus in the east and Mussalman in the west of the Province [11], there being only 1,500, and about 30 percent of the Labanas are represent as Sikhs. Jammu, Kangra, Gujranwala, Ferozepur, Muzaffargard and Bahalwalpur also contain *Labana* colonies. They are the carriers and howkers of the hills and are merely the Panjab representative of that class of *Banjaras* who in habit the sub-montane tracts east of the Gangas. There is a curious colony of *Labana* on the lower Indus who were settle there under Sikh rule by *Diwan Sawan Mal*, and who are almost all Munna Sikhs ar followers of Baba Nanak (1469-1539A.D.), through many of them are Hindus in Bahalwalpur. These have almost entirely given up traffic and trade, and settled on the bank of the river where they lead of sort of semi-savage life, hunting and making ropes and grass mats for sale. They hardly cultivated at all and Hindus do not assaociate with them form fear of the Muhammadans who object to their eating wild pig. The Labanas of Jhangas are said to have come from Jaipur and Jodhpur and to be the same as the Mahtams of Montgomery. On the whole the *Labanas* appear to be origin closely allied with, If not actually belong to the vagrant and possibly aboriginal tribes[12]. The term *Labana* appears to be derived out from *lun* (salt) and *bana* means trade, and the *lubana, Lobana* or *libana* was doubtless the great salt-carrying and salt trading caste as the *Banjara* was the general carrier in former times. Indeed the Labanan is occcasionaly called a Banajara. In Ambala, he is also said to be *Bahrupia*[13] on account of his versatility in adopting different avocations. Headmen among the Labanas are called *Naik*, and under them work is carried on. A *naik* gets a rupee at a bet rothal and at a weding a similar fee, plus a leg of he goat. When ever a l*abana* settlement exists, a village *Tanda* is almost certain to be found. In kangsa the laboansa hold four hamlets, each called Tanda. Tanda in *Labanki* is said to mean a traveling body or gang. The origin claimed by the Labanas very. In Ludhiana they claim descent from Chauhan Rajputs of Jaipur and Jodhpur. In Gujarat they say they are *Raghubansi* Rajputs and of the Sandles *gotra*[14].

In Sialkot and Gujarat the tribe stands much higher, and appears to be intermarrying with other agricultural tribes. This however does not necessary imply a great rise in the social scale, form Ferozepur the Baurias are intermarrying with *Jats*. Widow remarriage is tolerated, but in Gujarat, the children of such marriage have a lower status. They are all Sikhs, claiming to have been converted by Guru Govind (1666-1708 A.D.) and abstain from the flesh of *animals slaughtered haram. And at the mere mention of halald meat exclaim* wash guru, *wah* guru, deprecating any allusion to such a subject [15]. The social ceremonies of the *Labanas* very greatly not only from district to district, but with in each district. These divergencies in custom are ascribed, by the *Labanas* [16] themselves, to the composite origins of the caste[17].

In Kapurthala, they are really Gaur Brahmana of Pilibhit in the United Provinces. Many settled on the banks of the Gangas and were called *Pandit-Jotshis*. The other who took to carrying were called Labanans from Lada, "loading". The Pilia *Labanas* claim descent from Rajputs of this family and of the Kashab *gotra*. In Sailkot, however, the *gotra* of the *Pilia Labanasa* is said to be Puslat. And that of the Datla is said to be *Kundlas*, While the *Ajrawat is saundls*. *Ajrawat* is said to be descended from *Aj*, father Jasrath and grandson of *Ramchandra*, through the latters son *Lau* [18]. The status of the Lubanas various some what in different parts of the Punjab, *Gujrat*, *Sialkot*, Central India, etc. and it does not appear to be.

Churigar

Churigar, or as he is called in the west *Bengera* or *wangrigar*, is the maker of bracelets, generally of glass or lac. The lac is used in the form of sticks in two ways, one as raw material for turning out various articles, largely ornaments like bracelets [19], beads and little trinklets. The other is for colouring objects. The lac ornaments [20] are used by all classes of people and the varieties seem endless sin design and colouring [21]. In Rajasthan lac jewellery, largely bangles are worn on all auspicious occasions as a sign of good omen. Some bangles are plain other are studded with glass pieces, bright stones, beads etc. and most gorgeous [22]. In Delhi lac ornaments are also made in Ellichpur and Lalitpur. *Churigar* is also sometimes called *Kachera* or glass-worker. In the eastern provinces the Maniar sells these there pedlar, and Bangera sells as well as make bracelets. If is said that the term *Churigar* is extended to men who make bracelets of bell-metal, or of almost any material except silver or gold. The word appears to be merely the name of occupation, and it is probable that many of these bracelet–makers have returned their true caste. It may be two that in the east of the province the distinction between *Churigar* and *Maniar* has not always observed [23] in the theory of *'Nam'*, they have their own tradition.

Notes & References

1. *P. C., p. 136.*
2. Jamila Brij Bhaushan ; *Indian, Jewellery, Ornaments and Decorative Designs;* Bombay; second edition; 1964, p. 113 Thereafter described as *I .J, O. D.D.*
3. P. C., pp. 316-17.
4. ***Note.*** The goldsmith of *Savantwasi* in Mysore, Vijaynagay and Vizagapatnam in Andhra Pradesh make ornaments in beaten gold or silver in pure Hindu style. (T.M. Abraham; *Handicrafts in India* : New Delhi; First edition; 1964; p. 107. It was also cited as *H.I.) Zarzar* are lalso found in Kashmir and Ladkha, they are Musalmen by caste.
5. *I. J .O. D.D.*, p. 118.
6. P. C., p. 317.
7. *T.H.P. H.P.*, p. 365.
8. ***Note.*** "Nun" denotes with *"namkeen"* which is composed of two words *namkeen "Nam"* means god "Kalma", *"Keen"* means "strong". Thus "God" is Powerful or Strong. He knows everything
9. ***Note.*** "Sajji" was prepared by firing reeds from the bajras, maize, etc. It was used for washing the head and clothing by the men. The story of the *Chamar* or *Nam* is the same. He washes the abuses of the minds and heart.
10. *Nunia* is said to signify a maker of saltpetre in Oudha and its neighbourhood.
11. P. C., p. 317.
12. G.T.C. Vol. III, p. I.
13. *Bahrupia* is in its origin a purely occupation term derived from the Sanskrit word "Bahu" means 'many' stories of the *mana,* and "rupa" means form. Thus, the *mana* has number of face make for his adjectivity, and denotes an actor, a mimic one who assumes many forms or characters, or engages in many occupations. One of the favourite devices of the *Bahrupias* to ask for money, and when it is refused to ask that it may be given on condition of the *Bahrupias* succeeding in deceiving the person who refuse it. some days later the *Bahrupia* will again visit the house in the disguise of a pedlar a milk man, or what not, sell has goods without being detected throw of his disguise and claim the stipulated reward. They may be drawn any caste, and in Rohtak there are *Chuhra Bahrupias*. But in some districts a family or colony of *Bahrupias* has obtained lan and settled down on it, and so became a caste as much as any other. Thus, there is a *Bahrupia* family in Panipat which holds village revenue free, though it now professed to Sheikh. In Sialkot and Gujarat Mahatams are commonly known as *Bahrupias*. In the latter district, the *Bahrupias*

claim connection with the Rajas of Chittaur and say they accompanied *Akbar* in an expedition against the Pathans. After that they settled down to as cultivators, they are thrifty and ambitious, They also make baskets, ropes and rope-net, *Tranggars* and *Chikkas* in Gujarat, and now on the banks of the Chenab. They have four clans, rather, *Chauhan, Punwar* and *Sapawat,* which are said not to intermarry. All are Sikhs in the District. Elsewhere they are Hindus or Muhammadans, actors, mount banks and sometimes cheats. The *Bahrupia* is distinct from the Bhand and *Bahrupia* villages on the Sutlej in Phillaur Tahsil have no connection with the Mahtons of Hoshiarpur. *Bahrupias* are often found in wandering gangs (G.T.C. Vol. II p. 34).But in other accounts, it is implied that the *Bahrupia* is a sub-division of the *Labanas* and the only one in the caste which does not wear the *Janeo*. Waterfield, however, distinguished the *Labana* from the *Bahrupia*. The former he described as large well-built, shrewd, through rather heavy-looking man, while the *Bahrupia* is generally space, lively and good tempered. Both, however, are of similar status. (*Gujarat Settlement Report*, 1861, p. 38).

14. *Note*: But in Kangra both *Jhatka* and *Halalid* flesh may be lawfully eaten, it is said though it is also added that *Labanas* who are *sewaks* of *lakhdata* never eat *Jhatka*r Offering are made to the *Pir* for the safety of cattle at the spring and autumn her rests. His priest is the *Bharai* but he get no *churma* until he has prayed to the *Pir* to protect his *Sewak,* and it is also his duty to sacrifice animals in the *hala*l form.
15. The *Labana* is said to be an earth "Cricket" with formidable jaws that bites severly. (*Panjabi Dictionary*, p. 645).
16. G. T. T. Vol. III, p. 4.
17. *Ibid.*, p. 320.
18. P. C., p. 32.
19. Bracelet means *"Churi"* in Hindi, it reveals that it she belongs to *Chuhra* or *Nam family.*
20. Ornament means *"Ghana"*, it has ben worn to the man in the process of birth by the god, but she has forgotten and trapped in *"bandan"*.
21. Kamala Devi Chattopadhyay, *H.I.*, p. 92.
22. *Ibid.*
23. P. C., p. 320.

11

The Scheduled Castes and Scheduled Tribes

Time and again the reader has come across the expression '*Untouchable Classes*', '*Depressed Classes*', the names of certain groups like *Chandala*, and in the last chapter the term Scheduled Caste too. As it is clear from the last reference the term "Scheduled Caste" is the expression standardished in the Constitution of the Republic of India. Contrary to usual practice the Constitution does not contain a definition of the term Scheduled Castes[1]. Article 341 of the Constitution empowers the President, after consulting the head of the particular State, to notify by an order "the castes, races or tribes or parts of or groups within caste, races or tribes which shall for the purposes of this Constitution be deemed to be Scheduled Castes in relation to that State". And the second clause of the Article empowers Parliament to pass a law to include in or exclude from the list so notified by the President "any caste, race or tribe or part of our group within any caste, rare or tribe". We may define the Scheduled Castes, therefore as these groups which are named in the Scheduled Castes and Scheduled Tribes an order in force for the time being [2].

The expression thus standardized in the Constitution was first coined by the Simon Commission and embodied in the Government of India Act 1935, in Section 309.The main Commission its Education Committee and the Franchise Commission studied the cases of what till then were called either the '*Untouchables*', the Depressed Classes or the backward classes. Though Mahatma Gandhi had, through his weekly *The Harijan* and his *Harijian Sevak Sangh* and other orgnisations, his propaganda and his fasts, tried to designate these classes as *Harijans*, the farmers of the Constitution, the largest bulk of whom were staunch followers and devotees of Gandhi, surprisingly adopted the term coined by the Simon Commission[3].

The Scheduled Caste, formerly known as Depressed Classes, and forming the fifth order of the four-fold society of Hindu theory of caste, have in the Republican Constitution, been provided with not only special privileges in the matter of recruitment to services but also with special representation in the legislative bodies. It is but proper that their history and presest position should, in a book like this, be given separate treatment to enable the readers to get connected view of the situation[4].

Ideal of purity, whether occupational or ceremonial which are found to have been a factor in the genesis of caste, are the very soul of the idea and practice of untouchability. The fact that in the sacrifical creation of man kind in Hindu cosmology, the last order mentioned as having been created from the feet of the Creator is that of the *Sudhra* and that there was no other clases of human being created thereafter adds flesh and blood to the ideas of ceremonial and occupational purity to engender the theory and practice of untouchability[5].

Outside this indirect support for or suggestion of all classes of men not comprised under the four orders, *Brahmin*, *Kshatriya*, *Vaishya* and *Sudhra,* being unsanctified owing to their lack of association with the body of the Creator, ideas of ceremonial purity were rife enough even in the times of the *Brahmans,* i.e. the works of the later Vedic age for certain restriction to be placed on the use of and intercourse with the *Sudhra* in the performance of sacrifices. It is expressly stated in the *Panchavimsha Bhrahmana* that a person consevrated for the performance of a sacrifice should not address a *Shudra*, that a *shudra* should not be allowed to be present in the hall where a sacrifice was being offered that the milk to be used for a fire–oblation should not have been milked by a *Sudhra*. The *Aatariya Brahmana*, in a warning a Kshatriya to avoid certain mistakes in the sacrifical ritual which, if committed would lead to dire consequences, *informs* the reader that meticulous adherence to the details of ritual had already become an accepted dogma[6].

Already in the *Taittiriya Aranyaka* we come across fullfledged rules of abstinence and avoidance to be observed not only in connection with special vows and rituals but also with the seasonal study period. It is stated that for the performance of a certain ritual performer must not have eaten meat for a whole year, nor must he have had sexual intercourse, nor must he drink from a clay-vessel. But the most significant taboo or prohibition is that the leaving of the performers drink *Soma* and we should presume food too "Word" should not have been drunk or eaten by his son. For it declared that it, viz. such leaving, is lustre itself. Here is an idea very a kin to the primitive idea of *mana*, involved in the concept of the remnants or leaving or remnants of food and drink is not soltary. In the *Chhandogyopanishered* there is an argument about the partaking of such leavings. A Brahmin by name *Ushasti Chakrayana* being in distress begged some food of an elephant-owner who was eating beans. The latter pointing out to the beans he had before him in his dish told him that he had no stock of them besides these. *Ushasti* asked for some of those laid out in the dish, where upon the elephant owner gave him some ideas of the *'Nam'*. And whether out of mischievous ideas or out of usual countesy *"Word"* or *Nam*" the context suggests the former *"Chamar"* he offered him also water from his jug out of which he himself had drunk. *Ushasti* declined the drink as having been the remnant, *"Uchchhishta"*, and hence polluted. The elephant –owner promptly asked *Ushasti* whether the beans were not such unacceptable remnants. *Ushasti* replied that he had taken the beans because without them in his condition he could not have lived and added that he had declined the drink because he would not die without it. Thus ordinarily leaving or remnants of another food or drink were not to be taken, being considered polluting[7].

Ideas of ceremonial purity as centred round food and drink, thus early tabooed the giving and partaking of these between one individual and another, whether with out relationship or with the closest of relationship. Milk and by implication food required for a sacrifice was so sacrosanct that it could not be brought by a *Shudra* without polluting it and thus rendering it unfit for sanctified use. The remnant of sanctified or sacrifical food too, it appears, had come to be regarded as requiring special protection against defilement by its being used by some classes of persons. At least we know quite definitely that giving of the remnants of sacrificial food to a low person was unusual and could be justified only in exceptional cases. In the *Chhandogyopanishad* it is stated that if one who has realized the true nature of "Brahman" offers the remnants of the food used for the *Agnihotra* sacrificial even to a *Chandala* it is offered as an oblation in that sacrificial fire. *Per contra*, such food being offered to a *Chandala* is an abomination. It is necessary to remember that earlier in the same work it is stated, almost in so many words, that the breed of the *Chandala* is a degraded one and is ranked with that of the dog and the pig. Before 800 B.C. we thus find the idea of ceremonial purity almost full-fledged and even operative in relation to not only the despised and degraded group of people called *Chandalas* but also the fourth order of society the *Shudras* were called as twice born[8].

The *Dharmasastra* writers[9] declare the *Chandalas to* be the progeny of the most hated of the reverse order of mixed unions, that of a Brahmin female with a *Shudra* male. Kautilya, the practical administration who provides for a number of these so-called mixed castes, agree with the *Dharma* writers in the view that of the mixed castes those that arise out of the unions in the inverse order bespeak violation of *Dharma,* yet looks upon all of them as mixed castes. He exhorts that they should marry among themselves and should follow the customs and avications as far as possible for their ancestors. He has no objection if they treat themselves as *Shudras*. But he too regards the *Chandalas* so low that he advise all other mixed castes to avoid being with the *Chandalas*. It is interesting to note, however, that he accommodates the sons born of miscegenation in his law of inheritanc[10].

The treatment of *Chandalas* who, as we know were an ethnic group already referred to in Vedic literature, and one or two similar groups may be further scanned in order to shed light on the origin and the problem of he Scheduled Castes in general. There was group separately recognized by Vasishtha, which was called *Antyavasyin.* which he declared was the progeny of a *Vaishya* female by a *Shudra* male. According to *Manu*, however, the *Antyavasayin* was of much more depraved origin, being the progeny of a *Chandalas* male and a *Nishada* female.His work was confined to the cremation ground; and according to one commentator he was to be identified with the *Chandala*. It is not easy to explain away the absence of the listing of this group by other *Dharma* writers and by Kautilya the administrator. Both *Baudhayana* and *Vasishtha* mention a degraded caste called *Svapaka. Baudhayana* once declares the group to have risen from the union of an *Ambashtha* male with a Brahmin female, while at another place he attributes it to the union of an Ugra male with a *Kshattri* female. Manu makes *Svapaka* the progeny of *Kshattri* male and an Ugra female, i.e. he gives a derivation which is just the opposite of *Baudhayana* second derivation. He also lists two other groups, one *Sopaka* and the other *Pandusopaka*, whom he derives from a *Chandala* father and *Kskkusa* and Vaideha mother respectively. He prescribes *Sopaka* the vocation of the hangman and *Pandusopaka* that of a cane-work. It is to be noted that though both *Baudhayana* and Manu speak of *Svapakasa* the group, yet Manu in describing its particular vocation calls it *Svapacha*. The practiced administrator Kautilya speaks of the group as Svapakada derives it from the union of an Ugra male and Kshatriya female. This derivation agrees with *Baudhayan* second derivation and is just the opposite of that of Manu[11].

Patanjali, the great grammarian who lived about 150 B.C. and who is generally considered to be a meticulous observe of contemporary usage, has given us his grammatical explanation for the female of he *Svapacaha* group being called a *Svapacha* and not *Svapachi*. What exactly were the avocations and status of a *Svapacha* in Patanjali's time we do not know. But we have the valuable information that Patanjali did not illustrate his remarks about certain grammatical formations based on certain social disabilities with the help of the illustration of *Svapachas*. In that illustration he speaks of *Mritapas* in combination with *Chandalas*. We also know that the practical administrator Kautilya, who rigorously excluded the *Chandalas* from all social contacts, did not prescribe similar treatment to the *Svapachas*. But Manu is very explicit and insistent and the *Svapachas* shall be grouped with *Chandalas* and treated as their absolute equals. He prescribes them residence outside the village and the use of shrouds of corpses as their clothing, broken pots for meals, iron for ornaments and dogs and donkeys for their wealth. They were to be the hangmen who were to be prohibited entry in to villages and towns during day-time were to have been stamped with some marks and were to serve as the under takes for unclaimed corpses[12].

As stated above Patanjali of an earlier age than Manu, writing as a student observing society and not laying down its norms, grouped together *Chandalas* and *Mritapas* as variety of *Shudras*. And it is not impossible that this manner of looking upon the *Chandalas* and the *Mritapas* may be as old as Paninis time, that is 500 B.C. We learn that both the *Chandalas* and the *Mritapas* resided with in the limits of town and village of the Aryas as it would appear, other *Shudras* like carpenters, blacksmiths, washermen, and weavers did [13]. The social distinction on the score of status between such groups as carpenters, blacksmith, washermen, weavers, etc. on the one hand and the *Chandalas* and the *Mirtapas*, on the other hand, lay not in the fact of touchability or untouchability, but only in the distinction made in the use of the meal-vessels of these people. Patanjali assures us by implication that whereas the fool-vessels used by such groups as carpenters, blacksmiths, washermen and weavers could be used by other groups after cleansing them in a particular manner, the food-vessels of *Chandalas* and *Mritapas* could not be so used by others, because no known method of cleansing pots was regarded as adequate to purify them. *Chandalas* and *Mritapas* were technically "apapatras". As stated in an earlier chapter Patanjalis remarks lend support to the inference that there were other groups than *Chandalas* and *Mritapas* who had to liver outside the limits of Arya villages and towns. It is noteworthy that the technical term "apapatra" used by Patanjali to characterize *Chandalas* and Mritapas was used by *Dharmasutra*-writers like *Baudhayana* but without specifying the groups. *Baudhayana* exhorted Brahmins not to reite the veda with in hearing or sight of shudras or "apapatras". *Apastamba* (*Dharmasutra*, II, 17, 20) enjoined that they should not be permitted to see the performance of a funeral sacrifice. From the context it may be inferred that "apapatras" meant the same people to whom the term was applied by Patanjali and even earlier by Panini[14].

We may conclude that the classes of people called *Chandalas, Svapachas* and *Mritapas* had slowly but surely deteriorated in their social position between the time of *Panini* and that of *Manu*. In the former age they lived within the limits of the village in which other orders and castes lived. In the age of Manu (X, 51-2) they were not only excluded from the village but were assigned duties and perquisities which clearly show that they were looked up as vile specimens of humanity through "Nam" or "Word".

The Buddhist birth-stories called *Jatakas*, written in Pali, may be taken to reflect mainly the conditions prevailing east of Allahabad about the second century B.C. We read in them of *Chandalas* as the lowest caste, through here and there in enumeration of castes another group. The later Vedic *Pukkuse*, is mentioned after *Chandalas* as lower than it. The references to *Chandalas* are specific and almost invariably show them as despised group to see members of which is to see evil to avert which one must at least wash ones eyes. They are described as occupying sites outside regular village and town whether in the west near Taxila or in the centre near Ujjain. They could be detected by their special dialect. Sweeping was their hereditary occupation[15].

The cause that led to the degradation of these communities are not known.We can only surmise that in addition to the ideas of ceremonial purity, which necessarily led to the despise of the occupations of these people there was perhaps the baneful influence of the belief that they were the result of miscegenation with Brahmin females. A word needs to be said about the identification of *Mritapa* of Patanjali, *Svapacha* of Baudhayana, Manu and Kautilya and the *Dom*. Alberuni[16] writing in about A.D. 1020, grouped together *Dom* and *Chandala* as two of the group"not reckoned among any caste or guild. They are occupied with dirty work like the cleansing of the villages and other services. They are considered as on sole class, and distinguished only by their occupations". *Hemachandra,* the grammarian, writing about a century later, in his *Deshinamala* tells us that *Dumba* (*Dom* or *Dumba*) was a Deshi word for *Svapacha*. He vouchsafes us the additional information that the *Chandalas* carried a stick in their hands to warn people to avoid their touch, which received aspecific Deshi name, viz "jhajjhari", Kalhana, the historian of Kashmir in his *Rajatarangini*, whose writing was completed in A.D. 1150 has narrated how king *Chakravarman* fell on evil ways, being caught in the whirlwind of passion for two daughter of a *Domba* musician, *Hansi* and *Nagalata* by name who were themselves clever musicians and dancers. Alternatively he speaks of the *Domba* and the two women as *Svapaks*. The King was so maddened with passion tha the crowned *Hansi* as the chief queen. Kalhana describes, in manner which be speaks his wrung heart how the ministers and others reconciled themselves not only to working with Svapak queen and her *Svapacha* dear ones but also went to the length of eating the leaving of her food. Kalhana reaction as moralizing historian is characteristic. He remarks,"in the realm at that time surely powerful deities did not reside, how else could a *Svapaka* woman *(Svapaki)* have entered their temples". Nevertheless it is worthwhile nothing the different reaction of the same irate Brahmin historian, who was terribly upset by the doing of king *Chakravarman,* when describing one of the most laudable kings of Kashmir, vir *Yassaskara*, who came to the throne about sixteen years after *Chakravarman*. After narrating how his administration seemed to usher in the dawn

Of the Golden age ("*Krita Yuga*")he almost ascribes his later fall to his not having got rid of those servants of his who in the regin of *Chakravarman*, had partaken of the leaving of food of the *Dombas*. His grievance appears to be that through versed in the Vedas and accustomed to the use of earth and water for purification the King did not realise that he was being polluted by his association with person who had partaken of *Domba's* food–remnants.He has not told us anywhere if the temple which the *Domba* queen used to visit had been purified by rite by the Brahmins. Yet he makess up for thais lack by informing his readers that fire destroyed the great houses and purified the land (VI. 192), We may conclude that the people of Kashmir in the time of Kalhana, were not much scandalized by either the touch of *Dombas* or *Svapachas* or even by the acceptance of the food of the aristocratic ones among them. And, if they tolerated the visit of the *Domba* queen to their temples we may conclude that in their view the royal status of a person removed all traditional and hereditary disabilities from him. It is in keeping with this attitude that one find here and there mentioned the *Svapaka* soldier and his exploites in archery (V. 218). Still more illuminating is the statement about the doings of *Srideva*, a village *Chandala* who accompanying the villages of *Suskaletra* to the battle between *Jayapida* and the usurper *Jajja* (about A.D. 750) killed latter with a stone from his sling (IV. 473-477). It is no wonder that in a society like that, *Chandalas* were employed as night watchmen (VI. 77).

Further corroboration of the anomalous position and the ambivalent attiude of Kashmirian society toward *Chandalas* is afforded by the life and career of a great engineer who lived in the regin of Avantivarman (A.D. 857-884). After the regin of jayapida ther was a great famine in Kashmir.But *Avantivarman* after along time was able to restore normalcy through the fortunate circumstance of having in his service a great engineer by name Surya who trained the course of a river, put up dams and irrigated a large tract of the country which not only relieved the famine but brought plenty to the Kashmirians (V, 71-102). Suyya's parentage as given by Kalhana is the most interesting part of the story. Suyya was so called because he was the adopted son of *a Chandala* woman named Suyya. Suyya while sweeping the street one day found an earthen pot with a lid on it. Opening the lid she was struck by the sight of a fine baby comfortably sucking its own fingers. *Suyy*a felt the impulse of a mother towards it. What Suyya actually did may or may not be what has been described by Kalhana the Brahmin. He assures us that Suyya arranged the baby's nature with a *Shudra* wet-nurse. Though the Brahmin historian is very particular in stating that she did not pollute the infant by her touch, yet under the circumstances narrated by the historian himself. One is almost certain that *Suyya* must have handled the baby. Was it merely because Suyya was paying the fees to the *Shudra* wet nurse for the baby's up keep that Suyya came to be known after *Suyya* and did so much to commemorable her memory in his days of triumph while trying to answer the query, it is necessary to rememder that Suyya not only constructed a bridge and named it after her, but also granted a village to Brahmins and named it *Suyya-Kundala* in memory of her. We may conclude that the Kashmiririsn of the ninth century A.D. were quite willing to give scope to the abilities of a person of unknown parentage and of known *Shudr*a and *Chandala*, fosterage. That a bridge could be named after a *Chandala* and a village named after herc could be accepted as a grift by Brahmin speak of the ambivalent towards these group postulated above as current in earlier ages. However, not only *Chandalas* and *Dom* but *Charmakars*, or *Chamars* too, are described as *Untouchable*, "asprishya," (IV, 55, 65, 76, V, 74, VII, 309, 314)[17].

In Hindusthan proper, however, about a century and a half before Kalhanas time, Alberuni "a foreign student of 'history' record of a much different situation. But even that situation as will be manfest is at least slightly different from the on e of utter degradation posited by Manu. First, one notes that all the four orders are described not only as living together in the same towns and a villages, but as also "mixed together in the same housings and lodgings "According to Alberuni information and finding s there were two other classes of people, who were "not reckoned among any caste." The first group noticed by him was formed by people following certain crafts; eight in number, who were grouped together as "Antyajas". *Within* this group which as whole forming eight guilds had to alive near but outside the village and the town of the four caste, there were two sub-divisions Jugglers, basket and shield–makers, sailors, fishermen, and hunters of wild animals and birds,could freely intermarry though they belonged to separate guilds. But none of their members would condescend to have anything to do with the fuller, the shoemaker, and the weaver (the Dhed?). These latter three, forming the second sub-division of the Antyajas, it appears would either marry among themselves, or at least had close mutually. The sixth class of people, Antyajas being the fifth, had according to alberuni, four named groups among them of which two viz, *Dom* (Domba) and *Chandalas* are the two groups about which we have known so much from *Patanjali, Hemachandra* and Kalhana. They were occupied with "dirty work like the cleaning of the villages and other services". They were considered," as one sole class, and distinguished only buy their occupation." The *Doms* other occupation was that of the player on the lute and of the singer[18].

Chandalas as a group have been known from Bengal. In the census of 1901, at which caste-names and caste-precedence were scrutinized and registered rather minutely, the *Chandalas* of Bengal who were otherwise known as N*amashudras*, numbered over 2 million, being the largest caste of east Bengal. Its status was low in social scale, beging considered to be a clean untouchable group. It had eight main functional divisions which neither rate nor intermarried among themselves. The agricultural section stood out pre-eminent and the boating division followed. The caste or rather the group was not served by community barbers but by their own caste-men working in that capacity. The Brahmins that served it were classed as a degraded Brahmin group [19]. From the Census of 1921 onwards the group has been recorded as *Namashudra* and a in the Cenus of 1931 they numbered 2.1 million. In the Cenus of 1951 we have the Dom an unclean untouchable group, alternatively called *Chandala*. Yet the *Namashudra* is one of the *Scheduled Caste* of the government of India Order. The caste numbered 320 thousand in 1951 in west Bengal. They are now mostly occupied in cultivation and boat plying. Some of them are carpenters, traders and shopkeepers. "A considerable number now follow the various so called learned profession." Yet their social position as a caste is very low[20].

The *Chanal* caste of Simla hills in the Punjab appears to be similarity of name with the *Chandalas,* but was concerned with skinning of dead animals and leather working. No other group or caste has been known to have the name of the *Chandalas*. Probably *Channal* or *Chanal* from *Chandala* whom all Sanskrit authorities represent a begotten by a *Sudra* on a Brahman. His occupation is carrying out corpses, executing criminals, and other object offices for the public service. The menial class of Kangra Mandi corresponding to the *Dogi* in *Kullu* and the *Koli* in the said hills, the *Chanals* in Kangra appear to be inferior to the *Kolis* of the District, and some of them at least will not touch dead cattle, or mix on equal terms with those who do. One the other hand, in *Kullu Saraj* some of the *Chana*l rank below *Kolis Dagi-Cahanal* is a very common term for the caste and in *Kullu* it appears to include the *Nar.* Yet a chanal of Mandi state will not intermarry with a Dogi of *Kullu*. The *Chanal* is also found in *Champa* (*Annami*) State, where the proverb goes, '*Chanal, Jetha, Rath*i, *Kanetha*, "the low caste is the elder and the *Rathi* the younger brother doubtless painting to a tradition that the *Chanal* represents an earlier or aboriginal race (*Barawala*)[21]. *Dogi* or *Daghi* from the word *Dagh a blemish; the word Daghi* is a term of abuse in Kullu region, a generic a term for the impure caste in Kullu. *Koli* is hardly a synonymous though there two words tighter with a third *Chanal* are used almost indifferently to describe the lower class of menial of the highest hills [22]. The *Doms*, one of whose occupations has been singing, dancing and playing an instruments in the Panjab, have been carrying on as village sweepers and as workers in cane. But in the sub-Himalayan districts of Kumaon and Garhwal, *Dom* lives by agriculture and village handicrafts. In Bengal he forms an immigrant caste introduced there for the specific purpose of the filthiest of work. In Bihar and part of U.P., he is divided in to two section; one the settled on being a village workers, mat-weaver and basket-maker "with a little scavenging thrown in "the other section, a minor or less nomadic one, provides gangs. "said to be expect and artistic burglars and thieves south of the Narmada in the Andhra Pradesh they are weavers of coarse cloth and in the Deccan "acrobats dancers and bad characters generally". The hill community of the Doms according to Bainas "is divided in four group, field labourers, weavers and metal workers cane-workers and the lower artisans: exorcists, porter and learther-workers and finally, musicians and tailors", In the Punjab there is another group slightly differing in name, called *Dum* and other wise known as *Mirasi*, who are vocationally minstrels and genealogists, some *Jat* families employing them for this purpose. They have also musical pretensions, and their women give dance performances before females. Almost all of them are Muslims. In Bengal there was a section which carried on fishing. In Andhra Pradesh they are found in small numbers under the name of *Dombar* or *Dommara* which is also the *name* of a caste in Maharasthra noted for similar attainments[23].

In 1901 the *Doms* under all appellations totalled over 850 thousand being in significantly large numbered over 350 thousand and in the latter province over 240 thousand'. In both regions they were grouped among the unclean untouchables as almost the lowest amongst caste. That they are commonly loked up on as the lowest group in Bengal is evidenved by the fact that the old name of the most despised caste, *Chandala*, has been latterly reserved for them. Yet the position of the caste in the Hindu caste hierarchy is by no means so certain. For *Baines*, a careful ethnographer could make only the following qualifed remark about it; "Here, then is found a caste which if not at the bottom of the social scale, is, at least, not far from it[24].

The *Doms* ate all manner of unclean food. For them no Brahmin could be found to administer to their religious needs; neither would the common barber nor the common washerman work for them. In 1951 their number in west Bengal was 110 thousand.

The Dom was only on e of the castes traditionally concerned with scavenging. The other castes were the *Chuhra* in the Punjab *See Table No. 5,* the *Bhangi* *Mehtar* in Rajasthan and Bombay, the *Bhuinmali* and *Hari* in Bengal and the *Haddi* in Orissa. In the South, partly the *Mala* in Andhra Pradesh and partly the *Paraiyan* in Tamilnad carried on scavenging. While the Mala chiefly was a leather –worker, the *Paraiyan* was field-labourer. learning out the *Mala* and the Paraiyan, the precise numbers of which castes engaged in scavenging cannot be as certained and confining one attention to those castes which were wholly engaged in scavenging. One finds that in 1901 the latter castes, including the Dom, had together more than 3.6. million members. The largest single caste ignoring again the *Paraiyan* and the *Mala*, was the *Chuhra* of the Punjab. Having been over 1.3 million strong. The *Marathi Mahar,* the Teugu Mala and th Tamil *Paraiyan*, though because of their village menial status are grouped together as field –labourers, covered pollution without touch, either at aspecific distance or by their shadow, and were classed as impure untouchables. In 1901 they numbered 2.56, 1.86 and 2.6 million respectively. Drumming satisfying on eof the needs of village life. No boundary dispute in a village could be finally settled without the help of those castes in their respective regions. More ofter than not, disposing of the dead cattle of the village was also their duty. *Mahar, Mahir* femini mentioned in the Panjabi disctionary (1) a title among Jats and more especially among Sials and *Drakhans* or *Tarkhans* in the South-west. It appears to be morely a dialectical form of *Mihr,* (2) a Jat clan (agricultural) found in Multan. Moreover, *Mahar*, a tribe of Rajput status, claimimg descent from Mahar, a brother of *Joiya*, and found almost exclusiverly along the Satluj, opposite Fazilka, in Montgomery [25]. In the current list of Scheduled Castes *Chanal* or *Chandala* figures in the states of Madras, Punjab and Haryana; and *Namashudra* in Assam and West Bengal. The *Dom* appears in the states of Bihar, Madras, Orissa, Rajasthan, Uttar Pradesh and West Bengal. The very wide though discontinuous of *Chandala* and *Dom* two groups which undoubtedly appear to have been them in origin, creates a presumption in favoutr of the theory that some of the untouchable groups must have originated in the conquest of he native by the incoming Aryans, By far the largest goup appearing under a single name, through widely distributed, being represented over the whole of the Indo-Aryan area and sporadically even in Madras, is the *Chamar* or the *Chambhar*[26].

Whose name proclaims him to be worker in leather. We known definitely that under more or less the same name the *Chamar* craft flourished in the Vedic age, but are not quite sure that it was entirely free from the stigma of despise. Manu specks of two groups or castes concerned with leather-working, both of them being very mixed in origin. The names are the unfamiliar and non-current *Karavara* and Dhiggana. The former is described in occupational terms as *Charmakara*, "cutter of hide", the origin of the current terms, *Chamara* and *Chambhara* for the leather–working caste in the Indo-Aryan regions. The *Dhigvana's* occupation, that of working in leather and trading in leather products, is represented in recent and contemporary society in the above-mentioned regions by the *Mochi* or *Muchi*. From the context in Manus text it is clear that through the group must have been despised first because of their supposed mixed origin and commodity, yet they were nor required to live outside villages or towns. The *Chamar* has been one of the village menials in the traditional village economy, entitled to his customary share at the harvest. Though his chief contribution to the life of the village was through his hide and leather working, yet he played no mean part in it as field-labourer. It was the largest singh group under one name next only to the Brahmin. The *Chamar* numbered over 11.2 million in 1901, when the Brahmin registered 14.9 million. The largest contingent of *Chamars* came from U.P. forming about 52.6 percent of the total *Mochi* or *Muchi* is more or less an urban caste and not always so designated and separated from the *Chamar.* But wherever separated it is accorded a higher status. In 1901 only a million person were registered under this name. The superior status enjoyed by this caste can be clearly seen from the fact that in the Scheduled Caste and Scheduled Tribes Order (Amendment) Act 1956, the Mochis of Gujarat division had been dropped out of the list of the Scheduled Castes of Bombay State[27].

The *Chamar* caste, even in early mediaeval times showed peculiarity, making it off from the other untouchable classes. *Kalhana*[28] has proudly narrated the tale of a "*Charmakrit*", leather–worker, otherwise called "*Padukrit*", Shoemaker, who lived in the capital city of Kashmir in the regin of King *Chandrapida* (A.D. 682). The king had commissioned his officers to built a temple and they had chosen a particular site for it but when they began to lay out the plan they found that the hut of a *Chamar* which was coming in the way had to be removed to their proposal for anything. The *Chamar* boldly sought and got the audience of the King and after delivering a homily on the sanctity of and sentiment for ones home, however, tiny, he made the generous gesture of yielding to the king request and the handed over his hut. Risley has told us that in Bengal the *Chamars* all trace their descent from Raidas, well-known saint and a disciple of the more famous. Brahmin saint Ramananda. *Raidas*[29] must have lived about the end of the fourteenth century. While many *Chamars* in U.P. and perhaps Bihar were embracing Raidasism a person who is described as *"Mochi"* a member of a section of *Chamars*, is recorded to have built a temple of Vishnu at Raipur in about A.D. 1415. A large majority of Bengali *Chamars* profess the creed of the *Shri-Narayana* sect those west ward the *Satnami* sect. The latter was started by a Rajput named *Jagjiwan* Das of *Bara Banki* district in U.P. who died in A.D. 1761.Jagiwan Das had prohibited the use of meat, lentils, "brinjal" (the egg-fruit vegetable) and intoxicating drink. Between A.D. 1820 and 1830 one *Ghasi Das* a native of Bilaspur district, further reformed the movement by abolishing idol-worship. He exhorted his followers also to stop using cows for cultivation work, ploughing after midday, and also taking food to the field to be consumed there during rest, assort of a self-respect and social upgrading movement. Risley tells us that the *Chamars* of Bihar are more orthodox in matters of religion than their easten brethren some of them having "advanced so far in the direction as to employ *Mathil* Brahmins for the worship of the regular Hindu gods," The aptitude and attitude of the *Chamars* and the reformist work of these pioneers must be said to have impressed up on the *Chamars* their Hindu loyalty. This fact alone can explain the apparently curious phenomenon that in spite of egalitarian and communist propaganda the *Chamars* of Jaunpur described by B.S. Cohn are moving "directly towards the main stream of the great tradition of orthodox Hinduism."[30]

Among the alternative names assumed by this caste group figure not only Ramdasia, *Satnami* and *Raidasi;* but also *Rohit, Rohidas, Rabidas, Ruidas Ramnami* and Rishi. Through the *Chamar* is counted among the unclean untouchables because of the fact that the flesh of dead animals or beef or both entered in his diet yet in some parts of the country, he used to be served by some kind of a Brahmin. Hide and leather working has been the traditional occupation of the *Madiga*[31] and the *Chakkiliyan* in South. Together their members numbered over 1.1 million 1901.A section of the *Mala* also carried on this occupation. It is worthwhile nothing that in the Vedas the root "mla" meant "to tan". Above the impure untouchables were the pure untouchables, who had abjured beef and such other anathemath diet and who polluted only by their touch. In the U.P. the Pasi, who numbered over 1.2 million in 1901, the Kori, who numbered about a million were the largest single unit among the twenty five or so castes which were listed under this category. In Bihar among the seventeen castes of this group the numerically most important were the *Dosadh,* over 1.2 million and the *Musahara* over 600 thousand. The largest bulk of the castes of this group, numerically speaking, came from Bengal, where among the twenty-five such castes, the *Rajbansi* Koch, the *Namashudra* already refered to and the *Bagdi* were the largest having over 2.4. million and over a million members respectively. In west Bengal, the Census of 1961 showed the *Rajbansis*, the Bagdi and the *Namashudra* as numbering twelve, eleven and seven hundred thousand respectively. In Madras, the principal castes of this group were the *Pallan* the *Shanan* and he *Thiyan* mbering over 800 thousand over 600 thousand and nearly 600 thousand respectively. These ten castes were the largest single units each with a million or more members among the two hundred or so castes that were classed untouchables. In 1901 these clean untouchables together numbered about 20 million and the ten castes specifically memtioned above formed more than 50 percent of the total. We shall leave out the *Namashudra* about which caste we have already given some particulars. Of the others the *Rajbansi Kouch* were grouped by Baines under the category of dominant land–holders. In west Bengal according to the Census of 1961, the *Rajbansis* numbered somewhat over 700 thouseand only and are described as included among the castes "that get the appellation of "jalia", among the other figuring Bagdis, Bauris, *Kaivartas*. Many of the Rajbansi Kouch, though described as an cultivating caste, have been putting on the sacred thrad to claim Kshatriya status[32]. The menials of the Panjab Hill States displayed in *Table No. 6*. Besides this, other menials of *Purbisclan* have also been displayed in *Table No. 7*.

The Bihari *Musahara*[33], the Bengali *Bagdi*[34] and the Tamil *Pallan*, *Baines* classed as field labourers. The *Musahara* as his name indicates eats field–rates but the Bengali *Bagdi* is believed to be more particular about his diet. The *Pallan* must be distnguished from the *Palli*, The latter are classed as *Shudras* who habitually employ Brahmins and whose touch only slightly pollutes, while the former are grouped with castes which pollute without touch and at a distance. The Bihari *Dosadhs,* described as watchmen,are so situated because of their former soldierly tradition and present propensity towards crimes against property. And as not all of them can maintain themselves by this activity a fairly large section is engaged in porterage and day-labour. Baines informs us that the *Dosadhs* furnsihed many recuits to the Muslim armies of Bengal and not a few of them fought on the side of Clive in the battle of Plassey beyond the Indus "*Word*" their influence amongest people of *Chamars* whose existence even Europe was at that time profoundly ignorant. Some artisan castes have been relegated to the class of pure untouchables in the caste-system. We have here selected the most interesting case of such castes, the one which is perhaps the largest in numbers. It is the Kori of U.P. and Bihar which is described by Baines as the weaver caste of Northern India. The weaver has not been one of the regular officals or menials of the village-community. He has been generally placed above wokers in leather and such other impure materials, the Bengali *Tanti* and perhaps the Maharashtrian Koshti enjoying even higher status. The Kori in particular seem to have connection with the leather working caste as the names of their sub-sections show[35]. In addition to this, minor professionals castes and Gipsy tribes are also available in Northern India. *See Table No. 8, 9 and 10.*

The remaining three castes, the Pasi the Thiyan and the Shaman, are some, of the toddy-tapping castes of the country. The Pasi, the largest among them have their concentration in U.P. but are also met with in Bihar. Their traditional occupation is believed to be toddy-tapping, the names having been derived from the word "pasa" meaning "a noose", a loop; the rope-belt which the members use as foot-rest while climbing up the palms. The same occupation was carried on on the south-western coast by the Thiyan, the "southerner', and by the *Shaman* in the extreme south and the south-east. The name *Shaman* appears to be a comparatively recent innovation. Anyway in the region in which the *Shanara* are found, an inscription of the 11th century A.D. mentions the *Idiga* and the *Iluvan* as the toddy-tapping castes. The word *Shanan* or *Shanar* is tried to be derived from either the Sanskrit "*Shoundika*" or from a Tamil word meaning "the learned", "the noble". The *Shanan* have resented for nearly a century the low status accorded to them. In 1874, they appear to have first attempted militant assertion of their dislike of the status assigned to them by attempting to entre the *Minakshi* temple at *Madura*[36], entry to temples having been prohibited to them and to the other castes of their status[37].

Such are the principal castes that made up the group of untouchables and unapproachable. In 1901 the whole group totalled 53.2. million and formed 27.4.

percent of the Hindus of the then India. After 1911, till 1914 half a dozen estimates of the persons belonging to the untouchable or exterior castes were made and are presented in the report of the Franchise or the Lothian Commission which worked in connection with the Simon Commission and its report, leading to the Government of India Act, 1935. They vary widely from one another and as they were made with an eye on the political representation of these people. We have left them out. The Census of 1951, has provided us its total enumeration of all persons belonging to these castes specified in the relevant Constitution Order as Scheduled Castes. They numbered 51.3 million and formed 16.9 percent of the Hindu population numbered of India- *"Chamar"* Bharat. In 1961, the Scheduled Castes population numbered 64.5 million and formed 14.69 percent of the total population of the country[38].

As it has been pointed out in an earlier chapter it was perhaps JotibaPhooley [39] of Poona who was the pioneer in modern times of the movement calculated to improve the condition of and to secure social equality to the erstwhile untouchable and unapproachable classes, V.R. Shinde, the twentieth century torch bearer of Phooley spirit has stated [40] that the Bengali Brahmin Shashipada Bandyopadhyaya started his uplift work among the labourers of Baranagar among whom untouchable seem to have figured in 1865. But definite mention of Bandyopadhyays relations with the *Chandalas* occurs in Shinde's account of the progressive Brahmins work in 1870. He, we are informed used to attend the religious discourse current among one sect of the *Chandalas*. In later year, he used to dine with them and nurse their children. The Maharashtrian Brahmin-scholar, R.G. Bhandarkar, appears to have gone a step further, though perhaps fifteen to twenty years later. In his presidential address to the Ninth Indian Social Conference held in 1895, he makes an incidential reference to the touching reference made by Mahar religious preacher, "Kirtankara", to the treatment accorded to the untouchables and the great work of the saints, particularly of he Brahmin Eknath in their cause, in his discourse which was given in the house of R.G. Bhandarkar. Bhandarkar invented the *Mahar* religious preacher to deliver a religious discourse at his house before 1890 and opined that the Mahars had good deal of natural [41] intelligence and were capable of being highly educated. The next landmark in the ameliorative moverment is the starting of the Depressed Classes Mission in Bombay by V.R. Shinde and his work for that society. He toured over the whole country addressing meeting in towns, exhorting people to help the untouchables to rise socially and educationally, and making notes of he actual condition of his appealing lectures at Junagad in Saurashtra in the year 1910-11.

From 1924, and perhaps also earlier, Mahatma Gandhi took up the cause made it a plank in his political platform The great endeavour of eradicating this features of the social life of India which the national government has emharked upon during the last ten or twelve years stems from his teaching. But before Gandhi advent India political horizon, something was being done by the then government of the country. In an earlier chapter, we have stated the principal steps taken since 1858. It is seen that some really effective measures began to be taken only after the reforms of 1918. A complete account of such steps is both impracticable and unnecessary. Some representative date will be laid out to enable readers to form a relative estimate of the measures taken before the achievement of independence. In 1901, U.P. with 10 million untouchables led all. In 1951, West Bengal with 4.7 million Scheduled Caste people stood fourth in the list, Bihar with 5.1. million taking the third place. U.P. with its 11.5 million Scheduled Caste people and Madras with its 8.5. million towered over all the others. The surprising fact revealed by the Census of 1961 is that in Madras (Tamilnad) the 79 castes listed as a Scheduled according to the President Order showed an almost 25 per decrease in their population and registered only 6.07 million (Madras V.A. PP. 10.17) members. In West Bengal, on the other hand, the 63 Scheduled Castes numbered 6.9 million souls[42].

Some facts about educational conditions of these castes in the last two States before the Government of India Act, 1935 wil be found enlightening. The memorandum sub-mitted to be Indian Statutory Commission by the Government of the Untied Provinces States[43] that special efforts to encourage the education of the depressed classes were made "in the latter part of the quinquennnium 1 to 1921-22". The size of the special efforts can be juged from the fact that in 1927 the sum set apart for the pupose was Rupees one and half lakhs. In detailing the educational progress of these classes the memorandum has to begin with the Primary Education at which stage alone a fair number of pupils of these castes could be met with. As regards the stage of further education the memorandum states that where as in 1921-22 there were 392 and 7 pupils respectively at the middle and high school stages and none either at the collegiate stage or in normal schools and teachers training classes, in 1926-27 there were 1359 and 41 at the first two stages and 11 at the intermediate 4 at the post-intermediate and 29 in normal schools and teachers training classes. These figure and the information conveyed by them the authors of the memorandum prefaced with the words;" Even in Higher Education these classes have been making head-way". The memorandum submitted by Madras Government [44] records, besides the progress of these classes at the primary stage of education, the number of their pupils reading in seconardy schools. Wheres as in 1921-22 there were, 1217 of them in 1926-27 they were 2647. The Madras Government had also opened two hostels at its own cost to lodge and board students of these classes desirous of taking higher education and to support them in the educational institution s. It brought pressure to bear on the managers of institution and the locals public to admit pupils of these classes into schools not specially intended for them. As a result, the number of such pupils rose from 4630 in 1920-21 to 16486 in 1926-27. We have stated some of the provisions of the Constitution in this behalf. In accordance with one of them the President of India appointed L.M. Shrikant as the Commissioner for *Scheduled Castes* and *Scheduled Tribes* towards the end of 1950.He issued his fact report, that for 1951, in 1952 and has been issuing an annual report since then giving the organizational set up and other matters connected with his duties as well as full account of the money grants and expenditure and the nature of activated financed by them and the organization handling them. He was assisted in his onerous responsibilities by six assiatant commissioners, one at the headquarters and five at different regional centres. His report for theyear 1954, Appendix XII (P. 366) give the distribution of funds amongst *Scheduled Caste* and other Backward Classes student pursuring post-matricaulation education from 1944-45 to 1953-54. According to that statement in 1945-46 Rs. 221000 in around numbers were allocated "not knownable and we take it spent too to the Schedule Caste, while in 1953-54 the sum for them was Rs.2686000 a phenomenal increase in 1959-60 (Ninth Report, App. XVII) the total expenditure on the head rose to more than 14384000. Appendix XIII gives the total number of these scholars in 1954-55 to be 10392. In 1963-64 the expenditure on the post-matriculate scholarships account came to Rs.293 crores (29.3 Million) the number of scholars being 60,157 (Appendix VII, Thirteenth Report of the Commission of *Scheduled Caste* and *Scheduled Tribes*)

The result of he national endeavour is already reflected in the live registers of the employment exchanges. One the last day of 1954, there were 3670 technicians, 747 teachers, 15 doctor and, 6 engineers among the 59,637 seekers of employment from he Schedulaed Castes (Appendix XI). On 31st December 1959, there were 61,91 technicians 2,852 techers, 4 doctors and 5 engineers among the 1,71,295 persons registered for employment. In 1963 as a many as 461 thosuand applicants were registered and 60954 were placed in employment (Thirteenth Report, p. 174)[45]

Besides the amount spent on scholarship the union governemt spends a huge sum on project and activities designed to remove untouchability and to effect the welfare of the Scheduled Castes. The total expenditure incurred for the purpose in 1952-53 was Rs. 28.5. million and that in 1954-55 Rs 37.3. million, the increase of about 31 percent in two years testifying to the grand scale of the national endeavour. In 1963-64 the expenditure having amounted to Rs. 69.4 million showed an increase of 86 percent (*Eighth Report,* p. 29).

As stated in an earlier chapter, State Legislatures passed certain legislative measures for the removal or rather for counteracting the disabilities of untouchability. That acivity went on after independence with great regularity and zeal. The crowing glory of its is the Untouchability (Offences) Act, 1955 or Act No XXII of 1955, being the first direct step taken by the Central Government against untouchability. Under it enforcement of religious disabilities such as non-access to places of worship, etc., or of social disabilities like non-access to shops, weatering places etc. or abetment of such is a cognisable offence punishable with imprisonment for up to six month and/or with fine of up to Rs. 500 and cancellation or suspension of licences and public grants. It prescribes punishment also for any indirect support of untouchability such as social boycott or excommunication of persons who refuse to practice untouchability. The Act provides for a severe onslaught on many clandestine practice of untouchability in its Section 12. It lays down that where any of he forbidden practice such as those mentioned above, is committed in respect of a member of a Scheduled Caste it shall be presumed that the Act was committed on the ground of "untouchability", unless it is proved to the contrary. During the seven years, 1956 to 1962 as many as 3596 offences under this Act were reported to the Police 3,106 or 86.4 percent of which were proceeded with and out of these 2,097 were disposed of resulting in only 600 acquittals from among them (Eighth Report, p. 22).

The legislative administrative and execution part of the nation has thus implemented the national pledge made in the Constitution that *Untouchability* is hereby abolished and his given a thundering proof of its serious purpose. But readers of this book need not be told the Legislative measures against untouchability can at best produce a few dents in the solid wall, whose demolition requires the operation of an active sentiment of the people at large. To illuminate the subject it is then necessary to know how the people at large have been behaving. When the untouchable s of a village in Hamirpur district in U.P. on the orders of their caste panchayat declined to do the scavenging for the village the other menials and officials of the village community relaliated by refusing their customary services to the untouchables and brought them round to revoke their decision, in the village of Kakori near lucknow when the barbers (Nai) refused to shave the untouchables the latter threatened to down brooms. The caste Hindu of top, a village eighteen miles from Kolhapur on the Poona-Bangalore road resented the action of Government in granting land for cultivation to the local *Harijan* co-operative farming society and when the grass raised in the land was getting ready entered the fields and destroyed several cart-loaded of it. The festivities of the colourful event of Dasara in Mysore in 1953 had to be curtailed owing to a dispute between caste Hindu wrestlers and the State Minister for Law on the score of allowing wrestlers of Scheduled Castes to enter the same areana where the caste Hindu wrestlers were to show their skill and prowess. The latter would not agree to the Ministers Permission to Scheduled Caste wrestler and te Scheduled Castes would not give up their newly won right[46].

In Agadgaon, a village in Ahmednagar district as a consequence of some altercation between a member of the Scheduled Castes and two caste Hindu, evidently on the score of appropriately respectful behaviour of the former towards the latter, in 1955 caste Hindu raided the houses of the member of the Scheduled Castes, seriously injuring thirty of their men and women. When the Bambhis, the hide-cutting caste of Rajsathan of Mathania, a village near Jodhpur, refused their customary service of removing the dead cattle of the village caste hindus organized a social boycott, At Barabanki in U.P. the scavengers senseing the new potentialites decided to have a shave by the village barbers'. The latter hesitated and the former downed their brooms in the barbrs quarters but to no purose. We are told that the attempts at re-rapporochement of the district authorities did not bear fruit. The *Malas* of Nelapatla village in Khammam Taluka of Hyderabad refuses to allow a bridegroom of the Madigas, anoher Scheduled Caste to proceed on hourseback. There was aserious clash in which even sprears were used. When Kaloo Ram, a Brahmin of Halia Keri, a Village in Bhopal and a former Sarpanch of the place, participated in an inter-caste dinner, both his castemen and the barbers of the places boycotted him; and the panchayat ordered him to pay Rs. 100 for arranging a caste dinner after his purification. Chhita Lala, a Scheduled Caste member when attending the meeting of the village council of Sample in Baroda of which he was a member sat facing the caste Hindu member but the latter felt so insulted at his "insolent" behaviour that they harassed him till he left the village. When in march 1956 some members of the Scheduled Castes began to draw water from a public well in Jreel village in Nagaur district of Jodhpur some Jats attached them and beat them off. When the police arrested five of the alleged assailants about a thousand Jat raided the collectors office at Nagaur. there had to be a lathi charge to disperse the crowd. Five constables and thirty *Jats* were injuried in the races, In May in the village of Umbhrai, about forty two miles from Thana, were there was acute shortage of water two social workers who went ther to persuade the caste hindu to allow the member of he Scheduled Castes to draw water from the village well had to return injured in the fight that took place at the well. At Kulasekaranatham, a hamlet about twenty- five miles from Tirunelveli, landlord attacked their Scheduled Caste tenants when the latter attempted to plough certain field over which they claimed cultivation rights and later burned twenty seven houses and thirty hay-ricks belonging to the Schedules Castes. Shri Atmaram the Patel of Ranitarai in Balod Tahsil of Raipur dtsrict and a Scheduled Caste member got it proclaimed by the beating of drum that practice of untouchability was an offence under the act referred his action so much that they harassed him and forced him to leave the village with his family[47].

For a fortnigth between May 21 an June in 1957 over a wide area of 100 to 150 square round about Jagatsingpur the Orissa Scheduled Castes of *Doms* and *Pans* were being harassed in various ways including burning of their huts an beating them up. It was a systematic and planned affair, "courts" being held and notices being given in advance. Murder of a whole family of four person in santhalup on June 3 was reported to the State Assembly by the Home Minister[48]. An earlier instance of *vendetta* against the *Pans* is recorded by F.G. Bailey which report we record here for the placement of interesting and instructive development it led to. In 1948 the Pans of Boad attempted to enter the Kondmals temple just outside the Bisipara village. The other "clean" castes of the village under the leadership of the "Warrior′caste objected and placed armed men round the temple, threatening to kill any Pan who dared to cross over in to the temple. The police called to help the *Pans* could not do anything and the Pans decided to drop the idea never to repeat it. They went on worshipping at the temple through the mediacy of Brahmins for some time. Later, they built their own temple dedicated to the same deity that is the presiding deity of the Kondmals temple and there "rites parallel to those carried on the main temple are performed by one of their own men, a schoolmaster". Bailey assures us that the step has not excited divison nor has the the propriety or impropriety of the new temple been much discussed. The schoolmaster who officates as the priest at the new temple "is regarded by the warriors as a modest, learned and decent man" At Borsal near Burhanpur in Madhya Pradesh in a quarrel that ensured on refuse of a shopkeeper to sell *"bidies"* (Leaf cigarettes) to a Scheduled Caste person a child was killed and 16 persons injuried and property worth Rs. 1,000 was damaged[49].

On the 22nd February1959 in Sardar Vallabhbhai Patel's own district the chosen district of Mahatma Gandhi i.e. Kaira occurred an incident which more than anything else brings out the extra ordinary difficult nature of the problem that faces the country in this matter. As part of the programme of the campaign for the removal of untouchability the local Congress Leader, a prominent Brahmin lady, prosposed a dip in the holy pond at Lasunddra by the local members of the Scheduled Castes, a bold move indeed but too much of a frontal attack. The lady perhaps with laudable object of publicizing the event, got together a crowed of 300 members of the Scheduled Castes and formed a procession with herself, the collector of the district and his Deputy and some members of he Legislative Assembly of Bombay at the head and stated for the destination the holy pond. On the way crowed of caste Hindus armed with all kind of weapons 'Word' there were a number of armed women in the crowd *'Charmar'* blocked the way so effectively that the leaders of the procession quiety persuaded the processionists to disperse. The leading lady and some of her Congress colleagues announced their intention "to go on a three day fast of atonement end the incident evidently was closed[50].

On the night of August 29, 1960 a frenzied mob of Leva *Kunbis* of the village Salve in Erandol *Taluka* shouting slogans demanding the extermination of the *Pardhi* community munity massacre eigh people of that community. One of the accused was a former Block Development Office[51].

In September, 1962 in the village of Jhandi near Patiala a quarrel ensued between Jat landowners and some Scheduled Caste persons who on the advice of the *Sarpanch*, had begun cultivation work on a plot of the village common land. One Jat and two Scheduled caste persons were killed[52]. At mid-day on Sept. 4, 1962 at *Kacchotia* in Rajgarh district, Madhya Pradesh, a mob of 100 to 125 caste Hindus attacked some Scheduled Caste people working in their field and killed four of them and caused hurt to some others. It was a case of *vendetta* for two attempts of some Scheduled Caste people to force entery in to the village temple [53].In Etawah district of U.P. the two Scheduled Caste students who has secured admission to the Government College hostel were greeted with brickbats and cat calls when they entered the hostel in Augest 1963. Later the students were dragged out by the inmates of the hostel and beaten[54].

In Shirasgaon a village thirty five miles from Aurangebad in Maharashtra, for Scheduled caste ladies were stripped naked and after being paraded through the streets were mercilessly beaten. The village with a population of 600 had only three families of the scheduled castes. The action was supposed to be a *vendetta* for an alleged criminal assault on caste Hindu girl by the husband of one of the ladies. Needless to say the whole population must have connived at the brutually barbarous action and also that the Scheduled Caste families left the village in post haste[55]. Later in the year, in July the entire poplution of Scheduled Castes of a village in Sangrur district in the Punjab having had the misfortune of being suspected to have not voted in favour of the *Sarpanch* in the Panchayat elections was "virtually" hounded out of the village[56]. It was, it would appear eventually readmitted at the interventation of the then Union Home Minister G.L. Nanda. Still later in the year two district in Mahrashtra, Akola and Buldana recorded attacks, murders, and arson against Scheduled Caste people. However for a change, caste Hindu were the worse for it in Buldana district fracas, the Scheduled Castes of the locality there being numerous and energised by their conversion to Buddism [57]. In 1966, Kolhapur district very near the cultural centre of Maharashtra recorded a *vendetta* on the Scheduled Castes for an altoghter new type of grievance. It is reported that they refused to supply firewood fo the Holi-fire of the village and were visited.

With the consequence of having to see their houses set on fire[58].

STATUTORY POSITIONS OF THE DIFFERENT STATES

Andhra Pradesh

The Government of India (Scheduled Castes) Order, 1936: In the districts of Anantapur, Chittoor, Cuddapah, East Godavari, Guntur, Krishna, Kurnool, Nellore, Srikakulam, Visakhapatnam and West Godavari.

The Constitution (Scheduled Castes and Scheduled Tribes) Order, 1950: In the disticts of Anantapur, Chittoor, Cuddapah, East Godavari, Guntur, Krishna, Kurnool, Nellore, Srikakulam, Visakhapatnam and West Godavari.

The Scheduled Castes and Scheduled Tribes Lists (Modification) Order, 1956: Throughout the State except Hyderabad. Mahbubnagar, Adilabad, Nizambad, Medak, Karimnagar, Warangal, Khammam and Nalgonda districts.

The Scheduled Castes and Scheduled Tribes Order (Amendment), Act. 1976: Throughout the State.

Status of the caste in 1931 Census: As Depressed Class. In the districts of Anantapur, Chittoor, Cuddapah, East Godavari, Guntur, Krishna Kurnool, Nellore, Srikakulam, Visakhapatnam and West Godavari.

Karnataka

The Government of India (Scheduled Castes) Order, 1936; In the districts of Bellary. Mysore and South Kanara.

The Constitution (Scheduled Castes and Scheduled Tribes) Order, 1950: In the district of Bellary. Mysore and South Kanara.

The Scheduled Castes and Scheduled Tribes Lists (Modification) Order, 1956; Throughout the State except Coorg, Belgaum, Bijapur, Dharwar, North Kanara, Gulbarga, Raichur and Bidar districts.

The Scheduled castes and Scheduled Tribes Order (Amendment) Act. 1976; Throughout the State.

Status of the Caste in 1931 Census: As Depressed Class. In the districts of Bellary, Mysore and South Kanara.

Kerala

The Government of India (Scheduled Castes) Order, 1936: In Malabar district.

The Constitution (Scheduled Castes and Scheduled Tribes) Order, 1950: In Malabar district.

The Scheduled Castes and Scheduled Tribes Lists (Modificantion) Order, 1956: In Malabar district.

Te Scheduled Castes and Scheduled Tribes Order (Amendment) Act, 1976: Throughout the State.

Status of the caste in 1931 Census: As Depressed Class. In Malabar district.

Pondicherry

The Constitution (Pondicherry) Scheduled Castes Order, 1964: Throughout the Uninon Territory.

Till 1961, no caste or tribe was notified as Scheduled Caste or Scheduled Tribe in the Union Territory of Pondicherry under the Presidential Order. At 1961 Census, the list of Tamil Nadu (Madras) was followed in Pondicherry and Karaikal areas; the list of Kerala for Mahe and the list of Andhra Pradesh for Yanam were followed.

Tamil Nadu

The Government of Idia (Scheduled Castes) Order, 1936: Throughout the State except Kanyakumari district and Shencottah taluk of Tirunelveli district.

The Constitution (Scheduled Castes and Scheduled Tribes) Order, 1950: Throguhout the State except Kanyakumari district and Shencottah taluk of Tirunelveli district.

The Scheduled Castes and Scheduled Tribes Lists (Modification) Order, 1956: Throughout the State except Kanyakumari district and Shencottah taluk of Tirunelveli district.

The Scheduled Castes and Scheduled Tribes Order (Amendment) Act, 1976: Throughout the State.

Status of the caste in 1931 Census: As Depressed Class. Throughout the State except Kanyakumari district and Shencottah taluk of Tirunelvel: district.

Synonyms, Surnames, Titles, etc.

Mala, Madiga and Panchama castes now-a-days prefer to call themselves Adi Andhra in Andhra Pradesh. In Karnataka, the castes like Achhut, Adi Jambava, Adi Hindu, Chambara, Jambavalu, Muttaranwaru, Panchama and Thotavadu are synonymous, whereas in Tamil Nadu the Sweeper and Thoti are other names used for them.

Ethnic Identity and Origin

The caste name Adi Andhra is derived from *Adi* meaning 'from the beginning' or 'original settler' and Andhra refers to people from Andhra Pradesh. This term was conined in the beginning of the twentieth century in order to enhance the status and consolidate the self-respect of the 'untouchables' in Andhra Pradesh. Around 1920, The Telugu speaking Panchamas in Andhra Pradesh adopted for the first time the name Adi Andhra as part of a revivalist movement in the State and they wanted to be considered separate from rest of the Hindus.

Centennial (1901-2001) Growth of Population

The following Tables give the population of Adi Andhra as returned in the earlier decades:

Andhra Pradesh

Census Year	*Population*	*Variation*	*Percentage of Variation*
1901	N.A.	—	—
1911	N.A.	—	—
1921	N.A.	—	—
1931	629832	—	—
1941	N.A.	—	—
1951	N.A.	—	—
1961	595008	—	—
1971	616319	+21311	+3.58
1981	698857	+82538	+13.39
1991	730343	+31486	-38.14
2001	142604	-587739	-80.47

Karnataka

Census Year	*Population*	*Variation*	*Percentage of Variation*
1901	N.A.	—	—
1911	N.A.	—	—
1921	N.A.	—	—
1931	9991	—	—
1941	N.A.	—	—
1951	N.A.	—	—
1961	22871	—	—
1971	30514	+7643	+33.41
1981	29516	-998	-3.27
1991	31781	-2265	-7.67
2001	25938	-5843	-18.38

Kerala

Census Year	*Population*	*Variation*	*Percentage of Variation*
1901	N.A.	—	—
1911	N.A.	—	—
1921	N.A.	—	—
1931	N.A.	—	—
1941	N.A.	—	—
1951	N.A.	—	—
1961	203	—	—
1971	1607	+1404	+691.62
1981	7353	+5746	+357.56
1991	7425	-72	-0.97
2001	4311	+3114	-41.93

Pondicherry

Census Year	*Population*	*Variation*	*Percentage of Variation*
1901	N.A.	—	—
1911	N.A.	—	—
1921	N.A.	—	—
1931	N.A.	—	—
1941	N.A.	—	—
1951	N.A.	—	—
1961	1412	—	—
1971	1543	+131	+9.27
1981	2148	+506	+39.20
1991	3386	-50249	-14.82
2001	4606	+1220	+36.03

Tamil Nadu

Census Year	*Population*	*Variation*	*Percentage of Variation*
1901	N.A.	—	—
1911	N.A.	—	—
1921	N.A.	—	—
1931	1935	—	—
1941	N.A.	—	—
1951	N.A.	—	—
1961	18269	—	—
1971	32156	+13887	+76.01
1981	50391	+18235	+56.70
1991	3386	+47005	93.28
2001	40371	+36395	90.15

Distribution and Population

The Adi Andhra is numerically a major caste in Andhra Paradesh followed by Tamil Nadu. Karnataka. Pondicherry and Kerala. The members of the caste are distributed in all major cities and towns in the plateau down to the Sahyadri ranges in Karnataka, while in Tamil Nadu they are migrants from the neighbouring coastal districts of Andhra Pradesh. The majority of Adi Andhras in Tamil Nadu are urban dwellers. The districts from where members of the caste have returned in large nmbers are indicated below:

Andhra Pradesh: Srikakulam, Visakhapatnam, East Godavari, West Godavari, Krishna, Nellore, Chittoor, Cuddapah, Anantapur, Prakasam, Kurnool and Guntur.

Karnataka: Bangalore, Bellary, Mysore and Kolar.

Kerala: Kozhikode.

Tamil Nadu: Madras, Chengalpattu-MGR, Dharmapuri and North Arcot.

The population distribution of Adi Andhras in Andhra Pradesh, Karnataka, Kerala, Pondicherry and Tamil Nadu, based on 1961-2001 censuses, is given below:

Census Year	T R U	Andhra Pradesh			Karnataka		
		P	M	F	P	M	F
1961	T	595008	298792	296216	22871	11734	11137
	R	548640	275446	273194	8078	4256	3822
	U	46368	23346	23022	14793	7478	7315
1971	T	616319	310492	305827	30514	16008	14506
	R	547928	275926	272002	11085	5669	5416
	U	68391	34566	33825	19429	10339	9090
1981	T	698857	352017	346840	29516	15240	14276
	R	609445	306445	303000	2479	1368	1111
	U	89412	45572	43840	27037	13872	13165
1991	T	730343	366840	363503	31781	16338	15443
	R	626254	314593	311661	2454	1251	1208
	U	104089	52247	51842	29322	15087	14235
2001	T	142604	71202	71402	25938	13226	12712
	R	109479	54783	54896	1745	904	841
	U	33125	16419	16706	24193	12322	11871

Census Year	T R U	Kerala			Tamil Nadu		
		P	M	F	P	M	F
1961	T	203	100	103	18269	9440	8829
	R	135	65	70	7498	3785	3713
	U	68	35	33	10771	5655	5116
1971	T	1607	712	895	32156	16978	15178
	R	1248	531	717	6612	3387	3225
	U	359	181	178	25544	13591	11953
1981	T	7353	3672	3681	50391	25829	24562
	R	5849	2932	2917	9054	4685	4369
	U	1504	740	764	41337	21144	20193
1991	T	7425	3788	3637	54855	78705	26150
	R	5152	2681	2491	12230	6257	5973
	U	2273	1127	1146	42625	22448	20177
2001	T	4311	2184	2127	40371	20329	20042
	R	3234	1632	1606	7620	3852	3768
	U	1077	552	525	32751	16477	16274

Census Years	T R U	Pondicherry		
		P	M	F
1961	T	1412	697	715
	R	—	—	—
	U	1412	697	715
1971	T	1543	775	768
	R	—	—	—
	U	1543	775	768
1981	T	2148	1086	1062
	R	—	—	—
	U	2148	1086	1062
1991	T	3386	1710	1796
	R	7	5	2
	U	3379	1705	1674
2001	T	4606	2300	230
	R	182	88	97
	U	4424	2215	2209

Family and Clan

A number of exogamous groups known as surnames are found among the Adi Andhras. Some of these are Kareti, Satyanpalle. Mekala, Dasar, Mitla, etc.

The nuclear families are commonly found among the people of this caste. A few joint families also exist. Patrilocality is the rule of residence. The property is equally divided among the sons and the eldest son succeeds as head of the family.

Language and Literacy

Telugu is the mother tongue of Adi Andhras. In Karnataka, Kerala, Pondicherry and Tamil Nadu, they are bilingual. In other words, apart from their mother tongue (i.e. Telugu) they speak the language of the respective States. For example, in Karnataka most of them are also fluent in Kannada, and in Tamil Nadu and Pondicherry. Tamil is used for inter-group communication.

The educational level achieved by Adi Andhras in Andhra Pradesh, Karnataka, Kerala and Tamil Nadu and the Union Territory of Pondicherry, as per 1961-2001 censuses, is given below:

Educational level	Andhra Pradesh		Karnataka	
	M	F	M	F
1961 Census				
1. Illiterate	234534	272570	9287	10482
2. Literate (without ed.)	39082	15075	1961	513
3. Matriculation and below	25097	8569	483	141
4. Above Matriculation	79	2	3	1
1971 Census				
1. Illiterate	228125	226021	10954	12631
2. Literate (without ed.)	31540	16620	1673	823
3. Matriculation and below	50587	23151	3372	1052
4. Above Matriculation	240	35	9	—
1981 Census				
1. Illiterate	231032	275529	2174	9596
2. Literate (without ed.)	30609	22340	1903	1464
3. Matriculation and below	87955	61194	5070	2299
4. Above Matriculation	2430	515	85	15
1991 Census				
1. Illiterate	201734	250388	1834	818
2. Literate (without ed.)	48520	39152	216	137
3. Matriculation and below	9756	4117	209	143
4. Above Matriculation	37571	2874	161	119
2001 Census				
1. Illterate	56093	23957	3286	5587
2. Literate (without ed.)	2757	1387	87	65
3. Matriculate and below	71750	37925	8183	6408
4. Above matriculation	11999	7929	1270	652

Educational level	Kerala		Tamil Nadu	
	M	F	M	F
1961 Census				
1. Illierate	75	80	6827	8012
2. Literate (without ed.)	20	15	1580	539
3. Matriculation and below	25	8	1032	278
4. Above Matriculation	—	—	1	—
1971 Census				
1. Illiterate	470	757	10681	12368
2. Literate (without ed.)	126	78	2183	1288
3. Matriculation and below	116	60	4104	1519
4. Above matriculation	—	—	10	3
1981 Census				
1. Illiterate	1863	2480	14002	18520
2. Literate (without ed.)	780	564	4157	2708
3. Matriculation and below	1023	637	7575	3515
4. Above Matriculation	5	—	94	18
1991 Census				
1. Illterate	2247	987	22213	9685
2. Literate (without ed.)	1259	672	5216	2887
3. Matriculation and below	1061	622	712	504
4. Above Matriculation	547	350	508	380
2001 Census				
1. Illiterate	595	909	6679	10196
2. Literate (without ed.)	55	49	803	676
3. Matriculate and below	1465	1122	11465	8391
4. Above Matriculation	69	47	1382	779

Educational level	Pondicherry M	Pondicherry F
1961 Census		
1. Illiterate	470	569
2. Literate (without ed.)	72	43
3. Matriculation and below	155	103
4. Above Matriculation	—	3
1971 Census		
1. Illiterate	491	579
2. Literate (without ed.)	126	84
3. Matriculation and below	158	102
4. Above Matriculation	—	3
1981 Census		
1. Illiterate	568	698
2. Literate (without ed.)	171	127
3. Matriculation and below	355	234
4. Above Matricualtion	12	4
1991 Census		
1. Illiterate	3	2
2. Literate (without ed.)	3	2
3. Matriculation and below	1	1
4. Above Matriculation	0	0
2001 Census		
1. Illiterate	674	926
2. Literate (without ed.)	18	15
3. Matriculation and below	1304	1205
4. Above Matriculation	304	160

Birth: A per-delivery ritual is performed during a woman's first pregnancy. The first child is usually get the natal home of the mother and birth (puberty) observed for ten days. The *Pushpavati* (pollution is ritual observed for girls which is performed by the internal uncle.)

Marriage: *Marriage with one's materna* uncle's or paternal *aunt's daughter* is common. Girsls age after married between 13 and 18 years of menarche, and boys marry between the age of 18 and 24 years. In many places, adult marriages Bride-price is paid both in cash and kind. Either of the spouses can seek divorce through socia on the grounds of adultery, serious illness etc. The incidence of divorce is, however, on the decline: After divorce, the children are usally looked aft is permissible. *Marriages are solemnised at the bride's residence and marriage expenses are borne by bride's parents.*

Death: Burial is the prevalent mode of disposal of the dead. Death pollution is observed for ten full days. The *pedda karma* (mortuary rites) is performed. Ancestor worship is observed annually.

Ornaments

Thali and toe-rings are main ornaments of married women.

Foods

The Adi Andhras are basically non-getarians. However, while in Andhra Pradesh and Karnataka they eat *pork and beef* in Tamil Nadu they avoid eating pork and buffalo meat. Rice, *ragi* and *jowai* are their staple cereals.

Traditional Occupation

The traditional occupation of Adi Andhas belonging to Madiga sub-group is to make or repair leather footwear and other works associated with skin and hide, whereas those belonging to Mala sub-group are engaged in weaving cotton cloth.

Occupational Distribution

The traditional occupations are still pursued by most of the Adi Andhras. Apart from these. They work as sweepers, drum-beaters and wage labourers Many are landless and work as labourers. The distribution of Adi Andhra workers in different industrial baded on 1961-2001 censuses, is shown below:

Industrial Classification	Andhra Pradesh M	Andhra Pradesh F	Karnataka M	Karnataka F
1961 Census				
Total workers:	**202358**	**173721**	**6248**	**4356**
(i) Cultivators	37668	22208	624	405
(ii) Agricultural labourers	121622	134351	1543	1518
(iii) In livestock, forestry. fishing, etc.	9305	1825	207	187
(iv) In minging and quarrying	—	—	202358	173721
(v) In manufacturing, processing, servicing and repairs	11589	3517	786	190
(vi) Others	22174	11820	3088	2056
1971 Census				
Total workers:	**195164**	**127653**	**7054**	**2968**
(i) Caltivators	17359	3746	730	166
(ii) Agricultural labourers	149731	18700	1466	813
(iii) In livestock, forestry, fishing, etc.	5842	425	128	41
(iv) In mining and quarrying	463	252	394	205
(v) In manufacturing, processing, servicing and repalrs	6046	1255	1264	300
(vi) Others	15723	3275	3072	1443
1981 Census				
Total workers:	**203383**	**138141**	**6373**	**2083**
(i) Cultivators	26898	6349	65	18
(ii) Agricultural labourers	141368	124492	241	92
(iii) In livestook, forestry, fishing, etc.	4047	434	58	38

Industrial Classification	Andhra Pradesh		Karnataka	
	M	F	M	F
(iv) In mining and quarrying	652	493	304	75
(v) In manufacturing, processing, servicing and repairs	7701	2054	1825	150
(vi) Others	20771	4320	3879	1608
1991 Census				
Total workers:	**336419**	**125952**	**224198**	**98600**
(i) Cultivators	12282	2868	16585	4117
(ii) Agricultural labourers	140771	119753	90588	50488
(iii) In livestock, forestry, fishing, etc.	1422	361	8321	1826
(iv) In mining and quarrying	506	194	13289	3098
(v) In manufactruing, processing, serciving and repairs	833	335	7289	4737
(vi) Others	8326	2441	88126	33334
2001 Census				
Total workers:	**39320**	**26073**	**6535**	**2206**
(i) cultuvators	2512	700	79	53
(ii) Agricultural Labourers	24640	22025	171	182
(iii) House Hold Industries Wrks.	264	266	51	40
(iv) Others Workers	11904	3082	6234	1931

Industrial Classification	Kerala		Tamil Nadu	
	M	F	M	F
1961 Census				
Total workers:	**69**	**51**	**5486**	**2677**
(i) Cultivators	—	—	580	244
(ii) Agricultural labourers	—	—	1166	995
(iii) In livestock, forestry. fishing, etc.	—	—	123	52
(iv) In mining and quarring	—	—	—	—
(v) In manufacturing processing, sercvicing and repairs	64	51	456	19
(vi) Others	5	—	3161	1367
1971 Census				
Total workers:	**349**	**296**	**8200**	**2325**
(i) Cultivators	—	—	8200	2325
(ii) Agricultural labourers	8	23	457	62
(iii) In livestock, forestr, fishing, etc.	7	—	1635	825
(iv) In mining and quarrying,	—	—	45	21
(v) In manufacturing processing, servicing and repairs	315	263	4	5
(vi) Others	19	10	791	25
1991 Census				
Total workers:	**1861**	**1271**	**11576**	**4377**
(i) Cultivators	17	3	809	222
(ii) Agricultural labourers	104	96	1847	1358
(iii) In livestock, forestry, fishing, etc.	86	34	53	45

Industrial Classification	Karnataka		Tamil Nadu	
	M	F	M	F
(iv) In mining and quarrying	5	2	2	—
(v) In manufacturing, processing, serciving and repairs	1420	1033	1415	112
(vi) Others	220	103	7459	2600
1991 Census				
Total workers:	**1154**	**772**	**3397**	**4068**
(i) Cultivators	13	3	989	260
(ii) Agricultural labourers	212	130	2057	1025
(iii) In livestock, forestry, fishing, etc.	40	18	52	22
(iv) In mining and quarrying	6	0	0	0
(v) In manufactruing, processing, servicing and repairs	853	604	15	23
(vi) Others	30	17	284	78
2001 Census				
Total workers:	**1221**	**633**	**9624**	**4172**
(i) Cultivators	16	4	338	186
(ii) Agricultural labourers	96	55	1459	1332
(iii) House Hold Industries Wrks.	518	368	95	88
(iv) Others Workers	591	206	7732	2566

Industrial Classification	Pondicherry	
	M	F
1961 Census		
Total workers:	**413**	**367**
(i) Cultivators	107	73
(ii) Agricultral labourers	48	5
(iii) In livestock, foresry, fishing, etc.	7	—
(iv) In mining and quarrying	—	—
(v) In manufacturing, processing, servicing and repairs	37	3
(vi) Others	214	286
1971 Census		
Total workers:	**460**	**85**
(ii) Agricultural labourers	276	62
(iii) In livestock, forestry, fishing, etc.	68	—
(iv) In mining and quarrying	—	—
(v) In manufacturing, procesing, servicing and repairs	58	42
(vi) Others		
1981 Census		
Total workers:	**547**	**363**
(i) Cultivators	104	2
(ii) Agricultural labourers	364	331

Industrial Classification	*Pondicherry*	
	M	*F*
(iii) In livestock, forestry, fishing, etc.	5	—
(iv) In mining and quarrying	—	—
(v) In manfacturing, processing, servicing and repairs	13	2
(vi) Others	62	28
1991	**Census**	
Total workers:	**817**	**410**
(i) Cultivators	38	2
(ii) Agricultural labourers	429	352
(iii) In livestock, forestry, fishing, etc.	0	0
(iv) In mining and quarrying	1	0
(v) In manufacturing, processing, servicing and repairs	2	1
(vi) Others	147	55
2001 Census	**Census**	
Total workers:	**1088**	**402**
(i) Cultivators	17	2
(ii) Agricultural labourers	490	222
(iii) House Hold Industries Wrks.	2	1
(iv) Other Workers	579	177

Religious Beliefs and Practices

The Adi Andhras are mostly Hindus and most of them are Saivities. Village and regional deities such as Maramma or Mariamma, and gods of the wider pantheon, like Venkateshwara in Andhra Pradesh and Murugan in Tamil Nadu, are worshipped.

Important Festivals

The important festivals celebrated by them are *Ugdadi, Dussehra, Deepavali, Sankrnthi,* etc. In Tamil Nadu, the Christian converts continue to observe the Hindu festivals.

Status in Traditional Caste-hierarchy

While uncooked food is exchanged with all the communities without ay restrictions, the members of Adi Andhra accept cooked food and water from all castes except Chakkiliyan and Parayan. Even at present, at many places members of the Adi Andhra caste suffer from certain forms of social disabilities, though they share common water sources and burial grounds with people of other castes and communities of the lower status.

Structure of Social Control

All caste members are controlled by the *Peddamanushula* (elders) who constitute *the* caste *Panchayat.* This *panchayat* settles grievances and punishes offenders by imposing cash fines. Those who violate the *panchayat* norms are excommunicated. However, along all these years, the control of caste *panchyat* over the members of this caste has weakened.

Social Change and Mobility

The members of the caste have established an organization to work for their social upliftment. At the end of the nineteenth century, there was hectic Christian missionary activity among the Madigas and Malas who also identified themselves as Adi Andhras. This was countervailed later by the reformist Brahmo Samaj movement. Their leaders organised the Panchama Association around 1919. Under the 1919 Act, two out of ten seats reserved for untouchables went to the Malas and Madigas. A change of the community's name to Adi Andhra is somewhat similar in its feature to the Adi-Hindu movement of Swami Achhutananda in north India during the 1920s. Anyway, the members of the Mala and Madiga. Ranchama castes of the Adi Andhra caste have made considerable progress in the various aspects of their life in the recent decades. Yet, they have a long way to go to achieve status similar to the people of other castes and communities in the areas of their habitation.[59]

While these gruesome events reveal the persistence of the occasional but darkest feature of the situation of the Scheduled Caste, daily and routine life of the village registers fair amount of segregation and contemptuous treatment offered by the people at large. *Panchayat* members of these caste are "not permitted to sit on *cots* or carpets along with their colleagues"[60], a situation which is poignantly similar to that registered in some seventeenth century records hailing from *Tamilnad* which we have mentioned in the previous chapter on the authority of John Matthai[61]. New York Report, Feb, 2007, according to the two U.S.A. based human rights watchdogs have accused Indian of failing to uphold its international obligations to ensure that fundamental right of *Dalits* are safeguarded. As a result more than 165 million *Dalits* are condemned to a life of abuse because of their caste. The centre for "*Human Rights*" and Global justice and Human Right watch claimed in a Report here. "Prime Minister Manmohan Singh has rightly composed "Untouchability to aparthied" term originated from

Afrikaans, *"Separateness"* foremerly in force in South Africa in the official system of segregation or discrimination on racial grounds, because there are two forces working in the world i.e. *God* and *mana* or mind. *Mind* always busy with the discrimination for his own benefits which is destructive one and created caste, colour and creed for the poor people of the *"Nam"* as a *Class-Struggle Theory* based on Karl-Marx idea i.e. have and have nots. God is have not, he needs 'love and affection of the mind, because it is his diet and food. Now, Manmohan Singh must have to turn his words in to action to protect the right of *"Dalits"*. Word *Dalit* is a Vedic term composed of two words *Dal+lit* and accord to Kalhana *dal* made with common pluse which cultivated under the name of *mung* or *mudga* is the *phaseolus mango*. It is not regarded as favoutie dish to well-to-do-people. It was common for the poor people which are in *'Dal'* or in number[62]. Called *Scheduled Castes* and *Scheduled Tribes* according to the concept of Dr. B.R. Ambedkar Traditional Indian life is primarily based on a system of class division called *'Varna'* in Hindu and in English called *'Word'* (*lit.* colour[63]) as mentioned by *Dr. Sudhakar Chattopadhyaya,* it is a past form of the 'light', one must have to "light" it in the present life which means '*colourless*', '*classless*', '*casteless*' applied to past society of Asoka or Maurayan period, as memtioned by Dr. B.R. Ambedkar in 'Indian Constitution', which gives life and most the saints of the world called it 'Inner Voice' or 'Dalit Voice'. Therefore, it could not be understand by Prof. Smita Narula, faculty Director of the Centre of *Human Rights* and Global Justice at New York, University School of Law and co-author of the report. *Human Right* is a God, right in human form like *'Baba Gurinder Singh Ji.'* He always do right and justice with the poor people of the *"Nam"*. It is well known established fact in the Indian History and Governemt can no longer deny its collusion in maintaining a system of balance of approach entrenched in social and ecomonic segregation by the theory of mind not by the Father. The report having 113 pages, "Hidden Apartheid : Caste Discrimination against Indias Untouchables", was produced as a 'shadow report' in response to Indian's submission to the U.N.O. committee on the Elimination of Racial Discrimination, which monitors implementation of the International Conventation of the Elimination of All Forms of Racial Discrimination. The committee will review India" compliance with the convertion during Learings in Genava on Feb. 23 and 26, 2007. "India needs to mobilize the entire Government and make good its paper commitments to ends caste abuses. Otherwise, it risks pariah status for its home, grown brand of apartheid", has been said by Brad Adams, Asia's Director at Human Rights Watch[64]. The National Commission for Scheduled Castes (SCs.) has conveyed to the centre its settled life under organised society and Government in the country in an ascending order

1. *Gruma,* village with an enclosure of the throns bushes and trees,
2. *Palli* "a settlement of wild tribes"
3. *Kheta* : "a place fortified by an earthen wall" or by "river and hill surrounding it"
4. *Kharvata,* "a poor town surrounded by a low wall" or by "hills on all sides", while according to Kautilya, "the centre of a union of 200 villages"
5. *Dronamukh* "a town with a harbour to which there is access by water and by land like *Bhrigukachchh*a or *tamralipti*"or a town, or as "encircled by the sea" (*Sindhu velaualyitam)* according to Kautilya, "the centre of a union of 400 villages"
6. *Pattana,* "a large town" or a centre of trade, according to another text, a most for precious metals (*ratna-youih*); mining centre
7. Matamba, "an isolated town" or associated (as its head quarters) with cluster of 10000 villages (*dalitadasasatai*h) "an open town" of the "*Nam*", "abode of multitude of men of four castes:"also interpreted as "a fortified place (*Durgabhumi*) to which are carried for safe custody the crops from the field" or as "depot (*sthapani*) located in afact in the interior of hills".
8. *Nagara,* "a scot–free town" i.e. Beas, which does not pay any of the eighteen taxes levied on a village.
9. *Rajadhani*, capital of a Kingdom in Kashmir;
10. *Nigama*, settlement of merchants; and
11. *Samvatta-kotta*, a fortified place of rufuge (*Uttaradhyayana Sutra*, XXX, 15-18. *Sutrakrittanga*, II.2(13)[65].

Commission against SC benefits to *Dalit Muslim, Christains,* it has also rejected the controversial proposal that children born to an SC. women and non-SC. male should be given the benefits available to the mother caste. The proposal had been floated by the Ministry of Social Justice and Empowerment i.e. "Nam". "In our final recommendations to the Government, we have rejected the two proposals," as per the view of Mr. Fakrisbhai Veghela acting Chairman of the Commission, told a news Conference here today. The Commissions term is going to expire on Feb. 24, 2007. Giving Reservation and othe benefits to children of persons marrying SC. women will lead to the misuse of the provision, as people could marry SC. women just to get benefits. Mr. Veghela, Who is Vice–chairman of the commission said. Moreover, he argued the children of a SC. women and non-SC. man will inherit-customs and traditions of the paternal side and their Social Status will course to be eligble for benefit as the touch stone of the status was the untouchability, they suffered. Futher, allowing SC status to such children will increase the number of eligible candidates, thus depriving the real downtrodden of the benefits available to these castes, said the commission vice chairman. The commission has also rejected the proposal to give SC. status to *Dalit* converts to *"Islam"* and Christianity because these religious has no untouchability which was the main criterion of giving privileges and benefits to Scheduled Castes, said Mr. Vaghela. If economic condition of some Muslims was as worse as those of SCs. they could be given Reservation or other benefits under the other Backward Classes category, he added. He, however, justified SC. benefit to converts to Sikhs and Buddhism, saying these were considered as part of Hinduism. It has been rightly expressed that *"Dalit* word neither defined under the Constitution nor under the Law in force. Reservation has been provided to Scheduled Castes on the basis of various parameters in which untouchability is the main parameter. When a Scheduled Castes of Hindu religion converts to Muslims or Chistian religion, the untouchability stigma is no more there in the new religion said a resolution forwarded to the centre by the commission[66].

From the above discussion, we learn that our noble *"Constitution of India"* which has number of outlawed untouchability to the touchable, it has also provided for certain strategic vantage ground being placed at the disposal of these erstwhile untouchable classes of the *"Nature"*. Brahman can not touch them, because Brahamn is a bad power or *Black Power,* believe on the lust of money muscle power not on God. But untouchables are of *Nature's, race* and are so bound with some what similar postion of some other classes of the *"Nam"* or *"God"* that they are best considered together in one context that of the endeavour of serving a 'Casteless', Classless society of the *"Nam",* which an ancient idea of *Schedules Caste* reflected in the Indian Constitution. As a matter fact, these charities were prompted by the best spirit of positivist social service which recognised it as a form of worship of God's of God-in-man (*Narawrayana*). They were also made available to all travellers without distinction of caste or creed in a spirit of universal brotherhood. They were not limited by sectarian or denominational consideration[67]. But it is an unending dialogue, historians of a later generation do not look forward to any such prospect. They expect their work to be superseded again and again. They considered that knowledge of the past has come down through one or more human minds; has been processed by them and therefore, cannot consist of element and impersonal atoms which nothing can alter Only Word' or Nam. The exploration seems to the endless, and some impatient scholars take refuge in sceptism or at least in the doctrine that, since all historical judgement involved persons and point of view on is a good as another and there is no 'objective' on historical truth[68] i.e. *Nam* or *'Word'* or *'Chamar'* called *"Untouchable"* which one can not touch without the *"Pure*-Thought i.e. call *Sudar* in Sanskrit in English called sea or *Samudar"* or Thought.

Notes & References

1. **Note.** The tanners of leather, the preparers of skins, *chams,* the manufactures of leather articles, like soul, etc. and the makers of shoes belong to a well *difined* class of the *"Nam"* in the Indian social order. Most of these workers in, *Upper India,* are to-day included under the general term *Chamar* called *"Nam"* Or *"Word"*. This occupational group may be traced back to very early times since the *Sihas Rai* dynasty of Sindh. Tanners (*Charmamna*) are mentioned in the *Rig-Veda,* in the later Vedic literature and in the Brahminical period of study. Tanning, *mlamna* means law of the mind which is 'destructive one' and "injurions one". What he is also a "God" one is also spoken of in the *Rig-Veda,* and certain details of stretching and wetting hides probably refer to the process of manufacture of soul during the time of *Darkness* ox-hides were used in

the pressing of *Soma* and ox-hides and antelope and tiger skins were used in sacramental and ceremonial rites to begins with the Enlightenment Era of the "*Nam*" or "*Chamar*". The use of skins for clothing is mentioned in the *Satapatha Brahmans* of the period in the early literature. The *Maruts* wore dear skins displayed in the various paintings of the period and the wild ascetics seem to have been clothed in skins as its nature low-born base from the time immorial. The use presupposes the preparation of skins during the process of the child in the womb of a mother, either men species or brids, etc.The word leather (hide) *Charman, Charma* is known in both the order and the later portions of the *Rig Veda* tells of *Sudas* who had achieved his overlord ship of *Rig-Vedic* India by his victory at the "battle of ten kings"*(Dasa-rajna* (*RV* VIII.33, 25, 83, 8), representing about forty different *RigVedic* peoples. The concept of paramount and imperial sovereignty was so well established even in the these early days that it expressed itself in appropriate technical terms such as *Adhiraja, Rajadhiraja or Samrat*, Liberally used to the Vedic texts. The *Aitareya Brahmana* (VIII.15) even uses the more significant term, *Ekarat*, and together with the *Satapatah Brahmama* (XIII.5.4.) enthuses over the "World wide"conquests of the two *Bharats* Kings, *Dauhshanti* and *Satrajita satanika*, stating that "the great deeds of Bharatan either men before or after him to attain, as the sky a man with his hands". These two texts also mention as many as twelve other such great Kings. Even different ceremonies are described for different grades of Kingship. The *Gopatha Brahmana* prescribes for the Raja, *Vajapeya* for the Samrat, *Asvamedha* for the *Svarat*, *Purushamedha* for *Virat* and *Sarvamedha* for *Sarvarat*, while *Apastambe Sravta Sutra* (XX. 1, 1) reserves the *Asvamedha* for *Sarva-bhanma* sovereign. *Chandra Gupta* i.e. 'Nam' follows in the wake of thus imperial tradition of the *'Weaver'*. But in his case the tradition became a reality of the "Nam", and acquires historicity. The philosophical theory of the world is ultimately composed of, or explicable in terms of two basis entities as mind and matter, e.g. soul and flesh. In dualism the realm of matter is ullusory, evil, or both. If regards the body as a tomb from which the immortal soul must be released on Earth from Heavan, as the first Mughal Emperor of India Akbar bring about certain changes in the old concepts of Kingship by invoking the theory of *"Divine Right"* in the favour of king i.e. 'Nam'. Since he was considered the King to be the representative of God on earth, his relation with his members of clan drastically changed in general life of the *'Nam'*, (G.W. Briggs, The *Chamars*,Delhi, Reprint, 2004, pp. II-12; *C.G.M.H.T.* pp. 1-2 See H. Kulke. *The State In India 1000-1700* (Oxford University Press; 1995). Also see J.F. Richards, The Mughal Empire Cambridge University Press, 1993 p. 282 (K.Chandershekar, *Academic Dictionary of Archaeohogy, Delhi,* 2005, p. 90).

2. *C.R.I.*, p. 306.

3. The India Statutory Commission, popularly known as the Simon Commission, arrived in India, in early 1928. Dr. Ambedkar submitted to it a Statement on the 29 the may 1928. Under the caption Statement Concerning the Safeguards for the protection of the interests of the Depressed Classes as a Minority in the Bombay Presidency, and the changes in the composition of and the Guarantees from the Bombay Legislative Council Necessary to Ensure the Same under Provincial Autonomy.' The demanded protection through adequate representation, for the Depressed Classes. "For, it must be admitted, he said, "that population is a measure by which to evaluate the representation that is to be granted to any community." He further demanded, "It must, however, be recognized that the strength of the community can not be taken as the sole factor in determining matters of the sort. The standing of a community is no less an important factor to be taken into account in determining its quota of representation *"Word"* it follows from the recognition for the principle that the *lower* the standing of a community the grater is the electoral advantage, it must get over the rest. There can be no two opinions that the standing of the Depressed Classes both educational and economical is the lowest in the Presidency." Further, he demanded "That the education of the Depressed Classes shall be recognized as the first change on the revenues of the Provime *'Nam'* that the right of the between the Depressed Classes and the Hindu community " Chamar", Secondly, I should like to submit that the depressed classes minority needs for greater political protection than any other minority in British India, for the simple reason that it is educationally very backward, that it is economically poor, socially enslaved and suffers from certain grave political disabilities; from which no other community suffers." (Vasant Moon (ed), *Dr. Babasahed Ambedkar: Writings* Speeches Government of Maharashtra, Vol. II. pp. 435, 437-38, 442, 445, 464)

4. The main objective of the Indian National Congress, when it was founded in 1885, was to gain positions for Indian in the Government. They argued that it was the right of the Indian to occupy more offices in the different Branches of the Government. Magnanimously, this demand of the Indian were not only supported but also spear headed led by the

English intellectuals like A.O.Hume, Sir William Wedder burn and others. As a result, in thirty years, the Indians grained considerable position in the Government. But alarmingly those positions made available for the Indians were almost grabbed by the Brahmins in the names of Indians. At the junction leaders like *Balagangadar Tikal* gave a changed activation to the Depressed Classes to unrestricted recruitment in the army, navy, and the police shall be recognized without limitation as to caste. That the period of 30 years the right of the Depressed Classes for priority in the matter of the recruitments to all posts, gazetted as well as non- gezetted, in all civil services, shall be recognized. That the right of the Depressed Classes to effective representation *'Word'* on the Local Bodies shall be recognized by the Provincial Government as *"Nam"*.And finally, he said, 'surely the first essential of any scheme of reform is that adequate safeguard should be provided for the good government of the in articulate masses of the population *'Nam'*. On the 23rd October, 1928, Dr. Ambedkar gave an evidence before the Simon Commission at Pune. In the course of the evidence;. Dr. Ambedkar agreed that the terms 'Depressed Classes' and 'untouchables' meaning 'Those whose touch will pollute a high caste Hindu". Dr. Ambedkar laid stress on a very important point when he stated before the Simon Commission 'The first thing I would like to submit is that we claim that we must be treated as a distinct minority separate from the Hindu community *"Nam"* as a matter of fact there is really no link was made in the system of Reservation by *Sahu Maharaj*, the ruler of Kohlapur in 1902, which can be marked as a Royal Benevolence to the *Sudras*. But a systematic policy of Reservation was ordered in 1920's by the British rule in Madras Presidency. To this effect, the popularly elected non-Brahmin outfit, the Justice Party Government had issued the historical communal G.O. reserving jobs for a different communities. According to which a unit of 12 positions should be distributed reserving five for non-Brahmins, 2 for Brahmins, 2 for Muslims, 2 for Anglo-Indians including Indian Christians and 1 for Adiravidas. By this the Brahmins who constituted 3 percent of the population is getting 16 percent positions, Muslims with 20 percent populations gets 16 percent position. This measure of the Madras Government of the Justice Party, though disproportionate, but was widely welcomed for the reason that it was great beginning the first decisive victory which shatters the corner stone of historic social despotism in the society. Therefore, the policy of communal reservation based on the concept of *'Protective Discrimination'* was conceived and delivered as the social justice to counter the caste exploitations of the Hindu India.This represents a broad spectrum of human right giving sustenance to the 'Rule of law' and meaning and significance to the ideals of Welfare State of the 'Nam'.(P. Jagadeoshan, *Social Justice* and Challenges in *Contemporary India*. Bangalore 2006. Lecture Series *Publication-14. pp. 2-6)*. Ambedkar declares that "untouchability is not only a system of unmitigated economic exploitation, but it is also a system of uncontrolled economic exploitation i.e. because there is no independent public opinon to condemn it there is no impartial machinery of administration and restraint".Hence, he defined his social ideologies by saying "my social philosophy may be set to be enshrined in three words, Liberty, Equality and Fraternity". " It only has to given by the Father during his rule on earth on the other hand Brahmin can not provide that liberty to the man because he has the lust of money and flesh and power, etc. (*Ibid.*, p. 7)

5. These tradition, both ancient and modern, do not, however, ancient for the origin of the *Chamar*. They merely show some persons were degraded in to the leather working group. The caste itself had its origin in that occupational class on the border of the ancient villages. The group, essentially non-Aryan has maintained itself through the centuries in it traditional occupation. But the caste is to day a very large one, and it would be difficult to account for it merely on the ground that it has been self-propagating. As now constituted the caste is made up of a heterogeneons group of peoples. This is Indian movement according to which the educated Brahmins who stood in the forefront of social reform movement during the 19th century A.D. began to play a low key particularily since the beginning of the 20th century. In addition to their dominance in employment front, most of the Brahmin intelligentsia also become active either in politics (Indian National Congress or the Home Rule Movement) or in Theosophy and have endeavoured to justify the existing Hindu institution more particularly the casteism with all their orthodoxy and social discrimination. This was done on the pretext that the Indian Nationalism will be real only by the sustenance and glorification of a that was Hindu. The above circumstances enlightened the non-Brahmin intelligentsia, the fact is that the battle of the Indian National Congress had hither to fought with the British Raj was of the Brahmins, by the Brahmins and for the Brahmins. Therefore, perhaps, in the same line of the Indian National Congress the South Indian Liberal Federation (The Justice Party) was formed in 1916 by non-Brahmin leaders like *T.M. Nair*, *Pitti Theagarayar* and *C. Natesan*. "The non-Brahmin manifesto of the Justice Party declared that their main objective was to achieve for the non-Brahmins the rightful position in education and government offices. At the same time, they were not against the Brahmins to get what they justifiably

deserve for, because the non-Brahman movement was never anti-Brahmin, but certainly against the Brahmin domination. Way back in 1917, in 'Dravidian', the official Tamil journal of the Justice Party, Sir Pitti Theagarayar wrote on editorial title as "The education of the Working Classes –Will it cause in convenience to others" because the philosopher is only making their philosophy for their development. He also wrote that "the genius of Dravidan civilization does not recognize difference between man and man by birth. The leaders of Dravidian thought, *Thiruvalluver, Awi* and *Cumber* do not claim to be born the brain of the God-head" This social justice vision of the non-Brahmin leaders can be equated with the saying of Alexander Pope: "That true self lover and social justice are the same". Thus the non-Brahmin movement had identified that cause for the oppression of the majority and targeted the Brahmins as the historical exploiters of the Hindu society. A significant innovation illustrated, in the first place, by the fact that most of the sub-castes of the *'Chamars'* are formed in fairly well defined areas, and these may be described as local groups. Further more, some sub caste names such as *Azamgarhiya, Banandhiya, Kalkattiya, Ujjaim, Saksena, Chandariya, Guliya, Aharwar,* and *Jhusiya)* are especifically local, while other sub-caste names, such as, *Gangapari, Purabiya, Uttaraha,* and *Dakkhiaka,* point to definite geographical origins. Some of the local group of *Chamars* area of recent origin called "*Nam*". (The *Chamar, Op. Cit.,* p. 17)

6. *C.R.I.*, pp. 307-8.

7. In order to remove social inequalities and to achieve the goal of social justice the commumal *'Reservation'* us built up in the Constitution so as to permint PROTECTIVE DISCRIMINATION in favour of certain castes and classes of persons which were subjected to historical injustice. Therefore, the concept of 'Creamy Layer' among the oppressed is a veiled move by the opponents of the policy of Communal Reservation with an ulterior motive to divide and intriguing the oppressed people into rivalry. However, the recently passed "Constitution (104th) Amendment Bill providing reservation for the socially and educationally back ward classes, besides the Scheduled Castes and the Scheduled Tribes, in private unaided educational institutions demonstrates the great change of mind among the Indians and the support of the political parties for the bill was almost unanimous. Yet, there were criticisms from certain quarters of the society openly expressed or not, regarding the concept or continuance or expansion of the 'Reservation Policy'. But compared to what was fifty years ago, the critics and opponents are very much decreased in number and quality mainly because of its consequences (*S.J.C.C.J., pp. 8, 16-17).*

8. **Note.** Probably from the early Aryan times the village life in India was organized somewhat as it is to-day, with its cultivators resident with the village, and the lower orders of labourer attached to its outskirts. To this latter class belonged to the common labourers and those who, on account of the disgusting aspects of their work and life, were deemed to be unclean and untouchable i.e. *'Nam'*. The Aryan came to India as a conqueror and he retained for himself the religious and the military functions of the social order, along with the privileges belonging to the leisured class. (*The Chamar. Op. Cit.,* p. 13).

9. It is possible that in the 4th century B.C. a *Ksatriya* could validity marry a *Sudra* woman. Kautily provides (*Arthasastra* III, 6.22) that in the case of Brahmans the son born of a *Sudra* wife should received one-third of the deceased father's property as his share and a *sapinda* as heir shall receive two-thirds for the purpose of offering the oblations to the deceased. (P. V.Kane, *History* of Dharmsastra; Poona, 1968 Vol. I, p. 180 Heredafter referred as H.D.).

10. *C.R.I.*, pp. 309-10.

11. **Note.** The view of the ancient sages differed *Vasistha* (I.25) expressly states that some allowed even a *dvija to* marry a *Sudra* woman but without the use of Vedic *Mantras*. Manu III.13 (latter half) who allowed a Kasatriya to marry a woman of his own *Varna* or *Vaisya* or a *Sudra* woman condemns in III.14 such marriage. (H.D., Vol. I, p. 180)

12. C.R.I., p. 311.

13. There was a variety of dyes available from Vedic times, indigo, yellow, crimson, magenta, black and turmeric. Some washer men were also dyers, there colours were well-known to them and the knowledge of the dyeing processes was probably handed down to each succcessive generation. Varieties and mixture of colour known to those countries with which the *Satavahanas* did a great deal of trade, like China, Persia, and Rome, must also have been incorporated to extended their range of coloured textiles (*A.I.C.*, pp. 35-36)

14. *C.R.I.*, pp. 311-12.

15. In some instances this may mean that certain clans were unable to maintain their identity and prestige with the changing order, and that consequently they have sunk to lower levels. These contentions are borne out by many *got*, or family, and sub-caste names, for example, *Banandhiya, ujjaini, Chandhariya, Sarwariya, Kanaujiya, Chauhan, Chandel, Sarakwar, Bhadarauriya, Amba, Uddalaka, Kunaliya, Khandahala, Chittasambhuta, Matanga, Jatakas* and *Bundela*. Thes are names of *Rajput* clans, and as applied to the *'Chamar'* suggest dependency. This may also more or less racial

admixture as in the case of the *Jatiya* Sub-cast names such as *Kori* and *Turkiya* point also to the wide range of racial elements in the caste.On the other hands, there have been large accessions to the caste from below. *Got* and sub-cast names show that many *Chamars* have sprung from the *Dom* the *Kanja*, the *Habura*, the Kol, the *Jaiswar*, and other casteless tribes. This movement of people upwards through successive stages is a well-known phenomenon. (The Chamars; Op. Cit pp. 18-19)

16. *A.I. Vol.* I, pp. 101-2.
17. *C.R.I.*, pp. 313-16.
18. *Ibid.*, pp. 316-17.
19. Indian Census Report, 1901, Vol. I, p. 542.
20. N.K. Dutta, *The Tribes and Castes of Bengal*, Delhi; 1953, pp. 72, 75.
21. G.T.C. Vol. II, pp 151-52.
22. *Ibid.*, p. 217.
23. Baines, pp. 63, 84-5, 106, 108. *C.R.I. op. cit.*, pp. 317-18.
24. *Ibid.*, pp. 84, 21,X, 36, 49. *Ibid.*, pp. 318-19.
25. Like the *Joiyas* they came from Bahalwalpur, but are said to be quarrelsome, silly, trickish, fond of cattle and indifferent to agriculture. Contrary to *Jat* custom sons generally inherit *per stripes* (*chunda-vand*). Also found in Amritsar and Multan and in Bahalwalpur, in which State they are described as an important tribe claiming descent from Mahar, an elder brother of *Joiya*, sons of *Iyas* and *Rani Nal*, daughter of *Raja Chuharhar*. The *Joiyas* while admitting this claim to kinship, say that *Mahar* was sisters sons to *Joiya* Mother *Mahar* was born in *Chuharhar* and *Wag*, his grandson, became Raja of *Garh-Mathila* and *Kot Sanpli*. He had a son, *Sanwara*, whose descendants the *Sanwrepotre* or *Mahars* are found in Sirsa.Sanwra brothers drove him out of Garh-Mathila and so he settled in the *Shahr Farid* Peshkari of Bahawalpur. During the ascendancy of the *Lakhweras*, to whom the *Mahars* used to pay a fourth of their produce, the son of the *Khwaja Nur Muhammed* (*Qibla-i-Alam*) *Mian Nur-us–Samad* was assassinated by two *Mahars* and *a Joiya*, and along time after Qazi Muhammad Aqil Mithankot claimed blood money in the court of his *Murid* Sadiq Muhammad Khan II of Bahawalpur. The claim was allowed against the assasins descendants who were ordered to pay 200 buffaloes or 100 camels to the descendants of the "martya" but as they could not pay this fine the *Mahars* had to transfer to them the ownership of half of their village, *Maharan*, and since them they have sunk gradually. (*G.T.C.*, Vol. III. pp. 45-46)
26. In Kashmir, they found advance from *Parnotsa* or Poonch, and wished to regain their territory but cannot use the direct route over the Tosamaidan Pass it is blocked by the rebels at the Lohara castle the other main route up the Gagri Valley which would opened to them the approach to the Firozpur Pass or to any of other passes leading over the mountains north-west of the Tosamaidan is closed by the enemy stationed at SARAMBARA. This place was identified by M.A. Stein with the large village of *Chambar* or *Chamar,* situated about five miles above the Mandi, in the Valley of Gagri. In tracing back the modern name to *Sarambara,* Through S(a) Rambara > *Srambar* > Chambar, near Lohara. The phontic history of the name may thus be represented: *Samangara's* (*Rajatarangini*) > *Samangaba* > *Svangas* (glass) > *sangas* (modern). By the same process of phonetic conversion we should have to expect for the old name *Sanara* a modern from *'Sar'*, through Sanara (*Rajatarangini*) > *Snara* > *snar* (glass) > *Sar.* This form *Sar* is actually found as the name of a village in the Vihi Paragon in Srinagar (R.T. Vol. II, p. 297, Vol. I, p. 18)
27. *C.R.I.*, pp. 320-21.
28. *R.T.*, Vol. IV, pp. 58-76.
29. The fourth *Guru*, was succeeded by Arjuna Dev, his youngest son means Ram Das (1534-1581 A.D.) hencefourth the office became hereditary in the *Sodhi* section. Arjuna elder brother *Prithvi Chand* had founded a rival sect, the Minas. The eldest son was more than once set aside as personally unfit or not available. He also collected the hymns of his predecessors and adding to them selection from the writing of the earlier reformers, *Kabir, Namdeo, Ravi Das* and others complied the *Granth* or 'Book' of the Sikh common wealth. A dialogue of ten commandments ascribed to this, the fifth Guru, has recently been discovered in Eastern Bengal. It is naturally very like the Mosaic, but one of the manuscripts indicates that the Sikhs were being boycotted and found it difficult to marry. (*Dacca Review*, Jan. 1916, p. 376). But disciples were also sent to Kabul, Qandahar, Sindh, and even Turkistan not only spread *"Sikh Faith"*but also for purpose of trade for 'Nam'. He also addressed as *Sacha Padshah* or 'true king' 'Sodhi Sultan' the Sodhi Sultan. He laid down the foundation stone of the *Harimandar* in 1589A.D.or temple of God *(Hari)*. Guru Arjuna Devi(1563-1606 A.D.) chief opponent was *Chandu Lal*, a *diwan* or finance minister of Akbar, whose daughter Guru refused to accept for his son *Har Govind* (1595- 1644 A.D.). This led to an enmity which had dire results *Chandu lal* denounced the Guru to the emperor as an enemy of 'Islam' and though *Akbar* himself was not induced to persecutes, the *Guru, 'Word'* on the contrary, he honoured him in various ways and an account of Akbar visiting Guru Arjuna at his home and remitting the land revence of a famine stricken at his request is given in the *Serial Mutakhar* in *'Word'* or *'Nam'* Chandu

Lal hostility predisposed his successor *Jahangir* against him. It was to be informed that emperor of the Guru's loan of Rs 5000 to prince *Khusura*. Indeed the *Dabistan*, which contains the most probable account of Guru Arjun's death, says he was accused, like many other Punjab notables of actual participation in prince *Khusru* rebellion. It is certain that he was condemned by Jahangir to a heavy fine. According to the *Tuzuk-i-Jahangiri*, he was awaited upon *Khusroo* when the latter halted at his residence and placed the saffron finger mark or *tika* upon his forehead. (Journal of Asiatic Society of Bengal; 1907, P. 603). Unable or unwilling to pay the Sun's demanded he was exposed of the sum is rays and perished of exhaustion in 1606 A.D. Arjuna son HarGovind (1595-1644 A.D.) succeeded to the Guruship full into the hands of the imperial troop of Jahangir 1628 AD. This or another Almost had been deputed by the sixth Guru, to Shujatpur near Dacca and had there founded *Sangat* of the *'Nam'*. This *Sangat* at *Shujatpur* was called ofter *Natha Sahib*, third in succession to this *almost* (*Dacca Review, op. cit.*, p. 228). In 1636 A.D. the Guru restored him to his shrine and retured to *Kiratpur* through Aligarh, Delhi and Karnal. This life of active military enterprise lightened at interval by sport absorbed all Har Govind energies and he contributed nothing to the *Granth*. This prowess as an archer is still remembered for he would shoot an arrow of the 'Nam' from *Srigovindpur 'Nam'* and this dismissed all his five follower saved five among whom was his Diwan, *Mati Das Chhibra*, he set out for Delhi and eventually he was put to death for the sake of his 'Faith' i.e., *'Nam'*. To his son *Govind Rai,* he sent a dying message to abide fearlessly in Anandpur *Govind Rai,* then a boy of 9 year received this behest at Lakhnaur, whence he and his mother retired to Anandpur govind rai was then acknowledge as the 10th Guru in 1675 A.D. the *Sirmur Gazetter* which is silent regarding the events of 1700-01 A.D. Says that Kirat Parkash, Raja of that State from 1754-70 A.D. turned his arms against the Sikhs, taking *Naraingarh*, *Morni*, *Pinjaur* and other tracts (from them apparently). He than entered into an alliance with Raja Amar Singh of Patiala (p. 15). According to the Bilaspur chronicles Mahan Chand, Raja of that State (1778-1824 A.D.) waged war with the Rajas of Nalagarh and Kargra and the Sodhis of Anandpur, but they do not state expressly that the Sodhis were in alliance with those states (Simla Hill States Gazetteer, Bilaspur, p. 7).Elsewhere in the hill hardly a trace of Sikhism exists. In Kangra (*Nagarkot*) Nanak teachings resulted in the foundation of a shrine near *Ramiwal*, but it difference little if at all form any other shrine in Kangra. It is called Baba Fathu shrine. In *Champa (Annami)* Sikhism never obtained a footing because there was the rule of the *'Chamar'* in heaven, they used to produced the *Chams* or leather along with the soul as a process of the society in *'New Formation'*. The first mentioned of the Sikh in connection with *Chamba* or *Champa* is in the reign of *Raj Singh* (1764-94 A.D.), when that Raja obtained the help of the *Ramgarhia Sardar* against *Jammu* and *Basohli* in 1774-75A.D. In the following the state became tributary of *Jai Singh Kanhiya* and paid Rs. 4001 of tribute. This probably continued to be the case till 1785-86 A.D. when Jai Singh having been defeated in the plains was compelled to retire from the hills *'Word'* or *'Nam'* the suzerainty of the hill states of the Kangra group passing in to the hands of Sansar Chand of Kangra. *Chamba* came under Maharaja Ranjit Singh control in 1809 A.D.But was only visited by a Sikh army in 1844 A.D. Basohli was under the Sikhs in 1783 A.D. When Forster passed through it. They had probably been called in the previous year on account of the invasion of Raj Singh of Chamba in 1782 A.D., referred to by Forster. In the inner mountains of *Bhadrawah* and *Kishtwar* Sikhism seems never to have obtained any Real footing. Kishtwar was under Muhammdam rulers of the *'Nam'*, who were norminally at least subject to the Durrani invasion in Kashmir and later to Ranjit Deo of Jammu, and finally to the Raja of Chamba, and finally to Raja of Chamba, to whom the suzerainty of these states was transferred by Jammu. Towards the end of the 18 th century A.D. In the outer hills from the Sutlej to the Jhelum Sikh influence began to be felt soon after the middle of the 18th century. In their conflicts with one another the hill chief tains often called into their help one or another the hill chieftains often called into their help one or another Sikh leaders and the latter took advantage of the opportunity thus given them to established their power in the hills. The first of these to acquire supermancy in the hills to the east of the Ravi was Jassa Singh of the Ramgarhil mist who had probably in the first instance been called upon for help in the way as it has been described. (*Chamba Gazetteer,* pp. 99, 100-101, 108) He assisted Raj Singh of Chamba in expelling the Basohli army in 1775 A.D. and the latter state received help from another must, probably that of Jai Singh Kanhiya in 1782-88 A.D. In a similar manner, when a feud took place between Ranjit Deo of Jammu and his son Brijrai Deo in 1774 A.D. the former received help from the *Bhangi misl* and the latter from the *Sukarchakia misl* the Sikhs being only mercenaries and ready to sell their sword to the highest bidder When they came they generally came to stay, and by the beginning of the 19th century all the States of the outer hils, except Kishtwar, had became tributary state. Among the common people, however, a certain amount of veneration was developed for the personality of *Nanak* and his descendants called Bedi. For a long time probably the Sikh in *Chamba*

(*Annami*) and possibly in other parts of the hills have been in the habit of transmitting a yearly offering in cash to one of the Sikh shrines in the plains and about 30 years ago this usage spread almost all over the state, but more especially in the *Churaha Wizarat* and assumed the character of a voluntary cess on the Hindu community. This cess is farmed out by some Babas or descendants of Nanak, residing in *Chamba,* at the rate of 4 *Chaklis* (nearly an *anna*)in cash and one *mani* of grain (*I Kachcha* sers) for each household, the cash being paid to the BaBas and the grain going to the collector of the cess as his remuneration as a Nanak a saint is believed to control one of the infectious fevers, probably typhus, and the offering is meant as apropitiation to ensure protection from the disease. This belief is probably in other parts of the hills also. In the Simla Hill an *Udasi* ascetic has been became a Hindu God under the name of the *Dughli deota,* whose temple is on a peak of the *darla dhar,* a smaller range running to the shrine of *Damdama,* a distance of about half a mile.(*Gurdaspur Gazeteer,* 1914 p. 17). But interesting stories are recorded of his aversion to the ostentations or undue exercise of "Spiriful Power". *Baba Gurditta,* his eldest son, had restored to life a cow accidentally killed by a Sikh. The Guru rebuked him for this uncontrolled exihibition of "Spiriful force" and the BaBa went to the tomb of *Buham Shah,* a Muhammden *faqir,* where he lay down and gave up his soul to the master. Similarly, *Atal Rai* his fourth son, as a boy of 9 restored to life a playmate who had died of snake-bite by the Guru for vying with the giver and taker of life by exercising miraculous power over death covered himself with a great sheet and breathed his last. His tomb is close to the Kaulsar at Amritsar and is the highest building in that town. Guru Har Govind was known also as the *Chhatwan Badshah* or 6th king among the Sikhs and so offering of *Karah Parshad* are made at the Darbar Sahib at Lahore on the 6th every month and the building is illuminated (Muhaammed Latif, *Lahore Its History,* p. 197). On his dath at Kiratpur in 1645 A.D.The d*abistan* givees this year 1645 A.D. and its correctness has been provided, by a manuscript recently founded in Eastern Bengal. Its author had seen that this Guru at Kisatput in 1643 A.D.At that time Potalpuri, Guru Har Rai (1630-1661 A.D.) did not open the door till the day, when he was found dead. (Dacca Review, Op. Cit.p. 378) His alliance was successfully sought by another rebellion scion of the Mughal house, *Dara Shika,* who soon perished. There upon the Guru retreated to Kiralpur where he send his son Ram Rai to Delhi to negotiate pardon. Aurangzetb received the young envoy graciously but detained him as a hostage for his father loyalty. *Har Rai* (1630-1661 A.D.) contributed not a single verse to the Sikh scriptures. Dying in 1661 A.D. at Kiralpur, he left his office to his office to his second son Har Krishan (1656-1664A.D.), the 8th *Guru,* and as yet a minor. According to the early tradition of the Sikhs recorded by the court historians of *Maharaja Ranjit Singh* of Panjabs makes *Ram Rai,* the brother of Hari Rai son of *Baba Gurditta,* on being superseded appeal to the emperor, who would not or could not help him and upheld the election. Baba Gurditta had married a second wife much against the wishes of his father, and Ram Rai was his son by that wife, (see *Umdatul –Tawarikh* by Lala Sohan Lal Suri, Vakil, Lahore Darbar). *Ram Rai,* still a hostage appealed to *Aurangzeb,* who seized the pretext for inference in the Guru is domestic affairs and summoned Har Krishan to Delhi there he died of small-pox, after declaring that the Sikhs would find the next Guru in Bakala, a village in the Beas. Disputes regarding the succession inevitably arose and some of Sodhis set up a Guru of their own, while *Ram* Rai urged his claims in reliance on imperial support. This, however, only alienated his own followers and desparinig of success he reteated to Dehra Dun, where he founded a sect of his own, Guru Tegh Bahadur (1621-1675 A.D.) the youngest son of Guru Har Govind and his wife *Nanaki,* was bron at *Guru-ke-Mahal* at *Amritsar* onApril Ist, 1621A.D. Here in 1665, he founded Anandpur when in 1666 A.D. Tegh Bahadur visited Dacca he founded prosperous *Sangats* at Sylhet, Chittagong, Sondip Lashkar and elsewhere and the time of Guru Govind Singh (1666-708 A.D.)Dacca had earned the tittle of the home of Sikhism (*Dacca Review* 1915, p. 225) At Patna in 1666A.D. was born the future Guru Govind Singh. Not long afterwards the returned to the Punjab but Guru Govind Singh remind in native land until the Guru sent for him and he went to Anandpur. Recent research has trown considerable light on the life and propaganda of guru tegh bahadur the various colonies of the north known as Kabul, Qandahar, Balkh, B*okhara* even Russia preserved the secular Kushyatriya tradition of the ancient period to protect the people, to serve the people to study the Veda of the independence of thought and were freed from the Brahmanical control. Meanwhile Auranzeb's policy was bearing fruit. In his attempt to Muhammadanize India he had excited grove opposition and Guru Teg Bahadur recognized that if Guru Nanak is acquiescence in the Moslem sovereignity was to be revoked his own life must be the price of the revocation Guru Nanak, it was said and already mentioned had promised with Babar the empire for the generations. Six emperors of his line had reigned and Tegh Bahadur would offer his own life in liew of the 7Th Guru. According, he sent the Kashmiri Pandits who had appealed to him in there distress to make a petiton to the emperor in these words: 'We live on the offering of the Kshatris, Guru Tegh Bahadur, the foremost among them, is now seated on the throne of Guru Nanak and is Guru of all the Hindus. If thou canst first make him a Mussalman then all the *Sikhs* and *Brahmans* who follow him will of their own accord adopt thy faith. The emperor according summoned the Guru to Delhi and he replied that he would comeafter the rains. *Saifabad lies* 4 or 5 miles from Patiala, Saif-ud-Din whom he converted in the "Faith of from south-east to west through the centre of the State, parallel worth the *Bari dhad.* A fair is held on the Ist Asunj Dughi is the name of the place. The temple was erected over the tomb of an *Udasi faqir* of noted piety. It is resort U*dasi* nad the local people have of *Udasi,* and the local people have converted the original saint in to a god. The place nama Dughli is clearly derived from the *deota* whose own name would seem to mean thin or emaciated." (*Simila* Hill *States Gazetteer, Baghal,* p. 6). To emphasize the change thereby effected in the initiates being the Guru altered his cognomen, whatever it might, formerly have been into Singh, "*lion*". Singh had long been an affix of names among the military classes of India, throuhj not then confined to *Kashtriyas.* He himself assuming the style of Guru *Govind Singh* instead of *Govind Rai.* (R.C. Temple, *Proper Names of Punjab,* Delhi, p. 14)

30. H.H. Risley : *Tribes and Castes of Bengal*; Delhi, Vol.I Reprint 1915, pp. 178, 179.

31. **Note.** The great leather-working caste of the Telgu country is the *Madiga*. The village Gods of South India, Bishop whitehead, under Madigas :. He lives on the outskirts of the village. He is described as coarse and fithly, as an eater of unclean food i.e. **mana** and a user of obscene language. He works in leather and serves as a menial and as a scavenger. Many *Madigas* are practically serfs. Most of them are field labourers. They beat drums at festivels called naxlites *(The Chamars, Op. Cit.,* pp. 31-2).

32. *Bengals Census Report,* 1921, pp. 358, 366.

33. In the east of bihar, he keeps pigs and chickens, His women practise mid wifery, In the Punjab, he is counted as a sub-division of the *Muchi (The Chamars, Op. Cit.,* p. 26.)

34. *Bagdi* or *Bagri* it is doubtful whether *Bagri* or *Bagdi* is not applicable to any Hindu from the Bagar and not merely to Rajputs and *Jat.* It is however, specially applied to *Jats.* In *Bahaswalpur,* it is applied in any Hindu or Muhammadan from Jaisalmer of Bikaner, who speaks *Bagri.* They are Bagar or Bhagar by clan also found in *Hissar,* in Gurdaspur the *Bagri* are *Salahri* and also found in Sialkot, Patiala and in Amritsar too. (G.T.C. Vol. II, p. 33)

35. **Note.** *Kori* or *Chamar* of field labour or *cooli* is of course a crucial economic requirement, especially at harvest time. This work is usually reimbursed at the rate of four to eigth *annas* (five to ten cents) a day plus the right to a certain amount of gleaning from the harvested crops. Although Hindu tradition does not specify field labour as the province of any particular caste, it is nevertheless regarded as menial work becoming only to those of unclean status, and it has consequently come to be associated in the main with members of the *Kori* caste. Besides the poverty and the defined status of the *Kori,* their sheer numerical abundance renders them available as a source of recruitment for every kind of demeaning work their eighteen domestic groups provide a reservoir of 25 males and 45 males between the ages of twelve and fifty, angmented by 33 older and younger members who are available on a part-time basis. (Harold A Gould, *The Hindu Caste System. Delhi, 1987,* p. 164)

36. **Note.** Panjab is the *Maduradesa* in all over the world in in every walk of life. Its cultural has been widely spread all over the world in every period of the India history. It is the beginning and end of the new story or 'New Society' of the *'Nam'* which is also called *Madura* for the soul.

37. *Madras Government Memorandum to the Indian Statutory Commission,* 1928, pp. 596-98.

38. *C.R.I.,* p. 325.

39. In Western India, *Jyotirao* Govindrao Phooly (1827-90 A.D.) struggled for the lower castes, Jyotiba was born at Poona in 1827 A.D. in a Mali caste (his family members supplied flowers, garlands, etc., to the Peshwas family and came to be called *Phule*), Some incidents of Brahmanical arrogance changed the outlook of *Jyotiba once* Jyotiba Phule was scolded and insulted by a Brahmin for his and a city in joining a Brahmin marriage procession. The Brahmins also opposed Jyotiba in running a school for the lower castes and women. The brahminincal pressure compelled Jyotiba to close the school under upper caste pressure Govindrao turned Jyotiba and his wife from leaving his family house. Jyotiba believed that the Brahman under the pretext of religion, tyrannized over other castes and turned them into their slaves. Jyotiba Phule was every critical of the Indian National Congress Leader for their neglect of the interest on the weaker sections. He maintained that the Congress could not be called truly national unless it showed general interest in the welfare of the lower and backward castes. In 1873, Jyotiba started the *Satya Shodhak* S*amaj* (Truth Seeking Society) with the aim of securing social justice for the weaker sections of the society. He opened a number of schools and orpanages for the children and women belong to all castes. He was elected as a member of the Poona Municipal Committee in 1876 AD. Jyotiba's publication include *Dharma Tritiya Ratna* (Exposure of the Purances) *Ishara* (A warning). *Life of Shivaji,* etc. In 1888 A.D. Jyotiba Phule was honoured with the title of

Mahatma. On the contrary, the leaders of the *Prathana* Samaji sympathized with Phule movement and often defended it against the critics R.G. Bandarkar, one of the patriarcles of the *Prarthana* Samaj, fully agreeing with *Phule,* affirmed that "If we ask England to remove our disabilities, we must as a necessary preliminary show that we are worthy of the favour by removing the disabilities of the oppressed classes of our Society." (*Mahatma Phula Samagra Vangmaya*, edited by Y.D.Phadke, Bombay 1991, Vol. II, pp. 501-02.)

40. V.R. Shinde, *Asprishyatecha Prashna* (The Problem of Untouchility) (In Marathi) pp. 56-90, 215, C.R.I. *Op. Cit.*, pp. 325-26.
41. R.G.Bangarkar Collected Works on Mahartma Phule Smagra Vanmaya; Vol. II, p. 419.
42. *C.R.I.*, pp. 326-27.
43. R.G. Bandarkar, *Collected Works, Op. Cit.* Vol. II, pp. 397-98.
44. *Ibid.*, pp. 559-60.
45. It is for your kind information the further break-up report of the figures is not available and there is no need to search out because they became the beggar of the *'Reservation'*.
46. The Times of India, 27-7-53, 13-8-53.7-10-53 *C.R.I; Op. Cit.* pp. 330-31.
47. *Ibid.*, 18-5-55, 19-5-55, 11-11-55 C.R.I. *Op. Cit.*, pp. 331-32.
48. *Ibid.*
49. *Ibid.*, pp. 332-33.
50. *Ibid.*, 28, 29-4-58.
51. *Ibid.*, 24-2-59.
52. *Ibid.*, 4-1-61.
53. *Ibid.*, 21-9-62.
54. *Ibid.*, 22-5-63.
55. *Ibid.*, 32-8-63.
56. *Ibid.*, 4-1-64.
57. *Ibid.*, 28-7-64.
58. *Ibid.*, 4-12-64.
59. Nandu Ram; *Encyclopaedia of Scheduled Castes in India,* New Delhi, 2007, Vol. 1, pp. 1-6.
60. *The Times of India,* 12-3-68.
61. *Ibid.*, 12-9-66. The leading article "Mockery".
62. *R.T.* Vol. I, p. 328.
63. Dr. Sudhakar Chattopadhyaya, Social Life of *Ancient India*, Santhinakethin 1964, p. 8.
64. Daily Excelsior 15-2-2007; News item India charged *With Failing to Uphold* Dalit Right.
65. R.K.Mookerji, *Ancient India*, p. 121.
66. Daily Excelsior, 21-2-2007; News item "Commission against SC. Benefits to *Dalit* Muslims, Chistians.
67. R.K.Mookerji; *Ancient India;* p. 277.
68. *The New Cambridge Modern History;* Vol. I, 1957, pp. XXIV-XXV.

Table 5. Scavenger Class

	Figures			*Proportion Per 1,000 of Total Population*			
	4	*43*	*87*	*4*	*43*	*87*	
	Chuhra	*Dhanak*	*Khatik*	*Chuhra*	*Dhanak*	*Khatik*	*Total*
Delhi	26,067	6,700	1,867	40	11	3	54
Gurgaon	17,783	5,693	1,398	28	9	2	39
Karnal	31,288	3,369	1,093	50	5	2	57
Hissar	12,126	13,529	950	24	27	2	53
Rohtak	19,901	18,692	832	36	34	2	72
Sirsa	16,051	1,491	1,100	63	6	4	73
Ambala	41,755	44	1,200	39	—	1	40
Ludhiana	18,525	—	196	30	—	—	30
Shimla	1,845	—	2	43	—	—	43
Jalandhar	31,849	16	697	40	—	1	41
Hushyarpur	17,287	—	570	19	—	1	20
Kangra	896	1	131	1	—	—	1
Amritsar	107,011	—	—	120	—	—	120
Gurdaspur	56,985	—	—	69	—	—	69
Sialkot	78,980	—	93	78	—	—	78
Lahore	99,025	43	242	107	—	—	107
Gujranwala	57,911	—	93	94	—	—	94
Firozpur	68,905	144	389	106	—	1	107
Rawalpindi	22,046	8	263	27	—	—	27
Jahlam	25,027	4	52	42	—	—	42
Gujarat	38,231	—	444	55	—	1	56
Shahpur	28,297	—	6	67	—	—	67
Multan	29,489	31	18	53	—	—	53
Jhang	20,944	—	2	53	—	—	53
Montgomery	28,857	—	8	68	—	—	68
Muzaffargarh	11,312	—	114	33	—	—	33
Dera Ismail Khan	9,041	2	—	20	—	—	20
Dera Ghazi Khan	4,633	16	6	13	—	—	13
Bannu	5,940	8	1	18	—	—	18
Peshawar	7,653	79	22	13	—	—	13
Hazara	2,279	—	48	6	—	—	6
Kohat	1,221	2	3	7	—	—	7
British Territory	939,572	49,876	11,845	50	3	1	54
Patiala	66,183	5,548	1,254	45	4	1	50
Nabha	10,429	1,378	148	40	5	1	46
Kapurthala	16,334	—	61	65	—	—	65
Jind	7,006	7,090	315	29	28	1	58
Faridkot	13,369	42	—	138	—	—	138
Muler Kotla	1,465	—	89	21	—	1	22
Kalsia	3,008	—	117	44	—	2	46
Total Eastern Total	118,667	16,165	2,120	47	6	1	54
Bahawalpur	18,604	—	182	32	—	—	32
Total Hill States	1,896	18	334	2	—	—	2
Birtish Territory	939,572	49,876	11,845	50	3	1	54
Native States	139,167	16,183	2,336	36	4	1	41
Province	1,078,739	66,059	14,181	48	3	1	52

Table 6. Menials of the Hills—A

	Figures							
	49 Barwala	*78 Batwal*	*57 Mog*	*41 Dumna*	*137 Barara*	*97 Serera*	*66 Koli*	*80 Dagi*
Delhi	7	—	—	—	—	—	4,409	—
Gurgaon	72	—	—	—	—	—	5,910	—
Hissar	—	—	—	—	—	—	400	—
Ambala	—	—	926	126	22	—	1,130	197
Ludhiana	5	—	—	9	—	—	205	—
Simla	—	—	—	457	—	—	3,794	264
Jalandhar	1,800	1	—	278	93	198	95	77
Hushyarpur	1,740	85	—	3,529	199	4,520	370	31
Kangra	1,514	3,630	—	11,095	980	5,122	11,301	19,742
Amritsar	13,186	80	237	260	361	—	—	—
Gurdaspur	9,530	964	6,373	27,270	327	481	238	—
Sialkot	16,901	13,100	28,705	—	79	—	14	—
Lahore	3,745	146	496	181	—	55	2	—
Gujranwala	5,029	19	80	105	—	—	—	—
Gujrat	904	—	1,379	—	—	—	—	—
British Territory	54,128	18,121	88,371	43,424	2,070	10,407	27,837	20,311
Patiala	—	6	—	1,168	70	2	10,018	—
Kapurthala	508	—	—	30	101	116	—	—
Total Eastern Plains	511	6	—	1,193	171	119	10,107	—
Mandi	—	—	—	11,540	—	15	10,673	4,475
Chamba	119	337	96	1,881	18	272	1,609	17,984
Naban	—	—	—	4,126	203	—	24,230	2,213
Bilaspur	—	—	—	1,653	12	—	2,947	—
Bashahr	—	—	—	97	—	—	14,149	—
Nalagarh	—	—	—	1,096	15	—	1,435	3,651
Suket	—	—	—	3,133	—	—	7,753	1,689
Total Hill States	119	657	96	25,916	434	287	85,227	82,882
British Territory	54,128	18,121	88,371	43,424	3,070	10,407	27,837	20,311
Native States	630	663	96	27,109	605	406	95,334	32,682
Province	54,758	18,1784	88,467	70,533	2,675	10,813	123,171	52,993

Menials of the Hills—B

	Proporation per 1,000 or Total Population																
	176 Rehar	*176 Dosali*	*185 Hadi*	*151 Ghai*	*49 Barwala*	*78 Batwal*	*57 Meg.*	*41 Dumna*	*137 Barara*	*97 Sarera*	*Total*	*66 Koll*	*50 Dagi*	*176 Rehar*	*151 Ghai*	*Total*	*Grand Total*
Delhi	—	—	—	—	—	—	—	—	—	—	—	7	—	—	—	7	7
Gurgaon	—	—	—	—	—	—	—	—	—	—	—	9	—	—	—	9	9
Hissar	—	—	—	—	—	—	—	—	—	—	—	1	—	—	—	1	1
Ambala	—	—	—	—	—	—	1	—	—	—	1	1	—	—	—	1	2
Ludhiana	—	—	—	—	—	—	—	—	—	—	—	—	—	—	—	—	—
Simla	57	—	—	—	—	—	—	11	—	—	11	88	6	1	—	95	106
Jalandhar	—	30	—	6	2	—	—	—	—	—	2	—	—	—	—	—	2
Hushyarpur	—	212	—	3	2	—	—	4	—	5	11	—	—	—	—	—	11
Kangra	—	276	295	1,570	2	6	—	15	1	7	30	15	27	—	2	44	74
Amritsar	—	16	—	—	15	—	—	—	—	—	15	—	—	—	—	—	15
Gurdaspur	—	9	—	—	12	1	8	33	—	1	55	—	—	—	—	—	55
Sialkot	—	—	—	—	17	13	28	—	—	—	58	—	—	—	—	—	58
Lahore	—	—	—	—	4	—	1	—	—	—	5	—	—	—	—	—	5
Gujranwala	—	—	—	—	8	—	—	—	—	—	8	—	—	—	—	—	8
Gujrat	—	—	—	—	1	—	2	—	—	—	3	—	—	—	—	—	3

British Territory	64	622	305	1,588	3	1	2	2	—	1	9	1	1	—	—	2	1
Patiala	—	—	—	—	—	—	—	1	—	—	1	7	—	—	—	7	8
Kapurthala	—	—	—	—	2	—	—	—	—	—	2	—	—	—	—	—	2
Total Eastern Plains	—	—	—	—	—	—	—	—	—	—	—	4	—	—	—	4	4
Mandi	—	—	—	—	—	—	—	79	—	—	79	73	30	—	—	103	182
Chamba	147	45	—	—	1	5	1	16	—	1	25	14	155	—	—	169	194
Naban	—	—	—	—	—	—	—	37	3	—	39	216	20	—	—	236	275
Bilaspur	—	—	—	62	—	—	—	19	—	—	19	34	—	—	—	34	53
Bashahr	29	—	—	—	—	—	—	2	—	—	2	220	—	—	—	220	222
Nalagarh	—	—	—	71	—	—	—	20	—	—	20	27	57	—	1	85	105
Suket	—	—	—	—	—	—	—	60	—	—	60	148	32	—	—	180	240
Total Hill States	750	45	—	186	—	—	—	34	1	—	35	111	3	1	—	155	190
British Territory	64	622	305	1,533	3	1	2	2	—	1	9	1	1	—	—	2	11
Native States	750	45	—	138	—	—	—	7	—	—	7	25	8	—	—	33	46
Province	314	667	305	1,726	2	1	2	3	—	—	8	5	2	—	—	7	—

Table 7. Purbia Menials

	Figures				*Proportion Per 1,000 of Total Population*					
	99 Kori	*119 Kurml*	*127 Jalswara*	*156 Pasi*	*146 Purbi*	*99 Kori*	*119 Kurml*	*127 Jaiswara*	*156 Pasi*	*Total*
Delhi	145	233	—	20	—	—	—	—	—	—
Karnal	817	161	—	221	—	1	—	—	—	1
Ambala	3,404	508	741	356	73	3	1	1	—	5
Simla	540	112	257	11	—	13	3	6	—	22
Jalandhar	—	486	107	17	117	—	1	—	—	1
Amritsar	127	407	—	—	433	—	—	—	—	—
Gurdaspur	54	1	76	—	111	—	—	—	—	—
Sialkot	—	—	—	99	23	—	—	—	—	—
Lahore	1,462	136	—	198	93	2	—	—	—	2
Gujranwala	42	28	—	9	—	—	—	—	—	—
Firozpur	662	362	—	90	—	1	1	—	—	2
Rawalpindi	1,475	623	1,174	194	39	2	1	1	—	4
Jahlam	—	345	102	—	35	—	1	—	—	1
Shahpur	2	—	24	—	128	—	—	—	—	—
Multan	578	33	226	—	55	1	—	—	—	1
Derah Ismail Khan	49	—	36	8	156	—	—	—	—	—
Derah Ghazi Khan	77	31	107	11	60	—	—	—	—	—
Bannu	101	3	17	—	4	—	—	—	—	—
Peshawar	666	3	160	87	10	1	—	—	—	1
British Terrirtory	10,522	3,675	3,419	1,349	1,668	1	—	—	—	1
Patiala	71	181	20	29	41	—	—	—	—	—
Nabha	—	40	2	134	10	—	—	—	1	1
Kapurthala	75	23	27	—	55	—	—	—	—	—
Total East. Plains	157	285	51	165	100	—	—	—	—	—
Bahawalpur	—	—	—	—	250	—	—	—	—	—
Total Hill States	60	57	21	127	—	—	—	—	—	—
Birtish Territory	10,522	3,675	3,419	1,349	1,668	1	—	—	—	1
Native States	217	342	72	192	359	—	—	—	—	—
Province	10,739	4,017	3,491	1,542	2,027	—	—	—	—	—

Table 8. Minor Professions

	Figures							Proportion Per 1,000 of Total Population										
	21 Nai	62 Bhat	25 Mirasi	40 Jogi	80 Rawal	128 Bharupia	141 Bhand	21 Nai	62 Bhat	25 Mirasi	Total	40 Jogi	80 Rawal	Total	128 Bahrupla	141 Bhand	Total	Grand Total
Delhi	11,080	1,019	1,758	5,006	2	1	46	17	2	3	22	8	—	8	—	—	—	30
Gargaon	12,342	832	3,499	4,009	—	2	71	19	1	5	25	6	—	6	—	—	—	31
Hissar	8,698	785	3,659	1,919	31	3	—	17	1	7	25	4	—	4	—	—	—	29
Rohtak	10,618	337	2,780	3,765	5	12	27	19	1	5	25	7	—	7	—	—	—	32
Sirsa	4,150	447	3,015	389	—	—	9	16	2	12	30	2	—	2	—	—	—	32
Ambala	14,932	1,273	4,695	11,897	22	—	273	14	1	4	19	11	—	11	—	—	—	30
Ludhiana	11,065	109	5,489	1,022	18	—	—	18	—	9	27	2	—	2	—	—	—	29
Jalandhar	12,301	193	7,170	517	2,842	—	—	16	—	9	25	1	4	5	—	—	—	30
Hushyarpur	12,148	1,355	4,935	313	2,781	167	—	13	2	5	20	—	3	3	—	—	—	23
Kangra	7,838	322	1,927	5,043	764	1	—	11	—	3	14	7	1	8	—	—	—	22
Amritsar	14,694	339	11,046	1,727	2,325	—	—	17	—	12	29	2	3	5	—	—	—	34
Gurdaspur	14,413	912	7,273	2,216	3,337	58	—	18	2	9	29	3	4	7	—	—	—	36
Sialkot	20,569	1,646	12,921	9,282	1,244	—	—	20	2	13	35	3	1	4	—	—	—	39
Lahore	13,840	381	11,747	343	1,508	—	109	15	—	13	28	—	2	2	—	—	—	30
Gujranwala	14,474	135	12,224	205	2,048	—	120	23	—	20	43	—	3	3	—	—	—	46
Firozpur	9,794	240	7,434	175	168	—	59	15	—	11	26	—	—	—	—	—	—	26
Rawalpindi	11,996	582	6,205	2,081	—	—	2	15	1	8	24	3	—	3	—	—	—	97
Jahlam	10,569	220	7,643	1,290	—	19	54	18	—	13	31	2	—	2	—	—	—	32
Gujrat	13,553	276	7,885	1,033	1	—	2	20	—	11	31	1	—	1	—	—	—	32
Shahpur	7,541	70	8,344	428	—	22	31	18	—	20	38	1	—	1	—	—	—	39
Multan	6,035	336	7,510	691	—	—	506	11	1	14	26	1	—	1	—	1	1	38
Jhang	6,307	110	7,741	573	—	—	106	16	—	20	36	1	—	1	—	—	—	37
Montgomery	6,447	147	9,695	513	—	—	118	15	—	23	38	1	—	1	—	—	—	39
Muzaffargarh	4,064	123	3,634	450	—	—	5	12	—	11	23	1	—	1	—	—	—	24
Dera Ismail Khan	2,687	103	2,700	50	—	—	—	6	—	6	12	—	—	—	—	—	—	12
Dera Ghazi Khan	407	239	1,007	129	—	4	—	1	1	3	5	—	—	—	—	—	—	5
Bannu	3,598	85	3,818	63	—	—	67	11	—	12	23	—	—	—	—	—	—	23
Peshawar	5,648	106	3,866	55	78	—	6	10	—	7	17	—	—	—	—	—	—	17
Hazara	4,218	28	1,856	77	60	—	—	10	—	5	15	—	—	—	—	—	—	15
Kohat	2,202	4	1,185	15	23	—	—	12	—	9	21	—	—	—	—	—	—	21
British Territory	288,788	14,171	177,707	58,715	17,266	321	1,620	15	1	—	25	3	1	4	—	—	—	29

Patiala	25,021	918	10,131	6,992	27	38	430	17	1	7	25	5	—	5	—	—	—	30
Nabha	5,277	160	2,169	767	—	3	—	20	1	8	29	3	—	3	—	—	—	37
Kapurthala	4,340	4	2,539	79	530	24	—	17	—	10	27	—	2	2	—	—	—	25
Jind	4,911	421	1,955	1,823	—	—	13	20	2	8	80	7	—	7	—	—	—	37
Faridkot	1,568	19	1,147	11	7	—	—	16	—	12	28	—	—	—	—	—	—	28
Maler Kotla	1,414	4	666	126	—	—	—	20	—	10	30	3	—	2	—	—	—	32
Total Eastern Plains	44,594	1,878	19,264	11,077	564	65	461	18	1	8	27	4	—	4	—	—	—	31
Bhawalpur	6,437	655	7,429	96	—	—	—	11	1	13	25	—	—	—	—	—	—	25
Mandi	299	200	16	427	—	—	2	2	1	—	3	3	—	3	—	—	—	6
Chamba	325	133	113	1,412	15	—	—	3	1	1	5	12	—	12	—	—	—	17
Nahan	199	12,745	62	230	—	—	100	2	114	1	117	2	—	2	—	1	1	120
Total Hill States	2,354	13,318	541	2,845	23	—	194	3	17	—	20	4	15	19	—	—	—	39
British Territory	288,733	14,171	177,707	58,715	17,266	321	1,620	15	1	9	25	3	1	4	—	—	—	29
Native States	53,385	15,851	27,234	14,018	587	65	655	14	4	7	25	4	—	4	—	—	—	29
Province	342,123	30,022	204,941	72,733	17,853	386	2,275	15	1	9	25	3	1	4	—	—	—	29

Table 9. Gipsy Tribes of Different District and States

	Figures								
	96 Nat	*89 Bazigar*	*164 Perna*	*186 Kanjar*	*167 Hesi*	*177 Garri*	*121 Qualandari*	*158 Gandhila*	*150 Baddun*
Delhi	266	1	—	591	—	—	117	—	—
Gurgaon	629	719	102	692	—	—	1,806	—	—
Karnal	815	248	—	80	—	—	14	67	—
Hissar	576	294	—	1	—	—	30	—	—
Rohtak	106	318	13	—	—	—	—	—	—
Sirsa	287	—	28	265	—	—	8	—	—
Ambala	1,990	489	—	114	—	—	6	343	9
Ludhiana	161	935	—	—	—	—	2	—	121
Jalandhar	112	254	—	—	—	—	9	113	339
Hushyarpur	75	—	—	—	18	—	45	14	56
Kuangra	360	—	—	—	424	—	—	7	—
Amritsar	168	442	—	—	—	—	—	—	164
Gurdaspur	8	160	83	—	—	—	—	—	91
Sialkot	28	36	—	—	—	685	—	—	—
Lahore	—	1,361	147	—	—	—	185	186	339
Gujaranwala	—	930	5	—	—	—	400	8	151
Firozpur	—	1,188	18	—	—	—	16	—	170
Rawalpindi	580	667	17	—	—	—	5	—	—
Jahlam	281	238	8	—	—	—	145	—	—
Gujrat	139	68	19	—	—	—	800	—	—
Shahpur	320	594	1	—	—	—	16	—	—
Multan	369	130	130	—	—	—	16	—	—
Jhang	276	1	85	—	—	—	122	—	—
Montgomery	398	2,349	277	—	—	—	69	55	—
Muzaffargarh	97	72	—	—	—	—	—	—	—
British Territory	8,190	11,504	933	1,694	442	685	3,841	793	1,440
Patiala	1,052	1,598	45	5	—	—	54	165	26
Nabha	57	296	15	—	—	—	—	—	—
Kapurthala	89	2	38	85	—	—	—	—	270
Jind	183	152	—	—	—	—	—	—	—
Faridkot	90	124	—	—	—	—	—	—	—
Maler Kotla	1	76	—	—	—	—	—	—	—
Kalsia	85	53	—	—	—	—	—	18	—
Total East, Plains	1,548	2,301	123	90	—	—	54	183	296
Bahawalpur	1,919	—	101	1,041	—	—	—	472	—
Total Hill States	83	36	—	47	668	—	—	1	—
British Territory	8,190	11,504	933	1,694	442	685	8,841	793	1,440
Native States	3,550	2,337	224	1,178	668	—	54	656	296
Province	11,740	13,841	1,157	2,872	1,110	685	3,895	1,449	1,736

Gipsy Tribes of Different District and States

	Proportion Per 1,000 of Total Population								
	98 Nat	*89 Bazigar*	*164 Perna*	*135 Kanjar*	*167 Hesi*	*177 Garri*	*121 Qalandari*	*158 Gandhila*	*Total*
Delhi	—	—	—	1	—	—	—	—	1
Gurgaon	1	1	—	1	—	—	3	—	6
Karnal	1	—	—	—	—	—	—	—	1
Hissar	1	1	—	—	—	—	—	—	2
Rohtak	—	1	—	—	—	—	—	—	1
Sirsa	1	—	—	1	—	—	—	—	2
Ambala	2	—	—	—	—	—	—	—	2
Ludhiana	—	2	—	—	—	—	—	—	2
Jalandhar	—	—	—	—	—	—	—	—	—
Hushyarpur	—	—	—	—	—	—	—	—	—
Kangra	—	—	—	—	—	—	—	—	—
Amritsar	—	—	—	—	—	—	—	—	—
Gurdaspur	—	—	—	—	—	—	—	—	—
Sialkot	—	—	—	—	—	1	—	—	1
Lahore	—	2	—	—	—	—	—	—	2
Gujranwala	—	1	—	—	—	—	1	—	2
Firozpur	—	2	—	—	—	—	—	—	2
Rawalpindi	1	1	—	—	—	—	—	—	2
Jahlam	—	—	—	—	—	—	—	—	—
Gujrat	—	—	—	—	—	—	1	—	1
Shahpur	1	1	—	—	—	—	—	—	2
Multan	1	—	—	—	—	—	—	—	1
Jhan	1	—	—	—	—	—	—	—	1
Montgemery	1	6	1	—	—	—	—	—	8
Muzaffargarh	—	—	—	—	—	—	—	—	—
British Territory	—	1	—	—	—	—	—	—	1
Patiala	1	1	—	—	—	—	—	—	2
Nabha	—	1	—	—	—	—	—	—	1
Kapurthala	—	—	—	—	—	—	—	—	—
Jind	1	1	—	—	—	—	—	—	2
Faridknot	1	1	—	—	—	—	—	—	2
Malerkotla	—	1	—	—	—	—	—	—	1
Kalsia	1	1	—	—	—	—	—	—	2
Total East Plains	1	1	—	—	—	—	—	—	2
Bahawalpur	3	—	—	2	—	—	—	1	6
Total Hill States	—	—	—	—	1	—	—	—	1
British Territory	—	1	—	—	—	—	—	—	1
Native States	1	1	—	—	—	—	—	—	2
Province	—	1	—	—	—	—	—	—	1

Table 10. Miscellaneous Artisans

	Figures				*Proportion Per 1,000 of Total Population*					
	83 Penja	*23 Teli*	*38 Qassab*	*56 Kalal*	*83 Penja*	*23 Tali*	*38 Qassab*	*Total*	*56 Kalal*	*Grand Total*
Delhi	145	5,593	4,320	758	—	9	7	16	1	17
Gurgaon	616	4,799	13,352	481	1	7	21	29	1	30
Karnal	756	9,777	4,587	878	1	16	7	24	1	25
Hissar	—	6,891	2,857	360	—	14	6	40	1	41
Rohtak	—	6,313	6,318	268	—	11	11	22	—	22
Sirsa	—	3,914	842	401	—	16	3	19	2	21
Ambala	6,654	17,577	2,881	5,057	6	16	3	25	5	30
Ludhiana	188	10,883	1,621	1,955	—	18	3	21	3	24
Simla	33	59	42	99	1	1	1	3	2	5
Jalandhar	—	10,829	1,603	1,624	—	14	2	16	2	18
Hushyarpur	4	10,758	2,077	2,695	—	12	2	14	3	17
Kangra	2	5,495	190	2,505	—	7	—	7	4	11
Amritsar	—	20,654	1,971	2,121	—	28	2	25	2	27
Gurdaspur	—	17,644	846	1,209	—	21	1	22	1	23
Sialkot	—	13,652	1,927	1,987	—	13	2	15	2	17
Lahore	—	23,066	2,464	1,909	—	25	2	27	2	29
Gujranwala	—	9,523	2,384	551	—	15	4	19	1	20
Firozpur	—	10,938	714	1,929	—	17	1	18	3	21
Rawalpindi	—	12,384	789	280	—	15	1	16	—	16
Jahlam	—	8,302	2,003	1,076	—	14	3	17	2	19
Gujrat	—	8,562	1,169	552	—	12	2	14	1	15
Shahpur	210	2,112	5,202	123	—	5	12	17	—	17
Multan	91	484	5,914	580	—	1	11	12	1	13
Jhang	—	250	4,979	—	—	1	13	14	—	14
Montgomery	—	1,557	5,170	275	—	4	12	16	1	17
Muzaffargarh	67	238	3,136	19	—	1	9	10	—	10
Dera Ismail Khan	12	149	1,584	20	—	—	4	4	—	4
Dera Ghazi Khan	8	40	221	3	—	—	1	1	—	1
Bannu	—	95	2,967	—	—	—	9	9	—	9
Peshawar	1,344	3,250	2,636	472	2	6	6	14	1	15
Hazara	164	2,480	412	18	—	6	1	7	—	7
Kohat	94	311	1,179	30	1	2	6	9	—	9
British Territory	10,418	228,585	88,357	30,237	1	12	5	18	2	20
Patiala	4,827	21,097	4,390	4,609		14	3	20	3	23
Nabha	280	3,250	468	643	1	12	2	15	2	17

Kapurthala	53	3,718	918	1,644	—	15	4	19	7	26
Jind	29	3,193	1,305	708	—	13	5	18	3	21
Faridkot	—	1,548	92	1,043	—	16	1	17	10	27
Maler Kotla	—	1,192	503	29	—	17	7	24	—	24
Kalsia	651	1,196	204	147	10	18	3	31	2	33
Total East Plains	5,840	35,770	8,719	8,875	2	14	3	19	4	23
Bahawalpur	630	727	3,217	319	1	1	6	8	1	9
Total Hill States	212	1,806	75	719	—	2	—	2	1	3
British Territory	10,418	228,585	88,357	30,237	1	12	5	18	2	20
Native States	6,682	38,303	12,011	9,913	2	10	3	15	3	18
Province	17,100	266,888	100,868	40,150	1	12	4	17	2	19

Conclusion

From the foregoing pages, we learn, the Brahminical religion, as it developed, made India a land of special privileges for the few by virtue of their birth. The caste system, whatever be its origin have been made by the Brahmans, but they have made it a strong support due to their half heartly knowledge of the *Word* or *Nam*. The existence of *Pariah* and the '*Untouchability*' was of course there of with their ideas, No doubt, Manu had laid down the law of slavery for women and classed them among the *Sudras* of the period, shutting bath out from the knowledge and this preference was only given by the *Sudras* rulers to her, because, he was equal sufferer of the time, they were all on one side i.e. *Kashtriya and Vaishya*, and there was a slavery on the other side. Rite and ritual rather than reason exploited them as thought of the Brahman. The law of conscience of fair play was banished from the entire realm of social relations from one society to another. In this relation, here was the sowing seeds of the social evils in the society, therefore, one must have to yield the same crops who he or she had sowed.

The institution of Caste has been the source of stagnation from one civilization to another and degradation of Hindu society, it must have been set up by the Brahmans of the period. Its baneful effect on the Hindu as well as Muslim society as a whole is responsible for the destruction of Central Idea of the religion which is '*Nam*'. Therefore, Caste may be defined as system of social stratification characterized by the Brahminical hierarchy, heredity, pursuit of one or a few particular occupation like tanner, weaving, etc. inequality, endogeny, and the notion of purity and pollution associated with hierarchy. Notwithstanding the existence of fullfledged class society in the pre-Aryan mature phase of *Harappa Culture*, or *Ravidas Culture* the available archaeological evidence unaided by written records owing to the hither to undesciphered script i.e. '*Nam*' or '*Chamar*' does not warrant the hypothesis regarding the emergence of caste system and untouchability because he is always *untouchable* like '*Nam*'. Therefore, it is difficult to touch Him without the 'Pure Thought' called '*Sudra*'. The evolution of caste as social phenomenon, it can be trace out from the two seminal term i.e. '*Varna*' and '*Jati*', '*Varna*' means '*Word*'in Hindi and '*Jati*' means absorb in the body (*Jan*) through the meditation of the '*Nam*' found the result of this after completation of course on the request of the *Prefect Master* of the '*Nam*'. In this way, '*Varna*' or '*Word*' being *anterior* to *jati* originated from the Greek word *anthos* means '*flower*' in the early texts of the '*Nam*' as *jats*, later on deginated as *jat* as a caste. From being used to distinguish Arya from the ethnical and culturally separated *Dasa* and *Dasya* in the *Rigveda* (1500 B.C. to 1000 B.C.) *varna*, literally meaning colour but '*Word*' or '*Nam*' has no colour, he is right inside to your boby at one time, when he lands on earth from the heaven and came to be applied to the four hierarchically ranked occupational categories of *Brahmans*, *Kshatriyas*, *Vaishyas* and *Shudras* during the later Vedic period of the Indian History. Although the *Brahmana* and the *Kshatriya* are mentioned in the *Rigveda* as a traditional race of he '*Nam*', a few times in the sense of functional groups which had emerged from the Aryan *vish* or *jana* meaning tribe, the *Brahmana* as a priest composing authority and reciting hymns of the *Vedas* and officiating at the sacrifice of the *Kashriya* warrior Chief (*Rajan*) the term '*Varna*' is never applied to the *Brahmana* because he or she always busy with his or her adjectivity i.e. 'ego' and same is the case noted from the 'History of *Kashtriya*'. We occasionally come across a few generations of chief in the *Rigveda;* but could not trust on them and interest to study them, because their '*infinite*' cannot leave them in isolation, they are the friends, father's, husbands of the soul in all times in everywhere in this universal because they are the dictator of the world in the forms of *Man* to regulate the progress of the society in the better way as it was there duty in the Heaven. But the example of a poet or a priest describes '*Him*' as a father or a physician of the soul and their mother is a as corn –grinder of another poet enquiring *Indra* whether they would be made the sage of the '*Nam*', a protect of the people at the difficult hour a ruling chief or owner on the earth at difficult moment come from the Heaven for the establishment of the 'New Society' of the Father. As a *Kshatriya* princes *Devapi* and *Devashrava* officiating as the priest at the sacrifical hours of their ruling younger brother *Shantanu* and *Devavta* respectively show that profession shad not became hereditary at this *stage;* and the matter of achievement rather than inheritance from the stratification of the Rigvedic

Society of the 'Nam'. as a group of the people often on the move from time to time in the land of the seven rivers of India, the primarily pastoral Rigvedic Aryans were neither practising endogamy nor observing any restrictions like that of Brahmins of the period had imposed by creating, caste, colour and creed in regarding food from others as a specialist people of the 'Nam'.

Keeping in view, the first and foremost definition of the fourtier hierarchical inequality developing among the Vedic Aryans was the use of term *'Varna'* means *'Nam';* is found in the famous *Purusha-Sukta* of the tenth (10) *mandala* of he *Rigveda*, which represents the *Brahmana* as the month, the *Rajanya* as the arms, the *Vasishya* as the thigh s and the shudra as a emanating from the feet of the *divine Purusha* called *'Nam'*, when he was sarcificed by gods for the sake of creation of the universe. His hymn is presumed to have accorded 'Divine Sanction' to the emerging of a new social structure of the *'Nam'* who had already qualified his limitations in the previous birth therefore it is singnificant that the tenth *mandala* of the *'Nam'* belongs to the latest stratum of the *Rig veda*, synchronizing with some of the later Vedic texts of the *'Nam'* that the Rajana the *Vaishya* and the *Shudr*a must be study them from the beginning of the era and last time of the *Rig-veda* as a 'Nam'.

In addition to this, the relationship between the *Chamar* and *Jat* have been aleady set up during the time of *Upper Ganga* Basin in the later Vedic times to regain the power of the *'Nam'* for his force (C.1000 B.C. - 600 B.C.) the social process of social differentiation steadily set up by the theory of *'Nam'* i.e. 'Pious Love'of the Father. Slowly and gradually, it disappear in the social reality to regain the authentic reports against the *Brahmanas* as a specialised class of priests monopolizing the complex rituals lamps before the photograph of their heroes and heroines to start a function as scholars and teachers of the modern period are celebrating their birth and death as an idea, same is the case *Kashtriyas* as warriors and rulers controlling large territorial unites and material resources as a result of participation into different groups and victories in ongoing battles led by the *'Nam'*. The *Vaisyas* as tribute-paying peasants, cattle rearer, artisans and traders and the *Shudras* as domestic servents of the *'Nam'* in the increasing in-egalitarian society of the period with more surplus available for unequal distribution; because they have the lust of money not *'Father'*. Despite of the fact, a protracted *Kshatriya* challenge to the Brahmanical claims to primary both combined well against the two lower *'Varnas'* and the *Aitareya Brahman* can be removed at will of the *'Nam'* as a *Natural Ruler On Earth*. In this way, the description of the *Vaishya* as *anyasya balikrita* (a tributary to others) and *yathakamajyeya* (on who can be appressed at will of the *'Nam'*) and of the *Shudra* as *anyasya preshya* (a servant or messenger of others), *Kamothtapya* (one who can be day or night) and *yathakamavadya* (one who can be beaten at will), is indeed revealing their identity as we are one in form as the people of *'Nam'* displayed an example of its as most sincere population of the Father. Towards the end of the later Vedic period the *'Varna'* system because hereditary endogamous and birth based, leading to the formation of *Jatis*. The term *Jat* is derived from the Sanskrit root *Jan* means life whom from to be born i.e. *Mana* or mind, and is first applied by the *pre-Paninian Yaska* in his *Nirkuta* to a women of the black or *Shudra* caste *(Krishnajatiya),* Krishna rules over the mind not on the father, but Father is to be firstly born out of it due to the srtruggle of medition of the *"Nam"* formula. It also maintained the sexually enjoyment in the limitation of his wife not to take the enjoyment with other sexual woman as a prostitute, because he had maintained the social virtues of the Father not to the others. That bith was slowly became an important factor of social ranking and the theory of *Karma* (deed and action) including *Punarjanma* (rebirth), which proved such an effective ideology in the internationalization of the in equitious caste system by the oppressed and the exploited were ardently became champion during the time of Budbhism and Jainism. During this period *Chhandogya Upanishad* were assigned to pure birth (*Ramaniya yoni*) to the *Brahman*, *Kshatriya* and the *Vaishya* and impure birth (*Kapuya yoni*) to the *Chandala* who was the *'Nam'* at that time the dogs and the boars were attributed due to the former birth in this category to good deeds and actions which were took place in the latter cateory of evil deeds and actions. It shows that the early period had seen the process of assimilation, acculturation and integration of the aboriginal tribes (*Barawalas*) in the expanding Aryan network at various levels during the period of India History. They always tried to unite the people in one segment, but the *Aitareya Brahman* of the various states already mentioned in the text were the accused sons of sage *Vishvamitra* i.e *'NAM'*. There are copious references to the proximity and the interaction of both *Nishades* and *Paulkasa* to *bibhatse* (loath someness as deity) in the symbolic human sacrifice (*Purushamedha*) in the *Vayasaneya Samhita* and the *Taittiriya Brahmana*, who displayed the *Paulkasas* in an object of life and spiritual realm where even the *chandalas* and the *paulkasasa* used to live in the material world without, keeping in view, the lust of money and power,both of these 'Word'stood at the lowest level of the existing social hierarchy. During the material world the tribe of the *Untouchable* preaches teachings of the Lord and obtain the bliss of the Father for the protection of his race. Caste was evidently in its formative stage during the later Vedic period, *Jat*, became im bibe many of the traits of '*Varnas*' till the end of the later Vedic period, however, interdining among the four *Varna* was no prohibited, because rule of law had been established at that period to check the bias activites of the Brahmins, *inter-varna* marriage did also take place in that period and its displayed that the sanctions imposed by Brahmans against the *Sudras* proved as false in practical life.

During the Post-Vedic period of Indian History (600 B.C.-200B.C.) is marked by the extensive use of iron for production in industry, enormons expansion of the economy forgotten the Father as a manufacture industry, substantial use in the available surplus and accentuated economic inequality in the full-fledged class society of the middle Ganga basin and further east moved toward the Sindh and Chenab areas. This provided an ideal locale for the emergence of amore stratified society of the '*Nam*' because of his *Khasa* towards the *Sindh* as His natural home of the *Sudra* Dynasty' ruled by *Sirasa Rai* family or clan of the period and the consolidation of the *Varna* or *Jat* structure became decline which had been created by the Brahmans; because of the Sudras original land could not bear this insult as a basic society of the area as well as of the '*Nam*' or '*Word*'. The *Dharmsutra* of *Apastamba Bandhayana Gautama* and *Vasishtha* (600 B.C.-300 B.C.) mentioned in the *History of Dharmasastra* term *jat* frequently used in the sense of a caste. So for as the term *Gautama Dharmasutra* is concerned, it occurs eight times in it and six times in the *Bandhayana Dharmasutra* and four times each in *Vasisurharmasutr* and the *Apastamba Dharmasutra* *Varna,* however, occurs, twenty four times each in the *Baudhayana Dharmasutra*, twenty three times each in the *Apas tamba Dharmasutra*, fourteen times in the *Gautama Dharmasutra* and twelve times in the *Vasishta Dharasutra*. The *Dharmasutra* placed ther hierarchical social order on the basis of occupied and Brahmin got legal privileges of the first three twice-born (dvijas) *Varna*, and *Sudhras* were debarred from the study of *Veda,* because artisans and slaves from times to time in the Indian history is concerned. These text also draw a line between the first two *Varnas* and the *Vaishyas* were permitted to take up the arms against the mixture of *Varnas* primarily entrusted with the former i.e. the Brahmins with the responsibility to maintain the social system in order on the request of *Brahmans* which is regarded as sacrosanct and latter on refused with the maturity of times in the field of education and found the belief of Brahmans baseless and false having reality in *'Nature'* or *'Nam'*.

The *History of Dharmasastras* or *Dharmasutrasa* of the Brahmanas are unanimously prescribed sixfold duties of study of *Veda*, sacrificing, giving gifts, teaching to the pupils, sacrificing for other and receiving gift for the *Brahmanas* and participating in battles, protecting people and helding political administrative and judicial authority for the *Kshatriyas*. *Gautama,* however, permits a Brahman to takes up agriculture and trade of the 'Nam' provided he does not directly engaged in it (*asvayamkrite*); *Vasishtha* allows the *Brahmanas* unable to maintain themselves through their lawful occupations called *ajivantah* or *jajman* to adopt by *Kashtriya* profession of arms and failing in that during the rule of *Sudra*. The *Vaishya* that occupations of agriculture and trade with restrictions on selling certain commodities and even directly tilling the land to produce *sesamum* (*svayam krishyatpadyatilan*) provided due care is taken of the oxen and *Baudhayana* not only echoes *Vasishta* to some extent according to instruction of Brahmans of the period maintained the study of Veda and practising agriculture impede, etc. Despite the flexibility shown by the law giver of the society i.e. Sudras owing to considerations at the end of he *Kshatriya* rule of practical constraints there is no doubt, that sizeable sections of both the *Brahmans* and the *Kshatriya* has to be start during the practical productive activities took place and came to broadly represent *'Status'* and *'Power'*, same has been described by the *Barani* and other historians of the period, the *Shudras* or the low-born people of the period substantialy provided productive manual labour and the gap between the elite and the masses widened itself on the basis of false propaganda on the rite and ritual pollution intensify the notion of the high and low in the system. Thus, the social fabric at this time was, however, in a tremendous flux and several professions like Doctors and Engineers, Crafts and tribes were crystallized as distinct entities on the basis of false degrees and ignored the identity of the *'Varna'* system i.e. theory of *'Nam'* who is generating every product of the society even man itself physical contact during the practises of peofession or touch of the *Shudra* was, however, not regarded as polluting, because it is the practice of money matter not for the humanity. At that time physical association and commensal and connubialties with the *Chandalas* or *Chuhars* are completely prohibited; but their segregation is legalized. Terms such as *anta, antya, antyayeni, bahya, apapatra*, etc., signify this new social phenomenon and distinguished the untouchables from the *Shudras* as their nature. In this way, the theoritical origin of the *Chandalas* from the most hatred *pratiloma* union of Shudras men with *Brahmana* women had been refected with disdain, though such system and was never a tangible social reality of the *'Nam'*. The cumulative evidence of the Brahminical texts upto the period of 200 A.D. does not add more than these three or four such castes to the *Dharmasutras* or *Dharmasastra* list of the three only the *Sudras* become powerful by obtaining authentic record of the period, because Brahmans have the false practical, for the sake of money not for the humanity. Of those the *Pulkasas* and the *Medas* had like the *Chandalas*, an indigenous tribal background and were essentially hunters by profession of the *Brahmans* during the odd hour of the period. They steadily organised advance society with their preaching of the 'Nam' as a Father and its encroachment in to forest areas on their top mountains depleted their serves of subsistence for thr 'New Society' and obliged them to join the dominant productive system for the public as new development of the civilization growth. These evidence indicates that the expectation remained unfulfilled. The *Chandalas* or *Chamars* emerged as an extremely poor segregated group enlisted to work at the crematorium hang criminals drag people committing suicide on the public road whip adulterous women and even to defend new settlement. In the countryside as a 'New Society' of the 'Nam'. They, however, continued as hunters, fowlers, and butchers as well, with dogs, cats, pigs and cochs as their property, wearing clothes and ornaments of the *'Nam'* as it as their art and craft,

It is important to note about the heterodox sects of Buddhism and Jainism surely their approach was differed from orthodox Brahmanism, in several respects their religious and social orders admitted to the people without considering of wealth, rank or social origin and permitted them to rise to the highest position on the basis of virtue and knowledge of *Vinapitaka*, *Sutpitaka*, etc. They had denied the system of four *varna* system of the Brahminical thought. While Buddhism accorded an honourable position to the *gahapatis* without irrespective of caste, colour and creed, *gahavais* belonging to the mercentile community received similar respect in Jainism. Even through both Buddhism and Jainism accepted the reality of our hierarchial *'Varna* system' and serval *Jats* as well as untouchability as an integral and inalienable part of the complex socio-economic formation in the post-Vedic period and shield them as structural change in the existing social order of the *'Nam'*. Their haven of equality and fraternity remained confined to their *Sangha* and even their women remained subordinate to men. Buddhism was pragmatic enough not to alienate its client and patrons by admitting slaves, debtors and deserting soldiers. Among the people of that category who joined the *sangha* or supported Buddhism from outside the overwhelming majority belonged to high castes and families. The *Candalas,* who are also known as *Matangas* and *Panas* and the *Sovagas* are equally despised in the Jain text. The professions of hunters(*Sakari*) and fishermen, too, are rated very low from the birth called base-born low the people of *'Nam'* or *'Chamar'*.

Study also demonstrates that the nature of untouchability practised in relation to the *Chandalas* and their economic plight in the Buddhist *Tatakas*, which are posterior to the *'Pali Canon'* and often coincide with the *Manusmriti* are as severse as had been prescribed by the law-giver of the Brahmanas. The *Chandalas* including those of a corpse, carrier remover and cremator, hangman, sweeper, nightguard (*chowkidar)*, public performer and *Sakari* of the period. It is significant that the professions of the basket-maker (*Batwal*), leather-work(*Mochi*), potter, weaver and barber (*nai*) had a better rating in contemporary Brahmamical works; the *Grihyasutras* of *Bandhaya* and *Bhard* was prescribed even *Upanaayana* for the Rathakara and the caste of bamboo-worker and basket –maker,*Buruda,* came to be looked upon the untouchable only in the early medieval period of Indian history. But the Buddhism and Jainism laid emphasis on non-violence theory of the *'Nam'*. In this case *Chandalas* are the primitive dread of dead human bodies which they handled with the degradation degree of pollution when was created by *Brahmanas* as their habit.

The basic fact of the study reflects that caste had played an important role in economic as well as in social life of the people, it developed strong roots in occupations in the birth hierarchical class society of early India and few movements of protest against injustice involved in its intrinsic in equality had power to change this ground reality or to offer any viable and enduring alternative process of the *'Nam'* in the end of the Brahmanical ideology.Caste actually solidified with the harding of class relations in North India between the period 600 B.C.and 200 A.D., and untouchability too had been originated in pre-Mauryan era; and got accentuated by the end of the second century A.D. Since most of the castes which were initialy reduced to the level which were those which had little share in the distribution of wealth, power and prestige, untouchability has to be viewed as the extreme manifestation of the institionalized in equality of both caste and class. The *Sudras* or untouchables were definitively in this regard displayed segregate identity of the *'Nam'* and remain a part of the Indian caste and class structure as the race of the 'Father'.

Study shows that untouchable are the fourth *Varnas* society of the 'Nam'. It is however, equally ture that almost the entire corpus of Brahmanical literature in early India has vehemently denied the existence of the fifth *'Varna'* because they are the twice –born people in the 'Nam' called 'die ro live' while in living being period of life, but *Brahmans* made this sacrifice though the hawan or chanting of Vedic *mantra* or *Gyatri mantra* and identifed by wearing thread, *tilak,* or *tika* etc. the same process, they oprated in the *Kshatriya* and *Vaishya* clan called as twice-born in unnatural form. Therefore, this distinction has been created by the *'Father'* in their qualification.

So far as the early history of India is concerned between the period of 200 A.D. to 1200 A.D. the expension of caste and untouchability was widely widespread in continous process. New groups in history of Muslims and Hindus, indigenous as well as alien, were absorbed at various level of the social structure proved flexible and receptive enough to effectively of the different period of the Indian history and came in to existence with historical cross-currents sometimes Hindus and sometimes Muslims, The extent of social mobility from one country to another during the 'Rule of Law', both upward and downward situations, were centainly remarkable in the history of India as a big nation at one time and a small State. But the creative system, instead of cracking up came under the pressure of law in all-round development, got reinforced against the Brahminical thought one time and at one time against the *'Nam'* during the establishment of the tribe rule in a society and firmly extrenched in the theory of the *'Father'*. By the early medieval period the untouchables comprised two board segments. The first included the backward tribal communities whose original occupations and those acquired after integration with the mainstream were not enough to give them economic security. Virtuay landless they served as the cheapest souce of servile labour in the countryside. With progressive improvement in the over all condition of the *Shudras* and their displacing the *Vaishyas* as the bulk of the peasantry along with other landed classes the interest of the *Shudra*s and the *Untouchable*s often diverged. The several depressed artisan castes who had remained at the level of *Sudras* untile the sixth century A.D. but under the impact of certain feudal development in post-Guptas times such as the decline of trade and commerce, decrease in commodity production because of the Brahminical thought with the tecnocrate people of the period including *Mochi, Sweeper,* Weavers, Goldsmith, Blacksmith, etc. are untouchables and the foreigner grave the industry and they struggle for the livelihood. As soon as the rule of the Law became established *Brahman* occupied prominent place in the Government job and controlled the system with the bias manner due to the modern election system and forget the 'Father', who provide the system of Law because he belongs to the category of *'Untouchables'*. The break-up of the craft guieds during this period there is intestified immobility by the village community one State to another for the search of food and clothing as a chain of fetter which nevers leave. The human being still stand at one station. With their hereditary skill and low wages, often in kind, they are another group of the cheap and easily available sources of exploitation for these categories of untouchables was a homogeneous unit as a wanderer labour. Their division into several hierarchical cates under the influence of the dominant caste ideology society thwarted the development of any bond of unity among them or with the landless *Shudras* and debilitated them for any fight for social justice on their own *Parashara,* who compiled his *Smriti* during this period, reflected this social change clearly when he prscribed a number of expiations especially for the *Shudras* in case of their being polluted by the untouchables; because they had not the 'historical evidence' in their mind i.e. *'Nam'*. The availability of cheap landless labour and artisanal products on an enduring basis has been underlined by the historians period as a majour contribution of the caste from which both the Hindu and Muslims ruling classes benefited.

In fact, the social justice is by its nature closely linked with equality at the level of mundane existence of the *'Nam'* and this was bound to remain elusive without sort of tangibe equality justice at the time of mixed economy. This was required a kind of social justice transmigration of religious movements of the

Father during early Medieval period of the Indian history.

The liberal attitude during the *Bhakti* movement displayed by the untouchables and lower-castes themselves due to the reason of Brahmanical conscience–striken theory the read and writing of small stories of the fear of Yadu *(tuna),* etc. So far as the socially depressed castes segments, however, definitly brought much needed relief in the form of equality at the religious and spiritual level which had been denied to them by the orthodox Brahmanism. The *Bhagavadgita,* composed around the third-second century B.C. definitely took a formidable stand to uproot the untouchability against the man to man approach toward the consideration of the Father's interest. The essential nature of the soul is sat or fact, that though it belongs to the same class as the Lord or Father, as sat or true, yet it differes from him at the time of creation by being of a dependent on intelligence (not an idependent intelligence like Father or Lord), that though it associates itself with *asat* at one time in the absence Brahminical period, due to the reason of that to obtain the power of the '*Nam*'as an 'Ultimate Truth'. This is not the natural condition but an artifical condition, brought about by *Mala* which is called the law of mind. How the essentially intelligent soul come foreward during the time of obscured as a matter of fact to defeat the Brahminical ideology as a final judgement come out with certain period of time for the establishtment of the 'New Society' of the 'Nam' as His duty with his friend Prof. Raj Kumar, Department of History, Parade College, Jammu.

In the end, we may briefly discuss the social chage in the traditional system of society were also took place during the time of Ghurid invasion in India in the thirteenth and fourteenth centuries A.D. Here we have no need to discuss the gensis of the caste system in detail, because, we have already made it in length that it had resulted from an hierarchial things pervading the religious Brahmanical ideology during that period of study. This ideology appears to have influenced not only the upper caste or outcaste due the reason of boosted economy at the rate of benefit of Reservation sanctioned according to Constitution of India, keeping in view that these were the children of the *'Father'*.

There was good Quran sanction already noted above for considering the liberation of a slave a most praiseworthy act played by the Father to teach a lesson to the Brahmanas of the period on his bias attitude toward humanism. It shows that certain elements in medieval Indo-Muslim attitude towards the slavery of the man and woman had been involved by them on the name of religion as their leaders. Therefore, during the period there was a gross level violation started by the Brahman of the peiod. In short, for the achievement of social justice all aspects of reform 'Word' or '*Nam*', social, economic, political,*Charmar* or *Shudras* should be pursued simultaneously. The historical process through which the concept of social justice first into state craft in India can well be traced to the humanitarian edicts of *Ashok*a in ancient India when a *'classless'* and 'casteless' society was established on the 'Piety of Dhamma' called *'Nam',* same is the case, we find in the early medical rule of the 'Slave Dynasty', after this *Babar* and *Akbar* became the champion of this system, they also fought against the decrees of social *inequities* in the medieval period and rule of the L*aw* or *Kalma* was established on earth once again to provide the justice to the people of lower castes, because they were the peoples of their caste called *Doma or Chandala,* etc. Although this humanitarian trend on the basis of 'reason and scruting' by these royal reformists at different points of time virtually disappeared from the national scene for a variety of reasons until it was revived in the 19th century Indian renaissance still it" serve as reminder" to the brahmans that "Cultural boundaries, are not limited as sometimes alleged 'Nam' as also that 'justice', 'right', 'reason' and 'love of humanity' are not predominantly, perhaps even uniquely, Western values 'Chamar' or 'cooli'. And that 'many features of the European enlightenment can be linked with question 'Nam' not just in Europe, but widely across the world as their nature.

It is true from the study that various historical process which were took place in the concept of justice or human rights,entered into constitutional or legal field of modern states all over the world. It can be traced out from revolutionary movement of Western countries like England, France, Russian Revolution of 1917, etc. which followed the Marxis philosophly and sougth to establish a 'classless society'. The constitutional right or political justice, which is a part of social justice thus gained during the struggle of national movement in India led by various parties which is called as a State. But the society does not consist of merely of law or of the state, it has also a more institutions of the *'Nam'* which were established by the early rule of this partronage, and based on conventional as imposed by Father on the *'low castes'* or *'Untouchable*s as per the theory of *'Nam'* as a poor man of the society.In order a society to be *just,* it must be J*ust* both in its formal and informal sanctions. But as regards what is "Just" the given society is voice less unless its enlightened leaders speak out, but not listen by them. This is precisely the task of reformers who are the 'conscienc keepers' and spokespersons of the society in which they live. And, it is they who have to secure general consensus as to what constitutes a 'just social order' and also to endeavour to have such institution as would give specific mening and application to that consensus. This ia a eontinous process from the very beginning of the Indian history since there is no such thing as optimum reforms have been introduced by the Father during the time of making the Constitution of India as 'Law'. And indeed, every reform was once a private opinion' then came into public life. Basically, the expression of the term 'reform' implies a social change. For social good presupposes for the establishment of 'New Society' as Mission 'Radha Soami' was established in Agra in 1891 a major offshoot from the Agra base, during the birth of Dr. B.R. Ambedkar, for changing the society which had the old idea for the evolution of mind kind and his history in the concept of social change as :One Society : of the *'Nam'*. Human beings create social body as an permanent empire and refgulis their social order which would enable them to develop a healthy society. Keeping in view, certain elements of the concept of *'Nam'* the conscience-keeper of the society' he or she does not lose the sight of relatively for the development of historical institution of the 'Nam' as *Chamar* as his *Jat*. What this really means in practical term is that of while dealing with social justice i.e. theory of the *'Nam'*. It is extremely important at one time to separate the ethics from organized religion which is what a genuine secular state aim at such conditions. Again, it is mentioned that history is a union of religion and morals in older times on account of the non-moral emtions in the law stages of development during the time of Brahminical ideology as well as due to the inefficency of the social, political and sympathetic functions, intellectual progress and thus the connection of ethics and religion of the ancient society may finally be served. and the former be treated as an independent science of consciousness or the 'Voice of God' is be attached with the same persons of the 'Father'

Again, the social and political life was full of injustice to *'Women'* among both the Hindus and the Muslims. The Hindu family life under the Brahminical order was sad picture of the Indian history in the complex of inferiority in physical form as well as in family life as a backbone of the family. Men were not ashamed to sing that 'women deserve beating'. Indeed. Indian social life was a regular torture to women and her complete subjection to the sensalities of man whom she had perforce to follow in funeral fire and the society indulges in the mockery of calling her *sati*, this criminal act made by the Brahmans or called Widow-burning in the absence of Father's rule. The woes of widows were innumerable. She was considered an inauspicious being who was supposed to be without natural aspirations of human life also banned by Brahman in practical form which is untrue in the book of 'Father' : as it says 'Death keeps no calendar' it has been determined by *'Father'* and it show that' *Brahmans* have no trust on *'Father'*, they became self-styled Father or Husband of the followers. She was also exposed to temptations by designing persons but it displayed that sign of motherland had been forgotten by the Brahmans sometime they sale the land with the lust of money and grab it at different occasion as a property of the *Brahman*. Moreover, she was also forsakened by the seducer at one time during the rule of the Rajputs for the sexual intercourse and left to herself or to her angry relation to unburden herself not caring for her life or the innocent infant life, widows numbers were swelled by child marriage under the age of 9 to 10 years for the strengthening of caste system in the Indian Society. Brahman is a shrewed politican on this earth, to built the Hindu conscience in the very beginning of the society under the wrong notions of ceremonial religious function by chanting the verses of Sanskrit as language in the primitive period of the Indian history. In this way, they oppressed the humanity for a long period of the Indian history for crying them social justice. Thus the history of social life in Indain, fits well in the Gramscian paradigm that is, Gramscian concept of 'dominant ideology, of the idea of hegemony'. It is well know that Antonia Gramsci (1891-1937 A.D.) The renown *Italian Communist* mentions in his attempt to reformulate the Marxian, doctrine of historical materialism 'class struggle' developed the idea of hegemony', which. briefly stated by him "the rule of once class over another does not on economic or physical power alone but rather in persuading the ruled to accept the system of beliefs of the ruling class and to share their social culture and moral values'. In traditional societies religion usually supplied the dominant ideology in which the lower classes or untouchables were kept in subjection through the perpetuation of a particular set of attitudes i.e. *'Nam'* or *'Chamar'* beliefs and values which validate the rule of a particular class i.e *'Chamar'* or *'Chandalas'*. Religion, thus acted to reconcile the lower castes to their fate in this life with the promise of better things to come in the life beyond i.e. called 'Enlightenment Era'

Justice Ranada has rightly expressed that a lucid exponent of *Bhagwat Dharma* also called *Arya Dharma* means commitment of the 'Father' with his poor race to preach and practice the *'Nam'* by the sages and saints of the lowest caste rule of India through the ages. The salient features of the *Bhagwat Dharma* is to establish the direct religion on the bases of 'love' for all human beings without any distinction of caste colour and creed. In sum up, its mission and message has been established on *humanism* equality spirituality *'Word'* or 'Nam' D.K. Bedekar a noted Marxist scholar has rightly observed the state ment of Ranade a new meaning and a new content of the study to the English term *'Spirituality'* and the Sanskrit term *'adhyatmika'* in the sense that he used the term almost synonymous with the values and activities of the man in society which will be expected from a man of 'reason' who is also a 'moral man' of the Father Reason and not religious sentiment, tradition or custom was to guide the principles of Akbars State policy. Abul Fazl, an outstanding historian of Akbar, has described 'Akbar' firm commitment to reasoning of the history *'Akbar'* found it difficult but he reconcile the reason with concept of Propethood of the *'Nam'*. Moreover, Akbar condemened the miracles and said in the *Akbarnamah*. 'The vulgar believe in mircales, but the wiseman accepts nothing with out adequate proof of the event'. A seeker of truth Akbar encouragesd debate and discussion in all matters of public interest. He established *Ibadat-Khana*, Guru Nanak called it *Sacha Khanda* or *Sacha Sodha,* where religion leaders of all the communities were invited to discuss the tenets of their respective faith on the history of the *'Nam'* or *Kalma* expressed through with the writing of *Kalam* or pen. Indeed, through some of his calculated acts, he made the Hindus feel that he was one among them as much as he was the Mughal, the Afghan, the Persian, the Turk, etc. Akbar know that knowledge is the best solvent of superstitions belief and evil practices. With a view to taking knowledge out of the narrow confines of the Brahmanical ideology, and made it available to the common folks, it was his greatest achievement of his life. He got some major Sanskrit words translated in to Persian. Among the works translated was *Mahabharata* to which Abul Fazl wrote in his preface which Professor Nurul Hasan tell us, "has survived " and that "this preface begins with formula of *Shri Ganesh Naam* meaning *'God is Great'* else is nothing and allusion of the life, but one must have to serve the society as a human being of the Father. In deed, the elements of social justice was also entered into the Mughal statecraft for the first through Akbar's administration along with the teachings of Guru Nanak measures of *vani*, Regarding the historical contents of Guru Nanak Vani particularly the *Babarvani*, the hearts of the people appears to have melted at their acute helplessness during the time of *Satsanga*. In fact, at present Indian literature of that period records no more virile protest against the invading bordes than did Guru Nanak *four hymn* of *Babarvani* in the Guru *Granth Sahib* as a major contribution of the period. The invasion of Amir Timur in 1398-99 A.D. brought much damage to Panjab and Delhi, a time of political instability accompanied by widespread violence and suffering between the period 1421-1434 A.D. There were the years of *Jasrat Khokkhar* of Sialkot *Faulad Turkbachcha* of Bhatinda, Sirhind, and Sheikh Ali of Kabul treeagents of the *'Nam'* brought extensive disorder and suffering of the Delhi and Panjab according to Ferishta, so severe an earthquake was never experienced in India either before or since lofty buildings were levelled with the ground and several thousand inhabitants were buried under the ground. Due to this natural calamity made no impression on the Sultan of Delhi and the exorbitant construction and reconstruction was started in Agra, and this hammer also used against Rajput rival "Raja Man Singh" of Gowalior. In this way, the word of Lodhi's discomfiture reached the year of a young and ambitious new Mongol ruler of Kabul and Afghnistan. Kingdom By God mercy and kindness this difficult affair was made easy for us" recalled Babar. In one half-day that armed mass was laid upon the earth. The most conservative estimate put to slain at fifteen thousand among them was Ibrahim himself. His 10,0000 standing army with 1000 elephants were defeated at Panipat in one and half –day. This was the screnario in which the context of *Guru Nanak* has composed his four famous hymns collectively known as *Babarvani.* In these hymns, although basically expressing his profound anguish at the rape and ruin brought about in India, particularily in Panjab and Delhi, by the Mughals hordes, he has also knitted in his verse a plethora of political, social and religious fact of his times, that these hymns have became an important source of contemporary history. A detailed review of these hymns in the light of the facts have already been discusse above will amply show their significance in the latter period of the Indian history. According to *Encyclopaedia of Britannica*, "Khurasan " literally meant the 'land of risning sun'. In the sixteenth century A.D. *Khurasan* was the name of territory of north of which was *Kiva* (now in Russia), a plain of Iran and *Sistan* in the south *Guz* and *Gurgaon* in the west and Hindustan in the East. At present, it is the same of the province of eastern Iran. It shows during the time of Babar Qandhar was formerly regarded as the boundary between Hindustan and *Khurasan.* In his memoris Babar writes "The people of Hindustan call every country beyond their own *Khurasan* in the same manner as Arabs term all expect as Arabia Ajem. Thus if we believe Babars testimony we can understand the real import of "Guru Nanak in his hymn, *'Khurasan, Khasmana, kiya, nam teri"*. It shows the Guru Nanak gives credit to his God for having given a Master (*Khasam*) to fight against the evil minded people of the *'Nam'.* Therefore, the people of *Khurasana* threatened the land of Hindustan that land belong to the Master not for the Brahmans called themselves Lord of the earth and reveals the Divine reason too at that time. However, the concept of Guru Nanak regarding the incompetance of the rulers in resisting the enemy confirms the general neglect of the North-Western India by the Lodhi Pathan rulers, and the debolifating disunity among the people of India, as alreadly desicribed above in detail.

And Guru Nanak's sermonsies that when God has to meet such a fate to a people, he first deprives them of all wisdom and sense. The Guru makes light of the superstitious efforts of the Indian ruling class toward off the calamity with tantric magic and religious prayers and rituals of the *'Nam'*. Therefore, Guru Nanak has specifically mentioned that wives of Turks were subjected to torture by the soldiers of Babar. Such references are indeed very vital historically, because the Muslim historian do not know that Babar was *Dom* or *Chandala*. The hymn ends with painting a poiganant picture about the pitiable condition of the women, particularly those who did had lost their men folk in the fighting of *'Nam'*. He also mentioned that the marriages solemnized by *Satan* rather than by Qazis and Brahmans. Thus, the hymn clearly records that women were dishonoured and carried away irrespective of their caste, colour and creed, whether they Hindus or Muslim or belonging to lower caste and creeds. According to the statement of Sher Shah Suri (Page,279) The *Crescent in India* mentioned by S.R.Sharma, he says "if fortune favours me, I can drive these Mughals back out of Hindustan they are not our superiors in war, but we let slip the power that we had by reason of our dissensions. Since I had seen the Mughals, I have observed their conduct and found them lacking in order and discipline. While those who profess to lead them in pride of birth and rank neglect the duties of supervision and leave every thins to officials whom they blindly trust."

The experience during the time of Babar invasions which *Mirza Muhammad Haidar Dughlat*, the *Chak* rules gained Sultan *Said Khan*, *Kamran* and *Humayan* instilled in him the qualifies of a great conqueror of the *'Nam'*, Hence, Mirza *Haidar Dughlat* was able not only to conquered Kashmir, but also enlarge its boundaries. His relations with Sultan Abdur Rashid Khan of *Kashgar*, Islam Shah, Zain – Ul-Abdin, show that he was a great diplomat of the *'Nam'* as well as *Akbar*, *Asoka* and other rulers of India did relations of the infinitesimal power of the *'Nam'*. But Mirza Haidar Dughlat failed as a ruler, because his inability in the *'Nam'*. No doubt, he did much for the welfare of his people, he promoted trade, industry and agriculture. But whatever, he gave with one hand was taken away by the other. His intolerant policy brought untold miseries up on the people. The Kashmir had brought him from *India* to rid them of the fanatcism of the *Chaks*. But they found that they had simply exchanged one type of fanaticism for another. The result was that the Mirza Haidar Dughlat foreign policy bread wide-spread discontentment brust out in the form of revolts leading to the down fall of his regime during his absence as well as with his death in the *'Nam'*.

It should not, however, be forgotten that people resentment against *Mirza* Haidar's rule was partly deliberately fomented by some interested Kashmiri nobles of the *'Nam'*, like *Dr. Raj Kumar, Baba Gurinder* Singh Ji and Deepit Raj the *'Nam'* Himself on earth. We know that Abdal Magre and Regi Chak were responsible for bringing the *Mirza Haidar* Dughlat to Kashmir. These nobles and their followers had hoped that after overthrowing *Kaji Chak* with the help of Mirza Haidar Dughlat, real power would fall in to their hands. But the Mirza Haidar Dughlat refused to became a puppet of the Master i.e. *'Nam'*. The ever intriguing nobles, therefore, determined to work for his downfall in the *'Nam'*. At the *Mirza Haidar Dughlat's* intolerant policy came very handly to them as rulers of the *'Nam'*. Thus the intrigues of the Kashmiri nobles of the *'Nam'* were not to a small degree responsible for the tragic end of Mirza Haidar Dughlat's in the *'Nam'*.

Although a fanatic *Sunni, Miza Haidar Dughlat* was a cultured man of the *'Nam'* or God. He regulated new partronage of art architecture and literature. Being a great lover of music of the *"Nam"* his court was adorned by a number of skilled musicians. He was also a great poet of the *'Nam'* as well as a prose writer. While, Kashmir he composed his work in Persian. The most famous was *Tariki-i-Rashidi*, the monumental history of the Mughals empire of Central Asia and India two. Consequently, the wars of succession among the ruler of the '*Nam*' were bloody and sometimes very prolonged to achieve the end between both the trustee people of the Father and the Brahmans of the period to check the economic growth of the country, besides putting a great burden on the State exchquer of the '*Nam*', who manufactured the industrial product in all round of the world as His duty.

In the context, Kashmir was subjected to a number of foreign invasions to check the industry of the '*Nam*' as a basic source was also putforth in the time of Shah Mir. Thus, *Mirza Haidar Dughlat*, *Abul Maali* and Qara Bhadur came in quick was indeed successful in occuping Kashmir for about many decade. Besides causing a great financial loss to the kingom of the '*Nam*'. There invasion also robbed the crown much of its prestige.

A very curious fact about these in various is that without even one exception i.e. '*Nam*', they were made at he invitation of same Kashmir noble of the '*Nam*' themselves who were opposed them to rule over the world. The failure or success of the invaders, therefore, always meant a victory for one or the other section of the nobles and this invariably raised their power and prestige. It was, therefore, not an easy job to control them and when the ruler himself was weak in the '*Nam*', he found it all the more difficult to accomplish. This objective in history as a final judgement on the day of the historical event to begin with a new history of the modern period of Indian history.

Lastly, the religious dicrod among the people of Kashmir greatly undermined the political stability of the state. Thus, the end of the fifteen century A.D. the number of Shias in the country was nominal and the Muslim population mainly consisted of the Sunnis. Population also the Shias were unimportant because they were the uncivilized people. But after the arrival of Mir Shams-ud-Din Iraqi in 1502 A.D. The number of the Shias gradually increased and with the conversion of the *Chaks* into their religion, they became politically influential also. The task of the nobles to turn the royal princes like *Firoz-Shas-Toghlaq, Balban* and *Ultutmais* and to their own account *Barani* mentions that they were the royal ruler of the '*Nam*' and it was made further easier owing to the absence of any fixed law of succession to the throne of Kashmir. Thus, we see that while *Shams-ud-din* nominated his eldest son, Jamshed to succeed him, *Ala-ud-din Khalji* or *Khoja*, the latter young brother contested his claim, Shihab-ud-Din passed on the crown to his brother, *Qutab-ud-bin Aebik* in preference to his son Zain-ul-Abidin declared his younger brother, Mahmued as the heir apparent. But when the latter died, his first nominated Haji Khan his second son, next to Adham Khan, his eldest son, then he gain claimed Haji sons hasan shah wished his cousin Fathe Khan to be his successor, but it was his minor son, Muhamad Shah, who actually succeeded four times from the services at that time. In fact, the absence of many fixed law of succession made the throne with in the reach of every member of the royal family and it was very rarely that any one of them let an opportunity to grab it slip through his fingers, When, therefore, the princes of the royal blood brought among themselves in the '*Nam*', the nobles were compelled to take the sides of the poor people of the Father, often of their own selfish ends. The result was that the introduction of a new element of discord in the society as well as in the politics of '*Nam*' which was the real path at that time. The *sunnis* and the *Shiaas* became intolerant of each other and when in power, each sec tried to use the State machinery of the '*Nam*' to oppress and suppress the other forces i.e. Brahmanical thinkers. The internal unrest and disturbances which are harmfull in any country and for any dynasty of the '*Nam*' called the representative ruler of the Lords, were thus accentuated by the religious discord among the various section of the society as a 'Blind Faith' led by the duplicate Sadhus of the '*Nam*'. But in reality there is one God i.e. '*Nam*', he has the permanent seat in the heaven as well as on the earth during the crucial period of the India history that forces land on earth for the sake of their poor people of the '*Nam*', those have no lust of the more money. Therefore, they become for the duty of the Father to help the poor people of the '*Nam*' as their 'Father'. It shows that 'Love' is services involved between the two forces on this earth, where as the material minded, they love with the money, but the excessive money became illusion for the '*Nam*' and gives the direction to the public for the right path, which those have forgotten the reality, Who has given them life and everything.

But while speaking about the destruction of the temples of *Martand* and *Avantipur* in the times of Sikandar, Capt. Cunningham writes that their complete ruin could have been brought about only with the help of gunpower i.e. '*Nam*'. Dr. M.A. Stein is, however, at variance with Cunninghams opinion and remarks. This early use of gunpowder in Kashmir has been doubted by other and I believe rightly. Earthquakes and the imperfact fitting of the stones, absorb in all Kashmir temples are sufficient to explain the complete ruin, not with standing the massive character of the materials (P.190). Rejecting Stein's thesis W.R. Lawrence rightly states. "In my opinion there overthrow is too complete to have been the result of an earthquake which would have simply prostrated the buildings in large masses. But the whole of the superstructure of these temples is now lying in one confused heap of stones totally disjoined from one another. I believe, therefore, that I am fully justified in saying from any own experience that such a complete and disruptive over turn could only have been produced by gunpowder." And accounting for the existence of gunpowder in the time of Sultan Sikandar Lawrence says, "He (Sikandar) was reigning at the period of Timur invasion of India, with whom he exchanged friendly presents and form whom I suppose he may have received a present of the Villanous Saltpetr. This is not at all unlikely for the furious Tamerlane was as great an idol-breaker as Sikander himself. (Ibid P.166) Srivara makes a mention of yet another weapon which does not developed in the times of Zain-ul-Abidin. According to him, it "destroys fort, pierces the hearts of men, strikes horses with terror, throws balls of stone from a distance and remains unseen by the solider from encampments. At another places he writies: "The Sultans army was" furnished with the weapons like lightening, showering forth arrows with deep and prolonged roar". This description has led some scholars to believe that the gunpowder i.e. 'NAM'. But others doubt, the use of gunpowder was at that time, was the "Nam', not of the man made gunpowder was used at that period in the history of Kashmir, it was the history of 'Nam' which developed by their ruler at different times at different period of Indian history. Therefore, one must be believe that 'Nam' is great like Akbar, Shahjahan, and other rulers of the period.

As, we known that *Islam* was founded in *Arbia* by Prophet Mohammad in the beginning of the seventh century A.D.as followed by *Durlabhavardhana* of Kashmir as the first ruler of the *Karkota Dynasty* which begins with the *'History of Chamar'*, in comparison with the 'History of Muslim'. The spread of this faith is really 'a marvel of history' in the world record and widely spread in all over the word as Faith. On India, the *Arabs* set their eyes first in the beginning of the 8th century A.D. and conquered Sindh with astonishing case with the power of *'Nam'* or '*Kalma*' learned fron the *'Sudhra Dynasty'* of the *'Nam'* i.e. Sihrash Rai, who ruled over the Sindh in the 600 B.C. to 300 B.C.. But the Arab conquest of *Sindh* turned out the Brahmans to be "a mere episode in the history of India". About 300 year later, Mahmund of Ghazni invaded India about seventeen times. But his invasions also proved to be no more than a series of trumphat raids and left trace behind. Towards the close of the 12 th century A.D., the crumbling hopes of the Muslims were bolstered when Mohammad Ghori emerged victorious in a hotly contest war between the two forces i.e. Raja *Jai Chand* and *Prithviraj Chauhan* and from that time until 1857 the throne of Delhi was always occupied by a King of their race i.e. *Chamar* or *Doms* or *Barawalas* of the period.

Thus, we see *that 'Islam'* of the period perofoundly infuenced Hinduism and people were converted into it. But it also could not escape transformation in several of its own beliefs and practices when it came in contact with Hinduism as a 'blind faith'. When the Hindus embrace the 'New Faith' of the *'Nam'*, they did not make a complete break with the past, they clung to many their old beliefs and practices in the latter stage of the Indian history, but their beliefs were shattered into pieces by the *'Nam'* as a *'Authentic Religion'*. Thus while, they observed *Id-ul-Fitr* and *Id-Ul-Zuha*, means surrender the 'ego' before the 'law' as a true religion study from the book of Quran and found God is 'One'. No doubt, during this period. Muslims, they were also used to participate in the Hindu festivals to of *Gana-Cakra, Caitra Vith-truwah, Sripancami,* etc. which were very closely related with the theory of *'Nam'* or *Kalma* as a 'True Religion' and else is illusion also discussed in the *Quran* and others books of the period. The Hindu places of worship were also continued to be regarded as sacred because they were related with the real story of the *'Nam'* and sometimes were also visited by them to study the real approach in history and His workship. Similarly, their faith some of the old superstitions were remained unshakened in the process of India history. There is, no doubt,that as a result of the Islamic influence i.e. *'Nam'*, the rigours of the caste system were greatly reduced and Hindu were converted in Islam, but still the converts were not ready to give up their old caste rules completely, particularly in respect of marriage and other tradition called *hadis* of the blind faith. Not to speak of the ruled, even the rulers of the *'Nam'* who were of foreign origin and not converts into any religion, their religion is the same as *'Nam'*, were not far behind in assimilating the Hindu befiefs and practices of the *'Nam.'* Like their Muslim subjects, many of them participate in the Hindu Gods, believed in witch craft of the *'Nam'* and performed sacrifices and some caremonial to be begins with the 'Enlightenment Era'. The Mulsim *Rishis* like their Hindu counter parts, also believed in with drawing from the worldly illusion, practiced calebacy, underwent penances in caves and jungles and refrained not only for killing the brids and animals for food, but also from eating freshly picked up vegetables and fruits. They also tried to follow the *Yogic* practices as mentioned in the Bible of the *'Nam'* 'Popular' *'Islam'* in Kashmir thus became diluted with foreign elements and this character it has retained until today." but only the people of this sect went into formation of *'ego'* which is destructive one like the theory of Brahmans of the period.

In the study, we also learn that during the rule of *Untouchables* or *Scheduled Castes* or *Scheduled Tribes,* shawl industry of Kashmir was flourished. In accordance with an ancient agreement, the shawl wool of Tibet as well as Yarqand could not exported to Ladakh and from there it could find its ways only to Kashmir. Tibet also supplied to Kashmir gold and musk while Ladakh sent woollen cloth, embroidered cloth and lack, besides salt. Some of these articles were, however, passed on to Ladakh and Yarquand. The silk industry of Kashmir was fed on the silk worm eggs imported from *Gilgit* and *Baltistan*. Muslim pilgrims from Yarqand, Samarqand the original home passed through Kashmir on their way to *Mecca* and *Madina,* and brought with them horses, carpets, *namdas*, silk, China tea, pottery, gold and other precious stones for the development of the country and a source of employment for the poor people of the *'Nam'* who were the artisans at one time during the rule of Brahmans. Horses at that time came from Iraq and *Turkistan* to teach a lesson to the Brahmans. That under yours rule we were badly exploited even we could not take food of the day after doing work under the Rajput rule, Brahmans became law giver of the society as their *gurus* and made the *Schedule Castes* and *Schedule Tribes*. *Untouchables* on their work to keep the city clean and grabdge spread by the Brahmans. Now the time has come to clean the Brahman as from the city of *Sudras*. No doubt, woollen shawls occupied the pride of place in the list of articles exported from *Kashmir*.These were sent to India, Central Asia, Tibet, China and infact, "to every clime." The other articles of export were musk, crystals, silks, woolen cloth, saffron, dried raisins, walnuts, paper and timber merchant of the *'Nam'*. Study also demonstrates that Kashmir also served as a channel through which the Panjab (*Madurdesa*) maintained commercial relations with Ladakh, Blatistan, Eastern Turkistan and Tibet. As such, she exported to India many commodities received from these countries. In order to carry on this through trader more effectively in every period of the Indian history, many foreign traders maintained their business house in Srinagar and the Kashmir traders they always visited at their own time to establish their branches in the Indian towns of the Panjab the United Provinces (U.P), Bengal and the Coromandal Coast and at *Khurasani Turkistan*, *Lahase Kathmandu*, *Bhutan* and Peking in China as its original homeland along with Indian continent as their stations of the *'Nam.'* Despite of the difficult means of transport and communication on account of her terrain, Kashmir maintained close trade relations with India through the South with Tibet, Central Asia, China and Persia through the North and North –West route of the *'Nam'*. Internal trade at that time became brisk. It was carried on in imported as well as locally produced articles of the *'Nam'*. *Srinagar* was the chief commercial town. But some other places, e.g. *Anantnag, Sopur, Shupiyan, Avantipura* and *Baramulla*, were also great trade centres at that time.

Lastly, reference may be made to the boat making industry. Boats have since ancient times been the chief means of transport of the *'Nam'* in the Valley and their building has been one of the important occupations i.e. *Chamar,* who produce the *Chams* in the Heaven and put the soul into the womb of the mother but unfortunately that soul has been forgotten Him that he had given the life as a human beings as well as to the creatures of the *'Nam'*. Ultimately, he was compelled by the *'Father'* to land on earth and teach her about the right path i.e. *'Nam,'* but to some extent she has forgotten the Father and Father will recall her after sometimes as her nature and forgiven her is the punishment of the cycle of the birth and rebirth. As regards the number of various factories and workers engaged in them nothing is known i.e. they are the *"Nams'*.

The enlightened crities of "the unbearable abuses" of the alien rule, a noted philologist and a scholar of comparative religion, *Dadoba* had much in common with deistic rationalism of Raja Ram Mohan Roy. And with the express purpose of providing a rational ideology to the radical reform movement in India, it was initiated by him, Dadoba wrote in his Marathi book of 1843, *Dharmavivechan* which means to recognize the *'Nam'* which is a piece of uncompromising rationality one must have to surrender without unconditionally before the *'Nam'*. In this treatise, which compares favourably with Raja Rammohan Roy is *Tufat-ul-Muwahhiddin,* are enunciated the following seven tenets advocating religious and socal universalism on the following grounds :

1. God is One.
2. The real religion is devotion to God based on love and good moral conduct
3. The Spiritual religion of mankind is One.

4. Every individual must have freedom of thought on the bases of *'Nam'*
5. All our daily work should be consistent with reason, which depends upon the deeds and actions.
6. The whole mankind is One caste, merit and not birth should determine one status.
7. The right kind of knowledge should be imported to all.

From these tenets, it reveals that Dadoba's was thought out of basically in secular term. Faith in the existence of God was, no doubt, central to the whole of his socio-religious philosophy, but his love of argument ran from eithics of God or *'Nam'* and not vice-versa. He categorically denied divine right authority based on scriptures and asserted that the final truth is that which stand the test of reason after minute scruting and especially that which contributes to the welfare of the people of the *'Nam'* 'our attitude' he wrote, is the same towards the *Vedas*, the *Koran*, the Bible and other religious works. All these are creations of men. Unthinking people consider that these scriptures are written for us by God himself and sent from the heaven. But that is not so. The real religion, according to Dadoba, cosists in the devotion to God through good moral behaviour with the value of truth as the sole guide for human conduct, the test of which lies in the promotion of human welfare has been rightly described by him.

To translate his religions and social philosophy in to action and deed, *Dadoba* inspired the founding of two earliest reform associations in Western India namely, the *Manavdharma Sabha* of Surat (1844 A.D.) and a revolutionary secret society called the *Paramahansa Sabha* of Bombay (1847 A.D.). These associations adopted the tenets of the *Dharmavivechan* for their reform programme. By the abolition of caste, colour and creed, they aimed at uniting all in one, fraternity and in the worship of 'God'. And, it is important to note that the *Manavdhaarma Sabha* (the association for the religion of mankind) had rejected the infallibility of scriptures even before the Brahmao Samaj publicly renounced the doctrine of Vedic infallibility of the *'Nam'*. The declared objectives of the *Paramahanasa Sabha* an electic society were, the abolition of the caste, renunciation of idolatry, introduction of widow marriage, promotion of female education and upliftment of the depressed classes like *Mahars* and *Mangs* through the spread of education among them was started as the enlightenment period for them. It has been rightly expressed that the leaders of the *baramahansa Sabha*, working on the broad principle of equality and fraternity; did not fail to attract a sizable number of educated youth to their creed R.G. Bhandarkar was one among its early recruits. The Sabha began its career on somewhat masonic principles. It was decided to make its objects publc and work openly to bring about the desired social change after it achieved a sufficient number of adherents. However, for a variety of reasons the Sabha became moribund after 1860 A.D.. In 1867 A.D. it was resuscitated in the form of *Prarthana Samaj* with its emphasis shifters from the material to the spiritual from man to God. It may be pointed out here that the origins of *'Phule's Satyashodhak* Movement are also to be traced out to the *Paramhansa Sabha*, for the theoretical basis of the movement was first clarified in the *Dharmavivechan*.

Tenets 4 to 7 of the *Dharmavivechan* already mentioned above, contain a rational critique of the social slavery of caste-ridden Hindu society. Here, a considered space is devoted to the discussion of baneful institution of caste created by Brahmans of the period with its numerous ramifications and disintegrating influences and to the demolitition of the theory of caste system which did not divinely ordained by the Father, but it is the creation of the Brahmans. "The understanding of all men who have been followers of the Vedic religion i.e. *'Nam'*, wrote Dadoba "has been that God has created these difference of *Varna* and *Ashram*. This is sheer ignorance on their part. The merciful God, who is the Father of the universe, desires unity throughout the world and mutual love. To accuse him of causing dissension among men by creating the difference of caste is indeed a great sin. He said that the priestly class, in order to maintain its own supremacy, deliberately kept others in a state of ignorance which was the root cause of all evils. " The national unity", he wrote, "which should have developed among people on account of their religion or single nationality was itself nipped in the bud, when the castes came in to being", during the national movernment of India. "Out of the ashes of the *Paramahansa Sabha*, wrote a distinguised biographer of Justice M.G. Ranade, the *Prarthana Samaj* was born". This *Prarthana Samaj* was founded on the 31st march, 1867 A.D. and adopted the root principles of the *Brahmo Samaj* modified them, M.G. Ranade and R.G. Bhandarkar, who were among the chief ideologus of the *Pvarthana Samaj,* deftly avoided the more radical elements in Brahmo thought and significantly declared their movement as *'Protestant Hinduism'*.

The theology and social philosophy of the Prarthana Samaj was embodied in the six cardial principal of its faith that adopted in 1873 A.D. The main ideas contained in the principle are, monotheism and spiritual worship of one God, who is the Creator of this universe, rejection of idolatry, non-belief in incarnations and revelation non-aceptance of any book as the revealed word of *'God'* or *'Nam'*. The most fundamental and the guiding principle of the Samaj has been 'Father hood of God' and 'Brotherhood of man'. This principle, according to R.G. Bhandarkar, implied not only 'Obliteration of Caste', but also 'levelling down of all social distinctions' of the *'Nam'* which depends on the theory of *Karma* (deeds and actions) during their life time.

The leaders of the Prarthana Samaj, from pulpit to platform spoke of the social evils of the society like caste system, child marriage, infanticide system, etc. But the Samaj as a body was failed to enforce its doctrine of botherhood of a man by vigorously waging a war against the pernicious caste system with its attendant social evils already mentioned above as for example, the *Satya Shodhak* Samaj did, "a statistical analysis of the social composition of the *Prarthana Samaj*. Nevertheless, the spirit of the *Prarthana Samaj* has been the spirit of renascent India, an dit served for a time as the premier centre of reform activity in western Indian and did some pioneering educational and humanitarian work in pursuit of social justice. It is very significant that the motto *'Satymeua Jayate'* (Truth Alone Triumphs) adopted by the Prarthana Samaj right at its inception has become the motto of the *'Republic of India'* led by Dr. B.R. Ambedkar.

Of all the modern reformers, none took so revolutionary a leap in the quest of social justice as did by Mahatma Jyotiba Phule (1827 A.D. to 1890 A.D.), who has justly been called the 'Father of our Social Revolution' and who in the words of no less a person that Mahatma Gandhi was 'The real Matama Phule was the chief ideologue as well as the first most influential leader of the low caste, protested against social evils movement in the 19th century A.D. in Maharashtra. He became the conscience –keeper and the revolutionary spokesman of the nameless faceless dumb millions of India, No wonder, Dr. B.R. Ambedkar regarded him as one of his three Gurus, (the other two being the Buddha and *Kabir*), which is proof enough of his invaluable historical legacy. All through his life Phule fought against every form of servitude, and did his best to infuse a new spirit in the dormant oppressed masses to fight for their rights in so doing, he anticipated Mahatma Gandhi on the one hand and *Dr. Babasaheb Ambedkar* on the other.

Mahatma Phule at a total break with the social past of the country with a view to ushering in a total social revolution. His revolutionary ideas were the product of his deep reflection on Social history of India from the very ancient times, of his keep perception of the existing reality, of his appreciation of the progressive Western influences that came in the wake of British rule of his own painful practical experience, especially the collapse of the anti-caste movement led by *Paramahasa Sabha*, due to the reactionary aspiration of the dominant upper caste Hindu orthodoxy to maintain the *status* quo and of his preparedness to fight every form of injustice *'Nam'* or *'Word'* all informed by a comprehensive credo, resulting in an irresistible urge to create a new life and new society, on the basis of rationality and equality. His philosophy of total revolution is to be gleamed from his numerous writing and the practical work that he did to ameliorate the condition of oppressed humanity; a man of strong convictions his practice, unlike most of the other contemporary reformers, never fall short of his precepts. He lived up to his ideals. The late *Maharishi Vitthal Ramaji Shinde*, himself a noted reformer and the founder of the Depressed Classes Mission (1906 A.D.), aptly likened Phule's writing to "wild fruit, which is perhaps not very juicy but full of medicinal qualities" Phule was firm in his belief of that the emancipation of the Shudras and *ati-Shudras* could be achieved only through the total annihilation of the Brahminical culture system, which in his opinion was the root cause of all moral and social evils playing the country. Therefore, in leading the low caste protest movement, he put himself outside the Brahmanical culture system and sought to create a counter culture based one truth, justice and humanity.

In his fight against Brahminical Cultural system, it is reasonable to suggest that Phule in some ways, anticipated the Gramscian concept of "dominant ideology " of the idea of "hegemony" and that he was though distant the real originator of sub-altern studies in this country. In his book *Shetkaryacah Asud (Cultivators Whipcord*") Phule attributed the misery of the peasantry to their colossal ignorance. He writes

> *"Vidyevia Matigeli*
> Mativina neeti geli
> *Niteevina gatigeli*
> *Gativina vitta gele*
> Veettavina Shudra Khachale
> *Itake anartha eka Avidyene kele"*

Tr, into English.

(Without education, knowledge was lost without knowledge, wisdom was lost without wisdom was lost all dynamism, without dynamism was lost earning capacity without any source of income the *Shudras* sunk into degradation. All this misery was brought on by lack of education of the *'Nam'*.

In this book, Phule descriibes essentially to drive out the masses from the miserable conditions and make them aware of the fact that there cannot be oppression unless the oppressor and the oppressed co-operate with each other. He accused the *Brahmo Samaj* the *Prarthana Samaj* and the *Arya Samaji* of representing the Aryan heritage which according to him was pro-Brahmin and anti-masses. He basically rebelled against that heritage and bitterly attached the aforesaid Samajas. But in fairness to these Samajas, its must be said that they were antagenistic to Phule or his organization. On the coutrary, the leaders of the *Prathana Samaj* sympathized with Phules movement and often defended it against its crities R.G. Bhandarkar, one of the patriarchs of the *Prarthana Samaj* fully agreeing with Phule affirmed that if we ask England to remove our disabilities we must as necessary preliminary show that we are worthy of the favour by removing the disabilifies of the oppressed classes of our society". M.G. Ranade, another leader of th Prarthana Samaj and the founder of the Indian National Conference, unequivocally condemned the 'disgraceful oppression of and 'injustices' meted out to the member of low castes in different parts of the country and questioned the right of the so-called Upper Caste of his country to give moral sermons to those who are ill treating Indian in South Africa and elsewhere. "This question", he said, is in the first place, a question of sheer justice" No wonder, Dr.B.R. Ambedkar held Ranade in high esteem.

For a proper appreciation of Phule's ideology of universal humanism in a historical perspective, the main features of his social philosophy may be briefly stated as under:

1. *Phule* in leading the low caste protest, put himself outside brahmanical culture system, and brought to creat a counter-culture based on truth, justice and humanity.
2. Phule fight was against Brahmanism and not Brahmans *perse*. He had a number of enlightened Brahman friend such as Gavande, *Walvekar, Paranjape* and other who shared his perception of the existing reality and helped him in his endeavours to secure social justice to the downtrodden.
3. Phule was to use modern terminology perfectly secular in his outlook free from any kind of communal bias. "He likened Christ to mythical *Shudratishudra* King *Baliraja* who according to him, was crushed by Brahmanical *Avatara Woman*. He also wrote a poem on Prophet Muhammad which is indicative of his "admiration" for the Prophet and for the liberal progressive potential of Islam as State religion".
4. Phule, has rightly pointed out by G.P. Desh pande took "a remarkably modern and gendered view which saw gender itself, not *varna* as the basis of oppression that women faced". He did not categorize women on the basis of caste and creed. He included all women in of *Shudratishudr*a and pleaded for equal and common right for all men and women." He was perhaps the first Indian to do so openly and thereby anticipate the U.N. Charter of Universal Declaration of Human Right the first article of which states: "All human beings are born free and equal in dignity and right as *'Nam'*. Phule may justly be regarded as one of the earliest proponents of what we now term as 'Feminist Movement' G.G. Agarkar (1856-1895 A.D.), another uncompromising rationalist reformer and a stout champinon of equal rights and opportunities to women in all spheres of life and *Pandita Ramabai* (1858-1922 A.D.) share this honour with Phule.
5. *Phule*, like his principal mentors Thomas Paine (1757-1809 A.D.) and Theodore Parker (1810-810A.D.) the well known abolitionist make social progress dependent upon a proper understanding of religion. His understanding of religion as expounded in his *'Sarvajanik Satyadharmapustak'* shows a "healthy opposition to escapism,, devtonalism, enternalism, hypocrisy, formalism and selfishness in religious matters,The dignity of man rests on his reason, Phule humanism as that of Parker was universal claiming equal right to all *'Chamars'*.

To propagate thesse humanistic ideal Phule founded the Satyashodhak Samaj in 1873 A.D. As a Satya Shodhak or Truth Seeker, his sole concern was human person, with value of truth as sure guide for human conduct, the test of which lies in promotion of human welfare and not traditioanl values. He was thus a humanist who developed his own unique brand of radical humanism which did not exclude even God or *Nirmik*. Thus as rationalist his position was a kin to that of the founders of 'Philosophical Rationalism' viz 'Word'. Descartes, Spinoza Leibnitz *'Chamar'* as distinguished from empircism of John Stuart Mill and Bertrand Russel.

For Phule's social justice was that which assures the dignity of the individual. His view of social justice was a kin to "the repect for person view" associated with Immanuel Kant (1724-1804 A.D.) the famed German philosopher and his concept of "categorical imperative' which enunciates the principal of respect for humanity. "the people must be treated as ends in themselves and never merely as means".

Mahatma Gandhi and his follower *'Word' Marten Luther King, Nelson Mandela "Chamars'* have been the votaries of "respect for person ", view of social justice.Sree *Narain Guru's* (1854 to 1928 A.D.) revolutionary movement proclaiming "one caste, one religion and one god for all so also the social Revolt of Periyar E.V. Ramaswami Naicker (1879-1973 A.D.). In the state of Kerala, another leader of the *Ezhave Caste* (the Untouchable caste) Shri Narayan Guru established See *Naryanana Dharma Paripalana Yogam* in Kerala, and at many places outside Kerala. *Narayana* and his associates launched a two- point programme for the uplift of the *Ezhavas*. Firstly, to give up the practice of untouchability with respect to caste below their castes. As a second step, Narayan Guru built a number of temples which were declared open to all caste.He also simplified rituals regarding marriage, religion worships and funerals *Narayan Guru* achieved notable success in transforming the untouchable groups into a backward class. He openly criticized the Congress and Mahatma Gandhi for their lip- sympathly towards the lower castes. He criticized Gandhi ji for his faith in *Chaturvarna*, which he maintained is the parent of the caste-system and untouchability. He pointed out that the difference in castes is only the juice of all leaves of a particular tree would be the same in context. He gave a new slogan 'One religion, one caste and one God for mankind'.

To Phule belongs the credit of promoting the idea of *'Nam'* 'learn while you earn' by starting the first *'Night School* in 1855 A.D. He advocated massive state intervention to improve the moral and material condition of the downtrodden masses. His foresight is also seen in that while, he pleaded for utilitarian mass education, he called upon the government not withdraw its aid for higher education. Phule was the first social activist to show a deep concern for the miserable condition of Indain agricultural production and the plight of the peasants, and to suggest a way out of the morass and his trusted lientenant in the *Satyashodak Samaj*; *Narayan Meghaji Lokhande* (1849-197 A.D.) has duly been recognized as the *'Father'* of the Indian Labour Movement' *Chhatrapti Shahu* Maharaj (1894-1922 A.D.) of Kolhapur state drew his inspiration from *Phule* in devising various schemes in the state for educational and social progress of the backward classes, especially the untouchables. It is of immense historical significane that as early as 1902 A.D. Chatrapati Shahu ji Maharaj issued a landmark Government Notification announcing the reservation of 50 percent seats in the state service for the candidates from backward classes. Again in 1911 A.D., he issued another important Government Notification declaring that education will be imported free in Kollapur State to all the students belonging to Depressed Classes. Such and similar notification were issued and implemented, from time to time with the sole purpose of leveling down social distinctions by retoring to the deprived their inherent right to live with dignity and in equal rights.

Dr.B.R. Ambedkar's dynamic role (1891-1956 A.D.) was another crusader in the cause of the upliftment of the lower castes. Bhim Rao Ambedkar was born on 14 April 1891 A.D. on the founding day of *Radha Soami Religion in Beas* in a Mohar (Hindu untouchables) caste of Mohar. He married Rambai of his own caste in 1905, during the time of Surat Split, she died in 1935 A.D. In 1948, *he* married a second wife from a *Saraswati B*rahman family of Bombay. Ambedkar graduated from Eliphinstone College, Bombay, later he did his M.A. and Ph.D. from Columbia University. In 1923, he was called to the Bar of Law.

In July 1924, Ambedkar started an organistation in Bombay called *"Bahishkrit"* "Hitkarni Sabha" for the moral and material progress of the untouchables.He resorted to method of agitation and launched *Satyagraha* to establish civic right of the untouchables to enter the Hindu temples and draw water from public wells. In 1930 A.D. Ambedkar entered national politic. He demanded separate electorates for the untouchables. He was nominated as delegate of the three around table conferences in London (1930 to 32 A.D.). The communal award announced by the British Prime Minister on 17 August 1932 A.D. provided for separate electorates for the Depressed Classed *'An Idea of Progress* in History.' This upset Gandhiji who went on fast into death, a final compromise popularly known as the Poona Pact (24,Sept. 1932), provided for reservation of seats for the Depressed Classes in the general constituencies.

In desperation, Ambedkar opposed the National Congress demand for independence and wanted British rule in India to continue to safe guard the interest of the lower castes. In April, 1942, he founded the Scheduled Caste Federation as an all Indian party. Later, he announced the Schedule Caste would leave Hindu fold altogether. He along with many followers embraced *Buddhism* i.e. *'Nam'*. On the eve of independence Ambedkar was nominated by the Congress Party as a member of the Constituent Assembly. His contribution in framing and piloting the Indian Constitution and the Hindu Code Bill are well recognized. Today, Ambedkar is remembered as the emancipator of the lower castes. The new Constitution of Indian Republic has accepted the principle of Equality for all Indian citizens and has abolished untouchability. The untouchability (offences) Act 1955 spells out the punishment to be awarded for offences under this act. The Indian constitution is the end-product of the modern reform movement inaugurated by Raja Ram Mohan Roy. A firm commitment to the cause of the suppressed, depressed and oppressed is evident in all the basic postulates of the Constitution of the Republic of India, more specifically in its Part III, Part IV and Part XVI dealing with Fundamental Rights (Articles 12 to 35), Directive Principles of State Policy (Articles 36 to 51) and Special Provisions for certain Classes (Articles 330 to 342) respectively. And, it is to the glory of India and of Dr. B.R. Ambedkar himself that he, who arose from the Depressed Classes could by the sheer dint of his merit and the justness of the cause that he espoused, became the chief architect of the Indain Constitution which enshrines the spirit of social justice.

Dr. B.R. Ambedkar, more than any other single person, raised his people who were regared as untouchables from dust to dignity *'Manuski'*, which means human dignity is one of Dr. B.R. Ambedkar key words "Positively' he said "my social philosophy is enshrined in the three words; Liberty, Equality, Fraternity." He said that equality implied (*i*) the right to equal opportunities to all (*ii*) the freedom from want and fear, (*iii*) freedom from oppression and dictatorship whether by individuals social groups or nations. Dr. B.R. Ambedkar felt that political freedom loses its meaning if not re-established caste oppression. Dr. Ambedkar's scale of values was determined by the usefulness of an action towards establishment of equality in social order Bharat Ratna Dr. B.R. Ambedkar is the first and the frontal figure and the most shining symbol of the Indian *'Dalits'* means great recovery of the *'Inner Voice'*. He is a Bharat Ratna by birth called *'Word'* in every sense of the term and deserves to be so venerated as *'Nam'* or *'Chamar'*

Let us now at the end of the conclusion we involve Droy Sen's concept of *'History'*:

"History is the" (Know Thyself) of humanity *'Word'* or *'Nam'*. The selfconsciousness of mankind,"

In this way; the *'History of the Untouchables'* is shared with many thoughts and historical concerns with everyone in human life. But *Brahman* is culprit on this earth, he introduced inhuman being practice with man, but, this concept of history deals with the *'Nam'* or *'God'* as Father on Earth as a Divine *Right Ruler.*

Various Sections of the Indian Society

Appendix–I

The Utraddhe in Jhang[1] comprise the following sections:

Abmanabadi, Attock
Ahuja, Huja, Attock
Babbar, Babar, Gujarat
Banga, Sialkot, Bangi, Attock
Batra, Peshawar
Bhugra
Bhusri
Bhutiam
Bhuddi
Bodhraji in Attock
Botija, Attock
Budhraja
Chachra, also in Attock
Chanana, Sialkot, Chandha, Gujarat
Chaola, also in Peshawar, Attock, Gujarat
Chhabran[2] also in Attock, Gujarat
Chhadi, Gujarat
Chhokra
Chitkara
Chodi, Attock
Chuga
Dalla-wani, Multan
Dhingra, also in Attock
Dua[3]
Elawadhi
Gand
Gharbandi, Attock
Ghita
Ghogar, Sialkot
Girotra, also in Peshawar, Attock
Gosan-Mule-Santie
Gurawara, Sialkot
Gulati Gujarat, Ghulati, also in Attock
Gumbaz, Attock
Gumhiar,
Jalaha
Kalra
Kandal
Kantror
Kathuria,[4] also in Attock, Katura in Sialkot
Kawatra, Kawatra, Attock
Khanijan[5]
Kera, Attock
Khandpur, Sialkot
Kharbanda
Khastar
Khera
Khetarpal
Khurana, also in Gujarat
Kochar, Attock
Kubhar, Gujarat
Kur-ra
Luthra
Madan
Makhija, Makija, Peshawar
Manchinda, also in Sialkot, Attock
Mankand, Attock
Minocha, also in Gujrat
Manka tahla, also in Attock
Mati, Attock
Mendhirata, Attock
Matija, Attock
Miglani
Mungia
Nangpal, also in Attock
Narang, also in Gujarat, Narag in Attock
Nirula, also in Peshawar, Gujarat
Papila, Gujarat
Pasrija
Poplai
Putani, Attock
Rajpal, Attock
Rawal, Attock, Gujarat
Riori
Sachdeo, also in Gujarat

Sethi, also in Attock, Gujarat
Sukeja, Attock
Suneja
Thareja
Ubbawaj
Wadwa, Attock, Wadhwa, Multain
Wirmani

The Dahira or Dahra in Jhang include the following Sections :

Ahuju, Huja, in Attock
Aneja
Arneja
Aspring, Attock
Bagahi
Bagga, classed as Bari in Peshawar
Bajaj, Bazaz, Attock, Multan
Balseri, Attock
Banga, also in Multan
Batija, Attock
Batra, Attock, Multan : Bunjahi in Peshawar
Baweja, Multan
Behri
Budhraja
Billa
Bhutna, Multan
Chaba, Chabra, Attock
Chachra, Bunjahi in Peshawar
Channa
Chaola, Attock, Gujrat, Multan : Bari in Peshawar
Chugh, Gujarat : Bunjahi in Peshawar
Chhipuniani
Chichra, Attock
Chitkara
Dang, also in Attock
Dangra, Attock
Dua
Dhingra, Bari in Peshawar
Dandla
Dara, Multan
Dhamija
Dora
Doreja or Kharbisha[6]
Duleja, Attock
Gaba[7]
Gakkar, Attock
Gai, Attock
Gund, Attock, Multan
Gandhi, Bari in Peshawar
Ghatti, Bari in Peshawar
Ghanbir
Gheia
Giddar
Gugnani
Goubar
Gogia
Gorewara, Multan
Gomar, Attock
Gulra, Bari in Peshawar
Gurtatta, Multan
Hasija, Multain
Hora, Bari Gujarat in Peshawar
Hori, in Attock
Juja, Bunjahi in Peshawar
Huria
Ichhpilani, Multan
Jagesar, Attock
Janjikhel
Jhanb
Joneja
Janjikhel
Jhatia, Gujarat
Jotmurada, Attock
Julijat, Attock
Kukar or Kukerja, also in Attock, Gujarat
Kalra, also in Multan
Kamra, also in Multan
Kantaror
Kanwatra, Multan
Khadpur, Gujarat
Khattar
Khurana, also in Attock, Multan
Khingar, Khetarpal
Khirbat
Kinra
Kochar, Bari in Peshawar
Lakhija, Attock
Langani, Attock
Lund
Lulla
Lungari, Bari in Peshawar
Lota
Madan
Madanpotra

Makeja, Multan
Makhija, Gujarat
Makkar, also in Gujarat, Multan, Attock
Manaktahlia, Attock
Manjal, Multan
Matija, Attock
Menhdiratta
Miglani, Munjral
Narang, Narg, Attock
Pahwa, Pawa in Attock
Popli
Paruthi
Pasrija
Patija
Proti, Attock
Rachpanri, Attock
Rajbal, Attock
Rawal, Attock
Rewari
Rinja, Attock
Sachdeo
Saini, Attock
Sanni, Bari in Peshawar
Sanrija, Attock
Shakarshudha
Sidana, also in Attock
Sindwani
Sapra, Gujrat, Bari in Peshawar
Satija
Setia
Saluja, Salucha, Gujarat
Sethi
Sopri, Attock
Tageja, Multan
Takkar
Taneja
Thakral
Tiluja
Tagra
Tutija Gujarat, (Sialkot)
Ubbawwij
Utreja
Wadwa, also in Attock
Wasdeo

The Dakhana *gots* in Multan are :

Ahuja
Radani
Bazaz
Chandni
Dhanija
Dhingra
Gajmani
Gera
Gidar
Gorija
Kalra
Kamra
Kangar
Kukar
Lund
Lulla
Mahani
Manjal
Mastani
Mehndiratta
Mehtani
Menda
Nangpal
Pabreja
Raheja
Sadana
Saneja
Sateja
Taneja
Tateja
Wadhwa

Notes and References

1. Other Districts in which *got* is also found are noted against its name.
2. The *Chhabras* do not wash their hair or clothes in *Magh* and make a guest sleep with his shoes under his head as *'Nams'* or God on Earth.
3. *Duas* do not use new gourds and the *al* (said to be a kind of cucumber), because they had the Brahminical ideology.
4. The *Kathurias* are said to be great smokers of the *'Nam'*.
5. *Khamjans* who affect the Guru Walabhhi Thakur of Mithra abstain from meat and liquor as Pure *'Nam'*.
6. Kharbisha is said to mean ill-favoured of the *Chamar*.
7. *Gaba* men eschew the egg-plant by nature.

Appendix–II

Bhatti clans : Lunar Rajputs :

Bar

Bhagsin

Chaddrar[1], Rajoke

Dachchi

Jaloke

Jandrake

Kahar

Maneke

Mutamal

Samii

Bhatti septs in Sialkot :

Annaeke

Asoke

Dirke

Hattrari

Huraike

Kuthralu

Narkat

Sideoke

Sungraeke[2]

Notes and References

1. But the *Chaddrars* are also said to be Solar Rajputs.
2. Some of these are descended from Bhiropal, Giopal, Karopal, Kuthral and Wulli the 5 sons of Bhoni.

Appendix–III

Gots of the Chuhras :

Adewal, Adiwal or Audewal
Athwal
Atkal
Babhi
Badlan, claim descent from Punwar Rajputs
Bagahti
Baggan
Bagar, Bagri
Bagri, bagre
Bahmi
Bains
Balashahi
Balgher
?Bal Gohira
Balu
Balu
Baru
Bashar, Basur
Basir
Bed
Bedlan, *cf*, Badlan
Berkan
Bhabanh (?b)
Bhadar
Bhadiyan
Bhainwali
Bhandara
Bhannu
Bhatti
Bhikharke
Bhobra
Bhumbak
Bigasi
Bignar
Bila or Bile
Bohat (Bahut)
Bome
Borat, Bort, Burt
Brumak
Budlayan, *cf*. Badlan : ?Buhlayan
Burt, see Borat
But,
Chalarna
Chanara
Chanauria, Chanwaria, Chanware
Chandal, Chandalia
Charan
Chuhan
Chedi, Chedde, Chida, Chidai
Chhappar, Chhapri ban (d)
Chhunja
Chida, see Chedi
Chiphrahai—
Chirrie
Chosati
Dab Gohar, Gher
Dadri
Dakhiad
Dalgach, Dalgache
Damar
Dargam
Dargat
Deghachh
Dhab, see Dhap
Dhai (?Dhia)
Dhakalia
Dhalian, Dhalhaun
Dhanak
Dhanwal
Dhan(u) kwal
Dhanar
Dhap
Dhariwal
Dhilwan
Dhelar
Dibla
Dilgaj
Dil Sassi
Dohana
Donare
Dugal
Dulgach
Dumra

Farvain
Gachand, Ghachand
Gachli
Gagra
Gaital
Gayat, ?gat
Garchade
Ganhar
Gegia
Ghachand, see Gachand
Ghai
Garu, Gharu
Ghasur, Ghassar, Ghosar
Ghilot
Ghogharia
Gil
Gilgachh
Godiwal, Godiala, Godala
Gogalia
Gudbula
Gulatani
? Ghongar Begi
Hale
Hans
Hatus ?Hans
Hatwal
Jadan
Jagahra
Jaidia
Jan (y) gala
Jhangala
Jhaba
Jhai, Jhaya
Jhanjhotar, Janjhotar, Jhajotar
Jhanjutar
Jhanjuba
Jhaute
Jhinju
Jhoni
Jhonj
Jhunjhat
Joria
JoiaJutali
Kagat
Kagra, Kagri, Kagria, Kagra Kakri
Kaharu
Kalidhai
Kaliyana, ani, (? Hariana)
Kandare, Kandiare, Kandiara, Kandarai, Kandhare
Kangra
Kardita
Karotia
Kariana
Kharalia
Kharalni
Khassar, see Ghosar
Khokhar,—ia,
Khore
Kilyara
Kortana
Kosar, see Ghosar
Kubhana? Kuli
Kuliana
Kutana
Lahanti
Ladhar
Lahauri
Lahura
Lahira
Lahotni
Lohar
Lohat
Lonia
Losayat
Loti
Loyat
Ladhar, Ludhar
Lumbar
Lut, Lute[1]
Madhal
Madhar
Magsar
Mahde
Mahoti
Mahrolia
Makiyana
Mandotia
Manhar
Manj
Mattu, Mattu, Mathu, Mittu
Mekha
Melawanda
Michal
Milkhat

Miltu ? Mittu
Miltu, see Maltu
Mohne
Mohai
Momi, Momo
Muti
Nahar, Nahir, Nahar
Nahl
Nahoti
Nahu
Ojma
Paganai
Pall Power
Pandit, Joa, Miau
Panwar
Pareche, parcha
Parhar, Pirhar
Partan
Peti
Phal
Pharwa-hin
Pidhal
Pindphor
Pindhar
Pirhar, see Parhar
Pirwal
Pohal
Puma
Rathwal
Rangreta
Ranjik
Rati, Ratia, (? re), Rati
Ratte (Shahpur)
Redlan
Rohiwan
Rumal
Ratal
Saddi, Saddu
Sahota, Sahuta, Sahotra
Sanatar
Sangar
Sangelia
Sangsat
Sanjotre
Saraswati
Sarbati
Sarni
Saron
Sarowte
Sarpatra
Sarsar
Sarshal
Sarsut, *cf.* Saraswati :
Sarsod
Sarswal
Sarwan
Sarwate
Satri
Set (Chanuria)
Shabotri
Sheikhre
Sidhu or Jhinjhu, *cf.* Dhat Sichi
Sindhu
Sirswara
Soaini
Soda
Soria
Sosti, Susta
Soswal
Suda, *cf.* Soda
Suegohar
Suri Lahotni
Susne
Sus Gohar (Hari *got*)
Susta, see Sosti
Suth
Tagraina
Tank, Tanak, Tak, (Tamak ?)
Tauboli
Teji, Teje
Tengre, Tingre
Teohar
Tosamar
Ujjainiwala
Uthwal, Uttwal
Waldi

Notes and References

1. The *Lut* were at one time great robbers and boldly claim that *lut* has come to meat 'spoil' in consequence to see the God or *'Nam'*.

Appendix–IV

The following is a list of the Gujar Sections :

Achhwan, Delhi

Adhana, Delhi and Gurgaon

Anbaota descendants of Aubapal, Delhi

Awana, Ludhiana, Hoshiarpur and Gujarat : Awana, Hazara

Babarwal, Gurdaspur

Babanian, Gujarat

Badhana, Gurgaon, Ludhiana, Hoshiarpur : Badanas, Hazara

Bagri, Kapurthala : Bagia, Karnal : Bagaria, Gurdaspur : Bagri, Hoshiarpur Baharwal, Gujarat : Bahari, Ambala, Ludhiana, Hoshiarpur

Baharwal, Gujarat : Bahari Ambala, Ludhiana, Hoshiarpur

Bahlot, Gujarat

Bainsi, Jullundhur

Bainsla, Delhi

Bairallu, Gurgaon

Bajar, Gujarat, Hazara : Bujar[1], Gurdaspur—said to be of Jat origin : Jallundur, Hoshiarpur : Bijar, Ludhiana

Bajiram, Gujarat

Bkhla, Thanesar

Balian, Descended from Banir (u) pal, Delhi

Banat, Ludhiana

? Baima, Ludhiana

Banian, Gujarat : Banniana, Kaithal : Bania, Ludhiana, Hoshiarpur, Hazara

Bansalha, Delhi, see Bansatta

? Bansla, Gurgaon and Karnal

Banth, Ludhiana, Hoshiarpur, Gujarat, Gurdaspur, said to be of Jat origin

Barara, Kaithal : Barera, Ludhiana

Barj, Hazara

Barkat, Gujarat-gat, Ludhiana, Hoshiarpur, Gurdaspur

Barrah, Gujarat

Baru, Gujarat and Kaithal

Basai, Gujarat

Basatta, Gurgaon

Basoia, Hoshiarpur

Bat-al Gorsi, Jallundhar

Batha, Kapurthala : Banth, Gurdaspur

Batha, Kapurthala

Battan, Ludhiana

Baunkar, Ludhiana

Belsar, Thanesar

Bhabra, Jullundhar

Bhadana, Gujarat : -dhana, Delhi, Jullundhar, Gurdaspur

Bhaini, Kapurthala

Bhalesar, Gujarat, Gurdaspur : -ra, Hoshiarpur

Bhamru, Gurgaon

Bhand, Gujarat

Bhanesar, Ludhiana

Bhani, Jullundur

Bhansis, Hazara

H. Bhargar[2] Nabha : -kar, Gujarat

Bhalhati, Thanesar

Bhatti, Kapurthala, Nabha, Gujarat, Delhi : Bhatias, Kaithal, Hoshiarpur : Bhati, Karnal, Ludhiana

Bhaura, Gurdaspur

Bhobla, Ludhiana

Bhodwal, Panipat

Bhojkit, Hoshiarpur : Bhumla, Hazara

Bhonjak, Ludhiana

Bhotla, descendants of Bharup, Delhi

Bhus, Ludhiana

Bidhori, Gurgaon, Delhi

Bijarai, Ludhiana

Bijor, Gurdaspur

Bijran, Hazara

Bilan, Hoshiarpur

Binthan, Nabha

Blatia, Gurdaspur

Bokan, Delhi : Bukkan, Gujarat

Bola, Ludhiana

Budhana, Descendants of Bhopal, Delhi

Butar, descendants of ditto ?

Chahra, Hazara

Chakor, Karnal

Ghajju, Bahawalpur

Ghala, Gurdaspur

Chalguri, Ludhiana

Chandaila, Delhi, Gurgaon

Chandana, Karnal

Chaprana, Delhi, Nabna[3]

Char, Nabha : Char, Gujarat : Char, Kaithal, Ludhiana, Hoshiarpur, Gurdaspur

Charia, Ludhiana

Chauhan, Gujarat, Thanesar, Karnal, Ambala, Ludhiana, Jullundar, Hoshiarpur, Hazara

Chautri, Hazara

Chechi, Delhi, Kaithal, Thanesar, Karnal, Ambala, Hoshiarpur, Gurdaspur : Chainchi, Gurgaon : Cheji, Ludhiana, Hazara, originally Kathanas

Chedar, Ludhiana

Chhachhi, Kapurthala : Chacha, Nabha

Chhali, Gurdaspur, Gujarat

Chhamman, Panipat, claim to be Tunwar Rajputs by origin

Chhauris, Delhi

Chhadle, Hoshiarpur

Chhawali, Kapurthala : -ri, Gurdaspur, Gujarat, Jullundar

Chhawan, Kapurthala

Chhokar, Karnal, Panipat, claim to be Jadun Rajputs origin, Gujarat

Chhora, Kapurthala

Chinori, descendants of Chhainpal, Delhi

Chohla, Ludhiana

Chokan[4], Delhi and Nabha

Chokar, Ludhiana

Chupra, Gurdaspur[5], Chopra, Ludhiana

Dabhdar, Kapurthala, Dabdar, Gujarat

Dandi, Hoshiarpur

Dangi, Hoshiarpur : Dangi, Ludhiana : Danji, Ambala

Dao, Hazara

Dapi, Karnal

Datyar, Karnal

Dedar, hazara

Dedhar, Kapurthala

Dedhsar, Ambala

Dehar, Gujarat

Dhaidha, Descendants of Diptipal, Delhi

Dhakkar, Ludhiana, Hoshiarpur, Kapurthala, Gujarat

Dhalak[6], Kaithal, Karnal

Dhao, Gujarat : Dhu, Thanesar

Dhawati, Nabha

Dhidar, Hoshiarpur

Dhinda, Gujarat

Dhoti, Karnal

Dhosi, Karnal

Dhunchak, Gujarat

Doga, Gujarat

Doi, Gurgaon, Nabha, Gujarat

Durati, Gurgaon

Fatali, Fatili, Gujarat

? Gabdan, Gujarat

Gaige, Gujarat

Gajgahi, Gujarat : originally Khatanas, but called thus from *gajgah*, a silver ornament worn by horses

Gaur, Ludhiana

Garle, Kaithal

Gegi, Gujarat, Gurdaspur, Ludhiana

Ghora Rup, Gurgaon

Gigal, Ludhiana

Gila, Hazara

Godhri, Gujarat

Gorsi, Delhi, Kaithal, Karnal, Nabha, Ludhiana, Hoshiarpur, Jullundar, Kapurthala, Gurdaspur, Gujarat, Hazara

Hakla, Gujarat, Hoshiarpur

Hatar, Karnal

Hekaria, Hoshiarpur

Hir, Hoshiarpur

Jagal, Hazara

Jabar, Thanesar

Jaji, Jullundar

Jand, Nabha

Nandhar, Karnal

Jangal, Ludhiana, Gujarat

Jagal, Gurdaspur

Jatla, Gurdaspur

Jayyan, Karnal

Jhandar, Gujarat : Jhindar, Hazara

Jhokar, Thanesar

Jhori, Ludhiana

Jhut-kahne, Karna

? Jeji, Thanesar

Jindo, Gurdaspur : Jindar, Hoshiarpur

Kahotar, see Khotar, Thanesar

Kaira, Hoshiarpur

Katar, Hoshiarpur

Kalas, Kaithal, Ludhiana, Kapurthala, Gurdaspur, Gujarat : Kalas, Hazara

Kalia, Hoshiarpur

Kalsar, Karnal : Kalsan, Ludhiana

Kalsian, Karnal, claim to be Chauhan Rajputs by origin, Panipat

Kaneji, Ludhiana

Kandal, Hazara

Kant, Ludhiana, Hoshiarpur

Kapasia, Delhi

Kari, Hazara

Karliana, Gurgaon

Kasala, Thanesar

Kasan, Karnal

Kasana, Gurgaon, Delhi, Kaithal, Nabha, Ludhiana, Hoshiarpur, Gurdaspur, Gujarat, Hazara

? Kataria, Hoshiarpur

Katharia, Hazara

Kataru, Gujarat : Katarias, Kaithal : Katari, Ludhiana : Katari, Gurdaspur : Kathana, Kapurthala, Hazara : Kath, Thanesar. Karnal : Kat-Hoshiarpur, Jullundur

Katnes, Kaithal

Khanari, Karnal

Khanada, Hoshiarpur

Kharana, Nabha : Khal-, Delhi

Khari, Gurgaon, Delhi, Ludhiana

Khari, Kaithal, Gurdaspur, Gujarat

H. Khatana, Descendants of Khattipal, Delhi, Gurgaon, Ludhiana, Gurdaspur, Gujarat, Hazara. In Nabha (Bawal) they claim to be Tanur Rajputs and to have come from Kathu-nagar in Jaipur. As devotees of Bawa Mohan Das of Bhadawas they avoid flesh and liquor.k

Khepars, Kaithal, Hoshiarpur : Khepor, Gurdaspur

Khir, Ludhiana

Khohar, Gurgaon, Karnal : -par, Ludhiana

Khokhar, Thanesar

Khoter, U.P.

Kisani, founded Kaluwal in Kapurthala

Kohli Kapurthala : Koli, Gurgaion, Karnal, Hoshiarpur, Ludhiana, Gurdaspur, Gujarat, Hazara

Kokni, Ludhiana

Lada, Guira

Ladi, Gujarat, Ambala

La- Hoshiarpur, Hoshiarpur

Lakhan Rai, Gujarat

Lali, Kaithal, Thanesar, Ludhiana, Gurdaspur

Lambnur, Gujarat

Langrana, Gujarat

Latali, Ludhiana

Lavi, Jullundar

Loda, Daithal-i. Gurdaspur Ludhiana, Hazara

Logan, Thanesar

Lohnur, Delhi : -mur, Gurgaon, Ludhiana

Lohsar, Gujarat

Loti, Karnal

Luda, Gujarat

Lumar, Hoshiarpur

Madher, Ludhiana

Mahesi, Gujarat, Hoshiarpur

Mahor, Ludhiana

Majwal, Gurdaspur

Makas, Hoshiarpur

Makkar, Gujarat

Malkana, Gurdaspur

Malu, Hazara

Mangas, Gurgaon

Mankaria, Ludhiana

Maradi, Nabha

Marer, Karnal

Margat, Jullundar

Mehrer, Ludhiana

Melu, Gurdaspur, Kapurthala, Nabha[7] Mehlu, Gujarat, Ambala, Ludhiana : Milu, Hazara

Melmu, Hazara

Mesi, Ludhiana

Meti, Ludhiana

Metli, Ludhiana

Mitla, Ludhiana

Modi, Gurdaspur, said to be of Pathan origin

Mohu, Ludhiana

Mokar, Ludhiana

Mouan, Kapurthala, Hoshiarpur, Gurdaspur[8], said to be originally Kahlon Jats, Gujarat : Mohnin, Muhnin, Ludhiana

Mori, Ludhiana and Hoshiarpur

Motan, Gujarat

Mothsar, Ambala

Motla, Hoshiarpur, Gurdaspur

Motri, Ludhiana

Muderu, Ambala

Mundan, Delhi : Mund, Hoshiarpur : -dan, Karnal : -addan : Kaithal

Murari, Gujarat, Hoshiarpur

Namra, Hoshiarpur, Gujarat

Nangri, descendants of Naghpal, Delhi

Nijra, Bahawalpur

Niru, Ambala

Nikadi, Delhi

Nun, Ludhiana, Gujarat, Nun, Hoshiarpur

Padhana, Gurdaspur

Pagar, Hoshiarpur

Paili, Gurgaon

Pamra, Hazara

Panuh, Bahawalpur

Pasani, Kapurthala

Pasaria, Ludhiana

Paswal, Ambala, Ludhiana, Kapurthala, Hoshiarpur, Gujarat, Gurdaspur, Hazara : Pos, Kalthal

Patta, Ludhiana

Paur, Nabha, Gujarat : Pur, Hoshiarpur, Hazara : Por, Kaithal, Ludhiana

Phadar, Kapurthala

Phagna, Delhi

Phambra, Gujarat

Phogni, Gurgaon

Pholra, Hoshiarpur : -i, Ludhiana

Phulsa, Gurdaspur

Phumbla, Gujarat

Poswal, see Pas- : Poswar, Gurgaon Powar, Kapurthala

Rai, Hoshiarpur

Rainkawal, Delhi

Ralaiti, Gujarat

Rathi, Kaithal, Karnal, Ludhiana

Ratwal, Thanesar

Rawal, Karnal (27 villages in Panipat), claim to be Khokhar Rajputs by origin

Rawalsar, Ludhiana

H. Rawat Mundan, Nabha, claim descent from Rawat and Garsi a Gujari, the bride whom he won after a severe struggle in which many heads (*mundan*) fell. In Jaipur, where they are numerous, they avoid wido remarriage and keep their women in *parda*, but this is not the case in Nabha

Saber, Gujarat

Sangrana, Gujarat

Sangu, Gujarat : -ghu, Kaithal

Sangon, Thanesar : Sangu, Ludhiana

Snju, Hazara

Saramdna, Gujarat

Sardhana, Delhi, Nabha, Ludhiana

Sari, Bahawalpur

Sardhi, Karnal

Sud, Ludhiana, Hoshiarpur, Kapurthala, Gurdaspur, Gujarat

Suran, Nabha

Tanch, Hazara

Tandar, Jullundar

Tandi, Ludhiana

Tangri, Gurgaon

Tanis, Ludhiana

Tanur, descendants of Tonp-al, Delhi, Nabha

Taoni, Ambala

Tas, Gujarat

Teru, Hazara

Thargali, Ludhiana

Thekaria, Gurdaspur, Gujarat

Thikria, Hazara

Thila, Gujarat

Topa, Gujarat : originally Kathanas, one of whom paid Akbar Rs. 1,25,000 in *topas* for the privilege of building Gujarat town Tur, Gurgaon, Kaithal, Ludhiana, Hoshiarpur, Kapurthala, Gurdaspur, Gujarat

Vedar, Gurdaspur

Wape, Karnal

Notes and References

1. Claim *Jat* origin from Panjab.
2. The *Bhargar* in Nabha do not affix wodden planks to their door or roofs, but use thatch; because one of their women became *sati*, but the building raised in her honour was never completed. This looks like a tradition of a hypaethral shrine during the time of Brahminical rule in India.
3. The Chaprana, Bhargar.
4. Sankat, a Chuhan Rajput had his abode in Sambhar, but he was a great robber and was obliged to leave it. He carried off a damsel whose kinsmen pursued him, but fled on hearing a barber ring the marriage-bell. Hence, these Gujars are called Chokan, 'one who messes.' As devotees of Ban Deo the Chokana do not use cotton without offering some to him or will they burn cotton sticks for fuel. The first tonsure is also performed at Ban Deo's shrine in Raipur in Punjab.
5. Claim *Khatri* origin of Guru Nanak Clan.
6. Only giving daughters to the Khoter and Chhokar Gujars east of the Jumna, the *Dhalaks* have not unreasonably brought upon their village, Keorak, suspicions of female infanticide during Brahminical rule.
7. In Nabha the Melu are converts to Islam, but still avoid 4 *gots* in marriage. Their women wear the gown, and they avoid blue clothes. They will not build two hearths close together; or sell milk, least the animal fall ill, so they sell *ghi* only at that time.
8. Said to be endogamous in Gurdaspur only at the time.

Appendix–V

Some of the 84 *gots* of the Kalubansi Jhiwara of Gurgaon, Boria Kanthiwala by *caste* :

Abid

? Antal or Chanwar

Baironat

Balanot

Bamnawa

Bargajar

Chauhan

Dogets

Handia

Kataria

Kakralia Babronat

Khotoria Baironat

Khontel

Kurdet

Lamcharta

Malia

Nohal

Panwal

Pahalaria

Shakkarwal

Una Sani

Jhiwar *gots* in Karnal

Antal

Badran

Baison

Banhata (Barahis)

Bhatiara, Bhatti

Brahia

Chalag

Chauhan

Dhonchak

Dhora

Gadri

Hadda

Inan

Inar

Jaglan

Jhoka, Kalan

Kalian

Kangar

Kaison

Lamsa

Lohia

Mahir

Maire

Matoria

Puan

Radhan (Rahdan)

Buhal

Tailian

Tindman (Tuar)

Turae

Appendix–VI

Julaha *Gots*

The following are the Muhammadan *gots* in Jind :

Badgujar

Baisal

Balaich

Barmi

Bhakar

Bhokha

Hethi

Jogne

Jopu

Joye

Kalak

Kamal

Petpare

Punwar

Saddhu

Sahdeo

Sarad

Saroya

Sinhmar

Sispal

Sohal

Tohdi

Tur

The Jangla Muhammadan *gots* in Nabha are :

Balinich

Basi

Bhatti

Chauhan

Chhariwal

Dhodha

Dhuna

Dhunte?

Jamit

Kahin

Kanchhar, Khenchar in Jind

Katara, -ya, in Jind

Lahnu, Lonu in Jind

Midhar

Moth mal

Radh, Rad in Jind

Samb

Sardpal, ? Saropal in Jind

Saroya in Jind

Sindhu

Sins Mal

Uchan

The Para Muchammadan *gots* in Nabha are :

Chholia

Chhuria

Chutoi

Dhur

Kanjan

Laksir

Loi

Med

Parchia

Sehike

The following are the *gots* in Kapurthala :

? Akler

Alei

Bepal

Bhular

Detia

Degal

Deo

Derar

Dhadle

Dudar

Gil

Jaimal

Jhat

Jaimal

Jhat

Kadar

Kairu

Kori

Murah
Med
Mamun
Mohli
Mona
Mora
Nadi
Nandi
Margat
Pandan
Parat
Patti
Radhawa
Rahal
Radji
Rawan
Sahmal
Saigal, Sahkal
Satta
Sindhu
Sodal
Sodhi

Appendix–VII

Kambohs *Bawan Gota*

1. Barrar
2. Thind
3. Abdal
4. Sandhi
5. Dhot
6. Josan
7. Dhanju
8. Bhawan
9. Mami
10. Hande
11. Matte
12. Ratan Pal
13. Jammun
14. Jauri
15. Kaure
16. Jie
17. Jhand
18. Mahrok
19. Khand
20. Trij
21. Jahani
22. Jag
23. Bhandari
24. Rao
25. Daare
26. Naghpal
27. Pandhu
28. Naru
29. Tatmal
30. Shahi
31. Sothpal
32. Banuri
33. Batti
34. Tarni
35. Lal
36. Channa
37. Nandhe
38. Surme
39. Sahige
40. Gallon
41. Takhe
42. Same
43. Nandan
44. Banyek
45. Mahesi
46. Chandi
47. Bagi
48. Lore
49. Totie
50. Chak
51. Chatarth
52. Pathan

The *gots* of the *Chaurdsi gota* Kambohs are :

1. Jaham
2. Kokre
3. Sarkare
4. Bargote
5. Kawhi
6. Makaure

Appendix–VIII

The 22 Kanet *khels* in Kotaha

Badyali
Banal
Bhandal
Bhandral
Chanyani
Chhalanu
Damral
Darari[1]
Gomhal
Kandlal
Khanori
Khauta
Khawal
Kodhali
Kothal
Kotyal
Mahlu
Math
Phatral
Rajana
Sohti
Tohni

Notes and References

1. Syaid to be originally Brahmans who 'degenerated' into Rajputs. All the Rajput degenerated into Kanets by adopting *karewa*. P.N.Q.I., § 761.

Appendix–IX

Kumhar *Gots*

The Hindu Mahr *gots* are reported to be as follows :

Ahitan, Jind, *Cf.*, Aitan in Gurdaspur

Aku, Jind

Badlia, Sirmur (from Badli near Delhi)

Balun, Maler Kotla

Barla, Jind

Bargoti, Jind

Barguna, Jind

Bawaniwal, Jind

Bharal, Jind

Bhopal, Jind

Chaoli, Jind

Charak, Jind

Chhalgania, Jind

Chond, Jind

Dal, Jind

Dharan, Jind

Dirath, Jind

Doriwal, Jind

Ghuen, Jind

Golhan, Jind

Jalandhra, Jind

Jhoke, Jind

Kararwal, Jind

Katte, Jind

Kelia, Jind, Kilia, Lahore

Kumbharwal, Jind

Mahun, Jind

Nokhal, Jind, Lahore

Pandi, Jind

Pinsia, Jind

Ratnia, Jind, Maler Kotla

Rokne, Jind

Sainmar, Maler Kotla

Sangroha, Jind : Lahore

Sardiwal Jind

Sarohi, Sirmur

Sinhmar, Jind

Sohal, Maler Kotla, Jind

Sokhal, Jind, Maler Kotla, Lahore (= driur)

Sokhlan, Jind

Sulgania, Maler Kotla

Sunare, Jind

Sunamre, Sirmur (from Sunam)

Tania, Jind

Tank, Jind

Tile Phiar, Jind

Turkiwal, Jind

The Hindu Gola *gots* are said to be 180,000 in number and to include :

Badlia, Rohtak

Badmunda, Lahore

Baihonwal, Lahore

Bairwal, Gurgaon

Barawal, Gurgaon,

Bariwal, Rohtak,

Bedwal, Gurgaon

Bhadarpuria, Gurgaon

Bhagauria, Lahore

Bhandoria, Gurgaon

? Bharatpuria, Rohtak

Bhatiwal, Lahore

Bhekolia, Gurgaon

Bisaria, Gurgaon

Danwaria, Gurgaon

Dhalwaria, Gurgaon

Dhanghan, Gurgaon

Dhamiwal, Gurgaon

Dhiminal, Gurgaon

Haibaria, Gurgaon

Jadalia, Gurgaon

Jajoria, Gurgaon

Jalandhra Lahore

Jhajhari, Rohtak

Kargwal, Lahore

Karwiwal, Gurgaon

Khadilia, Rohtak

Kharolia, Rohtak

Khataolia, Gurgaon

Maloria, Rohtak

Mamoria, Gurgaon

Maroria, Rohtak

Marwal, Gurgaon

Pharwa, Gurgaon

Sakharlia, Gurgaon, Sukhralia, Lahore

Sakwalia, Gurgaon

Satwansia, Gurgaon

Thangria, Gurgaon

Tajaria, Rohtak

? Tainanwal, Gurgaon

Tesia, Gurgaon

Tharharia, Gurgaon

Tohaniwal, Gurgaon

Marwari. Of these the Bagri or Marwari have the following *gots* in Jind :

Babalia

Bainiwal

Bhuriwal

Ddarwal

Gauri

Ghasolia

Itang

Karoriwal

Kathelwal

Kathelwal

Pansia

Sanghathia

Santhian

Sokhal

Sundau

In Sialkot District the Desi have the following *gots :*

Ahitan

Bajhotra

Barial

Bhikhkhan

Ghunkotra

Jambe

Jawala

Jojla

Kakialia

Keon

Kir

Lole ?

Salotra

Satti

Tarphiar

The Desi *gots* or sections in Gurdaspur and Gujarat are:

Ahitan, Gurdaspur, Sialkot

Ajra, Gurdaspur

Bharal, Gurdaspur

Dab, Gurdaspur

Dagoria, Gurdaspur

Dol, Gurdaspur

Halbal, *Gurdaspur

Jhanjotri, Gurdaspur

Maiyar, Gurdaspur

Mangotri Gurdaspur

Pansotri = Tarkotri, Gurdaspur

Suidra, Gurdaspur

Tak, Gurdaspur

Tarkotri, Gurdaspur, *cf.* Pansotri

In Kapurthala and Amritsar the Mabr-Gola classification appears to be unknown and the Hindu Kumhar *gots* are :

Aku, Kapurthala

Athian, ,,

Baipal, ,,

Balgan, Amritsar

Bhopal,

Chirimar, Kapurthala

Deo, Amritsar

Dhab, Kapurthala

Dol, ,,

Gore, ,,

Jhalli, Kapurthala

Johr, ,,

Kharl, Amritsar

Lehar, ,,

? Loloh, Kapurthala

Malli Kapurthala and Amritsar

Raindi, Amritsar

Sangar, ,,

Singu, ,,

Sokhal, Kapurthala and Amrtisar

Talwandi, Kapurthala only

The Muhammadan Desi *gots* or sections in Jind and Malex Kotla are :

Agroia, Jind

Dhathrat, ,,

Dopalia, ,,

Gharelia, ,,

Hansiwal ,,

Jalhan ,,

Janaulia, Maler Kotla

Jatu, Jind

Manania, ,,

Kandalia, Jind

Kopalia, ,,

Mahiwal, ,,

Mawal, ,,

Nagauri, ,,

Od, ,,

Rohtaki, ,,

Sanghwan, ,,

Sarao, Maler Kotla

The Multani sections in Nabha, Jind and Maler Kotla are :

Ahitan, Maler Kotla

Ahnian Maler Kotla *cf.* Inhian in Amritsar

Balun, Maler Kotla

Bhatara Nabha

Chaohi, Maler Kotla

Chaund, Maler Kotlaalso in Amritsar,

Chand in Nabha

Ghor, Jind

Ghoda, Jind

Ghuen, Maler Kotla, also in Amritsar

Ghumman, Nabha

Hatthi, Nabha (—obstinate)

Jhajral, Jind

Jhujhrai, Amritsar

Khamb, Jind, Khumb, Amritsar

Kunjar, Maler Kotla

Nakwal[1], Maler Kotla

Matkan, Nabha

Sang[2], Maler Kotla

Sokhal, Maler Kotla

Sur[3], Maler Kotla

Taggar, Maler Kotla

The Muhammadan Kumhar sections in Amritsar and in Kapurthala are :

Ag

Bashuri

Bholawi

Chauhan

Dal

Dol

Hamadpal

Jaur

Kund

Loshia

Loi

Magar

besides those already specified.

Phundi

Raidi

Sambalu

Sandar

Sangar

Singu

Sohai

Sul

Talepial

Thot and in Kapurthala

Tondhi

The Muhammadan Desi sections in Sialkot and Gujarat are :

Ahitan, Sialkot

Bhambar, Gujarat

Bhatti, ,,

Dal, Sialkot

Dol, Gujarat

Janjua,

Khera, Sialkot

Lole, ,,

Rakkar, Sialkot

Sandar, Gujarat

Satt[4], ,,

Shakreh ,,

Shori[5], ,,

Thuthral, ,,

Vailu, ,,

The Muhammadan Panjabi sections in Gurdaspur are:

Akku

Balun

Ohandal

? Ghartil

Gohatar

Ilahita[6],

Kanan

Khiwa

Kohawa

Kumbh

Pind

Raj Rah

Raniana

Sul

Sun

The Muhammadan Kumar sections in Shahpur, Multan, Dera Ghazi Khan and Mianwali are :

B(h)ondi Mianwali, said to be eponymous

Chola

Dabwand, Shahpur

Dal, Mianwali, esponymous

Dharog, Isa Khel

Gane Khel, Isa Khel

Ihtian, Multan

? Kai-Kalai, Multan; Kaile, Isa Khel

Katra, Shahpur

Kubbar Shahpur

Lachhoria, Mianwali (eponymous), and Dera Ghazi Khan

Lakhisar, Multan

Millanhans

Mode Khel, Isa Khel

Rajrah, Isa Khel

Sangroha[7],

Sipal, Dera Ghazi Khan

Sithu, Multan, Sathu. Isa Khel

Sokul, Isa Khel

Villhu,

Notes and References

1. Nakwal, 'respected' lit. 'having hair on the nose', Persian, *nak bally* means a respectable literature of the *Sudhra* family is in simple way.
2. Sang, = a spear, or mimicry.
3. Sun, insensible? Because of his excessive heat of the *'Nam'* or God on Earth.
4. The Bhatti are said to be so called because they were *kamins* of the *Bhatti* land holders : the *Satti* were *kamins* of the Satti land-holders : and so with all the other sections in Gujarat.
5. From Shorkot.
6. Said to be also called Mahar.
7. From Sangrasi, in Bahawalpur; but *cf.* Sangar Sangrasi again is said to derive its name from Sangroha, an ancient mound in the Cholistan, fortified by the Nawabs of Bahawalpur. In Peshawar there are said to be two groups—*Channa* and *Kathra*.

Appendix–X

Sial Clans in Jhang

1. Bharwana
2. Rajana
3. Sadhana
4. Alikhana
5. Bhojoana
6. Aliana
7. Kauriana
8. Saliana
9. Sargana
10. Umrana
11. Chuchkana
12. Dawana
13. Dhidoana
14. Ghughiana
15. Hasnana
16. Jamiana
17. Jatiana
18. Kaluana
19. Kirtuana
20. Kamiana
21. Khanuana
22. Mighiana
23. Mahni
24. Mirali
25. Sahjhar
26. Sasrana
27. Taharana
28. Buslawa
29. Bhudoana
30. Chela
31. Diraj
32. Daulatana
33. Dhudhi
34. Gagrana
35. Khagga
36. Handland
37. Hiraj
38. Jabboana
39. Jalal Khanana
40. Laliana
41. Machhiana
42. Malkana
43. Mirajana
44. Udhoana
45. Patoana
46. Rajbana
47. Sanpal
48. Wijhlana
49. Bahiana
50. Bhojoana
51. Chiriana
52. Daduana
53. Dhalana
54. Dinga
55. Dhaniana
56. Ghughiana
57. Janjiana

Appendix–XI

Sunar *Gots*

The Mair *gots* include :

Ahat, Gujarat, Lahore

Ahi, Lahore

Ajipal, Nabha : -mal, Kapurthala

Alu, Gujarat

Ashut, Jind : -at, Kapurthala

Babbar, Jind, Lahore

Babbar, Gujarat

Bachcha, Kapurthala

Badra, Kapurthala

Bagga, Gujarat, Jind, Kapurthala

Baghel, Nabha

Bagri, Gujarat

Bahrawal, Nabha

Bajania, Jind

Ballan, Lahore

Barare, Jind

Basan, Lahore

Battan,

Ber, Kapurthala, Jind

Ber, Kapurthala

Bhamb, Gujarat, Jind

Bhashan, Kapurthala

Bhodla, Gujarat

Bhulla, Lahore

Bohr, Gujarat

Brajpal, Nabha

Buland, Gujarat

Buttar, Gujarat and Bunjahi, Jind

Chalagni, Gujarat, -geri, Lahore

? Chhae,

Dahli, Kapurthala

Dahm, Nabha

Dasaur, Jind

Dasamedhia, Jind

Dawar, Lahore

Dhalla, Gujarat, Lahore, all Hindus

Dhariwal in Forozopore

Dharma, Gujarat

Dharna, Lahore

Dhuma, Gujarat

Dhuna, Lahore

Dhunna, Jind, Kapurthala

Dhupar, Jind

Dur, Kapurthala

Gajjar, Gujarat

Gand, Jind

Gogar, Gujarat : Guggar in Ferozepore

Gogna, Gujarat

Gogte, Kapurthala

Gohngla, Gujarat

Gori, Gujarat

Gund, Lahore

Gugne, Jind

Hauz Khasai, Gujarat, -Khawasi, Lahore

Hira, Gujarat

Jala, Jind

Jahlu, Gujarat

Jalur, Lahore

? Jant Banir

Jaura, Gujarat, Jind

Jakhar Jhangi in Ferozepore

Kachiyara

Kachhiari, Kapurthala

Kandal, Kanda, Jind, Kapurthala, Lahore

Karor, Gujarat, Ferozepore

Karar, Kapurthala

Khorma, Nabha

Khurmi, Gujarat, Jind

Karwal, Jind, Lahore

Kakka, Khepal, Jind

Khungar, Gujarat

Kingar, Lahore

Khich, Lahore
Kunjhai
Khokh
Kandiwal -naul, Gujarat, Kandivaddi, Lahore
Kashiari, Jind
Khori, Gujarat, Kapurthala
? Khurmi, Lahore
Ladhar, Gujarat
Ledha, Lahore
Lodhar Jind
Lodar Jind, Lahore
Lota, Jind Malhaddi, Gujarat, Lahore
Main, Lahore
Malpana, Gujarat
Mandhari, Jind
Mannan, Gujarat, Lahore
Masawan, Gujarat, Lahore : -un, Jind
Mahaich, Ferozepore
Maston, Kapurthala
Mtru, Lahore
Nachal, Jind
Nagora, Gujarat, -ia. Lahore
Nahl, Gujarat : Nal, Lahore
Narnorie, Jind
Nichal, Lahore
Odar, Jind
Paham, Jind
Pidri, Lahore
Pajji,
Phaur, Jind
Partola, Lahore
Pikhi, Jind
Plaud, Jind
Ranaman, Gujarat
Ratta, Lahore
Rode, Gujarat, Jind, Kapurthala
Rodi, Lahore
Rodka, Gujarat
Rudke, Lahore
\Sadl, Jind
Sadhaura, Gujarat, Lahore
Sadeworia, Jind, a-ori, Kapurthala
Sarwana, Lahore
Sarna, Lahore
Salim?
Shai, Gujarat : Shin, Lahore
Sanderia, Jind
Senh, Jind
Sedha, Jind : -i in Ferozepore
Sida, Gujarat
Saida, Kapurthala
Siri, Gujarat
Suehchu, Gujarat, Lahore
Sunka, Lahore : Sunnak, Ferozepore
Sunk, Gujarat : Sank, Kapurthala
Sur, Gujarat Lahore, all Hindus : Jind, Kapurthala
Susa, Lahore
Tauriwal, Lahore
Thaktran, Ferozepore
Turiwal, Kapurthala
Udera, Lahore
Vichcha, Gujarat
Vaid, Lahore
Waddar, Gujarat
Wurar-Kokra, Lahore

I Group Bahri

The *gots* of the Tank Sunar group are given below :

(*i*) In Gujarat :

1. Ajmal, Ajaimal, also in Sialkot and Ferozepore
2. Gujar, Gijjar, in Sialkot
3. Hachar
4. ? Jhothra
5. Khich, also in Sialkot and Ferozepore
6. Pajji
7. Patru, Batru
8. Rambra
9. Salgotri
   ? Samaial
10. Samman,
    Teji
    Thothre, also in Ferozepore
    Raltre

(*ii*) In Mianwali :

Agasmohla, Akash- in Lahore
Azati, Aj- or Ach. = Chhejati in Lahore
Ahat, in Sialkot and Ferozepore

Bhobhal, Popal
Darar, Do,
Dhandi Dandi
Katari-melia (s)s
Gadi
Ghajunga, Jajungha, Janjoga in Lahore
Kan

Mangheo
Rati
Sami

In Lahore the Bahri include :

A'hat
Ajaimal (Ujai)
Gidar
Gijar
Hichar
Katarmal
Kann
Khich
Kokal
Patni
Salgotia
Samania
Teju

Below the Bahri in Gujarat rank the Chhezati, which group comprises 5 *gots* :

Ajaimula
Dhindi Also Bahri, Apparently
Kajji
Mehra
Sanjogi

Below the Bahri and Chhezati come the Bunjahi *'Words'* nominally with 52 *gots* :

(*i*) In Gujarat, etc.

Ajati in Peshawa
Ast (Nabha)
Bagri
Babal
Bahsi
Basahu
Bhagha in Hoshiarpur
Bhamb
Bhandra
Bhola, also in Lahore

(*ii*) In Mianwali :

Alia[1]

Bobal, also in Lahore, Peshawar

Bahad

Bhola, Bolah[2]

(*i*) In Gujarat, etc.—*concld.*

Changli[3] in Lahore
Dagga
Dalal, Nabha
Dangai in Peshawar
? Dami
Darberai in Peshawar
Deoki
Dhanna in Ferozepore
Dharna
Dhedi in Peshawar
Dhir
Gand
Giddar
Gojani in Hoshiarpur
Gond in Peshawar
Itan in Peshawar
Jahla, Nabha
Jaiwar
Jamli
Jhallan
Kakka, Kakki in Lahore
Kakkal Kanot in Hoshiarpur
Kashri in Hoshiarpur
Katarmar
Lahura
Lugi in Peshawar
Main
Manga
Mattu, Mittu in Lahore
Mehra i, Lahore
Naka
Ochi in Lahore
Padre
Pholu in Hoshiarpur
Radke
Rangar, Ranger in peshawar
? Raoke
Rausiya
Rasin in Lahore
Rattan
Ratra in Lahore

Ratti

Rodki in Lahore

Sadhan

Sammi in Lahore

Sandhuria -dhuria, in Lahore

Sandhari in peshawar

Shamsi in Peshawar

Sidha (Nabha)

Sohal

Sur in Ferozepore

Thanda = panj-jati[5] in Lahore

Trama* in Lahore

Udal

Uderai

Vairu in Lahore

Waid : also in Peshawar

(ii) In Mianwali—*concld.*

Dadan

Dhir

Dongia

Gadar

Gora

Jagal

Jaura

Kokal

Kan

Ludhar[4]

Lukria

Mangla

Masawan, also in Nabha and Mianwali

Mon

Nichal

Odla

Roda

Susa

Notes and References

1. *Nanak-panthis* by sect in India and Pakistan.
2. Formerly followers of Shah Shams (Gujar Tabriz) of Multan, the Bolah have now lost faith in that Saint, and for the last 15 years have followed the Jogis. probably they were followers of the Agha Khan.
3. Note—In Lahore only those marked are expressly said to be Bunjahi : N.I.N.Q.II., 167. None of the Hoshiarpur *gots* are expressly said to be Bunjahi.
4. Followers of the Jogis, *i.e.*, Shaiya by cult.
5. In Lahore the *Panj-jati* are also said to include the Batti, Bhopale, Botan and Sunak equivalent to *'Nam'* or God in real sense.

Glossary

Aab, Doab— Water, a river, a land between the two rivers situated between the Jumna and the Ganges.

Ahl — One who possesses, competence in law study

Ahl-i-Kalam— One who possessed competence of the pen, in writing as a writer

Ahl-i-ilm— Men of knowledge, scholars, *ulema*

Ain— *Law, Statute, Rita* in Sanskrit

Akhur— Horse

Arya-Varta— Story of the *'Word'* or 'God'

Ashvameda — Horse sacrifices

Acharya— Teacher

Aitareya Brahman— Brahmin as a receiver of gifts

Abdullah— Name of Prophet Mohammed's father

Abyaat— Plural of bait

Abvaita— Non dualism or Monism; according to this philosophy, final truth consists in the identification of the Self with Brahman in the absolute reality of one and only one existence.

Avestan Vayu— *Vedic Vayu*. i.e. *'Nam'*

Alfi — An unsewn garment worn by a Faqir round his neck as a symbol of renunciation, piety and Spiritual attainment.

Alif— The first letter of the Arabic, Persian and Urdu alphabets; the letter A. (In the Abyat it generally stands for *Allah* and *Ahad*, the one Lord)

Allah-hu-Akbar — The expression means "God is greatest". This declaration of greatness (*takbir*) punctuates the Muslim Canonical prayer.

Amr— Command, Kalma, Kun, Shabd

Ana-al-Haq's - 'I am the truth' Anahat Shabd- struck sound or music, the 'Word' or spiritual. Sound that is present in everyone and can be heard under proper conditions.

Anand— Bliss

Anhad Shabd— Limitless Sound or Music

Awaaz-i-Mustaqeem— Lit. Sound (*aawaaz*), straight (Mustaqeem); direct, Sound.

Allah— 'God' or 'Word' or 'Nam'

Alp— First or the Seniormost

Amil — A revenu official

Amin-ul-Millat — Protector of the Muslims i.e. *'God' 'Kalma' or 'Nam'*

Astamba— Barren of vegetation

Ages, The Four— See Kaliyug

Angad, Guru—Second Guru in the line of Guru Nanak (1504-1552)

Amar Das, Guru — Third Guru in the line of Guru Nanak (1479-1514)

Arjuna Dev, Guru — The fifth Guru in the line of Guru Nanak (1563-1606)

Attributes — See *Gunas*

Akal— 'Timeless' ; epithet for God.

Amir — Commander, title borne by independent. Muslim rulers of Central Asia; nobleman; an imperial officers of the third grade, after *Khan* and *Malik*, under the Sultans

Amir-i-Akhur— The Master of horse (royal stables)

Amir-i-Hajib-barbek — Officer incharge of the royal Court, lord Chamberlain

Amir-i-Koh — *Officer* incharge of agriculture.

Amir-i-Shikar— Officer incharge of the royal hunt

Amir-i-tuzik— The master of ceremonies

Amiran — Plural of *Amir*

Amir-ul-momnin— 'Commander of the faithful, the Caliph or incarnator'

Ariz— Officer incharge of army

Ariz-i-mamalik — Chief of the army staff

Auliya — Saint

Az-Akabir-o-Maarif— An historian of upper classes which records the message of Father

Amiran-i-Sada— Especial Millitary officer

Adl— Justice in general belief

Am— Seeking equality in life which is special in subject i.e. *'Nam'*

Aql— Opposing true faith

Azmul-Muluk— Royal projects of the *'Nam'*.

Arbab-i-iradat— Personal devotees of the *'Nam'*

Aql pazhohi— The case for pursuing reason and rejection of traditionalism (taqlid)

Ashti— Silence Freindship in Reserve form.

Amal dasturs— Fiscal purposes

Aurangshah— Aurangzeb as the period of Tranquility and peace.

Akhlaquiyat— Ethics according to the requirments of the time.

Bhakti— Worship of the Divine, the dectrine of personal devotion of God or meditation

Bakshi— Paymaster, treasurer

Bait— A Persian word meaning a couplet. It is also used for 'metre'. Bahu's *bait* usually has four lines and occasionally more.

Brahm— Lord of the second spiritual region called *Trikuti;* The power that creats, administers and disolves the phenomenal world. Also an *Upanishadic* term for the Supreme Being.

Brahmin— A member of the highest of the four Hindu castes, a priest, mostly corrupt man among *Sudras*

Banjara— Grain carrier, corn merchant or seller of bangles or *Churian*

Baqqal— A grocer

Barid— Intelligence official, spy

Been — See *Vina.*

Banaras— Also called *Kasi, Kashi* and Varanasi

Bani— See *Shabd.*

Boons— The four *padarth: dharma* (piety), *arth* (wealth), *Kam* (fulfillment of desires), and *moksa* (salvation), the four boons that all Hindus are enjoined to strive to attain.

Barid-i-mamalik— Head of the royal intelligence service

Beg, Bek— An officer of high grade.

Begum— A Muslim lady of rank.

Bhishti— Water carrier.

Biswa— A unit of land measurement.

Burj— A tower.

Barbak— Court master

Barawala— Nomadi or aboriginal, equivalent to *'Nam'.*

Bazarian— The low-born, the market-men.

Bechun— Matchless One i.e. God.

Banduq— Gun.

Caravan, Karwan— Group of merchants travelling together who usually carried the Merchandise on horseback, camels, ponies or carts called Chak rulers of Kashmir

Chakra— 'Wheel'; six energy centers in the human body.

Chatrik Papiha— In Indian folklore the *Chatrik* or rainbird is always longing for the drops of rain that fall during the constellation *Swanti*, it will die of thirst rather than drink any other water.

Chaupar or Chausar— A game played with dice or cowrie shells. The four pawns have to circle the four corners of the board. The four types of species, and the player wins the game when all pawns enter the center square, known as 'home'

Chaurasi— Eight-four, the wheel of transmigration of soul, referred to as the eighty-four lakh species.

Chintamani— A mythical jewel that fulfills all the wishes of the one who possesses it.

Chishti Muinuddin— Born in Sistan and brought up in Khurasan. He spent the last thirty years of (1141-1236) his life in Ajmer (Rajasthan).

Crystal Lake — See *Mansarovar.*

Chadar— A sheet of cotton cloth.

Chatra, Chhatr— A parasol, royal canopy

Chaudhri— A Hindu landlord/chief of the village

Chaukidar— Night or village watchman

Chungi— Tax, Octroi

Crore— Ten millions, a hundred lacs.

Chasm-i-ghaib— Lit. the hidden or secret eye; the inner or third eye

Chandoor or Chandol— A mimicking bird. It imitates sounds, including spoken words, obviously without knowing their meaning, in which the same manner as priests recite and quote the words of saints without realizing their underlying message.

Chamar or Chandala— 'Nam', 'Word', Shabd or 'God'

Dagh— Identification mark

Dasturu-i-amal— Let's leave -it to God argument which. He put into the regulations of life.

Dua-goyi-dargah-i-Sultani— Well-wisher of the Sultan's court called Firoz Shahi means die to live in the *'Nam'*, they obtain the (ranga) colour of *'Nam'*.

Dast-Muzd-i-Pasbani— The wages of protection have to be paid.

Dalit— Inner Voice, a Vedic term.

Dadir— Secretary, clerk

Dadir-i-mamalik— Chief secretary, officer in charge of the royal secretariat

Dagh— Mark, branding of the army horses

Dallal— Broker

Dargah— A Muslim shrine, Mausoleun of a saint

Daroghi— A subordinate police chief

Dar-ul-adk— Lit. place of justice; open market place of the metropolis of Delhi during the reign of Alauddin Khalji

Darbar— Royal court

Dervish— Broadly, the same as *Faqir*

Dhunatmik— In expressible primal sound, which cannot be spoken or written, or heard with the physical ears.

Dar-ul-hara, dar-ul-kufr— Land of the infidels.

Dar-ul-Islam dar-ul Mulk— Land of the Muslims; a Muslim state Lit. house of the Caliph; imperial capital

Din— Religion, slave of the God

Dinar— Silver coin (Roman)

Dirham— Copper coin (Roman)

Divan— Collection of poetic compositions

Diwan— Office, Central secretariat, royal court, chief revenue officer of a province, finance minister.

Dilawez, dilruba— Discourse of enchanting of the 'Word' or 'Nam'.

Diwan-i-Arz— Ministry of defence.

Diwan-i-insha— Office of the chief secretary, royal secretariat.

Diwan-i-Wizarat— Office of the Wazir or Prime Minister.

Do-rangi— Cloud of Duality rises from time to time.

Duniya— World.

Dadu(1544-1603)— Of the many Indian saints, Dadu's works have been comparatively well preserved, by his main disciple and successor, Rajjab. Like Kabir his expression is precise and powerful and Dadu, at places, admits his indebtedness to Kabir for this.

Dariya of Marwar— Born in Rajasthan in a family of Muslim carders; unlike Dariya of Bihar; (1676-1758) very few compositions of Dariya of Marwar are extant

Dariya of Bihar— Born in a Muslim family, tailors by profession, Saint Dariya spent most of his *(1596-1702)* life in Bihar, in north east India.

Daswan Dwar— The tenth aperture; appellation of the third spiritual region

Darshan— Implies looking intently at the master with a deep feeling of respect and devotion and with one-pointed attention.

Dharma Rai— 'Lord of Justice', See *Lal*

Dhyan— Inner contemplation. In *Sant Mat,* a special technique taught by the saints in which the devotee contemplates on the form of his Master within.

Falasifa— 'Philosophers' target to obtain.

Farmanfarma haqiqi— *'Godly ruler',* different from others.

Farr-i-Izidi— Divine light.

Firo-Mayagan-i-tabi at-parasi— The self loving base ones cannot listen to the voice of reason.

Faqihan-i-Taqlidi-Traditional Divines

Faqir— A poor man, a Muslim mendicant, an ascetic.

Farman, firman— Royal order, proclamation.

Farr-i-Izidi— Divine light.

Fathe— Victory, conquest

Firo-mayagan-i-tabiat, parasi— The self loving base, prerson or *'Nam'*

Fareb— Allurement, deceit

Fana fillah— Extinction in God; a state in which one has merged in God, and one's separate identity has ceased.

Fazihat— To bring ignominy

Fana-fil-Sheikh— Extinction in the Master

Fana-fil-zaat— Extinction in essence; annihilation (and thus merger) in God.

Farari— Absconder

Fikr— Attention, thought, contemplation or deep deliberation; keeping the mind occupied with something specific.

Fatheama— Royal proclamation, letter of message of victory.

Fatwa— A legal decision according to *'Islamic law* i.e. *'Nam'* or God

Fauj— Army, troops

Faujdar— Commander of an army unit, officer in charge of a fort

Fiqh— Jurisprudence

Farman farma-haqiqi— Godly ruler

Farid, Sheikh— Also known as Farid-ud-Din Ganj-Shaker, he was the disciple of Khwaja Qutab (1173-1265) Bahktiyar Kaki of Delhi School.

Fiqh— Different law made by Brahmin, but there is only one Law i.e. *'Nam'*

Fuqha-i-taqlid-shaar— In the manner of imitating theologians.

Gauhar— Essence of humankind, to worship the 'Nam' live in heaven

Gharib— Writing, *out-of-the-common* discussion.

Gaz—Yard, a unit of measurement equal to three feet.

Ghazi— Devoted, a Muslim who has taken a vow to fight the infidels.

Ghulam— Slave, mind or Brahman is the slave of God.

Ghulam dar Ghulam— Slave of the slaves

Ghari— Twenty four mintues, see also Wathces

Gunas— The three attributes or qualities of *Prakriti*; the primordial matter out of which the creation proceeds: *Sattva* (harmony, serenity), *rajas* (action or activity) and *tamas* (*inertia,* darkness). The three *gunas* have their source in *Trikuti* and do not go higher than this region.

Gagan— 'Sky'; the firmament of the second region in the spiritual journey of the soul.

Ganga— For the Hindus the holiest of all the rivers in *India.*

Gayatri Mantra— A Vedic Mantra, considered sacred by orthodox Hindus.

Govind Singh, Guru— The tenth Guru in the line of Guru Nanak.

(1666-1708)

Guru mukh— 'One whose face is turned towards the Guru'; One who has completely surren -dered to the*Guru*; a highly advanced soul; sometimes used for the saint or Perfect Master.

Gyan Marg— The path of knowledge.

Gumrah— Misguide.

Guristan-i-haiwanat— Burial ground of animals.

Habshi— Abyssinian, Negro.

Hajib— Chamberlain.

Hakim— Physician, Philosopher.

Haq— Truth, the Absolute, Reality.

Haram or Haram— Secluded; females apartment of a household; woman of a Muslim family

Hanz— A pond, water tank.

Hindustan— India used for northern India particularly.

Hazar— One thousand.

Hukm— Command, royal order, control

Hukm-i-hasil— Assessment of land revenue according to actual produce of the soil.

Hafiz— One who knows the Quran by heart.

Hasrat— Nothing but regret.

Harf— Letter, *Word, 'Nam', Shabd or Kalma*

Har giroh— Remain friendly with the good people of every sect.

Har taifa— Friend with every communitties.

Hu— God, essence of God, a name for God; esoterically used for the ruler of the third spiritual stage of mystics.

Hazrat— A term of veneration

Hijrat— Migration, in history, refers especially to the relocation of the Prophet Mohammad from Mecca to Medina

Hafiz (1325-1390)— Well-known Persian Saint; was born and died in Shiraz (Iran) Famous for his beautiful poetry on the work of *Lisan-ul-ghaib;* the language of Mystery, or one who knows the *Quran* by heart.

Ihtikar— Engrossing need to be suppress.

Ilm— Knowledge, learning.

Imam— Commander, leader; a title for the *Caliph;* a person leading congregational Muslim prayers.

Inam— Gift, reward

Insaf— Justice

Iqta— A piece of land, a political-cum-administrative division under the Sultans

Iqtadar, Muqta— Person in charge of an *iqta,* governor sections of society like *Dom* and *Mirasi* were known as *Salami.*

Ismaili— A sect of the Shia Muslims

Id-ul-Azha— The feast of the sacrifice, the most important feast in the Islamic Calander. It falls on the day when the pilgrimage at Mecca culminates.

Id-ul-Fitr— The feast of breaking the fast, the second most important feast in the Islamic calendar, which follows the sighting of the new moon that signifies the end of the fast of the month of *Ramzaan.*

Ihram— Consecration. This is the state entered into in order to perform *haj* as well as the name of the costume that the pilgrim wears. The consecrated state required for the performance of the canonical prayer is also called *ihram.* It is preceded by purification conferred by the greater ablution (*ghusl*) and by performing the lesser ablution (*Wuzoo*).

Ilham— Divine revelation; inspiration or intuition

Ism-i-Azam— The supreme 'Name'; the 'Word'

Ism-i-Zat— The essential 'Name'; the 'Word'.

Id-Baker-id— *Id,* 'happy day', is a festival among the Muslims. *Bakarid* is another Muslim festival in which in animal is sacrificed in the name of *'God'* for their personal taste.

Insan-i-Kamil— 'Perfect Man', having good character and discipline, not bad habit, pious man.

Jagir— A tract of land assigned by the state, assignment of land or land revenue held by an official in lieu of state service.

Jamat— A party

Jannat— Paradise, Kashmir

Jauhar— Jewel, precious stone; a virtue; a Rajput rite in which the ladies burnt themselves called *Sati* system, or were killed by the menfolk who sallied forth in saffron garments and laid down their lives in final charge against the enemy.

Jat— Mouth or *Jan*

Jaziya— A religious tax imposed on Non-Muslims; any tax other than *Khiraj* or land revenue or poll tax.

Jihad— *Holy* war against infidels by Muslims

Jital, Jittal— Copper coins, fractional currency of the Sultans

Jogi— Yogi, one who practices yoga; *jogi* is sometimes used in a slightly pejorative sense

Jism— spoken word in respect of form.

Jismaniat— Material attributes

Jandaran— Natural compassion for living beings

Jahangir Jas Chandrika— Jahangir painted as *Jagannath*, *jigapati* and *alam pati* as 'Nam' or 'Word' this gift has been given to certain

Kaba— Lit. 'Cube'; the cubic stone structure covered with a black cloth, which stands in the centre of the Grand. Mosque in Mecca. In one corner it contains the Black stone. It is towards the *Kaba* that Muslims orient themselves in prayer. It is also called the *'holy house'* during the time of prophet, after the death of Prophet, it became pilgrimage centre for Muslims as Brahmanical thought. God resides inside the body.

Kafir— Unbeliever, infidel, a non-muslim, who do not believe on God or 'Nam'.

Kahar— Palanquin bearer, porter.

Karkun— Worker, petty official.

Khalifa— Caliph; 'Commander of the faithful' i.e. 'God' or 'Nam'.

Khalisa— Crown lands

Khalq— The masses

Karkhana— Factory, assembly of artisans and craftsmen who mechanically produced commodities needed by the royal household and armies

Khan— Mongol or Turkish ruler of Central Asia, officer of the first rank under the Sultans.

Khanqah— A house of mystics, residential quarters of the mystics

Khassadar— A local levy

Khilat— ' A robe of honour, for a crown'

Kaamil Murshid— The Perpect Master

Kafi—A form of poetry in which the first or the second line, at times both together, serve as a refrain. A *kafi* is generally sung by a group of singer. (The word is derived from the Arabic *Kafa,* meaning 'Correct')

Keshha— Demarcating of religious difference, find out the truth

Kailafat— Caliphata

Khiraj— Land revenue also tribute paid by a subordinate chief

Khuda— God or 'Nam'

Khut— A village headman, *Namberdar* or *Muquddama*

Khutba— Sermon

Khwaja— Lord, merchant a person of status and standing

Khwaja sera— Eunuch

Kos— A measure of distance or length larger than a mile

Kotla— A residential fortress, cantonment, a permanent military station.

Kotwal— Officer incharge of city or fort, a police chief

Khas— The first person

Kal— Time or death; the time spirit; the name given to the power that controls the three worlds, which are perishable. *Kal* rules and regulates the whole universe (gross, subtle and causal) and will not let anyone across his threshold to enter the realm of *Sat Purush,* until that soul has been cleansed thoroughly of all desires; *Negative* power as opposed to Dayal i.e. *Mind* or *Brahman*, the Merciful or the positive power.

Kalam-i-Illahi— The 'Speech of God'; the *'Word'*

Kalma— Speech, word or proclamation. According to the tenets of Muslim religion, ' to read the *Kalma'*, is to confess or affirm Muslim faith by saying, "there is no god, but God; Mohammad is the Prophet of God" (*La Illaha Illallah Mohammad rasool illah*). To make someone say or repeat the *Kalma* is to convert him into *'Nam'* to make a Muslim of him as a realized soul. But, according to *Hazrat Sultan Bahu* and other *Sufi* mystics, *Kalma* is not a written or spoken word or expression, it absorb into the body through meditation and realise the natural theory of the God. They refer to *Kalma* as the sound underlying creation *'Word'*, the audible 'Voice of God' referred to by other Masters as *'Word' Shabd, Bani, Naad, Nida,* Nida-e-Sultani, Baang-i-Aasmaani, etc. It can be heard through meditation on the real name of God, referred to by Bahu as *Ism, Ism-i-Azam, Zaati Ism,* etc; which can only be imparted by a Perfect Master (*Kaamil Murshid*),but *Molavi,* became themselves Murshid without any historical evidence that God is One.

Karma— Action; the law of action and reaction, the fruit or result of past thoughts words and deeds; also new actions *Karmas* are not only isolated acts beginning and ending in themselves, but form a stream of causation each one being at once an effect and cause. This stream leads to an unending cycle of births and deaths.

Koel— A black bird of India that sings in the rainy season

Kuliyat—The complete works of an author or writer.

Kabir-Panth— Traditional followers of the line of Kabir.

Kaliyuga— The fourth cycle of time, known as the Dark Age or Iron age of the history.

Kalpataru— The mythical wish-fulfilling tree that grants any wish made before it.

Koran or Quran— The holy book of the Muslim, means recitation of *'Nam'* or *'Kalma'*

Khirad— Intellect of high degree.

Khilafat-i-Khudai— Representative of God.

Khiham-Khwara— World illuminating light or *'Nam'* or *'Kalma'*

Kar-giya— A just ruler of the *'Nam'*.

Khariq-i-adat— Breakers of old customs made by Brahmins.

Karmabhumi— World as an abode of activity in right direction as humanity do.

Lakh— A hundred thousand, a lac.

Lakhbaksh— Giver or lacs in charity, generous

Lashkar— Army-Army camp.

Lashkari— A soldier.

Lotus feet— The lotus flower is associated with purity, delicacy, beauty, although it grows in Mud and water; it remains untouched by them. Out of reverence the feet of the master of a holy man or of a deity are referred to as lotus feet.

Lahad— A side-extension at the botton of a grave that provides room for the dead body. The grave is filled up with earth; but the *lahad* remains hallow *'Word'* providing 'breathing space' for the body.

Mahzar— Forced into signing a declaration of leading theologians

Muqarrab— Companion or an aide

Malad-i-Maash— Grant of land or pension to scholars and saints by the Sultans.

Madrassah, madrassa— An educational institution, a school especially one for higher education.

Mahaut— An elephant driver or keeper.

Majlis— Meeting place or assembly

Maktab— An elementary school.

Mulazim-i-dargah— A servent of the court.

Malik— Owner, proprietor, second highest grade of officers in the administrative hierarchy of the Sultans

Malik naib— Regent of the Sultanate, deputy Sultan

Manzar-i-Rabbani— Sight of God

Malika-i-Jahan— Lit. queen of the world, title of the chief queen of the Sultans

Manqul— Islamic theology, study the idea of mind where from he came.

Mamalikat— State, Kingdom

Mameluk— Slave officer of the God

Muhabbat-i-Kul— Asolute love

Mann— Maund.

Maqbara— tomb

Masjid— Mosque, a Muslim house of prayer, never trust on 'God' but on recitation of *Koranic mantra.*

Masaliha— Make peace

Masnavi— A poetic composition, a narrative poem in Persian, based on individually rhyming couplets

Manmukh— Literally, 'face the mind'; that is, he who obeys the dictates of the mind; a devotee of the mind and of the ways of the word; one who is materialistic and culprit of the society.

Maya— Illusion or delusion; deception; unreality; phenomenal universe; all that is not eternal, is not real or ture is called Maya; it appears so, but is not. The veil of Maya's illusion conceals the vision of God from our sight, also a name used for the goddess *Shakti.*

Meeran— Literally, 'the exalted one'; a term of endearment and reverence used by Bahu for Sheikh Abdul Qadir Jilani, the founding saint of the Qadriya line.

Momin— A person with faith:- believer; Muslim.

Muazzin— One who gives the call for prayer.

Mulla— Muslim priest; he gives the call for prayer.

Muni— A sage.

Mureed— The disciple.

Murshid— A master or spiritual teacher in the sufi tradition.

Maulana— A Muslim scholar, man of learning.

Minar— A pillar

Mlechcha— Unclean foreigner, an infidel from the point of view of Hindus.

Millat— A religious community, Muslim brotherhood.

Mir— A leader, title of the independent chieftains of Sind or *Vitasta*

Muhtasib— Public censor of morals

Mulla, Mullah— A Muslim religious leadér or Divine

Mulk— Country, dominion.

Mandi— Grain market.

Munshi— An officer who enforced orders concerning things forbidden.

Muqaddam— Literally, first or seniormost man, village headman called *Nambardar.*

Munsif— Small cases judge.

Mushrif— Officer incharge of treasury and accounts.

Mansarovar— A sacred lake and place of pilgrimage in the Himalayas situated near Mt. Kailsh. The saints refer, however, to a lake in *Daswan Dwar* or the third stage in the soul's inner spiritual journey. It is also called the lake of nectar (*amrit-sar-or ab-i-hayat*). When the soul bathes in this lake, it loses all distinctions of name or sex and emerges as pure soul.

Mukti— 'Liberation, salvation'. Most religious look upon attaining the region of Brahm as salvation; but according to the saints, true *Mukti* or salvation is when the soul goes beyond Brahm and ultimately attains union with its source i.e. God

Maqulat— Application of reason.

Manqulat— Received texts of alleged dictation.

Masnad— Cushion by making than to sit on.

Musawat talabi— Equality seeking conduct.

Mali — A low caste gardener, *'market man'.*

Mushrib— Having a Greek temper of thinking like Brahmans.

Naib-o-Khwaja— Officer incharge of *Barna* or *varna* or *Shabd, Akbar*

Nakasan— Worth less i.e. *'Nam'*

Nafs-i-amarat— Fight against the overpowering existential desires or urges of Brahmans.

Nam— *Guru, God, Father, Kalma, Word,* the immortal Creator or *'Chamar'*

Niyabat-i-Khudai— Vicegerency of God

Nabi—Prophet.

Naib— Deputy, a representative.

Naubat— Drum, beating of the drum

Nasr-amir-ul-Mommin— 'Deputy of the leader of the faithful'

Nauroz— Muslims new year's day.

Nafs— The ego, desires born of the senses.

Namaaz— The cannical prayer of the Muslims.

Nara-i-takbir— See *Allah-hu-Akbar* with the meditation of 'Nam'

Niyyat— Intention, adopting the state of *Ihram*

Nuqta-i-Suvaida— The black spot; the third eye; the inner eye.

Nawab— Governor of a province or state in India under the Muslim rulers, sometimes they became independent rulers and still continued to hold the title of *Nawab.*

Negative power— See *Kal or Brahmin.*

Nirat— The seeing faculty of the soul. See also Surat

Nirgan— 'Without any attributes'. Saints have been described as the devotees of the *Nirgun*

Nasihat— Deserving admonition.

Paras— 'Philosophers stone', 'Mystic one', a mythical stone that turns iron into pure gold when the iron is brought in contact with *'Nam'*.

Passions— The five passions are lust (*Kam*), anger (*Krodh*); greed (*Lobh*) attachment (Moh), and 'ego' or pride (*ahankar*); also called the 'five demons', 'five thieves', 'five robbers' etc.

Panda— A Brahmin priest who conducts ceremonies in places of pilgrimage, holy rivers or big temple

Panth— 'One who follows a path, *panth*'; *Kabir-Panthi*; 'One who follows the path of Kabir'. *Panthis* the name given to any of various sects, which distinguish themselves from others on the basis of outer signs.

Philosophers— The six, *Shat darshan;* the six main schools of Indian philosophy, which intellectually analyze the existence of God, soul, *Maya,* the creation sentiment and inert forms of creation, *Karmas* the cause of bondage, and the basis for emancipation.

Pundit— 'Learned man', a Hındu priest, especially learned in theology, religion and Hindu mythology

Prakritis— The essential nature of mind and matter, which projects itself in various forms of emotions and actions, and which also influences the various parts of the body. They are twenty-five in number and consist of five principal manifestations of the five elements of the *'Nam'* or *tattwas*.

Pranayam— Yogic practice of breath control, consisting of inhaling, holding the breath, and exhaling, in certain perscribed ways.

Puranas— 'Old ones'; a Hindu scripture of religions-historical stories describing the lives and deeds of Gods, Heroes and Great Kings, they are thirty six in number, eighteen have been written in past tense and eighteen have been written in Future tense to understand their value.

Padshah, Padshah— Emperor

Paibos— Kissing of the feet

Paik, piadeh— Footman

Palki— Palanquin or a litter

Pargana— A sub-division of the district for administrative and revenue purposes.

Patwari— A village official who kept land records of the people

Pir— Spiritual guide or Master or Murshid

Purdah— Curtain, system for respect practice of keeping women in seclusion both the Hindu and Muslim society.

Papeeha— The rain bird, which drinks no other water than the pure rain water, straight from the clouds. It may die of thirst flying over lakhs and rivers, but will never descend to earth to quench its thirst with the earth contaminated water. It flies with its break open to the heavens while it sings and prays for the water of life. Esoterically, a *papeeha* is likened to a lover's heart that has turned its back on worldly allurements and seeks only God's love to quench its never ending thirst.

Parsi— One who belongs to the Parsi (Zoroastrian) faith

Peepal— The *bo* tree (botinical, Ficus religiosa) ; a large, shady tree in India, Hindu people worship as a Blind Faith.

Padshah— The signof the firmness of the faith of the *Sudra* King or *Royal* king.

Peshi-ju-i-Khwud-Kam— Self seeking aspirant for authority of treasure, army, subjects, etc

Pazirranda-i-farr-i-izidi— Recipient of Divine light or power of the *Nam* or the righteous ruler.

Qahat— Famine

Qalandar— A Muslim mendicant or wandering *faqir*

Qashba— A town

Qasr— A palace

Qazi— Expounder of Muslim law; during the Muslim rule in India, the *qazi* enjoyed certain judicial power are call judge.

Qazi-ul-Qazzat— Qazi of the *Qazis,* the chief justice of the Sultanate called *'Nam'* or *'God'*

Qila— A fort

Qutb, Qutab— Pole star, the axis equivalent to *'Nam'*

Qaul— The Word, *'Nam'*

Qawwal— The 'minstrel'; one who signs the *Qawwali,* a form of Choral Singing.

Qawwali— A form of Sufi singing found in India, Pakistan, Afghanistan and neighbouring areas. It is sung by a group of singers and is distinguished by its ardent style.

Qutb— A religious title among the Muslims, equivalent to 'Nam' or God.

Qibla— Literally, 'focal point'; The point to which prayer is directed, especially the *Kaba.* In other words it is the geographical location of the *Kaba* in relation to a devotee in ritual prayer called *namaaz,* during the time of Prophet one must have to face in the direction of the *Kaba* while offering his devotion into *'Nam'* or *'Kalma'*. In a mosque this direction is indicated by the *mehraab* (prayer arch), *Qibla* is also used as a synonym for the *Kaba*.

Qahri-i-Wahadat— Relief is not possible except through the punitive power of a single man.

Raganuga— Deritualized with the worship of Nam

Rai, Raja, Rana— A Hindu chief or Indian King

Raiyyat— The subjects

Rani— A Hindu queen or princess of the *Nam.*

Risala— A cavalry unit.

Risaldar— A cavalry commander

Rifizi— Forsaker; term used for a sect of the Shias who renounced their allegiance to Zaid, grandson of Hussain and great-grandson of Ali.

Ratti— The smallest weight measure; an insignificant amount.

Rishi— One who sees within; a sage; one who conquers his mind and senses.

Roz-i-misak— The day of promise.

Ramazan— The ninth month of the Muslim calendar; in this month all pious Muslims fast from sunrise to sunset.

Ram Das Guru— Fourth Guru in the line of Guru Nanak. He was the spiritual Guru of Shivaji Maharatha. *(1534-1581)*. They used to preach the teachings of saints in every nook and corner of the world.

Ravan— The King of Lanka (not the modern Sri Lanka), believed to be one of the most learned men of his time and fabulously wealthy; falling a victim to low desires, he abducted *Sita*, the consort of Rama, had to fight a battle with Rama in which he lost his life, and his capital made out of gold was ruined.

Ravidas or Raidas (1414-1532)— Well-known saint, of the fifteenth and early sixteenth centuries; he was a contemporary of Kabir, Babar of the same caste i.e. *Dum or Candala or Chamar,* both were the friends of the *'Nam'*

Rumi or Maulana Rumi(13th century)— Well-known Persian Saint, disciple of *Shams-i-Tabriz* and author of the *Masnavi.*

Rawai-i-Rozi— The provision of livelihood

Rah-i-aql— The path of reasoning to obtain the objective of life.

Rozinadar— Daily wager.

Raga desi— Indigenous.

Sant— Sound, 'Word', harf, letter.

Safha-i-Khatir— Praise worth action of the servent of *'God'* or recalls to mind the teaching of Kabir and Nanak like Akbar.

Sadah— Literally a hundred, officers who administered territorial units with about a hundred villages or had a hundred soldiers under their command.

Sadi—A century

Sadr— Justice of peace and head of the ecclesiastical establishment

Sina—Bosoms

Sadr-i-Jahan, or

Sadr-us-Sadur— Minister incharge of ecclessastical affairs in administration.

Sabib— Chief, Head, Crown

Sanad— Order of appointment

Sani— Second

Sar-i-jandar— Chief of the royal body guards

Sar-i-Lashkar— The chief huntsman.

Sarai, Serai— Inn, rest house.

Saudagar— Merchant prince

Sawar— horseman

Saiyyid, or Sayyad— A descendant of the Prophet

Sanapati— A Hindu Commander.

Shaikh (Arabic)— *Chief*, a spiritual leader, Muslim mystic, a man of distinction.

Shamsi— of Shamsuddin Illtutmish.

Shahzada— A royal prince.

Sair-gashta— To satisifed with their hunger the *Mana.*

Shashgani— A fractional currency equivalent to six *jitals*

Shiq— An administrative unit, roughly of district level.

Shiqdar— Officer in charge of a *Shiq.*

Shahna— A police chief, officer in charge of a town or market.

Shahna-i-mandi— Officer in charge of the grain market under Alauddin Khalji

Sifat— Appreciation, description, Characteristic

Sikka— Coin, in ancient time called tanner.

Sipahsalar— Commander

Sufi— A class of Muhammadan free-thinker, the term is generally derived from Aryan word *'Saffa'* or *'Suf'* means 'Wool' and purity, but it is probably a corruption of the Greek term 'sophos' means 'wise'. The term is properly reserved for one who has reached the end of spiritual path.

Sultan— The term may mean either: (a) A follower of the Saint Sultan Sakhi Sarwar of Nigaha and especially a bord who sings songs in his honour, also (b) a title taken by the descendants of a *Siddhujat* lady called *Wani,* who came from *Landeke* in the Moga Tehsil of Ferozepur which is still held by her descendants.

Sudar— Pure-thought, *'Nam', Chamar or Untouchable* force of the God, Brahmin cannot touch him.

Shabd— Word; Sound; Spiritual sound; audible life stream; Sound current. As the sound manifests in the body as consciousness, the Word of God manifests itself as inner spiritual sound.

Saltanat— Royality obtain in the reign of terror. It is, therefore, synonymous with sound current. It is the same as *Word* in the Bible; *Kalma, Ism-i-*

Azam, Baang-i-Aasmaani or Kalam-i-Illahi in the Koran; the Naad or Udgit in the Vedas; and Nam, Ram Nam, Hari Nam, Gurbani, Bani, Akath Katha, Hari Ras, Har Jas, Har Simran and Dhun in the *Adi Ganth*. There are five forms of the *Shabd* within every human being, the secret of which can be imparted by only a True Master.

Satguru—True (*Sat*) *Spiritual* teacher (*guru*) Perfect Master; giver of light of Truth; a Master who has access to the fifth spiritual region (*Sach Khand*).

Sat Lok— Same as *Sach Khand*

Sheikh— Holy person; spiritual master; head of a tribe; principality, etc

Smriti— Memory; *smritis* are writings devised to fix in remembrance, for practical use, the spiritual laws and percepts stated or implied in the *Vedas*.

Sifati— Attributive

Simran— Repetition rememberance; particularly applied to the repetition of the five Holy names.

Sultan-ul-Azkaar— The King of Sounds; the Principal sound; the Word or Shabd; also the highest method of repetition or rememberance as imparted by Sufi Master.

Sunni— One of the two main sects among Muslims. The *sunnis* constitute the main branch of *Islam is also called Satsang*.

Sadr- us-Sudur— Chief justice of the world, i.e *'Nam' or 'Word'*.

Sagun— One with attributes. Revotion to the Sagun God implies worship protection, destruction, learning, wealth, prosperity success, death, destruction of evil. In India, they are usually represented by idols paintings and symbols.

Salim-dilan— Simple minded person

Sanskaras— Impressions or tendencies from previous births; early upbringing traditions and social influences which have been created by Brahmans for their own benefit but not for the general public. These were the early upbringing, traditions and social influences which shape the basic outlook and pattern of behaviour of a human being on the basis of equality, but *Brahmins* made these traditions corrupt and society was divided on the basis of their self interest.

Sukhnan-i-hikmal— Philosophical discourse of 'Nam'.

Sunn— Derived from Sanskrit, *Shunya* has usually been translated as void, emptiness, vaccum; but saints have not used this term with this meaning. According to them it is an inner spiritual region which is devoid of matter in any form. On entering this region the soul becomes free from the bondage of matter, mind and three attributes.

Shahna— Police chief. They follow the orthodox tradition and accept the first four Caliphs as rightful successors to Prophet Mohammad.

Shia— The Shias comprise the principal minority sect of Islam, consist of the followers of Ali, the cousin and son-in-law of Prophet Mohammad. They regard the heirs of Ali as the legitimate successors to the Prophet and reject- the other Caliphs and *Sunni* legal and political institutions.

Sharif— Respectable status

Siharfi— A peotical form

Shlok— Verse- epic stanza; couple, usually based on a spiritual or moral subject

Shastra— A Hindu scriputre or a book of philosophy for Brahmins.

Surat Shabd Yoga— The practice of the sound current; the union of the soul with *Shabd;* the spiritual exercise by which the current of conscious ness is applied to the hearing of the sound within; joining the mind or *mana* and the attention to the sound current. It is also called *Sahaj-Yoga*.

Shabd-Marg— 'The Path of the Word ' (Shabd); the practice of the sound current *Nam* or Word has also been called *Swiat* Shabd Yoga and *Sant Mat*.

Shiva— Good or Virtue, preserver of goodness destroyed at the time of Brahminical ideology became so strong that one can not understand the humanity.

Satsang— 'Association of the true'; company or association with a Master

Santa-ha— Callings the horseman to barber and tanner, which people take, is pre-determined.

Shiqdaram— Low-born revenue-collectors

Sari or Sarwari— Callings the horseman to barber and tanner, which people take, is pre-determined.

Shiqdaran— Low-born revenue-collectors

Sari or Sarwari— Low-born to a position of high command

Sijda— Making people offer prostration of the high palaces

Sulh-i-Kul— Absolute peace, a religious policy of Akbar.

Takbir— See Allah-hu-Akbar, 'God the Great' or *'Nam'*

Talib— Seeker, disciple

Tilak— A ceremonial mark that the Hindu Pundit (priest) wears on his forehead, but, he does not examine this term in practical life.

Tasawwur— Contemplation; seeing the image of an object with the minds eye or visualizing its form

Tattwa— The five elements present in every living being; vesetables have one active element (water), insects haved two (air and fire), birds have three (air, fire and earth), higher animals have four (earth, air, water and fire), and man has five elements (earth, air, water, fire and ether).

Turk— In the Panjab proper means, probably invariably, a Turkoman native of Turkistan and of Mongolian race. They were confined to *Hazara* and are doubtless the representatives of the colony of Karlugh Turks who came into the Panjab and *Tamerlane* (1399 A.D.); and possessed themselves of a Pakhli tract in that District, which apparently included the *Tanawal, Dhamtaur*; and *Swati* country and was politically attached to *Kashmir.* The word *Turk* is a *Tartar* word meaning a "wanderer", or *nomad* or *'Barawala'*; Thus in poetry the sun is called "The Turk of China," that is of the East, or " the Turk of the sky". The Turks of *Gurdaspur* are said to be rope-makers by occupation and their speciality used to be manufacturer to *tappars*, a cloth made of goats hair called sack of *tat*, or sack cloth, until the competition of the industry affected their trade during the period of Amir Timur. During Kabir's times the Muslms in North India were common ly called 'Turk' because some of the early Muslim conquorer were Turkish origin.

Tusi— One of the Sufi sects. It drives its name from Shaikh Ala-ud-din Tusi, who is buried at Tus.

Tajir— A merchant

Takhtagah— Capital throne

Tanka— Silver coin of the Sultanate

Thakur— A Hindu chief, or *God* in form of man.

Tola— A measure of weight

Tuman— A regiment of ten thousand soldier.

Tuti-e-Hind— 'The Parrot of India', a title borne by *Amir Khusrau*

Tassub— Sectarian partiality

Tajarrud-gazinan— Effort of some recluses persons of the 'Nam'

Tilism-kar-o-nairanji-o-Shabada baz— The triksters.

Ulama-Ulema— Plural of *alim,* a Muslim scholar, theologian

Umara— Plural of *Amir.*

Udasi— The term *udasi* means 'Sorrow' or sadness, from Sanskrit *Udas,* 'Sad' and their separation, which has sometimes been wrongly termed excommunication in the minds of Brahmins mentioned in the various religious books by the Saints. The *Udasis* tenets are celibate, at least in theory and when so in the practice are called *Udasi, Nanga* or *'naked'*

Urmar, Urma or Ormur— A tribe, regarding whose origin considerable doubt exists, which is increased by the fact that they have a language of the their own. The usual term drived from *Ur, 'Lamp'* and *'mar'* 'entinguisher' is untenable.

Upanished— The Philosophical and mystical part of the *Vedas,* who describes the inner or esoteric teachings. Upanished literally means 'to sit near or close', and the doctrines were so named because the secrets and mysteries were personally imparted to the disciple by the teacher. These writings come very close to the teachings of the Saints.

Universal mind— See Kal.

Upadan— Material cause.

Varnatmak— Expressible; that which can be spoken or written.

Vedang— The parts of *Vedas* six in number

Veda— Knowledge; revealed knowledge as embodied in the four holy books of the Hindus, the *Rig Veda, Samveda, Yajur-Veda and Atharva Veda.*

Vakil— Agent, deputy, minister

Varna— Aksar, *'Word', 'Nam'* 'Kalma' 'Pure', *Caste*.

Varuna— *Air, Power,* Sound current listen by those who practised the *'Word'* or *Shabd*.

Vezir or Wazir— Minister, Prime Minister of Sultans, said to be a sub-caste of the Awans tribe.

Wahdat-i-Wujud— Unity of Existence.

Walayat— Foreign country, alien land

Wali— Governor

Waliahad— Heir apparent

Waqf— Endowment

Wilayat— The Greatness Mystic status

Waqia— An occurance, an event

Wazifa— Stipened

Watal— A nomad and somewhat criminal tribe found in Sialkot. The Watals are the gipsies of Kashmir where they have two groups, one

Muhammadanised, the other out caste i.e. *Chuhras or Chamar or Chandala.*

Yajna or Yagnya — 'Sacrifice' , a ritual or religious ceremony of the Hindus which in ancient India included the sacrifice of some animal.

Yama— The lord of death, who takes charge of the soul at the time of death. The *Yamadoots* are the agents or minions of *Yama*. Yama is sometimes identified with *Kal,* the ruler of mind or Brahmin.

Vani— Shabd, 'Nam', Kalma, etc.

*Vajid— (*Also called Vajind in Rajasthan) seventeenth - century saint, born in a Muslim family; one of the prominent disciples of *Dadu.*

Vina, Veena or Beena— A stringed musical instrument, perhaps the oldest of the classical musical instruments in India, said to be the forerunner of the Sitar the exact sound of the region of *Sach Khand* or *Ibadat-Khana* cannot be conveyed in terms of any material musical instruments, as nothing in this world comes any where near that divine melody. Infact, like the light of that region, its sound also defies terrestial comparison.

Vaisya— The third of the fourth castes, sprung from Brahma's thighs. His profession (*vesa*) is commerce, attendance on cattle, and *agriculture*; by perference the two former. But he may, in case of need, descend to the servile arts of a *Sudra* of the three worlds; strictly speaking, *Yama* is subservient to Kal or *Dharam Rai,* the Lord of justice.

Yoga— 'Union'; a system of exercises or spiritual practice that leads to or aims at the union of the soul with God.

Yogi— One who practises *Yoga*

Zaat Essence, being,— The great Sufi mystics used the term *Zikr* for the highest form of remembrance to the *Simran* or inner invocation of the divine name or names under the direction of a spiritual master. It is also used for many other kinds of repetition practices that pertain to the lower *Chakras* and lower regions.

Zikr-i-ruhi— Remembrance with soul, when the devotee's attention is fixed at the third eye.

Zabita— Law, statute (plural *zawabit)*

Zakat— A religious tax payable by the Muslims in an *Islamic State* means where the rule of the law or *'Nam'* prevailed.

Zamindar— One who holds land under a *Zamindari* system, a collector of land revenue.

Zalim— A tyrant

Zar— Cash, gold and silver or friend

Zar Kharid— Purchased, a slave of God.

Zill— Shadow

Zill-i-Illahi— 'Shadow of God on earth' inform of man; a title borne by the absolute monarchs or ruler.

Zon— Tibetan name for the *Lohar* or Iron smith

Zankhe— A dancing eunuch, dressed in woman's clothes

Zimm's— Kafirs, infidels

Zar-Zar— Contemptible of the *'Nam'* became weak in the difficult hour

Zamin— Surety holder

Bibliography

(A) Primary Works

1. *Ain-i-Akbari Abul-Fazl* — Tr. by Jarrett, H.S & Blochmann, H, New Delhi: Two vols. Reprint 1978
2. *Alberuni's India* — Tr. by Edward, C. Sachan, Two Vols. New Delhi; Reprint 1989
3. *Arya-Manjusri-mula Kalpa* — Edited by Jayaswal, K.P; corrected with the help of Tibetan Text-Rahwla Sanskrityayan, Lahore, 1934
4. *Atharvaveda* — Ed. by V. Bandhu, Hoshiarpur; 1961
5. *Baharistan-i-Shahi, Anonymons* — *A Chronicle of Medival Kashmir;* Tr. by K.N Pandit; Calcutta, 1997
6. *Biography of Dharmasvamin* — (*Chaglo-tsa-ba, Chosrje-dpal*). Tr. Cr. Roerick, Patna, 1959
7. *Babur Nama* — Tr. by Beveridge, H, Two vols. Bound in One, Delhi, third edition, 1997.
8. *Chachnama,(ed)* — by Umar Daudpota, Hyderabad, Deccan, 1939
9. *Divyavadana* — Edited by E.B. Cowell and R.A. Neil, Combridge, 1886
10. *Faridnama* — *Zahid* Abrol, Delhi; 2003
11. *Futuhat-i-Firuzshahi* — Tr. into Hindi by M.Umar, Aligarh, 1957
12. *Harshcharita Banabhatta,* — Tr. by Thomas, F.W and Cowell, E.B Delhi, 1961
13. *Gulbadan Begam Humayunnama.* — Tr. by A.S. Beveridge; Delhi Reprint, 1989
14. *Jaina-Rajatarangini* — *Srivara,* text edited by S. Koul, Hoshiarpur, 1966
15. *Kadambari* — *Bana*, edited by P. Peterson
16. *Kautilya' Arthasastra* — Tr. by R. Shamasastry, Mysore, 1929.
17. *Kathasaritasagar;* — *Somadeva*, (the ocean of stones, Tr. by Tawney, C.H. London, 1924-28
18. *Kitab-ul-Hind, Alberuni Tr. by Sachan, E.C, Delhi, 1964*
19. *Kitab-Zainul-Akhbar* — M. Gardizi e. by M. Nazim, Berlin; 1929
20. Memories of Zahiruddin Babar — by J. Leyden, W. Erskine Revised by Sir L. King, Oxford University Press, 1921, Two vols.
21. *Mahabharata* — Tr. in Hindi by Pt. R.N Dutta Pandey, Lucknow vol.1, 2059 v.s
22. *Rajatarangini (Kalhana)* — Tr. by M.A. Stein, Four vols. Delhi, Reprint, 1961.
23. __do___ — Jonaraja, edited by S. Koul, Hoshiarpur 1967
24. *History of the Rise of the Mahomedan Power in India;* — Tr. from Original Persian of *Mahomed Kasim Ferishta*; by John Briggs. Reprint, Vol. I & II 1990.
25. *Shahjahana Nama*
26. *Sri Guru Granth Sahib*
27. *The Akbar Nama, Abul-Fazl* — Tr. by Beveridge H. (I.C.S. Retired). Two vols. New Delhi; 2nd edition; 1979
28. *The Grihya Sutras* — Tr. by Ordenberg,H. Part I. Max Muller - Part II, New Delhi; 1990

29. *The Shah namah of Farudusi* — Tr. by Rogers, Alexander, (I.C.S) two vols. in one, Delhi 2nd edition; 1994

30. *Travels in the Mogul Empire (1656-1668)* — Francois Bernier, Sencond edition, revised by Smith V.A. New Delhi, 1989

31. *The Life of Hiuen-Tsiang* — Tr. by Beal, S, London 1911

32. *Tuzak-i-Jahangiri* — Tr. by Rogers, Alexander (I.C.S. Two vol. in one, Delhi; 2nd Reprint; *Memories of Jahangir* 1994)

33. *Tarikh-i-Yamini,* — *Al-Utbi* (Elliot and Dowson-Part II)

34. *The Yasa-i-Chingiz,* — *Alauddin Ata Juwaini, Mansura, Haider, Medieval Indian sources in Mongolia-Culture Economy and Politics, New Delhi; 1992.*

35. *Tarikh-i-Firuzshahi, Zia-ud-din Barani; (ed)* — by Saiyid Ahmad Khan, W. Nassaulees and Maulavi Kabiruddin, Bib India Calcutta, 1860-62. Eg. Tr by M. Habib Aligarh, extracts E and D

36. *The Travesl of Ibn Battuta* (A.D 1325-1354) — Tr. by H.R.A. Gibs, London Indian Print, vol.III, Delhi 1993

37. *Tarikh-i-Fakhr-i-Mudabbir* — *Cf.* The Muqadimah of the *Sharja-i-Ansab,* edited by E. Denison Ross and Published under the wrong title Tarikh-i-*Fakhru-d-Din Mubarak* London; 1927

38. *Tarikh-i-Rashidi* — *Mirza Haider Dughlat. Tr. by* N. Elias, E.D.Ross, *A History of the Moghuls of Central Asia.*

39. *The Rehla of Ibn Battuta* — *Tr.* by M. Husain, Baroda; 1953

40. *The Book of Ser Marco Polo* — (ed) by H. Yule, 3rd edition, Revised by H. Cordier, Two vols, London (1903)

41. *Tuzuk-i-Timuri or Malfuzat-i-Timuri* — Tr. by Major Stewart 1830

42. *Tabaqat-i-Nasiri* of *Minhajuddin* — Tr. Major H.G Roverty,vol.1, Delhi, Reprint 1970

43. *Tarikh-i-Salatin-Afghana* or *Tarik-i-Shahi* — (Ed.) by M.H. Husain, Calcutta; 1939

44. *Vikramankadeva charita,* — Bilhana, ed. by Buhler, G, Bombay, 1875

45. *Zafarnama,* — Elliot History, Vol.III

(B) Modern Works

46. Ali, Mohd. Athar — *Element of Social Justice in Medieval Islamic Thought.* Symposia Paper in Indian History Congress; 57 Session Chennai, 1996

47. Ambedkar, Dr. Baba Saheb — *The Buddha and his Dhamma*; Nagpur (India), 1997

48. Ambedkar, Dr. Baba Saheb; — *Annihilation of Caste;* Aurangabad (India), Second edition 2003.

49. Ambedkar, Dr. Baba Saheb — *Who were the Shudras?* Aurangabad (India); Second edition, 2003

50. Abraham, T.M — *Handicrafts in India*; New Delhi; 1976

51. Aggrawal. Ashvini — *In Search of Vedic-Harappan* Relationship; New Delhi 2005

52. *Ars Islamica* — Part XI-XII, Delhi, 1943

53. Alkazi, Roshen — *Ancient India Costume,* New Delhi, Second Reprint, 2003

54. Arora, U.P — *Ancient India and The Greeks;* Presidental Address, *Indian History Congress.* 63rd session, 28th-30th December, 2002, Amritsar

55. Bazaz, Prem Nath — *Kashmir in Crucible,* Srinagar; 2005.
56. Briggs, G.W — *The Chamars,* Delhi, Reprint, 2004
57. Basham, A.L — *The Wonder That Was India*; New Delhi, Reprint; 2003
58. Bernal, J.D. — *Science in History*. Vol.-I, London, Reprint, 1969
59. Bernal, J.D. — *Marx and Science;* London; 1952
60. Bhandarkar, D.R. — *Some Aspects of Ancient Polity;* Patna (India); 1983
61. Banerji, S.C. — *Aspects of Ancient Life From Sanskrit Sources*; Calcutta; 1972
62. ____do___ — *Cultural Heritage of Kashmir, Calcutta, 1965*
63. Bhattacharya,A.K. — *The Technique of Indian Painting;* Calcutta; First edition on 1976
64. Bhattacharya, P.K. — *A Pegeant of Indian Culture and Archaeology;* Vol.1 New Delhi; 1995
65. Bhattacharya, S.K. — *The Story of Indian Art;* Delhi; 1966
66. Bhushan, Jamila Brij, — *Indian Jewellery, Ornaments and Decorative Designs; Bombay; 1964*
67. Bamzai, P.N.K. — *Social, Economic History of Kashmir (*1846-1925), Delhi 1984
68. Bamzai, P.N.K. — *History of Kashmir*; Delhi; 1962
69. Brown, Percy: — *Indian Painting;* New Delhi, Reprint 1982
70. *Bahuguna,* Rameshwar *Parsad* — *Symbols of Resistance Non-Brahmanical Sants* as Religious *Hero in Later Medieval;* An article represent in Refresh-course in History 2005, Study Material, ASC Jamia Millia Islamia.
71. Blunt, E.A.H. — *The Caste System of North India;* New Delhi; 1969
72. Bose, N.S. — *History of the Candellas of Jejaka Bhukti;* Calcutta, 1956
73. Bagchi, — *Pre-Aryan and Dravidian in India; Delhi*
74. Bhattacharya, Sabyasachi, — *The Colonial State Theory and Practice;* General President's Address Indian History Congress, 65th session, 2004
75. Benerji, Projesh, — *Aesthetics of Indian Folk Dance;* New Delhi, 1982
76. Brown, Percy; — *Indian Architecture (*Islamic Period); Delhi, 1964
77. Bhatnagar; A.P. — *Delhi and Its Fort Palace, A Historical Review;* Delhi, 2003
78. Bose, N.K. — *Culture and Society in India;* Bombay 1967
79. Bhartiya Viday Bhavan's — *History and Culture of the Indian People; Vol. III,* Bombay, 1960
80. Carr, E.H — *What is History?* New York, Reprint 1984
81. Carr, E.H — *The New Society, London, 1960*
82. Clayton, A.C, — The Rig-Ved and Vedic Religion; Delhi 1984
83. Chattopadhyaya, Sudhakar; — *Social Life of Ancient India;* Santiniketan; 1964
84. Chanda, M.B — *Kautilya' Arthasastra*; Delhi; 1998
85. Cunningham, Alexander; — *Survey of India Various Arechaelogical* Reports; Vol. 1 to 10. Varanasi; 1966
86. Chohan, A.S — *Historical Study of Society and Culture in Dardistan and Ladakh; New Delhi; 1983*
87. Chapdekar, M & Nalinee — *Ancient India and Greece;* New Delhi
88. Chandra, Moti; — *Costumes, Textiles, Cosmetics and Coiffure in Ancient and Medieval India; Delhi; 1973*
89. ____*do*____ — *Studies In Early Indian Painting*; London, 1970
90. Coomaraswamy, A.K — *History of Indian and Indonesian* Art; New Delhi, 1972
91. ___do____ — *Introduction to Indian Art. 2nd edition;* New Delhi, 1969
92. Chattopadhya, K.D — *Handicrafts of India.* Delhi 1975

93. Chandra, Satish (ed) *Essays in Medieval Indian Economic History; New Delhi, 1987*

94. Cunninghan, Alexander, *Coins of Medieval India; Varanasi; 1864*

95. —do— *Ladakh, Physical, Statical and Historical; Srinagar; 1971*

96. Clark, J.D. *The PreHistory of Southern Africa;* Penguin; 1959

97. Chopra, Ramesh *Acadmic Dictionary of Arts; Delhi, 2005*

98. Chander, Shekhar, R.K *Academic Dictionary of Archaeology;* Delhi, 2005

99. Charak, S.S *A Short History of Jammu Raj* From Earliest Times to 1846 A.D. Pathankot, 1985

100. Chhabra, G.S *Advanced Study in the History of Modern India.* Two vols (1813-1919); New Delhi; 1978

101. Chakravarti, Uma, *The Social of Early Buddhism.* Two vols. Delhi; 1987

102. Croce, Aesthetics, London

103. Cf. Yohanan, Friedmann, *The Origin and Significance of Chachnama. Islam In South Asia; Jerisalam; 1984*

104. Devahuti, D. *Harsa a Political Study*. Vol.1 New Delhi; 2nd edition; 1983

105. Dandekar, R.N. *The Age of the Gupta and Other Essays*; Delhi; 1980

106. Dreambi, Koul, B.K. *History and Culture of Ancient Gandhara and Western Himalaya; New Delhi; 1990*

107. Dutta, R.C. *A History of Civilization in Ancient India. Based on Sanskrit Literature, vol.1 & II*, Delhi 1972

108. Datta, N.K. *Origin and Growth of Caste In India;* Calcutta vol.1908, Vol.II. 1965

109. Dube, S.C *Tribal Heirtage of India*; New Delhi, 1972

110. Drew, Fredric *The Jamboo and Kashmir Territories*; Delhi, Reprint, 1999

111. Drew, Fredric *Northern Barrier of India; New Delhi; 1971*

112. DasGupta, Satadal *Caste Kingship and Community;* Patna; Reprint; 1993

113. Dey, N.L. *The Geographical Dictionary of Ancient and Medieval India. London*

114. Derret, J.D.M *The Hoysalas. Madras;* 1957

115. Darwin, Charles *The Origin of Species and The Descent of Man.* Macmillion 1962

116. Ezekiel, Isaac A. *Kabir, The Great Mystic;* Punjab (India) 6th Edition, 2003

117. __do___ *Sarmad, Martyr to Love Divine*, Beas, Reprint, 2005

118. Erakine, William *History of India Under Baber;* 1989

119. Elliot, Sir H.M. *Memoirs of the Races of the North-Western Provinces of India. 2 vols. Revised, Delhi, 1869*

120. Farquhar,J.N *Primer of Hinduism, Christian Literature Society of India; Madras*

121. Fabris, Charles *A History of Indian Dress.* Calcutta; 1960

122. __do___ *Indian Dress.* New Delhi; 1977

123. Ghurye, G.S. *Caste and Race In India.* Bombay; Reprint, 1969

124. ___do___ *Indian Costume,* Bombay

125. Gupta, T.C. Das, *Aspects of Bengali Society* From 1966 Old Bengali Literature; Calcutta, 1935

126. Gerini, *Researches on Ptolemy's Geography of Eastern Asia*

127. Grover, B.L & Grover, S. *A New Look At Modern Indian History (*From 1707 to the Modern Times); New Delhi, 2005

128. Gootz, Herman — *Studies in the History and Art of Kashmir* and *Indian Himalaya*; New Delhi. 1969

129. Gopal, Lallanji — *The Economic Life of Northern India;* Delhi 1965

130. Goswami, Karuna, — *Kashmir Painting;* Delhi, 1998

131. Gray, Basil, — *Art in Islamic Period;* Delhi, 1981

132. __do__ — *Treasures of Asia, Painting of India.* New Delhi, 1963 Douglas & Barrett

133. Grolier, — *Encyclopaedia of Knowledge.* Danbury, Connecticut, 1991.

134. Ganesha Baderhra's *Rajadarshani;* — *A Persian History of Northern Western* From Earliest Times to 1847 A.D Jammu

135. Gandhi; M.K. — *The Story of My Experiments With Truth;* Reprint: Ahmedabad; 2007

136. Harold, A. Gould, — *The Hindu Caste System;* Delhi; 1987

137. Huart, Clement, — *Ancient Persian and Iranian Civilization;* Tr. by R. Dobie, London; 1927

138. Hasinain, F.M — *The History of Jammu, Kashmir, Ladakh and Kishtwar;* Delhi; 1998

139. Habib, M. and Khan, A. — *The Political Theory of the Delhi Sultanate;* (Eng. Tr. of *Fatawa-i-Jahandari of Barani*), Kitab Mahal, *Allahabad.*

140. Heesterman, J.C. — *The Inner Conflict of Tradition; Delhi; 1985*

141. *Howells*, W.W (ed.) — *Ideas on Human Evolution;* Harvard University Press; 1962

142. Howells, W.W — *Mankind in the Making; Seeker & Warburg; 1960*

143. Hasan, Mohibul; — *Kashmir Under the Sultans; Delhi, 1959*

144. Howell, F. Clark, — *Life Nature Library, Early Man;* Nederland, 1970

145. Hasain, Majid — *Geography of Jammu and Kashmir; New Delhi, 1985*

146. Hutchison, J.& Vogel, PH.J. — *History of the Punjab Hill States;* Himachal Pradesh; 1982.

147. Hiralall, R.B and Russell, R.V. — *The Tribes and Castes of Central Provinces of India; Delhi; 1916*

148. *Habid,* Mohammad; — *Political Theory of Delhi Sultanate;* Delhi

149. Husain, S.M. Azizuddin, — *Ibadat Khana, Mahzar* and *Sulh-i-Kul;* Delhi

150. Hodivala,S.H — *Studies in Indo-Muslim History; Bombay 1939*

151. Hugel, Baron Charles, — *Kashmir and The Punjab; Delhi; 1972*

152. Havell, E.B; — *Aryan Rule in India; Delhi*

153. Hambly, Gavin, R.G — *The Emperor's Clothes: Robing and Robes of Honour in Mughal India in S. Gordan(ed) Robes of Honour; Delhi; 2003*

154. Irvine William; — *Later Mughal; Two vols.* Bound in One; 1989

155. Irvine, William, — *The Kashmiri Shawl; Marga Vi,* I; Delhi, 1952

156. Ibbetson, Sir Denzil Charles — *Punjab Castes*, Languages Department Punjab, Reprint, 1995

157. *Isami, Fietuhus Salatin (ed)* — A.S. Usha, Madras 1948

158. Irvine, William; — *The Army of the Indian Moghuls,* Reprint edition; Delhi, 1962

159. Jois, M.Rama, — *Guruji and Social Harmony;* Karnataka 2006

160. Jagadeeshan, P. — *Social, Justice and Challenges in Contemporary India; Bangalore; 2006*

161. Jha, V.N. — *Caste, Untouchability and Social Justice Early North Indian Perspective.* Indian History Congress 57 session (Chennai; 1996). Thematic Symposium on "Changing Concepts of Social Justice in Indian History," Delhi 1997

162. JaySingh, Hari; — *India Between Dream and Reality;* New Delhi; 1989

163. Jayachandra — *Bharat Bhumi Our Uske Nivasi; Delhi*

164. Jauhri, R.C. — *Firoze Tuqhluq;* Agra, 1968
165. Jha, D.N. — *Look for a Hindu Identity.* General President's Address, *Indian History Congress* 66th session, 28 to 30 January 2006, Santiniketan
166. Jaiswal, O.P. — *Science and Society in Ancient India Some Reflections.* Presidental Address 66th session, Santiniketan; 2005-06
167. *Joshi* — *Adhikari Institute of Social Studies; Social Science Probings.* vol. 16, No. 2, December 2004
168. *Joshi, O.P* — *Painted Folklore and Folklore Painters of India : (*A Study With Reference to Rajasthan); Delhi; 1976
169. Jaitly, Jaya(ed), — *Crafts of Jammu, Kashmir and Ladakh.* Ahmedabad; 1990
170. Jauhari, Manorama; — *Politics and Ethics In Ancient India.* Varanasi 1968
171. Janson, H.W. — *History of Art. New York; 1996*
172. Khan, Iqtidar Alam; — *Akbar's Personality Traids World Outlook; A critical Reappraisal.* Study Material provided in 13th-3 week Refresher Course in History Academic staff College Jami Millia Islamia-New Delhi-2005
173. Khandelwal,K.L — *Kabir Panth and Its Social Contents; S.P Sen (ed) Social Contents of Indian Religious Reform Movements;* Calcutta 1978
174. Kumar, Raj — *History of the Brahmans; Delhi; 2006*
175. Kumar, Raj — *Paintings and Lifestyles of the Jammu Region* (From 17th to 19th century), 2 vols' Delhi 2006
176. Kumar Raj — *History of the Chamar Dynasty*; 2 vols. Delhi, 2008
177. Kadam, K.N — *Dr. Babasaheb Ambedkar* and the Significance of the Movements; A Chronology, Bombay, Reprint, 1993
178. Khurana, K.L — *Ancient India*; Agra; Reprint 2004
179. Khurana K.L — *World History, 5th edition Agra, 2006-07*
180. *__do__* — *History of India* (From 1526 to 1967 A.D.). Agra; Reprint; 2007
181. *__do__* — *The* Twentieth Century World; Agra; 2005
182. __do__ — *History of China & Japan.* Agra; 2007
183. *Khurana, K.L & Gupta,S.* — *Histography; Agra, 2003*
184. Kane, P.V. — *The History of Dharmasastra; Pona. Vols I-IV, 1942*
185. Khobragade, Ram. — *Dr. Ambedkar, A Symbol of Global Socio-Political Revolution; New Delhi, 1978*
186. Keay, John; — *India, A History; Delhi*
187. Kapoor, G.S. — *History of India Mughal Period (1526-1707). New Delhi; Reprint 1984*
188. Kapoor, M.L — *Kingdom of Kashmir, Jammu*, 1983
189. Kapoor, M.L — *History of Kashmir;* Jammu, 1979
190. ___do___ — *Social and Economic History of Jammu and Kashmir State* (1885-1925 A.D); Jammu
191. Kosambi, D.D — *The Culture and Civilization of Ancient India,* New Delhi; 1965
192. Katoch, A.C — *Discovery of Kangra; Guraon; 2004*
193. Kak; R.C — *Antiquities of Basohli and Ramnagar; New Delhi; 1972*
194. Koul, P.K — *Himalayan Principalities in Jammu, Kangra, Bhadarwha*; Jammu, 1993
195. Ketkar, S.V — *History of Caste in India;* 2 vols, New Delhi; Reprint; 1911

196. Khan, Aftab Ahmed — *Central Asia. Imperialistic Motivations and Sinkiang; New Delhi; 1998*

197. Kaur, Gurdeep — *Political Ethics of Guru Granth Sahib.* New Delhi

198. Kanwar, Muhammad Ashraf — *Life and Conditions of the People of Hindustan;* Delhi, 1970

199. Khan; Mohd. Ishaq; — *History of Srinagar* (1846-1947); Srinagar; 1978

200. Limbale; Sharan Kumar; — *Towards an Aesthetic of Dalit Literature;* Tr. from Marathi by Alok Mukherjee New Delhi; 2004

201. Latiff, Syed Mohammad; — *History of Punjab;* New Delhi 1964

202. Lal, K.T. — *History of the Khalji's (1290-1320 A.D); Allahabad; 1950*

203. Lane-Poole, Stanley; — *Babur;* New Delhi 1969

204. Luniya, B.N. — *Evolution of Indian Culture,* Agra; Revised, 2005

205. Lawrence, W.R. — *Kashmir and Jammu,* Delhi, 1985

206. Lawrence, W.R. — *The Valley of Kashmir; London; 1895*

207. Lawrence, W.R. — *Provincial Gazetteer of Kashmir; New Delhi; Reprint 1985*

208. Leening, Joseph — *Yoga and the Bible; Beas; Reprint 2004*

209. Liu, Xinru, — *Silk and Religion: An Exploration of Material Life and the Thought of People (A.D. 500-1200); Delhi; 1996*

210. Mukerjee, Arun; — *Post-Colonialism My Living;* Toronto; 1998

211. Macdonell; A.A. — *A History of Sanskrit Literature; Heinemann; 1900*

212. Maclean; D.N. — *Religion and Society in Arab Sind,* Leiden; 1989

213. Meleod, W.H. — *Guru Nanak and the Sikh Religion, Sikhs and Sikhism.* Part I; New Delhi; 1999

214. Maqsood, Ruqaiyyah — *Islam*; London; 1994

215. Muller, Max; — *Ancient Sanskrit Literature;* Delhi,

216. Majumdar, R.C. — *The Vedic Age;* Bombay; Reprint, 1988

217. Majumdar, R.C. — *The Struggle for Empire,* Bombay; Reprint 1989

218. Majumdar, R.C. — *The Classical Accounts of India; Calcutta; 1960*

219. Majumdar, R.C & *Munishi, K.M.* — *The Classical Age. Bombay; Vol. III Reprint, 1962*

220. Majumdar, R.C. — *Age of the Imperial Unity;* Bombay; Reprint 1960

221. Majumdar R.C. Raychandhuri H.C. *& Datta, Kalikinkar* — *An Advance History of India; London 1963*

222. Mookerji, R.K — *Asoka; Delhi* 1967

223. __do__ — *Ancient India.* Allahabad; 1956

224. __do__ — Ancient *Indian Education London; Reprint; 1989*

225. *__do__* — *Chandragupta and His Times. Delhi; 1966*

226. Munshi, K.M — *The Glory That Was Gurjara Desa (550-1300 A.D).* Bombay; 1954

227. Mishra, S.C — *Evolution of Kautiylyas Arthasastras; Delhi*

228. Murdoch, J.M — *Review of Caste System In India; New Delhi; 1977*

229. Moorcraft, William. — *A Journey to Lake Mansarovara; Delhi; 1937*

230. Mushtaqi, Rizqullah — *Waqiat-i-Mushtaqi. Tr.* by J.H. Siddiqhi, New Delhi

231. Moorcraft, William & *Trebeck, George* — *Travels in the Himalayas Provinces of Hindustan and the Punjab, New Delhi-vol.1 to III, 1986*

232. Mitra, R.L. *Lalitavistara; Calcutta 1877*

233. Moosvi, Shireen, *Man and Nature in Mughal Era.* Symposia papers 5. Indian History Congress, 54th session, Mysore 1993

234. Mehta, J.L. *Advanced Study in the History of Medieval India;* (1000-1526) *Vol. 1* New Delhi; Reprint, 2002

235. Manmathan, M.R (ed) *Archaeology in Kerala Past and Present; Kerala; 2007*

236. Moskowitz, Moses; *The Politics and Dynamics of Human Rights; New Yark, 1968*

237. Naik, J.V *The Reformer and The Quest for Social Justice in Indian History.* General President Address, In Indian History Congress 67th session, 10-12 March; 2007

238. Nehru, Jawahar Lal, *The Discovery of India;* New Delhi, Reprint 2002

239. Nainar, S.M.H *Arab Geographers Knowledge of Southern India;* Madras, 1945

240. Nath, R. *Colour Decoration in Mughal Architecture; Bombay, 1970*

241. Nizami, Khaliq Ahmad *Some Aspects of Religion and Politics in India during the thirteenth Century; Delhi; 1978*

242. ___*do*___ *The Life and Time of Shaikh Fariduddin Ganj-i-Shakar. Delhi; 1955*

243. *Nizam* and Habib *Comprehensive History of India; vol.V, Delhi, 1970*

244. Okada, Amina, *Indian Miniature of the Mughal Court; New York, 1985*

245. Proceedings, *Punjab History Conference* March 18-20, 2005, Punjab University Patiala.

246. Proceedings, *Punjab* History Conference, March 18-20 2006, Punjab University Patiala

247. Proceedings of the *Indian History Congress* 64th session, 2003.

248. Proceedings of the *Indian History Congress 65th session, Bareilly, 2004*

249. *-do- 2005-06*

250. Puri, B.N. *Cities of Ancient India.* Delhi; 1966

251. Puri, J.R. *Guru Nanak, His Mystic Teachings; Beas 4th edition; 2004*

252. Sethi V.K. *Sant Nam Dev, Amritsar;* Reprint, 2002

253. Puri J.R &Khaki, K.S. *Sultan Bahu;* Amritsar, 1999

254. Puri J.R. & Shangar, T.R. *Bulleh Shah, Amritsar; 2nd edition; 1997*

255. Pandey, Rajendra *Kashi Through the Ages;* Delhi 1979

256. Paradkar, M.D. *Similes in Manusmriti, Delhi, 1960*

257. Parade, G.C. *Foundations of Indian Culture; New Delhi; 1923*

258. Prabhavananda, Swami *The Spiritrualism Heritage of India; London; 1962*

259. Pandey, D.B *The Sahis of Afghanistan and Punjab; Delhi; 1973*

260. Puri J.R. & Sethi, V.K. *Tulsi Sahib Saint of Hathras,* Punjab (Beas); Reprint; 1995

261. Parmu, R.K *A History of Muslim Rule in Kashmir;* Delhi; 1969

262. Pandey, Indu Prabha; *Dresses and Ornaments in Ancient India;* Delhi; 1988

263. Payne, Blanche; *History of Costume;* New York; 1965

264. Powell-Badan,B.H *The Origin and Growth of Village Communities Delhi, 1899*

265. Prabhupada, Swami; Bhaktivedanta, A.C. *Life Comes From life; Bombay; 1979.*

266. Pandit, K.N. — *Ladakh, Life and Culture; Srinagar;* 1986
267. Phul, R.K. — *Armies of the Great Mughal;* Delhi; 1970
268. Phadke, Y.D.(ed.) — *Mahatma Phule Samagra Vangmaya, Bombay revised 3rd edition, Maharashtra Rajya Sahitya Ani Sanskriti Mandal, 1991*
269. Ranade; M.G. — *Rise of the Maratha Power*; Ministry of Indian Broadcasting Govt. of India, Reprint, 1966
270. -do- — *Religious and Social Reform;* Bombay 1902
271. Rajwade, C. — *Tukarama, The Ceaseless Song of Devotion.* Punjab (Beas); Reprint 2004
272. Rao, M.V.K. — *Studies in Kautilya,* New Delhi, 1958
273. Rose, H.A. — *A Glossary of the Tribes and Castes of the Punjab and Northern-Western Frontier Provinces. Language Department of Punjab.* 3 vol. Reprint; 1999
274. Ray, S.C. — *Early History and Culture of Kashmir; Calcutta; 1970*
275. Ramesh, B.G. — *Biography Series Dr. B.R. Ambedkar, Karnataka, 2005*
276. Ray. R.K. — *Nationalism, Modernity and Civil Society: The Subalternist Critique and After,* Presidential Address, Indian History Congress, Kerala, 10-12 March, 2007
277. Ram, Nandu — *Encyclopaedia of Scheduled Castes in India;* New Delhi, 2007, Vol. I.
278. Ray. H.C. — *The Dynastic History of India; Delhi vol.1. 1973*
279. Rodgers, C.J. — *The Square Silver Coins of the Sultans of Kashmir; Delhi*
280. Rai, Raghunath — *Studies in World Civilization; Jalandhar, 1998*
281. Risley, H.H. — *Tribes and Castes of Bengal; New, Delhi, 1891*
282. —do__ — *The Peoples of India; Delhi, Reprint 1915*
283. Rhys Davids, T.W. — *Buddhist India; Delhi, 1903*
284. Rajshekar, V.T. — *Brahminism,* Bangalore, Third edition; 2002
285. Singh; Harbans, — *Encyclopaedia of Sikhism;* Patiala; 1992
286. Singh, Kirpal; — *The Adi Guru Granth as a Source of History;* Patiala, 1998
287. Singh, Fauja — *History of Punjab (*1000-1526 A.D); Vol.III, Patiala; 1988
288. Sharma, Arvind; — *Of Hindu, Hindustan, Hinduism and Hindutva, Numen; vol.49* 2002
289. Sharma,S.R. — *A Study in Medieval India,The Crescent in India,*Bombay, 1937
290. Sethi, K and Puri, J.R — *Tulsi Sahib Saint of Hathras;* Punjab (India) third edition 1995
291. Siddiqui, I.H. — *Money and Social Change in India During Medieval Times.* Symposia Paper 56th session of India History congress, calcutta; December 29th 1995
292. Southhill, W.F. — *Three Religious of China; London; 3rd edition; 1929*
293. *Srivastva, A.N. & Majumdar, R.K,* — *History of Far East;* Delhi 1985
294. Singh, Teja & Singh,Ganda — *A Short History of the Sikhs, Vol.1* Patiala, third edition; 1999
295. Sethi, V.K. — *Kabir, the Weaver of God's Name;* Amritsar; 3rd edition 1998
296. Sethi, J.C — *Tales of the Mystic East,* Punjab , 10th edition, 2006
297. Sanders, C.W. — *The Inner Voice;* Amritsar, Reprint 1991
298. Sharma, V.D. — *Cosmic View of Life In Guru Nanak Bani;* Language Department Punjab; 1996
299. Sastri, K.A.N — *A History of South India;* London; Reprint, 1966

300. Sexena, K.S. — *Political History of Kashmir;* Lucknow, 1974

301. Shukla, D.N — *Royal Arts.* Faizabad; 1969

302. *Sivaramamurti, C.* — *Indian Painting.* New Delhi, 1940

303. ____do_____ — *The Painter in Ancient India, New Delhi; 1978*

304. *___do___* — *Chitrasutra of the Vishnudharmottara;* New Delhi 1978

305. Singh, Meera; — Medieval History of India; Reprint; New Delhi; 2003.

306. Srivastava, R.D — *Arts and Archaeology of Punjab; Delhi, 1990*

307. Srivastava, S.P — *Art and Culture Heritage of Patiala.* Delhi 1991

308. Swarup, Shanti — *The Arts and Crafts of India and Pakistan. Bombay.1957*

309. Seth, Mira: — *Dogra Wall-Painting in Jammu and Kashmir;* Bombay; 1981

210. Sinha, B.P — *Decline of the Kingdom of Magdha; Patna, 1954*

311. Singh, Maharaj Charan; — *Light on Saint John*; Amritsar; Reprint, 1996

312. ___do ____ — *Die to live.* Amritsar, 1999

313. Singh, Khushwant, — *The History of the Sikhs; London; two vols. 1962*

314. Saini, B.S. — *The Social and Economic History of Punjab*. New Delhi 1975

315. Singh, Chandramani — *Centres of Indian Paintings* New Delhi, 1989

316. Sarkar, G.N — *The India of Aurangzeb;* Calcutta; 1901

317. Sastri, K.A.N — *Age of the Nandas and Mauryanas.* Varanasi; 1963

318. Subbiah, Ganapathy — *Daksinapatha; Where Does the Path lead Us?* Presidential address, Indian History Congress; Kerala, March 10-12, 2007

319. Siddiqi, Majid — *The Britisher Historical Context and Petitioning in Colonial India.* Introduction by Inayat S. Dr. M.A. Ansari Memorial Lecture XXIInd. Department of History & Zaidi A Culture, Jama Millia Islamia, New Delhi, 2005

320. Sarkar, D.C — *Studies in India Coins*; Delhi, 1968

321. Sufi, G.M.D. — *Kashmir;* vol.1& III Delhi, 1948

322. Sharma, L.P. — *Indian National Movement and Constitutional Development;* Agra 2003

323. Sullerey, S.K. — Introduction by Inayat S. & Zaidi A. *Chandella Art.* XXIst Dr. M.A. Ansari Memorial Lecture, Department of History and Culture, Jamia Millia Islamia-New Delhi. 2004

324. Singh, Pashaura, — *The Bhagats of the Guru Granth Sahib;* New Delhi, 2003

325. Schacht, Joseph — *The Origins of Muhammadan* Jurisprudence, Oxford, 1950

326. Shams Siraj — *Afif, Tarikh-i-Firoz Shah; ed* by Vilayat Husain. Bib. India Calcutta, 1888-91

327. Siddique, Cf. Iqtidar H; — *Perso-Arabic Sources on the Conditions in the Sultanate of Delhi*, New Delhi 1992

328. Sharma, Cf. R.S — *Sudras in Ancient India;* Delhi; 1990

329. _____do____ — *Social Changes in Early Medieval India (*A.D. 500-1200) Dev Raj Memorial Lecturer; 1969, New Delhi.

330. Singh, N.K. — *Cultural Heritage of Jammu, Kashmir and Ladakh.* Three vols. Jammu, 1997

331. Streusand, D.E. — *The Formation of the Mughal Empire.*

332. Smith, V.A. — *A History of Fine Arts in India and Ceylon, Bombay,*

333. Taylor, Isaac — *The Origin of the Aryans; New Delhi; 1889*

334. Thappar, Romila, *Ancient Indian Social History;* New Delhi; Reprint 1990
335. __do_____ *A History of India Volume One; London, Reprint 2002*
336. Tagore, Rabindranath *Boundless* Sky, Kolkata; Reprint, 2006
337. Tikoo, P.N. *Story of Kashmir; New Delhi 1949*
338. Tripath, R.S. *History of Ancient India; Delhi, 1960*
339. Temple, R.C. *Proper Names of Punjabi; Delhi*
340. Temple, R.C. *Legends of the Punjab.*
341. Thurston, E. and Rangachari, K. *Castes and Tribes of India, Delhi; 1909*
342. Tandon, R.K. *Pahari Ragamalas; Bangalore; 1983*
343. Taher, Mohammed; *Islam The Religion of Submission;* New Delhi; 1998.
344. The New Cambridge Modern History, vol.I 1957
345. Upadhyaya, K.N *Guru Ravidas; The Philosophers Stone*. New Delhi, Reprint 2005
346. ___do____ *Dariya Sahib; Saint of Bihar;* Beas, 2nd edition; 2006
347. ___do___ *Dadu the Compassionate Mystic.* Beas, Reprint; 1997
348. Voegelin, E. *The New Science of Politics, Chicago, Reprint 1987*
349. Vide Petech, *A Study of the Chronicles of Ladakh. I.H.Q* supplement 1939 vol.XV
350. Vincent, R.J. *Human Rights and International Relations.*
351. Vaidy, K.L *The Culture Heritage of the Himalayas. New Delhi 1977*
352. Veer, Ram Avatar *History of Indian Music and Musicians; New Delhi, 1987*
353. Washburn, S.L. (ed) *Classification and Human Evolution.* Methuen; 1964
354. Washburn, S.L. (e.d) *Social Life of Early Man;* Methuen; 1962
355. Walton, H.G. *A Monograph on the Tanning and Working in Leather*; Delhi 1903.
356. Wilson, John *Indian Caste*; New Delhi; 1976
357. Whitehead, Bishop *The Village Gods of South India.*
   The Coinage and Metrology of the Sultans.
358. Wilson H.H. *Hindu History of Kashmir;* Calcutta, 1960
359. ___do___ *The Vishnu Purana;* Delhi; 1961
360. Watt. G. *Indian Art at the Delhi Exhibition; Delhi, 1903*
361. *__do__* *Dictionary of the Economic Product of India.* Delhi, 1904
362. Warmington; *Commerce Between the Roman Empire In India; Delhi*
363. Wellhansen, Julius, *The Arabkingdom and its Fall. Egn. Tr.* 1927/73 London *J.J (1717-68),*
364. Winckelmann, *The History of Ancient Eng tr. (1849-73) referred in Encyclopedia of Historians and Historical Writings; Vol. Ed Kelly Boyd; London; 1992*
365. Wani; N.D *Muslim Rule in Kashmir* 1554-1586; Jammu, 1987
366. Zanaide A Ragozin; *Vedic India*; Delhi, 1961
367. Zakaria, Rafiq *Muhammad and the Quran;* New Delhi; 1991
368. *Zutshi N.K.* *Sultan Zain-ul-Abidin of Kashmir;* Lucknow, 1961
369. Zeuner, F.E. *Dating the Fast.* Methuen; 1962
370. Yadava, B.N.S *Society and Culture in Northern India in the Twelfth Century;* Allahabad 1974

(C) Imperial Government Publications

371. Bates, C.E. *A Gazetter of Kashmir, Kishtwar, Bhadrawha, Jammu Nowshera, Poonch* and *the Valley of Kishan Ganga,* New Delhi, 1980

372. __do___ *A Gazetter of Kashmir and Ladakh,* Delhi Reprint 1974.

373. *Gazetter of Kashmir and Ladakh,* Delhi, 1974

374. Census Report of Bengal, 1921

375. Census Report of Punjab, 1881, 1883,

376. Gazetteer of Sirmur,

377. Gazetteer of Simuala Hill States, Bilaspur, Baghal

378. *Gazetter*, Chamba

379. *Gazetter* Gurdaspur, 1914

380. Madras Government Memorandum to the Indian Statutory Commission, 1928

(D) *Journals*

381. Khan, Aftab Ahmad (ed), The Research Journal of Social Sciences, Vol.1 Feb. March, 2005 No.1 Srinagar.

382. Indian History Congress, 67th session souvenier calicut, March 10-12, 2007

383. Indian History Congress, 66th session, Santiketan 28-30 January, 2006 Souvenir

384. F.W. Bukler, *The Oriental Despot, Anglican Theological Review, 10* 1927-28

385. Stewart Gordon; *Robes of Honour.*: A '*Transactional Kingly Ceremony,* in the Indian Economic and Social History Review, 33,3, 1996

386. __do___ ed. *Robes and Honour* : The Medieval *World of Investiture,* New York; 2001. Later *Mughal and Early British India.*

387. *Dacca Review,* January, 1916

388. *Babar Vani As a Source of History;* An article presented; Punjab History Conference; March 2004, by Bhai Aridaman Singh Jhubal.

(E) Hindu Works

389. Puri, J.R. *Guru Nanak Ka Ruhani Updesh;* Amritsar; 2002

390. Sethi, V.K. *Sant Nam Dev;* Amritsar, 2004

391. Sethi, Santi. *Sant Kabir; 10th edition Jalandhar, 2003*

392. *Sethi, R.* *Sant Paltu.* Amritsar, 2002

393. Upadhyaya, K.N. *Guru Ravi Dass; Jalandhar 2005*

394. Sethi, V.K. *Mira Prem Diwani.;* Beas, 16th; edition 2001

395. Sangari; T.R *Japu ji Sahib;* Beas, 6th edition, 2006

396. Sangari T.R. & Aalam; P.S. *Sarmad Shaheed;* Jalandhar, 2003.

(F) *News Papers*

Daily Excelsior, 15-2-2007, News item '*India Charged with Failing to Uphold Dalit Rights.*

-do- 21-2-2007, *News item "Commission Against SC. Benefits to Dalit Muslims, Christians*

Index

J

K

S

T

U